Handbook of Research in Second Language Teaching and Learning

Senior Acquisitions Editor:	Naomi Silverman
Assistant Editor:	Erica Kica
Cover Design:	Kathryn Houghtaling Lacey
Textbook Production Manager:	Paul Smolenski
Full-Service Compositor:	TechBooks
Text and Cover Printer:	Hamilton Printing Company

This book was typeset in 10/11.25 pt. Palatino, Italic, Bold, and Bold Italic. The heads were typeset in Palatino and Americana, Bold, Italics, and Bold Italics.

Lawrence Erlbaum Associates, Inc., Publishers
10 Industrial Avenue
Mahwah, New Jersey 07430
www.erlbaum.com

Library of Congress Cataloging-in-Publication Data

Handbook of research in second language teaching and learning / edited by Eli Hinkel.
    p. cm.
    Includes bibliographical references and indexes.
    ISBN 0-8058-4180-6 (casebound: acid-free paper)—ISBN 0-8058-4181-4 (pbk. : acid-free paper)
    1. Second language acquisition. 2. Language and languages—Study and teaching.
3. English language—Study and teaching—Foreign speakers.   I. Hinkel, Eli.
    P118.2.H359 2005
    418—dc22   2004023636

Books published by Lawrence Erlbaum Associates are printed on acid-free paper, and their bindings are chosen for strength and durability.

Printed in the United States of America
10 9 8 7 6 5 4 3 2 1

Handbook of Research in Second Language Teaching and Learning

Edited by

Eli Hinkel
Seattle University

LAWRENCE ERLBAUM ASSOCIATES, PUBLISHERS

2005   Mahwah, New Jersey   London

This book is dedicated to the memory of
David Ellsworth Eskey
May 22, 1933, to October 19, 2002

David's contribution to the study and teaching of language and second language has played an important role in expanding the knowledge of thousands of teachers and graduate students, who read and benefited from his work. David was an excellent scholar and teacher, whose dedication to his students and the cause of reading remained unfailing, heartfelt, and sincere. Among applied linguists and reading researchers, David continually advanced that scarce variety of intellectual thought known as common sense. He will be greatly missed.

Contents

List of Contributors

Dennis E. Ager
Aston University

Neil J. Anderson
Brigham Young University

María Estela Brisk
Boston College

Richard B. Baldauf, Jr.
University of Queensland

Annie Brown
University of Melbourne

Anne Burns
Macquarie University

Michael Byram
University of Durham

Patricia Byrd
Georgia State University

Suresh Canagarajah
Baruch College
City University of New York

Susan Carkin
Lane Community College

Marianne Celce-Murcia
University of California
    Los Angeles

Micheline Chalhoub-Deville
The University of Iowa

Carol A. Chapelle
Iowa State University

KimMarie Cole
State University of New York
    Fredonia

Susan Conrad
Portland State University

Alan Davies
University of Edinburgh

Robert DeKeyser
University of Pittsburgh

Craig Deville
The University of Iowa

Dan Douglas
Iowa State University

Patricia A. Duff
University of British Columbia

Catherine Elder
Monash University

Rod Ellis
University of Auckland

David E. Eskey
University of Southern
    California

Anwei Feng
University of Durham

Sandra Fotos
Senshu University

Lis Grove
University of Melbourne

ZhaoHong Han
Teachers College
Columbia University

Linda Harklau
University of Georgia

Margaret R. Hawkins
University of Wisconsin–Madison

John S. Hedgcock
Monterey Institute of
    International Studies

Kathryn Hill
University of Melbourne

Eli Hinkel
Seattle University

Georgette Ioup
University of New Orleans

Noriko Iwashita
University of Melbourne

Alan Juffs
University of Pittsburgh

Yamuna Kachru
University of Illinois

Robert B. Kaplan
University of Southern California
    (Emeritus)

Gabriele Kasper
University of Hawaii, Manoa

Antony John Kunnan
California State University
    Los Angeles

James P. Lantolf
Pennsylvania State University

Anne Lazaraton
University of Minnesota

Constant Leung
King's College
University of London

Anthony J. Liddicoat
Griffith University

Tom Lumley
University of Melbourne

Numa Markee
University of Illinois at
    Urbana-Champaign

Peter Master
San Jose State University

Stephen May
University of Waikato

Sandra Lee McKay
San Francisco State
    University

Tim McNamara
University of Melbourne

Denise E. Murray
Macquarie University

I.S.P. Nation
Victoria University of Wellington

David Nunan
University of Hong Kong

Elite Olshtain
Tel Aviv University

Teresa Pica
University of Pennsylvania

Thomas Ricento
University of Texas
    San Antonio

Celia Roberts
King's College
University of London

Carsten Roever
University of Melbourne

Michael Rost
University of California Berkeley

Sandra J. Savignon
Pennsylvania State University

Larry Selinker
New York University

Marguerite Ann Snow
California State University
    Los Angeles

Merrill Swain
The Ontario Institute for Studies
    in Education
The University of Toronto

Elaine Tarone
University of Minnesota

Brian Tomlinson
Leeds Metropolitan University

Theo van Els
Radboud University Nijmegen

Leo van Lier
Monterey Institute of
    International Studies

Terrence G. Wiley
Arizona State University

Jessica Williams
University of Illinois at Chicago

Jane Zuengler
University of Wisconsin–Madison

Introduction

You taught me language, and my profit on't
Is, I know how to curse. The red plague rid you
For learning me your language!

Shakespeare, Caliban, in *The Tempest*,
act 1, sc. 2, l.

A great deal of research on second language (L2) learning has been carried out since the end of World War II. Over time, as researchers have come to recognize the enormous complexity of L2 learning and its many facets, investigations into this domain of knowledge have become a great deal more diverse and sophisticated. Whereas, for example, in the 1940s and 1950s, learning L2 was seen as a "habit" that learners were expected to develop and maintain, today, L2 studies undertake to gain insight into social, political, cultural, psychological, cognitive, and interactional processes entailed in learning a L2.

With the expanding influence of English as lingua franca and more recently with the emerging ubiquity of technology, the number of L2 English learners has been continuing to grow dramatically worldwide. However, the rising numbers of English language learners do not merely result in teaching second or foreign languages (FL) to more people. The evolving complexities of human societies, political structures, and the ever-increasing pace of globalization have also led to the emergence of new types of learners and learning needs, adding new dimensions to recent research and heightening the need for new knowledge in and about L2 teaching and learning.

This *Handbook of Research in Second Language Teaching and Learning* brings together a broad-based, state-of-the-art overview of current knowledge and research into the following domains of second language teaching and learning: social contexts of L2 learning; research methodologies in L2 learning, acquisition, and teaching; contributions of applied linguistics to the teaching and learning of discrete and inextricably intertwined L2 skills; L2 processes and development; and teaching methods and curricula; second or foreign language testing and assessment; and language planning and policies.

The *Handbook* is intended for the diverse range of professionals that populate the L2 universe: researchers, graduate students, and faculty in teacher education and applied linguistics programs, teachers, teacher trainers, teacher trainees, curriculum and materials developers, or others who are curious about the field.

The learning of another language inevitably brings forth the intricate issues that are bound up in language and its use, such as learners' first and second culture, identity, and varied perspectives on the very activity of L2 and FL teaching. Other crucial factors in L2 teaching, learning, and their institutional functions concern assessment and testing, as well as research into language policies and language rights—as they have direct implications for social structures, schooling, teacher training, and prestige planning.

To illustrate the exponential growth of the English teaching enterprise, it may be interesting to note that at present, the number and geographic reach of professional associations in the field and their growing memberships. For example: the Australian Association for the Teaching of English includes 8 territorial branches, the International Association of Teachers of English as a Foreign Language is comprised of 13 Special Interest Groups and maintains close ties with approximately 30 Associate organizations in various countries, and the TESOL membership consists of 20 Interest Sections and 6 Caucuses, with nearly 90 affiliate organizations on all habitable continents. Worldwide, the rate of regularly scheduled professional meetings, such as conventions, conferences, symposia, colloquia, and the like, is higher than six per month (i.e., one every 5 days year round).

The sheer number of the professional organizations and meetings evinces the need for the development and promulgation of knowledge about L2 teaching and learning. A great deal of work in L2 research and pedagogy is published annually in hundreds of journals and books, as the body of the disciplinary knowledge expands and deepens.

Another important reason to mention the diversity of interests among L2 professionals is that in practically any compendium of articles it would be very difficult (if at all possible) to cover the research on all the factors that directly or indirectly affect L2 teaching and learning, regardless of how long a particular book is or how many volumes a set of such books may include. Thus, a collection such as this of overviews of what is known, important, useful, relevant, influential, productive, or controversial and conflicting in L2 teaching and learning fills an important need by including most or many (but certainly not all) research areas.

The selection of the topics and areas of research for inclusion in a handbook of any kind is a difficult and sometimes precarious business. In a discipline as enormously diverse as the teaching and learning of English or other types of second languages around the world, it would be difficult to identify common characteristics that without exception apply to all types of humans that populate the L2 universe.

Speaking broadly, to determine how the profession of L2 researchers and practitioners defines itself and how L2 professionals of all types and in many world regions identify the areas of importance and usefulness, it was necessary to take a look at the topics of research and interest among the professional associations and research organizations around the world.

Thus, a three-pronged approach was adopted:

1. As a point of departure, the divisions, affiliates, special interest groups, and content and topic areas in various professional associations and organizations in dozens of countries and across continents were compiled to ensure the breadth of research topics, content areas, and values.
2. To focus on currency and relevance, the themes highlighted at research and professional conferences, meetings, gatherings, academies, presentations, and in-progress workshops were similarly collected.
3. Most important, a thorough and extensive review of the L2 research published in the past two decades played a central role.

As a result of this substantial examination, possible themes for the *Handbook* began to emerge and were subsequently narrowed down to eight main research areas reflected in the book. The book chapters set out to highlight the major findings and the advancements of knowledge that have taken place in the past several decades and across regions, political borders, and continents. This tome includes eight parts, each divided into 5 to 13 chapters, depending on its topics and contents. For example, it seems necessary to take stock of the research on classic L2 skills and processes involved in learning to speak, listen, read, and write in another language. Similarly, an overview of other L2 facets account for more narrowly focused domains of research that play a crucial role in much of what takes place in the world of L2 teaching, learning, and the learner.

In general terms, an inclusion or exclusion of a particular theme or topic in this already huge compendium of overviews reflects its prominence in L2 research literature, as well as the importance of the topic to the profession. This post hoc approach seems rather fitting because the *Handbook* has the goal of reviewing the current L2 research as it exists today. The task of identifying new research venues is best left to the researchers with active research programs. It is important to note, however, that the research areas of interest and value may vary greatly across geographic locations and the human contexts in which L2 is taught, learned, and researched.

A Caveat Emptor: In any single book, no matter how large, it is not possible to include chapters on all L2 topics or issues that are important to all (or even most) individuals or cohorts of individuals. Furthermore, it does not seem to be likely that every reader would benefit from reading or can be expected to read the vast amount of material covered in this book. A more reasonable expectation is that interested readers will simply select the chapters that are of greater relevance to them and their specific contexts.

After much deliberation, and many discussions, debates, and consultations with prominent L2 researchers, the following research areas are not covered in this *Handbook*, not because they are not important but for the reasons noted above:

- The political, economic, and attitudinal issues that accompany the hiring and employment of non-native ESL/EFL teachers.
- The legal, governmental, and political issues associated with the status of refugees.
- The special concerns and the many complexities in L2 learning by the deaf.
- The many important local, governmental, economic, and funding considerations entailed in teacher training, preparation, and education in various regions and countries around the world. However, from a broad perspective, the entire *Handbook* represents a contribution to teacher education and professional preparation.
- The research on L2 learning and motivation/attitudes is covered in the specific chapters to which it is directly relevant (e.g., see chapters 7, 31, 42, and 49), rather than in a separate chapter, for example, in the case of many new immigrants, motivation usually comes from the need to eat and earn a living.

To be sure, some of the topics of the chapters included in this book may not be immediately and directly tied to the research on L2 teaching and learning. For example, none of the prevalent L2 research methods were specifically developed for investigating L2 teaching, learning, or acquisition, and all were created and perfected in other disciplines, such as anthropology, education, psychology, or sociology. Nonetheless, research methods directly impact why, how, and when L2 research is conducted. Thus, it seems that a respectable handbook on research has to include overviews of the research methods by means of which the profession attains new knowledge of L2 teaching, learning, and acquisition because how something is investigated directly affects the nature, types, usability, and applicability of the findings.

Systematic research into language teaching and learning is a relatively new enterprise, but for thousands of years, in the actual practice of L2 teaching and learning, development and refinement of the methods has been carried out experientially, experimentally, and intuitively. In this regard, language teaching can be compared to cooking. Due to the advances of science, much has been learned about the nutritional content of various food substances, and nutritious meals certainly take into account the beneficial qualities of their ingredients. However, delicious meals are not necessarily nutritious and vice versa. A scientifically sound approach to L2 teaching and learning does not necessarily make for the most enjoyable language course, and in many cases, the teaching that is to be both beneficial and enjoyable has to supply both elements to make L2 learning nutritious and delicious at the same time. All this is to say that, in many cases of the practice of L2 teaching and learning carried out by real people in real life, clearly delineating the boundary between research and practice may not be possible in all cases, nor does it seem to be always necessary. However, in cooking and eating, as in L2 teaching and learning, one does have to be mindful of the delicious empty calories, as well as highly nutritious but barely edible foods. The knotty issues associated with clear-cut distinctions between research and practice may not be resolved in the foreseeable future, although many may disagree.

THE ORGANIZATION OF THE BOOK

The book is organized into eight thematic parts, and an introduction is included in each. In all, the book contains 57 chapters.

The people, for example, L2 learners and users, who populate the L2 universe are at the heart of the research on L2 teaching and learning. Much L2 research is geared toward finding out as much as possible about the societal matrices in which second and foreign languages are taught and learned. Hence, **Part I, Important Social Contexts in Research on Second Language Teaching and Learning,** begins with the research about many different types of L2 learners that have different language learning needs and goals within the social contexts of their lives. The nine chapters in this section of the book focus on the people who set out to learn a second and foreign language in various locations, institutions, and political and educational systems with an immediate goal of attaining different types of L2/FL proficiencies in order to achieve their educational, vocational, academic, professional, career, and communicative objectives.

The methods for research in how second languages are taught and learned represent the second theme. These are discussed in **Part II, Methods in Second Language Research**. In L2 research, each research method has its strengths and weaknesses, and each of the five methods presented in the chapters discuss markedly different approaches to gathering and analyzing data. What specifically can be learned through research crucially depends on the method of collecting data and making conclusions from the analysis.

The many contributions of applied linguistics to research on L2 teaching and learning represent the focus of **Part III, Applied Linguistics and Second Language Research**. The eight chapters included in this part cover such divergent domains of study as Second Language Acquisition (SLA), sociolinguistics, language socialization, pragmatics, sociocultural research and theory, conversation analysis, contrastive rhetoric, and corpus studies. In this regard, the findings of applied linguistics research can shed a great deal of light on various L2 phenomena, such as the processes of language learning and use.

The 12 chapters in **Part IV, Research in Second Language Processes and Development**, represent an extension of the theme of applied linguistics research in Part III. The findings of the research into the connections between age, cognition, fossilization, and output and L2 learning are directly tied into key areas of applied linguistics research. Similarly, the development of essential L2 skills, such as speaking, listening, literacy, grammar, reading, vocabulary, and writing is bound up with mental and physiological processes of learning and maturation. To a large extent, the division of the 20 chapters in Parts III and IV has the goal of easing the reader's path along the book's contents.

It would be no exaggeration to say that in the practice of L2 teaching, there are as many methods as one would like to name and count. For this reason, the eight chapters in **Part V, Methods and Curricula in Second Language Teaching**, attempt to deal only with a few prominent exemplars widely adopted in various geographic locations and social contexts around the world. For example, the preeminence of the communicative method in many countries can be compared only to the undaunted popularity of traditional grammar-based methods. The chapter on L2 learning strategies highlights the applications of strategies for language learning across all methods and approaches. It is important to note, however, that in all likelihood, Part V excludes at least as many methods as it includes, and the importance of the "beyond methods" movement is not to be underestimated.

The six chapters in **Part VI, Second Language Testing and Assessment**, are probably insufficient to discuss in any depth the many important human and institutional issues entailed in measuring L2 proficiency. However, the goal of the chapters in Part VI is to underscore the vexing complexity of language testing and assessment, as it is closely tied to L2 learning, learning processes, and inferential measurements of L2 competence, proficiency, and skill. Thus, the chapters in Part VI present brief overviews of the sociopolitical contexts of language assessment, considerations of validity and the history of testing, research methods, testing of language for specific purposes, and classroom-centered language assessment.

The theme of **Identity, Culture, and Critical Pedagogy in Second Language Teaching and Learning** is taken up in **Part VII**. Research into the direct connections between language learning and the social identity, culture, and the ways in which second or foreign languages are taught demonstrates that these constructs combine to impact the social group and the individual within the fabric of the society and its political and educational systems. The study of how learners' identities can be bound up with culture and language pedagogy relies in a wide range of macro- and microanalytic approaches, discussed in Part VII.

The six chapters in **Part VIII, Language Planning and Policy and Language Rights** present an overview of the important directions in the research of language policy and planning, and the impact of these on minority language rights. The introductory chapter outlines a number of key issues and terms and a general framework for the types of activities that define the field. The next five chapters discuss the classic activity types and focus on the important recent research specifically geared toward language teaching and learning.

THE STRUCTURE OF CHAPTERS

In this *Handbook*, as in any other large book that consists of dozens of chapters written by five or six dozen authors and co-authors, the contributions are not likely to be very similar in character. To a large extent, the chapters reflect the diversity of the research into second and foreign language teaching and learning, the contexts in which it is taught and learned, and the individuals who teach and learn. In this regard, the chapters can be seen as a somewhat idiosyncratic microcosm of L2 research.

As has been mentioned, systematic research into L2 teaching and learning draws on research findings and methods in a conglomeration of other disciplines. Some of the L2 research venues place high value on dense information content, innovative research directions, full surveys of the field, and thorough examinations of seminal publications. Other researchers attribute great importance to discursive interpretations, historical developments, or narrowly focused theoretical perspectives. To add to the mix, some chapters deal with concrete and well-defined topics or argue for the validity of particular research findings, teaching methods, or language learning theories, and others cover abstract research areas or seek to balance disparate research undertakings.

Nonetheless, despite the great diversity of the field, the research, and the disciplinary perspectives, every effort has been made to make the chapters consistent in style, tone, and the depth of material coverage. For this purpose, all contributors were requested to construct their chapters along a similar outline:

- An explanation of how the topic discussed in the chapter fits into a larger picture of the domain of L2 research.
- Important developments, trends, and traditions in the discipline, as well as current controversies and the reasons that they have arisen.
- A detailed examination of the current research findings presented in the chapter.
- A section on conclusions and/or future research directions.
- A substantial list of references that can assist interested readers in backtracking seminal and relevant works.

Each chapter represents a stand-alone examination of research in a specific L2 sub-domain, yet, the book as a whole seeks to reflect the major trends in the current investigations into the people and the contexts where and how second and foreign languages are taught and learned.

ACKNOWLEDGMENTS

I owe a debt of gratitude to my colleagues whose wisdom, guidance, and advice were vital. I am sincerely and deeply grateful to my friends of many years for giving generously of their knowledge, experience, and assistance (in alphabetical order):

Susan Carkin, Lane Community College
Marianne Celce-Murcia, University of California, Los Angeles
Rod Ellis, University of Auckland
David Eskey, University of Southern California
Sandra Fotos, Senshu University
Linda Harklau, University of Georgia
Robert B. Kaplan, University of Southern California

Naomi Silverman, Senior Editor at Lawrence Erlbaum Associates, has been a insightful, supportive, and patient friend. The *Handbook* was Naomi's idea, and this tome owes her its very existence.

Paul Bruthiaux, Texas A&M University, Peter Lowenberg, San Jose State University, and more than a dozen additional reviewers who chose to remain anonymous helped shape the contents of individual chapters. My heartfelt thanks to them: The book could not have proceeded without their knowledge and expertise.

My devoted comrade and sole member of the in-house IT department, Rodney Hill, created and maintained logistics software employed in making this book a reality. His pain and suffering will be amply rewarded in another life.

Handbook of Research in Second Language Teaching and Learning

I

Important Social Contexts in Research on Second Language Teaching and Learning

Introduction

During the decades of the formalization of English teaching and the growth of research into how second and foreign languages are learned, language professionals have come to recognize that among other crucial factors:

- Learners in different locations and contexts have different needs and different language learning abilities.
- Different learners have different levels of education and literacy.
- Individual learners or groups of learners can be distinct in terms of their ages, socioeconomic backgrounds, and sociolinguistic variables.

In addition, research into second and foreign language teaching and learning has come to recognize that:

- Educational and schooling systems differ widely around the world.
- Some educational bodies are centralized and others are relatively independent.
- Teaching materials and curricula can be prescribed or developed locally.
- In some systems teachers are better trained than in others.
- Some learners undertake language study as a hobby and others need to learn the language to earn their livelihoods.
- Teaching can be carried out more intensively over long periods of time or less intensively in short-term courses.
- Second language research, teaching, and learning can be as diverse as the multitudes of human life paths, living environments, living conditions, societies, and cultures, as well as the economic, geographic, political, legal, and power-based circumstances.

In short, today the science and practice of second or foreign language (L2/FL) teaching and learning has come to recognize that learners and the contexts of language learning are myriad.

A Caveat Emptor. For the purposes of this Handbook or any other single book for that matter, it is clear that no thorough description of all the types of humans that carry out L2/FL learning is possible. Thus, it is necessary to limit the discussion of learning contexts to those that are likely to represent the largest populations involved in L2/FL learning. The word "likely" is necessary here because no one knows with any degree of certainty or even with a degree of approximation how many types of learners or individual learners study L2 or FL within any given context.

The topics of chapters included in Part I are based not on the actual sizes of populations involved in learning L2/FL, but rather on the body of research and other scholarly work published about a particular cohort of learners. However, as the title of Part I indicates, this measure of the importance of a particular language learning context in effect says little about its importance to any one person or group of persons. The title "Important Contexts of Research on Second Language Teaching and Learning" simply speaks to the quantity of publications and research studies carried out within particular contexts in which L2s and/or FLs are learned, with an implication that a larger or smaller number of researchers consider it to be of interest.

The prominent areas of L2/FL research include, for example:

- School-age children in bilingual education systems and schools in many countries around the world.
- Elementary and high school students who are immigrants or children of immigrants or other types of populations who change languages, communities, and countries in search of work or safe places to live.
- Immigrants, who can include skilled and unskilled workers, trained and educated professionals, as well as employees in multinational companies.
- Adult learners in adult education, vocational, and junior college programs.
- Learners who learn another language for the sake of learning it or those who aspire to entering universities or those who pursue academic degree studies in countries other than their home countries.
- College/university students who study English as a Foreign Language (EFL) primarily (and sometimes exclusively) in the classroom.
- Residents of multilingual countries, regions, and communities, all of whom use English as a lingua franca in the course of their daily interactions.

Among these people, different types of second language learners and users have different reasons for learning and using another language. Their learning goals invariably influence the development of their L2 skills. For instance, the L2 learning processes and aims of adult immigrants who need to secure employment and rebuild their social networks are clearly distinct from those of school-age children attending school, or international students enrolled in colleges and universities in English-speaking countries. In effect, it is the goals for which a second or foreign language is used that determine where and how it is learned. Thus, the focus on the contexts for language use and language learning attempts to encompass the many types of people that inhabit the L2/FL universe regardless of specific geographic locations.

Chapter 1, by **Maria Estela Brisk**, takes a broad perspective on the implementation of multilingual and bilingual education programs in various parts of the world. The chapter highlights the fact that bilingual education is extraordinarily widespread and that it can take many different forms. Brisk emphasizes that not all students who attend bilingual education programs are bilingual when they start nor are they all from language minorities. Brisk also explains that ideology accounts for popular beliefs that surround bilingual education. Bilingual programs, in fact, largely share one important characteristic of using two or more languages for instruction but the extent of their uses may vary, as do their educational foci.

Chapter 2, by **Margaret Hawkins**, focuses on research on second language teaching and learning in elementary schools. The discussion promotes the view that language learning and schooling are social processes situated in the social worlds of the learners and the institutions, and include a vast range of connections among students' languages, learning, cultures, and identities. The chapter also examines second language teaching and learning as a construct within the power relations that shape the learning and interactions in language and schooling. These power relations, although played out through local and situated interactions, are formed through larger discourses at play in institutions and societies.

Chapter 3, by **Patricia Duff**, is devoted to many models and program designs for English as a Second Language (ESL) instruction at the secondary school level. One overall finding of much research reviewed in the chapter is that the challenges facing secondary school students and their teachers are quite enormous and that they range from basic socialization and settlement to oral language development and the development of academic literacies. In addition, these students often experience extreme social isolation and disappointment at their academic and linguistic development, often because their own expectations or those of their family and school were very high. According to Duff, however, many recent resources provide helpful venues for the support that can be given to these students during their initial and ongoing language and literacy development.

Chapter 4, by **Denise Murray**, explores the many difficult issues that have been identified in adult and vocational education of immigrant populations in various countries. Murray reviews the educational delivery systems that differ considerably across English-speaking countries, resulting in different perceptions of the adult learner, as well as different foci in research agendas for adult ESL education. A review of extant literature also indicates that, in many cases, the adult ESL learner is invisible in national policies and almost invisible on the agenda of academic researchers.

Chapter 5, by **Susan Carkin**, examines the findings of research in English for academic purposes (EAP), generally housed in formal academic contexts. EAP status within L2/FL teaching and learning includes English language use by students, professionals, and nonprofessional workers in vocational contexts. EAP is taught across multiple disciplines and includes learning and study skills components of broadly relevant academic skills. Overall, EAP concerns itself with the development of and the transition from pedagogic genres (e.g., essay exams and term papers) to increasingly authentic genres associated with various disciplines. This focus on learning academic language through academic tasks, texts, and content is the basis for claims that EAP instruction represents a highly pragmatic approach to learning, encompassing needs analyses, evaluation, academic skills, disciplinary content, and tasks in support of student learning in tertiary educational contexts.

Chapter 6, by **Peter Master**, reviews a great deal of work published in English for Specific Purposes (ESP). The chapter reviews the current research and data-based studies in ESP, as well as descriptions of ESP programs and contexts. The largest representative of an international movement known as Languages for Specific Purposes (LSP) is also briefly examined to highlight the current research trends in the LSP movement. Research in ESP thus occurs within the overlapping domains of English language education for specific purposes and discourse/genre analysis.

Chapter 7, by **Celia Roberts**, describes second language teaching and learning in the workplace. In the context of employment, the workplace represents the curriculum for L2/FL teaching and learning. For learners, the stakes in learning are high because the central goal of instruction is not just an improvement in workers' language skills, but the possibility of changing the communicative patterns and assumptions of staff at all levels. Research in L2/FL in the workplace necessitates an examination of organizational talk and writing and language practices that can become potential disadvantages in a multilingual workplace. Roberts points out that when the workplace is the curriculum, then language education may grow in range and scope to include issues from new technologies to competency standards.

Chapter 8, by **Brian Tomlinson**, provides a broad overview of English as a Foreign Language (EFL) contexts. EFL is learned by people who already use at least one other language outside the learning environments and who live in a community in which English is not used in the course of people's daily lives. Thus, the social, cultural, and linguistic norms of the community in which EFL is learned invariably influence the teachers' and learners' expectations of the language learning processes and their outcomes. Based on his overview, Tomlinson concludes that no particular pedagogical procedure can be used effectively without some modification from context to context, but a procedure that proves effective in one context of learning can be potentially effective in other contexts of learning, as well.

Chapter 9, by **Yamuna Kachru**, outlines explicitly the perspective of researchers studying varieties of English around the world. Kachru emphasizes the fact that English has acquired a range and a depth unparalleled in human history. However, vigorous debate has accompanied the status of Outer and Extended Circle varieties and the characterization of what is meant by "standard" in relation to varieties used in all the Circles. The concept of Standard English and its relevance for World Englishes (WEs) is also addressed in the chapter. In the summation of her outline of issues that have surrounded WEs for several decades, Kachru underscores that the WE research community is anticipating a paradigm shift in the teaching and learning of English in the Inner, Outer, and Expanding Circles and that the change in perspectives on the teaching and learning of English will bridge the gap between sociolinguistic reality and prevailing myths about English. Kachru emphasizes the need for inclusiveness of the global fellowship of the English-speaking populations.

1

Bilingual Education

María Estela Brisk
Boston College

The terms "bilingual students" and "bilingual education" are often confused. Students are bilingual because they know and use at least two languages even if their fluency and use of the languages vary. Some are fluent in both, others are stronger in one, yet others are literate in only one of their languages. Bilinguals use both languages to different degrees. Some converse, read, and write both daily; others find occasional use for one of their languages. Angélica was raised speaking Spanish and English. She was fluent in both languages when she entered an English-medium school. Soon she switched to function only in English, retaining adequate listening and reading ability in Spanish. She studied French in high school. In college, a special course on writing Spanish and extensive reading of Spanish materials in preparing a thesis on Latin American films helped her regain fluency and strengthened her abilities to read and write in Spanish. As an adult, she uses English with her husband and English and Spanish with her children and at work. Occasionally she uses French. Every bilingual presents a different pattern of proficiency and use over their lifetime (Grosjean, 1989; Mackey, 1968; Romaine, 1995).

This chapter explores how multilingual and bilingual education programs are implemented throughout the world. Examples illuminate not only how widespread but also how varied such education is. Several encyclopedias explore such programs (C. Baker & Prys Jones, 1998; Cummins & Corson, 1997). Bilingual students are found in both "bilingual" and "monolingual" schools. Similarly, some bilingual students attend bilingual education programs whereas others maintain language skills outside the classroom. Not all students who attend bilingual education programs are bilingual when they start nor are they all from language minorities.

In this chapter, the term "native language" refers to the language used in raising a child and "second language" as the one learned at a later stage, often in their first excursions from the home environment, through media, in schools, and with peers. "Heritage languages" are those used by students' ethnic group, whereas "societal language" is the predominant language for communication in the students' nation.

This chapter starts with definitions followed by models and purposes of dual language and multilingual programs. The third section surveys bilingual education programs around the world. The chapter concludes with an analysis of concerns and practices related to implementation.

DEFINITIONS

Bilingual education, broadly defined, is the use of two languages as media of instruction. This simple definition is not what most people have in mind when they think of bilingual education. Ideology accounts for common beliefs that bilingual education involves just one language or requires absolutely equal use of both languages for instruction. For example, critics of bilingual education often attack a "straw man" by assuming that bilingual education is, simply, "instruction in the native language most of the school day for several years" (Porter, 1994, p. 44). Some proponents of bilingual education maintain, on the other hand, that only "dual language programs" consisting "of instruction in two languages equally distributed across the school day" are acceptable (Casanova & Arias, 1993, p. 17). The reality is that bilingual education comes in many forms, influenced by particular circumstances, student needs, and resources. They all use two or more languages for instruction but their use may vary proportionately and may also focus on different purposes over the course of students' education. Some prefer the label bilingual/bicultural education because culture[1] is an important component of bilingual programs, "based on the premise that the language and culture children bring to school are [both] assets that must be used in their education" (Nieto, 2000, p. 200).

Migration patterns and the need for mastery of regional or international languages gave rise to programs that use more than two languages for instruction. Multilingual education programs "aim for communicative proficiency in more than two languages" (Cenoz & Genesee, 1998, p. viii).

Some language programs are mislabeled bilingual education because students achieve a certain degree of bilingualism. In these programs only one language is the medium of instruction and the other is taught as a subject. Such programs are designed to develop fluency in either an international language, the language of a prominent ethnic group in the country, the heritage language of guest workers or immigrants, or the societal language in schools where the minority is the language of instruction. For example, schools in European countries with two dominant groups offer instruction in one of the major languages and teach the other as a subject matter. In the Flemish region of Belgium, Dutch is the language of instruction and French is offered as a subject after fifth grade. The pattern is reversed in French-speaking regions of Belgium, whereas parents in Brussels choose between Dutch and French schools (Glenn & De Jong, 1996).

MODELS AND PURPOSE

Dual models differ according to their goals, type of students served, and how languages are used in the curriculum. They can be implemented as a program within a school or apply to an entire school. Some programs have as a major goal fluency in two languages whereas others strive for fluency in a second language, usually the societal language. These programs serve either minority or majority populations. Only two-way and integrated programs include both groups. Programs differ in the way languages are used in the curriculum for literacy and content area instruction. Some models introduce both languages simultaneously, others gradually, yet others switch after a certain number of grades. Some continue teaching both languages through the length of the program. Others teach in the first language for a short period of time. Table 1.1 include the various dual language models specifying goals, target populations, languages used, and sources where detailed descriptions of such programs can be found.

National education programs, school districts, and individual institutions provide bilingual education programs for a variety of purposes such as enrichment,

TABLE 1.1

Dual Language Models

Model	Goal	Target Population	Language	Sources
Two-way	Bilingualism	Majority and minority	L1 and L2	Lindholm-Leary, 2001; Center for Applied Linguistics, 2002
Maintenance	Bilingualism	Minority	L1 and L2	McCarty, 2002
Mainstream bilingual education	Bilingualism	Majority; international	L1 and 2	Mackey, 1972
Bilingual immersion	Bilingualism	Majority	L2 then L1 added	Lambert & Tucker, 1972; Johnson & Swain, 1997
Bilingual programs for the deaf	Bilingualism	Deaf students	Sign Language and L2	Gibson et al., 1997
Sequential bilingual education	Bilingualism	Majority (speaks a language other than the official)	L1 and Official language	Obondo, 1997
Transitional bilingual education (TBE)	L2 learning	Minority	L1 and then L2	Ovando & Collier, 1998
Pull-out TBE	L2 learning	Minority	L2 with some L1 support	Brisk, 1998
Integrated TBE	L2 learning	Minority with majority	L2 and L1 for a limited amount of time	Glenn & De Jong, 1996
Bilingual structured immersion	L2 learning	Minority	L2 with limited L1 support	Gersten et al., 1998

Gersten, Baker, & Keating, 1998; Lindholm-Leary, 2001; Mackey, 1972; McCarty, 2002; and Ovando & Collier, 1998.

maintenance, educational assistance for language diverse populations, language re-vitalization, education of the deaf, serving transient populations, and serving bilingual communities or countries.

A bilingual program is said to have *enrichment* as a goal when the students do not learn the language because of need but because parents want them to be fluent in a second language. In Hungary, bilingual education programs were created to develop fluency in English, German, Russian, Italian, or Spanish. History, mathematics, physics, biology, and geography are subjects often taught in the foreign language for at least three academic periods. The goal is to master the content area in both Hungarian and a foreign language (Duff, 1997).

Bilingual programs are created when political unity achieved under a dominant language leaves minority languages in a precarious situation. In the United States, Australia, and many other countries such programs are usually created either to *maintain* the heritage language of such groups or to *assist* the speakers of these languages while they acquire the societal language. In Slovenia, Italian and Hungarian minorities have the right to bilingual education in Slovenian and either Italian or Hungarian to maintain fluency in the heritage language (Novak Lukanovic, 1995). A variety of dual language models exist to help minority populations acquire fluency in the societal language. Transitional bilingual education (TBE), pull-out TBE, integrated TBE, and bilingual structured immersion programs temporarily use the heritage language while the students learn the societal language. Such programs are common in Australia (Gibbons, 1997), Africa (Bunyi, 1997), and the Americas (Faltis, 1997).

Bilingual programs are created to *revitalize* languages that are close to disappearing. Such efforts are springing up around the world with varying degrees of success (Christian & Genesee, 2001; Cummins & Corson, 1997; Johnson & Swain, 1997). Bilingual immersion programs in Catalonia serve Catalan and Spanish-speaking students. Catalan is the medium of instruction from kindergarten to third grade in all schools. Beginning in third grade, one and then two content area courses are offered in Spanish (Artigal, 1997).

Bilingual programs for the *deaf* employ both signing and the written form of the societal language. The purpose of these programs is to educate deaf learners in the language that is most natural to them (i.e., a sign language) while they also gain access to material written in the societal language. These programs promote the culture of the deaf as well as the larger societal culture (Gibson, Small, & Mason, 1997). A two-way preschool bilingual program was established in Southern California to help deaf, hard of hearing, and hearing children with deaf family members learn in both ASL and English (Allen, 2002).

Bilingual international schools serve *transient* populations the world over often using English and the national language for instruction. Nationals often enroll children in these programs to encourage their bilingualism. L'Ecole Bilingue in Cambridge, Massachusetts, attracts both European speakers of French and native English-speaking Americans. Preschool and kindergarten are taught completely in French with 1 hour of English a day. From first through sixth grade teaching-time is equally divided between English and French. (The French-American International School of Boston, 2002). In India, a country of over 1,000 languages, children of transient government employees are educated in Hindi and English. Usually Hindi is used for the humanities and English for the sciences and mathematics (Sridhar, 1991).

Bilingual communities create programs to promote fluency in the languages they use and need. In much of Africa where multiple languages are used, schools often implement sequential bilingual programs. Tribal languages are used for the very early years and then the language of education switches to the official language (Obondo, 1997). Hong Kong has a similar system. Chinese is used in elementary education and English at the secondary level except for Chinese and Chinese history (Johnson, 1997).

Multilingual programs have as a goal fluency in more than two languages. They serve the population in communities that for historical reasons use several languages or transient populations of varied nationalities. The international value of English has increased the emergence of multilingual programs among those communities that already promote dual language education.

In a number of countries or regions, all students participate in multilingual programs (see Table 1.2). The heritage language is often used during the early years whereas the others are introduced later. Second or third languages are usually taught as a subject before becoming a language of instruction. Such systems are established to respond to the multilingual nature of countries. In Luxemburg the goal is to develop trilingual citizens in Luxemburgish, French, and German. Schools teach in Luxemburgish, the native language of all citizens, in preschool and first grade; in German, the language of the media and church, during the rest of elementary school; and in French, the government language, in high school (Hoffman, 1998).

TABLE 1.2
Multilingual Models

Model	Goal	Target Population	Language	Sources
Multilingual educational systems	Multilingualism	Whole country	L1, L2, and L3	Hoffman, 1998
European schools	Multilingualism	European Union officials' children	L1, L2, and L3 (L4 optional)	Hoffman, 1998; Housen, 2002
Double immersion	Multilingualism	Religious/cultural group	French, English, Hebrew	Genesee, 1998
Dual language + English	Multilingualism	Minority and majority	L1, L2, and English	Cenoz, 1998

The European School model serves the children of European Union officials. As they move within the union, they continue their education without disruptions. Students' heritage language, the medium of instruction at least until Grade 8, continues as a subject until Grade 12. Foreign language (French, English, or German) learning starts in the first year of primary school. This language becomes a primary language of instruction in secondary school. A third language is introduced in Grades 8 to 10. Students can choose a fourth language in the final 2 years of schooling (Housen, 2002).

Parents and educators in dual-language programs often want children to develop fluency in English, the international language of the moment. Such programs are found in Europe, Israel, and other countries with national languages other than English. The Lauro Ikastola school, in the Basque region in Spain, houses a trilingual program. Students include both Spanish-speakers and Basque-speakers. The goals are competency in Basque and Spanish as well as oral and written proficiency in English beyond survival skills (Cenoz, 1998).

A unique trilingual model for the purpose of introducing a language related to the heritage, although not the first language of the students, is double immersion education. Following the bilingual immersion model, private schools in Montreal catering to upper- and middle-class English-speaking Jewish children implement different versions of this model. The goal is to develop trilingualism in Hebrew, French, and English (Genesee, 1998).

BILINGUAL EDUCATION IN THE WORLD

Bilingual education is an educational practice with an ancient history and worldwide application. Most countries in the world offer bilingual programs in either public or private schools and often in both. Typically the national or official language is used for instruction, whereas the other language can be indigenous (aboriginal languages in Australia), another official language (Quechua in Peru), regional (Catalan in Spain), the language of immigrants (Ukranian in Canada), the language of guest workers (Turkish in Denmark), an international language (English in Indonesia), or the language of sojourners (Japanese in the United States).

Bilingual education dates from 3000 B.C. when scribes in Mesopotamia were taught in both Sumerian and Akkadian (Lewis, 1977). The specific languages used in bilingual programs have changed over time in different countries but the rationale for bilingual education has not changed much. Bilingual education is employed to meet two objectives: educational goals and sociopolitical concerns. Educational systems and families often create bilingual education programs to promote fluency in a second language that enjoys prestige or economical importance. Multilingual nations, mass migrations, colonization, official status of languages, and concerns for language minorities also call for bilingual education.

Elite Bilingual Education

Elites the world over have fostered prestigious languages. Romans promoted the learning of Greek until Latin was considered "the sole safeguard of man's store of culture, science and faith" (Lewis, 1977, p. 27). French dominated the European high culture for several centuries. From England to Russia, poets and authors used French as their preferred language (Lewis, 1977). The growth of science in Germany during the 19th and early 20th centuries spurred teaching of German among budding scientists in Europe and North America.

English is the language of prestige of the moment. It is one of the main or official languages in more than 60 countries. About 400 million people speak English as a first language, whereas 350 million speak it as a second language. It is currently the preferred foreign language of study in the world. English is considered a key to global communication in many fields such as science, technology, medicine, mass media, the World Wide Web, research, and transnational business (Baker & Prys Jones, 1998; Brutt-Griffler, 2002).

Elites recognize that limited teaching of a language, as in foreign language programs, seldom results in high levels of fluency. In many countries bilingual education programs that include the national language and a language of prestige are common in schools, especially in private schools frequented by children from affluent homes (Baker & Prys Jones, 1998).

The present trend toward globalization sparks interest for bilingual abilities. Ironically, at a time that bilingual education is under fire in the United States, educated middle-class parents increasingly pressure public school systems to offer two-way and second language immersion programs. At least 260 two-way bilingual programs have developed in the United States mostly in the past 10 years. In these programs, English speakers and speakers of another language learn side-by-side in both languages. The majority is in Spanish at the elementary level. Other languages used are French, Chinese, Korean, and Navajo. A few expand to the high school level (Center for Applied Linguistics, 2002).

During the mid-60s, English-speaking parents in St. Lambert, Quebec, realizing that economic survival in Quebec would require proficiency in French, supported changes in the way schools taught French. As a result, a new model of bilingual education, French immersion, appeared. French immersion programs, which started as a pilot experiment, are presently an educational option throughout Canada. Adaptations of this model have spread worldwide as a way to educate middle- and upper-class non-native speakers in a language that has prestige or economic value (Swain & Johnson, 1997).

An Educational Option for Language Diverse Groups

Political entities have always included speakers of different languages. In a world of about 200 countries and 6,000 languages, multilingual nations are the rule not the exception. Colonization, wars, and migration changed the linguistic landscape. In the 19th century, universal education turned schools into a tool to impose and spread the use of the languages (and language varieties) of those with power.

Language education policies in multilingual nations are complex and vulnerable to ideological changes. Those who speak a high-status language and want to maintain power, promote use of their language in education. They claim that speakers of languages or language varieties with low-social status are best educated in their (high status) language. They feel that this knowledge will give them a fair chance to compete in society (Porter, 1996; Rodriguez, 1982). Others argue that different linguistic communities have a right to education in their language (Skutnabb-Kangas, 1988) or that initiating instruction in home language accelerates literacy in all languages (Cummins, 1984; Modiano, 1968).

For many years nations tended to require education in a language based on national needs. Accordingly, the official language or the language of power in a nation is often viewed as the natural vehicle for instruction. The result was that many children were educated in their second language. A pioneering study conducted by the United Nations Educational, Scientific and Cultural Organization (UNESCO) revealed that children educated in their second language experienced difficulties in school and that the home language is critical because it is the vehicle through "which a child absorbs the cultural environment" (UNESCO, 1953, p. 47). As a result of this report, the second half of the 20th century witnessed a resurgence of interest in using students' mother tongue for instruction.

Colonization spread the power of the European languages around the world as they became fundamental for government and education. Upon gaining independence, countries where the colonizers became the majority (the Americas, Australia, and New Zealand) through massive migration, brutal conquest, and imported diseases, colonial languages became societal languages. As a result, indigenous populations now represent only a small percentage of such countries' population. Economic and political immigration of the past two centuries complicated the linguistic and demographic composition of these countries.

Educational policies in these countries belatedly considered indigenous populations; however, non-indigenous populations were overlooked or merely offered temporary educational assistance. The United States and Canada are exceptions. In these two countries large populations of native speakers of Spanish or French exerted pressure to establish bilingual education. Their work inspired and supported bilingual education for other non-indigenous groups. Bilingual programs for indigenous populations exist in these two countries, but their numbers are small when compared to services for immigrant populations (Begay et al., 1995; Heimbecker, 1997; Jacobs & Cross, 2001).

In New Zealand and Latin America, after years of imposing colonial languages in education and government, new appreciation for the languages of indigenous populations sparked some policy reversals. In New Zealand, Maori, the sole indigenous language, was endangered when, in 1970, Maori-medium schools opened. By 1997, 19.3% of the Maori students were enrolled in Maori–English bilingual programs and 18.1% were learning Maori as a subject (Benton, 2001; Durie, 1997). Similarly in Bolivia, a country where 63% of the population are native speakers of indigenous languages (primarily Aymara and Quechua), bilingual education programs emerged, also in the 1970s. Bolivia's education reform plan of 1994 requires public schools to use indigenous languages as the medium of instruction or at least offer it as a language class in addition to Spanish (Hornberger & Lopez, 1998).

Bilingual education for both immigrants and indigenous populations exists in Australia whose federal government more readily supports programs for the aborigine than for the immigrant (Gibbons, 1997). An interesting feature of the Australian situation is that many aborigine children do not speak their ancestral languages used in the bilingual programs. Instead their native language is either aborigine English or Kriol, languages that have low status even among the aborigine elders who oppose their use in education (Harris & Devlin, 1997).

The colonial legacies in Africa and Asia are, of course, quite different because European migration was not nearly as massive and the indigenous populations survived, almost intact. The European population, which constitutes a small minority in Africa and Asia, nevertheless successfully imposed their languages on government and business elites. In the process of decolonization, many independent countries replaced the artificially imposed European languages with traditional languages as the official language. Others, for commercial or other reasons, actually continued the metropolitan practice of advancing European languages over local ones. Bilingual education has been used in both settings, that is, where local languages dominate as well as where colonial languages retain their place.

In Kenya, Kiswahili—an African language widely used in West Africa—was added as a main language of instruction. Both Kiswahili and English are taught from first grade. Tribal languages are also used for instruction where there is a substantial concentration of speakers. Beginning in Grade 4, English becomes the sole language of instruction (Bunyi, 1997). Although 22 out of 34 African countries reported using indigenous languages in education, "practices in many African countries show a trend toward the increasing use of colonial languages as media of instruction" (Obondo, 1997, p. 26).

Shifts in language policies appeared also in Asia. Upon formation of the federation of Malaysia in 1957, schools taught in either Malay, Tamil, Chinese, or English at the elementary level and Malay and English at the secondary level. The increase in power of indigenous populations promoted Malay as the predominant language of instruction. Whereas relatively few schools use Tamil or Mandarin as a medium of instruction, English has been relegated to the status of a foreign language.

India faces the greatest linguistic challenge with hundreds of local languages, 15 regional official languages, a national official language (Hindi), and English, which remains widely used. "One aim of Indian education is for children to become competent in their native language plus Hindi and English" (Baker & Prys Jones, 1998, p. 464). In reality, students are educated in their native or regional language in the early grades. In Hindi-speaking regions, this language is favored, whereas in non-Hindi regions English is preferred (Schiffman, 1999; Sridhar, 1991).

China, the one remaining empire in the world, includes Tibetan, Mongolian, Kazak, and Korean speakers among many others. China eluded European colonization, except in Macao and Hong Kong. Its educational policies toward language minorities have fluctuated between pluralism to monolingualism aimed at imposing Mandarin. The current stance, once again, embraces both Mandarin and another language as media of instruction. Some schools use only one as the medium of instruction and the other language taught as a subject. Use of a writing system and extending bilingual education to the university level, among other topics, are still being debated (Zhou, 2001).

Shifts in boundaries between countries, economic conditions, and political changes complicate the linguistic composition in European countries. Different linguistic groups survive within countries. Bilingual education emerged to satisfy the educational and identity needs of these groups. Ancient groups like the Frisians in the Northern Netherlands preserved their language as either a medium of instruction or taught as a language in all schools of the region so that teacher preparation in regional programs at the university level must offer Frisian (Gorter, 1997). Bilingual programs for majority students develop language proficiency in the languages of important minority groups. In Finland, Finnish/Swedish immersion programs serve Finnish speakers and an increasing number of bilingual families resulting from mixed marriages (Bjorklund, 1997). Other programs aim at revitalizing languages on the brink of extinction as in the case of Wales. About one fifth of all elementary and secondary schools in Wales are now bilingual. In other schools, Welsh is taught as either a first or second language (Baker, 1997).

The influx of guest workers and immigrants during the past century present new challenges, especially in Europe. Europeans, used to dealing with language policy and education with respect to their own populations, assumed responsibilities for children of foreign laborers. Some countries created mother tongue language programs presuming, sometimes hoping, that the families would return to their place of origin and children would need to function in their own countries. Other countries created transitional programs where students' heritage language is used temporarily. In the Netherlands students spend a year in the program where the native language is used for instruction and orientation to the new school system. Other schools created "consolidated" programs integrating immigrant students with nationals (Glenn & De Jong, 1996).

Political changes alter the status of languages in a society and their use in education. The end of Franco's dictatorship in Spain featured recognition of the major languages, including Catalan, Basque, Valencian, and Galician. Both Catalunia and the Basque provinces have since experimented with schools using Spanish and their regional language. The dissolution of the Soviet Union and the retreat of colonial powers in Asia and Africa necessitated changes in language policy. In 1992, Estonia's newly independent Ministry of Education established Estonian as the language of instruction for all levels of education. Under the Soviet regime, Russian had been the main language of instruction.

PRESENT TRENDS IN BILINGUAL EDUCATION

In the 21st century language policies in education are influenced by two contradictory policies: promotion of bilingual education for the majority students and rejection of bilingual education for minority students. Economic and political connections across the planet influence language policies. To prepare their citizens to participate in global affairs, schools support bilingual programs to develop high levels of proficiency in foreign languages.

Increasing immigration to developed nations often produces xenophobic responses including rejection of bilingual instruction for those who are not native speakers of the national language. Bilingualism and maintenance of the heritage language is considered subversive and unpatriotic, whereas proficiency in the national language is imperative. What is problematic is that "such unitary linguistic philosophy is taken as the most natural state of affairs" (Lewis, 1977, p. 25) rather than as a more recent historical development. The rise of middle classes, industrialization, and the development of the European nation–state established the importance of local national languages. The move to universal education further encouraged imposition of the language of those in power on the masses. Those who oppose bilingual education because, they claim, it subverts political unity do not seem to be aware that there is no evidence that a "uniformist language policy does safeguard the integrity of a linguistically diverse state" (Lewis, 1977, p. 25).

Such opposition to bilingual education for language minorities is reflected in the English-only movement that has been sweeping the United States since the 1980s. This movement promoted English as the official language. Although legislation at the federal level has not succeeded, 23 states have passed such legislation (Crawford, 2000).[2] Recently attacks have been directed to bilingual education proper. Since 1998 California, Arizona, and Massachusetts voters approved a referendum requiring replacement of bilingual education by 1 year of English immersion followed by immediate integration into mainstream classrooms (Crawford, 2002b). Little public understanding of bilingual education contributed to the passage of such measures. Opponents of bilingual education are presently moving their efforts to other states.

Although at the federal level, the No Child Left Behind Act of 2001 supports bilingual programs, it also places great emphasis on assessment in English language proficiency and content areas. Schools feel increasing pressure to focus on English at the expense of heritage languages. Notably, the term "bilingual education" disappeared from the language of the legislation and offices supporting its implementation. The new term "English language acquisition," reflects the sentiment toward promotion of English only.

Throughout the world bilingual programs serving non-indigenous people are in jeopardy. Attacks are less often directed at programs that serve indigenous people. For example, Proposition 203 in Arizona does not affect American Indian students within or even outside reservations. In Australia bilingual programs for Aborigine receive more support than programs for immigrant populations. In many countries in Europe, controversies over bilingual education for guest workers contrast with the emergence of bilingual programs for indigenous minorities, such as the Welsh, Frisians, Basques, and others.

The implementation of bilingual education over time throughout the world has varied in form and support. When it was implemented as an enriching educational program, it received much support. Families cherish these schools because of their high quality. But proposals to implement bilingual education for minorities change depending on the ideology of those in power. These changes make programs unstable with negative consequences on students' educational success (Gibbons, 1997).

IMPLEMENTING BILINGUAL PROGRAMS

The actual implementation of bilingual programs involves a number of complex decisions with respect to personnel, status of the program within the school, specific language, literacy, and content area curriculum, instructional practices, and assessment measures. To coordinate all these components takes time. Consistent support during development and availability of resources affect ultimate implementation.

The process of implementation of programs has differed widely with noticeable effects on their success. Programs established after research and planning carried out by coalitions of administration, staff, families, and experts have a better chance to succeed from the very beginning. Coral Way in Dade County, Florida, a pioneer program in the United States, was initiated after research, planning, and curricula and staff development (Mackey & Beebe, 1977).

Once established, these programs monitor students' progress to test the soundness of their practices. From the first year of implementation, a team of linguists assessed language and academic skills as well as cognitive achievement of students enrolled in the French immersion program in St. Lambert school in Montreal (Lambert & Tucker, 1972). The Amigos program in Cambridge, Massachusetts, enlisted some of these same researchers to follow the progress of their students (Cazabon, Lambert, & Hall, 1993).

Programs responding to legislated mandates are typically developed in a rush without much time for planning, recruitment, and preparation of staff, development of curriculum, or acquisition of materials. The progress of students often goes unmonitored or, if it is assessed by district-mandated measures, the performance of students in bilingual programs is frequently not disaggregated. Such results are of little use to teachers or administrators seeking to gage the effectiveness of the program (Torres-Guzman, Abbate, Brisk, & Minaya-Rowe, 2002). It usually takes years of strong leadership for these programs to succeed. Only 12% of the students in the Rachel Carson School in Chicago were scoring at the state average when Kathleen Mayer became principal. Seven years later more than half of the students had reached or surpassed state standards. Yearly awards prove the continuous progress made by this school (Portraits of Success, 2002).

Shared Features of Successful Programs

Choosing an appropriate model does not ensure success.

> Programs that work almost invariably have a small set of very well-specified goals ... a clear set of procedures and materials linked to those goals, and frequent assessments that indicate whether or not students are reaching the goals. Effective programs leave little to chance. They incorporate many elements, such as research-based curricula, instructional methods, classroom management methods, assessments, and means of helping students who are struggling, all of which are tied in a coordinated fashion to the instructional goals. (Fashola, Slavin, Calderón, & Durán, 2001, p. 49)

Research on bilingual education demonstrates that successful programs share a number of features with respect to the school climate, curriculum, instruction, and assessment.

Successful bilingual programs exist in school environments that promote respect for the students and their families. Their languages and cultures are valued and incorporated in the curriculum. Students are well known by the staff, they are expected to achieve, and are supported in this effort. Families are welcome in the school and are considered partners in the education of the students. These schools embrace the bilingual program and consider it an important component of their educational mission. Three major characteristics support the quality and stability of good programs: strong and knowledgeable leadership, clear goals for the program, and quality personnel willing to help students succeed (Brisk, 1998; Carter & Chatfield, 1986; Lucas, Henze, & Donato, 1990).

Models, to a degree, determine the uses of the languages for instruction. Successful programs develop both languages and use them to promote academic achievement and sociocultural integration. Regardless of the language policy adopted, consistency of language use and cross-grade articulation help students' development. (Christian, Montone, Lindholm, & Carranza, 1997). Cultural considerations are essential in implementing sound curricula, choosing materials, interacting with and disciplining students, and understanding different ways to demonstrate knowledge. Quality bilingual programs offer a full range of curricular options and expanded possibilities for equal participation in extracurricular activities and other educational offerings in the school. Successful bilingual programs keep up to date with the research on curriculum and instruction. They seek to implement research-based practices (Fashola et al., 2001).

Good programs continually monitor their students' progress in both languages using multiple measures. For bilingual students assessment needs to include language and content. Evaluation of language proficiency and content knowledge need to be separated when carried out in the second language.

Controversial and Unresolved Practices

Despite general agreement on optimal practices, many implementation choices are still controversial or unresolved. Among them are:

- Language goals.
- Measuring academic achievement.
- Promoting sociocultural integration.
- Uses of language in the curriculum including a) language of literacy introduction, b) teaching language through content area, c) separation of languages in instruction.
- Incorporating culture.

- Grouping students by ability within grade level and by L2 proficiency across grade levels.
- Educating students with interrupted schooling.
- High-stakes testing.
- Segregating versus not segregating students.
- Native and instructional language of teachers.
- Parent involvement.

To be truly successful, bilingual programs must meet three basic goals for their students: Develop language and literacy, encourage academic achievement, and promote sociocultural integration (Brisk, 1998). Agreement, in theory, on these goals often obscures controversies regarding priorities and implementation.

The *language goals* of bilingual programs are an obvious source of controversy. "Bilingual instruction generally aims for [competing] goals: to transition students from a language they know to another language, or to add a language or languages so that students become bi- or multilingual" (Christian & Genesee, p. 1).

Emphasis on transition can result in what Lambert (1977) calls "subtractive bilingualism," students learn a second language at the cost of losing their first language. He believes bilingual programs should have "additive bilingualism" as a goal. To be successful, programs should promote the acquisition and development of both languages. In the United States all legislation supporting bilingual education gives a priority to the acquisition of English. Title III of the No Child Left Behind Act of 2001 states as its purpose "to help ensure that children who are limited English proficient, including immigrant children and youth, attain English proficiency, develop high levels of academic attainment in English" (The National Clearinghouse for Bilingual Education, 2001, p. 1).

Although there is no disagreement as to the need to promote *academic achievement*, educators and policymakers often disagree on how to measure it. The accountability movement sweeping the United States narrows the definition of academic success to passing standardized tests usually in English. Many educators believe that academic achievement should be demonstrated in a variety of ways, including performance in long-term projects that reflect skills required in real life situations (Sizer, 1992, 1995).

Issues of cultural identity have often been addressed in research on bilingual individuals (Portes & Rumbaut, 2001; Suárez-Orozco & Suárez-Orozco, 2002). Bilingual programs have been less purposeful in their goal of helping individuals define their cultural affiliation. Few programs explicitly address the goal of *sociocultural integration*, that is, adjustment to the new cultural environment while able to function in the heritage culture (Cazabon et al., 1993; De Jong, 2002).

There are still different approaches to the *use of the languages* and many unresolved or controversial issues such as the choice of language for initial literacy, use of content area for language instruction, and separation of languages for instruction. Bilingual programs often initiate students to literacy in their native language. Canadian immersion programs, however, do it in the students' second language, whereas other programs introduce literacy in both at the same time. All claim success in spite of their different approaches. When students' native language is a major language, such as Japanese in Japan, methods that introduce literacy in the second language work (Lambert & Tucker, 1972). When the native language is vulnerable, achieving literacy first in that language is essential (Cummins, 1984; Garcia, 2000). Despite research supporting the value of native language instruction, especially for literacy initiation, some parents and educators question its usefulness. In communities in Africa and Asia, European languages are essential to communicate globally. There is much resistance to introducing literacy in the local languages. A minority of parents and educators support initial education in the native languages as they are concerned by students' failure when educated in a foreign language, particularly in rural areas where the European languages have little use (Baker, 2002).

Some educators maintain that teaching content through a second language facilitates acquisition of a second language. Others point out that explicit language objectives must be included in the content lessons if language learning is to occur (Freeman & Freeman, 1998). Some programs strictly separate languages as a requirement for second language development. Other researchers emphasize the value of using both languages in literacy and content area teaching (Jacobson, 1990). Literacy development in the second language is often supported by the use of students' native language. Use of two languages helps develop skills writing, reading comprehension, and clarifying vocabulary (Lucas & Katz, 1994).

How *culture* is defined differs. Some schools believe that culture is introducing historical facts, highlighting traditions, and exhibiting artifacts (Nieto, 2000). In a deeper sense, culture influences many aspects of education such as curriculum content, assumptions about background knowledge, teaching approaches, classroom interaction and management, school routines, and parental participation. Schools that embrace this broader definition of culture have successfully educated children of diverse cultural backgrounds (Saravia-Shore & Arvizu, 1992).

Grouping students for instruction triggers controversy. Bilingual students vary among themselves in language proficiency and cognitive abilities, making grouping very complex. There are valid arguments for heterogeneous as well as homogeneous grouping. Heterogeneous grouping challenges students, whereas homogeneous grouping helps address specific needs (Radencich et al., 1995). Some programs group bilingual students for second language instruction by English ability across grade level. This type of grouping impedes integration of language with content instruction (Met, 1994).

An increasing educational problem faced by bilingual programs serving immigrant and refugee populations is *students with limited schooling*. Economic and political problems often interrupt schooling. Children leave school to help their families or they find themselves for months in refugee camps where little instruction takes place. Upon moving, if they are enrolled in school according to their age, they may be unable to cope with the curriculum. At issue is the language of instruction. Some question the wisdom of instructing them in their native language when they have so much to catch up and they need the language of school to further their education. Others maintain that, as with younger learners, the native language is an important tool for literacy and academic learning (Mace-Matluck, Alexander-Kasparik, & Queen, 1998).

Assessment of bilinguals is particularly controversial. In many countries, the *high-stakes nature of tests* creates barriers for language minority students in their progress through school. Often these students are retained, placed in special education classes, or drop out of school (Haney, 2002). In the United States, to cope with this predicament, schools have experimented with accommodations or have exempted bilingual learners from tests. Policies of accommodations (such as extended length of testing time, breaking up the tests, assessing in the native language or in both, providing dictionaries, reading items aloud, and others) are promoted by some but opposed by others (August & Hakuta, 1997; Rivera, Stansfield, Scialdone, & Sharkey, 2000). Of greater concern is the practice of exempting students. Although it sounds fair, the motivation is not to help students but to help raise the districts' total scores (Suárez-Orozco & Suárez-Orozco, 2002). Failing to monitor such students' performance can, in the long run, jeopardize their academic development.

Bilingual programs struggle with the dilemma of *segregation and integration*. Bilingual students have needs that require specialized attention requiring some level of segregation. Yet integration of language minorities with mainstream populations is essential for their education and social acceptance and enhances the education of majority students (Brisk, 1991; De Jong, 1996; Glenn & De Jong, 1996). Two-way programs have been questioned as to whether they serve minority students. Some believe that higher status of majority students is still reflected in these programs (Freeman, 1998). Some claim that language and academic needs of the majority students take priority in programmatic decisions (Valdez, 1997). The Barbieri two-way program in Framingham, Massachusetts, through assessment of students and changes in curriculum and language of instruction, addresses such concerns (De Jong, 2002).

Successful *bilingual teachers* need to be both academically prepared and able to function as advocates for bilingual students. The criterion for language fluency still stirs controversy. Some believe teachers should only teach in their native language. Yet, non-native speakers of either language can make significant contributions. In Australia, the bilingual programs for aborigenes assigned teachers to instruction strictly along native language lines. Over time, aborigene teachers acquired fluency in English and began taking over the instruction in English. The strategy led to strengthening the control of the programs by aborigene people (Harris & Devlin, 1997). On the other hand, having majority culture teachers as bilingual teachers often helps bridge the gap with school administrators (Brisk, 1991).

Parent participation in education is a cornerstone of student success. For many years most researchers assumed that this participation must include attending school meetings and other traditional mainstream ways of participation. Research among families of various cultures challenges these assumptions, demonstrating that participation in education can take different forms with comparable success. The problem lies in the misunderstandings between schools and home as to what constitutes parental participation in education (Trumball, Rothstein-Fisch, Greenfield, & Quiroz, 2001).

CONCLUDING THOUGHTS

Bilingual education programs have in common the use of two or more languages for instruction, but that is where the similarities end. The reasons for developing programs are varied, the models are multiple, and the specific ways of implementing each component pit researchers against each other. Programs are mostly developed either to enhance the education of students or to support a language policy. Programs created to educate students and provide them with the advantage of bilingualism usually require combined efforts of communities and educators, sometimes supported by the local education system. Most common are programs established to develop language skills of students in entire regions or countries. The need for such programs emerges from the multilingual nature of countries, the establishment of an official language or languages, the need to develop a common language for broader communication, and the affirmation of ethnic groups.

Programs developed by edict to educate students in particular languages ostensibly have an educational goal but, in reality, follow a political agenda to impose or support a particular language, with much less attention to the needs of individual students. Such is the case of transitional programs that aim at imposing languages of power in a nation, programs for guest workers in the language of their country regardless of the native language of the students, and revitalization programs in a language that children never spoke. The creation of such programs often has a credible rationale. Nations want their citizens to share a language, whereas communities are concerned with the rapid extinction of their heritage languages. Proponents should never lose sight that the goal of education is to develop children and not to defend languages. Such programs require strong leaders and caring teachers who never forget that their main charge are the students. Monitoring students' academic and linguistic development, as well as patterns of sociocultural affiliation, are better measures of success than whether a particular language dominates the curriculum.

Controversies surrounding bilingual education are often reflected in contradictory research promoted to defend various stances. Unfortunately, research is too often manipulated to support particular ideologies. Moreover, educational policy sadly disregards research in bilingual education and imposes the governmental ideology of the moment. Neither bilingual education programs nor the controversy about them will ever go away. Great variation in models, changes in policies, and disagreements about specific implementation practices illustrate the variability and changing nature of bilingual education implementation. The quest for the perfect model is unrealistic and misguided. Children are best served with research that looks at specific practices leading to educating families and teachers on ways that children develop and learn in different languages. To best serve a defined group of students research must be contextual and implementation should bring together families, schools, and policy-makers.

NOTES

1. As defined by Nieto (2000) "consists of the values, traditions, social and political relationships, and worldview created, shared, and transformed by a group of people bound together by a common history, geographic location, language, social class and/or religion." (p. 139).
2. For frequent updates check Crawford, 2002a.

REFERENCES

Allen, B. M. (2002). ASL-English bilingual classroom: The families' perspectives. *Bilingual Research Journal, 26,* 1–20.

Artigal, J. (1997). The Catalan immersion program. In K. Johnson and M. Swain (Eds.). Immersion education: International perspectives (pp. 133–150). Cambridge: Cambridge University Press.

August, D., & Hakuta, K. (1997). *Improving schooling for language-minority children: A research agenda.* Washington, DC: National Academy Press.

Baker, C. (1997). Bilingual education in Ireland, Scotland, and Wales. In J. Cummins & D. Corson (Eds.), *Encyclopedia of language and education* (Vol. 5, Bilingual Education, pp. 127–141). Dordrecht, The Netherlands: Kluwer Academic.

Baker, C., & Prys Jones, S. (1998). *Encyclopedia of bilingualism and bilingual education.* Clevedon, UK: Multilingual Matters.

Baker, V. (2002). *Native language versus national language literacy: Choices and dilemmas in school instruction medium.* Retrieved June 3, 2003 from http://www.literacyonline.org/products/ili/webdocs/ilproc/ilprocvb.htm

Begay, S., Sells Dick, G., Estell, D. W., Estell, J., McCarty, T. L., & Sells, A. (1995). Change from the inside out: A story of transformation in a Navajo community school. *Bilingual Research Journal, 19*(1), 121–139.

Benton, R. A. (2001). Balancing tradition and modernity: A natural approach to Maori language revitalization in a New Zealand secondary school. In D. Christian & F. Genesee (Eds.), *Bilingual education* (pp. 95–108). Alexandria, VA: Teachers of English to Speakers of Other Languages.

Bjorklund, S. (1997). Immersion in Finland in the 1990s. A state of development and expansion. In R. K. Johnson & M. Swain (Eds.), *Immersion education: International perspectives* (pp. 85–101). Cambridge, UK: Cambridge University Press.

Brisk, M. E. (1991). Toward multilingual and multicultural mainstream education. *Journal of Education, 173*(2), 114–129.

Brisk, M. E. (1998). *Bilingual education: From compensatory to quality schooling.* Mahwah, NJ: Lawrence Erlbaum Associates.

Brutt-Griffler, J. (2002). *World English. A study of its development.* Clevedon, UK: Multilingual Matters.

Bunyi, G. (1997). Language in education in Kenian Schools. In J. Cummins & D. Corson (Eds.), *Encyclopedia of language and education* (Vol. 5, Bilingual Education, pp. 33–43). Dordrecht, The Netherlands: Kluwer Academic.

Carter, T., & Chatfield, M. (1986). Effective schools for language minority students. *American Journal of Education, 97,* 200–233.

Casanova, U., & Arias, M. B. (1993). Contextualizing bilingual education. In M. B. Arias & U. Casanova (Eds.), *Bilingual education: Politics, practice and research* (pp. 1–35). Chicago: University of Chicago Press.

Cazabon, M., Lambert, W. E., & Hall, G. (1993). *Two-way bilingual education: A progress report on the Amigos program.* Santa Cruz, CA: The National Center for Research on Cultural Diversity and Second Language Learning.

Cenoz, J. (1998). Multilingual education in the Basque Country. In J. Cenoz & F. Genesse (Eds.), *Beyond bilingualism. Multilingualism and multilingual education* (pp. 175–191). Clevedon, UK: Multilingual Matters.

Cenoz, J., & Genesee, F. (1998). Introduction. In J. Cenoz & F. Genesee (Eds.), *Beyond bilingualsim: Multilingualism and multilingual education* (pp. vii–x). Clevedon, UK: Multilingual Matters.

Center for Applied Linguistics. (2002). *Directory of two-way bilingual immersion programs in the U.S.* Retrieved 05/15/02 from http://www.cal.org/twi/directory/

Christian, D., & Genesee, F. (2001). Bilingual education: Context and programs. In D. Christian & F. Genesee (Eds.), *Bilingual education* (pp. 1–7). Alexandria, VA: Teachers of English to Speakers of Other Languages.

Christian, D., Montone, C., Lindholm, K., & Carranza, I. (1997). *Profiles in two-way immersion education.* McHenry, IL: Center of Applied Linguistics and Delta Systems.

Crawford, J. (2000). *At war with diversity: U.S. language policy in an age of anxiety.* Clevedon, UK: Multilingual Matters.

Crawford, J. (2002a). *Language legislation in the U.S.A.* Retrieved December 10, 2002 from http://ourworld. compuserve. com/homepages/JWCRAWFORD/langleg.htm

Crawford, J. (2002b). *Proposition 203: Anti-bilingual initiative in Arizona.* Retrieved 06/05/02 from http:// ourworld.compuserve.com/homepages/JWCRAWFORD/az-unz.htm

Cummins, J. (1984). *Bilingualism and special education: Issues in assessment and pedagogy.* Clevedon, UK: Multilingual Matters.

Cummins, J., & Corson, D. (Eds.). (1997). *Encyclopedia of language and education* (Vol. 5, Bilingual Education). Dordrecht, The Netherlands: Kluwer Academic.

De Jong, E. J. (1996). Integrating language minority education in elementary schools. Unpublished dissertation. Boston University, Boston, MA.

De Jong, E. (2002). Effective bilingual education: From theory to academic achievement in a two-way bilingual program. *Bilingual Research Journal, 26*(1), 65–86.

Duff, P. (1997). Immersion in Hungary. An EFL experiment. In R. K. Johnson & M. Swain (Eds.), *Immersion education: International perspectives* (pp. 19–43). Cambridge, UK: Cambridge University Press.

Durie, A. (1997). Maori–English bilingual education in New Zealand. In J. Cummins & D. Corson (Eds.), *Encyclopedia of language and education* (Vol. 5, Bilingual Education, pp. 15–23). Dordrecht, The Netherlands: Kluwer Academic.

Faltis, C. (1997). Bilingual education in the United States. In J. Cummins & D. Corson (Eds.), *Encyclopedia of Language and Education* (Vol. 5, Bilingual Education, pp. 189–197). Dordrecht, The Netherlands: Kluwer Academic.

Fashola, O. S., Slavin, R. E., Calderón, M., & Durán, R. (2001). Effective programs for Latino students in elementary and middle schools. In R. E. Slavin & M. Calderón (Eds.), *Effective programs for Latino students* (pp. 1–66). Mahwah, NJ: Lawrence Erlbaum Associates.

Freeman, R. D. (1998). *Bilingual education and social change.* Clevendon, UK: Multilingual Matters.

Freeman, Y. S., & Freeman, D. E. (1998). *ESL/EFL teaching: Principles for success.* Portsmouth, NH: Heinemann.

French-American International School of Boston. (2002). Retrieved 6/6/02 from www.ecolebilingue.org

Garcia, G. E. (2000). Bilingual children's reading. In M. L. Kamil, P. B. Mosenthal, P. D. Pearson, & R. Barr (Eds.), *Handbook of reading research* (Vol. III, pp. 813–834). Mahwah, NJ: Lawrence Erlbaum Associates.

Genesee, F. (1998). A case study of multilingual education in Canada. In J. Cenoz & F. Genesse (Eds.), *Beyond bilingualism. Multilingualism and multilingual education* (pp. 243–258). Clevedon, UK: Multilingual Matters.

Gersten, R., Baker, S., & Keating, T. (1998). El Paso programs for English language learners: A longitudinal follow-up study. *READ Perspectives, 1,* 4–28.

Gibbons, J. (1997). Australian bilingual education. In J. Cummins & D. Corson (Eds.), *Encyclopedia of language and education* (pp. 207–215). Dorderecht, The Netherlands: Kluwer Academic.

Gibson, H., Small, A., & Mason, D. (1997). Deaf bilingual bicultural education. In J. Cummins & D. Corson (Eds.), *Encyclopedia of language and education* (Vol. 5, Bilingual Education, pp. 231–240). Dordrecht, The Netherlands: Kluwer Academic.

Glenn, C. L., & De Jong, E. J. (1996). *Educating immigrant children: Schools and language minorities in twelve nations.* New York: Garland.

Gorter, D. (1997). Bilingual education in Friesland. In J. Cummins & D. Corson (Eds.), *Encyclopedia of language and education* (Vol. 5, Bilingual Education, pp. 117–125). Dordrecht, The Netherlands: Kluwer Academic.

Grosjean, F. (1989). Neurolinguists, beware! The bilingual is not two monolinguals in one person. *Brain and Language, 36,* 3–15.

Haney, W. (2002). Revealing illusions of educational progress: Texas high-stakes tests and minority student performance. In Z. Beykont (Ed.), *The power of culture: Teaching across language differences* (pp. 25–42). Cambridge, MA: Harvard Education.

Harris, S., & Devlin, B. (1997). Bilingual programs involving aboriginal languages in Australia. In J. Cummins & D. Corson (Eds.), *Encyclopedia of language and education* (Vol. 5, Bilingual Education, pp. 1–14). Dordrecht, The Netherlands: Kluwer Academic.

Heimbecker, C. (1997). Bilingual education for indigenous groups in Canada. In J. Cummins & D. Corson (Eds.), *Encyclopedia of language and education* (Vol. 5, Bilingual Education, pp. 57–65). Dordrecht, The Netherlands: Kluwer Academic.

Hoffman, C. (1998). Luxembourg and the European school. In J. Cenoz & F. Genesse (Eds.), *Beyond bilingualism. Multilingualism and multilingual education* (pp. 143–174). Clevedon, UK: Multilingual Matters.

Hornberger, N., & Lopez, L. E. (1998). Policy, possibility and paradox: Indigenous multilingualism and education in Peru and Bolivia. In J. Cenoz & F. Genesee (Eds.), *Beyond bilingualism. Multilingualism and multilingual education* (pp. 206–242). Clevedon, UK: Multilingual Matters.

Housen, A. (2002). Processes and outcomes in the European schools model of multilingual education. *Bilingual Research Journal, 26*(1), 44–64.

Jacobs, K. t. A., & Cross, A. n. E. J. (2001). The seventh generation of Kahnawá:ke: Phoenix or dinosaur. In D. Christian & F. Genesee (Eds.), *Bilingual education* (pp. 109–121). Alexandria, VA: Teachers of English to Speakers of Other Languages.

Jacobson, R. (1990). Allocating two languages as a key feature of a bilingual methodology. In R. Jacobson & C. Faltis (Eds.), *Language distribution issues in schooling* (pp. 3–17). Clevedon, UK: Multilingual Matters.

Johnson, R. K. (1997). The Hong Kong education system. Late immersion under stress. In R. K. Johnson & M. Swain (Eds.), *Immersion education: International perspectives* (pp. 171–189). Cambridge, UK: Cambridge University Press.

Johnson, R. K., & Swain, M. (1997). *Immersion education: International perspectives.* Cambridge, UK: Cambridge University Press.

Lambert, W. E. (1977). The effects of bilingualism in the individual: Cognitive and sociocultural consequences. In P. A. Hornby (Ed.), *Bilingualism: Psychological, social, and educational implications* (pp. 15–27). New York: Academic Press.

Lambert, W. E., & Tucker, R. (1972). *Bilingual education of children: The St. Lambert experiment.* Rowley, MA: Newbury House.

Lewis, E. G. (1977). Bilingualism and bilingual education: The ancient world to the Renaissance. In B. Spolsky & R. Cooper (Eds.), *Frontiers of bilingual education* (pp. 22–93). Rowley, MA: Newbury House.

Lindholm-Leary, K. J. (2001). *Dual language education.* Clevedon, UK: Multilingual Matters.

Lucas, T., Henze, R., & Donato, R. (1990). Promoting the success of Latino linguistic minority students in high schools. *Harvard Educational Review, 60,* 315–340.

Lucas, T., & Katz, A. (1994). Reframing the debate: The roles of native languages in English-only programs for language minority students. *TESOL Quarterly, 28,* 537–561.

Mace-Matluck, B., Alexander-Kasparik, R., & Queen, R. (1998). *Though the golden door. Educational approaches for immigrant adolescents with limited schooling.* McHenry, IL: Center for Applied Linguistics.

Mackey, W. F. (1968). The description of bilingualism. In J. A. Fishman (Ed.), *Readings in the sociology of language* (pp. 554–584). The Hague: Mouton.

Mackey, W. F. (1972). *Bilingual education in a binational school.* Rowley, MA: Newbury House.

Mackey, W. F., & Beebe, V. N. (1977). *Bilingual schools for a bicultural community: Miami's adaptation to the Cuban refugees.* Rowley, MA: Newbury House.

McCarty, T. (2002). *A place to be Navajo: Rough Rock and the struggle for self-determination in indigenous schooling.* Mahwah, NJ: Lawrence Erlbaum Associates.

Met, M. (1994). Teaching content through a second language. In F. Genesee (Ed.), *Educating second language children: The whole child, the whole curriculum, the whole community* (pp. 159–182). Cambridge, UK: Cambridge University Press.

Modiano, N. (1968). National or mother tongue language in beginning reading: A comparative study. *Reasearch in the Teaching of English, 2,* 32–43.

National Clearinghouse for Bilingual Education. (2001). No Child Left Behind Act of 2001. Washington, DC: Author.

Nieto, S. (2000). *Affirming diversity: The sociopolitical context of multicultural education.* New York: Longman.

Novak Lukanovic, S. (1995). Overlapping cultures and plural identities. Rapport on the Conference of June 19–29, 1994, Ljubljana Slovenia. Ljubljana: National Commission for UNESCO, Institute for Ethnic Studies.

Obondo, M. A. (1997). Bilingual education in Africa: An overview. In J. Cummins & D. Corson (Eds.), *Encyclopedia of language and education* (Vol. 5, Bilingual Education, pp. 25–32). Dordrecht, The Netherlands: Kluwer Academic.

Ovando, C. J., & Collier, V. P. (1998). *Bilingual and ESL classrooms: Teaching in multicultural contexts* (2nd ed.). Boston: McGraw-Hill.

Porter, R. P. (1994, May 18). Goals 2000 and the bilingual student. *Education Week,* 44.

Porter, R. P. (1996). *Forked tongue. The politics of bilingual education* (2nd ed.). New Bruswick, NJ: Transaction.

Portes, A., & Rumbaut, R. G. (2001). *Legacies: The story of the immigrant second generation.* Berkeley: University of California Press.

Portraits of Success. (2002). *Rachel Carson elementary, transitional bilingual education.* Retrieved 6/13/02, 10/14/2000 from http://www.lab.brown.edu/public/NABE/portraits.taf?_function=detail&Data_entry_uid1=3

Radencich, M. C., McKay, L. J., Paratore, J. R., Plaza, G. L., Lustgarten, K. E., Nelms, P. et al. (1995). Implementing flexible grouping with a common reading selection. In M. Radencich & J. L. McKay

(Eds.), *Flexible groupings for literacy in the elementary grades* (pp. 43–65). Needham Heights, MA: Allyn & Bacon.

Rivera, C., Stansfield, C. W., Scialdone, L., & Sharkey, M. (2000). *An analysis of state policy for the inclusion and accommodation of English language learners in state assessment programs during 1998–1999.* Arlington, VA: The George Washington University Center of Equity and Excellence in Education.

Rodriguez, R. (1982). *Hunger of memory: The education of Richard Rodriguez.* Boston, MA: D. R. Godine.

Romaine, S. (1995). *Bilingualism.* Boston: Basil Blackwell.

Saravia-Shore, M., & Arvizu, S. (1992). *Cross-cultural literacy: Ethnographies of communication in multiethnic classrooms.* New York: Garland.

Schiffman, H. (1999). South and southeast Asia. In J. A. Fishman (Ed.), *Language and ethnic identity* (pp. 431–443). Oxford, UK: Oxford University.

Sizer, T. (1992). *Horace's school: Redesigning the American high school.* Boston: Houghton Mifflin.

Sizer, T. (1995, January 8). What's wrong with standard tests. *Education Week,* 58.

Skutnabb-Kangas, T. (1988). Multilingualism and the education of minority children. In T. Skutnabb-Kangas & J. Cummins (Eds.), *Minority education* (pp. 9–44). Clevedon, UK: Multilingual Matters.

Sridhar, K. K. (1991). Bilingual education in India. In O. García (Ed.), *Bilingual education* (Vol. I, pp. 89–106). Amsterdam: John Benjamins.

Suárez-Orozco, C., & Suárez-Orozco, M. M. (2002). *Children of immigration.* Cambridge, MA: Harvard University Press.

Swain, M., & Johnson, R. K. (1997). Immersion education. A category within bilingual education. In R. K. Johnson & M. Swain (Eds.), *Immersion education: International perspectives* (pp. 1–18). Cambridge, UK: Cambridge University Press.

The National Clearinghouse for Bilingual Education. (2001). *No Child Left Behind Act of 2001. Title III: Language instruction for limited English proficient and immigrant students.* Washington, DC: National Clearinghouse for English Language Acquisition.

Torres-Guzman, M. E., Abbate, J., Brisk, M. E., & Minaya-Rowe, L. (2002). Defining and documenting success for bilingual learners: A collective case study. *Bilingual Research Journal, 26*(1), 1–22.

Trumball, E., Rothstein-Fisch, C., Greenfield, P. M., & Quiroz, B. (2001). *Bridging cultures between home and school.* Mahwah, NJ: Lawrence Erlbaum Associates.

UNESCO. (1953). *The use of vernacular languages in education.* Paris: Author.

Valdez, G. (1997). Dual-language immersion programs: A cautionary note concerning the education of language-minority students. *Harvard Educational Review, 67*(3), 391–429.

Zhou, M. (2001). The politics of bilingual education in the People's Republic of China since 1976. *Bilingual Research Journal, 25*(1), 46–68.

2

ESL in Elementary Education

Margaret R. Hawkins
University of Wisconsin–Madison

INTRODUCTION

This chapter focuses on research on second language acquisition (SLA) in elementary schools. Although the discussion centers primarily on English language acquisition as it relates to schools and classrooms, it also promotes a view of language learning and schooling as situated social processes. In order to fully understand how languages are acquired in schools, we must explore the social worlds of the learners and the institutions and uncover the vast range of connections between students' languages, learning, cultures, and identities.

Within the field of second language acquisition, there has been a gradual shift in perspectives. Early research, beginning in the 1970s, focused on psycholinguistic views of language learning, placing the locus of learning inside the individual learner, and focusing on formal features of language. Typical topics addressed in such research were the order of morpheme acquisition, pronunciation, optimal age of acquisition, and interlanguage development[1] (Krashen & Terrell, 1983; Long, 1990). As the field began to embrace sociolinguistic perspectives, researchers began to look more at language as a communicative tool, with language use a way to negotiate meaning between interactants in social encounters. Thus, language use is seen as always situated in particular and specific contexts, occurring between interlocuters who bring to the interaction (and represent) their own meanings and understandings. Interaction itself thus becomes the locus of meaning and learning, with researchers focusing on understanding what shapes interactions in situated encounters, and what effects they in turn produce. This has given rise to research looking at topics such as cultural norms in and for communication (and mismatches between cultural groups), differing linguistic codes as appropriate to and used within specific social contexts, and relationships between learners' cultures, identities, and language use. Most recently, there has been a move toward critical applied linguistics, which overtly claims that language cannot be understood outside of the power relations that shape the interactions within which it occurs. These power relations, although played out through local and situated interactions, are formed through larger discourses at play in institutions and societies.

Commensurate with shifts within the field of SLA, new understandings have been emerging within the larger fields of education as to how we define learning, teaching, literacies, and classrooms. Learning, once looked at primarily as the transference of knowledge from the knower to the learner, is being reframed as social apprenticeship, where the learner comes to appropriate new forms of knowledge (and language and literacies) through social activities in specific local environments. Lev Vygotsky, a Russian psychologist whose work is currently being taken up broadly in education, has called this the "zone of proximal development" (ZPD), wherein learners come to new understandings and practices through apprenticeship to more knowledgeable others (Vygotsky, 1986). Forms of language and literacy practices in schools are viewed as specific situated discourses, as are modes of teaching and learning. Different cultures value and privilege different practices and modes, thus rendering schools as sites where multiple and often conflicting cultural models of language use, teaching practices, and forms of literacy are enacted.

This calls for a shift in our perceptions as to what SLA research might look like in classrooms and schools and calls into question what we are researching and how. It reinforces the need for a comprehensive and coherent framework—a view of classrooms as sites of learning that defines what language and literacy mean to the local participants and how acquisition occurs. This chapter provides an articulation of this paradigm shift, the impact on research agendas into the schooling of young second language learners, and an overview of the research areas and findings to date.

TERMINOLOGY

Within the field of English language teaching and learning there are a number of acronyms and terms that call for explanation. The field itself has been referred to as ESL, TESOL (Teaching English to Speakers of Other Languages), ESOL (English as a Second or Other Language), and TESL (Teaching English as a Second Language). Criticisms of these terms range from feelings of false assumptions (that English is a student's second language, whereas in many instances it may be their third, fourth, etc.) to the bulkiness of the terms themselves. More recently proffered are the acronyms EAL (English as an Additional Language) and ELT (English Language Teaching), which, although preferable, have not thus far been widely taken up.

Students who come from language backgrounds other than English and are in the process of learning English have been referred to as LES (Limited English Speaking), LEP (Limited English Proficient), and NNES (Non-Native English Speakers). Criticisms of these stem from perceptions of indications of deficiency (that students are lacking something, as opposed to being advantaged by knowing multiple languages). Alternatives are, again, using bulky phrases such as "students from diverse linguistic and cultural backgrounds," or the more recent ELLs (English Language Learners). This chapter will use EAL to refer to the field, and ELLs to refer to the students, as these terms are the most inclusive of the current options.

A FRAMEWORK FOR UNDERSTANDING CLASSROOMS

The previous discussion begins to explicate a shift in the way classrooms and learning are viewed and understood. One major goal of this chapter is to closely articulate this emerging perspective and why it is important, then to situate current research within this new paradigm. I have elsewhere identified seven key constructs, which taken together form a cohesive framework for understanding language and literacy development in classrooms (Hawkins, 2004). In brief, these are:

- Communities of Learners/Communities of Practice
  A view of classrooms as environments that promote "scaffolded interaction," where "communities of learners" engage in cultural practices, with participants

taking on various and different ("asymmetrical") roles over time. Knowledge is distributed across the community, not in the possession of any one individual member, thus available to all through activity-based interactions. (Brown, 1994; Lave, 1996; Rogoff, 1994)

- Zone of Proximal Development/Apprenticeship
  Learning as a process of "apprenticeship" where apprentices collaborate in (mediated) social practices with teachers and more expert peers, thus affording scaffolding, or support, in the process of acquiring/constructing new forms of interaction, language, and thinking. (Vygotsky, 1978, 1986; Wertsch, 1998)
- Identities/Positioning
  The socially situated identities participants in social interaction take on at any given time are a complex integration of their diverse sociocultural experiences, the sociocultural experiences of others in the interaction, the structure and flow of language, participation and negotiation in the interaction, and the larger cultural and institutional settings within which the interactions take place. (Bernstein, 1990; Edwards & Potter, 1992; Fairclough, 1992; Hanks, 1996; Schegloff, Ochs, & Thompson, 1996)
- Power/Status
  Meaning and social relationships are interdependent. Social interactions are situated in specific local contexts, which are always part and parcel of larger social, institutional, and community contexts. Embedded are ideologies, beliefs, and values, which are carried out and reproduced through the unfolding social interactions. (Foucault, 1980; Lemke, 1995)
- Multiple (Social) Languages
  No language exists as a general thing. Rather, each language is comprised of many different "social languages," that is, different styles of language that communicate different socially situated identities (who is acting) and socially situated activities (what is being done). Every social language communicates in use, as it creates and reflects specific social contexts, socially situated identities integrally connected to social groups, cultures, and historical formations. (Bakhtin, 1981; Gee, 1996)
- Multiple Literacies
  Literacies are defined as the requisite knowledge and skills to send and interpret messages through multiple media and modes in (rapidly changing) local and global contexts—and to align meanings within situated social practices. (Cope & Kalantzis, 1999; Kress & Van Leeuwen, 2001)
- Classroom-as-Ecology
  Classrooms viewed as ecological systems—the co-dependence of factors that together construct and define the nature of the learning that takes place.

These constructs taken together provide a view of classrooms as complex ecological systems. Learning is no longer seen as merely a matter of transmitting context-independent knowledge. Traditional notions of "knowledge," "language," "literacy," and "learning" are challenged and complexified. Learning occurs as people engage in (socially situated) activities with others, and knowledge is distributed among all participants (with the value of what counts as "knowledge" being contextually determined). The activities themselves carry social meanings largely through the forms of language and literacies used to negotiate the interactions. What counts as "knowledge" and which forms of language and literacy practices are privileged are in large part determined by the larger societal and institutional contexts within which the site of learning is situated, but also susceptible to being in part shaped by the local interactions themselves (see Hawkins, 2000). Thus, in order to understand how language and literacy learning works in schools, it is not enough to delineate and explore discrete categories such as "curriculum," "materials," "methods," "learning styles," or

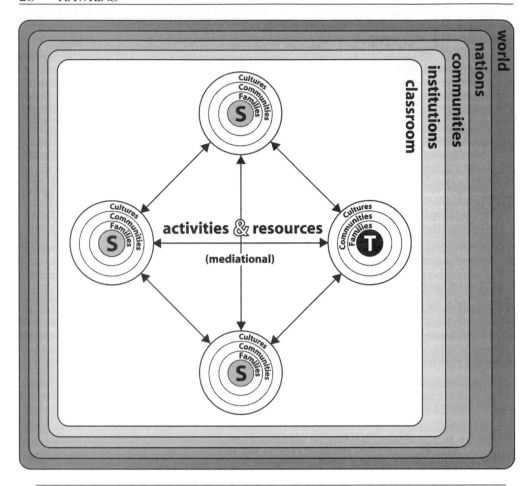

FIG. 2.1. Interrelationships between the classroom's ecological systems.

"vocabulary" to research as independent variables, we must now look at how meanings (and ideologies) are represented through and carried by these media, and the negotiations that occur around them within the specific site.

Figure 2.1 attempts to represent the interrelationships between these complex dynamics. Each participant in the classroom (with students represented by "s" and the teacher by "t") embodies and represents larger discourses into which they have been socialized. These are represented by the circles labeled "families," "communities," and "cultures." Interactions in classrooms are a dance in which the diverse beliefs, values, and practices from each are constantly being negotiated by the learner and among learners (around specific school-based activities). But this is not happening in a space devoid of its own ideologies and practices. It is happening in a classroom, which itself is situated in larger institutional, cultural, and societal contexts. These are represented by the rings around the classroom. And the culturally valued ways of knowing, learning, and communicating are filtered through the system and bear significant weight on classroom interactions and practices too.

Figure 2.1 accounts for factors at play in classroom ecologies. What is not represented, however, is the fluidity and movement of change. The diagram is static, representing factors and interactions as fixed. But an ecological system is a living thing—constantly shifting, with forces aligning and realigning to shape new landscapes.

Thus, just as learner forms of language are not fixed but shift and develop through time, so do all other components within the ecology, constantly redesigning the inter-relations between them and the meanings assigned to them. What this means, then, is that we cannot account for, say, a participant's "culture," or "identity," without acknowledging that at best we are describing interpretations at a particular moment in time.[2]

Thus, research into English language learning in classrooms must account for not only discrete variables and components of language and language learning, but for ways in which these "pieces" come together to form a whole—an ecology within which it is the dynamics between and among variables that accounts for the learning that takes place.

LEARNING ENGLISH IN ELEMENTARY SCHOOLS

Thus far, our conversation about languages and learning has been general and ap-plicable to learners of any age in almost any formal setting. This chapter, however, is specifically dedicated to looking at young learners. How does (and should) research differ when learners' ages are taken into account?

In U.S. schools, the practice of teaching English to young learners is becoming increasingly complex. The number of newcomers is growing rapidly. Data from the United States Department of Education show that the number of students with "lim-ited English skills" in U.S. schools has doubled in the last decade, with the current count at 5 million. In the 1999–2000 census, 1 out of every 12 students was identified as Limited English Proficient (Crawford, 2000). The backgrounds of the students are becoming increasingly diverse, and the politics around "best programs" and "best practices" are shifting. Teachers are serving new populations with little guidance as to how best to do so. In other countries language policies are changing as well, and many are implementing English classes at earlier grade levels in schools. Since 1999, for example, Taiwan has extended the teaching of English to the elementary level as standard curriculum, and the government is now working on a bilingual policy and law to make both the Mandarin dialect of Chinese and English the official languages in 2010. What such policies mean is that curriculum will have to be developed and teachers trained in pedagogy and methods for young children. Thus, we need to know what is particular about young learners, and what we need to know to support their acquisition of English.

Young children are at the nexus of multiple social worlds and realities and are in the formative stages of developing schemata about them. They are apprenticing to the social worlds and practices of school as well as to those of their homes and communities. For children whose home languages and cultures differ significantly from those of the school, they must learn to negotiate very different social worlds, with differing norms, rules, expectations, and value systems. This means not only acquiring a linguistic system that they may not have access to at home, but also the sociocultural competence to successfully negotiate an identity as a "learner" in school.

A number of early studies have shown that children come to school embedded in culturally specific language and literacy practices (Cazden, 1988; Heath, 1983; Lee, 1993; Michaels, 1981). They have different understandings of how and when to partic-ipate in group interactions, exposure to different forms of texts, and differing ways of interacting with text and print. One implication of this is that in early grades in school, although many of the children have emergent literacy skills, the resources, strategies, and experiences that mainstream children bring may resonate more closely with those represented and valued in the school setting, thus enabling them to more readily ac-cess and engage with school-based forms of language and literacy.

REVIEW OF RESEARCH

We now turn to research that has been conducted on English language learning and teaching in elementary schools. We do so, however, with two caveats. The first is that there has been much written about language learners in elementary schools and best practices that does not represent original empirical research. Although these publications may be helpful to further awareness of issues, they will not be reviewed here. The second is that there have been relatively few empirical studies, to date, carried out on English language learning in elementary classrooms, particularly in the very early years of schooling. Diane August and Kenji Hakuta edited a review of research on the education of language minority students in 1998. They summarize what has been learned, but also point to many issues not yet adequately addressed. They claim:

> Research is needed . . . to examine effective educational practice for special populations:
> (1) the effects of instructional interventions and social environments on the linguistic,
> social, and cognitive development of young children. (p. 85)

In addition to a sparse number of studies, many existing studies focus on a specific issue within narrow limited boundaries. Although there is certainly a need for greater information into the discrete components of language use and learning, this is perhaps a necessary but not sufficient condition for understanding language learning and teaching dynamics. Within the context of the framework previously explicated, we need not only to identify the individual components but also the complex ways in which they interact within the ecology of the classroom to support language development. August and Hakuta claim:

> An important contribution to understanding variability in second-language acquisition
> would be an enhanced understanding of the components of English proficiency and how
> these components interact. Also important is the question of how proficiencies in the two
> languages of bilinguals are interrelated and how language and other domains of human
> functioning interact. (p. 19)

Thus, in the ensuing discussion we will address and describe the existing research, keeping in mind that we must not only understand the discrete points being made, but also the connections between the areas of inquiry.

Effective Instruction

As our understandings of language learning in and for classrooms has evolved, the issues surrounding instruction have become ever more complex. In 1986 Jim Cummins presented a theoretical model in which he distinguished between Basic Interpersonal Communication Skills (BICS) and Cognitive Academic Learning Skills (CALPS). The significance of this distinction is that there is a difference in the language needed to communicate interpersonally on an informal basis and that needed to successfully participate in school-based learning. This aligns with our earlier discussion of languages being not unitary entities, but having multiple forms. Successful language users must recruit the appropriate form for the specific interaction/discourse in which they are attempting to participate. Cummins' and subsequent research has shown that it takes 1 to 3 years for learners to acquire BICS, and 3 to 7 to acquire CALPS (Collier, 1987; Cummins, 1986; Thomas & Collier, 1997). Thus, with the underlying assumption that the role of teachers is to support children to be successful in school, researchers have looked into the specific forms of language required for participation and how to scaffold acquisition for students. In an early study Lily Wong Fillmore analyzed talk in third and fifth grade classrooms across subject areas to identify language functions used in instructional activities. She says:

> Students who are able to participate in lessons with self-initiated informative sequences . . . and to provide explanations, descriptions, and narrations, appear to get more out of instructional activities . . . They also need to provide a variety of request forms- in order to get the teacher's attention or to get a turn, to ask for help, permission, information, clarification, or individual attention or help. (Wong Fillmore, 1982, p. 154)

She claims that the ability to produce such structures as relational statements, definitions, summaries, and exemplifications serve two purposes: they provide access for the student to the instruction and content matter; and they construct the teacher's perception as to whether the student is participating successfully, both of which are necessary conditions for school success.

More recently, Wong Fillmore (2001) has addressed the area of academic English, claiming, "what all students, including ELLs must have to deal with the new expectations (curriculum and assessment reforms, benchmark testing, etc.) is a mature understanding of the English used in texts and in academic settings" (p. 2). She claims that academic English "tends to be more precise and specific in reference than everyday English, be more complex syntactically, and be more dependent on 'text' than on 'context' for interpretation" (p. 2). Thus, effective instruction means teaching that focuses not on development of decontextualized vocabulary and grammatical features, but that supports students' abilities to engage with the multiple forms of language, literacies, and texts represented and valued in schools.

Content Area Learning

Currently researchers both within and outside the field of EAL are focusing on content-specific forms of knowledge and the language necessary to represent and claim that knowledge. This work has been done primarily in the areas of math, science, and social studies, which in addition to English/language arts are considered the "core" areas that students must master to be successful in school. Questions being asked are: How is it that scientists (or mathematicians or historians) talk, think, and act in order to successfully participate in the discourse community of the discipline? And how do we socialize students to talk, think, and act like scientists (or mathematicians or historians)? This aligns with the shift to conceptualizing classrooms as communities of learners apprenticing to new discourse communities and to the attendant forms of language. Within EAL, researchers have explored ways of using language specific to math, science, and social studies to identify the specific forms of language attendant to these areas and where they may present difficulties to ELLs. Although much of this research has been conducted at upper grade levels, researchers have identified disciplinary-specific properties and language structures that bear on early instruction as well. For example, in the area of math, there are:

- Explanations without concrete references.
- Narrow context, few cues or referents, little redundancy.
- Terms with specialized meanings (e.g., table, altogether).
- Combination and complex strings of words with specialized meaings (e.g., square root, least common denominator).
- Word problems (combinations of language comprehension and computation).
- Differences (from students' native cultures) in math symbols.
- Writing verbal input in numerical and symbolic code.

(Derived from Chamot & O'Malley, 1994; Secada & Carey, 1990.)

For social studies, potential difficulties arise from:

- Explanations without concrete referents.
- High literacy level required.
- Requirement of conceptual understanding of time, chronology, distance, and differing ways of life.
- Specialized vocabulary, often with words representing complex set of ideas (e.g., democracy, representation).
- Long sentences, multiple embedded clauses.
- Tense forms and markings relative to the period being studied, using complex structures such as "had had," or "supposed to have had."
- Cause-and-effect statements common and often inverted (sentences begin with "Because...").

(Derived from Chamot & O'Malley, 1994; Eschevarria, Vogt, & Short, 2000; McKeown & Beck, 1994.)

In the area of science, there has perhaps been more attention paid by researchers to young learners than in the areas of math or social studies. Difficulties can be caused by:

- Expository discourse.
- Expectation of ability to make inferences from given facts.
- Developing hypotheses.
- Structuring experiments.
- Classification systems.
- Noting and describing (experiments).
- Multiple-step directions.
- Complex grammatical forms (passive voice, multiple embeddings, long noun phrases, if–then constructions).

(Derived from Chamot & O'Malley, 1994; Eschevarria, Vogt, & Short, 2000.)

Identifying specific forms of language used in individual content areas highlights differences between home- and school-based language, which, as discussed earlier, is more divergent for children from nonmainstream backgrounds. It informs us as to the importance of differentiating between "social" and "academic" language; of the teacher's responsibility to address and incorporate specific language forms, features, and functions into instruction; and of the necessity of socializing children into content-specific language practices beginning in the early years of schooling. To amplify this discussion, we will turn to current research and conversations in the area of science.

There is a small but growing body of work on science exploration in elementary schools specifically as it relates to diverse learners. Researchers are exploring the relationships between "everyday language" and science processes (Michaels & Sohmer, 2000, Warren et al., 2000; Warren & Rosebery, 2000), focusing on identifying ways in which the child's first language can be recruited as an "intellectual resource." Much of this work looks at the disparity between culturally embedded communicative styles and those valued in schools and explores instructional approaches designed to maximize and validate home- and community-based speech and interaction styles (Fradd & Lee, 1999) in service of science inquiry. Fradd and Lee's (1999) study of fourth-grade science students points to teachers' tacit assumptions about students' prior knowledge. They claim, "By the time students arrive in fourth grade, many skills are assumed and therefore not taught" (p. 19). Yet some students had never seen basic measurement instruments (such as thermometers, rulers, and scales). They had no experience with measuring and recording information, with tables and charts, nor with "accurate descriptions" or explanations of occurrences. These are all gatekeepers and even by fourth grade are indicators of school success versus failure. Although prior knowledge and experience must be recruited to scaffold comprehension of new concepts (and language), students also need knowledge and skills in using the forms of language and literacy specific to the study of science in school, which utilizes concepts, vocabulary, tools and processes not necessarily represented in home- or community-based discourses. Thus, more attention must be paid to exploring processes of "bridging" what students bring with what they are required to do to claim academic competence in school.

Reading and Writing

The areas of reading and writing together are often referred to as "literacy." For the sake of clarity this chapter will not use that term in this way because the term "literacies" has already been used to signify a broader range of skills and knowledge needed to communicate through multiple media and technologies.[3] In addition, reading and writing have been historically separated in the research of young ELLs in schools, with reading being perhaps the most researched single area of focus (and less having been done in the area of writing), though August & Hakuta claim, "With regard to reading instruction in second language, there is remarkably little direct relevant research" (1998, p. 20). In the following discussion of the teaching and learning of reading and writing in schools, a foundational assumption will be that the ideal outcome of schooling for ELLs is full bilingualism and biliteracy; that is, the ability to function fluently (across all skill areas) in both languages.

One of the most heated debates internationally in the education of young children who are being schooled in a language other than their mother tongue centers on the language of instruction. Nowhere is this more evident than in discussions on reading instruction. Reading is often viewed as the foundation for all other areas of schooling. Reading instruction should be guided by solid information as to the relationships between language proficiency and the acquisition of reading skills, and guidance as to how best to manage the two languages in instruction. Geva & Verhoeven (2001) state:

> In deciding on the best approach to teaching bilingual children to read, three main educational approaches can be distinguished. Children can be totally immersed in an L2 literacy curriculum, they can initially be instructed in the native language (in which case the transition to the L2 is made after a period of time), or they can be given bilingual literacy instruction from the onset. (p. 2)

There are two major modes of research into this issue. One compares achievement of children's reading ability as "products" of the different approaches by comparing achievement of specific discrete reading skills and strategies. The other explores the effects on children's reading ability of factors relating to their home, cultural, and linguistic knowledge and skill base.

The first type tends to divide reading into discrete (measurable) components. The primary subsets of skill areas involved in reading have been identified as phonemic awareness, phonics, vocabulary development, reading fluency (including oral reading skills), and reading comprehension strategies (Antunez, 2002). Examples of this type of research are international studies looking at children's acquisition of French plural morpheme markers (English/French; Cormier & Kelson, 2001), word decoding efficiency (Dutch/English; Verhoeven, 2001), and phonemic and phonological awareness and word recognition (English/Hebrew; Spanish/English; Durgunoglu, Nagy & Hancin-Bhatt, 1993; Wade-Woolley & Geva, 2001). One major focus of this type of research is transfer—that is, the degree to which discrete skills in reading in the first language transfer to the second language. These skills are not examined as relational to other factors, such as the literacy practices engaged in at home or prior schooling experiences. These studies have a relatively consistent finding that can inform decision making as to language of instruction: Young English learners at the same grade level and from the same language background who are instructed in reading in their first language have roughly equivalent reading skills (as measured by acquisition of discrete components) in reading in English as those who are given reading instruction in English. Those who receive reading instruction in English do have slightly more advanced skills in listening and speaking in English. But those instructed in the first language have more advanced reading and comprehension skills in the first language. There is ample evidence that reading skills do transfer across languages. The children's reading comprehension in English is affected by their proficiency in English and by the levels of literacy in their first language, but not by the language of instruction. (August, Calderon, & Carlo, 2000; Carlisle, & Beeman, 2000; Kendall, LaJeunesse, Chmilar, Shapson, & Shapson, 1987).

The second approach tends to contextualize the subsets of skills and strategies attributed to reading proficiency. This limited body of research looks at the prior knowledge students bring to school and to reading tasks, familiarity with the format of literacy activities and tests, instructional design, strategies students use to access texts, and attitudes toward reading. A key shift is that these studies do not locate the acquisition of reading skills within the learner—that is, a child's success in learning to read in English may not be (solely) a product of his or her innate linguistic and cognitive skills and abilities. Consistent with the metaphor of an ecology, it is the interaction of a multitude of factors that constitute the learning/acquisition of reading skills.

Jimenez, Garcia, and Pearson (1995) state that "additional research needs to focus on understanding how the reading of bilingual students of varied reading proficiencies, languages, and ages differs from that of their monolingual counterparts" (p. 93). In two studies (1995, 1996) they examined factors contributing to the reading proficiency (in English) of Latino children. They investigated learners' strategies, text interactions, transfer of skills across languages, and attitudes. In comparisons between successful and less successful readers, they found that more successful (Anglo and Latino) readers "could access well-developed networks of relevant prior knowledge" (1996, p. 91) and encountered fewer unfamiliar vocabulary words and concepts, thus enabling them to attend more to comprehension. They also found that learners who could explicitly recruit language and reading strategies fared better, leading them to recommend a more explicit focus in instruction on awareness of language features and learning strategies. They conclude that "students may possess untapped potential that is limited by models of reading based entirely on the thinking and behavior of monolingual Anglo readers" (1996, p. 93). These themes of what learners bring and the strategies they use resonate with the work of Garcia (1991). His study focused on the reading test performance of Hispanic children, also at the fifth and sixth grade levels. He noted that:

> their test performance was adversely affected by their limited prior knowledge of certain test topics, their poor performance on the scriptally implicit questions (which required use of background knowledge), their unfamiliarity with vocabulary terms used in the test questions and answer choices. (p. 371)

There have been several studies of the development of reading and writing skills in young children, all of which look at the histories and cultural practices children bring to school. Edelsky (1986) conducted an early study of children's writing in a Spanish–English bilingual program in the United States that took into account features of their writing (code-switching, spelling, punctuation, etc.) but also contextual factors relating to the classroom, home, and communities of the children. A more recent study by Masny & Ghahremani-Ghajar (1999) examined "literacy events" in the classroom and the homes of Somalian children in Canada, noting that the identities and voices children brought to school were not validated in school practices of reading and writing. Both studies call for pedagogical practices that incorporate the histories, knowledge, and voices of the children. Similarly, a recent study by Pransky and Bailey (2002) looks at the "mismatches" between classroom and home language and communication practices of the students, calling for teachers to take on investigatory roles in assessing classroom literacy events. In a study of instructional practices in reading for ELLS conducted at the second-grade level, Leu (1997) showed how the design of reading instruction (e.g., ability grouping, methods of instruction based on mainstream students' acquisition of reading, inappropriate materials, low teacher expectations) negatively impacted students' progress.

What these studies indicate is a serious mismatch for ELLs between the knowledge and experiences children bring to school and those represented in curriculum and texts; the negative impact of being expected to engage through text with vocabulary and concepts not yet acquired in the target language; and lack of familiarity (for ELLs) with the scripts and genres of school reading practices. These are similar to the issues identified in the earlier discussion of content learning.

The research illuminates how far we have yet to go in understanding how best to scaffold English language learners in acquiring reading skills. Both research and theory must explore connections between learners' backgrounds and cultural knowledge and the discourses and practices of schooling, how these play out in classroom interactions and literacy events, and how they are aligned within larger societal discourses. One useful way of conceptualizing this has been proffered by Gutierrez, Baquedano-Lopez, & Tejada (1999) and taken up further by Manyak (2001; 2002). They use the term "hybrid" when referring to the intermingling of cultural and linguistic codes in classroom and literacy practices. Manyak (2002) defines hybrid as a construct "to conceptualize new cultural forms, practices, spaces, and identities created from a synthesis of diverse elements" (p. 423). The research of Gutierrez, Baquedano-Lopez, Alvarez, & Chiu (1999) demonstrates how embracing hybridity led to the construction of a "culture of collaboration" in the classroom, and a reassignation of meaning and value to the discourses. Manyak looks at code-switching, language used as scaffolding (Spanish to scaffold English), and indices to home cultures and communities as resources for comprehension and engagement. In both sets of studies the researchers begin to conceptualize the complex nature of literacy learning in classrooms, the ways in which the dynamics between various factors (such as forms of languages, forms of literacies, school practices, and social and cultural resources) shape interactions and the ways in which the interactions shape and define the learning.

Use of Two Languages

In addition to discussions of language choice in the field of reading, there has been some inquiry into the distribution of languages in the broader classroom setting. Reverting to the earlier discussion of classrooms as situated social spaces, the choice of language use (when to use which language for what purpose) is in part determined by policies and beliefs in the larger institutional and societal contexts in which the classroom is situated. In many countries there are national policies about language use, designating a specific language as the language of schooling. In the United States there is a growing trend, and in some states legislation, toward limiting the use of another language in instruction. Yet many states still have statutes mandating bilingual instruction. Distribution of language use in schools is often, perhaps usually, dependent on the program model the school (or district) adopts. (For a full discussion of program models, see Brisk, this volume.) Even when teachers have choices, and have the ability to communicate in the primary language of schooling and the home language/s of the students, the choices of language use are not always consciously made.

There are few studies looking specifically at the language distribution in bilingual classes for young learners. Nonetheless, those that exist present relatively consistent and compelling findings. Ernst-Slavin's (1997) account of first-grade children of Mexican descent in the United States uncovers exclusion of the children's variety of Spanish in the bilingual classroom and discusses the impact of linguistic and cultural exclusion. Irujo's (1998) year-long ethnographic study of an elementary bilingual second grade classroom (Spanish/English in the United States) points to a lack of conscious choice in the determination of language use by the teacher, though there were consistent patterns of and triggers for code-switching. English was accorded higher status in the classroom community, as evidenced by practices such as new arrivals being rewarded for using English. The study documents the students' differential perceptions of the two languages and their appropriation of attitudes that place higher value on English. Shannon's (1990) exploration of a fourth grade classroom mirrors these findings. She found that instruction was almost solely delivered in English, but the children spoke Spanish almost exclusively when interacting around academic tasks or socially with each other. Further, she identified less rigorous instructional standards and lower expectations for the children who received more Spanish reading and language arts instruction because they had less English proficiency. She claims:

> English is the "high" language of instruction, and Spanish is the "low" language, the language of informal peer interaction. Furthermore, I have demonstrated that when Spanish is used as an instructional language, its status is clearly lowered. (p. 45)

Shannon also indicates divisive social relations between the children who primarily interact in Spanish and those who utilize more English.

These studies demonstrate how, in a classroom ecology, the ways in which languages are allocated and used contribute to the shaping of social relations, the culture of the classroom, and opportunities for and access to academic achievement. They unanimously identify inequitable language practices that lead to differential statuses being conferred on the forms of language represented in the classroom (with the home language of the ELLs in each case relegated to lower status) and social divisions based on language use that result in differential statuses being conferred on the children themselves. This raises deep concerns about the messages being sent to children about their languages, heritages, and thus their identities in schools. It also brings into question issues about engagement with learning. If children are not receiving academic content in a language that is accessible to them and cannot participate equally in academic activities because of language and social barriers, what are they "learning" in school?

In a later study Shannon (1995a) explores another fourth grade bilingual classroom in which she claims, "the hegemony of English is recognized, challenged, and resisted" (p. 185). She analyzes classroom practices to discover the processes by which this happens. She points primarily to the teacher's explicit attempts to confer high status to Spanish by ensuring that the two languages were equally represented in the communicative practices and material resources in the classroom, by explicitly drawing students' attention to issues of dual language use, and by the hybrid nature of language practices in the classroom. This represents an important step toward research that identifies ways in which languages can best be utilized in classrooms to scaffold positive social relations and learning and to result in full participation in the classroom community for all students.

Home/School Connections

There has been a consistent theme throughout this chapter of the mismatches between the communicative and cultural practices of ELLs' homes and communities and those of school. As mentioned earlier, these have been well documented in early work on cross-cultural communication patterns and the impact on children's learning in school (Au, 1980; Collier, 1987; Heath, 1983; Michaels, 1981; Phillips, 1983). This is consistent with a conceptualization of classrooms as spaces where multiple and diverse beliefs, practices, and discourses come into contact, and through moment-by-moment negotiations and interactions shape the classroom ecology, including the roles and identities of the participants. The few studies of home/school connections with young English language learners as subjects that exist can be categorized as two distinct (but interrelated) strands of research exploring ways to foster positive connections between families and schools and to bridge the linguistic and cultural divide. One of these focuses on documenting the language and literacy practices of the home and exploring differences from those of school; the other focuses on the direct inclusion of families and family literacies in the classroom.

Notable and influential in the first category is the work of Luis Moll and his associates (Moll, Amanti, Neff, & Gonzalez, 1992; Moll & Greenberg, 1990), in which they explore the "funds of knowledge" that students bring to school. These he describes as, "historically accumulated and culturally developed bodies of knowledge and skills essential for household or individual functioning and well-being" (Moll et al., 1992, p. 31). He further conceptualizes and identifies:

> how families develop social networks that interconnect them with their social environments (most importantly with other households), and how these social relationships facilitate the development and exchange of resources, including knowledge, skills and labor, that enhance the household's ability to survive or thrive. (Moll et al., 1992, p. 31)

This conceptualization assists in understanding that family and community networks of knowledge and resources can differ substantially, and that those assumed in teachers' expectations about what children bring to school and what the family's role is in supporting their children's educations, may not have a universally unified meaning or be shared. This is well supported by other studies of Mexican origin elementary-age children and their families (Carlisle & Beeman, 2000; Delgado-Gaitan, 1990; Schecter & Bayley, 1997; Valdes, 1996). All three of these studies document extensively the families' home language and literacy practices, their views about education and schooling, and their engagement with their children's schooling. They suggest that the language and literacy practices and funds of knowledge from students' homes need to be represented and validated in the school curriculum and pedagogical practices. This accounts for a necessary, but one-way, flow of information—that is, it calls for teachers and schools to better understand, represent, and speak to the everyday lives of students. Although it calls for negotiation of culture, language, and identities within the classroom environment between the students and school staff, it does not actively recruit the participation of parents.

In a body of research that contributes significantly not only to our understandings of home–school relations, but of possible ways in which to respond pedagogically to the challenges this work presents, a trio of educators have worked together to foster school–home collaborations and research their impact (Willett, Solsken, & Wilson-Keenan, 1998; Wilson-Keenan, Willett, & Solsken, 1993). Their initiatives include home visits and also multiple ways to bring parents into the classroom and involve them in the school lives of the children, thus creating "a classroom where hybridity was invited and valued" in an effort to "re-imagine both instructional and research practices that strive to transform existing relations of power and privilege" (Willett et al., 1998, p. 167). They claim their work "can help us to find creative ways to open up hybrid spaces for negotiating across differences and to include different voices in the classroom and in research" (p. 207). Thus, they have created research and pedagogical designs that not only include parents' voices and views, but that create hybrid spaces in which home and school discourses and practices are both represented, and in which negotiations of voices and identities can occur.

VOICES IN RESEARCH

An issue that has historically plagued research is that of the research–practice divide. This is, in essence, an argument that those conducting the research are not the classroom practitioners; thus, do not have the local understandings of the practitioners; nor are they producing findings and representing them in ways useful to practitioners. One of the key design features of the research by Willett, Solsken, and Wilson-Keenan (1998) is that the research site is Wilson-Keenan's classroom, and she is a full participant in all phases of the research process (see also Hawkins & Legler, 2002). Her voice is fully represented and explored.

There are, as well, other accounts of teacher research. These are written by classroom teachers and articulate the reflections and perceptions (and often the struggles) of teachers. For the teacher, they provide a medium for close observation and exploration of their students and classroom practices and an opportunity to reflect on how that information shapes and integrates with their curriculum design and pedagogy. For the reader, they provide a close-up view from an insider's perspective (a fully participating member of the classroom community), and often include details of instruction and classroom events and how these are connected to particular philosophies and beliefs, which are not otherwise available.

> Cynthia Ballenger, a teacher of young Haitian children, articulates this: in many ways this book is an exploration ... [of] the tension between honoring the child's home discourse as a rich source of knowledge and learning itself, and yet wishing to put that discourse into meaningful contact with school-based and discipline-based ways of talking, acting, and knowing. ... they helped me to see the assumptions I brought to my work together as well as those that they did. This is a book about what counts as knowledge in the classroom and my own attempts to evaluate this in light of daily encounters. (Ballenger, 1999, p. 6)

In other examples, Gonzalez et al. (1993) take up the notion of "funds of knowledge" and conduct visits to their students' homes, then explore how their changed understandings of their students' funds of knowledge impacted their curriculum. Urdinavia-English (2001) explores her practices teaching social studies to ELLs, identifying points of difficulty for access, and ways to connect curriculum and instructional approaches to the students' lives. These initiatives are especially significant in that the researchers, in their roles as teachers, are in a position to directly and immediately utilize the discoveries the research yields to re-design practice. Thus, the research itself becomes part of the classroom ecology, affecting subsequent interactions.

Another under-represented voice in educational research on young children is that of the children. Although, in one sense, their voices are certainly represented—that is, the adult researcher often focuses much of the analysis on the actual speech of the children—the children are not asked about their understandings and interpretations of events and relationships. Their understandings, in fact, are most often interpreted by others and assigned to them. Thus, one component missing from analyses of social interactions in classrooms is the self-articulated perspectives of the children.

Researchers, as outside observers or at best peripheral participants, can offer valuable interpretations. But, to parallel the previously discussed argument, only through strengthening understandings of local "insider" perspectives can we hope to map out the ecologies of classrooms.

PULLING IT ALL TOGETHER

This chapter promotes a view of classrooms as ecologies, wherein the dynamics between all constituent parts construct the whole, as the whole influences the dynamics between the constituent parts (and thus the meanings and values assigned to and claimed by the individual parts). One pervasive notion has been that of "hybridity," used in various contexts to denote the evolving nature of cultures and practices (including but not limited to language practices) as they come into contact and interact with each other. This notion is helpful for conceptualizing these contacts not as binaries—that is, an oppositional either/or relationship where one set of practices/beliefs must take precedence—but as ongoing processes in which practices/beliefs continually shift and are redefined through the negotiations.

In closing, then, we point to some studies of language and learning in classrooms that conceptualize classroom and school practices, social relations, and identity construction as co-determinous and as central to the learning and schooling process. These studies investigate the practices and routines of classrooms and the discourses of schools, demonstrate how they ultimately construct identities and positions for ELLs, and show how identity positions afford or constrain access to classroom practices.

Willett (1995) conceives of the classroom as a community of learners and explores ways in which L2 learners' interactions around the routines and practices of the classroom helped shape the construction of their identities as learners, while being in turn shaped by the "micropolitics" of the classroom, thus demonstrating the reciprocity of these relationships. Shannon (1995b) also utilizes a community of learners perspective and focuses on how the classroom culture socializes ELLs to be engaged, participate, and assume identities as ELLs. Hruska (2000) identifies discourses around bilingualism, gender, and friendship across formal and informal school events. She considers contributing factors, thus situating school practices in larger institutional and societal discourses and power dynamics. She ultimately connects these discourses to the school identities constructed by bilingual children in a kindergarten classroom and shows how they affected their self-esteem and motivation and their investment in school. Shannon's focus is primarily on the teacher's construction of the learning environment and Hruska's on the way in which school discourses shape learners' identities, engagements, and investments, whereas Willett investigates links between the environment and interactions, and ascribes agency to the children. She claims, in fact, that the learners she observed purposely manipulated language and practices in bids for identities, that they "strategically enacted and elaborated culturally shaped interaction routines to construct their social, linguistic, and academic competence (as locally defined)" (Willett, 1995, p. 499). Thus, she shows interrelationships between these facets, presenting them not as distinct, but as dynamic. These three studies place centrality on incorporating a focus on social relations in understanding how language development and learning occur in classrooms.

In a more elaborate study that is inclusive of all of the components of the framework presented in this chapter, Kelleen Toohey (2000) claims, "Classrooms . . . organize particular ways for children and teachers to talk, read, write and listen, which differ from discursive practices in other communities." (p. 125). Her longitudinal study of young children in Canada (1996; 1998; 2000), framed by a "community of learners" perspective, explored discursive practices in kindergarten through second grade and how they shaped the identities and participation of six second language learners. She looked at the languages, literacies, practices, and "resources" of the classroom, and the children's social interactions, exploring ways in which the children's identities and positions were formed (with the concomitant social status), and the effects of these formations. She claims "that children had most opportunities for appropriating classroom language in situations when they could speak from desirable and powerful identity positions" (Toohey, 2000, p. 125).

All four of these studies represent an emergent focus in the field of second language acquisition and demonstrate a shift in perspective about language learning and schooling as it pertains to young children. Who children are, the languages they speak, and the cultures they embody are interdependent and intertwined. How and what they learn in school is a complex negotiation between what resources they bring to the learning situation; what belief systems, values, and practices are represented in the learning site; and who they can be and how they can communicate in the situated interactions there. If the goal of educational research is to inform us as to how to best design and manage learning environments and instruction to support children's social, linguistic, and academic development, it must help us to understand the ecology of the classroom—to identify the components, map the complex interactions between them, and provide frameworks for understanding the ways in which they shape the lifeworlds of the inhabitants. This calls for further exploration of these environments, especially with an explicit inclusion of all the diverse voices represented therein, and a close accounting of the role of language in the reciprocal relationship between the social dynamics and learning.

NOTES

1. Interlanguage was originally defined by Selinker (1972) as "a separate linguistic system based on the observable output which results from a learner's attempted projection of a TL (target language) norm" (p. 214, parenthetical clarification mine). Ellis (1997) elucidates further by saying, "...the systematic knowledge of an L2 that is independent of both the target language and the learner's L1" (p. 140).
2. My thanks to Suban Keowkanya, Jina Lee, Sara Michael Luna, Mattanee Palungtepin, Joao Rosa, Amy Sharpe, and Chung Pei Tsai for bringing this point to my attention.
3. There has, in fact, been an argument made that the sorts of "literacy" taught in schools has not kept up with the rapidly changing forms of literacies existent in the larger social environment and may not adequately prepare children to participate in the new global economies (DiSessa, 2000; Gee, 1999; Hawkins, in press; Kress & Van Leeuwen, 2001).

REFERENCES

Antunez, B. (2002). Implementing reading first with English language learners. *Directions in Language and Education* (No. 15). Washington, DC: National Clearinghouse for English Language Acquisition & Language Instruction Educational Programs.

Au, K. H. (1980). Participation structures in a reading lesson with Hawaiian children: Analysis of a culturally appropriate instructional event. *Anthropology and Education Quarterly, 11,* 91–115.

August, D., Calderon, M., & Carlo, M. (2000). *Transfer of skills from Spanish to English: A study of young learners. Report for Practitioners, Parents, and Policy Makers.* Washington, DC: Office of Bilingual Education and Minority Languages Affairs, U.S. Department of Education.

August, D., & Hakuta, K. (Eds.). (1998). *Educating language minority students.* Report from Commission on Behavioral and Social Sciences and Education, National Research Council. Washington, DC: National Academy Press.

Bakhtin, M. (1981). *The dialogic imagination.* Austin: University of Texas Press.

Ballenger, C. (1999). *Teaching other people's children: Literacy and learning in a bilingual classroom.* New York: Teachers College Press.

Bernstein, B. (1990). *The structuring of pedagogic discourse. Vol. IV: Class, codes, and control.* London: Routledge.

Brown, A. L. (1994). The advancement of learning. *Educational Researcher, 23*(8), 4–12.

Carlisle, J., & Beeman, M. (2000). The effect of language of instruction on the reading and writing achievement of first-grade Hispanic children. *Scientific Studies of Reading, 4*(4), 331–354.

Cazden, C. (1988). *Classroom discourse: The language of teaching and learning.* Portsmouth, NH: Heinemann.

Chamot, A., & O'Malley, M. (1994). *The CALLA handbook.* Reading, MA: Addison-Wesley.

Collier, V. (1987). Age and rate of acquisition of second language for academic purposes. *TESOL Quarterly, 21*(4), 617–641.

Cope, B., & Kalantzis, M. (Eds.). (1999). *Multiliteracies: Literacy learning and the design of social futures.* London: Routledge.

Cormier, P., & Kelson, S. (2001). The roles of phonological and syntactic awareness in the use of plural morphemes among children in French immersion. *Scientific Studies of Reading, 4*(4), 267–294.

Crawford, J. (2000). *Making sense of Census 2000.* Retrieved October 29, 2003 from www.asu.edu/educ/epsl/ LPRU/ features/article5.htm

Cummins, J. (1986). Empowering minority students: A framework for intervention. *Harvard Educational Review, 56*(1), 18–36.

Delgado-Gaitan, C. (1990). *Literacy for empowerment: The role of parents in children's education.* Bristol, PA: Falmer.

DiSessa, A. A. (2000). *Changing minds: Computers, learning, and literacy.* Cambridge, MA: MIT Press.

Durgunoglu, A., Nagy W., & Hancin-Bhatt, B. (1993). Cross-language transfer of phonological awareness. *Journal of Educational Psychology, 85*(3), 453–465.

Edelsky, C. (1986). *Writing in a bilingual program: Habia una Vez.* Norwood, NJ: Ablex.

Edwards, D., & Potter, J. (1992). *Discursive psychology.* Newbury Park, CA: Sage.

Ellis, R. (1997). *Second language acquisition.* Oxford, UK: Oxford University Press.

Ernst-Slavin, G. (1997). Different words, different worlds: Language use, power, and authorized language in a bilingual classroom. *Linguistics and Education, 9,* 25–48.

Eschevarria, J., Vogt, M., & Short, D. (2000). *Making content comprehensible for English language learners.* Needham Heights, MA: Allyn & Bacon.

Fairclough, N. (1992). *Discourse and social change.* Cambridge, UK: Polity Press.

Foucault, M. (1980). *Power/Knowledge: Selected interviews and other writings 1972–1977.* Brighton, UK: Harvester Press.

Fradd, S., & Lee, O. (1999). Teachers' roles in promoting science inquiry with students from diverse language backgrounds. *Educational Researcher (28)6,* 14–20

Garcia, G. (1991). Factors influencing the English reading test performance of Spanish-speaking Hispanic children. *Reading Research Quarterly, 26*(4), 371–392.

Gee, J. P. (1996). *Social linguistics and literacies: Ideology in discourse* (2nd ed.). London: Taylor & Francis.

Gee, J. P. (1999). New people in new worlds: Networks, the new capitalism and schools. In W. Cope & M. Kalantzis (Eds.), *Multiliteracies: Literacy learning and the design of social futures* (pp. 43–68). London: Routledge.

Geva, E., & Verhoeven, L. (Eds.). (2001). The development of second language reading in primary children— Research issues and trends. *Scientific Studies of Reading, 4*(4), 261–267.

Gonzalez, N., Moll, L., Floyd-Tenery, A. R., Rivera, A., Rendon, P., Gonzalez., R., & Amanti, C. (1993). *Teacher research on funds of knowledge: Learning from households* (Educational Practice Report: 6). Washington, DC: National Center for Research on Cultural Diversity and Second Language Learning.

Gutierrez, K., Baquedano-Lopez, P., Alvarez, H. & Chiu, M. (1999). Building a culture of collaboration through hybrid language practices. *Theory Into Practice, 38*(2), 87–93.

Gutierrez, K., Baquedano-Lopez, P., & Tejada, C. (1999). Rethinking diversity: Hybridity and hybrid language practices in the third space. *Mind, Culture and Activity, 6*(4), 286–303.

Hanks, W. F. (1996). *Language and communicative practices.* Boulder, CO: Westview.

Hawkins, M. (2000). The reassertion of traditional authority in a constructivist pedagogy. *Teaching Education, 11*(3), 279–295.

Hawkins, M. (2004). Researching English language and literacy development in schools. *Educational Researcher, 33*(3), 365–384.

Hawkins, M. (in press). Social apprenticeships through mediated learning in language teacher education. In M. Hawkins (Ed.), Language learning and teacher education: A sociocultural approach. Clevedon, UK: Multilingual Matters.

Hawkins, M., & Legler, L. (2002). *Collaboratively researching language in a kindergarten classroom.* Paper presented at TESOL, Salt Lake City, UT.

Heath, S. B. (1983). *Ways with words: Language, life and work in communities and classrooms.* Cambridge, UK: Cambridge University Press.

Hruska, B. (2000, April). *Bilingualism, gender and friendship: Constructing second language learners in an English dominant kindergarten.* Paper presented at the annual meeting of the American Association for Applied Linguistics, Vancouver B. C., Canada.

Irujo, S. (1998). *Teaching bilingual children: Beliefs and behaviors.* Pacific Grove, CA: Heinle & Heinle.

Jimenez, R., Garcia, G., & Pearson, P. D. (1995). Three children, two languages, and strategic reading: Case studies in bilingual/monolingual reading. *American Educational Research Journal, 32*(1), 67–97.

Jimenez, R., Garcia, G., & Pearson, P. D. (1996). The reading strategies of bilingual Latino/a students who are successful English readers: Opportunities and obstacles. *Reading Research Quarterly, 31*(1), 90–112.

Kendall, J., LaJeunesse, G., Chmilar, P., Shapson, L., & Shapson, S. (1987). English reading skills of French immersion students in kindergarten and grades 1 and 2. *Reading Research Quarterly, 22*(2), 135–159.

Krashen, S., & Terrell, T. (1983). *The natural approach: Language acquisition in the classroom.* Oxford, UK: Pergamon.

Kress, G., & Van Leeuwen, T. (2001). *Multimodal discourse: The modes and media of contemporary communication.* London: Edward Arnold.

Lave, J. (1996). Teaching, as learning, in practice. *Mind, Culture, and Activity: An International Journal, 3*(3), 149–164.

Lee, C. D. (1993). *Signifying as a scaffold for literary interpretation: The pedagogical implications of an African American discourse genre.* Urbana, IL: National Council of Teachers of English.

Lemke, J. (1995). *Textual politics: Discourse and social dynamics.* Bristol, PA: Taylor & Francis.

Leu, S. (1997, March). *The dilemmas of English as second language children learning to read in an all-English mainstream classroom.* Paper presented at the Annual Meeting of the American Educational Research Association, Chicago, IL.

Long, M. (1990). Maturational constraints on language development. *Studies in Second Language Acquisition 12,* 251–285.

Manyak, P. (2001). Participation, hybridity, and carnival: A situated analysis of a dynamic literacy practice in a primary-grade English immersion class. *Journal of Literacy Research, 33*(3), 423–465.

Manyak, P. (2002). Welcome to Salon 110: The consequences of hybrid literacy practices in a primary-grade English immersion class. *Bilingual Research Journal, 26*(2), 421–442.

Masny, D., & Ghahremani-Ghajar, S. (1999). Weaving multiple literacies: Somali children and their teachers in the context of school culture. *Language, Culture and Curriculum, 12*(1), 72–93.

McKeown, M., & Beck, I. (1994). Making sense of accounts of history: Why young students don't and they might. In G. Leinhardt, I. Beck, & C. Stainton (Eds.), *Teaching and learning in history* (pp. 1–26). Hillsdale, NJ: Lawrence Erlbaum Associates.

Michaels, S. (1981). "Sharing time": Children's narrative styles and differential access to literacy. *Language in Society (10),* 423–442.

Michaels, S., & Sohmer, R. (2000). Narratives and inscriptions: Cultural tools, power, and powerful sense-making. In B. Cope & M. Kalantzis (Eds.), *Multiliteracies: Literacy learning and the design of social futures* (pp. 267–288). London: Routledge.

Moll, L., Amanti, C., Neff, D., & Gonzalez, N. (1992). Funds of knowledge for teaching: Using a qualitative approach to connect homes and classrooms. *Theory Into Practice, 31*(2), 132–141.

Moll, L., & Greenberg, J. (1990). Creating zones of possibility: Combining social contexts for instruction. In L. Moll (Ed.), *Vygotsky and education.* Cambridge, UK: Cambridge University Press.

Philips, S. U. (1983). *The invisible culture: Communication in classroom and community on the Warm Springs Indian Reservation.* New York: Longman.

Pransky, K., & Bailey, F. (2002). To meet your students where they are, first you have to find them: Working with culturally and linguistically diverse at-risk students. *The Reading Teacher, 56*(4), 370–383.

Rogoff, B. (1994). Developing understanding of the idea of communities of learners. *Mind, Culture, and Activity: An International Journal, 1*(4), 209–229.

Schecter, S., & Bayley, R. (1997). Language socialization practices and cultural identity: Case studies of Mexican-descent families in California and Texas. *TESOL Quarterly, 31*(3), 513–541.

Schegloff, E. A., Ochs, E., & Thompson, S. A. (1996). Introduction. In E. A. Schegloff, E. Ochs, & S. A. Thompson (Eds.) *Interaction and Grammar,* Cambridge, UK: Cambridge University Press. Pp. 1–51.

Secada, W., & Carey, D. (1990). *Teaching mathematics with understanding to limited English proficient students.* Urban Diversity Series NO. 101, ERIC Clearinghouse On Urban Education, Institute On Urban and Minority Education. October 1990. ERIC Document Reproduction Service, Alexandria, VA. New York: ERIC Clearinghouse on Urban Education.

Selinker, L. (1972). Interlanguage. *International Review of Applied Linguistics, 10,* 209–231.

Shannon, S. (1990). An ethnography of a fourth-grade bilingual class: Patterns of English and Spanish. In D. Bixler-Marquez, G. Green, & J. Ornstein-Galicia (Eds.), *Mexican-American Spanish in its societal and cultural contexts* (pp. 35–47). Brownsville, TX: Pan American University.

Shannon, S. (1995a). The hegemony of English: A case study of one bilingual classroom as a site of resistance. *Linguistics and Education, 7,* 177–202.

Shannon, S. (1995b). The culture of the classroom: Socialization in an urban bilingual classroom. *The Urban Review, 27*(4), 321–345.

Thomas, W., & Collier, V. (1997). *School effectiveness for language minority students.* Washington, D.C.: National Clearinghouse for Bilingual Education.

Toohey, K. (1996). Learning English as a second language in kindergarten: A community of practice perspective. *The Canadian Modern Language Journal, 52*(4), 549–576.

Toohey, K. (1998). "Breaking them up; taking them away": ESL students in grade one. *TESOL Quarterly, 32,* 61–84.

Toohey, K. (2000). *Learning English at school: Identity, social relations and classroom practice.* Clevedon, UK: Multilingual Matters.

Urdinavia-English, C. (2001). Whose history? Social studies in an elementary English class for speakers of other languages. *Social Studies, 92*(5), 193–198.

Valdes, G. (1996). *Con respeto: Bridging the distance between culturally diverse families and schools.* New York: Teachers College Press.

Verhoeven, L. (2001). Components in early second language reading and spelling. *Scientific Studies of Reading, 4*(4), 313–330.

Vygotsky, L.V. (1978). *Mind in society: The development of higher psychological processes.* Cambridge, MA: Harvard University Press.

Vygotsky, L.V. (1986). *Thought and language.* Cambridge, MA: MIT Press.

Wade-Woolley, L., & Geva, E. (2001). Processing novel phonemic contrasts in the acquisition of L2 word reading. *Scientific Studies of Reading, 4*(4), 295–312.

Warren, B., Ballenger, C., Ogonowski, M., Rosebery, A., & Hudicourt-Barnes, J. (2001). Re-thinking diversity in learning science: The logic of everyday sense-making. *Journal of Research in Science Teaching, 38*(5), 529–552.

Warren, B., & Rosebery, A. (2000). *On being explicit: Toward a new pedagogical synthesis in science.* Manuscript submitted for publication.

Wertsch J. V. (1998). *Mind as action.* Oxford, UK: Oxford University Press.

Willett, J. (1995). Becoming first graders in an L2: An ethnographic study of L2 socialization. *TESOL Quarterly, 29*(3), 473–503.

Willett, J., Solsken, J., & Wilson-Keenan, J. (1998). The (im)possibility of constructing multicultural language practices in research and pedagogy. *Linguistics and Education, 10*(2), 165–218.

Wilson-Keenan, J., Willett, J., & Solsken, J. (1993). Focus on research: Constructing and urban village: School/home collaboration in a multicultural classroom. *Language Arts, 70,* 204–214.

Wong Fillmore, L. (1982). Language minority students and school participation: What kind of English is needed? *Boston University Journal of Education, 11,* 143–156.

Wong Fillmore, L. (2001, May). *Language issues in teacher education: What's academic language?* Paper presented at Preparing for Culturally and Linguistically Diverse Classrooms workshop, Madison, WI.

3

ESL in Secondary Schools: Programs, Problematics, and Possibilities[1]

Patricia A. Duff
University of British Columbia

INTRODUCTION: THE IMPACT OF RECENT IMMIGRATION ON ESL IN SECONDARY SCHOOLS

The demographics in English-speaking countries such as Canada, the United States, Australia, and England have changed dramatically in recent years, primarily as a result of immigration. Canada, for example, admits on average 200,000 to 225,000 immigrants each year, the majority of whom are not native speakers of either of Canada's official languages, English and French. Proficiency in either—or both—English or French has not, until very recently, been a crucial factor in the acceptance of either immigrant or government-assisted refugees in Canada, and as a result, many of those admitted have only limited knowledge of either language.[2] With the steady influx of newcomers arriving over the past 2 decades, unprecedented numbers of English language learners (ELLs)[3] have been entering elementary and secondary schools, to the point where in many cities, not only in Canada but in the United States, the United Kingdom, and Australia as well, ELLs now constitute the majority, not minority of students.

In the United States between the mid-1980s and mid-1990s, there was a nearly 70% increase in the number of school-age children and youth whose home language was not English (TESOL, 1997). TESOL (1997) reported that in 1993 there were more than 2.5 million ELLs in U.S. public schools, and it was expected that "by the year 2000 the majority of the school-age population in 50 or more major U.S. cities [would] be from language minority backgrounds" (p. 1).[4] Lindholm-Leary's (2001) estimates are even larger; she reports nearly 10 million of 45 million school-age children (of whom 6 million are Hispanic) come from homes in which languages other than English are spoken, based on 1996 U.S. Census Bureau population statistics. California alone had an estimated 2.2 million language-minority students in 1999[5] (half of all students), followed by Texas (1.4 million), New York (nearly 1 million), Florida, Illinois, New Jersey, Arizona, and Pennsylvania (at least a quarter million language-minority students each) according to research reported by Lindholm-Leary (2001, p. 11). It is difficult to get accurate statistics about numbers because of the various reporting systems that are used, which also may just reflect enrollments on one particular day of the year; there are also differences in reporting systems across states. The largest Anglo-Canadian cities (Toronto and Vancouver) have comparable proportions of English language learners across elementary and secondary schools, on average 50% of total enrollments, although in general the number of Hispanic students is much smaller in Canada.

Similar changes are also happening in areas traditionally less populated either by new immigrants or by bilingual native-born Americans. According to a recent *New York Times* article entitled "Wave of Pupils Lacking English Strains Schools" (Zhao, 2002), the number of ELLs in school districts in the American South, Midwest, and Northwest (e.g., Idaho, Nebraska, Wisconsin, South Carolina, and Georgia) has at least tripled since 1993, with a five-fold increase in North Carolina alone, whose farms and factories have attracted especially large numbers of Latino immigrants.

Newcomers and their families face many challenges upon settlement. For school-age children, learning the target language of the community and becoming integrated into mainstream programs at school is a primary concern. For their parents and older siblings, gaining access to social networks, education, employment, and other activities and services in the wider community may be paramount. Learning the official local language, generally English, is often a crucial aspect of families' social integration into the wider English-speaking community in these contexts (Toohey, 2000).

Students entering secondary school specifically—comprising Grades 7 to 12, 8 to 12, or 9 to 12, depending on the country, state/province, and school district—must adapt to the linguistic, sociocultural, discursive, and academic norms and practices in content areas, and school personnel must find ways to effectively meet the minority students' linguistic, academic, and cultural needs, and to communicate effectively with students' families.[6] Whereas the pressures and challenges for domestic *native-English-speaking* (NES) adolescent students at the secondary school level are often considerable, for *non-native* English speakers (NNESs) the challenges are often insurmountable.

In this chapter, I review research that has been done in connection with ESL students at the secondary level. The themes to be examined here are:

- Previous research on ESL learners in secondary school.
- English program types and requirements, and language and content integration.
- ESL and secondary school content areas—the case of social studies.
- Standards movements, initiatives, and guidelines.
- Assessment issues at the secondary level.
- Second language socialization in secondary school.
- ESL versus mainstream learning contexts—cultural and affective issues.
- ESL students at risk—secondary school drop-out or "push-out."
- Secondary school-to-college transitions.

More research on English teaching and learning in secondary EFL contexts is badly needed as well as on ESL, especially as new policies are implemented internationally to introduce English earlier in national language curricula, often without clear articulation between elementary and secondary curricula, goals, and assessment measures. The stakes to learn English are becoming higher than ever. However, EFL educational settings and issues are beyond the scope of this chapter.

PREVIOUS RESEARCH ON ESL LEARNERS IN SECONDARY SCHOOL: ENDURING ISSUES

Until the mid-1990s, there was little published research on secondary-level immigrant or minority-L1 bilingual students in mainstream school curricula in the United States or Canada, despite the growth in this population and the numerous challenges they encounter in the school system (Faltis, 1999). Because of the urgency of providing a robust and equitable education for immigrant children and youth, new research has begun to examine their experiences in ESL classes, in mainstream classes, in their successful or unsuccessful completion of high school requirements, and their subsequent transition to postsecondary education.

It has long been acknowledged that it takes English language learners many years to attain the academic language proficiency required to succeed in such content areas as social studies, English literature, mathematics, biology, and chemistry (Collier, 1989, 1995; Cummins, 1981, 2000; Hakuta, Butler, & Witt, 2000; Srole, 1997), with estimates ranging from 4 to as many as 10 years to reach English-peer norms. Added to the linguistic pressures of complex, and often abstract, decontextualized vocabulary, syntax, and other features of oral language, the academic content itself is comprehensive and often difficult, and the literacy requirements and genres can also be extremely demanding. Furthermore, general and discipline-related cultural knowledge, such as intertextual allusions to other texts (biblical, literary, historical, pop-culture) or events in English literature or in social studies discourse is crucial but is often not part of new immigrant ELLs' cultural or textual schemata (Duff, 2001). Furthermore, students must often negotiate complex family, peer-group, and other social pressures that typically face adolescents, whether ELLs or not (Eckert, 1989; Phelan, Davidson, & Yu, 1998). Their academic program choices, extracurricular activities, social alliances, and identities—which may or may not converge with the preferences of their parents—may have a significant impact on students' subsequent prospects and trajectories for higher education and for their careers. For immigrant ELLs who may have experienced years of interrupted education, trauma, culture shock, and so on, succeeding academically in English contexts requires systematic and sustained intervention and such success is by no means assured. On top of their academic load, students may need to serve as language and cultural brokers for their extended family and take on other extracurricular roles as well. However, refugee-status or low-income immigrants and students who arrive from other countries during their teenage years with relatively low levels of English language proficiency may face the greatest obstacles of all (Gunderson, 2000).

It is often assumed that students who immigrate as young children are assured a much higher rate of success with mainstreaming and succeeding on a par with their local peers. However, ESL learners who arrive in the early grades of elementary school and are quickly mainstreamed also apparently face major disadvantages relative to their Canadian-born L1-English-speaking peers on standardized exams many years later, such as on provincial or state Grade 12 English examinations, despite their English fluency and their ability to obtain passing grades in their secondary school courses (Roessingh & Kover, 2002). Even in otherwise ideal educational and social circumstances, as in the program context outlined by Collier (1995), ESL students with excellent previous education in their L1 and 6 years of American education in English "had not yet reached the 50th percentile in English language arts, reading, science, and social studies by the time of graduation" (p. 10). The process of becoming fully integrated is therefore arduous for many ELLs, regardless of the level at which they enter school.

ESL PROGRAM TYPES AND REQUIREMENTS: LANGUAGE AND CONTENT INTEGRATION

Educational programs designed to assist English language learners with their academic language needs typically provide intensive language instruction in the early stages of their schooling, often with subsequent sheltered or content-based language instruction (CBLI), prior to the transition to mainstream coursework (Davison, 2001). The actual number of years for which students are eligible for ESL support and the form(s) that support takes is usually determined by state or provincial governments and is therefore quite variable from one region, year, and governing political party—and whim—to the next; that is, it is often determined more by political expedience than educational wisdom. In many regions of England, Australia, and Canada currently, ESL students are being mainstreamed more quickly than before and ESL teachers are losing their jobs (a growing trend in Western Canada, for example, as government policies and economic exigencies force the closure of some ESL programs by reducing provincial support for ESL students); alternatively, in more positive situations, the role of ESL teachers is being refashioned so that they work more closely with content teachers in mainstream courses (e.g., in England and the state of Victoria in Australia; Clegg, 1996a; Davison, 2001; Leung & Franson, 2001). The focus in such programs is the role of *language in education* or *language-across-the-curriculum*, and not just decontextualized *language education*. The goal is to help *all* learners and teachers gain a greater understanding of how language and literacy practices, including lexical-grammatical structures and different types of discourse markers and text types function within particular content areas to convey particular types of meanings.

There are many models and program designs for ESL instruction at the secondary school level. Carrasquillo and Rodriguez (2002) describe four such program types in the United States, which have counterparts in other countries.

- Free-standing ESL programs, with students from many different L1s who have immediate communication needs and little English proficiency; sheltered content instruction may be provided as well as language instruction but not at the beginning levels.
- Intensive remedial ESL programs, particularly at the high school level, with an emphasis on vocabulary, idiomatic expression, and basic reading and writing skills for students with virtually no English.
- "Pull-out" ESL programs, with 45- to 60-minute lessons during language arts classes, for example; these classes occur in separate ESL classrooms comprised of students from different grades and programs and with designated ESL teachers, who may travel throughout a school district to provide this support.
- ESL/bilingual education programs, with content gradually introduced in English as students become more proficient. There are other variants on this theme, however, including: transitional bilingual education, maintenance bilingual education, immersion education, structured English immersion, two-way (or dual-language) immersion, and newcomer programs (see Christian, 1996; Lindholm-Leary, 2001; Peregoy & Boyle, 1997).

Other alternatives to these four program types exist, such as programs that address the language and content needs of ESL students in mainstream classes by having appropriately trained content teachers make necessary accommodations for ESL students during regular lessons; or by means of adjuncted ESL classes specifically linked to content courses, giving students credit for both dealing with the language and content of the subject area (Snow & Brinton, 1988). In some school districts, students are allowed to attend high school only up to a certain age (e.g., age 18 or 19) and then must leave high school, they are "pushed out." If they have not completed graduation requirements by that time, they must seek graduation equivalency courses at community colleges or through other programs.

As an example of an adjunct program in Canada, Roessingh (1999) describes an ESL course that was successfully adjuncted to a sheltered Grade 10 English Literature course at a high school in a city in Alberta. The 23 Grade 10 students in the courses came from Pacific Rim regions and had typically immigrated around the age of 16. Their English reading was assessed to be at the 4.5 grade equivalent (GE) when they arrived but after their year of adjuncted instruction, they were reportedly reading at the 6 to 7 GE, as determined by the Gates MacGinitie reading test (MacGinitie & MacGinitie, 1992); Roessingh suggests a minimum threshold level of 7 GE should precede placement into an unsheltered, unadjuncted Grade 10 academic English course. All 23 students reportedly passed both courses and the English exam taken by all Grade 10 students at the end of the year and many continued to do well in their subsequent Grade 11 academic English course.

Many approaches have been developed for the integration of ESL students in specific content areas in the United States, Australia, England, and Canada, and for successfully combining language and content instruction (e.g., Chamot & O'Malley, 1994; Christie, 1992; Crandall, 1987; Martin, 1993; Mohan, 1986; Short, 1994; see also, Davison & Williams, 2001; Ovando & Collier, 1998; Stoller & Grabe, 1997). These approaches highlight the syntactic, lexical, and rhetorical structures and genres associated with academic disciplines and with particular types of texts; they also stress the importance of providing corresponding graphic support, cultural connections, and study skills and strategies. At the secondary level, students need to have a sophisticated command of English grammar and vocabulary, and must have control over a range of different written genres and registers and the discourse features associated with them. Reading and listening comprehension requirements are considerable, exacerbated by the amount of background knowledge or cultural schemata needed to access certain subjects. ESL students might have a vocabulary of 5,000 to 7,000 words, a reading speed (narratives) of approximately 100 wpm, and reading grade equivalent of Grade 6 or 7 in comparison with NESs in Grade 10 or higher, who are likely to have a 40,000-word vocabulary and a reading speed of approximately 300 wpm (Roessingh, 1999). Oral presentations, written reports and projects related to academic content, and quizzes and tests are common at this level, in addition to reading assignments and the need to comprehend teachers' lectures and explanations as well as classmates' discourse in class (Duff, 2001).

Much successful language and content (L&C) integration takes place in theme-based ESL or "sheltered" social studies, mathematics, or science courses designed to cover academic content but normally reserved for ESL students (e.g., Evans, 1996; Filson, 1996; McKean, 1996). Explicitly combined L&C instruction is less frequently found in mainstream content courses unless major reforms initiated by ESL specialists have been successfully implemented, often because of a lack of coordination between ESL and content specialists, little or no applied linguistics training among the latter, and the (misguided) notion that ESL students' needs are not the responsibility of content specialists, even though they may constitute more than half the students in a course. Nevertheless, some content teachers are finding ways of effectively accommodating the needs of their ESL students (e.g., Clegg, 1996a, 1996b; Mohan, Leung, & Davison, 2001; Snow & Brinton, 1997), usually with input from language teachers. Several sources document approaches to facilitating L&C integration and instruction in social studies, mathematics, and/or science (e.g., Carrasquillo & Rodriguez, 2002; Chamot, 1995; Crandall, 1987).

For notoriously difficult courses such as English literature with a high "linguistic threshold" that may be required for both high school graduation and university entrance, Roessingh and Field (2000) discuss the importance of the timing and sequencing of coursework in the academic mainstream, based on a consideration of students' "readiness," their L1 academic background (which was relatively high in their study), and the availability of adjuncted ESL support for students for English literature courses. Thus, they recommended that newcomers should first concentrate on subject areas in which they have strength, such as mathematics and chemistry before attempting to take social studies and English literature courses. The authors and several research participants in the study also recommended that courses like social studies be taken during summer school as a way of reducing the intensity of academic coursework during the regular academic year.

ESL AND SECONDARY SCHOOL CONTENT AREAS—THE CASE OF SOCIAL STUDIES

Rather than review ESL research in all secondary-level academic domains, here I provide a summary of research conducted in the content area I am most familiar with, social studies. Deborah Short and her colleagues have produced excellent sample curriculum guides, materials, and professional development feedback forms for middle-school teachers of ELLs learning social studies, often in sheltered ESL courses (Echevarria, Vogt, & Short, 2000; Short, 1994, 1997, 1999), based on their experiences as teachers, curriculum and materials developers, teacher educators, and researchers. They stress vocabulary, terms, concepts, and tasks specifically associated with social studies, as well as more general language functions, such as being able to define terms, retell events in sequence, and compare outcomes of events, and then perform various kinds of assignments, oral and written. With respect to reading comprehension, Short (1997) found that social studies textbooks, often the basis for lectures, were difficult: texts had various cohesion and coherence problems, limited explanations about key vocabulary (e.g., 10 or fewer words explained per chapter), and confusing displays, headings, and sidebars. Beck and McKeown's (1991) earlier analysis of social studies texts at lower grade levels also revealed that they were problematic because, among other things, they assume levels of background knowledge that students often lack (see also Carrasquillo & Rodriguez, 2002). Duff (2001) reviews some other research that has been conducted on L&C integration in social studies.

In my qualitative research on ELLs in mainstream high school social studies courses (Duff, 2001, 2002a, 2002b), I also found that students often lacked the linguistic, cultural, and geographical knowledge to interpret both oral and written texts, and the content with which they did have expertise, familiarity, or personal experience, such as Chinese history, was missing from the local curriculum. The courses in my research were at the Grade 10 level, at which the primary focus is Canadian history, economics, and society. The curriculum also expected students to interpret historical events and texts in a more critical, personal, and narrative way than had generally been required of them in other countries. Besides occasional essay writing or multiple choice tests, students had to take part in debates and role plays and produce in-class oral presentations, tasks that they were often uncomfortable with or ill-equipped for. The curriculum followed a multimodal approach that is currently promoted in social studies (Case, 1997; Seixas, 1997a, 1997b; Short, 1997; Singer & Hofstra Social Studies Educators, 1997). In many secondary mainstream classes, as in those I observed over a 2-year period, ESL students actually produced very little oral or written English, either during teacher-fronted instruction and discussions or on assignments. Assignments might include writing postcards home, from the perspective of a Canadian settler, or doing a poster representing the front page of a newspaper from a particular historical era. Working in small groups, ESL students often used their L1 and worked with classmates from similar linguistic backgrounds. This observation is not a critique of such L1 practices, however it does suggest that opportunities for L2 use may be reduced in contexts both inside and outside of school where large numbers of students share the same L1. Furthermore, both ESL students and local students said it was difficult for them to understand one another's English speech in class, which added to ESL students' reticence to participate actively in class—they couldn't respond to or build on one another's utterances in discussions because they couldn't hear or comprehend one another. This problem did not seem to impede local students, however. In addition, references to contemporary local issues, events, pop culture items, role models, and personal interests were commonplace. On the one hand, this practice made the classroom discourse potentially more interesting to the (local) students if not the whole class; on the other hand, it made it that much more difficult for newcomers to comprehend and contribute to.

Although integrated L&C instruction emphasizes the role of language in learning and the genres and syntactic structures used to convey particular types of meaning (e.g., Echevarria et al., 2000), social studies classes in my research contained very little explicit attention to text structures and vocabulary that students read, heard, or were asked to produce, or other kinds of scaffolding that scholars claim is beneficial for both ESL and local students (see e.g., Mohan, 2001). Similarly, graphic organizers and other visual aids and even use of the blackboard to write down important phrases or to illustrate the relationship among pieces of information (e.g., cause–effect, sequence, evaluation, classification) were used relatively infrequently. Similar findings were reported for social studies classes observed by Harklau (1994, 1999a) in California, although in the school where she did her research, there were fewer than 100 ESL students out of a student body of 1,600. In both our research contexts, ELLs' overt participation in mainstream classroom discourse was therefore impeded by a variety of social, educational, and discursive factors. Finally, as previously mentioned briefly, students were expected to produce relatively little extended expository writing, such as essays more than just a few paragraphs in length. As a result, students had relatively little practice and experience producing the kinds of essays or term papers that would be required in certain fields of higher education.

STANDARDS MOVEMENT, INITIATIVES, AND GUIDELINES

Prepared by leading scholars and other professionals in TESOL, *ESL Standards for Pre-K–12 Students* (TESOL, 1997) aims to describe the needs of ELLs across grade levels in the United States and provides a set of graduated goals and standards for students at beginning, intermediate, or advanced levels of English proficiency, or those who have limited previous formal schooling and have special needs as a result (e.g., literacy, understanding the culture and organization of schooling). Regardless of grade or proficiency level, the *Standards* document provides a set of three goals related to students' use of English for general communication, for communication connected to their academic content areas, and for pragmatically or sociolinguistically appropriate language use, both oral and written. For the first goal, to use English to communicate in social settings, Grades 9 to 12 standards emphasize that students are expected to participate in social interactions using English; use both oral and written English for personal enjoyment; and use various learning strategies to improve their communication skills. For the second goal, to use English to achieve academically in all content areas, students are expected to use English for classroom interaction, and to convey and construct both oral and written subject matter; and use learning strategies in relation to academic knowledge. Finally, for the third goal, to use English in socially and culturally appropriate ways (i.e., sociolinguistic and pragmatic aspects of language use), students are expected to use English and nonverbal communication appropriately according to the expected genre, register, and so on. Throughout the *Standards* document, students are encouraged to negotiate meanings with teachers and classmates cooperatively and effectively using various strategies, including the use of their L1. Sample progress indicators linked to the various goals and standards for Grades 9 to 12 students are shown in Table 3.1. Standards 1 to 3 do not appear to be sequenced in such a way that addressing Standard 2, for example, implies that Standard 1 has been mastered. Rather, the standards focus on different aspects of language use: the use of English in social interaction generally (Standard 1); the specific kind of communication and information involved in various tasks (Standard 2); and relevant learning strategies (Standard 3). Similarly, the three goals deal with different aspects of language use (basic interpersonal communication, academic language, and pragmatics). Although Goal 2 may indeed be more complex than Goal 1, it does not seem to imply prior mastery of the earlier goal, and it is not necessarily less complex than Goal 3.

Table 3.2 provides an example of how a task could be modified for different proficiency levels in secondary school. Here the task is for students to research the development of a (hypothetical) neighborhood toxic waste dump and the position they will take on the issue.

The goals and standards reflect the need for students to develop what Cummins (1979) refers to as oral and written basic interpersonal communication skills (BICS) and cognitive academic language proficiency (CALP; see Cummins, 2000, for a history of the BICS/CALP distinction and critiques of it); also stressed is the importance of sociolinguistic and discursive factors such as the social context in which language is to be used and the discourse registers and genres required. This model is consistent with Canale and Swain's (1980) description of communicative competence, which in their model comprised linguistic (code) competence, discourse competence, sociolinguistic competence, and strategic competence although it did not explicitly refer to academic proficiency.

In addition to *Standards* statements and initiatives such as these, many helpful resources for teachers and teacher educators dealing with secondary ESL students have been published over the past decade that provide both theoretical foundations, case studies, and highly practical model lessons, assessment tools, and lists of other resources (e.g., Cloud, Genesee, & Hamayan, 2000; Coelho, 1998; Hernandez, 1997; Scarcella, 1990). Several emphasize the importance of affirming students' cultural backgrounds and building on their existing knowledge. Other shorter guidelines have also been published to promote immigrant students' access to and engagement in secondary schools. Walqui (2000), for example, provides "ten principles of effective instruction for immigrant students," (pp. 1–2) including the following:

1. The culture of the classroom fosters the development of a community of learners, and all students are part of that community.
2. Good language teaching involves conceptual and academic development.
3. Students' experiential backgrounds provide a point of departure and an anchor in the exploration of new ideas.
4. Teaching and learning focus on substantive ideas that are organized cyclically.
5. New ideas and tasks are contextualized.
6. Academic strategies, sociocultural expectations, and academic norms are taught explicitly.
7. Tasks are relevant, meaningful, engaging and varied.
8. Complex and flexible forms of collaboration maximize learners' opportunities to interact while making sense of language and content.

TABLE 3.1

TESOL Goals, Standards, and Selected Sample Progress Indicators

Description of Standards for Each Goal	Sample Progress Indicators
Goal 1, Standard 1 Use English to interact in the classroom.	Make an appointment, write personal essays, describe feelings and emotions after watching a movie . . . (p. 109)
Goal 1 Standard 2 Interact in, through, and with spoken and written English for personal expression and enjoyment.	Discuss preferences for types of music, book genres, and computer programs; recommend a game, book, or computer program; listen to, read, watch, and respond to plays, films, stories, books, songs, poems, computer programs, and magazines . . . (p. 113)
Goal 1, Standard 3 Use learning strategies to extend their communicative competence.	Make notes in preparation for a meeting or interview; ask someone the meaning of a word; tell someone in the native language that a direction given in English was not understood; practice recently learned words by teaching a peer . . . (p. 117)
Goal 2, Standard 1 Use English to interact in the classroom.	Ask a teacher or peer to confirm one's understanding of directions to complete an assignment; negotiate cooperative roles and task assignments; use polite forms to negotiate and reach consensus; ask for assistance with a task . . . (p. 121)
Goal 2, Standard 2 Use English to obtain, process, construct, and provide subject matter information in spoken and written form.	Compare and classify information using technical vocabulary; write a summary of a book, article, movie, or lecture; research information on academic topics from multiple sources . . . (p. 127)
Goal 2, Standard 3 Use appropriate learning strategies to construct and apply academic knowledge.	Practice an oral report with peer prior to presenting in class; skim chapter headings, and bold print to determine the key points of a text; verbalize relationships between new information and information previously learned in another setting . . . (p. 135)
Goal 3, Standard 1 Use the appropriate language variety, register, and genre according to audience, purpose, and setting.	Select topics appropriate to discuss in a job interview; interpret and explain a political cartoon, situation comedy, or a joke; recognize irony, sarcasm, and humor in a variety of contexts; write business and personal letters; make polite requests . . . (p. 139)
Goal 3, Standard 2 Use nonverbal communication appropriate to audience, purpose, and setting.	Compare gestures and body language acceptable in formal and informal settings; maintain appropriate level of eye contact with audience while giving an oral presentation; use appropriate volume of voice in different settings . . . (p. 145)
Goal 3, Standard 3 Use appropriate learning strategies to extend their sociolinguistic and sociocultural competence.	Evaluate different types of communication for effectiveness in making one's point; rehearse different ways of speaking according to the formality of the setting . . . (p. 149)

Note. Adapted from *ESL Standards for Pre-k–12 Students* by TESOL, 1997, Alexandria, VA: TESOL.

TABLE 3.2

Sample Vignette: Goal 2 (Academic English)

Goal 2, Standard 2	Beginning	Intermediate	Advanced	Limited Formal Schooling
Goal 2: To use English to achieve academically in all content areas. **Standard 2:** To use English to obtain, process, construct, and provide subject matter information in spoken and written form.	Survey neighbors to learn if they are for or against a potential dump site and represent results in a graph.	Illustrate in a chart the advantages and disadvantages of various waste management options.	Using a computer model, generate a graph on the decomposition of different waste material over time and summarize.	Create a photo essay or magazine picture collage to reflect the pros and cons of a dump site and write captions.

Note. Adapted from *ESL Standards for Pre-k–12 Students* by TESOL, 1997, Alexandria, VA: TESOL.

9. Students are given multiple opportunities to extend their understandings and apply their knowledge.
10. Authentic assessment is an integral part of teaching and learning.

ASSESSMENT ISSUES AT THE SECONDARY LEVEL

The tenth principle concerns assessment, a ubiquitous and very political topic in education. Assessment of English language learners' L2 ability and/or their content knowledge at the secondary level covers the usual range of approaches, from locally developed content-based assignments or tests, to portfolios and performance-based assessment and a variety of other "in-house" English language assessment measures. Scholars recommend multiple sources of information about ELL students' abilities (Carrasquillo & Rodriguez, 2002), including teacher-made tests, teachers' observations, students' works (e.g., lab reports), collective group work, questionnaires or home surveys, standardized tests, portfolios of students' work, and students' self-assessments. The assessment may be for diagnostic, formative, summative, or other purposes, such as for program evaluation or for funding agencies, such as governments. According to Carrasquillo & Rodriguez (2002), who cite U.S. Department of Education statistics, oral English proficiency tests and home language surveys are the most common approaches used by school districts to assess students' language proficiency. However, they also note that many such measures of proficiency fail to take into account students' academic language proficiency, and many use a multiple-choice format.

Criterion-referenced assessment, as opposed to standardized, norm-referenced testing, needs to be contextualized meaningfully within the curriculum. Leung (2001) describes criterion-referenced task-based approaches to assessment and evaluation for secondary students. Tasks are closely related to the curriculum and to teaching and learning objectives, and language items are examined for their functionality within their immediate discourse context.

Another approach previously alluded to involves the use of nationally standardized curricula and tests, such as those associated with the English (subject) National Curriculum in England, described by Leung and Franson (2001). Students' performance is evaluated on an 8-level scale (designed originally for English speakers ages 5–14). However, as Leung and Franson point out, problems exist with using standardized tests for purposes they were not intended for, including those normed on and developed for English-L1 learners or for younger or older populations.

In a renewed neo-conservative political culture stressing educational accountability, students and teachers may be required to achieve certain scores on statewide examinations to proceed to the next grade level or continue on to college or university (no matter how well- or ill-conceived these examinations and measures might be or their suitability and thus validity for diverse populations). For example, since 1997 all students in New York State, including ELLs, must pass the Regents Comprehensive Examination in English to obtain a high school diploma (Carrasquillo & Rodriguez, 2002).

One of the ongoing difficulties in assessing ELL students' writing in content areas is the difficulty of conducting an integrated assessment of language and content (Mohan & Low, 1995; Short, 1993). Many content-area instructors seem to focus on content primarily and tend not to provide feedback on linguistic aspects, perhaps because of the enormity of the task, their lack of training in doing this, and uncertainty about whether providing such feedback makes any difference in students' development of ESL literacy. However, without some kind of systematic feedback on linguistic aspects of their performance, students may have reduced opportunities to focus on formal aspects of their language development that may otherwise remain underdeveloped and may continue to plague them at higher levels of education (e.g., Harklau et al., 1999). Mohan and Low discuss some of the benefits of collaborative teacher assessment of ESL writers, for which teachers agree on the criteria to be used in assessment.

In California, according to Hakuta et al. (2000), the IPT or IDEA Proficiency Test is used to distinguish English learners from those who are Fluent-English Proficient; sample oral skills for each follow:

- Identify content area vocabulary; use superlatives and past tense; understand and name opposites; ask past tense questions; discriminate differences in closely paired words; describe and organize the main properties of common objects (limited English-speaking EL, IPT level E).
- Use conditional tense verbs; discriminate fine differences in closely paired words; comprehend and predict the outcome of a story; recall and retell the main facts of a story; share meaningful personal experiences (fluent-English-speaking, IPT level F). (Hakuta et al., 2000, p. 20)

In contrast to the local, highly contextual, discourse-bound approach to assessment is standardized testing that is not linked to any particular curriculum contexts. Few international standardized ESL tests are specifically designed to test secondary level ELLs. One exception is the Secondary Level English Proficiency (SLEP) Test developed by the Educational Testing Service in New Jersey, which targets this age group. The test is normed on American English-speaking secondary students and some of the listening comprehension items include scripted conversations among American high school students. The test is often used to test ELLs in international English-medium schools (e.g., Duff, 1991). The SLEP Test includes listening and reading comprehension components only, with 75 multiple choice items in each, arranged according to their difficulty level. The test was envisioned as a precursor to the Test of English as a Foreign Language (TOEFL), in terms of its level of difficulty and intended population of test-takers, and ETS has published correlations between the SLEP Test and TOEFL (SLEP Test Manual, 1987).[7]

SECOND LANGUAGE SOCIALIZATION IN SECONDARY SCHOOL

One research approach for examining the experiences and needs of language-minority students at the secondary level is framed in terms of language socialization, discourse socialization, or academic literacies (see review in Zuengler & Cole, this volume), although there is relatively little research that examines adolescent learners' experiences specifically. Socialization, L&C, and language/literacy acquisition research have much in common; however, language socialization tends to focus less on micro skills, vocabulary, grammar, learning strategies, and elements of best practice in teaching and more on cultural practices and group membership, rituals and verbal routines, and changes in newcomers' degree of participation in local communities of learning over time and the social factors that support or scaffold increased participation (Lave & Wenger, 1991; Wenger, 1998). The difference in focus stems mainly from the origins of research on language socialization in linguistic anthropology rather than in education (Schieffelin & Ochs, 1986). More applied linguists and sociolinguists working in educational contexts are now applying language socialization perspectives to their ethnographic and discourse analytic work in secondary schools as well, in a variety of ways, and examining different issues (e.g., Bayley & Schecter, 2003; Duff, 1995, 1996, 2002a; Freeman, 1998). Topics examined include variable levels of affiliation with L1 and L2 communities of practice and their sociolinguistic behaviors and issues of social/academic integration, often but not always contextualized within a larger sociopolitical setting. Some current second language socialization research, such as my own (e.g., Duff, 2002a), examines how teachers and students co-construct classroom discourse that positions classroom members in certain ways—as cultural insiders or outsiders, as experts or novices, as full-fledged, competent participants or citizens in a given learning community, or as only peripheral or marginal members. Other research examines how from early on in their education, students are inducted into the practices associated with particular disciplines, such as science (Cole & Zuengler, 2003). L2 socialization research on adolescents has also focused on non-overt participation or silence on the part of some ESL students and how nonverbal and verbal behaviors are connected variably with different learner identities, aspirations, and possibilities (e.g., Pon, Goldstein, & Schecter, 2003; see also Morita, 2002, for similar work with university students).

ESL VERSUS MAINSTREAM LEARNING CONTEXTS—CULTURAL AND AFFECTIVE ISSUES

Several recent studies have examined differences in learning environments for secondary-level immigrant students in ESL classes versus mainstream courses (e.g., Duff, 2001; Harklau, 1994; Miller, 2000). The research usually involves interviews with students about their experiences at school as well as researchers' ethnographic observations of classroom contexts. Harklau (1994, 1999a, 1999b, 2000) conducted a multi-year ethnographic study in a northern Californian community that tracked four "newcomer" high school students of ethnic Chinese backgrounds in their transition from ESL to mainstream courses; she later examined their school-to-college transitions. In an Australian study with a similar population of ethnic Chinese immigrant students, Miller (2000), like Harklau, found that ESL speakers typically had "more real opportunities to use English [in an ESL reception program] than in their mainstream high schools" and "[in the mainstream] they found they were neither heard nor understood" (p. 96). Harklau's (1994) study reported that the tracking system used in schools further increased the differences between ESL and mainstream environments, particularly for ELLs placed in low-track mainstream programs.

Canadian studies of secondary-level ESL students (e.g., Duff, 2001, 2002a, 2002b; Gunderson, 2000; Kanno & Applebaum, 1995; Liang, 1998; Roessingh & Kover, 2002) reveal a commonly reported tension: ELLs and their parents often seek expedited mainstreaming and thus removal from physically and socially isolated groups of ESL students—and then experience frustration and disappointment with lower-than-expected grades and/or with social alienation once they are mainstreamed. Social, linguistic, and academic support is typically inadequate after students enter the mainstream. Parents who have the financial means often rely on after-school classes staffed by private tutors who use students' L1 and/or L2 to help ensure their success. Seeking additional coaching after school or on weekends is also a cultural practice in many countries with highly competitive education systems. Some students meet with private tutors for several hours each week to help them with their most troubling academic subjects and assignments. Unfortunately, students whose families lack the financial resources, access to qualified tutors, or the ability to provide academic support themselves have fewer options and may be at a considerable disadvantage.

ESL courses, beyond providing students with necessary training and practice in the L2 and in L2-content integration, also provide students with crucial social networks that they may find difficult to establish in the mainstream with local students (Duff, 2002a). In addition, the ESL classes often provide opportunities for students to express themselves orally and in writing, revealing aspects of their interests, histories, identities, aspirations, and personalities that may be completely masked in mainstream courses. The validation and recognition they receive from such opportunities can be invaluable and may be unavailable to them in the mainstream. However, to the extent that ESL classes are perceived merely as "fun-and-games" and as personal revelation, they become viewed as irrelevant to the academic goals of students (and their parents). Finally, as McKay & Wong (1996) demonstrate in their study of ethnically Chinese secondary students in California, students may be simultaneously negotiating multiple "Discourses," often including multiple sets of expectations, cultures, desires, and social positionings by themselves and by others. Thus, the contrast between ESL and mainstream cultures is just one cultural divide that students must cross on a regular basis. Harklau (1999b, 2000) and Valdés (1998) have written about issues of multiple and sometimes contradictory forms of representation of ELLs that they must then negotiate or endure during and beyond secondary school and some of the affective consequences of students' complex and evolving identities and ways of being positioned.

ESL STUDENTS AND HIGH SCHOOL DROP-OUT RATES

The linguistic and academic difficulty of secondary school coursework—especially in the senior years—and feelings of frustration and marginalization in mainstream environments contribute to high rates of dropout or attrition among minority-language students. There may also be important economic and social considerations for their attrition, such as the need for teens to enter the job market relatively early to earn money for the family, to take care of family members, and so on. Several recent studies (e.g., Derwing, Decorby, Ichikawa, & Jamieson, 1999; Roessingh & Kover, 2002; Watt & Roessingh, 2001) have documented patterns of dropout among ESL students in Canada; some American states also keep statistics on annual dropout rates across ethnic groups (e.g., California; see http://www.cde.ca.gov). Watt and Roessingh (2001) described a longitudinal study of 540 ESL students at an urban high school in Western Canada from 1988 to 1997, and budget cuts in the early 1990s that affected levels of provincial ESL support. They reported that dropout rates for ESL students remained quite consistent over the years, at 74%, but that "accelerated integration into academic mainstream courses has had a detrimental impact on the educational success of in-termediate level ESL students" (p. 203). More of the students who completed high school were opting for vocational tracks than academic tracks because they lacked the linguistic support and foundation for academic matriculation. The authors stated that, in contrast to the ESL rate, the general high school dropout rate was about 30 to 35%, based on federal, provincial, and municipal government sources. Derwing et al. (1999), conducting research in a different city in the same relatively affluent province, also found a low level of completion among students: 54% among 486 ESL students, of whom only 40% completed all high school graduation requirements; the rest dropped out, completed 100 credits toward graduation but did not receive a diploma, or were "pushed out" because of their age. (Others could not be tracked because they had moved from their school district.)

SCHOOL-TO-COLLEGE TRANSITIONS FOR SECONDARY STUDENTS

Finally, successful completion of high school, for those ELLs who attain that mile-stone, does not ensure their seamless admission into university or college and their successful graduation several years later. In fact, a generation of immigrants at least partly schooled in English-speaking countries now entering college or university are often dismayed to find themselves still being placed in postsecondary ESL compo-sition courses once in college, rather than in freshman English composition courses. Their instructors, moreover, are at a loss of how best to respond to the unique linguistic needs of this group, now commonly dubbed "Generation 1.5 students" (Harklau et al., 1999). Placement in remedial ESL courses is seen to be a particularly discouraging out-come for those ELLs previously viewed as "model" students in high school who may paradoxically find themselves stigmatized or struggling in courses at university be-cause of their undeveloped English essay writing skills (Harklau, 2000; Harklau et al., 1999). Therefore, a number of recent studies have examined the writing instruction received by ELLs in secondary school and the degree to which it prepares them for higher education and other literacy purposes, such as community, workplace, and per-sonal purposes (e.g., Lay, Carro, Tien, Niemann, & Leong, 1999). Hartman and Tarone (1999) reported that writing instruction for secondary ESL students in the Minnesota contexts they researched tended to focus on sentence- to paragraph-level grammar and mechanics, with an emphasis on grammatical accuracy. There was little or no prewriting activity such as concept mapping and brainstorming, little drafting and freewriting of the type encouraged in process writing approaches, and little emphasis on content. For higher-level ESL writing, modeling was considered important by one teacher, and she emphasized the correct suppliance of words found in readings, verb tenses, and other grammatical usage.

In contrast, in mainstream English classes at the same grade levels, a process ap-proach to writing was used that included prewriting activities, such as freewriting, journaling, and brainstorming, in order to elicit or activate students' background knowledge about topics. Weekly assignments in the latter context might include book reviews, literary criticism, character studies, and so on, in which students were expected to take a position of some sort and provide arguments in support of it. Gram-mar and mechanics were relatively minor concerns. One Grade 12 college preparatory English teacher, lamenting the lack of academic literacy preparation on the part of mainstreamed ESL students, of the sort required on test essays, said: "For crying out loud, spend some time tutoring them before you throw them to the wolves, as it were. I can't slow up!" (Adger & Peyton, 1999, p. 107). Content teachers in other areas (e.g., history, social studies, economics), for their part, reported that short-answer questions and essays were required in their courses, but they did not provide explicit instruction on writing; their primary concern was students' knowledge of subject matter, critical thinking, and the communication of ideas. Teachers reported on problems with the ESL students' logic and idea development in their writing and their paragraph development. It is natural that the ESL classes and mainstream English or other content classes would have somewhat different emphases and, thus, should be seen as complementary, because they have historically dealt with different populations and different priorities. That is, newcomers need to understand the basics of English before being asked to produce creative or complex works in their undeveloped second language. However, some conclusions drawn by Hartman and Tarone were that: (a) ESL students need to spend more time engaged in appropriate literacy instruction before being mainstreamed; (b) ESL students need to focus more on organization and content in their ESL writing instruction and not primarily on grammar and vocabulary (which may or may not transfer when doing more open-ended writing tasks); (c) inclusion on more process writing in ESL classes would not only better prepare ESL students for mainstream writing requirements in high school and beyond but would also help them develop and learn to communicate their ideas in English before attempting to write about them; (d) more emphasis should be placed on content and on a wider range of text types and genres; and (e) individual tutoring in writing would be beneficial for many students.

In a case study of three Latino middle school students' experiences with writing instruction across ESL and mainstream contexts, Valdés (1999) also points out that in ESL classes teachers approached writing instruction in various ways: (a) through a controlled composition approach (or guided composition) with a narrow emphasis on sentence-level grammatical accuracy and little room for creative expression on the part of students; (b) a more creative, generative process approach that for low-level students yielded pieces not easily understood by readers; (c) process writing and direct instruction, which had students work on longer pieces of writing, with multiple drafts, conferencing, instruction about organization, and a focus on students' own lives. Thus, students being mainstreamed and then proceeding to higher education may have had highly variable experiences with early L2 (and L1) literacy instruction, experiences that may years later continue to either help or haunt them. Across several studies in the Harklau et al. (1999) volume, ELLs were very surprised by the rigorous demands at the university level, for which high school simply left them unprepared. Therefore, the development of appropriate academic writing skills must remain a priority for both research and intervention with secondary-level ELLs.

CONCLUSION

This chapter reviewed some of the burgeoning research on ESL students at the secondary level from a number of perspectives: demographic, political, educational, social, and cultural. I have also attempted to balance descriptive, prescriptive, and research approaches to schooling at this level. One overall finding is that the challenges facing these students and their teachers are quite enormous, ranging from basic socialization and settlement, to oral language development and the development of academic literacies appropriate not only for secondary and higher education, but also for new standardized tests being imposed on many school districts. Students often experience extreme social isolation and disappointment at their academic and linguistic development, often because their own expectations or those of their family and school are overly ambitious. Another common theme is that many secondary level programs do not provide adequate content-based language and literacy instruction for students, resulting in difficulties for them once they are mainstreamed. However, despite these many challenges, many sources cited in this chapter provide suggestions about how students can be supported through their initial and ongoing language/literacy development in secondary school and how their academic interests and needs can be met in a deliberate, integrated fashion. More longitudinal research now needs to be conducted on the students' transitions from school to work or higher education. Rather than view secondary ESL students and their learning in isolation, they must be viewed in the context of their prior and subsequent learning, both inside and outside of English-medium schooling in order to understand more fully the effectiveness of their education and possibilities for the future.

NOTES

1. This research and preparation of this paper were supported by standard research grants from the Social Sciences and Humanities Research Council of Canada.
2. Canada's immigration policies and priorities and, in particular, the point system used to determine immigrants' eligibility were revised in 2002, placing new emphasis on proficiency in both languages.
3. I refer to English learners in schools, interchangeably, as ESL students, English language learners, newcomer students, and non-native English speakers. However, I recognize that these terms (and others, like *limited English proficient* students, *minority-language* students) may be problematic, potentially stigmatizing students because of their deficits in English rather than focussing on their L1 resources, repertoires, and emergent bilingualism. Interestingly, the California Dept. of Education has just changed its way of classifying students into English Learners (ELs) or EL students, and Fluent-English-Proficient (FEP) (http://www.data1.cde.ca.gov/dataquest/). Naturally, such terms do not adequately reflect the vast differences among students in either category, their years of residence in the English-dominant country, or their other characteristics.
4. The same is true in many British and Australian cities. Furthermore, many other non-English-dominant countries in Europe and elsewhere have similarly large numbers of new immigrants, often from a different range of source countries and needing to learn target languages other than English in their new host country.
5. There were over 1.5 million English learners in California public schools alone in Spring 2001, of whom 83.4% were Spanish-L1, with 1-3% of the remainder falling into the following major L1 groups, in descending order: Vietnamese, Hmong, Cantonese, Pilipino/Tagalog, Korean, and Khmer/Cambodian (according to 2001 statistics reported in http://www.cde.ca.gov). In comparison, there were about 188,000 fewer English learners just 5 years earlier. Among the 844,387 "Fluent-English-Proficient" in California public schools in Spring 2001, 65% were also from Spanish backgrounds, followed by those from Pilipino/Tagalog, Vietnamese, Cantonese, Korean, Mandarin, Khmer, Farsi, and Armenian backgrounds, representing in total 23% of the remainder.
6. Secondary school is contrasted with elementary school, but some school districts divide secondary school into middle or junior high school (e.g., grades 7–9) and senior high school (e.g., grades 10–12).
7. The SLEP Test is also commonly used in program contexts and with populations vastly different from those it was designed for, which is obviously problematic for reasons of test validity. In British Columbia, for instance, it is used for ELL adults in some healthcare programs and in other kinds of ESL/vocational programs with adults.

REFERENCES

Adger, C. T., & Peyton, J. K. (1999). Enhancing the education of immigrant students in secondary school: Structural challenges and directions. In C. J. Faltis & P. Wolfe (Eds.), *So much to say: Adolescents, bilingualism, and ESL in the secondary school* (pp. 205–224). New York: Teachers College Press.

Bayley, R., & Schecter, S. R. (Eds.). (2003). *Language socialization in bilingual and multilingual societies.* Clevedon, UK: Multilingual Matters.

Beck, I. L., & McKeown, M. G. (1991). Social studies texts are hard to understand: Mediating some of the difficulties. *Language Arts, 8,* 482–490.

Canale, M., & Swain, M. (1980). Theoretical bases of communicative approaches to second language teaching and testing. *Applied Linguistics, 1,* 1–47.

Carrasquillo, A. L., & Rodriguez, V. (2002). *Language minority students in the mainstream classroom* (2nd ed.). Clevedon, UK: Multilingual Matters.

Case, R. (1997). Elements of a coherent social studies program. In R. Case & P. Clark (Eds.), *The Canadian anthology of social studies* (pp. 9–15). Burnaby, British Columbia: Simon Fraser University.

Chamot, A. U. (1995). Implementing the Cognitive Academic Language Learning Approach: CALLA in Arlington, Virginia. *The Bilingual Research Journal, 19*, 379–394.

Chamot, A. U. & O'Malley, J. M. (1994). *The CALLA handbook: Implementing the cognitive academic language learning approach.* Reading, MA: Addison-Wesley.

Christian, D. (1996). Two-way immersion education: Students learning through two languages. *The Modern Language Journal, 80*, 66–76.

Christie, F. (1992). Literacy in Australia. *Annual Review of Applied Linguistics, 12*, 142–155.

Clegg, J. (1996a). Introduction. In J. Clegg (Ed.), *Mainstreaming ESL* (pp. 1–35). Philadelphia: Multilingual Matters.

Clegg, J. (Ed.). (1996b). *Mainstreaming ESL.* Philadelphia: Multilingual Matters.

Cloud, N., Genesee, F., & Hamayan, E. (2000). *Dual language instruction: A handbook for enriched education.* Boston: Heinle & Heinle.

Coelho, E. (1998). *Teaching and learning in multicultural schools.* Clevedon, UK: Multilingual Matters.

Cole, K. M., & Zuengler, J. (2003). Engaging in an authentic science project: Appropriating, resisting, and denying "scientific" identities. In R. Bayley & S. Schecter (Eds.), *Language socialization in bilingual and multilingual societies* (pp. 98–113). Clevedon, UK: Multilingual Matters.

Collier, V. P. (1989). How long: A synthesis of research on academic achievement in a second language. *TESOL Quarterly, 23*, 509–531.

Collier, V. P. (1995). *Promoting academic success for ESL students.* Jersey City, NJ: NJTESOL-BE.

Crandall, J. (Ed.). (1987). *ESL through content area instruction: Mathematics, science, social studies.* Washington, DC: Center for Applied Linguistics.

Cummins, J. (1979). Cognitive/academic language proficiency, linguistic interdependence, the optimal age question and some other matters. *Working Papers on Bilingualism, 19*, 121–129.

Cummins, J. (1981). The role of primary language development in promoting educational success for language minority students. In California State Department of Education, *Schooling and language minority students: A theoretical framework* (pp. 3–49). Sacramento: California Department of Education.

Cummins, J. (2000). *Language, power and pedagogy.* Clevedon, UK: Multilingual Matters.

Davison, C. (2001). Current policies, programs and practices in school ESL. In B. Mohan, C. Leung, & C. Davison (Eds.), *English as a second language in the mainstream* (pp. 30–50). New York: Longman/Pearson.

Davison, C., & Williams, A. (2001). Integrating language and content: Unresolved issues. In B. Mohan, C. Leung, & C. Davison (Eds), *English as a second language in the mainstream* (pp. 51–70). New York: Longman/Pearson.

Derwing, T., Decorby, E., Ichikawa, J., & Jamieson, K. (1999). Some factors that affect the success of ESL high school students. *Canadian Modern Language Review, 55*, 532–547.

Duff, P. (1991). Innovations in foreign language education: An evaluation of three Hungarian–English dual-language programs. *Journal of Multilingual and Multicultural Development, 12*, 459–476.

Duff, P. (1995). An ethnography of communication in immersion classrooms in Hungary. *TESOL Quarterly, 29*, 505–537.

Duff, P. (1996). Different languages, different practices: Socialization of discourse competence in dual-language school classrooms in Hungary. In K. Bailey & D. Nunan (Eds.), *Voices from the language classroom: Qualitative research in second language education* (pp. 407–433). New York: Cambridge University Press.

Duff, P. (2001). Language, literacy, content and (pop) culture: Challenges for ESL students in mainstream courses. *Canadian Modern Language Review, 58*, 103–132.

Duff, P. (2002a). The discursive co-construction of knowledge, identity, and difference: An ethnography of communication in the high school mainstream. *Applied Linguistics, 23*(3), 283–288.

Duff, P. (2002b). Pop culture and ESL students: Intertextuality, identity, and participation in classroom discussions. *Journal of Adolescent and Adult Literacy, 45*, 482–487.

Echevarria, J., Vogt, M., & Short, D. J. (2000). *Making content comprehensible for English language learners: The SIOP model.* Boston: Allyn & Bacon.

Eckert, P. (1989). *Jocks & burnouts: Social categories and identity in the high school.* New York: Teachers College Press.

Evans, R. (1996). Content-based language teaching: Geography for ESL students. In J. Clegg (Ed.), *Mainstreaming ESL* (pp. 179–197). Philadelphia: Multilingual Matters.

Faltis, C. J. (1999). Introduction: Creating a new history. In C. J. Faltis & P. Wolfe (Eds.), *So much to say: Adolescents, bilingualism, and ESL in the secondary school* (pp. 1–9). New York: Teachers College Press.

Filson, A. (1996). Environmental studies for ESL students: School skills, literacy and language. In J. Clegg (Ed.), *Mainstreaming ESL* (pp. 156–178). Philadelphia: Multilingual Matters.

Freeman, R. (1998). *Bilingual education and social change.* Clevedon, UK: Multilingual Matters.

Gunderson, L. (2000). Voices of the teenage diasporas. *Journal of Adolescent and Adult Literacy, 43*, 692–706.

Hakuta, K., Butler, Y. G., & Witt, D. (2000). How long does it take English learners to attain proficiency? (The University of California Linguistic Minority Research Institute, Policy Report 2000-1). Retrieved May 25, 2002, from http://www.cde.ca.gov/el/hakuta2.pdf

Harklau, L. (1994). ESL versus mainstream classes: Contrasting L2 learning environments. *TESOL Quarterly, 28*(2), 241–272.

Harklau, L., Losey, K., & Siegel, M. (Eds.). (1999). *Generation 1.5 meets college composition.* Mahwah, NJ: Erlbaum.

Harklau, L. (1999a). The ESL learning environment in secondary school. In C. Faltis & P. Wolfe (Eds.), *So much to say: Adolescents, bilingualism, and ESL in the secondary school* (pp. 42–60). New York: Teachers College Press.

Harklau, L. (1999b). Representing culture in the ESL writing classroom. In E. Hinkel (Ed.), *Culture in second language teaching and learning* (pp. 109–130). New York: Cambridge University Press.

Harklau, L. (2000). From the "good kids" to the "worst": Representations of English language learners across educational settings. *TESOL Quarterly, 34*, 35–67.

Hartman, B., & Tarone, E. (1999). Preparation for college writing: Teachers talk about writing instruction for Southeast Asian American students in secondary school. In L. Harklau, K. Losey, & M. Siegal (Eds.), *Generation 1.5 meets college composition* (pp. 99–118). Mahwah, NJ: Lawrence Erlbaum Associates.

Hernandez, H. (1997). *Teaching in multilingual classrooms*. Upper Saddle River, NJ: Prentice-Hall.

Kanno, Y., & Applebaum, S. D. (1995). ESL students speak up: Their stories of how we are doing. *TESL Canada Journal, 12*, 32–49.

Lay, N. D. S., Carro, G., Tien, S., Niemann, T., & Leong, S. (1999). Connections: High school to college. In L. Harklau, K. Losey, & M. Siegal (Eds.), *Generation 1.5 meets college composition* (pp. 175–190). Mahwah, NJ: Lawrence Erlbaum Associates.

Lave, J., & Wenger, E. (1991). *Situated learning: Legitimate peripheral participation*. New York: Cambridge University Press.

Leung, C. (2001). Evaluation of content-language learning in the mainstream classroom. In B. Mohan, C. Leung, & C. Davison (Eds), *English as a second language in the mainstream* (pp. 177–198). New York: Longman/Pearson.

Leung, C., & Franson, C. (2001). Mainstreaming: ESL as a diffused curriculum concern. In B. Mohan, C. Leung, & C. Davison (Eds), *English as a second language in the mainstream* (pp. 165–176). New York: Longman/Pearson.

Liang, X. (1998). *Dilemmas of cooperative learning: Chinese students in a Canadian school*. Unpublished doctoral dissertation, University of British Columbia.

Lindholm-Leary, K. (2001). *Dual language education*. Clevedon, UK: Multilingual Matters.

Martin, J. (1993). Genre and literacy: Modeling context in educational linguistics. *Annual Review of Applied Linguistics, 13*, 141–172.

MacGinitie, W., & MacGinitie, R. (1992). *Gates-MacGinitie readings tests, (2nd ed.), levels E and F*. Scarborough, Ontario, Canada: Nelson.

McKay, S., & Wong, S-L. C. (1996). Multiple discourses, multiple identities: Investment and agency in second-language learning among Chinese adolescent immigrant students. *Harvard Educational Review, 66*, 577–608.

McKean, R. (1996). A sheltered history course for ESL students. In J. Clegg (Ed.), *Mainstreaming ESL* (pp. 136–155). Philadelphia: Multilingual Matters.

Miller, J. (2000). Language use, identity, and social interaction: Migrant students in Australia. *Research on Language and Social Interaction, 33*, 69–100.

Mohan, B. (1986). *Language and content*. Reading, MA: Addison-Wesley.

Mohan, B. (2001). The second language as a medium of learning. In B. Mohan, C. Leung, & C. Davison (Eds), *English as a second language in the mainstream* (pp. 107–126). New York: Longman/Pearson.

Mohan, B., Leung, C., & Davison, C. (Eds.). (2001). *English as a second language in the mainstream: Teaching, learning and identity*. New York: Longman/Pearson.

Mohan, B., & Low, M. (1995). Collaborative teacher assessment of ESL writers: Conceptual and practical issues. *TESOL Journal, 5*(1), 28–31.

Morita, N. (2002). *Negotiating participation in second language academic communities: A study of identity, agency, and transformation*. Unpublished doctoral dissertation, University of British Columbia.

Ovando, C., & Collier, V. (1998). *Bilingual and ESL classrooms: Teaching in multicultural contexts* (2nd ed.). Boston: McGraw-Hill.

Peregoy, S. F., & Boyle, W. F. (1997). *Reading, writing, and learning in ESL* (2nd ed.). New York: Longman.

Phelan, P., Davidson, A. L., & Yu, H. C. (1998). *Adolescents' worlds: Negotiating family, peers, and school*. New York: Teachers College Press.

Pon, G., Goldstein, T., & Schecter, S. (2003). Interrupted by silences: The contemporary education of Hong Kong-born Chinese Canadians. In R. Bayley & S. R. Schecter (Eds.), *Language socialization in bilingual and multilingual societies* (pp. 114–127). Clevedon, UK: Multilingual Matters.

Roessingh, H. (1999). Adjunct support for high school ESL learners in mainstream English classes: Ensuring success. *TESL Canada Journal, 17*, 72–85.

Roessingh, H., & Field, D. (2000). Time, timing, timetabling: Critical elements of successful graduation of high school ESL learners. *TESL Canada Journal, 18*, 17–31.

Roessingh, H., & Kover, P. (2002). Working with younger-arriving ESL learners in high school English: Never too late to reclaim potential. *TESL Canada Journal, 19*, 1–19.

Scarcella, R. (1990). *Teaching language minority students in the multicultural classroom*. Englewood Cliffs, NJ: Prentice-Hall/Regents.

Schieffelin, B. B., & Ochs, E. (1986). *Language socialization across cultures*. Cambridge, UK: Cambridge University Press.

Seixas, P. (1997a). Making sense of the past in a multicultural classroom. In R. Case & P. Clark (Eds.), *The Canadian anthology of social studies* (pp. 163–170). Burnaby, British Columbia: Simon Fraser University.

Seixas, P. (1997b). The place of history within social studies. In I. Wright & A. Sears (Eds.), *Trends and issues in Canadian social studies* (pp. 116–129). Vancouver, British Columbia: Pacific Educational Press.

Short, D. (1993). Assessing integrated language and content instruction. *TESOL Quarterly, 27*, 627–656.

Short, D. (1994). Expanding middle school horizons: Integrating language, culture, and social studies. *TESOL Quarterly, 28*, 581–608.

Short, D. J. (1997). Reading and 'riting and ... social studies: Research on integrated language and content in secondary classrooms. In M. A. Snow & D. M. Brinton (Eds), *The content-based classroom* (pp. 213–232). White Plains, NY: Addison-Wesley/Longman.

Short, D. (1999). Integrating language and content for effective sheltered instruction programs. In C. Faltis & P. Wolfe (Eds), *So much to say: Adolescents, bilingualism, and ESL in the secondary school* (pp. 105–137). New York: Teachers College Press.

Singer, A. J., & Hofstra Social Studies Educators, Hofstra University. (1997). *Social studies for secondary schools: Teaching to learn, learning to teach*. Mahwah, NJ: Lawrence Erlbaum Associates.

SLEP Test Manual. (1987). Princeton, NJ: Educational Testing Service.

Snow, M. A., & Brinton, D. M. (1988). Content-based language instruction: Investigation the effectiveness of the adjunct model. *TESOL Quarterly, 22*, 553–574.

Snow, M. A., & Brinton, D. M. (Eds.). (1997). *The content-based curriculum*. White Plains, NY: Addison-Wesley/Longman.

Srole, C. (1997). Pedagogical responses from content faculty: Teaching content and language in history. In M. A. Snow & D. M. Brinton (Eds.), *The content-based curriculum* (pp. 104–116). White Plains, NY: Addison-Wesley/Longman.

Stoller, F. L., & Grabe, W. (1997). A six-T's approach to content-based instruction. In M. A. Snow & D. M. Brinton (Eds.), *The content-based classroom* (pp. 78–94). New York: Addison-Wesley/Longman.

TESOL (1997). *ESL standards for pre-k–12 students*. Alexandria, VA: TESOL.

Toohey, K. (2000). *Learning English at school: Identity, social relations and classroom practice*. Clevedon, UK: Multilingual Matters.

Valdés, G. (1998). The world outside and inside schools: Language and immigrant children. *Educational Researcher, 27*(6), 4–18.

Valdés, G. (1999). Incipient bilingualism and the development of English language writing abilities in the secondary school. In C. J. Faltis & P. Wolfe (Eds.), *So much to say: Adolescents, bilingualism, and ESL in the secondary school* (pp. 138–175). New York: Teachers College Press.

Walqui, A. (2000). *Strategies for success: Engaging immigrant students in secondary schools.* (Report No. EDO-FL-00-03), Washington, DC: ERIC Clearinghouse on Languages and Linguistics/Center for Applied Linguistics.

Watt, D., & Roessingh, H. (2001). The dynamics of ESL drop-out: Plus ça change... *Canadian Modern Language Review, 58*, 203–222.

Wenger, E. (1998). *Communities of practice: Learning, meaning, and identity*. New York: Cambridge University Press.

Zhao, Y. (2002, August 5). Wave of pupils lacking English strains schools. *New York Times*, p. 36.

4

ESL in Adult Education

Denise E. Murray
Macquarie University

That the title of this chapter is ESL in adult education and not one of the possible alternatives such as teaching English to adults or ESL for adults is significant in two ways. The title situates the chapter within the contested dichotomy of ESL versus EFL. Further, it frames this ESL instruction within adult education, that is, those systems established in English-dominant countries such as Australia, Canada, Great Britain, New Zealand, and the United States to provide high school subjects to adults who did not graduate from high school or to provide general interest subjects such as conversational Spanish or computer literacy. In other words, this framing differentiates between non-immigrant adults learning English (such an in intensive English programs) and immigrant/refugee adults learning English. Therefore, the focus of this chapter is on the teaching of English to adult immigrants and refugees. However, the chapter focuses on issues of particular interest to this population—issues of curriculum, program evaluation, particular learner characteristics, and assessment of learning. Although many other topics, such as reading strategies, learner identity, and task-based learning, are topics relevant to ESL in adult education, these topics will be dealt with in other chapters of this Handbook. The choices have been made based on providing readers with an overarching framework of ESL in adult education in English-dominant countries.

The delivery systems differ considerably across these countries, resulting in different perceptions of the adult ESL learner and instructional delivery as well as different research foci on what an agenda for research into ESL in adult education might entail. Consequently, there is no coherent body of research literature on adult ESL education; rather we have fragmentary, context-specific research, often with findings that are not generalizable. Even demographic research is scattered and inconsistent. A review of extant literature indicates that in most countries, the adult ESL learner is invisible on the national policy agenda and consequently program delivery and research are mostly nonfunded or underfunded. Thus, the adult ESL learner is almost invisible on the agenda of academic researchers—because of the lack of funding. The exceptions have been the long-term program and research funding in Australia and the recent alignment of ESL with literacy through the National Centre for ESL Literacy Education (NCLE) in the United States.

GLOBAL CONTEXTS FOR ESL IN ADULT EDUCATION

Although adult ESL learners across these countries may share similar backgrounds, experiences, and immigration or refugee status, because the context for their learning of English varies as a result of differences in program delivery systems, the adult education context for each country needs to be explained.

Australia

Australia has a more than 50-year history of encouraging English language learning as part of the settlement process of immigrants and refugees (Martin, 1999). Australian policies focus on the provision of language training and interpreter and translation services, along with coordination of welfare, labor market, health, and other social services to ensure immigrants' access to services. These services are coordinated through the National Integrated Settlement Strategy, a planning framework that fosters cooperation between all levels of government. English language provision is administered by the Adult Migrant English Program (AMEP) within the Department of Immigration and Multicultural and Indigenous Affairs.[1] Immigrants and refugees for whom English is not a first language and who have been assessed as not having functional English language skills are entitled to 510 hours of English language instruction. Provision within the AMEP is via state and territory organizations that are funded by the Commonwealth Government through a competitive tendering process every 5 years. In addition to formal face-to-face courses, a variety of other delivery modes are funded: distance learning, home tutoring, and self-paced learning through Independent Learning Centres (usually within the organizations that provide classes). For those learners not eligible for the AMEP or who have reached their 510 hour limit, courses are available through Institutes of Technical and Further Education, community groups, private language schools and other Commonwealth-funded programs linked to literacy and/or vocational training, some of which are fee-for-service and some offered free.

Because the AMEP is a nationally conducted program, the program has features unique to Australia: a national curriculum framework that meets the settlement needs of learners, a national research centre to coordinate and conduct research across the program, a collaborative approach between the Commonwealth and providers, and the professionalism of AMEP teachers. During the 53 years of the AMEP, instructional practice has changed as a result of research into best practice and into language learning and as a result of government policy. In the 1980s, as a result of research conducted in Australia and also a general direction toward learner-centeredness in TESOL, the AMEP "adopted a highly decentralised, learner-centred and needs-based curriculum planning philosophy" (Burns, 1995, p. 11). To operate such a bottom-up planning process that expected teacher autonomy, required teachers to become curriculum developers and researchers. During this period, a culture of professionalization and collaborative research developed, especially of action research. However, the action research models were collaborative and institutionally grounded (see, for example Brindley, 1990). In the early 1990s the program underwent major curriculum and policy changes, changes that are still in place today. These included the development of a national curriculum framework that is text-based and the certification of learner progress through the assessment of competencies.

Canada

Canada also has a nationally funded language program, Language Instruction for Newcomers to Canada (LINC), which provides free basic instruction in English and

French to facilitate adult immigrant and refugee integration into Canadian society. This comprehensive, uniform national program, however, was not instituted until 1992. Prior to that, language delivery to immigrants, although funded federally, was characterized by localized programs across a range of sectors, with variable curricula, teacher qualifications, and expected learner outcomes. The national nature of this funding does, however, reflect the Canadian acceptance that language instruction is part of immigrant and refugee settlement[2] and is a federal responsibility. As in Australia, LINC is managed through the federal department responsible for immigration, currently Citizenship and Immigration Canada, established in 1994 to "link immigration services with citizenship registration, to promote the unique ideals all Canadians share and to help build a stronger Canada" (Citizenship and Immigration Canada, 2002). However, unlike Australia, although the curriculum and assessment framework is national, program delivery is more devolved, funded annually through grants, and there is no national center to coordinate research, professional development, and resources.

Great Britain

Until 2002, the United Kingdom had not considered the learning of the national language for adult immigrants and refugees to be the responsibility of government. Indeed, even the conferring of citizenship for immigrants does not require demonstration of proficiency in English, Welsh, or Scottish Gaelic if the immigrant or refugee is married to a British citizen. However, two recent initiatives are changing the face of adult ESL in the United Kingdom. In 2002, the Home Secretary, David Blunkett, (2002) published a White Paper, "Secure Borders, Safe Haven: Integration with Diversity in Modern Britain," which proposes that language skills (along with knowledge about British society) become a requirement of citizenship. Meanwhile, the Department For Education and Skills included ESOL in its list of core skills that required curriculum development; Consequently, in 2001, the new Adult ESOL Core Curriculum was published, a core curriculum aligned with the national standards for adult literacy.

New Zealand

New Zealand, like the United Kingdom, is reconsidering how it addresses the needs of immigrants and refugees.

> Historically, the combination of high employment levels and a focus on English-speaking migrants meant the need for specific settlement services was low. The only large wave of non-English speaking background migrants in the period from 1945 to 1991 was that of Pacific Islands peoples in the 1960s and 1970s. This group was encouraged to migrate to fill semi-skilled job vacancies. Language proficiency was not considered a high priority in such employment (Fletcher, 1999).

Thus, New Zealand has no national curriculum framework for English (or Maori) language instruction for adults. More recently, New Zealand has focused on business migration, while still admitting family and humanitarian (refugee) migrants, the latter not being provided with language training after arrival. Immigrants and refugees can, however, enroll in private language schools and institutions on a fee-for-service basis.

United States

In contrast to Australian and Canada, ESL provision in the United States is a fragmented, locally delivered enterprise. Crandall (1993) vividly captures the minority status of adult ESL provision in the United States as follows:

> Large multilevel classes, limited resources, substandard facilities, intermittent funding, limited contracts with few benefits: This is the context in which ESL literacy practitioners work. Adult education is a stepchild of K–12 education and an afterthought in U.S. educational policy. That fact is made obvious each time a public school which is no longer needed is reassigned to adult education (often with the same small, children's desks inside) or when adult education classes are conducted in inappropriate facilities that during the day have other functions as elementary or secondary classrooms (p. 497).

In 1917, an immigration literacy test was introduced, primarily with the intention of restricting immigrants, especially from southeastern Europe. Later court decisions overturned much of this legislation, but sustained English literacy as a requirement for naturalization, a situation still in force today. The first Federal Act for teaching adult immigrants English was enacted in 1964. But this and later acts did not institutionalize a coherent policy for delivering English language instruction to immigrants, resulting in provision that is fragmented, financially unstable, marginalized, and spread across a number of sectors—adult literacy, cultural diversity, vocational education, community colleges, and community-based organizations. Federal funding comes through adult education, job-related federal grants, and block grants to the states. The only period in U.S. history when delivery of adult English language was tied to settlement was after the influx of Southeast Asian refugees. As there was no existing community to receive these immigrants and because of the United States' involvement in the Vietnam War, a comprehensive program was established for these refugees, involving the Departments of Education, Health and Human Services, and State. Yet the education of refugees has always been with the goal of their becoming self-sufficient, which really means that they no longer need social services, even if the wages they bring in are minimum and barely subsistence level. With this goal in mind, programs are designed to move learners into the workforce as quickly as possible, leading to curricula that focus on "survival."

IMPORTANT DEVELOPMENTS/TRENDS/TRADITIONS IN THE DISCIPLINE

Curricular Frameworks

In the United States, Australia, and the United Kingdom, recent approaches to adult education at the policy level have focused on adult literacy. In this policy context, ESL practitioners have had to argue for how ESL differs from adult literacy (see, for example, Moore, 1995; Davison, 1996) and/or include literacy (and sometimes even numeracy) as a language teaching focus in order to secure recognition and funding.

In the United States, the establishment of the National Center for ESL Literacy Education (NCLE) reflected a more national approach to the language education of immigrants, but with the focus on literacy. Although this innovation has led to more coordinated research and resource dissemination, the lack of a generally accepted definition of literacy gives programs freedom to develop their own views of and goals for literacy education (Wrigley & Guth, 1992), a freedom that results in a number of different approaches to adult ESL instruction. According to Crandall and Peyton (1993) adult ESL educators describe five different approaches used in the United States: Freirean, whole language, language experience approach, learner writing and publishing, and competency-based education.

The Freirean approach, sometimes called a participatory approach, is based on the political view that literacy is of value only if it helps people liberate themselves from the social conditions of oppression. Thus, the goal is social change. To achieve this, teachers act as facilitators and co-learners. Learners identify their own problems and develop solutions, producing texts that describe their problems, and seek to change their situations (see, for example, Ullman, 1999). In programs that use a whole language approach, written language is not broken apart, nor are rules or conventions discussed. Learners interact with texts they and others have written in a community of learners. The language experience approach, which can be used in a whole language program, is a technique in which learners dictate their own experiences, the experiences are transcribed, and then the transcriptions are used as reading material. The teacher's role is transcriber until learners can do it themselves. Teachers do not correct student errors, although students may do so themselves. Learner writing and publishing may actually be used in any of the other approaches, but programs with this focus value learners' own experiences and authentic audiences for writing. As students write for a real audience (their peers), they can reflect on what constitutes good writing. Competency-based ESL curricula often stress job-related tasks and include topics such as filling out forms, calling in sick, or developing listening skills to identify procedures to follow, but not the language needed for managerial or supervisory functions or for developing critical literacy for examining their roles and for reading texts in a variety of ways. Or, they may focus on personal survival competencies such as using public transportation or buying stamps at the post office. The goal is to help students to function in their new society.

The underlying philosophies of these different approaches are quite similar at the highest level—all seek to empower learners through literacy—yet, what we teach and how we teach it sends powerful and very different messages to learners. For example, competency-based education can lead learners to view literacy as only work-related and that their roles in the United States are as workers, not as critical thinkers. The other approaches can lead learners to believe that form doesn't matter. Only the Freirean approach recognizes explicitly the ideological nature of literacy. After the National Literacy Act of 1991, adult ESL programs and much of the ESL literature on adult ESL began to use "literacy" almost as synonymous with "ESL." Most recently, with federal legislation advocating welfare to work through initiatives such as the Workforce Investment Act of 1998, adult ESL providers are adopting a competency-based, vocational skills model in order to secure funding.

In Australia, in contrast to the United States, a national curriculum framework, the Certificates in Spoken and Written English (1998), at four levels (CSWE I, II, III, and IV) is mandated by the Commonwealth Government. In addition to the four levels, learners are placed in one of three bands, based on their learning pace; Band A being for learners with limited formal learning experiences, with low levels of literacy in their L1 and often with an L1 using a non-Roman script, whereas Band C is for students literate in their L1 and with some post-secondary education or technical skills training. The curriculum also offers different learning foci such as vocational English, further study, and community access. The framework is based on a text-based approach to curriculum design and a competency-based approach to assessment of outcomes. In a text-based approach (see, for example, Feetz, 1998), language is seen as a resource for making meaning through whole texts[3], and language learning involves learning how to choose among the different meaning making linguistic systems to communicate effectively in different contexts (see, for example, Certificates in Spoken and Written English, 1998; Feetz, 1998; Halliday, 1985). The curriculum includes literacy as a key competency, in response to both learner needs in a highly literate society, and in response to government policies and debates in the 1990s concerning the literacy crisis in Australia (see the following). The curriculum document itself consistently refers to "English language and literacy" as the curriculum's goal. In response to research into learner needs (e.g., McPherson, 1997), modules on numeracy training are included in the curriculum. The Certificates in Spoken and Written English (CSWE) curriculum was adopted in 1992, in response to a 1985 review of the AMEP in Australia (Campbell, 1986), a review that recommended a national key centre and a curriculum that had clearly defined learner pathways (see below for details of this review). From 1977, the AMEP had been generously funded to provide a variety of English language programs to meet the needs of different learners, which included programs in the workplace for professionals, using home tutoring, offered through, distance learning, for newly arrived immigrants and refugees and for long-term residents. During this period, the AMEP had adopted learner-centered approaches, in which learner needs were the starting point for syllabus design, the syllabus was negotiated with the learner, and the teacher was seen as curriculum developer (see Nunan, 1988).

Within the CSWE curricular framework, however, language providers and teachers have flexibility in the syllabus and instructional approach they use. However, common across the system is a focus on texts, both written and oral, and the explicit teaching of their structure (see, for example Feetz, 1998). Most AMEP teachers use the five-stage teaching-learning cycle developed through extensive research into language teaching in Australia, especially in disadvantaged K–12 schools (see, for example, Callaghan & Rothery, 1988). The diagram below summarizes this approach:

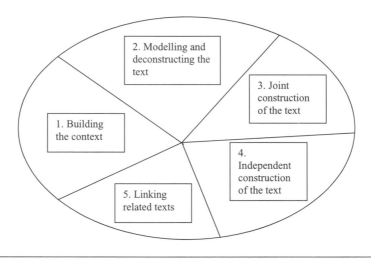

FIG. 4.1. *Source:* Feetz, 1998, p. 28.

In the United Kingdom, the new Adult ESOL Core Curriculum is based on the core curriculum for adult literacy, a focus required by the Qualifications and Curriculum Authority that developed the 2000 national standards for adult literacy. The national curriculum was developed as part of a national strategy on literacy and numeracy, in response to the findings of a 1999 government-sponsored report (Department for Education and Employment, 1999), a report that defined literacy and numeracy as "the ability to read, write and speak in English and to use mathematics at a level necessary to function at work and in society in general" (p. 7). For ESOL, literacy has been defined as the ability to speak, listen and respond, read and comprehend, and write to communicate (The Adult ESOL Core Curriculum, 2001). The Adult ESOL Core Curriculum offers a framework for English language learning, defines the skills, knowledge, and understanding that ESOL learners need to demonstrate their achievement of the national standards, and provides a reference tool for ESOL teachers in a variety of different settings (The Adult ESOL Core Curriculum, 2001).

The curriculum covers three levels across the four skills of listening, speaking, reading, and writing, but advocates an integrated approach. The overarching framework for the teaching of reading and writing comes from the National Literacy Strategy and includes:

- Text level addresses overall meaning of the text, the ability to read critically and flexibly, and write in different styles and forms.
- Sentence level deals with grammar, sentence structure, and punctuation.
- Word level looks at the individual words themselves, their structures, spelling and meaning (The Adult ESOL Core Curriculum, 2001, p. 11).

The curriculum suggests that although teachers might draw learners' attention to discrete parts of texts, the goal is understanding whole texts. However, no particular linguistic or pedagogic model is suggested as the basis for the curriculum framework. However, in describing how to use the curriculum, the writers indicate that teachers might want to begin with context that has been negotiated with learners (e.g., job search skills) and build tasks around the content that include required functions, grammar, and vocabulary; yet, in later sections it recommends starting syllabus development with a set of functions, topics, skill, or grammatical items (p. 21). It seems then, to be recommending a mixed syllabus (see Feetz, 1998).

In Canada, the benchmarks, firmly established within the disciplines of ESL, have been developed independently of adult literacy curricula. The national English-language benchmarks were developed through a working group of ESOL learners, teachers, administrators, immigrant service providers, and government officials (Pierce & Stewart, 1997). The benchmarks provide a descriptive scale of ESOL proficiency; they are not a syllabus. However, curriculum developers can use the benchmarks as a guide in syllabus design.

Program Evaluation

In 1994, the U.S. Department of Education completed a national evaluation of federally supported adult education programs to determine program effectiveness toward improving literacy, English language proficiency, and high school completion. Although this evaluation was of all adult programs, it provides useful data on ESL provision, in which 50% of all adult learners are enrolled (Office of Vocational and Adult Education, 1999).[4] ESL has been identified as the fastest growing area in federally funded adult programs (National Center for Educational Statistics, 1997), with 38% of national adult education enrollment being in ESL. This national evaluation found that the majority of clients in ESL classes were Hispanic (69%) and Asian (19%), lived in major metropolitan areas in the western region of the United States, were literate in their home language (92%), but spoke little English (87%). Almost half were employed while attending ESL adult classes. Class size was larger for ESL classes (median of 20) than for other adult programs (for example, Adult Basic Education had a class size median of 12) and ESL learners stayed in classes three to four times as long as did adults in other literacy/basic education programs. Retention (persistence) was found to be greater for learners who used support services such as counseling, attended day classes, and who engaged in independent study and/or computer-assisted learning. In other words, clients who used support services, attended during the day (rather than at night), and who engaged in independent and/or computer-assisted learning were more able to sustain their participation. In a telephone follow-up survey, the evaluation found that the majority of clients who left the program for reasons other than having completed the program or having achieved their goals, left because of change in work or because of family responsibilities. Interestingly, client cost per hour was not a predictor of persistence, but was a predictor of learning gains (Young, Fitzgerald, & Morgan, 1994).

Sixty percent of learners indicated that adult ESL had helped them improve their English skills, a finding supported by results on the standardized assessment (CASAS).[5] After 120 hours of instruction, adult ESL learners achieved an average gain of 5 scale points on the CASAS reading test;[6] increasing amounts of ESL instruction and increasing financial investment in ESL programs contributed directly to literacy gains in English. Additionally, learner employability improved—both initial employment and obtaining a better position. The report also notes that "the current adult education system is unable to keep up with the high demand for ESL services in spite of the important results being achieved by ESL literacy education" (Fitzgerald, 1995, p. 3).

In Australia, the AMEP has undergone a series of program evaluations, usually in response to external political pressures and/or changes of government. A 1978 report from a government-initiated review (Galbally, 1978) called for:

- The establishment of a wide range of post-arrival services for adult immigrants, including unlimited entitlements to free educational and settlement services. Provision of tuition to English language instruction was seen as an essential aspect of nation building.
- Stable triennial funding through state/territory organizations (AMES[7]).
- Increased job security for teachers through state education departments providing permanent AMES teaching positions.

These measures led to the rapid expansion of AMEP programs, including for newly arrived, long-term residents, home tutor, workplace, academic and professional, and distance learning programs. The stable and expanding environment for ESL teaching led to the professionalization of the field through a greater availability of graduate certificate, diploma, and masters programs. Unlike in the United States where such programs primarily lead to overseas positions, in Australia, the professionalization of the field was through the adult ESL sector.

In 1985, the Commonwealth Government commissioned an extensive review of the AMEP (Campbell, 1986), in particular focusing on the appropriateness of the curriculum model, which, at that time, was a learner-centered, learner-negotiated model. The review found that, although teachers supported the principles behind such a curriculum, in practice they found it placed tremendous demands on their time and expertise. In addition, the review found that there was a perceived lack of continuity in the program (Nunan, 1987). A key recommendation, therefore, was to develop curriculum guidelines or frameworks with clear learner pathways; in other words, to reduce the reliance on teachers as curriculum developers and provide a less negotiated syllabus. These frameworks were taken up at state level, where groups of teachers, working with colleagues assigned the role of curriculum coordinators, developed curricula for local use. Eventually, one such state (NSW AMES[8]) developed an integrated curriculum document, tested it with their own teachers and learners, had it accredited within the Australian vocational education system, and eventually had it adopted as the curriculum framework for the entire AMEP. This framework is the Certificates in Spoken and Written English (CSWE) referred to earlier.

Since tendering, the AMEP in Australia is measured on three criteria—reach, retention, and results. In 2000, research was conducted into both reach and retention of adult immigrants eligible for AMEP classes. This research, based on 1996–1998 data, found that 28% of clients left the program for one term or more without completing 510 hours or achieving functional English. The largest withdrawal rates were for Family Migration clients in general, young women in specific Vietnamese and Arabic communities, older adults in the Chinese groups, young adults in the former Yugoslavia groups, and young adult men in the Arabic group. Reasons clients cited for withdrawal included gaining employment, family or childcare responsibilities, fast pace of class, discouragement at slow progress, wanting a single-sex class, and lack of understanding of their entitlement (Noy, 2001a). A complementary study on why eligible clients did not begin English language classes found that the principle reason for not registering was that the client gave priority to meeting other needs such as finding employment. Other reasons included misunderstanding the regulations regarding registration and entitlement, not having access to culturally appropriate childcare, and lack of confidence in their ability to cope with formal learning because of their limited educational background (de Riva O'Phelan & Mawer, 2002).

In 2000, a National Client Satisfaction Survey was conducted through interviews with 3,203 clients, representing 87% of AMEP students contacted. This high participation rate was attributed to the survey methodology: Initial contact letters and the survey itself were conducted in 16 home languages, and service providers had discussed the upcoming survey in classes in advance. Overall, students were satisfied with the services provided, with dissatisfaction on individual survey items being less than 10% of clients. Survey questions covered a broad range of issues, including whether staff at their language center made them feel welcome, whether their English classes were enjoyable, how useful English was to them in their day-to-day life, and their initial assessment and placement. Seventy-nine percent of clients found the AMEP to be very helpful or helpful in assisting them to feel more confident about living in Australia, whereas 17% found it a little helpful. Clients from some backgrounds (Somalis, Turks, and Persians) were less comfortable in mixed classes; students were less happy with their outcomes in writing English than in speaking, reading, and understanding English.

Although there is no comparable national program in New Zealand and therefore no comparable governmental impetus for program evaluation, a recent study (Watts, White, & Trlin, 2002) examined learners' English language learning experiences, both formal and informal, and also the service providers' perceptions of learner needs. This study found that more than half (61.7%) of the participants had joined English classes in their first year in New Zealand. However, learners also indicated that they wanted greater levels of English language support from their own community, from government, and from the wider Kiwi community. Whereas they wanted classes from the first two groups, they wanted "opportunities to take part in and learn from conversational interaction" (Watts, White, & Trlin, 2002, p. 89). However, they also recognized that immigrants and refugees must take responsibility for their own learning of the host language. Among providers, "the strongly expressed view was that immigrants and refugees have diverse cultural, educational and linguistic needs and require flexible learning arrangements to meet their individual circumstances" (p. 90). They, like in Australia, found a number of factors that prevented some immigrants and refugees from participating, mostly lack of confidence, family attitudes, and religious belief. Providers also felt that government should play a larger role, especially in providing resources for (free) ESL provision. This report calls for the New Zealand government "to establish a national policy to coordinate the present fragmented system" (p. 96), citing the coordinated mechanisms of both Australia and Canada as models.

Like New Zealand, because there is no central government oversight of adult ESL, no government-sponsored program evaluations have been conducted. However, research was carried out in 1989 in 13 adult education ESOL centers around the United Kingdom, with the goal of providing:

> a detailed profile of the ESOL learners' socioeconomic, linguistic, and cultural back-
> ground. As well as analysing the migrants' attitudes and motivation towards English
> and their desire to maintain their mother tongues or heritage languages, the book de-
> scribes how the ESOL teachers and supervisors design their curriculum, produce teaching
> materials and evolve the tools and procedures to evaluate the progress made by learners
> (Khanna, Verma, Agnihotri, & Sinha, 1998, p. vii).

Their informants were fairly representative of the migrant groups in the United Kingdom, except for underrepresentation of African and Middle Eastern groups. They
found that the majority of learners were female; between the ages of 16 and 45;
attended classes in church halls, schools, clinics, or community centers; and were
in classes held twice a week and of 2 hours duration. They further found that the
Pakistanis, though sharing positive social and linguistic stereotypes with Indians,
had much higher levels of proficiency because their age at arrival in the United Kingdom was half that of the Indians. A majority of teachers are part time or voluntary
White teachers with brief training of 10 hours spread over 5 to 6 weeks. Among their
recommendations were the use of bilingual classes, female teachers for South Asian
women, a non-assimilationist approach to ESOL, more professionalism among teaching staff, an ESOL program sensitive to the socioeconomic, cultural, and linguistic
backgrounds of the ESOL learners, and "a national strategy for ESOL teaching which
recognises the sociolinguistic and pedagogic value of the development of skills in
both mother tongue and English" (Khanna et al., 1998, p. 103).

Learner Needs

Learner needs have been researched both in the microcosm of the learner and in the
broader context of the effect of language proficiency on immigrant and refugee settlement and integration. The former research issue has been of interest primarily to
teachers and program administrators as they attempt to develop programs that meet
the needs of the learners in their classes. The latter research issue is the concern of receiving governments who use such research to determine immigration policy. Because
these two strands of research are usually conducted by different researchers coming
from different research paradigms, the fact that what learners need and governments
want are in conflict is usually not addressed.

Research in a number of countries shows that host country language proficiency of
immigrants and refugees has a large positive effect on their earnings and labor mar-
ket/occupational status. In the United States and Canada, those proficient in English
have earnings 17% and 12% higher respectively than those not proficient in English
(Chiswick & Miller, 1992), whereas in Australia the reduction in earnings is around
10% (Stromback, 1988). Similarly, immigrants with higher levels of host country language proficiency have higher participation rates in the labor force and therefore lower
unemployment rates; language proficiency level is particularly important for immigrants in highly skilled occupations (see, for example, Wooden, 1994 for Australia;
Boyd, DeVries, & Simkin, 1994 for Canada; and Chiswick, Cohen, & Zach, 1997 for
the United States). Whereas oral language proficiency in English is required for initial
employment, literacy in English is needed for promotion and more advanced levels of
work (National Institute for Literacy, 2000). Less research has been conducted on the
effects of language proficiency on integration, and most of the researchers have used
interview or qualitative survey data. The studies that have been conducted identify
language/communication difficulties as being a serious issue for social interaction,

accessing services, and confidence in interacting in the wider community (see, for example, Ip, Wu, & Inglis, 1998 for Australia; Lidgard, Ho, Chen, Goodwin, & Bedford, 1998 for New Zealand).

Learner Characteristics

Learners With Special Needs.   Although each population of ESL learners will include learners with special needs, this issue has been addressed less in the adult sector. McPherson (1997) found that teachers and learners identified the groups that have special learning needs as aged learners, learners with low levels of literacy in L1, learners with no formal education background, students from non-Roman script backgrounds, and survivors of torture and trauma. Some studies have been conducted on survivors of torture and trauma (e.g., McPherson, 1997; Welaratna, 1985), learners with limited schooling and/or limited or no L1 literacy (e.g., Er, 1986; Hood & Kightley, 1991; McPherson, 1997; Weinstein, 1998), different learning styles (Willing, 1988), and older learners (Er, 1986, McPherson, 1997; Scott, 1994).

McPherson (1997) found that "classes formed on the basis of a range of characteristics which indicate a slow pace of learning will often result in such a disparate group that their very different language and literacy needs will not be effectively met" (p. 42). McPherson found further, that learners in Band A (that is, those with limited formal education and usually low levels of literacy in their L1) needed courses characterised by:

- Assessment and referral schemes that can identify special needs at entry into the program.
- Bilingual assistance for course information, goal clarification, language, learning.
- Lower intensity courses.
- A teaching methodology that has as explicit goals the development of language learning strategies and spoken and written language for community access.
- Teachers trained to identify special needs and develop appropriate strategies to meet them.
- Recognition within the certificates in Spoken and Written English (CSWE) for achievement of language goals related to settlement needs, and the need for further education and training. (p. 43)

For survivors of torture and trauma, McPherson's research identified the need for a uniquely designed learning context to accommodate their physical, psychological, and social needs, a finding supported by other research on such learners. Herman (1992) and the Canadian Centre for Victims of Torture (2000) note that such learners are often overwhelmed by their past experiences and feel a lack of control over their lives, a lack of connection and lack of meaning, and often have memory loss and poor concentration. Yet, language learning requires connection, control, concentration, and meaning-making. Research in this area has recommended that the language learning environment be flexible by providing opportunities for learners to share their experiences (but only if they so wish) and to choose their level of participation in classes. They also recommend that teachers focus on learners' strengths, including using L1, and help learners access community resources (see, for example, Canadian Centre for Victims of Torture, 2000; Florez, 2000; Isserlis, 1996, 2000; Rivera, 1999). Other adult ESL publications refer to the variety of language learners and strategies for teaching learners with particular needs (see, for example, The Adult ESOL Core Curriculum, 2001; Canadian Centre for Victims of Torture, 2000), but are based on experience and intuition, rather than on research or at least research reported in the publication.

In Australia, as a result of McPherson's recommendations, Department of Immigration and Multicultural and Indigenous Affairs agreed to provide an additional

100 hours of instruction for refugee clients, recognizing their special circumstances—often victims of torture and trauma, facing psychological and other barriers in their initial year of settlement. This program, called the Special Preparatory Program (SPP; Noy, 2001b):

- Provides a bridge from initial settlement and learning difficulties linked with past trauma to formal AMEP learning by establishing routine, structure and social networks.
- Allows extra time in a formal AMEP program to settle in and learn to begin to learn.
- Provides a supportive, nonthreatening environment (an additional support system) through relevant personal contact.
- Provides connections/information about support and settlement services (links and referral processes).

The SPP was evaluated in 2000 (Noy, 2001b), an evaluation that found that the vast majority (87.5%) of SPP clients made a successful transition to regular AMEP classes and that their initial progress in these classes compared favorably with that of other clients, demonstrating that the SPP assisted them to adapt to the learning environment and to learn successfully. SPP students generally withdrew from the AMEP for similar reasons to other students, although slightly more SPP than other students withdrew because of health and family reasons. Both this research and the original investigation into learners with special needs noted that learners with special needs require more than 510 hours to achieve functional English, in particular, written competencies.

Willing's 1988 study was the first and only major investigation of learning styles and strategies among the adult ESL population. The study involved interviews with teachers and learners and a questionnaire to which 517 learners responded. The questionnaire consisted of 30 items in the form of statements with which the respondent could answer "no," "a little," "good," and "best." In this study he found that:

> The learner's sense of satisfaction, his [sic] perceived achievement in a learning arrangement, and his perseverance in remaining in that learning arrangement, have been shown to be correlated with his perception of a compatibility between his own basic learning style and the teaching methods used. This suggests that the cognitive (and personality) tendencies of the individual should be prime factors in deciding teaching methodology in a given instance, rather than the teaching method, and choice of materials, being based on an a priori commitment of any kind. (p. 162)

The learners in his study exhibited styles along a continuum from analytical, structure-seeking (often authority oriented) to a concrete, communication orientation. To accommodate such a variety of styles, he suggested professional development of teachers, assessment of student learning styles, student awareness of learning styles, and teachers' willingness to change their own strongly held beliefs about effective language learning. Students, for example, frequently stated (Bako, Gazy, Gunn, Luchich, & Tongan, 2002; Willing, 1988) that they wanted a textbook with a clear progression in course structure, rather than lots of apparently unrelated "bits of paper" (handouts).

Assessment

Assessment issues have become of increasing concern as educational institutions have come under pressure from legislators to be more accountable. This accountability is often defined as measuring outcomes and demonstrating cost-effectiveness. Although there have been legislative requirements for such accountability systems in many countries (for example, the National Reporting System for Adult Education as required by the Workforce Investment Act in the United States), assessment reform needs to begin with clear, researched content standards, standards that articulate what adult ESL learners need to know and be able to do. In Australia, Canada, and more recently, the United Kingdom, such standards are articulated through the curriculum frameworks. In both Australia and Canada, outcomes-based assessment is an integral part of the curriculum—in Australia, measured through attainment of competencies required for the four certificate levels; in Canada, measured through 36 benchmarks that describe the competencies learners should demonstrate at that benchmark. In both cases, outcomes are measured by learners performing tasks. The tasks themselves are not mandated, but the situations and language required for the task are specified. The Canadian Benchmarks underwent a vigorous field testing before their implementation. Because the Australian CSWE is accredited by the NSW Vocational Education and Training Accreditation Board, it is subjected to revision when the Certificates are submitted for re-accreditation every 5 years. This revision includes input from the field through surveys and through ongoing moderation conducted by the organization that holds the copyright to the curriculum framework. In contrast, in the United Kingdom, assessment of student learning has been informal (Khanna, Verma, Agnihotri, & Sinha, 1998); however, now that there is a curriculum framework in place, assessment frameworks may follow.

However, in Australia, there has also been an ongoing research program into the validity, reliability, and feasibility of the tasks teachers use to assess their learners, which has, in turn, assisted in the revisions of the framework. This program has included investigating task comparability and difficulty (Brindley, 2000; Brindley & Slatyer, 2000; Wigglesworth, 2000), rater consistency (Brindley, 2001; Smith, 2000), washback (Burrows, 2001), and task moderation (Claire, 2001). This program of research has identified several issues of concern in teacher assessment of learner competencies: "moderation practices and rating patterns are shown to vary across teachers and locations;" "teachers' concerns about the increased workload involved in designing and administering their own assessment tasks" (Burrows, 2001, p. 8). As a result of these findings, the AMEP Research Centre engages teachers in professional development in task design and, through this process, has developed an online bank of assessment tasks and procedures that have been rigorously field tested.[9]

In the United States, as a result of a survey that identified the lack of skills among job seekers for the jobs they were applying for, the U.S. Department of Labor convened a group of business and education leaders to determine what schools could do to better prepare students for the workforce (Secretary's Commission on Achieving Necessary Skills, 1991).[10] The National Reporting System for Adult Education (2001) lists five core measurable outcomes: educational gain, employment, employment retention, placement in postsecondary education or training, and receipt of a secondary school diploma or equivalent. For ESL, educational gain is described in terms of competencies at six levels. Programs assess learners at intake and then after instruction, using the descriptors for each competency. Assessments can be either competency-based standardized tests such as CASAS Life Skills Test or performance assessments; however, the procedure must be the same for all programs in the state. Although research has been conducted on adult ESL assessment in the United States, most has centered around comparing ESL-specific tests with general adult basic education tests (see, for example, Adult Learning Resource Center, 1991). Because the assessment focus in the United States has been on external, standardized tests, there has not been the same sort of research program into the relation between outcomes assessment and the curriculum, the professional development of teachers, or the need for the development of tasks. The focus has been on the reliability and validity of the standardized tests. This is not surprising, given that in contrast to Australia, development of adult ESL content standards and therefore clearly defined learner outcomes has, until recently, been devolved to the state level (see, for example, California Department of Education, 1992). Recently, TESOL, the international professional ESL association, developed standards for adult ESL programs, but because the standards cover all aspects of programs, content standards are skeletal (Program Standards for Adult ESOL Programs, 2000). Thus, there is no agreement on what skills and proficiencies should be taught and then assessed and for what purposes.

Because of this lack of coherence among learner outcomes, syllabus design, and assessment, ESL experts have asserted that assessment instruments are inadequate. In *Adult ESL Language and Literacy Instruction: A Vision and Action Agenda for the 21st Century* (2000), adult ESL experts conclude that:

> Many states are having difficulty implementing assessments that meet the federal accountability requirements of the National Reporting System. Some standardized tests in use do not adequately measure gains by beginning English language learners with minimal literacy proficiency, or those made by English language learners at more advanced proficiency levels. Some tests in use do not measure gains in the acquisition and use of oral communication skills (the primary goal of many learners) and progress in nonlinguistic understandings and skills necessary to make these gains. (p. 9)

In Canada, the Canadian Language Benchmarks (1996) provide a useful document for creating assessment tasks. These benchmarks, a descriptive scale of ESOL levels, identify 12 benchmarks across three levels of proficiency in the three skills areas of listening/speaking, reading, and writing. Benchmarks are written in performance language, describing what a learner can do and under what conditions. The document includes sample tasks that could be used for assessment. Complementing the benchmarks document is the Canadian Language Benchmarks Assessment, designed to assist in placement and assessment of learners. There are three instruments, one for each of the skills areas of the benchmarks: the listening/speaking is an interview that takes 10 to 30 minutes to administer; the reading and writing instruments can be administered to individuals or groups and take a further 1 to 2 hours to administer. Development is still underway and the assessment is not considered high stakes because it does not determine future jobs or study (Pierce & Stewart, 1997).

CURRENT CONTROVERSIES AND THE REASONS THAT THEY HAVE ARISEN

One could list many controversies, ones that range from classroom practice to government policy. However, I have chosen to discuss only four controversies, ones that have the potential for major impact on learners' lives: ideology, literacy or ESL?, provision, and assessment.

Ideologies in English Language Delivery

As both Tollefson (1991) and Auerbach (1985) have argued, ESL curricula often reflect deeply held ideologies such as that work leads to economic success, that welfare dependence results from being lazy, English binds the nation, and education creates equality of opportunity. Thus, inequity, either social or economic, must be the result of individual's language and literacy problems, all of which can be remedied through education and hard work on the part of the immigrant. These ideologies play out in a society in which the dominant group and culture has imposed its values and beliefs through language (and literacy) requirements, but often as guises for race, color or religion according to Leibowitz, 1971. This has been even more evident in the K–12 sector.

Therefore, we see that adult ESL programs' goals are often at odds with those of their learners—learners want to learn English literacy in order to get a better job; the program, on the other hand, may be measured by the rate of job placement so that their goal becomes *any* job. This latter focus of funding and consequently programs, guarantees a workforce suitable for menial labor, despite the previous job history or skills of the immigrant. Thus, doctors work as janitors, teachers work as hotel maids, engineers work as busboys. Learners' identities and status are defined by their competency in the English language. There is a not-so-subtle irony in the fact that while on the one hand the ideology underlying policy formation in the United States views hard work as leading to economic success, on the other hand, despite immigrants' hard work in their jobs, economic success is usually not assured until linguistic competency is achieved. Even then, economic and social success may be unachievable because of race, color or religion.

ESL/Literacy

The title of McKay's 1993 book says, "Agendas for Second Language Literacy." All the stakeholders have different agendas in teaching English to new adult immigrants. This is exacerbated by competing agendas, both political and theoretical, between ESL and adult. In Australia, the 1991 policy document that established the Australian Language and Literacy Policy (Department of Employment Education and Training, 1991) defined literacy in such a way that it became equated with English, language, or even oracy (see Davison, 1996, for an extensive discussion). Traditionally, adult ESL teachers had considered themselves to be language teachers and that literacy was a part of the language they were teaching. But, they also recognized important distinctions between first and second language acquisition, a distinction lost in the Australian Language and Literacy Policy definition and subsequent provision. This conflation of terms has led to many organizations describing themselves as language and literacy providers—which may be true in terms of provision; they provide both literacy instruction to native English speakers and ESL to learners with a mother tongue other than English. In reality, however, it blurs the distinction in the minds of the public and of politicians. A similar positioning has occurred in both the United Kingdom and the United States. Although the United Kingdom curriculum does include speaking and listening, its being framed within the national literacy strategy demonstrates how literacy and ESL have been conflated in the United Kingdom, just as was attempted in Australia and is often assumed in the United States. In the United States, adult ESL language and literacy is the current terminology. Although the ESL field may have made pragmatic decisions by adopting literacy as part of the ESL agenda—to secure funding, to ensure more than the spoken language is taught, to describe multiprogram organizations—definitions are vital in any field as they help define that field. Although we may want to insist on including literacy as part of ESL provision, if ESL or language is considered synonymous with literacy, the very distinctions between first and second language acquisition are lost. Becoming literate in ones' first language is not the same as becoming literate in a second or third.

Provision

A controversy peculiar to Australia, but with important ramifications elsewhere, is the length of provision of ESL classes. In Australia, newly arrived immigrants and refugees without functional English are entitled to 510 hours of free classes in the AMEP, after which they may continue their study through community programs or the regular Technical and Further Education sector. The number of hours was arrived at by looking at the average number of hours learners stayed in programs. This limit of free tuition is hotly contested in Australia, with teachers and providers recognizing that learners take varying paths and times to acquire English. Most recently govern-ment, too, has recognized the need of some learners for additional hours (see previous SPP discussion). That a program that was once freely available to learners of varying proficiency in English and with varying focuses of instruction (see previous discussion on Galbally report), indicates that the adult ESL field must be eternally vigilant on be-half of our learners. When we consider the lack of coordinated provision in the United States, New Zealand, and the United Kingdom, we see that the field of adult ESL is de-professionalized, despite the number of immigrants entering these countries.

Assessment

Assessment remains a controversial issue in adult ESL. As Van Duzer and Berdan (1999) note:

> Learners want to know how well they are progressing in learning English. Teachers want feedback on the effectiveness of their instruction. Program administrators want to know how well they are meeting program goals and how they can improve their services. Those funding the programs as well as the general public want to know whether funds spent are yielding results. Policymakers want to know what specific practices are successful so they can establish guidelines for allocating future funds. A single approach to assessment may not provide enough useful information to satisfy each of these demands. (p. 201)

Although teachers and learners want assessments to determine their progress, they are resistant to high-stakes assessments that will determine their futures—either in the workforce or in further education. Whereas many current measures are not suffi-ciently valid or reliable to be used for such determinations, this situation can actually act to the disadvantage of learners. For example, the Australian Certificates, although accredited within the vocational education sector, are not aligned with other voca-tional education programs or instruments so that holding a CSWE Certificate does not guarantee the learner access to jobs or further education. Similarly, in the United States, the lack of a coherent system means learners do not have a coherent pathway through ESL programs to vocational or academic programs. In Canada, developers are resisting using their assessments for such high-stakes purposes.

FUTURE DIRECTIONS FOR RESEARCH

In 1998, NCLE published its research agenda for adult ESL (in the United States), an initiative designed to focus the attention of policymakers, funders, and researchers on improving the effectiveness of adult ESL programs and thereby the lives of learners. The research areas identified by learners, instructors, program administrators, policy-makers, and researchers suggest five general areas around which research questions in the field of adult ESL cluster:

- The learners themselves.
- Program design and instructional content and practices.
- Teacher preparation and staff development.
- Learner assessment and outcomes.
- Policy.

Priority issues are:

- Assessment of adult ESL learner progress and achievement.
- Measurement of the impact of participation in adult ESL programs on the lives of participants. (Van Duzer, Peyton, & Comings, 1998)

In 1990, Brindley articulated a research agenda for TESOL in Australian adult ESL that identifies research approaches, examples of research questions, and procedures for conducting research. The framework focuses on collaborative research as the most appropriate approach that would allow "investigation of research questions from the perspective of teachers, policy makers, administrators and of learners themselves" (p. 7).

The research questions and issues raised in both these agendas are as relevant now as when they were originally published. From the overview presented in this chapter, it can be seen that although research has been conducted over the intervening period, it has often been tied so closely to institutions or in response to particular policies (e.g., literacy subsuming ESL) that the goals of improving programs and thereby improving learners' lives have not been met. Even in Australia, with an almost 2-decade history of comprehensive research into adult ESL, much of the research is not generalizable. Although the action research projects provided important professional development and insights for the teachers involved in the projects and quite often important feedback to organizations about program delivery, the voice of learners, policymakers, and administrators is either eclipsed or seen through the voice of teachers. Additionally, as will all self-reported research methodologies, the lack of triangulation means that the perspective of the observer is also not heard. It seems then, that Brindley's call for collaborative research using a variety of research tools and techniques is required so that the research would serve the needs of the different stakeholders: learners, teachers, administrators, and policymakers.

> A greater emphasis on research of the collaborative kind would have a number of advantages. Apart from the most obvious benefit of improving our collective understanding of second language teaching and learning and the contexts in which they take place, it would enable problems to be investigated from multiple perspectives, thus increasing the likelihood of systematic follow-up of research results (Brindley, 1990, p. 25) and so improve the lives of learners.

NOTES

1. This is the current name for the department. Over the past 50 years the department has had a variety of different names, but English language provision has always been the responsibility of the AMEP section within the department responsible for immigration and settlement. Traditionally immigrants to Australia have been referred to as migrants; hence, the name Adult Migrant Education Program.
2. The 1976 Canadian Immigration Act created a separate class for refugees to distinguish them from immigrants, and established Canada's first refugee determination system. The June 2002 Immigration and Refugee Protection Act replaced this act.
3. This curriculum model is based on Systemic Functional Grammar, where text refers to a stretch of language, whether spoken or written, that coheres through meaning and is embedded in the social contexts in which it is used.
4. In 1992, when the National Evaluation of Adult Education Programs was conducted, 51% of participants in adult programs were in ESL programs, a 268% increase over the 12 years since the previous 1980 national survey (Fitzgerald, 1995).
5. CASAS, the Comprehensive Adult Student Assessment System, "is the only adult assessment system of its kind to be approved and validated by the U.S. Department of Education in the area of adult literacy" according to the CASAS website (http://www.casas.org). The system uses a competency-based approach to assessing language, literacy, and numeracy in real-life domains and is used extensively throughout the United States in ESL programs to assess learners' competency at the beginning, during, and at the end of instruction.
6. CASAS scores range from 150 to 260. CASAS suggests four levels of literacy: Beginning Literacy (below 200); Basic Literacy (200–214); Intermediate Literacy (215–224); High School Literacy (225 and above).
7. AMES or Adult Migrant Education Services were the state organizations that provided the English language instruction for the national AMEP.
8. The organization offering adult ESL in the state of New South Wales.

9. To ensure security of the test items, the task bank is only accessible to teachers in the AMEP and is password protected.
10. This commission identified specific skills needed by the workforce, the set of skills becoming known as SCANS (Secretary's Commission on Achieving Necessary Skills).

REFERENCES

Adult ESL language and literacy instruction: A vision and action agenda for the 21st century. (2000). Retrieved January 30, 2002, from http://www.cal.org/ncle/vision.htm

The Adult ESOL Core Curriculum. (2001). Retrieved August 29, 2002, from http://www.dfes.gov. uk/readwriteplus/ESOL

Adult Learning Resource Center. (1991). *Correlation study of adult English as a second language and adult basic education reading tests*. Des Plaines, IL: Author. (ERIC Document Reproduction Service No. ED352849)

Auerbach, E. R. (1985). The hidden curriculum of survival ESL. *TESOL Quarterly, 19*, 475–494.

Bako, M., Gazy, S., Gunn, M., Luchich, O., & Tongan, C. (2002). New perspectives on bilingual support. Panel presentation, AMEP National Forum, Adelaide, Australia.

Blunkett, D. (2002). *Secure borders, safe haven: Integration with diversity in modern Britain*. Retrieved March 8, 2002, from http://194.203.40.90/news.asp?NewsID=123

Brindley, G. (1990). Towards a research agenda for TESOL. *Prospect, 6*(1), 7–26.

Brindley, G. (2000). Task difficulty and task generalisability in competency-based writing assessment. In G. Brindley (Ed.), *Studies in immigrant English language assessment, Volume 1* (pp. 125–157) Sydney, Australia: NCELTR.

Brindley, G., & Slatyer, H. (2000). Task difficulty in ESL listening assessment. Paper presented at the 34th Annual TESOL Convention, Vancouver, British Columbia.

Brindley, G. (2001). Investigating rater consistency in competency-based language assessment. In G. Brindley & C. Burrows (Eds.), *Studies in immigrant English language assessment, Volume 2* (pp. 59–91). Sydney, Australia: NCELTR.

Boyd, M., DeVries, J., & Simkin, K. (1994). Language, economic status and integration. In H. Adelman, A. Borowski, M. Burstein, & L. Foster (Eds.), *Immigration and refugee policy: Australia and Canada compared. Volume I & II* (pp. 549–577). Melbourne, Australia: Melbourne University Press.

Burns, A. (1995). Teacher researchers: Perspectives on teacher action research and curriculum development. In A. Burns & S. Hood (Eds.), *Teachers' voices: Exploring course design in a changing curriculum* (pp. 4–19). Sydney, Australia: NCELTR.

Burrows, C. (2001). Searching for washback: The impact of assessment in the Certificate in Spoken and Written English. In G. Brindley & C. Burrows (Eds.), *Studies in immigrant English language assessment, Volume 2* (pp. 95–187) Sydney, Australia: NCELTR.

California Department of Education. (1992). *English-as-a-second-language model standards for adults education programs*. Sacramento, CA: Author.

Callaghan, M., & Rothery, J. (1998). *Teaching factual writing: A genre-based approach*. Sydney, Australia: Department of School Education, Metropolitan East Disadvantaged Schools Program.

Campbell, W. J. (1986). *Towards active voice*. Report of the Committee of Review of the Adult Migrant Education Program, Canberra: Australian Government Publishing Service.

Canadian Centre for Victims of Torture. (2000). Torture and second language acquisition. Retrieved August 30, 2002, from http://www.icomm.ca/ccvt/intro.html

Canadian Language Benchmarks. (1996). *English as a second language for adults; English as a second language for literacy learners*. Ottawa, Ontario: Ministry of Supplies and Services.

Certificates in Spoken and Written English. (1998). Sydney, Australia: New South Wales Adult Migrant English Service.

Chiswick, B. R., & Miller, P. W. (1992). Language in the labour market: The immigrant experience in Canada and the United States. In B. R. Chiswick (Ed.), *Immigration, language and ethnicity: Canada and the United States.* (pp. 229–290). Washington, DC: American Enterprise Institute Press.

Chiswick, B. R., Cohen, Y., & Zach, T. (1997). The labour market status of immigrants: Effects of the unemployment rate at arrival and duration of residence. *Industrial and Labour Relations Review, 50*(2), 289–303.

Citizenship and Immigration Canada. The department. Retrieved August 27, 2002, from http://www.cic.gc.ca/english/department/index.html

Claire, S. (2001). Assessment and moderation in the CSWE: Processes, performances and tasks. In G. Brindley & C. Burrows (Eds.), *Studies in immigrant English language assessment, Volume 2* (pp. 15–57). Sydney, Australia: NCELTR.

Comprehensive Adult Student Assessment System. (1996). *CASAS Life Skills Test*. San Diego, CA: Author.

Crandall, J. (1993). Professionalism and professionalization of adult ESL literacy. *TESOL Quarterly, 27*, 497–515.

Crandall, J., & Peyton, J. K. (Eds.) (1993). *Approaches to adult ESL literacy instruction*. McHenry, IL and Washington, DC: Delta Systems and Center for Applied Linguistics.

Davison, C. (1996). The multiple meanings of literacy in the TESOL and adult literacy professions: Problems of perspective? *Prospect, 11*(2), 47–57.

de Riva O'Phelan, J., & Mawer, G. (2002). *'More of the same' won't do the trick: Increasing the reach of the Adult Migrant English Program.* Sydney, Australia: NCELTR.

Department for Education and Employment. (1999). *A fresh start—improving literacy and numeracy.* (The report of the working group chaired by Sir Claus Moser). London: DfEE.

Department of Employment Education and Training. (1991). *Australia's language: The Australian language and literacy policy.* Canberra, Australia: Australian Government Printing Service.

Er, E. (1986). *A survey of the English language learning needs of elderly illiterate Chinese migrants.* Sydney, Australia: NSW AMES.

Feetz, S. (1998).*Text-based syllabus design.* Sydney, Australia: NCELTR.

Fitzgerald, N. B. (1995). ESL instruction in adult education: Findings from a national evaluation. Washington, DC: Clearinghouse on ESL Literacy Education. Retrieved May 30, 2002, from http://cal.org/ncle/DIGESTS/FITZGERA.HTM

Fletcher, M. (1999). Migrant settlement: A review of the literature and its relevance to New Zealand. New Zealand Department of Labour. Occasional Paper 1999/3. Retrieved August 12, 2002, from http://www.lmpg.govt.nz/opapers.htm

Florez, M. C. (2000, June/July). Native languages in the beginning adult ESL classroom: To use or not to use. *WATESOL News, 30*(4), 1, 10.

Galbally, F. (1978). *Migrant services and programs: Report of post-arrival programs and services for migrants.* Canberra: Australian Government Publishing Service.

Halliday, M. A. K. (1985). *Language, context and text: Aspects of language in a social semiotic perspective.* Geelong, Australia: Deakin University Press.

Hood, S., & Kightley, S. (1991). *Literacy development: A longitudinal study.* Sydney, Australia: NSW AMES.

Herman, J. (1992). *Trauma and recovery.* New York: Basic Books.

Ip, D., Wu, C-T., & Inglis, C. (1998). Settlement experiences of Taiwanese immigrants in Australia. *Asian Studies Review, 22*(1), 79–97.

Isserlis, J. (1996). Women at the centre of the curriculum. In K. Nonesuch (Ed.), *Making connections: Literacy and EAL curriculum from a feminist perspective* (pp. 13–14). Toronto: Canadian Congress for Learning Opportunities for Women.

Isserlis, J. (2000). Trauma and the adult English language learner. *ERIC Digest.* Retrieved August 19, 2002, from http://www.cal.org/DIGESTS/trauma2.htm

Khanna, A. L., Verma, M. K., Agnihotri, R. K. J., & Sinha, S. K. (1998). *Adult ESOL learners in Britain: A cross-cultural study.* Clevedon, UK: Multilingual Matters.

Leibowitz, A. H. (1971). *Educational policy and political acceptance: The imposition of English as the language of instruction in American Schools.* City: Publisher. (ERIC Document Reproduction Service No. ED047321).

Lidgard, J., Ho, E., Chen, Y-Y., Goodwin, J., & Bedford, R. (1998). Immigrants from Korea, Taiwan and Hong Kong in New Zealand in the mid-1990s: Macro and micro perspectives. Population Studies Centre Discussion Paper (29). Hamilton, New Zealand: University of Waikato.

Martin, A. (1999). *New life, new language: The history of the Adult Migrant English Program.* Sydney, Australia: NCELTR.

McKay, S. (1993). *Agendas for second language literacy.* Cambridge, UK: Cambridge University Press.

McPherson, P. (1997). *Investigating learner outcomes for clients with special needs in the Adult Migrant English Program.* Sydney, Australia: NCELTR.

Moore, H. (1995). Telling the history of the 1991 Australian Language and Literacy Policy. *TESOL in Context, 5*(1), 6–20.

National Center for Educational Statistics. (1997). *Participation of adults in English as a second language classes: 1994–5.* Washington, DC: U.S. Department of Education.

National Client Satisfaction Survey Report. (2000). Retrieved September 6, 2002, from http://www.immi.gov.au/amep/reports/clientsurvey.htm

National Institute for Literacy. (2000). *Equipped for the future content standards: What adults need to know and be able to do in the 21st century.* Washington, DC: Author.

National Reporting System for Adult Education. (2001, March). *Measures and methods for the National Reporting System for Adult Education: Implementation guidelines.* Washington, DC: U.S. Department of Education, Office of Vocational and Adult Education, Division of Adult Education and Literacy.

Noy, S. (2001a). *Competing priorities: Retention patterns in the Adult Migrant English Program.* Sydney, Australia: NCELTR.

Noy, S. (2001b). *The special PREP program: Its evolution and its future.* Sydney, Australia: NCELTR.

Nunan, D. (1987). *The teacher as curriculum developer.* Adelaide, Australia: NCRC.

Nunan, D. (1988). Learner-centred curriculum: A study in second language teaching. Cambridge, UK: Cambridge University Press.

Office of Vocational and Adult Education, U.S. Department of Education, Division of Adult Education and Literacy. August (1999). *State administered adult education program 1998 enrollment.* Retrieved October 16, 2000, from http://ed.gov/offices/ovae/98enrlbp.html

Pierce, B. N., & Stewart, G. (1997). The development of the Canadian language benchmarks assessment. *TESL Canada, 14*(2), 17–31.

Program Standards for Adult ESOL Programs. (2000). Alexandria, VA: TESOL.

Rivera, K. (1999). *Native language literacy and adult ESL instruction.* ERIC Digest. Washington, DC: National Center for ESL Literacy Education.

Scott, M. L. (1994). Auditory memory and perceptions in older adult second language learners. *Studies in Second Language Acquisition, 16*(3), 49–58.

Secretary's Commission on Achieving Necessary Skills. (1991). *What work requires of schools" A SCANS report for America 2000.* Washington, DC: U.S. Department of Labor.

Smith, D. 2000. Rater judgments in the direct assessment of competency-based writing assessment. In G. Brindley (ed.) Studies in immigrant English language assessment, Vol 1 (pp. 159–189). Sydney, Australia: NCELTR.

Stromback, T. (1988). Migrants, ethnic groups and the labour market: Policy options paper Canberra, Australia: Office of multicultural Affairs.

Tollefson, J. W. (1991). *Planning language, planning inequality: Language policy in the community.* London: Longman.

Ullman, C. (1999). Between discourse and practice: Immigrant rights, curriculum development, and ESL teacher education. *TESOL Quarterly, 33,* 513–528.

Van Duzer, C., Peyton, J. K., & Comings, J. (1998). *Research agenda for adult ESL.* Retrieved August 11, 2002, from http://www.cal.org/ncle/agenda/

Van Duzer, C. H., & Berdan, R. (1999). Perspectives on assessment in adult ESOL instruction. In Comings, J., Garner, B., & Smith, C., (Eds.), *Annual Review of Adult Learning and Literacy* (pp. 200–242). San Francisco: Jossey-Bass.

Watts, N., White, C., & Trlin, A. (2002). Immigrant and provider perceptions of ESOL learning environments. *The TESOLANZ Journal, 9,* 84–96.

Welaratna, U. (1985). Cambodian refugees: Factors affecting their assimilation and English language acquisition. *The CATESOL Journal, 1*(1), 17–26.

Weinstein, G. (1998). Family and intergenerational literacy in multilingual communities. ERIC Q & A. Retrieved August 8, 2002, from http://www.cal.org/ncle/digests/FamLit2.htm

Wigglesworth, G. (2000). Issues in the development of oral tasks for competency-based assessments of second language performance. In G. Brindley (Ed.), *Studies in immigrant English language assessment, Vol 1* (pp. 81–123). Sydney, Australia: NCELTR.

Willing, K. (1988). *Learning styles in adult migrant education.* Sydney, Australia: NCELTR.

Wooden, M. (1994). The labour market experience of immigrants. In M. Wooden, R. Holton, G. Hugo, & J. Sloan (Eds.), *Australian immigration: A survey of the issues* Canberra: Australian Government Publication Service.

Workplace Investment Act of 1998, Pub L. No. 105-220, § 212.b.2.A, 112 Stat. 936 (1998).

Wrigley, H. S., & Guth, G. J. A. (1992). *Bringing literacy to life: Issues and options in adult ESL literacy.* San Diego, CA: Dominie Press.

Young, M. A., Fitzgerald, N., & Morgan, M. A. (1994). *National evaluation of adult education programs. Fourth report: Learner outcomes and program results.* Washington, DC: U.S. Department of Education.

5

English for Academic Purposes

Susan Carkin
Lane Community College

INTRODUCTION

English for academic purposes (EAP), a subdomain of English for specific purposes (ESP), is generally housed in formal academic contexts. EAP shares subdomain status with English for occupational purposes (EOP), which includes English language use by both professionals (e.g., in medicine, business, law) and by nonprofessional workers (in vocational contexts). EAP itself is further subdivided into two emphases: EGAP, English for general academic purposes, and ESAP, English for specific academic purposes, a distinction first articulated by Blue (1988; cited in Dudley-Evans & St. John, 1998). The principal difference between these two subdivisions of EAP is one of scope. EGAP emphasizes "common core" skills and activities where English is taught for general academic purposes, across multiple disciplines, and includes learning and study skills components of broadly relevant academic skills. Thus, the general purpose approach is largely associated with lower-level EAP courses in which students are preparing for later work in disciplinary contexts. In contrast, ESAP emphasizes higher order skills, student development, and authentic texts and features while working within specific epistemological traditions associated with different disciplines. Overall, whether the emphasis is ESAP or EGAP, EAP concerns itself with the development of English for academic purposes and the transition from "pedagogic genres" (e.g., essay exams and term papers; see Johns, 1997) to increasingly authentic genres associated with various disciplines. This focus on learning academic language through academic tasks, texts, and content is the basis for claims that EAP instruction represents a highly pragmatic approach to learning, encompassing needs analyses, evaluation, academic skills, disciplinary content, and tasks in support of student learning in tertiary educational contexts.

This chapter begins with an overview of the range of contexts in which EAP is taught. It includes needs assessment, critical EAP, and a review of literate skills, competencies, and principal genres associated with EAP.

THE DOMAIN AND RANGE OF EAP: A BRIEF HISTORY

In his intellectual history of EAP, one of its most prominent scholars, John Swales (2001), fixes the date of its appearance in the 1960s. At that time, language for academic purposes appeared quite distinct from the more prominent literary uses of language. Swales notes that early EAP studies differed from traditional literary studies in their descriptive (as opposed to stylistic) goals, their representation of "normal" scientific genres, and their synchronic focus, among other differences (p. 44). A seminal book by Halliday, McIntosh and Strevens (1964) is often cited as providing the basic rationale underlying EAP, namely, descriptions of language, particularly vocabulary and syntax, "as used in specific target situations" (Flowerdew & Peacock, 2001, p. 11), that is, disciplines and occupations, and analyzed through statistical comparisons. Studies of language variation have grown increasingly refined over the years. Where early studies worked with relatively broad academic language categories, including English for Science and Technology (EST, e.g., Lackstrom, Selinker, & Trimble, 1970, 1973), later studies became more focused on limited sets of features in highly particular registers, examining, for example, the uses of the passive in two astrophysics articles (Tarone, Dwyer, Gillette, & Icke, 1981). As more disciplines and texts were studied, the domain of EAP broadened. Swales (2001) characterizes the change in focus and increased emphasis on context and situation as "multi-modal . . . [with] relationships between texts and contexts. . . much richer and more complex" (p. 49). He further notes that as discoursal studies, genre and register analyses, cultural influences, contrastive rhetoric, and social-construction theories influenced EAP, there have been substantial gains in our understanding of academic discourse. (For other perspectives on the history of EAP, see Benesch, 2001; Bhatia, 2002; Hyland and Hamp-Lyons, 2002; Jordan, 1997; Swales, 2000).

The implementation of an EAP program involves needs assessment, evaluation, analysis of student goals and skills, and a determination of the particular language features, vocabulary, organizational structures, discoursal patterns, and genres associated with the varieties of English found in university texts and classrooms. In the United States and other English-dominant countries, EAP largely resides in preuniversity and "bridge" programs. Such programs are associated with intensive and semi-intensive formats, and with particular language classes linked to content courses in which disciplinary faculty collaborate with ESL instructors (Brinton, Snow, & Wesche, 1989; Johns, 1992, 1995, 1997; Snow, 1997; Snow & Brinton, 1992). Where non-native speakers (NNSs) possess the requisite language proficiency to enter a university directly, EAP instruction is often limited to a composition course or sequence. Such writing courses assist second language (L2) students in acquiring the writing skills needed for successful work in higher education.

EAP is also taught in a variety of international settings to students who have various reasons for studying academic English and where English itself has different functional ranges. Dudley-Evans and St. John (1998) identify four types of EAP "situations" in tertiary levels of study. First, EAP is taught in higher education settings in English-speaking countries, like the United States, United Kingdom, Canada, and Australia. The students in this setting are primarily international students coming for graduate and undergraduate degrees as well as for short-term campus- or field-based programs. Second, EAP is taught in countries where there may be several native languages, but English has official recognition as the language of education throughout the schools, as in Zimbabwe and Singapore. Students in these settings may have a long history of English study in school but use their native language for ordinary communication and transactions. Third, EAP is taught in countries where specialty subjects are tied to English, such as medicine, technology, engineering, and science, while a national language is used for other subjects for which there are adequate texts in the native language, as in Jordan, where some majors are studied in Arabic and others in English. Finally, EAP exists in countries in which all tertiary education is taught in the L1 with English recognized as an auxiliary language, benefiting some students who may need to read cutting edge studies found only in English, as in many South American countries. Students studying within these four different situations can be expected to have different levels of proficiency in English, different EAP needs, distinct uses for EAP, and different interfaces between English and their major fields of study. Such variety in English preparation and purpose in tertiary settings is one reason for EAP's strong emphasis on needs assessment tied to particular contexts and populations prior to developing materials and setting goals.

NEEDS ANALYSIS AND ASSESSMENT IN EAP

Even though EAP is associated with tertiary educational settings, its international range, as well as graduate and undergraduate levels, make needs assessment a "cornerstone," critical for "the process of establishing the *what* and *how* of a course" (Dudley-Evans & St. John, 1998, p. 121). EAP students can be expected to vary by country, culture, institution, and academic goals, as well as by ethnic background, level of academic literacy in their L1s, English language development, rhetorical styles, and even their attitudes toward knowledge (Ballard & Clanchy, 1991). Needs assessment of the diverse learners in EAP underlies syllabus design, materials development, text selection, learning goals and tasks, and, ultimately, evaluation of students and course or program success.

The needs of EAP students in educational contexts have been investigated in a number of ways. Studies in the 1980s and 1990s largely surveyed and interviewed university professors, compiling their responses to catalogue and analyze skills (writing, reading, listening, speaking, vocabulary, strategies, etc.) and task demands (course reading and writing assignments, test formats, group work, etc.) of various disciplinary classrooms (cf. Braine, 1989; Bridgeman & Carlson, 1984; Ferris & Tagg, 1996a, 1996b; Horowitz, 1986; Johns, 1981, 1988; Santos, 1988; Waters, 1996; West, 1994). Such studies have investigated a range of skills and tasks across different disciplines as well as across undergraduate and graduate levels. These studies have highlighted the wide range of variability surrounding task demands, that is, differences by task type, by level, and by discipline. Classroom and learning tasks for engineers and business majors are very different, as are tasks typical of humanities and social sciences. Other studies have surveyed college instructors to determine their tolerance of student errors (e.g., Johns, 1981; Santos, 1988; Vann, Meyer, & Lorenz, 1984), information that can inform EAP curricula.

A common criticism of faculty surveys is that they rely narrowly on faculty and their perceptions of ESL student problems, leaving the students, their experience, and their perceptions out of the investigation (Nunan, 1988). A second criticism has to do with the predetermined categories into which responding faculty must place their answers, thus, disallowing potentially useful responses outside the domain of the survey.

Other studies examine the academic texts that students must be able to process, in particular, academic lectures and written texts. These studies focus on the use and distribution of discourse characteristics and linguistic features (e.g., Biber, Conrad, Reppen, Byrd, & Helt, 2002; Carkin, 2001; Chaudron & Richards, 1986; Flowerdew & Tauroza, 1995).

A study of writing tasks by Educational Testing Services in 1996 (Hale, Taylor, Bridgeman, Carson, Kroll, & Kantor) collected as data actual classroom materials and assignments given to undergraduate and graduate students in eight North American universities across five disciplines. Among the findings from the ETS project was the favoring of short tasks (less than one half page of writing) by the physical sciences group and preference for longer tasks (more than one page) by the social sciences group.

In contrast with needs analyses that look largely to faculty evaluation of ESL student performance, a few studies have put students under the investigative lens. Leki and Carson (1994) survey students for their perceptions of writing needs, whereas Leki (1995) interviews five students on a weekly basis for her analysis of the successful repertoire of coping strategies used in completing writing assignments during their first term of university work. Complementing Leki and Carson's work with ESL students is Silva's (1993) stance on the ethical treatment of ESL writers. Silva's position on respect for ESL writers, their texts, and their differences is aimed at those who judge student writing, ostensibly content area faculty who have responded to surveys of error gravity and found ESL lacking over the years.

CRITICAL EAP

The primacy and narrowness of faculty perceptions surrounding ESL student performance along with the unequal power relations created by English's hegemony as a world language are elements of the movement led by Fairclough (cf. 1989, 1995) that has given rise to critical EAP (Benesch, 1996, 2001; Pennycook, 1994, 1997, 1999). Critical EAP scholars look beyond issues of preparing students for academic success in language and disciplinary settings; rather, they focus on a participatory approach that is also transformative, allowing power to be shared in the curriculum, in the negotiation of topics and syllabi, in the teaching and mastery of the genres of power, and through the EAP curriculum to "offer the prospect of change" (Pennycook, 1999, p. 346).

Benesch (2001) is also critical of EAP's long-standing pragmatic focus on methods and materials to the exclusion of students' participation in curricular decisions and their use of language to transform their study and lives. Benesch argues for critical needs and rights analysis (1999, 2001) in which students' responses (e.g., their objections or suggestions) to assignments are taken into account in ongoing needs analyses.

Overall, the benefit that critical EAP brings to ESL students and their classrooms is that of helping students understand academic power relations, question how decisions are made that affect their education, and encourage them to address issues and ideas that can contribute to the improvement of their own academic lives and classrooms (Benesch, 1999; Canagarajah, 2002).

ACADEMIC LITERACIES AND ACADEMIC COMPETENCIES

In her 1997 book, subtitled "Developing Academic Literacies," Johns defines literacy as a plural concept which involves:

> an understanding that [reading and writing] skills are influenced by each other as well as by speaking and listening ... ways of knowing content, languages, and practices ... strategies for understanding, discussing, organizing, and producing texts ... the social context in which a discourse is produced and the roles and communities of text readers and writers ... learning processes as well as products. (p. 2)

Johns argues for the plural term, academic literacies, because of the wide range and diverse purposes associated with literacy in different academic traditions (e.g., humanities versus sciences), with the ongoing changes that occur in the literate orientation of individuals, and with the variety of theories about literacy possessed by students and teachers in classrooms.

Others conceive of academic literacy more traditionally, as the reading and writing demands of the university (e.g., Chase, Carson, & Gibson, 1991). Spack (1997) addresses the concept of literate practice in reading, writing, and listening to university texts, suggesting that it is achieved over several years for NNSs. Based on her longitudinal case study, Spack concludes that academic literacy is acquired not only through the formal study of language, but also when "language (or literacy) is viewed as a vehicle to understand and construct knowledge" (p. 49), an opportunity that requires involvement in a variety of courses over several semesters.

Academic literacy embraces the particular skills, abilities, varying levels of expertise, and strategies held by student learners and known as academic competencies. These competencies include proficiencies in the traditional four skills, including lexicogrammatical knowledge and discourse competence. The variety of strategies students employ to comprehend texts and lectures, as well as those used to produce academic texts, are associated with academic success in general. Studies of competency generally investigate NNS performance against that of competent native speakers (NSs), inferring degrees of competence (or lack thereof) in the measured difference from NS norms (e.g., Hinkel's 1995 study on modal verbs). Academic competency figures prominently into EAP needs analysis, including placement testing, in which the learning needs of students with varying levels of expertise are taken into account for program and course development.

The concern with academic literacy and learner competencies has given rise to numerous studies of the skills associated with academic success in EAP contexts. The next section of the chapter examines writing, listening, speaking, and reading and vocabulary development in EAP contexts.

ACADEMIC LANGUAGE AND ACADEMIC SKILLS

School-based language has been broadly characterized as increasingly decontextualized, that is, disembedded from immediate "here-and-now" contexts associated with informal conversation, as students advance through an educational system. A second broadly acknowledged characteristic of academic language is its explicitness relative to language used at home, in social settings, and in face-to-face conversation. A large number of EAP studies revolve around the nature of academic language and students' interface with it, seeking to clarify elements of this complex set of relations. The literate skills of reading and writing can draw on findings from numerous L1 studies of academic literacy, including reading processes and development, sociocultural contexts, and a large field of composition research, all having varying degrees of relevance to L2 and EAP contexts. L2 listening and speaking, however, as relatively developed skills in L1 students, lack the strong research background of developmental L1studies of literate skills and dispositions.

EAP WRITING

The composing processes and products of university students have received a great deal of attention in L1 research. In particular, the process-oriented approach to writing in L2 is a reflection of L1 composition research. The process approach emphasizes personal and expressive writing at the expense of skills and attitudes needed by academically bound ESL students with limited lexical and linguistic repertoires, as well as limited exposure to the kinds of writing required in various university classrooms (cf. Hinkel, 2002; Horowitz, 1986; Reid, 1984a, 1984b; Zamel, 1984). Overall, the process approach has not advantaged EAP students, and it calls into larger question the uncritical application of L1 studies to L2 learners in EAP and other contexts.

Early studies of the reading and writing demands encountered by university students were often surveys that focused on the identification and analysis of tasks associated with courses that enrolled relatively high numbers of L2 students. Thus, surveys of writing assignments in university departments provided information about topics and genres across a variety of disciplines (often science versus humanities contrasts) and levels, that is, first year through graduate school (e.g., Braine, 1995; Bridgeman & Carlson, 1983; Horowitz, 1986; Johns, 1981, 1990; Rose, 1983). These studies were clear improvements on teacher intuition, unexamined textbooks, and stereotypical assignments accomplished by providing useful information about actual writing tasks and academic expectations. Such information assists EAP writers with a more clearly delineated target and EAP professionals with a basis for curricular decisions.

EAP LISTENING: ACADEMIC LECTURES

One of the most frequently studied features of academic lectures is the discourse signaling class of features known as macromarkers, a category of words, phrases, and clauses that signal relationships within the discourses and assist students in setting expectations and confirming or disconfirming predictions as they listen. Such words as *however, moreover, nevertheless, so, now, because* and phrases like *in addition, my point is that*, and *let's turn to* are examples of macromarkers studied by a number of researchers (e.g., Chaudron & Richards, 1986; DeCarrico & Nattinger, 1988; Dunkel & Davis, 1994; Flowerdew & Tauroza, 1995) who used different categorizations of the feature as well as different sources (e.g., naturalistic vs. actual lectures), thus making cross-study comparisons and conclusions problematic. Other important areas of lecture discourse have been investigated. Flowerdew (1992), for example, examines definitions in lectures to EFL undergraduate science students. He found simple definitions (single sentences) to be a pervasive speech act in his set of academic lectures, occurring on average of one definition every 1 minute and 55 seconds. Strodt-Lopez (1991) analyzes asides in lecture discourse, determining that they contribute to overall lecture coherence.

Studies of academic lectures employ a variety of treatments, variables, categories, definitions, texts, topics, contexts, and methods (e.g., Dudley-Evans, 1994; Olson & Huckin, 1990; Tauroza & Allison, 1994), with results often impossible to generalize beyond the texts studied. These studies do not yet form a coherent picture of lecture discourse. Our understanding of academic lectures is relatively fragmentary—a patchwork of interesting if discrete findings that cannot be integrated and from which it is largely impossible to generalize. Studies of single linguistic features or categories of features provide bits of useful descriptive information, but generally are limited to a description of a particular variable along a single parameter of variation No single parameter, however, can adequately describe the complex or multidimensional nature of communication in lecture (or human) discourse (cf. Biber, 1988).

EAP READING AND VOCABULARY

Reading and word knowledge cannot be separated in the context of fluent reading. It is estimated that in order to read fluently, a reader must know a minimum of about 95% of the words on a page (Grabe & Stoller, 2002; Nation, 2001), an unlikely quota for most L2 students. In addition to vocabulary needs, EAP readers need knowledge of the academic texts they will read. Academic texts vary by level, such as survey textbooks that typically introduce a discipline and simultaneously fulfill a general education goal (Carkin, 2001). Academic texts also vary by discipline, for example, including such elements as case studies for business, applications and technical reports for engineering, classification schemes based on structure and function for biology, charts and graphs for description and prediction in economics, and so on (cf. Hyland, 1999a).

A significant contribution to the study of academic vocabulary has been made over the years by Nation and his students and colleagues as they produced increasingly refined and topical vocabulary lists through corpus-based analyses (Nation, 1990, 2001; Nation & Hwang, 1995; Xue & Nation, 1984). Working in this research tradition, Coxhead (2000) has contributed the Academic Word List (AWL), a corpus-based study that yielded a list of 570 head words found in university texts in four major knowledge divisions and 28 specified subfields. Coxhead notes that over "82% of the words in the AWL are of Greek or Latin origin" (pp. 228–9). Their distribution over the 28 subject areas (94% of the words occur in at least 20 of the 28 subfields) as well as their low occurrence in nonacademic texts attests to their representation across academic texts. The AWL is an important resource for EAP students and teachers; knowledge of AWL words can facilitate academic reading. (See also work on vocabulary by Coady & Huckin, 1997; Schmitt, 2000; Schmitt & McCarthy, 1997).

Reading also facilitates vocabulary acquisition, as studies of extensive reading have shown (e.g., Elley, 1991). Benefits of extensive reading develop over time, however, whereas university students in EAP contexts change classes and texts after a term, suggesting that extensive reading is probably best cultivated as a strategic and individual skill.

EAP students are challenged not only by limited vocabulary when compared to their L1 classmates, but also by reading speed. In university classes undergraduates are typically assigned 25 to 60 pages of weekly reading in many academic subjects (Carkin, 2001). Graduate students read considerably more pages of more difficult texts. Managing the reading workload can be assisted by EAP instruction that is content based, attends to academic genres, integrates reading and writing, and helps students develop relevant academic vocabulary used across a range of disciplines (cf. Coxhead, 2000).

EAP SPEAKING IN EDUCATIONAL CONTEXTS

The study of speaking in EAP contexts has not been directly studied, having taken a back seat to the comprehension-based research on reading and listing as primary ways of obtaining information in academic settings. However, the national prominence of the "foreign TA problem" (Bailey, 1982, 1984) associated with International Teaching Assistants (ITAs) in the early 1980s motivated a number of studies of how professors and TAs announced topics and transitions, made explanations and examples, elaborated on student comments, asked questions, and created solidarity in the classroom (cf. volumes by Bailey, Pialorsi, & Zukowski/Faust, 1984; Pica, Barnes, & Finger, 1990; see also Rounds, 1987).

Although ITA studies helped those ESL students who received graduate assistantships, they were not directly applicable to the speaking needs of international students in undergraduate and graduate classrooms. In their 1996 studies, Ferris & Tagg surveyed faculty across multiple disciplines in four universities, determining that faculty were "most concerned with ESL students' ability to express themselves fluently in class discussions and to give clear, coherent answers" (1996b, p. 311). The faculty also expressed concern with NNS' ability to interact with peers in classrooms. Interestingly, and despite the plethora of pronunciation texts, the faculty in Ferris and Tagg's study did not find much problematical with their students' pronunciation in classroom discourse.

Speaking demands in academic classrooms receive short investigative shrift in part because of the many large lectures that students face in their first 2 years of college. In lecture halls of 200 and more students, bolder students speak up, question the professor, or offer comments. Rarely are such students NNSs. The opportunities for interactive talk—between professor and students or among students—on academic issues seems a characteristic closely aligned to class size and to level of study. Thus, studies that examine forms of talk in relation to class size and type, opportunities for interaction, level of study, and discipline are needed to refine our understanding of the academic demands on NNS speaking. Recognizing the ongoing need for description of spoken academic language, Biber, Conrad et al. (2002), working under the aegis of the Educational Testing Service (TOEFL 2000), have collected spoken data from a variety of academic and social settings in four regional universities. The ongoing analysis of this corpus holds promise for more refined descriptions and analyses of the spoken language used in academic contexts.

ACADEMIC GENRES

Genres are conventionalized communication events that share some set of communicative purposes "recognized by expert members in the parent discourse community" (Swales, 1990, p. 58), and are thereby shaped in terms of style, structure, content, and intended audience, that is, the members of the discourse community to which the text is addressed (Marco, 2000). Bhatia (2002) elaborates on the concept of genres, noting that they are associated with "relatively stable structural forms and ... constrain the use of lexico-grammatical resources" that are "not static" (p. 23). Genres are important for EAP because knowledge of genre provides what Johns (1997) calls "a shortcut for the initiated into the processing and production of ... texts" (p. 21). Additionally, research has shown that in higher education settings, the goals of advanced literacy are tied to academic success generally and to disciplines and their diverse ways of making meaning specifically. Academic success depends in large measure on NNSs' negotiation of three primary genres—lectures, textbooks, and research articles—which are used in undergraduate and graduate levels and found across virtually all disciplines (cf. Johns, 1997, 2002). The next section of the chapter summarizes some of the prominent language characteristics of genres critical to EAP, touching on academic lectures while focusing on textbooks and research articles. Collectively, these three types of texts are ubiquitous as sources of academic content to students in universities and display a modest record of investigation by EAP/ESP researchers. The research done on these academic genres is addressed by selected studies that examine variation by genre, discipline, discourse, and lexico-grammar.

Academic Lectures

Lectures are a time-honored method of information transmission from experts to learners, what Benson (1994) calls higher education's "central ritual" (p. 181) and a primary informational genre for EAP study. Research on lecture discourse includes studies that examine a wide range of particular lexical and grammatical structures, categories of structures (e.g., interpersonal pronouns, hedges, discourse-signaling cues), collocations, and speech acts (e.g., topic announcements, definitions, asides), as well as organizational patterns and argumentation structure (e.g., problem-solving, point-driven). In his edited volume on academic lectures, Flowerdew (1994) surveys research on academic lectures and concludes that "the majority of the work raises more questions than it answers" (p. 25), calling, not unexpectedly, for more research specific to lectures. Among the reasons for Flowerdew's assertion are the wide range of lecture variables that have been studied, including categories of features, disciplines, content, levels (beginning through advanced undergraduate, graduate), and so on. Also important is the issue raised by Flowerdew and Tauroza (1995) regarding the findings from a number of studies of lecture comprehension based on nonauthentic (i.e., controlled or manipulated) discourse.

Academic Textbooks

Textbooks, like lectures, are primary informational genres found in virtually all formal educational contexts. In tertiary settings, textbooks are used in both undergraduate and graduate levels, becoming increasingly specialized as they represent more of the core issues of a discipline. Introductory textbooks, those used in general education courses during the first year or two of university study, are typically broad survey texts designed for students with little or no background in the field. Especially in introductory general education classes, textbooks are often the only source of readings required of students (Carkin, 2001). Myers (1992) describes textbooks as "the repositories of codified knowledge" (p. 4). Hyland (1999b) describes introductory textbooks specifically as providing "a coherently ordered epistemological map of the disciplinary landscape ... [which] can help convey the norms, values and ideological assumptions of a particular academic culture" (p. 3). Textbooks are frequently characterized as presenting factual information, representing the consensus of disciplinary experts, and displaying a limited sampling of the repertoire of conventions and functions of disciplinary practice (Geisler, 1994).

Despite the increasing number of EAP studies focusing on academic language, there is no holistic or comprehensive picture of variation in textbooks, either by discipline or through an academic career, from freshman through graduate school. Current understanding of academic textbooks is fragmentary and characterized by studies of particular features or categories of features in a limited number of texts or even passages of texts. Nevertheless, numerous discrete studies have increased our understanding of ways textbook writers use particular sets of features to help students understand the text (Hyland, 1999b; Myers, 1992). Love (1991, 1993), for example, is concerned with the ways in which introductory college textbooks "acculturate" students into a disciplinary field Her examination of textbooks shows that they exhibit "process–product" discourse cycles that employ a heavily nominalized style as a consequence of events that take place over time (e.g., geological processes), which are then "subjected to mental processes which categorize them, relate them to each other, and generally 'bring them to order'" (Love, 1993, p. 202). Her analysis offers valuable insights into the relationship between an introductory textbook, its student readers, and particular lexico-grammatical features that "reflect and ... construct the epistemology of the discipline (1993, p. 217). However, Love produces no counts or distribution patterns for some of her more quantifiable features (e.g., nouns and nominalized processes in subject position), so we cannot know how pervasive or how representative her findings are.

Hyland (1999b) focuses on the use of metadiscourse in introductory textbooks. He notes that textbook authors "are unable to invoke community knowledge as the novice [student] lacks experience of the linguistic forms which give coherence and life to that knowledge" (p. 6). He finds that, on average, compared to published research articles, textbooks employ over twice as many textual as interpersonal forms of metadiscourse to organize the text. Textbooks display a more frequent use of textual forms (connectives, code glosses, endophoric markers) to assist comprehension, whereas research articles display more frequent use of interpersonal forms (hedges and person markers) to assist persuasion (p. 10). Overall, textbooks display limited instances of interpersonal and textual metadiscourse, with some disciplinary variation, suggesting that learning in a discipline through textbooks does not allow students into the "full range of conventions within which the socio-cultural system of the discipline is encoded" (p. 22). Students reading textbooks do not systematically encounter forms of argument, uses of citations, relational markers specific to their disciplines, although textbooks provide a "glimpse" of such elements.

Overall, our understanding of textbooks, especially the range of those used in higher education, is arguably the weakest link among what is known about written academic genres. Although there are many critical analyses that focus on the relationship between the text and "underlying critical concerns of power and politics of language use, domination, and empowerment..." (Bhatia, 2002, p. 21), such studies have questionable value to EAP students who need English to accomplish fairly instrumental goals. EAP has focused on describing the way textbooks work, seeking to connect the textbook genre with the academic goals and disciplinary practices that surround it. EAP research has, thus, concentrated on studies of genre in relation to academic discourse (Flowerdew, 2002; Swales, 1990), a wide range of diverse linguistic and discoursal features found within such genres (cf. Biber et al., 2002), and classroom applications of genre (cf. Hyon, 2002; Johns, 1995, 2002).

Research Articles

In contrast to the number of studies on academic textbooks, research articles (RAs) are extensively investigated. Flowerdew (2002) calls RAs "the pre-eminent academic genre—in terms of its role as a vehicle for the generation of knowledge ... and because of its gatekeeping function as an indicator of academic achievement and professional success" (p. 5). Swales (1990) devotes a chapter in his book to the English RA, and offers an "overview of the textual studies of the English RA" (pp. 131–132) from 1972 to 1988. He observes "considerable variation" shown in the papers investigating RAs on a number of fronts: scale of research, level of analysis, methodological and linguistic approaches, fields (discipline), feature(s) investigated, etc. (p. 130). Most of the RAs investigated are from science and technology disciplines.

In EAP, RAs have been investigated for pedagogical purposes, to help graduate students understand how such genres work to deliver information that is situated within disciplines and constructed among experts. Thus, some studies have investigated sociohistorical accounts of a discipline's development through its writing and writers (e.g., Atkinson, 1996; Bazerman, 1988), demonstrating the evolution of modern genres. Other studies examine patterns of citation, integral or nonintegral, as important persuasive elements that serve to emphasize the relative importance of the message or writer (Hyland, 2000; Swales, 1990). Many studies have focused on particular components of RAs, such as abstracts (Hyland, 2000; Salager-Meyer, 1992; Swales, 1981, 1990), which represent summaries of entire articles with the purpose of persuading time-pressed professionals that the entire article is worthwhile reading. Other studies have investigated particular features such as reporting verbs and tense choices, showing that article writers select among features to identify or distance themselves from assertions.

As one of the most-studied genres, RAs offer a wealth of information to EAP professionals who would assist graduate students in understanding and writing them. The most comprehensive examination of such articles to date is Swales (1990). As more studies are added to the ever-growing literature, there is a need for integration of the wide range of studies across disciplines, as well as a need for in-depth studies of particular disciplines, charting how the RA in microbiology, for example, differs from those in other disciplines.

DIRECTIONS FOR THE FUTURE

The demand for English language education is a global phenomenon because of its dominance in international business, technology, and science (Nunan, 2001; Swales, 1971; Trimble, 1985) and the volume of research articles published in English from numerous countries around the world. The study of academic English is key to accessing new technologies, to creating new knowledge, and to distributing the contents of scholarship in journals that are increasingly converting from national languages to English (Swales, 2000). EAP is international in scope because of the preeminence of English in publications of scholarship, science, technology, and business. Swales observes that over the last 20 years "there has been a massive conversion . . . from other-language journals to English-medium ones, and . . . almost all of the new journals that have been springing up have an English-only submission policy" (p. 67). The hegemony of the English language, especially with regard to RAs, is not without negative consequences in terms of its effect on the loss of research registers in other languages, as Swales (2000) explains. The relationship between academic English and the access, production, and distribution of information provides a rich research tableau for the foreseeable future.

In attempting to characterize EAP, the fragmented and checkered nature of research findings becomes apparent. In his review of research on needs of EAP students for the TOEFL 2000 Project, Waters (1996) notes, "in research terms, we simply lack a coherent overall picture of what EAP proficiency in North American higher education involves" (p. 52). However, EAP is also marked by incremental progress toward an increasingly refined description of particular elements and discourse patterns over the last 3 decades. Swales (2001) notes that although EAP is a long way from "full accounts of *any* genre" largely due to the "complexities arising from disciplinary variation" (pp. 50–51), steady progress is being made.

Because of the highly specific nature of EAP—the relation of academic language to particular audiences with specific academic purposes, as well as to disciplinarity, genre, register, and level of generality—studies targeting meaning-making elements of its specificity, like those mentioned herein, will continue to provide incremental information. Such studies need to be complemented with more comprehensive and holistic perspectives examining larger patterns of use. Textbooks and lectures, common academic genres that constitute the formal input to most students throughout their undergraduate careers, deserve a greater share of the EAP research effort. Similarly, the study of academic conversations in higher education, as well as the study of the range of written genres students encounter across the disciplinary curriculum through various levels of study, afford ample opportunity for ongoing EAP research.

In the foreseeable future, research on disciplinary variation within, between, and across spoken and written EAP texts and genres will continue to inform the profession. Through such studies, EAP professionals, as well as those interested in academic language used in diverse disciplines, will benefit from increasing refinements in disciplinary discourses in particular, and academic language in general.

REFERENCES

Atkinson, D. (1996). The philosophical transactions of the Royal Society of London, 1675–1975: A sociohistorical discourse analysis. *Language in Society, 25*, 333–371.

Bailey, K. (1982). *Teaching in a second language: The communicative competence of non-native speaking teaching assistants*. Unpublished doctoral dissertation, UCLA.

Bailey, K. (1984). The "Foreign TA problem." In K. Bailey, F. Pialorsi, and J. Zukowski/Faust, *Foreign teaching assistants in U.S. universities* (pp. 3–15). Washington, DC: National Association of Foreign Student Affairs.

Bailey, K., Pialorsi, F., & Zukowski/Faust, J. (1984). *Foreign teaching assistants in U.S. universities.* Washington, DC: National Association of Foreign Student Affairs.

Ballard, B., & Clanchy, J. (1991). Assessment by misconception: Cultural influences and intellectual traditions. In L. Hamp-Lyons (Ed.), *Assessing second language writing in academic contexts* (pp. 19–35). Norwood, NJ: Ablex.

Bazerman, C. (1988). *Shaping written knowledge: The genre and activity of the experimental article in science.* Madison: University of Wisconsin Press.

Benesch, S. (1996). Needs analysis and curriculum development in EAP: An example of a critical approach. *TESOL Quarterly, 30,* 723–738.

Benesch, S. (1999). Rights analysis: Studying power relations in an academic setting. *English for Specific Purposes, 18*(4), 313–327.

Benesch, S. (2001). *Critical English for academic purposes: Theory, politics and practices.* Mahwah, NJ: Lawrence Erlbaum Associates.

Benson, M. (1994). Lecture listening in an ethnographic perspective. In J. Flowerdew (Ed.), *Academic listening: Research perspectives* (pp. 181–198). Cambridge, UK: Cambridge University Press.

Bhatia, V. (2002). A generic view of academic discourse. In J. Flowerdew (Ed.), *Academic discourse* (pp. 21–39). Harlow, UK: Pearson Education.

Biber, D. (1988). *Variation across speech and writing.* Cambridge, UK: Cambridge University Press.

Biber, D., Conrad, S., Reppen, R., Byrd, P., & Helt, M. (2002). Speaking and writing in the university: A multidimensional comparison. *TESOL Quarterly, 36*(1), 9–48.

Biber, D., Reppen, R., Clark, V., & Walter, J. (2001). Representing spoken language in university settings: The design and construction of the spoken component of the T2K-SWAL Corpus. In R. Simpson & J. Swales (Eds.), *Corpus linguistics in North America* (pp. 48–57). Ann Arbor: University of Michigan Press.

Blue, G. (1988). Individualising academic writing tuition. In P. Robinson (Ed.), *Academic writing: Process and product* (pp. 129–148) (ELT Documents 129). London: MET and British Council.

Braine, G. (1989). Writing in science and technology: An analysis of assignments from ten undergraduate courses. *English for Specific Purposes, 8*(1), 3–15.

Braine, G. (1995). Writing in the natural sciences and engineering. In D. Belcher & G. Braine (Eds.), *Academic writing in a second language* (pp. 113–134). Norwood, NJ: Ablex.

Bridgeman, B., & Carlson, S. (1983). *Survey of academic writing tasks required of graduate and undergraduate foreign students* (TOEFL Research Report No. 15). Princeton, NJ: Educational Testing Service.

Bridgeman, B., & Carlson, S. (1984). Survey of academic writing tasks. *Written Communication, 1,* 247–280.

Brinton, D., Snow, M., & Wesche, M. (1989). *Content-based second language instruction.* New York: Newbury House.

Canagarajah, S. (2002). Multilingual writers and the academic community: Towards a critical relationship. *Journal of English for Academic Purposes, 1*(1), 29–44.

Carkin, S. (2001). *Pedagogic discourse in introductory classes: Multidimensional analysis of textbooks and lectures in macroeconomics and biology.* Unpublished doctoral dissertation. Northern Arizona University, Flagstaff.

Chase, N., Carson, J., & Gibson, S. (1991, April). *Texts, notes, and lectures: Perceptions of reading purposes and demands in four college courses.* Paper presented at the 41st annual meeting of the National Reading Conference. Palm Springs, CA.

Chaudron, C., & Richards, J. (1986). The effect of discourse markers on the comprehension of lectures. *Applied Linguistics, 7,* 113–127.

Coady, J., & Huckin, T. (Eds.). (1997). *Second language vocabulary acquisition.* Cambridge, UK: Cambridge University Press.

Coxhead, A. (2000). A new academic word list. *TESOL Quarterly, 34*(2), 213–238.

DeCarrico, J., & Nattinger, J. (1988). Lexical phrases for the comprehension of academic lectures. *English for Specific Purposes, 7*(2), 91–102.

Dudley-Evans, A. (1994). 'Genre analysis: an approach to text analysis for ESP'. In M. Coulthard (Ed.), *Advances in Written Text Analysis,* (pp. 219–299). London: Routledge.

Dudley-Evans, T., & St. John, M. (1998). *Developments in ESP.* Cambridge, UK: Cambridge University Press.

Dunkel, P., & Davis, J. (1994). Effects of rhetorical signaling cues on the recall of English lecture information by speakers of English as a native or second language. In J. Flowerdew (Ed), *Academic listening: Research perspectives* (pp. 55–74). Cambridge, UK: Cambridge University Press.

Elley, W. (1991). Acquiring literacy in a second language: The effect of book-flood programs. *Language Learning, 41,* 375–411.

Fairclough, N. (1989). *Language and power.* London: Longman.

Fairclough, N. (1995). *Critical discourse analysis.* London: Longman.

Ferris, D., & Tagg, T. (1996a). Academic oral communication needs of EAP learners: What subject-matter instructors actually require. *TESOL Quarterly, 30*(1), 31–58.

Ferris, D., & Tagg, T. (1996b). Academic listening/speaking tasks for ESL students: Problems, suggestions, and implications. *TESOL Quarterly, 30*(2), 297–320.

Flowerdew, J. (1992). Definitions in science lectures. *Applied Linguistics, 13*(2), 202–224.

Flowerdew, J. (Ed.). (1994). *Academic listening: Research perspectives.* Cambridge, UK: Cambridge University Press.

Flowerdew, J. (Ed.). (2002). *Academic discourse*. Harlow, UK: Longman.

Flowerdew, J., & Peacock, M. (2001). Issues in E.A.P: A preliminary perspective. In J. Flowerdew & M. Peacock (Eds.) *Research perspectives on English for academic purposes* (pp. 8–24). Cambridge, UK: Cambridge University Press.

Flowerdew, J., & Peacock, M. (Eds.). (2001). *Research perspectives on English for academic purposes*. Cambridge, UK: Cambridge University Press.

Flowerdew, J., & Tauroza, S. (1995). The effect of discourse markers on second language lecture comprehension. *Studies in Second Language Acquisition, 17*(4), 435–458.

Geisler, C. (1994). *Academic literacy and the nature of expertise*. Hillsdale, NJ: Lawrence Erlbaum Associates.

Grabe, W., & Stoller, F. (2002). *Teaching and researching reading*. Harlow, UK: Longman.

Hale, G., Taylor, C., Bridgeman, B., Carson, J., Kroll, B., & Kantor, R. (1996). *A study of writing tasks assigned in academic degree programs*. Research Report 54. Princeton, NJ: Educational Testing Service.

Halliday, M., McIntosh, A., & Strevens, P. (1964). *The linguistic sciences and language teaching*. London: Longman.

Hinkel, E. (1995). The use of modal verbs as a reflection of cultural values. *TESOL Quarterly, 29*(3), 325–343.

Hinkel, E. (2002). *Second language writers' texts: Linguistic and rhetorical features*. Mahwah, NJ: Lawrence Erlbaum Associates.

Horowitz, D. (1986). What professors actually require: Academic tasks for the ESL classroom. *TESOL Quarterly, 20*, 445–462.

Hyland, K. (1999a). Disciplinary discourses: Writer stance in research articles. In C. Candlin & K. Hyland (Eds.), *Writing: Texts, processes and practices* (pp. 99–121). London: Longman.

Hyland, K. (1999b). Talking to students: Metadiscourse in introductory coursebooks. *English for Specific Purposes, 18*(1), 3–26.

Hyland, K. (2000). *Disciplinary discourses: Social interactions in academic writing*. Harlow, UK: Pearson Education.

Hyland, K., & Hamp-Lyons, L. (2002). EAP: Issues and directions. *Journal of English for Academic Purposes, 1*, 1–12.

Hyon, S. (2002). Genre in ESL reading: A classroom study. In A. Johns (Ed.), *Genre in the classroom: Multiple perspectives* (pp. 121–141). Mahwah, NJ: Lawrence Erlbaum Associates.

Johns, A. (1981). Necessary English: A faculty survey. *TESOL Quarterly, 15*, 51–57.

Johns, A. (1988). The discourse communities dilemma: Identifying transferable skills for the academic milieu. *English for Specific Purposes, 7*(1), 55–59.

Johns, A. (1990). L1 composition theories: Implications for developing theories of L2 composition. In B. Kroll (Ed.), *Second language writing: Research insights for the classroom* (pp. 24–36). Cambridge, UK: Cambridge University Press.

Johns, A. (1992). What is the relationship between content-based instruction and English for specific purposes? *CATESOL Journal, 5*(1), 71–75.

Johns, A. (1995). Teaching classroom and authentic genres: Initiating students into academic cultures and discourses. In D. Belcher & G. Braine (Eds.), *Academic writing in a second language* (pp. 277–291). New York: Ablex.

Johns, A. (1997). *Text, role and context: Developing academic literacies*. Cambridge, UK: Cambridge University Press.

Johns, A. (Ed.). (2002). *Genre in the classroom: Multiple perspectives*. Mahwah, NJ: Lawrence Erlbaum Associates.

Jordan, R. (1997). *English for academic purposes*. Cambridge, UK: Cambridge University Press.

Lackstrom, J., Selinker, L, & Trimble, L. (1970). Grammar and technical English. In R. Lugton (Ed.), *English as a second language: Current issues* (pp. 101–133). Philadelphia: Center for Curriculum Development.

Lackstrom, J., Selinker, L., & Trimble, L. (1973). Technical rhetorical principles and grammatical choice. *TESOL Quarterly, 7*(1), 127–136.

Leki, I. (1995). Coping strategies of ESL students in writing tasks across the curriculum. *TESOL Quarterly, 29*(2), 235–260.

Leki, I., & Carson, J. (1994). Students' perception of EAP writing instruction and writing needs across the disciplines. *TESOL Quarterly, 28*(1), 81–101.

Love, A. (1991). Process and product in geology: An investigation of some discourse features of two introductory textbooks. *English for Specific Purposes, 10*, 89–109.

Love, A. (1993). Lexico-grammatical features of geology textbooks: Process and product revisited. *English for Specific Purposes, 12*(3), 197–218.

Marco, M. (2000). Collocational frameworks in medical research papers: A genre-based study. *English for Specific Purposes, 19*(1), 63–86.

Myers, G. (1992). Textbooks and the sociology of scientific knowledge. *English for Specific Purposes, 11*(1), 3–17.

Nation, P. (1990). *Teaching and learning vocabulary*. Rowley, MA: Newbury House.

Nation, P. (2001). *Learning vocabulary in another language*. Cambridge, UK: Cambridge University Press.

Nation, P., & Hwang, K. (1995). Where would general service vocabulary stop and special purposes vocabulary begin? *System, 23*, 35–41.

Nunan, D. (1988). *Syllabus design*. Oxford, UK: Oxford University Press.

Nunan, D. (2001). English as a global language. [Research Issues, P. Duff & K. Bailey, Eds.] *TESOL Quarterly*, *35*(4), 605–606.

Olson, L., & Huckin, T. (1990). Point-driven understanding in engineering lecture comprehension. *English for Specific Purposes, 9*, 33–47.

Pennycook, A. (1994). *Cultural politics of English as a international language*. London: Longman.

Pennycook, A. (1997). Vulgar pragmatism, critical pragmatism, and EAP. *English for Specific Purposes, 16*(4), 253–269.

Pennycook, A. (Guest Editor). (1999). Special topics issue: Critical approaches to TESOL. *TESOL Quarterly, 33*(3).

Pica, T., Barnes, G., & Finger, A. (1990). *Teaching matters: Skills and strategies for international teaching assistants*. Rowley, MA: Newbury House.

Reid, J. (1984a). Comments on Vivian Zamel's "The composing processes of advanced ESL students: Six case studies." [The Forum]. *TESOL Quarterly, 18*(1), 149–153.

Reid, J. (1984b). The radical outliner and the radical brainstormer: A perspective on composing processes. [The Forum]. *TESOL Quarterly, 18*(3), 529–534.

Rose, M. (1983). Remedial writing courses: A critique and a proposal. *College English, 45*, 109–128.

Rounds, P. (1987). Multifunctional personal pronoun use in an educational setting. *English for Specific Purposes, 6*(1), 13–29.

Salager-Meyer, F. (1992). A text-type and move analysis study of verb tense and modality distribution in medical English abstracts. *English for Specific Purposes, 11*(2), 93–113.

Santos, T. (1988). Professors' reactions to the academic writing of nonnative speaking students. *TESOL Quarterly, 22*, 69–90.

Schmitt, N. (2000). *Vocabulary in language teaching*. Cambridge, UK: Cambridge University Press.

Schmitt, N., & McCarthy, M. (Eds.) (1997). *Vocabulary: Description, acquisition and pedagogy*. Cambridge, UK: Cambridge University Press.

Silva, T. (1993). Toward an understanding of the distinct nature of L2 writing: The ESL research and its implications. *TESOL Quarterly, 27*(1), 657–677.

Snow, M. (1997). Teaching academic literacy skills: Discipline faculty take responsibility. In M. Snow & D. Brinton (Eds.), *The content-based classroom*, (pp. 290–304). New York: Addison-Wesley/Longman.

Snow, M., & Brinton, D. (1992). Content-based instruction [Special themed issue]. *The CATESOL Journal, 5*(1).

Spack, R. (1997). The acquisition of academic literacy in a second language. *Written Communication, 14*(1), 3–62.

Strodt-Lopez, B. (1991). Tying it all in: Asides in university lectures. *Applied Linguistics, 12*(2), 117–140.

Swales, J. (1971). *Writing scientific English*. Walton-on-Thames, UK: Nelson.

Swales, J. (1981). Aspects of research article introductions (Aston ESP Research Reports No. 1). Birmingham, UK: University of Aston.

Swales, J. (1990). *Genre analysis: English in academic research settings*. Cambridge, UK: Cambridge University Press.

Swales, J. (2000). Languages for specific purposes. *Annual Review of Applied Linguistics, 20*, 59–76.

Swales, J. (2001). EAP-related linguistic research: An intellectual history. In J. Flowerdew & M. Peacock (Eds.), *Research perspective on English for academic purposes* (pp. 42–54). Cambridge, UK: Cambridge University Press.

Tarone, E., Dwyer, S., Gillette, S., & Icke, V. (1981). On the use of the passive in two astrophysics journal papers. *English for Specific Purposes, 1*, 123–140. Updated for publication in 1998 in *English for Specific Purposes, 17*(1), 113–132.

Tauroza, S., & Allison, D. (1994). Expectation-driven understanding in information systems lecture comprehension. In J. Flowerdew (Ed.), *Academic listening: Research perspectives*, (pp. 35–54). Cambridge, UK: Cambridge University Press.

Trimble, L. (1985). *English for science and technology*. Cambridge, UK: Cambridge University Press.

Vann, R., Meyer, D., & Lorenz, F. (1984). Error gravity: A study of faculty opinion of ESL errors. *TESOL Quarterly, 18*, 427–440.

Waters, A. (1996). *A review of research into needs in English for academic purposes of relevance to the North American higher education context* (TOEFL Monograph Series, MS-6). Princeton, NJ: Educational Testing Services.

West, R. (1994). Needs analysis in language teaching. *Language Teaching, 27*, 1–19.

Xue, G., & Nation, P. (1984). A university word list. *Language Learning, 3*, 215–229.

Zamel, V. (1984). The author responds . . . [The Forum]. *TESOL Quarterly, 18*(1), 154–158.

6

Research in English for Specific Purposes

Peter Master
San Jose State University

INTRODUCTION

The domain of English for Specific Purposes (ESP) has had a strong research tradition since its inception in the 1960s. This chapter delineates the current research concerns of ESP in order to gain a sense of the direction in which the field is moving, with a special focus on the years 2000–2002. The information is gleaned primarily from the pages of the flagship journal of the field, *English for Specific Purposes*, which editors of the journal have often used as an indicator of major trends in the field (e.g., Dudley-Evans, 2001; Hewings, 2002; Master, 2001). The chapter surveys data-based studies as well as descriptions of ESP programs and environments, such as shadowing a business manager. It then examines current issues that concern the field and concludes with an investigation of the most significant research question that can be asked about ESP: Does it work?

RESEARCH DOMAIN

ESP is a division of English Language Teaching (ELT), the only other member of which is English for General Purposes (EGP; Master, 1997a; Strevens, 1988). Johns and Dudley-Evans (1991) provide a broad definition of ESP as "the careful research and design of pedagogical materials and activities for an identifiable group of adult learners within a specific learning context" (p. 298) whose principal distinguishing characteristics are needs assessment and discourse analysis, though Brown (1995) maintains that discourse analysis is a requirement for determining the needs of any language education enterprise. Discourse Analysis is a field unto itself, comprising an important discipline within the field of Linguistics. In terms of ESP, where it seeks to weigh the importance of various elements in the genuine language situations English language learners will encounter, discourse analysis is concerned with microlinguistic elements such as frequency counts (i.e., tense/aspect, mood, information structure, and other text linguistic devices) as well as macrolinguistic concerns such as genre, levels of discourse in rhetorical subsections of texts (e.g., Swales' notion of "moves" or steps that "make a paper coherent to genre-experienced readers," 1990, p. 190), and learner interactions with discourse within specific disciplines.

English for Specific Purposes also comprises the largest representative of an international movement known as Languages for Specific Purposes (LSP). The current concerns of the LSP movement are exemplified by a recent call for papers for an international conference on the subject. The topics of the 6th International Conference on Languages for Specific Purposes (http://www.upc.es/eupvg/cilfe6/index.htm, retrieved 9-26-02), held in Spain in early 2003 and entitled "The Role of Information Technology in LSP Research and Pedagogy," included the use of networks (especially the Internet) and multimedia in LSP teaching; E-learning applications and experiences; information technology in educational research; interaction in virtual learning environments; information technology and materials development; information technology and learner autonomy; lexicology, lexicography, and terminology; translation; and discourse and genre studies (corpus-based studies). The primary difference between LSP and ESP is the former's inclusion of translation, which ESP is obviously not concerned with.

Research in ESP, thus, occurs within the overlapping domains of English language education for specific purposes and discourse/genre analysis.

DEVELOPMENTS, TRENDS, AND TRADITIONS

In an analysis of research trends in four western Applied Linguistics (AL) journals between 1985 and 1997, Gao, Li, & Lü (2001) found that there has been a general shift in AL to qualitative methods such that "qualitative research has gained essentially an equal footing with quantitative research as a major research paradigm" (p. 10). In the *TESOL Quarterly*, one of the four journals Gao, et al. analyzed, the qualitative research over the 12-year period consisted of ethnography (32%), verbal reports (25%), text analysis (22%), narrative accounts (17%), and classroom interaction analysis (3%). In the other three journals (*Applied Linguistics*, *The Modern Language Journal*, and *International Review of Applied Linguistics*), text analysis was the dominant subtype.

Gao et al.'s (2001) data provide a useful comparison for research in ESP. Hewings (2002) provides an overview of ESP research as reflected in *English for Specific Purposes*, published by Elsevier. Table 6.1 shows the topics of published papers over the 20+ year history of the journal. It is clear from Table 6.1 that text/discourse analysis has dominated the pages of the journal since its inception and continues to increase into the present decade. Program descriptions, on the other hand, sharply diminished after

TABLE 6.1
Topics of Papers (Hewings, 2002)

Topic	Vol. 1–5 1980–1986	Vol. 6–10 1987–1991	Vol. 11–15 1992–1996	Vol. 16–20 1997–2001
Text/discourse analysis	34	33	51	49
Program description	36	11	14	10
Needs analysis/syllabus design	11	12	6	9
Materials/methods	5	8	9	6
Argument/discussion (no data)	0	12	4	8
Testing	2	3	4	6
Teacher training	5	1	1	3
Other	7	7	10	9

1986, primarily because submissions in this category were too often descriptions of local programs without sufficient generalizability to other ESP contexts in the world. (When I was a co-editor of the journal between 1995 and 2002, the most common rejection letter I wrote concerned the lack of universal application of the description of a local program). Needs analysis and syllabus design also decreased in the 1990s after it had been made clear early in the decade that the views of the students (clients or subjects) being taught ESP comprised an essential element of the needs analysis. Materials and methods, on the other hand, continue to be developed in response to specific needs analyses.

Hewings (2002) also shows the ESP sub-area represented by articles published in *English for Specific Purposes*, which apply to some degree to ESP research as a whole. Over the 20-year history of the journal, English for Science and Technology (EST) and English for Academic Purposes (EAP) have dominated and continue to dominate, whereas articles concerned with General ESP have fallen from 20% in the early years of the journal to less than 5% in recent years. English for Occupational/Professional Purposes (EOP/EPP) continues to hover around 10%. Hewings notes that, although the interest in Business English has dramatically increased in the last decade (accounting for almost 20% of what foreign students study in the United States; cf. Open Doors, 2002), the Business English research base is still in its infancy and will remain underrepresented in the pages of the journal until it is taught in universities.

Hewings also provides a closer analysis of the text/discourse analysis category, including mode of communication and concern with professional versus student products. Mode of communication refers to whether the data analyzed were written or spoken. Between 1997 and 2001, analyses of written text comprised 86% of this category, the remaining 14% spoken. In the early 1980s, the ratio was 73% written to 27% spoken, the spoken variety decreasing steadily ever since. Hewings believes this may be partially due to the fact that written text is easier to analyze, even though it is clearly more important for the ultimate user of ESP to be able to speak than to write. It is also partially due to the increasing importance of genre analysis to the field, which tends to focus on written rather than spoken genres. Similarly, there has been a much greater concern with professional products (most recently 75% professional, 15% student, and 10% interaction between professional and student in generating a product), though analyses of interactions have increased slightly over the years. Hewings believes this is a natural state of affairs because professional product data has a far wider application in ESP than does data gained from student products or their interactions with professionals in producing them.

One of the strengths of research in ESP is its international character. Hewings shows that there has been a steady increase in the number of international authors published in *English for Specific Purposes* with a concomitant decrease in the percentage of authors from the United Kingdom and the United States. In the period from 1997 to 2001, international authors accounted for 69% of the articles, with 19% from the United States and 12% from the United Kingdom, whereas in the early 1980s, the ratio was 39% from the United States, 25% from the United Kingdom, and 36% from other countries. Hewings believes this is a testament to the growing acceptance of ESP around the world and, consequently, its validity as a subject for research. It also reflects the fact that ESP is generally more likely to be carried out in non-English-speaking countries than in English-speaking ones and that ESP goes under different guises in the United States, such as content-based instruction (CBI) or Workplace ESL (Master, 1997b). Hewings shows that the 1990s were marked by a substantial increase in papers from two regions of the world outside the United States and the United Kingdom: Central and South America, and China and Hong Kong.

The gender of authors in *English for Specific Purposes* is also of interest. In the last decade, female authors have been slightly better represented than males, most recently

55% female and 45% male, the percentage of females rising from a low of 42% at the beginning of the 1980s. Hewings notes, however, that the authors cited in *English for Specific Purposes* articles are overwhelmingly male.

Hewings concludes his overview of *English for Specific Purposes* by speculating on what the future holds for the field of ESP. He believes that although increasing specificity is a primary characteristic of ESP research today, the field will have to become more concerned with English as an International Language. "The growing use of English as the means of communication in interaction between non-native English speakers seems likely to have a major impact on the kinds of ESP programmes we provide and the type of research needed to underpin those programmes" (Hewings, 2002, unpaginated). Similarly, Dudley-Evans and St. John (1997) believe that cross-cultural issues will be increasingly important research issues, especially "what language is culturally appropriate in different situations" (p. 232). They also think that critical approaches to research will affect the development of ESP as they question the norms of ESP teaching.

With regard specifically to English for Academic Purposes (EAP), Jordan (1997) states that future research will undoubtedly focus on genre analysis at different levels, computer- assisted language learning (CALL), disciplinary cultures (i.e., the "insider" culture of specific discourse communities), learner independence, and collaboration between EAP teachers and subject specialists (pp. 279–280). These categories are also of interest to ESP, and topics such as genre analysis, CALL, and learner independence are concerns of the entire ELT teaching profession.

CURRENT RESEARCH

The primary focus of current ESP research is specificity, that is, detailed explications of the nature of the language used or required to communicate in specific academic and occupational settings, usually accompanied by specific pedagogical applications for non-native speakers of English. Current research in ESP as reflected in *English for Specific Purposes* continues to be concerned with specificity in three broad areas of focus: (a) macro-linguistic concerns such as writing, authenticity, and oral communication, (b) microlinguistic elements such as vocabulary and grammatical categories, and (c) descriptions of various types of ESP programs. In the articles published in the last three volumes of the journal (2000, 2001, and 2002), as shown in Table 6.2, 60% had a macrolinguistic focus, 21% had a microlinguistic focus, and 19% dealt with program descriptions. The categories of ESP that these articles are concerned with are described in Table 6.3.

Table 6.3 shows that articles concerning academic, science/technology, and business topics continue to dominate the journal, accounting for more than two thirds (69%) of the articles published. It should be noted that English for occupational/

TABLE 6.2
Focus in *English for Specific Purposes* 2000–2002

Year	Vol No.	Macrolinguistic	Microlinguistic	ESP Programs
2000	19	11	3	3
2001	20	13	6	4
2002	21	10	3	4
Total		34	12	11
Percent		60%	21%	19%

TABLE 6.3

Topics of ESP in *English for Specific Purposes* 2000–2002

Year	EAP (Academic)	EST (Sci/tech)	EOP/EPP (Occup/prof)	EBE (Business/econ)	EMP (Medical)	ELP (Legal)
2000	3	4	3	3	3	1
2001	10	4	4	2	3	0
2002	4	5	2	3	1	2
Total	17	13	9	8	7	3
Percent	30%	23%	16%	14%	12%	5%

professional purposes includes six Business/Economics articles and one on a new area of focus in EOP: English for textile and clothing merchandisers.

The topics and the results of these studies are summarized by category in the next section. They provide a detailed view of the research focus in ESP over the last 3 years.

English for Academic Purposes (EAP)

The macrolinguistic concerns in EAP included academic assessment, authenticity, data gathering, negotiating in the classroom, writing, and use of the Internet. Macdonald, Badger, and White (2000) questioned the validity of authentic materials in EAP classes, finding relevant texts less motivating than interaction with a speaker, and EAP instructors' live simulations of lectures more effective than taped authentic lectures. Okamura and Shaw (2000) analyzed letters accompanying papers submitted for publication and found that academics, both native-English speakers (NES) and non-native English speakers (NNES), used appropriate rhetoric and language, but that undergraduate students and overseas English teachers used inappropriate rhetoric and language, suggesting that the status of the learner must be considered in the teaching of writing. Braine (2001) reported on the difficulties encountered in acquiring data on undergraduate writing tasks in Hong Kong, apparently because of the sources' uncertainty about their levels of English proficiency. Feak and Salehzadeh (2001) described a video listening placement assessment for EAP courses at the University of Michigan. Gao, Li, and Lü (2001) compared recent trends in research methods in applied linguistics in China and the West, as described earlier. Hyon (2001) found that genre-based instruction was remembered to some extent over time but noted that certain approaches to genre may not aid students' understanding of genre variation and complexity. Mavor and Trayner (2001) designed a genre-aligned framework for teaching EAP courses in a Portuguese university. Vassileva (2001) examined English and Bulgarian linguistics research articles and found that they were similar in the quantity of hedging and boosting but different in the distribution of hedges and the degree of deference to the discourse community. Basturkmen (2002) focused on the negotiation of meaning in the language of interaction in college classrooms. Paltridge (2002) suggested broadening the range of thesis/dissertation types analyzed in teaching EAP students to generate the genre. Slaouti (2002) argued for the inclusion of critical awareness regarding authority and academic status in teaching college students to use the World Wide Web.

The microlinguistic concerns in EAP included academic use of lexicogrammatical items and agency. Green, Christopher, and Mei (2000) analyzed a corpus of academic texts written by Chinese speakers for the use of topic-fronted devices and sentence initial logical connectors and found an overproduction of marked themes, leading to an overly emphatic tone. Lindemann and Mauranen (2001) analyzed the roles of *just* in spoken academic discourse and found that the mitigating sense of the word involved a phonologically reduced version, whereas the sense of "exactly" tended to use a full vowel and be stressed, supporting the need for phonetic detail in EAP. Moore (2002) researched the frequency and type of agentive elements (Halliday, 1994) in sociology, physics, and economics textbooks and found economics to be closer to physics than to sociology (even though economics is considered a social science), perhaps to give it scientific credibility.

The academic courses focused on architecture, reading, and the use of textbooks. Spector-Cohen, Kirschner, and Wexler (2001) developed an EAP reading program at the University of Tel Aviv in Israel. Swales, Barks, Östermann, and Simpson (2001) described an EAP course for Master's of Architecture students at the University of Michigan. Yakhontova (2001) discussed the use of a U.S.-based EAP textbook in a Ukrainian university course.

English for Science and Technology (EST)

The macrolinguistic concerns in EST included scientific/technical reading, writing, and use of transparencies. Chimbganda (2000) reported that first year Bachelor of Science students who used risk-taking strategies, such as restructuring discourse to clarify the intended meaning, wrote better than those who used other strategies. Diaz-Santos (2000) described the advantages of reading "technothrillers" such as *Jurassic Park* in EST classes as a basis for orienting students, to the concerns of the scientific discourse community. Halimah (2001) compared the Arabic and English scientific writing of 100 Arabic-speaking students and found that the mechanics were acceptable but not the rhetorical style, which he attributed to the lack of focus on such matters in the classroom. Ward (2001) found evidence that Thai engineering students evaded reading English language textbooks by concentrating only on the applications, especially the examples (so that they could pass examinations), while ignoring the background knowledge of physical systems that is essential for an engineer. Lahuerta (2002) found rhetorical organization to play a significant role in English as a Foreign Language (EFL) students' comprehension of EST text. Rowley-Jolivet (2002) noted the importance of slides and transparencies in structuring the discourse at international scientific conference presentations. Samraj (2002) analyzed the introductions of research papers in wildlife behavior and conservation biology using Swales' CARS (create a research space) model, in which she found variation and the need to modify the model (see also Swales (1990b)).

The microlinguistic concerns in EST included the scientific/technical use of grammar, lexical phrases, and self-reference. Gledhill (2000) examined the collocations of high-frequency words in introductions to cancer research articles, revealing that semi-preconstructed phrases (e.g., *patients who received drug X*) abound in scientific writing. Hyland (2001) investigated the occurrence of self-reference (self-citation and first person pronouns) in 240 research articles in the hard and soft sciences, finding that self-reference occurs at points where the authors "are best able to promote themselves and their individual contributions. Their intrusion helps to strengthen both their credibility and their role in research, and to help them gain acceptance and credit for their claims" (p. 223). Martinez (2001) looked at transitivity in the physical, biological, and social sciences, finding that the revelation and concealment of agency allows the author to negotiate the tension between objectivity and personal impact on the scientific community. Soler (2002) analyzed adjectives in scientific research articles, which are far less frequent than nouns and verbs, and found them to occur most often in the discussion section, where they play an important role in modulating objectivity, certainty, and evaluation.

The scientific/technical courses focused on teaching in South Africa and Malaysia. Parkinson (2000) described a theme-based language course for EST students at a South African university. Chien Ching (2002) reported on an EST writing course at a Malaysian university.

English for Occupational/Professional Purposes (EOP/EPP)

The macrolinguistic concerns in EOP/EPP included professional/occupational authenticity, oral and written communication, and workplace needs. Brett (2000) questioned the use of authentic materials when students using a CD-ROM based on authentic spoken Business English (BE) lost enthusiasm for self-study on computers and questioned the relevance of the materials. Gimenez (2000) compared email and formal business letters from the same company and found that the standard business letter format taught in Business English classes would not prepare students to generate appropriate email correspondence. Li and Mead (2000) focused on the workplace needs of textile and clothing merchandisers for EOP courses at two educational institutions in Hong Kong. Gimenez (2001) analyzed cross-cultural non-native-speakers of English engaged in business negotiations, finding that "[t]he way which prices are negotiated appeared to be more related to the status-bound behaviour of the negotiator than to culture" (p. 183). Henry and Roseberry (2001) analyzed a computerized corpus of 40 job application letters at the level of strategy rather than move or genre register and found a range of discourse and syntactic features that were not described in textbooks on the genre. Upton and Connor (2001) used a hand-tagged computerized learner corpus analysis to determine the politeness-strategy "moves" in professional job application letters in three cultures (U.S., Belgian, and Finnish), finding that the U.S. writers were more formulaic, the Belgians more individualistic, and the Finns exhibited both traits to lesser degrees. The study supports the need for computer investigations that go beyond lexico-grammatical patterning. Louhiala-Salminen (2002) shadowed a Finnish international corporation manager, revealing the interplay between speaking and writing and how English functioned as the medium of communication in a multinational environment. Pinto dos Santos (2002) analyzed the rhetorical moves in business letters of negotiation.

The single microlinguistic concern in EOP/EPP was the use of occupational/professional metaphors. Charteris-Black and Ennis (2001) studied linguistic and conceptual metaphors in financial reports in Chilean and British newspapers, finding the former to prefer psychological health metaphors and the latter nautical metaphors.

English for Business and Economics (EBE)

The macrolinguistic concerns in EBE included business authenticity, metaphoric awareness, student socialization into the field, and written and spoken communication. Boers (2000) found that enhanced metaphoric awareness in reading economics texts helped students to remember figurative expressions to recognize their inference patterns. Charteris-Black (2000) made a case for basing ESP vocabulary teaching for economics students on words that reflect the underlying metaphors of economics, with animate metaphors (e.g., *growth*) to describe the economy and inanimate ones (e.g., *slide*) to describe movements of the market. Hemais (2001) found that marketing journals depend to a greater extent on insights from practice than they do from research. Northcott (2001) was concerned with the socialization of international students into a business program at the University of Edinburgh. Crosling and Ward (2002) questioned the focus on formal business presentations in university business classes when the primary need in the business world is for communication in informal contexts.

The single microlinguistic concern in EBE was the business use of anticipatory *it*. Hewings and Hewings (2002) used computerized corpora to analyze anticipatory *it* in published business research articles and L2 student business dissertations and found the latter did not sufficiently modulate their knowledge claims.

The business courses focused on teaching in Botswana and Hong Kong. De Beaugrande (2000) reported on a pilot project to teach business at the University of Botswana. Jackson (2002) compared the use of case studies in two business courses at the Chinese University of Hong Kong.

English for Medical Purposes (EMP)

The single macrolinguistic concern in EMP was medical communication. Frank (2000) studied the language and communication problems between international students and university student health center staff members, which they found to derive primarily from medical vocabulary and from pragmatic difficulties arising from differing cultural and procedural expectations and affective notions such as prejudice, manner of speaking, and the value of patience and kindness.

The microlinguistic concerns in EMP included medical collocational frameworks and communication. Marco (2000) studied collocational frameworks such as *the __ of*, *a __ of*, and *be __ to* in mediscal research papers and found the collocates that fill these slots to be genre-dependent. Ferguson (2001) examined *if*-conditionals in medical discourse and found that in spoken consultations they allow politeness and sensitivity, whereas in research articles they provide operational definitions. Ibrahim (2001) analyzed the questions that doctors in the Arabian Gulf countries use in consultations and argued for consideration of the cultural underpinnings of doctor-centeredness.

The medical courses focused on teaching in Cuba, Hong Kong, and the United States. Maclean, Betancourt, and Hunter (2000) described the 15-year evolution of an EMP program in Cuba. Shi, Corcos, and Storey (2001) used videotapes of clinical training sessions to help medical students acquire oral communication skills in an EMP course at the University of Hong Kong. Bosher and Smalkowski (2002) described an EMP oral communication course at the College of St. Catharine in Minnesota.

English for Academic Legal Purposes (EALP)

The macrolinguistic concerns in EALP included legal writing and the use of computer-mediated materials. Feak, Reinhart, and Sinsheimer (2000) argued that EALP (English for Academic Legal Purposes) students should learn to write legal research papers ("notes") rather than primary research reports as preparation for working in legal contexts. Candlin, Bhatia, and Jensen (2002) justified the need for a computer-mediated resource bank of language and discourse-based materials for teaching EALP because they found the 37 EALP books currently available to be too context-specific and of little use outside that context.

There was no microlinguistic focus in the EALP articles, and the single legal course focused on teaching in Hong Kong. Bruce (2002) reported on an EAP course for first-year law students at Hong Kong University.

This survey of articles makes it clear that specificity is the primary focus of ESP research, manifesting in a variety of macro- and microlinguistic concerns in the six major areas of ESP. Other areas of ESP, such as English for the Arts/Art and Design, English for Sociocultural Purposes, and Vocational ESL (Master, 2000) have seldom been represented in the journal, but it is hoped that research in these areas will appear in the future.

CURRENT CONTROVERSIES

Current controversies in the field of ESP include the extent of subject knowledge the ESP practitioner needs to have, the value of genre-based instruction, and the charge that EAP is "accommodationist." A major concern, although one that has not yet been labeled a controversy as such, is the efficacy of ESP itself.

Subject-Matter Knowledge

The question of how much subject-matter expertise the ESP practitioner must have has been a controversy since the early days of ESP. Schachter (1981), representing one extreme of a continuum of views on this matter, believed that EST teachers were primarily ESL teachers making good use of content-specific materials in order to impart communicative competence in English. As a result, she saw teacher knowledge of content as a potential obstruction to the teacher's true role and even recommended that EST instructors stop teaching a particular area of science or technology after a certain time because they would be unable to resist the temptation to teach content. The other extreme is an entirely content-based curriculum in which linguistic knowledge is subordinated to subject content instruction. Mackay (1981), for example, noted that "some major ESP projects prefer to hire teachers of science who also happen to have some ELT [English Language Teaching] experience or training" (p. 122).

The issue was aired in two articles in the "Issues in ESP" column in *TESOL Matters.* Taylor (1994) argued that "given a solid base of ELT experience, the critical factors for the ESP teacher are attitude and interest, not content knowledge" (p. 14). She believed that "ultimately, helping students express themselves in a content area is easier for an outsider than for a content expert, who usually takes linguistic and content knowledge for granted and has difficulty seeing his or her discipline from the non-English-speaking student's point of view" (p. 14). Troike (1994), on the other hand, maintained "It is far easier, and more efficient, to train subject-matter specialists in the basics of ESL than to try to train ESL teachers in the technical content of the ESP subject" and "if we try, or even pretend, to teach ESP without knowing the subject matter, we are seriously fooling ourselves or shortchanging our students, or both" (p. 7).

In my view, the degree of expertise of the ESP practitioner depends on the nature of the ESP being taught. In most academic and occupational settings, I side with Taylor's belief that the ESP instructor is usually better prepared to deal with the real needs of the ESP student than a content instructor. However, in highly technical contexts, such as air traffic control or CAT scan technology, a trained subject-matter specialist is essential, especially when human lives are at stake. Team teaching (Johns & Dudley-Evans, 1991), that is, the presence of both a content and a language instructor in the classroom, is an effective way to resolve the issue, but it is generally too expensive a solution and not widely practiced, though a successful example is described in Master (2000).

The Value of Genre-Based Instruction

Since the publication of John Swales's *Genre Analysis* in 1990a, considerable attention has been devoted to the notion of genre in the field of ESP. The issue concerns not the value of genre as a construct but whether or not genre specifications should be explicitly taught. The American New Rhetoric position is that they should not. With its detailed ethnographic descriptions of genres in science, medicine, and business, this school focuses on genre as social action (cf. Miller, 1984) and "provide[s] the field of ESL with rich perspectives on what actions genres perform in various communities and how these groups come to value certain text types" (Hyon, 1996, p. 713). It is the understanding of these social contexts that is important, and not the specifications of the genre. "[W]hat has to be attended to ... are features of the situation. ... Knowing the gross surface features is the easy part, and insufficient on its own" (Freedman & Medway, 1994, pp. 11–12, cited in Hyon, 1996, p. 690). Teaching applications are therefore not emphasized, though some New Rhetoricians are beginning to work out means of applying their theories in the classroom, for example, by having university students specify the purpose, audience, and circumstances of writing a text at the top of an assignment and then assessing how well the writing responds to this context (Coe, 1994, cited in Hyon, 1996).

The Australian school of systemic functional linguistics, on the other hand, believes that genre specifications should be explicitly taught. Based on Halliday's (1978) notion that language form is shaped by social context (i.e., the activity going on, the relationships among participants, and the channel of communication), Martin, Christie, and Rothery (1987; cited in Hyon, 1996) describe genres as structural forms used by cultures for various purposes in certain contexts. The Australian school was concerned that immigrant primary and secondary students (and now adult migrants in the workforce) were not being given the school genres required for social success.

The two schools of thought are aimed at different populations. The New Rhetoricians are concerned with helping university students and professionals to function in sophisticated academic and professional milieus, whereas the Australian school aims to foster the survival of immigrant children and adult migrants in the school and the workplace. ESP practitioners have tended to apply the Australian notion of genre to all non-English-speaking students, including those in academic and professional contexts, leading to accusations in some quarters that the teaching of genre specifications stifles creativity, and raising the issue of whether genre teaching is ultimately a scaffold or a straitjacket.

Accommodation in EAP

Critical theory is concerned with "questioning the status quo to probe beyond conventional explanations of why things are the way they are" (Benesch, 2001, p. 64). Inspired by Freire (1998) and Foucault (1988), critical EAP encourages students to "assess their options in particular situations rather than assuming they must fulfill expectations" (p. 64). In this light, the longstanding effort of EAP practitioners to aid their students by helping them to learn the requirements of the disciplines and develop their academic communicative competence (Swales, 1990a) has been called accommodationist (Benesch, 1993) and assimilationist (Pennycook, 1994) by critical EAP theorists. Allison (1994) challenged these theorists, calling them ideologist and imperialistic in their effort to dominate other viewpoints and arguing that EAP pragmatism did not presume an unexamined status quo. Ultimately, the EAP pragmatists agreed that criticism could be constructive (Allison, 1996), whereas the critical theorists acknowledged the struggles EAP practitioners have had in trying to develop better programs for academic non-native speakers (Benesch, 2001).

In my view, all educational enterprises, although especially those within the English teaching profession (including not just EAP but the entire field of ESP), need to constantly and rigorously question themselves. Not to do so is to run the risk that, while benignly helping students to acquire access to better job opportunities and greater academic success, ESP practitioners are unwittingly promoting the interests of those already in power (Master, 1998). Widdowson (1980) warned of the danger of providing a servant with just enough language ability to serve a master, describing it as "the curse of Caliban." Critical EAP theorists have reminded the field of ESP that education is a political act no matter how innocently pragmatic we claim to be.

For this reason, language teachers have to "remain vigilant in regard to all voices, including their own" (Fiumara, 1990, paraphrased in Master, 1998, p. 724).

The Efficacy of ESP

When statistical analysis appeared in the 57 published articles summarized in the previous section, it was invariably of the descriptive variety, that is, "a set of concepts and methods used in organizing, summarizing, tabulating, depicting, and describing collections of data" (Shavelson, 1981, p. 9). More than half of the articles used simple descriptive statistics such as percentages, means, and in one case standard deviations; two reported chi square values; and two reported correlation coefficients.

The category of research that appears to be missing in ESP research is quantitative studies, that is, experimental or quasi-experimental designs supported by inferential statistics. The most obvious topic that such research might be applied to is the efficacy of ESP itself. Calls for such research have been made for over 30 years. Mackay (1981), for example, noted that "the euphoria of the innovative phase in ESP programs has died down" (p. 108), leaving the field open to several questions of accountability:

- Do these ESP/EST programs work?
- Are they more effective than previous programs aimed at general language proficiency?
- If so, in what ways are they more effective?
- Are there any ways in which they are less effective?
- Can the expense be justified?
- Should we spend money on continuous quality control of ESP courses?
- Is there any evidence that syllabus planners are performing at least as well now, in terms of serving their clients' needs, as they were prior to the ESP epoch?
- Are there any unintended or unforeseen outcomes resulting from the use of any given ESP program? (cited in Master, 2000).

Johns and Dudley-Evans (1991) found that, even though the case for ESP had been accepted internationally, "few empirical studies have been conducted to test the effectiveness of ESP courses" (p. 303). They described the principal areas of concern in ESP to be how specific ESP courses should be, whether they should focus on a particular skill or integrate them all, and whether an appropriate ESP methodology could be developed. They noted that EAP was still dominant internationally, but that as ESP moved from its traditional EAP base, there would be "an increasing need for research into the nature of discourse, written or spoken, that must be produced or understood by those enrolled in ESP courses" (p. 307).

One of the few attempts to seriously address the efficacy of ESP instruction was the Reading in EST (REST) Project (under the auspices of UCLA) at the University of Guadalajara in Mexico (Hudson, 1991; Lynch, 1992; 1996). Lynch (1992) found that a group of third-year chemical engineering students (Pretest $n = 111$; Posttest $n = 103$) who received an EST reading curriculum that focused on previewing, sampling, comprehending, and analyzing the rhetorical and grammatical structure of "authentic chemical engineering texts that were being used in the students' other courses" (p. 65) over a 4-month period made statistically significant improvement ($p = .000$) on an English language test (the UCLA English as a Second Language Placement Examination, or ESLPE, whose reliability value for the Kuder-Richardson 21 formula [KR_{21}] ranged between .71 and .81 for the four administrations) compared to a control group (Pretest $n = 61$; Posttest $n = 54$) of pharmacobiology students at the same university who received "no English instruction whatsoever, not even traditional EFL classes" (p. 90). In the editors' postscript to Lynch (1992), Alderson and Beretta (1992) described the study as "one of the first thorough attempts to evaluate an EST programme in a university setting" (p. 96). Unfortunately, as the author notes, the absence of a treatment for an equivalent control group "reduce[s] the question of treatment effect to 'is the REST curriculum better than nothing?'" (p. 90) and thus, allows no empirical proof of the efficacy of ESP to be drawn.

In another promising study based on the same program, Hudson (1991) investigated the effect of EST content (reading) comprehension on general language acquisition. The content, also drawn from the field of chemical engineering, was based on journal articles concerned with such themes as materials and properties, electronics, and physical and mechanical processes. Using a test that examined reading grammar, reading comprehension, and general reading ability (with KR_{20} reliability coefficients ranging from .84 to .90 for the three forms of the test), Hudson found significant improvement in all three areas after the experimental group ($n = 152$) had received 2 years of academic instruction compared to a control group ($n = 212$) that had received no instruction (labeled "uninstructed" in Tables 1 and 2, Hudson, pp. 93–4). The absence of a treated control group means that this study also provides no evidence of the efficacy of ESP, nor of content-based instruction (CBI), athough it had the potential to do both.

Brown (1995) used an EST program (also conducted under the auspices of UCLA) begun in 1980 at the Guangzhou English Language Center (GELC) at Zhongshan University in Guangdong Province in the People's Republic of China as one of two examples (the other is the University of Hawaii) of a systematic approach to program development. In the chapter on program evaluation at GELC, Brown stated, "It turned out, in general terms, that students who learn English for science and technology appear to gain systematically in their overall proficiency as measured by tests like the TOEFL" (p. 240). On further examination, I was not able to ascertain any additional information supporting this conclusion.

Kaspar (2000) provided indirect evidence for the improved performance of high-intermediate to advanced EAP students who were given sustained content-based instruction using the Internet as a resource in either business or environmental science compared to the rest of the ESL program at the same level (who presumably did not receive sustained content-based instruction). Based on reading and writing examinations, 73.3% of the treatment group were able to skip a level (i.e., from ESL 91 to ESL 93, bypassing ESL 92) and move to ESL 93, a course for both native and non-native speakers, whereas only 21.4% of the students at this level "in the program overall" (p. 67) were able to do this (chi-squared = 28.47; $p < .001$). Unfortunately, because the study was not designed as an experiment, the data are entirely post hoc. No pretest score was reported to provide an assessment of the level of the students prior to the treatment, and the number of subjects is not indicated. The testing instrument is not described, statistically or otherwise, nor are the criteria for skipping a level. Finally, it appears that the treatment group was included as part of the control group in the comparison. These factors remove the possibility of empirical results.

Despite these potentially promising leads, empirical proof of the efficacy of ESP thus remains elusive. Echoing the need for research into ESP, Duff (2001) cites Jordan (1997) and Zamel and Spack (1998) in maintaining that "insufficient research has examined language learning, discourse socialization, and assessment at more advanced levels of secondary and postsecondary education for various academic or occupational purposes" (p. 606). She provides four major research questions to address what she finds to be lacking. Those that best reflect the issue of the efficacy of ESP are (p. 607):

- What kinds of preparation, intervention, and assessment are most effective in assisting ESL learners in these [i.e., ESP] settings to attain their own goals as well as reach established external standards?

- What factors contribute to underachievement or attrition among particular Ethnolinguistic groups of L2 students in academic/occupational programs, and what interventions might improve completion rates and other desired outcomes for these groups?
- What is the impact of ESL program completion on participants' language abilities and identities within their academic and professional communities?

Dudley-Evans (2001), in his farewell editorial, notes how focused and specific ESP work has become.

> The specificity I have noted is not necessarily of a subject-specific nature; it is rather that, as ESP research becomes more sophisticated and the range of its activity much broader, it has inevitably developed a much more focussed approach that looks at more detailed questions. (p. 311) [A]lready in 10(1) [1991] the trend in *English for Specific Purposes* towards articles presenting analysis rather than pedagogical issues and syllabus design was apparent.... While not in any way rejecting the need for theory and analysis in ESP, I do feel that we are reaching a stage where we need to consider how effective the courses that are developed from this research are. Are we really delivering in the ESP classroom? Are students in ESP classes more motivated than those in General English classes? I look forward to reading some more papers on these topics in future issues." (p. 312)

In short, despite 30 years of calls for empirical research demonstrating the efficacy of ESP, not a single published study has appeared to this end. All we really have is what Bowyers (1980, cited in Johns and Dudley-Evans, 1991) called "war stories and romances."

CONCLUSIONS AND FUTURE DIRECTIONS

ESP has enjoyed more than a 30-year history of acceptance based on anecdotal successes and the obvious motivational inspiration it provides for English language learners, not only in academic and occupational settings but also in sociocultural contexts such as literacy and citizenship programs, prisons, and AIDS programs (Master, 1997b). It needs to heed the repeated calls to establish its empirical validity as a viable means of second language acquisition. There is also a dire need for research in the occupational and sociocultural aspects of ESP as well as the training of ESP practitioners.

The field will no doubt continue to provide detailed descriptions of specific instantiations of ESP like those that have characterized the last 3 years of *English for Specific Purposes*. In this regard, Hewings (2002) believes that China and Hong Kong will continue to be substantial contributors to the journal in the coming years, along with Eastern Europe and Spain, where ESP is becoming of particular interest at the university level.

It is hoped, too, that the field will begin to see the publication of experimental studies based on inferential statistics. Although it is difficult to measure the effects of syllabi and methodologies, one can imagine controlled studies in which non-native speakers (NNSs) are taught skills using field-specific material and comparing their performance to a similar group using non-field-specific material. For example, NNS science majors could be taught reading skills based on journals in their fields (like the REST study) while a control group of NNS science students is taught reading skills using English literature or material from some other field such as psychology; their performance on a common reading test could then be measured and compared. An EOP example might be teaching a group of NNS manufacturing employees a Vocational ESL/English for Occupational Purposes (VESL/EOP) class based on a careful needs analysis of their on-the-job language requirements while a similar group receives general instruction in survival English, and comparing their performance on a number of measures, such as a language test, a criterion-referenced skills test, or an objective measure such as number of reported "rejects" (i.e., flawed products that must be discarded) by each group on the manufacturing line over a given period of time.

At the same time, it is hoped that the field will continue to remain keenly aware of the power of the double-edged sword ESP practitioners wield in representing the most powerful nations on the planet while addressing the increasing demand for instruction in English as the lingua franca of the learning and working world.

REFERENCES

Alderson, J. C., & Beretta, A. (1992). Editors' postscript to Lynch. In J. C. Alderson & A. Beretta, (Eds.), *Evaluating second language education* (pp. 96–99). Cambridge, UK: Cambridge University Press.

Allison, D. (1994). Comments on Sarah Benesch's "ESL, ideology, and the politics of pragmatism": A reader reacts. *TESOL Quarterly, 28,* 618–623.

Allison, D. (1996). Pragmatist discourse and English for academic purposes. *English for Specific Purposes, 15,* 85–103.

Basturkmen, H. (2002). Negotiating meaning in seminar-type discussion and EAP. *English for Specific Purposes, 21,* 233–242.

Benesch, S. (1993). ESL, ideology, and the politics of pragmatism. *TESOL Quarterly, 27,* 705–717.

Benesch, S. (2001). *Critical English for academic purposes: Theory, politics, and practice.* Mahwah, NJ: Lawrence Erlbaum Associates.

Boers, F. (2000). Enhancing metaphoric awareness in specialised reading. *English for Specific Purposes, 19,* 137–147.

Bosher, S., & Smalkowski, K. (2002). From needs analysis to curriculum development: Designing a course in health-care communication for immigrant students in the USA. *English for Specific Purposes, 21,* 59–79.

Bowyers, R. (1980). War stories and romances. In *Projects in materials design* (ELT Documents Special, pp. 71–82). London: British Council.

Braine, G. (2001). When professors don't cooperate: A critical perspective on EAP research. *English for Specific Purposes, 20,* 293–303.

Brett, P. (2000). Integrating multimedia into the Business English curriculum: A case study. *English for Specific Purposes, 19,* 269–290.

Brown, J. D. (1995). *The elements of language curriculum.* Boston: Heinle & Heinle.

Bruce, N. (2002). Dovetailing language and content: Teaching balanced argument in legal problem answer writing. *English for Specific Purposes, 21,* 321–345.

Candlin, C., Bhatia, V. K., & Jensen, C. H. (2002). Developing legal writing materials for English second language learners: Problems and perspectives. *English for Specific Purposes, 21,* 299–320.

Charteris-Black, J., (2000). Metaphor and vocabulary teaching in ESP economics. *English for Specific Purposes, 19,* 149–165.

Charteris-Black, J., & Ennis, T. (2001). A comparative study of metaphor in Spanish and English financial reporting. *English for Specific Purposes, 20,* 249–266.

Chien Ching, L. (2002). Strategy and self-regulation instruction as contributors to improving students' cognitive model in an ESL program. *English for Specific Purposes, 21,* 261–289.

Chimbganda, A. B. (2000). Communication strategies used in the writing of answers in biology by ESL first year science students of the University of Botswana. *English for Specific Purposes, 19,* 305–329.

Coe, R. M. (1994). Teaching genre as process. In A. Freedman & P. Medway (Eds.), *Learning and teaching genre* (pp. 157–169). Portsmouth, NH: Boynton/Cook.

Crosling, G., & Ward, I. (2002). Oral communication: The workplace needs and uses of business graduate employees. *English for Specific Purposes, 21,* 41–57.

De Beaugrande, R. (2000). User-friendly communication skills in the teaching and listening of business English. *English for Specific Purposes, 19,* 331–349.

Diaz-Santos, G. (2000). Technothrillers and English for science and technology. *English for Specific Purposes, 19,* 221–236.

Dudley-Evans, T. (2001). Editorial. *English for Specific Purposes, 20,* 311–312.

Dudley-Evans, T., & St. John, M. J. (1997). *Developments in English for Specific Purposes: A multidisciplinary approach.* Cambridge, UK: Cambridge University Press.

Duff, P. A. (2001). Learning English for academic and occupational purposes. *TESOL Quarterly, 35,* 606–7.

Feak, C. B., Reinhart, S. M., & Sinsheimer, A. (2000). A preliminary analysis of law review notes. *English for Specific Purposes, 19,* 197–220.

Feak, C., & Salehzadeh, J. (2001). Challenges and issues in developing an EAP video listening Placement assessment: A view from one program. *English for Specific Purposes, 20,* 477–493.

Ferguson, G. (2001). If you pop over there: A corpus-based study of conditionals in medical discourse. *English for Specific Purposes, 20,* 61–82.

Fiumara, G. C. (1990). *The other side of language: A philosophy of listening.* London: Routledge.

Foucault, M. (1988). On power. In L. D. Kreitzman (Ed.), *Politics, philosophy, culture: Interviews and other writings, 1977–1984.* New York: Routledge.

Frank, R. (2000). Medical communication: Nonnative English speaking patients and native English speaking professionals. *English for Specific Purposes, 19,* 31–62.

Freedman, A., & Medway, P. (1994). Introduction: New views of genre and their implications for education. In A. Freedman & P. Medway (Eds.), *Learning and teaching genre* (pp. 1–22). Portsmouth, NH: Boynton/Cook.

Freire, P. (1998). *Pedagogy of freedom: Ethics, democracy, and civic courage.* Lanham, MD: Rowman & Littlefield.

Gao, Y., Li, L., & Lü, J. (2001). Trends in research methods in applied linguistics: China and the West. *English for Specific Purposes, 20,* 1–14.

Gimenez, J. C. (2000). Business e-mail communication: some emerging tendencies in register. *English for Specific Purposes, 19,* 237–251.

Gimenez, J. C. (2001). Ethnographic observations in cross-cultural business negotiations between non-native speakers of English: An exploratory study. *English for Specific Purposes, 20,* 169–193.

Gledhill, C. (2000). The discourse function of collocation in research article introductions. *English for Specific Purposes, 19,* 115–135.

Green, C. F., Christopher, E. R., & Mei, J. L. K. (2000). The incidence and effects on coherence of marked themes in interlanguage texts: A corpus-based enquiry. *English for Specific Purposes, 19,* 99–113.

Halliday, M. A. K. (1978). *Language as social semiotic: The social interpretation of language and meaning.* London: Edward Arnold.

Halliday, M. A. K. (1994). *An introduction to functional grammar* (2nd Ed.). London: Edward Arnold.

Halimah, A. M. (2001). Rhetorical duality and Arabic speaking EST learners. *English for Specific Purposes, 20,* 111–139.

Hemais, B. (2001). The discourse of research and practice in marketing journals. *English for Specific Purposes, 20,* 39–59.

Henry, A., & Roseberry, R. L. (2001). A narrow-angled corpus analysis of moves and strategies of the genre: 'Letter of Application.' *English for Specific Purposes, 20,* 153–167.

Hewings, M. (2002). A history of ESP through English for Specific Purposes. *English for Specific Purposes World.* Retrieved December 22, 2002, from http://www.esp-world.info/Articles_3/Hewings_paper.htm

Hewings, M., & Hewings, A. (2002). "It is interesting to note that . . .": A comparative study of anticipatory 'it' in student and published writing. *English for Specific Purposes, 21,* 367–383.

Hudson, T. (1991). A content comprehension approach to reading English for science and technology. *TESOL Quarterly, 25,* 77–104.

Hyland, K. (2001). Humble servants of the disciple? Self-mention in research articles. *English for Specific Purposes, 20,* 207–226.

Hyon, S. (1996). Genre in three traditions: Implications for ESL. *TESOL Quarterly, 30,* 693–722.

Hyon, S. (2001). Long-term effects of genre-based instruction: A follow-up study of an EAP reading course. *English for Specific Purposes, 20,* 417–438.

Ibrahim, Y. (2001). Doctor and patient questions as a measure of doctor-centeredness in UAE hospitals. *English for Specific Purposes, 20,* 331–344.

Jackson, J. (2002). The China strategy: A tale of two case leaders. *English for Specific Purposes, 21,* 243–259.

Johns, A., & Dudley-Evans, T. (1991). English for Specific Purposes: International in scope, specific in purpose. *TESOL Quarterly, 25,* 297–314.

Jordan, R. R. (1997). *English for Academic Purposes: A guide and resource book for teachers.* Cambridge: Cambridge University Press.

Kaspar, L. F. (2000). Sustained content study and the Internet. In M. Pally (Ed.), *Sustained content teaching in academic ESL/EFL* (pp. 54–71). Boston: Houghton Mifflin.

Lahuerta, A. (2002). Empirical examination of EFL readers' use of rhetorical information. *English for Specific Purposes, 21*(1), 81–98.

Li So-Mui, F., & Mead, K. (2000). An analysis of English in the workplace: The communication needs of textile and clothing merchandisers. *English for Specific Purposes, 19,* 351–368.

Lindemann, S., & Mauranen, A. (2001). "It's just real messy": The occurrence and function of *just* in a corpus of academic speech. *English for Specific Purposes, 20,* 459–475.

Louhiala-Salminen, L. (2002). The fly's perspective: Discourse in the daily routine of a business manager. *English for Specific Purposes, 21,* 211–231.

Lynch, B. K. (1992). Evaluating a program inside and out. In J. C. Alderson & A. Beretta, (Eds.), *Evaluating second language education* (pp. 61–96). Cambridge, UK: Cambridge University Press.

Lynch, B. K. (1996). *Language program evaluation.* Cambridge, UK: Cambridge University Press.

Macdonald, M., Badger, R., & White, G. (2000). The real thing?: Authenticity and academic listening. *English for Specific Purposes, 19,* 253–267.

Mackay, R. (1981). Accountability in ESP programs. *The ESP Journal, 1,* 107–122.

Maclean, J., Betancourt, Z. S., & Hunter, A. (2000). The evolution of an ESP programme in Cuba. *English for Specific Purposes, 19,* 17–30.

Marco, M. J. L. (2000). Collocational frameworks in medical research papers: A genre-based study. *English for Specific Purposes, 19,* 63–86.

Martin, J. R., Christie, F., & Rothery, J. (1987). Social pressures in education: A reply to Sawyer and Watson (and others). In I. Reid (Ed.), *The place of genre in learning: Current debates* (pp. 46–57). Geelong, Australia: Deakin University Press.

Martinez, I. (2001). Impersonality in the research article as revealed by analysis of the transitivity structure. *English for Specific Purposes, 20,* 227–247.

Master, P. (1997a). Content-based instruction vs. ESP. *TESOL Matters, 7,* 10.

Master, P. (1997b). ESP teacher education in the USA. In R. Howard & G. Brown, (Eds.), *Teacher Education for LSP* (pp. 22–40). Clevedon, UK: Multilingual Matters.

Master, P. (1998). Positive and negative aspects of the dominance of English. *TESOL Quarterly, (32),* 716–727.

Master, P. (2000a). English and computers: A modified adjunct course. In P. Master, (Ed.), *Responses to ESP* (pp. 165–169). Washington, DC: U.S. State Department.

Master, P. (2000b). The future of ESP. In P. Master, (Ed.), *Responses to ESP* (pp. 23–26). Washington DC: U.S. State Department.

Master, P. (Ed.). (2000c). *Responses to ESP.* Washington, DC: U.S. State Department.

Master, P. (2001). Editorial. *English for Specific Purposes, 20,* v–vi.

Mavor, S., & Trayner, B. (2001). Aligning genre and practice with learning in higher education: An interdisciplinary perspective for course design and teaching. *English for Specific Purposes, 20,* 345–366.

Miller, C. (1984). Genre as social action. *Quarterly Journal of Speech, 70,* 151–167.

Moore, T. (2002). Knowledge and agency: A study of "metaphenomenal discourse" in textbooks from three disciplines. *English for Specific Purposes, 21,* 347–366.

Northcott, J. (2001). Towards an ethnography of the MBA classroom: A consideration of the role of interactive lecturing styles with the context of one MBA programme. *English for Specific Purposes, 20,* 15–37.

Okamura, A., & Shaw, P. (2000). Lexical phrases, culture, and subculture in transactional letter writing. *English for Specific Purposes, 19,* 1–15.

Open Doors. (2002). *What foreign students study.* Retrieved December 22, 2002, from http://www.opendoorsweb.org/Press/fast_facts.htm#foreign students study

Paltridge, B. (2002). Thesis and dissertation writing: An examination of published advice and actual practice. *English for Specific Purposes, 21,* 125–143.

Parkinson, J. (2000). Acquiring scientific literacy through content and genre: A theme-based language course for science students. *English for Specific Purposes, 19,* 369–387.

Pennycook, A. (1994). *The cultural politics of English as an international language.* London: Longman.

Pinto dos Santos, V. B. M. (2002). Genre analysis of business letters of negotiation. *English for Specific Purposes, 21,* 167–199.

Rowley-Jolivet, E. (2002). Visual discourse in scientific conference papers. A genre-based study. *English for Specific Purposes, 20,* 19–40.

Samraj, B. (2002). Introductions in research articles: Variations across disciplines. *English for Specific Purposes, 21,* 1–18.

Schachter, J. (1981, March). Teach ESP—Me? No, thanks. Paper presented at the Fifteenth Annual TESOL Convention, Detroit, MI.

Shavelson, R. J. (1981). *Statistical reasoning for the behavioral sciences.* Boston: Allyn & Bacon.

Shi, L., Corcos, R., & Storey, A. (2001). Using student performance data to develop an English course for clinical training. *English for Specific Purposes, 20,* 267–291.

Slaouti, D. (2002). The World Wide Web for academic purposes: Old study skills for new? *English for Specific Purposes, 21,* 105–124.

Soler, V. (2002). Analyzing adjectives in scientific discourse: An exploratory study with educational applications for Spanish speakers at advanced university level. *English for Specific Purposes, 21,* 145–166.

Spector-Cohen, E., Kirschner, M., & Wexler, C. (2001). Designing EAP reading courses at the university level. *English for Specific Purposes, 20,* 267–291.

Swales, J. M. (1990a). *Genre analysis: English in academic and research settings.* Cambridge, UK: Cambridge University Press.

Swales, J. M. (1990b). Nonnative speaker graduate engineering students and their introductions: Global coherence and local management. In U. Connor & A. M. Johns, (Eds.), *Coherence in writing: research and pedagogical perspectives* (pp. 187–208). Washington, DC: TESOL.

Swales, J. M., Barks, D., Ostermann, A. C., & Simpson, R. C. (2001). Between critique and accommodation: Reflections on an EAP course for Masters of Architecture students. *English for Specific Purposes, 20,* 439–458.

Strevens, P. (1988). ESP after 20 years: A reappraisal. In M. Tickoo, (Ed.), *ESP: State of the art* (pp. 1–13). Singapore: SEAMEO Regional Language Centre.

Taylor, M. (1994, Feb/Mar). How much content does the ESP instructor need to know? *TESOL Matters, 4,* 14.

Troike, R. (1993, Dec/1994, Jan). The case for subject-matter training in ESP. *TESOL Matters, 3,* 7.

Upton, T., & Connor, U. (2001). Using computerized corpus analysis to investigate the textlinguistic discourse moves of a genre. *English for Specific Purposes, 20,* 313–329.

Vassileva, I. (2001). Commitment and detachment in English and Bulgarian academic writing. *English for Specific Purposes, 20*, 83–102.

Ward, J. (2001, March). EST: Evading scientific text. *English for Specific Purposes, 20*, 141–152.

Widdowson, H. (1980). *English for specific purposes: The curse of Caliban.* Plenary address given at the Fourteenth Annual TESOL Convention, San Francisco, CA.

Yakhontova, T. (2001). Textbooks, contexts, and learners. *English for Specific Purposes, 20*, 397–415.

Zamel, V., & Spack, R. (Eds.). (1998). *Negotiating academic lteracies: Teaching and learning across languages and cultures.* Mahwah, NJ: Lawrence Erlbaum Associates.

7

English in the Workplace

Celia Roberts
King's College, University of London

INTRODUCTION

It is hard to find any aspect of this topic, including the words to describe it in this title, that is not contentious. At one end of the spectrum is the assumption that the workplace is a good context in which to teach English as a Second Language. It is assumed that workers need and want to learn English and that provided time and space can be negotiated with the employer, workplace English is relatively unproblematic. At the other end of the spectrum are two different but contrastive positions. One is a practical and organizational view that employees will only make real progress in using English if courses are tied to wider employer concerns and initiatives that can benefit the workforce in several ways. Within this view, workplace educators take on different roles and titles that may not include either "English" or "teaching." The second position takes a more critical and ideological stance. It raises questions about who benefits from English courses, whether language audits disadvantage the less communicatively competent and questions the hegemony of English in multilingual workplaces. For most researchers and practitioners in the workplace, these different views have to be held in tension. Negotiating the scope, roles, and relationships of workplace educators is part of a larger struggle in which the purposes, methods, and scale of their work are implicated. In this review of research into language education in the workplace, these tensions have to be acknowledged.

In this chapter, I will first describe some of the distinctive characteristics of English in the workplace and associated research, then discuss some of the general theoretical moorings of workplace research. I then focus on current research theories and methodologies and illustrate these through five workplace studies. Finally, I consider future directions in research and ways in which it needs to reflect the changing and widening role of English in the workplace interventions, while acknowledging the tensions between workplace priorities and critical perspectives.

DISTINCTIVE CHARACTERISTICS OF ENGLISH
IN THE WORKPLACE

Unlike many of the other contexts described in this book, the workplace is a vast and unwieldy canvas on which to create a picture of second language learning. Here the context for second language learning is not the classroom but the whole communicative environment. As Mawer (1999) puts it, "the workplace is the curriculum" (p. 60). What is at stake is not just the improvement in language ability of individual workers but the possibility of changing the communicative patterns and assumptions of staff at all levels. This entails looking at how the organization is held together by talk and writing and how these practices reflect or contest the potential for disadvantage and discrimination in a multilingual workplace. If the workplace is the curriculum, then a whole range of issues from new technologies to competency standards may become part of the language educators remit.

The workplace context is particularly challenging because it is in such a state of change. Although these changes seem to be overwhelming at this historical moment, ever since workforces shifted from being monolingual to multilingual they have been subject to multidimensional change (Ford, Anderson, Hull, Phelan, Read, Robson, & Wingrove, 1976). The current changes include increasing use of technology, more flexible work practices, more multitask working, flatter structures, and allied to all of these, more language and literacy demands (Belfiore, 1993; Mawer, 1999). The "new work order" (Gee, Hull, & Lankshear, 1996) may provide new opportunities for workers, or it can be a means of controlling and excluding, or indeed a combination of both.

Changing the communicative environment of the workplace involves interventions that affect staff at various levels within the organization. Since the 1970s, research and practice have included what has variously been described as "cultural awareness," "cross-cultural training," and "diversity training." The assumption that those with least communicative power—non-English speakers—should not bear the brunt of any changes led to the development of courses for, initially, supervisors, trade unionists, and managers on issues of intercultural communication. These, in turn, have led to quite an extensive research and development program in North America, the United Kingdom, and Australia in which the "gatekeeper" as guardian of scarce resources has been targeted. In these settings, the workplace is the service encounter or assessment interview where the communicative abilities of linguistic minority clients or applicants are judged and where they are either let through the gate or not. These gatekeeping encounters are also the only sites where some minority speakers may have any chance to use English (Bremer, Roberts, Vasseur, Simonot, & Broeder, 1996).

These two types of workplaces—the multilingual company and the institution as a gatekeeping site (and of course the company also includes gatekeeping activities)—are both contexts in which English may be used rather than acquired. Although thousands of English language courses have been run in workplaces, it is the opportunity to *use* the workplace environment as a continuing site of language development that is central to most workplace projects. This focus on language use rather than on acquisition chimes well with theories of second language socialization. The "novice" English speaker learns to use language as a social practice and through language learns the sociocultural knowledge that is "wired into" (Agar, 1994) language use (see Zuengler & Cole, this volume).

Second language socialization theories underpin research and practice in workplace English. Language is seen as a social phenomenon or more precisely, a set of practices that are relative to particular groups' ways of being and acting. Allied to this linguistic and cultural relativity is the acknowledgement that there is a linguistic dimension to discrimination and exclusion (Roberts, Davies, & Jupp, 1992). The methodology for this research is drawn from a fairly elastic bag of discourse theories that include Hallidayan functionalism, conversation analysis, pragmatics, and interactional sociolinguistics. Combined with these and central to researching the workplace is ethnography or, more precisely in many cases, ethnographic techniques (Green & Bloome, 1997).

Because, as Hymes (1980) has suggested, ethnography is a kind of common sense that we are born with (but tend to forget as we grow up), ethnographic tools are an obvious means for trying to understand the unfamiliar and seemingly hostile contexts of the workplace. It has been commonplace for workbased programs to undertake some initial ethnographic investigation in order to, at the least, design a relevant course. Because ethnographic studies are a kind of systematic common sense making, it is difficult to know whether to count such initial investigations as research or not. The databases of workplace reports in North America, Australia, New Zealand, and, until 15 years ago in the United Kingdom, represent a large body of practitioner research. They combine detailed descriptions of workplaces with conceptual knowledge and evaluations in ways that break down the barriers between research and not-research (Cochran-Smith & Lytle, 1993). So research in this chapter will include both more formal studies and will also draw on practitioner research in which the teacher is not just an "articulator of some brought-in curriculum, but . . . [is] an active ethnographer of the workplace, one whose professional investigations and tasks are always to be set in the context of an appreciation of the structures and relations of power in the workplace in question, in particular in respect of its channels, modes and practices of decision-making" (Candlin, 1999, xiv).

Even if we take this expanded view of research, there is still relatively little research on workplace English outside of the more general research on talk and the professions and the "gatekeeping" research previously mentioned. There are a small number of books that deal with the practice of teaching and learning language and literacy in the workplace and its wider social implications in Canada (Belfiore & Burnaby, 1984), the United Kingdom (Roberts, Davies, & Jupp, 1992), the United States (Hull, 1997), and Australia (Mawer, 1999) and a few monographs such as Goldstein (1997), Clyne (1994), and Willing (1992), but there have been surprisingly few articles in well-known refereed journals. There are several possible reasons for this. The manufacturing and service workplaces are not easy places to research compared with the classroom. There are many constraints from management, the environment is noisy, the courses are often short, and any improvements perceived or measured narrowly are tied to very specific workplace goals (Belfiore, 1992; Goldstein, 1993; Katz, 2000).

CONNECTIONS WITH RELATED RESEARCH

English in the workplace research has its theoretical moorings in Hymesian notions of communicative competence and the ethnography of communication. It also draws on systemic grammar and the literature on pragmatics. To this extent, it shares an approach with most teaching and research within the tradition of communicative language teaching. Most English language courses and related research and evaluation combine language and literacy teaching and draw on literacy research particularly within the "new literacies" tradition (Barton, Hamilton, & Ivanič, 2000; Cope, Pauwels, Slade, Brosnan, & Neil, 1993; Street, 1995) and adult workplace literacy (Benseman, 1998; Holland, Frank, & Cooke, 1998; Smith, Mikulecky, Kibby, Drecher, & Dole, 2000).

The wider context of training in the workplace draws on the literature of adult learning more generally and on research and policy around the changing workplace.

The different approaches to adult learning are usefully summed up in Mawer (1999). She discusses the development from relatively reductionist adult training to a more holistic, humanistic learning approach, quoting Ford (1991), "dogs are trained, people learn." With this approach, the focus is on a more dialogic process in which learners are involved in first understanding the new context in which they will have to operate and in learning how to learn. Learning processes are embedded in what has been called "the learning company" (Peddler, Bourgoyne, & Boydell, 1991) in which all aspects of the system are expected to be critical and self-reflecting. As Mawer admits, however, much of this visionary work remains at the level of rhetoric and is hard to reconcile with the outcomes-orientated approach to rethinking vocational training based on a narrow view of competencies.

This accusation of narrowness can also be laid at the door of some workplace language and literacy schemes and their underlying theoretical assumptions. However communicatively competent workers might become as a result of workplace courses, research has shown that this is not a panacea for all the difficulties and inequalities of the multilingual workplace (Cullity, 1998; Hull, 1993; Mikulecky, 1984). Many of the problems can be attributed to inefficient or poor management, inappropriate styles and expectations, and a range of other social and individual factors related to gender, class, commitment, responsibility, and so on (Mawer & Field, 1995). Some of these issues can begin to be addressed by focusing on those who interact with workers from non-English speaking backgrounds.

The research on intercultural awareness and related training is part of the growing body of research on talk and discourse at work. This research examines communicative practices from the fine-grained level of interaction to the macro-ideological level of institutional order. Drawing on Goffman's "interaction order" (1974) and Giddens (1991), a fundamental assumption of these studies is that the wider social order is not a given but is actively produced in and through interaction. In other words as participants interact together (and with those not physically present) they are actively *structuring* the situation that feeds into social structures (Goffman, 1974).

There is a long tradition of discourse-based sociolinguistic and sociological studies of professional communication. The majority of these have been in healthcare and education and some in business and law (Bhatia, 1993; Cameron, 2000; Coleman, 1984, 1985, 1989; Fisher & Todd, 1983; Gibbons, 1987, 1994; Mehan, 1979). Some of the early studies drew on speech act theory (Labov & Fanshel, 1977) to explicate language patterns. More recently, while retaining a central interest in the relation of language and context, sociolinguistic studies have focused on more institutional themes such asymmetrical power relations and decision-making processes (Cicourel, 1992; Fisher & Todd, 1986; West, 1984).

Within sociology, Conversational Analysis (CA) has come to dominate the research on talk at work. The most relevant studies for this chapter concern healthcare and medicine (Atkinson & Heath, 1981; Drew & Heritage, 1992; Heritage, Chatwin, & Collins, 2001; Maynard, 1991; Heath, 1992; Peräkylä, 1995) and business and decision making (Boden, 1994; Firth, 1994). Within CA, talk *is* social action so there is no distinction made between language and its context and outcomes. This talk (and non-verbal communication) is designed to be accountable both to the speaker and to what has gone before in the interaction. So interaction is made up of connected sequences of actions that appear to have stable patterns. The patterns of communication and the fact that they are jointly accomplished is the rationale for workplace programs to have training for native and fluent speakers of English in positions of power, as well as English language training. Central to the research and teaching of gatekeepers is the assumption that their contributions help to construct the performance of interviewees. Although workplace English can draw on the general tenets of CA, there is still little research that is "pure" conversation analysis of intercultural communication (see Firth, 1994; Wagner, 1995 for exceptions). Given that CA relies on the speakers and the analysts sharing the practical reasoning processes that make sense of interaction, CA of intercultural communication can only be done where the analyst is fully bilingual and bicultural (see also Gumperz & Levinson, 1996).

These discourse-based studies cover a wide spectrum of ideological positions. One of the most powerful, and one to which most recent workplace English research subscribes, can be described, broadly, as critical. Workplace literacy and gatekeeping studies and to a lesser extent language research have engaged with issues of power relations, with asking how structural inequalities—including the unequal access to English as the language of power—come to be produced and with a commitment to helping students to "engage critically with the conditions of their working lives" (Cope et al., 1993, p. 26). This general critical stance is realized in three areas relevant to the workplace: critical linguistics, in particular critical discourse analysis (CDA), critical or "new" literacies, and critical pedagogy. CDA has tended to focus on the discourses of work and institutional life and how these are constructing new work roles and identities (Fairclough, 1989, 1992; Farrell, 2000; Sarangi & Slembrouck, 1996) For example, many of the discourses of work are being colonized by competing discourses (Fairclough, 1992; Wodak, 1996) which, these authors argue, for example, turn gatekeeping interviews into "little chats" and ethically questionable capitalist practices into morally uplifting missions.

The discourses of the "new capitalism" have come under heavy attack from critical literacy. These new capitalist discourses are "imperialistic" (Gee, Hull, & Lankshear, 1996) as they take over discourses from religion, communities, and universities in order to persuade workers of their core vision. The need to constantly change products and customize them to survive in the globalized market place requires workers to become increasingly flexible and take more responsibility. This new work order "empowers" workers to work harder, be more communicatively skillful, and to have less job security. There are new work genres, many of them new types of meetings where hierarchies are blurred, and new work and professional identities have to be constructed and negotiated (Farrell, 2000; Hull, 1997; Iedema & Scheeres, 2003; Schellekens, 2001).

Critical literacy also has an impact at the level of workplace courses. Here it links with critical pedagogy and with the transformative goals of Paulo Friere (1972). Whereas a skills approach may give some individuals opportunity, a critical pedagogy aims to help students re-assess their position in society and review critically their working lives (Auerbach & Wallerstein, 1987).

This brief review of some of the associated research in language and literacy, in talk and interaction at work, and in broader issues of workplace learning and training suggests both the breadth and the potential for controversy and tension in the research on and for workplace English. The next section will review aspects of research that are directly related to workplace education in the United States, Canada, the United Kingdom, Australia, and New Zealand with some reference to studies of other languages.

DEVELOPMENTS AND CURRENT ISSUES IN RESEARCH

Compared with the large body of research on language and discourse in professional institutions, there has been relatively little research on industrial workplaces or on multilingual settings in work contexts more generally. For this reason, it is important to include in this review both research that has informed teaching and assessment practice and the numerous reports and accounts that have been published and/or fed into resource banks such as the National Centre for English Language Teaching and

Research, Macquarie University, Australia; the ERIC Clearinghouse on Adult, Career and Vocational Education, United States and Canada; Workbase in New Zealand; and the now defunct National Centre for Industrial Language Training in London in the United Kingdom. Other reports have been published by government-funded programs such as the Workplace English Language and Literacy Programme in Australia; the Multicultural Workplace Programme in Canada; the National Workplace Literacy Program in the United States.

Much of the research on English in the workplace has derived from practitioner involvement. For this reason, research is dependent on opportunities for workplace education that are highly dependent on political and commercial imperatives (Wyse, 1997). Whereas the United Kingdom, the United States, and Canada were developing workplace programs and related research in the 1970s and early 1980s, by the late 1980s the United Kingdom project was being scaled down. During this time, Australia took the lead in developing English in the workplace and associated research. Recently, the political scene in Australia has been less hospitable to this area, and in the United Kingdom a new National Research and Development Centre for Adult Literacy and Numeracy has been set up that includes ESL research and ESL employees as one of its key target populations. Inevitably research in this area has followed the political imperatives of different countries and governments as issues of language, literature, and ethnicity are constructed as relatively important or not to a particular country's economic and social well-being.

Turning now to specific research projects, we can identify four main approaches used in the research on and for English in the workplace that have been particularly influential: textual analysis of discourse, interactional sociolinguistics, pragmatics, and ethnography.

The textual analysis of discourse has drawn on Halliday's (1973) systemic/functional model of language. This was particularly influential in the early analysis of workplace texts (Roberts et al., 1992). Halliday's focus on the relatively patterned and predictable habits of meaning that develop within particular groups (1973) and the significance of prosodic systems (1967) in making meaning fed into both the development of language materials and awareness courses (Byrne & Fitzgerald, 1996; Gumperz, Jupp, & Roberts, 1979; Roberts, 1998). Later developments of Hallidayan linguistics in genre theory (Martin, 1984; Bhatia, 1993) have been used to highlight the rule-governed nature of speech and written genres.

Some of the criticisms of the systemic/functional model—that it is overly prescriptive and does not take account of the locally designed and jointly accomplished nature of interaction—have been answered by studies in interactional sociolinguistics. Macro issues of inequality, institutionalization, and discrimination and sociological notions of ethnicity, social identity, networks, and gatekeeping are linked to micro issues of discourse coherence, CA ideas of sequential organization, and concepts of face and frame (Gumperz, 1982; 1997; 1999). Within this framework, small interactional moments can have large social consequences. Where speakers do not share the same way of interacting, inferential processes, or conditions for negotiating, there is always the potential for misunderstanding and negative social evaluation—what Erickson (1985) calls "clinical labelling."

Central to the ways in which people make sense to each other moment by moment is the notion of contextualization (Auer & di Luzio, 1992; Cook-Gumperz & Gumperz, 1976). It is impossible for speakers to understand each other without a context, but contextualization goes further than this in showing that language and paralinguistic signs or cues actively create and shape the interaction moment by moment. These "contextualization cues" (Gumperz, 1982; 1992a; 1992b) signal what is to be expected in an exchange, what can be understood rather than explicitly conveyed, and how interpersonal relations and social identities are to be managed (Gumperz, 1996, p. 396). The most important cues and, paradoxically, the most hidden ones are prosodic cues. These function to show cohesiveness, to signal speaker involvement and perspective, to show emphasis and contrast, and to show what is old or new information. Where speakers do not share the same prosodic systems, both sides can misjudge the other and this can lead to negative stereotyping. Using both naturally occurring and role-played encounters, intercultural awareness training, based substantially on the studies of interactional sociolinguistics, has been implemented in a range of industrial and professional settings (Belfiore & Heller, 1992; Cope, Pauwels, Slade, Brosnan, & Neil, 1993; McGregor & Williams, 1984; Pauwels, 1994; Roberts et al., 1992).

Early developments in workplace English drew heavily on the Pragmatics literature. Speech act theory, with its emphasis on speaker intention and social context, drove much of the functional approaches to language teaching and some early work-based materials such as the doctor–patient communication project (Candlin, Leather, & Bruton, 1974). Levinson (1983) has shown that there are systematic pragmatic constraints that largely determine how speakers make inferences from each others' contributions. Rather than some general idea of appropriate behaviour, language learners can trace evidence of these constraints in naturally occurring encounters. Gricean maxims that assume that speakers are motivated by rational efficiency (Grice, 1989) and politeness theories that assume that people are motivated by "faces," wants, and needs (Brown & Levinson, 1987) constrain language performance and guide inferential processes. Because they consist of both universal and culturally specific elements, their use as analytic tools was significant in both language courses and intercultural awareness training. Together with interactional sociolinguistics, Pragmatics continues to provide important insights into differences of communicative style and misunderstandings (Li, 2000). However, its focus on individual speaker intention as the locus of analysis and on oral communication rather than multimodality puts some limitations on its usefulness.

The final approach in this section is a method rather than a theory. Ethnography is the detailed investigation of the cultural and social patterns of interaction and the values, beliefs, and assumptions that account for such interaction. Participant observation is the defining technique of ethnography and, in Agar's term, to do this requires being "a professional stranger" (Agar, 2000). This term is a kind of oxymoron, reflecting the paradox in ethnography between just being an outsider—someone defined by their lack of knowledge and familiarity—and being a professional—someone defined by their knowledge and skills. Workplace educators find themselves in even more of a contested situation than the professional ethnographer. This is because of the tensions between trying to understand all the conflicting issues of the workplace from the inside and meeting the demands of the company, which often expects quick-fix solutions (Mawer, 1999). All the research studies discussed in the following have used ethnography, either as an extended study in the tradition of anthropological ethnography (Wallman, 1979; Westwood & Bachu, 1988), as micro-ethnography (Erickson & Schultz, 1982), or as a set of ethnographic tools (Green & Bloome, 1997).

REVIEW OF ENGLISH IN THE WORKPLACE STUDIES

This section reviews five studies that illustrate the four main areas just discussed. The majority of research sites are in manufacturing industry rather than in professional contexts or service industries, although studies from these contexts will also be referred to. They have been selected on the basis that the workplace is the curriculum and rather than discuss research that looks at how individuals or one group go through the process of language socialization (see Zuengler & More, this volume) these studies look at language and literacy use across a range of settings within the wider imperatives of the workplace.

Pragmatics

The first of these is Michael Clyne's study of English as a lingua franca in multilingual workplaces in Australia (Clyne, 1994). Most of the data were collected in two car factories, a textile factory, an electronics factory, and the catering section of a hostel. The corpus consists of audiotaped data of routine work communication supplemented by video and audio data of formal meetings (182 hours in total). A pragmatic analysis of the data draws on the literature on cross-cultural pragmatics (Blum-Kulka, House, & Kasper, 1989) and pragmatic failure (Thomas, 1983) and concentrates on the speech acts of complaints, commissives, directives, and apologies and also looks at "small talk" (see also Holmes, 2000) in order to examine cultural variation in discourse. The approach is a contrastive one in which different ethnic groups are compared and gender and power relations are taken into account in discussing the extent to which cultural differences cause communication breakdowns.

Clyne discusses systematic differences in the ways in which speech acts are realized and how these relate to larger interactional concerns to do with turn-taking and negotiating. For example, he argues that the European workers tend to have "well-developed schemata intended to persuade others of their viewpoint" whereas the Southeast Asian group negotiates as little as possible and says what is expected (Clyne, 1994, p. 125). These differences are part of contrasts in overall communicative style between the different groups. Three different communicative styles are identified: Style A represented by European speakers and Spanish speaking Latin Americans, Style B speakers from South Asia, and Style C speakers from Southeast Asia. The latter group is claimed to be at a disadvantage in intercultural communication in the Australian workplace because they are less likely to assert themselves and directives and complaints addressed to them tend to be longer and more explicit than those directed to other groups (p. 153).

Clyne concludes that discourse patterns vary considerably between ethnic groups and that these differences can be attributed to "sociocultural interactional parameters" such as harmony, uncertainty avoidance, and individuality and to "discourse-cultural parameters" such as orientation to content and the degree of linearity (Clyne, 1994, p. 203). These patterns vary as much across different minority ethnic groups as they do between these groups and the majority or dominant Anglo-Australian group. Given this conclusion, Clyne argues that English in the workplace programs need to include some support in dealing with the different communicative styles of the typical multilingual workplace, and these should focus on discourse and pragmatic breakdowns (see also Duff, Wong, & Early, 2000; Li, 2002; and Roberts et al., 1992).

Another major study that has been substantially influenced by pragmatics but also draws on Halladayan and interactional sociolingusitic work is Willing's research on professional problem solving (Willing, 1992; 1997). As with Clyne's study, problems in communication in a linguistically diverse workplace are often based on culturally specific styles of communicating. In white-collar problem solving, there are a range of subtle linguistic skills that make the speaker relatively persuasive or not. For example, speakers have to convey and listeners have to infer the degree of cognitive commitment to the assessments and suggestions put forward and these depend crucially on their use and understanding of modality. Willing argues (1997) that it is difficult to distinguish clearly between epistemic and politeness modality and recommends that there should be more concentration on modality in language courses.

Interactional Sociolinguistics

The second study draws on the interactional sociolinguistic literature and on some of the tools of ethnography. It is a case study of how formal assessment and gatekeeping procedures shed light on the linguistic dimension of discrimination. This is part of a wider practical and research concern about the relationship between competence at a job and the linguistically complex demands of being trained and assessed for doing the job (Brindley, 1994; Mawer & Field, 1995; McNamara, 1997; ProTrain, 1993; Sefton, Waterhouse, & Deakin, 1994). The case study arose out of consultancy work undertaken by the National Centre for Industrial Language Training in the United Kingdom and was part of a formal investigation by the Commission for Racial Equality (CRE) into the promotion procedures in a large engineering company (Brierley, Dhesi, & Yates, 1992).

The question was: Had the company indirectly discriminated against applicants of South Asian origin, who had applied to become foreman, because of an over-reliance on the formal interview as a method of selection? The task, therefore, was to compare the communication skills required to pass the foreman-selection procedures with the skills required to do the job.

In addition to observation and audio recordings on the shopfloor and simulated interviews, foremen were interviewed using ethnographic interviewing techniques (Spradley, 1979). The simulated job interviews were based on the company's procedures and assumptions: The event was characterized by indirectness and by a stylized truthfulness in which issues of face are paramount. The idea that candidates are expected to "sell themselves" but in deprecatory ways is quite different from selection interviews in the Indian subcontinent that are designed to find out about any general weaknesses in character. A comparison of the promotion interview and the communication that foremen had to deal with on the shopfloor showed that they were, not surprisingly, very different and the pragmatic and discourse skills required of the interview were far more complex.

Whereas the South Asian foremen handled shopfloor communication well, their performance in the interviews was rated as less assured along a number of dimensions. First, in terms of self-presentation they tended to come across as either over-emphatic or too indirect. Second, the South Asian groups' responses were not seen as displaying immediate relevance either because their answers lacked lexical cohesion or because their use of prosody differed systematically from that used by native English speakers. Finally, this group had more difficulty being persuasive in their line of argument. This was partly because of relatively more syntactically complex questions—for example, demanding a hypothetical answer or, again, because of systematic differences in the relative use of syntax and prosody between native English speakers and those whose English is influenced by North Indian languages.

The researchers concluded that the selection interview was discriminatory because Asian applicants who could communicate clearly on the shopfloor were put at a disadvantage by the linguistic demands and implicit conventions of the interview. Language training alone might address some of the symptoms but not the cause of discrimination and would only serve to reinforce the existing and erroneous deficit view of the South Asian applicants' abilities as shopfloor communicators. As a result, the company was served with a legal notice from the CRE requiring them to change their promotion procedures.

This case study illustrates one of a number of cases in the United Kingdom, Australia, and the United States (Hull, 1993; 1997; Wonacott, 2000) where it has been assumed that the language and literacy competence of workers is directly related to their job competence and potential. As we have seen, this is not just an educational matter but has ramifications in the industrial and legal world. This study is also an example of the close connection between research and practical relevance that is typical of so many projects related to English in the workplace.

Ethnography

The third set of studies take a broader ethnographic and critical perspective. The first of these (Goldstein, 1997) concerns language choice and the role of English in a Canadian multilingual factory. The second focuses on literacy practices within the "new work order" in the high-technology electronics companies in Silicon Valley, California, and in the service industries. Goldstein's study arose out of her experiences as a workplace English teacher. It challenges the assumption that English competency is necessary to communicate in the workplace and for equal opportunities and promotion. Drawing on the theoretical work of feminist sociolinguists Susan Gal, Jane Hill, and Kathryn Woolard on the political economy of language choice and use, Goldstein's ethnography is a study of Portuguese factory workers and their relationship with supervision and quality assurance staff.

Language choice, whether Portuguese or English, and attitudes to learning English depend not only on practical matters such as getting the job done or getting a better job but on the symbolic value of language and the structural positions of the workers. Portuguese serves as a means of maintaining ethnic identity and solidarity in what is construed as the Portuguese manufacturing "family." Language choice helps to maintain boundaries and to manage social roles with code-switching used strategically to cross boundaries, but because most of the workers prefer to stay on the line, Portuguese is, paradoxically, endowed with authority. It is the language of friendship and of economic survival in this factory.

Workplace English, Goldstein argues, gives access to English but not necessarily to promotion because a high level of education is required for jobs such as quality controllers. English language training may help the company, but the question is how necessary or helpful is it for the individual? Goldstein concludes that English classes in the workplace are worthwhile provided that they are underpinned by an acknowledgement that "language boundaries are part of people's working and personal lives" (Goldstein, 1997, p. 83). If language training is only part of the hegemonic process that gives English absolute dominance and further marginalizes limited speakers of English, then it needs to be challenged. An alternative to most of the discourses of ESL training is a critical pedagogy that, in the Frierian tradition, aims to help students to think critically about their conditions of work and their position in society (Belfiore & Burnaby, 1984; Bell, 1982). English can be empowering as long as it does not undercut Portuguese values.

Hull's studies of literacy practices also combine a critical perspective with practical relevance. The new work order is characterised by "the shift towards high-technology manufacturing, service-orientated industries, and new forms of organisation such as self-directed teams" (Hull, 1997, p. 20). The restructuring of workplaces and the new technologies require new literacy skills both on the production line and in training (Farrell, 1999; Holland et al., 1998; Moore, 1999) . As with other studies mentioned, attempts to assess literacy can label workers as less competent and skilled than they are in doing the job and blocks promotion prospects (Hull, 1996; 1997; Katz, 2000). Hull argues for new frameworks for understanding literacy in relation to the restructured workplace and shows how finely tuned oral language abilities are also necessary.

The company rhetoric of empowerment through self-directed teams is critiqued in Hull's study of the training required for team work and the team meetings that are meant to show self-direction in action (Gee, Hull, & Lankshear, 1996, chapters 4 and 5). Neither the training nor the meetings took into account the language and literacy needs of the workers, many of whom had no voice in the proceedings. Indeed, the realities of training and work practices were far removed from the celebratory discourses of diversity and empowerment of the new work order.

The new requirements in literacy, which have arisen as a result of new industry standards and work organization, such as self-directed learning, demand changes in workplace educators (see Mawer, 1999). To meet some of these demands, research data from the Silicon Valley companies has been used to build a multimedia database for workplace literacy tutors (Hull, 1996). This is a new departure from a tradition that has developed in workplace English and intercultural communication programs in which the research data is transformed into learning materials.

The final study is, again, a case study that shows the extent of involvement of workplace English educators and the range of skills and responsibilities they can have and is typical of a growing number of projects in Australia, the United States, and Canada. Mawer's study of Aus Tin, a medium size packaging/printing business also illustrates a company whose workers were affected by the new work order when mulitiskilling and team-based approaches to work design were introduced (Mawer, 1999). Because it was clear that many workers were concerned about the changes and that recent training for them had been inappropriate, a communication skills audit was undertaken. Such an audit can give an overall picture of language backgrounds and abilities in a company (Sefton & O'Hara, 1992), but there is also the danger that it can be used to label workers negatively, as already discussed. Research methods for an audit combine audio and video recordings and collection of written texts with an ethnographic perspective using interviews and more informal means of participant observation to provide a description of the institutional processes and structures as well as a more "insider" perspective from workers, management, and the unions. Criterion-referenced assessments of oral and literacy abilities validated by workplace personnel and self-assessments were also used in the Aus Tin audit (Mawer, 1999, p. 92).

The communication skills audit was widened out beyond the needs of a specific group of employees to look at the whole communicative context of the workplace in light of restructuring and to document the skills and experience of workers so that unrecognized overseas qualification and hidden skills could be recognized. The audit showed that although nearly half the workforce did not have the necessary language skills to manage the demands of the restructured workplace, there was a broad base of technological knowledge and strong motivation to improve both computer and language skills. Recommendations to the company and the consultative committee were wide ranging. They included literacy and trainer training, a review of training programs, the integration of communication skills within enterprise competency standards, and a greater use of skilled overseas qualified employees. In contrast to the quick-fix approach often expected by companies, the recommendations were implemented over a 3 year period.

Mawer describes the range and level of language and literacy courses offered. There was the typical tension between company expectations based on difficult economic conditions and the prevailing work culture, on the one hand, and, on the other, the commitment to meet the expressed language training needs of the workers. An innovative component of the first course was to allow participants to gain work experience in one of the other departments to widen their skills base. A further innovation was language support on the line in which informal learning took place as workers learned to fill out the new forms. After a number of further courses, an appointment was made of a full-time enterprise-based teacher who was able to consult much more fully with supervisors and workers. The teacher was also involved in integrating the language and literacy demands into the new competencies for each industrial task.

The workplace teachers were also involved in helping to develop a set of training modules that were to be part of the skills-based pay system. The case study illustrates some of the resistances to this goal and highlights again the conflictive nature of many workplace projects. Accompanying the development of new modules was a training-the-trainers course that, like the on the line literacy training, was largely carried out through informal learning. The final element in the case study was the role of the teacher in facilitating a new enterprise agreement to replace the traditional industrial award system.

Evaluation Studies

There is a final set of studies, most of them based on evaluation reports on training and other interventions in a particular company. These reports assess the value of the workplace educator involvement, look at some of the differences of opinion among the different stakeholders over issues such as levels of language competence, and raise questions about the role and positioning of workplace educators. Attempting to assess the impact of courses on the workplace is notoriously difficult. Whereas it is possible to test before and after and present some persuasive figures to show language development, this type of assessment may have little impact on the company's attitude or commitment to greater changes. An ambitious project such as that at Aus Tin previously described may have an impact in a range of different areas, but it may be difficult to assess the overall impact. In some cases (for example, Mawer, 1994) a very focused course can have large implications. A course for teaching calculator skills to workers on the packing line had an immediate impact on productivity, but it also raised awareness of the needs and potential for literacy development much more broadly. Other evaluations have concentrated on the benefits to workers. For example, some studies suggest that language courses can provide some level of economic protection and improve chances of new employment (Belfiore, 1993; Goldstein, 1993) and that they can reduce reliance on language brokers, who are often in a supervisory position, and help workers cope with situations where there are conflicts over production (Pierce, Harper, & Burnaby, 1993). Other studies have concentrated on the voices of the workers and their perceptions of benefits (Benseman, 1998) both for themselves and their families. Benefits to companies are well summed up in an Australian government evaluation of ESL and literacy training in the workplace (Department of Employment, Education and Training 1996). These are: direct cost savings, access to and acceptability of further training, participation in teams and meetings, promotion, job flexibility, and the value of training.

Added to a critical stance on English in the workplace discussed previously, are evaluations that question the benefits of courses in terms of job prospects (Bell, 1995; Katz, 2000) and give further impetus to the argument that intercultural awareness training is also necessary to bring about change. Other critical evaluations question the role and positioning of the workplace educator previously discussed. Farrell (1999, 2000) discusses the construction of new working identities in contemporary workplaces and how these are designed to accommodate to the new work order. Workplace-based teachers are implicated in the social and political processes of these new identities and types of knowledge. Finally, there are some studies that highlight some of the differences among government, management, and staff. For example, in a survey on apprenticeship schemes, workers were more positive than employers about the skills they already had (O'Neil & Gish, 2001). Similarly, in an assessment of target language skills for engineers and nurses, there was a discrepancy between government policy on language levels and employers' preferences (Hawthorne, 1997).

The studies reviewed here are representative of the formidable range of English in the workplace issues. They also reflect the fluid boundary between research and practice that action research and the reflective practitioner approaches have also engaged with. The variety of studies theoretically, ideologically, methodologically, and in terms of their status as research and the breadth of research sites is one of the themes that I now turn to in the last section.

FUTURE DIRECTIONS FOR RESEARCH ON AND FOR ENGLISH IN THE WORKPLACE

Research related to English in the workplace will no doubt continue to depend on political and economic trends as they affect policy and provision in this area. Although some research independent of these trends may be undertaken, as it has been in the past (Clyne, 1994; Willing, 1992), it seems likely that most research, especially practitioner-led research, will ebb and flow as workplace programs and the funding for them do. Although these programs have been vulnerable to the changing shifts in policy and to the priority given to training and development in manufacturing and service industries, the links between research and action remains one of the strengths of workplace English. So, when there is an active policy to promote workplace English, there is a tendency also for a resurgence in research in this area.

Workplace English studies have always looked at learning beyond the classroom and to this extent they have drawn on the language socialization studies not only in reconceptualizing language as a social practice, but in focusing on language *use* in routine interactions. The reality of multilingual work contexts makes the apprenticeship model a much less straightforward one (Clyne & Ball, 1990; Duff et al., 2000) and one direction in which research could go is in looking at how English as a lingua franca provides a context for developing English competence. There is a case here for more longitudinal studies along the lines of the European Science Foundation's Natural Language Acquisition Project (Perdue, 1993).

The scope of much of the research on and for English in the workplace has mirrored the scope of workplace projects during the 30 years since they first began. Early studies focused on shopfloor language needs analysis and post-course evaluations. More recently, as the studies mentioned have shown, the scope has widened considerably so that the whole communicative environment of the workplace is now under scrutiny (Hull, 1993).

> Rather than focusing on those with "low language and literacy levels"—as identified by some general proficiency scale of dubious predictive validity—a holistic, integrated approach is likely to involve an educational, support role with key people such as workplace managers, team leaders and trainers. It may, for example, involve helping to develop relevant and accessible vocational curriculum, facilitating effective teamwork, influencing assessment systems and having input into the development of standards or training plans. (Mawer, 1999, p. 64)

Research on the workplace as a communicative environment raises questions of methodology. Recordings of naturally occurring interactions within a discourse analysis tradition remain central to any research on the interactive patterns of work talk. But without ethnography, there is the danger that:

> a researcher's decision to tape-record conversation or discourse creates a contextual frame that limits what is to be identified as relevant data, their organisation, and the kinds of analysis and inferences to which these data will be subjected. (Cicourel, 1992, p. 293).

As Hak (1999) asserts, the recorded data becomes the text—the object of our study—and everything else is merely context. He does not argue that we should try to record the whole because this is impossible, but rather that we should think about what we are trying to find out. He suggests bracketing out interest in discourse and communication and instead try to understand what the particular environment we are studying looks like from the perspectives of those who work in it (p. 447). This leads us to ethnography and to the goal that any recording of discursive events should be embedded in an ethnographic method. "Ethnography" is an overused and often mis-understood term but applied linguistics and sociolinguistics are increasingly using ethnographic method to pursue a linguistic ethnography in which the communica-tive ecology of the workplace (or other institution) is produced out of a dialogue of close discourse analysis and ethnographic illumination. In the fraught and often con-flictive environments of the shopfloor, the meeting room, or the hospital ward, the "lurking and soaking" (Werner & Schoepfler, 1989) of the professional ethnographer is not an easy task. And workplace researchers should never underestimate the po-tential distrust, embarrassment, and anxiety that their presence as investigators may produce.

Nevertheless, ethnography harnessed to the concerns of at least most of the in-formants in the workplace is both methodologically and practically worthwhile. At least, the workplace researcher has the new work order rhetoric of "participation," "the learning organization," and "self-directed learning" to align with in striving for some common ground from which to initiate the ethnographic project.

At the beginning of the chapter, I emphasized some of the tensions in workplace English between employer/skills-orientated research and practice aimed at under-standing, harmony, competence, and productivity (see Department of Employment, Education and Training, 1996) and educationally orientated goals aimed at critical awareness. These tensions are most sharply defined when critical theorists reflecting on workplace English come up against practitioner/researchers working from the inside in a particular company, as in the reports and papers previously discussed. For example, Tannock (1997) critiques a course in a U.S. canning factory in which, it is argued, the workers were more aligned to management values and priorities than to a more emancipatory literacy project. Mawer, in discussing this critique, points out that a discursive account of the literacy class has overlooked some of the structural factors to do with the aims and length of the course that was to lead to accreditation for two key jobs. Perhaps the workers were more concerned with getting skills for the job than doing a critical analysis of the company mission? (Mawer, 1999, p. 284).

In practice, these differences—liberal versus critical—co-exist and are held in ten-sion by individual researchers. They argue for the importance of using the work con-text as a site for learning, recognize that this entails building up trust and confidence with management as well as employees, but also look for ways of developing criti-cal understanding of course participants' working lives (Goldstein, 1993; Kalantzis & Brosnan, 1993; Pierce, 1989; Pierce et al., 1993). Typical of the argument here is the ques-tion of whether basic work-related English language training is a benefit or a means of cornering migrant workers in unskilled, low-paid jobs (Auerbach & Wallerstein, 1987; Tollefson, 1991).

One area of research where a critical stance sits comfortably with the goals of an organization is where research is done on issues of access, assessment, and selection in a range of gatekeeping settings. This is where the workplace researcher and ed-ucator meets the reflective employer who is aware that their own procedures may be discriminatory. Concerns about institutional racism may galvanize employers to call in discourse specialists to look at practices and procedures. Of course, in some cases, the employer is beaten into a changed awareness by a legal stick, as previously illustrated (Brierley et al., 1992) and in the many other cases in North America, the United Kingdom, and Australia. But in most instances the reflective employers have been from the service industries—health, employment, housing, police, and the civil service—where there has been more of a tradition of equal opportunities.

It is this type of discourse research that seems likely to grow in the future. Typically it combines pragmatics, interactional sociolinguistics, critical discourse analysis, and elements of Hallidayan functionalism to shed light on a range of problems concerning language and disadvantage. These may be, for example, in legal or police settings (Eades, 1994; Gibbons, 1987; 1994), in job selection interviews (Adelsward, 1988; Auer, 1998; Sarangi, 1994a), or in examinations within the health field (McNamara, 1994; 1997; Roberts & Sarangi, 1999). Methodologically, it has much in common with the studies on intercultural communication in the workplace of the type exemplified by Clyne and his associates (Clyne, 1994; Clyne & Ball, 1990). But recent work has been more critical of the approach that takes cultural background or ethnicity for granted and then examines differences in communicative style (Sarangi, 1994b). Such an approach assumes that cultural differences are privileged and are the reason why misunderstandings occur. There are two major strands of criticism here. One is a criticism of ethnic groups having fixed or essential characteristics (Hall, 1992). Rather, identities are constructed out of communicative practices (Hanks, 1996) and similar communicative experiences as Gumperz suggests: "It is long-term exposure to similar communicative experience in institutionalised networks of relationships and not language or community membership as such that lies at the root of shared culture and shared inferential practices" (Gumperz, 1997, p. 15). So, for example, most of the female workers that Goldstein (1997) studied were part of an institutionalized network of relationships, but there were workers of Portuguese origin whose communicative practices were relatively different and who styled different identities out of their interactions with other non-Portuguese groups.

Another criticism is that what characterizes communication between participants with different language backgrounds is not so much cultural difference as the ability to make one's actions seem sensible, plausible, and attuned to the particular task. For example, Day's analysis of multicultural workplaces in Sweden suggests that people's identities as members of particular work groups was more significant than their belonging to a certain national group. In meetings what mattered was the ability to make the activity into a meeting rather than any particular cultural take on its content (Day, 1992). This criticism is similar to Wagner's study of business meetings in which he argues that interactants do not have to agree on the precise nature of the problem or necessarily be aligned in order for them to find a solution (Wagner, 1995). In other words, just as culture may not be salient as some researchers have argued, perhaps precise understanding and agreement may not be so necessary either. And this point contributes to the larger debate in workplace English about the danger of exaggerating language difference and deficit and of looking at workplace problems through the prism of language. However much language feeds into the structuring of workplace social life and holds it together, it does not account for *all* the conditions of working life. Any researcher of workplace language has to remember this.

Compared with many other themes covered in this book, for example, the research on second language acquisition, the output of English in the Workplace research remains small, not least because of the contested nature of its aims and objectives. However, its strength and its potential in the future, lie in its practical relevance, its engagement with the real world of the workplace, and its capacity to incorporate issues that go beyond any narrow conceptualization of language skills development.

REFERENCES

Adelsward, V. (1988). Styles of success. On impression management as collaborative action in job interviews. In *Linköping Studies in Arts and Sciences* (pp. 140–163). Linköping, Sweden: Linköping University.
Agar, M. (1994). *Language shock.* New York: Morrow.
Agar, M. (2000). *The professional stranger.* (2nd ed.) New York: Academic Press.

Atkinson, P., & Heath, C. (Eds.). (1981). *Medical work : Realities and routines.* Farnborough, UK: Gower.

Auer, P. (1998). Learning how to play the game: An investigation of role-played job interviews in East Germany. *Text, 18*(1), 7–38.

Auer, P., & di Luzio, A. (Eds.). (1992). *The contextualization of language.* Amsterdam: Benjamins.

Auerbach, E., & Wallerstein, N. (1987). *ESL for action: Problem posing at work.* Reading, MA: Addison-Wesley.

Barton, D., Hamilton, M., & Ivanič, R. (2000). *Situated literacies.* London: Routledge.

Belfiore, M. (1992). *The changing world of work research project.* Toronto: Ontario Ministry of Citizenship.

Belfiore, M. (1993). The changing world of work research project. *TESL Talk, 21,* 2–20.

Belfiore, M., & Burnaby, B. (1984). *Teaching English in the workplace.* Toronto: OISE Press/Hodder and Stoughton.

Belfiore, M., & Heller, M. (1992). Cross-cultural interviews: Participation and decision making. In B. Burnaby & A. Cumming (Eds.), *Socio-political aspects of ESL* (233–240). Toronto: OISE Press/Hodder and Stoughton.

Bell, J. (1982). The Levi-Strauss project: Development of a curriculum. *TESL Talk, 13*(4), 83–91.

Bell, J. (1995). Canadian experiences of training linguistically diverse populations for the workplace. *Australian Review of Applied Linguistics, 18*(1), 35–51.

Benseman, J. (1998). *Voices for the workplace.* Auckland, New Zealand: The National Centre for Workplace Literacy and Language.

Bhatia, V. (1993). *Analysing Genre: Language use in professional settings.* London: Longman.

Blum-Kulka, S., House, J., & Kasper, G. (Eds.). (1989). *Cross-cultural pragmatics.* Norwood, NJ: Ablex.

Boden, D. (1994). *The business of talk: Organizations in action.* Cambridge, UK: Polity Press.

Bremer, K., Roberts, C., Vasseur, M., Simonot, M., & Broeder, P. (1996). *Achieving understanding: Discourse in intercultural encounters.* London: Longman.

Brierley, C., Dhesi, S., & Yates, V. (1992). Ethnographic and linguistic analysis applied: A case study. In C. Roberts, E. Davies, & T. Jupp, Language and discrimination: A study of communication in multi-ethnic workplaces (pp. 224–245). London: Longman.

Brindley, G. (1994). Competency-based assessment in second language programmes: Some issues and questions. *Prospect, 9*(2), 41–55. Sydney, Australia: Macquarie University, National Centre for English Language Teaching and Research.

Brown, P., & Levinson, S. (1987). *Politeness: Some universals in language usage.* Cambridge, UK: Cambridge University Press.

Byrne, M., & Fitzgerald, H. (1996). *What makes you say that?* Canberra, Australia: Special Broadcasting Services.

Cameron, D. (2000). *Good to talk? Living and working in a communication culture.* London: Sage.

Candlin, C. (1999). General Editor's Preface. In G. Mawer, Language and literacy in work place education: Learning at work (pp. vii–xv). London: Longman.

Candlin, C., Leather, J., & Bruton, C. (1974). *English language skills for overseas doctors and medical staff: Work in progress.* (Reports 1–4). Lancaster, UK: University of Lancaster.

Cicourel, A. (1992). The interpenetration of communicative contexts: Examples from medical encounters. In A. Duranti & C. Goodwin (Eds.), *Rethinking context: Language as an interactive phenomenon* (pp. 291–310). Cambridge: Cambridge University Press.

Clyne, M. (1994). *Inter-cultural communication at work: Cultural values in discourse.* Cambridge: Cambridge University Press.

Clyne, M., & Ball, M. (1990). English as a lingua franca in Australia, especially in industry. *ARAL, 7,* 1–15.

Cochran-Smith, M., & Lytle, S. (1993). *Inside/outside: Teacher research and knowledge.* New York: Columbia Teachers College.

Coleman, H. (Ed.). (1984). Language and work 1: Law, industry and education. (Special Issue). *International Journal of the Sociology of Language, 49.*

Coleman, H. (Ed.). (1985). Language and work 2: The health professions. (Special Issue). *International Journal of the Sociology of Language, 51.*

Coleman, H. (Ed.). (1989). *Working with language: A multi-disciplinary consideration of language use in work contexts.* Berlin: Mouton de Gruyter.

Cook-Gumperz, J., & Gumperz, J. (1976). *Context in children's speech.* (Papers on Language and Context. Working Paper 46). Berkeley, CA: Language Behaviour Research Laboratory.

Cope, B., Pauwels, A., Slade, D., Brosnan, D., & Neil, D. (1993). *Local diversity, global connections: Six approaches to cross-cultural training.* Canberra, Australia: Office of Multi-cultural Affairs.

Cullity, M. (1998). *A case study of employees' motivation to participate in a workplace language and literacy programme.* Churchlands, Australia: Edith Cowan University.

Day, D. (1992). Communication in a multicultural workplace: Procedural matters. In H. Crischel (Ed.), *Intercultural Communication: Proceedings of the 17th International L.A.U.D. Symposium.* Duisberg, Germany.

Department of Employment, Education and Training. (1996). *More than money can say—The impact of ESL and literacy training in the Australian Workplace.* Canberra, Australia: DEET.

Drew, P., & Heritage, J. (Eds.). (1992). *Talk at work: Interaction in institutional settings.* Cambridge, UK: Cambridge University Press.

Duff, P., Wong, P., & Early, M. (2000). Learning language for work and life: The linguistic socialization of immigrant Canadians seeking careers in health care. *Canadian Modern Language Review, 57*(1), 9–57.

Eades, D. (1994). A case of communicative clash: Aboriginal English and the legal system. In J. Gibbons (Ed.), *Language and the law* (pp. 234–264). London: Longman.

Erickson, F. (1985, June 29). *Listening and speaking*. Paper presented at Georgetown University Round Table on Linguistics, Washington, DC.

Erickson, F., & Schultz, J. (1982). *The counselor as gatekeeper*. New York: Academic Press.

Fairclough, N. (1989). *Language and power*. London: Longman.

Fairclough, N. (1992). *Discourse and social change*. Cambridge, UK: Polity Press.

Farrell, L. (1999). "Working knowledge" and "Working identities": Learning and teaching the new word order of the new work order. Paper presented at the Australian Association for Research in Education Conference, Melbourne, November.

Farrell, L. (2000). Ways of doing, ways of being: Language, education and "working" identities. *Language and Education, 14*(1), 18–36.

Firth, A. (1994). Talking for a change: Commodity negotiating by telephone. In A. Firth (Ed.), *The discourse of negotiation: Studies of language in the workplace* (pp. 183–222). Oxford: Pergamon.

Fisher, S., & Todd, A. (1983). *The social organization of doctor–patient communication*. Washington, DC: Center for Applied Linguistics.

Fisher, S., & Todd, A. (1986). *Discourse and institutional authority: Medicine, education and law*. Norwood, NJ: Ablex.

Ford, G., Anderson, G., Hull, D., Phelan, G., Read, V., Robson, P., & Wingrove, B. (1976). *A study of human resources and industrial relations at the plant level in seven selected industries*. Canberra: Australian Government Publishing Service.

Friere, P. (1972). *Pedagogy of the oppressed*. Harmondsworth, UK: Penguin.

Gee, J., Hull, G., & Lankshear, C. (1996). *The new work order: Behind the language of the new capitalism*. Sydney, Australia: Allen and Unwin.

Gibbons, J. (1987). Police interviews with people from non-English speaking backgrounds: Some problems. *Legal Services Bulletin, 12*(4), 183–184.

Gibbons, J. (1994). Introduction: Language and disadvantage before the law. In J. Gibbons (Ed.), *Language and the law* (pp. 195–198).

Giddens, A. (1991). *Modernity and self-identity in the late modern age*. Cambridge, UK: Polity Press.

Goffman, E. (1974). *Frame analysis: An essay on the organization of experience*. New York: Harper & Row.

Goldstein, T. (1993). The ESL community and the changing world of work. *TESL Talk, 21*, 56–64.

Goldstein, T. (1997). *Two languages at work: Bilingual life on the production floor*. Berlin: Mouton de Gruyter.

Green, J., & Bloome, D. (1997). Ethnography and ethnographers of and in education: A situated perspective. In J. Flood, S. B. Heath, & D. Lapp (Eds.), *Handbook of research on teaching literacy through the communicative visual arts*. New York: IRA/Simon & Schuster/Macmillan.

Grice, P. (1989). *Studies in the ways of words*. Cambridge, MA: Harvard University Press.

Gumperz, J. (1982). *Discourse strategies*. Cambridge, UK: Cambridge University Press.

Gumperz, J. (1992a). Contextualisation and understanding. In A. Duranti & C. Goodwin (Eds.), *Rethinking context: Language as an interactive phenomenon* (pp. 229–252). Cambridge, UK: Cambridge University Press.

Gumperz, J. (1992b). Contextualization revisited. In P. Auer & A. di Luzio (Eds.), *The Contextualization of language* (pp. 39–54). Amsterdam: Benjamins.

Gumperz, J. (1996). The linguistic and cultural relativity of conversational inference. In J. Gumperz & S. Levinson (Eds.), (1996). *Rethinking linguistic relativity* (pp. 374–406). Cambridge, UK: Cambridge University Press.

Gumperz, J. (1997). A discussion with John J. Gumperz. In S. Eerdmans, C. Previgagno, & P. Thibault (Eds.), *Discussing communication analysis 1: John Gumperz* (pp. 6–23). Lausanne, Switzerland: Beta Press.

Gumperz, J. (1999). On interactional sociolinguistic method. In S. Sarangi & C. Roberts (Eds.), *Talk, work and institutional order* (pp. 453–472). Berlin: Mouton de Gruyter.

Gumperz, J., Jupp, T., & Roberts, C. (1979). *Crosstalk*. London: National Centre for Industrial Language Training.

Hak, T. (1999). "Text and "con-text": Talk bias in studies of health care work. In S. Sarangi & C. Roberts (Eds.), Talk, work and institutional order: Discourses in medical management and mediation settings (pp. 389–400). Berlin: DeGruyter.

Hall, S. (1992). The question of cultural identity. In S. Hall, D. Held, & T. McGrew (Eds.), *Modernity and its futures* (pp. 222–237). London: Lawrence & Wishart.

Halliday, M. (1967). *Intonation and grammar in British English*. The Hague, The Netherlands: Mouton.

Halliday, M. (1973). *Exploration in the functions of language*. London: Edward Arnold.

Hanks, W. (1996). *Language and communicative practices*. Boulder, CO: Westview Press.

Hawthorne, L. (1997). Defining the target domain: What language skills are required for engineers and nurses? *Melbourne Papers in Language Testing, 6*(1), pp. 3–18.

Heath, C. (1992). The delivery and reception of diagnosis in the general-practice consultation. In P. Drew & J. Heritage (Eds.), *Talk at work* (pp. 235–267). Cambridge, UK: Cambridge University Press.

Heritage, J., Chatwin, J., & Collins, S. (2001). Conversation analysis: A method for research into interactions between patients and health care professionals. *Health Expectations, 4*, 58–70.

Holland, C., Frank, F., & Cooke, T. (1998). *Literacy and the new work order.* Leicester, UK: National Institute of Adult and Continuing Education.

Holmes, J. (2000). Talking English from 9 to 5: Challenges for the ESL learners at work. *International Journal of Applied Linguistics, 10*(1), 85–140.

Hull, G. (1993). Hearing other voices: A critical assessment of popular views on literacy and work. *Harvard Education Review, 63*(1), 20–49.

Hull, G. (1996). *Changing work, changing literacy. A study of skills requirements and development in a traditional and a restructured workplace. Final Report.* Berkeley, CA: National Center for the Study of Writing and Literacy.

Hull, G. (Ed.). (1997). *Changing work, changing workers: Critical perspectives on language, literacy and skills.* Albany, NY: SUNY Press.

Hymes, D. (1980). *Language in education: Ethnolinguistic essays.* Washington, DC: Center for Applied Linguistics.

Iedema, R., & Scheeres, H. (2003). From doing work to talking work: renegotiating knowing, doing and identity. *Applied Linguistics, 24*(3), 316–337.

Kalantzis, M., & Brosnan, D. (1993). *Managing cultural diversity.* Sydney, Australia: Centre for Workplace Communication and Culture, University of Technology.

Katz, M. (2000). Workplace language teaching and the intercultural construction of ideologies of competence. *Canadian Modern Language Review, 57*(1), 144–172.

Labov, W., & Fanshel, D. (1977). *Therapeutic discourse: Psychotherapy as conversation.* New York: Academic Press.

Levinson, S. (1983). *Pragmatics.* Cambridge, UK: Cambridge University Press.

Li, D. (2002). The pragmatics of making requests in the L2 workplace. *Canadian Modern Language Review, 57*(1), 58–87.

Martin, J. (1984). Language, register and genre. In *Children writing reader.* Geelong: Deakin University Press.

Mawer, G. (1994). *Language, literacy and numeracy at Merck Sharp and Dohme Pty Ltd: Evaluation report of an integrated approach.* Sydney, Australia: Foundation Studies Division TAFE NSW and Merck Sharp and Dohme.

Mawer, G. (1999). *Language and literacy in workplace education: Learning at work.* London: Longman.

Mawer, G., & Field, L. (1995). *One size fits some! Competency training and non-English speaking background people.* Canberra, Australia: AGPS.

Maynard, D. (1991). Perspective-display sequences and the delivery and receipt of diagnostic news. In D. Boden & D. Zimmerman (Eds.), *Talk and social structure* (pp. 164–192). Cambridge, UK: Polity Press.

McGregor, A., & Williams, R. (1984). Cross-cultural communication in the employment interview. *Australian Review of Applied Linguistics, 7*(1), 203–219.

McNamara, T. (1994, July). The assessment implications of competency standards. Paper presented at Language Expo Australia, Sydney.

McNamara, T. (1997). Problematizing content validity: The occupational English test (OET) as a measure of medical communication. *Melbourne Papers in Language Testing, 6*(1), 19–43.

Mehan, H. (1979). *Learning lessons.* Cambridge, MA: Harvard University Press.

Mikulecky, L. (1984, December). Preparing students for workplace literacy demands. *Journal of Reading,* 253–257.

Moore, R. (1999). Empowering the ESL worker within the new work order. *Journal of Adolescent and Adult Literacy, 43*(2), 142–152.

O'Neil, S., & Gish, A. (2001). *Apprentices' and trainees' English language and literacy skills in workplace learning and performance: Employer and employee opinion.* Leabrook, Australia: National Centre for Vocational Education Research.

Pauwels, A. (1994). Applying linguistic insights in intercultural communication to professional training programmes: An Australian case study. In A. Pauwels (Ed.), *Cross-cultural communication in the professions* (pp. 195–212). Special issue, *Multilingua, 13*(1/2).

Peddler, M., Bourgoyne, J., & Boydell, J. (1991). *The learning company.* Maidenhead, UK: McGraw-Hill.

Peräkylä, A. (1995). *AIDS counselling: Institutional interaction and clinical practice.* Cambridge, UK: Cambridge University Press.

Perdue, C. (Ed.). (1993). *Adult language acquisition: Cross-linguistic perspective. Vols. 1 & 2.* Cambridge, UK: Cambridge University Press.

Pierce, B. (1989). Toward a pedagogy of possibility in the teaching of English internationally: People's English in South Africa. *TESOL Quarterly, 23*(3), 401–420.

Pierce, B., Harper, H., & Burnaby, B. (1993). Workplace ESL at Levi Strauss: Dropouts speak out. *TESL Canada Journal, 19*(2), 9–32.

ProTrain (1993). *Access evaluation.* Sydney, Australia: Tourism Training.

Roberts, C. (1998). Awareness in intercultural communication. *Language Awareness, 7*(2 & 3), 109–127.

Roberts, C., Davies, E., & Jupp, T. (1992). *Language and discrimination: A study of communication in multi-ethnic workplaces.* London: Longman.

Roberts, C., & Sarangi, S. (1999). Hybridity in gatekeeping discourses: Issues of practical relevance for the researcher. In S. Sarangi & C. Roberts (Eds.), Talk, work and institutional order: Discourse in medical, management and mediation settings (pp. 473–503). Berlin: DeGruyter.

Sarangi, S. (1994a). Accounting for mismatches in intercultural selection interviews. In A. Pauwels (Ed.), *Cross-cultural communication in the professions.* Special Issue. *Multilingua, 13*(1/2), 163–194.

Sarangi, S. (1994b). Intercultural or not? Beyond celebration of cultural differences in miscommunication analysis. *Pragmatics, 4,* 409–427.

Sarangi, S., & Slembrouck, S. (1996). *Language, bureaucracy and social control.* London: Longman.

Sarangi, S., & Roberts, C. (Eds.). (1999). *Talk, work and institutional order: Discourse in medical, management and mediation settings.* Berlin: Mouton de Gruyter.

Schellekens, P. (2001). English Language as a barrier to employment, training and education. London: Department for Education and Employment.

Sefton, R., Waterhouse, P., & Deakin, R. (Eds.). (1994). *Breathing life into training—A model of integrated training.* Melbourne, Australia: National Automotive Industry Training Board.

Sefton, R., & O'Hara, L. (1992). *Report of the workplace education project.* Melbourne, Australia: Victorian Automative Industry Training Board.

Smith, C., Mikulecky, L., Kibby, M., Drecher, M., & Dole, J. (2000). What will be the demands on literacy in the workplace in the next millenium? *Reading Research Quarterly, 35*(3), 378–383.

Spradley, J. (1979). *The ethnographic interview.* New York: Holt, Rinehart & Winston.

Street, B. (1995). *Social literacies: Critical approaches to literacy development, ethnography and education.* London: Longman.

Tannock, S. (1997). Positioning the worker: Discursive practice in a workplace literacy program. *Discourse and Society, 8*(1), 85–116.

Thomas, J. (1983). Cross-cultural pragmatic failure. *Applied Linguistics, 4*(2), 91–112.

Tollefson, J. (1991). *Planning language, planning inequality: Language policy in the community.* London: Longman.

Wagner, J. (1995). "Negotiating activity" in technical problem solving. In A. Firth (Ed.), *The discourse of negotiation* (pp. 223–246). Oxford, UK: Pergamon.

Wallman, S. (1979). *Ethnicity at work.* London: Macmillan.

West, C. (1984). *Routine complications: Troubles in talk between doctors and patients.* Bloomington: Indiana University Press.

Westwood, S., & Bachu, P. (Eds.). (1988). *Enterprising women.* London: Routledge.

Werner, O., & Schoepfler, G. (1989). *Systematic field work. Vols. 1 & 2.* Newbury Park, CA: Sage.

Willing, K. (1992). *Talking it through: Clarification and problem-solving in professional work.* Sydney, Australia: National Centre for English Language Teaching and Research.

Willing, K. (1997). Modality in task-orientated discourses: The role of subjectivity in "getting the job done." *Prospect, 12*(12), 33–42.

Wodak, R. (1996). *Disorders of discourse.* London: Longman.

Wonacott, M. (2000). Preparing limited English proficient persons for the workplace. Columbus, OH: Clearinghouse on Adult, Career and Vocational Education.

Wyse, L. (1997). From where to where?—A look at workplace education. *Fine Print, 20*(4), 18–20.

8

English as a Foreign Language: Matching Procedures to the Context of Learning

Brian Tomlinson
Leeds Metropolitan University

INTRODUCTION

This chapter provides a critical overview of the issues related to the learning and teaching of English as a Foreign Language (EFL) in different social contexts. It asks whether there are universally applicable principles and procedures or whether approaches should vary in relation to the distinctive features of different social contexts.

ENGLISH AS A FOREIGN LANGUAGE (EFL)

EFL is learned by people who already use at least one other language and who live in a community in which English is not normally used. This community is inevitably influenced by norms that are not those of English-speaking countries and those norms influence the teachers' and learners' expectations of the language learning process.

SOCIAL CONTEXTS

Most learners of EFL learn it in school together with a large class of peers of similar age and proficiency. They typically have a coursebook, they are preparing for an examination, and they are taught by a teacher who is not a native speaker of English. However, there are many variations on this EFL scenario. The size of the class can vary from 10 to 100. The school might have no electricity and no books (for example, on some islands I have visited in Vanuatu) or it might have a computer room, a library, and a language laboratory. The teacher might or might not be trained, fluent, experienced, and a native speaker. Or they could be learning English in a language school, at university, or at work. Whatever the social context of their learning, it will affect their expectations and behaviour. For example, I have observed in Indonesia and Japan different learner behaviour by the same students in their morning class and in their afternoon club.

METHODOLOGY AND MATERIALS

Surprisingly much of the literature on EFL methodology seems to disregard contexts of learning. For example, Duquette (1995) outlines very useful procedures for applying theory to practice in order to implement a communicative approach but does not relate the procedures to varying contexts of learning. Also it seems that many of the global EFL coursebooks are written by qualified, native-speaker teachers whose experience of EFL has been primarily in well-resourced language schools teaching small classes of motivated learners. And yet most of the users of these books experience EFL in very different social contexts, the majority in large classes of unmotivated learners with inadequate resources and unqualified teachers. This situation persists despite criticism of methodology imposed from "the West" (e.g., Holliday, 1994) and of global materials written with "Western" classrooms in mind (e.g., Padwad, 2002). However, there is an increasing recognition that, "Language teaching as lived out in the classroom is always a local phenomenon"(Tudor, 1996, p. 210) and that, "Classrooms operate within a cultural context which to a large extent determines not only what is to be learned, but also how it is to be learned" (McKay, 1992, p. 47). This implies that teachers and materials writers should at the very least be aware of the "culture of learning" (i.e.,"what people believe about the 'normal' or 'good' learning activities and processes" [Coleman, 1996, p. 230]).

LEARNING PRINCIPLES

There is much controversy among second language acquisition (SLA) researchers and methodologists as to the optimum ways to learn a foreign language, but there does seem to be general agreement on the basic principles of language acquisition (Tomlinson, 1998a). What we need to know though is which, if any, of the generally agreed principles can be applied to any social context in which English is learned as a foreign language. Can teachers, in Asia, for example, establish a relaxed atmosphere in the classroom, involve learners affectively in the learning process (Arnold, 1999; Tomlinson, 1998b), and help learners to make decisions about their learning?

APPARENT CULTURAL DIFFERENCES

Flowerdew (1998, p. 323) asks, "Why is it that when one poses a question to a group of Arab students the whole class is clamouring to answer, while a question addressed to a class of Chinese learners may elicit no response, followed by a stony silence . . . ?" The answer is that cultural norms can determine learning behaviour. But it could be that students can modify behaviour if they perceive potential value in doing so. Likewise teachers asked to implement innovative methodology might initially be disturbed but eventually become accustomed. Dat (2002, p. 272) refers to Karavas-Doukas (1998, p. 36), who says that teachers need time to come to grips with new ideas and reflect on their implications until both skill and confidence help develop a sense of ownership of those ideas. Dat quotes a teacher in one of his communicative experiments in Vietnam as saying, "Some strategies don't work because I am simply not familiar with employing them. These will have to take time to develop into my own techniques (p. 272)."

THE CASE FOR CONTEXTUAL VARIATION OF PROCEDURES

Local Conditions

Most methodologists seem to agree that "language teachers must pay attention to local conditions rather than taking a set of ideas" around the world with them (Stubbs, 2000, p. 16). Benson (2000) comments that Harold Palmer's "enthusiasm for phonetics and direct teaching suffered badly when he was confronted by the realities of institutional language teaching in Japan" (p. 47) and Maingay (1997) reports mistakenly assuming that all the participants on a multinational teachers' course would come to appreciate the tutor's process-oriented approach and "go back to their countries ready to use the same approach with their trainees (pp. 120–121)."

Many researchers seem to agree that both curriculum and methodology should only be determined after a consideration of local conditions. For example, Byram & Cain (1998) describe an experiment in which learners of French in English schools and learners of English in French schools were helped to acquire "cultural competence." Although the principles, aims, and objectives were the same in both countries, the methods had to be different because "the teaching contexts prevailing in each country were entirely different" (p. 32).

Richards (2001) points out that, "curriculum planners draw on their understanding both of the present and long-term needs of learners and of society, as well as the planners' beliefs and ideologies about schools, learners and teachers" (p. 113). And Kleibard (1986) reports that, "we find different interest groups competing for dominance over the curriculum and, at different times, achieving some measure of control depending on local as well as general social conditions" (p. 8). It is arguable that, if the groups are local, their view of the curriculum will reflect local cultural values, whereas if they are outsiders, their view will reflect culturally distant values. Richards (2001) offers academic rationalism as a culture-free approach to curriculum development, which "stresses the intrinsic value of the subject matter and its role in developing the learner's intellect, humanistic values and rationality" (p. 114). But perhaps the curriculum ideology that is appropriate in most cultural contexts is "cultural pluralism," which argues that schools should prepare students to participate in several different cultures and to develop cross-cultural competence. No cultural group is seen as superior and the first language is valued and used (Auerbach, 1995).

Another perspective on this issue is provided by Pennycook (1994) who argues that "English language teaching must start with ways of critically exploring students' cultures, knowledge and histories in ways that are both challenging and at the same time affirming and supportive" (p. 311), and by Phillipson (1992) and Rodgers (1989) who argue for greater consideration of sociopolitical factors when developing language teaching programs.

Universal Conditions

While working in Indonesia, Japan, Nigeria, Singapore, the United Kingdom Vanuatu, and Zambia, I have heard claims about the uniqueness of social and educational cultures. In each country the social cultures are distinctively different, but the educational cultures seem to be remarkably similar. One of the main objectives of educational systems seems to be to maintain the status quo and to train students to become obedient and responsible citizens (LoCastro, 1996). Classroom pedagogy is essentially teacher-centered (Mitchell & Lee, 2003), the curriculum is dominated by knowledge to be transmitted, and the emphasis is on convergence of behaviour and thought. And in some countries the school culture of conformity and control is reinforced by social norms of reverence for authority (Tomlinson, 1988). In Singapore, for example, many teachers seem reluctant to encourage learners to express individual views (even though critical thinking is emphasized in the curriculum).

Who can blame teachers for maintaining control? Often it is the pressure of their examination culture and the resultant need to transmit huge amounts of knowledge that determines their methodology. This is a point made by LoCastro (1996) with reference to the introduction of a new, more communicative curriculum in Japanese high schools when she says that, "classroom teachers are under pressure to teach 'exam English.' Unless the university examination system is changed, many feel that the new curriculum will be virtually ignored, particularly at the senior high school level" (p. 47). Be (2003) makes a similar point in relation to textbook innovation in Vietnam.

Learner Differences

Treating every student in the same way benefits some and handicaps others. Treating Korean students like Spanish students, for example, would certainly penalize the Korean students. But treating all Korean students in the same culturally appropriate way would penalize those Korean students whose personalities and learning style preferences do not conform to stereotypical Korean norms.

Expectations.   Learners have expectations about how they will be taught EFL that are shaped by cultural norms and by previous experience. For example, Dat (2002) reports problems in Vietnam when the teacher breaks all expectations by acting as a co-communicator. And Karavas-Doukas (1998) reports how a number of EFL innovation projects failed because they attempted to "introduce practices within school cultures that promote a different type of social order in the classroom" (p. 49). Often though, if a teacher persists with an innovation, such phenomena of "temporary culture" (Holliday, 1994, p. 23) as classroom patterns and expectations are changeable. Having expectations broken does not necessarily inhibit language learning, and I have found that learners can quickly adjust their expectations if the novel activities are introduced on trial and if they find the activities to be enjoyable and useful. We have to be careful though that we do not assume that learners will share teacher perceptions of what facilitates the learning of a foreign language. McDonough (2002) claims that learners and teachers inhabit different worlds. She reports administering a questionnaire on the value of learning activities to teachers and to learners of Greek and French and finding big discrepancies in their responses (e.g., only 20% of the teachers considered grammar practice to be useful compared to 81% of the learners). Likewise, Spratt (1999) reports only a 50% correlation in an experiment in Hong Kong between learner preferred activities and teacher perceptions of their preferences; Nunan (1988) reports a mismatch between learner and teacher perceptions of the usefulness of different activities in Australia; and Barkhuizen (1998) reports a similar situation in South Africa. McDonough (2002) finds that her own views as a learner and as a teacher of differ considerably and she points out that, "Every class is unique and dynamic. It develops and changes over time as all participants adapt, usually cooperatively to build an individual classroom culture" (p. 410).

Needs and Wants.   The value of relating actual classroom procedures to the learners' reasons for learning English has long been recognized (Carter & Nunan, 2001). For example, learners whose major need for English is to enable them to read articles and books are unlikely to respond to a methodology that focuses on oral interaction in groups (e.g., students in universities in Indonesia in which the medium of instruction is Bahasa Indonesia but much of the literature they are referred to is in English). Often, though, what learners "need" to do in the classroom conflicts with what they want to do. For example, Canagarajah (1999) stresses that in Sri Lanka "not all students want to follow the curriculum offered by local universities, which tend to be heavily oriented to English for academic purposes" (p. 94). If learner wants are not satisfied, learning will be inhibited. For example, I well remember a group of Saudi Arabian pilots who tired of focusing on English for aviation and wanted to develop their ability to participate in social interaction. Learner wants are very rarely researched or taken into consideration, but on a textbook project in Namibia the learners were asked what they wanted English for and then such wants as writing love letters were catered to in the resulting coursebook (Tomlinson, 1995)

Attitudes.   The attitudes of learners toward pedagogic procedures undoubtedly affects their effectiveness. For example, many studies suggest that group interaction "has a role in engaging learners in the process of negotiating meaning, or constructing knowledge jointly" (Tin, 2000, p. 186). However, these studies are mainly of "students from Western cultural and educational backgrounds" and "we need to consider whether the way group work works in these settings is the same as in other settings" (p. 186). Tin found that in group work British students behaved reactively, whereas Malaysian students behaved in an additive way.

In an ongoing multicountry research project investigating learner and teacher attitudes, Tomlinson and Masuhara (2004) have found both differences and similarities between high school learners of English in different cultures. For example, Spanish students ($n = 189$) liked and valued both pair and group work, whereas Chinese students ($n = 236$) did not. However, both the Spanish and the Chinese students liked affective, experiential, and interactive activities best but valued individual, analytic activities the most. Both the Spanish and the Chinese students valued activities that are often discredited by methodologists (e.g., translation, dictation, and grammatical explanation). Both the Spanish and the Chinese students rated reading stories as useful, and they both quite liked doing it. One possibility Tomlinson and Masuhara are considering is that there is a universal predisposition to learn a foreign language in enjoyable and experiential ways but also a universal belief that you need to learn a foreign language in primarily analytical ways. If this is true, which of these tendencies should materials and methodology attempt to match?

Learning Styles.   It is generally accepted that determinations of methodology should take into consideration the learning style profile of the learners (Oxford, 1990, 1995, 1996; Wenden, 1991). There is evidence of cultural differences in preferred learning styles and Oxford (1996) is convinced that, "Cultural background affects *strategy* choice" (p. xi). She claims that "many Hispanic ESL/EFL students choose particular learning strategies, such as predicting, inferring . . . avoiding details, working with others rather than alone," whereas "many Japanese English as a Second Language (ESL)/EFL students reflectively use analytic strategies aimed at precision and accuracy, search for small details, work alone, and base judgments more on logic than on personal interactions" (p. xi). An important point though is made by Bedell and Oxford (1996) when they say that "culture should not be seen as a strait jacket, binding students to a particular set of learning strategies all their lives. Strategy instruction can help students see the value in 'new' language learning strategies that are not necessarily within the limits of their cultural norms" (p. 60).

It is self-evident to anyone who has taught English in different countries that within any classroom in any country there will be individual variations of preferred learning styles (Lewis, 1996). Some learners will be predominantly analytical and will prefer to learn the language by studying it, whereas most will be predominantly experiential and will prefer to learn a language through exposure and use. Some learners will prefer to process the new language visually, some aurally and many kinaesthetically. But there is general agreement that current curricula, methodologies, coursebooks, and examinations favor analytically inclined learners (Tomlinson, Dat, Masuhara, & Rubdy, 2001), and it is possible that they influence the prevailing methodologies throughout the world more than local cultures do.

Teacher Differences

Attitudes.   Many researchers have concluded that the main variable in determining the success of methodological innovation is teacher attitude. If teachers view a change as threatening, they will resist it; if they see it as enhancing their role or facilitating their performance, they will support it.

The most significant attitude of teachers seems to be one that asserts the need for continuity. As Louden (1991) says, "Until those of us who look for improvement and change in education learn to approach teachers with more respect for the power of continuity in their work, we are likely to continue to be disappointed with the progress of educational reform" (p. xiv). Other researchers have focussed on this problem of encouraging teachers to do what they are not used to and not comfortable doing. For example, Sercu (1998) says, "Belgian teaching is largely dominated by the knowledge dimension of learning, and teachers feel uneasy having to deal with affective or behavioural aspects of the learning process" (p. 200) Urmston (2001) concludes that, "Preliminary findings suggest that English teachers in Hong Kong as a group are quite cohesive and not open to change, as evidenced by the widespread resistance to government initiated innovations such as a task-based curriculum" (p. 179).

Liu (1998) complains that the conditions that face EFL teachers in China (e.g., large class sizes, poor resources, a didactic tradition) mean that they cannot teach in the same "process or discovery-oriented" ways as their counterparts who teach small, well-resourced classes where "interaction, group work and student-centeredness are the order of the day" (p. 5). But I did manage to achieve interaction, group work and student centeredness in classes of 90 without any audio-visual aids and with an expectation of a didactic, product-oriented and teacher-centered approach in a traditional university in Japan. Such an approach suited my teaching style preferences and maintained my continuity of approach, and I was asked to demonstrate it in a workshop and in an article (Tomlinson, 1991) to the other members of the department. A few younger members found my approach suited to their preferred teaching styles and modified their classroom pedagogy, but most of the staff, while appreciating my approach theoretically, continued to teach English in the more didactic ways with which they felt comfortable.

Although respecting the need for teacher continuity, we need to consider whether it might be unfairly conflicting with learner needs and wants and act ultimately against the interests of the learners. This might be especially so when teachers justify resisting change by stating that it is not compatible with what learners need, want, and expect. Dat (2002) describes experiments in Vietnam in which normally reticent students proved the prophecies of their teachers wrong (e.g., "You don't know them, they just won't speak") by expressing themselves in English during cooperative activities (p. 256). He also reports how some teachers when experimenting with new methodologies still teach according to their own set of standards and beliefs. Other researchers have warned against the danger of accepting teachers' views about learners' inclinations and capabilities. For example, Kubanyiova (2002), reports on enthusiastic student participation in drama activities at Assumption University, Bangkok, despite warnings by teachers ("who have inhibitions about acting") that Thai students are "too shy" to participate in drama activities (p. 179).

Teacher attitudes are usually amenable to change, providing the teachers are given incentives to change them, as on the PKG English Programme in Indonesia (Tomlinson, 1990) when teachers were encouraged to change their attitudes by being given more responsibility and scope for initiative. As Karavas-Doukas (1998) says, "Teacher attitude change is a key aspect of the teacher training process ... Developing changed perspectives is a long and arduous process yet it is the first and necessary step toward real change" (p. 37). On the PKG Programme many teachers did gradually change their attitudes as a result of reflection on their current practice and of sanctioned opportunities to experiment and to take initiative in deciding for themselves what approaches and materials to use.

There is some evidence that what many teachers want is not radically different from what SLA researchers and methodologists would recommend (Masuhara, 1998; Tomlinson, 1990). For example, a 10-country research project I conducted for a British publisher revealed that what teachers (and learners) want most from coursebooks is interesting texts.

Teaching Styles.   It is possible to characterize culturally typical teaching styles (for example, overt transmission of knowledge in Korea), but I have found that within any one culture there is a great variety of teaching styles. Some teachers are very serious, whereas others make use of humor; some are quietly low key, whereas others prefer to perform. Obviously teaching styles are influenced by culture, training, and experience, but ultimately they are determined by personality. And, if teaching methodologies do not cater to teaching style differences, they will not help learners to learn. Strong versions of methods have little chance of engaging the full support of all the teachers being told to use them. Flexible weak versions of pedagogic approaches, which encourage teacher variation within a recommended framework, have a much better chance of helping teachers to help their learners to learn.

Course Materials

There is evidence that what teachers and learners actually do in the classroom is determined principally by what the coursebook tells them to do. Be (2003), for example, reports a project in which 478 students and their 28 teachers in two schools in Vietnam revealed they were using the textbook as a script rather than as a resource. Current thinking is that textbooks should be written and evaluated with reference to their context of use and that such variables as sociocultural background, attitudes to learning, previous language-learning experience, and expectations of the learning process should be considered when making decisions about materials that will determine what goes on in the classroom. McGrath (2002, pp. 17–22) provides an overview of the literature relating to such factors and refers to Skierso (1991), Matthews (1991), McDonough and Shaw (1993), Cunningsworth (1995), and Masuhara (1998). Tomlinson (2003b) also deals with these factors.

INEVITABLE ADAPTATION

Ellis (2002) claims that methodological variation is inevitable because "the way English is taught implicitly disseminates the cultural values of the person doing the teaching" (p. 1), and Block (2002) says the impact of a guest teaching culture is inevitable. An example of this is the influence of the large number of American and British teachers of English in Japanese private institutions; although McKay (1992) points out that "although private institutions can often encourage a wider range of methods, students may be hesitant to use them because of their prior experience in public institutions" (p. 121). That foreign teachers necessarily import foreign teaching approaches is true, but we must beware of assuming that all teachers from a culture will teach in the same way as its stereotypical teacher.

Many researchers argue that cultural accommodation should be deliberately and sensitively undertaken rather than left to chance. Harvey (1985), for example, stresses the importance of considering the prevailing culture when deciding what and how to teach. He argues for "a balanced approach and the use of existing potential" and says that "the needs and skills of the learner cannot be ignored" (p. 186). He describes a course to upgrade the skills of science lecturers at Tianjin University and concludes that "Chinese learning methods cannot simply be dismissed as 'primitive,' 'old-fashioned,' or 'misguided.' There are a number of obvious historical, pedagogical and psychological reasons for them" (p. 186).

Many researchers advocate focusing on features of methodologies that coincide with local cultural values. For example, Shamin (1996) says, "An innovation, if it clashes radically with the culture of the community, should be adapted to the local culture before being introduced" (p. 119) and Flowerdew (1998) "advocates the use of group work for a group of learners from a Chinese cultural background, where, to some extent, Confusian values still prevail" (p. 323). Flowerdew refers to her own experience teaching tertiary students in Hong Kong, and to the research of Cortazzi and Jin (1996), Lam (1997), Nelson (1995), and Wong (1996), to support her claims that students should be helped to learn in ways that match their cultural values and that group work matches the values of Chinese learners of English. Flowerdew (p. 327) supports Cortazzi's (1990) stressing of the need for teachers "to acquire knowledge of, and sensitivity towards, learners' cultural and educational backgrounds, and perhaps consider adjusting their own expectations accordingly" (p. 63), and she concludes that teachers should "consider adjusting their teaching style so that it is congruent with the students' cultural background" (p. 63).

There is also evidence that attempts to innovate from within a culture often involve compromise between the innovative procedures being advocated and the procedures typically followed in that culture. Shamin (1996), for example, reports how she had to modify her innovative methodology by reverting to a more authoritarian role to overcome student resistance to her "communicative" approach in her classroom in Pakistan. And LoCastro (1996) points out that the new high school courses in Japan, whilst aiming to be "communicative," actually reflect "the underlying attitudes held by the Japanese educational system about language and language learning" by retaining a "content-oriented—specifically grammar-oriented—" curriculum (p. 44). I have encountered this phenomenon myself while writing coursebooks for Singapore secondary schools (Tomlinson, Hill, & Masuhara, 2000; Tomlinson, Hill, Masuhara, & Ying, 2002; Tomlinson et al., 2003). Our brief was to write for the new English Language Syllabus 2001 (which aims at the development of independent and critical thinking skills), but we were constrained by the need for our books to be approved by Ministry officials still driven by the content and modelling norms of the prevailing educational culture (Singapore Wala, 2003).

THE CASE FOR THE UNIVERSAL APPLICATION
OF PRINCIPLED PROCEDURES

Beginning to Learn a Foreign Language

Both the European Science Foundation (ESF) Project (Myles, 2000; Perdue, 1984, 1993a, 1993b) and the theoretically opposed Universal Grammar (UG) research have provided evidence of learner similarity regardless of cultural background. For example, the ESF Project has concluded that there are three initial stages shared by all learners, that "pragmatic and semantic universals play an important part in the shaping of early interlanguages" (Myles, 2000, p. 80) and that, "in spite of the fact that the ESF research design was conceived in order to highlight differences . . . it ended up showing very convincingly how similar the early language systems are in all learners, whatever their background" (p. 80). UG also claims that all learners, regardless of first language or culture, exhibit very similar characteristics (especially at the beginning stages). There are a number of differing UG hypotheses (see Myles, 2000, p. 76), but it seems that all of them are supported by research evidence that demonstrates universality in the beginning stages of learning a foreign language. If this is true, procedures for helping learners in one culture would seem to be useful for helping learners in another.

SLA Research

Most reports of second language acquisition (SLA) research seem to share an assumption that the principles (if not the procedures) of successful language acquisition are universal (see Ellis, 1994, and Scovell, 1998, for overviews). However, a number of applied linguists have questioned the universal validity of research that has been conducted mainly by Western researchers in Western cultures. For example, Kachru (1994, p. 796) complains that most of the data has been taken from immigrants and international students studying in North America, Britain, or Australia and that little effort has made to collect information from other contexts in the rest of the world. And Sridar (1994) points out that the dominant L2 acquisition paradigm "leaves out vast millions of L2 users who learn and use second languages in their own countries" (p. 801). These complaints are undoubtedly valid and more research is needed comparing SLA acquisition between equivalent populations in different cultures. However, nobody seems to have come up with any evidence suggesting that the basic principles of successful language acquisition vary from culture to culture.

Evidence of Successful Changes of Approach

Dat (2002) describes how in Vietnam a conservative, traditional practitioner teaching a deeply reticent class managed to encourage his very quiet class to speak in English by moving from a habitually authoritative role toward a more flexible innovative approach. This example is typical of the experience I have had as a teacher trainer in many different cultures where I have found that students and teachers are willing to experiment with methodological change if the changes are justified to them and if the changes are perceived as potentially valuable. There are also many examples in the literature of such willingness to change and of pedagogic procedures being valuable irrespective of the culture they are used in. For example, Fu (1995) says that "What and how teachers do and say things greatly affects the atmosphere of the class community. Teachers' sharing of their own stories is an important way to set an intimate tone for their classes and is a good model for a learning community of equal partners" (p. 199). Davies (2002) also recommends teachers using their own lives and views as material to, "focus upon the personal experiences of the teacher in relation to particular sociocultural themes" (p. 369), and McDonough (2002) reports that 100% of the learner respondents in her survey rated the teacher talking about herself as useful. Fu argues that teachers should not be "afraid of doing something incongruent with the ways students were raised, as every culture has room for improvement and every nation progresses by adopting other strengths for its own benefit" (p. 199) This position is endorsed by Lewis and McCook (2002), whose study of 14 high school teachers' journals on an in-service training course in Vietnam revealed that, "the teachers stated their roles in terms of both communicative and traditional language learning principles" (p. 151). In other words, they did what many teachers have done in my experience. Instead of rejecting culturally unusual approaches outright, they tried them, evaluated them, and eventually adapted them in ways that suited their culture and their personality. Of course, they only did this if the new ways were introduced as potentially valuable additions to their repertoires, and they justifiably resisted methodologies that were imposed on them as compulsory replacements for their normal practice.

Many researchers have found that students and teachers are especially willing to accommodate change if the new approaches mirror features in their social culture that have not previously been exploited in their educational culture. For example, Cheung (2001) suggests that the teacher-centered, accuracy-focused approaches typical of the Hong Kong classroom do not help students to apply what they have learned to real life situations and advocates an innovative learner-centered approach that uses Hong Kong popular culture to help students to learn English. Also group activities have been found to be particularly suitable for EFL learners in many collectivist cultures where a sense of belonging to the group is important (Rodgers, 1988, p. 7; Fu, 1995, p. 199; Williams & Burden, 1997, p. 79).

It has also been found that many learners do not expect or even want foreign teachers to imitate local cultural norms when teaching a foreign language. Guest (2002), for example, concludes that, "While students may hold preconceptions as to how a 'normal' class operates within their own culture, isn't it likely that they will automatically readjust their expectations when a foreign teacher appears on the scene?" (p. 159).

Many researchers have stressed the importance of the teacher in determining what actually happens in the classroom (Masuhara, 1998). If the teacher values a methodological change, it will be reflected in a significant change in classroom activity. If the teacher is resistant, the changes will be at the best cosmetic. The teachers' own beliefs can affect classroom action more than a particular methodology or coursebook (Williams & Burden, 1997). For example, as Piper (1998) observes, the reason why conversational skills fail to develop in the classroom is because many teachers tend to control learner talk not by helping it to meet the learners' purpose but by directing it to the teacher's purpose (p. 245). And, as Howe (1993) says, whether students are "passive" or "active" in class depends more on their teachers' expectations than on culturally based learning styles. Many researchers have reported on the positive effects of teachers changing their beliefs and expectations, but there are also reports in the literature of teachers endorsing Kenny and Savage's view (1997) that:

> All human systems tend to seek stability and hence preserve themselves from undesirable or unnecessary change. Except in dire situations where it is a choice between changing and perishing, it is much easier to stay the same. (pp. 291–292)

For example, Lamb (1995) compared in-service content on a project in Indonesia with classroom practice 1 year later. He found that only a few teachers reported fundamental change in their classroom practice, whereas most reported "no uptake," "confusion," and "adaptability and rejection." Hird (1995), likewise, reports on the results of an in-service course in Huangzhou after which teachers "saw only limited possibilities for the use of Western methodology in their teaching" (p. 22).

Breaking the Norm

Tennant (2001) outlines a course on Japanese art that was taught to a group of second-year students at a Japanese university using English as the medium of instruction. The project approach used by Tennant combined an universal approach with local content. It was unusual in Japanese cultural terms in that it set challenging tasks and required initiative and independent research, but it seemed to have been very successful. Such an approach constitutes an increasingly common way of breaking the norm by combining culturally familiar features with features that are so culturally divergent that they might otherwise be resisted.

Holliday (2001) demonstrates "the standard appropriate methodology combination of capitalizing on existing cultural resources to motivate people in innovatory educational settings—or using cultural information to engineer effective change" (p. 4). He gives the example of a group of professors in the University of Damascus whose "desire for L1 medium lectures in formal grammar was seen not as a constraint but as a cultural resource" (p. 4), and who were therefore given texts on grammar with Arabic translations as their texts on their reading course. Another example of a covert approach is given by Coleman and Ainscough (2001) who describe how groups of Japanese students on the Foundation Course at the University of Kent are taught "a course that has, for the students, the face validity of a content-based course, but which is delivered using methodologies and materials which teach, in a covert fashion, the EAP skills they need" (p. 9).

Culture Stretching

Reid (1987) claims that learners benefit from "style-stretching," that is, learning through styles that are not necessarily their own preferred dominant styles. It is likely that learners gain in similar ways from culture stretching.

Dat (2002) describes experiments in Vietnam in which normally reticent students proved the prophecies of their teachers wrong by expressing themselves in English during cooperative activities. The experiments stretched their culture, and they benefited from it. But Dat says many learners are denied this chance because "By refusing to believe in learners' potential to express themselves in English and their willingness to participate in English, many practitioners form self-fulfilling beliefs about their students' incompetence that leads to habits of accepting the status quo and preventing change from happening" (p. 256).

A number of projects have stretched the participants' culture without any apparent problem. For example, Beretta and Davis (1985) evaluated the Bangalore/Madras Communicational Teaching Project positively without any reference to problems encountered because of the cultural unfamiliarity of the approach. And Parish and Brown (1988) describe a teacher training program for teachers of English in Sri Lanka (PRINSETT) without once mentioning cultural unfamiliarity as a problem. Instead they assert that:

> Participants are engaged in language tasks and methodological analysis that they have never been exposed to. The active-participatory approach is non-traditional and completely novel in their experience. The work is demanding but the response is extremely positive. (p. 27)

Tomlinson (1990) reports that:

> The PKG English Programme (in Indonesia) has been successful in getting the teachers on its courses to question their standard practice and to develop new approaches to teaching English. This has been achieved by first of all helping them to develop their own confidence and skills as users of English, and by inviting them to compare the methodology which helped them with the methodology which they use with their students. (p. 32)

The School Culture

There seems to be a universal school culture of conservatism and control that encourages convergence and conformity and that rewards hard work and analytic skill (Tomlinson, 1988). This culture is reflected in global EFL coursebooks (Tomlinson,

1996; Tomlinson et al., 2001) and in particular in beginners' EFL coursebooks (Islam, 2001; Tomlinson, 1999). Islam demonstrates how beginners' coursebooks in Japan and in Spain are very similar in their bias "towards the learning preferences of analytic, studial, left brain learners at the expense of global, experiential, right-brain learners" (p. 16). He then demonstrates how using a Total Physical Response (TPR) Plus Approach (Tomlinson, 1994) was successful in motivating Japanese beginner learners of English despite (or maybe because of) it being very different from what they were used to. Tomlinson (2002) also reports how students in a secondary school in Spain said they wanted to do different things in English lessons from what they were used to doing in other lessons, and Coleman and Ainscough (2001) say, "Most of our students, having been exposed to many hours of grammar-focused lessons in Japan, resist such lessons at Chaucer College" (p. 9).

Breen and Littlejohn (2000a) include reports on projects that have involved successful negotiation between learners and teachers and between learners and the syllabus in school cultures in which such negotiation is far from the norm. For example, Slembrouck (2000) reports how he overcame objections from a "sceptical department head" at Ghent University in Belgium and was eventually given "carte blanche to try out a negotiated syllabus" (pp. 139–140).

The "Good" Language Learner

Most descriptions of what a "good" language learner does are culture free and assume the procedures are universal. For example, Rubin and Thompson (1983) list 13 things that a "good" language learner does, including:

- Good learners find their own way.
- Good learners are creative and experiment with language.
- Good learners learn to live with uncertainty and develop strategies for making sense of the target language without wanting to understand every word.

If such tendencies do facilitate language acquisition, then learners in school cultures that inhibit individuality, initiative, creativity, and experimentation are at a considerable disadvantage. As Breen and Littlejohn (2000b) say: "In classrooms that require conformity to externally determined decisions . . . students have to try to make sense of the curriculum covertly as best they can or withdraw into surviving as an individual not wishing to appear out of place" (p. 21).

The "Good" Teacher

Dat (2002) says:

> It is uncommon to see a class getting bored and uncooperative when working with a cheerful, approachable and dedicated teacher. . . . Conversely, a teacher who cares about maintaining hierarchy tends to prevent language tasks from developing into dynamic interaction. (p. 269)

Dat was talking about teachers in Vietnam. Is what he says universally true? Is there such a thing as a good teacher who, regardless of the cultural norms of the society and the school, manages to facilitate language acquisition through being "cheerful, approachable, and dedicated?" My experience of teaching or observing in classrooms in more than 40 countries supports Dat's hypothesis and suggests that the "good" language teacher is also positive, supportive, and sympathetic and, above all, has a good sense of humor. It would be very interesting to see the results of research that sets out to investigate the phenomenon of the universally "good" teacher.

Universal Likings

Some approaches to teaching EFL mirror universal tendencies and preferences and are suitable for use in any classroom regardless of its culture. For example, I have used humor, achievable challenge, fiction, and incongruity in classrooms in cultures as supposedly different as the British, the Japanese, and the Ni-Vanuatu. What was perceived as funny or incongruent or as a narrative norm varied from culture to culture. However, very few students were resistant to activities that were based on narrative and that involved the learners in doing something unusual, challenging, and funny. On the Indonesian PKG project we developed an approach called TPR Plus (Tomlinson, 1990, 1994), which incorporated these features, and I have developed this approach and used it without resistance in cultures as different as those to be found in Brazil, Botswana, Namibia, Turkey, Singapore, Spain, and Vietnam. I have also found that listening to and reading stories is a universally popular and useful way of learning a foreign language. "Narrative is the universally preferred means of learning about life and throughout the world both children and adults have always learned more effectively from narrative than from any other way." (Tomlinson, 2003a, p. 14). It is very interesting that just about all the literature on research into the effects of extensive reading projects reports positive effects on language acquisition in many different countries regardless of local cultural norms (Day & Bamford, 1998; Davis, 1995; Elley, 1991).

Cook (2000) points out the importance in language learning of universal likings and says, for example, that, "It may be that the adult liking for fiction is in part due to the freedom of interpretation which it allows, and the absence of negative consequences when one individual's interpretation diverges from those of other's" (p. 54). He also says that, "The human response to incongruity in verbal humour . . . seems to be built upon some general innate liking for incongruity in general" (p. 74).

Cultural Variability

It is obviously reductionist to talk about Western culture and oriental culture or American culture and Chinese culture. Each human being belongs to many different cultures and is conditioned by membership in them. But "we are also distinct from each other because we each diverge in what we typically think, feel, believe and do" (Tomlinson, 2000, p. 5). To assume that a learner of a foreign language will automatically conform to the generalized norms of their national, racial, religious, or peer group cultures is misleadingly simplistic. In my experience, most learners are quite willing to add their own version of the foreign language culture (and of a novel way of learning it) to their cultural portfolio and in doing so they perceive little threat to their cultural identity. Kramsch (2001) supports this view of cultural variability and pluralism when she says, "Today, many studies in cross-cultural psychology seem simplistic because they ignore the cultural diversity within a given nation-state and the increasing potential for change within a global economy" (p. 203).

Who are the native speakers of a language and what are the cultural norms they represent? According to Kramsch (1998) the native speaker is a stereotype who is "a mono-lingual, mono-cultural abstraction; he/she is one who only speaks his/her (standardized) native tongue and lives by one (standardized) national culture. In reality, most people partake of various languages or language varieties and live by various cultures and sub-cultures" (p. 80).

The main point is that we should be aware of the dangers of cultural over-generalizations and should remember that in the classroom we are teaching EFL to a class of diverging individuals rather than to a convergent group of cultural stereotypes.

Research Procedures

The research projects reported in this chapter were almost all action research projects that set out to investigate the effects of pedagogic interventions in real classrooms in actual social settings by using such procedures as case studies, interviews, questionnaires and observations (Burns, 1999; Kemmis & McTaggart, 1988; Mingucci, 1999). Consequently, most of the research has been qualitative, rather than quantitative, and it has been indicative rather than conclusive. However, many of the projects have included an element of deliberate experimentation and have focused their inquiry on specific variables while acknowledging the impossibility of controlling all the variables in a real environment. For example, on the PKG Project in Indonesia (Tomlinson, 1990) the classes of the participating teachers on the In-On Service Programme became experimental classes that followed a locally determined version of the communicative approach. On the Bangalore Project (Beretta & Davies, 1985) a number of classes followed a task-based approach rather than the locally normal approach, and on the Book Flood Project in Fiji (Elley, 1991) experimental classes were chosen to follow an extensive reading approach once a week.

CONCLUSION

It seems that no particular pedagogical procedure can be used effectively without some modification from context to context but also that a procedure that proves effective in one context of learning has the potential to be effective in other contexts of learning too.

The basic principles of SLA appear to be universal, as do the principles of interlanguage use. What seem to differ from culture to culture are the typical procedures through which these principles are most effectively applied. However, these procedures are more flexible and amenable to modification than is generally acknowledged; and ultimately most teachers and learners are willing to experiment with change providing that the change is nonthreatening and potentially beneficial. What seems to really matter is that there is an initial negotiation between teachers and students to find "ways to accommodate the cultural differences that exist" (McKay, 1992, p. 51). That way modified versions of most approaches can become acceptable to most students.

In my view, EFL teachers, wherever they are, should teach in ways that suit their beliefs and personality while being sensitive to the needs and wants of their learners and to the prevailing norms of the cultures in which they are teaching.

REFERENCES

Arnold, J. (1999). *Affect in language learning*. Cambridge, UK: Cambridge University Press.

Auerbach, E. R. (1995). The politics of the ESL classroom: Issues of power in pedagogical choices. In J. Tollesfon (Ed.), *Power and inequality in language education*. (pp.) New York: Cambridge University Press.

Barkhuizen, G. P. (1998). Discovering learner's perceptions of ESL classroom teaching/learning activities in a South African context. *TESOL Quarterly, 32*(1), 85–108.

Be, N. (2003). *The design and use of English language teaching materials in Vietnamese secondary schools*. Unpublished doctoral dissertation. Victoria University, Wellington, New Zealand.

Bedell, D. A., & Oxford, R. L. (1996). Cross-cultural comparisons of language learning strategies in the People's Republic of China and other countries. In R. L. Oxford (Ed.), *Language learning strategies around the world: Cross-cultural perspectives* (pp. 47–60). Manoa, University of Hawaii Press.

Benson, M. J. (2000). The secret life of grammar-translation. In H. Trappes-Lomax (Ed.), *Change and continuity in applied linguistics* (pp. 120–148). Clevedon, UK: British Association of Applied Lainguistics/Multilingual Matters.

Berretta, A., & Davies, A. (1985). Evaluation of the Bangalore Project. *ELT Journal, 39*(2), 121–127.

Block, D. (2002). Communicative language teaching revisited: Discourse in conflict and foreign national teachers. *Language Learning Journal, 26*, 19–26.

Breen, M. P., & Littlejohn, A. (Eds.). (2000a). *Classroom decision making*. Cambridge, UK: Cambridge University Press.

Breen, M. P., & Littlejohn, A. (2000b). The significance of negotiation. In M. P. Breen & A. Littlejohn (Eds.), *Classroom decision making*. Cambridge, UK: Cambridge University Press.

Burns, A. (1999). *Collaborative action research for English language teachers*. Cambridge, UK: Cambridge University Press.

Byram, M., & Cain, A. (1998). Civilisation/Cultural studies: An experiment in French and English schools. In M. Byram & M. Fleming, *Language learning in intercultural perspectives: Approaches through drama and ethnography* (pp. 32–44), Cambridge, UK: Cambridge University Press.

Canagarajah, A. S. (1999). *Resisting linguistic imperialism in English teaching*. Oxford, UK: Oxford University Press.

Carter, R., & Nunan, D. (Eds.). (2001). *The Cambridge guide to teaching English to speakers of other languages*. Cambridge, UK: Cambridge University Press.

Cheung, C. (2001). The use of popular culture as a stimulus to motivate secondary students' English learning in Hong Kong. *ELT Journal, 55*(1), 55–61.

Coleman, H. (1996). *Society and the language classroom*. Cambridge, UK: Cambridge University Press.

Coleman, J., & Ainscough, V. (2001). EAP as the hidden agenda. *FOLIO, 6*(2), 914.

Cook, G. (2000). *Language play, language learning*. Oxford, UK: Oxford University Press.

Cortazzi, M. (1990). Cultural and educational expectations in the language classroom. In B. Harrison (Ed.), *Culture and the language classroom* (pp. 54–65). London: Modern English Publications.

Cortazzi, M., & Jin, L. (1996). Cultures of learning: Language classrooms in China. In H. Coleman (Ed.), *Society and the language classroom* (pp. 169–206). Cambridge, UK: Cambridge University Press.

Cuningsworth, A. (1995). *Choosing your coursebook*. Oxford, UK: Heinemann.

Dat, B. (2002). *Understanding reticence: An action research project aiming at increasing verbal participation in the EFL classroom in Vietnam*. Unpublished doctoral dissertation, Leeds Metropolitan University, UK.

Davies, A. (2002). Using teacher-generated biography as input material. *ELT Journal, 56*(1), 368–375.

Davis, C. (1995). Extensive reading: An expensive extravagance? *ELT Journal, 49*(4), 329–336.

Day, R. R., & Bamford, J. (1998). *Extensive reading in the second language classroom*. Cambridge, UK: Cambridge University Press.

Duquette, G. (1995). *Second language practice*. Clevedon, UK: Multilingual Matters.

Elley, W. B. (1991). Acquiring literacy in a second language: The effect of book-based programs. *Language Learning, 41*(3), 375–411.

Ellis, R. (1994). *The study of second language acquisition*. Oxford, UK: Oxford University Press.

Ellis, R. (2002, March). Cultural attache. *EL Teaching Matters, 1*, p 1.

Flowerdew, L., (1998). A cultural perspective on group work. *ELT Journal 52*(4), 323–329.

Fu, D. L. (1995). *My trouble is my English: Asian students and the American dream*. Portsmouth, NH: Boynton/Cook and Heinemann.

Guest, M. (2002). A critical "checkbook" for culture teaching and learning. *ELT Journal, 56*(2), 154–161.

Harvey, P. (1985). A lesson to be learned: Chinese approaches to language learning. *ELT Journal, 39*(3), 183–186.

Hird, B. (1995). How communicative can language teaching be in China? *Prospect, 10*(3), 21–27.

Holliday, A. (1994). *Appropriate methodology and social context*. Cambridge, UK: Cambridge University Press.

Holliday, A. (2001). Appropriate methodology in using materials: Ideology and artefact. *FOLIO, 6*(2), 4–8.

Howe, S. (1993). Teaching English in Vietnam. *Interchange, 22*, 29–32.

Islam, C. (2001). A different beginner textbook. *FOLIO, 6*(2), 15–19.

Kachru, Y. (1994). Monolingual bias in SLA research. *TESOL Quarterly, 28*(4), 795–800.

Karavas-Doukas, K. (1998). Evaluating the implementation of educational innovations: Lessons from the past. In P. Rea-Dickins & K. P. Germaine (Eds.), *Managing evaluation and innovation in language teaching: Building bridges* (pp. 25–55). London: Longman.

Kemmis, S., & McTaggart, R. (1988). *The Action Research Planner*. Geelong, Victoria, Australia Deakin University Press.

Kenny, B., & Savage, W. (Eds.). (1997). *Language and development—Teachers in a changing world*. London: Longman.

Kleibard, E. (1986). *The struggle for the American curriculum, 1983–1958*. Boston: Routledge/Kegan Paul.

Kramsch, C. (1998). *Language and culture*. Oxford, UK: Oxford University Press.

Kramsch, C. (2001). Intercultural communication. In R. Carter & D. Nunan. *The Cambridge guide to teaching English to speakers of other languages* (pp. 201–206). Cambridge, UK: Cambridge University Press.

Kubanyiova, M. (2002). Drama with Thai students (a couple of tried ideas on how to start). *The English Teacher: An International Journal, 5*(2), 178–180.

Lam, P. (1997). Culture, learning and teaching style in the EOP classroom. In S. Ho & C. Carmichael (Eds.), *Exploring language* (pp. 63–71). Hong Kong: Language Centre, Hong Kong University of Science and Technology.

Lamb, M. (1995). The consequences of INSET. *ELT Journal, 49*(1), 72–80.

Lewis, R. (1996). Indonesian students' learning styles. *Elicos Association Journal, 14*(2), 27–32.

Lewis, M., & McCook, F. (2002). Cultures of teaching: Voices from Vietnam. *ELT Journal, 56*(2), 146–153.

Liu, D. (1998). Ethnocentrism in TESOL: Teacher education and the neglected needs of international TESOL students. *ELT Journal, 52*(1), 3–10.

LoCastro, V. (1996). English language education in Japan. In H. Coleman (Ed.), *Society and the language classroom* (pp. 40–58). Cambridge, UK: Cambridge University Press.

Louden, W. (1991). Understanding teaching: Continuity and change in teachers' knowledge. New York: Cassell.

Maingay, P. (1997). Raising awareness of awareness. In I. McGrath (Ed.), *Learning to train: Perspectives on the development of language teacher trainers* (pp. 58–72). Hemel Hempstead, UK: Prentice Hall International.

Masuhara, H. (1998). What do teachers really want from coursebooks? In B. Tomlinson (Ed.), *Materials development in language teaching* (pp. 239–260). Cambridge, UK: Cambridge University Press.

Matthews, A. (1991). Chosing the best available textbook. In A. Matthews, M. Spratt, & L. Dangerfield (Eds.), *At the chalkface* (pp. 202–206). London: Nelson.

McDonough, J. (2002). The teacher as language learner: Worlds of difference? *ELT Journal, 56*(4), 404–411.

McDonough, J., & Shaw, C. (1993). *Materials and methods in ELT*. Oxford, UK: Blackwell.

McGrath, I. (2002). *Materials evaluation and design for language teaching*. Edinburgh, Scotland: Edinburgh University Press.

McKay, S. (1992). *Teaching English overseas*. Oxford, UK: Oxford University Press.

Mingucci, M. (1999). Action research in ESL staff development. *TESOL Matters, 9*(2), 16.

Mitchell, R., & Lee, J. H. (2003). Sameness and difference in classroom learning cultures: Interpretation of communicative pedagogies in UK and Korea. *Language Teaching Research, 7*(1), 35–64.

Myles, F. (2000). Change and continuity in second language acquisition research. In H. Trappes-Lomax (Ed.), *Change and continuity in applied linguistics* (pp. 68–81). Clevedon, UK: British Association of Applied Linguistics Multilingual Matters.

Nelson, G. (1995). Cultural differences in learning styles. In J. Reid (Ed.), *Learning styles in the ESL/EFL classroom* (pp. 3–18). Boston: Heinle & Heinle.

Nunan, D. (1988). *The learner centred curriculum*. Cambridge, UK: Cambridge University Press.

Oxford, R. L. (1990). *Language learning strategies: What every teacher should know*. Boston: Heinle & Heinle.

Oxford, R. L. (1995). *Patterns of cultural identity*. Boston: Heinle & Heinle.

Oxford, R. L. (Ed.). (1996). *Language learning strategies around the world: Cross-cultural perspectives*. Manoa: University of Hawaii Press.

Padwad, A. (2002). Review of teaching and learning in the language classroom. *The English Teacher: An International Journal, 5*(2), 191–193.

Parish, C., & Brown, R. W. (1988). Teacher training for Sri Lanka: PRINSETT. *ELT Journal, 42/1*, 21–27.

Pennycook, A. (1994). *The Cultural politics of English as an international language*. London: Longman.

Perdue, C. (1984). *Second language acquisition by adult immigrants: A field manual*. Rowley, MA: Newbury House.

Perdue, C. (Ed.). (1993a). *Adult language acquisition: Cross-linguistic perspectives*. Vol. 1. Cambridge, UK: Cambridge University Press.

Perdue, C. (Ed.). (1993b). *Adult language acquisition: Cross-linguistic perspectives*. Vol. 2. Cambridge, UK: Cambridge University Press.

Phillipson, R. (1992). *Linguistic imperialism*. Oxford, UK: Oxford University Press.

Piper, T. (1998). *Language and learning—The home and school years*. (2nd ed.). Columbus OH: Merrill.

Reid, J. (1987). The learning styles and preferences of ESL students. *TESOL Quarterly 21*, 87–111.

Richards, J. (2001). *Curriculum development in language teaching*. Cambridge, UK: Cambridge University Press.

Rodgers, T. (1988). Co-operative language learning: What's new? In K. D. Bikram (Ed.), *Materials for language learning and teaching*, (pp.). Anthology Series 22. Singapore: SEAMO Regional Language Centre.

Rodgers, T. S. (1989). Syllabus design, curriculum development and polity determination. In R. K. Johnson (Ed.), *The second language curriculum* (pp. 24–34). Cambridge, UK: Cambridge University Press.

Rubin, J., & Thompson, I. (1983). *How to be a more successful Language learner*. New York: Heinle & Heinle.

Scovell, T. (1998). *Psycholinguistics*. Oxford, UK: Oxford University Press.

Sercu, L. (1998). In-service training and the acquisition of intercultural competence. In M. Byram & M. Fleming, *Language learning in intercultural perspectives: Approaches through drama and ethnography* (pp.). Cambridge, UK: Cambridge University Press.

Shamin, F. (1996). Learner resistance to innovation classroom methodology. In H. Coleman (Ed.), *Society and the language classroom* (pp. 105–122). Cambridge, UK: Cambridge University Press.

Singapore Wala, D. A. (2003). Publishing a coursebook: Completing the materials development circle. In B. Tomlinson (Ed.), *Developing Materials for Language Teaching* (pp. 58–71). London: Continuum.

Skierso, A. (1991). Textbook selection. In M. Celce-Mercia (Ed.), *Teaching English as a second or foreign language* (pp. 432–453). Boston: Heinle & Heinle.

Slembrouck, S. (2000). Negotiation in tertiary education: Clashes with the dominant educational culture. In M. P. Breen & A. Littlejohn (Eds.), *Classroom decision making* (pp. 133–149). Cambridge, UK: Cambridge University Press.

Spratt, M. (1999). How good are we at knowing what learners like? *System, 27*(2), 141–155.

Sridar, S. N. (1994). A reality check for SLA theories. *TESOL Quarterly, 28*(4), 800–805.

Stubbs, M. (2000). Society, education and language: The last 2,000 (and the next 20?) years of language teaching. In H. Trappes-Lomax (Ed.), *Change and continuity in applied linguistics* (pp. 15–37). Clevedon, UK: British Association of Applied Linguistics/Multilingual Matters.

Tennant, S. (2001). Teaching English as a foreign language by exploring the art and culture of the students own culture. *The English Teacher: An International Journal, 5*(1), 35–50.

Tin, T. B. (2000). Looking at changes from the learner's point of view: An analysis of group interaction pasterns in cross-cultural settings. In H. Trappes-Lomax (Ed.), *Change and continuity in applied linguistics* (pp. 63–83). Clevedon, UK: British Association of Applied Linguistics/Multilingual Matters.

Tomlinson, B. (1988). Conflicts in TEFL: Reasons for failure in secondary schools. *ILEJ Journal, 4,* 103–110.

Tomlinson, B. (1990). Managing change in Indonesian high schools. *ELT Journal, 44*(1), 25–37.

Tomlinson, B. (1991). English education in Japanese universities. *Kobe Miscellany 17.* Kobe, Japan: University of Kobe Press.

Tomlinson, B. (1994). Materials for TPR. *FOLIO, 1*(2), 8–10.

Tomlinson, B. (1995). Work in progress: Textbook projects. *FOLIO, 2*(2), 26–30.

Tomlinson, B. (1996). New directions in materials development. *Arena, 11,* 24–25.

Tomlinson, B. (Ed.) (1998a). *Materials development in language teaching.* Cambridge, UK: Cambridge University Press.

Tomlinson, B. (1998b). Affect and the coursebook. *IATEFL Issues, 145,* 20–21.

Tomlinson, B. (1999). Developing criteria for evaluating L2 materials. *IATEFL Issues, Vol. 153* 10–13.

Tomlinson, B. (2000). Talking to yourself: The role of the inner voice in language learning. *Applied Language Learning, 11*(1), 123–154.

Tomlinson, B. (2001, June). Seeing more between the lines. *Learning English. The Guardian Weekly, June* 21–27, 5.

Tomlinson, B. (2002). Matching methodology to the context of learning. Paper presented at AILA Conference, Singapore.

Tomlinson, B. (2003a). Stories to tell: Storybooks as coursebooks. *FOLIO, 7*(1), 14–18.

Tomlinson, B. (Ed.). (2003b). *Developing materials for language teaching.* London: Continuum Press.

Tomlinson, B., Hill, D. A., & Masuhara, H. (2000). *English for Life 1.* Singapore: Times Media.

Tomlinson, B., Dat, B., Masuhara, H., & Rubdy, R. (2001). EFL courses for adults. *ELT Journal, 55*(1), 80–101.

Tomlinson, B., Hill, D. A., Masuhara, H., & Ying. L. P. (2002). *English for Life 2.* Singapore: Times Media.

Tomlinson, B., Appleton, J., Barnes, H., Barnes, J., Birch, S., Masuhara, H., & Timmis, I. (2003). *Life Access 4.* Singapore: Times Media.

Tomlinson, B., & Masuhara, H. (2004). *Matching methodolgy to the context of learning.* Manuscript in progress.

Tudor, I. (1996). *Learner-centredness as language education.* Cambridge, UK: Cambridge University Press.

Urmston, A. W. (2001). Learning to teach English in Hong Kong: Effects of the changeover in sovereignty. *Language Teaching Research, 5*(2), 178–179.

Wenden, A. L. (1991). *Learner strategies for learner autonomy.* Englewood Cliffs, NJ: Prentice-Hall.

Williams, M., & Burden R. L. (1997). *Psychology for language teachers—A social constructivist approach.* Cambridge, UK: Cambridge University Press.

Wong, W. (1996). *How do Hong Kong students learn? Implications for Teaching 13.* Hong Kong: Educational Technology Centre, Hong Kong University of Science and Technology.

9

Teaching and Learning of World Englishes*

Yamuna Kachru
University of Illinois

INTRODUCTION

The unprecedented spread of one language, English, all across the globe has raised issues that need urgent study and action, as they affect all domains of human activity from language in education to international relations. The first such issue is to understand the role that English plays, the status that it has, and the purposes it serves in different contexts—contexts that are different from where the language originated and assumed its present form.

In order to study what English means and does, it may be useful to look at a particular construct suggested in B. Kachru (1985) according to which the English-using world can be divided into three concentric circles. This conceptualization is based not only on the historical context of English but also on the status of the language and its functions in various sociocultural domains in different regions. The Inner Circle consists of the native English-speaking countries, e.g., Australia, Canada, New Zealand, the U.K. and the U.S.A. The language originated in the UK and was taken to the other countries of the Inner Circle by population migration, i.e., English-speaking people moving to these regions. The Outer Circle comprises the former colonies or spheres of influence of the U.K. and the U.S.A., e.g., India, Kenya, Nigeria, the Philippines, Singapore, among others. There was no large-scale movement of English-speaking populations to these countries, instead, a small number of administrators, educators and missionaries were responsible for language spread among the indigenous population in these countries. Now, the nativized varieties of English in these countries have achieved the status of either an official language, or of an additional language widely used in education, administration, legal system, etc, although the indigenous languages continue to be used in many domains of activity. The Expanding Circle consists of cuntries which, though not directly colonized, gradually came under Western influence and where English is fast becoming a dominant second language in academia, business and commerce, higher education, media, and science and technology, e.g., in the Arab world, China, European countries, Japan, Korea, and many countries in South and Central America. In these areas of the world, English does not have an official status.

The varieties of English used in all these Circles are referred to as world Englishes, the justification being that *Englishes* in the three Circles display variation in form, function, literary creativity, and acculturation in the new contexts. The acculturation of the language is at all levels—phonology, lexicon, syntax, discourse and literary creativity.[1]

The aim of this paper is to present a brief survey of the state of research on World Englishes (WEs) from the point of view of teaching and learning of English around the world. Because the area of study known as second language acquisition (SLA) is intimately related to the teaching and learning of English globally, I will also look at how research on WEs connects with research in SLA. Finally, I will discuss the motivations for and advantages of teaching and learning world Englishes in all the Circles of English.[1] This obviously has serious implications for institutions involved in four domains of activity: teacher training programs such as the Masters in Teaching English to Speakers of Other Languages (MATESOL) and teacher certification in Teaching English to Speakers of Other Languages (TESOL); professional organizations dedicated to the theoretical, methodological, and pedagogical concerns of English Language Teaching (ELT) professionals; journals dedicated to the same concerns; and the vast English language textbook, reference book, and language testing industry. I mention these in particular as they have the most significant impact on ELT practices across all the Circles.

I will begin with some background observations. It is essential to outline explicitly the perspective of researchers studying varieties of English around the world before considering in what domains of research the study of WEs either does or does not intersect with research in SLA. That English has acquired both a *range* and a *depth* unparalleled in human history is uncontroversial. By *range* is meant the functional allocation of the language in intimate, social, and professional domains by its users, and by *depth* is meant the penetration of the language in various strata of society across cultures and languages (B. Kachru, 1986a; B. Kachru & Nelson, 1996). That English has developed a number of varieties in its diaspora is also beyond debate. However, there is vigorous debate on the status of Outer and Extended Circle varieties and how to characterize what is meant by "standard" in relation to varieties used in all the Circles. The debate on standards and varieties, as researchers in WEs believe, has just as much to do with attitudinal and ideological positions with regard to status of the varieties as to an unwillingness to face the linguistic and acquisitional realities (Sridhar, 1994). One clear evidence of attitudinal bias is provided by the instruments of testing proficiency in English developed in the United Kingdom and the United States and used around the world (see Davidson, 1994; Lowenberg, 1992, 1993, 2001). The concept of Standard English and its relevance for WEs is addressed in more detail a little later in this chapter.

EMERGENCE OF VARIETIES IN DIASPORA

The diaspora of English, as B. Kachru (1992c), suggests is of two types. The first arose as a consequence of the migration of the English-speaking people and comprises Australia, North America, and New Zealand. The second resulted from the diffusion of English among speakers of diverse groups of languages in Asia, Africa, the Caribbean, and other parts of the world. These two diasporas have distinct historical, linguistic, sociological, pedagogical, and ideological contexts.

The English language has undergone a number of linguistic processes—some similar, some quite different—in both types of diaspora. These processes were set in motion as a result of the physical context and patterns of settlement, for example, in the Inner Circle in North America and Australia. Populations from various parts of Europe and later from other regions of the world arrived and settled down next to each other in these countries of the Inner Circle. A composite language and culture grew out of this various population that gave the varieties of the first Diaspora their characteristic structure. The evidence for this can be found, for instance, in the many features of African, Native American, and Hispanic idioms, metaphors, and discourse strategies that have become a part of American English. It is clear that varieties of Inner Circle English, such as American, Australian, Canadian, and New Zealand emerged because of the processes set in motion by language contact. The same factors are responsible for what occurred in the Outer Circle varieties such as Indian, Nigerian, and Singaporean.

In the early 20th century, American English gave rise to the same attitudinal prejudices that are now directed against the Outer Circle varieties, as is clear from the following quote from *New Statesman* (June 25, 1927) in Mencken (1936, p. 33)[2]:

> [T]hat their [America's] huge hybrid population of which only a small minority are even racially Anglo-Saxons should use English as their chief medium of intercommunication is our misfortune, not our fault. They certainly threaten our language, but the only way in which we can effectively meet that threat is by assuming—in the words of the authors of "The King's English" [by H. W. and F. G. Fowler, Oxford, 1908] that "Americanisms are foreign words and should be so treated."

The only difference in the emergence of the two types of Diaspora varieties is that in the case of the first, the language was brought in by a significant number of immigrants from the Mother country and adopted by other immigrants, initially mainly from Europe. In case of the second Diaspora, the language was brought in, one might say, by a handful of users of English, not all of them English-speakers,[3] and transplanted in Africa, East, South, and Southeast Asia and other so-called Anglophone regions of the world. This one difference, however, leads to very different historical, sociocultural, and canonical contexts of development of varieties and their literatures in the second Diaspora.

AIMS AND FOCUS OF RESEARCH

Researchers in WEs are interested in all aspects of the emergence, grammars, sociolinguistics, ideological issues, creative literatures, and teaching and learning of WEs (see the collected papers in B. Kachru, 1986a, 1992a; Smith, 1987; Thumboo, 2001). They have worked on the historical background of the dissemination of English in the world (e.g., Bamgbose et al., 1995; Bautista, 1997; B. Kachru, 1983; Pakir, 1991a, 1991b, 2001; K. Sridhar, 1989; among others). They are involved in studying the linguistic processes that are responsible for variety-specific characteristics as well as common features among varieties of the language in different regions of the world. These include phonological, lexical, and grammatical processes, discourse strategies, and textual properties (see, Bokamba, 1992; B. Kachru, 1983, 1986a; Lowenberg, 1986, 1991; Smith, 1987; Smith & Forman, 1997; Thumboo, 2001). In addition, they are interested in investigating the sociocultural contexts of use of English, particularly in the second Diaspora (see, B. Kachru, 1986a, 1992a; Y. Kachru, 1993, 1995a, 1995b, 1997a; Nelson, 1992; K. Sridhar, 1991; Tawake, 1993, 1994; Valentine, 1988, 1991, 1995, 2001; among others).

It has been demonstrated beyond controversy that all Outer Circle varieties have a standard, or "acrolectal," form, which is mutually intelligible among all English-using populations. The characteristic features of the acrolectal forms within regions/national boundaries—whether they have been codified or not—are widely attested in highly literate domains of use, for example, the domains of academia, creative literature, diplomacy, higher administration, media, etc. (Bautista, 1997; B. Kachru, 1983; Pakir, 1991a, 2001).

In view of the differing conventions of use and usage, intelligibility among the varieties is another topic that has been explored to some extent. Several studies have been conducted to determine if the claim regarding superior intelligibility of Inner Circle varieties can be sustained on the basis of empirical investigations (Frenck & Min, 2001; Smith, 1992; Smith & Christopher, 2001; Smith & Nelson, 1985; Smith & Rafiqzad, 1979). Another aspect of the intelligibility issue is that of the intelligibility of indigenized varieties in their native settings (see B. Kachru, 1992b; Sridhar, 1994; Sridhar & Sridhar, 1986, 1992). As Sridhar (1994) observes, accent, transfer from substratum languages, code-mixing and switching, etc. are enriching resources in stable multilingual communities with shared verbal repertoires. They are not an impediment to intelligibility; instead, they are as natural as style or register switching in monolingual communities (p. 802).

Language contact and convergence in these regions have not only affected English, they have also had an impact on the local languages. Therefore, researchers in WEs are interested in looking at the two-way interaction between English and local languages to understand the effects of contact and convergence. The interface of contact and convergence has been termed "nativization" (of English) and "Englishization" (of local languages). Englishization of local languages has been discussed in studies such as Baik (2001), Hsu (1994a, 1994b, 2001), B. Kachru (1979), and Shim (1994).

Most users of English in these regions (i.e., Africa, Asia) are bilinguals, or even multilinguals (I will subsume "bilingual" under "multilingual" and will use "multilingual" to indicate both categories henceforth). A great deal of WE research focuses on the language use of multilinguals. For example, considerable work has been done on code repertoire of multilinguals and the phenomena of code-mixing and switching (Bautista, 1990, 1991; T. Bhatia & Ritchie, 1989; Bhatt, 1996; B. Kachru, 1978; Kamwangamalu, 1989; Kamwangamalu & Li, 1991; Pandey, 2001; among others).

The teaching and learning of English in the Outer and Expanding Circles is one sub-topic within the range of topics that WE research is concerned with (Brown, 1993, 2001; Brown & Peterson, 1997; B. Kachru, 1995c, 1997b; Y. Kachru, 1985a, 1985b, 1997b). This research is informed by the findings of the fields of first and second language acquisition (FLA and SLA), ethnography of communication, literacy, psycholinguistics, multilingualism, neurolinguistics, and other relevant fields. A large body of research is devoted to how fluent, proficient users of the varieties use them in administration, business, diplomacy, education, law, literary creativity, politics, religion, and other spheres of human activity (see, e.g., papers in Baumgardner, 1996a; V. Bhatia, 1997; B. Kachru, 1992a; Smith, 1987; Thumboo, 2001).

All institutionalized varieties have a body of literature that is useful for teaching language as well as the culture of the region. For readers across languages and cultures one resource for gaining familiarity with the varieties of English in the second diaspora is the literature created in them. Appreciation of literary creativity in world Englishes makes it hard to maintain prejudicial attitudes toward what is perceived as "non-standard" because it is unfamiliar. Some research has been devoted to classroom utilization of world English literatures for raising consciousness about the multicultural identity of world Englishes (see, e.g., Courtright, 2001; B. Kachru, 1986b, 1995a, 1995b, 2001; Nelson, 1992; Smith, 1992; Tawake, 1994; Thumboo, 1985, 1986, 1988, 1991, 1992).

There is, of course, variation within regional varieties, such as South Asian English or West African English, and national varieties, such as Singaporean English, just as there is dialectal and diatypic variation within the English-speaking populations of Australia, Canada, New Zealand, the United Kingdom, and the United States (McArthur, 1992). The basilectal, or pidgin-like forms, and the mesolectal, or colloquial forms, which may or may not be mixed with substratum language forms, are used for various purposes in the Outer and Expanding Circles, just as various speaker and speech types are used by Inner Circle speakers and writers. The focus of research, however, is not on just this variation and relating it to theories of acquisitional deficiency. Rather, the interest is in the functional allocation of the varieties within the English-using communities (see, e.g., Bamiro, 1991; B. Kachru, 1986a; Taiwo, 1976; Tay, 1993).

A great deal of attention is directed toward the communicative needs of the users that underlie the observed linguistic differences between the Outer and Expanding Circle varieties as compared to the Inner Circle ones (see the discussions in the sphere of literary creativity in Dissanayake, 1985, 1990; B. Kachru, 1992b, 1995a, 1995b; Y. Kachru, 1988b; Thumboo, 1985, 1986, 1992).

WORLD ENGLISHES AND INTERLANGUAGE (IL)

The world varieties of English have been labeled variously as "interference" varieties (Quirk et.al., 1985) and interlanguages (Selinker, 1992). To characterize these standard forms of the Outer Circle as Interlanguage is unjustified on several grounds, including that of the definition of IL from Selinker (1992):

> An "interlanguage" may be linguistically described using as data the observable output resulting from a speaker's attempt to produce a foreign norm, i.e., both his errors and non-errors. (p. 231)

Users of standard Indian, Nigerian, or Singaporean English are NOT attempting to produce a "foreign" norm; they are functioning in their own variety. As the famous Nigerian writer, Chinua Achebe, has observed:

> Most African writers write out of an African experience and of commitment to an African destiny. For them that destiny does not include a future European identity for which the present is but an apprenticeship. (Jussawalla & Dasenbrock, 1992, p. 34)

Confusing attitudes with sociolinguistic reality is not new in linguistic research. There are Americans, just as there are Indians or Singaporeans, who think their own variety is not as "pure" or "elegant" as British English or some other "foreign" norm. That, however, does not lead to questioning the existence of a standard variety of American English, nor should it result in denying the status they deserve to the standard varieties of the Outer Circle.

One major issue, related to this point, is that of input. Most of the input the learners of English receive in the Outer (and Expanding) Circle is from internal sources (Sridhar & Sridhar, 1986). No need is felt, certainly in many of the Outer Circle countries, for making either American or British English input available to a large majority of learners. Therefore, defining input in terms of external norms and making judgments about acquisitional deficiency is irrelevant and unjustifiable. The entire theoretical conceptualization of data and analysis are challenged by these realities (B. Kachru, 1995c, B. Kachru & Nelson, 1996; Y. Kachru, 1994; S. N. Sridhar, 1994).

As regards the characterization of the features of Indian, Nigerian, or Singaporean varieties as fossilization, that is not applicable to these varieties either. Again, this is justifiable on the basis of the definition of fossilization from Selinker (1992): "[F]ossilization names the real phenomenon of the permanent non-learning of [target language] TL structures, of the cessation of IL learning (in most cases) far from expected TL norms" (p. 225).

In case of the institutionalized varieties, the TL norms are the internal norms. There is no evidence to suggest that educated users of national or regional varieties differ among themselves with regard to their linguistic and communicative competence any more than their counterparts in the Inner Circle do. Individual variation in competence and performance is a universal phenomenon and applies regardless of the context of Inner or Outer Circle.

The arguments with regard to incompleteness are equally irrelevant in the context of institutionalized varieties. The "Bloomfieldian duplicative model of bilingualism, one in which the ideal bilingual has a native-like command of both languages each complete in itself... is naive. Bilingualism, typically, does not duplicate L1 competence; it complements it... a bilingual acquires as much competence in the two or more languages as is needed and... all of the languages together serve the full range of communicative needs" (pp. 801–802). It is neither necessary nor to be expected that multilinguals would use the same language for all their communicative needs as the monolinguals do (see, e.g., the discussion in Lavendra, 1978, where Italian immigrants in Argentina are shown to use Italian and Spanish as style/register variants). A bilingual person is not two monolingual persons joined at the hips, with two separate nervous systems; he or she is one whole person with two linguistic, and sometimes, two cultural conventions that are sometimes in harmony, sometimes in conflict.

IDEOLOGICAL ISSUES

One major consideration that is left out of the discussion on WEs in the SLA literature is that of sociocultural identity. As Crystal (1985) aptly observes, "[A]ll discussion of standards ceases very quickly to be a linguistic discussion, and becomes instead an issue of social identity" (p. 9). There is enough evidence in sociolinguistic literature to show that users of institutionalized varieties are secure in their identities and do not wish to acquire the identity of either an American or a British speaker of English.

Research on world Englishes has focused attention on theoretical concepts of native speaker, data, and norm. Sociolinguistic and attitudinal factors have been highlighted to reveal the ideological biases in what Pennycook (1994) calls the discipline of linguistics, applied linguistics, and the teaching of the language. Pennycook claims that:

> With the spread of English across the empire, the issue of the standardization of English became not merely one of cultural politics within Great Britain but increasingly one of imperial cultural politics. (p. 110)

That there are now several centers of power that compete in promoting several native models of English and market distinct methodologies cannot be denied. The motivation is clearly the exploitation of the economic, power of English, as is obvious from the following quote: "As the director of a dynamic worldwide chain of English language schools puts it, 'Once we used to send gunboats and diplomats abroad; now we are sending English teachers'" (Phillipson, 1992, p. 8).

The question of standards brings in the related issues of ideology and economic interests. An American or a British model brings in tremendous cultural, economic, and political advantages to the mother country of the target model in the areas of the job market for ELT professionals, publishing industry, and testing business.

It is interesting to note that the entire notion of a standard language is a relatively recent phenomenon in the history of the English language (McArthur, 1998).[4] The term "standard" was first used for the flag of the English monarch and later transferred to weights and measures and the royal assets. Much later, in the 18th century, it came to be associated with literature and language (McArthur, 1998, p. 161). Still later, when British colonialism spread to different parts of the world, under the influence of the Roman tradition laid down by Cicero for Latin, the "foreign usage" was accorded the least quality and prestige.

Researchers in WEs examine the issue of standard English from the perspectives of linguistics, education, sociolinguistics, critical theory, and ideology (Bhatt, 2001; B. Kachru, 1986a; Pakir, 2001). Ultimately, their concern is with sociolinguistic realities that the learners and teachers of English confront in the various global contexts of the ELT trade.

Having stated the research concerns of the field of World Englishes, let me now very briefly outline the research concerns of investigators of SLA before pointing out the relevance of the former area of studies to the latter.

AIMS AND FOCUS OF SLA RESEARCH

There is widespread consensus among scholars that SLA emerged as a distinct field of research in the late 1950s to early 1960s (e.g., Larsen-Freeman & Long, 1991; Mitchell & Myles, 1998; Ritchie & T. Bhatia, 1996). There is also a high level of agreement that the following sets of questions have attracted the most attention of researchers in this area:

- Is it possible to acquire an additional language in the same sense as one acquires a first language? If yes, are the two processes similar? If not, what is the difference between acquisition and learning?
- Is there a critical or sensitive period for additional language acquisition as there seems to be for first language acquisition?
- What is the explanation for the fact that adults have more difficulty in acquiring additional languages than children have?
- What motivates people to acquire additional languages? Is the motivation primarily integrative or is it instrumental? Is there a difference between the end results of the process of language acquisition depending on the nature of motivation?
- What is the role of instruction (i.e., language teaching) in the acquisition of an additional language?
- What sociocultural factors, if any, are relevant in studying learning/acquisition of additional languages?

From an examination of the literature of the field it is clear that all the approaches adopted to study the phenomena of SLA so far have one thing in common: The perspective adopted to view the acquiring of an additional language is that of an individual attempting to do so. Whether one labels it "learning" or "acquiring" an additional language (Krashen, 1981, 1985), it is an individual accomplishment and what is under focus is the cognitive, psychological, and institutional status of an individual. That is, the spotlight is on what mental capabilities are involved, what psychological factors play a role in the learning or acquisition, and whether the target language is learnt in an instructional setting or acquired through social interaction with its natural populations. Generalizations are presented in terms identical to individual language acquisition rather than taking into account the communicative needs of the community in using the additional language within its social and cultural context. This is as true of the morpheme acquisition studies (e.g., Bailey, Madden, & Krashen, 1974; Dulay & Burt, 1974; Krashen, Butler, Birnbaum, & Robertson, 1978; Larsen-Freeman, 1976), as it is of studies inspired by properties of universal grammar, although the latter have utilized several approaches.

The approaches based on linguistic universals have drawn on theoretical models such as Principles and Parameters (e.g., Flynn, 1987; Flynn & O'Neil, 1988; Marthohardjono, 1993; White, 1989) and Minimalist Programs (e.g., Archibald, 2000; T. Bhatia & Ritchie, 1996; Herschensohn, 2000). Models that exploit typological and implicational universals have utilized the notion of Accessibility Hierarchy (Keenan & Comrie, 1977), and the notion of markedness resulting from accessibility hierarchy (e.g., Eckman, Bell, & Nelson, 1988; Rutherford, 1984). These models, naturally, approach language acquisition from the perspective of the I-grammar, an abstraction that represents the linguistic competence of an idealized native speaker–hearer (Chomsky, 1986).

There are studies that claim to be based on sociolinguistic model(s) of second language acquisition (e.g., Preston, 1989); however, the individualistic orientation of learning/acquisition is maintained in these studies. Even studies that claim to take into account notions from pragmatics and communicative competence exhibit the same characteristics (see, e.g., discussions of interlanguage pragmatics in Blum-Kulka, House, & Kasper, 1989; Kasper & Blum-Kulka, 1993). Although research in pragmatics is based on speaker intentions, research on second or foreign language pragmatics neglects speaker intentions and analyzes second language speaker utterances solely from the perspective of the hearer, who is presumed to be a native speaker of the language under focus. This leads to notions of "pragmatic failure," which has no theoretical sanction if viewed from the perspective of speaker intentions. According to the Gricean cooperative principles (Grice, 1975), speakers and hearers are assumed not to intend misleading each other, unless they intentionally violate the maxims. It is hardly the case that in a majority of the contexts the users of a second or foreign language in communicating their intentions are deliberately misleading their interlocutors.

There is no recognition of the fact in SLA research that additional languages are learnt/acquired in bilingual and multilingual contexts. The uses and functions of the additional language are determined by the needs of the community, that is, the competence in the target language that a multilingual acquires in such contexts is largely a function of the niche the additional language occupies in the linguistic repertoire of the community. An almost total disregard of this fact has resulted in the neglect of a variety of issues that need to be raised in the context of the learning or acquisition of languages of wider communication, especially English. These are precisely the questions that research in world Englishes raises and attempts to answer.

One major difference between WEs and classical SLA perspectives is that unlike research in WEs, which is informed by research findings in a variety of fields, SLA research so far, by and large, has neglected to incorporate in any serious sense the insights of ethnography of communication, literacy studies, multilingualism, and, of course, research on WEs (see, however, Brisk, 2000 and Pavlenko, 2001). It is not the case that there is a lack of awareness of multilingualism, issues of identity, and other issues in the field of language education in general (see, e.g., Grosjean, 1982; Hakuta, 1986; Mohan, Leung, & Davison, 2001; Ogulnick, 2000). The theorizing in SLA, however, has not transcended the bounds of ideologically entrenched bias that has been pointed out in WE literature (B. Kachru, 1997a; Y. Kachru, 1994; Sridhar, 1992, 1994; Sridhar & Sridhar, 1986).

RELEVANCE OF WEs TO SLA

Theoretically, research in SLA could benefit from reevaluating the usefulness of the concepts of native speaker, linguistic competence, transfer, interlanguage, and fossilization in the context of acquisition of additional languages. The pronounced monolingual bias in SLA research has so far excluded a large population of multilingual speakers of languages from playing any role in such research. As Pennycook (1994) observes:

> [T]hought on linguistics from Saussure through to Chomsky and beyond has taken monolingualism to be the norm, a view clearly rooted far more in the language myths of Europe than in the multilingual contexts in which most people live. (p. 121)

Current paradigms of research are hardly conducive to producing scientific knowledge of SLA constrained as they are by the "language myths of Europe." They inhibit generation of alternative perspectives on SLA that multilingual contexts provide (Y. Kachru, 1994). To take just one example, many languages of wider communication (LWC), including English (in the Outer Circle), modern standard Hindi (in India), and Swahili (in East Africa) are used essentially by populations who are almost exclusively multilinguals.[5] SLA theories at this point have hardly anything relevant to say about the acquisition of these LWCs (Y. Kachru, 1996b), because they have a large number of speakers but no well-defined body of "ideal native speakers." The question naturally arises as to how we can afford to ignore such a widespread phenomenon and still claim to formulate "universal" theories.

Claims of universalism in SLA theories at this point, therefore, are meaningless. It is a greater pity because a wealth of data is available in Outer and Expanding Circle Englishes for the unbiased researchers to formulate adequate theories of SLA. As Sridhar (1994) observes, "[w]hat we need is a more functionally oriented and culturally authentic theory, one that is true to the ecology of multilingualism and views the multilingual's linguistic repertoire as a unified, complex, coherent, interconnected, interdependent, organic ecosystem, not unlike a tropical rain forest" (p. 803). As B. Kachru (1990) points out, world Englishes provide the most extensive "laboratory" to date for applied linguistic and sociolinguistic research. Observation and analyses in this laboratory could bring important SLA concepts and claims into focus and also bring serious gaps to light.

LEARNING AND TEACHING OF WORLD ENGLISHES

In any context of language learning and teaching, the issue of what to learn or to teach is bound to rise. In the case of ELT, the debate in recent decades has been about which English to aim for. For a majority of ELT experts in the Inner Circle as well as in some members of Outer and Expanding Circle the competing standards are still British or American English. Other members of the Outer Circle, however, have started challenging the exocentric norms and rethinking the question of standards (see Bamgboṣe, 1992; Gill & Pakir, 1999; B. Kachru, 1985, 1991; Pakir, 1991b, 1997).

The observations relevant to the debate are the following. Contrary to the myth that people in China or India or Japan or Nigeria learn English to interact with users of English from the Inner Circle, English is basically used by people of Outer and Expanding Circle interacting with each other within or outside their respective Circle. In an overwhelming majority of contexts, no one from Inner Circle is either involved or even relevant.

The fear that development of multiple endocentric norms would result in a Tower of Babel is also unfounded. The American, Australian, British, Canadian, and New Zealand norms differ significantly in some respects, yet, the observed and documented differences present no barrier to mutual interaction.

In recent years the trend in intellectual fields related to language study has been toward a shift from communicator to message to receiver to context (Dissanayake, 1997; Pakir, 1997). Pluricentric languages such as Chinese, English, French, and Spanish are likely to give rise to different norms in different geographical regions (Clyne, 1992). The sociolinguistic profile of WEs suggests that just as the Inner Circle shows a range of variation in its regional and social dialects, so do the Outer and Expanding Circles. And these varieties have functions within their sociocultural contexts. Therefore, it is neither possible nor desirable to impose any rigid linguistic norm on the entire world. Pakir (1997) describes the situation in Singapore; similar phenomena can be and have been documented for South Asia, Africa, and other parts of the English-using world (e.g., Bamiro, 1991; B. Kachru 1986a; Owolabi, 1995).

The question naturally arises: If each region using English for its purposes develops its own variety of English, how can there be any mutual intelligibility among them? Research has shown that no particular variety is in a privileged position as far as mutual intelligibility is concerned. The more varieties one is exposed to, the more one learns how to accommodate the differences in accent, lexicogrammar, and discoursal strategies (Smith, 1992). And it is becoming easier to get acquainted with more and more varieties of English through the media as the new century advances. The resources of Internet and cable news are examples of two channels through which one can get exposure to almost all varieties of English.

Research studies in the fields of grammatical description (e.g., Baumgardner, 1993, 1996b; Bautista, 1997; Cheshire, 1991; B. Kachru, 1983; Lowenberg, 1984; Platt & Weber, 1979; Rahman, 1990; Simo-Bobda, 1994, among others) are documenting the phonological lexical, and grammatical features of world Englishes. Dictionary-making has woken up to the usefulness of documenting the immense impact of language contact on the lexicon of English, and there are several attempts at incorporating items from different regional Englishes into the mainstream dictionaries of Inner Circle varieties (*Encarta World English Dictionary*, 1999, had consultants for East Africa, Hong Kong, Hawaii, Malaysia-Singapore, South Africa, South Asia, U.K. Black English, and U.S. African American English; *The Macquarie Dictionary*, 1997, has lexical items from Southeast Asian Englishes, for example, Malaysia, Singapore, and The Philippines). Dictionaries and partial lexicons of different World Englishes are also being compiled and published for wider dissemination (e.g., Allison, 1996; Baumgardner, 1996a; Butler, 1997; Hawkins, 1984; B. Kachru, 1973, 1975; Lewis, 1991; Muthiah, 1991; Pakir, 1992; Rao, 1954, among others).

The international corpus of English (ICE) project, initiated in late 1980s (Greenbaum, 1990, 1991; Greenbaum & Nelson, 1996) will, it is projected, result in several descriptive studies of World Englishes on the basis of corpora gathered in eighteen different countries from the three Circles (Nelson, 2004).

Studies on discourse conventions—spoken as well as written—are yielding valuable insights into how English is used as a medium of communicating different sociocultural practices (J. Bhatia, 1992; D'souza, 1988; Gumperz, 1982; Y. Kachru, 1987, 1991, 1993, 1995a, 1995b, 1996a, 1997a, 1998a, 1999, 2001a, 2001b, 2001c, 2003; Nwoye, 1992; Valentine, 1988, 1991).

Finally, English teachers are looking at literary works created in African, Indian, Singaporean, and other varieties for making participants in their classes aware of the cultural meanings of World Englishes (Courtright, 2001; B. Kachru, 1986b; Tawake, 1993, 1994).

The survey above and studies such as B. Kachru (1997b) suggest that there are enough resources for imaginative use in the teaching and learning of world Englishes. For instance, Hannam University and Open Cyber University in Korea have introduced and are developing the Internet as a resource for teaching WEs to Korean learners of English (Jung & Min, 2002; Shim, 2002). Both sets of teachers are collecting materials from the websites of all the three Circles of English and preparing appropriate units for language teaching based on these materials.

There is, however, a great deal of work to be done before all those involved in ELT worldwide feel comfortable with the paradigm shift that teaching and learning WEs signals. Applied linguistics and ELT professionals have yet to take a principled stand and prepare themselves to incorporate the world Englishes perspective into their academic practices. These then will have an effect on the education policymakers, and educational authorities will then be able to adopt an appropriate stance toward the teaching and learning of English.

One of the key areas to bring about a change in the current practices of ELT profession is that of EL teacher training. Almost no teacher training program in the Inner

Circle at this point has a component of making trainees aware of world varieties of English (B. Kachru, 1997a; Vavrus, 1991). A pilot project started at Portland State University throws interesting light on what the consequences are when a serious component of world Englishes is introduced in a certificate or master's program of training teachers in English as a second language or TESOL (Brown & Peterson, 1997). The aim of the project was to see how the prior knowledge structures of trainees in such programs undergo modification as a result of their introduction to the key areas of research on world Englishes.

First, a list of concepts was developed on the basis of existing research on WEs. These fell into four sets: theoretical, pedagogical, ideological (status of varieties), and descriptive (description of grammars of varieties). The 27 concepts that were developed were used as labels and printed out on 2 × 3 cards. These consisted of labels such as American English, British English, Indian English, Nigerian English, German English, Japanese English, etc., categories such as English as a Second Language (ESL), English as a Foreign Language (EFL), concepts such as monolingual, bilingual, interlanguage, nativization, standard English, and others, and ideological positions such as the native speakers being the best teachers of English in any context. Trainees enrolled in a three-quarter, nine-credit course were asked to sort out the cards before and after taking two types of courses: one that exposed them to a 4-hour unit on issues in world Englishes and another that was a quarter-long, three-credit course. All of them had completed a required methodology sequence with a 4-hour unit of terminology and issues in world Englishes.

For each administration of the sorting task, the resulting sorts were transformed into 27 × 27 matrices representing all 351 possible pairings of labels. Each cell of the matrices represented a pairing of two concepts and the values in the cells indicated how many students placed any two labels together during a sorting task. The similarities of co-occurrences were treated as similarity measures. Four analytical procedures were used to compare the results of the sorting tasks (Brown & Peterson, 1997, p. 36).

The findings of the project made it obvious that before and after the 4-hour exposure to world Englishes concepts, the students had a very simplistic conceptual structure of the phenomenon. The future teachers of English ready for the world market for TESOL jobs categorized the labels into two groups: one containing examples of varieties of English and the other containing theoretical, pedagogical, and ideological concepts. The two groups contained two subgroups each. The varieties cluster showed clear native/non-native grouping, that is, it distinguished the three traditionally recognized varieties—American, Australian, and British—from all others, for example, Brazilian, German, Indian, Japanese, Nigerian, and Singaporean. The concepts clusters showed, on the one hand, the grouping of norms, monolingualism, preference for native speaker teachers,[6] nativization misidentified with native speakers or the process of making someone nativelike, and, on the other hand, grouping of ESL/EFL, bilingualism, interlanguage, creativity, and liberation, signaling a positive attitude toward bilingualism in English.

After the quarter long, three-credit course, however, the sortings show a much richer conceptual structure. The trainees show awareness of the three Circles of English and their three different historical and sociocultural contexts of development. Within each Circle they are able to sort corresponding theoretical, pedagogical, and ideological concepts, for example, English as a native language is associated with the Inner Circle, ESL with the Outer Circle, and EFL with the Expanding Circle. Standard English, restrictive, monolingual, preference for native speakers as teachers are all associated with the Inner Circle, which is the prevalent ideology of the ELT profession. On the other hand, bilingual, liberating, creativity, differences (from Inner Circle Englishes) and no preference for native speaker teachers are associated with Outer and Expanding Circle varieties, which corresponds to the stance of researchers in WEs.

The other noticeable fact is the nature of the conceptual structures. The Multi-Step Graphic Scaling diagrams (Brown & Peterson, 1997, pp. 40–41) show the simplistic organization of knowledge structures in trainees exposed to just 4 hours of WEs. In contrast, the conceptual structure of trainees with exposure to a three-credit course shows a much richer network of interlinked concepts. That is to say, the trainees in the TESOL program at the end of their course gained much more awareness of the sociolinguistic realities of the spread of English and the theoretical, pedagogical, and ideological issues raised by the global diffusion of the language.

Many of the trainees come to the TESOL programs from language and literature departments, as TESOL is not generally an undergraduate program. More language and literature departments, therefore, have to incorporate WE literatures (or various Spanish, French, Portuguese, or Chinese literatures, as the case may be) in their undergraduate curricula to sensitize students to the issues raised by LWCs. Universities in India have started including WE literatures in their undergraduate English literature curricula, and several universities in the United States have made options available in "ethnic" literatures (e.g., African American, African, Asian American, Indian, or South Asian). Awareness of differences resolves many issues of prejudice and resistance to variety and myths about standards and "ownership" of the language (Widdowson, 1994).

CONCLUSION

In conclusion, the WE research community is anticipating a paradigm shift in the teaching and learning of English in the Inner, Outer, and Expanding Circles that will bridge the gap between sociolinguistic reality and prevailing myths about English, and the "native" speakers and "other" users of English. The emphasis is on inclusiveness of the global fellowship of the English-using populations. The aim is to make users of English aware of and responsive to the following (see also B. Kachru 1997b):

1. Sociolinguistic profile of the English users in largely monolingual and complex multilingual communities.
2. Variation within varieties and their societal function.
3. Attitudinally neutral investigation of variety-specific characteristics of regional Englishes (not only of less well-studied Inner Circle varieties such as Australian, Canadian, and New Zealand Englishes, but also those of Outer and Expanding Circles.
4. Similar investigation of stylistic, discoursal, and genre-related differences and innovations in specific sociocultural contexts.
5. In-depth study of literary creativity and canons of English literatures.
6. Attitudes and experiences that facilitate intelligibility across varieties.
7. Awareness of factors that promote the teaching and learning of English in various contexts instead of promoting belief in the "myths" of "native speaker," "natural [to the Inner Circle] input," "authentic [from the Inner Circle] materials for teaching," "pragmatic failure," and others (B. Kachru, 1995c).

Learning and teaching world Englishes does not mean learning and teaching of each regional variety to everyone in the Inner Circle classrooms or everyone learning English in Brazil, China, Japan, Saudi Arabia, or Southern Africa. It means making learners aware of the rich variation that exists in English around the world at an appropriate point in their language education in all the three Circles and giving them the tools to educate themselves further about using their English for effective communication across varieties. The burden of communication, when the opportunity arises, is not on just the users of Outer and Expanding Circle varieties. It is equally on the speakers of Inner Circle varieties, as success in communication depends on cooperation between interlocutors. The applied linguistics and ELT professions have a responsibility to equip learners of English to meet the challenge of globalization. World Englishes is one of the most effective instruments that could be employed to meet this challenge.

It is encouraging to see the awareness of the complex issues of contexts, cultures, identities, etc. involved in the development of world Englishes in some recent work. This awareness is reflected in studies that deal with descriptions of English as an international language (e.g., Jenkins 2000) and those that emphasize the communicative language teaching methodologies based on the relationship between context and communicative competence in particular social and cultural settings (e.g., Berns, 1990; Savignon, 2002).

NOTES

* I am grateful to my friend and colleague, Cecil Nelson, for reading an earlier draft of this paper and commenting on it, and to Wooseung Lee for checking and rechecking the citations and references in the paper.
1. For a succinct description of the conceptualization of world Englishes, see B. Kachru (1997b). See also Kachru, B. & Smith (1986). For acculturation of English in Asia and Africa, see the references cited in appropriate sections of this paper.
2. *New Statesman* was reacting to an International Conference in English that was held in London, but the call for it had come by the American side of the Atlantic.
3. Many of the agents of the spread of English in the former colonies came from various parts of the British Isles and Western Europe. Many English medium schools were and are still run by Belgian, Dutch, and other missionary organizations all over the world. As Mesthrie (1992) observes, the South African Indian English (SAIE) developed as a distinct variety as a result of several factors, including "the teaching of English by a French-speaking missionary to Tamil-speaking children via the medium of a Zulu-based pidgin" (p. 29).
4. In the Indian tradition, there was a distinction made between *sanskrit* ("cultured, refined") and *prakrit* ("natural, unsophisticated") forms of language beginning in the pre-Buddhist times (i.e., prior to 500 BC). In the Greek and Roman tradition (McArthur, 1998), Greek spoken by the upper class in Attica, including Athens, was the language of oratory and, thus, the focus of teaching oratory; the common dialects of the non-Attic populations was not highly valued. Cicero made a distinction among city usage, country usage, and foreign usage, where the first had the most quality and prestige, the second less so, and the last one was "to be deplored" (McArthur, 1998, p. 163).
5. In many parts of the Chinese-speaking world, a majority of the population speaks one of the dialects (e.g., Cantonese, Hokkien, Taiwanese) but learns and functions in Mandarin Chinese. In the Hindi belt of India, people speak one of the dialects of the Hindi region, for example, Awadhi, Bhojpuri, Braj, Garhwali, Kumauni, Magahi, etc., at home and in their intimate domains, but are educated and function in the larger context in modern standard Hindi. These so-called dialects of the Hindi area are mutually unintelligible and have very different grammars from each other and from Standard Hindi.
6. The belief, contrary to reality on the ground, that native speakers are the best teachers of ESL and EFL, still persists in the TESOL profession, and prevailed in Singapore and most Anglophone Outer Circle regions until very recently. China, Japan, Korea, and other Expanding Circle regions continue to subscribe to this view although a majority of English teachers in these countries are local users of English. See Canagarajah (1999) for a detailed discussion of this attitude in the ELT profession.

REFERENCES

Allison, R. (Ed.). (1996). *Dictionary of Caribbean English usage.* Oxford, UK: Oxford University Press.

Archibald, J. (Ed.). (2000). *Second language acquisition and linguistic theory.* Malden, MA: Blackwell.

Baik, M. J. (2001). Aspects of Englishization of Korean discourse. In E. Thumboo (Ed.), *The three circles of English* (pp. 181–193). Singapore: National University of Singapore, Unipress.

Bailey, N., Madden, C., & Krashen, S. (1974). Is there a "natural sequence" in adult second language acquisition? *Language Learning, 21,* 235–243.

Bamgbose, A. (1992). Standard Nigerian English: Issues of identification. In B. Kachru (Ed.), *The other tongue: English across cultures* (pp. 148–161). 2nd ed. Urbana: University of Illinois Press.

Bamgbose, A., Banjo, A., & Thomas, A. (1995). *New Englishes: A West African perspective.* Ibadan: Masuro.

Bamiro, E. O. (1991). Nigerian Englishes in Nigerian English literature. *World Englishes, 10*(1), 7–17.

Baumgardner, R. J. (1993). *The English language in Pakistan.* Karachi: Oxford University Press.

Baumgardner, R. J. (1996). Innovations in Pakistani English political lexis. In Baumgardner, 1996. 175–188.

Baumgardner, R. J. (1996a). Innovations in Pakistani English political lexis. In R. J. Baumgardner (Ed.), South Asian English: Structure, use and users (pp. 175–188). Urbana: University of Illinois Press.

Baumgardner, R. J. (Ed.). (1996b). *South Asian English: Structure, use and users*. Urbana: University of Illinois Press.

Bautista, M. L. S. (1990). Tagalog-English code-switching revisited. *Philippine Journal of Linguistics, 21*(2), 15–29.

Bautista, M. L. S. (1991). Code-switching studies in the Philippines. *International Journal of the Sociology of Language, 88*, 19–32.

Bautista, M. L. S. (Ed.). (1997). *English Is an Asian Language: The Philippine Context*. Sydney, Australia: Macquarie Library Pvt. Ltd. [First printing 1996]

Berns, M. (1990). *Contexts of competence: Social and cultural considerations in communicative language teaching*. New York: Plenum Press.

Bhatia, T. K. (1992). Discourse functions and pragmatics of mixing: advertising across cultures. *World Englishes 11*, 2/3, 195–215.

Bhatia, T. K., & Ritchie, W. C. (Eds.). (1989). *Code-mixing: English across languages* [Special issue]. *World Englishes, 8*(3).

Bhatia, T. K., & Ritchie, W. C. (1996). Bilingual language mixing, universal grammar, and second language acquisition. In W. C. Ritchie, & T. K. Bhatia (Eds.), *Handbook of second language acquistion* (pp. 627–688). New York: Academic Press.

Bhatia, V. K. (1997). (Guest Ed.) *Genre analysis and world Englishes*. Special issue of *World Englishes 16*(3).

Bhatt, R. M. (Guest Ed.). (1996). Symposium on Constraints on code-switching. *World Englishes, 15*(3).

Bhatt, R. M. (2001). Language economy, standardization, and world Englishes. In E. Thumboo (Ed.), *The three Circles of English* (pp. 401–422). Singapore: National University of Singapore, Unipress.

Blum-Kulka, Shoshana, House, J., & Kasper, G. (Eds.). (1989). *Cross-cultural Pragmatics: Requests and Apologies*. Norwood, New Jersey: Ablex.

Bokamba, E. (1992). The Africanization of English. In B. Kachru (Ed.), *The other tongue: English across cultures* (pp. 125–147). Urbana: University of Illinois Press.

Brisk, M. (2000). *Literacy and bilingualism: A handbook for all teachers*. Mahwah, NJ: Lawrence Erlbaum Associates.

Brown, K. (1993). World Englishes in TESOL programs: An infusion model of curricular innovation. *World Englishes, 12*(1), 59–73.

Brown, K. (2001). World Englishes and the classroom: Research and practice agendas for 2000. In E. Thumboo (Ed.), *The three circles of English* (pp. 371–382). Singapore: National University of Singapore, Unipress.

Brown, K., & Peterson, J. (1997). Exploring conceptual frameworks: Framing a world Englishes paradigm. In L. Smith and M. Forman (Eds.), 32–47. *World Englishes* 2000. Honolulu, HI: University of Hawaii Press.

Butler, S. (1997). "World English in the Asian context: Why a dictionary is important," in Smith and Forman (eds.), 1997. 90–125.

Canagarajah, A. S. (1999). Resisting linguistic imperialism in English teaching. Oxford, UK: Oxford University Press.

Cheshire, J. (Ed.). (1991). *English around the World: Sociolinguistic perspectives*. Cambridge, UK: Cambridge University Press.

Chomsky, N. (1986). *The knowledge of language: Its nature, origin and use*. New York: Praeger.

Clyne, M. (1992). *Pluricentric languages: Differing norms in different nations*. Berlin: Mouton de Gruyter.

Courtright, M. S. (2001). *Intelligibility and context in reader responses to contact literary texts*. Unpublished doctoral dissertation. University of Illinois at Urbana-Champaign.

Crystal, D. (1985). Comment on Quirk (1985). In R. Quirk, & H. Widdowson (Eds.), *English in the world: Teaching and learning the language and literatures* (pp. 9–10). Cambridge, UK: Cambridge University Press.

Davidson, F. (1994). The interlanguage metaphor and language assessment. *World Englishes, 13*(3), 377–386.

Dissanayake, W. (1985). Towards a decolonized English: South Asian creativity in fiction. *World Englishes, 4*(2), 233–242.

Dissanayake, W. (1990). Self and modernism in Sri Lankan poetry in English. *World Englishes, 9*(2), 225–236.

Dissanayake, W. (1997). Cultural studies and world Englishes: some topics for further exploration. In Smith and Forman 1997. 126–145.

Dulay, H., & Burt, M. (1974). Natural sequence in child second language acquisition. *Language Learning, 24*, 37–53.

D'souza, J. (1988). Interactional strategies in South Asian languages: Their implications for teaching English internationally. *World Englishes, 7*(2), 159–171.

Eckman, F., Bell, L., & Nelson D. (Eds.). (1988). *Universals of second language acquisition*. Rowley, MA: Newbury.

Encarta World English Dictionary. (1999). New York: St. Martin Press.

Flynn, S. (1987). *A parameter-setting model of second language acquisition*. Dordrecht, The Netherlands: Reidel.

Flynn, S., & O'Neil, W. (Eds.). (1988). *Linguistic theory in second language acquisition*. Dordrecht, The Netherlands: Kluwer.

Frenck, S., & Min, S. (2001). Culture, reader and textual intelligibility. In E. Thumboo (Ed.), *The three Circles of English* (pp. 19–34). Singapore: National University of Singapore, Unipress.

Gill, S. K., & Pakir, A. (Eds.). (1999). Symposium on standards, codification and World Englishes. *World Englishes, 18*(2), 159–274.

Greenbaum, S. (1990). Standard English and the international corpus of English. *World Englishes, 9*(1), 79–83.

Greenbaum, S. (1991). ICE: The international corpus of English. *English Today, 28*(7.4), 3–7.

Greenbaum, S., & Nelson. G. (Guest Eds.). (1996). *Studies on international corpus of English.* [Special issues] *World Englishes, 15*(1).

Grice, H. P. (1975). Logic and conversation. In P. Cole and J. L. Morgan, (Eds.), *Syntax and semantics 7: Speech acts* (pp. 41–58). New York: Academic Press.

Grosjean, F. (1982). *Life with two languages: An introduction to bilingualism.* Cambridge, MA: Harvard University Press.

Gumperz, J. J. (Ed.). (1982). *Language and social identity.* Cambridge, UK: Cambridge University Press.

Hakuta, K. (1986). *Mirror of language: The debate on bilingualism.* New York: Basic Books.

Hawkins, R. E. (1984). *Common Indian words in English.* Delhi, India: Oxford University Press.

Herschensohn, J. R. (2000). *The second time around: Minimalism and L2 acquisition.* Amsterdam: Benjamins.

Hsu, Jia-Ling (1994a). Language change in Modern Chinese: Some aspects of Englishization. *World Englishes 13*(2), 167–184.

Hsu, Jia-Ling (1994b). *Language contact and convergence: Englishization of Mandarin Chinese in Taiwan.* Ph.D. Dissertation, University of Illinois at Urbana-Champaign, Urbana, Illinois.

Hsu, Jia-Ling (2001). The sources, adapted functions, and the public's subjective evaluation of the Englishization of Mandarin Chinese in Taiwan. In Thumboo, 2001. 241–256.

Jenkins, J. (2000). *World Englishes: A resource book for students.* London: Routledge.

Jung, K., & Sujung M. (2002). Web-based world Englishes learning program. Paper presented at the Ninth Annual Meeting of the International Association of World Englishes., 2002, at the University of Illinois at Urbana-Champaign, October 18–20, 2002.

Jussawalla, F., & Dasenbrock, R. W. (1992). *Interviews with writers of the post-colonial world.* Jackson: University of Mississippi Press.

Kachru, B. B. (1973). Toward a lexicon of Indian English. In B. B. Kachru, R. B. Lees, S. Saporta, A. Pietrangeli, & Y. Malkiel, (Eds.). *Issues in linguistics: Papers in honor of Henry and Renee Kahane* (pp. 352–376). Urbana: University of Illinois Press.

Kachru, B. B. (1975). The New Englishes and old dictionaries: Directions in lexicographical research on non-native varieties of English. In L. Zgusta (Ed.), *Theory and method in lexicography* (pp. 71–101). Chapel Hill, NC: Hornbeam Press. [Also in Kachru 1982].

Kachru, B. B. (1978). Code-mixing as a communicative strategy in India. In J. E. Alatis (Ed.), *International dimensions of bilingual education.* (pp. 107–124). Washington, DC: Georgetown University Press. [Reproduced in Richards, Jack C. (Ed.), *New Varieties of English: Issues and Approaches.* Singapore: Regional Language Center].

Kachru, B. B. (1979). The Englishization of Hindi: Language rivalry and language change. In I. Rauch, and G. F. Carr (Eds.), *Linguistic method: Papers in honor of H. penzl* (pp. 199–211). The Hague, The Netherlands: Mouton.

Kachru, B. B. (1983). *The Indianization of English: The English language in India.* Delhi, India: Oxford University Press.

Kachru, B. B. (1985). "Standards, Codification and Sociolinguistic Realism: The English Language in the Outer Circle." In Quirk, Randolph and Widdowson, Henry (Ed.), *English in the World, Teaching and Learning the Language and Literatures.* 11–30. Cambridge: Cambridge University Press.

Kachru, B. B. (1986a). *The alchemy of English: The spread, functions and models of non-native Englishes.* Oxford: Pergamon.

Kachru, B. B. (1986b). Nonnative literatures in English as a resource for language teaching. In C. J. Brumfit, & R. A. Carter (Eds.), *Literature and language teaching* (pp. 140–149). Oxford UK: Oxford University Press.

Kachru, B. B. (1990). "World Englishes and Applied Linguistics." *Studies in the Linguistic Sciences 19*:(1), 127–152. Also published in *World Englishes 9*(1); In Halliday, M. A. K., et al. (Eds.). *Learning, Keeping and Using Language.* Amsterdam: John Benjamin, 1990. 203–229 and in *South Asian Language Review 1*(1), 1–32.

Kachru, B. B. (1991). Liberation linguistics and the quirk concern. In *Proceedings of the 24th Mid-America Linguistic Conference.* Also in *English Today, 7*(1), 1–13, Cambridge University Press. Reprinted in Tickoo, M. L. (Eds.), *Languages and Standards: Issues, Attitudes, Case Studies.* Singapore: SEAMEO Regional Language Center. 206–226.

Kachru, B. B. (Ed.). (1992a). *The other tongue: English across cultures* (2nd ed.). Urbana: University of Illinois Press.

Kachru, B. B. (1992b). Meaning in deviation: Toward understanding non-native literary texts. In B. Kachru (Ed.), *The other tongue: English across cultures* (pp. 301–326). Urbana: University of Illinois Press.

Kachru, B. B. (1992c). The second Diaspora of English. In T. W. Machan & S. T. Scott (Eds.), *English in its social contexts: Essays in historical sociolinguistics* (pp. 230–252). New York: Oxford University Press.

Kachru, B. B. (1995a). The speaking tree: A medium of plural canons. In J. A. Alatis (Ed.), *Educational linguistics, crosscultural communication, and global interdependence* (pp. 6–22). Georgetown University Roundtable on Language and Linguistics, 1994. Washington, DC: Georgetown University Press.

Kachru, B. B. (1995b). Tanscultural creativity in world Englishes and literary canons. In G. Cook, & B. Seidlhofer (Eds.), *Principle and practice in applied linguistics*, (pp. 271–287). Oxford, UK: Oxford University Press.

Kachru, B. B. (1995c). Teaching world Englishes without myths. In S. K. Gill, (Eds.), *INTELEC '94: International English language education conference, national and international challenges and responses* (pp. 1–19). Bangi, Malaysia: Pusat Bahasa Universiti.

Kachru, B. B. (1996). The paradigms of marginality. *World Englishes, 15*(3), 241–255.

Kachru, B. B. (1997a). Past-imperfect: The other side of English in Asia. In L. E. Smith, & M. Forman (Eds.), *World English, 2000* (pp. 68–89). Honolulu: University of Hawaii Press.

Kachru, B. B. (1997b). World Englishes 2000: Resources for research and teaching. In L. E. Smith, & M. Forman (Eds.), *World Englishes 2000* (pp. 48–67). Honolulu, HI: University of Hawaii Press.

Kachru, B. B. (2001). World Englishes and culture wars. In C. K. Tong, A. Pakir, K. C. Ban, & R. B. H. Goh (Eds.), *Ariels: Departures & returns—Essays for Edwin Thumboo* (pp. 391–414). Singapore: Oxford University Press.

Kachru, B. B., & Larry E. Smith (eds.) (1986). *The power of English: Cross-cultural dimensions of literature and media*. Special issue of *World Englishes 5*, 2–3.

Kachru, B. B., & Nelson, C. (1996). World Englishes. In S. L. McKay, & N. H. Hornberger (Eds.), *Sociolinguistics and language teaching* (pp.). Cambridge, UK: Cambridge University Press.

Kachru, Y. (1985a). Discourse analysis, non-native Englishes and second language acquisition research. *World Englishes, 4*(2), 223–232.

Kachru, Y. (1985b). Discourse strategies, pragmatics and ESL: Where are we going? *RELC Journal, 16*(2), 1–30.

Kachru, Y. (1987). Cross-cultural texts, discourse strategies and discourse interpretation. In L. E. Smith (Ed.), *Discourse across cultures: Strategies in world englishes* (pp. 87–100). London: Prentice-Hall International.

Kachru, Y. (Guest Ed.). (1991). *Symposium on speech acts in world Englishes. World Englishes, 10*(3), 299–306.

Kachru, Y. (1993). Social meaning and creativity in Indian English. In J. E. Alatis (Ed.), *Language, communication and social meaning* (pp. 378–387). Georgetown University Roundtable on Languages and Linguistics, 1992. Washington, DC: Georgetown University Press.

Kachru, Y. (1994). Monolingual bias in SLA research. *TESOL Quarterly, 28*(4), 795–800.

Kachru, Y. (1995a). Cultural meaning and rhetorical styles: Toward a framework for contrastive rhetoric. In B. Seidlhofer, & G. Cook (Eds.), *Principles and practice in applied linguistics: Studies in honor of Henry G. Widdowson* (pp. 171–184). Oxford, UK: Oxford University Press.

Kachru, Y. (1995b). Lexical exponents of cultural contact: Speech act verbs in Hindi-English dictionaries. In B. B. Kahre & H. Kachru (Eds.), *Cultures, ideologies, and the dictionary: Studies in honor of Ladislav Zgusta*, (pp. 261–274). Tuebingen, Germany: Verlag.

Kachru, Y. (1996a). Language and cultural meaning: Expository writing in South Asian English. In R. J. Baumgardner (Ed.), *South Asian English: Structure, use and users* (pp. 127–140). Urbana: University of Illinois Press.

Kachru, Y. (1996b). Culture, variation and languages of wider communication: The paradigm gap., In J. E. Alatis, C. A. Straehle, M. Ronkin, & B. Gallenberger (Eds.), *Linguistics, language acquisition, and language variation: Current trends and future prospects*, (pp. 178–195). Georgetown University Round Table on Languages and Linguistics 1996. Washington, DC: Georgetown University Press.

Kachru, Y. (1997a). Culture and argumentative writing in world Englishes. In L. E. Smith & M. Forman, (Eds.), *World Englishes 2000* (pp. 48–67). Honolulu, HI: University of Hawaii Press.

Kachru, Y. (1997b). Culture, variation and English language education. In S. Cromwell, P. Rule, & T. Sugino, (Eds.), *On JALT 96: Crossing borders* (pp. 199–210). The Proceedings of the JALT 1996 Conference on Language Teaching and Learning. Tokyo.

Kachru, Y. (1998a). Culture and speech acts: Evidence from Indian and Singaporean English. *Studies in the Linguistic Sciences, 28*(1), 79–98.

Kachru, Y. (1998b). Context, creativity, style: Strategies in Raja Rao's novels. In R. L. Hardgrave (Ed.), *Word as mantra: The art of Raja Rao* (pp. 88–107). New Delhi, India: Katha.

Kachru, Y. (1999). Culture, context and writing. In E. Hinkel (Ed.), *Culture in second language teaching and learning* (pp. 75–89). Cambridge, UK: Cambridge University Press.

Kachru, Y. (2001a). Communicative styles in world Englishes. In C. K. Tong, A. Pakir, K. C. Ban, Kah Choon, & R. B. H. Goh (Eds.), *Ariels: Departures and returns—Essays for Edwin Thumboo* (pp. 267–284) Oxford, UK: Oxford University Press.

Kachru, Y. (2001b). Discourse competence in world Englishes. In E. Thumboo (Ed.), *The three circles of english* (pp. 341–355). Singapore: University of Singapore Unipress.

Kachru, Y. (2001c, Winter). World Englishes and rhetoric across cultures. *Asian Englishes: An International Journal of the Sociolinguistics of English in Asia/Pacific*, 54–71.

Kachru, Y. (2003). Conventions of politeness in plural societies. In R. Ahrens, D. Parker, K. Stierstorfer, & K. K. Tom (Eds.), *Anglophone cultures in South-East Asia: Appropriations, continuities, contexts* (pp. 39–53). Heidelberg, Germany: University of Heidelberg Press.

Kamwangamalu, N. (1989). A selected bibliography of studies on code-mixing and code-switching (1970–1988). *World Englishes, 8*(3), 433–440.

Kamwangamalu, N. & Li. C. L. (1991). Mixers and mixing: English across cultures. *World Englishes, 10,* 247–261.

Kasper, G. & Blum-Kulka, S. (Eds.). (1993). *Interlanguage pragmatics.* Oxford University Press.

Keenan, E. & Comrie, B. (1977). Noun phrase accessibility and universal grammar. *Linguistic Inquiry 8,* 63–99.

Krashen, S. (1981). *Second language acquisition and second language learning.* Oxford: Pergamon.

Krashen, S. (1985). *The input hypothesis: Issues and implications.* London: Longman.

Krashen, S., Butler, J., Birnbaum, R., & Robertson, J. (1978). Two studies in language acquisition and language learning. *ITL: Review of Applied Linguistics, 39/40,* 73–92.

Larsen-Freeman, D. (1976). An explanation for the morpheme acquisition order of second language learners. *Language Learning, 26,* 125–134.

Larsen-Freeman, D., & Long, M. (1991). *An introduction to second language acquisition research.* London: Longman.

Lavendra, B. R. (1978). The variable component in bilingual performance. In J. E. Alatis (Ed.), *International dimensions of bilingual education* (pp. 391–409). Georgetown University Round Table on Language and Linguistics 1978. Washington, DC: Georgetown University Press.

Lewis, I. (1991). *Sahibs, Nabobs and Boxwallahs: A dictionary of the words of Anglo-India.* Delhi, India: Oxford University Press.

Llamazon, T. (1969). *Standard Filipino English.* Manila, The Philippines: Ateneo University Press.

Lowenberg, P. H. (1986). Non-native varieties of English: Nativization, norms, and implications. *Studies in Second Language Acquisition, 8*(1), 1–18.

Lowenberg, P. H. (1991). Variation in Malaysian English: The pragmatics of languages in contact. In J. Cheshire (Ed.), *English around the world: Sociolinguistic perspectives* (pp. 364–375). Cambridge, UK: Cambridge University Press.

Lowenberg, P. H. (1992). Teaching English as a world language: Issues in assessing non-native proficiency. In B. Kachru (Ed.), *The other tongue: English across cultures* (pp. 108–121). Urbana: University of Illinois Press.

Lowenberg, P. H. (1993). Issues of validity in tests of English as a world language: Whose standards? *World Englishes, 12*(1), 95–106.

Lowenberg, P. H. (2001). Creativity, context and testing. In E. Thumboo (Ed.), *The three circles of English* (pp. 383–400). Singapore: The National University of Singapore, Unipress.

The Macquarie dictionary (3rd ed.). (1997). Sydney, Australia: Macquarie University.

Marthohardjono, G. (1993). *Wh-movement in the acquisition of a second language: A cross-linguistic study of three languages with and without movement.* Unpublished doctoral dissertation, Cornell University, Ithaca, NY.

McArthur, T. (1998). *The English languages.* Cambridge, UK: Cambridge University Press.

McArthur, T. (Ed.). (1992). *The Oxford companion to the English language.* Oxford, UK: Oxford University Press.

Mencken, A. L. (1936). *The American language.* New York: Knopf.

Mesthrie, R. (1992). *English in language shift: The history, structure, and sociolinguistics of South African Indian English.* Cambridge: Cambridge University Press.

Mitchell, R. & Myles, F. (1998). *Second language learning theories.* London: Edward Arnold.

Mohan, B., Leung, C., & Davison, C. (Eds.). (2001). *English as a second language in the mainstream: Teaching, learning, and identity.* New York: Longman.

Muthiah, S. (1991). *Words in Indian English: A reader's guide.* Delhi, India: HarperCollins.

Nelson, C. (1992). My language, your culture, whose communicative competence? In B. Kachru (Ed.), *The other tongue: English across cultures* (pp. 327–339). Urbana: University of Illinois Press.

Nelson, G. (Ed.). (2004). Special issue on International Corpus of English. *World Englishes, 23*(2).

Nwoye, O. G. (1992). Obituary announcements as communicative events in Nigerian English. *World Englishes, 11*(1), 5–27.

Ogulnick, K. L. (Ed.). (2000). *Language crossings: Negotiating the self in a multicultural world.* New York: Teachers College Press, Columbia University.

Owolabi, K. (Ed.). (1995). *Language in Nigeria: Essays in honor of Ayo Bamgbose.* Ibadan: Group Publishers.

Pakir, A. (1991a). The range and depth of English-knowing bilinguals in Singapore. *World Englishes, 10*(2), 167–179.

Pakir, A. (1991b). The status of English and the question of "standard" in Singapore: A sociolinguistic perspective. In M. L. Tickoo (Ed.), *Languages and standards: Issues, attitudes, case studies* (pp. 109–130). Singapore: SEAMEO Regional Language Center.

Pakir, A. (Ed.). (1992). *Words in a cultural context.* Proceedings of the Lexicography Workshop, Singapore: UniPress.

Pakir, A. (1997). Standards and codification for world Englishes. In L. E. Smith & M. Forman, (Eds.). *World Englishes 2000* (pp. 169–181). Honolulu: University of Hawaii Press.

Pakir, A. (2001). Bilingualism in Southeast Asia and the evolution of a new English language ecology. In C. K., Tong, A., Pakir, K. C., Ban, & B. H. K. Goh (Eds.), *Ariels: Departures & returns—Essays for Edwin Thumboo* (pp. 415–429). Singapore: Oxford University Press.

Pandey, A. (2001). Code alteration and Englishization across cultures. In E. Thumboo (Ed.), *The three circles of English* (pp. 277–300). Singapore: National University of Singapore, Unipress.

Pavlenko, A., et al. (Eds.), (2001). *Multilingualism, second language learning, and gender.* New York: Mouton de Gruyter.

Pennycook, A. (1994). *The cultural politics of English as an international language.* London: Longman.

Phillipson, R. (1992). *Linguistic imperialism.* Oxford, UK: Oxford University Press.

Platt, J. & Weber, H. (1979). *English in Singapore and Malaysia,* Kuala Lumpur, Malaysia: Oxford University Press.

Preston, D. (1989). *Sociolinguistics and second language acquisition.* Oxford, UK: Blackwell.

Quirk, R., Greenbaum, S., Leech, G., & Svartvik, J. (1985). *A comprehensive grammar of the English language.* London: Longman.

Rahman, T. (1990). *Pakistani English: The Linguistic Description of a Non-Native Variety of English,* NIPS Monograph Series III. Islamabad: National Institute of Pakistan Studies.

Rao, G. S. (1954). Indian words in English: A study of Indo-British cultural and linguistic relations. Oxford, UK: Clarendon.

Ritchie, W. C. & Bhatia, T. K. (Eds.). (1996). *Handbook of second language acquisition.* New York: Academic Press.

Rutherford, W. (Ed.). (1984). *Typological universals and second language acquisition.* Amsterdam: Benjamins.

Savignon, S. J. (ed.). (2002). *Interpreting communicative language teaching: Contexts and concerns in teacher education.* New Haven, CT: Yale University Press.

Selinker, L. (1969). Language transfer. *General Linguistics, 9*(2), 67–92.

Selinker, L. (1992). *Rediscovering interlanguage.* London: Longman.

Shim, Rosa J. (1994). Englishized Korean: Structure, status and attitudes. *World Englishes 13*(2), 233–244.

Shim, Rosa J. (2002, April 6). The Internet as a resource of materials for teaching English as a world language. Paper presented at the American Association of Applied Linguistics Annual Conference. Salt Lake City, Utah.

Simo-Bobda, A. (1994). *Aspects of Cameroon English phonology.* Berne: Peter Lang.

Smith, L. E. (1992). Spread of English and issues of intelligibility. In B. Kachru (Ed.), *The other tongue: English acress cultures* (pp. 75–90). Urbana: University of Illinois Press.

Smith, L. E. (Ed.). (1987). *Discourse across cultures: Strategies in world Englishes.* London: Prentice-Hall International.

Smith, L. E. & Christopher. E. M. (2001). Why can't they understand me when I speak English so clearly? In E. Thumboo, (Ed.), *The three circles of English* (pp. 91–100). Urbana: University of Illinois Press.

Smith, L. E. & Forman, M. L. (Eds.). (1997). *World Englishes 2000.* Honolulu, HI: University of Hawaii Press.

Smith, L. E. & Rafiqzad. K. (1979). English for cross-cultural communication: The question of intelligibility. *TESOL Quarterly, 13,* 371–380.

Smith, L. E., & Nelson, C. E. (1985). International intelligibility of English: Directions and resources. *World Englishes, 3,* 333–342.

Sridhar, K. K. (1989). *English in Indian bilingualism.* New Delhi, India: Manohar.

Sridhar, K. K. (1991). Speech acts in an indigenized variety: Sociocultural values and language variation. In J. Cheshire (Ed.), *English around the world: Sociolinguistic perspectives* (pp. 308–318). Cambridge, UK: Cambridge University Press.

Sridhar, K. K. & Sridhar, S. N. (1986). Bridging the paradigm gap: Second language acquisition theory and indigenized varieties of English. *World Englishes 5*(1), 3–14.

Sridhar, S. N. (1992). The ecology of bilingual competence: Language interaction in the syntax of indigenized varieties of English. In L. E. Smith, and S. N. Sridhar, (Guest Eds.), *The extended family: English in global multilingualism,* (pp. 141–150). Special Issue.

Sridhar, S. N. (1994). A reality check for SLA theories. *TESOL Quarterly, 28*(4), 800–805.

Sridhar, S. N. & Sridhar. K. K. (1992). The empire speaks back: English as a non-native language. In P. Nelde (Ed.), *Plurilingua XIII: It's easy to mingle when you are bilingual* (pp. 187–198). Bonn: Dummler.

Taiwo, O. (1976). *Culture and the Nigerian novel.* New York: St. Martin's Press.

Tawake, S. K. (1993). Reading *The Bone People*—cross-culturally. *World Englishes, 12* (3), 325–333.

Tawake, S. K. (1994). Culture and identity in literature of the South Pacific. *World Englishes, 9,* 205–213.

Tay, M. W. J. (1993). *The English language in Singapore: Issues and development.* Singapore: National University of Singapore, UniPress.

Thumboo, E. (1985). Twin perspectives and multi-ecosystems: Tradition for a commonwealth writer. *World Englishes, 4*(2), 213–221.

Thumboo, E. (1986). Language as power: Gabriel Okara's "The Voice" as a paradigm. *World Englishes, 5*(2-3), 249–264.

Thumboo, E. (1988). The literary dimension of the spread of English: creativity in a second tongue. In P. H. Lowenberg (Ed.), *Language spread and language policy: Issues, implications and case studies,* (pp. 385–415). Washington, DC: Georgetown University Press.

Thumboo, E. (1991). The pragmatics of meaning: Language as identity in new English literature. In L. F. Bouton & Y. Kachru (Eds.), *Pragmatics and language learning* (Monograph Series, Vol. 2, pp. 203–222). Urbana: University of Illinds, Division of English as an International Language.

Thumboo, E. (1992). The literary dimension of the spread of English. In B. Kachru (Ed.), *The other tongue: English across cultures* (pp. 255–282). Urbana: University of Illinois Press.

Thumboo, E. (Ed.). (2001). *The three circles of english.* Singapore: National University of Singapore, Unipress.

Valentine, T. M. (1988). Developing discourse types in non-native English: Strategies of gender in Hindi and Indian English. *World Englishes, 7*(2), 143–158.

Valentine, T. M. (1991). Getting the message across: Discourse markers in Indian English. *World Englishes, 10*(3), 325–334.

Valentine, T. M. (1995). Agreeing and disagreeing in Indian English discourse: Implications for language teaching. In M. L. Tickoo (Ed.), *Language and culture in multilingual societies: Viewpoints and visions* (Anthology Series 36, pp. 227–250). Singapore: SEAMEO Regional Language Center.

Valentine, T. M. (2001). Women and the other tongue. In E. Thumboo (Ed.), *The three circles of English* (pp. 143–158). Singapore: National University of Singapore, Unipress.

Vavrus, F. K. (1991). When paradigms clash: The role of institutionalized varieties in language teacher education. *World Englishes, 10*(2), 181–195.

White, L. (1989). *Universal grammar and second language acquisition.* Amsterdam: Benjamins.

Widdowson, H. G. (1994). The ownership of English. *TESOL Quarterly, 26*(2), 337–389.

II

Methods in Second Language Research

Introduction

Throughout the history of learning another language (and therefore the history of human mobility and migration), many research projects and experiments have been carried out to shed light on how second languages are learned and used. Many good examples of these can be found in the famous book by A. P. R. Howatt (A History of English Language Teaching, Oxford University Press, 1984/2004), who describes many studies conducted in the early 20th century on the teaching and learning of English in various parts of the world.

However, in the 1950s when applied linguistics arrived on the scene as a formal discipline, it was a latecomer among the human sciences, such as anthropology, behavioral sciences, educational theory, psychology, sociology, and their numerous subdomains, such as the sociology of learning. Thus, applied linguistics and its attendant research into second language (L2) processes had the advantage (or disadvantage, depending on the point of view) of the scientific research paradigms and methods developed for the purposes of gathering knowledge in other human disciplines. Although at the present several research methodologies are widely employed in applied linguistics and L2 learning, none is specifically unique or was specifically developed for language studies.

For this reason, the methods employed in L2 research and discussed in Part II necessarily draw on those that had already been designed, established, and refined elsewhere among other data-driven disciplines. In the research in social and behavioral sciences, all methods of empirical data gathering and, by outcome, all collected data is social in nature and fundamentally depends on the processes and methods by which it is gathered, interpreted, and used. The canonical methods of data gathering find a large number of classifications, depending on the disciplines where they were designed and developed. For example, the methods commonly called ethnography and participant observation were originally created in anthropology, survey-based and experimental research have long served the needs of psychology and the social sciences, and archival research methods have benefited history and political science.

Each research method has a foundational basis in paradigmatic procedures and logical progression. The types of hypotheses researchers set out to test determines the data gathering tools and, therefore, the types of analysis that can be applied to particular data. For instance, Quantitative research methods are crucially distinct from Qualitative because quantitative data is very difficult to gather naturalistically.

The means of data analysis fundamentally depends of the type of data gathering methods and the kinds of the data that are valued. For instance, while individuals' personal histories and narratives can be valued in one domain of research, quantitative data may be believed more valid and generalizable in another. In many cases, the methods for collecting data can be combined, resulting in dual or triple approaches to research design. In some disciplines, such as psychology, experimental data is considered to be of great merit, and in anthropology, the data gathered in naturally occurring contexts is probably considered to have the highest credibility.

Numerous methods for data gathering and analysis have become recognized in social sciences and, by extension, in L2 research. However, practically in all cases, the type of collected data determines the applicable methods of analysis. The quantitative data gathered from relatively large population samples in experiments or naturalistically can be analyzed numerically and/or statistically, but the information obtained in a small number of representative cases requires qualitative and/or interpretive analytical research procedures. Each has a number of advantages and disadvantages, and strengths and flaws, and each is strongly preferred or dispreferred by particular groups of or individual researchers in L2 processes. There are, of course, exceptions among researchers, and it is possible to find those who conduct qualitative and quantitative studies, but they are infrequent. In this regard, an individual's belief in the validity and merits of particular research methods, the types of data considered to be representative and analyzable, and the methods of by which the data can be analyzed can be a matter of religion.

The chapters in Part II discuss the prevalent methods in L2 research. Although Ethnographic/Qualitative and Case Study research methods and Quantitative research methods draw on the classical and fundamental research paradigms, others, such as Classroom and Action research, represent adaptations of these methods *to narrow and specific contexts of L2 teaching*.

- Chapter 10, by **Linda Harklau**, presents an overview of the Ethnographic Research methodology, also called Qualitative. Participant or nonparticipant observation represents the coin of the qualitative studies' realm, and all ethnographic data require a researcher's interpretation. In the case of qualitative studies, researchers usually do not set out to test a particular hypothesis but gather the data in naturalistic contexts.
- Chapter 11, by **Leo van Lier**, discusses Case Studies, which are a very common approach to qualitative data collection in second language research. As with other ethnographic methods, one of the most important advantages of case study research is that it allows the researcher to note the specific contexts in which L2 processes occur and to track and document changes over time.
- Chapter 12, by **Anne Lazaraton**, provides an overview of the types of quantitative studies carried out in L2 research and compares their popularity to qualitative methods. In general terms, quantitative data are gathered by means of carefully designed experiments and are analyzed statistically, provided of course that the sample involved in data gathering is sufficiently large.
- Chapter 13, by **David Nunan**, reviews the methods commonly adopted in Classroom Research, as well as the purposes and uses of its findings. The main goal of Classroom Research is to shed light on the relationship between classroom teaching, including instructional methods and tasks, the role of the teacher's input, learner language gains and sequences, and interactions among learners and the teacher. David Nunan points out that in terms of data gathering methods, researchers have debated the merits of experimental versus naturalistic approaches to data collection and analysis and the merits of collecting data in classroom rather than in non-classroom settings.
- Chapter 14, by **Anne Burns**, discusses the methods and applications of Action Research that primarily represents a systematic and self-reflective inquiry by the participants with the goal of improving their own practices and situations. One of the major distinctions between formal paradigmatic research and Action Research is that the latter has the primary objective of addressing participants' own practical concerns. An example of application of Action Research to L2 teaching can be a practical and data-driven decision of whether to change a language-based curriculum or a teaching method in a particular school or location. As Anne Burns notes, Action Research data gathering can allow teachers to have a voice.

10

Ethnography and Ethnographic Research on Second Language Teaching and Learning

Linda Harklau
University of Georgia

The term ethnography refers to a range of diverse and ever-changing research approaches (Atkinson, Coffey, Delamont, Lofland, & Lofland, 2001) originating in anthropological and sociological research and characterized by first-hand, naturalistic, sustained observation and participation in a particular social setting. The purpose of ethnography is to come to a deeper understanding of how individuals view and participate in their own social and cultural worlds.

Over the past 25 years, ethnography has become a major approach to research on second language learning and teaching. The epistemological assumptions and methods favored by individual researchers often depend on the scholarly communities into which they are socialized (Davis, 1995). Nevertheless, in spite of the ethnographic principle of self-examination, few researchers explicitly articulate the intellectual ancestry of the approaches they use. This review contextualizes ethnographic research on second language (L2) learning in three diverse scholarly communities that have shaped its development: cultural anthropology and sociology; linguistic anthropology and sociolinguistics; and ethnographies of teaching and learning.

CULTURAL ANTHROPOLOGY AND SOCIOLOGY

Ethnography originated as the primary research methodology of the emerging discipline of anthropology in the 1870s to the 1920s (Goldschmidt, 2001; Lenkeit, 2001). Heavily influenced by the work of Boas (Salzman, 2001), its aim was to counter social Darwinist claims of human differences as biologically and racially determined through empirical documentation of the diversity of human cultures (Goldschmidt, 2001). In North America, early ethnographies were conducted among Indian tribal communities (Goldschmidt, 2001) and non-industrialized cultures abroad (Brewer, 2000). Ethnography was also the dominant methodology of the Chicago School of sociology established in the 1920s and 1930s. Drawing on G. H. Mead's work and symbolic interactionism, it sought to document urban life (Deegan, 2001; Goldschmidt, 2001). In Britain, early influences in anthropology and sociology included Malinowski and Radcliffe-Brown's Durkheimian notions of social structure (Kuper, 1996). Early British ethnography often focused on cultures in colonies abroad. It documented the functions of political institutions, rituals and mythology, and social networks such as kinship systems (Kuper, 1996). Post-World War II interaction among anthropologists and sociologists blurred the distinctions among U.S. ethnographic traditions (Goldschmidt, 2001; Wolcott, 1999). Ethnoscience and cognitive anthropological approaches influenced by the structural linguist Pike (1967) were prevalent in the 1960s and 1970s (Barfield, 1997). In Britain, Levi-Strauss led a movement toward structuralism with influences from French linguistic and sociological theory (Kuper, 1996).

Methodologies

Ethnographies typically focus on small societies or small bounded units (e.g., a town) within broader social units. Therefore, although not all case studies are ethnographic or even qualitative, all ethnographic research involves case study (Brewer, 2000, p. 77). Because of the particularity of case study, ethnographers disagree on the extent to which it is feasible or desirable to generalize from ethnographic findings.

Although some ethnographers resist codification of their procedures (Brewer, 2000, p. 9), it can be said that the hallmark of "classical" ethnographic methodology is participant observation. This traditionally has meant residing or spending considerable lengths of time interacting with people in everyday naturalistic settings, observing and recording their activities in extensive fieldnotes, and interviewing and conversing with them to learn their perspectives, attitudes, beliefs, and values (Salzman, 2001). A major portion of the participant observer's work is to generate a descriptive corpus of fieldnotes as a contemporaneous record of events and experiences as they unfold. Data are ideally gathered from most participants—or "informants"—in the setting, but may be chosen with random samples or based on individuals' particular knowledge, skills, and insights (Lenkeit, 2001). Key informants work most closely with the ethnographer. Ethnographers typically conduct informal interviews with informants in the setting (Brewer, 2000, p. 63; Lenkeit, 2001) entailing open-ended questions that evolve *in situ*. More formal interviews, consisting of a schedule of questions, may be conducted as the research continues. Often formal interviews are audio-recorded and transcribed. Ethnography may incorporate other field methods including life histories (Darnell, 2001), narrative analysis (Cortazzi, 2001), photography and videotape (Lenkeit, 2001; Nastasi, 1999), archeological data, written documents (Brewer, 2000), or other data documenting historical trends, and surveys (Salzman, 2001). Some (e.g., Brewer, 2000, p. 74) include studies of natural language in field methods.

Another distinctive feature of ethnographic work is comparison across multiple data sources, commonly known as "triangulation." Although varying by researchers' underlying epistemological stance and training, data analysis tends to be distinguished by an inductive process initiated in the course of data collection (Brewer, 2000, p. 107). Data are ultimately organized into patterns, categories, or themes that are compared against negative or disconfirming data and, thus, evolve as data collection proceeds. Often this process entails uncovering the implicit "commonsense" sociocultural knowledge, beliefs, and practices of participants (Herzfeld, 2001). In later stages of analysis and writing, meaning is attached to the data by theorizing the meaning of and relationships among categories.

Epistemological Stances

The epistemological status of ethnographic knowledge has been debated in recent years. In early work, researchers conferred the status of science on ethnographic knowledge and tended to take their findings as self-evident, de-emphasizing the role of researcher's training, background, and preexisting theories (Goldschmidt, 2001; Salzman, 2001). Some continue to see ethnography as contributing to a science of the social (e.g., Bernard, 2002). Although these researchers acknowledge that ethnographers can never be completely objective, at the same time they believe that careful attention to methodology, study replication, and comparing across settings—or "ethnology"—can result in the training of subjectivity and uncovering of replicable findings about cultural patterns. Contemporary ethnographies in this vein often incorporate quantifiable data and statistical analyses (Lenkeit, 2001; Salzman, 2001, p. 8).

Other theorists take interpretivist or phenomenological stances. They contend that anthropological facts are inseparable from the concepts, categories, and theories of the ethnographer and are therefore necessarily interpretations (Salzman, 2001). From this perspective, ethnographies are guided by general or "heuristic" theories that direct attention to certain factors but do not predetermine results (Salzman, 2001). Ethnographies in this vein have been influenced by a strand of philosophical thought suggesting that human beings and the social world are fundamentally different in nature and behavior than physical and inanimate objects because of the capacities for language and meaning making. Therefore, the social world cannot be reduced to what can be observed but rather is created, perceived, and interpreted by people themselves. To gain knowledge of the social world, one must gain access to actors' own accounts of it (Brewer, 2000, p. 35).

Work in Britain by Evans-Pritchard (1962) and in the United States by Geertz (1966/1973) anticipated a dramatic shift away from a focus on cultural structures and their functions and toward cultural symbols and their meaning. In the 1980s proponents of postmodern approaches including Marcus and Fischer (1986), Clifford and Marcus (1986), and Van Maanen (1988) drew on trends in literary criticism to explicitly reject scientific epistemology and instead portray ethnography as a literary-like interpretive enterprise (Goldschmidt, 2001). These scholars challenged whether there is an objective or knowable "real" world that can be accurately described (Brewer, 2000, p. 47). Postmodern ethnography thus rejects any possibility of scientific notions of validity, reliability, and generalization. It also questions the ethnographer's claim to privileged status or knowledge. It requires that researchers practice "reflexivity," exploring their own subjectivity as well as informants' (Tedlock, 2000). The central role of the researcher in what is found is made clear (Salzman, 2001), and the circumstances and contingencies surrounding the production of data are addressed explicitly (Brewer, 2000). Postmodernism has also spurred experimental forms of writing and ways of presenting ethnographic results (Tedlock, 2000).

Postmodernism has precipitated a major epistemological divide in ethnographic theory (Brewer, 2000; Darnell, 2001; Salzman, 2001). Some (e.g., Brewer, 2000, p. 26; Herzfeld, 2001; James, Hockey, & Dawson, 1997) attempt to steer a middle path, reconciling postmodern critiques and notions of representation with more traditional ethnographic realist modes of inquiry and writing. Epistemological divisions are further overlaid with a number of "schools" (Salzman, 2001) or "styles" (Brewer, 2000, p. 5) of ethnographic research, each drawing on its own theoretical perspectives that in turn affect methods and reporting. For example, neo-Marxist critical realist approaches (e.g., Harris, 1979) explain processes of social and cultural change by identifying material conditions that underlie them (Salzman, 2001). These may include a moral dimension of advocacy for oppressed and exploited peoples (Scheper-Hughes, 1995). Ethnographers working from feminist perspectives have made claims for the uniqueness of their contributions to ethnography (see, e.g., Behar & Gordon, 1995; Lather, 1991). In the "contemporary carnivalesque diversity of standpoints, methods and representations" (Atkinson et al., 2001, p. 3), no single philosophical or theoretical orientation can lay exclusive claim to correct or true ethnography.

LINGUISTIC ANTHROPOLOGY AND SOCIOLINGUISTICS

Linguistics as a discipline originated in early anthropological work. Over time, however, the interests of linguists and anthropologists diverged (Lenkeit, 2001). In the 1950s and 1960s several linguistically and interactionally-oriented schools of anthropological and sociological inquiry reinvigorated the links between ethnography and language. These included the sociology of language, ethnography of communication, and interactionist sociolinguistics.

Sociology of Language

Fishman (1968) first coined the term "sociology of language" to designate a strand of scholarship utilizing traditional ethnographic methods to document language choices and use in multilingual workplace, school, and community settings (Dorian, 1999). Sociologists of language also link language use with macro-level national language and education policies (e.g., Davis, 1994; Francis & Ryan, 1998; Goldstein, 1997b; Hornberger, 1988; Zentella, 1997). They may incorporate quantitative analyses of audio recorded language and code-switching data, and elicited self-report data such as questionnaires.

Ethnography of Communication

Hymes (1964) first proposed the notion of ethnography of speaking, later dubbed the ethnography of communication. Based on the work of European linguist Jacobson, Hymes and colleague Gumperz (Gumperz & Hymes, 1964) proposed that the speech act replace the linguistic code as the primary unit of study and analysis in linguistics. Hymes suggested that the appropriate methodology for this work was ethnography of communicative events, with a multi-faceted description of the setting, participants, purposes, topics, codes, and channels of speech acts and speech events (Hornberger, 2000). Hymes and Gumperz initiated an innovative strand of ethnographic work that has remained highly influential over the past 35 years.

   The primary focus of ethnography of communication studies has been face-to-face interaction. Initial work in this vein tended to be taxonomic, aimed at creating inventories of community speech practices and recurrent routines (Keating, 2001). Most ethnography of communication research features samples of audio- or videorecorded interactions selected from a larger corpus. These are exhaustively analyzed with reference to turns at talk, speech acts, sequences of speech acts, interactional encounters, speech events, social occasions, speech situations, and other aspects of communicative practices (Keating, 2001). Thus, ethnography of communication can be distinguished in method and emphasis from ethnographic approaches in cultural anthropology and sociology where audio and video recordings of behavior have been regarded as supplemental to participant observation and fieldnotes (see, e.g., Nastasi, 1999).

Interactionist Sociolinguistics

Several approaches to the study of interaction emerged in American sociology in mid-20th century (Pollner & Emerson, 2001). Reacting against sociological approaches focusing on a priori social structures, Garfinkel's (1967) pioneering work on ethnomethodology focuses instead on how shared but implicit competencies, assumptions, and knowledge of interactants within a cultural setting produce and sustain order in social life (Pollner & Emerson, 2001). Subsequent work in this vein included Cicourel's (1973) "cognitive sociology" and conversation analysis (Atkinson & Heritage, 1984). Goffman (1974), a sociologist in the symbolic interactionist tradition

(Deegan, 2001, p. 21), also produced ethnographic work aimed at developing elaborate and highly theorized abstractions about "interaction rituals" and "frames" of linguistic and social behavior in given social contexts. Contemporary theorists in this vein include Gubrium and Holstein (1997) and Silverman (1993).

Although interactionist approaches share some methodological attributes of ethnography of communication, there are also significant disagreements between them in desirable scope, focus, and modes of investigation (Gubrium & Holstein, 1997; Pollner & Emerson, 2001). Whereas ethnography and ethnography of communication tend to focus on the emic (Pike, 1967) *substance* of participants' worldviews, understandings, and experiences, ethnomethodologists instead focus etically on the linguistic and interactional *procedures* through which people construct social realities (Gubrium & Holstein, 1997). Ethnomethodology thus rejects ethnographic methods for eliciting participant perspectives such as interviews (Pollner & Emerson, 2001) as subjective, focusing instead on close analysis of observable and recordable verbal and nonverbal behavior (Gubrium & Holstein, 1997). Audio or video recording of interaction is often essential to this work. Although advocates argue that recordings' reviewable nature makes possible more empirically verifiable assertions, others argue that researcher perspective nevertheless affects what is taped and how it is transcribed, coded, analyzed, and interpreted (Nastasi, 1999).

In spite of theoretical and methodological differences, ethnography of communication and interactionist approaches have been intertwined throughout their development (Wieder, 1999). For example, subsequent to his founding work in the ethnography of communication, Gumperz (1981) drew on Goffman's work to develop "interactional sociolinguistics," examining how "contextualization cues" such as intonation, speech rhythm, and lexical, phonetic, and syntactic choice interact with participants' background knowledge.

The scope and focus of interactionist approaches in the past decade has been affected by the increasing influence of neo-Marxist and critical perspectives. Theorists (e.g., Gal, 1989; May, 1997) argue that these approaches have focused too exclusively on the immediate context of talk and have not given adequate consideration to how language as a symbolic system operates in power, domination, and global political economy. Gal (1989), for example, rejects the notion that there is an unproblematic reality that researchers reveal. Instead, because language in part structures reality in society, it must be seen simultaneously as an ideologically laden form of social representation and action (Duranti, 1994). Although understanding the origins of inequality among speakers was an original goal of the ethnography of communication (Hymes, 1973), in recent years there has been increasing impetus toward "locating linguistic practices as parts of larger systems of social inequality" (Hornberger, 2000, p. 363).

ETHNOGRAPHIES OF TEACHING AND LEARNING

American sociologists had conducted ethnographic research in schools since the Chicago School era (Bogdan & Biklen, 1998). The late 1940s and 1950s marked the entrance of U.S. anthropologists onto educational terrain (see, e.g., Spindler, 1955). The publication of Glaser & Strauss' 1967 volume on "grounded theory" marked a growing discontent with the dominance of positivism and experimental methods throughout the social sciences (Hammersley & Atkinson, 1993, p. 12). Qualitative approaches to research—especially ethnography—began to appear in education and other fields including nursing and health studies, business and the organization of work, science and technology, human geography, social psychology, cultural and media studies, and education (Atkinson et al., 2001), and have gained in prominence ever since (Gilmore & Glatthorn, 1982; Spindler, 1982).

Most classroom-based ethnographic research conducted over the past 3 decades has theoretical roots in ethnomethodology, phenomenology, and symbolic interactionism (Gordon, Holland, & Lahelma, 2001). These include Mehan's (1979) "constitutive ethnography" and Erickson's (1975) "microethnography." Like other interactionally-oriented work, these approaches adopted video recording as a primary data collection method in order to record subtleties of naturally occurring face-to-face interactions. These approaches therefore shared a tendency toward intensive etic analysis of interaction and de-emphasis on participant observation and emic participant perspectives (Bogdan & Biklen, 1998).

The ethnography of communication, with a broader focus on school and communities (Watson-Gegeo, 1997), also figured prominently in the developing field of educational ethnography. Hymes and Gumperz both played early and active roles in the establishment of a community of scholars in educational ethnography (Cazden, John, & Hymes, 1972; Gumperz, 1981). The civil rights movement and desegregation in the 1960s provided increasing impetus for ethnographic studies of disadvantaged and academically unsuccessful students and schools (Bogdan & Biklen, 1998). New attention focused on ethnolinguistic and racial minority students. Paralleling the development of work on child language socialization in linguistic anthropology (e.g., Schiefflin & Ochs, 1986), a major thrust of early educational ethnographic work was to document child language socialization and cultural transmission in language minority communities in North America (Keating, 2001). Research demonstrated that classroom interactions in Western-style schools have strong, culturally based, and often implicit expectations for interaction among students and teachers. Scholars showed that there were significant discontinuities or mismatches between these communicative norms and those in language minority students' homes and local communities (Gal, 1989), and that institutional processes of power create differential school outcomes through interactions and texts.

The use of ethnography in educational circles was also promoted by scholars taking Vygotskian and Bakhtinian sociocultural perspectives who sought to document how learning and development are situated in sociocultural contexts (e.g., Scribner & Cole, 1981; Tharp & Gallimore, 1988). Ethnography of communication and sociocultural perspectives were also drawn on by literacy scholars seeking to counter cognitively and innativist perspectives on reading and writing development. These scholars have sought to document literacy practices—the ways in which reading and writing are used in particular sociocultural contexts—as well as the beliefs and attitudes about literacy that underlie these practices (Athanases & Heath, 1995; Barton, 1994; Cook-Gumperz, 1986; Cope & Kalantzis, 2000; Hornberger, 2000; Lam, 2000; Street, 1984; Szwed, 1981).

From its beginnings, ethnographic work on language and communication has been eclectic, borrowing from diverse disciplinary and intellectual traditions (e.g., Cazden, John, & Hymes, 1972; Fishman, 1968; Gilmore & Glatthorn, 1982; Green & Wallat, 1981; Gumperz & Hymes, 1964; Spindler, 1982). Epistemological and methodological distinctions among ethnography of communication, interactionist sociolinguistic methods such as ethnomethodology, and discourse analytic methods deriving from conversation analysis and Hallidayan systemic functional linguistics have been obscured as these intellectual traditions have borrowed from one another (Duff, 2002). Many first and second language and literacy educators (e.g., Ernst, 1994; Freeman, 1998; Green & Bloome, 1997; Lin, 1999; Rymes, 2001; van Lier, 1988; Watson-Gegeo, 1997; Willett, 1995) do not differentiate among these traditions or characterize their work as a combination of approaches.

Other ethnography draws its methodological and epistemological roots from social anthropology and sociology. For example, Ogbu (1987) and colleagues' (e.g., Gibson &

Ogbu, 1991) "cultural ecological" thesis argues that although interactionally oriented approaches can explain *how* processes of minority school failure and language learning unfold, they cannot explain *why*. Influenced by Durkheimian sociology and neo-Marxist work on class structures (Gordon et al., 2001), Ogbu looks instead to broad sociohistorical and political forces shaping particular minority groups' "folk models" of their place in society. Other work in this tradition has focused at the institutional or community, rather than classroom, level (e.g., Gebhard, 1999; Goto, 1997; Lee, 2001; Levinson, Foley, & Holland, 1996; Olson, 1997; Trueba & Bartolomé, 2000; Weis & Fine, 2000). Ethnographers in the past 2 decades have increasingly portrayed the immediate context of face-to-face interaction and the broader contexts of school, community, and society as mutually constitutive (e.g., Davidson, 1996; Phelan, Davidson, & Yu, 1998; Weis & Fine, 2000).

Paralleling other areas, critical approaches have gained influence in educational ethnographic inquiry in recent years (see, e.g., Canagarajah, 1993; Goldstein, 1997a; Gordon et al., 2001; Toohey, 1995; Trueba & Bartolomé, 2000; Watson-Gegeo, 1997). These share some philosophical affinities with longstanding traditions of participatory ethnography conducted in collaboration with or by participants such as teachers (see, e.g, Gonzales & Moll, 1995) and ethnography utilized as a pedagogical tool to learn inductively about students' own or target cultures (e.g., Allen, 2000; Roberts, Byram, Barro, Jordan, & Street, 2001). Ethnographies of teaching and learning language have not been immune from incursions of poststructuralism that have influenced other ethnographic efforts in recent years (Duff, 2002), with particular scrutiny given to the anthropological and ethnographic concept of "culture" (e.g., Atkinson, 1999; Holliday, 1999).

CONTEMPORARY ETHNOGRAPHIES OF ADDITIONAL LANGUAGE TEACHING AND LEARNING

The rising popularity of ethnography in social science research was noted in several early articles in *TESOL* (e.g., Hannerz, 1973; McLeod, 1976). Many ethnographic studies of classroom processes—including some focusing on bilingual students (e.g., Saravia-Shore & Arvizu, 1992; Trueba, Guthrie, & Au, 1981)—have appeared since the mid-1970s. However, only after the mid-1980s have a significant number focused on second language learners and second language learning per se (Watson-Gegeo, 1988). By 1995, Lazaraton found a small but increasing proportion of this research in applied linguistics journals. In the past 15 years, ethnography has become a recognized research tradition on L2 teaching and learning representing a wide diversity of perspectives and findings.

Topics

Ethnographies of second language learning span instructional settings from elementary (e.g., Dagenais & Day, 1998; Edelsky, 1986; Ernst, 1994; Huss-Keeler, 1997; Toohey, 2000; Willett, 1995), to middle grades (e.g., Gomes & Martin, 1996; Katz, 1996; Lin, 1999; McKay & Wong, 1996; Toohey, 2000; Toohey, Waterstone, & Jule-Lemke, 2000; Valdés, 2001), to secondary (e.g., Duff, 1995; Duff, 2002; Goldstein, 1997c; Guerra, 1996; Harklau, 1994; Harklau, 2000; Heller, 1999; Ibrahim, 1999; Rampton, 1995; Terdal, 1993; Vollmer, 2000), to adult education and college (e.g., Atkinson, 2003; Atkinson & Ramanathan, 1995; Benson, 1989; Burnett, 1998; Canagarajah, 1993; Flowerdew & Miller, 1995; Losey, 1997; Morita, 2000; Nelson & Carson, 1996; Nunan, 1996; Ramanathan, 1999; Spielmann & Radnofsky, 2001; Warshauer, 1998). Other ethnographies address workplace (Goldstein, 1997b; Holliday, 1995; Katz, 2000; Li, 2000) and community settings (Dagenais & Day, 1999; Norton, 2000; Trosset, 1986; Valdés, 1996; Vasquez, Pease-Alvarez, & Shannon, 1994; Weinstein, 1997).

Classroom-based ethnographic studies of L2 learning in recent years have focused on a wide range of topics including teacher perspectives on lesson plan adjustments (Nunan, 1996) and lectures (Flowerdew & Miller, 1995), student perspectives on lecture comprehension (Benson, 1989; Flowerdew & Miller, 1995), dialog journals (Holmes & Moulton, 1995), cross-cultural expectations on parent involvement in school (Huss-Keeler, 1997), experiences of learners in English as a Second Language (ESL) (Gomes & Martin, 1996) and mainstream classrooms (Duff, 2002; Willett, 1995), student accommodation and resistance to learning English in a post-colonial context (Canagarajah, 1993), the relationship of gender and language learning (Losey, 1997; Woolard, 1997), the effects of computers on foreign language classroom interaction (Burnett, 1998), the experiences of multilingual children in French immersion programs (Dagenais & Day, 1998), microanalyses of ESL and English as a Foreign Language (EFL) classroom interactions (Duff, 1995; Ernst, 1994; Nelson & Carson, 1996; Toohey et al., 2000) and oral presentations in graduate seminars (Morita, 2000).

Several studies harness ethnographic methodology in order to conduct needs analyses (Holliday, 1995; Northcott, 2001) or to describe and evaluate bilingual and L2 curricula and programs (Edelsky, 1986; Freeman, 1998; Guthrie, 1985; Shaw, 1996; Terdal, 1993). Holliday (1994) advocates an "ethnographic action research" approach in order to develop and evaluate context-sensitive L2 curricula. Other program and curriculum-focused ethnographies include an analysis of contrasting programmatic cultures and expectations in L1 and L2 college composition programs (Atkinson & Ramanathan, 1995), tensions among Anglophone and Francophone teachers at a Canadian French immersion school (Cleghorn & Genesee, 1984), the role of race and gender in study-abroad program experiences (Siegal, 1996; Talburt & Stewart, 1999), and influences on computer use in an ESL composition classroom (Warshauer, 1998).

At the institutional level, ethnographic studies have focused on interethnic peer communication at an English high school (Rampton, 1995), Latino youth involvement in gangs (Katz, 1996), sociopolitical factors in English learning in postcolonial contexts (Atkinson, 2003; Lin, 1999; Ramanathan, 1999), the influence of race on English language learning (Ibrahim, 1999), and language learning anxiety in an intensive French program (Spielmann & Radnofsky, 2001). Other studies have aimed to describe holistically the experiences of additional language learners in settings including a Canadian French immersion high school (Heller, 1999), North American English-medium elementary schools (Toohey, 2000), middle schools (McKay & Wong, 1996; Valdés, 2001), and high schools (Goldstein, 1997c; Harklau, 1994; Vollmer, 2000).

Yet other ethnographies take place in a wide range of community and workplace settings. Goldstein (1997b) and Katz (2000) utilize critical ethnography to illustrate underlying assumptions in workplace ESL. Li (2000) looks at cross-cultural communication styles in the workplace. Norton (2000) and Trosset (1986) document adult language learning across community settings. Several studies document the home and community lives and language practices of children, youth, and adults in order to contrast them with classroom contexts (Dagenais & Day, 1999; Guerra, 1996; Moore, 1999; Valdés, 1996; Vasquez et al., 1994; Weinstein, 1997).

Methods

In addition to participant observation, fieldnotes, recordings, and interviews, ethnographies of L2 teaching and learning have also incorporated a variety of other data sources including teacher lecture notes and handouts (Benson, 1989), annotated lesson plans (Nunan, 1996), samples of textbooks and student-written materials (Canagarajah,

1993; Dagenais & Day, 1998; Flowerdew & Miller, 1995; Harklau, 1994; Huss-Keeler, 1997), participant diaries and journals (Flowerdew & Miller, 1995; Katz, 1996; Norton, 2000; Shaw, 1996), dialog journals (Holmes & Moulton, 1995); elicited writing on target language attitudes (Canagarajah, 1993); participant life history narratives (Guerra, 1996); participant commentary on video recordings (Morita, 2000; Nelson & Carson, 1996) and other member checks (Moore, 1999), focus groups (Flowerdew & Miller, 1995; Talburt & Stewart, 1999), and questionnaires (Canagarajah, 1993; Holmes & Moulton, 1995; Morita, 2000; Northcott, 2001). Many studies focus on one (Benson, 1989) to several (Dagenais & Day, 1998; Harklau, 1994; Holmes & Moulton, 1995; Katz, 1996; Li, 2000; Losey, 1997; Moore, 1999; Norton, 2000; Toohey, 2000) focal participants within the study context.

Studies may also incorporate ethnographic principles and techniques in pseudo-experimental, case study, discourse analytic, and survey research designs (see, e.g., Blanton, 1998; Gomes & Martin, 1996; Harklau, 2000; Lam, 2000; Liebman-Kline, 1987; Liou, 1997; Rivers, 2001; Siegal, 1996; Takashima, 1992; Taylor, 1992; Tella, 1992). Others tap ethnographic techniques such as interviews or written reflections in exploratory research and pilot studies (see, e.g., Bartelt, 1997; Goldstein, 1997c).

Weaknesses and Controversies

Paralleling other applied fields such as education (see, e.g., Athanases & Heath, 1995; Rist, 1980; Spindler, 1982), there is an ongoing tension in the second language research community between codifying what constitutes "good" ethnography and yet honoring diverse scholarly traditions and perspectives. Sociologists and anthropologists until recently relied on disciplinary apprenticeship (Deegan, 2001, p. 20) and rarely articulated their methods formally. The spread of ethnography into other disciplines without established ethnographic traditions in the 1970s generated new textbooks and handbooks (e.g., Bogdan & Taylor, 1975; Lofland, 1971). Much of the impetus to standardize and formalize ethnographic conventions still comes from applied fields, particularly education (see, e.g., Denzin & Lincoln, 2000; Hammersley & Atkinson, 1993; Wolcott, 1999).

One difficulty is that the proliferation of ethnographic approaches in applied fields has had a homogenizing influence, folding ethnography into a broader and often undifferentiated category of "qualitative research." Some (e.g., Edge & Richards, 1998; Watson-Gegeo, 1997; Wolcott, 1999) continue to caution that not all qualitative approaches are in fact ethnographic. For example, Atkinson et al. (2001) note that although in-depth interviews, focus groups, and the collection of textual materials may be valuable methods of qualitative inquiry, they do not constitute ethnography when collected independent of participant observation. Likewise, in applied linguistics, Lazaraton (1995) has pointed out that TESOL Quarterly's original qualitative research guidelines confounded the disparate approaches of ethnography and conversation analysis.

The lack of clear definitions also leads to concerns about the misapplication of the term "ethnography" to inadequately conceptualized or designed research (e.g., Watson-Gegeo, 1988). Mindful of the dominance of quantitatively-oriented positivist and postpositivist perspectives in applied linguistics, ethnographers worry that a lack of clear standards will reinforce a "default assumption" that qualitative studies lack rigor (Davis, 1995, p. 432). Nevertheless, as Atkinson et al. (2001) and Wolcott (1999) acknowledge, there remains considerable debate on what may be called ethnography.

The level of methodological reporting and detail varies widely in ethnographic research reports in applied linguistics. A lack of detail in some publications—for example, amounts and types of data collected—is problematic because many (but not all) scholars assess studies' rigor, validity, or credibility by their methodology. That being said, the overall amount of data and variety of data sources in ethnographic studies of additional language learning and teaching appear to be increasing. Whereas some ethnographic studies of second language acquisition (SLA) may still involve as little as 5 weeks of fieldwork (e.g., Talburt & Stewart, 1999), it is no longer unusual for ethnographies to span multiple years (e.g., Flowerdew & Miller, 1995; Harklau, 1994; Heller, 1999; Toohey, 2000; Valdés, 1996).

A final difficulty is that ethnographic work remains limited primarily to White Anglophone researchers in English-speaking countries. There remains a paucity of ethnographic work on language learning outside of North America and Britain (but see Atkinson, 2003; Canagarajah, 1993; Duff, 1995; Flowerdew & Miller, 1995; Lin, 1999; Moore, 1999; Ramanathan, 1999; Siegal, 1996; Talburt & Stewart, 1999; Woolard, 1997). English remains the target language in the vast majority of studies (but see Burnett, 1998; Dagenais & Day, 1998; Dagenais & Day, 1999; Moore, 1999; Spielmann & Radnofsky, 2001; Trosset, 1986; Woolard, 1997). Although McKay & Wong (1996) argue that researcher ethnicity and linguistic background are crucial in what ethnographic data are collected and how they are analyzed, much of the ethnographic work in applied linguistics neither takes a reflexive stance on researcher subjectivities nor explicitly articulates epistemological positionings. By its absence, this suggests the predominance of realist orientations. Researchers taking critical and post-structuralist perspectives (see e.g. Canagarajah, 1993; Goldstein, 1997b; Harklau, 2000; Ibrahim, 1999; Katz, 2000; Lin, 1999; McKay & Wong, 1996; Norton, 2000; Toohey, 2000; Vollmer, 2000) tend to be more explicit regarding their epistemological stances toward ethnographic knowledge.

CONCLUSION

As this review has suggested, there are some hallmarks of ethnographic research common to most studies. For example, virtually all approaches are marked by firsthand, naturalistic, sustained participant observation in the social setting(s) under study. Multiple sources of data are also deemed desirable by most ethnographers, as well as an iterative, in-depth, and systematic process of data collection and analysis. In addition, there appears to be an emerging consensus that micro-level processes of interaction are embedded in or mutually constitutive with macro-level institutional and societal economic, cultural, and political structures, even though in actual practice researchers focus at particular contextual levels (Duff, 2002; Scollon, 1995). Beyond these commonalities, however, we run into vastly different notions of what constitutes ethnography. Nevertheless, second language researchers often use the term ethnography generically without situating their work in specific intellectual and methodological traditions. Even fewer articulate contrasts among ethnographic traditions.

Perhaps one reason for this is that ethnographic schools of thought tend to be defined in opposition to other modes of inquiry rather than against each other. For example, well into the 1990s qualitative research methodologies in applied linguistics were typically only discussed insofar as they contrasted with psychometric, post-positivist approaches, neglecting contrasts within qualitative traditions (Lazaraton, 1995). Likewise, linguistic anthropologists have tended to contrast ethnography of communication against structuralist linguistics (Gal, 1989; Watson-Gegeo, 1997) or experimental social psychology (Wieder, 1999) rather than against other ethnographic traditions. Hence, they have tended to emphasize its historical links with other ethnographic traditions (Keating, 2001) and downplay differences in approach and emphasis.

Another reason is the often implicit influence of these ethnographic communities of practice on one another. All ethnography entails a tension between representations of participants' emic perspectives and the abstractions and interpretations layered on them by the ethnographer's etic perspective (Watson-Gegeo, 1988). However, as this review indicates, schools of ethnographic inquiry also vary significantly in their overall focus, be it the traditional anthropological emically-oriented *what* of participant understandings and experiences, or the interactional sociolinguist's etically-oriented *how* participants structure social realities through interaction. The epistemological and methodological disparities underlying these foci were quite salient to early educational ethnographers but have received less attention over time. Although both foci are equally worthy and enlightening, research in second language studies would benefit from more awareness and explicit differentiation about the differing assumptions, premises, data collection, and methods of analysis guiding ethnographic approaches.

Ethnographers and other qualitative researchers in second language studies no doubt still contend with misunderstandings and questions about their work from psychometrically- and experimentally-oriented colleagues. Yet this review has traced an ethnographic tradition within studies of second language learning and bilingualism that extends back more than 30 years, and a century-long tradition of ethnography underlying that. It also indicates both emerging and longstanding strands of scholarship in which ethnography has been the predominant methodological frame. The long history and current vitality of ethnographic work in second language studies suggests that it should no longer be necessary to legitimize ethnographic approaches in applied linguistics. A defensive stance contributes to prescriptivism and hampers applied linguists from joining the lively and contentious conversation taking place among other ethnographers and qualitative researchers regarding the nature and form of ethnographic knowledge.

Given the varying approaches associated with ethnography, I believe it is undesirable or even impossible to develop absolute pronouncements for what ethnography is or should be in studies of second language learning. After all, as Moore (1999) argues, agreement would preclude the sort of self-reflexive and critical stance that is advocated across much of the field. Rather, what this review suggests is that we must ultimately judge the utility and quality of ethnographic work by researchers' ability to situate their work within a particular ethnographic and intellectual tradition (see Davis, 1995 for a similar argument) and to show how their work makes a novel or useful contribution to scholarship in that tradition.

REFERENCES

Allen, L. Q. (2000). Culture and the ethnographic interview in foreign language teacher development. *Foreign Language Annals, 33*(1), 51–57.

Athanases, S. Z., & Heath, S. B. (1995). Ethnography in the study of the teaching and learning of English. *Research in the Teaching of English, 29*, 263–287.

Atkinson, D. (1999). TESOL and culture. *TESOL Quarterly, 33*, 625–654.

Atkinson, D. (2003). Language socialization and dys-socialization in a south Indian college. In R. Bayley & S. R. Schecter (Eds.), *Language socialization in bilingual and multilingual societies* (pp. 147–162). Philadelphia: Multilingual Matters.

Atkinson, D., & Ramanathan, V. (1995). Cultures of writing: An ethnographic comparison of L1 and L2 university writing/language programs. *TESOL Quarterly, 29*, 539–568.

Atkinson, J. M., & Heritage, J. (1984). *Structures of social action: Studies in conversation analysis.* Cambridge, UK: Cambridge University Press.

Atkinson, P., Coffey, A., Delamont, S., Lofland, J., & Lofland, L. (2001). Editorial introduction. In P. Atkinson, A. Coffey, S. Delamont, J. Lofland, & L. Lofland (Eds.), *Handbook of ethnography* (pp. 1–7). London: Sage.

Barfield, T. (1997). *The dictionary of anthropology.* Malden, MA: Blackwell.

Bartelt, G. (1997). The ethnography of second language production. *IRAL: International Review of Applied Linguistics in Language Teaching, 35*(1), 23–36.

Barton, D. (1994). *Literacy: An introduction to the ecology of written language.* Cambridge, MA: Blackwell.

Behar, R., & Gordon, D. A. (Eds.). (1995). *Women writing culture.* Berkeley: University of California Press.

Benson, M. J. (1989). The academic listening task: A case study. *TESOL Quarterly, 23*, 421–445.

Bernard, H. R. (2002). *Research methods in anthropology: Qualitative and quantitative approaches* (3rd ed.). Walnut Creek, CA: AltaMira.

Blanton, L. L. (1998). *Varied voices: On language and literacy learning*. Boston: Heinle & Heinle.

Bogdan, R. C., & Biklen, S. K. (1998). *Qualitative research for education: An introduction to theory and methods*. (2nd ed.). Boston: Allyn & Bacon.

Bogdan, R. C., & Taylor, S. J. (1975). *Introduction to qualitative research methods: A phenomenonological approach to the social sciences*. New York: Wiley.

Brewer, J. D. (2000). *Ethnography*. Buckingham, UK: Open University Press.

Burnett, J. (1998). Language alternation in a computer-equipped foreign language classroom: The intersection of teacher beliefs, language, and technology. *Canadian Modern Language Review, 55*, 97–123.

Canagarajah, A. S. (1993). Critical ethnography of a Sri Lankan classroom: Ambiguities in student opposition to reproduction through ESOL. *TESOL Quarterly, 27*, 601–626.

Canagarajah, A. S. (1995). Functions of code-switching in ESL classrooms: Socialising bilingualism in Jaffna. *Journal of Multilingual and Multicultural Development, 6*, 173–195.

Cazden, C., John, V., & Hymes, D. (Eds.). (1972). *Functions of language in the classroom*. New York: Teachers College Press.

Cicourel, A. V. (1973). *Cognitive sociology: Language and meaning in social interaction*. Harmondsworth, UK: Penguin.

Cleghorn, A., & Genesee, F. (1984). Languages in contact: An ethnographic study of interaction in an immersion school. *TESOL Quarterly, 18*, 595–625.

Clifford, J., & Marcus, G. E. (Eds.) (1986). *Writing culture: The poetics and politics of ethnography*. Berkeley: University of California Press.

Cook-Gumperz, J. (Ed.). (1986). *The social construction of literacy*. New York: Cambridge University Press.

Cope, B., & Kalantzis, M. (Eds.). (2000). *Multiliteracies: Literacy learning and the design of social futures*. New York: Routledge.

Cortazzi, M. (2001). Narrative analysis in ethnography. In P. Atkinson, A. Coffey, S. Delamont, J. Lofland, & L. Lofland (Eds.), *Handbook of ethnography* (pp. 384–394). London: Sage.

Dagenais, D., & Day, E. (1998). Classroom language experiences of trilingual children in French immersion. *Canadian Modern Language Review, 54*, 376–393.

Dagenais, D., & Day, E. (1999). Home language practices of trilingual children in French immersion. *Canadian Modern Language Review, 56*(1), 99–123.

Darnell, R. (2001). *Invisible geneologies: A history of Americanist anthropology*. Lincoln: University of Nebraska Press.

Davidson, A. L. (1996). *Making and molding identity in schools: Student narratives on race, gender, and academic engagement*. Albany: State University of New York Press.

Davis, K. A. (1994). *Language planning in multilingual contexts: Policies, communities, and schools in Luxembourg*. Philadelphia: Benjamins.

Davis, K. A. (1995). Qualitative theory and methods in applied linguistics research. *TESOL Quarterly, 29*, 427–453.

Deegan, M. J. (2001). The Chicago School of ethnography. In P. Atkinson, A. Coffey, S. Delamont, J. Lofland, & L. Lofland (Eds.), *Handbook of ethnography* (pp. 11–25). London: Sage.

Denzin, N. K., & Lincoln, Y. S. (Eds.). (2000). *Handbook of qualitative research*. Thousand Oaks, CA: Sage.

Dorian, N. C. (1999). Linguistic and ethnographic fieldwork. In J. A. Fishman (Ed.), *Handbook of language and ethnic identity* (pp. 25–41). New York: Oxford University Press.

Duff, P. (1995). An ethnography of communication in immersion classrooms in Hungary. *TESOL Quarterly, 29*, 505–537.

Duff, P. A. (2002). The discursive co-construction of knowledge, identity, and difference: An ethnography of communication in the high school mainstream. *Applied Linguistics, 23*, 289–322.

Duranti, A. (1994). *From grammar to politics: Linguistic anthropology in a Western Samoan village*. Los Angeles: University of California Press.

Edelsky, C. (1986). *Writing in a bilingual program: Había una vez*. Norwood, NJ: Ablex.

Edge, J., & Richards, K. (1998). May I see your warrant, please? Justifying outcomes in qualitative research. *Applied Linguistics, 19*, 334–356.

Erickson, F. (1975). Gatekeeping and the melting pot: Interaction in counseling encounters. *Harvard Educational Review, 45*(1), 44–70.

Ernst, G. (1994). "Talking circle": Conversation and negotiation in the ESL classroom. *TESOL Quarterly, 28*, 293–322.

Evans-Pritchard, E. E. (1962). *Essays in social anthropology*. Oxford, UK: Oxford University Press.

Fishman, J. A. (Ed.). (1968). *Readings in the sociology of language*. The Hague, The Netherlands: Mouton.

Flowerdew, J., & Miller, L. (1995). On the notion of culture in L2 lectures. *TESOL Quarterly, 29*, 345–373.

Francis, N., & Ryan, P. M. (1998). English as an international language of prestige: Conflicting cultural perspectives and shifting ethnolinguistic loyalties. *Anthropology and Education Quarterly, 29*, 25–43.

Freeman, R. D. (1998). *Bilingual education and social change*. Philadelphia: Multilingual Matters.

Gal, S. (1989). Language and political economy. *Annual Review of Anthropology, 18*, 345–367.

Garfinkel, H. (1967). *Studies in ethnomethodology*. Englewood Cliffs, NJ: Prentice-Hall.

Gebhard, M. (1999). Debates in SLA studies: Redefining classroom SLA as an institutional phenomenon. *TESOL Quarterly, 33*, 544–556.

Geertz, C. (1973). *The interpretation of cultures*. New York: Basic Books. (Original work published 1996).

Gibson, M. A., & Ogbu, J. U. (Eds.). (1991). *Minority status and schooling: A comparative study of immigrant and involuntary minorities*. New York: Garland.

Gilmore, P., & Glatthorn, A. A. (Eds.). (1982). *Children in and out of school: Ethnography and education*. Washington, DC: Center for Applied Linguistics.

Glaser, B. G., & Strauss, A. L. (1967). *The discovery of grounded theory: Strategies for qualitative research*. New York: Aldine de Gruyter.

Goffman, E. (1974). *Frame analysis: An essay on the organization of experience*. New York: Harper & Row.

Goldschmidt, W. (2001). Historical essay. A perspective on anthropology. *American Anthropologist, 102*, 789–807.

Goldstein, T. (1997a). Language research methods and critical pedagogy. In N. H. Hornberger & D. Corson (Eds.), *Encyclopedia of language and education. Volume 8: Research methods in language and education* (pp. 67–77). Dordrecht, The Netherlands: Kluwer Academic.

Goldstein, T. (1997b). *Two languages at work: Bilingual life on the production floor*. New York: Mouton de Gruyter.

Goldstein, T. (1997c). Bilingual life in a multilingual high school classroom: Teaching and learning in Cantonese and English. *Canadian Modern Language Review, 53*, 356–372.

Gomes, B. A., & Martin, L. (1996). "I only listen to one person at a time": Dissonance and resonance in talk about talk. *Language in Society, 25*, 205–236.

Gonzales, N., & Moll, L. C. (1995). Funds of knowledge for teaching in Latino households. *Urban Education, 29*, 443–471.

Gordon, T., Holland, J., & Lahelma, E. (2001). Ethnographic research in educational settings. In P. Atkinson, A. Coffey, S. Delamont, J. Lofland, & L. Lofland (Eds.), *Handbook of ethnography* (pp. 188–203). London: Sage.

Goto, S. T. (1997). Nerds, normal people, and homeboys: Accommodation and resistance among Chinese American students. *Anthropology and Education Quarterly, 28*, 70–84.

Green, J., & Bloome, D. (1997). Ethnography and ethnographers of and in education: A situated perspective. In J. Flood, S. B. Heath, & D. Lapp (Eds.), *Handbook of research on teaching literacy through the communicative and visual arts* (pp. 181–202). New York: Simon & Schuster/Macmillan.

Green, J. L., & Wallat, C. (Eds.). (1981). *Ethnography and language in educational settings*. Norwood, NJ: Ablex.

Gubrium, J. F., & Holstein, J. A. (1997). *The new language of qualitative method*. New York: Oxford University Press.

Guerra, J. (1996). "It's as if my story repeats itself": Life, language, and literacy in a Chicago comunidad. *Education and Urban Society, 29*(1), 35–54.

Gumperz, J. J. (1981). Conversational inference and classroom learning. In J. L. Green & C. Wallat (Eds.), *Ethnography and language in educational settings* (pp. 3–23). Norwood, NJ: Ablex.

Gumperz, J. J., & Hymes, D. (Eds.). (1964). The ethnography of communication. [Special issue]. *American Anthropologist, 66*(6, Part 2).

Guthrie, G. P. (1985). *A school divided: An ethnography of bilingual education in a Chinese community*. Hillsdale, NJ: Lawrence Erlbaum Associates.

Hammersley, M., & Atkinson, P. (1993). *Ethnography: Principles in practice* (2nd ed.). New York: Routledge.

Hannerz, U. (1973). The second language: An anthropological view. *TESOL Quarterly, 7*, 235–248.

Harklau, L. (1994). ESL and mainstream classes: Contrasting second language learning contexts. *TESOL Quarterly, 28*, 241–272.

Harklau, L. (2000). From the "good kids" to the "worst": Representations of English language learners across educational settings. *TESOL Quarterly, 34*, 35–67.

Harris, M. (1979). *Cultural materialism: The struggle for a science of culture*. New York: Random House.

Heller, M., with Campbell, M., Dalley, P., & Patrick, D. (1999). *Linguistic minorities and modernity: A sociolinguistic ethnography*. New York: Longman.

Herzfeld, M. (2001). *Anthropology: Theoretical practice in culture and society*. Malden, MA: Blackwell.

Holliday, A. (1994). *Appropriate methodology and social context*. New York: Cambridge University Press.

Holliday, A. (1995). Assessing language needs within an institutional context: An ethnographic approach. *English for Specific Purposes, 14*(2), 115–126.

Holliday, A. (1999). Small cultures. *Applied Linguistics, 20*, 237–264.

Holmes, V. L., & Moulton, M. R. (1995). A contrarian view of dialogue journals: The case of a reluctant participant. *Journal of Second Language Writing, 4*, 223–251.

Hornberger, N. H. (1988). *Bilingual education and language maintenance: A southern Peruvian Quechua case*. Berlin: Mouton de Gruyter.

Hornberger, N. H. (2000). Afterward. In M. Martin-Jones & K. Jones (Eds.), *Multilingual literacies: Reading and writing different worlds* (pp. 353–367). Philadelphia: Benjamins.

Huss-Keeler, R. (1997). Teacher perception of ethnic and linguistic minority parental involvement and its relationship to children's language and literacy learning: A case study. *Teaching and Teacher Education, 13*(7), 171–182.

Hymes, D. (1964). Introduction: Toward ethnographies of communication. *American Anthropologist, 66*(6), 1–34.

Hymes, D. (1973). On the origins and foundations of inequality among speakers. *Daedalus, 102*(3), 59–86.

Ibrahim, A. E. K. (1999). Becoming Black: Rap and hip-hop, race, gender, identity, and the politics of ESL learning. *TESOL Quarterly, 33*, 349–369.

James, A., Hockey, J., & Dawson, A. (1997). Introduction: The road from Santa Fe. In A. James, J. Hockey, & A. Dawson (Eds.), *After writing culture: Epistemology and praxis in contemporary anthropology* (pp. 1–15). New York: Routledge.

Katz, M.-L. (2000). Workplace language teaching and the intercultural construction of ideologies of competence. *Canadian Modern Language Review, 57*, 144–172.

Katz, S. R. (1996). Where the streets cross the classroom: A study of Latino students' perspectives on cultural identity in city schools and neighborhood gangs. *Bilingual Research Journal, 20*, 603–631.

Keating, E. (2001). The ethnography of communication. In P. Atkinson, A. Coffey, S. Delamont, J. Lofland, & L. Lofland (Eds.), *Handbook of ethnography* (pp. 285–301). London: Sage.

Kuper, A. (1996). *Anthropology and anthropologists: The modern British school* (3rd ed.). New York: Routledge.

Lam, W. S. E. (2000). L2 literacy and the design of the self: A case study of a teenager writing on the Internet. *TESOL Quarterly, 34*, 457–482.

Lather, P. (1991). *Getting smart: Feminist research and pedagogy with/in the postmodern*. New York: Routledge.

Lazaraton, A. (1995). Qualitative research in applied linguistics: A progress report. *TESOL Quarterly, 29*, 455–472.

Lee, S. J. (2001). More than "model minorities" or "delinquents": A look at Hmong American high school students. *Harvard Educational Review, 71*, 505–528.

Lenkeit, R. E. (2001). *Introducing cultural anthropology*. New York: McGraw-Hill.

Levinson, B. A., Foley, D. E., & Holland, D. C. (1996). *The cultural production of the educated person: Critical ethnographies of schooling and local practices*. Albany: State University of New York Press.

Li, D. (2000). The pragmatics of making requests in the L2 workplace: A case study of language socialization. *Canadian Modern Language Review, 57*, 58–88.

Liebman-Kline, J. (1987). Teaching and researching invention: Using ethnography in ESL writing classes. *ELT Journal, 41*(2), 104–111.

Lin, A. M. Y. (1999). Doing-English-lessons in the reproduction or transformation of social worlds? *TESOL Quarterly, 33*, 393–412.

Liou, H.-C. (1997). The impact of www texts on EFL learning. *Computer Assisted Language Learning, 10*, 455–478.

Lofland, J. (1971). *Analyzing social settings: A guide to qualitative observation and analysis*. Belmont, CA: Wadsworth.

Losey, K. M. (1997). *Listen to the silences: Mexican American interaction in the composition classroom and community*. Norwood, NJ: Ablex.

Marcus, G. E., & Fischer, M. (1986). *Anthropology as cultural critique*. Chicago: University of Chicago Press.

May, S. (1997). Critical ethnography. In N. H. Hornberger & D. Corson (Eds.), *Encyclopedia of language and education. Volume 8: Research methods in language and education* (pp. 197–206). Dordrecht, The Netherlands: Kluwer Academic.

McKay, S. L., & Wong, S.-L. C. (1996). Multiple discourses, multiple identities: Investment and agency in second-language learning among Chinese adolescent immigrant students. *Harvard Educational Review, 66*, 577–608.

McLeod, B. (1976). The relevance of anthropology to language teaching. *TESOL Quarterly, 10*(2), 211–220.

Mehan, H. (1979). *Learning lessons: The social organization of classroom behavior*. Cambridge, MA: Harvard University Press.

Moore, L. C. (1999). Language socialization research and French language education in Africa: A Cameroonian case study. *Canadian Modern Language Review, 56*, 329–350.

Morita, N. (2000). Discourse socialization through oral classroom activities in a TESL graduate program. *TESOL Quarterly, 34*, 279–310.

Nastasi, B. K. (1999). Audiovisual methods in ethnography. In J. J. Schensul, M. D. LeCompte, B. K. Nastasi, & S. P. Borgatti (Eds.), *Enhanced ethnographic methods: Audiovisual techniques, focused group interviews, and elicitation techniques* (pp. 1–50). Walnut Creek, CA: Altamira Press.

Nelson, G. L., & Carson, J. G. (1996). ESL students' perceptions of effectiveness in peer response groups. *Journal of Second Language Writing, 7*, 113–131.

Northcott, J. (2001). Towards an ethnography of the MBA classroom: A consideration of the role of interactive lecturing styles within the context of one MBA programme. *English for Specific Purposes, 20*, 15–37.

Norton, B. (2000). *Identity and language learning: Social processes and educational practice*. Harlow, UK: Pearson Education.

Nunan, D. (1996). Hidden voices: Insiders' perspectives on classroom interaction. In K. M. Bailey & D. Nunan (Eds.), *Voices from the language classroom: Qualitative research in second language education* (pp. 41–56). New York: Cambridge University Press.

Olson, L. (1997). *Made in America: Immigrant students in our public schools*. New York: New Press.

Ogbu, J. U. (1987). Variability in minority school performance: A problem in search of an explanation. *Anthropology and Education Quarterly, 18*, 312–324.

Phelan, P., Davidson, A. L., & Yu, H. C. (1998). *Adolescents' worlds: Negotiating family, peers, and school*. New York: Teachers College Press.

Pike, K. (1967). *Language in relation to a unified theory of the structure of human behavior.* The Hague, The Netherlands: Mouton.

Pollner, M., & Emerson, R. M. (2001). Ethnomethodology and ethnography. In P. Atkinson, A. Coffey, S. Delamont, J. Lofland, & L. Lofland (Eds.), *Handbook of ethnography* (pp. 118–135). London: Sage.

Ramanathan, V. (1999). "English is here to stay": A critical look at institutional and educational practices in India. *TESOL Quarterly, 33,* 211–231.

Rampton, B. (1995). *Crossing: Language and ethnicity among adolescents.* New York: Longman.

Rist, R. (1980). Blitzkrieg ethnography: On the transformation of a method into a movement. *Educational Researcher, 9,* 8–10.

Rivers, W. P. (2001). Autonomy at all costs: An ethnography of metacognitive self-assessment and self-management among experienced language learners. *Modern Language Journal, 85,* 279–290.

Roberts, C., Byram, M., Barro, A., Jordan, S., & Street, B. V. (2001). *Language learners as ethnographers.* Tonawanda, NY: Multilingual Matters.

Rymes, B. (2001). *Conversational borderlands: Language and identity in an alternative urban high school.* New York: Teachers College Press.

Salzman, P. C. (2001). *Understanding culture: An introduction to anthropological theory.* Prospect Heights, IL: Waveland.

Saravia-Shore, M., & Arvizu, S. F. (Eds.). (1992). *Cross-cultural literacy: Ethnographies of communication in multiethnic classrooms.* New York: Garland.

Scheper-Hughes, N. (1995). The primacy of the ethical: Propositions for a militant anthropology. *Current Anthropology, 36,* 409–420.

Schieffelin, B., & Ochs, E. (Eds.). (1986). *Language socialization across cultures.* New York: Cambridge University Press.

Scollon, R. (1995). From sentences to discourses, ethnography to ethnographic: Conflicting trends in TESOL research. *TESOL Quarterly, 29,* 381–384.

Scribner, S., & Cole, M. (1981). *The psychology of literacy.* Cambridge, MA: Harvard University Press.

Shaw, P. A. (1996). Voices for improved learning: The ethnographer as co-agent of pedagogic change. In K. M. Bailey & D. Nunan (Eds.), *Voices from the language classroom: Qualitative research in second language education* (pp. 318–337). New York: Cambridge University Press.

Siegal, M. (1996). The role of learner subjectivity in second language sociolinguistic competency: Western women learning Japanese. *Applied Linguistics, 17*(3), 356–382.

Silverman, D. (1993). *Interpreting qualitative data: Methods for analysing talk, text and interaction.* London: Sage.

Spielmann, G., & Radnofsky, M. L. (2001). Learning language under tension: New directions from a qualitative study. *Modern Language Journal, 85,* 259–278.

Spindler, G. D. (Ed.). (1955). *Education and anthropology.* Stanford, CA: Stanford University Press.

Spindler, G. D. (Ed.). (1982). *Doing the ethnography of schooling: Educational anthropology in action.* New York: Holt, Rinehart & Winston.

Street, B. V. (1984). *Literacy in theory and practice.* New York: Cambridge University Press.

Szwed, J. F. (1981). The ethnography of literacy. In M. F. Whiteman (Ed.), *Writing: The nature, development, and teaching of written communication. Volume 1. Variation in writing: Functional and linguistic-cultural differences* (pp. 13–23). Hillsdale, NJ: Lawrence Erlbaum Associates.

Takashima, H. (1992). Transfer, overgeneralization and simplification in second language acquisition. *IRAL: International Review of Applied Linguistics in Language Teaching, 30*(2), 97–120.

Talburt, S., & Stewart, M. A. (1999). What's the subject of Study Abroad?: Race, gender and "living culture." *Modern Language Journal, 83,* 163–175.

Taylor, S. (1992). Victor: A case study of a Cantonese child in early French immersion. *Canadian Modern Language Review, 48,* 736–759.

Tedlock, B. (2000). Ethnography and ethnographic representation. In N. K. Denzin & Y. S. Lincoln (Eds.), *Handbook of qualitative research* (pp. 455–486). Thousand Oaks, CA: Sage.

Tella, S. (1992). The adoption of international communications networks and electronic mail into foreign language education. *Scandinavian Journal of Educational Research, 36,* 303–312.

Terdal, M. S. (1993). Watching whole language work. *TESOL Journal, 2*(3), 25–29.

Tharp, R. G., & Gallimore, R. (1988). *Rousing minds to life: Teaching, learning, and schooling in social context.* Cambridge, UK: Cambridge University Press.

Toohey, K. (1995). From the ethnography of communication to critical ethnography in ESL teacher education. *TESOL Quarterly, 29,* 576–581.

Toohey, K. (2000). *Learning English at school: Identity, social relations and classroom practice.* Tonawanda, NY: Multilingual Matters.

Toohey, K., Waterstone, B., & Jule-Lemke, A. (2000). Community of learners, carnival, and participation in a Punjabi Sikh classroom. *Canadian Modern Language Review, 56,* 421–437.

Trosset, C. S. (1986). The social identity of Welsh learners. *Language in Society, 15,* 165–192.

Trueba, E. T., & Bartolomé, L. I. (Eds.). (2000). *Immigrant voices: In search of educational equity.* Lanham, MD: Rowman & Littlefield.

Trueba, H. T., Guthrie, G. P., & Au, K. H.-P. (Eds.). (1981). *Culture and the bilingual classroom: Studies in classroom ethnography.* Rowley, MA: Newbury House.

Valdés, G. (1996). *Con respeto: Bridging the distances between culturally diverse families and schools. An ethnographic portrait.* New York: Teachers College Press.

Valdés, G. (2001). *Learning and not learning English: Latino students in American schools.* New York: Teachers College Press.

van Lier, L. (1988). *The classroom and the language learner: Ethnography and second-language classroom research.* New York: Longman.

Van Maanen, J. (1988). *Tales of the field: On writing ethnography.* Chicago: University of Chicago Press.

Vasquez, O. A., Pease-Alvarez, L., & Shannon, S. M. (1994). *Pushing boundaries: Language and culture in a Mexicano community.* New York: Cambridge University Press.

Vollmer, G. (2000). Praise and stigma: Teachers' constructions of the "typical ESL student." *Journal of Intercultural Studies, 21*(1), 53–66.

Warshauer, M. (1998). Online learning in sociocultural context. *Anthropology and Education Quarterly, 21,* 68–88.

Watson-Gegeo, K. A. (1988). Ethnography in ESL: Defining the essentials. *TESOL Quarterly, 22,* 575–592.

Watson-Gegeo, K. A. (1997). Classroom ethnography. In N. H. Hornberger & D. Corson (Eds.), *Encyclopedia of language and education. Volume 8: Research methods in language and education* (pp. 135–144). Dordrecht, The Netherlands: Kluwer Academic.

Weinstein, G. (1997). From problem-solving to celebration: Discovering and creating meanings through literacy. *Canadian Modern Language Review, 54,* 28–48.

Weis, L., & Fine, M. (Eds.). (2000). *Construction sites: Excavating race, class, and gender among urban youth.* New York: Teachers College Press.

Wieder, L. (1999). Ethnomethodology, conversation analysis, microanalysis, and the ethnography of speaking: Resonances and basic issues. *Research on Language and Social Interaction, 32*(1/2), 163–171.

Willett, J. (1995). Becoming first graders in an L2: An ethnographic study of L2 socialization. *TESOL Quarterly, 29,* 473–503.

Wolcott, H. F. (1999). *Ethnography: A way of seeing.* Walnut Creek, CA: AltaMira.

Woolard, K. A. (1997). Between friends: Gender, peer group structure, and bilingualism in urban Catalonia. *Language in Society, 26,* 533–560.

Zentella, A. C. (1997). *Growing up bilingual: Puerto Rican children in New York.* Malden, MA: Blackwell.

11

Case Study

Leo van Lier
Monterey Institute of International Studies

WHAT ARE CASE STUDIES?

As a research methodology, case study research has been extremely influential in shaping the way we talk about education, yet it has traditionally been regarded as somewhat of a soft and weak approach when compared to studies that have been deemed more rigorous, randomized, or experimental in nature. In general education we can cite Wolcott's classic case study of "The man in the principal's office" (1973)[1]; in language acquisition theory, Halliday's study of Nigel (1975); and in second language learning, Schmidt's study of Wes (1983). These and many other case studies have shaped discussion and research in their respective fields of focus in forceful and productive ways. This chapter aims to examine the case study as a valuable tool to examine educational reality.

Case study research is primarily a form of qualitative and interpretive research, although quantitative analyses are sometimes used if they are deemed relevant. It relates in various ways to other kinds of research, such as action research, ethnography, and experimental research. This chapter describes what case study research is, how and why it is done, and evaluate its impact on the field over the past 2 or 3 decades.

Case study research has become a key method for researching changes in complex phenomena over time. Many of the processes investigated in case studies cannot be adequately researched in any of the other common research methods, such as laboratory experiments, cross-sectional process-product research (such as pretest–treatment–posttest measures), and direct testing. But how do we know when a case study is the best way to approach a certain area of investigation and when another method might be more effective? I will try to answer that question in this introduction.

Among the advantages of the case study approach are the attention to context and the ability to track and document change (such as language development) over time. In addition, a case study zeros in on a particular case (an individual, a group, or a situation) in great detail, within its natural context of situation, and tries to probe into its characteristics, dynamics, and purposes.

When a case study is about an individual, we want to understand how that individual functions in the real context in which he or she lives or works. As Johnson says:

case studies can provide rich information about an individual learner. They can inform us about the processes and strategies that individual L2 [second language] learners use to communicate and learn, how their personalities, attitudes, and goals interact with the learning environment, and about the precise nature of their linguistic growth. (1992, p. 76)

So, case studies focus on context, change over time, and specific learners or groups. In other words, when we want to understand how a specific unit (person, group) functions in the real world over a significant period of time, a case study approach may be the best way to go about it.

One of the classic texts on case study research is Yin (1989). He defines case study as, "an empirical inquiry that:

- investigates a contemporary phenomenon within its real-life context;
- when the boundaries between phenomenon and context are not clearly evident; and in which
- multiple sources of evidence are used."(p. 23).

Yin's definition establishes some proposed features of the notion of case: a phenomenon in a real-life context (as opposed to, presumably, a laboratory setting), but one in which the notion of "boundaries" between phenomenon and context may be somewhat blurred. Let's explore this a bit further. Merriam (1988/1998) defines a case as "a single instance, phenomenon, or social unit" (p. 27). Other authors likewise struggle with this notion of boundedness. For Smith (1978), a case is a "bounded system." Stake (1995) calls it an "integrated system." Miles and Huberman (1994) call a case "a phenomenon of some sort occurring in a bounded context" (p. 25). These quotes point to a major problem area, which we can sum up in the question: What are the boundaries of a case? Merriam admonishes us that, "if the phenomenon you are interested in studying is not intrinsically bounded, it is not a case" (p. 27). On the other hand, Miles and Huberman suggest that intrinsic boundedness may not be so easy to establish. They agree that the case must be the unit of analysis, in which there is a "heart" or focus of the study, but then there is a "somewhat indeterminate boundary defining the edge of the case: what will not be studied" (1994, p. 25).

We can see in this argument some kind of struggle about defining what a case really is. Of course, if it is one person, the boundary—in a relatively trivial sense—is the skin around the body. But this merely sidesteps the social, distributed side of behavior, cognition, and interaction. The point here is that if the case study draws the boundary rigidly, it may oversimplify and isolate the case.

Having looked at the characteristics of the notion of "case" and its boundedness in the larger context, we can proceed to identify different kinds of cases. In the first place, a case can be a single individual, such as a second language learner. However, a case can also be a group of individuals with a common context, set of goals, or some kind of institutional boundedness. Examples are a classroom, a foreign language department, a program, a school, or an administrative office. Clearly, all of these examples, from individual to group to institution, are bounded in some way, but in none of the cases are the boundaries impermeable or watertight.

Another approach to specifying the notion of case is L. S. Shulman's classification of the use of cases and case methods in education. He distinguishes seven common types of cases:

1. *Case materials*: the raw data that are used (diaries, interview data, transcriptions).
2. *Case reports*: first-person accounts, usually in narrative form.

3. *Case studies*: third-person accounts, the most common way in which cases are reported.
4. *Teaching cases*: case studies that are edited for training or teaching purposes, for example, those commonly used in business schools.
5. *Case methods of teaching*: a methodology developed for teaching by means of teaching cases.
6. *Casebooks*: collections of cases, for example, for teacher education (J. H. Shulman, 1992).
7. *Case-based curriculum*: a curriculum built around the use of cases, casebooks, etc. (J. S. Shulman, 1992, p. 19).

In second language acquisition (SLA), most of the time we will be referring to case studies (the third category above), that is, descriptive third-person accounts of a learner or a group of learners. However, as I will illustrate, below, we can also use case studies as input in SLA courses (including book-length autobiographical novels, as suggested in Pavlenko & Lantolf, 2000), and we can, of course, also use teaching cases in preservice or inservice professional development for language teachers.

THE PLACE OF CASE STUDY RESEARCH IN SLA THEORY AND PRACTICE

This section places case study research within the larger topic of research in SLA and applied linguistics and discusses how it can contribute to the knowledge of the field. As mentioned in the introduction, case study research is usually qualitative and interpretive (even though there is no argument that precludes quantification, see Yin, 1989). Case studies are contextual forms of research, and as we have seen, one of the inherent problems is to draw the boundaries around the case. Another variable concerns the degree of intervention in the setting that is designed into the study. At the least-intervention end research is more ethnographic, and at the more intervention end research becomes action research.

These observations mean that ethnographies and action research are in a sense case studies because they fall within the scope of Yin's definition quoted above. In Fig. 11.1 the variables "individual–collective" (i.e., one person or a group) and

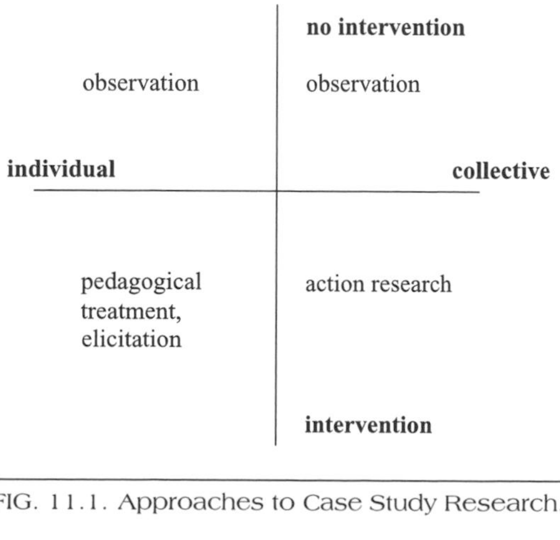

FIG. 11.1. Approaches to Case Study Research.

"no intervention–invention" (i.e., if some kind of treatment or change is involved) are juxtaposed to show how case studies may take varying approaches in practice.

In the past, case studies have often been accorded less status than more rigorously controlled experimental or process-product studies because, as the argument often goes, case studies are not generalizable. However, this criticism is unwarranted. It is probably true that it is difficult to generalize from an individual (or a group) to an entire population without the presence of strict controls to account for environmental variables. However, there is also a form of generalization that proceeds not from an individual case to a population, but from lower-level constructs to higher-level ones. Futhermore, in the practical world in which case studies are conducted, *particularization* may be just as important—if not more so—than *generalization*. By particularization I mean that insights from a case study can inform, be adapted to, and provide comparative information to a wide variety of other cases, so long as one is careful to take contextual differences into account. Furthermore, if two cases provide apparently contradictory information about a certain issue, such as social and psychological distance in the cases of Alberto (Schumann, 1978) and Wes (Schmidt, 1983), this contrast can provide much food for thought and further research, thus being of great benefit to the field.

If we look at the history of our field, it is no exaggeration to say that several famous case studies have played a large role in shaping the knowledge base that we now have. In first language acquisition we have the well known case study of Nigel by M. A. K. Halliday (1975). This study was instrumental in shaping Halliday's perspective on functional grammar and his view of language as *social semiotic*. In applied linguistics, seminal case studies include the already mentioned study by Schumann of Alberto (1978) a Puerto Rican immigrant to the United States, and Schmidt's two case studies, one of Wes (1983) a Japanese painter living in Hawaii, and the other of R (Schmidt himself, as a learner of Portuguese in Brazil; Schmidt & Frota, 1986). The latter is also a first-person diary study, and thus illustrates a different genre within case study.

These case studies helped to shape these researchers' theoretical positions, and they have also helped to shape the entire field in quite substantial ways. Schumann developed his notions of social and psychological distance on the basis of the Alberto study, and from these ideas he constructed the *acculturation model*, which to this day is a prominent topic of discussion in the field. Schmidt, on the other hand, in his case study of Wes, pointed to certain problems with Schumann's model, and looked in detail at the construct of communicative competence to suggest some ways in which the acculturation model might have to be reevaluated. In the later study on R, Schmidt focused on attention and noticing and used the case study findings to make detailed proposals about the role of consciousness in a number of later studies. We can thus conclude that, far from being marginal studies of merely anecdotal value, case studies have played a key role in shaping the knowledge base of SLA.

Also worth mentioning is the value of case study as a vehicle for apprenticing students in the field (in preservice and postgraduate programs). There are two particular ways in which case studies are used (and are useful) as inductions into the field. First, given the bewildering variety and complexity of the issues involved in SLA (from the perspective of the novice), a well written case study can bring to life many key issues and illustrate their relevance in dramatic, contextualized ways, something that a textbook or a controlled experimental research study cannot do. Second, it can be very valuable for graduate students in SLA to conduct a small case study as part of their introduction to the research community. Once again, such hands-on contextualized work can be instrumental in bringing to life the questions and problems discussed in the theoretical textbooks and research reports.

THE HISTORY OF CASE STUDIES IN SLA

This section summarizes some of the major case studies that have been conducted and shows how they have been influential in the field. For convenience I will divide them into studies of adult and child L2 development.

Case Studies of Adult SLA Development

I already mentioned the case studies by Schumann (1978) and Schmidt (1983; Schmidt & Frota, 1986), and indicated how these studies have contributed tremendously to some of the core discussions in our field. There have been a number of other case studies of adult learners, and I will give just a brief overview here of some of the most well known ones.

One of the major longitudinal studies was conducted under the auspices of the European Science Foundation (ESF) over a period of 10 years, in five different European countries (France, Germany, The Netherlands, Sweden, and the United Kingdom). Participants were adult immigrants speaking a variety of minority languages: Punjabi, Italian, Turkish, Arabic, Spanish, and Finnish. The study is actually a hybrid between a crosslinguistic data collection project and a contextualized observational project. It is perhaps due to this tension between controlled elicitation and participant observation, the study has resulted in several publications that are quite different in nature. Linguistic sequences and interlanguage grammars are carefully traced and documented in, for example, Klein and Perdue (1992), whereas a more interpretive, ethnographic perspective (i.e., a more traditional case study approach, with strong narrative elements) was taken in Bremer, Roberts, Vasseur, Simonot, and Broeder, 1996.

As discussed in the following, the ESF study led to the description of a "basic variety" of language, sufficient for minimal survival purposes, but one that immigrants often cannot get beyond. One the other hand, the ESF study also showed the need to study language development in its social context (see also Norton Peirce, 1995), and to focus on issues of understanding, awareness, identity, and power.

Some other case studies of adult SLA, for example, Huebner (1983), Ioup, Boustagui, El Tigi, and Moselle (1995), include detailed and meticulous documentation of linguistic development. Huebner's study of a Hmong immigrant in Hawaii tracks, for example, the development of the article system over an extended period of time, and Ioup et al. study the learning histories and the nativelike performance (including syntactic and phonological) of two successful learners of Egyptian Arabic.

Case Studies of Child Second Language Development

There have been a large number of studies of first and second language acquisition of children. The first well known effort was Leopold's study of the acquisition of German and English by his daughter Hildegard, conducted over a number of years beginning in the 1930's (Hatch, 1978). Another major effort is Slobin's edited series of crosslinguistic studies of first and second language acquisition in five volumes (so far 1985–1992). This contains case studies in a number of different countries and languages.

In addition, Elisabeth Bates, Brian MacWhinney, and associates (MacWhinney & Bates, 1989) have conducted a series of studies from the perspective of the *competition model* of language acquisition, and more recently, the *emergentist* perspective (MacWhinney, 1999). In these case studies the argument is made that the environment plays a crucial role in language acquisition, thus contradicting the perspective of nativist researchers in the Chomskyan tradition who, by and large, consider the environmental contribution to be limited, minimal, or even just trivial (Pinker, 1994).

Given the great variety of child language acquisition studies, I will take one crucial topic in SLA and see how case studies have dealt with it. This is the topic of sequences of acquisition, that is, the stages that learners go through in the acquisition of the second language. This issue is very important because educators, politicians, parents, and all other stakeholders continually debate the question of how long it takes English language learners to reach a level of proficiency that allows them to profit from mainstream education (Hakuta, 1986; Hakuta, Butler, & Witt, 2000; van Lier, 1999).

SEQUENCES IN SLA—A CASE IN POINT

L2 learners, especially young children, often begin their learning career with a silent stage, which can last for several months. During this stage, which Itoh and Hatch (1978, p. 78) call the "rejection stage," learners don't speak, and it is unclear how much they absorb. It often appears to be a rather traumatic period, during which learners have problems adjusting in the new setting, especially in immersion contexts.

Once learners begin to speak, they tend to use formulaic expressions for conversational interaction and acquire basic vocabulary. Most case studies report that grammatical structures used in these early stages are "unanalyzed," that is, they cannot be used to produce new utterances. Rather, they are acquired as whole chunks, as if they were one word. An example would be "I dunno," which contains a subject pronoun (I), an auxiliary verb (DO), a negator (NOT) and a lexical verb (KNOW), but learners do not know this at this formulaic stage (Fillmore, 1976). It is only later that they begin to distinguish verbs, negators, etc., and auxiliary verbs are acquired even later than that. So, a child may say, "I dunno" (or "adunno," more precisely) after a few months of learning English, and only later begin to realize that this is a phrase consisting of four words. In addition, something that was said correctly at one stage, such as an irregular verb form (*gave, came*) may at a later stage be changed to an incorrect form (*gived, comed*) due to the powerful influence of a rule that is beginning to be learned. This phenomenon is known as the U-shaped learning curve (Kellerman, 1985), where learning new structures involves breaking apart conversational chunks that were learned earlier as unanalyzed units.

A more psycholinguistic or cognitive science approach to the issue of developmental processing is illustrated in the recent work of Manfred Pienemann (Pienemann, 1998). The processability theory developed by Pienemann posits that there are certain stages of cognitive complexity and processing constraints in language that lead to a clearly identifiable progression in acquisition. Without going into the complex details of Pienemann's theory, at every stage there are certain prerequisites that need to be met for further progress to be possible. For example, rich lexical information needs to be available before a progression to complex syntactic patterns is possible.

Returning to the case studies, in most instances data are collected for about 6 months or less to a year or a bit more, and they report little grammatical development beyond the formulaic level (Fillmore, 1976; Itoh & Hatch, 1978). Some of the longer case studies, those that last for more than a year (Hakuta, 1975; Sato, 1990) report at the end of their study a level of grammatical mastery that is still very simple. Syntactic features such as third-person *s* (she walks), auxiliary verbs, modals, past tense, subordination, and relative clauses, and so on, are rarely developed after 1 year of exposure to English.

In case studies of adults, which are often longer than 1 year, sometimes up to 3 or 5 years long (Huebner, 1983; Ioup et al., 1995; Klein & Perdue, 1992; Schmidt, 1983; Shapira, 1978), a picture of great variability emerges. It appears that adults (say, learners19 and older; see also Bialystok & Hakuta, 1994) have a far greater range of variation in terms of speed of acquisition and ultimate achievement than do younger learners. One plausible reason for this is that younger people are in a relatively homogeneous school environment, and the range of expectations and peer contexts is similar. At least this applies to those younger people who are or remain in the school environment, and who therefore are available to be tested.

Many studies of adults (e.g., Huebner, 1983; Schmidt, 1983; Schumann, 1978) show very little grammatical improvement over time, and even studies of exceptionally successful learners show a process that takes several years (Dietrich, Klein, & Noyau, 1995; Ioup et al., 1995). Klein and Perdue, in their extensive study of second language development (the European Science Foundation project previously mentioned), report that all learners (at least untutored learners) begin by developing a "basic variety" that is grammatically very simple, but versatile and flexible for use in everyday conversation (Klein & Perdue, 1992). This basic variety is similar to what Schumann called "pidginization," and it may involve "fossilization" (Schumann, 1978). These latter terms refer to cases in which the learner stays at this simple grammatical stage indefinitely, a phenomenon Klein and Perdue also report for many of the learners studied in their multiyear, multicountry project (Klein & Perdue, 1992). However, Klein and Perdue also report cases of learners who, after 1 ½ or 2 years (there is great variability) begin to move out of the basic variety and begin to develop more complex grammatical structures, which gradually allow them a wider range of linguistic comprehension and expression.

To illustrate the issue of sequences in second language acquisition, the following are some brief summaries of some of the classic case studies:

• Hakuta (1976): Hakuta studied the acquisition of English of Uguisu, the 5-year-old daughter of a visiting scholar from Japan. Data were collected for a period of 60 weeks (roughly 1 year and 2 months), after Uguisu had had 5 months of exposure to English. The first 5 months (before data collection began) appear to have been a silent period. At the end of the data collection period (after data sample 30), the following grammatical (morphosyntactic) features are reported as not having been acquired:

3rd person s
irregular past
regular past
plural s

Although Uguisu achieved criterion (that is, 90% correct use for articles around week 40; Hakuta argues, through an analysis of correct use, that full semantic control of the article system is not acquired until much later).

• Yoshida (1978): A 3.5-year-old Japanese boy, Mikihide, was observed over a period of 7 months to study vocabulary development. The Peabody Picture Vocabulary Test (PPVT) was administered twice. During the first 3 months the subject produced one-word utterances. Comprehension was far superior to production. In 7 months, he acquired about 260 words, in many cases aided by recognition of English loanwords in Japanese. In production, his pronunciation was not always recognized by native speakers of English, and "iz" was used as a generic verb.

• Itoh and Hatch (1978): A Japanese child, Takahiro, 2.6 years old, was observed for 6 months in naturalistic context (observations, recordings). Itoh and Hatch identified three stages of language development over the period of the study:

rejection stage (3 months)
repetition stage (end of 3rd month)
spontaneous speech stage (4th month)

The repetition stage began when Takahiro's aunt came to visit and began to play a "repeat after me" game with pictures. At the end of the study, verb acquisition was quite limited in comparison to nouns. He did not mark sentences for tense. There was no evidence of 3rd person s, or of development of AUX (auxiliaries). His utterances were not highly developed, but he could carry on conversations quite easily with others.

• Sato (1990): Sato studied two Vietnamese brothers, 10 and 12, living with an English-speaking family. The length of the study was 1 year and 3 months. The participants went to school but received no native language support and no English as a Second Language (ESL) classes. The oldest, Thanh, was placed in sixth grade, the younger brother, Tai, in a third/fourth grade combination class. Sato focused on past tense reference and found very little evidence of syntacticization and minimal improvement over time. No consistent inflected past verbs were observed. Next, Sato discussed complex propositions and their syntactic encoding (predication, argument structure) and found very little evidence of the acquisition of complex propositions. Development of subordination, complementation, relative clauses, etc., was also minimal. At the end of the study the brothers were only just beginning to use logical connectors.

• Butterworth and Hatch (1978): This study focused on a 13 year-old Colombian, upper-class boy. He had had grammatical instruction in English in Colombia. He had been in school in the United States for 2 months when the study began. The study lasted 3 months, hence, final reports cover a 5-month span. Ricardo had problems adjusting to America. He did not develop tense or aspect, did not use DO-support, did not develop objective or possessive case for pronouns. Butterworth and Hatch hypothesized that the tremendous pressure Ricardo was under to express complex meanings resulted in reduction and simplification of both input and output. Overall, he showed very little improvement over the period.

• Fillmore (1976): The study looked at the L2 development of five Latino children over a period of 1 school year, from September to March. During that period, two of the children went back to Mexico for up to several months. Note, this is an issue that needs to be reckoned with: many students miss substantial portions of the school year because their families take extended trips back home, especially around Christmas time. Fillmore reported little solid progress in terms of structural development and cited a wide variation in conversational strategies used by the children to join games in the playground, etc.

To summarize, if we use case studies to address the question of how long it takes for children to acquire a second language, no clear answer emerges because the case studies are too short to provide the full picture. However, it does become clear that second language acquisition, even for children (who are popularly supposed to just "pick it up"), is a protracted affair, taking much longer than is commonly assumed. Children do give the impression early on of surprising conversational ability, but the case studies show that this impression is created by clever use of conversational phrases.

Following from this conclusion, it should come as no surprise that when English language learners reach a stage in their schooling (from fourth grade upward) when cognitive and academic language skills become of paramount importance, they hit a wall of complexity that their basic conversational skills cannot penetrate, and at that point they fall further and further behind (a phenomenon Dutch researchers have called *divergence*, see Verhoeven, 1990), unless specific steps are taken to develop their academic-linguistic competence. Superficial examinations of these learners' language skills (often by linguistically naïve/untrained counselors) suggest that this is not a language problem, and these learners are then simply shunted into low expectation streams or tracks. Politicians and other public figures who know little or nothing about language acquisition are able to claim, on the basis of hearsay about the linguistic precocity of some children who, using a reduced basic variety, are able to impress adults with their apparent fluency, that children can learn a second language within a year, and that this is sufficient for mainstreaming in the school system. There are no reliable data of any kind that could possibly support such claims or practices, which therefore must be regarded as wholly irresponsible and unprofessional.

Case studies are a powerful way of showing some of the complexities of acquiring a second language. Many more such studies are needed that document the acquisition of academic discourse at the middle and secondary school level, to find out precisely what the difficulties are that students face at that point and to develop strategies that work (Gibbons, 2002; Nystrand, 1997).

CURRENT ISSUES

Currently a great deal of educational research focuses on longitudinal, situative (contextualized), and ecological studies, ideal topics for a case study approach. In general education, an ongoing debate is that between cognitivist and situative research paradigms (Anderson, Reder, & Simon, 1997; Greeno, 1997). Issues that are debated include the role of social context (and social activity) in the acquisition of skills and knowledge and, relatedly, the extent to which abilities acquired in one task context can be transferred to another context. This notion of the relative situatedness of knowledge and skills is also important in SLA. Proficiency is variable, and the conditions that govern this variability are not at all well understood (Tarone, 1983). van Lier and Matsuo (2000) take a conversation analytical approach to variation in L2 proficiency, but it is likely that carefully documented case studies can also shed much further light on this area (Norton, 2000).

Another area much in need of case study research is the role of technology in SLA for example, case studies of Computer-Mediated Communication (CMC; Warschauer & Kern, 2000). Questions addressed include the similarities and differences between face-to-face interaction and CMC, issues of motivation and autonomy in online learning contexts (Wegerif, 1998), and the challenges of building collaborative communities of learners online. One area of great urgency is the so-called Digital Divide, the notion that access to technology is inherently unequally distributed among different social groups, genders, schools, countries, and so on. One approach taken to this issue by politicians, administrators, and business leaders is to provide "free" (nothing is ever really free, of course) hardware and wiring to poor neighborhoods and schools. However, cursory inspection suffices to reveal that, even if equipment and wiring are identical, access is not thereby magically equalized. For example, it is frequently observed that in poorer schools students tend to do mind-numbing "drill-and-kill" types of work, whereas in wealthier schools students will be designing websites, movies, electronic portfolios, and so on (Crook, 1994; Merrow, 1995). Case studies can do much to illuminate the ingredients of inequality in schools and to dispel the notion that the Digital Divide is basically about hardware and software. It is much more basically about pedagogy, professional preparation, and curriculum.

A further area in which the case study approach can be very useful is in teacher education, both pre-service and in-service. I already suggested that in graduate SLA courses students can profit from studying the prominent case studies in the field and also from conducting their own small case study. In addition, teacher professional development benefits from the use of case descriptions, either as small vignettes or as longer narrative descriptions of specific settings. Examples of this include Bailey, Curtis, & Nunan (2001), Clandinin and Connolly (1995), and Shulman (1992).

Finally, critical applied linguists (Pennycook, 2001) and critical discourse analysts (Auerbach, 1992; Clark & Ivanic, 1997; Fairclough, 1995) take an overtly ideological stance that aims to bring about social and educational change in the settings in which we work. They basically take the perspective that language is a political tool, often used as a form of control, persuasion, exclusion, and discrimination. Literacy, writing, and general language classes can focus on the sources and processes that produce these forms of linguistic inequality and assist learners in developing an awareness of the uses and abuses of language and propose strategies to counteract them. Case studies such as those conducted by Norton (1995, 1997, 2000), Heller and Martin-Jones (2001), Sarangi (1999), and Coupland (1997) can highlight such issues as racial discrimination, ageism, gender inequalities, stereotyping, the denigration of specific accents and dialects (such as "Ebonics"), and so on. Such cases can speak strongly to teachers, students, and policymakers, illustrating linguistic struggles in more vivid ways than any textbook treatment or lecture can accomplish.

FUTURE DIRECTIONS

There is an unmistakable direction in the social sciences toward a greater scrutiny of contextual factors in our efforts to understand complex phenomena such as language learning. After decades of research dominated by Cartesian (nomothetic) reductionism, in which complex phenomena are broken down into small pieces that are then investigated in controlled laboratory conditions, most researchers now acknowledge the need to take contextual factors into account. This does not mean the abolishment of nomothetic research, but it does mean the acceptance, broadly speaking, of contextualized forms of research as an equal contributor to our stock of knowledge.

This acceptance requires the development of new research approaches. A crucial element in this development is the examination of earlier pioneers who worked in contextual ways, but whose achievements were drowned out by the experimental, controlled, and causal claims of psychometricians and researchers looking for statistical significance. Thus, the work of Vygotsky (1978; van der Veer & Valsiner, 1994), Lewin (1943), Bruner (1986), Bateson (1979) and many others is experiencing a renaissance. Simultaneously, the traditional "hard" sciences such as mathematics, physics, and biology are experiencing a ground shift. Quantum theory, chaos and complexity theory, and systems theory are transforming our view of the entire physical world (Capra, 1996). These changes will also transform the way the educational and second language community does its research, and the way it builds its ontology and epistemology. For example, when I discussed the problems with boundaries in the introduction, I could have added a discussion on complex adaptive systems, self-regulating systems, dissipative structures, and other concepts that derive from complexity theory (Larsen-Freeman, 1997; van Lier, 2004). Clearly, the old order will no longer do. Even if it continues its tradition of using the hard sciences (which turn out to be much softer than we previously assumed) as an ideal to be emulated, it will have to come to grips with a shift of focus toward context rather than isolation, understanding rather than proof, and relations rather than objects.

With this renewed importance of context in mind, what are some topics that future case studies might address? A few possibilities are:

- *Activity theory.* One model of activity theory has been illustrated by Engeström (1966) in an investigation of medical clinics in Finland. It may be a useful contextual model for case studies in language learning contexts that systematically examine practices and institutional structures alongside the activities of learners.
- *Academic language development for mainstreamed English language learners.* What

are the difficulties that students face and how do they and their teachers deal with them? Also, the role of the student's native or other language(s) in the acquisition of academic English abilities needs much more scrutiny than it has hitherto received.

- *Ecological validity in research and assessment practices.* Contextualized case studies of large-scale standardized testing compared with case studies in settings in which authentic, performance-based forms of assessment are used (such as portfolios).
- *Project-based approaches to language learning,* with a focus on the use of various technologies. How do learners adapt to a learning situation that is not transmission-based but in which they have choices and basically construct their own learning environment?
- *Systems theory as a model for contextualized research.* In addition to Engeström's activity theory model previously mentioned, there are other contextual research models that can be usefully applied in case study research. These include Bronfenbrenner's nested ecosystems (1979, 1993) and Checkland's soft systems model (1981; van Lier, 2004).

Contextualized research such as case study research is complex and messy. Some theory of connecting context and case is necessary, regardless of how the boundaries of the case are drawn. I have mentioned just three models of context: Engeström's activity theory, Bronfenbrenner's nested ecosystems, and Checkland's soft systems approach. Which particular model is used is perhaps less important than the realization that a consistent and systematic view of context and a clear connection between person and context are necessary. This is particularly so when the case study is an *intrinsic* rather than an *instrumental* one, to use a distinction made by Stake (1995). In an intrinsic case study the case itself is the focus of attention, the case (a student, a class, a group, etc.) is intrinsically interesting to the researcher. In such a case contextual factors are, as previously argued, of key importance. If, on the other hand, the motivation for the case study is a particular research question, the focus will be on gathering the relevant data rather than on the case itself. This type of study is called an instrumental case study by Stake (1995). In practice, however, it is often not easy to distinguish particular studies so easily, because they usually combine both intrinsic and extrinsic or instrumental interests, either from the outset, or because certain interesting phenomena emerge during the study. But Stake's general point is well taken: "The more the case study is an intrinsic case study, the more attention needs to be paid to the contexts" (1995, p. 64).

CONCLUSION

Cases are specific persons, places, or events that are interesting and worthy of intensive study. The case is a real-life entity that operates in a specific time and place. Whether or not the contextual boundaries can be easily drawn, case study is contextual study, unfolding over time and in real settings. Often the phenomena of interest become visible as the case study proceeds, surprising facts come to light and demand attention.

Case studies have often been regarded as somewhat marginal compared to more experimentally controlled types of study. I have tried to show in this chapter that, in fact, case studies have played a crucial role in shaping our field, and that their importance as ways of doing research is likely to increase over the near term, as the importance of contextual analysis is realized more and more.

A number of resources containing advice about doing case studies exist. In the general educational field, some of the major sources are Merriam (1998), Miles and Huberman (1994), Stake (1995), and Yin (1989). In the applied linguistics and language learning field, sources include Johnson (1992) and Nunan (1992).

One of the inherent problems in doing case studies is the drawing of boundaries, in time and space, around the case. How long? How many different places? How many people and influences? Some contextual framework is needed, and I suggested three: Engeström's activity model (1996), Bronfenbrenner's nested ecosystems (1979), and Checkland's soft systems method (1981). Any one of these models, or other systematic models of context, can help the case researcher navigate the contextual chaos that seems to surround every interesting case.

Once the case and its contexts are drawn as a rough sketch or framework, a major task of the case study researcher is that of telling the story of the case. Descriptive and narrative skill are essential to bring the crucial points across in vivid and realistic ways to the audience for whom the case study is intended. Once again, such narrative reporting has at times been sneered at for being subjective and unscientific. However, recent work has forcefully established narrative (or discursive) work as potentially rigorous and frequently highly incisive and revealing (Harré & Gillett, 1994; McEwan & Egan, 1995; Wortham, 2001).

In addition to contributing in major ways to the field, case studies can be useful in at least two other ways: as an induction to the field for graduate students in educational linguistics, both in terms of studying the classic case studies and in terms of conducting their own small studies; and as tools in teacher education and development (Bailey, Curtis, & Nunan, 2001; Clandinin & Connolly, 1995).

It is perhaps appropriate to finish with a quote from Stake. It may sound somewhat lofty, but it is a useful antidote to an educational and political culture that at times seems to find significance and value only in rankings of people and schools based on standardized test scores.

> Finishing a case study is the consummation of a work of art. A few of us will find case study, excepting our family business, the finest work of our lifetime. Because it is an exercise in such depth, the study is an opportunity to see what others have not yet seen, to reflect the uniqueness of our own lives, to engage the best of our interpretive powers, and to make, even by its integrity alone, an advocacy for those things we cherish. The case study ahead is a splendid palette (1995, p. 136).

NOTES

1. Wolcott calls his study an ethnography, but it is at the same time a case study, under the definitions discussed in this chapter.

REFERENCES

Anderson, J. R., Reder, L. M., & Simon, H. A. (1997). Situative versus cognitive perspectives: Form versus substance. *Educational Researcher, 26*(1), 18–21.

Auerbach, E. (1992). *Making meaning, making change: Participatory curriculum development for adult ESL literacy.* McHenry, IL: Delta Systems.

Bailey, K. B., Curtis, A., & Nunan, D. (2001). *Pursuing professional development: The self as source.* Boston: Heinle & Heinle.

Bateson, G. (1979). *Mind and nature: A necessary unity.* London: Fontana.

Bialystok, E. & Hakuta, K. (1994). *In other words: The science and psychology of second-language acquisition.* New York: Basic Books.

Bremer, K., Roberts, C., Vasseur, M. T., Simonot, M., & Broeder, P. (1996). *Achieving understanding.* London: Longman.

Bronfenbrenner, U. (1979). *The ecology of human development.* Cambridge, MA: Harvard University Press.

Bronfenbrenner, U. (1993). The ecology of cognitive development: Research models and fugitive findings. In R. H. Wozniak & K. W., Fischer (Eds.), *Development in context: Acting and thinking in specific environments* (pp. 3–44). Hillsdale, NJ: Lawrence Erlbaum Associates.

Bruner, J. (1986). *Actual minds, possible worlds.* Cambridge, MA: Harvard University Press.

Butterworth, G. & Hatch, E. (1978). A Spanish-speaking adolescent's acquisition of English syntax. In E. Hatch (Ed.), *Second language acquisition: A book of readings* (pp. 231–245). Rowley, MA: Newbury House.

Capra, F. (1996). *The web of life: A new scientific understanding of living systems*. New York: Anchor Books.

Checkland, P. (1981). *Systems thinking, systems practice*. New York: Wiley.

Clandinin, D. J., & Connolly, F. M. (1995). *Teachers' professional knowledge landscapes*. New York: Teachers' College Press.

Clark, R., & Ivanic, R. (1997). Critical discourse analysis and educational change. In L. van Lier & D. Corsen (Eds.), *Encyclopedia of language and education* (pp. 217–227). Norwell, MA: Kluwer Academic.

Coupland, N. (1997). Language, ageing and ageism: A project for applied linguistics? *International Journal of Applied Linguistics, 7*(1), 26–48.

Crook, C. (1994). *Computers and the collaborative experience of learning*. London: Routledge.

Dietrich, R., Klein, W., & Noyau, C. (1995). *The acquisition of temporality in a second language*. Amsterdam: Benjamins.

Engeström, Y. (1996). Developmental studies of work as a testbench of activity theory: The case of primary care medical practice. In C. Chaiklin & J. Lave (Eds.), *Understanding practice: Perspectives on activity theory* (pp. 64–103). Cambridge, UK: Cambridge University Press.

Fairclough, N. (1995). *Critical discourse analysis: The critical study of language*. London: Longman.

Fillmore, L. W. (1976). *The second time around: Cognitive and social strategies in second language acquisition*. Unpublished doctoral dissertation, Stanford University, Palo Alto, CA.

Gibbons, P. (2002). *Scaffolding language, scaffolding learning: Teaching second language learners in the mainstream classroom*. Portsmouth, NH: Heinemann.

Greeno, J. G. (1997). On claims that answer the wrong questions. *Educational Researcher, 26*(1), 5–17.

Hakuta, K. (1975). Becoming bilingual at age five: The story of Uguisu. Unpublished senior honors thesis, Harvard University, Cambridge, MA.

Hakuta, K. (1976). A case study of a Japanese child learning English as a second language. *Language Learning, 26,* 321–351.

Hakuta, K. (1986). *Mirror of language: The debate on bilingualism*. New York: Basic Books.

Hakuta, K., Butler, Y. G., & Witt, D. (2000). How long does it take English learners to attain proficiency? Retrieved April 15, 2001, from http://www.stanford.edu/~hakuta/Docs/HowLong.pdf .

Halliday, M. A. K. (1975). *Learning how to mean*. London: Edward Arnold.

Harré, R., & Gillett, G. (1994). *The discursive mind*. Thousand Oaks, CA: Sage.

Hatch, E. (Ed.). (1978). *Second language acquisition*. Rowley, MA: Newbury House.

Heller, M., & Martin-Jones, M. (Eds.) (2001). *Voices of authority: Education and linguistic difference*. Norwood, NJ: Ablex.

Huebner, T. (1983). *A longitudinal analysis of the acquisition of English*. Ann Arbor, MI: Karoma.

Ioup, G., Boustagui, E., El Tigi, M., & Moselle, M. (1995). Reexamining the critical period hypothesis. *Studies in Second Language Acquisition, 16,* 73–98.

Itoh, H., & Hatch, E. (1978). Second language acquisition: A case study. In E. Hatch (Ed.), *Second language acquisition: A book of readings* (pp. 76–88). Rowley, MA: Newbury House.

Johnson, D. (1992). *Approaches to research in second language learning*. New York: Longman.

Kellerman, E. (1985). If at first you do succeed. . . . In S. Gass & C. Madden, (Eds.), *Input in second language acquisition* (pp. 345–353). Rowley, MA: Newbury House.

Klein, W., & Perdue, C. (1992). *Utterance structure: Developing grammar again*. Amsterdam: Benjamins.

Larsen-Freeman, D. (1997). Chaos/complexity science and second language acquisition. *Applied Linguistics, 18*(2), 141–165.

Lewin, K. (1943). Defining the "field at a given time." *Psychological Review, 50*(3), 292–310.

MacWhinney, B., & Bates, E. (Eds.). (1989). *The crosslinguistic study of sentence processing*. Cambridge, UK: Cambridge University Press.

MacWhinney, B. (Ed.). (1999). *The emergence of language*. Mahwah, NJ: Lawrence Erlbaum Associates.

McEwan, H., & Egan, K. (Eds.). (1995). *Narrative in teaching, learning, and research*. New York: Teachers College Press.

Maturana, H. R., & Varela, F. J. (1992). *The tree of knowledge: The biological roots of human understanding*. Boston: Shambhala.

Merriam, S. B. (1998). *Case study research in education: A qualitative approach*. San Francisco: Jossey-Bass. (Original work published 1988)

Merrow, J. (1995). Four million computers can be wrong! *Education Week XIV*(27), 52, 38.

Miles, M. B., & Huberman, A. M. (1994). *Qualitative data analysis*. Thousand Oaks, CA: Sage.

Norton Peirce, B. (1995). Social identity, investment, and language learning. *TESOL Quarterly 29,* 9–31.

Norton, B. (1997). Language, identity, and the ownership of English. *TESOL Quarterly, 31,* 409–429.

Norton. B. (2000). *Identity and language learning: Gender, ethnicity and educational change*. New York: Longman.

Nunan, D. (1992). *Research methods in language learning*. Cambridge, UK: Cambridge University Press.

Nystrand, M. (with Gamoran, A., Kachur, A., & Prendergast, C.) (1997). *Opening dialogue: Understanding the dynamics of language and learning in the English classroom*. New York: Teachers College Press.

Pavlenko, A., & Lantolf, J. (2000). Second language learning as participation and the (re)construction of selves. In J. Lantolf (Ed.), *Sociocultural theory in language learning* (pp. 155–178). Oxford, UK: Oxford University Press.

Pennycook, A. (2001). *Critical applied linguistics*. Mahwah, NJ: Lawrence Erlbaum Associates.

Pienemann, M. (1998). *Language processing and second language development: Processability theory*. Amsterdam: Benjamins.

Pinker, S. (1994). *The language instinct*. New York: Morrow.

Sarangi, S. (1999). Talk, work and institutional order. In M. Heller & R. J. Watts (Eds.), *Language, power and social processes*. Berlin: Mouton de Gruyter.

Sato, C. (1990). *The syntax of conversation in interlanguage development*. Tuebingen, Germany: Gunther Narr.

Schmidt, R. (1983). Interaction, acculturation, and acquisition of communicative competence. In N. Wolfson & E. Judd (Eds.), *Sociolinguistics and second language acquisition* (pp. 137–174). Rowley, MA: Newbury House.

Schmidt, R., & Frota, S. (1986). Developing basic conversational ability in a second language: A case study of an adult learner of Portuguese. In R. Day (Ed.), *"Talking to learn": Conversation in second language acquisition* (pp. 237–326). Rowley, MA: Newbury House.

Schumann, J. (1978). Second language acquisition: The pidginization hypothesis. In E. Hatch (Ed.), *Second language acquisition: A book of readings* (pp. 256–271). Rowley, MA: Newbury House.

Shapira, R. G. (1978). The non-learning of English: Case study of an adult. In E. Hatch (Ed.), *Second language acquisition: A book of readings* (pp. 246–255). Rowley, MA: Newbury House.

Shulman, J. H. (Ed.). (1992). *Case methods in teacher education*. New York: Teachers College Press.

Shulman, L. S. (1992). Towards a pedagogy of cases. In J. H. Shulman (Ed.), *Case methods in teacher education* (pp. 1–30). New York: Teachers College Press.

Slobin, D. (Ed.). (1985–1992). *The crosslinguistic study of language acquisition*. Hillsdale, NJ: Lawrence Erlbaum Associates.

Smith, L. M. (1978). An evolving logic of participant observation, educational ethnography and other case studies. In L. Shulman (Ed.), *Review of research in education* (pp. 316–377). Chicago: Peacock.

Stake, R. E. (1995). *The art of case study research*. Thousand Oaks, CA: Sage.

Tarone, E. (1983). On the variability of interlanguage systems. *Applied Linguistics, 4*, 143–163.

van der Veer, R., & Valsiner, J. (Eds.). (1994). *The Vygotsky reader*. Oxford, UK: Blackwell.

van Lier, L. (1999). What we know from case studies of structural development. Report prepared for the Office of Bilingual Education and Minority Languages Affairs (OBEMLA). Washington, DC: U.S. Department of Education.

van Lier, L. (2004). *The ecology and semiotics of language learning: A sociocultural perspective*. Boston: Kluwer Academic.

van Lier, L., & Matsuo, N. (2000). Varieties of conversational experience: Looking for learning opportunities. *Applied Language Learning, 11*(2), 265–287.

Verhoeven, L. (1990). Language variation and learning to read. In P. Reitsma & L. Verhoeven (Eds.), *Acquisition of reading in Dutch* (pp. 105–120). Dordrecht, The Netherlands: Foris.

Vygotsky, L. (1978). *Mind in society*. Cambridge, UK: Cambridge University Press.

Warschauer, M., & Kern, R. (Eds.). (2000). *Network-based language teaching: Concepts and practice*. Cambridge, UK: Cambridge University Press.

Wegerif, R. (1998). The social dimension of asynchronous learning networks. *JALN, 2*,(1). Retrieved September 23, 2001, from http://www.aln.org/

Wolcott, H. F. (1973). *The man in the principal's office: An ethnography*. New York: Holt, Rinehart & Winston.

Wortham, S. (2001). *Narratives in action: A strategy for research and analysis*. New York: Teachers College Press.

Yin, R. K. (1989). *Case study research: Design and methods (Rev. Ed.)*. Thousand Oaks, CA: Sage.

Yoshida, M. (1978). The acquisition of English vocabulary by a Japanese-speaking child. In E. Hatch (Ed.), *Second language acquisition: A book of readings* (pp. 91–100). Rowley, MA: Newbury House.

12

Quantitative Research Methods

Anne Lazaraton
University of Minnesota

INTRODUCTION

In 1995, Ron Scollon (citing Goodwin, 1994) remarked that "research methodology is a cover term for day-to-day practices which are often less well formed than our final research reports suggest" (Scollon, 1995, p. 381). This is problematic, in the sense that "the validity of any discipline is predicated on the assumption that the research methods used to gather data are sufficiently understood and agreed upon" (Gass, Cohen, & Tarone, 1994, p. xiii). For the discipline of applied linguistics, a fundamental change in perspective (if not practice) would appear to be underway in its research, from an essentially unquestioned reliance on and preference for quasi-experimental studies employing parametric statistics in the 1980s, to a broader, multidisciplinary perspective on research methodology, as well as the nature of research itself, in the 1990s and to the present time. The field seems to be struggling with a redefinition of its research goals, methods, and paradigms, as can be seen in terms of our growing acceptance of qualitative methods (e.g., Lazaraton, 1995), our increasingly pointed questions about the significance of our research (e.g., Hamp-Lyons, 1998; Rampton, 1997), and our continuing explorations of alternatives in our research (e.g., Cumming, 1994). This chapter proposes to analyze the status of quantitative research in applied linguistics by:

- Overviewing the nature of quantitative research in second language learning and teaching in the last 20 years by surveying the literature on research methodology published in four applied linguistics journals (*Language Learning, Modern Language Journal, Studies in Second Language Acquisition*, and *TESOL Quarterly*) and in scholarly books to ascertain what applied linguists are and have been saying about quantitative research methods.
- Summarizing the results of an empirical study that analyzed the published research studies in these same journals over an 11-year period (1991–2001) to determine what the actual research methods employed were.

It is hoped that this information will be useful for understanding our own choices (and biases) in research methodology, for reflecting on how we go about training students in those research methods, and for appreciating, if not embracing, the methodological choices of others in their own research endeavors.

BACKGROUND: A HISTORICAL OVERVIEW

Perhaps the best place to start this retrospective is in 1982, with the landmark publication of Hatch and Farhady's *Research Design and Statistics for Applied Linguistics*. Grotjahn (1988) observed that it "filled a gap in applied linguistics, where a book on research design and statistics was sorely lacking" (p. 64). The authors wrote the beginner book to "demystify" statistics and to make the procedures covered easy to carry out. Basic concepts in research design and research report formatting are covered, as are a number of parametric statistical procedures, from *t*-tests to ANOVA to regression. Although now outdated (and out of print), the book teaches some basic computer commands for and explains printouts from mainframe SPSS (using punch cards!) to let the computer "do the work for you." End of chapter exercises require readers to solve problems that require statistical calculations.

In the next several years, two more texts, Butler's (1985) *Statistics in Linguistics* and Woods, Fletcher and Hughes's (1986) *Statistics in Language Studies* also appeared. Butler's book (which followed and is similar to Anshen's 1978 text, *Statistics for Linguists*) provides a solid introduction to statistics for linguists, using problems with linguistics data. The book (which is out of print) is aimed at beginners and covers statistical concepts, research design, and various parametric and nonparametric statistical tests. Woods et al., in contrast, is a high-level text that teaches the reader how to evaluate and to use statistics. Examples are also based on linguistic data, and there is a heavy emphasis on understanding probability and statistical inference (but little on research design). Advanced, multivariate procedures such as cluster analysis, MANOVA, principal components analysis, and factor analysis are covered. End of chapter exercises require the reader to compute statistics; an appendix explains how to do these computations with a computer.

In 1986, Henning published an article in *TESOL Quarterly* to define quantitative research methods and to analyze the kinds of articles that were being published in the field at that time. He defined quantitative research as an endeavor in which quantities of data are tallied, manipulated, or systematically aggregated. He looked in two journals—*TESOL Quarterly* and *Language Learning*—over 5-year periods from 1970 to 1985, and found an increase in the number of quantitative articles: In *TESOL Quarterly* there was an increase from 12% to 61%, and in *Language Learning* from 24% to 92%. He viewed this as "a positive development—a kind of coming of age of a discipline" (p. 704).

At about the same time, Lazaraton, Riggenbach and Ediger (1987) conducted a survey of 300 professionals working in the field, asking them about their attitudes toward statistics and empirical research and their knowledge in these areas. Of the surveys sent out, 121 were returned, mostly by university faculty working in North America. The majority of the respondents indicated that they had taken, at most, one or two courses in research design and statistics, a number most felt was insufficient for the work they were doing or for the kind of advising they were being asked to do in their jobs. The second area surveyed was the respondent's ability to use and to interpret 23 statistical terms (such as mean or median) and statistical procedures (such as correlation or *t*-test). On a 4-point scale, respondents reported a mean of less than 2 for terms like power, Rasch model, and Scheffé test.

Brown's *Understanding Research in Second Language Learning: A Teacher's Guide to Statistics and Research Design* appeared in 1988. The text, designed for teachers with no statistics background, focuses on the critical *evaluation* (in contrast to production) of statistical research. In other words, Brown aims for "research literacy" by covering the basics of research design, simple statistical procedures, and approaches to research evaluation. End of chapter review and application questions reinforce the material.

One year later, Seliger and Shohamy (1989) published *Second Language Research Methods*, a guide to research methods and design, rather than statistical procedures themselves. They focus on the process of both experimental and naturalistic research (planning, data collection, analysis, report write-up) and the principles underlying it. Readers are not taught how to do data analysis (in the one chapter devoted to it), but are given examples to read and to process. End of chapter exercises reinforce chapter concepts.

The results of the Lazaraton, Riggenbach and Ediger (1987) study led us to conclude that applied linguistics professionals felt limited in their ability to carry out the empirical work they were doing. One outcome of this survey was the decision by Evelyn Hatch to write a revision of Hatch and Farhady's 1982 book, *Research Design and Statistics for Applied Linguistics*. This resulted in *The Research Manual: Design and Statistics for Applied Linguistics* (Hatch & Lazaraton, 1991), which is twice as long as the original and includes information on nonparametric statistics. Since the survey respondents reported trouble interpreting research terms and procedures, actual research summaries for readers to critique are included, a unique feature of the text that I consider extremely useful. Additionally, the book aims toward statistical literacy as well as productivity. Not all applied linguists engage in statistical research, but most need to have access to the professional literature, and without some basic knowledge of research design and statistics, they are unable to read the majority of articles in professional journals. A separate computer supplement (Lazaraton, 1991), which is now outdated (and out of print, like *The Research Manual*), explains using mainframe SAS and SPSS to solve end-of-chapter problems in the manual itself.

The same year, Nunan (1991) authored an article in *Studies in Second Language Acquisition* that analyzed 50 published empirical investigations over the previous 25 years. He attempted to characterize the studies in terms of the environment in which the data were collected, the rationale for the research done, the design and method of data collection, the type of data collected, and the type of analysis conducted. He found that 35 out of 50 studies were conducted in classrooms or under laboratory conditions, whereas only two were conducted naturalistically. Unfortunately, he notes, the insistence on conducting research in classrooms or under experimental conditions limits the generalizability of findings, since elicited data may or may not be consistent with data collected in more natural environments. Nunan found that 18 studies were experiments, (32 were not), 10 were carried out by observation, 9 were conducted by analyzing transcripts, and 25 used elicited data. Questionnaires, interviews, diary studies, and introspection were rare. Nunan concluded his article by suggesting that more classroom-based research be done, since the studies he had looked at were narrow in scope and focus and failed to acknowledge the social context in which learning foreign languages takes place.

Two additional texts appeared in 1992. The first, Johnson's *Approaches to Research in Second Language Learning* (now out of print), serves as a guide to six research approaches (correlational, case-study, survey, ethnographic, experimental, and large-scale). The emphasis is on issues and interpretation in these research approaches (rather than statistical procedures themselves), and concepts are reinforced by extended sample studies that are critiqued using evaluative questions developed for each approach. No exercises are included, but extensive references conclude each chapter. The second book, Nunan's (1992) *Research Methods in Language Learning*, assumes no prior knowledge of research design and statistics. It strives to help readers understand and critique empirical research studies rather than produce them. He, like Johnson, covers a range of research methods—experimental, ethnographic, case study, classroom, introspective, and interaction analysis. Sample studies are included in each chapter, which help readers understand the concepts, as do end of chapter activities.

A valuable contribution to the topic of research methods is Cumming's 1994 edited article in *TESOL Quarterly*, "Alternatives in TESOL Research: Descriptive, Interpretive and Ideological Orientations." He asked various researchers to write a short piece on alternative approaches to research, including *descriptive* approaches (looking at learner language, analyzing verbal reports, and undertaking text analyses), *interpretive* approaches (classroom interaction analysis and ethnography), and *ideological* approaches (critical pedagogical research and participatory action research). However, although these are alternative orientations that one might choose in doing research, the analyses that result are still heavily quantitative. Tarone (1994a), the author of the piece on analyzing learner language, says that "researchers typically agree, in theory, that both qualitative and quantitative methodologies are essential to the accurate description and analysis of learner language" (p. 676), yet goes on to remark that "quantitative methods of research have probably been overdominant in attempts to analyze learner language, as well as in suggesting implications of language analysis research for the ESL classroom" (p. 678). This comment is certainly in line with what I found in the journal, *Studies in Second Language Acquisition*, where analyses of learner language frequently appear and where over 90% of the articles from 1991 to 1997 were quantitatively based; this number was 100% from 1998 to 2001 (see the following). Pennycook, in his piece on critical pedagogical approaches to research, makes a similar point: "This lack of published work [in critical pedagogical research in education], however, reflects not so much a paucity of critical work into questions concerning ESL in the workplace, ESL and gender, ESL and antiracist education, and so on, but rather the difficulty in getting such work published" (p. 691).

Several other research-related issues that have arisen recently should at least be highlighted here. The proper study, scope, method, and data of second language acquisition has been hotly debated in *Modern Language Journal* (e.g., Firth & Wagner, 1997, 1998; Gass, 1998; Long, 1997). Tarone (1994a), among others, reminds us that the emphasis on elicited data and lab-like conditions in second language acquisition (SLA) research means that we really have no idea of how people deal with language, with language learning, and with the demands of using language in *real* contexts. Along these lines, Nicholson and Bunting (2001) argue that there is a serious mismatch between, on the one hand, the language learners studied and reported on in our scholarly journals (primarily university students), and the characteristics of the adult ESL learner population at large, on the other.

Additionally, mention must be made of several developments in *TESOL Quarterly* over the last decade or so. The first was the debut of the edited *Research Issues* column in the Winter 1990 issue of the journal. Twenty topics (see Appendix B for a complete list), discussed by two scholars each, have dealt with both qualitative and quantitative research issues such as multiple *t*-tests (Winter 1990), the use of verbal protocols (Summer 1998), and sources of bias in SLA research (Winter 1994). Second, *TESOL Quarterly* has been at the forefront of setting out guidelines for statistical research (instituted in the Summer 1993 issue), for qualitative research (Winter 1994), and for informed consent (Spring 1999). It is heartening to see one of our journals take the lead in suggesting standards against which both journal submissions and published research can be judged. I would be remiss in not pointing out that *Language Learning*, in its September 2000 (Volume 50, Issue No. 3) issue, began requiring submitting authors "to provide a measure of effect size, at least for the major statistical contrasts they report" (Ellis, 2000, p. xii). I applaud this effort to steer writers (and readers) away from putting too much stock in significant *p* values, which are highly dependent on sample size.

Finally, it is worth remarking that no more *widely used* textbooks on research design and/or statistics have been published since 1992, although several more specialized books have appeared: for example, Scholfield's *Quantifying Language* (1995), which covers the types and analyses of quantifiable data; McDonough and McDonough's *Research Methods for English Language Teachers* (1997), which provides an introduction to qualitative and quantitative research methodology and data collection for classroom research; Wray, Trott, and Bloomer's *Projects in Linguistics* (1998) covers research topics, tools, and techniques for 10 areas of linguistics, such as SLA, accent and dialects, and language and gender; and Porte's *Appraising Research in Second Language Learning* (2002), which teaches the critical analysis of quantitative research studies. In any case, the interested reader should consult Appendix A for a feature comparison of the 12 books mentioned in this section.

Thus, we have seen that a number of major textbooks, various journal articles, and several journalistic decisions have shaped the current thinking on research methodology in applied linguistics. But how well does actual practice reflect these thoughts, opinions, and edicts? It is also worth considering research methodology articles that appear in our scholarly journals; furthermore, we should not overlook the contributions that the journals themselves make in setting or delimiting a research agenda and its consequent methodological choices. The next section attempts to answer this question.

THE STUDY: METHOD

I made a careful analysis of all the data-based, empirical research articles in four applied linguistics journals over an 11-year period (1991–2001). The methodology employed was in line with a survey by Thomas (1994) of four refereed journals spanning a 5-year period. Although she was interested in definitions of second language (L2) proficiency, our goals are the same. She points out that the journals that we both reviewed "prominently mention research on L2 acquisition in their statements of editorial policy. Although their readerships probably overlap, they have differing histories, institutional affiliations and theoretical perspectives" (p. 311). The four journals were: *Language Learning*, subtitled "A Journal of Research in Language Studies"; *Modern Language Journal*, which is "Devoted to research and discussion about the learning and teaching of foreign and second languages"; *Studies in Second Language Acquisition*, whose editorial policy states that it is "devoted to problems and issues in second and foreign acquisition of any language"; and *TESOL Quarterly*, which "represents a variety of cross-disciplinary interests, both theoretical and practical" and which addresses "implications and applications of this research to issues in our profession."

A number of articles appearing in these journals were excluded from the study. First, articles in special topics issues were not included as these were guest-edited and therefore not necessarily an accurate reflection of normal editorial policy or normal submissions to the publication. Second, I only analyzed articles that reported first-hand results of research; meta-analyses and replications of previous studies were omitted. I also excluded conceptual and theoretical articles, position pieces that didn't report empirical research, book reviews, special edited columns, and solicited articles. My goal was to get an idea of the "regular" articles published in these journals.

For each issue of each journal, I started by tallying the number of qualitative and quantitative articles in order to get a rough idea of the kinds of research being published. Those that statistically analyze data are clearly quantitative, whereas those that report that, for example, the work is an ethnography using field notes and quotes from respondents, are clearly qualitative. In some cases it was unclear how to categorize approximately seven articles; in these cases, the data were analyzed quantitatively, but the majority of the article consisted of quotes from learners, transcripts etc. These articles were categorized as "mixed."

TABLE 12.1

Totals Across All Journals

Articles	1991	1992	1993	1994	1995	1996	1997	1998	1999	2000	2001	Total
Qualitative	38	52	45	36	46	41	34	37	40	39	42	450 (86%)
Quantitative	0	6	4	3	9	7	4	7	7	9	11	67 (13%)
Mixed	0	(1)	(2)	(2)	0	(1)	(1)	0	0	0	0	(7) (1%)
Total	38	59	51	41	55	49	39	44	47	48	53	524

Results

Table 12.1 shows that a total of 524 empirical articles were analyzed: 450 (86%) were quantitative in nature, 67 (13%) were qualitative, whereas the remaining 7 (1%; shown in parentheses in Tables 12.1 and 12.2) were a mixture of both:

However, these results are somewhat misleading, as shown by a breakdown by journal in Table 12.2:

These data indicate that, with the exception of *TESOL Quarterly*, in the other journals, over 85% of the published articles employ quantitative research procedures (*Language Learning*, 96%; *Modern Language Journal*, 87%; *Studies in Second Language Acquisition*, 95%). Only in *TESOL Quarterly* was there anything approaching a balance in research approaches, and still, nearly 60% of the articles were quantitative, whereas just over 40% were qualitative. *Modern Language Journal* shows a trend in this direction, in that 15 of the 22 (68%) qualitative articles were published in the last 4 years of the 11-year period. It seems that *TESOL Quarterly* (and perhaps *Modern Language Journal*) would be the primary journal of the four to which one would consider sending a qualitative research report, as there would seem to be little chance of it being published in the other refereed journals through the normal blind review process.

In the next stage, I looked at the statistical procedures used in the quantitative research articles and tallied the number of times each procedure was used per year over the four journals. These results appear in Table 12.3.

The most common procedures were those labeled as "descriptive," where frequencies, percentages, means, and standard deviations are presented. Although 76% (*Language Learning*) to 90% (*TESOL Quarterly*) of the articles in all four journals presented descriptive statistics, I found it surprising that this number was not 100%. This was particularly noticeable in *Modern Language Journal*, where even ANOVA source tables were missing. It is my belief that all statistical analyses should be accompanied by the descriptive statistics on which they are based. It should be noted that even some of the qualitative studies presented descriptive statistics, contrary to the belief that qualitative researchers never count. A couple of the published ethnographies presented tables of frequency counts or percentages.

I found it particularly interesting to see that Analysis of Variance (ANOVA) accounted for over 40% of the statistical analyses in the articles I examined. Clearly, a lot of applied linguistics research is focused on the *effect* that a variable (or variables) has on some outcome measure. Specifically, ANOVA was employed in almost 50% of the articles in *Language Learning* and in over 50% in *Studies in Second Language Acquisition*. This is somewhat troubling because the Lazaraton, Riggenbach and Ediger (1987) survey found that ANOVA was not ranked among the easier procedures to interpret or to carry out. As *The Research Manual* (Hatch & Lazaraton, 1991) points out, ANOVA has a number of fairly stringent assumptions related to it, and my guess (but not a fact, since I did not analyze this specifically) is that at least some of studies that used ANOVA did so in violation of at least some of the assumptions of the procedure.

TABLE 12.2

Data-based Studies By Year and Journal

Language Learning

Article	1991	1992	1993	1994	1995	1996	1997	1998	1999	2000	2001	Total
Qualitative	13	14	13	15	13	14	14	11	13	13	15	148 (96%)
Quantitative	0	1	0	0	1	0	0	1	2	0	1	6 (4%)
Mixed						(1)						(1)
Total	13	15	13	15	14	15	14	12	15	13	16	155

Modern Language Journal

Article	1991	1992	1993	1994	1995	1996	1997	1998	1999	2000	2001	Total
Qualitative	11	19	22	9	17	16	6	14	17	10	9	150 (87%)
Quantitative	0	2	0	1	2	2	0	2	3	5	5	22 (13%)
Mixed				(1)								(1)
Total	11	21	22	11	19	18	6	16	20	15	14	173

Studies in Second Language Acquisition

Article	1991	1992	1993	1994	1995	1996	1997	1998	1999	2000	2001	Total
Qualitative	8	9	8	8	8	8	8	9	8	10	11	95 (95%)
Quantitative	0	0	0	0	0	0	0	0	0	0	0	0
Mixed		(1)	(2)	(1)			(1)					(5) (5%)
Total	8	10	10	9	8	8	9	9	8	10	11	100

TESOL Quarterly

Article	1991	1992	1993	1994	1995	1996	1997	1998	1999	2000	2001	Total
Qualitative	6	10	2	4	8	3	6	3	2	6	7	57 (59%)
Quantitative	0	3	4	2	6	5	4	4	2	4	5	39 (41%)
Total	6	13	6	6	14	8	10	7	4	10	12	96

TABLE 12.3

Statistical Procedures By Year and Journal

Procedure		1991	1992	1993	1994	1995	1996	1997	1998	1999	2000	2001	Total
Descriptive	LL	8	10	8	13	11	17	9	8	11	10	8	113/148 (76%)
	MLJ	7	15	19	9	14	14	5	14	14	8	8	127/150 (85%)
	SSLA	6	6	8	7	7	6	9	7	8	9	11	84/95 (88%)
	TQ	6	9	2	4	6	3	5	3	2	6	7	53/59 (90%)
	Total	27	40	37	33	38	40	28	32	35	33	34	377/450 (84%)
Procedure		1991	1992	1993	1994	1995	1996	1997	1998	1999	2000	2001	Total
ANOVA	LL	8	5	6	7	6	7	7	6	5	9	5	71/148 (48%)
	MLJ	4	6	7	5	6	6	2	8	10	4	4	62/150 (41%)
	SSLA	3	3	4	5	6	6	3	4	5	6	5	50/95 (53%)
	TQ	2	5	0	0	3	0	1	1	1	0	3	16/59 (27%)
	Total	17	19	17	17	21	19	13	19	21	19	17	199/450 (44%)
Procedure		1991	1992	1993	1994	1995	1996	1997	1998	1999	2000	2001	Total
Pearson	LL	4	6	3	3	4	3	3	2	6	6	2	42/148 (28%)
	MLJ	4	5	7	4	4	5	1	4	10	2	5	51/150 (34%)
	SSLA	1	3	0	2	3	1	3	2	2	2	4	23/95 (24%)
	TQ	2	1	0	0	2	0	1	0	0	2	2	10/57 (18%)
	Total	11	15	10	9	13	9	8	8	18	12	13	126/450 (28%)

Procedure	1991	1992	1993	1994	1995	1996	1997	1998	1999	2000	2001	Total
t-test												
LL	4	2	5	2	4	3	3	3	2	3	2	33/148 (22%)
MLJ	5	2	4	1	5	5	2	3	3	1	4	35/150 (23%)
SSLA	1	1	3	3	3	1	3	3	1	1	2	22/95 (23%)
TQ	1	1	0	0	2	0	1	1	0	3	3	12/57 (21%)
Total	11	6	12	6	14	9	9	10	6	8	11	102/450 (23%)

Procedure	1991	1992	1993	1994	1995	1996	1997	1998	1999	2000	2001	Total
Regression												
LL	4	3	2	1	3	2	1	1	3	2	2	24/148 (16%)
MLJ	3	6	2	0	2	1	0	1	0	1	3	19/150 (13%)
SSLA	0	0	0	2	1	0	1	2	1	0	2	9/95 (9%)
TQ	0	3	0	0	1	0	1	0	0	0	1	6/57 (11%)
Total	7	12	4	3	7	3	3	4	4	3	8	58/450 (13%)

Procedure	1991	1992	1993	1994	1995	1996	1997	1998	1999	2000	2001	Total
Chi-square												
LL	1	2	0	0	1	5	2	0	1	2	0	14/148 (9%)
MLJ	2	1	2	0	0	0	0	1	1	0	1	8/150 (5%)
SSLA	3	0	1	1	2	2	0	0	3	1	0	13/95 (14%)
TQ	2	2	1	1	2	1	0	1	0	1	2	13/57 (23%)
Total	8	5	4	2	5	8	2	2	5	4	5	48/450 (11%)

While many of the 199 ANOVA studies examined had large sample sizes (the largest being 89,620 for a *Language Learning* study on TOEFL test takers), one study in *Studies in Second Language Acquisition* had a sample size of 12 and ANOVA was run; *Modern Language Journal* published a factor analytic study with an $N = 41$. In any case, one implication of this finding is that if applied linguists are to learn to carry out and/or to interpret just one statistical procedure, that procedure should be ANOVA. Otherwise, they will be unable to read and evaluate the results in half of the empirical studies in these journals.

The next most common statistical procedure was Pearson correlation, which was employed in 28% of the studies. So, more than one fourth of the published research was searching for *relationships* among variables. Following correlation, *t*-test was the next most common procedure, applied in 23% of the articles. Rounding out the list were regression analysis (13%) and then Chi-square (11%). Chi-square is a procedure for analyzing frequency data, which are quite common in applied linguistics research, so I expected to see it employed more often. On the other hand, Chi-square is often *misapplied*, given that it has strong independence assumptions that data in our field do not usually meet.

A number of procedures were used in less than 10% of the articles. For example, multiple analysis of variance (MANOVA) was employed in 31 articles, factor analysis in 27, and analysis of covariance (ANCOVA) in 25 articles. Each of these procedures has very stringent assumptions and usually have very high sample size requirements. Appendix C presents a complete tally of the procedures that were less frequently employed. Nonparametric procedures (excluding Chi-square) were reported 58 times (or in 13% of the articles), which is not a particularly notable number, but I hope that is an improvement from the situation before *The Research Manual* (which covered a number of statistical procedures) was published, where the rate might have been only 2%.

DISCUSSION

Clearly, a number of limitations are evident in this study. First, my analysis of the articles was "telescopic"—I attempted to aggregate information and present an overall picture of research methodology in the field. A more hybrid approach, perhaps supplementing these macro-observations with an in-depth analysis of a subset of articles would be more revealing. I did not look at whether the procedures used in each article were carried out *appropriately*, either by the type of research questions posed or by the type of data collected, nor did I look at the research orientations that Cumming (1994) describes. An in-depth analysis would lend itself to investigating these issues.

Second, I only looked at four journals. While it can be argued that *TESOL Quarterly* and *Modern Language Journal* have broad readerships across the second and foreign language teaching professions, perhaps *Language Learning* and *Studies in Second Language Acquisition* are more "niche" journals (such as *Language Testing, Journal of Second Language Writing,* or *SYSTEM,* for example) that are not representative of applied linguistics in the broad sense. A journal that was obviously overlooked is *Applied Linguistics*—the reason being that, in my experience, it is not widely available in U.S. universities. Perhaps a broader range of research methodologies is being used to conduct studies that are reported in these or other journals, which may, or may not, be applied linguistics journals. Or, perhaps these studies are not being published in journals at all, or perhaps they are being presented at conferences but are not being written up.

What are the implications of so much published applied linguistics research employing fairly sophisticated analytical procedures? One result is that a great deal of the research becomes obscure for all but the most statistically literate among us. Page after page of ANOVA tables in a results section challenges even the most determined reader, who may still give up and head right for the discussion section. In this way, journal articles, especially those in niche journals can (unconsciously) promote an "in group/out group" mentality. A second outcome is that using high-powered parametric procedures may tempt one to overgeneralize results to other contexts or to other language users, when, in fact, many research designs do not use random selection from a population or random assignment to groups, but rather employ intact groups of a very limited demographic profile. Tarone (1994b) insightfully notes:

> crucially, it is then the responsibility of the researcher who is using a particular research approach to restrict the claims that are made to the appropriate domain of that research approach. The researcher must not only *know* the strengths and weaknesses of the methodology being used, but must also constrain the conclusions he or she draws at the end of the paper by framing those conclusions in light of those strengths and weaknesses. In general, the temptation is very great for a researcher to make grand claims regarding his or her findings, claims that far exceed what is permitted by their methodological underpinnings. (p. 326)

Finally, the appeal, or sexiness, of these procedures may tempt one to ask questions that can be answered using these procedures, a sort of "wag the dog" syndrome. In other words, we ask questions or collect data that lend themselves to sophisticated statistical analyses, rather than collecting data first, and then seeing what questions emerge, and what sorts of appropriate analyses can be used to answer them.

CONCLUSION

In a recent *New York Times* editorial entitled, "The Last Sociologist," Orlando Patterson (2002) sadly observes, "the rise in professional sociology of a style of scholarship that mimics the methodology and language of the natural sciences ... anxious to achieve the status of economics and the other "soft" sciences, the gatekeepers of sociology have insisted on a style of research and thinking that focuses on the testing of hypotheses based on data generated by measurements presumed to be valid" (p. WK 15). Patterson believes that this approach works well for only very limited aspects of social life. I believe the same can be said for applied linguistics. Certainly, there is an important, perhaps even a central, role for quantitative empirical research in applied linguistics, but not for all research questions, in all social contexts, with all language users.

Although I continue to find myself somewhat disillusioned by these results (see my comments in Lazaraton, 1998, 2000), they do seem to be useful in gauging where the field is at, in deciding where to send my own future work, and in advising my students where to send theirs. While the findings suggest that parametric statistical procedures still "reign supreme," I would hope that more care would be taken in applying *all* statistical procedures appropriately as per their underlying assumptions. And this can only occur if researchers and graduate students seek out educational opportunities for training in research design and statistics. Perhaps the next frontier in applied linguistics research should be developing alternatives to parametric statistics for small-scale research studies that involve limited amounts of dependent data. Finally, I would also hope that we would see more studies that combine qualitative and quantitative research methods, since each highlights "reality" in a different, yet complementary, way.

REFERENCES

Anshen, F. (1978). *Statistics for linguists*. Rowley, MA: Newbury House.
Brown, J. D. (1988). *Understanding research in second language learning: A teacher's guide to statistics and research design*. Cambridge, UK: Cambridge University Press.
Butler, C. (1985). *Statistics in linguistics*. Oxford, UK: Basil Blackwell.

Cumming, A. (Ed.). (1994). Alternatives in TESOL research: Descriptive, interpretive, and ideological orientations. *TESOL Quarterly 28*, 673–703.

Ellis, R. (2000). Editor's statement. *Language Learning 50*, 3, xi–xiii.

Firth, A., & Wagner, J. (1997). On discourse, communication, and (some) fundamental concepts in SLA research. *Modern Language Journal 81*, 285–300.

Firth, A., & Wagner, J. (1998). SLA property: No trespassing! *Modern Language Journal 82*, 91–94.

Gass, S. (1998). Apples and oranges: Or, why apples are not orange and don't need to be: A response to Firth and Wagner. *Modern Language Journal 82*, 83–90.

Gass, S. M, Cohen, A. D., & Tarone, E. E. (1994). Introduction. In E. E. Tarone, S. M. Gass, & A. D. Cohen (Eds.), *Research methodology in second-language acquisition* (pp. xiii–xxiii). Hillsdale, NJ: Lawrence Erlbaum Associates.

Grotjahn, R. (1988). Introducing (applied) linguists to statistics: A review of two books and some general remarks. [Review of the books, *Statistics in Linguistics* and *Research Design and Statistics for Applied Linguistics*]. *Studies in Second Language Acquisition 10*, 63–68.

Hamp-Lyons, L. (1998). What counts as significant research? *TESOL Research Interest Section Newsletter 5(1)*, 1–2.

Hatch, E., & Farhady, H. (1982). *Research design and statistics for applied linguistics*. Rowley, MA: Newbury House.

Hatch, E., & Lazaraton, A. (1991). *The research manual: Design and statistics for applied linguistics*. Boston: Heinle & Heinle.

Henning, G. (1986). Quantitative methods in language acquisition research. *TESOL Quarterly 20*, 701–708.

Johnson, D. M. (1992). *Approaches to research in second language learning*. New York: Longman.

Lazaraton, A. (1991). A computer supplement to *The Research Manual*. New York: Newbury House.

Lazaraton, A. (1995). Qualitative research in TESOL: A progress report. *TESOL Quarterly 29*, 455–472.

Lazaraton, A. (1998). Research methods in applied linguistics journal articles. *TESOL Research Interest Section Newsletter 5(2)*, 3.

Lazaraton, A. (2000). Current trends in research methodology and statistics in applied linguistics. *TESOL Quarterly 34*, 175–181.

Lazaraton, A., Riggenbach, H., & Ediger, A. (1987). Forming a discipline: Applied linguists' literacy in research methodology and statistics. *TESOL Quarterly 21*, 263–277.

Long, M. H. (1997). Construct validity in SLA research: A response to Firth and Wagner. *Modern Language Journal 81*, 318–323.

McDonough, J., & McDonough, S. (1997). *Research methods for English language teachers*. London: Edward Arnold.

Nicholson, M., & Bunting, J. (2001, January). Mainstream TESOL research and under-represented populations. *TESOL Research Interest Section Newsletter, 8(1)*, 4–5.

Nunan, D. (1991). Methods in second language classroom-oriented research: A critical review. *Studies in Second Language Acquisition 13*, 249–274.

Nunan, D. (1992). *Research methods in language learning*. Cambridge, UK: Cambridge University Press.

Patterson, O. (2002, May 19). The last sociologist. *The New York Times*, p. WK 15.

Pennycook, A. (1994). Critical pedagogical approaches to research: In A. Cumming (Ed.), *Alternatives in TESOL research: Descriptive, interpretive, and ideological orientations. TESOL Quarterly, 28*, 690–693.

Porte, G. K. (2002). *Appraising research in second language learning: A practical approach to critical analysis of quantitative research*. Amsterdam: Benjamins.

Rampton, B. (1997). Second language research in late modernity: A response to Firth and Wagner. *Modern Language Journal 81*, 329–333.

Scholfield, P. (1995). *Quantifying language: A researcher's and teacher's guide to gathering language data and reducing it to figures*. Clevedon, UK: Multilingual Matters.

Scollon, R. (1995). From sentences to discourses, ethnography to ethnographic: Conflicting trends in TESOL research. *TESOL Quarterly 29*, 381–384.

Seliger, H. W., & Shohamy, E. (1989). *Second language research methods*. Oxford, UK: Oxford University Press.

Tarone, E. (1994a). Analysis of learner language. In A. Cumming (Ed.), *Alternatives in TESOL research: Descriptive, interpretive, and ideological orientations. TESOL Quarterly Special Issue, 28*, 676–678.

Tarone, E. E. (1994b). A summary: Research approaches in studying second-language acquisition or "If the shoe fits..." . In E. E. Tarone, S. M. Gass, & A. D. Cohen (Eds.), *Research methodology in second-language acquisition* (pp. 323–336). Hillsdale, NJ: Lawrence Erlbaum Associates.

Thomas, M. (1994). Assessment of L2 proficiency in second language acquisition research. *Language Learning 44*, 307–336.

Woods, A., Fletcher, P., & Hughes, A. (1986). *Statistics in language studies*. Cambridge, UK: Cambridge University Press.

Wray, A., Trott, K., & Bloomer, A. (1998). *Projects in linguistics: A practical guide to researching language*. London: Edward Arnold.

APPENDIX A

Feature Comparison for Twelve Research/Statistics Books

Text	Organizing principle	Research design	Statistics explained	Computer guidance	Critique guidelines	Reader activities/ Answer key	Research report format	Other features
Hatch & Farhady 1982	Statistical procedures/ research design	yes	1–5, 7–10, 12–14, 18, 19	yes	no	yes/no	yes	Statistical tables, list of formulas
Butler 1985	Basic statistical concepts/ procedures	no	1–8, 10, 22, 28	1 chapter	no	yes/yes	no	Statistical tables, flow charts to choose procedures
Woods, Fletcher, & Hughes 1986	Statistical concepts/ procedures	no	1–5, 7–8, 13–19, 22, 23	Appendix	no	yes/no	no	Statistical tables, chapter summaries
Brown 1988	Research reading/ critique skills	yes	1–5, 7, 14	no	yes	yes/no	yes	
Seliger & Shohamy 1989	Steps in research process	yes	1–5, 7, 14, 17, 18	2 pages	no	yes/no	yes	
Hatch & Lazaraton 1991	Statistical procedures/ research design	yes	1–5, 7–14, 16, 18–30	separate text	no	yes/yes	yes	Statistical tables; list of formulas, journals, test assumptions; pretest
Johnson 1992	Research in experimental approaches chapter		none	no	yes	no/no	yes	List of journals, large list of references
Nunan 1992	Research in experimental approaches chapter		1–5, 7	no	yes	yes/no	yes	Glossary
Scholfield 1995	Types/analyses of quantifiable data	no	1, 2, 7	no	no	no/no	no	Quality checks on measurement

(continued)

Appendix A (*Cont.*)

Text	Organizing principle	Research design	Statistics explained	Computer guidance	Critique guidelines	Reader activities/ Answer key	Research report format	Other features
McDonough & McDonough 1997	Research methods	no	1, 2, 7	1 page	features of good research	no/no	no	Addresses of organizations, journals; discussion notes
Wray, Trott, & Bloomer 1998	Topics, techniques, tools for linguistics research	no	1 chapter	1 chapter	no	no/no	no	250 project ideas
Porte 2002	Research paper	yes	1–5, 7, 8, 13, 14	no	yes	yes/no	yes	Glossary, flow chart to choose procedures, statistical test assumptions, statistical tables

Statistical procedures

1. Mean
2. Standard deviation
3. Chi-square
4. *t*-test
5. ANOVA
6. z-test
7. Pearson correlation
8. Spearman rank order correlation
9. Point biserial correlation
10. Phi coefficient
11. Kendall's W
12. Implicational scaling
13. Linear regression
14. Multiple regression
15. Cluster analysis
16. ram
17. Discriminant analysis
18. Factor analysis
19. Principal components analysis
20. Path analysis
21. Loglinear
22. Mann-Whitney U Test (Rank Sums)
23. Sign test
24. Median test
25. Kruskal-Wallis ANOVA
26. Friedman test
27. McNemar's test
28. Wilcoxon matched-pairs signed-ranks test
29. Fisher's exact test
30. Eta^2

APPENDIX B

Research Issues Columns in *TESOL Quarterly*

Winter 1990:	Research issues debuts; Multiple *t*-tests
Spring 1991:	The role of hypothesis testing in qualitative research
Winter 1991:	Power, effect size, and second language (SL) research
Autumn 1992:	Validity and reliability in qualitative research in SLA
Spring 1992:	Regression models in an ESL context: Issues in onstruction and interpretation
Spring 1993:	Ethics in TESOL research
Winter 1993:	Using Likert scales in L2 research
Winter 1994:	Sources of bias in SLA research
Winter 1995:	Research on the (writing) rating process
Summer 1995:	Methodological challenges in discourse analysis
Summer 1996:	Gender in research on language
Spring 1997:	The politics of transcription
Summer 1997:	Standards for teacher research
Winter 1997:	Approaches to observation in classroom research
Summer 1998:	The use of verbal protocols in L2 research
Winter 1998:	Research on the use of technology in TESOL
Summer 1999:	Poststructural approaches to L2 research
Winter 2000:	Interview research in TESOL
Summer 2001:	Corpus-based research in TESOL
Winter 2001:	*Research Issues* column on identifying research priorities
Summer 2002:	Narrative research in TESOL

APPENDIX C

Statistical Procedures Used in Fewer Than 10% of Articles
(number indicates actual frequency)

Procedure	Frequency
MANOVA	31
Factor analysis	27
ANCOVA	25
Mann-Whitney U Test (Rank Sums)	18
Spearman rank order correlation	10
Kruskal-Wallis ANOVA	9
Path analysis	9
LISREL/Structural equation modeling	7
Bonferroni adjustment	5
Fisher's exact test	5
Wilcoxon matched-pairs signed-ranks	5
Loglinear	4
Discriminant analysis	3
IRT/Rasch	2
Kendall's Tau B	2
Kendall's W	2
McNemar's test	2
Multidimensional scaling	2
VARBRUL	2
Binomial test	1
Bryant-Paulston procedure	1

(continued)

Appendix C (*Cont.*)

Procedure	Frequency
Cluster analysis	1
Friedman test	1
G Theory	1
Implicational scaling	1
Kolmorgorov-Smirnov test	1
Logit model	1
MANCOVA	1
Mantel-Henzel	1
Mauchy sphericity	1
Maximum Likelihood Estimate	1
Median test	1
Multitrait-Multimethod	1
Point biserial correlation	1
Rule-space	1
Sign test	1
Uncorrelated proportions	1
z-test	1

13

Classroom Research

David Nunan
University of Hong Kong

DEFINING CLASSROOM RESEARCH

In order to provide a comprehensive, state-of-the-art overview of classroom research, it is necessary to define the terms "classroom" and "research." These terms, which at first sight might seem unproblematic, turn out to be surprisingly difficult to articulate.

Most of us probably imagine that the concept of classroom is so familiar that it does not need defining. A classroom is a room in which teachers and learners are gathered together for instructional purposes. Thus, in 1983, Allwright wrote:

> Classroom-centered research is just that—research centered on the classroom, as distinct from, for example, research that concentrates on the inputs to the classroom (the syllabus, the teaching materials) or the outputs from the classroom (learner achievement scores). It does not ignore in any way or try to devalue the importance of such inputs and outputs. It simply tries to investigate what happens inside the classroom when learners and teachers come together. (p. 191)

Some years later, van Lier broadened the characterization somewhat, suggesting that "The L2 [second language] classroom can be defined as the gathering, for a given period of time, of two or more persons (one of whom generally assumes the role of instructor) for the purposes of language learning" (van Lier, 1988, p. 47).

More recently, with the rapid evolution of information technology and the development of "virtual" classrooms, the notion of the classroom as a place where people gather together has come under challenge. (I will look at this issue of redefining the concept of the classroom later in the chapter.)

Elsewhere, I have defined research as a "systematic process of inquiry consisting of three elements or components: (1) a question, problem or hypothesis, (2) data, and (3) analysis and interpretation" (Nunan, 1992, p. 3). To these three components, I would add that the activity should be capable of meeting tests of validity and reliability and that the results should be published. (Here, I am using "publish" in the broad sense of "to make public.")

Another distinction that needs to be drawn is between classroom research and classroom-oriented research. Classroom research includes empirical investigations carried out in language classrooms (however the term classroom might be defined).

Classroom-oriented research, on the other hand, is research carried out outside the classroom, in the laboratory, simulated or naturalistic settings, but which make claims for the relevance of their outcomes for the classrooms. In 1991, I carried out a detailed review of classroom and classroom-oriented studies. Of 50 studies reviewed, only 15 were classroom based (Nunan, 1991a).

THE PLACE OF CLASSROOM RESEARCH WITHIN APPLIED LINGUISTICS RESEARCH

Applied linguistics is a broad interdisciplinary field of scholarship that encompasses theoretical, empirical, and practical work in diverse areas including first language education, second language acquisition, language pathology, speech and hearing, and language use in social and professional contexts.

Research in second language acquisition can be broadly divided into naturalistic and instructed acquisition. From a psycholinguistic perspective, the following questions currently preoccupy researchers:

1. What cognitive structures and abilities underlie the L2 learner's use of his or her L2?
2. What properties of the linguistic input to the L2 learner are relevant to acquisition?
3. What is the nature of the L2 learner's capacity for attaining the cognitive structures and abilities referred to in (1)? Here we may distinguish the following subquestions:
   a. What is the nature of the L2 learner's overall capacity for language acquisition?
   b. How is that capacity deployed in real time to determine the course of second language acquisition (SLA)?
   c. How are the L2 user's two (or more) languages represented in the brain?
4. What changes in brain structure, if any, underlie changes in the capacity for language acquisition across the life span of the individual?

(Adapted from Ritchie and Bhatia, 1996, p. 19)

Turning to the more specific issue of instructed acquisition, the focus has been on identifying *how* instruction makes a difference in the acquisition of a second language. Some key questions here are (Nunan, 1996):

- Is there a distinction between conscious learning and subconscious acquisition?
- Is learning a second language like learning a first?
- Why do some learners fail to acquire a second language successfully?
- How can we account for variation (a) between learners (b) within learners?
- What modes of classroom organization, task types, and input facilitate second language development?

The last question brings us directly to the focus of this chapter, namely, what classroom research has to tell us about the relationship between what goes on in the classroom and second language acquisition. This research is reviewed in the next section.

TRENDS AND TRADITIONS

This section deals with both substantive and methodological issues. Substantive issues have to do with the "what" of research, methodological issues with the "how." Substantive research seeks to identify relationships between language acquisition and variables such as instructional methods and task types, teacher input (e.g., input, questions, corrective feedback), and aspects of learner behavior such as acquisitional sequences and learner–learner interaction. Methodologically, researchers have debated the merits of experimental versus naturalistic approaches to data collection and analysis, and the merits of collecting data in classroom rather than non-classroom settings.

Substantive Issues

The Methods Comparison Studies.   In the 1960s, classroom research was dominated by the so-called "methods comparison studies." As the name implies, these large-scale, highly expensive studies compared different methods, teaching techniques, and programs in order to determine which were more effective. For example, Scherer and Wertheimer (1964) set out to investigate whether audiolingualism, which was then coming in to vogue, was superior to the traditional grammar-translation approach. Using a classical experimental design, the researchers divided their subjects (college students studying German as a foreign language) into two groups. One group was instructed using a grammar-translation method, while the other group was taught through audiolingualism, which emphasized listening and speaking and adopted an inductive approach to grammar.

The study was unable to show the superiority of one method over another. Students' strengths reflected the relative emphasis of the method through which they were taught. The grammar-translation students were significantly better at reading and translation, whereas the audiolingual students were significantly better at listening and speaking.

Almost 20 years later, another psychometric study provided a clue as to the relative indeterminacy of the methods comparision studies. In this study, Swaffar, Arens and Morgan (1982) compared audiolingualism with cognitive code learning. However, they made a key modification to the psychometric design utilized by other methods studies—they added a classroom observation element to the study. This enabled them to provide an explanation for the inconclusive outcome from their study. (As with earlier research, this study was unable to establish a clear-cut superiority of one methodology over the other.) When they looked at the moment-by-moment realities of the classroom, they found that the teachers used a range of different, overlapping practices that rendered methodological differences meaningless. They concluded that methodological labels such as "audiolingualism" and "cognitive code learning" are illusory because they refer to a range of classroom practices utilized by all teachers regardless of the methodology they were supposed to implement.

Focus on the Teacher: Input Factors.   According to Tsui (2001, p. 121) classroom research has focused on three different aspects of the pedagogical environment: input factors, interaction, and output.

> Input refers to the language used by the teacher, output refers to language produced by learners, and interaction refers to the interrelationship between input and output with no assumption of a linear cause and effect relationship between the two.

Input factors that have been investigated include the amount and types of teacher talk, teacher speech modifications, questions, instruction, and error correction and feedback. (For a detailed, book-length review of the research, see Chaudron, 1988).

In the field of general education, numerous studies have documented the ratio of teacher talk to student talk. These studies have revealed that teachers tend to talk, on average, twice as much as students, although some studies put the figure as high as 80%. (See, for example, Legarreta's (1977) study of bilingual classrooms, and Tsui's

(1985) investigation of Hong Kong classrooms in which over 80% of the talk came from teachers.) Despite a growing recognition of the importance of student output for acquisition (see the following), the persistence of teacher-dominated classrooms is a concern. Another concern is that in classes containing first and second language speakers, the great majority of the utterances (and therefore the pedagogical attention by teachers) are directed to the first language speakers.

Studies of teacher-to-student speech show that teachers attempt to make their speech more comprehensible by speaking slower, using simpler structures, clearer articulation and more repetition, and by using more basic vocabulary than when interacting with native speakers. Whether these modifications are helpful or not is not at all clear. Research findings have led researchers "to question whether the modification of input by teachers alone is sufficient to make the input comprehensible, and whether they ought to examine the interaction between teacher and learners" (Tsui, 2001, p. 121).

Questions are a teacher's stock-in-trade, and it is therefore not surprising that these have been extensively studied. A particular focus of interest is the effect of the type of questions teachers ask on student output. When comparing display questions (those to which the teacher knows the answer) with referential questions (those to which the teacher does not know the answer), the length and complexity of the student's response, as well as instances of negotiation of meaning (see the following) increased. Unfortunately, without specific training, teachers tend to restrict the questions they ask exclusively to those of the display variety. Brock (1986) found that in classrooms where the teachers were not trained to ask referential questions, only 24 out of 144 questions were referential. After training, out of a total of 194 questions, 173 were referential. The significance of the study was that learners in classrooms where more referential questions were asked gave significantly longer and more complex responses. Brock concluded:

> That referential questions may increase the amount of speaking learners do in the classroom is relevant to at least one current view of second language acquisition (SLA). Swain (1983), in reporting the results of a study of the acquisition of French by Canadian children in elementary school immersion classrooms, argues that output may be an important factor in successful SLA. (Brock, 1986, p. 55)

(I will review the literature on the input/output controversy in the next section of the chapter.)

The next substantive issue I would like to review is teachers' treatment of errors. A number of different terms have been used for verbal responses given to learners in the face of an incorrect utterance. These include "correction," "feedback," and "repair." In relation to classroom instruction, questions that researchers have posed include:

- Which errors do teachers correct?
- How do teachers correct errors?
- When do teachers correct errors?
- What effect does error correction have on subsequent learner output?

The last question, attempting to establish a causal relationship between error correction and acquisition, is the most important. It is also the most difficult to address, which probably accounts for the relative paucity of studies in the area. As Ellis (1994) notes:

> Opinions abound about what type of error treatment is best, but there is little empirical evidence on which to make an informed choice. Currently, two recommendations seem to find wide approval. One is that error treatment should be conducted in a manner that is compatible with general interlanguage development (for example, by only correcting

errors that learners are ready to eliminate). The other is that self-repair is more conducive to acquisition than other-repair, as it is less likely to result in a negative affective response. (p. 586)

Focus on the Learner.   In the 1970s a series of studies was carried out that became known as the "morpheme order studies" (Dulay & Burt, 1973, 1974). The main aim of these studies was to seek evidence relating to the contrastive analysis hypothesis. This hypothesis makes predictions about acquisition orders based on contrasts between a learner's first and second languages. It also predicts that the order in which particular grammatical items are acquired will differ according to the first language of the learner. What the studies found, however, was that second language learners from strikingly different backgrounds (in the first instance, Chinese and Spanish) acquired a set of target English language morphemes in virtually the same order, that this order did not reflect the frequency with which items appeared in the input, and that the order was very similar for both children and adults.

As a result of this research, the investigators proposed a "natural order of acquisition" that was determined by the nature of the target language and that was independent from the first language. Shortly thereafter, in a series of classroom studies, researchers attempted to see whether they could upset this natural order through instruction. (They could not!) For a review of this research and a discussion of its pedagogical implications, see Krashen (1981, 1982).

It was out of this research, that Krashen developed his distinction between conscious learning and subconscious acquisition, arguing that the methodological focus in the classroom should shift from learning to acquisition. He further argues that the SLA process itself was very similar to first language acquisition, and that teachers should strive to replicate those conditions in the classroom. Central to his methodology was the importance of a focus on meaning rather than form, along with the notion that comprehensible input, that is, understanding messages in the target language, was the necessary and sufficient condition for successful language acquisition.

This "acquisitionist tradition" (Nunan, 1991b) spawned numerous methodologies, including the Natural Approach, developed by Krashen himself, along with Terrell (see Krashen & Terrell, 1983) and the Total Physical Response (TPR; Asher, 1988). Both methods purportedly rested on principles derived from insights into first language acquisition. These included a focus on meaning rather than form, a focus on comprehension rather than production, particularly at the early stages of instruction, and an adherence to the "here and now" principle. TPR also advocated providing input to learners by getting them to carry out commands couched in the imperative.

Although these methodological principles grew out of SLA research, relatively little research exists into their effectiveness in the classroom. An exception is TPR. Asher claimed empirical support for the approach, arguing that TPR students significantly outperformed students in regular classrooms. However, the research on which the claim rested was called in to question by Beretta (1986):

> In the 1972 report [comparing TPR with regular classroom instruction], one of the stories used in classroom training in the TPR group is presented as an example; it is entitled "Mr. Schmidt goes to the office." Later in the report, we are informed that one of the criterion measures used to compare experimental (TPR) and control (regular) groups is a listening test involving a story entitled "Mr. Schmidt goes to the office." In view of this, it is hardly astonishing that the experimental students dramatically out-performed controls ($p = .0005$). On a reading test, no significant differences were found. (p. 432)

The two central tenets of the acquisitionist approach—focus on meaning not form and the comprehensible input hypothesis—came under attack from a number of fronts. Swain, a longstanding critic of the comprehensible input hypotheses (see, for example, Swain, 1985, 1993, 1997), has argued that, while input was necessary, it was not sufficient for second language acquisition. The conclusion was reached after a series of classroom studies into French immersion programs in Canada showing that students in input-rich classrooms did not develop native-like proficiency. Swain proposed, instead, the "comprehensible output" hypothesis. This hypothesis argues that in comprehending input, learners can "bypass" the syntactic system and go straight for meaning. However, in producing and speaking, the learner must "syntacticize" his or her utterance in order to be understood.

> In listening, semantic and pragmatic information assist comprehension in ways that may not apply, or may apply differently in production, in that the semantic and pragmatic information can circumvent the need to process syntax. With output, however, learners need to move from the semantic, open-ended, strategic processing prevalent in comprehension to the complete grammatical processing needed for accurate production. Output, then, would seem to have a potentially significant role in the development of syntax and morphology, a role that underlies the functions output may have in the learning of a second language. (Swain, 1997, p. 5)

A growing body of classroom-oriented research has looked at modified interaction and the role that such modified interaction might play in second language acquisition. The term "interactional modification" or "conversational adjustment" refers to those instances during a conversation in which the speaker restructures an utterance in order to make it more comprehensible. The assumption behind the research is that pedagogical tasks that maximize opportunities for interactional modifications will be beneficial for second language acquisition. However, to date none of this research has actually established a direct relationship between such modifications and acquisition. Rather, the relationship is an indirect one and is predicated on the comprehensible input hypothesis, as Long (1985) points out:

> Step 1: Show that (a) linguistic/conversational adjustments promote (b) comprehensible input.
> Step 2: Show that (b) comprehensible input promotes (c) acquisition.
> Step 3: Deduce that (a) linguistic/conversational adjustments promote (c) acquisition. Satisfactory evidence of the a → b → c relationships would allow the linguistic environment be posited as an indirect causal variable in SLA. [The relationship would be indirect because of the intervening "comprehension" variable.] (p. 378)

Interestingly, Long's chapter positing comprehensible input as a major causal variable in SLA appears in the same collection as Swain's chapter on comprehensible output. Of course, the two are not mutually exclusive, and it is not unreasonable to assume that in interactional classroom work both are fuelling the acquisition process.

In a recent study, Martyn (2002) investigated the influence of certain task characteristics on the negotiation of meaning in small group work. One interesting methodological aspect of Martyn's work is that she conducted the research in intact classrooms rather than in laboratory settings. The research is therefore genuinely classroom-based rather than classroom-oriented.

Variables investigated by Martyn include:

- Interaction relationship: whether one person holds all of the information required to complete the task, whether each participant holds a portion of the information, or whether the information is shared.
- Interaction requirement: whether the information must be shared for successful task completion, or whether it is optional.

- Goal orientation: whether the task goal is convergent or divergent.
- Outcome options: whether there is only a single correct outcome, or whether more than one outcome is possible.
- Cognitive demand: the processing load on the subject brought about by the complexity of task content and processes.

Martyn's research reveals the complexity of the relationship among task-type, interactional modification, and language acquisition. The two task variables that emerged as significant were information exchange requirements and cognitive demand. Tasks with high-information exchange requirements generated significantly more instances of negotiation than did tasks with low-information exchange requirements. Tasks that placed high-cognitive demands on the subjects generated significantly higher density of negotiation (defined as extended negotiation sequences) than did low-cognitive demand tasks. In a qualitative analysis of her data, Martyn found that learners provided one another with conditions for second language acquisition by drawing attention to meaning/form relationships in negotiation of meaning sequences.

Although required information exchange and cognitive demand had a significant effect on the amount of negotiation on meaning, there was also a range of other interpersonal and interactional variables that were only revealed because the study was carried out in a genuine classroom setting. Her research showed how complex the learning environment is and also how difficult it is to isolate psychological and linguistic factors from social and interpersonal ones. (For an excellent overview of theoretical and empirical work on tasks, see Skehan, 1998).

Methodological Issues

Like most social sciences, a distinction is traditionally drawn between qualitative and qualitative approaches to research. In his book on classroom research, Chaudron (1988) elaborates this with four-way distinction (see Table 13.1).

This four-way distinction is somewhat misleading, because interaction and discourse analysis are techniques rather than traditions. In fact, the two techniques can be used within either of the other two traditions in the table.

TABLE 13.1

Comparing Different Research Traditions

Tradition	Typical Issues	Methods
Psychometric	Language gain from different materials and methods	Experimental method—pre- and post-treatment tests with experimental and control groups
Interaction analysis	Extent to which learner behavior is a function of teacher-determined interaction	Coding of classroom interactions in terms of various observation systems and schedules
Discourse analysis	Analysis of classroom discourse in linguistic terms	Study classroom transcripts and assign utterances to predetermined categories
Ethnographic	Obtain insights into the classroom as a "cultural" system	Naturalistic "uncontrolled" observation and description

Note: Adapted from *Second language classrooms: Research on teaching and learning* by C. Chaudron, 1988, Cambridge, UK: Cambridge University Press.

The distinction between qualitative and quantitative traditions has been criticized by Grotjahn (1987) as being too crude. He points out that the qualitative/quantitative distinction can refer to three different aspects of the data collection and analysis process. These are the overall design (whether data are collected through an experiment or nonexperimentally), the type of data (whether the data are qualitative or quantitative), and the type of analysis (whether the data are analyzed statistically or interpretively). Mixing and matching these variables gives us two "pure" research paradigms—the exploratory-interpretative, based on a nonexperimental design, yielding qualitative data that are analyzed interpretively, and the analytical-nomological based on an experimental design yielding quantitative data that are analyzed statistically. However, they also provide us with six "hybrid" research forms.

Bailey (1999) accepts the notion that there are two dominant traditions, the experimental and the naturalistic, and adds a third—action research. The defining characteristic of action research is that it is carried out by classroom practitioners rather than outside researchers. (Action research is discussed in some detail in the next section of the chapter.)

A major methodological dilemma that has bedeviled classroom research for years is how to capture differences in what goes on at the level of the classroom. Work already described, by researchers such as Swaffar, Arens, and Morgan (1982) demonstrated the importance of documenting and quantifying classroom processes if differences in learner output are to be adequately explained. Formal experiments that only measured input and output (so-called "black box" research; Long, 1980) failed in this respect.

The need for ways of documenting and quantifying classroom interaction led to the development of observation instruments of different kinds. The most comprehensive description and analysis of such schemes is by Chaudron (1988), which, unfortunately is somewhat dated. Chaudron analyzed 23 different systems according to a number of criteria. These include whether the observer codes a particular behavior every time it occurs or only whether or not it occurs in a specific time period, whether the items that are coded are high or low inference, the number of categories involved, whether multiple codings are possible, whether the coding happens in real-time, whether the system is based on an explicit theory of language or pedagogy, whether the instrument was developed for research or teacher training purposes, whether the unit of analysis is an arbitrary time period or an analytical unit such as a move or an episode, and the range of behaviors and events sampled.

One of the most comprehensive systems of analysis (which was developed subsequent to Chaudron's analysis) is the Communicative Orientation of Language Teaching (COLT) Scheme (Spada & Frohlich, 1995). Apart from it comprehensiveness, COLT is of interest because it is both theoretically and empirically motivated, being based on an explicit theory of language teaching (communicative language teaching), and a psycholinguistic theory of acquisition.

> One of the primary motivations for developing COLT was a desire to respond to [the concern that observation instruments have theoretical and empirical validity]. We wanted to identify those features of instruction which communication theorists and L2 researchers consistently referred to as contributors to successful learning. We also wanted to identify features of communication and interaction which were believed to be important contributors to successful language learning in the L1 research literature. And, most importantly, we wanted to define our instructional categories in such a way that these hypotheses could be tested in process-product research. (Spada & Frohlich, 1995, p. 6)

The scheme itself consists of two parts. Part A focuses on the description of classroom activities and consists of five major parts: the activity type, the participant organization, the content, student modality, and the materials used in the classroom. Part B focuses on communicative features and identifies seven characteristics, namely,

TABLE 13.2

Questions Relating to the Principal Features of the COLT Scheme

Feature	Questions
PART A: Classroom Activities	
Activity type	What is the activity type—e.g. drill, role play, dictation?
Participant organization	Is the teacher working with the whole class or not?
	Are students in groups or individual seat work?
	If group work, how is it organized?
Content	Is the focus on classroom management, language (form, function, discourse, sociolinguistics) or other?
	Is the range of topics broad or narrow?
	Who selects the topic—teacher, students, or both?
Student modality	Are students involved in listening, speaking, reading, writing, or combinations of these?
Materials	What types of materials are used?
	How long is the text?
	What is the source/purpose of the materials?
	How controlled is their use?
PART B: Classroom Interaction	
Use of target language	To what extent is the target language used?
Information gap	To what extent is requested information predictable in advance?
Sustained speech	Is discourse extended or restricted to a single sentence, clause or word?
Reaction to code or message	Does the interlocutor react to code or message?
Incorporation of preceding utterance	Does the speaker incorporate the preceding utterance into his/her contribution?
Discourse initiation	Do learners have opportunities to initiate discourse?
Relative restriction of linguistic form	Does the teacher expect a specific form or is there no expectation of a particular linguistic form?

Note: Adapted from *Research methods in language learning* by Nunan, 1992, Cambridge, UK: Cambridge University Press.

the use of the target language, information gap, sustained speech, reaction to code or message, incorporation of preceding utterance, discourse initiation, and relative restriction of linguistic form.

Table 13.2, adapted from Nunan (1992), sets out the key questions that an observer would need to answer in relation to the different features of the scheme. The questions clearly reveal the theoretical and empirical bias evident in the scheme.

One of the advantages of the scheme is that it enables an observer to quantify classrooms interaction and make comparisons across intact classes. (By intact, I mean classroom 5 that were constituted primarily for pedagogical purposes rather than to serve the purposes of an experiment.)

CURRENT CONTROVERSIES

The Effect of Instruction—The Morpheme Order Studies/Recent Focus on Form Research

A longstanding controversy in the field concerns the place of formal instruction in the classroom. The research by Krashen and others (previously discussed), in the early 1980s called into question the place of formal instruction. In recent years, however, formal instruction has made something of a comeback. For example, two academics who have done extensive research on the subject recently wrote:

> Our view is that some degree of carefully timed and delivered focus on form is likely to be appropriate in most cases of L2 learning difficulty.... we believe that leaving learners to discover form-function relationships and the intricacies of a new linguistic system wholly on their own makes little sense. This does not mean, however, that we advocate a constant focus on all forms for all learners all the time. (Doughty & Williams, 1998, p. 11).

Doughty and Williams support their claim by reporting several classroom-based focus on form studies. Focus on form refers to the practice of explicitly drawing students' attention to linguistic features within the context of meaning-focused activities. In other words, communication comes first, and a focus on form comes second. The advantage of this reorientation is that "the learner's attention is drawn precisely to a linguistic feature as necessitated by a communicative demand" (Doughty & Williams, 1998, p. 3). Learners are therefore more likely to see the relationship between language form and communicative function than if they are presented with grammar explanations and exercises out of context.

A related concept is that of "consciousness raising" (Fotos & Ellis, 1991). Consciousness-raising is a type of focus on form approach to grammar teaching. According to Larsen-Freeman (2001, pp. 39–40), these exercises do not require students to produce the target structures. Instead, students are made aware of the target grammatical item through discovery-oriented tasks.

The current interest in focus on form has grown out of research questioning the idea that as teachers all we need to do is to create opportunities for learners to be immersed in and to communicate in the target language, and that it is unnecessary to focus on form at all. Work carried out in immersion classrooms in Canada and elsewhere has shown that when a focus on form is entirely absent, the learners do not develop an adequate mastery of certain grammatical features. In fact, they appear to end up with a kind of classroom pidgin language.

Controlling the Research Agenda

One controversy that has persisted for a number of years concerns the issue of who should control the research agenda. The controversy has emerged in the face of teacher-initiated action research. This section looks at the reasons for the emergence of action research, which places control of the research agenda in the hands of the practitioner, and briefly reviews the pros and cons of the movement.

One of the problems with a great deal of research is that it "has little to do with [teachers'] everyday, practical concerns" (Carr & Kemmis, 1985, p. 8). As Beasley and Riordan (1981) pointed out quite a few years ago:

> the gulf between research bodies and the teaching profession has ensured that many research programmes are not related to professional concerns and interests of teachers and students. Priorities for research often reflect the interests of academic researchers or central office administrators, not school people. Teachers and students in the classroom are rarely actively engaged in the research. (p. 60)

Since these remarks were made, action research has emerged as a possible way of bridging this gap between research and practice and between researchers and practitioners. Action research contains similar ingredients as other forms of research—specifically, questions, data, and interpretations/analysis. However, what makes it unique is that it centers on questions or problems that confront teachers in their day-to-day work, and it is carried out by teachers. The research therefore:

- Begins with and builds on the knowledge that teachers have already accumulated.
- Focuses on the immediate interests and concerns of classroom teachers.
- Matches the subtle, organic process of classroom life.
- Builds on the "natural" processes of evaluation and research which teachers carry out daily.
- Bridges the gap between understanding and action by merging the role of the researcher and practitioner.
- Sharpens teachers' critical awareness through observation, recording and analysis of classroom events and thus acts as a consciousness-raising exercise.
- Provides teachers with better information than they already have about what is actually happening in the classroom and why.
- Helps teachers better articulate teaching and learning processes to their colleagues and interested community members.
- Bridges the gap between theory and practice. (Beasley & Riordan, 1981, p. 36)

Despite these purported benefits, action research has not escaped criticism. Some researchers argue that while action research might lead to more reflective practice, it does not qualify as research, that the average classroom practitioner does not have the knowledge and skills to conduct the research in a way that would guard it against threats to reliability and validity.

FUTURE DIRECTIONS

A Sociocultural Approach to Language Acquisition

Until recently, the psycholinguistic tradition has dominated research into language acquisition in instructional contexts. However, there is some evidence that this is beginning to change. Recently, several studies and a collection of articles (Lantolf, 2000) have appeared that are devoted to sociocultural theory and second language learning. Underpinning this work is the Russian psychologist Vygotsky's theory of mediated cognition. In this theory, language is a cognitive tool through which humans are able to act upon and change the world in which they live.

Classroom research features prominently in applications of sociocultural theory to second language acquisition. The Lantolf volume consists of 11 chapters. Two of these are theoretical, whereas nine are empirical. Of these nine, seven are classroom-based. The titles of these seven chapters give a flavor of the orientation of this research and highlight the challenge it offers to prevailing psycholinguistic/interactionist models of SLA (see Table 13.3).

Given her work within the psycholinguistic tradition, the chapter by Swain is particularly interesting. Swain conducted an intensive analysis of classroom transcripts collected by her and other researchers using the Vygotskian notion that output is a socially constructed cognitive tool. The following extract and analysis provide a flavor of this kind of analysis.

Classroom Extract
In this extract, two students are collaborating in writing a story based on a set of pictures. The are trying to work out how to finish a sentence beginning *Yvonne se regarde dans le miroir* ... (Yvonne looks at herself in the mirror.)
Kathy: Et brosse les cheveux.
(and brushes her hair.)
Doug: Et les dents.
(and her teeth.)
Kathy: Non, non, pendant qu'elle brosse les dents et ...

(No, no, while she brushes her teeth and . . .)
Doug: Elle se brosse . . . elle SE brosse
(She brushes . . . she brushes [emphasizes the reflexive pronoun].)
Kathy: Pendant qu'elle se brosse les dents et peigne les cheveux.
(While she brushes her teeth and combs her hair.)
Doug: Ya!
Kathy: Pendant qu'elle . . . se brosse . . . les cheveux, I mean, no, pendant qu'elle se PEIGNE les cheveux.
(While she . . . brushes . . . her hair, I mean, no, while she COMBS her hair.)
Doug: Ya.
Kathy: et se brosse . . .
(And brushes . . .)
Doug: Les dents.
(Her teeth.)
Kathy: Pendant qu'elle SE peigne les cheveux et SE brosse les dents.
(While she combs her hair and brushes her teeth [emphasizes the reflexive pronouns].)
(Adapted from Swain & Lapkin, 1998. Reproduced in Swain, 2000, p. 111).
Commentary
[Here] we see Kathy and Doug co-constructing the second half of the sentence that Kathy is writing down. They end up with the correct, *pendant qu'elle se peigne les cheveux et se brosse les dents* (while she combs her hair and brushes her teeth), but not without struggling with which verb goes with which noun, and the reflexive nature of the particular verbs they are using. . . . This dialogue between Doug and Kathy serves to focus attention and to offer alternatives. Through dialogue they regulate each other's activity, and their own. Their dialogue provides them both with opportunities to use language, and opportunities to reflect on their own language use. Together their jointly constructed performance outstrips their individual competencies. (Swain, 2000, p. 111)

This type of analysis is very different from the quantification and statistical analysis of instances of interactional modifications typical of much recent classroom-based and classroom-oriented research. Ultimately, the researchers want to demonstrate how these collaborative conversations provide opportunities for second language learning.

Broadening the Range of Methods/Triangulation

Another trend is a broadening of the range of research tools and techniques. Classroom researchers appear to be increasingly reluctant to restrict themselves to a single data

TABLE 13.3

Classroom Research Drawing on Sociocultural Theory

Researcher	*Title of Study*
Donato	Sociocultural contributions to understanding the foreign and second language classroom
Kramsch	Social discursive constructions of self in L2 learning
Ohta	Rethinking interaction is SLA: Developmentally appropriate assistance in the zone of proximal development and the acquisition of L2 grammar
Swain	The output hypothesis and beyond: Mediating acquisition through collaborative dialogue
Roebuck	Subjects speak out: How learners position themselves in a psycholinguistic task
Sullivan	Playfulness as mediation in communicative language teaching in a Vietnamese schoolroom
Verity	Side affects: The strategic development of professional satisfaction

collection technique, or even a single research paradigm. The collection of original studies in the edited volume by Bailey and Nunan (1996) bears this out. Although not all of the qualitative studies in this collection are classroom-based, the majority of them do draw on data from the classroom. Data include classroom transcripts, interviews, retrospective protocols, journals and diaries, reports, curriculum accounts, and ministerial documents.

One study from the collection illustrating the value of triangulation is that by Block (1996). Block wanted to capture the complexities of classroom events by looking at them from different angles. In particular, he wanted to investigate similarities and differences in the accounts given by teachers and learners of day-to-day classroom events and to compare these interpretations with his own as a researcher. The data-base included classroom observation, oral diaries, and interviews.

Block found widely differing interpretations by different participants in the study. He concluded his study by making the following observation on the research methodology he employed:

> one might further investigate the idea of individual differences in data provision among informants. Just as many authors have suggested that there are different types of language learners (e.g., Oxford, 1990; Willing, 1988), it might well be the case that there are different types of informants. We might even ask ourselves if there is a correlation between the way an informant approaches data provision and the way he or she approaches language learning. For example, is an analytical informant such as Alex [one of Block's informants] equally analytical in his choice of learning strategies? (Block, 1996, p. 192)

Extending the Concept of the "Classroom"

At the beginning of this chapter, I provided two characterizations of a classroom. In the first, by Allwright, it was suggested that a classroom is a room in which teachers and learners are gathered together for instructional purposes. The second characterization, by van Lier, suggested that a classroom exists when two or more people (one of whom is assumed to be a teacher) are gathered together for the purposes of teaching and learning. Although they do not say so explicitly, both commentators imply that the people are involved in face-to-face interaction.

However, with the increasing mobility of millions of individuals for employment, educational and leisure purposes, the emergence of information technology, and the rapid growth of e-learning, we can no longer make the assumption that language learning will involve face-to-face interaction, nor that it will take place in a space that looks anything like a classroom as traditionally conceived. As Legutke notes, "These changes challenge our self-concept as foreign language teachers, because, much more than in the past, we are now called upon to redefine our roles as educators, since we need to mediate between the world of the classroom and the world of natural language acquisition" (Legutke, 2000, p. 1).

What does this mean for classroom research? Does it mean that such research is dead? I think not. In fact it opens up many exciting new research possibilities. At the same time, it forces those of us involved in classroom research to redefine our agenda, our methods, and our assumptions.

By way of example, I will mention some ongoing research being conducted by me and a colleague, Mary Ann Christison (Christison & Nunan, 2001). This research grew out of our involvement with GlobalEnglish, an Internet-based language school. Part of the research involved a discourse analysis of the virtual, text-chat classroom, which we compared with face-to-face conversation classes. When conducting our analysis, we found that the analytical tools that we would normally employ in conventional face-to-face classrooms were only partly useful, and that outcomes that were well established in traditional classroom research were only partially replicated. For example, in relation to discoursal "moves" and topicalization, we drew the following conclusions:

1. All of the pedagogical functions identified in face-to-face classroom interaction are evident in synchronous teacher-hosted chat.
2. Choosing the appropriate "responding" move is crucial, both to pedagogy and also the ongoing interaction.
3. The "responding" move enables the teacher to build a pedagogical interaction.
4. The multilayering of discourse in chat is even more complex than in face-to-face interaction (the "Russian Doll" syndrome).
5. Text chat may have pedagogical advantages over voice chat.

Legutke (2000) concludes his paper by speaking, not of the classroom, but of "the learning environment." He suggests that redesigning the language classroom is not an all or nothing thing in which we jettison the old and embrace the new. Rather, "the question is how the various old and newly emerging facets fit together, how the design features and their related roles and actions interplay: the training ground and the studio for set production, the communication center and the research laboratory, and, of course, the traditional classroom" (Legutke, 2000, p. 21). In researching and evaluating the classroom, or "learning environment" of the future, he suggests that we confront seven criterial questions:

1. Does our learning environment provide for situated practice and meaningful communication? What is worth communicating about?
2. Does our learning environment allow for interaction with an authentic audience?
3. Does our learning environment involve our learners in meaningful tasks?
4. Are learners encouraged to use a variety of representational resources to create meaning and play with language?
5. Do students have access to these resources and have they learned how to use them?
6. Are learners encouraged to turn mindfully to their own learning process and become responsible for their own learning?
7. Do learners have a chance to cooperate in co-creating the learning environment? Does the physical space allow for such cooperative behavior? (Legutke, 2000, p. 22)

CONCLUSION

The aim of this chapter has been to review the topic of classroom research: past, present, and future. I began the chapter by offering some definitions before situating classroom research within the broader discipline of applied linguistics. The bulk of the chapter is devoted to a review of substantive and methodological issues in classroom research. In the final part of the chapter I touch on several current controversies before looking ahead to what I see as future trends.

REFERENCES

Allwright, D. (1983). Classroom-centered research on language teaching and learning: A brief historical overview. *TESOL Quarterly, 17*(2), 191–204.
Asher, J. (1988). *Learning another language through actions: The complete teacher's guidebook.* Los Gatos, CA: Sky Oaks.
Bailey, K. (1999). *What have we learned in twenty years of classroom research?* Featured speaker presentation at the March 1999 TESOL Convention, New York.

Bailey, K., & Nunan, D. (Eds.). (1996). *Voices from the Language Classroom*. Cambridge, UK: Cambridge University Press.

Beasley, B., & Riordan, L. (1981). The classroom teacher as researcher. *English in Australia, 55*(1), 36–42.

Beretta, A. (1986). Program-fair language teaching evaluation. *TESOL Quarterly, 20*(3), 431–444.

Block, D. (1996). A window on the classroom: classroom events viewed from different angles. In K. Bailey, & K. Nunan (Eds.). *Voices from the Language Classroom* (pp. 168–194). Cambridge, UK: Cambridge University Press.

Brock, C. (1986). The effect of referential questions on ESL classroom discourse. *TESOL Quarterly, 20*(1), 47–59.

Carr, W., & Kemmis, S. (1985). *Becoming critical: Knowing through action research*. Victoria, Australia: Deakin University Press.

Chaudron, C. (1988). *Second language classrooms: Research on teaching and learning*. Cambridge, UK: Cambridge University Press.

Christison, M. A., & Nunan, D. (2001). *Pedagogical functions in synchronous elearning interaction: The online conversation class*. Paper presented at the 2001 TESOL Convention, St. Louis, MO.

Donato, R. (2000). Sociocultural contributions to understanding the foreign and second language classroom. In J. Lantolf (Ed.), *Sociocultural theory and second language learning* (pp. 27–51). Oxford, UK: Oxford University Press.

Doughty, C., & Williams, J. (Eds.). (1998). *Focus on form in classroom second language acquisition*. Cambridge, UK: Cambridge University Press.

Dulay, H., & Burt, M. (1973). Should we teach children syntax? *Language Learning, 23*, 235–252.

Dulay, H., & Burt, M. (1974). Natural sequences in child second language acquisition. *Language Learning, 24*, 253–278.

Ellis, R. (1994). *The study of second language acquisition*. Oxford, UK: Oxford University Press.

Fotos, S., & Ellis, R. (1991). Communicating about grammar: A task-based approach. *TESOL Quarterly, 25*(4), 605–628.

Grotjahn, R. (1987). On the methodological basis of introspective methods. In C. Faerch & G. Kasper (Eds.), *Introspection in second language learning* (pp. 54–81). Clevedon, UK: Multilingual Matters.

Kramsch, C. (2000). Social discursive constructions of self in L2 learning. In J. Lantolf (Ed.), *Sociocultural theory and second language learning* (pp. 133–153). Oxford, UK: Oxford University Press.

Krashen, S. (1981). *Second language acquisition and second language learning*. Oxford, UK: Pergamon.

Krashen, S. (1982). *Principles and practice in second language acquisition*. Oxford, UK: Pergamon.

Krashen, S., & Terrell, T. (1983). *The natural approach*. Oxford, UK: Pergamon.

Lantolf, J. (Ed.). (2000). *Sociocultural theory and second language learning*. Oxford, UK: Oxford University Press.

Larsen-Freeman, D. (2001). Teaching grammar. In M. Celce-Murcia (Ed.), *Teaching English as a Second or Foreign Language* (pp. 251–266). Boston, MA: Heinle.

Legareta, D. (1977). Language choice in bilingual classrooms. *TESOL Quarterly, 11*, 9–16.

Legutke, M. (2000, December). *Redesigning the foreign language classroom: A critical perspective on information technology (IT) and educational change*. Plenary presentation, International Language in Education Conference, University of Hong Kong.

Long, M. (1980). Inside the "black box": Methodological issues in classroom research on language learning. *Language Learning, 30*, 1–42.

Long, M. (1985). Input and second language acquisition theory. In S. Gass & C. Madden (Eds.), *Input in second language acquisition* (pp. 377–393). Rowley, MA: Newbury House.

Martyn, E. (2002). *The effects of task type on negotiation of meaning in small group work*. Unpublished doctoral dissertation, University of Hong Kong.

Nunan, D. (1991a). Methodological issues in classroom research. *Studies in Second Language Acquisition, 13*, 2.

Nunan, D. (1991b). Language teaching methodology. London: Prentice-Hall.

Nunan, D. (1992). *Research methods in language learning*. Cambridge, UK: Cambridge University Press.

Nunan, D. (1996). Issues in second language acquisition research: Examining substance and procedure. In W. Ritchie & T. Bjatia (Eds.), *Handbook of second language acquisition* (pp. 349–374). New York: Academic Press.

Ohta, A. (2000). Rethinking interaction in SLA: Developmentally appropriate assistance in the zone of proximal development and the acquisition of L2 grammar. In J. Lantolf (Ed.), *Sociocultural theory and second language learning* (pp. 51–78). Oxford, UK: Oxford University Press.

Oxford, R. (1990). *Language learning strategies: What every teacher should know*. Rowley, MA: Newbury House.

Ritchie, W., & Bhatia, T. (1996). Introduction and overview. In W. Ritchie & T. Bhatia (Eds.), *Handbook of second language acquisition*. (pp. 1–42). New York: Academic Press.

Scherer, G., & Wertheimer, M. (1964). *A psycholinguistic experiment in foreign language teaching*. New York: McGraw-Hill.

Roebuck, R. (2000). Subjects speak out: How learners position themselves in a psycholinguistic task. In J. Lantolf (Ed.), *Sociocultural theory and second language learning* (pp. 79–95). Oxford, UK: Oxford University Press.

Skehan, P. (1998). *A cognitive approach to language learning*. Oxford, UK: Oxford University Press.

Spada, N., & Frohlich, M. (1995). *Communicative orientation of language teaching observation scheme: Coding conventions and applications*. Sydney, Australia: NCELTR.

Sullivan, P. (2000). Playfulness as mediation in communicative language teaching in a Vietnamese schoolroom. In J. Lantolf (Ed.), *Sociocultural theory and second language learning* (pp. 113–131). Oxford, UK: Oxford University Press.

Swaffar, J., Arens, K., & Morgan, M. (1982). Teacher classroom practices: Redefining method as task hierarchy. *Modern Language Journal, 66,* 24–33.

Swain, M. (1985). Communicative competence: Some roles of comprehensible input and comprehensible output in its development. In S. Gass & C. Madden (Eds.), *Input in second language acquisition* (pp. 235–256). Rowley, MA: Newbury House.

Swain, M. (1993). The output hypothesis: Just speaking and writing aren't enough. *The Canadian Modern Language Review, 50,* 158–164.

Swain, M. (1997). The output hypothesis, focus on form and second language learning. In V. Berry, B. Adamson & W. Littlewood (Eds.), *Applying linguistics: Insights into language in education* (pp. 1–21). Hong Kong: University of Hong Kong.

Swain, M. (2000). The output hypothesis and beyond: Mediating acquisition through collaborative dialogue In J. Lantolf (Ed.), *Sociocultural theory and second language learning* (pp. 97–114). Oxford, UK: Oxford University Press.

Swain, M., & Lapkin, C. (1998). Interaction and second language learning: Two adolescent French immersion students working together. *The Modern Language Journal, 83,* 320–338.

Tsui, A. (1985). Analyzing input and interaction in second language classrooms. *RELC Journal, 16,* 8–32.

Tsui, A. (2001). Classroom interaction. In R. Carter & D. Nunan (Eds.), *The Cambridge guide to teaching English to speakers of other languages* (pp. 120–125). Cambridge, UK: Cambridge University Press.

van Lier, L. (1988). *The classroom and the language learner: Ethnography and second language research.* London: Longman.

Verity, D. (2000). Side affects: The strategic development of professional satisfaction. In J. Lantolf (Ed.), *Sociocultural theory and second language learning* (pp. 179–197). Oxford, UK: Oxford University Press.

Willing, K. (1988). *Learning strategies in adult migrant education.* Sydney, Australia: NCELTR.

14

Action Research

Anne Burns
Macquarie University

INTRODUCTION

This chapter begins by positioning action research (AR) in relation to other better known paradigms of research and outlines shifts in the way it has developed and been realized philosophically and practically. The second half focuses on how AR has been taken up in English Language Teaching (ELT) contexts and highlights some of the current debates around its validity as a research approach. Examples of three different forms of current AR reporting are discussed. Predictions about its potential to inform socioconstructivist and sociopolitical perceptions of language pedagogy and practice are suggested.

Despite many varying definitions of AR (e.g., Bogdan & Biklen, 1982; Ebbutt, 1983; Elliot, 1981; Halsey, 1972; Rapoport, 1970), one common thread is that participants in a given social situation classroom are themselves centrally involved in a systematic process of enquiry arising from their own practical concerns. This is the major distinction between AR and other forms of applied research, in which participants investigate issues considered theoretically significant in the field (Burns, 2000; Crookes, 1993).

Although interpretations and definitions of AR are still very much under development, one of the most frequently cited is from Carr and Kemmis (1986, p. 162):

> Action research is simply a form of self-reflective enquiry undertaken by participants in order to improve the rationality and justice of their own practices, their understanding of these practices and the situations in which the practices are carried out.

Thus, other central characteristics of AR are the enhancement of practice, the development of new theoretical understandings, and the introduction of change into the social enterprise.

Although not exactly new, AR is still (re)emerging as a branch of research in education generally and is now gaining growing currency in the field of ELT. Its scope, however, extends well beyond these fields to industry (Argyris & Schön, 1978), health (Kember, 2001), and community (Batliwala & Patel, 1997) settings. In this chapter I trace the history of AR, the various ways it has been conceptualized, and how it has been taken up in the field of ELT. I discuss some of the criticisms leveled against this form of inquiry and point to some possible future directions. As the scope of the AR literature is large, I confine my discussion in the second half of the chapter to the ELT field.

THE ORIGINS OF ACTION RESEARCH

The sources of AR are located within "a quiet methodological revolution" (Denzin & Lincoln, 1998, p.vii) that has been taking place over at least the last 50 years in research in the social sciences and humanities. It is part of a movement toward qualitative, interpretive, and participative research paradigms that expanded dramatically during the 20th century to contest the dominant positivist, scientific worldview that originated in the 15th century with the Enlightenment. Reason (1998, pp. 261–262), although acknowledging the role of positivist research in releasing society from "the bonds of superstition and Scholasticism," sees as its major limitation the narrowing and monopolization of knowledge by an elite few, so as to " . . . place the researcher firmly outside and separate from the subject of his or her research, reaching for an objective knowledge and for one separate truth" Reason, 1998, pp. 261–262.

Participative, "naturalistic" inquiry with its exploratory–interpretive approaches (Grotjhan, 1987, p. 59) is fuelled by democratic, egalitarian, and pluralist principles. It has been broadly influenced by philosophical concepts of humanistic psychology (Rogers, 1961), liberationist education (Freire, 1970) social phenomenology (Schutz, 1967), social constructivism (Berger & Luckman, 1966; Cicourel & Kitsuse, 1963), critical theory (Habermas, 1972) and feminist studies (Lichtenstein, 1988). It is with this paradigm that AR is associated.

One of the early antecedents of AR in the field of educational inquiry was John Dewey (e.g., 1904), who set out his agenda for research in terms of the centrality of educational practices as the source of data and the ultimate test of the validity of research findings. The concept of a distinctive focus on *practice* was both a challenge to established forms of academic research and a democratization of the scope of research, including as it did the possibility that practitioners themselves might become included in addressing common pedagogical problems (McTaggart, 1991). Although in contrast with the dominant themes of the time, Dewey's insistence on the practical linked to an intellectual tradition that can be traced back to Aristotle and was to become extremely influential in educational inquiry in the 1940s.

Much of the current representations of AR is attributed to the work of the social psychologist Kurt Lewin (1946, 1948). He is generally regarded as "the father of action research" (Marrow, 1969; McNiff, 1988; McTaggart, 1991), although Corey (1953) argues that the concepts and terminology had already appeared in the writings of Collier, U.S. Commissioner for Indian Affairs, who argued for a joint approach by researchers and administrators that was "action-research, research-action" (1945, p. 300). Lewin's scientific experiments on the problems of social groups served as a basis for his conceptualization of research as a cyclical, action-based model that included planning, reconnaissance, fact-finding, action, and analysis. His experimentation in "group dynamics" emerged from a postwar era where research into social problems was of urgent interest at a time of great societal upheaval. What distinguished this perspective, from the predominant focus on the *application* of research results to practice, was the unification of theory and action. As Carr and Kemmis (1986, p. 44) put it, it was a view that "regards theory and practice as dialectically related, with theory being developed and tested by application in and reflection on practice." Lewin was above all else "a practical theorist" (Marrow, 1969) whose interests lay in theories of the *facilitation* of AR.

SHIFTS IN CONCEPTUALIZATIONS OF AR

McTaggart (1991, p. v) characterizes the history of AR in education as a "struggle to sustain action research practice." The story of its development from the initial impetus of Lewin's work is perhaps best portrayed as three broad movements (cf. McKernan, 1996), during which its fortunes as a recognized research position have risen and declined: the *technical-scientific*, the *practical-deliberative*, and the *critical-emancipatory*. Elements of all three approaches still exist in current interpretations of AR (cf. Crookes, 1993).

Technical-Scientific

Corey's (1949, 1952, 1953) work with teachers in the United States represented the first attempts to define and popularize educational AR. However, paradoxically, his aims to make it scientifically "respectable"—by arguing for its capacity to generate "hypotheses to be tested" (1949, p. 512), and by contrasting it with "fundamental research" seeking to "generalize" and "discover the 'truth'" (1949, p. 509)—were also the seeds of its demise. His case for AR portrayed it as essentially a technical activity through which teachers could seek improvements to their practice. Although proposals for AR were also developed by advocates such as Taba and Noel, they had, according to Kemmis (1982), lost the cyclical interactions among reconnaissance, problem-identification, and evaluation proposed by Lewin, and turned into a sequence of steps "which it is wise not to reverse" (Taba & Noel, 1957, p. 12).

The critiques of AR by Hodgkinson's (1957) and others as "amateur," "unsophisticated," and "ungeneralizable," and the advent in the United States, and later in Britain, of large-scale Research, Development, and Diffusion models of educational research meant that by the late 1950s AR was effectively marginalized in the United States.

Practical-Deliberative

The resurgence in educational AR in the 1960s and 1970s was motivated by the emergence of curriculum as a field of inquiry. In particular Schwab's (e.g., 1969) work in the United States and Stenhouse's (e.g., 1971) in Britain put *practical deliberation* (Reid, 1978) at the heart of the curriculum enterprise:

> Practical deliberation responds to the immediate situation which is deemed problematic from a moral perspective—there is a sense in which curriculum action must be taken to put things right. The practical is also connected with the *process* rather than the *products* of enquiry. (McKernan, 1996, pp. 20–21)

Stenhouse's work in the Humanities Curriculum Project (1967–72), extended by that of his colleagues, Elliott and Adelman in the Ford Teaching Project (1972–74), placed localized, school-based cycles of action and inquiry by teachers at the core of curriculum development, together with the hermeneutic aspects of inquiry for *understanding*. "The idea is that of an educational science in which each classroom is a laboratory, each teacher a member of the scientific community" (Stenhouse, 1975, p. 143). Elliott (1985, 1991) argued that teaching is a moral and theoretical activity defined in terms of the realization of practitioners' context-bound values. The subsequent publication of Schön's concepts of the *Reflective Practitioner* (1983) reinforced the centrality of the cognitive, the reflective, and the deliberative in processes of curriculum practice. Signs of a renewed interest in action (van Manen, 1984) and participatory (Hall, 1979) research in the United States also emerged at this time (see also Bissex & Bullock, 1987; Goswami & Stillman, 1987; Wallat, Green, Conlin, & Haramis, 1983).

Critical-Emancipatory

From the mid-1980s, new ways of thinking about AR were developed by Kemmis and his colleagues at Deakin University in Australia, influenced by the writings of critical theorists including Habermas (1972), Freire (1982), and Fals Borda (1979).

Carr and Kemmis (1986, p. 203) argued that, in contrast to practical AR that focused on individualistic judgments, "the form of action research which best embodies the values of a critical educational science is *emancipatory* action research." Individual practice should be seen as socially constituted and reflective of broad social, educational, and political interactions within the school. Through AR, a collaborative and dialectic relationship could be created between individual and group responsibility toward the production and implementation of common educational policies and practices. This was a transformative, resistant, and activist form of AR where "the practitioner group itself takes responsibility for its own emancipation from the dictates of irrationality, injustice, alienation and unfulfillment" (p. 204). By examining taken-for-granted habits, rituals, customs, and precedents, as well as bureaucratic control structures and constraints, the group could empower itself to realize in practice its own fundamental educational values (cf. Kincheloe, 1991; Whitehead and Lomax, 1987). Kincheloe (1991) articulates the alternative position taken by critical-emancipatory theorists:

> When the critical dimension of teacher research is negated, the teacher-as-researcher movement can become quite a trivial enterprise. Uncritical educational action research seeks direct applications of information gleaned to specific situations—a cookbook style of technological thinking is encouraged... Such thinking does not allow for complex reconceptualizations of knowledge and as a result fails to understand the ambiguities and the ideological structures of the classroom. [In this way] teacher research is co-opted, its democratic edge is blunted. (p. 83)

Kemmis and McTaggart's model, with its four "moments," reinvigorated Lewin's theory of AR as a self-reflective spiral or loop:

- *Plan*—prospective to action, forward looking and critically informed in terms of the recognition of real constraints, and the potential for more effective action.
- *Action*—deliberate and controlled, but critically informed in that it recognizes practice as ideas-in-action mediated by the material, social, and political "struggle" toward improvement.
- *Observation*—responsive, but also forward looking in that it documents the critically informed action, its effects, and its context of situation, using "open-eyed" and "open-minded" observation plans, categories, and measurements.
- *Reflection*—evaluative and descriptive, in that it makes sense of the processes, problems, issues, and constraints of action and develops perspectives and comprehension of the issues and circumstances in which it arises.

(Based on Kemmis & McTaggart, 1986, pp. 11–14)

In carrying out AR, practitioners draw extensively on *qualitative methods*, such as case studies, interviews, journals, and classroom observations. However, quantitative procedures are not excluded; as Elliott and others point out, AR should not be defined in terms of its methods (Elliott, in Introduction to McKernan, 1996, p. ix).

ACTION RESEARCH IN THE FIELD OF ELT/APPLIED
LINGUISTICS: MAIN RESEARCH FINDINGS

The burgeoning interest in AR in the field of ELT is essentially a phenomenon of the 1990s. Although the field was not immune to trends in educational research, by the late 1980s, as van Lier (1988) notes, AR had "not so far received much serious attention as a distinct style of research in language teaching" (p. 67). Nevertheless, calls for the participation of teachers in classroom-centered research (CCR) were mounting (Allwright, 1988; Jarvis, 1983; Long, 1983; van Lier, 1988), whereas observational and other features of AR were already evident in research related to the classroom (e.g., Allen, fröhlich, & Spada, 1984; Allwright, 1980; Brown, Anderson, Shillcock, & Yule, 1984; Long, Adams, Mclean, & Castanos, 1976). At the same time, the expansion of AR activity was predicted in Breen and Candlin's (1980) proposals that curriculum evaluation should be an integral aspect of classroom teaching and learning; Breen's (1985) argument that the classroom was better considered not an "experimental laboratory" for second language acquisition (SLA) research, but as a "social context for language learning"; and van Lier's (1988) call for "ethnographic monitoring" of classroom curriculum processes.

Nunan's publication, *Understanding Language Classrooms* (1989a), drew substantially on this work, but explicitly generated an "an altered stance"(Candlin, in General Editor's Preface) toward AR. Subtitled *A Guide for Teacher-Initiated Action*, it projected research by language teachers not just as a worthwhile recommendation, but as a serious possibility by offering:

> ... a particular focus on ways and means whereby teachers might investigate their own classrooms. The intention is to provide a serious introduction to classroom research to language professionals who do not have specialist training in research methods... it is aimed specifically at the classroom teacher and teachers in preparation. (p. xi)

Nunan's endorsement of teacher research was underpinned by the recognition from the late 1970s that communicative language teaching significantly altered the role of the teacher in the curriculum process (cf. Connelly & Clandinin, 1988). The concepts of "the learner-centered curriculum" (Burton, 1987; Nunan, 1988) and "the teacher as curriculum developer" (Nunan, 1987) and "course designer"(Nunan, 1985) were perhaps then most strongly articulated in the Australian Adult Migrant English Program (AMEP; cf. Tudor, 1996, p. 21), where AR became from the late 1980s a by-word for integrating a research orientation into the work of practitioners (Brindley, 1990; Burton, 1998; Burns, 1999; Nunan, 1990).

A further impetus to the ethos of teacher research in the ELT field came from the distinctions made between teacher *training* and teacher *education* (Larsen-Freeman, 1983; Richards, 1987/90). Teaching as "discrete and trainable skills, such as setting up small-group activities, using strategies for correcting pronunciation errors, using referential questions... " reflected a low-inference, micro-perspective, in contrast to a holistic, macro-approach of the autonomous professional capable of "clarifying and elucidating the concepts and thinking processes that guide the effective second language teacher" (Richards, 1990, p. 14). The reflective and research-oriented proposals for teacher professional development contained in the collection edited by Richards and Nunan, (1990; e.g., Pennington, 1990) were echoed by Wallace (1991), drawing on the work of Schön (1983). Wallace drew a distinction among (1) a craft model of teaching, where novices learn by imitating master teachers; (2) an applied science model based on a separation of research and practice, where teachers are assumed to implement the findings of scientific research; and (3) a reflective model, which is a combination of "received" and "experiential" knowledge, where professional competence is mediated through cycles of practice and reflection. Wallace aimed to build a coherent framework for reflective practice, of which AR could be "an extension" (p. 57). The notion of the reflective language practitioner is now strongly endorsed (if not universally practiced) in most discussions of language teacher development (cf. Gebhard, 1996; Richards & Lockhart, 1994), whereas related branches of research have focused on teacher learning (Freeman & Richards, 1996), knowledge (Freeman, 1996), and cognition (Woods, 1996).

CURRENT DEBATES: ACTION RESEARCH IN ELT

In a significant and frequently cited article, Crookes (1993) argues that two kinds of AR are of import to the second language field. The first, underpinned by "the teacher as researcher " movement in education (cf. Cochran-Smith & Lytle, 1990; Strickland, 1988), is a (nominally) value-free and conservative version; the second follows a more radically progressive, critical, and emancipatory line (Carr & Kemmis, 1986; Gore & Zeichner, 1991). Research of the second kind, Crookes states, "has gone almost without representation in SL [second language] discussions of this topic" (p. 133).

An analysis of much of the published literature on AR over the last decade confirms Crookes' argument. Although this is perhaps a facet of the newness of action research in the field and uncertainty, or even rejection, of its viability as a valid research approach (cf. the discussions on the status of qualitative research in general in the field of SLA, e.g. Lazaraton, 1995; McCarthy, 2001), the majority of publications are concerned with outlining various versions of the AR process and/or providing (usually individually based) illustrative case studies (e.g., Bailey & Nunan, 1996; Edge & Richards, 1993; Nunan, 1989b; Wallace, 1998). Where collaboration between researchers and teachers takes place, there is a tendency for it to be of the "flying visit" (Breen, Candlin, Dam, & Gabrielsen, 1989) variety. Also, despite the arguments that action research provides a "voice" for teachers, collective accounts of AR written by classroom teachers, who would not also consider themselves academics or teacher educators, do not yet figure prominently, with some exceptions (e.g. the reports in Burns & Hood, 1995, 1998; Burns & de Silva Joyce, 2000; Edge, 2001; Richards, 1998).

Allwright (1993, p. 125), for example, has argued for "exploratory teaching" (cf. Allwright & Bailey, 1991) as an alternative to action research. He suggests that in the rush to advocate AR, "teachers face the risk of discovering the hard way that research can be an unacceptable burden to add to those they are already suffering from in their daily lives as classroom teachers" (p. 25). He argues that exploratory teaching is capable of greater sustainability than AR. Exploratory teaching differs by exploiting normal pedagogical activities to explore issues that "puzzle" teachers and learners. The focus is on *understanding* to promote more effective teaching, rather than on *problem-solving*. His work with teachers in Brazil (Allwright & Lenzuen, 1997) generated a series of procedures: 1) identify a puzzle area, 2) refine your thinking about that puzzle area, 3) select a particular topic to focus on, 4) find appropriate classroom procedures to explore it, 5) adapt them to the particular puzzle you want to explore, 6) use them in class, 7) interpret the outcomes, 8) decide on their implications and plan accordingly. However, Allwright's model appears to follow fairly closely some of the major processes of action research, while at the same time apparently disallowing the status of research to teachers' investigative activities.

Freeman's (1998, p. ix) discussion of teacher research is also influenced by his work in Brazil, as well as in Masters' programs he taught in the United States. Like Allwright, he examines how research can fit within the work of teaching and transform it through increased understanding. His aim is to "connect the 'doing' of teaching with the 'questioning' of research" (p.ix). Although he raises the possibility that "teachers will redefine the territory of their work," Freeman's interest presents as essentially individualist—the "presentation of how teacher-research can be done, and ... the assertion that teacher-research has a fundamental role in redefining the knowledge-base of teaching" (pp. ix–x). Nevertheless, the publication is among one of the first full-length treatments of the topic to be interspersed with a series of accounts of action research written by teachers (see also Wallace, 1998).

Publications by Wallace (1998) and Burns (1999) are the first book-length treatments in ELT to explicitly foreground the term "action research" in their titles. Wallace's discussion builds from his earlier theme (1991) of "reflection on our professional practice" (p. 1), but its focus is on providing concrete procedures for the individual teacher-researcher:

> If you are a practicing teacher with a keen interest in professional development you might like to consider the action research approach presented here. If you do, hopefully you will find certain of the techniques described to be of some practical use. (Wallace, 1991, p. 1)

In line with Crookes' argument, there are strong echoes here of the technicist and practical versions of teacher research. Burns attempts to depart from this approach and to shift toward a more critical stance by illustrating how AR can be integrated into ongoing collaborative teacher development processes that can create the conditions to support and influence institutional change. It also departs from other versions of researcher–teacher collaboration in that the participating researchers can be said to share "member's competence" (Linde, personal communication, cited in Woods, 1996) with the teachers, since they all work within the same Australian educational system. Roberts (1998), commenting on earlier work (Burns & Hood, 1995) that led to this publication, notes that:

> ... it shows the need for teachers' curriculum inquiry to be a genuine part of their work, and for their insights to be seen to contribute to larger-scale change. It would seem to be highly consistent with our preferred framework for [language teacher education] ... in that it highlights the exchange between individual development and its social context; positive relationships and opportunities for critical dialogue; and a consistent link between a person's work and the landscape in which it takes place. (p. 288)

Nevertheless, this work—in common with other examples, such as the AR carried out with Indian teachers investigating pedagogical change within moves to a communicative curriculum (Mathew & Lalitha Eapen, 1996), with Australian foreign language teachers' researching their classroom practice (Mickan, 1996), and with secondary teachers in Hong Kong aiming to develop greater professional competence and status (Tinker Sachs, 2000)—is probably closer to what Kemmis (1993) describes as co-operative AR.

According to Kemmis it is possible to identify a continuum of types of collaboration: *co-option* relationships, where the research is owned by the researchers; *co-operative*, where teachers work with researchers who share an interest in and facilitate their practice and often report it collaboratively; and *collaborative*, where researchers and teachers (or teachers working together) participate equally in the research agenda and are both the agents and the objects of the research. The latter type is still rare in current activities in the ELT field, although participatory research of the type conducted by Auerbach, Arnaud, Chandler, & Zambrano (1998), where researchers worked in a university–community collaboration with immigrants and refugees who became adult ESL and native language literacy instructors in their own communities, offers an example (see also Auerbach, 1994). While not explicitly called AR, this example perhaps comes closest to what could be considered both fully collaborative and critical-emancipatory in orientation in the language teaching field.

Elements of a more critical orientation to AR, located within a holistic and ecological interpretation of language education, are also to be found in van Lier's (1996) discussion of awareness, autonomy, and authenticity in the language curriculum. Van Lier argues that actions in the *cyclical stages of action research* and the purposes for which they were developed:

> ... beg large questions which are likely to take action research in critical directions, particularly if the teacher researcher moves from a problem-solving ... to a problem-posing approach, which looks at the classroom as a historically evolving and culturally embedded system. (p. 34)

Advocating a critical rather than a technical approach, Van Lier aligns his position with that of Candlin (1993), who distinguishes between "weak" and "strong" versions of AR, and Crookes (1993). He views supportive collaboration between teacher researchers as central, together with an interactive interpretation of the cyclical nature of AR where cycles and steps are "simultaneous strands that are braided together as one goes along" (p. 34; cf. Burns, 1999). A further conceptual point is that reflection is not a one-off event but a process that pervades AR activity—a "way of working" (Kemmis & McTaggart, 1986) rather than a time-bound project.

As this brief description implies, current interpretations of action research vary along a *practical–critical* continuum. Both types are valuable to the field of language teaching, but it is arguable that the radical and collaborative forms of action research are likely to have the greater impact on renewing practice at its "grass-roots" (cf. Crookes, 1989; van Lier, 1996). This point will be further elaborated in the final section of this chapter.

The Scope of Action Research Studies

Published studies of AR in ELT are still relatively small in number. In general two types of accounts are the most common: those written by academic researchers who have introduced action research as a component of BATESOL/MATESOL (Bachelor's and Master's in Teaching English to Speakers of Other Languages) and other university programs and who sometimes report on action research on behalf of their students or colleagues; and those written by individual teacher-researchers, sometimes as the result of projects carried out for tertiary qualifications. A third, and less common type, is the reporting by teachers of AR conducted for their own professional development within a larger collaborative grouping.

Tsui (1996) exemplifies the first type. Tsui worked with 38 practising ESL teachers enrolled in the Postgraduate Certificate in Education program at the University of Hong Kong. The teachers video or audio recorded their lessons and reviewed the tapes to identify their own problem areas for investigation. More than 70% identified student reticence and anxiety about responding in English in the classroom as a major issue. The teachers tried out different strategies, kept a diary of their observations and reflections, and wrote evaluative reports. Other examples of this type of AR are Thorne and Qiang (1996), Markee (1997), and Crookes and Chandler (1999).

A study conducted by Cowie (2001) illustrates the second category of reporting. Cowie describes a 3-year process during which he investigated the most effective ways to teach writing in his undergraduate classes in the liberal arts faculty of a Japanese public university. His investigations led him to revise his teaching approaches, but also to deepen his knowledge about conducting research. Calling his approach "not action research, but I'm getting there," his account highlights the nature of the processes and insights that can become significant for teacher researchers. Brousseau (1996) and Gersten and Tlusty (1998) also exemplify studies of this second type.

McPherson's (1997) study illustrates action research carried out as part of a large-scale collaborative AR process on disparate learner groups involving 26 Australian teachers. She traces the evolution of her understanding of the social dynamics operating in the classroom that initially impeded effective communicative teaching and learning. Through three successive cycles of AR, the intervention strategies she introduced enabled more effective student–teacher relationships and classroom activities. McPherson points out that the collaborative elements of the research were a crucial factor in its cyclical development. Mathew (2000) and Tinker Sachs (2002) provide further examples of this type.

While not specifically drawing on the conceptual frameworks of AR or labeling themselves as such, many other studies published over the last decade in more pedagogically oriented journals, such as the English Language Teaching Journal, English Language Forum or TESOL Journal, could be classified as action research, as could several of the studies regularly reported in collections of papers, such as the Hong Kong Working Papers in ELT or Die Unterrichtspraxis/Teaching German. Many of the short teacher-research studies published in Richards (1998) that illustrate how teachers identify and resolve a teaching issue reflect a very strong action research orientation. The latter publication is of interest in that it is unlikely that these localized and small-scale studies would have seen the light of day had they not been solicited for publication by the editor (through the International TESOL Association).

CRITIQUES OF ACTION RESEARCH (AND SOME POSSIBLE RESPONSES)

I have portrayed AR in positive terms and, indeed, evidence of the positive effects of action research in teachers' professional lives is growing, as exemplified in the following:

> The collaborative approach to the project provided regular contact with peers and opportunities to share idea and experiences. This aspect of the project cannot be undervalued. The project provided me with an opportunity to examine my teaching practices and revisit some to the practices I used in the past whose value I had forgotten. (O'Keeffe, 2001, p. 57)

However, as a form of research it is not without critics. Jarvis (1981) voiced early doubts about the capacity of teachers to do research, arguing that it was an activity best left to specialists and that, in any case, action research was without academic prestige. The latter argument still dogs AR, although its more recent prominence in the field is causing a gradual reevaluation of its status (cf. Richards, 2001). Part of the reason for lack of prestige are doubts about its rigor:

> Certainly research by teachers, for teachers, on their processes of teaching can only be a good thing. But if obtaining a clearer understanding of teaching processes requires care and rigour in other modes of research, there is no good argument for action research producing less care and rigour unless it is less concerned with clear understanding, which it is not. (Brumfit & Mitchell, 1989, p. 9)

Brumfit and Mitchell's points provoke a number of key questions: What are the standards by which AR is to be judged and should these be the same as for other forms of research? Should it conform to existing academic criteria? What ethical considerations need to be brought to bear on research that is highly contextualized in practice? How should action research be reported? What tensions exist between the quality of action research and its sustainability by practitioners? (See Allwright, 1997 and Nunan, 1997 for recent discussion of these issues.)

Even promoters of action research, sometimes seem to have doubts about its status. Wallace (1991) states, "'Research' of this kind is simply an extension of the normal reflective practices of many teachers, but it is slightly more rigorous and might conceivably lead to more effective outcomes (p. 17)."

Although it might be unintended, the use of scare quotes positions AR in contrast to "real" research, albeit as preferable to more usual unstructured forms of thinking about teaching. Wallace's more recent account (1998) situates action research in relation to the reflective cycle as a component of "professional development strategies (excluding 'conventional research')" (p. 14). As with case study and other forms of qualitative research, issues of the legitimacy (cf. Bourdieu, 1991) of action and practitioner research are likely to go on being contested for some time.

A possible response to some of these questions is provided by Crookes (1993) and Freeman (1998), who argue that accurate and fair ways of representing what teachers find in their research will require unconventional new discourses and genres. In developing them, it will be the meaningfulness and trustworthiness (Mishler, 1990) of the research that becomes paramount. A central question will be: To what extent does this research resonate with my understandings of practice and have meaning in my context? Similarly, Bailey (1998) suggests that AR should not be judged by the traditional criteria of random selection, generalizability, and replicability, as its goals are to establish local understandings. In short, it is likely that AR practitioners will need to confront the challenge "to define and meet standards of appropriate rigor without sacrificing relevance" (Argyris & Schön, 1978, p. 85).

Other concerns and critiques relate to the over-involvement of the action researcher, leading to personal bias; the time constraints posed by longitudinal research; the double burden of teaching and research; the lack of models and procedures for data analysis (cf. Winter, 1989); and question marks over accountability in experimentation with learner subjects (cf. Hitchcock & Hughes, 1995; Tinker Sachs, 2000).

Perhaps one of the strongest features of action research that can contribute to enhancing rigor is its iterative, or cyclical, nature. Iterations in the cycle, where initial insights and findings give way to new, but related, questions and data collection can serve to (a) build on evidence from previous cycles; (b) expand the scope of the study; (c) triangulate the data across different episodes, sites, and subjects through multiple data sources; (d) test new findings against previous iterations of the cycle; and (e) avoid the bias inherent in cross-sectional research. The iterative aspect becomes particularly powerful when research is conducted collaboratively, as findings and outcomes can be cross-referenced across multiple activities.

FUTURE DIRECTIONS

Second language acquisition studies have been a major force in the field of ELT. However, over the last few decades the focus of SLA research has been predominantly on theoretical concerns (see the discussions in the thematic issues of *Applied Linguistics*, 1993). More recently, calls have been made from those both within and outside the SLA field for a shift to research generated from the classroom and from the perspective of practitioners. This, it is argued, will raise "the silent voices" of teachers and shape SLA research more realistically in the direction of actual practice (Zephir, 2000). Ellis, himself a major figure in SLA research, has recently stated the case for AR, describing his own shifts in thinking:

As I left the classroom . . . I began to treat SLA as an object of enquiry in its own right. That is I began to pay less attention to how the results of research . . . might aid language pedagogy and more attention to trying to produce good research . . . Increasingly, though, I have had to recognize that the gap between what second language acquisition researchers do and what teachers do has grown wider and that the former spend an increasing amount of time talking to each other in a language only they understand. (Ellis, 1997, pp. vii–viii)

There are two major ways in which AR can potentially invigorate the field of ELT: the first can be termed *socioconstructivist* and the second *sociopolitical*.

Action research offers a means for teachers to become agents rather than recipients of knowledge about second language teaching and learning, and thus to contribute toward the building of educational theories of practice (Bourdieu, 1990). Changes in the cultures of teaching and learning English, themselves the subject of global changes in industrialized societies, means that, in the near future at least, the relevance of AR is set to expand. The nature of knowledge as abstract, decontextualized, and propositional is increasingly being questioned in this field as elsewhere. Illustrations of collaborative AR as a process of literate knowledge building within a collaborative "community of inquiry" have been offered by Wells & Chang-Wells (1992), whose work with school teachers in Canada over a period of 3 years led to significant changes in teachers' practices. Thinking about teaching as communal, inquiry-oriented action rather than as individual classroom practice represents a significant shift for current models of teacher education.

In the future, professional knowledge building in teacher education is also likely to connect the practical and theoretical skills needed by teachers with their underpinning morals and values. AR allows for a *social-constructivist* approach, that is, one that integrates the individual development of teachers' knowledge with the specific social situations and local contexts in which they work. This is an approach embedded in an ecological perspective (see van Lier, e.g. 1997) where close attention is paid to contextual analysis, the actions, discourses, and perceptions of the people in the context and the patterns that connect them, as well as the "nested ecosystems" (Bronfonbrenner, 1979) that move analysis from the micro contexts of the classroom to the macro contexts beyond.

Aligned with these broadened contextual perspectives are the political possibilities for AR, (although it would be naïve in the extreme not to acknowledge the potential for AR to be co-opted for bureaucratic or political purposes). As teacher researchers gain a voice, the *socio-political* and critical aspects of their work may also be strengthened. McNiff (1988, p. 72) sees this as an inevitable consequence—"politics will intrude." Although this development may well set action researchers at odds with established educational systems, it could also be a powerful force for changing and improving existing unsatisfactory language teaching situations. For example, Ferguson (1998) describes how she lobbied for continuation of her adult ESL class in the face of previously unrevealed bureaucratic decisions to cut funds. Although not specifically termed critical AR, her comments on her newly gained political insights might well be:

We, as ESL practitioners, can look at our field of work and easily say, "It's hopeless!" The inadequacies in the field are great: in recognition of the need for ESL service for adults, in funding for service delivery, in amount of services available, in employment opportunities for teachers and so on and on. However, we can just as easily say, "It's wide open!" There is so much room for improvement that small actions towards building political visibility can be significant. Any expertise we gain is valuable. Any progress we make is laudable. (p. 13)

To whatever extent future trends in AR incorporate some of the directions foreshadowed here, it seems inevitable that it will become instrumental in forging new relationships between academic researchers and teachers in our field, and in giving rise to new paradigms for research in which practitioners will have a much greater role to play.

CONCLUSION

This brief overview of the philosophical and theoretical antecedents, developments, and central characteristics of AR inevitably covers only some of the ground. As an approach that appears to excite and stimulate teachers and teacher educators alike, it will be of great interest to the field of ELT to see how AR contributes to professional development and research in the coming decades. It is hoped that, we can look forward to stronger and more genuinely collaborative partnerships between teachers and researchers, and as teachers gain confidence in their research skills, to a greater number of accounts of practitioner research in the ELT literature.

ACKNOWLEDGMENTS

I am very grateful to Kathi Bailey, Graham Crookes, and Leo van Lier for their invaluable comments and suggestions on an earlier version of this chapter.

REFERENCES

Allen, J. P. B., Fröhlich, M., & Spada, N. (1984). The communicative orientation of language teaching: An observation scheme. In J. Handscombe, R. A. Orem, & B. Taylor (Eds.), *On TESOL '83: The question of control* (pp. 231–252). Washington, DC: TESOL.

Allwright, D. (1980). Turns, topics and tasks: Patterns of participation in language learning and teaching. In D. Larsen-Freeman (Ed.), *Discourse analysis in second language research* (pp. 165–187). Rowley, MA: Newbury House.

Allwright, D. (1988). *Observation in the language classroom.* London: Longman.

Allwright, D. (1993). Integrating "research" and "pedagogy": Appropriate criteria and practical possibilities. In J. Edge & K. Richards (Eds.), *Teachers develop teachers research* (pp. 125–135). London: Heinemann.

Allwright, D. (1997). Quality and sustainability in teacher-research. *TESOL Quarterly, 31*(2), 368–370.

Allwright, D., & Bailey, K. (1991). *Focus on the language classroom.* Cambridge, UK: Cambridge University Press.

Allwright, D., & Lenzuen, R. (1997). Exploratory practice. Work at the Cultura Inglesa, Rio de Janeiro, Brazil. *Language Teaching Research, 1*(1), 73–79.

Argyris, C., & Schön, D. (1978). *Organizational learning.* Reading, MA: Addison-Wesley.

Auerbach, E. (1994). Participatory action research. *TESOL Quarterly, 28*(4), 693–697.

Auerbach, E., Arnaud, J., Chandler, C., & Zambrano, A. (1998). Building community strengths: A model for training literacy instructors. In T. Smoke (Ed.), *Adult ESL: Politics, pedagogy and participation in classroom and community programs* (pp. 209–228). Mahwah, NJ: Lawrence Erlbaum Associates.

Bailey, K. & Nunan, D. (Eds.). (1996). *Voices from the language classroom.* Cambridge, UK: Cambridge University Press.

Bailey, K. (1998). Approaches to empirical research in instructional settings. In H. Byrnes (Ed.), *Perspectives in research and scholarship in second language teaching* (pp. 123–178). New York: The Modern Language Association of America.

Batliwala, S., & Patel, S. (1997). A census as participatory research. In R. McTaggart (Ed.), *Participatory action research* (pp. 263–277). Albany, NY: State University of New York Press.

Berger P. L., & Luckman, T. (1966). *The social construction of reality.* Garden City, NY: Doubleday.

Bissex, G., & Bullock, R. (Eds.). (1987). *Seeing for ourselves: Case study research by teachers of writing.* Portsmouth, NH: Heinemman.

Bogdan, R., & Biklen, S. K. (1982). *Qualitative research for education: An introduction to theory and methods.* Boston: Allyn & Bacon.

Bourdieu, P. (1990). *The logic of practice.* Stanford, CA: Stanford University Press.

Bourdieu, P. (1991). *Language and symbolic power.* Cambridge, MA: Harvard University Press.

Breen, M. P. (1985). The social context for language learning—a neglected situation? *Studies in Second Language Acquisition, 7,* 135–158.

Breen, M. P., & Candlin, C. N. (1980). The essentials of a communicative curriculum in language teaching. *Applied Linguistics, 1,* 89–112.

Breen, M. P., Candlin, C. N., Dam, L., & Gabrielsen, G. (1989). The evolution of a teacher training program. In R. K. Johnson (Ed.), *The second language curriculum* (pp. 111–135). Cambridge, UK: Cambridge University Press.

Brindley, G. (1990). Towards a research agenda for TESOL. *Prospect, 6*(1), 7–26.

Brumfit, C., & Mitchell, R. (1989). The language classroom as a focus for research. In C. Brumfit & R. Mitchell (Eds.), *Research in the language classroom.* (ELT Documents 133, pp. 3–15). London: Modern English Publications and The British Council.

Bronfonbrenner, U. (1979). *The ecology of human development: Experiments by nature and design.* Cambridge, MA: Harvard University Press.

Brown, G., Anderson, A., Shillcock, R., & Yule, G. (1984). *Teaching talk: Strategies for production and assessment.* Cambridge, UK: Cambridge University Press.

Brousseau, K. (1996). Action research in the second language classroom: Two views of a writing process class. *Carleton Papers in Applied Language Studies, 13,* 1–20.

Burns, A. (1999). *Collaborative action research for English language teachers.* Cambridge, UK: Cambridge University Press.

Burns, A. (2000). Action research and applied research: What are the relationships? *The Language Teacher, 24*(7), 3–5.

Burns, A., & Hood, S. (1995). *Teachers' voices: Exploring course design in a changing curriculum.* Sydney, Australia: National Centre for English Language Teaching and Research.

Burns, A., & Hood, S. (1998). *Teachers' voices 3: Teaching critical literacy.* Sydney, Australia: National Centre for English Language Teaching and Research.

Burns, A., & de Silva Joyce, H. (2000). *Teachers' voices 5: A new look at reading practices.* Sydney, Australia: National Centre for English Language Teaching and Research.

Burton, J. (Ed.). (1987). *Implementing the learner-centred curriculum.* Adelaide, South Australia: National Curriculum Resource Centre.

Burton, J. (1998). Professionalism in language teaching. *Prospect, 13*(3), 24–35.

Candlin, C. N. (1993). *Problematising authenticity: Whose texts for whom?* Paper presented at the TESOL Convention, Atlanta, GA.

Carr, W., & Kemmis, S. (1986). *Becoming critical: Knowing through action research.* London: Falmer.

Cicourel, A. V., & Kitsuse, J. I. (1963). A note on the use of official statistics. *Social Problems, 11,* 131–139.

Cochran-Smith, M., & Lytle, S. (1990). Research on teaching and teacher research: The issues that divide. *Educational Researcher, 19*(2), 2–11.

Collier, J. (1945, May). United States Indian administration as a laboratory of ethnic relations. *Social Research, 12,* 265–303.

Connelly, F. M., & Clandinin, J. D. (1988). *Teachers as curriculum planners: Narratives of experience.* New York: Teachers College Press.

Corey, S. (1949). Action research, fundamental research and educational practices. *Teachers College Record, 50,* 509–514.

Corey, S. (1952). Action research by teachers and the population sampling problem. *Journal of Educational Psychology, 43,* 331–338.

Corey, S. (1953). *Action research to improve school practices.* New York: Columbia University Teachers College Press.

Cowie, N. (2001). An "It's not action research yet, but I'm getting there" approach to teaching writing. In J. Edge (Ed.), *Action research* (pp. 47–63). Alexandria, VA: TESOL.

Crookes, G. (1989). Grassroots action to improve ESL programs. *University of Hawaii Working Papers in ESL, 8*(2), 45–61.

Crookes, G. (1993). Action research for second language teachers: Going beyond teacher research. *Applied Linguistics, 14*(2), 130–144.

Crookes, G., & Chandler, P. (1999). Introducing action research into post-secondary foreign language teacher education. *Foreign Language Annals, 34*(2), 131–140.

Denzin, N. K., & Lincoln, Y. S. (Eds.). (1998). *Strategies of qualitative enquiry.* Thousand Oaks, CA: Sage.

Dewey, J. (1904). *The relation of theory to practice in education.* Chicago: University of Chicago Press.

Ebbutt, D. (1983). Educational action research: Some general concerns and specific quibbles. In R. Burgess (Ed.), *Issues in educational research* (pp. 152–174). London: Falmer.

Edge, J. (Ed.). (2001). *Action research.* Alexandria, VA: TESOL.

Edge, J., & Richards, K. (Eds.). (1993). *Teachers develop teachers research.* London: Heinemann.

Elliot, J. (1981). *Action research for educational change.* Maidenhead, UK: Open University Press.

Elliott, J. (1985). Educational action research. In J. Nisbet (Ed.), *World Yearbook of Education 1985: Research, Policy and Practice* (pp. 231–250) London: Kogan Page.

Elliott, J. (1991). *Action research for educational change.* Maidenhead, UK: Open University Press.

Ellis, R. (1997). *SLA research and language teaching.* Oxford, UK: Oxford University Press.

Fals Borda, O. (1979). Investigating reality in order to change it: The Columbian experience. *Dialectical Anthropology, 4,* 33–55.

Ferguson, P. (1998). The politics of Adult ESL literacy: Becoming politically visible. In T. Smoke (Ed.), *Adult ESL: Politics, pedagogy and participation in classroom and community programs* (pp. 3–16) Mahwah, NJ.: Lawrence Erlbaum Associates.

Freeman, D. (1996). Redefining the relationships between research and what teachers know. In K. Bailey & D. Nunan (Eds.), *Voices from the language classroom* (pp. 88–122). Cambridge, UK: Cambridge University Press.

Freeman, D. (1998). *Doing teacher research. From inquiry to understanding.* Boston: Heinle & Heinle.

Freeman, D., & Richards, J. (Eds.). (1996). *Teacher learning in language teaching.* Cambridge, UK: Cambridge University Press.

Freire, P. (1970). *Pedagogy of the oppressed.* New York: Herder & Herder.

Freire, P. (1982). Creating alternative research methods: Learning to do it by doing it. In B. Hall, A. Gillette, & R. Tandon (Eds.), *Creating knowledge: A monopoly?* (pp._____). New Delhi, India: Society for Participatory Research in Asia.

Gebhard, J. (1996). *Teaching English as a second or foreign language. A self-development and methodology guide.* Ann Arbor: Michigan University Press.

Gersten, B. F., & Tlusty, N. (1998). Creating contexts for cultural communication: Video exchange projects in the EFL/ESL classroom. *TESOL Journal, 7*(5), 11–16.

Gore, J. M., & Zeichner, K. M. (1991). Action research and reflective teaching in preservice education: A case study from the United States. *Teaching and Teacher Education, 7*(2), 119–136.

Goswami, D., & Stillman, J. (1987). *Reclaiming the classroom: Teacher research as an agency for change.* Upper Montclair, NJ.: Boynton/Cook.

Grotjahn, R. (1987). On the methodological basis of introspective methods. In C. Faerch & G. Kasper (Eds.), *Introspection in second language research.* (pp._____) Clevedon, UK: Multilingual Matters.

Habermas, J. (1972). *Knowledge and human interests; Theory and practice; Communication and the evolution of society.* London: Heinemann.

Hall, B. L. (1979). Knowledge as commodity and participatory research. *Prospects, 9*(4), 393–408.

Halsey, A. H. (Ed.). (1972). *Educational priority: Volume 1: E.P.A. Problems and policies.* London: HMSO.

Hitchcock, G., & Hughes, D. (1995). *Research and the teacher.* (2nd ed.). London: Routledge.

Hodgkinson, H. L. (1957). Action research—a critique. *Journal of Educational Sociology, 31*(4), 137–153.

Jarvis, G. (1981). Action research versus needed research for the 1980s. In D. L. Lange (Ed.), *Proceedings of the National Conference on Professional Priorities* (pp._____). Hastings-on-Hudson, NY: ACTFL Materials Center.

Jarvis, G. (1983). Pedagogical knowledge for the second language teacher. In J. Alatis, H. H. Stern, & P. Strevens (Eds.), *Applied linguistics and the preparation of teachers: Towards a rationale* (pp._____). Washington, DC: Georgetown University Press.

Kemmis, S. (1982). *Action research. A short modern history.* Geelong, Victoria, Australia: Deakin University Press.

Kemmis, S. (1993). Action research. In M. Hammersley (Ed.), *Educational research—current issues* (pp. 235–245). London: P. Chatman.

Kemmis, S., & McTaggart, R. (Eds.). (1986). The *action research planner.* Geelong, Victoria, Australia: Deakin University Press.

Kember, D. (2001). *Reflective teaching and learning in the health professions.* Oxford, UK: Blackwell.

Kincheloe, J. (1991). *Teachers as researchers: Qualitative inquiry as a path to empowerment.* London: Falmer.

Larsen-Freeman, D. (1983). Training teachers or educating a teacher. In J. E. Alatis, H. H. Stern, & P. Strevens (Eds.), *Georgetown University Roundtable on Language and Linguistics.* Washington, DC: Georgetown University Press.

Lazaraton, A. (1995). Qualitative research in applied linguistics: A progress report. *TESOL Quarterly, 29*(3), 455–472.

Lewin, K. (1946). Action research and minority problems. *Journal of Social Issues, 2*, 34–46.

Lewin, K. (1948). *Resolving social conflicts.* New York: Harper & Row.

Lichtenstein, B. M. (1988). Feminist epistemology: A thematic review. *Thesis Eleven, 21*, 140–151.

Long, M. (1983). Training the second language teacher as classroom researcher. In J. E. Alatis, H. H. Stern, & P. Strevens (Eds.), *Applied linguistics and the preparation of teachers: Towards a rationale* (pp. 281–297). Washington, DC: Georgetown University Press.

Long, M., Adams, H., McLean, L., & Castanos, F. (1976). Doing things with words: Verbal interaction in lockstep and small group situations. In J. Fanselow & R. Crymes (Eds.), *On TESOL '76* (pp. 137–153). Washington, DC: TESOL.

Markee, N. (1997). *Managing curricular innovation.* Cambridge, UK: Cambridge University Press.

Marrow, A. (1969). *The practical theorist: The life and work of Kurt Lewin.* New York: Basic Books.

Mathew, R., & Lalitha Eapen, R. (Eds.). (1996). *The language curriculum dynamics of change. Teacher as researcher* (Vol. 2). Report of the International Seminar (August 1995). Hyderabad, India: Central Institute of English and Foreign Languages.

Mathew, R. (2000). Teacher-research approach to curriculum renewal and teacher development. In R. Mathew, R. L. Eapen and J. Tharu (Eds.), *The language curriculum: Dynamics of change. Volume I: The outsider perspective* (pp. 6–21). Hyderabad, India: Orient Longman.

McCarthy, M. (2001). *Issues in applied linguistics.* Cambridge, UK: Cambridge University Press.

McKernan, J. (1996). *Curriculum action research* (2nd ed.). London: Kogan Page.

McNiff, J. (1988). *Action research: Principles and practice.* London: Routledge.

McPherson, P. (1997). Action research: Exploring learner diversity. *Prospect, 12*(1), 50–62.

McTaggart, R. (1991). *Action research. A short modern history.* Geelong, Victoria, Australia: Deakin University Press.

Mickan, P. (Ed.). (1996). *Classroom language investigations.* Adelaide, Australia: National Languages and Literacy Institute of Australia.

Mishler, E. (1990). Validation in inquiry-guided research: The role of exemplars in narrative study. *Harvard Educational Review, 60*(4), 415–442.

Nunan, D. (1985). *Language teaching course design: Trends and issues.* Adelaide, Australia: National Curriculum Resource Centre.

Nunan, D. (1987). *The teacher as curriculum developer.* Adelaide, Australia: National Curriculum Resource Centre.

Nunan, D. (1988). *The learner-centred curriculum.* Cambridge, UK: Cambridge University Press.

Nunan, D. (1989a). *Understanding language classrooms: A guide for teacher-initiated action.* New York: Prentice-Hall.

Nunan, D. (1989b). The teacher as researcher. In C. Brumfit & R. Mitchell (Eds.), *Research in the language classroom.* (ELT Documents 133, pp. 16–32). London: Modern English Publications and The British Council.

Nunan, D. (1990). Action research in the language classroom. In J. C. Richards & D. Nunan (Eds.), *Second language teacher education* (pp. 62–81). Cambridge, UK: Cambridge University Press.

Nunan, D. (1997). Developing standards for teacher-research in TESOL. *TESOL Quarterly, 31*(2), 365–37.

Nunan, D., & Lamb, C. (1996). *The self-directed teacher.* Cambridge, UK: Cambridge University Press.

O'Keefe, J. (2001). The love of my life: A thematic approach to teaching vocabulary. In A. Burns & H. de Silva Joyce (Eds.), *Teachers' voices 7: Teaching vocabulary* (pp. 86–97). Sydney, Australia: National Centre for English Language Teaching and Research.

Pennington, M. (1990). A professional development focus for the language teaching practicum. In J. C. Richards & D. Nunan (Eds.), *Second language teacher education* (pp. 132–152). Cambridge, UK: Cambridge University Press.

Rapoport, R.N. (1970). The three dilemmas in action research. *Human Relations, 23*(6), 499.

Reid, W. A. (1978). *Thinking about curriculum: The nature and treatment of curriculum problems.* London: Routledge & Kegan Paul.

Reason, P. (1998). Three approaches to participative inquiry. In N. K. Denzin & Y. S. Lincoln (Eds.), *Strategies of qualitative enquiry* (pp. 324–339). Thousand Oaks, CA: Sage.

Rogers, C. (1961). *On becoming a person.* London: Constable.

Richards, J. C. (1990). The dilemma of teacher education in second language teaching. In J. C. Richards & D. Nunan (Eds.), Reprinted from *TESOL Quarterly, 21*, 209–226. Second language teacher education (pp. 3–15). Cambridge, UK: Cambridge University Press. (original work Published 1987)

Richards, J. C. (Ed.). (1998). *Teaching in action.* Alexandria, VA: TESOL.

Richards, J. C. (2001). Postscript: The ideology of TESOL. In R. Carter & D. Nunan (Eds.), *The Cambridge guide to teaching English to speakers of other languages* (pp. 213–217). Cambridge, UK: Cambridge University Press.

Richards, J. C., & Nunan, D. (Eds.). (1990). *Second language teacher education.* Cambridge, UK: Cambridge University Press.

Richards, J. C., & Lockhart, C. (1994). *Reflective teaching in second language classrooms.* Cambridge, UK: Cambridge University Press.

Roberts, J. (1998). *Language teacher education.* London Edward: Arnold.

Schön, D. A. (1983). *The reflective practitioner. How professionals think in action.* New York: Basic Books.

Schutz, A. (1967). *The phenomenology of the social world.* Evanston, IL: Northwest University Press.

Schwab, J. (1969). *College curricula and student protest.* Chicago: University of Chicago Press.

Stenhouse, L. (1971). The Humanities Curriculum Project: The rationale. *Theory into Practice, X*(3), 154–162.

Stenhouse, L. (1975). *An introduction to curriculum research and development.* London: Heinemann.

Strickland, D. (1988). The teacher as researcher: Toward the extended professional. *Language Arts, 65*(8), 754–764.

Taba, H., & Noel, E. (1957). *Action research: A case study.* Washington, DC: Association for Supervision and Curriculum Development, National Education Association.

Tinker Sachs, G. (2000). Teacher and researcher autonomy in action research. *Prospect: A Journal of Australian TESOL, 15*(3), 35–51.

Tinker Sachs, G. (Ed.) (2002). *Action research. Fostering and furthering effective practices in the teaching of English.* Hong Kong: City University of Hong Kong.

Tsui, A. (1996). Reticence and anxiety in second language learning. In K. Bailey & D. Nunan (Eds.), *Voices from the language classroom* (pp. 145–167). Cambridge, UK: Cambridge University Press.

Thorne, C., & Qiang, W. (1996). Action research in language teacher education. *ELT Journal, 50*(3), 254–261.

Tudor, I. (1996). *Learner-centredness as language education.* Cambridge, UK: Cambridge University Press.

van Lier, L. (1988). *The classroom and the language learner.* London: Longman.

van Lier, L. (1996). *Interaction in the language curriculum.* London: Longman.

van Lier, L. (1997). Observation from an ecological perspective. *TESOL Quarterly, 31*(4), 783–786.

van Manen, M. (1984). *Action research as theory of the unique: From pedagogic thoughtfulness to pedagogic tactfulness*. Paper presented at the American Educational Research Association Conference, New Orleans, LA.

Wallace, M. (1991). *Training foreign language teachers*. Cambridge, UK: Cambridge University Press.

Wallace, M. (1998). *Action research for language teachers*. Cambridge, UK: Cambridge University Press.

Wallat, C., Green, J., Conlin, S. M., & Haramis, M. (1983). Issues related to action research in the classroom—the teacher and researcher as a team. In J. Green & C. Wallat (Eds.), *Ethnography and language in educational settings* (pp. 89–113). Norwood, NJ: Ablex.

Wells, G., & Chang-Wells, G. L. (1992). *Constructing knowledge together*. Portsmouth, NH.: Heinemann.

Whitehead, J., & Lomax, P. (1987). Action research and the politics of educational knowledge. *British Educational Research Journal, 13*(2), 175–190.

Winter, R (1989). *Learning from experience*. London: Falmer.

Woods, D. (1996). *Teacher cognition in language teaching*. Cambridge, UK: Cambridge University Press.

Zephir, F. (2000). Focus on form and meaning: Perspectives of developing teachers and action-based research. *Foreign Language Annals, 33*(1), 19–30.

III

Applied Linguistics and Second Language Research

Introduction

Applied linguistics emerged as a separate discipline in the 1950s when, as some linguists believe, language teachers wanted to separate themselves from the teachers of literature, who had little to do with language learning and pedagogy. At the time, however, the study of linguistics was devoted to theoretical and formal features and models of language, and applied linguistics arrived on the scene with the goal of applying the findings of linguistics research to language use, development, and practice in the contexts of real-life communication. However, the research and findings of formal linguistics, which are by their very nature theoretical and abstract, cannot be easily applied to the enormous universe of language-related aspects of human functioning. Thus, at the outset, applied linguistics was established as a interdisciplinary study that necessarily draws on the experience, knowledge, and findings in sociology, anthropology, psychology, education, information sciences, and even political theory, in addition to those associated with formal linguistics.

Historically and to this day, a great proportion of applied linguistics research has dealt with and has been closely tied to language teaching and learning. It is important to note here, however, that stating so explicitly can be dangerous and somewhat tactless because there is a large number of applied linguists who believe that applied linguistics is a proper academic discipline of applied language study and that it should not and does not have to be associated with language learning and teaching. Nonetheless, the historical and contemporary reasons for the emergence and proliferation of applied linguistics research cannot be denied.

Over the years, applied linguistics has made an enormous contribution to second language (L2) pedagogy. A hypothesis based on the formal linguistic theories of first language acquisition stipulates that all language acquisition is innate and that the capacity of humans to acquire language is biological in nature. This innate ability is linked to physiological maturation that reaches its peak during puberty and then begins to decline. Researchers who study how second language is acquired set out to explore the applications of generative linguistic theories to the psychological and cognitive processes that permit children and adults to acquire second languages. To date, studies in Second Language Acquisition (SLA) have demonstrated that for adults the learning of a second language is dramatically distinct from the ways in which children learn the first language.

• Chapter 15, by **Teresa Pica**, examines the major findings and directions in second language acquisition (SLA) research. One of its objectives is to outline the aspects of theories that are based on its original applied and linguistic interests and clarify them by addressing questions about language acquisition processes. The findings of SLA research can find many applications to educational theories and shed light on the role of the learner's consciousness in the SLA process. The chapter also provides an overview of the nature of the learner's input needs and requirements with the goal of contributing to instructional decisions and informing the pedagogical practice.

Unlike the research in theoretical linguistics and SLA that are primarily concerned with psychological and behavioral processes in language acquisition, the study of sociolinguistics emphasizes that practically all language use and human communication are social in nature. To this end, the findings of research in sociolinguistics and its subdomains, such as language socialization, pragmatics, or sociocultural theory, have found many direct applications to the L2 teaching and learning.

- Chapter 16, by **Sandra McKay**, provides an overview of some of the major issues in Language and Society and relates these to L2 teaching and learning. Much sociolinguistics research deals with bilingualism and multilingualism, which have a great impact on language change and language use. In addition, the chapter discusses how variation in the use of linguistic forms across geographical locations, social classes, genders, and ethnic groups in English-speaking countries affect the teaching and learning of English.

Sociolinguistics is the study of language as a social and cultural phenomenon, and the research on language socialization and the development of L2 sociopragmatic and pragmatic competence are solidly rooted in its applications of the social and linguistic constructs to L2 teaching and learning.

- Chapter 17, by **Jane Zuengler** and **KimMarie Cole**, examines the processes of language socialization of children and novices to the linguistic forms and, through the use of language, to the values, beliefs, behaviors, and practices of a community. The fundamental principle of language socialization is that language practices are the means through which linguistic and sociocultural knowledge is created and maintained in social activities. The research on language use establishes important links between interactions among speakers and the broader cultural contexts in which this language use is situated.
- Chapter 18, by **Gabriel Kasper** and **Carsten Roever**, looks at pragmatics as a domain of sociolinguistic research that determines how context affects meaning. In research on L2 teaching and learning, pragmatics is defined as the ability to act and interact by means of language. For L2 and foreign language (FL) learners, this is a necessary and frequently daunting learning task because the contextual meaning of an utterance or an expression can be and often is dramatically different from its literal meaning. Kasper and Roever review central issues and findings in L2 developmental pragmatics, discuss the effects of instruction on L2 sociopragmatic and pragmatic competence, and provide an overview of data collection methods.

Other venues in applied linguistics research that have had a great deal of influence on what is known about second language teaching and learning include such areas of study as Sociocultural Theory, Conversational Analysis, Contrastive Rhetoric, and Corpus-based Studies of spoken and written text in English. Chapters 19 through 22 discuss these domains of applied linguistics inquiry and explain how the findings in each can be used and useful in enhancing second language teaching and elucidating learning.

- Chapter 19, by **James Lantolf**, explains the sociocultural theoretic approach to L2 development and its major premise that SLA and L2 learning are by definition a social and cultural enterprise. Sociocultural Theory proposes that humans attain the capacity to voluntarily control or regulate their memory, attention, perception, planning, learning, and development as they appropriate culture and its attendant norms, as well as language. Furthermore, as people learn language, they are brought into culturally specified and organized activities that are in effect the essential features of human functioning.

• Chapter 20, by **Numa Markee**, approaches Conversational Analysis as an area of research in the connections between language, social interaction, and micro-features of conversational discourse. Markee's examination briefly takes a look at the ethnomethodological approach to conversation analysis to highlight the main issues and questions investigated by means of conversation analysts. This overview is followed by an explication of how conversational transcripts that are prepared according to the widely adopted analytical conventions can be used in SLA and classroom research to develop useful microanalyses of second language learning activity.

• Chapter 21, by **Robert Kaplan**, is devoted to the conceptual framework developed in the research on Contrastive Rhetoric. The foundational premise of Contrastive Rhetoric rests on the assumption that naturally occurring spoken and written discourses differ among communities and sociocultural paradigms, even though most Contrastive Rhetoric research has focused on written varieties. Contrastive Rhetoric is also concerned with divergent rhetorical constructs and discourse structuring as they are directly connected to literacy. Contrastive Rhetoric represents the first serious contemporary study of L2 writing and the only early paradigm that gave prominence to cross cultural research.

• Chapter 22, by **Susan Conrad**, discusses corpus linguistics as an approach to research and teaching that relies on the computer-assisted analyses of language as it is used in real life. Central to the corpus-based research is the philosophical tenet that language study is primarily an empirical endeavor, and, thus, descriptions of language and theories about language should be developed on the foundation of real language behavior. Conrad points out that the contributions of corpus linguistics to L2 teaching deal with three descriptions of language that lead to principled pedagogical decisions about what to teach in second language classes, uses of corpus linguistics methods in the classroom for L2, and studies of language produced by learners.

A Caveat Emptor: Applied linguistics research has addressed a vast number of language-related issues, language uses in an immense number of contexts, and language features of practically any variety. In fact, as has been mentioned, although many applied linguists believe that applied linguistics as a discipline dedicated to language analysis has little to do with L2 teaching and learning, equally many (if not more) are convinced that virtually all facets of the L2 business are derived from or benefited by research in applied linguistics, which originally led to the emergence of applied linguistics per se.

The chapters in Part III do not include a range of studies in applied linguistics research because many of these have found direct applications to L2 teaching and learning and have evolved from research in applied linguistics to that in the second language enterprise.

The following areas of applied linguistics research have NOT been covered in Part III. However, the direct applications of research findings are located in other Parts of this book in their related L2 incarnations.

1. Phonetics and pronunciation. See Chapter 27 on L2 speaking and the attendant language skills in Part IV.
2. Psycholinguistics (predominantly concerned with how children learn their first languages). See Chapter 15 in this section, as well as Chapters 23 and 24 on age in L2 development and cognitive considerations in L2 learning in Part IV.

3. Discourse analysis. See Chapter 40 on applications of the findings and methods of discourse analysis to L2 teaching in Part V.
4. Text linguistics. See Chapter 22 on corpus studies in this Part and Chapter 34 in Part IV on applications of text linguistics to L2 research and teaching
5. Ethnography of communication. See Chapter 10 on ethnography in L2 teaching and learning in Part II, as well as Chapter 18 on pragmatics in this section.
6. Language attitudes. See Chapters 49 and 50 on identity in L2 learning and intercultural competence in Part VII.
7. Second language testing and assessment and language policy and planning occupy their own separate sections of the book—see Parts VI and VIII, respectively.

15

Second Language Acquisition Research and Applied Linguistics

Teresa Pica
University of Pennsylvania

The purpose of this chapter is to provide an overview of second language acquisition (SLA) research over the past several decades and to highlight the ways in which it has retained its original applied and linguistic interests, and enhanced them by addressing questions about acquisition processes. As the chapter will illustrate, SLA research has become increasingly bidirectional and multifaceted in its applications. As new theories and research have emerged on language, and even more so, on learning, their application *to* the study of SLA has been fruitful. It has led to long-needed explanations about developmental regularities and persistent difficulties and has opened up new lines of research on the processes and sequences of second language (L2) development.

The application of newer findings *from* the study of SLA to educational concerns has both informed and sustained long standing debates about the role of the learner's consciousness in the SLA process and about the nature of the learner's input needs and requirements. A modest, but increasing, number of SLA research findings have had direct application to instructional decisions. Most other findings have served as a resource to inform teaching practice. These many applications to and from the study of SLA reflect the robustness and vitality of the field.

DISCIPLINARY CONTEXTS

SLA Research and Applied Linguistics

The study SLA is a rich and varied enterprise, carried out by researchers, whose interests and training often lie in broader disciplines of linguistics, psychology, sociology, and education. Yet the field is most commonly associated with the domain of applied linguistics, reflecting a time when this latter field focused on practical problems and concerns in language teaching and attempted to resolve them through the application of linguistic theories. Both fields have expanded over the years. Their internal growth has enriched and elaborated their relationship.

Defining and describing research on SLA within the field of applied linguistics was once a straightforward task. Questions focused on practical concerns in language teaching and were addressed through linguistic principles and psychological theories of learning. At the time of its inception, the field of applied linguistics was guided by theories from linguistic structuralism and behaviorist psychology. Language was characterized as a system that could be classified into sounds and structures. Language acquisition was seen as habit formation, best served as students imitated and practiced these sounds and structures and were given positive reinforcement or corrective feedback as needed.

Very much an applied enterprise, this research followed an approach that came to be called "contrastive analysis" (Lado, 1957). Typically, a comparison would be made between the L2 to be learned and the first language (L1) of the learner. Drill, practice, and correction would follow on those areas of the L2 that differed from those of the L1 so that L1 "interference" could be avoided, and L2 habits could be formed. Unfortunately, this approach seldom worked, as learners did not appear to be developmentally ready to imitate many L2 structures they were given, and as linguists found it impossible to perform contrastive analyses on a feature-by-feature basis. Even after many years of practice, learners would wind up with little understanding of the L2 and limited ability to use it as a means of communication.

Both fields have broadened considerably over the years, as new views of language, the learner, and the learning process have inspired further research. Many of the issues that arose regarding L1 interference, drill, practice, and correction can now be viewed in light of later work in the field. Recent research findings have pointed to L1 contributions as downplayed L1 interference. They have redefined practice as learner-centered, knowledge-based activity, and revitalized the role of corrective feedback by identifying contexts in which it can be effective, possibly even vital, to success. (See respectively, research by Eckman, 1977; studies by DeKeyser, 1997; deGraff, 1997; and theoretical articles by Doughty, 2002; Long, 1996; Schmidt, 1990, 1992, 1995 and later parts of this chapter). This work has enriched the field of applied linguistics, and shed further light on the process of SLA.

SLA Research and Language Acquisition Studies

SLA research can also be placed within the domain of language acquisition studies, together with studies on bilingualism, as it relates to the acquisition of two languages within the course of primary language development. Also found in this domain is work on foreign language acquisition. Often referred to as foreign language learning, it is distinguished by a lack of access to the L2 outside the classroom and by factors surrounding an individual learner's motivation and goals.

The largest body of work in the domain of language acquisition studies focuses on child L1 acquisition (FLA) and developmental psycholinguistics. The studies on FLA that have had a major impact on SLA research are those that were carried out as views advanced by Chomsky (1965) on language, the learner, and the learning process supplanted those framed by theories of structuralism and behaviorism. Their application to the study of SLA influenced its initial research questions and provided it with data collection instruments and analytical categories. This work focused on the extent to which SLA was like FLA in its processes and developmental sequences. A great deal of descriptive data was thereby made available to the field. These data provide basic details on the systematicity, sequences, and processes of SLA, which have inspired future research and informed teaching practice.

The study of SLA is believed to provide a particularly fruitful area for insight into the process of language learning compared to the study of children acquiring their L1. This is because the cognitive, conceptual, and affective processes that characterize L1 development are not required of their older, L2 learning counterparts (see Gass & Ard, 1984). On the other hand, the L2 learner's cultural background, personality, and identity are unique resources that make the process of SLA an ever-present challenge to researchers. Fortunately, each of the fields has found a niche in the research endeavor, so there is little concern about whether the study of SLA or FLA is more central to questions on language acquisition. In the United States, this friendly coexistence seems especially confirmed by academic placement: Much of the academic study and research on FLA takes place in departments of psychology, whereas the study of SLA finds its place in departments of linguistics, applied linguistics, English as a Second Language, and education.

TRADITIONS, TRENDS, CONCERNS, AND CONTROVERSIES

Introduction

Studies of SLA have existed for as long as parents have been keeping diaries of their children's language development (see Leopold, 1939–1949, as an example, and Hatch, 1978 for an overview). However, many SLA researchers would argue that the formal study of SLA was launched in 1967, with Corder's publication, "The Significance of Learners Errors" (Corder, 1967). Its construct of "transitional competence," together with research on "interlanguage" (Selinker, 1972) and data description through "error analysis" (Richards, 1974), laid the groundwork for most of the early studies in the field and has had an impact that is felt to date.

Since that time, moreover, the field of SLA has grown at a remarkable pace, so much so that in the course of a single chapter, it is difficult to cover the enormous number of topics addressed, findings revealed, and factors considered in SLA research. Fortunately, many of these concerns and contributions are handled in other chapters throughout the volume and are detailed in a wide range of textbooks (see, for example, R. Ellis, 1994; Gass & Selinker, 1994; Larsen-Freeman & Long, 1991; Lightbown & Spada, 1999). Therefore, in the interest of observing a bidirectional perspective on the applications to and from SLA research and other fields, the chapter will focus on those areas in which such a perspective is clearly apparent: the "linguistic" and the "learning" dimensions of SLA. The chapter begins with a review of research on the linguistic sequences of interlanguage development.

Research on Interlanguage Development

Much of SLA research has focused on describing the learner's interlanguage and identifying sequences and patterns of development. The focus has been primarily on grammatical development. Because interlanguages are systematic, they follow rules and patterns that change over the course of L2 development, but do so in patterned ways.

When describing interlanguage development, researchers often cluster its patterns into interim grammars, which they refer to as developmental sequences or stages. Thus, learners are likely to omit grammatical morpheme endings in the early stages of learning, but overuse them at a later stage. For example, *We play baseball yesterday. We win.* might develop into *We played baseball yesterday. We winned* before past regular and irregular forms are sorted out. Learners are likely to utter *I don't understand* and *she don't understand* before they work through a negation system that includes *don't*, *doesn't*, and *didn't*. Although initial descriptions of interlanguage suggested that these errors were primarily, if not totally, developmental, there is now a great deal of support for the role of L1 transfer in error formation, as well as for the contributions made by universal strategies of communication and learning. Among the sentences above, for example, the learner's use of *play* in a context for *played*, are suggestive of processes of reduction or simplification, often used to manage emergent grammar or to communicate message content in the absence of morphosyntactic resources. *Played* and *winned* might reflect the learner's regularization of an emergent grammar, again for the purpose of its management or for communicating message meaning.

A great deal of the research on interlanguage development has focused on the learning of English, but there are also large bodies of work on French and German. Most interlanguage patterns are not language specific. Often they are referred to as "errors," but they are not isolated mistakes. Many reflect the learner's attempts at communication and learning or at managing and processing L2 input. Others reflect grammatical complexities or input frequencies that transcend individual L2s.

The most widely studied and reported developmental sequences are the accuracy order identified in English grammatical morphology, the developmental sequences of English verb and phrase negation and the formation of questions and relative clauses. Much of this work has been carried out through methods and perspectives of FLA research. In addition, there is a large database on developmental sequences for German L2. Its focus on the invariant sequence that German L2 learners follow in managing sentence constituent movement has lent considerable insight into the cognitive operations that underlie much of SLA. The sequences of L2 development, which will be described briefly in this section, provide a useful resource for teachers to apply to their attempts to understand their students' struggles, successes, and progress with respect to SLA. (See discussions by Lightbown, 1985, 2000; Pica, 1994a) Attempts to explain the sequences from the perspectives of linguistic and cognitive theories will follow in a later section.

Morpheme Accuracy Order.   Drawing on the work of Brown on morpheme orders in children learning English as their first language, Dulay and Burt (1973, 1974) asked to what extent L2 children reflected this sequence. Children from different L1 backgrounds, who were learning English in a variety of classrooms, were asked to describe pictures that provided contexts for their suppliance of grammatical morphemes such as plural -*s* endings and verb functors. As learners described their pictures, they revealed an "accuracy order," characterized by percentage of morpheme suppliance.

In follow-up studies, this order, which came to be known as an "average" or "natural" order (Krashen, 1977), held across spoken and written samples of children, adolescents, and adults, regardless of L1, whether or not formal instruction had been part of the learning experience. The "average" order was thus:

> progressive -ing
> noun plural -s
> copula
> article
> progressive auxiliary
> past irregular
> past regular
> 3rd person singular
> noun possessive -s

The grouping of morphemes reflects the variability within the order. For example, accuracy for progressive -*ing* was found to be somewhat higher than that for noun plural -s for some learners, whereas other learners were more accurate in their suppliance of copula compared to plural -s. Still, on average, all three morphemes were supplied more accurately than article or progressive auxiliary.

The consistency of the morpheme accuracy order led to the view that SLA was a matter of "creative construction," and therefore much like FLA. SLA was seen as an implicit learning experience, based not on rule knowledge, but rather, on an innate capacity for L2 learning. Controversies ensued over whether such consistency in the order was a function of the statistics used to correlate the data. Explanations were advanced for the kinds of errors revealed in the morpheme data. For many learners, omission of L2 copula could be attributed to the absence of this morpheme in their L1, or its lack of salience and semantic transparency in the L2. As later research would reveal, the errors could be attributed to each of these factors, and for many learners, focused input and intervention were required for their correction. This work has helped to offset the view that SLA is exclusively a creative, implicit process.

Verb and Phrasal Negatives.   Widely studied across many languages, negative structures appear to follow a similar sequence of development, which involves negative particle placement as well as verb tense and number marking. Initially, a negative particle, usually *no* or *not*, is placed next to the item it negates, as in *no like* or *I no like*. This juxtaposition reflects universal strategies of communication and grammar management. Thus, all learners exhibit this stage. Those whose L1 negation is consistent with the stage, for example, L1 Spanish or Italian learners, usually remain there longer than those whose L1 does not encode negation in this way (See Zobl, 1980, 1982). The next stage entails the use of an all-purpose, more target-like negator. In the case of English, this is usually *don't*. Later, the learner restructures *don't* for tense and number, so that *didn't* and *doesn't* appear.

Question Formation.   Learning to form questions involves multiple stages as well. As described in early case studies of children by Huang and Hatch (1978) and Ravem (1968), and in more recent work of Pienemann, Johnston, and Brindley (1988), the stages involve the acquisition of question type (yes/no and *wh* questions) as well as formation (inversion and fronting movements). Stage 1 is characterized by the use of single words and formulaic expressions, such as *a store?, what's that?* Many of these seem perfectly well formed, but they actually reflect learners' attempts to communicate or to manage their still developing grammar. In stage 2, the learner uses declarative word order. In Stage 3, fronting of *wh-* words and *do* begin to appear (*who you are?, do she like the movie?*), and by Stage 4, inversion of *wh* in copular questions (*who are you?*) and of copula and auxiliary in yes–no questions (*are you a student? was she driving the car?*) is seen. Stage 5 is characterized by the appearance of inversion in questions that require do-support to lexical verbs (*do you like movies? who is driving the car?*). Stage 6 is characterized by the appearance of complex or less frequently used question forms such as tags (*she's French, isn't she?*), negative questions (*didn't you like the movie?*), and embedded questions (*do you know what the answer is?*).

Relativization.   The acquisition of relative clause structures relates to both the different sentence positions in which relativization can occur as well as the way in which it is encoded through the use of relative pronouns such as *who, which, that*, in substitution for their referent pronouns. These operations are seen in *The woman helps me with my English. The woman is my neighbor.* Together, they can relativize into *The woman who helps me with my English is my neighbor.* Developmental sequences for relative clause formation follow a hierarchical order in which learners show greater accuracy for subject relativization (seen in the sentence just mentioned), than for direct object relativization (*The man bought a new car. The car has a sunroof. The car that the man bought has a sunroof*). This is followed by indirect object and object of preposition relativization (respectively, The woman *to whom* I gave the money was grateful and The man *from whom* I borrowed the book has moved away). This sequence has been shown to reflect language typology and instructional sensitivity. Both topics will be discussed shortly.

Word Order.   Finally, one of the most detailed and insightful studies of developmental sequences has been carried out on constituent movement and word order in German. Meisel, Clahsen, and Pienemann (1981) studied the untutored, non-instructed acquisition of German L2 by Gasterbeiter or guest workers, who had migrated to Germany from Eastern and Central Europe for short-term employment. They were native speakers predominantly of Romance languages and Turkish. Drawing from both longitudinal case studies and cross-sectional group data, Meisel *et al.* identified 6 stages:

Initially, the learners used individual words, phrases, unanalyzed formulas, and chunks. In stage 2, they moved on to simple sentence strings of sentence elements, usually subject-verb-object structures. In stage 3, they began to manipulate sentence constituents, seen mainly in adverbial movement from sentence final to sentence initial position. (*She could read the book yesterday* became *Yesterday she could read the book*).

Next the learners separated sentence elements. In keeping with standard German word order, they moved nonfinite lexical verbs from sentence internal to sentence final position. (*Yesterday she could read the book* became *Yesterday she could the book read*). The next stage was characterized by inversion, a more complex internal movement, as learners complied with German rules for verb initial placement in questions and adverbial phrases. (*Yesterday she could the book read* became *Yesterday could she the book read?*) In their final stage, the focus was on subordinate clauses, for which learners moved the finite verb to final position *Yesterday she could the book read* became *Although yesterday she the book could read*). Notably absent from the sequences are grammatical morphemes, as these appeared to vary according to a learner's age, contact with native speakers of the L2, and opportunities for L2 use. This invariant sequence of stages, together with the variability of accuracy and appearance of other features, have been referred to as the Multidimensional Model.

R. Ellis (1989) studied instructed learners of German L2 and found the same sequence of development. Pienemann and Johnston (1986) applied the sequence to English and cited the following stages: In stage 1, learners use single words and formulas. In stage 2, they use canonical word order. Stage 3 is characterized by fronting of "do" for questions and appearance of negative particles in verb constructions. In stage 4, inversion appears in yes–no questions. In stage 5, third person singular and do-support appear, motivated by the need for noun–verb agreement. Pienemann and Johnston have claimed that this is a sentence internal movement as it reflects the learner's management of both subject and verb structures. Complex structures such as question tags are seen in stage 6.

The Multidimensional Model has also been the focus of Pienemann's Teachability Hypothesis (Pienemann, 1989). He was able to show that learners could accelerate their rate of L2 learning if presented with rules for constituent movement that corresponded with their next stage of development. If taught the rules of stages beyond their current level, the learners would not be able to internalize what they were taught. This finding has tremendous implications and applications to teaching decisions. Yet, as Cook (2001) has noted, even the most widely used, up-to-date textbooks, fail to follow the sequences that Pienemann has identified.

In more recent research, the Multidimensional Model has come to be known as the Processability Model. This model is so named because it provides an explanation for stage progression and teachability predictions based on cognitive processing constraints. These are related to the complexity of production required for each movement across the stages. In developing the Processibility Model, Pienemann has drawn from Slobin's work on "operating principles" (Slobin, 1973, 1985), and from research on child FLA and bilingualism by Clahsen (1984). Recently, Pienemann has linked these processing strategies with Lexicalist-Functional grammar in a study of Swedish L2 developmental sequences (Pienemann & Haakenson, 1999). Pienemann's newer perspective on SLA is much more cognitive in its undergirding than his Multidimensional Model. Other cognitively oriented research on SLA will be addressed later in this chapter.

Research on Second Language Acquisition Processes: Overview

This introductory section will review current theories in linguistics and psychology that have been applied to questions on the SLA process. Later sections will highlight their application to data on the sequences of interlanguage development, discuss some of the new questions and studies that the theories have motivated, and attempt to sort out the controversies that have been created by their presence in the field.

As an applied enterprise, SLA research has looked to linguistics and psychology to guide its questions, shape its hypotheses, and explain its findings. As often noted and lamented, SLA has not been grounded in its own comprehensive theory that can account for its sequences and processes, predict its outcomes, single out its most influential factors (see Long, 1990, for a compelling discussion of this issue). As was discussed in the introduction to this chapter, early research on SLA was guided by theories from structural linguistics and behaviorist psychology. As generative theories of language and psycholinguistic theories of learning came to the forefront of linguistics and psychology, their research methods made it possible for SLA researchers to collect a great deal of the interlanguage data described in the previous section.

More recently, newer theoretical perspectives on language and learning have been applied to the study of SLA. From linguistics, theories on universal properties and principles of language have shed light on the regularities and constraints that characterize interlanguage grammars and have led to more principled research on the role of the L1 in the learning process. The nativist perspective on language acquisition that undergirds much of this research has served to invigorate the long-standing debate in the field as to the role of explicit rule learning in the SLA process and the need for explicit rule teaching in the classroom.

From psychology, cognitive theories have had a highly productive impact on SLA research and its applications. Cognitively informed studies have revealed the ways in which learners process L2 input and use it to build and restructure their interlanguage grammar. New findings on cognitive processes of attention, awareness, and practice have been used to explain the results of older studies. In addition, the interactions shown to promote these processes have revealed connections and applications to classroom practice.

Research on Linguistic Processes in Second Language Acquisition

The Role of Language Universals in SLA. The notion of a "universal" is not new to the field of linguistics but has provided both explanations of SLA sequences and predictions of SLA outcomes. Language universals reflect consistencies in the typological or surface properties of world languages. Surface features that are commonly found across languages, are perceptually salient in a language, and are transparent in their encoding of meaning or function are considered "unmarked." Those that are rare, difficult to perceive and to relate to meaning or function are considered "marked."

For example, voiceless alveolar stops such as (t) are considered "unmarked" as they are found among most languages, whereas interdental (th) is less commonly found and is therefore considered "marked."

The underlying assumption of language universals theory is that features that are less marked in a language are learned earlier than those that are marked. Thus, English L2 learners would be expected to acquire the unmarked (t) before the less common (th), and the -s that conveys plural meaning before the -s required for the more opaque third person singular.

Language universals also enter into implicational relationships. Thus, the presence of voiced alveolar stops such as (d) in a language implies the presence of voiceless alveolar stops, for example, (t). The voicing on (d) makes it more complex and marked than (t). Because more languages have unmarked than marked features, the presence of a marked feature implies the presence of its unmarked counterpart.

The typological universal that has had the strongest role in explaining SLA sequences of development is the Noun Phrase Accessibility Hierarchy (NPAH), in which relative clauses formation follows an order that is consistent with principles of markedness. Thus, across languages of the world, subject noun phrases are more accessible to relativization than are direct object noun phrases, which are more accessible than indirect object, object of preposition, and comparative noun phrases. These are implicationally ordered, so that if a language allows relativization of indirect objects, it also allows relativization of direct objects.

English allows relativization of all noun phrases on the NPAH. Other languages such as Chinese, allow relativization of fewer phrases, but they still observe the ordering implications. This relationship across languages of the world also holds within interlanguages of learners and can account for the order of acquisition of relative clause formation described in the previous section. As was shown, English L2 learners acquire the ability to form subject relatives before direct and indirect object relatives.

In addition to the explanatory role that the study of language universals has played in SLA research, it also has revealed predictive power. Several studies have shown that targeted instruction in relative clause formation at lower levels on the hierarchy, such as object of preposition, can generalize to acquisition at higher levels such as direct object (See Doughty, 1991; Eckman, Bell, & Nelson, 1988; Gass, 1982) This finding has not found its way into language curricula, despite its clear application to teaching practice.

The impact of the study of language universals on SLA research has also been seen in question formation. Again, Eckman (Eckman, Moravcsik, & Wirth, 1989) identified two typological universals that Wh-inversion (*who are you?*) implies Wh-fronting (*who you are?*) and that yes/no inversion (*do you like movies?*) implies *Wh* inversion. This implicational order revealed in typological studies is reflected in the developmental data on question formation at stages 3, 4, and 5, that was also described in the previous section.

The explanations and predictions offered through the perspective of language universals and the notion of markedness have given SLA researchers a fresh look at the role of transfer in SLA. As Eckman (1977) and Hyltenstam (1987) have shown, an L2 feature will be difficult if it is more marked linguistically in an absolute sense and even more so if it is more marked than its L1 counterpart. Thus, indirect object relativization or voiced stops would be more difficult to learn than subject relatives or voiceless stops, but would be even more difficult for those learners whose L1 was more limited in its scope of relativization or had only voiceless consonants. On the other hand, if the L2 feature were marked in the learner's L1, or even absent from it, its acquisition would not pose as much of a problem as long as the feature were unmarked in the L2. Thus, English learners of Chinese are able to suppress their L1 relative clause formation for objects of prepositions. English learners of German are able to suppress L1 voicing of final consonants in favor of unmarked, voiceless ones in German L2.

Principles of the construct of markedness, applied to interlanguage data development, can also explain why certain linguistic features are more difficult to notice than others, are less available in conversational input, and might qualify for focused instruction. These possibilities will be further explored in the discussion of cognitive processes.

The Role of Linguistic Universals in SLA.   Linguistic Universals reflect constraints on the form of human languages. The linguistic universals that have had the most impact on SLA research are the innate principles of Universal Grammar (UG) that are viewed as a genetic endowment or property of mind, and a binary system of options, known as parameters, each with marked and unmarked settings that configure into a "core" grammar. The construct of markedness, which is central to the work on universals of language typology, described in the preceding section, also plays a role in the study of linguistic universals. However, whereas language universals had to do with surface feature frequency across languages, linguistic universals have to do with underlying rules.

Everyone who has fully acquired an L1 has constructed a core grammar and has set the parameters of the core grammar in accordance with the L1. For example, individuals whose L1 is a "pro-drop" language must set this parameter into its simpler, unmarked setting. Thus, they might say *I have three cats ... are nice* because they have set the pro-drop parameter so that pronoun referents are not needed in subject position. Those individuals whose L1 is a non-pro-drop language need to set their parameter in a marked setting so that a subject pronoun is always needed, as in *I have three cats ... They are nice*. The marked parameter setting might be observed even in sentences where the subject pronoun held no meaning, as in *It is snowing* or *There are 24 hours in a day*. It is claimed that children begin learning their L1 as though the pro-drop and other parameters were in unmarked settings. Once confronted with marked input, they switch the parameters to marked settings.

There are three theoretical views on linguistic universals that have been addressed in studies of SLA. Many of these studies have focused on the principle of "subjacency," which has to do with *wh-* movement within sentences. Some languages allow more movement than others, and some do not observe the principle at all. Thus, studies of L2 learners whose L1 follows subjacency rules that are different from the L2 provide a good basis for determining the role of UG in SLA.

The strongest view is that SLA is like FLA, and learners have access to the principles and unmarked parameters of UG in much the same way that they did during FLA. They therefore begin interlanguage development through unmarked parameter settings, not through their parameterized core grammar. There is evidence in support of this view in research by Bley-Vroman, Felix, and Ioup (1988), who found that Korean L1 learners of English were able to recognize English sentences that followed the principle of subjacency for *wh-*movement, even though this principle is not observed in Korean. This finding illustrated that L2 learners are sensitive to universal principles, even when those principles have not been realized in their L1.

Another view is that L2 learners fall back on the parameterized core grammar of their L1 but are able to reset it for the L2, even when confronted with marked data that conflicts with their L1. Support for this position comes from White (1985). She found that Spanish L1 learners of English L2 relied initially on their L1 setting for pro-drop when making grammaticality judgments of English sentences, whereas French L1 learners of English did not appear to do so. In Spanish, the pro-drop parameter has an unmarked setting, but in English and French the setting is marked. Over time, however, the Spanish learners' grammaticality judgments were as accurate as those of the French learners. This result suggested that they were able to reset their L1 parameter for the marked English L2 setting.

Yet another view is that L2 learners are not able to draw on UG principles to reset the parameters of their core grammar, but instead rely on cognitive principles of learning and apply them to their L2 development. SLA is thus experienced as a conscious, problem-solving activity. Such a view accounts for the errors produced by L2 learners as they attempt to manage and control interlanguage grammar.

One of the most compelling reasons for application of linguistic universals to questions about SLA is that the principles and parameters represent constituents and operations that transcend individual languages. This offers excellent opportunities to further explore the role of transfer in L2 learning, to see how it affects aspects of grammar that are considered to be outside the UG core. Findings from such research can shed further light on current assumptions as to which principles and parameters are actually universal and which are subject to L1 constraints. Even more important is the fact that perspectives on linguistic universals provide SLA with both a theory of language and a theory of language learning.

However compelling they appear, though, theoretical views on linguistic universals pose several difficulties with respect to their application to SLA research. One difficulty is methodological. Most of the research involved with linguistic universals has asked learners to judge the grammaticality of sentences that reflect the linguistic principle or parameter under study. Usually they are asked to read or listen to sentences and give a *yes* or *no* judgment. Such an approach is in keeping with assumptions used throughout theoretical linguistics on the validity of native speaker intuition as a reflection of language competence. However, results of studies that use grammaticality judgment data are difficult to compare with those based on descriptive, interlanguage samples.

A second difficulty with linguistic universals lies in their perceived relevance to the study of SLA. Most consumers of SLA research are used to discussing it with reference to transcribed samples of interlanguage speech or frequency tables of interlanguage features. When they read about research findings on interlanguage, they expect reference to functional and inflectional features such as articles or tense markers. Yet, these are the very features considered peripheral to the core grammar. Further, when core grammar parameters are addressed, this is done through terms such as "subjacency" rather than through familiar terminology on *wh*-questions. This further limits comparison with data from other research.

A further difficulty with the application of perspectives on linguistic universals to SLA research relates to explanation of findings. Learner forms attributed to unmarked parameter settings can often be explained with reference to universal processes of simplification that have long held a place in interlanguage analysis. Thus, the question remains as to whether the learners who say *is raining* are doing so because they are observing the unmarked setting of the pro-drop parameter, have chosen to omit the semantically empty *it* as an agent in their message, or have not yet perceived it in the L2 input around them.

Many questions remain regarding linguistic universals as a driving force behind SLA questions and as an explanation of SLA data. Some of these pertain to competing findings within this perspective on SLA; others are related to terminological inconsistencies with studies across the field. Over time, and with persistence, these matters can open up opportunities for further study and new lines of research, which will lead to greater understanding of the SLA process.

Research on Cognitive Processes in Second Language Acquisition

The Role of Cognitive Processes in SLA.   Cognitive theories are concerned with mental processes used for skill building and skill learning. Thus, when SLA research is carried out within a cognitive perspective, the L2 is viewed as a skill, and its acquisition as a linguistic system is assumed to be built up gradually through processes of attention, conscious awareness, and practice.

To some researchers, a view of SLA that includes cognitive processes such as attention, awareness, and practice is inconsistent with theoretical assumptions of interlanguage research and with universal perspectives on language acquisition. This is because most researchers have viewed SLA as an implicit experience, guided by the learner's interaction with L2 input. To them, the cognitive process of attention is important, but mainly because it promotes understanding of meaning not because it facilitates skill learning. They associate cognitive constructs such as conscious awareness and practice with behaviorist theories of learning, dismissed from the field several decades ago.

Yet most SLA researchers who apply cognitive theories to inform their questions and methods do so under the assumption that SLA is indeed a largely implicit process. For them, cognitive theories are not alternate views on SLA. Instead, they are applied to research in order to better understand and to possibly explain why it is that, for many learners, an implicit experience of transacting L2 message meaning is not sufficient for achieving L2 grammatical competence.

Many L2 learners, for example, struggle with linguistic features that are difficult to notice in the messages they hear. These are often outside the scope of UG principles and parameters, and therefore can be affected by any number of internal and external factors, or never acquired at all. Other learners report that they can understand the meaning of a message without the need to focus on the many forms that encode it. Even young learners have been shown to have strong L2 comprehension, but lack grammatical proficiency. Some learners have internalized versions of the L2 that are functionally adequate for communicative purposes, but developmentally incomplete in form and structure. The consequences of this are nonstandard, stable, immutable, "fossilized" interlanguage varieties. These varieties were introduced to the field by Selinker in 1974, and have continued to challenge researchers, teachers, and, of course, fossilized L2 learners, to date. Fossilized learners of English, for example, might continue to position a negative particle next to the item it negates, as in *no like* or *I no like*, or *he don't like*, which reflects a developmental stage of negation learning, as well as a strategy of communication and grammar management.

Many of these concerns about SLA have been expressed as research questions about the quality and accessibility of L2 input that can best serve learners as data for their learning. Therefore, the remaining discussion of cognitive processes will focus primarily on research about their role in assisting learners to notice L2 input and apply it to their learning.

Comprehension, Input and Interaction.   That samples of L2 are needed by learners as a source of input for their learning has long been a basic assumption of SLA research. Corder (1967) distinguished between the input that is available to L2 learners and that which individual learners can actually use as intake for building interlanguage grammar, given their stage of development. Decades ago, Krashen argued that "comprehensible input" was necessary and sufficient for successful SLA (see, for example, Krashen, 1977). He described such input as understandable in its meaning, but slightly beyond the learner's current level of development with respect to its linguistic form. Both "intake" and "comprehensible input" were conceptually intriguing, but they did not lend themselves to testable hypotheses about SLA processes.

Long (1981, 1985) also argued that comprehensible input was crucial to SLA, but his research revealed that it was the learners' interaction with interlocutors that mattered as much as the input directed to them. Thus, when input was no longer comprehensible during interaction between L2 learners and interlocutors, they would modify the flow of the interaction and repeat, rephrase, or request help with the input until comprehension was achieved. It was claimed that the modified input directed toward the learners could assist their comprehension as well as their L2 learning.

Follow-up studies of such interaction, which Long referred to as the "negotiation of meaning," were carried out by Long and others (for example, Gass & Varonis, 1994; Mackey, 1999; Pica, Holliday, Lewis, & Morgenthaler, 1989; Pica, Holliday, Lewis, Berducci, & Newman, 1991). Their analyses revealed that as learners and interlocutors attempted to achieve comprehensibility, they repeated and rephrased initial messages, and extracted and highlighted words and phrases in patterned ways that often had developmental consequences. Pica *et al.* (1989, 1991) showed that the extent to which learners worked at these manipulations was directly related to the open endedness of the questions they were asked. Gass and Varonis (1994) showed that interlanguage items negotiated in an initial conversation would be accurately encoded in the learner's later production. Mackey (1999) revealed that learners' active participation in negotiation was closely connected to their development of L2 English question forms.

An analysis by Pica (1994b) showed that these extractions often revealed L2 grammatical relationships as they encoded message meaning. For example, in response to the learner's initial utterance that encoded a noun phrase in subject position (*the students watch the movie*), a listener might extract the noun phrase, topicalize and repeat it in object position (*the students? what did you say about the students?*). Such modifications appeared to give learners repeated access to L2 form as it encoded message meaning. This was the very kind of L2 input that could be used as intake for grammar building, restructuring, and internalization.

Because SLA was considered to be a subconscious, implicit process in terms of the learner's mental involvement, there did not seem to be a push to explore the cognitive side of the input–intake–internalization progression. SLA models based on information processing theory and cognitive processes (see, for example McLaughlin, 1978) were rejected by Krashen for their emphasis on the role of consciousness, which Krashen considered unnecessary for SLA, and possibly detrimental to the learner's progress.

Consciousness and Attention. Increasingly, researchers have come to observe that L2 learning is a much more conscious experience than was heretofore believed. Drawing on his own experience as a Portuguese L2 learner in and out of classrooms in Brazil, Schmidt and Frota (1986) found that cognitive processes such as attention and noticing were crucial to his L2 learning. The frequency with which he heard complex features of Portuguese and the salience of their form or position in input were two factors that helped Schmidt to notice them. Schmidt also found that in order to incorporate many features of Portuguese into his developing L2 grammar, he needed to "notice the gap" between such features as they were used by other speakers, and his own interlanguage production of these features. Here, too, his noticing was aided by the frequency and saliency of a feature, the communicative and cognitive demands of the situation in which he found himself, and his readiness to "notice the gap."

Schmidt's observations, along with findings on communicative, content-based classroom contexts considered rich in L2 input (Pica, 2002; Swain, 1985), have revealed that comprehensible input, however modified, might not be efficient, or even sufficient, for SLA. Thus, new questions have emerged about the kinds of input learners need to achieve a successful L2 outcome. Long addressed these questions in several publications, including Long (1996) and Long, Inagaki, & Ortega (1998). Drawing from not only Schmidt's arguments and findings, but also from FLA theory and research, and from studies of L2 form-focused instruction (such as those of Spada & Lightbown, 1993; White, 1991; White, Spada, Lightbown, & Ranta, 1991) and experimental intervention (Oliver, 1995), Long distinguished between input that provides positive evidence of relationships of L2 form, function, and meaning, and input that supplies negative evidence on forms and structures that are used by learners, but are not consistent with the L2 they are learning.

According to Long, sources of positive evidence include spoken and written texts that are in their authentic state, as well as those that have been modified for comprehensibility in ways previously described. Learners can access negative evidence through explicit corrective feedback or implicit feedback. Included among this latter are requests for learners to clarify or repeat utterances that can't be understood (for example, *Could you say that again?* or *Huh?*) and "recasts," which essentially repeat what a learner has just said (*I need pencil*) in a more accurate way (*You need a pencil*). The most effective recasts appear to be those that focus on only one grammatical feature over the course of a conversation or lesson (Doughty & Varela, 1998). When teachers recast a range of student misproductions, the students fail to distinguish them from other follow-up moves that teachers use to conduct their lessons. (Lyster, 1998).

Among the cognitively oriented interventions that appear to heighten the learner's access to L2 input for both positive and negative evidence are instruction on how best to process input for form and meaning (Van Patten & Oikkenon, 1996; Van Patten & Sanz, 1995), the learner's interaction with meaningful materials, enhanced both graphically and linguistically to highlight form and meaning relationships (Doughty, 1991), problem solving, information exchange and other goal-oriented, task-based activities (Pica et al., 2001; Pica, Kanagy, & Falodun, 1993), and activities that foster learners' communication about grammar (Fotos 1994; Fotos & Ellis, 1991; Loschsky & Bley-Vroman, 1993; Pica et al., 2001).

In addition to the positive and negative evidence that comes from modified input, feedback, and formal instruction, Swain has argued that learners' own production can provide a basis for learning of L2 relationships of form and meaning (Swain, 1985, 1995, 1998). Based on extensive observational data of learner exchanges, she has found that when asked to modify their message production toward greater comprehensibility or precision, they move from their rudimentary interlanguage grammar, in which relationships among sentence elements are often characterized by simple juxtaposition of relevant words (*Philadelphia live*) to more advanced, syntactic processing and message organization (*I live in Philadelphia*). Often their conversation engages them in discussion of the linguistic dimensions of their interaction, a process Swain refers to as "metatalk." Swain claims that learners' production also helps them to "notice the gap" between their output and input. Swain has placed her work within a collaborative, sociocultural perspective, whereas other output-focused researchers have found results consistent with hers and have been able to explain them in terms of cognitive processes (see, for example, deBot, 1996). Thus, there is strong support for the role of production in SLA, across social and cognitive perspectives.

L2 Knowledge.   Theoretical claims that L2 learning is a much more conscious process than was heretofore believed and an experience that can benefit from both input and feedback, have reactivated the long-standing debate in the field regarding L2 learning and its relation to L2 knowledge. This debate, once known almost exclusively as Krashen's "acquisition" vs. "learning" distinction (see again, Krashen, 1977, 1981, as well as Krashen's recent writings, for example, Krashen, 1994), centers on three positions regarding the interface of implicit and explicit L2 learning and resultant L2 knowledge.

The first position is a noninterface position, that is, that SLA is an altogether implicit activity. Although explicit L2 learning and explicit L2 knowledge are possible, they remain separate from the L2 competence that learners come to acquire. This position is consistent with nativist perspectives drawn from theories on linguistic universals (for example, Schwartz, 1993) and with Krashen's Monitor Theory (Krashen 1977, 1981), which have been used to account for the regularities of L2 development.

However, it does not account for the incomplete acquisition experienced by fossilized learners.

A very different position is the strong interface position, supported through studies by DeKeyser (1997), N. Ellis (1993, 1994), and Robinson (1997). This position, motivated by information processing theory (see McLaughlin 1978, 1996; O'Malley, Chamot, & Walker, 1987), holds that explicit L2 knowledge, attained through explicit learning, can become implicit L2 knowledge. This is generally achieved through practice in which learners deliberately focus their attention on L2 form as it encodes message meaning and work toward understanding and internalization. Many studies have shown support for this view. Carefully controlled in design, they tend to focus on very specific features and highly experimental conditions. Additional support has come from the meta-analysis and comparison or experimental and quasi-experimental studies on the effect of L2 instruction (Norris & Ortega 2001) on L2 learning. Together, individual studies and the meta-analysis of different kinds of studies indicate that the strong interface position is indeed a valid one, but might apply to context-specific dimensions of SLA.

Finally, there is a position known as the "weak" interface position, although it is much more robust than the other two positions in its number of supporters and supportive studies. Here, SLA is viewed as a predominantly implicit activity. However, it is believed that L2 knowledge can be built up through both explicit instruction and other interventions that enable learners to notice crucial relationships of L2 form and meaning that are difficult, if not impossible, for them to learn without such intervention. This is a view held by not only those who carry out research strictly within the cognitive perspective, but also among researchers associated with strategies of consciousness raising (Rutherford & Sharwood Smith, 1985) and those who work within a perspective that has come to be known as "focus on form." This work was initiated by Long (1991), and has been sustained by studies gathered in a volume edited by Doughty and Williams (1998; see, for example, chapters by DeKeyser, Harley; Lightbown; Long & Robinson; Swain; Doughty & Varela; and Williams & Evans).

The evidence in support of this "weak" position illustrates ways in which all three positions are correct, as each is conditioned by factors that are learner-related, stage-specific, language-related factors. Many of these factors need further exploration. Others have yet to be identified. Together with other needs across the field, they augur well for a solid future for SLA research. The chapter will therefore close with a brief look toward that future.

CONCLUSIONS AND FUTURE DIRECTIONS

This chapter has aimed to highlight the ways in which SLA research, across the past 3 decades, has retained its original applied and linguistic interests and enhanced them through greater attention to questions on acquisition processes. New research, carried out from the perspectives of linguistic and language universals and cognitive activities, has shed much light on the complexities of L2 development and the input and interactional needs of L2 learners. Application of findings from this research has rekindled old debates on the role of consciousness in L2 learning and uncovered new and necessary ways to study corrective feedback and L2 practice, beyond a behaviorist point of view.

Many questions remain unanswered. Others are in need of more complete answers. The three positions on the role of UG remain unresolved. Is each correct, according to the linguistic feature studied? Is one more relevant to UG; the others, more reflective of peripheral grammars? Continued research along these lines can contribute to a theory of L2 learning and inform theoretical linguistics as well. The study of the learner's L1 in relation to markedness and language universals has shown much promise. The classroom relevance of this research is already apparent, and that, in itself, should motivate additional studies.

Researchers need to continue to identify form-meaning relationships that defy the learner's grasp and yet are outside of UG and, therefore, not learnable from unmodified input or positive evidence alone. The construct of markedness can play a role in their identification. Those forms whose encodings of meaning are not salient, are infrequent or highly complex, or are embedded in specialized registers such as academic or professional discourse, are likely to require focused practice and repeated positive evidence, or various kinds of negative evidence to stimulate their learning. Future studies will need not only to identify the forms whose meaningful encodings are difficult to acquire, but also to design activities that help learners to notice them through focused input and negative evidence.

Researchers must also develop ways to operationalize and study processes of restructuring and internalization that occur after learners have noticed input and processed it as intake. The interventions designed to stimulate these processes will not only provide data on the input–intake–restructuring–internalization progression, but will serve as a basis for materials and activities that can be applied to classroom needs.

As new findings emerge on the role of consciousness and attention in the learning process, their relevance to the classroom is evident. However, there is an urgent need to operationally define these processes, lest they be misapplied to classroom practice in behaviorist rather than cognitive terms.

A consistent theme throughout SLA research has been the need for longitudinal data. The handful of longitudinal studies that have been carried out have made an impressive impact on the field. The most recent that of Schmidt and Frota (1986). The kind of longitudinal research needed at present must take the form of follow-up studies that check retention of features learned through instructional intervention and practice. Although it is clear that feedback and focused input can make a difference in the short term, their trusted application to classroom practice will require confidence in their long-term impact.

The relevance of classroom practice in informing SLA research and in being informed by its results will find SLA researchers and SLA practitioners working together to design studies and interpret their findings. This has already become apparent among classroom studies. Lingering linguistic questions, as previously described, suggest a need for teamwork with linguists as well. Opportunities for such research teams to collaborate, sharing and exchanging roles and responsibilities, as well as to work together in complementary roles, will bring greater efficiency as well as theoretical and pedagogical relevance to SLA research.

The field has increased in size and scope, yet it is still sufficiently focused on questions of learning and teaching for many voices and perspectives to be acknowledged. The fact that corrective feedback and focused practice are now viewed as cognitive processes and are at the forefront of research interest, suggests that the field is still open for a fresh look at processes once discarded or nearly forgotten, as long as the evidence to support them is abundant and convincing. That is how learner errors came to be seen as learning processes rather than as bad habits, and how communication and comprehension came to be acknowledged as insufficient for L2 competence. Lingering questions and concerns at present will continue to lead the way to future studies. New and currently unforseen directions will be taken. The richness and complexity of SLA as an learning process and a field of study suggest that there are many perspectives to apply and many more applications to be found.

REFERENCES

Bley-Vroman, R., Felix, S., & Ioup, G. (1988). The accessibility of Universal Grammar in adult language learning. *Second Language Research, 4*, 1–32.

Chomsky, N. (1965). *Aspects of the theory of syntax*. Cambridge, MA: MIT Press.

Clahsen, H. (1984). The comparative study of first and second language development. *Studies in Second Language Acquisition, 12*, 135–154.

Cook, V. (2001). *Second language learning and language teaching*. London: Arnold.

Corder, S. P. (1967). The significance of learners' errors. *International Review of Applied Linguistics, 5*, 161–169.

de Bot, K. (1996). Review article: The psycholinguistics of the output hypothesis. *Language Learning, 46*, 529–555.

deGraff, R. (1997). The eXperanto experiment: Effects of explicit instruction on second language acquisition. *Studies in Second Language Acquisition, 19*, 249–276

DeKeyser, R. (1997). Beyond explicit rule learning: Automatizing second language morphosyntax. *Studies in Second Language Acquisition, 19*, 1–39.

DeKeyser, R. (1998). Beyond focus on form: Cognitive perspectives on learning and practicing second language grammar. In C. Doughty & J. Williams (Eds.), *Focus on form in classroom second language acquisition* (pp. 42–63). New York: Cambridge University Press.

Doughty, C. (1991). Instruction does make a difference: The effect of instruction on the acquisition of relativization in English as a second language. *Studies in Second Language Acquisition, 13*, 431–469.

Doughty, C. (2002). Cognitive underpinnings of focus on form. In P. Robinson (Ed.), *Cognition and second language learning* (pp. 206–257). Cambridge, UK: Cambridge University Press.

Doughty, C., & Varela, E. (1998). Communicative focus on form. In C. Doughty & J. Williams (Eds.), *Focus on form in second language classroom* (pp. 114–138). New York: Cambridge University Press.

Doughty, C., & Williams, J. (Eds.). (1998). *Focus on form in second language classroom*. New York: Cambridge University Press.

Dulay, H., & Burt, M. (1973). Should we teach children syntax? *Language Learning, 23*, 245–258.

Dulay, H., & Burt, M. (1974). Natural sequences in second language acquisition. *Language Learning, 24*, 37–58.

Eckman, F. (1977). Markedness and the contrastive analysis hypothesis. *Language Learning, 27*, 315–330.

Eckman, F., Bell, L., & Nelson, D. (1988). On the generalizability of relative clause instruction in the acquisition of English as a second language. *Applied Linguistics, 9*, 1–20.

Eckman, F., Moravcsik, E. A., & Wirth, J. R. (1989). Implicational universals and interrogative structures in the interlanguage of ESL learners. *Language Learning, 39*, 138–155.

Ellis, N. (1993). Rules and instances in foreign language learning: Interactions of implicit and explicit knowledge. *European Journal of Cognitive Psychology, 5*, 289–319.

Ellis, N. (1994). Vocabulary acquisition: The implicit ins and outs of explicit cognitive mediation. In N. Ellis (Ed.), *Implicit and explicit learning of languages* (pp. 211–282). London: Academic Press.

Ellis, R. (1989). Are classroom and naturalistic acquisition the same?: A study of the classroom acquisition of German word order rules. *Studies in Second Language Acquisition, 11*, 305–328.

Ellis, R. (1994). *The study of second language acquisition*. London: Oxford University Press.

Felix, S. (1985). More evidence on competing cognitive systems. *Second Language Research 1*, 47–72.

Fotos, S. (1994). Integrating grammar instruction and communicative language use through grammar consciousness-raising tasks. *TESOL Quarterly, 28*, 323–351.

Fotos, S., & Ellis, R. (1991). Communicating about grammar: A task-based approach. *TESOL Quarterly, 25*, 605–628.

Gass, S. (1982). From theory to practice. In M. Hines & W. Rutherford (Eds.), *On TESOL '81* (pp. 120–139). Washington, DC: TESOL.

Gass, S., & Ard, J. (1984). Second language theory and the ontology of language universals. In W. Rutherford (Ed.), *Language universals and second language acquisition* (pp. 33–68). Amsterdam: Benjamins.

Gass, S., & Selinker, L. (1994). *Second language acquisition: An introductory course*. Mahwah, NJ: Lawrence Erlbaum Associates.

Gass, S., & Varonis, E. (1994). Input, interaction and second language production. *Studies in Second Language Acquisition, 16*, 283–301.

Harley, B. (1998). The role of focus-on-form tasks in promoting child L2 acquisition. In C. Doughty & J. Williams (Eds.), *Focus on form in second language classroom* (pp. 156–174). New York: Cambridge University Press.

Hatch, E. (Ed.). (1978). *Second language acquisition: A book of readings*. Rowley, MA: Newbury House.

Huang, J., & Hatch, E. (1978). A Chinese child's acquisition of English. In E. Hatch (Ed.), *Second language acquisition: A book of readings* (pp. 118–131). Rowley, MA: Newbury House.

Hyltenstam, K. (1987). Markedness, language universals, language typology and second language acquisition. In C. Pfaff (Ed.), *First and second language acquisition processes* (pp. 55–78). Cambridge, MA: Newbury House.

Krashen, S. (1977). Some issues relating to the monitor model. In H. D. Brown, C. Yorio, & R. Crymes (Eds.), *On TESOL '77: Teaching and learning English as a second language: Trends in research and practice* (pp. 144–158). Washington, DC: TESOL.

Krashen, S. (1981). *Second language acquisition and second language learning.* Oxford, UK: Pergamon.

Krashen, S. (1994). The Input Hypothesis and its rivals. In N. Ellis (Ed.), *Implicit and explicit learning of languages* (pp. 45–77). London: Academic Press.

Lado, R. (1957). *Linguistics across cultures: Applied linguistics for language teachers.* Ann Arbor: The University of Michigan Press.

Larsen-Freeman, D., & Long, M. (1991). *Second language research.* New York: Longman.

Leopold, W. F. (1939–1949). *Speech development of a bilingual child: A linguist's record, 1939, 1947, 1949, Vol. 1: Vocabulary growth in the first two years; Vol. 2: Sound learning in the first two years; Vol. 3: Grammar and general problems in the first two years; Vol. 4: Diary from age 2.* Evanston, IL: Northwestern University Press.

Lightbown, P. (1985). Great expectations: Second-language and classroom teaching. *Applied Linguistics, 6,* 173–189.

Lightbown, P. (1998). The importance of timing in focus on form. In C. Doughty & J. Williams (Eds.), *Focus on form in second language classroom* (pp. 177–196). New York: Cambridge University Press.

Lightbown, P. (2000). Anniversary article: Classroom SLA research and second language teaching. *Applied Linguistics, 21,* 431–462.

Lightbown, P., & Spada, N. (1999). *How languages are learned* (2nd ed.). London: Oxford University Press.

Long, M. (1981). Input, interaction, and second language acquisition. *Native and foreign language acquisition, Annals of the New York Academy of Sciences,* 259–278.

Long, M. (1985). Input and second language acquisition theory. In S. Gass & C. Madden (Eds.), *Input in Second Language Acquisition* (pp. 377–393). Rowley, MA: Newbury House.

Long, M. (1990). The least a second language acquisition theory needs to explain. *TESOL Quarterly, 24,* 649–666.

Long, M. (1991). Focus on form: A design feature in language teaching methodology. In K. deBot, R. Ginsberg, & C. Kramsch (Eds.), *Foreign language research in cross-cultural perspective* (pp. 39–52). Amsterdam: Benjamins.

Long, M. (1996). The role of the linguistic environment in second language acquisition. In W. C. Ritchie & T. K. Bhatia (Eds.), *Handbook of language acquisition: Vol. 2. Second language acquisition* (pp. 413–468). New York: Academic Press.

Long, M., Inagaki, S., & Ortega, L. (1998). The role of implicit negative evidence in SLA: Models and recasts in Japanese and Spanish. *The Modern Language Journal, 82,* 357–371.

Long, M., & Robinson, P. (1998). Focus on form: Theory, research, and practice. In C. Doughty & J. Williams (Eds.), *Focus on form in second language classroom* (pp. 15–41). New York: Cambridge University Press.

Loschky, L., & Bley-Vroman, R. (1993). Creating structure-based communication tasks for second language development. In G. Crookes & S. Gass (Eds.), *Tasks and language learning.* (Vol. 1; pp. 123–167). Clevedon, UK: Multilingual Matters.

Lyster, R. (1998). Recasts, repetition, and ambiguity in L2 classroom discourse. *Studies in Second Language Acquisition, 20,* 51–81.

Mackey, A. (1999). Input, interaction, and second language development. *Studies in Second Language Acquisition, 21,* 557–588.

McLaughlin, B. (1996). Information processing in second language acquisition. In W. C. Ritchie & T. K. Bhatia (Eds.), *Handbook of language acquisition. Vol. 2: Second language acquisition.* New York: Academic Press.

McLaughlin, B. (1978). The monitor model: Some methodological considerations. *Language Learning, 28,* 309–332.

Meisel, J., Clahsen, H., & Pienemann. M. (1981). On determining developmental stages in natural second language acquisition. *Studies in Second Language Acquisition, 3,* 109–135.

Norris, J., & Ortega, L. (2001). Does type of instruction make a difference? Substantive findings from a meta-analytic review. *Language Learning, 51,* 157–213.

Oliver, R. (1995). Negative feedback in child NS/NNS conversation. *Studies in Second Language Acquisition, 17,* 459–482.

O'Malley, J., Chamot, A., & Walker, C. (1987). Some applications of cognitive theory to second language acquisition. *Studies in Second Language Acquisition, 9,* 287–306.

Pica, T., Holliday, L., Lewis, N., Berducci, D., & Newman, J. (1991). Language learning through interaction: What role does gender play? *Studies in Second Language Acquisition, 13,* 343–76.

Pica, T. (1994a). Questions from the classroom: Research perspectives. *TESOL Quarterly, 28,* 49–79.

Pica, T. (1994b). Research on negotiation: What does it reveal about second language learning conditions, processes, and outcomes? *Language Learning, 44,* 493–527.

Pica, T. (2002). Subject matter content: How does it assist the interactional and linguistic needs of classroom language learners? *The Modern Language Journal, 85,* 1–19.

Pica, T., Billmyer, K., Julian, M. A., Blake-Ward, M., Buchheit, L., Nicolary, S., & Sullivan, J. (2001, February). *From content-based texts to form focused tasks: An integration of second language theory, research, and pedagogy.* Paper presented at the annual AAAL Conference, St. Louis, MO.

Pica, T., Holliday, L., Lewis, N., & Morgenthaler, L. (1989). Comprehensible output as an outcome of linguistic demands on the learner. *Studies in Second Language Acquisition, 11*, 63–90.

Pica, T., Kanagy, R., & Falodun, J. (1993). Choosing and using communication tasks for second language instruction. In G. Crookes & S. Gass (Eds.), *Tasks and language learning* (Vol. 1; pp. 9–34). Clevedon, UK: Multilingual Matters.

Pienemann, M. (1989). Is language teachable? Psycholinguistic experiments and hypotheses. *Applied Linguistics, 10*, 52–79.

Pienemann, M., & Haakenson, G. (1999). A unified approach towards the development of Swedish as L2: A Processibility account. *Studies in Second Language Acquisition, 21*, 383–420.

Pienemann, M., & Johnston, M. (1986). An acquisition-based procedure for language assessment. *Australian Review of Applied Linguistics, 9*, 92–112.

Pienemann, M., Johnston, M., & Brindley, G. (1988). Constructing an acquisition-based procedure for second language assessment. *Studies in Second Language Acquisition, 10*, 217–243.

Ravem, R. (1968). Language acquisition in a second language environment. *International Review of Applied Linguistics, 6*, 165–185.

Richards, J. C. (1974). *Error analysis*. London: Longman.

Robinson, P. (1997). Automaticity and generalizability of second language under implicit, incidental, enhanced, and instructed conditions. *Studies in Second Language Acquisition, 19*, 233–247.

Rutherford, W., & Sharwood Smith, M. (1985). Consciousness-raising and Universal Grammar. *Applied Linguistics, 6*, 274–282.

Schmidt, R. (1990). The role of consciousness in language learning. *Applied Linguistics, 11*, 17–46.

Schmidt, R. (1992). Psychological mechanisms underlying second language fluency. *Studies in Second Language Acquisition, 14*, 357–385.

Schmidt, R. (1995). Consciousness and foreign language learning: A tutorial on the role of attention and awareness in learning. In R. Schmidt (Ed.), *Attention and awareness in foreign language learning* (pp. 1–63). Honolulu: University of Hawaii Press.

Schmidt, R., & Frota, S. (1986). Developing basic conversational ability in a second language: A case study of an adult learner of Portuguese. In R. Day (Ed.), *Talking to learn: Conversation in second language acquisition* (pp. 237–326). Rowley, MA: Newbury House.

Schwartz, B. (1993). On explicit and negative data effecting and affecting competence and linguistics behavior. *Studies in Second Language Acquisition, 15*, 147–163.

Selinker, L. (1972). Interlanguage. *International Review of Applied Linguistics, 10*, 209–231.

Slobin, D. I. (1973). Cognitive prerequisites for the development of grammar. In C. A. Ferguson & D. I. Slobin (Eds.), *Studies of child language development* (pp. 175–208). New York: Holt, Rinehart & Winston.

Slobin, D. I. (1985). Crosslinguistic evidence for the language-making capacity. In D. I. Slobin (Ed.), *The crosslinguistic study of language acquisition (Vol. 2): Theoretical issues* (pp. 1157–1257). Hillsdale, NJ: Lawrence Erlbaum Associates.

Spada, N., & Lightbown, P. (1993). Instruction and the development of questions in L2 classrooms. *Studies in Second Language Acquisition, 15*, 205–224.

Swain, M. (1985). Communicative competence: Some roles of comprehensible input and comprehensible output in its development. In S. Gass & C. Madden (Eds.), *Input in Second Language Acquisition* (pp. 235–253). Rowley, MA: Newbury House.

Swain, M. (1995). Three functions of output in second language learning. In G. Cook & B. Seidlhofer (Eds.), *For H. G. Widdowson: Principles and practice in the study of language* (pp. 125–144). Oxford, UK: Oxford University Press.

Swain, M. (1998). Focus on form through conscious reflection. In C. Doughty & J. Williams (Eds.), *Focus on form in classroom second language acquisition* (pp. 64–82). New York: Cambridge University Press.

VanPatten, B., & Oikkenon, S. (1996). Explanation vs. structured input in processing instruction. *Studies in Second Language Acquisition, 18*, 495–510.

VanPatten, B., & Sanz, C. (1995). From input to output: Processing instruction and communicative tasks. In F. Eckman, D. Highland, P. W. Lee, J. Mileham, & R. R. Weber (Eds.), *Second language acquisition theory and pedagogy* (pp. 169–185). Mahwah, NJ: Lawrence Erlbaum Associates.

White, L. (1985). The "pro-drop" parameter in adult second language acquisition. *Language Learning, 35*, 47–61.

White, L. (1991). Adverb placement in second language acquisition: Some positive and negative evidence in the classroom. *Second Language Research, 7*, 122–161.

White, L., Spada, N., Lightbown, P., & Ranta, L. (1991). Input enhancement and L2 question formation. *Applied Linguistics, 12*, 416–432.

Williams, J., & Evans, J. (1998). Which kind of focus and on which kind of forms? In C. Doughty & J. Williams (Eds.), *Focus on form in second language classroom* (pp. 139–155). New York: Cambridge University Press.

Zobl, H. (1980). The formal and developmental selectivity of L1 influence on L2 acquisition. *Language Learning, 30*, 43–57.

Zobl, H. (1982). A direction for contrastive analysis: The comparative study of developmental sequences. *TESOL Quarterly, 16*, 169–183.

16

Sociolinguistics and Second Language Learning

Sandra Lee McKay
San Francisco State University

Countless decisions that L2 teachers make depend on sociolinguistic knowledge. When teachers decide which grammatical, pragmatic, and discourse standards to promote in their classroom, they need an awareness of the social dimensions of language use. When teachers grapple with how to productively use their students' mother tongue in the classroom, they must draw on sociolinguistic expertise. When teachers deal with students' attitudes toward language variation, they need sociolinguistic knowledge. This chapter highlights the importance of sociolinguistics for L2 pedagogy. In order to accomplish this goal, it is necessary to first examine the various ways in which sociolinguistics is defined.

TOWARD A DEFINITION OF SOCIOLINGUISTICS

Sociolinguistics is concerned with the relationship between language use and social factors. One of the major debates of sociolinguistics is whether to take social or linguistic factors as primary in investigations of this relationship. As evidence of this debate, Wardhaugh (1992) and others make a distinction between *sociolinguistics* and the *sociology of language*. Whereas sociolinguistics takes linguistic factors as primary in its investigations of language and society, the sociology of language investigates the manner in which social and political forces influence language use. Trauth and Kazzazi (1996), in the *Routledge Dictionary of Language and Linguistics*, make a similar distinction, noting that socolinguistics can have either a sociological or linguistic orientation. The dictionary, however, adds a third possibility, namely, an ethnomethodological orientation. Hence, three areas of sociolinguistic investigation are delineated:

> (a) A primarily sociologically oriented approach concerned predominately with the norms of language use (When and for what purpose does somebody speak what kind of language or what variety with whom?).... (b) A primarily linguistically oriented

approach that presumes linguistic systems to be in principle heterogeneous, though structured, when viewed within sociological parameters. . . . . (c) An ethnomethodolically oriented approach with linguistic interaction as the focal point, which studies the ways in which members of a society create social reality and rule-ordered behaviour. (p. 439)

In our discussion of sociolinguistics (McKay & Hornberger, 1996), we examine the field of sociolinguistics by differentiating a macrolevel and microlevel of social and linguistic analysis. Thus, in terms of the social context, sociolinguists can focus on larger social contexts like nations and communities or on more limited contexts like classrooms, restaurants, or medical offices. In reference to language, researchers can examine larger issues like the choice of one language over another or narrower concerns like the choice of one phonological feature over another. A macro and micro distinction then results in the following areas of sociolinguistic analysis.

Levels of Social Analysis

		Macro	*Micro*
Levels of Linguistic Analysis	*Macro*	Language and Society	Language and Culture
	Micro	Language and Variation	Language and Interaction

Each of the four areas supports a specific type of sociolinguisitic research. For example, in the area of Language and Society, sociolinguists examine the manner in which the social and political context influences a macrolevel of language use, investigating, for example, which language is used in which domains in a particular society or how social factors affect attitudes toward particular language varieties or language standards. Topics in this area include societal multilingualism, language planning and policy (see Part VIII, this volume), and language attitudes and motivation. In the area of Language and Variation, sociolinguists consider how social factors influence the choice of particular linguistic forms, considering, for instance, how geographical region, social class, or gender affect an individual's use of particular phonological, structural, or lexical features of a language. Topics that are considered in this area include regional, social, gender, and ethnic linguistic variation.

In the area of Language and Interaction, sociolinguists adopt a microlevel of social and linguistic analysis exploring, for example, how a specific social situation or role relationship affects the verbal and nonverbal communication of the participants. This area of sociolinguistics includes fields like conversational analysis (see Markee, this volume) and pragmatics (see Kasper, this volume). Finally in the area of Language and Culture, there is a microlevel of social analysis so that specific social situations, role relationships, or texts are examined, but a macrolevel of linguistic analysis is employed so that researchers make generalizations about how particular cultures and communities use language. This area of sociolinguistics includes the ethnography of communication and contrastive rhetoric (see Kaplan, this volume). Because other chapters in this book are devoted to an examination of Language and Interaction and Language and Culture, this chapter focuses on topics relevant to the area of Language and Society and Language and Variation. However, one major concern of Language and Society, namely, language planning and policy, will not be dealt with here because this topic is explored in depth in another section of the book.

To begin, we examine some of the major issues dealt with in the area of Language and Society and consider how these topics are related to second language (L2) teaching and learning. Because many English language learners today are acquiring English as an additional language rather than as a replacement for their first language, we will devote a good deal of attention to how bilingualism and multilingualism influence language change and language use. We will be particularly concerned with how the use of several languages in multilingual contexts can result in language loss, language change, code-switching, and the development of new codes. In the second section of the chapter we discuss major concerns of Language and Variation and examine how linguistic variation in the use of English in English-speaking countries can reflect the geographical region, social class, gender, and ethnicity of the speaker.

Two important sociolinguistic concerns will not be dealt with as separate sections but rather will be examined throughout the chapter because they are so central to L2 teaching and learning. The first is the issue of standards. Language change and language variation naturally raise questions of standards. Hence, as we deal with these topics, we will examine which standards to promote in English language learning and teaching. As we discuss the question of standards, we will emphasize the close relationship that exists between the promotion of standards and issues of power. A second concern that will be examined throughout the chapter is the issue of language attitudes. Frequently, particular linguistic variations engender positive or negative attitudes on the part of the listener. These attitudes can be significant in how individuals judge one another. Hence, it is important to address the question of attitudes in English language learning and teaching and to recognize how language attitudes, as with linguistic standards, are often related to issues of power. We turn now to discussion of multilingualism and its influence on language change and language use.

LANGUAGE AND SOCIETY

Multilingualism/Bilingualism

For some sociolinguists, multilingualism describes the use of two or more languages by a nation or by an individual. For other sociolinguists, however, the term *multilingualism* is used to refer specifically to nations and states, whereas the term *bilingualism* is used to refer to individuals. In this chapter we will adhere to the latter use of these terms.

Central to an understanding of multilingualism and bilingualism is the notion of a *speech community*. A speech community must share at least one *code*, that is, one language or one variety of a language. However, in addition to sharing a code, the members of a speech community must share a set of norms as to how to use this code. An individual can belong to a speech community based on a variety of factors such as gender, religion, ethnicity, or social class. Because an individual can belong to a variety of speech communities, the speech community one chooses to identify with can shift from one context to another. Hence, at one moment, an individual might wish to identify with members of his or her ethnic background, and at another time with members of his or her profession. The fact that an individual belongs to shifting and intersecting speech communities is especially significant for multilingual communities. Whereas monolinguals signal their shift in speech community by selecting the appropriate level of formality, lexical item, pronunciation, and so on, a bilingual can indicate a shift of speech community by selecting to use a particular language. We will return to this matter later when we consider code-switching.

Most language demographers agree that today there are more bilingual than monolingual speakers. Bilingualism may in fact become even more common as individuals acquire a language of wider communication, or *lingua franca*, to use in today's global culture. Today English appears to be the lingua franca of choice, leading many individuals to acquire English and become one of the growing number of bilingual speakers of English. In fact, the growth of bilingual speakers of English is so significant that

Graddol (1999) contends that in the next 50 years, the balance between native and non-native speakers of English will shift significantly. He maintains that:

> Based solely on expected population changes, the number of people using English as their second language will grow from 235 million to around 462 million during the next 50 years. This indicates that the balance between L1 [first language] and L2 speakers will critically change, with L2 speakers eventually overtaking L1 speakers. (p. 62)

The growth of bilingual speakers of English is significant for L2 pedagogy because it suggests that many learners of English today will be acquiring English as an additional language for use in their total linguistic repertoire. Hence, they exemplify what is referred to as *additive bilingualism* in which individuals add a second language to their repertoire. This situation is in contrast to many immigrants to English-speaking countries who undergo first language loss or *subtractive bilingualism*.

Given the tremendous interest that exists today in the learning of English, one may well ask, what are some reasons for the historical and present-day spread of English? One reason has been speaker migration; historically many individuals left their homes and migrated to English-speaking countries because of economic necessity, ethnic strife, and religious persecution. Such speaker migration, of course, continues today, but it is no longer the major reason for the spread of English. British and American colonialism has been another factor in the spread of English. Indeed, if one considers the many nations of the world today that give English some official recognition, many are former British or American colonies. Kachru (1989) refers to such countries as *outer circle countries* in contrast to *inner circle countries* like the United Kingdom and the United States in which most individuals are monolinguals speakers of English. A third reason for the spread of English has been annexation as, for example, when the United States annexed the Spanish-speaking areas of the southwest. Today, however, most individuals are acquiring English within their own country for economic, educational, and political reasons. This means that many users of English today will be making use of English within their own country for specific purposes or as a medium of international communication.

When most individuals in a country are bilingual, as exists in many outer circle countries, like the Philippines and Singapore, a situation of *diglossia* can develop. The term diglossia was first coined by Ferguson (1959) to describe a context in which two varieties of the same language are used by people of that community for different purposes. Normally one variety, termed the *high or H variety*, is acquired in an educational context and used by the community in more formal domains such as in churches or universities. The other variety, termed the *low or L variety*, is acquired in the home and used in informal domains like the home or social center to communicate with family and friends. As examples of diglossia, Ferguson points to situations like the use of classical and colloquial Arabic in Egypt or the use of Standard German and Swiss German in Switzerland. Later, Fishman (1972) generalized the meaning of diglossia to include the use of two separate languages within one country in which one language is used primarily for formal purposes and the other for more informal purposes. For example, in Singapore, English is generally used in education and government, whereas Hokkien, Malay, and Tamil are frequently used in the home and community.

In contexts like Singapore, India, and the Philippines in which English is the high variety in a multilingual country, there often exists a *cline of bilingualism* (Kachru, 1986) so that whereas some bilinguals in the country speak a standard variety of English, others speak a nonstandard variety. One can also speak of an individual's cline of bilingualism ranging from the variety he or she generally uses in the marketplace to the variety he or she typically uses in educational or business contexts. In some cases, an individual may have access to all the varieties spoken in a country from the most standard variety to the most colloquial variety. In other cases, however, an individual may have much more limited access to these varieties, often speaking only what is considered the L variety. Sridhar (1996) notes that many bilinguals have *selective functionality* in the languages they speak, that is, they develop competence in each of the languages to the level that they need it. What degree of competence in a language is necessary to be considered bilingual is, of course, difficult to determine. Hence, the term bilingual is often very loosely defined to describe an individual who makes use of more than one language (Clyne, 1997).

The fact that in many instances today bilingual speakers of English use English in multilingual contexts in which English is just one language in their total linguistic repertoire has important implications for English language pedagogy and research. It has often been assumed that the ultimate goal for English language learners is to achieve nativelike competence. Yet as more and more users of English come to use English alongside one or more other languages, their use of English will be significantly different from those bilinguals who learn English as a replacement for their L1, as is the case with many immigrants to English-speaking countries.

As Sridhar and Sridhar (1994) point out, for those bilingual users of English who make use of English in multilingual contexts, achieving nativelike competence in English can appear to some in the local community to be "distasteful and pedantic" and "affected or even snobbish" (p. 45). Furthermore, often English bilinguals in multilingual contexts are not exposed to a full range of styles, structures, and speech acts, which a good deal of L2 pedagogy assumes is necessary to acquire nativelike proficiency. Rather such individuals get "exposed to a subset of registers, styles, speech event types—mainly academic, bureaucratic, and literary" (pp. 46–47). Hence, in order to be most effective, L2 pedagogy in multilingual contexts needs to examine how English contributes to the overall communication pattern of the individual and the society. In many multilingual contexts in which English is used today, acquiring a formal register of English and in some cases developing reading and writing ability rather than listening and speaking may be the most appropriate language learning goals.

Language Contact and Language Loss

When a society has many individuals who are bilingual, two or more languages are often in daily in contact. One potential effect of this language contact is language displacement and potentially language loss. Language displacement frequently occurs in the case of speakers of minority languages abandoning their L1 language and replacing it with a language of wider communication. As Brenzinger (1997) points out:

> In all parts of the world, we observe an increasing tendency among members of ethno-linguistic minorities to bring up their children in a language other than their own mother tongue, thereby abandoning their former ethnic languages. These changes in language use by individuals might ultimately lead to the irreversible disappearance of the minority's original language. The new one, that is the replacing language, is in many cases one of the few fast-spreading languages such as English, Mandarin (Chinese), Russian, Hindi-Urdu, Spanish, Portuguese, Arabic, French, Swahili, and Hausa. (p. 273)

Brenzinger continues that there is no consensus as to how many languages are being lost today although several spectacular estimates have been made, with some contending that in the last 500 years at least half of the languages of the world have disappeared and others maintaining that only 10% of the present languages in the world today are not threatened by extinction.

Today, in many cases, English is the replacing language of minority languages. Brenzinger (1997), for example, points out that English is the replacing language for many Australian aboriginal languages, Indian languages in North America, and Celtic languages in Great Britain. In their investigation of local languages in rural, southern Nigeria, Schaefer and Egbokhare (1999) conclude that in this area, the spread of English is causing the abandonment of several indigenous, minority languages. In some instances, English is even replacing nonminority languages. Gopinathan (1998), for example, points to the increasing number of households in Singapore in which English is the principal household language, raising the possibility that the next generation of such households will be monolingual English speakers rather than bilingual Mandarin–English or Malay–English speakers.

Some argue that one of the primary reasons for English replacing other languages is due to the extensive promotion of English by English-speaking countries. One of the major exponents of this view is Phillipson (1992), who argues that the spread of English is a matter of deliberate policy on the part of English-speaking countries to maintain dominance. He has coined the term *linguistic imperialism* to describe a situation in which "the dominance of English is asserted and maintained by the establishment and continuous reconstitution of structural and cultural inequalities between English and other languages" (p. 47).

However, to assume that English itself or even the active promotion of English is the sole cause of a shift to English is to oversimplify the complexity of the spread of English. Many individuals are learning English today not because they have a love of the language nor because English is promoted by a growing private industry, but rather because they want access to such things as scientific and technological information, international relations, global economic trade, and higher education. Knowing English makes such access possible. Indeed Kachru (1986) in a book entitled, *The Alchemy of English,* contends that "knowing English is like possessing the fabled Aladdin's lamp, which permits one to open, as it were, the linguistic gates to international business, technology, science and travel. In short, English provides linguistic power" (p. 1).

Language Contact and Language Change

A second possible effect of language contact is language change. In this case the various languages used within the language contact context may undergo phonological, lexical, and grammatical changes as bilingual individuals make use of two or more languages on a regular basis. As a way of illustrating the type and extent of such changes, we will examine some of the changes that have occurred in the use of English in multilingual contexts.

Linguistic Varieties.   As was mentioned earlier, when English is used in multilingual contexts, there is a cline of bilingualism with some individuals speaking a standard variety of the region and others having much less proficiency in English. Tay (1982) and others refer to this cline of bilingualism as consisting of a *basilect, mesolect,* and *acrolect.* Although these terms were first used by Bickerton (1975) to describe variation within creoles, Tay uses the terms to discuss the range of English that is used in Singapore. In reference to Singapore, Tay points out that the acrolect has no significant grammatical differences from British English, differing primarily in terms of lexical innovation. The mesolect, on the other hand, has a number of unique grammatical features such as the dropping of some indefinite articles and the lack of plural markings on some count nouns. The basilect has more significant grammatical differences such as copula deletion and *do*-deletion in direct questions, along with more use of slang and colloquialisms.

In analyzing the varieties of English spoken in Singapore, Lick and Alsagoff (1998) point out that varieties of any language are associated with particular social groups and can be characterized by a specific set of linguistic variation. All of these varieties also exhibit regularity in their grammatical systems. From a linguist's point of view, all varieties of English are equal because they all are fully systematic and regulated by a set of rules. As an example, they point to a sentence from what is termed *Singlish*, a particular variety of English spoken in informal contexts in Singapore. The sentence, "She kena sabo by them," is equivalent to the standard English sentence, "She was sabotaged by them."

Lick and Alsagoff point out that this Singlish sentence is grammatical in a linguistic sense in that the sentence conforms to the grammatical rules of Singlish. If these words were arranged in any other order, they would not be considered grammatical by speakers of Singlish. In a linguistic sense, then, Singlish is a valid grammatical variety of English, linguistically equal to any other variety of English. When, however, Singlish was used on a local Singaporean television entertainment program, the use of Singlish led to tremendous controversy, with some Singaporeans urging the authorities to step in and regulate the use of Singlish on television so that children would not speak what they termed "bad English." Others, however, defended the use of Singlish, claiming that this variety of English was part of the Singaporean identity and that ordinary people could relate to this variety of English.

A controversy such as this highlights the fact that whereas all varieties of English are linguistically equal, they are not considered to be socially equal. The variety with the most prestige is typically referred to as standard English, with all other varieties generally labeled with pejorative terms such as substandard or nonstandard. As Lick and Alsagoff note:

> Generally, the variety spoken by the socially dominant group, which normally includes the rich and powerful, as well as the educated elite, has the most prestige. This variety is then institutionalized as the standard: it is used for governmental administration and on all formal occasions. It is taught in schools and used in the mass media (on television, radio, and in the press) and it serves as the model for those who wish to master the language. In contrast, the varieties used by people of lower social status, such as the poor and the uneducated, are tagged as *nonstandard*, sometimes derogatorily as *substandard*, synonymous with words such as *bad, corrupt,* and *offensive*. Such a standard–nonstandard division is basically a reflection of social inequality. (p. 282)

How then does a linguistic change come to be recognized as standard? Bamgbose (1998) delineates five factors that can be used to determine whether or not an innovation has become standardized. They are:

- Demographic (How many people use the innovation?)
- Geographical (How widely is the innovation used within the country?)
- Authoritative (Who uses the innovation?)
- Codification (Where is the usage sanctioned?)
- Acceptability (What is the attitude of users and nonusers toward the innovation?)

Bamgbose contends that the most important factors in determining if an innovation has become standardized is whether or not the innovation is codified in such things as dictionaries, coursebooks, or other manuals, and whether or not it is widely accepted.

Lexical Innovation. Perhaps the most interesting changes that have occurred in the use of English in multilingual contexts are lexical innovations. Because it is sometimes difficult to ascertain how widely used and accepted a lexical item is in a particular location, some lexicographers have begun to rely on corpus materials to determine the acceptability of particular lexical items. One project on lexical innovation that has taken this approach is the *Macquarie Dictionary* (Butler, 1999). The purpose of this dictionary project was to compile a dictionary of English that included generally accepted unique lexical items for various countries in southeast Asia. In order to reach this goal, the editors gathered a written corpus from representative countries that included fiction, nonfiction, and newspapers in English. This corpus was then checked against the words in an earlier edition of *The Macquarie Dictionary* that included essentially Australian English words. Words that did not exist in the earlier version were considered as possible items of a local variety of English.

Brown (1999) has compiled a dictionary of lexical innovation for the English used in Singapore. As is typical with lexical innovation for languages in contact situations, the lexical changes that are occurring in Singapore exemplify certain processes. First, there is *semantic extension*—when an English word takes on additional meanings in a local context. For example, the word *auntie* when used in Singapore has the traditional meaning of your mother's sister or your father's sister or an uncle's wife. However, it is also used to refer to any female friend of the family who is at least one generation older than the speaker. The use of the term *auntie* in this context is a way of demonstrating respect. A second common process of lexical innovation of languages in contact is the *borrowing* of a word from one language into another. For example, Malay words like *barang-barang* (meaning things) and Hokkien words like *chim* (meaning deep) are used by speakers of English in Singapore. Such borrowed items are not examples of code switching because these words are used by speakers of English in Singapore regardless of their first language. Furthermore, these items are generally single lexical items, often nouns, rather than a full range of lexical and syntactic structures as occurs in code switching. In addition, phonological changes can occur in the borrowed lexical item to reflect the phonological features of the language that incorporates the new word.

Although it is clear that lexical innovation is a vital part of the changes that are occurring in the spread of English, attitudes toward these changes differ significantly. Butler (1999), for example, in her survey of Filipino and Thai attitudes toward lexical innovation, found that most of the Filipino participants believed that local lexical items should take their place in a dictionary of Asian English. The primary concern of the Filipino participants was which words to include in the dictionary. The Thai participants, on the other hand, were much less likely to want to include any local English words in a dictionary of Asian English. Brown (1999) maintains that in Singapore attitudes toward lexical innovation form a continuum. For some, such lexical innovation suggests that Singapore has its own legitimate variety of English. For others, such changes reflect a deficiency in the speakers' use of English. The coining of new words, however, is not the only type of innovation that can occur in language contact situations. Grammatical changes are also developing, and it is this innovation that tends to cause the greatest concern among some educators in terms of preserving standards and intelligibility.

Grammatical Innovation.   A great many studies have been undertaken to determine the types of grammatical changes that are occurring in various multilingual contexts in which English plays a significant role. Frequently researchers begin by examining a written corpus of English of a particular multilingual context to determine what kinds of grammatical innovations exist and how acceptable these structures are to both native speakers of English and local speakers of English. In general, when investigations of language change use a written corpus of published English, only very minor grammatical differences are found. Shastri (1996), for example, found that there were no significant differences in the use of complementation in three comparable corpora—an American corpus, a British corpus, and an Indian corpus.

Lowenberg (1986) suggests that in many multilingual contexts, the kinds of grammatical changes that occur in published discourse tend to be minor differences such as variation in what is considered to be a countable noun (e.g., the standard use of *luggages* in the use of English in the Philippines and the use of *furnitures* in Nigeria) and the creation of new phrasal verbs (e.g., the use of *dismissing off* in the use of English in India and *discuss about* in Nigeria). Furthermore, even in the unpublished written discourse of educated bilingual speakers of English only very minor grammatical differences generally appear. Parasher, (1994), for example, found wide agreement among British, American, and Indian standard English speakers in judging the correctness of the written correspondence of educated professionals. However, there were some minor differences. Indian English speakers, for example, unlike American and British speakers, accepted as standard verbal patterns like the following: *We would appreciate if you could, I would not be able to revise the draft,* and *Funds have been received last year.*

What is perhaps most puzzling in the development of alternate grammatical standards in the use of English in multilingual contexts is that fact that whereas many accept lexical innovation as part of language change and recognize the legitimacy of such innovation, this tolerance is often not extended to grammatical innovation. In Widdowson's (1994) view, the reason for this lack of tolerance for grammatical variation is because grammar takes on another value, namely, that of expressing a social identity. As he puts it, "The mastery of a particular grammatical system, especially perhaps those features which are redundant, marks you as a member of the community which has developed that system for its own social purpose" (p. 381). Hence, when grammatical standards are challenged, they challenge the security of the community and institutions that support these standards.

It is also puzzling that whereas grammatical differences in the use of English among inner circle countries, like the United States and Britain, are generally accepted, with no one suggesting that this will lead to incomprehensibility, grammatical variation in multilingual contexts is often seen as a threat. Brutt-Griffler (1998), argues that such tolerance must be extended to all users of English. As she puts it, most inner circle countries:

> appear willing to meet on a common linguistic plane, accept the diversity of their Englishes, and do not require of one another to prove competence in English, despite the considerable differences in the varieties of English they speak and the cross-communication problems entailed thereby. . . . this situation must be extended to all English-using communities. (p. 389)

Presently, however, such tolerance is not extended to innovations that occur in the English used in multilingual contexts; rather some linguists argue that one variety of English must be promoted and a concerted effort must be made to teach standards. (See Quirk, 1990, for one example of this position.)

Language Contact and Language Use

As was demonstrated in the previous section, the fact that bilinguals make regular use of two or more languages can lead to linguistic changes in the languages they use. In addition, in language contact situations, bilinguals can shift from one language to another in what is termed *code switching*. Some sociolinguists make a distinction between *code switching* (i.e., switching languages at sentence boundaries) and *code mixing* (i.e., switching language within a sentence). However, we will use the term code switching to cover both situations.

One of the main questions addressed in research on code switching is what leads a bilingual individual to shift from one language to another. In answer to this question,

Blom and Gumperz (1972) posit two types of code switching. The first is *situational code switching* in which the speaker changes codes in response to a change in the situation such as a change in the setting or the speakers involved in the conversation. The second type is *metaphorical code switching* in which the shift in languages has a stylistic or textual function to mark a change in emphasis or tone. Some, like Poplack (1980) and Singh (1996), maintain that code switching is closely related to language proficiency. Singh, in fact, argues that this relationship can be summarized in the following aphorism: "A strong bilingual switches only when he wants to and a weak one when he has to" (p. 73).

One of the most comprehensive theories of code switching is Myers-Scotton (1993). She explains code switching in terms of a theory of rights and obligations. She proposes a markedness model of code switching that assumes that speakers in a multilingual context have a sense of which code is the expected code to use in a particular situation. Hence, for example, in an informal encounter in Singapore, two Chinese Hokkien speakers would in general greet one another in Hokkien. This then would be the unmarked code for informal contexts. In choosing to use Hokkien, the speakers would be signaling to one another that they belong to a common speech community of Chinese Singaporeans who share the Hokkien dialect. However, it is possible that one of the speakers could choose to use the marked code, in this case English. Myers-Scotton suggests several reasons why a speaker might make this choice as, for example, to increase social distance, to avoid an overt display of ethnicity, or for an aesthetic effect.

Myers-Scotton also points out that it is possible that code switching itself can be the unmarked code between individuals. Hence, again in Singapore, university students often regularly use code switching to signal their dual identity as English speakers and Malay, Hokkien, or Tamil speakers. Myers-Scotton contends that certain conditions need to exist for code switching to be the unmarked code. The speakers must be peers and relatively proficient in the two languages. They must also want to signal their dual membership in two communities.

Myers-Scotton's theory has several implications for L2 pedagogy. The first has to do with the use of the L1 in L2 classrooms. In natural language use, a particular code is generally viewed as the unmarked choice. For learners of English who share the same first language, the unmarked code to use with one another is typically the L1. Hence, language classrooms that encourage the exclusive use of English and in some instances even penalize the use of the first language are asking students to engage in a very unnatural type of language interaction. A more productive approach to learners use of English and their mother tongue would be for language teachers and researchers to examine how the two languages can best be used in the classroom to encourage language learning.

One study that attempts to do this is Hancock (1997). In his study of the use of the first language and the target language in an L2 classroom, Hancock argues that in the context of role playing, two types of discourse occur. One is the on-record discourse that is part of the role that the learner takes on in the activity. In on-record discourse, the target language is the unmarked code. The other is the off-record discourse that is not intended as part of the role play and generally is in the first language of the participants. In such instance the learners use their first language to accomplish such tasks as asking a language question (e.g., asking in the first language how you say something in the target language) or asking task-related questions (e.g., asking in the first language what the participants are supposed to do in the activity). Thus, such studies demonstrate that the first language can be productively used in language classrooms to aid in the practice of the target language.

A second implication of Myers-Scotton's theory for L2 pedagogy is that it is important for teachers to consider in which social situations in the community English typically serves as the unmarked code and select teaching objectives with this in mind. Hence, in multilingual contexts where English is often the unmarked code in more formal situations, it makes sense to focus on increasing students' proficiency in formal rather than informal registers of English use.

Language Contact and the Development of New Codes

Code switching can occur in language contact situations only in cases where speakers share two or more languages. In language contact situations in which speakers have no common language, one possibility, as was noted earlier, is for one individual to learn the language of the other speaker either through additive bilingualism or subtractive bilingualism. This is often the case in instances of speaker migration or colonialism. However, another option that can occur, particularly in contexts where individuals need to communicate for relatively limited purposes, is the development of a new linguistic code or *pidgin*. As Nichols (1996) points out, pidgins:

> come into being through the interaction of large numbers of people who speak several different languages and who have little reason or opportunity to learn another one of the many languages spoken in the contact situation. Typically, pidgins arise when people of many language backgrounds engage in extensive trading or forced labor, often in coastal areas near major seaports. They appear when massive population dislocation and movement take place. In these dynamic situations, there is too much going on for the small number of interpreters to cope with. (p. 98)

Because pidgins are used for limited communication between speakers, they typically have a simple vocabulary and uncomplicated morphological and syntactic structure. In general the language of the economically and politically more powerful group provides the lexicon (the superstrate language) and the less powerful (the substrate language) the syntactic and phonological structure. Technically, a *creole* is a pidgin that has native speakers, namely, children of pidgin speakers who grow up using the pidgin as their first language. Because the code is now the only language the speaker has available, the lexicon expands and the syntactic structure becomes more complex. However, as Rickford and McWhorter (1997) point out, creoles may also develop when adults who use the pidgin begin to use the code for more purposes and, thus, coin new words and develop more complex syntactic structures. In this way, the development of a pidgin into a creole is perhaps more accurately described not by the fact it has native speakers but that it comes to be used in a wider variety of contexts.

Why are sociolinguists interested in pidgins and creoles? Rickford and McWhorter (1997) provide several reasons. First, pidgins and creoles demonstrate the manner in which sociohistorical issues such as trade and enslavement can influence language development. Secondly, pidgins and creoles provide important data for investigating sociolinguistic variation and change in that they illustrate the manner in which language variation is related to social class, power, and identity. Third, pidgins and creoles raise important issues of applied sociolinguistics and language planning such as the feasibility and desirability of using them as languages of instruction. Finally, investigations of pidgins and creoles often produce what Rickford and McWhorter term "fractious energy" in that creolists are consistently arguing about theories and subtheories to account for the origin and development of pidgins and creoles.

One of the major debates undertaken by creolists is the origins of creoles. Originally the debate was between polygenetic theories, which assumed that individual creoles arose independently at different locations and times, and monogenetic theories, which assumed that most creoles developed from a small number of creoles that spread to other locations. However, more recently these theories have been replaced by a bioprogram theory of origin, instigated by Bickerton (1984), who argues that creoles develop from pidgins according to the demands of an innate human bioprogram that is relatively unaffected by conditions of the contact situations. For Bickerton, this is what accounts for the lexical and syntactic similarities that exist in many creoles of the world.

One of the major pedagogical issues surrounding the use of pidgins and creoles is to what extent they should be used in a classroom. In some contexts, creoles are used in initial literacy instruction under the assumption that early education is most successful if it is conducted in the child's first language. However, there is great resistance to this option particularly when a standardized version of the superstrate language exists in the same regions, as, it does, for example, in Hawaii. Often this resistance develops from negative attitudes toward the pidgin and creole rather than from any linguistic basis.

LANGUAGE AND VARIATION

Whereas in the previous section we focused on the ways in which multilingualism and bilingualism influence language use, in this section we will focus on the relationship between various factors of an individual's identity (e.g., gender, economic class, ethnicity, etc.) and the linguistic features of their language. Linguistic variation is central to the study of sociolinguistics. As Fasold (1984) notes:

> The essence of sociolinguistics, in my view, depends on two facts about language that are often ignored in the field of linguistics. First language *varies*—speakers have more than one way to say more or less the same thing. ... Second, there is a critical purpose that language serves for its users that is just as important as the obvious one. It is obvious that language is supposed to be used for transmitting information and thoughts from one person to another. At the same time, however, the speaker is using language to make statements about who she is, what her group loyalties are, how she perceives her relationship to her hearer, and what sort of speech event she considers herself to be engaged in. (p. ix.)

As will be evident from the following discussion, this variation is often a factor of geographical region, social class, ethnicity, and gender.

Language Variation and Geographical Region

The study of regional variation has the longest history of investigation, beginning in the 19th century with historical-comparative linguistics. One of the earliest and most intensive investigations of regional dialects in the United States was Kurath, Hanley, Bloch, and Lowman (1939–1943), whose fieldwork resulted in a comprehensive linguistic atlas of New England. More recently, a comprehensive fieldwork project of American regional dialects led by Cassidy (1985) resulted in a *Dictionary of American Regional Dialects*. In both projects, many fieldworkers were employed to interview individuals of various communities and age groups in order to map out specific features of dialect regions.

In the case of Cassidy's project, 2,777 individuals were interviewed in 1,002 communities using a standardized questionnaire. In order to not bias the responses of the subjects, the fieldworkers used indirect questions such as "What do you call the time early in the day before the sun comes into sight?" Various responses to this question are then plotted on a map so that *sunrise* would be plotted by one symbol and *dawn* by another. Next, lines are drawn on the map to separate the location of different variants.

The lines that separate lexical differences are called *isoglosses* and those that separate phonological differences are termed *isophones* Frequently, such plotting results in a combination of phonological, lexical, and grammatical differences that suggests a *dialect area*. Research has shown that dialects typically differ not only qualitatively, that is, dialect A uses *skillet* whereas dialect B uses *frying pan*, but also quantitatively in that one dialect may use a particular feature more frequently than another dialect.

There are several factors that can contribute to the development of a regional dialect. One is the settlement history of a particular area. For example, because many Dutch settled in Grand Rapids, Michigan, some features of this dialect area reflect a Dutch influence. A second factor that can contribute to the development of a regional dialect is migration pattern. Because the United States population shift has generally been from east to west, dialect boundaries in the United States are more likely to run horizontally than vertically. Finally, geographical and political boundaries can contribute to the development of regional differences. For example, in the United States, the Connecticut River parallels the boundary for some dialect differences.

What are the implications of regional variation for L2 pedagogy? To begin, if L2 learners are studying or living in an English-speaking country, it will be useful for them to have a receptive knowledge of some of the regional dialect differences that exist within the country. This knowledge can be developed by using listening materials that include a variety of regional dialects. In addition, learners need to be aware that, as with all linguistic variation, certain varieties will have more social prestige than others.

LANGUAGE VARIATION AND SOCIAL CLASS

The study of linguistic variation based on social class is a relatively recent phenomenon. The impetus for this focus came largely from the seminal work of Labov (1966a). In his study, Labov worked with a random sample of New Yorkers from the Lower East Side stratified into four socioeconomic classes based on occupation, income, and education. He investigated to what extent variables like *ing* vary in how they are pronounced based on an individual's socioeconomic class. Using interview data, Labov mapped the percentage of time that speakers dropped their *gs* (using "in" rather than "ing") in casual speech, careful speech, and reading style. What he found was a consistent pattern of the lower-working class using the reduced form more than the upper-middle class. However, like the upper-middle class, the lower-working class had a lower frequency in their use of the reduced form in the reading style than in the casual speech.

The methodology employed by Labov was significant in that he used naturalistic speech to make generalizations regarding linguistic variation. Even more important, the generalizations he made from this data demonstrated the relative frequency of a particular linguistic feature rather than the mere presence or absence of this feature. It is important to emphasize, however, that Labov's investigations illustrate a correlation and not a causal relationship. As Milroy and Milroy (1997) point out:

> It should not be assumed that to relate language variation to a social variable, such as social class, is to explain language variation as being *caused* by social class variation. There are several reasons for this caution, the chief of which is that there may be many aspects of social behavior that are not accounted for in a single social variable, and also underlying social factors that are subsumed under such a label as "social class" (such as educational level) which may sometimes yield more precise correlations than the main composite variable (in this case social class). (pp. 53–54)

The significance of social variation for L2 pedagogy is that once again there is a need for L2 learners to be aware that certain linguistic features will have more prestige than others and that, furthermore, both social and regional variants provide a mechanism for monolingual speakers of English to signal their membership in a particular speech community.

Language Variation and Gender

Research on the relationship between linguistic variation and gender demonstrates how language use is closely related to issues of power and prestige. Labov (1966b), for example, demonstrated that women of all classes and ages tend to use more standard variants than men (e.g., the use of "ing" rather than "in" in all styles of speech). Labov contends that women use prestigious forms to gain a better social position, reflecting their own linguistic insecurity. In contrast, Trudgill (1972) found that working-class men tend to use low-prestige nonstandard forms. To explain this phenomenon, Trudgill argued that the male use of these nonstandard forms is a type of covert prestige in which the use of nonstandard forms serve as a marker of masculinity and a way of signaling membership in a particular speech community.

In general, the early studies of language and gender in the 1970s supported what is termed a *dominance model* (Freeman & McElhinny, 1996) in that female language use was compared with male language use, which was considered to be more prestigious and desirable. This model is evident in Lakoff's (1975) book, *Language and Woman's Place*. Based solely on her own intuitions, Lakoff contended that women's speech has the following characteristics:

- Women use weaker expletives than men.
- Women's speech is more polite than men's.
- Women talk about more trivial topics than men.
- Women use more empty adjectives than men such as *charming* and *nice*.
- Women use more tag questions than men.
- Women often use rising intonation in statements signaling their uncertainty.
- Women use more intensifiers than men.
- Women use more hedges (e.g., "it's sort of) than men.
- Women use more correct grammar than men.
- Women don't tell jokes.

One of the major problem with Lakoff's characterization is that it links the use of these forms with an exclusively female identity. One early challenge to this assertion was a study by O'Barr (1982), who investigated the existence of Lakoff's features of women's language in the speech of courtroom witnesses. His study suggests that the use of these features is related to power and prestige rather than gender because females with high social status (e.g., doctors) used few of these features, whereas individuals with less status, whether male or female, made more use of the features of so-called women's language outlined by Lakoff.

Other research on language and gender supports what can be termed a *difference model*. Many of these studies focus primarily on the interactional style of women, contending that women tend to be more cooperative in their interactional style than men. (See Coates, 1991 and Troemel-Ploetz, 1992.) A recent popular account of this difference model is evident in Tannen's best-selling book, *You Just Don't Understand: Women and Men in Conversation*, in which she argues that men view the world as hierarchal so that in their conversations, they try to achieve the upper hand and not be put down; hence, in their conversation, they are often competitive. Women, on the other hand, approach the world as a network of connections so that they approach conversation as a cooperative endeavor in which they attempt to obtain intimacy.

Wodak and Benke (1997) critique most studies on gender and language use on two counts. First, they contend that frequently gender studies "have neglected the context of language behavior and have often analyzed gender by looking at the speaker's biological sex" (p. 128). They propose that instead studies of gender differences should employ a context-sensitive approach that regards gender as a social construct. In addition, they criticize the methodology of most existing studies on language and gender. They argue that a thorough investigation of language and gender necessitates a multimethod approach. They maintain that:

> Quantitative studies tend to simplify many phenomena; qualitative analyses, on the other hand, often rely on samples which are too small to draw general conclusions. Many categories are defined in a male-oriented way, male linguistic behavior is seen as unmarked, female linguistic behavior as deviating from the male norm. Most studies are undertaken in English-speaking countries, thus general explanations suffer from Anglo-European ethnocentrism. We would like to suggest a combination of methods, a multimethod... in which different aspects of the object under investigation are grasped by different quantitative and qualitative methods which complement and do not exclude each other. (p. 148)

Studies on gender variation support many of the generalizations made throughout the chapter, namely, that the use of specific linguistic features provide a mechanism for individuals to identify with a particular speech community. In addition, the attitudes that surround the use of particular features are frequently related to issues of power. For those learners who are studying English in English-speaking contexts, it is important for L2 classrooms to highlight the manner in which particular linguistic forms, such as the use of hedges and rising intonation in statements, can reduce the credibility and prestige of the speaker.

Language Variation and Ethnicity

A final important area of investigation of linguistic variation has been in reference to ethnicity. As Fishman (1997) notes, ethnicity is not an exact scientific term like "race," or "nationality," yet it has gained recent prominence. He defines it as signifying "the macro-group 'belongingness' or *identificational dimension of culture,* whether that of individuals or of aggregates per se. Ethnicity is both *narrower* than culture and more *perspectival* than culture" (p. 329). This perspectival attribute of ethnicity means that what constitutes a particular ethnicity tends to be subjective and variable.

In the United States, the most investigated relationship between language and ethnicity is that of African-American Vernacular English (AAVE). Not all African Americans speak AAVE and those who do, do not use the common features of the dialect all of the time. However, specific phonological and grammatical features tend to occur in the speech of many African Americans. For example, on a phonological level, there is often a simplification of word-final consonant clusters and stress on the first syllable rather than the second on words like *police* and *motel.* On a grammatical level, there is often an absence of the copula *is* and *are* and an absence of the third person present tense *–s.* The use of these features is often related to the gender of the speaker (males tend to use the features more frequently), the age of the speaker (younger individuals seem to use the features more frequently), the listener (the features are less frequently used with individuals of another ethnic background), and the linguistic environment of the feature (e.g., the copula deletion is more common with a pronoun subject than a noun phrase subject). (See Rickford, 1996, for a listing of various studies that document such variation.)

One debate that surrounds AAVE is the source of the dialect. Some contend that it developed from a creole, arising out of the conditions of slavery. Others maintain that AAVE is not unique because it shares many features with the speech of southern Whites in the United States (see Trudgill, 1974, for a full discussion of this debate). Another debate and one more relevant to L2 pedagogy is what is an appropriate pedagogy for speakers of AAVE. Some (e.g., Baratz, 1969; Stewart, 1969) have suggested that AAVE speakers should receive initial literacy instruction using dialect readers that include the spoken English forms of AAVE. Others (e.g., Stewart, 1964) have suggested that L2 teaching drills be used to help AAVE speakers recognize the differences between AAVE and standard American English and to acquire a standard variety. Perhaps the most reasonable alternative is that suggested by Rickford (1996) who argues that:

> The overarching need is that teachers recognize the regularity and integrity of the social dialects which children and adolescents employ in the classroom and in the schoolyard, that they appreciate the powerful attachment to such dialects which students often have— sometimes as a vital part of their social identity—and that they build on such dialects, where possible, in language arts and second language and foreign language instruction. (p. 184)

The instructional issues that arise out of AAVE are quite similar to those that surround the teaching of English in multilingual contexts in which children come to the classroom speaking a variety of English that is quite different from a standard variety of English. In such contexts, as Rickford points out, it is important for L2 teachers to recognize the regularity and integrity of these varieties and the manner in which the use of these varieties is often linked to social identity.

IMPLICATIONS FOR L2 PEDAGOGY AND RESEARCH

If we consider the four major domains of sociolinguistics delineated at the opening of the chapter, it is clear that some domains have yielded far more research that is relevant to L2 teaching and learning than others. As has been demonstrated in this chapter, in the area of Language and Society there has been a good deal of research regarding language attitudes, particularly in reference to varieties of English used by second language speakers of English. In contrast, the domain of Language and Variation has yielded far less research that is relevant to L2 teaching and learning. This is because such research typically investigates variation in English as exemplified by native speakers of English. On the other hand, as is evident from the Markee and Kasper chapters in this volume, the domain of Language and Interaction has produced a great deal of L2 research in discourse and conversational analysis as well as pragmatics. Finally, perhaps in response to the current spread of English to a great variety of social and cultural contexts, the domain of Language and Culture has recently produced a good deal of research on contrastive rhetoric (see Kaplan, this volume) as well as on the relationship between culture, identity, and language learning (see Lantolf; Ricento; and McCarty, this volume).

In closing, let me suggest three major implications of the sociolinguistic issues discussed in this chapter for L2 pedagogy and for needed L2 research. First, there is a need to recognize the social context in which many L2 learners are currently acquiring English. Because more and more learners of English will be acquiring English in multilingual contexts as one of several languages in their linguistic repertoire, more research is needed regarding how these learners make use of English in reference to the other languages they speak. Such research will be valuable in establishing classroom objectives that complement the students' use of English within their own speech community. In addition, in classrooms in multilingual contexts where teachers share a first language with their students, teachers need to carefully consider how they can best make use of their students' first language to further their competency in English.

Second, the teaching of standards should be based on sociolinguistic insights regarding language contact and language change. As was demonstrated in this chapter, language contact will inevitably result in language change. Because today many individuals are using English daily in contact with other languages, their use of English is changing, and they are in the process of establishing their own standards of English grammar and pronunciation. In general the research on these emerging varieties of English indicates that the codified and accepted standard of English that exists in these communities has few differences with other standard varieties of English. Hence, it is important for teachers to recognize the integrity and regularity of these varieties, to realize that they are important sources of personal identity, and to not promote negative attitudes toward such varieties.

Finally, L2 pedagogy should be informed by sociolinguistic research on linguistic variation. As was demonstrated earlier, the manner in which individuals use English will often vary based on geographical region, social class, gender, and ethnicity. For L2 learners who are studying English within English-speaking contexts, it is particularly important for teachers to develop materials that will raise students' awareness of such differences and to help them understand the manner in which these differences serve to indicate membership in a particular speech community. Although it is useful for students to have a receptive knowledge of linguistic variation, the productive target should in general be the variety that is the most standard and neutral variety of the community.

As was pointed out at the beginning of the chapter, many of the decisions that teachers make require sociolinguistic knowledge. In this chapter, we have focused primarily on the complexity of language use in multilingual contexts and the significance of linguistic variation for personal identity. We have done so in the belief that an understanding of these sociolinguistic concepts will contribute to teachers making informed classroom decisions regarding such important issues as the effective use of students' first language in the L2 classroom, the teaching of linguistic standards, and the promotion of linguistic attitudes that recognize the integrity of different varieties of English.

REFERENCES

Bamgbose, A. (1998). Torn between the norms: Innovations in world Englishes. *World Englishes, 17*(1), 1–14.

Baratz, J. C. (1969). Teaching reading in an urban Negro school system. In J. C. Baratz & R. W. Shuy (Eds.), *Teaching black children to read* (pp. 92–116). Washington, DC: Center for Applied Linguistics.

Bickerton, D. (1975). *Dynamics of a creole.* Cambridge, UK: Cambridge University Press.

Bickerton, D. (1984). The language bioprogram hypothesis. *Behavioral and Brain Sciences, 7*, 173–221.

Blom, J. P., & Gumperz, J. J. (1972). Social meaning in linguistic structures: Code-switching in Norway. In J. J. Gumperz & D. Hymes (Eds.), *Directions in sociolinguistics* (pp. 407–434). New York: Holt, Rinehart & Winston.

Brenzinger, M. (1997). Language contact and language displacement. In F. Coulmas (Ed.), *The handbook of sociolinguistics* (pp. 273–285). Malden, MA: Blackwell.

Brown, A. (1999). *Singapore English in a nutshell.* Singapore: Times Media.

Brutt-Griffler, J. (1998). Conceptual questions in English as a world language: Taking up an issue. *World Englishes, 17*(3), 381–392.

Butler, S. (1999). A view on standards in South-East Asia. *World Englishes, 18*(2), 187–198.

Cassidy, F. G. (1985). *Dictionary of American regional Dialects: Vol. 1. Introduction and A-C.* Cambridge, MA: Belknap.

Clyne, M. (1997). Multilingualism. In F. Coulmas (Ed.), *The handbook of sociolinguistics* (pp. 301–315). Malden, MA: Blackwell.

Coates, J. (1991). Women's cooperative talk: A new kind of conversational duet? In C. Uhlig & R. Zimmerman (Eds.), *Anglistentag 1990 Marburg proceedings* (pp. 296–311). Tübingen, Germany: Max Niemeyer.

Fasold, R. (1984). *The sociolinguistics of society.* New York: Basil Blackwell.

Ferguson, C. (1959). Diglossia. *Word, 15,* 325–340.

Fishman, J. (1972). *The sociology of language.* Rowley, MA: Newbury House.

Fishman, J. (1997). Language and ethnicity: The view from within. In F. Coulmas (Ed.), *The handbook of sociolingusitics* (pp. 327–344). Malden, MA: Blackwell.

Freeman, R., & McElhinny, B. (1996). Language gender. In S. L. McKay & N. H. Hornberger (Eds.), *Sociolinguistics and language teaching* (pp. 218–279). Cambridge, UK: Cambridge University Press.

Gopinathan, S. (1998). Language policy changes 1979–1997: Politics and pedagogy. In S. Gopinathan, A. Pakir, H. W. Kam, & V. Saravanan (Eds.), *Language, society, and education in Singapore* (pp. 19–44). Singapore: Times Academic Press.

Graddol, D. (1999). The decline of the native speaker. *AILA Review, 13,* 57–68.

Hancock, M. (1997). Behind classroom code switching: Layering and language choice in L2 learner interaction. *TESOL Quarterly, 31*(2), 217–235.

Kachru, B. B. (1986). *The alchemy of English.* Oxford, UK: Pergamon.

Kachru, B. B. (1989). Teaching world Englishes. *Indian Journal of Applied Linguistics, 15*(1), 85–95.

Kurath, J., Hanley, M. L., Bloch, B., & Lowman, G. S. (1939–1943). *Linguistic atlas of New England (Vols. 1–3).* Providence, RI: Brown University Press.

Labov, W. (1966a). *The social stratification of English in New York City.* Washington, DC: Center for Applied Linguistics.

Labov, W. (1966b). Hypercorrection by the lower middle class as a factor in sound change. In W. Bright (Ed.), *Sociolinguistics* (pp. 88–101). The Hague, The Netherlands: Mouton.

Lakoff, R. (1975). *Language and woman's place.* New York: Harper & Row.

Lick, H. C., & Alsagoff, L. (1998). Is singlish grammatical?: Two notions of grammaticality. In S. Gopinathan, A. Pakir, H. W. Kam, & V. Saravanan (Eds.), *Language, society and education in Singapore* (pp. 281–290). Singapore: Times Academic Press.

Lowenberg, P. (1986). Non-native varieties of English: Nativization, norms and implications. *Studies in Second Language Acquisition, 8,* 1–18.

McKay, S. L., & Hornberger, N. H. (Eds.). (1996). *Sociolinguistics and language teaching.* Cambridge, UK: Cambridge University Press.

Milroy, J., & Milroy, L. (1997). Varieties and variation. In F. Coulmas (Ed.), *The handbook of sociolinguistics* (pp. 47–64). Malden, MA: Blackwell.

Myers-Scotton, C. (1993). *Social motivation for codeswitching.* Oxford, UK: Clarendon.

Nichols, P. (1996). Pidgins and creoles. In S. L. McKay & N. H. Hornberger (Eds.), *Sociolinguistics and language teaching* (pp. 195–217). Cambridge, UK: Cambridge University Press.

O'Barr, W. M. (1982). *Linguistic evidence.* London: Academic Press.

Parasher, S. V. (1994). Indian English: Certain grammatical, lexical and sytlistic features. In R. K. Angihotri & A. L. Khanna (Eds.), *Second language acquisition: Socio-cultural and linguistic aspects of English in India* (pp. 145–164). New Delhi, India: Sage.

Phillipson, R. (1992). *Linguistic imperialism.* Cambridge, UK: Cambridge University Press.

Poplack, S. (1980). "Sometimes I'll start a sentence in Spanish y termino en espanol": Toward a typology of code-switching. *Linguistics, 26,* 47–104.

Quirk, R. (1990). What is standard English. In R. Quirk & G. Stein (Eds.), *English in use* (pp. 112–125). London: Longman.

Rickford, J. (1996). Regional and social variation. In S. L. McKay & N. H. Hornberger (Eds.), *Sociolinguistics and language teaching* (pp. 151–194). Cambridge, UK: Cambridge University Press.

Rickford, J., & McWhorter, J. (1997). Language contact and language generation: Pidgins and creoles. In F. Coulmas (Ed.), *The handbook of sociolinguistics* (pp. 238–257). Malden, MA: Blackwell.

Schaefer, R. P., & Egbokhare, F. O. (1999). English and the pace of endangerment in Nigeria. *World Englishes 18*(3), 381–91.

Shastri, S. V. (1996). Using computer corpora in the description of language with special reference to complementation in Indian English. In R. J. Baumgardner (Ed.), *South Asian English* (pp. 70–81). Chicago: University of Illinois Press.

Singh, R. (1996). *Lectures against sociolinguistics.* New York: Lang.

Sridhar, K. K. (1996). Societal multilingualism. In S. L. McKay & N. H. Hornberger (Eds.), *Sociolinguistics and language teaching* (pp. 47–71). Cambridge, UK: Cambridge University Press.

Sridhar, S. N., & Sridhar, K. K. (1994). Indigenized Englishes as second languages: Toward a functional theory of second language acquisition in multilingual contexts. In R. K. Agnihotri & A. L. Khanna (Eds.), *Second language acquisition: Socio-cultural and linguistic aspects of English in India* (pp. 41–63). London: Sage.

Stewart, W. A. (1964). *Foreign language teaching methods in quasi-foreign language situations.* Washington, DC: Center for Applied Linguistics.

Stewart, W. A. (1969). On the use of negro dialect in the teaching of reading. In J. C. Baratz & R. W. Shuy (Eds.), *Teaching black children to read* (pp. 156–219). Washington, DC: Center for Applied Linguistics.

Tannen, D. (1990). *You just don't understand: Women and men in conversation.* New York: Morrow.

Tay, M. (1982). The uses, users, and features of English in Singapore. In J. B. Pride (Ed.), *New Englishes* (pp. 51–72). Rowley, MA: Newbury House.

Trauth, G., & Kazzazi, K. (Eds.). (1996). *Routledge dictionary of language and linguistics.* London: Routledge.

Troemel-Ploetz, S. (1992). The construction of conversational equality by women. In K. Hall, M. Bucholtz, & B. Moonwomon (Eds.), *Locating power: Proceedings of the second Berkeley conference on women and language* (pp. 581–589). Berkeley, CA: Berkeley Women and Language Group, University of California.

Trudgill, P. (1972). Sex, covert prestige and linguistic change in the urban British English of Norwich. *Language in Society, 1,* 179–195.

Trudgill, P. (1974). *Sociolinguistics: An introduction to language use and society.* Middlesex, UK: Penguin.

Wardhaugh, R. (1992). *An introduction to sociolinguistics.* Cambridge, MA: Blackwell.

Widdowson, H. G. (1994). The ownership of English. *TESOL Quarterly, 28,* 377–388.

Wodak, R., & Benke, G. (1997). Gender as a sociolinguistic variable: New perspective on variation studies. In F. Coulmas (Ed.), *The handbook of sociolinguistics* (pp. 127–151). Malden, MA: Blackwell.

17

Language Socialization and Second Language Learning

Jane Zuengler
University of Wisconsin–Madison
KimMarie Cole
State University of New York at Fredonia

INTRODUCTION

In a recent review of language acquisition work, Roberts (1998) points out that although there have been calls for and attempts made to incorporate social and contextual issues into research in language acquisition, those elements have, in her words "a marginal role in language development" (p. 31). Roberts feels that it is not enough to simply label a context or identify features of a social setting. Instead, she argues that the social realm must be investigated as part of the way that learners are introduced to language, come to understand what it means, and learn how it can be part of their repertoire of communicative tools. She says, "Language socialisation rather than language acquisition better describes how learners come to produce and interpret discourse and how such learning is supported (or not) by assumptions of society at large about multilingualism and second language learners" (p. 31). Language socialization then becomes a useful framework for understanding the interactions that take place in classrooms and workplaces as second language learners enter into new discourse communities and gain expertise in their new languages and contexts of language use.

OVERVIEW OF FIRST LANGUAGE (L1) SOCIALIZATION RESEARCH

Language socialization is the practice by which children or novices to a community are socialized both to the language forms and, through language, to adopt the values, behaviors, and practices of that community (Schieffelin & Ochs, 1986). This central premise of language socialization is cited in almost all of the work that uses the framework, and often in these very terms, "socialization through the use of language and socialization to use language" (p. 163). This simple phrase works as a kind of theoretical shorthand, allowing those who use this perspective to succinctly express the value of this work in almost "sound bite" fashion. The lexical simplicity belies, however, the depth and breadth of what language socialization attempts to account for. As Ochs (1988) explains, "participants in verbal activities/practices draw on linguistic and sociocultural knowledge to create and define what is taking place. On the other hand, these verbal activities/practices are means through which aspects of linguistic and sociocultural knowledge are created and/or maintained" (p. 128). Ely and Berko Gleason (1996), in a review of language socialization in Western society, echo the need for a sociocultural or constructivist view in studying the ways that children learn language. This perspective embeds language and its use in the midst of social activities, offers important insights into the links between local moments of interaction and the broader "cultural" events in which this language use is situated, and provides a way to consider how *talk* works both as a method and a means to communicate and transmit the activities, values, and beliefs of a group.

Research into language socialization within applied linguistics has most often been used in the study of young children with their primary caregivers (see Schieffelin & Ochs, 1986a), where the traits and values of a given cultural group are described through the social practices participants engage in. These studies have looked at a variety of language features and contexts of use to develop an understanding of differences in socialization practices in different cultures. Ochs (1986), in her introduction to the volume, describes how the different studies work to demonstrate three different aspects of language socialization: the use of interactional routines; the role of language in helping children develop awareness of status, and how emotional language is appropriately used.

The insights made available by adopting a language socialization framework extend beyond the initial, domestic setting to "secondary" socialization settings as well, because the symbolic and tool-like features of language, which are the object of analysis in socialization work, are also used in the creation and maintenance of institutional social structures. Many of the studies that consider the language socialization of children in secondary settings have demonstrated the difficulties that some children have when home socialization is in conflict with the new expectations of school. (See, e.g., Delpit, 1995; Heath, 1983; Phillips, 1983.)

In some ways, this research highlights the usefulness of a language socialization perspective in uncovering the range of values and practices that can coexist within communities and highlighting how they inform us about differences in the ways that people gain expertise as they move through different communities. These studies also set the stage for recent research that has examined the language socialization practices for second language learners in schools and in the workplace. Understanding that language socialization is not only an experience of childhood opens the door to investigations of novices of different ages in a variety of settings as they are apprenticed to different facets of community membership. As Ochs (1988) reminds us, "socialization is a lifespan experience ... Throughout our lives, we are socializing and being socialized by those we encounter (including by our own children)" (p. 6). It is perhaps logical then that researchers would turn their attention to other questions of language socialization.

RESEARCH ON SECOND LANGUAGE (L2) SOCIALIZATION

The recognition that language socialization extends through one's life (Ochs, 1988; see also Bayley & Schecter, 2003) underscores the importance of understanding the processes that children, adolescents, and adults experience in settings outside the home, in places such as the school, the community, and the workplace.

Increasingly in the world, such settings are linguistically and culturally hetero-geneous, involving multi-or bilingualism, and for many, the acquisition of a second language.[1] In the review that follows, we draw from this more recent area of research to discuss, in particular, published studies that explicitly foreground the language social-ization framework in second language learning—that is, that they position themselves as L2 socialization research. In so doing, we focus this chapter on research in which the participants are neither monolingual nor proficient bilinguals, but who, implicitly or explicitly, are still in the process of acquiring a second language. However, this is not to imply that language socialization studies involving continuing acquisition can be easily distinguished from studies of proficient bi- or multilingual use. It is primarily a matter of degree as well as of representation. Drawing the boundary between one and the other focus of study proved to be a challenging and ultimately subjective decision in our effort to determine what work was relevant for review under the chapter theme, and what was not. As such, we recognize that other authors may draw the boundary differently.

Using our criteria of selection, we found 17 studies for discussion, the overwhelm-ing majority of which (i.e., 15) concern L2 socialization in educational settings. The other two are of workplace L2 socialization. In the review that follows, we will first con-sider the studies set in educational contexts, followed by the two studies of language socialization in the workplace. To the extent possible, findings will be summarized within and across sections of studies, highlighting outcomes of correspondence or contrast. It must be recognized, though, that language socialization theory considers the distinctive context and setting crucial for interpreting research findings, and much of this work has been ethnographic. That implies that comparisons across studies of differing contexts are potentially problematic. However, because all of the research is similar to some extent—that is, in having L2 in their settings, we offer cautious summaries that should illuminate both similarities and differences in focus, as well as findings regarding L2 socialization. In a final section of the chapter, we discuss issues that have been raised about language socialization in this literature; through-out the discussion, we offer recommendations for the direction of future research on L2 socialization.

SECOND LANGUAGE SOCIALIZATION IN EDUCATIONAL SETTINGS

It is perhaps not surprising that the large majority of studies of language socialization and second language learning, which we will review here, have examined the process in educational settings. It is well acknowledged that after the primary socialization of home and family, it is educational institutions that for many represent the major domain of "secondary" socialization. We organize the discussion of research following its educational age range, starting with a study of kindergartners and ending with one involving graduate students.

L2 Socialization in Kindergarten and Elementary/Primary School

Four of the five studies discussed in this section address elementary or primary school students, whereas only one focuses on children in kindergarten. There are a variety of L2s considered across a diverse range of educational settings. These studies examine, with a close or broader research lens, the language socialization dynamics in the class-room interactions between teachers and learners. In two of the studies, the classroom socialization is contrasted with the language socialization process as it takes place in the home or community.

The sole study of language socialization of L2 kindergartners, Kanagy's (1999) research followed a class of American English-speaking kindergartners through 1 year as they were beginning Japanese as a foreign language through enrollment in a Japanese immersion school. Kanagy chose three classroom routines to study in examining the children's socialization toward "L2 interactional competence." In choosing interactional routines, Kanagy joins five other studies to be reviewed, namely, Ohta (1999), Poole, (1992), Rymes (1997), Watson-Gegeo (1992), and Willett (1995). Similar to L1 socialization research, interactional routines serve as a rich site for L2 socialization. Routines are repetitive, with predictable behavior, and can serve as good locations for observing how socialization takes place (Kanagy, 1999). Given their predictability, learners are able to participate almost from the beginning. Researchers can document learners' development over time, because routines have relatively fixed patterns of participation and they frequently reoccur (Willett, 1995).

Employing an ethnographic method, Kanagy studied three routines over the course of the school year, what she called "greeting," "attendance," and "personal introduction." The children began by imitating what the teacher modeled and repeating in chorus, with more spontaneous performance emerging as time went on, displaying socialization "into interactional competence beyond their initial L2 ability" in Japanese (Kanagy, 1999, p. 1489). Kanagy points out, however, that the children did not appear to show L2 development in other respects such as word use. That they remained at the one-word level in their L2 Japanese is not necessarily a problem, according to Kanagy, as a single word is often appropriate in Japanese discourse (or for that matter, in other languages).

Socialization into interactional routines is not always successful or unproblematic, however. Willett (1995), one of four studies examining socialization at the elementary/primary school level, reports that for at least one of the children studied, his efforts to reshape or resist some aspects of classroom socialization led to his being negatively positioned, as (problematically) dependent, needy of more L2 instruction than others. Willett offers a case study of four English As a Second Language (ESL) learners in a mainstream U.S. first-grade class, focusing on routines and strategies. Taking a more general approach than Kanagy (who identified and named three interactional routines), Willett considered the learners' participation roles, their identities, and the ideologies that emerged in the classroom interactions, emphasizing with the last that social and political dynamics outside the classroom affect interactions within. Willett argues that children do not simply absorb knowledge and skills. They are agentive, because language socialization is a reciprocal, not an unilateral, process. Three of the focal students, all girls, appeared to develop strategies—for example, working together quietly at the back of the room—that rather than marginalizing them, led to their being considered positively by both teachers and other girls. (Whether remaining quietly at the back is ideologically and pedagogically unproblematic is outside the scope of this review; Willett does address this briefly.) For the one boy studied, socialization proved more immediately problematic. Although he appeared to have status with the other boys, the teachers constructed him as difficult and in need. Deciding that he required special ESL help, teachers arranged for him to leave the class for assistance. Because this meant he would be separated from the other boys, "Xavier" resisted the decision, but the more he did, the more the teachers saw his behavior as illustrative of his problems. Willett's study underscores that the complexity and reciprocity of socialization can lead to very different experiences for children in the same classroom. Willett makes the point that classroom communities are complex; individuals have multiple memberships whose agendas may be in conflict.

In her study of four classrooms in which children ages 4½ to 9 were learning Chinese as their heritage language, He (2003) echoes Willett to some extent in emphasizing that socialization requires collaboration and cooperation by the participants. Though she does not refer to resistance, as does Willett, He reminds the reader that confusion and differing expectations can occur in the process of socialization. He draws on Goffman (1981) in examining participation structures, which includes consideration of how and what interactional statuses are constructed, whether participants' contributions are ratified or not, and the coconstruction of hearer and speaker roles. In contrast to other language socialization studies (e.g., Willett, 1995; Kanagy, 1999) that take an ethnographic and/or longitudinal look at development over the school year, He undertakes a very close analysis of some classroom discourse, looking at "micro-interactional details." The data reveal how, in the socialization process, the teacher sometimes appropriates the students' contributions, preventing them from taking authorship. And on occasion, the teacher ignores what students say as a means of disciplining them. The common participation pattern constructed is one "in which the teacher makes sure that classroom interaction remains between two parties: the teacher and the class" (p. 12). Considering these findings, He questions whether the socialization patterns observed are a *cultural* dynamic in this Chinese heritage language classroom, or whether they are instead a *classroom* phenomenon. Given the lack of studies with data for comparison, He concludes that this cannot be answered.

The next two, elementary/primary level studies, use a broader lens than the preceding studies in considering whether and how L2 classroom socialization practices conflict with learners' home/community socialization in their L1. Watson-Gegeo's (1992) study is drawn from longitudinal, ethnographic research she conducted to address why Kwara'ae children in the Solomon Islands have had problems with achievement in L2 English-medium schools. Concentrated study of several families' L1 socialization practices revealed similarities with what is known about American middle-class caregiver interactions. That is, Kwara'ae adults often instructed their children orally, directly teaching certain skills, and actively, energetically drawing the children into interactional routines adjusted to their level of development. The L2 classroom discourse practices, however, were sites of difference and tension. In the language arts classes, practices appeared very formulaic, with unnatural, decontextualized English used to make a grammar or vocabulary point. Themes and topics were often alien to the children (e.g., "Ken is playing with ice cream" [p. 60] read to children who have not ever had ice cream). Though the children had developed strategies for memorizing and repeating the material, their engagement was superficial and comprehension questionable. An additional problem was the teacher's inadequate L2 proficiency due to insufficient language training. Such problematic L2 socialization practices for children who are used to stimulating L1 practices are a function of macrolevel forces, Watson-Gegeo argues, serving to reproduce the social order, ensuring that the rural poor, in particular, will remain so.

Documenting similar problems, Moore (1999) conducted an ethnographic study of L2 French classroom practices in the primary educational system in Cameroon. Moore was concerned to discover why many children leave school after attending for only several years. A great contrast existed between the home and community language norms and those of the L2 French-medium primary school classes. For example, although multilingualism and code-switching were supported and common outside of school, such language use was proscribed (and in fact, punished) within the classroom. Only French was permitted. Moore learned that the teacher imposed the French-only rule because he did not share any other language with the students and was afraid of losing classroom control otherwise. Another home–school conflict concerned expected and accepted interlocutors. In the community, children were expected to primarily interact with each other rather than with adults, whereas in the classroom, they were prohibited from speaking to each other. Like Watson-Gegeo (1992), Moore found that school practices involved heavy emphasis on form-focused, decontextualized, and unnatural L2 use. Unlike Watson-Gegeo, Moore does not point to social and political forces influencing school practice, but implies that a failure to understand the "communicative competencies" that students have already been socialized into in their communities can lead to classroom practices that not only fail to ratify the skills they possess but are obstructive to students' language socialization into the L2.

What emerges in four of these five studies is a profile of classroom language socialization as potentially problematic, tension producing, and unsuccessful. Students and teacher may have different and contrasting expectations (He); classroom practices may ignore or contradict students' home socialization (Watson-Gegeo, Moore); the method of socialization may be unengaging (Moore); or the teacher might not have the necessary competence to be viewed as an expert guide (Watson-Gegeo). Moreover, outcomes of socialization can differ from child to child in the same classroom (Willett).

At the same time, some of these studies argue that learners have agency in the socialization process. As the Willet and He research makes clear, socialization is a cooperative, reciprocal, and complex process. Learners can reshape, or resist, the socialization. Although the kindergarteners in Kanagy appeared to imitate and repeat in a one-way process directed by their teacher, other studies document learners more actively involved in coconstructing (or resisting) their socialization.

L2 Socialization in Secondary/High School

The reciprocity of socialization and agentive role of novices is even more salient in the research done at the high school level. Though the specific items of investigation or the units of analysis in these socialization studies differ—routines, in Rymes'1997 study; changing practices in Duff's 1996 research; varying participation in Duff and Early (1999) and Duff (2002); and representations of the immigrant students in Harklau (2003)—almost all of them consider societal dynamics and beliefs as infusing the local socialization processes in the classroom. Of the five studies to be reviewed, four examine North American settings, whereas one is conducted in Hungary. Duff, arguably the most prominent researcher in the area of second language socialization, has authored or coauthored three of the studies.

Duff's 1996 study in Hungary investigated how classroom discourse socialization changed—in L2 as well as L1—as a result of changes that the education system and the larger society underwent as they entered the post-Communist era. Duff conducted an ethnographic study of discourse practices in dual-language (Hungarian–English) schools that were in the process of moving away from traditional educational practices such as the *felelés*, a common, rather formal oral recitation by individual students that served as a means of knowledge assessment that also enforced conformity and discipline. Newer practices were implemented that engendered a more shared discourse, including small group work and discussions. Duff found that although the direction of change was consistent—newer practices were emerging in both the Hungarian-medium and English-medium classes, the role of the *felelés* was diminishing across the curriculum—one model of discourse socialization did not simply, entirely replace another. Instead, Duff found variation in the relationships between traditional and new practices; even in classrooms where the *felelés* had officially been discarded, it appeared in other activities such as lectures. Perhaps in tandem with the larger society, there was, in the classes observed, "a slipping and sliding along a continuum from highly controlled to more democratically distributed leadership and discourse" (p. 430). This was the case for the L1 Hungarian practices as well as those in the L2 English-medium classrooms.

Shifting to study of ESL students in mainstream classes in a Canadian high school, Duff and Early (1999) report research on how *perspective-taking* is socialized in English literature and social studies classes. In a classroom where the taking of multiple perspectives and supporting one's assertions were encouraged and supported, some students in each class engaged in active participation whereas many, on the other hand, remained on the periphery. The authors report that the ESL students remained largely silent, explaining that some of them chose not to participate in the style of argument that was being socialized, affiliating instead with their silent peers. However, the situation could not simply be explained as more complete socialization by the active participants and insufficient socialization for the silent ones (the ESL learners) who would remain "novices" on the margins. Duff and Early argue for a more complex interpretation, pointing out that the active participants did not necessarily display competence in the kind of supported reasoning or type of argumentation that were the intended goals. And though the ESL students may not have participated in the discussion, they could not simply be judged less competent, because many displayed academic success in their high achievement on tests, grade point averages, etc.

The difficulty of applying labels of "expert" and "novice" led Duff and Early to ask, "Who, then was socializing whom, and into what?" (p. 29). The authors conclude that language socialization is often a fluid, negotiated goal, rather than the officially stated and static goals of the curriculum. Moreover, for the culturally and linguistically diverse classes of their study, there appeared to be multiple, rather than just one classroom community.

Another study of ESL students in Canadian mainstream high school classes is Duff's (2002) examination of interactional participation in social studies discussions in which the teacher endeavors to construct respect for cultural difference. Using language socialization theory in conducting an ethnography of communication, Duff considers turn-taking and other manifestations of participation in classroom discussions of cultural difference. What she found is that although the ESL students, all of whom were ethnically Chinese, were not entirely silent, their contributions tended to be shorter, more cautious, and less audible than the turns taken by the "local" students (i.e., those who had been in Canada longer, some of whom were native English speakers). The ESL students did not offer much information to the others about themselves or their cultural allegiance; in fact, on some occasions, the local students were heard to speak for them when the teacher encouraged discussion of Chinese culture. Duff learned of multiple reasons for their reticence, due not simply to second language limitations, but including students' prior socialization, their discomfort at attention being directed to them, and their perceptions of outsiders and insiders.

The ESL students' relative silence was received negatively by the other students, who interpreted their behavior as showing a lack of interest or agency. Yet, these ESL students exhibited high academic achievement in other respects (as also reported in Duff & Early, 1999). Duff again raises the question of how to interpret variable participation in socialization practices, and relatedly, who the competent and the less competent are in these classrooms.

Harklau (2003) echoes Duff in asserting that socialization goals or targets must be recognized as fluid, multiple, and negotiable. In such a poststructural view, learners have agency, and the local and macro levels have a two-way relationship. Focusing on four L2 students in a case study within a larger ethnography, Harklau examines two aspects of socialization: how the immigrant students are represented in the classroom discourse and how students are socialized into the kind of multimodal language use that is common in high schools—that is, not just the face-to-face interaction that much of the language socialization research has focused on, but the multiple modes of writing, listening, and speaking that are required of students. Harklau found three representations of immigration to predominate in the classroom. One she referred to as a "colorblind" representation, in which ethnicity was discussed as a theory rather than with regard to the specific identities and backgrounds of the actual students in the class. A second and competing representation was a romanticized notion of immigration that Harklau calls the "Ellis Island" representation, whereas a third foregrounded the immigrant students as linguistically and perhaps cognitively challenged. As Harklau clarifies, all three representations circulate in the larger U.S. society's discourses about immigration and issues of multilingualism.

When Harklau considered the multiple modes of discourse, she found that there were often several representations constructed simultaneously, for example, the "colorblind" representation in face-to-face interactions but an "Ellis Island" representation encouraged in students' written work. It is necessary, Harklau concludes, to recognize that socialization is often complex not just with regard to language mode, but to the multiple and possibly conflicting messages that it conveys.

Although her study is also set in a U.S. high school, Rymes' (1997) is distinctive in its analysis of socialization routines in which L2 Spanish is used. However, it joins other studies (e.g., Duff, 2002; Duff & Early, 1999; Moore, 1999; Watson-Gegeo, 1992; Willett, 1995) in revealing how socialization processes can in fact have negative ramifications for second language use. Rymes takes a language socialization approach to illustrate how, in two conversations, routines conducted between native and non-native speakers of Spanish socialize negative attitudes about Spanish use. One conversation involves students talking to each other, whereas in the second, L1 Spanish-speaking students interact with school security guards who are L2 learners of Spanish. In each of the short interactions reported, the use of Spanish by the L1 Spanish-speaking students is turned into a metalinguistic/pedagogical focus by the L2 learners who ask for a translation of a Spanish word, or ask the L1 Spanish speakers to confirm something they have said in Spanish. Rymes describes the L2 learners' use of Spanish with the L1 Spanish speakers as primarily a display of their knowledge (rather than revealing an interest in communicating), with the result that the communicative potential of Spanish is undermined and, she argues, the L1 Spanish speakers are inhibited from further first-language use. In turn, the L2 learners have limited use of their Spanish.

Though different in orientation, the five studies just discussed are similar to the primary level studies by Watson-Gegeo (1992) and Moore (1999) in the ways they reveal how socialization in educational institutions is related to—or exists in tension with—values and beliefs outside the school, whether in the home, community, or society at large. Studies of L2 socialization are important sites for discoveries about the complex ways that identities and social setting influence and are influenced by language use and development. The likely endpoint of socialization is necessarily called into question when the L2 target of socialization is constructed as a denigrated variety (Rymes), or when the learners are constructed as immigrants in conflicting ways that represent societal rather than their own beliefs about themselves (Harklau).

These high school studies also add more evidence for a complex view of the socialization process. The very notion of an endpoint for socialization, for example, which is often assumed in L1 language socialization research, cannot be taken for granted. And in Duff and Early (1999), we discover that the socialization that the teacher intends can be different from the actual socialization that unfolds. In a focus different from the primary level studies, several of the high school studies seek to understand variable participation (i.e., Duff, 2002; Duff & Early, 1999), pointing out, for example, that the central participants in language socialization are not necessarily those whom the community would consider the most competent, whereas the more competent are actually those choosing to remain on the margins.

L2 Socialization at Post-Secondary Level

The five studies that are discussed in this section are similar in considering university or college students, but are quite heterogeneous with regard to geographical context, including Japan, Canada, the United States, and India. These differences continue to add richness to our understanding of the ways that language socialization can explain L2 development.

In focusing on two classes of ESL beginners in a U.S. university, Poole (1992) studied classroom routines to discover how they convey culture. At the same time, Poole emphasized (like Willett, 1995, among others) that cultural conveyance through socialization is not deterministic and that students, therefore, have the ability to reshape or resist the process. However, in this study, Poole primarily focused on the teacher's talk. Poole found accommodation toward the students, mitigation of the status imbalance between teacher and students, etc., which leads her to conclude that the classroom socialization process is similar to that found by Ochs for American middle-class caregivers and young children in their primary language socialization. In both cases, cultural information is being conveyed.

The next three studies, in focusing specifically on the socialization of pragmatic elements in the L2, examine language socialization within a narrower scope than the preceding studies. Yoshimi (1999) investigated the possible role of L1 (English) socialization in the pragmatic production of L2 learners of Japanese. The specific pragmatic element studied was the interactional use of *ne*, which conveys empathy and the "sharedness" of knowledge between the interlocutors. Employing a method quite different from the previously reviewed studies, Yoshimi conducted a qualitative discourse analysis of talk in quasi-experimental-like pairs created for the study.[2] Five L1 American English-speaking learners of Japanese in Japan were each paired with an L1 Japanese-speaking acquaintance and asked to have several conversations. The analysis specifically focused on the learners' nontargetlike (i.e., errorful) use of *ne*, to determine whether the learners' use reflected their L1-socialized assumptions about shared knowledge. The findings revealed that the majority of the learners' use of *ne* was considered appropriate in the L2. However, Yoshimi argues that the one third who were judged to be nontargetlike were reflective of L1 socialization to some extent. Yoshimi concludes with a call for examining L2 practices with a view to L1 socialization as a potential influence.

Matsumura (2001) looked at the socialization of L2 pragmatics by L1 Japanese learners of English, comparing one group of university students who were in Canada as L2 English learners and another group who remained in Japan learning English as a foreign language. Matsumura's is the only study of those reviewed that was quasi-experimental with quantitative analysis of language socialization effects.[3] Matsumura sought to determine, among the 340 participants, whether the L2 group in Canada showed more evidence of L2 socialization compared to the group remaining in Japan. This study looked at targetlike perceptions of social status and whether there was a corresponding growth in their ability to appropriately give advice to interlocutors of various statuses. Outcomes revealed that whereas the group in Japan only showed appropriate advice-giving language in English when hypothetically interacting with higher status persons, the students in Canada were more targetlike both in recognizing social status and in conveying advice appropriately to all three relative statuses. Matsumura concluded that their stay in Canada clearly socialized the learners toward more pragmatically targetlike use of English with respect to both perception of status and advice-giving.

Another study that looks at the socialization into L2 pragmatic use by university students is Ohta's (1999) research on a native-English-speaking learner over the course of a year in a Japanese as a foreign language class in the United States. Ohta focused on the learner's development in her ability to express conversational alignment via language socialization into two classroom routines—the initiation–response–feedback/follow-up (IRF) or initiation–response–equation (IRE; see Mehan, 1979; Sinclair & Coulthard, 1975) and a routine Ohta called "extended assessment activity." Ohta reports that the learner displayed, through her participation in the routines with the teacher and with her peers, a gradual linear increase in her ability to offer assessments and use other kinds of follow-up expressions in a targetlike manner in the foreign language. Such a smooth path certainly stands in contrast to the rather rocky road of socialization as unearthed in Duff (2002), Moore (1999), and the final study under review.

Atkinson (2003) is an ethnography of the language socialization of students at an English-medium college in southern India. The study reveals the effects of the formerly elite school's opening up to a broader cross-section of students, including those of Tamil rather than English-speaking backgrounds. Although the school has become more accessible to these students, the college's socialization process enforces norms that marginalize them, maintaining the centrality of the elite background "traditional" students. Coining the term "dys-socialization," Atkinson documents how instead of being successfully socialized into L2 English, the "nontraditional" students are, in fact, socialized toward feelings of inferiority and identitities as "non-English learners." The socialization serves as an *anti*-acquisitional process for L2 English and, at the same time, denigrates the students' Tamil language and culture. The result is a low degree of academic achievement by the "nontraditional" learners.

This set of studies of post-secondary learners builds on some of the previously discussed findings of research on L2 language socialization. The denigration of students' culture in their L1 that Atkinson documented echoes what Watson-Gegeos (1992) and Moore (1999) found in their studies. Perhaps due to their orientation, the other post-secondary studies do not portray problematic L2 language socialization processes. Yoshimi's, like Atkinson's, shares a connection to both Watson-Gegeo's (1992) and Moore's (1999) studies in his consideration of the impact of students' L1 socialization on their L2 socialization. Like Kanagy (1999), Ohta studied the acquisition of several routines in the L2 classroom, and like Kanagy, found that the routines were indeed successfully socialized. The two remaining post-secondary studies are to some extent distinctive from the others previously discussed—that is, Poole's research, in contrast to the others, focuses primarily on the teacher's discourse in socialization. And Matsumura's study was not only distinctive in using quantitative, quasi-experimental methodology, but in comparing an L1 with an L2 setting for socialization of L2.

LANGUAGE SOCIALIZATION IN THE WORKPLACE

Though there are a number of studies of language in the workplace (and especially of L1 use; see, e.g., Candlin & Candlin, 2002; Drew & Heritage, 1992; Katz, 2001, a study of L2 use; and Sarangi & Roberts, 1999), very few workplace-oriented studies have invoked language socialization as their primary theoretical framework. Two studies that adopt this framework are set in the United States and Canada. Each reports on the process by which L2 speakers, whether or not they received prior L2 language socialization, undergo informal language socialization on the job.

Li's (2000) ethnographic research reports an 18-month case study of a Chinese-speaking woman, "Ming," working in a filing department at a U.S. medical equipment company. Immigrants who are beginning a new job experience are experiencing what Li refers to as "double" socialization; besides being novices in their work environment, they are novices to the culture of the larger society. Additionally, there are several kinds of socialization that are germane to workplaces; citing Scollon and Scollon (1995), Li mentions the "formal" socialization of employment training, followed by the employee's more informal socialization through observation of others and their advice to the newcomer. It is the latter, informal socialization, which Li's study focuses on, in particular, Ming's socialization with regard to her L2 pragmatic development in making more targetlike *requests*.

Li documents Ming's growth in L2 competence toward more directness in requests, guided by watching how her colleagues interacted as well as by receiving explicit suggestions from them (e.g., "If you feel there is something, talk!" [p. 73]). Rather than simply following her colleagues' conduct, however, Ming made choices in her socialization. Faced with several American coworkers who Ming and several other non-native speakers felt were acting rudely to them (e.g., throwing rather than handing them items and using swear words when addressing them), Ming is reported to have helped organize a meeting with the coworkers and their boss, where she requested better treatment. After that, Ming enforced what she considered more polite behavior for her American colleagues; for example, if they continued to throw paper her way, she would respond, "Could you please, give me, you know, in the polite way? I don't think it's nice to do this" (p. 74). Ming's socialization experiences reveal not only that people have choices and can exhibit agency in the process, but can sometimes become the "experts" themselves.

In the second study of L2 socialization in the workplace, Duff, Wong, and Early (2000) followed 20 non-native English-speaking immigrants (primarily women) who were training to be healthcare aides in Canadian nursing homes, private homes, and hospitals. The trainees had completed their ESL and nursing preparation and were going into a first and then a second practicum experience. The researchers' primary orientation was on the trainees' informal, practicum-situated socialization experiences.

The two practica turned out to be very different sites of socialization. The trainees' first practicum took them to a city hospital where almost all of the residents were speakers of a Chinese dialect rather than of English. Though some were Chinese-speaking, none of the trainees spoke the dialect of the residents, and as a result, communication became very challenging. Trainees were surprised to discover that their nursing and medical English training were less important resources than the ability, urgently needed, to develop a means of communication with their patients. Throughout their practicum, trainees struggled to find ways of accommodating, by learning some words in the patients' language, and in many cases observing body language cues and using gestures.

Their second practicum, at a suburban residential facility in which residents were described as being financially comfortable, White English speakers, was one in which the trainees reported much more satisfaction. Rather than feeling that they primarily had to accommodate to the patients, they experienced more reciprocity of adjustment—a blurring, in socialization terms, of the functions of "experts" and "novices." Trainees were very positive about how much English they learned and practiced. Patients offered explicit advice on how to talk—what speech acts were appropriate, etc.—and trainees also took the opportunity to ask patients the meanings of words and unfamiliar expressions.

Each of these studies indicates that socialization occurs, often informally, in the workplace, and that job training does not necessarily provide sufficient, or relevant, socialization. Socialization on the job can take different shapes, and often, there are no clear or predicable expert–novice roles. In the Li (2000) study, Ming showed that she had agency, and, in fact, became the expert in socializing her L1 colleagues into what she considered appropriate workplace behavior. In the Duff et al. (2000) study, the L2 speakers encountered very different socialization experiences in each of their two employment sites. Discovering that many of the patients whom they needed to care for at the hospital were not English speakers, the L2-speaking caregivers made efforts to accommodate the patients. In this experience, neither was expert, but both were novices. At the nursing home, the patients were English-speaking; what developed was a reciprocal socialization. Although the caregivers' responsibilities were to care for the patients, the patients in turn helped the caregivers improve their English. Here, each was guided in some way by the other.

ISSUES IN AND FUTURE DIRECTIONS FOR RESEARCH ON L2 SOCIALIZATION

Recently, language socialization theory has received strong support in the field of applied linguistics. In a plenary talk at the Pacific Second Language Research Forum in 2001, Karen Watson-Gegeo argued that language socialization should become one of the major paradigms for research on second language acquisition, replacing the traditional cognitive-oriented models (see also Watson-Gegeo & Nielsen, 2003). And within the specific area of interlanguage pragmatics, Kasper (2001) considers language socialization to be one of four major approaches. Because language socialization concerns itself with natural, appropriate language use, Kasper finds the approach "eminently capable of examining how L2 pragmatic ability is acquired" (p. 519). And several of the L2 socialization studies we have reviewed, namely, Yoshimi (1999), Matsumura (2001), and Ohta (1999), focus on L2 pragmatic development. However, Schieffelin and Ochs (1986a) may disagree with Kasper, because they state that language socialization is concerned with a different (i.e., broader) scope of explanation than is interlanguage pragmatics.

Although the studies summarized in this chapter focus on different populations and arrive at somewhat different findings, they share a common feature in that they all draw on a language socialization perspective to frame their studies. This wealth of information leads us to pick up questions that have been asked before of language socialization work. The first is: what methodology or methodologies can best illuminate the "socialization to and socialization through language" that the researchers hope to account for? Turning back to Schieffelin and Ochs (1986a; 1986b), the answer is, at least in part, ethnography. In their discussions and Watson-Gegeo and Nielsen's (2003) more recent exploration of methodology, the authors point to the need for research tools that allow a consideration of both micro and macro structures in the research. (In fact, the issue of macro–micro is germane to the field of applied linguistics as a whole; see Pennycook, 2001.)[4] From a language socialization perspective, close investigation of actual talk and interaction is needed to see the socialization process in action. And, because larger cultural dynamics shape what is socialized and what it means within the community, there must be a way to account for the larger structures as well. van Lier (1996), using visual representation, emphasizes the multiple, interconnected layers of societal and institutional forces that can influence interaction in the classroom, and as the research we have reviewed here demonstrates, a variety of forces come into play in the discussions of language socialization in the schools. And certainly, a similar construct is also relevant for the workplace studies. Many of the researchers whose studies we have discussed do seem to address, in some way or another, these small and large (for lack of a better term) issues in their work.

Before declaring ethnography the sole way to conduct these studies, however, it is important to consider how one defines "micro" and "macro" and where one believes they can be located. As such, this becomes an epistemological question. Therefore, we must be careful about automatically dismissing research that does not include the kind of macro–micro linking as defined within ethnographic traditions. In fact, in mentioning a macro *and* a micro *link* or *connection between* them (e.g., Watson-Gegeo & Nielsen, 2003), one is assuming that they are separable components. There is, certainly, microanalytic research through which, it is argued, one can see the macro. Most notable is that of Conversational Analysis (CA), and in particular, the approach referred to as "applied CA" (Heap, 1997). One of the most prominent researchers using this approach, Kitzinger (e.g., Frith & Kitzinger, 1998; Kitzinger, 2000a, 2000b; Kitzinger & Frith, 1999), who does feminist/lesbian CA, argues that where "the political" is found is in the unfolding of mundane conversations. Similarly, He, whose study we discussed earlier, does not use longitudinal or large-scale ethnographic tools in her work, instead drawing on literature and a perspective that indicates that for any "macro" features to be relevant, they must be evident in the local interactions.

The language socialization work we present in this review offers important insights about language use and the socialization process. We recognize, along with Schieffelin and Ochs (1986a), the rationale for looking at both small and larger moments of cultural practice. Rather than calling for one research methodology and imposing a singular framework, though, we suggest instead that researchers must account for how they are addressing both aspects in their work. In so doing, their epistemological positions and corresponding assumptions about language learning and use will be made more transparent and accessible to critical consideration and may continue to expand our understanding of language socialization and its applications. Although we acknowledge, as Watson-Gegeo and Nielsen (2003) do, the difficulty in reporting qualitative findings within the structural limitations of journal articles, we still encourage authors to highlight the ways that their work can account for the entire socialization process and contribute to discussions of their epistemological positions in arriving at their conclusions.

A second issue to bring to a consideration of language socialization in L2 learning is a critique raised in several recent papers by Roberts (1998; 1999), namely, the question of whether the theory sufficiently accounts for power, ideologies, and positioning in the socialization process. As Roberts (1998) points out, understanding language to be social practice (as language socialization does) is a recognition that "practices" are not simply activities:

> In the case of literacy practices for example, they [literacy practices] include both the literacy event and the knowledge and assumptions about what this event is and what gives it meaning. For example, what counts as literacy in a subgroup is determined by those in dominant positions in a society. Literacy practices, therefore, are profoundly associated with identity and social position. (p. 36)

The critical linguistic literature has also argued that practices come with ideologies (Roberts, 1998, cites Fairclough, 1992; see also Gee, 1996, 1999, on "Discourses"). However, Roberts (1998; 1999) argues, early language socialization theory has not sufficiently accounted for the complex dynamics at play when people encounter, reshape, resist, etc, ideologies and take (and are given) certain positions within the interactions. The extension of language socialization to studying L2/minority language speakers, who, having already gone through primary language socialization, are now in complex, second language institutional settings such as education and the workplace, requires more problematizing of the process.

The issue of the recognition of power and ideology, as raised by Roberts, is without question a significant one for the theory to address. Several of the studies reviewed here, in fact, have in drawing on language socialization, foregrounded dynamics of power, ideology, identity, and positioning in the research they report (e.g., Atkinson, 2003; Duff, 2002; Duff & Early, 1999; Harklau, 2003; Rymes, 1997; Watson-Gegeo, 1992; Willett, 1995). Their results raise questions about power and ideology as well as show how these issues come into play even in defining the communities to which learners are being socialized. Language socialization is a framework that allows for these kinds of questions to be posed, considered, and deliberated alongside concerns with language forms and targetlike development. Because of the richness of this perspective, we encourage those who adopt this perspective to follow this lead in future research on language socialization and L2 learning. These concerns will undoubtedly cause researchers to question fundamental concepts of past language socialization work, as many of these studies have done. The questions and their answers will allow language socialization to become a more flexible tool for the study of second language development.

There is a third important issue that current language socialization research must consider. When research on language socialization focuses on children learning the practices, values, and beliefs of their homes, there are some questions that may not be posed because they are not relevant in those settings. When, however, the scope of this research is extended into institutional settings or to the socialization of multilinguals, these questions arise and provide a test for the explanatory power of language socialization. Roberts (1998), for example, questions to what extent the apprenticeship aspect of the language socialization model applies to workplace settings, because she has found that it is not possible for many immigrant workers to get into the interactions that lead to full membership in those communities. Without access to experts who engage learners in an extensive range of interactions in the second language, their language development will likely be limited as well. Such settings may be even more complex. This was documented in the Chinese-speaking hospital practicum for the ESL trainees in Duff et al. (2000). Duff et al., in fact, predict that shortly, such multilingual/multicultural workplace settings will be the norm rather than the exception.

Relatedly, we must question the assumption of a presumed end point of language socialization. In some cases, there may be multiple communities that are the targets of socialization or communities that discourage learners from seeking full membership. An additional concern is the assumption of neatly bounded categories of "expert" and "novice." As this group of studies demonstrated, these questions do not exist only for adults, but for the ways in which young "novices" contribute to and shape the socialization experience of those around them as well.

As it has been presented by Schieffelin and Ochs (1986a), language socialization certainly leaves room for these considerations. That is, members of a community are in fact socialized to different roles and statuses over their lifetimes as they enter or are denied entrance into particular interactions. In some ways, the investigation of institutional settings brings these lesser-studied aspects of the model into the light and provides ways for them to be analyzed in a manner that had been previously overlooked.

Shortly after we had written this discussion, Patricia Duff delivered a plenary address at the 2003 American Association of Applied Linguistics Conference in which she argued for a similar reconsideration of language acquisition theory. It is time, Duff said, that our field takes on a more complex consideration of language socialization in L2, one which recognizes that learners have agency, among other things, but that socialization for them is not always accessible, acceptable, or successful. We join Duff in looking forward to research that will further illuminate the complex processes and outcomes of L2 socialization.

NOTES

1. In using the term "second language," we follow much of the acquisition literature in considering it an umbrella term for both "second" and "foreign" language. When distinctions are relevant, they will be specified.
2. Such manipulated creation of and assignment into pairs, although supported in quasi-experimental paradigms, could be criticized as not embodying the need of language socialization research to examine

natural language within its context of socialization. We address the question of relevant methodology for language socialization theory in our discussion of issues later in the chapter. Because this study presented itself as one of language socialization, and because it met our other criteria for selection, we include it here.

3. This study contains both the same issue and the same reason for inclusion as in our preceding note.

4. According to Pennycook, "A central task for critical applied linguistics... is not only to find ways of thinking about relations between the micro contexts of everyday language use and the macro concerns of society, culture, politics, and power but also to go beyond this kind of dialectical two-tiered model" (2001, p. 172).

REFERENCES

Atkinson, D. (2003). Language socialization and dys-socialization in a South Indian college. In R. Bayley & S. R. Schecter (Eds), *Language socialization in bilingual and multilingual societies* (pp. 147–168). Clevedon, UK: Multilingual Matters.

Bayley, R., & Schecter, S. R. (2003). Introduction: Toward a dynamic model of language socialization. In R. Bayley & S. R. Schecter (Eds.), *Language socialization in bilingual and multilingual societies* (pp. 1–6). Clevedon, UK: Multilingual Matters.

Candlin, C. N., & Candlin, S. (Eds.). (2002). Expert talk and risk in health care [Special Issue]. *Research on Language and Social Interaction, 35*(2).

Delpit, L. D. (1995). *Other people's children: Cultural conflict in the classroom*. New York: New Press.

Drew, P., & Heritage, J. (Eds.). (1992). *Talk at work: Interaction in institutional settings*. Cambridge, UK: Cambridge University Press.

Duff, P. A. (1996). Different languages, different practices: Socialization of discourse competence in dual-language school classrooms in Hungary. In K. M. Bailey & D. Nunan (Eds.), *Voices from the classroom: Qualitative research in second language education* (pp. 407–433). Cambridge, UK: Cambridge University Press.

Duff, P. A. (2002). The discursive co-construction of knowledge, identity and difference: An ethnography of communication in the high school mainstream. *Applied Linguistics 23*(3), 289–322.

Duff, P., & Early, M. (March, 1999). *Language socialization in perspective: Classroom discourse in high school humanities courses*. Paper presented at the American Association for Applied Linguistics Conference, Stamford, CT.

Duff, P. A., Wong, P., & Early, M. (2000). Learning language for work and life: The linguistic socialization of immigrant Canadians seeking careers in healthcare. *Canadian Modern Language Review, 57*(1), 9–57.

Ely, R., & Berko Gleason, J. (1996). Socialization across contexts. In P. Fletcher & B. MacWhinney (Eds.), *The handbook of child language* (pp. 251–270). Oxford, UK: Blackwell.

Fairclough, N. (1992). *Discourse and social change*. Cambridge, UK: Polity Press.

Frith, H., & Kitzinger, C. (1998). "Emotion work" as a participant resource: A feminist analysis of young women's talk-in-interaction. *Sociology, 32*(2), 299–320.

Gee, J. P. (1996). *Social linguistics and literacies: Ideology in discourses*. London: Taylor & Francis.

Gee, J. P. (1999). *An introduction to discourse analysis: Theory and method*. London: Routledge.

Goffman, E. (1981). Footing. In E. Goffman, *Forms of talk* (pp. 124–159). Oxford, UK: Blackwell.

Harklau, L. (2003). Representational practices and multi-modal communication in U.S. high schools: Implications for adolescent immigrants. In R. Bayley & S. R. Schecter (Eds.), *Language socialization in bilingual and multilingual societies* (pp. 83–97). Clevedon, UK: Multilingual Matters.

He, A. W. (2003). Novices and their speech roles in Chinese heritage language classes. In R. Bayley & S. R. Schecter (Eds.), *Language socialization in bilingual and multilingual societies* (pp. 128–146). Clevedon, UK: Multilingual Matters.

Heap, J. L. (1997). Conversation analysis methods in researching language and education. In N. H. Hornberger & D. Corson (Eds.), *Research methods in language and education* (vol. 8, pp. 217–225). *Encyclopedia of Language and Education*. Dordrecht, The Netherlands: Kluwer Academic.

Heath, S. B. (1983). *Ways with words: Language, life and work in communities and classrooms*. New York: Cambridge University Press.

Kanagy, R. (1999). Interactional routines as a mechanism for L2 acquisition and socialization in an immersion context. *Journal of Pragmatics, 31*, 1467–1492.

Kasper, G. (2001). Four perspectives on L2 pragmatic development. *Applied Linguistics, 22*(4), 502–530.

Katz, M.-L. (2001). Engineering a hotel family language ideology, discourse, and workplace culture. *Linguistics and Education, 12*(3), 309–344.

Kitzinger, C. (2000a). Doing feminist conversation analysis. *Feminism & Psychology, 10*, 163–193. (Reprinted in P. McIlvenny (Ed.). (2002). *Talking gender and sexuality* (pp. 49–77). Amsterdam: Benjamins.

Kitzinger, C. (2000b). How to resist an idiom. *Research on Language and Social Interaction, 33*(2), 121–154.

Kitzinger, C., & Frith, H. (1999). Just say no? Using conversation analysis to understand how young women talk about refusing sex. *Discourse & Society, 10*(3), 293–316. (Reprinted in M. Wetherell, S. Taylor and

S. Yates (Eds.). (2001). *Discourse Theory and Practice: A Reader.* Buckingham, UK: The Open University Press.)

Li, D. (2000). The pragmatics of making requests in the L2 workplace: A case study of language socialization. *Canadian Modern Language Review, 57*(1), 58–87.

Matsumura, S. (2001). Learning the rules for offering advice: A quantitative approach to second language socialization. *Language Learning, 51*(4), 635–679.

Mehan, H. (1979). *Learning lessons.* Cambridge, MA: Harvard University Press.

Moore, L. C. (1999). Language socialization research and French language education in Africa: A Cameroonian case study. *Canadian Modern Language Review, 56*(2), 329–350.

Ochs. E. (1986). Introduction. In B. B. Schieffelin & E. Ochs (Eds.), *Language socialization across cultures* (pp. 1–13). New York: Cambridge University Press.

Ochs, E. (1988). *Culture and language development: Language acquisition and language development in a Samoan village.* New York: Cambridge University Press.

Ohta, A. S. (1999). Interactional routines and the socialization of interactional style in adult learners of Japanese. *Journal of Pragmatics, 31,* 1493–1512.

Pennycook, A. (2001). *Critical applied linguistics: A critical introduction.* Mahwah, NJ: Lawrence Erlbaum Associates.

Phillips, S. (1983). *The invisible culture: Communication in classroom and community on the Warm Springs Indian Reservation.* New York: Longman.

Poole, D. (1992). Language socialization in the second language classroom. *Language Learning, 42*(4), 593–616.

Roberts, C. (1998). Language acquisition or language socialization in and through discourse? Towards a redefinition of the domain of SLA. *Working Papers in Applied Linguistics, 4,* 31–42. London: Thames Valley University.

Roberts, C. (1999). Acquisition des langues ou socialization dans et par le discourse? Pour une redefinition du domaine de la recherché sur l'acquisition des langues etrangeres. *Langages, 134,* 101–115.

Rymes, B. (1997). Second language socialization: A new approach to second language acquisition research. *Journal of Intensive English Studies, 11*(2), 143–155.

Sarangi, S., & Roberts, C. (Eds.). (1999). *Talk, work and institutional order: Discourse in medical, mediation and management settings.* Berlin: Mouton de Gruyter.

Scollon, R., & Scollon, S. W. (1995). *Intercultural communication: A discourse approach.* Cambridge, MA: Blackwell.

Schieffelin, B. B., & Ochs, E. (1986a). Language socialization. *Annual Review of Anthropology, 15,* 163–191.

Sinclair, J. M., & Coulthard, R. M. (1975). *Towards an analysis of discourse: The English used by teachers and pupils.* London: Oxford University Press.

van Lier, L. (1996). *Interaction in the language curriculum: Awareness, autonomy and authenticity.* London: Longman.

Watson-Gegeo, K. A. (1992). Thick explanation in the ethnographic study of child socialization: A longitudinal study of the problem of schooling for Kwara'ae (Solomon Islands) children. In W. A. Corsaro & P. J. Miller (Eds.), *Interpretive Approaches to Children's Socialization* (pp. 51–66). San Francisco: Jossey-Bass City: Publisher.

Watson-Gegeo, K. A., & Nielsen, S. (2003). Language socialization in SLA. In C. Doughty & M. Long (Eds.), *Handbook of second language acquisition* (pp. 155–177). London: Blackwell.

Willett, J. (1995). Becoming first graders in an L2: An ethnographic study of L2 socialization. *TESOL Quarterly, 29*(3), 473–503.

Yoshimi, D. R. (1999). L1 language socialization as a variable in the use of *ne* by L2 learners of Japanese. *Journal of Pragmatics, 31,* 1513–1525.

18

Pragmatics in Second Language Learning

Gabriele Kasper
University of Hawaii at Manoa

Carsten Roever
University of Melbourne

Pragmatics, the ability to act and interact by means of language, is a necessary and sometimes daunting learning task for second and foreign language learners. This chapter will review central issues and findings in second language (L2) developmental pragmatics, examine the effects of instruction, and provide an overview of data collection methods.

DEVELOPING PRAGMATIC COMPETENCE

Sociopragmatic and Pragmalinguistic Competence

The challenge that learners face in acquiring the pragmatics of a second language is considerable because they have to learn (to paraphrase Austin, 1962) not only how to do things with target language words but also how communicative actions and the "words" that implement them are both responsive to and shape situations, activities, and social relationships. Following Leech (1983), these two intersecting domains of pragmatic competence are referred to as sociopragmatic and pragmalinguistic competence.

Sociopragmatic competence encompasses knowledge of the relationships between communicative action and power, social distance, and the imposition associated with a past or future event (Brown & Levinson, 1987), knowledge of mutual rights and obligations, taboos, and conventional practices (Thomas, 1983), or quite generally, the social conditions and consequences of "what you do, when and to whom" (Fraser, Rintell & Walters, 1981). Whereas sociopragmatics describes the interface between pragmatics and social organization, pragmalinguistics focuses on the intersection of pragmatics and linguistic forms (Leech, 1983). Hence, pragmalinguistic competence comprises the knowledge and ability for use of conventions of means (such as the strategies for realizing speech acts) and conventions of form (such as the linguistic forms implementing speech act strategies; Clark, 1979; Thomas, 1983). Becoming pragmatically competent can be understood as the process of establishing sociopragmatic and pragmalinguistic competence and the increasing ability to understand and produce sociopragmatic meanings with pragmalinguistic conventions. From cognitive-psychological and social-psychological perspectives, interlanguage pragmatics research has investigated how the process of becoming pragmatically competent in a second or foreign language is influenced by such factors as input, noticing and understanding, L2 proficiency, transfer, and individual differences. In contrast, theories of L2 (pragmatic) learning as social practice explore the interrelationship of sociopolitical contexts, social identities, and participation opportunities in L2 pragmatic learning (cf. Kasper, 2001b; Kasper & Rose, 2002).

Input

Analogous to other areas of second language learning, input is a necessary condition for developing L2 pragmatic knowledge. The importance of input has been shown in various studies. In a longitudinal study of international students' suggestions and rejections in academic advising sessions at a North American university, the students' sociopragmatic performance became increasingly more targetlike, whereas they showed little pragmalinguistic development (Bardovi-Harlig & Hartford, 1993), a result that the investigators attributed to the absence of modeling by peers (Bardovi-Harlig & Hartford, 1996). Japanese English as a Second Language (ESL) learners who were spending a year abroad in Canada consistently moved toward native speaker sociopragmatic norms, whereas the control group who stayed in Japan did not show any development (Matsumura, 2001). German English as a Foreign Language (EFL) learners improved rapidly in their knowledge of situational routines after even a short stay in a target language community, whereas learners who did not spend time abroad did not make any gains in their knowledge of routines regardless of overall proficiency or length of EFL instruction (Röver, 1996; Roever, in press). Korean ESL learners' performance of apologies and requests approximated native speaker performance more closely the more informal input they received (Kim, 2000).

However, although input opportunities are necessary to develop pragmatic ability, they are not sufficient. Despite extended time spent in the L2 speech community, learners' L2 pragmatics often remains distinctly nontargetlike (Bardovi-Harlig, 2001). This well-attested fact strongly indicates that learners' L2 pragmatic development may profit from support through instruction, as will be discussed later in this chapter.

Noticing and Understanding

According to psycholinguistic theory and research on second language learning, for input to be acquisitionally relevant, it has to be noticed, or detected under attention (Schmidt, 2001). One explanation why targetlike pragmatic ability does not develop despite ample input through exposure is that learners may not attend to relevant input features. In order to acquire pragmatics, attention must be allocated to the action that is being accomplished, the linguistic, paralinguistic, and nonverbal forms by which the action is implemented, its immediate interactional or textual context, and the dimensions of the situational context that are indexed by linguistic and pragmatic choices. Attending simultaneously to an input complexity of this order exceeds working memory space by far. This is one reason why input frequency plays a particularly important role in pragmatics. If attuned to these components of communicative action, learners can attend to subsets of them as they encounter contextualized instances of specific actions and, thus, build up pragmalinguistic and sociopragmatic knowledge incrementally and concurrently. But in addition to registering individual instances, learners have to understand their pragmatic, interactional, contextual, and sociocultural meanings and functions. As Schmidt (1995) proposes, understanding implies "the recognition of some general principle, rule, or pattern. Noticing refers to surface level phenomena and item learning, while understanding refers to deeper level(s) of abstraction related to (semantic, syntactic, or communicative) meaning, system learning" (p. 29). Registering that speakers of Indonesian use different address terms is a matter of noticing; figuring out how speakers index social relationships, define situations, and manage interaction by choosing particular address terms in particular discourse environments are all matters of understanding (DuFon, 1999).

Proficiency

Many studies relate learners' pragmatic ability to their overall grammatical (morphosyntactic and lexical) L2 knowledge. Some evidence suggests that learners' L2 pragmatic ability—both receptive and productive—progresses concurrently with their general L2 proficiency. In an early study, Carrell (1981) reported that comprehension of syntactically complex requests was proficiency-related, indicating a rather strong link between grammatical knowledge and request comprehension. Kerekes (1992) found increasingly nativelike perceptions of qualifiers in troubles talk as learners' ESL proficiency increased, and according to Koike (1996), advanced learners of L2 Spanish understood speech acts more successfully, produced more targetlike responses, and assigned different personal attributes to the speakers of stimulus material than lower level learners. Similarly, Cook (2001) reported that fourth year students of Japanese as a foreign language (JFL) were superior to second year JFL students in recognizing an inappropriate speech style in Japanese. Roever (in press) observed that ESL and EFL learners' comprehension of implicature was only negligibly affected by exposure to the L2 environment, whereas their implicature comprehension improved with increasing proficiency.

Several studies document that learners' production of speech acts improves with increasing L2 proficiency as well. Higher proficiency learners supplied more adjuncts and supportive moves in apologies and requests (Rose, 2000; Trosborg, 1995), suggesting that processing load decreases with higher proficiency. In terms of Bialystok's (1993) two-dimensional model of second language learning and use, the learners' increasing facility to produce longer and more complex realizations of speech act strategies indicates more effective control of processing. Similarly, as learners acquire more extensive knowledge of and control over conventions of form, targetlike realizations of refusals (Takahashi & Beebe, 1987) and conventionally indirect requests also occur more frequently (see Kasper & Rose, 2002).

But developmental trajectories do not necessarily evolve in a smooth and linear fashion. Blum-Kulka and Olshtain (1986) reported that in relation to L2 proficiency, learners' use of supportive moves in requests described a bell-shaped curve. Compared to native speakers of Hebrew, low-proficiency learners undersupplied supportive moves, intermediate-level proficiency learners oversupplied them, and high-proficiency learners' use resembled that of native speakers. Hassall (1997) observed a similar tendency in the production of requests by first language (L1) English speaking learners of Indonesian. Elided imperatives, a structurally simple request strategy, were only employed by the high-proficiency learners in Hassall's sample. Blum-Kulka and Olshtain (1986) and Hassall's (1997) findings are consistent with a well-attested tendency in less than advanced learners to design their speech acts in an overly explicit fashion (Kasper, 1981; Edmondson & House, 1991). Psycholinguistic and sociolinguistic explanations have been suggested to account for learners' verbosity or propositional explicitness; however, such explanations remain tentative at this point.

Studies demonstrating that pragmatic ability increases with formal L2 proficiency isolate grammar as a strong constraint on pragmatic development. But this does not imply that pragmatic ability emerges from grammar. Because adult L2 learners are fully pragmatically competent in at least one language, they can draw on pragmatic universals and L1 transfer of discourse, pragmatic, and sociolinguistic knowledge from the initial stages of L2 acquisition, long before their L2 grammar reaches the complexity and variability that are necessary in order to perform communicative action with target forms (Blum-Kulka, 1991; Koike, 1989). Research documenting how learners' pragmatics outperforms their grammar includes learners at beginning (Koike, 1989; Schmidt, 1983; Walters, 1980) and advanced proficiency levels (Eisenstein & Bodman, 1986, 1993). Conversely, it has also been shown that learners underutilize the pragmatic potential of available grammatical knowledge. For instance, Salsbury and Bardovi-Harlig (2000) identified a sequence for the emergence of modal verbs in interviews involving L2 learners, but when performing disagreements, the same learners relied on lexical expressions rather than modal verbs even though the grammaticalized forms were demonstrably available to them. The complex relationships between the development of specific grammatical and pragmatic knowledge are first beginning to be explored (Bardovi-Harlig, 1999; Kasper, 2001b; Kasper & Rose, 2002).

Pragmatic Transfer

Likewise, the interaction of proficiency and negative pragmatic transfer is far from straightforward. Consistent with research findings in second language acquisition generally, most interlanguage pragmatics studies have found an inverse relationship between negative pragmatic transfer and proficiency. In a study of apology production by Japanese ESL learners, intermediate proficiency learners showed more evidence of negative transfer than high-proficiency learners (Maeshiba, Yoshinaga, Kasper, & Ross, 1996). On the other hand, the reverse has also been noted: lower grammatical proficiency can work against pragmatic transfer (Cohen, 1997), whereas higher grammatical proficiency can enable it (Blum-Kulka, 1982, 1991; Hill, 1997; Olshtain & Cohen, 1989). Takahashi (1996) identified a proficiency effect on pragmatic transferability, defined as how functionally similar learners perceived L1 (Japanese) and L2 (English) request strategies to be. However, the direction of the effect could not be clearly determined. Probably because of its possible—though by no means inevitable—links to pragmatic misunderstandings, most studies have focused on negative rather than positive pragmatic transfer. But it is equally important to understand what aspects of learners' prior pragmatic knowledge that converge with L2 pragmatic practices are in fact transferred, what factors encourage or work against positive transfer, and how patterns of positive transfer change as L2 learning progresses.

Individual Differences

Many aspects of pragmatics are inseparable from sociocultural practices and values and may therefore involve learners more personally than grammar and morphology, which in turn may have an impact on how L2 pragmatics is learned. An early "individual difference" study found just that. In an investigation designed to test the Acculturation Model (Schumann, 1978), Schmidt (1983) observed how an adult L1 speaker of Japanese developed communicative competence in L2 English over a 3-year period. The learner exhibited low social and psychological distance to the host community, which appeared to be beneficial for his progress in discourse-pragmatic and strategic competence. But these factors did not influence his grammar, which showed little change toward target usage. A positive correlation between affiliation with the host community and pragmatic ability was also reported by Kim (2000), who found that the more strongly Korean ESL learners identified themselves as "very American," the higher the ratings of their apology and request performance. Japanese students at an international university in Japan indicated instrumental motivation to learn English and general willingness to accommodate to native speaker (NS) pragmatic practices, but their self-reports were not related to performance data (LoCastro, 2001). In a study examining how motivation may influence Japanese university students' learning of selected request strategies in English, Takahashi (2000, reported in Kasper & Rose, 2002) found that highly motivated students were more likely to notice discourse lubricants, idiomatic expressions, and discourse strategies than less strongly motivated students. Advanced EFL students whose exposure to the target language was limited to the educational setting displayed high sociopragmatic awareness, a finding that Niezgoda and Röver (2001) tentatively explained by referring to these students' strong (instrumental) motivation. In identity-theoretical perspective, it has been argued that learners' investment in learning the target language is shaped by their position in the target community, the activities they engage in, their stances to target community practices, and experiences in interactions with target community members (Norton, 2000; Siegal, 1996). An example of how learner subjectivity can influence learners' acquisition of L2 linguistic politeness was reported by DuFon (1999), who found that one learner of Indonesian purposefully continued to employ address terms that were too informal and not respectful enough to higher status interlocutors but whose use made the learner feel at ease. Conversely, another learner commented that paying proper respect to coparticipants was a great concern of hers, and she, therefore, took care to choose address terms according to Indonesian politeness conventions.

Research Design

Following investigative practices in first and second language acquisition research, studies of pragmatic development have adopted cross-sectional or longitudinal designs. Cross-sectional studies have typically examined how learners at different proficiency levels use speech act realization strategies. These studies have been rather narrowly focused on (one or more) speech acts, investigated by means of elicited data. A welcome development in a number of the more recent cross-sectional speech act studies is their considerably improved methodology. It is now standard procedure to develop the instrument for the main investigation on the basis of preliminary studies in order to choose relevant contexts, control and vary context variables, and select linguistic material in the case of comprehension and assessment studies (see Takahashi, 1995, and Tokuda, 2001, for examples). Although much remains to be done in order to further develop valid and reliable research methods for interlanguage pragmatics, the general direction toward more sophisticated designs and procedures promises well for future cross-sectional studies based on elicited data.

Compared to the cross-sectional research, longitudinal studies on pragmatic development span a much wider range. The pragmatic features examined include not only speech acts but also pragmatic routines, discourse markers, pragmatic fluency, and conversational ability—features that require study in a full discourse context. Most longitudinal studies examine learners at the beginning stages of pragmatic development, often (but not only) in second and foreign language classrooms. The wide scope of the longitudinal studies is reflected in a larger variety of research approaches and data types (see the following). Because most of them rely on data collected in authentic settings of language use, they have the potential to shed light on the relationship between social and institutional contexts and pragmatic development. Although the interaction of pragmatic and grammatical learning can be examined through different kinds of research approaches, longitudinal studies of socially situated authentic interaction provide privileged access to the relationship of social contexts and L2 pragmatic learning.

INSTRUCTED LEARNING OF PRAGMATICS

In educational perspective, a prime concern is whether pragmatics is teachable, and what instructional options are most effective for L2 learners' pragmatic development. Studies that have addressed these issues (Rose & Kasper, 2001) strongly suggest that most aspects of L2 pragmatics are indeed amenable to instruction, that instructional intervention is more beneficial than no instructional arrangements specifically targeted to pragmatic learning, and that for the most part, explicit instruction combined with ample practice opportunities results in the greatest gains. Interventional classroom-based research has examined a fairly broad range of instructional targets, a much narrower band of target language populations, and adopted a variety of teaching approaches and theoretical frameworks. Another line of classroom-based research has been observational, focusing on interaction processes in authentic classrooms and examining opportunities for and outcomes of pragmatic learning in different classroom arrangements and activities (Kasper, 2001a; Rose & Kasper, 2001). This chapter will report on interventional studies.

Teaching Goals

Interventional classroom research has targeted a fair variety of discursive, pragmatic, and sociolinguistic goals, such as discourse markers and strategies in English (House & Kasper, 1981; Wildner-Bassett, 1984), German (Wildner-Bassett, 1994), and Japanese (Yoshimi, 2001), pragmatic routines such as apologetic and attention getting routines in Japanese (Tateyama, Kasper, Mui, Tay, & Thananart, 1997; Tateyama, 2001), or mitigation in academic writing and computer-mediated discourse (Wishnoff, 2000). Many studies have focused on specific speech acts and their realization strategies, including apologies (Olshtain & Cohen, 1990), complaints (Morrow, 1996), compliments and compliment responses (Billmyer, 1990; Rose & Ng, 2001), refusals (Morrow, 1996), and requests (Takahashi, 2001). Fewer studies have examined instruction in overall discourse characteristics, such as sociostylistic variation in French (Lyster, 1994) and pragmatic fluency in English (House, 1996), and extended interaction, such as exchanges prompted by the "weekend question" in French (*"t'as passé un bon weekend?"*, Liddicoat & Crozet, 2001). Whereas most studies have concentrated on the production of the target features or their use in interaction, instruction specifically aiming at improving learners' pragmatic comprehension has received far less attention. An exception is a series of studies conducted by Bouton (1994, 1999) on ESL learners' comprehension of implicature in indirect responses.

Target Language and Students' L2 Proficiency

Reflecting the dominance of English as a target language in second language classroom-based research generally, by a wide margin, English has been the most frequently chosen target language in studies on instruction in pragmatics. Other target languages, such as Japanese, French, German, and Spanish, are only represented with less than a handful of studies each at the time of writing. There is an urgent need to expand the range of target languages, not least in order to better assess whether and to what extent findings from research on a particular target language may be transferable to other languages. It is noteworthy that the majority of studies were conducted in a foreign language rather than a second language environment, that is, in contexts where students had little benefit of L2 input and interaction outside the classroom.

One concern raised by language educators is whether pragmatics is teachable to beginning L2 learners. Studies by Wildner-Bassett (1994), Tateyama et al. (1997), and Tateyama (2001) demonstrate that short pragmatic routines are teachable to absolute beginners, indicating that such material can be learned before students develop analyzed L2 knowledge. This finding is consistent with research on the role of unanalyzed chunks in L1 and L2 acquisition, showing that routines allow learners to participate in conversation from early on and, thus, enable further opportunities for input, output, and interaction. For advanced learners, the question is whether instruction is at all necessary or at least facilitative. A solid body of research findings documents that advanced learners often do not successfully acquire particular L2 pragmatic practices without support through targeted instruction (Bardovi-Harlig, 2001). For the most part, pragmatic practices that appear difficult for advanced learners to acquire without instruction prove learnable through interventional measures (Bouton, 1994, 1999; House, 1996; House & Kasper, 1981; Olshtain & Cohen, 1990). The majority of studies have included learners of intermediate L2 proficiency. It is interesting that these studies have also produced the most mixed results: In some, students clearly profited from the offered instruction (Billmyer, 1990; Morrow, 1996; Wildner-Bassett, 1984), whereas in others, pre- and posttest results differed on only a few of several measures (Rose & Ng, 2001), no differences were found between treatment and control groups (Fukuya & Clark, 2001), only one of several treatments made a difference (Takahashi, 2001), or initial gains had disappeared at the time of a delayed posttest (Kubota, 1995). However, it is doubtful that the small or absent treatment effects were causally related to participants' L2 proficiency; rather, students' educational background and issues of research design and procedures appear to have contributed to these outcomes.

Teaching Approaches

Interventional research examines how effective approaches to instruction in pragmatics are, but it does so with varying specificity. Studies have sought to establish the following:

1. Whether the targeted pragmatic feature is teachable at all (Liddicoat & Crozet, 2001; Morrow, 1996; Olshtain & Cohen, 1990; Wildner-Bassett, 1994).
2. Whether instruction in the targeted feature is more effective than no instruction (Billmyer, 1990; Bouton, 1994, 1999; Lyster, 1994; Yoshimi, 2001).
3. Whether different teaching approaches are differentially effective.

Without exception, the teachability studies show that the targeted features are indeed teachable, that is, on the adopted postinstruction measures, students' performance improved appreciably. Likewise, the instruction vs. no-instruction studies demonstrate a clear advantage for instruction. The most revealing is the third group, studies comparing different approaches or treatment conditions. A number of studies have addressed the efficacy of metapragmatic instruction by comparing it to other teaching strategies, sometimes under the labels "explicit" and "implicit" teaching. Several investigations (House, 1996; House & Kasper, 1981; Pearson, 1998; Tateyama, 2001; Tateyama et al., 1997) have compared metapragmatic instruction with input and practice-only conditions. All of these studies (except for House, 1996, and Tateyama, 2001, each on one measure) found an advantage for explicit metapragmatic teaching. On the other hand, Rose and Ng (2001) reported that an inductive approach proved more effective for teaching pragmalinguistic aspects of complimenting, whereas a deductive approach was superior for sociopragmatic aspects of compliment responses.

One study (Takahashi, 2001) compared as many as four different approaches to teaching conventionally indirect request strategies to intermediate Japanese EFL students: (a) explicit teaching, in which students received metapragmatic explanation about form–function relationships of the target structures; (b) form–comparison, in which students compared their own request realizations with those of native speakers; (c) form–search, in which students identified the target strategies in provided request scenarios; and (d) a meaning-focused condition, in which students listened to aurally presented request events, read transcripts, and answered comprehension questions. Unlike in Rose and Ng (2001), the explicit group learned all four request strategies more successfully than the other three groups, who equally benefited little from the intervention. But as the explicit teaching was more in accordance with the instructional approach that the students usually experienced, it would be premature to conclude that the more inductive approaches are ineffective for teaching pragmalinguistic aspects of speech act realization.

Theories and Research Methods

Studies on instruction in pragmatics rely on two types of theories and research: theories of the instructional object and of the process of L2 learning and teaching. Theories of the teaching object include such approaches to discourse organization and management as Conversation Analysis and different types of discourse analysis, whereas studies focusing on speech acts are based in speech act theory and empirical findings on speech act realization. Theories of learning and teaching were initially limited to pedagogical approaches such as suggestopedia (Wildner-Bassett, 1984, 1986) and "functional-analytic" teaching (Lyster, 1994). But by engaging an information-processing model of skill acquisition to account for students' tasks in acquiring sociostylistically appropriate choices of French address pronouns, Lyster's study was also the first to draw on current cognitive approaches to second language learning. Takahashi's (2001) research on the effectiveness of different teaching approaches to request realization in English was theoretically anchored in the noticing hypothesis (Schmidt, 2001), a pragmatically adapted version of form-focused instruction (Doughty & Williams, 1998), and the psycholinguistically based technique of input enhancement (Sharwood Smith, 1993). Although observational studies on pragmatics in L2 classrooms have also engaged sociocultural theory and language socialization theory (e.g., Ohta, 1999, 2001), social practice theories of second language learning have not yet informed interventional studies. Effect-of-instruction research has apparently been viewed as most compatible with psycholinguistic theory and (quasi-, pre-) experimental design; however, interventional research on instruction in pragmatics could also be conducted under a social practice theory and engage different qualitative methodologies, including participatory methods such as action research. In fact, innovative instructional approaches to pragmatics may well be most effective when they are cooperatively developed in local teaching contexts.

Another methodological practice that interventional studies would be well advised to borrow from their observational counterparts is to conduct regular classroom observation, preferably including periods before, during, and after the intervention. Audio or video recordings, carefully transcribed and analyzed according to a specified discourse-pragmatic approach, provide essential documentation of how students and teachers implement the interventional agenda in classroom interaction and afford insights into the acquisitional potential of different classroom activities for learning the designated pragmatic practices.

COLLECTING DATA ON PRAGMATIC DEVELOPMENT

Data types in interlanguage pragmatics research can be categorized into three main groups (Kasper, 2000; Kasper & Rose, in press):

- Observational data of spoken interaction: authentic discourse, elicited conversation, and role plays.
- Self-reported questionnaire data: discourse completion, multiple-choice, and scaled-response.
- Oral and/or narrative self-reports: interviews, diaries, and think-aloud protocols.

All of these data types can be—and most of them have been—deployed in research on the development and instructed learning of L2 pragmatics. Studies illustrating these methods will be drawn from the literature in these subfields of interlanguage pragmatics.

Observational Data of Spoken Interaction

Data collection approaches in this category allow observing how participants produce and understand pragmatic information and how they interact in various settings. The three approaches we distinguish differ in the degree to which the researcher controls contextual parameters. In recording authentic discourse, the researcher attempts to avoid any manipulation of the natural setting. In elicited conversations, the researcher either sets a task for participants to accomplish but then lets the interaction run its course, or she or he assumes the role of an interviewer but does not require the participant to assume a pretended role. In role-plays, the researcher determines the setting of the interaction and asks participants to take on predefined roles in a pretense play.

Authentic Discourse.   One reason for choosing authentic discourse as data for the study of pragmatic development is the well-taken assumption that to a significant extent, pragmatic learning occurs *through* interaction and collaboration. Another reason is that much, though clearly not all, pragmatic learning is geared *toward* interaction; hence, it is crucial to obtain valid records of learners' progressing interactional ability. Spoken discourse in any authentic setting involves micro-designed and coordinated action, too complex and fleeting to commit to participants' or observer's memory, yet essential for the unfolding interaction and its outcomes. Therefore, audio- or videotaped records are crucial to collect valid and reliable interactional data (Peräkylä, 1997; Psathas, 1990). Although field notes may provide useful ethnographic information that can be desirable or necessary as a supplementary data source, electronic records and carefully prepared transcripts constitute the mainstay of pragmatic research based on authentic discourse data (Golato, 2003).

Authentic discourse has been observed to study pragmatic development in ordinary conversation (Achiba, 2002) and institutional encounters inside and outside of language classrooms. Classroom-based research includes longitudinal studies on learning how to request by two adolescent ESL learners (Ellis, 1992), on the (non)-development of interactional ability in Spanish as a foreign language (Hall, 1995), and on students' progress in using acknowledgment and alignment expressions in Japanese as a foreign language (Ohta, 2001). An example of institutional discourse outside of language classrooms is the academic advising sessions examined by Bardovi-Harlig and Hartford (1993, 1996) in a longitudinal study on students' performance of suggestions and rejections. Although access to institutions can be difficult to obtain and is sometimes subject to repeated renegotiation, institutional discourse has some clear advantages for the study of pragmatic development. Although institutional interaction is in large measure (although not entirely) prestructured by the goals of the activity and participants assume rather fixed roles in it, actions that are mandated by the activity occur repeatedly, such as question–answer sequences in interviews or suggestions–acceptances/rejections in the academic advising session. The relatively stable organization of institutional interaction allows comparisons of the same action sequences carried out by the same participants in one session and over time, and between different participants. Compared to ordinary conversation, institutional interactions provide a more stable environment that lends itself partic- ularly well to examine pragmatic development in authentic contexts. However, how learners develop conversational ability in ordinary interaction is an equally important research interest. Because authentic ordinary conversation is usually not prestructured by preset goals and its participation structure is negotiated *in situ*, comparing specific pragmatic practices within and across recordings can be a difficult proposition. In or- der to gain more control over the interaction, researchers therefore resort to different forms of elicited data.

Elicited Conversation.   In elicited conversations, informants are asked to carry out a conversation task or participate in an interview, but they do not assume a dif- ferent identity as they might in a role-play. Studies involving conversation tasks have investigated discourse transfer in conversational management (Scarcella, 1983) and backchanneling (White, 1989), and proficiency effects on expressions of advice or sympathy (Kerekes, 1992). Interviews as a vehicle for obtaining data on learners' L2 pragmatics are modeled on the sociolinguistic interview (Labov, 1972; Schiffrin, 1987; Kasper & Rose, in press). Interview-based studies have examined proficiency- related changes in repair organization (Færch & Kasper, 1982), retroactive transfer in backchanneling (Tao & Thompson, 1991), and the learners' acquisition of the Japanese sentence final particle *ne* (Sawyer, 1992). Salsbury and Bardovi-Harlig (2001) con- ducted a longitudinal interview study aimed at tracing ESL learners' development of modal expressions and disagreements. In order to offset the inherent asymmetry of interview interaction, this study included three participants, two learners and the native English speaking interviewer. In this way, learners engaged in different sta- tus relationships during the interview interaction (see Schiffrin, 1987, for a model of multiparty sociolinguistic interviews).

Often, researchers are interested in pragmatic actions and practices that are unlikely to come up in elicited conversation. Here, role-play provides an alternative.

Role-play.   Role-plays of various types are widely used for diagnostic, training, learning, testing, and research purposes throughout the social sciences. Closed role- plays consist of a single informant turn in response to a situational prompt and pos- sibly an opening turn by the interlocutor. This type of role-play has been used to elicit requests (Rintell, 1981; Rintell & Mitchell, 1989), apologies (Cohen & Olshtain, 1981; Rintell & Mitchell, 1989), and suggestions (Rintell, 1981). Open role-plays, on the other hand, can stretch over numerous turns, elicit a variety of speech acts, and allow the observation of a large number of discourse features. The researcher can struc- ture the role-play loosely by giving participants role-play instructions that define their roles and tasks, or it can be structured more tightly if a "confederate" follows a more or less detailed script. Because of the rich and varied discourse they elicit, open role-plays have been deployed frequently in interlanguage pragmatics research to investigate such actions and practices as requests (Hassall, 1997), expressions of grat- itude (Eisenstein & Bodman, 1993), refusals (Gass & Houck, 1999), apologies (García, 1989), complaints (Trosborg, 1995), face-threatening acts (Piirainen-Marsh, 1995), con- versational openings and closings (Kasper, 1981), discourse markers and strategies (Wildner-Bassett, 1984, 1994), pragmatic routines (Tateyama, 2001), and pragmatic fluency (House, 1996). Hudson, Detmer, and Brown (1995) used role-plays as an as- sessment instrument for the speech acts of apology, request, and refusal by Japanese ESL learners. The test takers' performance was assessed by raters watching a video recording of the role-plays. Yoshitake (1997) replicated this study with L1 Japanese learners of EFL and Yamashita (1996) with L1 English learners of Japanese as a Second Language (JSL).

Compared to authentic discourse, some speech events elicited through role-play have been found to be less complex and varied (Eisenstein & Bodman, 1993, Margalef-Boada, 1993). Role-plays also rank low on practicality (Brown, 2001a): They require (usually) dyadic interaction; they may elicit few instances of the desired pragmatic action or practice; the spoken discourse data must be transcribed and requires some form of discourse analysis. As role-play participants have to create a fictional world through their interaction rather than being engaged in a social activity embedded in, and consequential for, their lives outside of the simulation, the relationship of role-played interaction to authentic discourse remains an unresolved validity issue. On the positive side, open role-plays supply rich interactional data under controlled conditions; however, when practicality is a concern or a study requires quantitative treatment of a large body of data rather than an in-depth discourse analysis of a smaller data set, open role-play would not be an advisable choice.

Questionnaires

Questionnaires are a versatile type of instrument. Open-ended production (discourse completion) questionnaires serve to collect learner-produced pragmatic data in response to situation prompts; multiple-choice questionnaires elicit preferences for pragmatic options or interpretations of utterances; and scaled-response formats ask respondents to assess situational contexts and instances of speech acts or discourse according to predetermined variables. All types of questionnaires probe into "offline," self-reported states of knowledge or beliefs as respondents do not produce and understand linguistic and other vocal action under the time pressure and stimulus load of real-world interaction. Consequently, questionnaire data cannot provide valid representations of situated linguistic action in authentic activities, although it may bear some resemblance. But each questionnaire type imposes its own cognitive task demands. Discourse completion questionnaires, in which respondents have to actively construct responses, require free recall; choosing from presented stimuli in multiple-choice instruments involves recognition; and assessing characteristics of situational context or linguistic material by means of rating scales presents respondents with a judgment task.

Compared to role-plays, the administration and analysis of questionnaire data is far less resource demanding, especially when no analysis of production data is involved. But that does not mean that questionnaires are easy instruments that allow conducting a study fast. What is saved in time commitment at the data collection and analysis stage has to be invested prior to the data collection. Questionnaire design is a highly complex affair and requires that the researcher be well versed in the social research literature on the topic (e.g., Babbie, 2004; also Brown, 2001b, for an excellent practical guide to questionnaire design in language program surveys). Unless an already existing, well-developed questionnaire is an appropriate instrument for the purposes, population, and context of the study at hand, a new instrument has to be developed, which takes several cycles of piloting and pretesting. Existing instruments have to be validated for the population(s) participating in the new study. Because the quality of the data depends on the validity and reliability of the instrument, careful questionnaire development is as essential in pragmatics research as elsewhere in the social sciences.

Discourse Completion Questionnaires. In cross-sectional studies of pragmatic development (e.g., Blum-Kulka & Olshtain, 1986; Maeshiba et al., 1996; Rose, 2000; Takahashi & Beebe, 1987) and as assessment instruments in pre- and posttests in interventional classroom research (Olshtain & Cohen, 1990; Rose & Ng, 2001; Takahashi, 2001), discourse completion tasks or tests (DCTs) have been a frequently employed instrument. They have mostly been used to elicit productions of a specific speech act, usually as a one-turn response to a situational prompt. DCTs provide self-reports about past or hypothetical action, but they do not have the potential to represent situated (inter)action in its sequential development (Golato, 2003). However, DCTs are a useful format to provide knowledge displays of speech act strategies and linguistic forms. A number of DCT design issues have been examined, including the effect of rejoinders (Johnston, Kasper, & Ross, 1998) and their presentation (Kuha, 1999; Roever, in press), and the length of the situational prompt (Billmyer & Varghese, 2000).

Multiple Choice. In interlanguage pragmatics, multiple choice (MC) formats have occasionally been employed as a research tool, for instance to study the appropriateness of advice (Hinkel, 1997; Matsumura, 2001) and learners' progress in understanding implicature in English (Bouton, 1992). More frequently, MC has been deployed for pragmatic assessment, including tests of implicature comprehension and routines (Roever, in press) and the contextual appropriateness of speech act realizations (Hudson, Detmer, & Brown, 1995; Yamashita, 1996; Yoshitake, 1997), and as pre- and posttests in interventional classroom research (Bouton, 1994, 1999; Tateyama et al., 1997; Fukuya & Clark, 2001; Tateyama, 2001). Because MC presents respondents with a recognition task, the design of the response options is crucial and must be closely tied to the overall purpose of the MC. In MC questionnaires used for research, the response options are designed to represent possible respondent preferences from which they select the most preferred option. Consequently, all response options must be possible; whereas in a MC test used for assessment, all but one response option must be *im*possible, that is, except for one option, all others must be incorrect or inappropriate beyond a reasonable doubt. This differentiation has major consequences for task design: MC instruments for research purposes should be based on studies of naturally occurring language use; whereas for assessment purposes, they must contain distractors that are attractive to at least some members of the test-taker population. The extent to which these requirements can be fulfilled depends largely on the targeted pragmatic feature. Whereas MCs probing into learner preferences of alternative speech act realization strategies tend to achieve notoriously poor reliability scores (Brown, 2001a; Roever, in press), MCs for situational routines and implicatures can be constructed with satisfactory degrees of consistency (Roever, in press).

Rating Scales

Rating scales are well known as measures of "attitudinal objects" in social research and as elicitation formats for acceptability judgments in linguistics. In interlanguage pragmatics research, they have been deployed to investigate such issues as the use and placement of supportive moves in requests (Shimamura, 1993), the transferability of request strategies (Takahashi, 1996), or learners' perceptions of pragmatic and grammatical errors (Bardovi-Harlig & Dörnyei, 1998; replicated by Niezgoda & Röver, 2001). In a language testing context, Hudson et al. (1995) utilized rating scales to assess test-takers' pragmatic performance by external raters and for test-takers' self-assessment of their own pragmatic ability. Rating scales are suitable for sociopragmatic and pragmalinguistic assessment. One study that combined both assessment types is Shimamura (1993). For principles and practices to follow in the design of scaled response instruments, the sociometric and psychometric literature should be consulted (e.g., Bernard, 2000; Miller & Salkind, 2002).

Oral and Narrative Forms of Self-report

Compared to the data collection methods discussed earlier, forms of self-report that are not questionnaire-elicited have only been used sporadically in interlanguage pragmatics. Interviews, next to observation the most frequently employed data gathering procedure in the social sciences, have figured as one of several data sources in ethnographic studies of L2 pragmatic learning (DuFon, 1999; Siegal, 1994), but the research reports make only cursory mention of the interview data. In some studies of native speakers' pragmatic practices, interviews were the main data collection format (Boxer, 1996, on "indirect complaints") or were accorded equal weight as observations of pragmatic practices (Miles, 1994, on compliments). Interviews have a large and yet unexplored potential for shedding light on pragmatic development. As in the case of other research approaches, in order to conduct and analyze interviews effectively, it is essential to consult the (very large and theoretically diverse) literature on research interviews (e.g., Gubrium & Holstein, 2002; Silverman, 2001; Wengraf, 2001).

Diaries

Diaries have been imported into research on pragmatic development from second language acquisition research, where this format of narrative self-report has provided useful insights on learners' and teachers' experiences with using, acquiring, and teaching the target language. Apart from an early study by Schmidt and Frota (1986), in which journals served as one data source to trace Schmidt's learning of Brazilian Portuguese, diaries have not been employed much in interlanguage pragmatics research. In the only published diary study, Cohen (1997) describes his rather unsuccessful learning of Japanese pragmatics through a university course. For her study of the acquisition of politeness in L2 Indonesian by six sojourning learners during a study abroad program, DuFon (1999) asked her participants to keep a semi-prestructured diary journal. Comparing several data sources in her ethnographic study, DuFon reported that some pragmatic events were more recordable through particular methods than others. For instance, all learners commented in their journal entries on the use of address terms, but none provided any observations on experience questions. Cohen's and DuFon's studies illustrate two forms of diary: the self-study diary, in which the diarist and the researcher are the same person, and the commissioned diary, in which the researcher requests participants (often language learners or teachers) to keep a journal that is then submitted to and analyzed by the researcher. Both forms of diary produce narratives that shed light on the process of learning L2 pragmatics from the diarists' perspectives, and in case of multiple participants, they are also a valuable source of information about individual differences in pragmatic development, as the example from DuFon's study earlier in this chapter illustrates.

Verbal Protocols

Verbal protocols (Ericsson & Simon, 1993), also known as "think-aloud protocols," are respondents' reports of internal cognitive processes that occur as they are working on a task (concurrent verbal protocols) or their recollections of processes after the task has been completed (consecutive verbal protocols). Concurrent verbal protocols have the advantage of eliciting online reports, and they thereby synchronize task performance and reporting, but they may also produce reactivity, that is, they can interfere with doing the task. A further limitation, specific to verbal protocols of oral production, is that they exclude spoken tasks because participants cannot produce task-related talk and verbal protocol talk at the same time. Retrospective verbal protocols do not suffer from such conflicts but, because of memory limitations, they may reveal participants' recollections of their thoughts during task completion rather than what they actually were thinking. In interlanguage pragmatics research, concurrent verbal protocols have been collected by Robinson (1992) in conjunction with a DCT eliciting refusals and by Roever (in press) as a validation instrument in a study on pragmatic assessment. Cohen and Olshtain (1993) and Widjadja (1997) gathered retrospective protocols after participants engaged in role-plays (see Gass & Mackey, 2000, for retrospective protocols in second language research).

A particular concern about verbal protocols in interlanguage pragmatics is the language of reporting. The native speakers of Japanese in Robinson's (1992) study delivered their protocols in English, probably in deference to the English-speaking researcher. Roever (in press) instructed his participants explicitly that they should speak whatever language they felt most at ease with, and that protocols supplied in another language than the target language (English) would be translated. In response, participants conducted most of their reports in their L1, resulting in more complete, and presumably more valid, verbalizations especially in the case of the less proficient L2 speakers, but it also required that participants be limited to L1 groups for which translators were at hand. Verbal reports are particularly useful for instrument development because they provide researchers with valuable information about respondents' understanding of and interaction with stimulus material. They should, therefore, be used more regularly in interlanguage pragmatics research, especially for questionnaire design. At the same time, recent reconceptualizations of verbal reports from a sociocognitive perspective (Smagorinsky, 1998) strongly recommend a more critical understanding of verbal reports than the information-processing view subscribes to (for discussion with a view to interlanguage pragmatics, cf. Kasper & Rose, in press).

Conclusion

Research methods, and especially methods of data collection, potentially influence research outcomes in any area of study. But in an inherently context-sensitive domain of language use, possible method effects are a particular concern. In some investigative approaches, such as ethnographic studies and multitrait multimethod studies in quantitative research, engaging several methods of data collection is mandated. Examples of ethnographic studies in developmental L2 pragmatics are the work by Siegal (1994) and DuFon (1999); in the testing of pragmatics, the framework developed by Hudson, et al. (1995) and subsequent applications (Brown, 2001a; Hudson, 2001; Yamashita, 1996; Yoshitake, 1997) as well as Roever (in press); and several interventional classroom studies include multiple measures in their pre- and posttests (e.g., Lyster, 1994; Rose & Ng, 2001; Takahashi, 2001, Tateyama, 2001; Tateyama et al., 1997). Such studies not only enable investigators to triangulate research findings but also bring to the fore the potential and limitations of different research methods in the study of pragmatic development.

REFERENCES

Achiba, M. (2002). *Learning to request in a second language: Child interlanguage pragmatics*. Clevedon, UK: Multilingual Matters.

Austin, J. L. (1962). *How to do things with words*. Oxford, UK: Oxford University Press.

Babbie, E. (2004). *The practice of social research* (10th ed.). Belmont, CA: Wadsworth.

Bardovi-Harlig, K. (1999). Exploring the interlanguage of interlanguage pragmatics: A research agenda for acquisitional pragmatics. *Language Learning, 49*, 677–713.

Bardovi-Harlig, K. (2001). Empirical evidence of the need for instruction in pragmatics. In K. R. Rose & G. Kasper (Eds.), *Pragmatics in language teaching* (pp. 13–32). New York: Cambridge University Press.

Bardovi-Harlig, K., & Dörnyei, Z. (1998). Do language learners recognize pragmatic violations? Pragmatic vs. grammatical awareness in instructed L2 learning. *TESOL Quarterly, 32*, 233–259.

Bardovi-Harlig, K., & Hartford, B. S. (1993). Learning the rules of academic talk: A longitudinal study of pragmatic development. *Studies in Second Language Acquisition, 15*, 279–304.

Bardovi-Harlig, K., & Hartford, B. (1996). Input in an institutional setting. *Studies in Second Language Acquisition, 18*, 171–188.

Bernard, H. R. (2000). Social research methods. Thousand Oaks, CA: Sage.

Bialystok, E. (1993). Symbolic representation and attentional control in pragmatic competence. In G. Kasper & S. Blum-Kulka (Eds.), Interlanguage pragmatics (pp. 43–59). New York: Oxford University Press.

Billmyer, K. (1990). "I really like your lifestyle": ESL learners learning how to compliment. Penn Working Papers in Educational Linguistics, 6, 31–48.

Billmyer, K., & Varghese, M. (2000). Investigationg instrument-based pragmatic variability: Effects of enhancing discourse completion tests. Applied Linguistics, 21, 517–552.

Blum-Kulka, S., & Olshtain, E. (1986). Too many words: Length of utterance and pragmatic failure. Studies in Second Language Acquisition 8, 47–61.

Blum-Kulka, S. (1982). Learning to say what you mean in a second language. Applied Linguistics, 3, 29–59.

Blum-Kulka, S. (1991). Interlanguage pragmatics: The case of requests. In R. Phillipson, E. Kellerman, L. Selinker, M. Sharwood Smith, & M. Swain (Eds.), Foreign/Second language pedagogy research (pp. 255–272). Clevedon, Avon, UK: Multilingual Matters.

Bouton, L. F. (1992). Culture, pragmatics and implicature. AFinLa Yearbook 1992, 35–61.

Bouton, L. F. (1994). Conversational implicature in the second language: Learned slowly when not deliberately taught. Journal of Pragmatics, 22, 157–167.

Bouton, L. F. (1999). Developing nonnative speaker skills in interpreting conversational implicatures in English: Explicit teaching can ease the process. In E. Hinkel (Ed.), Culture in second language teaching and learning (pp. 47–70). Cambridge, UK: Cambridge University Press.

Boxer, D. (1996). Ethnographic interviewing as a research tool in speech act analysis: The case of complaints. In S. M. Gass & J. Neu (Eds.), Speech acts across cultures (pp. 217–239). Berlin: Mouton de Gruyter.

Brown, J. D. (2001a). Pragmatics tests: Different purposes, different tests. In K. Rose & G. Kasper (Eds.), Pragmatics in language teaching (pp. 301–325). Cambridge, UK: Cambridge University Press.

Brown, J. D. (2001b). Using surveys in language programs. Cambridge, UK: Cambridge University Press.

Brown, P., & Levinson, S. D. (1987). Politeness: Some universals in language usage. Cambridge, UK: Cambridge University Press.

Carrell, P. (1981). Relative difficulty of request forms in L1/L2 comprehension. In M. Hines, & W. Rutherford (Eds.), On TESOL '81 (pp. 141–152). Washington, DC: TESOL.

Clark, H. H. (1979). Responding to indirect speech acts. Cognitive Psychology, 11, 430–477.

Cohen, A. D. (1997). Developing pragmatic ability: Insights from the accelerated study of Japanese. In H. M. Cook, K. Hijirida, & M. Tahara (Eds.), New trends and issues in teaching Japanese language and culture (Technical Report #15; pp. 133–159). Honolulu: University of Hawaii, Second Language Teaching and Curriculum Center.

Cohen, A., & Olshtain, E. (1981). Developing a measure of sociocultural competence: The case of apology. Language Learning, 31, 113–134.

Cohen, A., & Olshtain, E. (1993). The production of speech acts by EFL learners. TESOL Quarterly, 27, 33–56.

Cook, H. M. (2001). Why can't learners of Japanese as a foreign language distinguish polite from impolite speech styles? In K. R. Rose & G. Kasper (Eds.), Pragmatics in language teaching (pp. 80–102). Cambridge, UK: Cambridge University Press.

Doughty, C., & Williams, J. (Eds.). (1998). Focus on form in classroom second language acquisition. Cambridge, UK: Cambridge University Press.

DuFon, M. A. (1999). The acquisition of linguistic politeness in Indonesian as a second language by sojourners in naturalistic interactions. Unpublished doctoral dissertation, University of Hawaii at Manoa.

Edmondson, W., & House, J. (1991). Do learners talk too much? The waffle phenomenon in interlanguage pragmatics. In R. Phillipson, E. Kellerman, L. Selinker, M. Sharwood Smith, & M. Swain (Eds.), Foreign/second language pedagogy research: A commemorative volume for Claus Færch (pp. 273–287). Clevedon, Avon, UK: Multilingual Matters.

Eisenstein, M., & Bodman, J. W. (1986). "I very appreciate": Expressions of gratitude by native and non-native speakers of American English. Applied Linguistics, 7, 167–185.

Eisenstein, M., & Bodman, J. W. (1993). Expressing gratitude in American English. In G. Kasper & S. Blum-Kulka (Eds.), Interlanguage pragmatics (pp. 64–81). Oxford, UK: Oxford University Press.

Ellis, R. (1992). Learning to communicate in the classroom: A study of two learners' requests. Studies in Second Language Acquisition, 14, 1–23.

Ericsson, K. A., & Simon, H. A. (1993). Protocol analysis. Verbal reports as data. Cambridge, MA: MIT Press.

Færch, C., & Kasper, G. (1982). Phatic, metalingual and metacommunicative functions in discourse: Gambits and repair. In N. E. Enkvist (Ed.), Impromptu speech (pp. 71–103). Åbo, Finland: Åbo Akademi University.

Fraser, B., Rintell, E., & Walters, J. (1981). An approach to conducting research on the acquisition of pragmatic competence in a second language. In D. Larsen-Freeman (Ed.), Discourse analysis (pp. 75–81). Rowley, MA: Newbury House.

Fukuya, Y., & Clark, M. (2001). Input enhancement of mitigators. In L. Bouton (Ed.), Pragmatics and language learning, Vol. 10 (pp. 111–130). Urbana-Champaign, IL: Division of English as an International Language, University of Illinois.

García, C. (1989). Apologizing in English: Politeness strategies used by native and non-native speakers. Multilingua, 8, 3–20.

Gass, S. M., & Houck, N. (1999). Interlanguage refusals: A cross-cultural study of Japanese-English. Berlin: Mouton de Gruyter.

Gass, S. M., & Mackey, A. (2000). *Stimulated recall methodology in second language research*. Mahwah, NJ: Lawrence Erlbaum Associates.

Golato, A. (2003). Studying compliment responses: A comparison of DCTs and recordings of naturally occurring talk. *Applied Linguistics, 24*, 90–121.

Gubrium, J. F., & Holstein, J. A. (Eds.). (2002). *Handbook of interview research*. Thousand Oaks, CA: Sage.

Hall, J. (1995). "Aw, man, where you goin'?": Classroom interaction and the development of L2 interactional competence. *Issues in Applied Linguistics, 6*, 37–62.

Hartford, B. S., & Bardovi-Harlig, K. (1992). Experimental and observational data in the study of interlanguage pragmatics. In L. F. Bouton, & Y. Kachru (Eds.), *Pragmatics and language learning monograph series* (pp. 33–52). Urbana, IL: DEIL.

Hassall, T. J. (1997). *Requests by Australian learners of Indonesian*. Unpublished doctoral dissertation, Australian National University.

Hill, T. (1997). *The development of pragmatic competence in an EFL context*. Unpublished doctoral dissertation, Temple University, Tokyo, Japan.

Hinkel, E. (1997). Appropriateness of advice: DCT and multiple choice data. *Applied Linguistics, 18*, 1–26.

House, J. (1996). Developing pragmatic fluency in English as a foreign language: Routines and metapragmatic awareness. *Studies in Second Language Acquisition, 18*, 225–252.

House, J., & Kasper, G. (1981). *Zur Rolle der Kognition in Kommunikationskursen*. [The role of cognition in communication courses.] *Die Neueren Sprachen, 80*, 42–55.

Hudson, T. (2001). Indicators for pragmatic instruction: Some quantitative measures. In K. R. Rose & G. Kasper (Eds.), *Pragmatics in language teaching* (pp. 283–300). Cambridge, UK: Cambridge University Press.

Hudson, T., Detmer, E., & Brown, J. D. (1995). *Developing prototypic measures of cross-cultural pragmatics* (Technical Report #7). Honolulu: University of Hawaii, Second Language Teaching and Curriculum Center.

Johnston, B., Kasper, G., & Ross, S. (1998). Effect of rejoinders in production questionnaires. *Applied Linguistics 19*, 2, 157–182.

Kasper, G. (1981). *Pragmatische Aspekte in der Interimsprache*. Tübingen: Narr.

Kasper, G. (2000). Data collection in pragmatics research. In H. Spencer-Oatey (Ed.), *Culturally speaking* (pp. 316–341). London: Continuum.

Kasper, G. (2001a). Classroom research on interlanguage pragmatics. In K. R. Rose & G. Kasper (Eds.), *Pragmatics in language teaching* (pp. 33–60). Cambridge, UK: Cambridge University Press.

Kasper, G. (2001b). Four perspectives on pragmatic development. *Applied Linguistics, 22*, 502–530.

Kasper, G., & Rose, K. R. (2002). *Pragmatic development in a second language*. Oxford, UK: Blackwell.

Kasper, G., & Rose, K. R. (in press). *Research methods in interlanguage pragmatics: A critical review*. Mahwah, NJ: Lawrence Erlbaum Associates.

Kerekes, J. (1992). *Development in nonnative speakers' use and perception of assertiveness and supportiveness in mixed-sex conversations* (Occasional Paper No. 21). Honolulu, HI: University of Hawaii at Manoa, Department of English as a Second Language.

Kim, I.-O. (2000). *Relationship of onset of age in ESL acquisition and extent of informal input to appropriateness and nativeness in performing four speech acts in English*. Unpublished doctoral dissertation, New York University.

Koike, D. A. (1989). Pragmatic competence and adult L2 acquisition: Speech acts in interlanguage. *Modern Language Journal, 73*, 279–289.

Koike, D. A. (1996). Transfer of pragmatic competence and suggestions in Spanish foreign language learning. In S. M. Gass & J. Neu (Eds.), *Speech acts across cultures* (pp. 257–281). Berlin: Mouton de Gruyter.

Kubota, M. (1995). Teachability of conversational implicature to Japanese EFL learners. *IRLT Bulletin, 9*, 35–67. Tokyo: The Institute for Research in Language Teaching.

Kuha, M. (1999). *The influence of interaction and instructions on speech act data*. Unpublished doctoral dissertation, Indiana University.

Labov, W. (1972). *Sociolinguistic patterns*. Philadelphia: University of Pennsylvania Press.

Leech, G. (1983). *Principles of pragmatics*. London: Longman.

Liddicoat, A. J., & Crozet, C. (2001). Acquiring French interactional norms through instruction. In K. R. Rose & G. Kasper (Eds.), *Pragmatics in language teaching* (pp. 125–144). Cambridge, UK: Cambridge University Press.

LoCastro, V. (2001). Individual differences in second language acquisition: Attitudes, learner subjectivity, and pragmatic norms. *System, 29*, 69–89.

Lyster, R. (1994). The effect of functional-analytic teaching on aspects of French immersion students' sociolinguistic competence. *Applied Linguistics, 15*, 263–287.

Maeshiba, N., Yoshinaga, N., Kasper, G., & Ross, S. (1996). Transfer and proficiency in interlanguage apologizing. In S. M. Gass & J. Neu (Eds.), *Speech acts across cultures* (pp. 155–187). Berlin: Mouton de Gruyter.

Margalef-Boada, T. (1993). *Research methods in interlanguage pragmatics: An inquiry into data collection procedures*. Unpublished doctoral dissertation, Indiana University.

Matsumura, S. (2001). Learning the rules for offering advice: A quantitative approach to second language socialization. *Language Learning, 51*, 635–679.

Miles, P. (1994). *Compliments and gender.* (Occasional Paper No. 26). Honolulu, HI: University of Hawaii at Manoa.

Miller, D. C., & Salkind, N. J. (2002). *Handbook of research design and social measurement* (6th ed.). Newbury Park, CA: Sage.

Morrow, C. (1996). *The pragmatic effects of instruction on ESL learners' production of complaint and refusal speech acts.*, Unpublished doctoral dissertation, State University of New York at Buffalo.

Niezgoda, K., & Röver, C. (2001). Pragmatic and grammatical awareness: A function of learning environment? In K. R. Rose & G. Kasper (Eds.), *Pragmatics in language teaching* (pp. 63–79). Cambridge, UK: Cambridge University Press.

Norton, B. (2000). *Identity and language learning.* Harlow, Essex, UK: Longman/Pearson Education.

Ohta, A. (1999). Interactional routines and the socialization of interactional style in adult learners of Japanese. *Journal of Pragmatics, 31*, 1493–1512.

Ohta, A. S. (2001). From acknowledgment to alignment: A longitudinal study of the development of expression of alignment by classroom learners of Japanese. In K. R. Rose & G. Kasper (Eds.), *Pragmatics in language teaching* (pp. 103–120). New York: Cambridge University Press.

Olshtain, E., & Cohen, A. D. (1989). Speech act behavior across languages. In H. Dechert & M. Raupach (Eds.), *Transfer in language production* (pp. 53–67). Norwood, NJ: Ablex.

Olshtain, E., & Cohen, A. (1990). The learning of complex speech act behavior. *TESL Canada Journal, 7*, 45–65.

Pearson, L. (1998). Spanish L2 pragmatics: The effects of metapragmatic discussion. Paper presented at the Second Language Research Forum, University of Hawaii, Manoa, October.

Peräkylä, A. (1997). Reliability and validity in research based on transcripts. In D. Silverman (Ed.), *Qualitative research* (pp. 201–220). London: Sage.

Piirainen-Marsh, A. (1995). *Face in second language conversation.* Jyväskylä, Finland: University of Jyväskylä.

Psathas, G. (1990). Introduction: Methodological issues and recent developments in the study of naturally occurring interaction. In G. Psathas (Ed.), *Interaction competence* (pp. 1–30). Washington, DC: International Institute for Ethnomethodology and Conversation Analysis and University Press of America.

Rintell, E. (1981). Sociolinguistic variation and pragmatic ability: A look at learners. *International Journal of the Sociology of Language, 27*, 11–34.

Rintell, E., & Mitchell, C. J. (1989). Studying requests and apologies: An inquiry into method. In S. Blum-Kulka, J. House, & G. Kasper (Eds.), *Cross-cultural pragmatics* (pp. 248–272). Norwood, NJ: Ablex.

Robinson, M. A. (1992). Introspective methodology in interlanguage pragmatics research. In G. Kasper (Ed.), *Pragmatics of Japanese as a native and target language* (Technical Report #3; pp. 27–82). Honolulu, HI: University of Hawaii at Manoa, Second Language Teaching and Curriculum Center.

Röver, C. (1996). Linguistische Routinen: Systematische, psycholinguistische und fremdsprachendidaktische Überlegungen, *Fremdsprachen und Hochschule, 46*, 43–60.

Roever, C. (in press). *Testing ESL pragmatics: Development and validation of a web-based assessment battery.* Frankfurt: Peter Lang.

Rose, K. R. (2000). An exploratory cross-sectional study of interlanguage pragmatic development. *Studies in Second Language Acquisition, 22*, 27–67.

Rose, K. R., & Kasper, G. (Eds.). (2001). *Pragmatics in language teaching.* Cambridge, UK: Cambridge University Press.

Rose, K. R., & Ng, C. (2001). Inductive and deductive teaching of compliments and compliment responses. In K. R. Rose & G. Kasper (Eds.), *Pragmatics in language teaching* (pp. 145–170). Cambridge, UK: Cambridge University Press.

Salsbury, T., & Bardovi-Harlig, K. (2001). "I know your mean, but I don't think so." Disagreements in L2 English. In L. F. Bouton (Ed.), *Pragmatics and language learning* (Vol. 10; pp. 131–151). Urbana, IL: University of Illinois, Division of English as an International Language.

Salsbury, T., & Bardovi-Harlig, K. (2000). Oppositional talk and the acquisition of modality in L2 English. In B. Swierzbin, F. Morris, M. Anderson, C. A. Klee, & E. Tarone (Eds.), *Social and cognitive factors in second language acquisition* (pp. 56–76). Somerville, MA: Cascadilla Press.

Sawyer, M. (1992). The development of pragmatics in Japanese as a second language: The sentence-final particle *ne.* In G. Kasper (Ed.), *Pragmatics of Japanese as a native and foreign language* (Technical Report #3; pp. 83–125). Honolulu, HI: University of Hawaii at Manoa, Second Language Teaching and Curriculum Center.

Scarcella, R. (1983). Discourse accent in second language performance. In S. M. Gass & L. Selinker (Eds.), *Language transfer in language learning* (pp. 306–326). Rowley, MA: Newbury House.

Schiffrin, D. (1987). *Discourse markers.* New York: Cambridge University Press.

Schmidt, R. (1983). Interaction, acculturation and the acquisition of communicative competence. In N. Wolfson & E. Judd (Eds.), *Sociolinguistics and second language acquisition* (pp. 137–174). Rowley, MA: Newbury House.

Schmidt, R. (1995). Consciousness and foreign language learning: A tutorial on the role of attention and awareness in learning. In R. Schmidt (Ed.), *Attention and awareness in foreign language learning* (pp. 1–63). Honolulu, HI: University of Hawaii, Second Language Teaching & Curriculum Center.

Schmidt, R. (2001). Attention. In P. Robinson (Ed.), *Cognition and second language instruction* (pp. 3–33). New York: Cambridge University Press.

Schmidt, R., & Frota, S. N. (1986). Developing basic conversational ability in a second language: A case study of an adult learner of Portuguese. In R. Day (Ed.), *Talking to learn* (pp. 237–326). Rowley, MA: Newbury House.

Schumann, J. H. (1978). *The pidginization process: A model for second language acquisition.* Rowley, MA: Newbury House.

Sharwood Smith, M. (1993). Input enhancement in instructed SLA: Theoretical bases. *Studies in Second Language Acquisition, 15,* 165–179.

Shimamura, K. (1993). *Judgment of request strategies and contextual factors by American and Japanese EFL learners* (Occasional Paper #25). Honolulu, HI: University of Hawaii at Manoa, Department of English as a Second Language.

Siegal, M. (1994). *Looking east: Identity construction & White women learning Japanese.* Unpublished doctoral dissertation, University of California at Berkeley.

Siegal, M. (1996). The role of learner subjectivity in second language sociolinguistic competency: Western women learning Japanese. *Applied Linguistics, 17,* 356–382.

Silverman, D. (2001). *Interpreting qualitative data* (2nd ed.). London: Sage.

Smagorinsky, P. (1998). Thinking and speech and protocol analysis. *Mind, Culture, and Activity, 5,* 157–177.

Takahashi, S. (1995). *Pragmatic transferability of L1 indirect request strategies perceived by Japanese learners of English.* Unpublished doctoral dissertation, University of Hawaii at Manoa.

Takahashi, S. (1996). Pragmatic transferability. *Studies in Second Language Acquisition, 18,* 189–223.

Takahashi, S. (2000). *The effects of motivation and proficiency on the awareness of pragmatic strategies in implicit foreign language learning.* Unpublished manuscript.

Takahashi, S. (2001). The role of input enhancement in developing pragmatic competence. In K. R. Rose & G. Kasper (Eds.), *Pragmatics in language teaching* (pp. 171–199). Cambridge, UK: Cambridge University Press.

Takahashi, T., & Beebe, L. (1987). The development of pragmatic competence by Japanese learners of English. *JALT Journal, 8,* 131–155.

Tao, H., & Thompson, S. A. (1991). English backchannels in Mandarin conversation: A case study of super-stratum pragmatic "interference". *Journal of Pragmatics, 16,* 209–223.

Tateyama, Y. (2001). Explicit and implicit teaching of pragmatics routines: Japanese *sumimasen.* In K. R. Rose & G. Kasper (Eds.), *Pragmatics in language teaching* (pp. 200–222). Cambridge, UK: Cambridge University Press.

Tateyama, Y., Kasper, G., Mui, L., Tay, H.-M., & Thananart, O. (1997). Explicit and implicit teaching of pragmatic routines. In L. Bouton (Ed.), *Pragmatics and language learning* (Vol. 8; pp. 163–177). Urbana, IL: University of Illinois at Urbana-Champaign.

Thomas, J. (1983). Cross-cultural pragmatic failure. *Applied Linguistics, 4,* 91–112.

Tokuda, M. (2001). L2 learners' perceptions of politeness in Japanese: The evaluations on non-native speaker in L2 Japanese. Unpublished doctoral dissertation, University of Hawaii at Manoa.

Trosborg, A. (1995). *Interlanguage pragmatics: Requests, complaints and apologies.* Berlin: Mouton de Gruyter.

Walters, J. (1980). Grammar, meaning, and sociological appropriateness in second language acquisition. *Canadian Journal of Psychology—Revue Canadienne de Psychologie, 34,* 337–345.

Wengraf, T. (2001). *Qualitative research interviewing.* London: Sage.

White, S. (1989). Backchannels across cultures: A study of Americans and Japanese. *Language in Society, 18,* 59–76.

Widjaja, C. S. (1997). A study of data refusal: Taiwanese vs. American females. *University of Hawaii Working Papers in ESL, 15*(2), 1–43.

Wildner-Bassett, M. (1984). *Improving pragmatic aspects of learners' interlanguage.* Tübingen, Germany: Narr.

Wildner-Bassett, M. (1986). Teaching and learning 'polite noises': Improving pragmatic aspects of advanced adult learners' interlanguage. In G. Kasper (Ed.), *Learning, teaching and communication in the foreign language classroom* (pp. 163–178). Aarhus, Denmark: Aarhus University Press.

Wildner-Bassett, M. (1994). Intercultural pragmatics and proficiency: "Polite" noises for cultural appropriateness. *International Review of Applied Linguistics, 32,* 3–17.

Wishnoff, J. R. (2000). Hedging your bets: L2 learners' acquisition of pragmatic devices in academic writing and computer-mediated discourse. *Second Language Studies, 19,* 127–157. (Working Papers of the Department of Second Language Studies, University of Hawaii.)

Yamashita, S. O. (1996). *Six measures of JSL pragmatics* (Technical Report #14). Honolulu, HI: University of Hawaii, Second Language Teaching and Curriculum Center.

Yoshimi, D. R. (2001). Explicit instruction and the use of interactional discourse markers. In K. R. Rose & G. Kasper (Eds.), *Pragmatics in language teaching* (pp. 223–244). Cambridge, UK: Cambridge University Press.

Yoshitake, S. S. (1997). *Measuring interlanguage pragmatic competence of Japanese students of English as a foreign language: A multi-test framework evaluation.* Unpublished doctoral dissertation, Columbia Pacific University, Novata, CA.

19

Sociocultural and Second Language Learning Research: An Exegesis[1]

James P. Lantolf
Pennsylvania State University

INTRODUCTION

Since the publication of Frawley and Lantolf (1985), there has been growing interest in the sociocultural theoretic approach to second language (L2) development (e.g., Lantolf & Appel, 1994; Lantolf, 2000c). The theory proposes that humans attain the capacity to voluntarily control or regulate their memory, attention, perception, planning, learning, and development, as they appropriate mediating artifacts, including language, as they are brought into culturally specified and organized activities.

Instead of reviewing yet again the literature on sociocultural theory and L2 research (see Lantolf & Pavlenko, 1995; Lantolf, 2000b; Lantolf, 2002), this chapter will focus on how the theory and its affiliated research have been interpreted and critiqued by scholars in the mainstream of second language acquisition (SLA). To do this, I will rely on several sources as representative of mainstream work that has addressed Sociocultural Theory (SCT) informed research—Atkinson (2002), Ellis (1997, 2003), Lightbown and Spada (1999), and Mitchell and Myles (1998). Although some of the criticisms of SCT research on L2 learning are on the mark and merit serious consideration by those working within this framework, others reflect a misunderstanding of the theory, and for this reason an exegesis is needed. The topics I will deal with here include the following: the zone of proximal development; SCT—a theory of language use or a theory of cognition; internalization and the autonomous learner; SCT and linguistic theory; rate and route of L2 acquisition; SCT and other social theories of SLA.

Some, such as Schinke-Llano (1995, p. 25) have remarked that "grappling with Vygotskian theory can sometimes be frustrating, much like dealing with a video camera that slips in and out of focus." I don't believe, however, that theory is as slippery as some might think. Its constructs and principles have not changed since they were originally laid down by Vygotsky, Luria, and Leontiev; but as with any theory worth its salt, the details have been debated and sharpened over the course of time. Indeed,

Vygotsky's collected works must be read as a struggle to clarify, modify, and develop the theory through the very activity of writing, which as Vygotsky argued, was a form of development.

ZONE OF PROXIMAL DEVELOPMENT

I will begin with the most well known construct of Vygotsky's theory, the *zone of proximal development* (ZPD). The ZPD emerged from Vygotsky's observation that for some children, schooling significantly increased their mental development, as measured by IQ tests (van der Veer & Valsiner, 1991). Briefly, the ZPD is a projection of a person's developmental future in the sense that what one can do in cooperation with others today one can do alone tomorrow (Vygotsky 1986, p. 188). Counter to Piaget's stance in which development lays down the pathway for teaching and learning to follow, for Vygotsky, "the only good kind of instruction is that which marches ahead of development and leads it" (Vygotsky, 1986, p. 188), and this is instruction that occurs in the ZPD. Learning, for Vygotsky, is assisted performance, whereas development is the ability to regulate mental and social activity as a consequence of having appropriated, or internalized, that assistance. This allows the individual to engage in activity that is independent of specific material circumstances (e.g., the language classroom).

Lightbown and Spada (1999, p. 44) point out that according to SCT, L2 "learners advance to higher levels of linguistic knowledge when they collaborate and interact with speakers of the second language who are more knowledgeable than they are." To be sure, this claim has indeed been made in the SCT L2 literature, but others, including Donato (1994), Swain and Lapkin (1998), and Ohta (2001) have shown that learners are able to collaboratively construct knowledge of an L2 in the absence of an expert knower. It is interesting to note that Lightbown and Spada present data from Donato (1994) as an illustration of how learning occurs in the ZPD. Moreover, missing from Lightbown and Spada's characterization of the ZPD is its orientation toward future development. At two different points in their text (p. 23 and p. 44) they essentially represent the ZPD as entailing assisted performance only, and although this is not inaccurate, it excludes the critical idea that what an individual (child or adult) can achieve with assistance, he or she will be able to achieve without assistance in the future.

According to Lightbown and Spada (1999) SCT differs from other interactionist perspectives in its assumption that "language acquisition takes place in the interactions of learner and interlocutor," instead of "internally and invisibly" as learners operate with the "linguistic raw material" offered by modified input (p. 44). Indeed, most L2 researchers seem to assume that SLA is "not directly observable" and can only be inferred on the basis of learner performance, including the production and comprehension of utterances and written texts (Carroll, 2001, pp. 16–17). As I will discuss later, I believe that it may very well be possible to observe L2 learning, at least in part, through analysis of private speech.

ZPD and Krashen's i + 1

Perhaps the most persistent and problematic aspect affiliated with the ZPD in L2 research is the mistaken assumption that it somehow equates to Krashen's notion of i + 1. Several recent papers have clearly demonstrated the incommensurability of these two constructs (de Guerrero, 1996; Dunn & Lantolf, 1998; Kinginger, 2001, 2002); therefore, I will forgo a detailed examination of the matter here. Nevertheless, it bears repeating, as Dunn and Lantolf (1998) argue, that the constructs are incommensurable because the underlying theoretical frameworks from which each emerges are themselves incommensurable. Krashen's theory is anchored in the information-processing model of cognition and communication and its underlying computational metaphor—a metaphor that privileges input—output relationships and abstract (unconscious) symbol manipulation along with the notion of an idealized autonomous knower. Vygotsky's theory rejects the notion of the autonomous individual (see the following) as well as the assumption that cognition is something that goes on exclusively, and invisibly, inside the head. Moreover, Krashen's hypothesis assumes a Language Acquisition Device (LAD) that is responsible for learning, whereas Vygotsky's theory insists that humans, not some LAD, are constantly developing the capacity to control/regulate their own mental activity. As Vygotsky put it *"man* [sic] *controls his brain and not the brain the man*... that without man his behaviour cannot be explained, that psychology cannot be expounded in terms of processes but only in terms of drama" (cited in Yaroshevsky, 1989 p. 230).[2] By drama, here, Vygotsky is referring to mediated social activity, which by its very nature is unpredictable; in essence, development is a drama without a definitive conclusion.

Krashen's is a model of language acquisition; Vygotsky's is a theory of human development. In fact, from Vygotsky's perspective it is inappropriate to speak of language acquisition, if it is assumed, as Krashen's model does, to be a sequential and predictable process. Vygotsky rejected this view of development in favor of a revolutionary perspective. Acquisition models see things as a "continuous, steady, and linear" flow without ruptures, regressions, and that result in predictable outcomes (Newman & Holzman, 1996, p. 134). Vygotksy sees development as a historical process with breaks, innovation, and unpredictability as the norm (see Belz in press; and Pavlenko & Lantolf, 2000).

The key to understanding the developmental activity that is the ZPD resides in Vygotsky's notion of imitation. Despite its unfortunate behaviorist baggage, "imitation is a critically important developmental activity, because it is the chief means by which children are *related to as other than*, and in advance of, who they are," as in the case of linguistic interaction where "adults relate to young children not as parrots, but as speakers" (Newman & Holzman, 1993, p. 151). For Vygotsky imitation is not a "mechanical activity" in which "anyone can imitate almost anything if shown how" (Vygotsky, 1986, p. 187); on the contrary, "to imitate, it is necessary to possess the means of stepping from something one knows to something new" and this can be accomplished with someone else's assistance (p. 187). It is here that Vygotsky saw the influence of instruction on development in the ZPD.

According to Tomasello (1999, p. 84), in imitative learning, children "attempt to place themselves in the 'intentional space' of the user—discerning the user's goal, what she is using the artifact [e.g., hammer, pencil, language] 'for'." Thus, through imitation in the ZPD, the child comes to see the "intentional affordances" of culturally constructed artifacts as well as the "intentional relations that other persons have with that object or artifact—that is, the intentional relations that other persons have to the world through the artifact" (Tomasello, 1999, pp. 84–85). Swain and Lapkin (in press) show that when interacting with others, L2 learners are intentionally able to imitate features of a second language that they do not yet understand, because the interlocutor gives meaning to the features, and in this way the learners come to understand what they initially did not.

Imitation is not simply mimicking, repeating, or parroting; it is a creative, transformative activity that only humans are genuinely capable of (Vygotsky, 1987; Tomasello, 1999). In symbolic play, for example, children "extract the intentional affordances of different objects and play with them" which often entails free interchange of their culturally intended use, such as when they use pencils as hammers, while at the same time "smiling at the adult in the process to signal that this is not stupidity but playfulness" (Tomasello, 1999, p. 85).

Although imitation is, especially in early childhood, transformative and revolutionary, once children enter school, it is frequently construed as cheating, and when it is encouraged, it is often construed as repetition and not transformation (Newman & Holzman, 1993, p. 152). This may not show up overtly, of course, but, for example, when taking tests, students are normally expected to (re)produce the correct answer, which usually has been previously supplied by the teacher or the textbook.

Some L2 researchers have argued SCT research concerned with the ZPD has failed to adequately distinguish unassisted learner performance from that which occurs with scaffolded assistance. In other words, if the ZPD is to be a useful construct in explaining L2 development, it must be clearly shown that although learners are *unable* to deploy specific linguistic forms and meanings independently, they are indeed *able* to do so with help from someone else (Ellis, 2003, p. 200). Moreover, to demonstrate that learners are capable of assisted performance in and of itself does not make the case for the relevance of the ZPD (p. 200). This is clearly a reasonable observation. However, the study by Aljaafreh and Lantolf (1994) shows precisely the kind of evidence required to illustrate the usefulness of the theoretical construct. The study examined the use of high frequency features of English (tense morphology, articles, model verbs, and prepositions) in the written performance of three English as a Second Language (ESL) learners. Each learner met individually with an expert tutor outside of her regular class meeting (the tutor was not the course instructor) once a week for an 8-week period. During each session the tutor would help the learner correct the grammar in her written assignment. The initial composition was not corrected as it served to develop a base profile of each learner's unassisted performance with regard to the four grammatical features under consideration. The researchers examined the kind of assistance offered by the tutor (e.g., explicit help in which the learner was provided with the correct form; or implicit clues, as when the learner was asked if she noticed anything wrong with a particular form) and the learners' uptake of that assistance. Development through the ZPD was documented over time as learners manifested greater independence from the tutor's guidance and enhanced accuracy in their use of the relevant forms. However, as Lantolf and Aljaafreh (1995) observed, learner development was not a smooth linear process; instead, it followed the type of irregular trajectory captured by Vygotsky's description of development as a revolutionary process. This showed up in either of two ways: from one tutorial session to the next a given learner required more instead of less explicit assistance to locate and correct an error; or a learner who produced the correct form for a particular feature (e.g., irregular past tense form, "took") for two or three compositions in a row, produced the form with regular past tense morphology (i.e., "taked").

Nassaji and Swain (2000), in a small-scale study of two learners, provide additional support for Aljaafreh and Lantolf's (1994) findings. They confirmed that other regulation that is sensitive to a learner's ZPD has a greater effect on learning than does randomly provided implicit or explicit assistance. In a somewhat different, but relevant study, Swain and Lapkin (2002) report that learners of French were able to use formal differences they noticed between their own written text and a version of the same text reformulated by a native speaker of the language. Although the learners noticed a high percentage of the reformulations, they frequently rejected those they had not noticed when pointed out to them on the grounds that the features did not jibe with their own rules of French grammar. The interesting finding was that the learners moved from unassisted performance (i.e., their original text) to performance mediated by the reformulated text to improve their future performance (i.e., their revised text). Thus, as Swain and Lapkin argue, the learners appropriated forms available in the reformulated text because they were within the learner's ZPD.

Mitchell and Myles (1998) note that SCT research on the ZPD has focused on conscious performance as when learners either produce written texts, as in the studies just considered, or when they formulate written scripts to prompt oral performance (e.g., Donato, 1994). Recently, however, Ohta (2001) has examined scaffolded performance in spontaneous speech. In what she calls "assisted performance in action," Ohta analyzes the ways in which adult classroom learners of Japanese scaffold each other through a variety of classroom tasks and exercises, including spontaneous oral performance. Included among the scaffolding strategies uncovered by Ohta are several that parallel those provided by the expert tutor in Aljaafreh and Lantolf (1994), including explicit correction and explanation as well as implicit prompts (elongation of a final syllable or repetition of a word). Another frequently used form of assistance was "waiting," which, according to Ohta (p. 89), is important "because assistance is only helpful when it is needed, not when it is redundant with the learner's established abilities." In other words, holding off on feedback offers learners the opportunity to gain fuller control of knowledge that immediate explicit assistance might not. Ohta also found that peers engage in language play (p. 107), not reported in Aljaafreh and Lantolf (1994), as a form of assistance. She notes that students carrying out joint tasks on occasion playfully manipulated the sounds occurring in certain Japanese morphemes (e.g., adjectival nouns) as a way of helping each other focus on the problematic aspects of these forms (see also Broner & Tarone, 2001).

Two important questions relating to the ZPD need to be addressed: "Do people who receive timely and effective scaffolding/means of mediation actually learn any faster than those who get less help ? Does intervention in the ZPD merely scaffold people more rapidly along common routes of interlanguage development, or can these routes be by passed/altered, by skilled co-construction ?" (Mitchell and Myles, 1998, p. 162). Although rate of learning is an important matter and clearly more research needs to focus on answering this question, it is the second question that is more interesting. Pienemann's (1998) processing model and related teachability hypothesis, for instance, claims that for certain sets of features in any given L2, a specific path must be followed by all learners and although teaching may affect the rate at which acquisition occurs, it does not influence the developmental sequence. SCT, on the other hand, because of its fundamental theoretical assumption that development is revolutionary and therefore unpredictable, have a good deal of difficulty with claims of universal predetermined developmental trajectories that are impervious to instructional intervention (Newman & Holzman, 1997, p. 73).

The pedagogical theory of P. Gal'perin, based on Vygotsky's principles, argues that instruction indeed plays a central role in shaping the route and rate of any type of mental development. Gal'perin and his associates have established a robust research program on classroom learning, including first and additional languages (see Carpay, 1974; Gal'perin, 1992; Karpova, 1977; Komarova, 1988, 1991; Markova, 1979; Talyzina, 1981). The key factor in Gal'perin's complex pedagogical model is the materialization and internalization of the object of study. For instance, Karpova (1977) implemented a successful program for teaching very young (2 to 3 years of age) Russian-speaking children the concept of a word through use of material support provided by differently colored plates, which enabled the children to easily perceive the individual words comprising simple sentences in Russian where before they were unable to distinguish words from phrases or even entire sentences. Markova (1979) discusses a 10-year, large-scale pedagogical project carried out with some three-thousand Russian students that was designed to enhance high levels of writing and speaking ability in their native language.

Carpay (1974) reports on a study designed to teach Russian speakers German adjective declensions and Dutch speakers Russian verbal aspect by first providing students with material models illustrating the meaning of the concepts of case and aspect in the respective languages. Following Gal'perin's framework, the students then verbalized privately in whispered and subvocal speech the relevant concepts in order to internalize these concepts. Moving from materialization to verbalization "is the crucial point in the passage from external to internal" (León, 2001, p. 274). Once internalization occurs, the knowledge can then serve the functional needs of the individuals independently of the particular circumstances in which it was appropriated. Swain (2000) reports on a study conducted by her doctoral student, S. Holunga, that shows that ESL learners instructed to verbalize specific metacognitive strategies such as predicting, planning, monitoring, and evaluating during collaborative tasks performed better on a posttest than did learners who were taught the same strategies but were not instructed to verbalize them.

Finally, a 15-week project by one of my own students, E. Negueruela (2003), implemented a Gal'pernian syllabus in an intermediate, university-level, Spanish L2 classroom. Negueruela argues that teaching students to understand conceptually the meaning of such grammatical features as tense/aspect, copula verbs, and clitic pronouns, followed by procedures aimed at materializing (e.g., diagrams, Silent Way rods), verbalizing, and internalizing these meanings, learners were able to perform at a more advanced level of ability than generally happens as a result of instruction that presents grammar as rules-of-thumb. In a rule-of-thumb presentation, found in virtually all current language textbooks, such features as tense/aspect are "explained" in the form of lists of unrelated surface descriptions: in Spanish for example—use the imperfect for telling time, for actions that are on going in the past, for background information in narratives, etc.; use the preterit for completed actions, for repeated actions, for the beginning of some action, etc. According to Negueruela, conceptual understanding, in Vygotsky's view the key to development in the school setting, requires instruction to present learners with coherent scientific knowledge of the type found in linguistic research. Although this appears to fly in the face of the assumptions of communicative language teaching where focus on form is to be backgrounded in favor of meaning negotiation, SCT argues that form needs to be brought to the fore, but with emphasis on the meaning of form in communication. Space does not permit further discussion of this perhaps controversial claim; nevertheless, the point is that when instruction makes it possible for learners to gain a conceptual understanding of a feature of language, or indeed a feature of any subject matter, it has a profound influence in shaping how development unfolds, both with regard to rate and route.

THE AUTONOMOUS KNOWER AND INTERNALIZATION

One of the basic assumptions of mainstream SLA theorizing is that despite the importance of communicative interaction, learning ultimately happens in the mind of the individual autonomous learner. This is not without its problems when it comes to the classroom setting. Ellis (1997) points out that belief in the autonomous knower and its affiliated "input metaphor" is that its asocial assumption "warrants the disassociation of teaching from the social contexts that shape how and what learners learn" (p. 242). In my view, the autonomous knower and input metaphors contribute to the general claim that teaching can only affect the rate and not the route of learning. These metaphors tend to deskill (my term) teachers because they reduce teaching to the provision of optimal input that will, theoretically at least, promote learning for all learners.

One of the reasons why the autonomous knower and input metaphors may be difficult to abandon is the assumption that overgeneralizations such as *eated cannot be explained through social interaction (Ellis 1997, p. 244). Thus, the dualism between embedded individuals (that is, real people involved in concrete real world activity) and the homogenized IDEAL learner—a universal and "lonely" (Atkinson, 2002, p. 536) being who is the same always and everywhere, must somehow be retained.

However, SCT as a monistic theory of mind that argues for a necessary dialectic relationship between the individual and the social (in fact, according to Vygotsky there can be no individuals independent of social and cultural circumstances) it is indeed possible to account for overgeneralizations without recourse to the social-cognitive split some, including Ellis (1997), Kasper (1997) and Atkinson (2002), want to sustain. I want to make it clear, because there does seem to be a good deal of misunderstanding among mainstream researchers, that SCT is not a sociolinguistic theory of language use; it is a psychological/psycholinguistic theory (see Leontiev, 1981) that explains human mental functioning on the basis of situated sociocultural activity that is mediated in large part by communicative practices.

According to Newman and Holzman (1996, p. 90) "to the extent that it [modern psychology] has ignored and attempted to eliminate from its investigations the essential sociality and historicality of human beings (including psychologists' own), it has focused on the isolated individual it has constructed." They note that despite its apparent "obsession with and glorification of the individual" (p. 76), psychology "has never been particularly concerned with individuals as individuals;" rather "its concern has been methodological—the individual is a useful construct in making knowledge claims about groups or formulating general laws of behavior" and has shown little interest in real concrete individuals in all of their "human diversity and uniqueness" (p. 74). Lave (1997, p. 64) suggests that although it might be possible to see laboratory experiments as what occurs when individuals "are asked to solve new problems in new circumstances," the problem is that the lab setting is unlike most mundane circumstances, usually requiring participants to perform tasks in a given timeframe while following a predetermined procedure. Moreover, according to Lave, "neither the experimenter nor the subject is likely to know how the situation is related to previous situations in which the subject has been routinely involved" and the experimenter is unlikely to pay much attention to the potential differences between the two circumstances (p. 65). SCT, on the other hand, recognizes the centrality of human individuals, but not as abstract, autonomous entities; rather, as continually active material and historical beings that dialectically emerge from, and at the same time remain part of, sociocultural communities (see Tulviste 1991, p. 85).

In the case at hand, what is at issue is not the form *eated* itself, but the (over) generalization process that gives rise to this form. Vygotsky argued that the key to overcoming the Cartesian dualism resides in the process of *internalization*. According to Kozulin (1990, p. 116), "the essential element in the formation of higher mental functions is the process of internalization." It is through internalization in the ZPD that activity between individuals or individuals and cultural artifacts is transformed into intramental activity (Vygotsky, 1978). It is important to keep in mind that internalization does not literally mean "'within the individual' or 'in the brain'"(Stetsenko, 1999, p. 245), exclusively, although certainly the brain is implicated in thinking (see the following). Rather it is a metaphor to capture the notion of the individual performing concrete and ideal activity "without the immediately present problem situation 'in the mind'" (Stetsenko, 1999, p. 245) and independently of others' "thoughts and understandings" (Ball, 2000, p. 250). It is in this process "of historically determined and culturally organized ways of operating on information that the social nature of people comes to be their psychological nature as well" (Luria, 1979, p. 45).

In L2 learning, learners construct mental representations of what was at one point physically (acoustic or visual) present in external form. This representation, in turn, enables them to free themselves from the sensory properties of a specific concrete situation. Again, to cite Stetsenko, the formation of intrapersonal processes "is explained as the transition from a material *object-dependent* activity (such as the actual counting of physical objects by pointing at them with a finger in the initial stages of acquiring the counting operation) to a material *object-independent* activity (when a child comes to be able to count the objects without necessarily touching them or even seeing them)" (1999, pp. 245–255).

Earlier I discussed the importance of imitation, a process, which for Vygotsky is the key to understanding *internalization*. Vocate (1994) notes that, as with social talk, self-talk is dialogic, but instead of an "I" talking to a "You," intrapersonal communication entails an "I" that makes choices on what to talk about and a "Me" that interprets and critiques these choices. The selection and interpretation process "is accompanied by entropic reduction and change" (Vocate, 1994, p.12). Importantly, it not only parallels, but is, in fact, derived from social interaction. Clark (1998, p.178) argues that our public language is ideally suited to be co-opted for intrapersonal functions, because, as with social communication, we lay open to inspection, critique, and modification ideas, concepts, and problems. Smith (1922, p. 84) writes that "when we think, we discuss things with ourselves; when we speak, we discuss things with others."

People, then, not only rely on others to mediate their learning and development, they also rely on themselves (i.e., self-mediation), but they do so in ways that are derived from their interpersonal experiences as sanctioned by their sociocultural communities and the specific activities they promote (Tulviste, 1991). Essentially, (over)generalization (i.e., prediction) is a process we internalize as we interact with other members of our communities, including parents, siblings, teachers, classmates, etc. It is normally a nonreflective process in the world of everyday activity. However, it can, and often does, become visible as it is presented to us in its "scientific" form during schooling (see Wells, 1999).

Internalization: Clarifying Some Issues

To further appreciate the claim that social interaction is the source of mental development and that the autonomous learner metaphor is not needed to account for psychological processes, I would like to consider in a bit more detail the process of internalization. Fodor (1980) argues that internalization is unable to explain how a less powerful mental state, represented by a child's current developmental level, can develop into a more powerful state, represented by some future mental, and possibly the adult steady, state. For Fodor the only way to account for a less to more powerful developmental trajectory is for the end state to be specified in the brain from the outset. In responding to Fodor's critique of Vygotsky, Newman, Griffin and Cole (1989) remind us that Fodor's conundrum is only a problem in the world of the autonomous, ideal knower. In the real world where people reside, the world of the social, a more powerful cognitive system can indeed develop from a less powerful one because of the assistance provided by other members of a community.

Recently, Atkinson (2002), in making a cogent case for a sociocognitive approach to SLA, expressed discomfort with what he perceived as the neo-Vygotskian claim that as a consequence of internalization, "language, is to some degree, gradually loosened from its moorings in social life" (p. 533). In other words as it moves from the inter- to the intramental plane, language "becomes substantially cognitive" (p. 537). Atkinson contends that language at any stage of development "never takes on an 'internal, truly mental function'" and is "always mutually, simultaneously, and co-constitutively in the head and in the world" (p. 538). I agree. J. V. Wertsch (1998), one of the leading contemporary SCT theoreticians, points out that many so-called cognitive functions (e.g., complex arithmetical computations carried out with a paper and pencil) are always distributed between the person and the world and as such never are completely inside-of-the-head processes. Indeed, as previously mentioned, internalization is not about something moving exclusively and completely inside of the head but is about an individual's ability to function independently of specific concrete circumstances. Van Oers (1998) refers to this ability as recontextualization, in which individuals are able to transfer and transform what they have appropriated in a specific social circumstance to other similar, though certainly not identical, social circumstances. On this view, there can be no such thing as decontextualized thinking, and by implication, decontextualized language activity. Rather, internalized forms of communicative semiosis constantly co-evolve with externalized social-interactive forms of languaging activity. Both are always and everywhere context-forming and context-formed, or as Cole (1996) puts it, are mutually constitutive elements of a co-weaving, distributed process.

Vygotsky, in my opinion, would most likely have been uneasy with the term "sociocognitive" because even though it represents an attempt to bring the social and the psychological into contact, it sustains the world/mind dualism that he saw as at the heart of the crisis in psychology (see Vygotsky, 1997). Contributing to the confusion over how SCT understands internalization is the fact that "cognitive" is normally construed in psychology as a process that goes on exclusively inside of heads. Vygotsky and other SCT researchers argued that cognition is not solely an inside-the-head process. As I have said, the brain must be involved in cognition; however, Vygotskians recognize the brain as a necessary, but not always a sufficient, condition for thinking to occur. Wertsch (1991, p. 33), referencing the work of Gregory Bateson, suggests that the concept of "mind goes beyond the skin" to encompass agents acting "with" (but I would change this to "through") mediational means. Vygotsky conceived of development as a social and cultural process—a process in which the person and the world are necessarily connected in a dialectic and inseparable relationship, and thus, while heads are clearly implicated in thinking, they do not do their thinking alone; rather they are part of what Luria (1973) refers to as a functional system formed by the person and the world—a system in which cognition is at its core distributed between brain(s), people, artifacts, and features of the environment (see Salomon, 1993). On this view, then, although brains are inside of heads, minds extend beyond the head and into the world of cultural artifacts and social relationships. It is not without relevance that Vygotsky himself used the term "cultural development" to capture the formation of uniquely human forms of thinking.

Internalization in L2 Learning

In a study of private speech among young (ages 3:3 to 8:3) ESL classroom learners, Saville-Troike (1988) noticed that several of the children entered a "silent period" in which they avoided speaking English socially, while at the same time privately imitating the linguistic affordances available in the classroom environment. In the following example, a 4-year-old Chinese L1 child privately[3] responded to the teacher's request to the class:

> Teacher: You guys go brush your teeth. And wipe your hands on the towel.
> Child: Wipe your hand. Wipe your teeth.
>
> (Saville-Troike, 1988, p. 584)

The child responds to the teacher's utterance with what from a conversational perspective is an inappropriate move. The child's utterance, however, is not intended as an interpersonal turn, but as an imitation of the teacher's language, resulting in an overgeneralization of the collocation constraint on "wipe." "Wipe your teeth" was created by the child from the ingredients made available by others.

In a study of the private speech of an adult classroom learner of Spanish, Lantolf and Yáñez-Prieto (2003) document a similar instance of overgeneralization. In explaining passives, the teacher points out that in constructions such as "The road is covered by snow" Spanish requires the copula verb *estar* (to be), an adjective derived from the past particle of *cubrir* (to cover) and the preposition *de* (of, with, by); hence, the correct rendering of the English sentence is*El camino está cubierto de nieve.* True passives in Spanish, as the teacher had previously explained, are rendered with the copula *ser* and the preposition *por* (by). In example (2), the teacher (T) presents the first part of the sentence and asks the students(s) to complete it with the correct passive construction.

T: *Mi pintura favorita* . . . My favorite painting . . .
S: *Fue pintada *de Monet ?* Was painted *of/by Monet ?
T: *Fue pintada . . .?*   Was painted (with rising intonation)
S: *De Monet ?*   Of/by Monet (with rising intonation)
T: *Por* . . . By
S: *POR, NO DE* (privately, while overlapping T's correction)
T: *Mi pintura favorita fue pintada por Monet.*
S: [while T moves on to work with other students] **FROM, FROM, FROM**

After telling herself that the correct preposition in passive constructions is *por* and not *de*, the student produces an interesting semantic overgeneralization. She communicates to herself privately that Spanish *de* means "from" in English, which of course it does, in some cases, but not in the constructions at issue, since *de* is also equivalent to "of," as well as "with" or even "by."[4]

SCT clearly is able to account for learning at the level of the individual without surrendering the theoretical claim that the individual is a sociocultural entity. Thus, the dualism, between the social and the cognitive that compels some SLA researchers to support the autonomous knower metaphor can be overcome. Having said all this, the burden remains for SCT researchers to empirically make the connection between L2 forms attested in private speech and the forms used by learners in their spontaneous public performances, either in speech or in writing. If this link can be established, it would mean that private speech provides, at least in part, access to L2 learning as it unfolds in real time.[5]

LONGITUDINAL STUDIES AND THE GENETIC METHOD

SCT L2 research has been critiqued for its apparent "lack of longitudinal studies" and for often "'rich' and unsupported interpretations of data collected at a single point in time" (Ellis 2003, p. 201). Mitchell and Myles (1998, p.162) also note that SCT research on L2 learning has so far failed to provide "long-term follow-up data." These critiques are all the more surprising given that Vygotsky (1978) proposed what is known as the "genetic method"—a method that privileges history (i.e., transformation)—to study mental processes.

It is important to appreciate how Vygotsky (1978) understood the role of time psychological research. He proposed four genetic domains as sites where psychologists can observe mental functioning: phylogenesis of the species, sociocultural development of specific cultures as well as human culture in general, ontogenesis of individuals, and microgenesis of particular processes. The latter two are the most relevant for L2 research (see Scribner, 1985, for a full discussion of Vygotsky's use of history). Whereas ontogenesis is concerned with the cultural development of the individual through the internalization social relationships and cultural artifacts, microgenesis focuses on "short-term formation of a psychological process" such as what occurs "when an investigator is trying to train a subject to criterion before beginning the 'real observations'" (Wertsch, 1985, p. 55). Essentially, one can consider microgenetic research a "very short-term longitudinal study" (p. 55). Thus, collecting data, at what appears to be a single point in time, from the traditional perspective of what constitutes a longitudinal study, may in fact entail genesis or history.

Ohta's (2001) previously mentioned study of L2 classroom learners of Japanese clearly meets the criterion of what is traditionally understood in SLA research as a longitudinal study. In her study, Ohta traces the social and private speech performance of 7 students over the course of 8 months. Aljaafreh and Lantolf's (1994) also qualifies as a longitudinal study in that it traces the development of 3 learners over approximately a 2-month time period. From the perspective of the individual learners, both of these studies fall within Vygotsky's ontogenetic domain. The latter study is also important for the way in which it characterizes development. Not only does it consider changes in the formal accuracy of learner performance, but it also documents with regard to the types of assistance the learners were able to utilize over the course time. That is, even though at certain points the learners' linguistic performance did not change with respect to its accuracy, the type of help required to guide their performance did. At some point, a given learner was only able to recognize and correct a particular form through direct and explicit intervention from the tutor, but at a later point, the same learner was able modify her production with minimal implicit assistance (e.g., raising an eyebrow or clearing the throat). This is a very important finding, which in my view, has not been adequately taken up by the field. It shows that learner performance, despite its external manifestation, can have a very different underlying psychological status that changes over time. In other words, an error corrected with explicit assistance does not have the same status as one corrected with an implicit hint. The latter clearly shows greater learner control over the feature than does the former. In addition, a large percentage of the SCT studies on L2 learning is situated within the microgenetic domain to the extent that they consider change in performance over very short periods of time. To be sure, most SCT researchers have failed to acknowledge this aspect of their work. Moreover, even though such changes in performance fall within Vygotsky's understanding of development as a revolutionary and therefore irregular process, owing to its instability, most SLA researchers would be hesitant to consider such change as genuine learning. Nevertheless, it is important to recognize microgenesis as a significant domain for the observation of learning because in some cases transformation is rapid and permanent, and because even when it isn't, the fact that learners are able to control the feature, if only briefly, indicates that it is within their ZPD.

ACTIVITY THEORY AND TASK-BASED LEARNING

According to Wertsch (1998), psychological research has traditionally aimed at answering two broad questions: Who does what? Even so, the "who" question is often assigned less saliency than the "what" question. SCT, because of its focus on people engaged in concrete activity, seeks not only to answer who is doing what, but also how, where, when, and above all why something is done. Although all six questions are relevant, the most important, and at the same the most difficult to uncover, is why people do what they do. This question, linked to the motives and goals of human actions, comprises the primary focus of activity theory.

Activity theory, based on the theorizing of Vygotsky, holds that all higher forms of human activity arise as a direct consequence of motives and goals. Activities, however, are inherently unstable and "what begins as one activity can reshape itself into another activity in the course of its unfolding" (Lantolf , 2000a, p. 11), as the motives and goals shift. Cobb (1998), for example, discusses a study in which school children start out playing shoe store, which required them to measure each other's feet, and then shift to an activity of measuring all kinds of objects in their environment (chairs, tables, blackboards, etc.); this, in turn, required them to discover a new set of measuring tools. As activities shift their focus (i.e., their goal) individuals often experience the need to seek out or develop new cultural artifacts (e.g., linguistic forms) to carry out the new activity. SCT studies that deal with learners' motives and goals (see Coughlan & Duff, 1994; Roebuck, 1998; Donato, 2000; Platt & Brooks, 1994; Platt & Brooks, 2002; Thorne, 2003) concur that learner performance on a given task is not predictable and that tasks should be seen as blueprints for activity and not as guarantees that specific types of activity will occur either at the same point in time by different people or even by the same people at different points in time or in different sites.

Given the unstable nature of activities and the unpredictable nature of learning outcomes, it seems that Activity Theory and task-based approaches to L2 research and teaching are incommensurable at least with regard to the latter's concern with determining which features of a L2 will be learned and which will not during the conduct of a particular task (see Ellis, 2003). This does not mean that tasks, as cultural artifacts, do not exert influence on learners as they undertake to carry them out. In fact, Ellis (2003), quite appropriately, in my view, critiques SCT researchers for not paying sufficient attention to the potential impact of task features on L2 learning. The only SCT study that I am aware of in which task features are taken account of is Thorne's (1999) dissertation on computer-mediated communication (cmc) in a French FL classroom. I hasten to point out, however, that even though Thorne showed how CMC interaction shapes learner behavior, his findings are not intended to be predicative, in the sense that specific types of CMC will foster specific types of learning.

The reason we cannot predetermine what learners will and will not learn in a given activity is that learning depends heavily on the significance individuals assign to the various activities they participate in. In others words, there are reasons why people learn (or not) what they learn, when they learn it, and how they will learn it (Lantolf & Genung, 2002). We can only compose the circumstances and conditions that promote learning. We cannot guarantee that it will happen at any given point in time or in any given way.

D. A. Leontiev (unpublished manuscript) proposes six principles aimed at coming to grips with the vagaries of human learning and development in activity. The first three humans share with other animals and the final three are unique to our species. Those that we share with animals include drive for gratification (e.g., the need to consume calories and reproduce), response to a stimuli (e.g., presence of an intruder); learned habits and dispositions (e.g., ring the bell and receive a food pellet; if you eat all of your spinach, you can have ice cream). Those that are unique to humans as cultural beings include social norms and expectations (e.g., everyone does it so I should as well); a life-world and meaning (e.g., because it matters to me and fits into my life story); free choice (e.g., why not ?). According to Leontiev, the last two principles are the most important in motivating human behavior. This is because humans are able "to relate their activity to their entire life-world rather than to an actual situation; their activity is determined by the world at large, as opposed to the immediate environment." Hence, reasons for human action emerge not just from the immediate circumstances, but from "far beyond the situation, including distant consequences and complicated connections". In essence, the final two principles reflect our ability to imbue activities with significance. Thus, humans can transcend "behavior determined both by internal impulses and learned programs, as well as by actual external stimulation. In other words, meaning offers a person a high degree of freedom from what is determined". In concrete human activity, it is rare that only one of the six regulating principles is in play. Most often they "merge into more or less complicated systems, where actual behavior is usually 'multi' controlled, except in some cases of pathology".

As I have said, although motives and goals are paramount in determining the outcome and process of learning, we cannot overlook the fact that the specific material circumstances in which the activity takes place also shapes the activity. Whereas activity carried out with material and symbolic tools not only imbues humans with their unique transformative capacity, the tools themselves can have considerable influence on how the activity itself is carried out. Thus, a shovel, which allows us to more easily dig bigger and better holes than our bare hands, at the same time compels us to make particular movements with our bodies that a saw does not, and under most circumstances we cannot substitute one set of motions for another (e.g., using a digging motion to saw a log). On the face of it, this appears to contradict the point I am trying to make about the unstable and unpredictable nature of activities and that, therefore, it should be possible to design tasks that indeed promote learning of specific target language features. After all, given the parallels between physical and symbolic tools, we would expect artifacts used in regulating mental activity to similarly influence the way that activity unfolds. I believe, however, that the work of Slobin on thinking-for-speaking sheds light on the situation.

In his research Slobin (1996) proposes that the "language or languages we learn in childhood are not neutral coding systems of an objective reality. Rather, each one is a subject orientation to the world of human experience, and this orientation **affects the ways in which we think while we are speaking**" (p. 91, bold in original). Categories such as verbal aspect and definiteness are categories made available by our language(s) that allow us, or said another way, constrain us, to adopt certain "points of view for the purposes of speaking" (p. 91). As with physical tools, these categories compel us to (symbolically) move in certain ways and not in others, and "once our minds have been trained in taking particular points of view for the purposes of speaking, it is exceptionally difficult for us to be retrained" (p. 91). Hence, L2 English speakers of L1 Italian, both tense-prominent languages, are able to use English past-tense to construct narratives as a sequence of "past events as seen from the present" (p. 90). In terms of the tool analogy, Italian speakers can carry out the same or similar movements in both languages with regard to tense marking. On the other hand, L1 speakers of Punjabi, an aspect-prominent language, deploy progressive to narrate events from the protagonist's point of view in L2 English, just as they would use the Punjabi imperfective to narrate events from the inside (p. 90). Hence, if these speakers want to narrate in English the same way as more experienced users of the language do, they need to learn to carry out new (symbolic) movements. On the other hand, they could opt to use the movements of their L1; however, such decisions are not without consequences (e.g., not doing well in exams such as TOEFL or OPI).

Despite the above, it seems that speakers have ways of bending their symbolic tools to meet their individual way of making sense of things (i.e., thinking-for-speaking). For instance, German L1 speakers participating in Slobin's "Frog Story" project tended to mark the first event in a sequence of events as completed rather than the second as continuing, as in the following example: *Der **ist** vom Baum **runtergefallen** und der Hund **läuft** schell weg*—'He [the little boy chasing his frog] **has fallen** down from the tree and the dog **runs** away quickly' [because a swarm of wasps were chasing it] (p. 81). Interestingly, one of the adult speakers in Slobin's study decided to mark the second event as continuing (i.e., aspect), even though German grammar supposedly does not allow for this option, through use of iteration: *Der Hund rennt rennt rennt*—"The dog runs runs runs" (p. 81). One might argue that the speaker was able to shape the language in a way that allowed him to talk about the event in an unbounded way; that is, he was able to mold the language tool to fit his way of making sense of the event. Even though language compels us to symbolically move in preferred ways, we are nevertheless able to shape the tool to meet our personal way of making sense of events—in essence, using a saw to dig a hole, which, of course, is difficult, but not impossible. Indeed, Markova (1979, p. 85), echoing Newman and Holzman (1993) when they decry the failure of schools to foment creative transformative learning, argues that development is not about learning the norms of speech activity; it is rather about "conscious (emphatic) infraction of received norms for the purpose of enhancing ones' effect; creation of new linguistic devices and their use in speech (speech creativity)."

It seems clear that the interaction between learner and task is not a one-way but a two-way street. Tasks as cultural artifacts should indeed have an effect on how learning activity emerges, but at the same time we should fully anticipate that learners will also shape the tasks in unexpected and creative ways to in order to make sense of their own learning activity.

SCT AND A THEORY OF LANGUAGE

As a final topic I would like to address the concern that SCT research on L2 has failed to "offer any very thorough or detailed view of the nature of language as a formal system" (Mitchell & Myles, 1998, p. 161). The concern that it has not situated "itself more explicitly with respect to linguistic theory" and has preferred instead to deal with "fragments of language" (p. 162). In many ways this is a legitimate critique and in what follows I will suggest a theory of language, which, in my view, at least, is quite compatible with SCT—Hopper's (1998, 2002) notion of *emergent grammar*.

Vygotsky proposed that the unit of analysis for a unified psychological theory of mind had to be a unit that was simultaneously mental and social (Minick, 1997, p. 122) and proposed that word meaning "is at one and the same time a unit of abstraction or thinking (i.e., a unit of mind) and a unit of communication or social interaction (i.e., a unit of behavior)" (Minick, 1997, p. 122). Although most contemporary SCT scholars argue that word meaning is too restricted a unit for understanding the mind, they nevertheless accept Vygotsky's principle claim that the appropriate unit of analysis must be linked to humans' meaning-making activity.

Hopper (2002) points out that the notion of grammar, the sine qua non of most linguistic theorizing, arose, in an interesting irony, from the pedagogical efforts of the Greeks to make "their language known to outsiders" as well as to impose "a degree of uniformity among its diverse users." In essence, grammar represented the Greeks' attempt to simplify for foreigners the complex process that native speakers go through as they learn the forms of their language "one by one, in specific contexts." Over the course of centuries, according to Hopper, the addition of layers of terminology (e.g., syntax, morphology, morphophonemics) has "successfully disguised the fact that rules and paradigms are in origin nothing but short cuts to language learning." For Hopper the grammar of theoretical linguistics is not the aprioristic construct that necessarily underlies communicative performance, but is "a by-product" of communication, an epiphenomenon; it is, in other words, "the name for certain categories of observed repetitions in discourse" (Hopper, 1998, p. 156). This, Hopper's calls, "emergent grammar," defined as a "perpetual process in which movement *toward* [italics in original] a complete structure of some kind is constant but completion is always deferred" (Hopper, 2002). On this view, "linguistic structure is intrinsically incomplete, a work in progress, a site under construction" (Hopper, 2002). Hopper's perspective on grammar is compatible with the general notion of process ontology, which claims that process "is fundamental, and entities [including structures of any kind, my insertion] are derivative or based in process" (Sawyer, 2002, p. 286). In Hopper's theory, the process is communication and the entity derived from this, by researchers, is grammar.

Hopper opposes emergent grammar to the so-called "fixed code" theory, which views language as a stable and complete linguistic system shared by everyone in a particular speech community. Hopper is careful to distinguish emergent from emerging. The former is "never fixed, never determined, but is constantly open and in flux" (Hopper, 1998, p. 157). The latter is understood as moving toward completion. Along similar lines, Vološinov (1973, p. 81) states that language "endures, but it endures as a continuous process of becoming," it flows and rather than being tossed like a ball from one generation to the next, each new generation enters into the stream of incessant communication. It is important to note that an a priori or fixed-code theory of grammar is necessarily monologic in that it postulates an ideal perfect knower in a homogeneous speech community (Hopper, 1998, p. 161). Vološinov (1973, p. 81), argues that the monologic tradition in linguistics reifies language and treats it as "if it were dead and alien" and, thus, moves it outside of "the stream of verbal communication." Hopper situates his theorizing squarely within the dialogic communicative perspective and, thus, stipulates that emergent grammar is not "a general abstract possession that is uniform across the community, but is an emergent fact having its source in each individual's experience and life history and in the struggle to accomplish successful communication" (Hopper, 1998, p. 164).

Emergent grammar is "a set of sedimented conventions that have been routinized out of the more frequently occurring ways of saying things" (Hopper, 1998, p. 163), and is assembled "fragment by fragment" as we increasingly participate more extensively and intensively in social activities. This does not mean that grammar is not systematic; however, its systematicity arises from memory of things past—a "collection of prefabricated particulars, available for use in appropriate contexts and language games" (p. 164). Development is constant and potentially unending. It is important to note that we mold and shape the language (as with Slobin's German speaker) as we move through various discursive activities, "relying on similarities to previous occasions of talk to keep us going, and accumulating stores of experience to be used the next time a similar occasion presents itself" (Hopper, 2002). Conceiving of language as emergent parallels closely Vygotsky's thinking on higher forms of consciousness. It is never complete, always (potentially) developing as we move into new activities.

As an example of emergent grammar, consider the pseudocleft structure. According to linguistic theory, pseudoclefts canonically use the following formula: WHAT + NP − subject (if *what* is not the subject) + verb + NP − object, as in "what this country needs is a good five-cents cigar" or "what they do in the afternoon is take long walks." Based on his analysis of a corpus of spoken English, Hopper (2002) *notes that so-called canonical pseudoclefts are rarel in actual communicative encounters*. Pseudoclefts are not derived from rules, but instead are formulaic and fragmentary. The verb in the WH clause is almost always *do* and *happen*, with *say* as a much less likely possibility. When other verbs are selected, they usually appear in fixed phrases such as "what I suppose is . . ." or "what I mean is . . ." In communication, the WH phrase is often followed by an entire sequence of phrases and clauses rather than an NP. Moreover, pseudoclefts may be listener- or speaker-centered, in that they may alert the listener to attend to the next piece of discourse, and frequently, impart an air of authority about what follows, and speakers often throw them in to gain processing time to construct an idea while staving off interruption from the interlocutor (Hopper, 2002). According to Hopper, the standard account of pseudocleft as a focusing feature is not sustained in corpora of spoken English. From the perspective of emergent grammar, then, learning an additional language is about enhancing one's repertoire of fragments and patterns that enables participation in a wider array of communicative activities. It is not about building up a complete and perfect grammar as a precondition for producing well-formed sentences.

Hopper's notion of emergent grammar is clearly situated within the broader view of language emanating from what Hanks (1996) refers to as the *linguistics of speaking* (see Lantolf & Thorne, in press for a fuller discussion). I encourage SCT researchers to explore the implications of the interface between Vygotsky's theory of mind and language theories such as Hopper's. It has the potential to change our understanding of language learning and teaching in profound ways.

CONCLUSION

In this chapter I have considered some, although not all, of the mainstream interpretations and critiques of SCT research on L2 learning and have attempted to explicate those areas in which there has been either misinterpretation or less than complete understanding of the relevant theoretical constructs. I have also pointed out areas where I believe SCT researchers need to consider seriously the critiques. In my view, the most important of these relates to the need for SCT informed research to pay closer attention to Hopper's theory of emergent grammar.

As the exegesis unfolded, several important differences between SCT and mainstream approaches to SLA emerged. To summarize these differences:. Mainstream researchers define language as a formal set of structures comprising an a priori grammar that must be acquired for speakers to be communicatively effective. Their primary research objective is to uncover the cause(s) of L2 learning. They posit an invariant route and rate of learning for all learners. Although learning happens in social environments, the autonomous knower is at the core of the learning process and therefore constitutes the primary focus of attention along with methodological individualism that privileges the experimental laboratory and its concern with defining and controlling variables. SCT, on the other hand, does not see language as a formal system with an a priori grammar but is instead an emergent system comprised of fragments that emerge and are shaped in the maelstrom of communicative interaction. It rejects the conduit metaphor that sees language not as the expression of thought and proposes that language is the symbolic artifact par excellence through which people complete thought, consequently, participating in a new sense-making system may potentially allow the person to develop new ways of mediating one's relationship to the world and to the self. The objective of SCT is not to discover the cause(s) of SLA but to uncover the reasons why people learn or do not learn a new language; as such it does not assume that learning does not follow the same route and rate for all people; these are shaped by the person's motives and goals and their ZPD; hence, human agency is highlighted. Finally, it rejects the individual/social dualism and argues instead that the individual and social form a dialectical unity.

NOTES

1. I would like to thank Merrill Swain and Steve Thorne for their invaluable comments and criticisms on earlier versions of this chapter.
2. According to Kozulin (personal communication, January 25, 2002), 'man' here is an inappropriate translation of the original Russian *chelovek* 'human being.'
3. Saville-Troike's (1988) criteria for distinguishing private from social utterances included the following: produced at a low volume that was likely "inaudible to anyone present without access to recording equipment," lack of eye contact lack of expectation of a response from an interlocutor (p. 573).
4. See Ohta (2001) for similar overgeneralizations among L2 classroom learners of Japanese.
5. According to Swain (personal communication, August 29, 2002), collaborative dialogue also provides real time access to learning.

REFERENCES

Aljaafreh, A., & Lantolf, J. P. (1994). Negative feedback as regulation and second language learning in the Zone of Proximal Development. *The Modern Language Journal, 78*, 465–483.

Atkinson, D. (2002). Toward a sociocognitive approach to second language acquisition. *The Modern Language Journal, 86*, 525–545.

Ball, A. F. (2000). Teachers' developing philosophies on literacy and their use in urban schools: A Vygotskian perspective on internal activity and teacher change. In C. D. Lee & P. Smagorinsky (Eds.), *Vygotskian perspectives on literacy research. Constructing meaning through collaborative inquiry* (pp. 226–255). Cambridge, UK: Cambridge University Press.

Belz, J. (in press). *Language learning in immigration: The literary testimonies of Werner Lansburgh.*

Broner, M. A., & Tarone, E. E. (2001). Is it fun ? Language play in a fifth grade Spanish immersion classroom. *The Modern Language Journal, 85,* 363–379.

Carpay, J. A. M. (1974). Foreign-language teaching and meaningful learning. A Soviet Russian point of view. *ITL, 25-26,* 161–187.

Carroll, S. E. (2001). *Input and evidence. The raw material of second language acquisition.* Amsterdam: Benjamins.

Clark, A. (1998). Magic words: how language augments human computation. In P. Carruthers & J. Boucher (Eds.), *Language and thought: Interdisciplinary themes* (pp. 162–183). Cambridge, UK: Cambridge University Press.

Cobb, P. (1998). Learning from distributed theories of intelligence. *Mind, Culture, and Activity: An International Journal, 5,* 187–204.

Cole, M. (1996). *Cultural psychology: A once and future discipline.* Cambridge, MA: Belknap.

Coughlan, P., & Duff, P. (1994). Same task different activity: analysis of a SLA task from an activity theory perspective. In J. P. Lantolf & G. Appel (Eds.) *Vygotskian approaches to second language research* (pp. 173–194). Norwood, NJ: Ablex.

deGuerrero, M. C. M. (1996). Krashen's i + l and Vygotsky's ZPD: Really two very different notions. *TESOL-Gram (The Official Newsletter of Puerto Rico TESOL), 23,* 9.

Donato, R. (1994). Collective scaffolding in second language learning. In J. P. Lantolf & G. Appel (Eds.), *Vygotskian approaches to second language research* (pp. 33–56). Norwood, NJ: Ablex.

Donato, R. (2000). Sociocultural contributions to understanding the foreign and second language classroom. In J. P. Lantolf (Ed.), *Sociocultural theory and second language learning* (pp. 27–50). Oxford, UK: Oxford University Press.

Dunn, W. E., & Lantolf, J. P. (1998). Vygotsky's zone of proximal development and Krashen's i + 1: Incommensurable constructs; incommensurable theories. *Language Learning, 48,* 411–442.

Ellis, R. (1997). *SLA research and language teaching.* Oxford, UK: Oxford University Press.

Ellis, R. (2003). *Task-based language learning and teaching.* Oxford, UK: Oxford University Press.

Engeström, Y., Miettinen, R., & Punamäki, R-L. (Eds.). (1999). *Perspectives on activity theory.* Cambridge, UK: Cambridge University Press.

Fodor, J. (1980). On the impossibility of acquiring "more powerful" structures. In M. Piatelli-Palmarini (Ed.), *Language and learning. The debate between Jean Piaget and Noam Chomsky* (pp. 142–162). Cambridge, MA: Harvard University Press.

Frawley, W., & Lantolf, J. P. (1985). Second language discourse: A Vygotskyan perspective. *Applied Linguistics, 6,* 19–44.

Gal'perin, P. Ia. (1992). Linguistic consciousness and some questions of the relationship between language and thought. *The Journal of Russian and East European Psychology, 30,* 81–92.

Hanks, W. (1996). *Language and communicative practice.* Boulder, CO: Westview Press.

Hopper, P. (1998). Emergent grammar. In M. Tomasello (Ed.), *The new psychology of language* (pp. 155–177). Mahwah, NJ: Lawrence Erlbaum Associates.

Hopper, P. (2002, July 10). *Emergent grammar: Gathering together the fragments.* Plenary lecture presented at the Summer Institute in Applied Linguistics, The Pennsylvania State University.

Kasper, G. (1997). "A" stands for acquisition: A response to Firth and Wagner. *The Modern Language Journal, 81,* 307–312.

Karpova, S. N. (1977). *The realization of the verbal composition of speech by preschool children.* The Hague, The Netherlands: Mouton.

Kinginger, C. (2001). i + ≠ ZPD. *Foreign Language Annals, 34,* 417–425.

Kinginger, C. (2002). Defining the zone of proximal development in US foreign language education. *Applied Linguistics, 23,* 240–261.

Komarova, L. (1988). The teaching strategy "A-K"∗ and its effect upon the appropriation of foreign language knowledge and ability. *Learning Activity, 1,* 21–28.

Komarova, L. (1991). Ein alternativer Weg des schulischen Fremdsprachenerwerbs. *Empirische Pädagogik, 5,* 47–61.

Kozulin, A. (1990). *Vygotsky's psychology. A biography of ideas.* Cambridge, MA: Harvard University Press.

Lantolf, J. P. (2000a). Introducing sociocultural theory. In J. P. Lantolf (Ed.), *Sociocultural theory and second language learning* (pp. 1–26). Oxford, UK: Oxford University Press.

Lantolf, J. P. (2000b). Second language learning as a mediated process. *Language Teaching, 30*(2), 79–98.

Lantolf, J. P. (Ed.). (2000c). *Sociocultural theory and second language learning.* Oxford, UK: Oxford University Press.

Lantolf, J. P. (2002). Sociocultural theory and second language acquisition. In R. Kaplan (Ed.), *The Oxford handbook of applied linguistics* (pp. 104–114). Oxford, UK: Oxford University Press.

Lantolf, J. P. (2003). Intrapersonal communication and internalization in the language classroom. In A. Kozulin, V. Ageev, S. Miller, & B. Grindis (Eds.), *Vygotsky's theory of education in cultural context* (pp. 349–370). Cambridge, UK: Cambridge University Press.

Lantolf, J. P., & Aljaafreh, A. (1995). Second language learning in the zone of proximal development: A revolutionary experience. *International Journal of Educational Research, 23,* 619–632.

Lantolf, J. P., & Appel, G. (Eds.). (1994). *Vygotskian approaches to second language research.* Norwood, NJ: Ablex.

Lantolf, J. P., & Genung, P. B. (2002). "I'd rather switch than fight:" An activity-theoretic study of power, success and failure in a foreign language classroom. In C. Kramsch (Ed.), *Language acquisition and language socialization. Ecological perspectives* (pp. 175–196). London: Continuum.

Lantolf, J. P., & Pavlenko, A. (1995). Sociocultural theory and second language acquisition. *Annual Review of Applied Linguistics, 15,* 108–124.

Lantolf, J. P. & Thorne, S. L. (in press). *Sociocultural theory and the genesis of second language development.* Oxford, UK: Oxford University Press.

Lantolf, J. P., & Yáñez-Prieto, M.-C. (2003). Talking into yourself in Spanish: Private speech and second language learning. *Hispania, 86,* 98–105.

Lave, J. (1997). What's special about experiments as contexts for thinking." In M. Cole, Y. Engestrm, O. Vasquez (Eds.), *Mind, culture and activity. Seminal papers from the laboratory of comparative human cognition* (pp. 57–69). Cambridge, UK: Cambridge University Press.

León, G. F. (2001). Toward a hermeneutical reconstruction of Gal'perin's theory of learning. In S. Chaiklin (Ed.), *The theory and practice of cultural-historical psychology* (pp. 260–282). Aarhus, Denmark: Aarhus University Press.

Leontiev, A. A. (1981). *Psychology and the language learning process.* Oxford, UK: Pergamon.

Leontiev, D. (Date). *The phenomenon of meaning: How psychology can make sense of it.* Unpublished manuscript.

Lightbown, P., & Spada, N. (1999). *How languages are learned.* (Rev. Ed.). Oxford, UK: Oxford University Press.

Luria, A. R. (1973). *The working brain.* New York: Basic Books.

Luria, A. R. (1979). *The making of mind. A personal account of Soviet psychology.* Cambridge, MA: Harvard University Press.

Markova, A. K. (1979). *The teaching and mastery of language.* White Plains, NY: M. E. Sharpe.

Minick, N. (1997). The early history of the Vygotskian school: The relationship between mind and activity. In M. Cole, Y. Engestrm, & L. Vasquez (Eds.), *Mind, culture, and activity. Seminal papers from the laboratory of comparative human cognition* (pp. 117–127). Cambridge, UK: Cambridge University Press.

Mitchell, R., & Myles, F. (1998). *Second language learning theories.* London: Edward Arnold.

Nassaji, H., & M. Swain. (2000). A Vygotskyan perspective towards corrective feedback in L2: The effect of random vs. negotiated help on the acquisition of English articles. *Language Awareness, 9,* 34–51.

Negueruela, E. (2003). *A sociocultural approach to the teaching-learning of second languages: Systemic-theoretical instruction and L2 development.* Unpublished doctoral dissertation. The Pennsylvania State University, University Park.

Newman, D., Griffin, P, & Cole, M. (1989). *The construction zone: Working for cognitive change in school.* Cambridge, UK: Cambridge University Press.

Newman, F., & Holzman, L. (1993). *Lev Vygotsky. Revolutionary scientist.* London: Routledge.

Newman, F., & Holzman, L. (1996). *Unscientific psychology. A cultural-performatory approach to understanding human life.* Westport, CT: Praeger.

Newman, F., & Holzman, L. (1997). *The end of knowing: A new developmental way of learning.* London: Routledge.

Ohta, A. S. (2001). *Second language acquisition processes in the classroom. Learning Japanese.* Mahwah, NJ: Lawrence Erlbaum Associates.

Pavlenko, A., & Lantolf, J. P. (2000). Second language learning as participation and the (re)construction of selves. In J. P. Lantolf, (Ed.), *Sociocultural theory and second language learning* (pp. 155–178). Oxford, UK: Oxford University Press.

Pienemann, M. (1998). *Language processing and second language development. Processability theory.* Amsterdam: John Benjamins.

Platt, E. J., & Brooks, F. B. (1994). The "acquisition-rich environment" revisited. *The Modern Language Journal, 78,* 497–511.

Platt, E. J., & Brooks, F. B. (2002). Task engagement: A turning point in foreign language development. *Language Learning, 52,* 364–399.

Roebuck, R. (1998). *Reading and recall in L1 and L2: A sociocultural approach.* Stamford, CT: Ablex.

Salomon, G. (Ed.). (1993). *Distributed cognitions. Psychological and educational considerations.* Cambridge, UK: Cambridge University Press.

Saville-Troike, M. (1988). Private speech: Evidence for second language learning strategies during the "silent period." *Journal of Child Language, 15,* 567–590.

Sawyer, R. K. (2002). Unresolved tensions in sociocultural theory: Analogies with contemporary sociological debates. *Culture & Psychology, 8,* 283–305.

Scribner, S. (1985). Vygotsky's use of history. In J. V. Wertsch (Ed.), *Culture, communication, and cognition. Vygotskian perspectives* (pp. 119–146). Cambridge, UK: Cambridge University Press.

Schinke-Llano, L. (1995). Reenvisioning the second language classroom: A Vygotskian approach. In F. R. Eckman, D. Highland, P. W. Lee, J. Mileham, & R. R. Weber (Eds.), *Second language acquisition theory and pedagogy* (pp. 21–28). Mahwah, NJ: Lawrence Erlbaum Associates.

Slobin, D. I. (1996). From "thought and language" to "thinking for speaking." In J. J. Gumperz & S. C. Levinson (Eds.), *Rethinking linguistic relativity* (pp. 70–96). Cambridge, UK: Cambridge University Press.

Smith, W. A. (1922). *The reading process.* New York: Macmillan.

Stetsenko, A. P. (1999). Social interaction, cultural tools and the zone of proximal development: In search of a synthesis. In S. Chaiklin, M. Hedegaard, & U. J. Jensen (Eds.), *Activity theory and social practice: Cultural historical approaches* (pp. 235–252). Aarhus, Denmark: Aarhus University Press.

Swain, M. (2000). The output hypothesis and beyond: Mediating acquisition through collaborative dialogue. In J. P. Lantolf (Ed.), *Sociocultural theory and second language learning* (pp. 97–114). Oxford, UK: Oxford University Press.

Swain, M., & Lapkin, S. (1998). Interaction and second language learning: Two adolescent French immersion students working together. *The Modern Language Journal, 82,* 320–337.

Swain, M., & Lapkin, S. (2002). Talking it through: Two French immersion learners' response to reformulation. *International Journal of Educational Research.*

Swain, M., & Lapkin, S. (in press). "Oh, I get it now!" From production to comprehension in second language learning. In D. M. Brinton & O. Kagan (Eds.), *Heritage language acquisition: A new field emerging.* Mahwah, NJ: Lawrence Erlbaum Associates.

Talyzina, N. (1981). *The psychology of learning.* Moscow: Progress Press.

Thorne, S. L. (1999). *An activity theoretical analysis of foreign language electronic discourse.* Unpublished doctoral dissertation. University of California, Berkeley.

Thorne, S. L. (2003). Artifacts and cultures-of-use in intercultural communication. *Language Learning and Technology, 7,* 38–67.

Tomasello, M. (1999). *The cultural origins of human cognition.* Cambridge, MA: Harvard University Press.

Tulviste, P. (1991). *The Cultural-historical development of verbal thinking.* Commack, NY: Nova Science Publishing.

van der Veer, R., & Valsiner, J. (1991). *Understanding Vygotsky. A quest for synthesis.* Oxford, UK: Blackwell.

Van Oers, B. (1998). The fallacy of decontextualization. *Mind, Culture, and Activity: An International Journal, 5,* 135–142.

Vocate, D. R. (1994). Self-talk and inner speech: Understanding the uniquely human aspects of intrapersonal communication. In D. R. Vocate (Ed.), *Intrapersonal communication. Different voices, different minds* (pp. 3–32). Hillsdale, NJ: Lawrence Erlbaum Associates.

Vološinov, V. N. (1973). *Marxism and the philosophy of language.* Cambridge, MA: Harvard Univeristy Press.

Vygotsky, L. S. (1978). *Mind in society. The development of higher psychological processes.* Cambridge, MA: Harvard University Press.

Vygotsky, L. S. (1986). *Thought and language.* (Newly revised & edited by A. Kozulin). Cambridge, MA: MIT Press.

Vygotsky, L. S. (1987). *The collected works of L. S. Vygotsky. Volume 1. The problems of general psychology. Including the volume Thinking and Speech.* New York: Plenum.

Vygotsky, L. S. (1997). The historical meaning of the crisis in psychology: A methodological investigation. In R. W. Rieber & J. Wollock (Eds.), *The collected works of L. S. Vygotsky. Volume 3. Problems of the theory and history of psychology* (pp. 233–344). New York: Plenum.

Wells, G. (1999). *Dialogic inquiry. Toward a sociocultual practice and theory of education.* Cambridge, UK: Cambridge University Press.

Wertsch, J. V. (1985). *Vygotsky and the social formation of mind.* Cambridge, MA: Harvard University Press.

Wertsch, J. V. (1991). *Voices of the mind. A sociocultural approach to mediated action.* Cambridge, MA: Harvard University Press.

Wertsch, J. V. (1998). *Mind as action.* New York: Oxford University Press.

Yaroshevsky, M. (1989). *Lev Vygotsky.* Moscow: Progress Press.

20

Conversation Analysis for Second Language Acquisition

Numa Markee
University of Illinois at Urbana–Champaign

INTRODUCTION

This chapter briefly reviews what an ethnomethodological approach to conversation analysis[1] (CA) is and outlines the main issues and questions that are of interest to conversation analysts. I then show how the use of transcripts that are prepared according to the transcription conventions of CA permit second language acquisition (SLA) and classroom researchers to develop highly detailed microanalyses of second language learning activity.

More specifically, using a fragment of talk drawn from a larger data set already published in Markee (1994, 2000), I show that CA transcription is a tool that potentially allows the emerging approach of conversation analysis for second language acquisition (CA-for-SLA; Kasper, 2002; Markee, 2003a) to explicate how learning activity is organized on a moment-by-moment basis. In addition, I demonstrate that when the same fragment of talk is retranscribed to yield an even more fine-grained transcript of the interaction, not only do we develop a more detailed analysis of the organizational structure of the learning activity under study, but we also develop a deeper substantive understanding of the socially distributed nature of human cognition and SLA. The chapter concludes with a discussion of how insights from such analyses may be incorporated into applied linguistics and SLA research and teaching.

CONVERSATION ANALYSIS

CA is a methodology for analyzing talk-in-interaction that seeks to develop empirically based accounts of the observable conversational behaviors of participants that are both minutely detailed and unmotivated by a priori, etic theories of social action (Heritage, 1988; Psathas, 1995; Schegloff, 1987). More specifically, CA aims to explicate how members orient (that is, observably pay attention) to certain behavioral practices as they co-construct talk-in-interaction in real time. These practices include the sequential organization of talk, turn taking, and repair (Markee, 2003b; Schegloff,

Koshik, Jacoby, & Olsher, 2002). Within these broad parameters, conversation analysts may focus more specifically on issues such as the sequential organization of various speech acts (Davidson, 1984; Drew, 1984; Pomerantz, 1975; 1978a; 1978b; 1984a; 1984b; Psathas, 1986; Schegloff, 1972), the construction of syntax-for-conversation (Goodwin, 1979; Lerner, 1991; Schegloff, 1979, 1996), reference (Sacks & Schegloff, 1979), and the structure of joke and story telling (Goodwin, 1984; Sacks, 1974; Stubbs, 1983).

There are two main types of talk-in-interaction that are studied by conversation analysts: *ordinary, mundane conversation* and *institutional talk. Ordinary conversation*, which is the default speech exchange system in all talk-in-interaction (Sacks, Schegloff, & Jefferson, 1974), may be thought of as the kind of everyday chitchat that occurs between friends and acquaintances, either face-to-face or on the telephone. Other speech exchange systems all involve various structural modifications to the sequential, turn-taking and repair practices of ordinary conversation. It is these modifications to the default practices of ordinary conversation that constitute a whole continuum of *institutional* varieties of talk (for example, debates, classroom talk, broadcast news interviews, press conferences, doctor–patient interactions, courtroom interactions, emergency calls on the telephone, etc.). Note that, the more distant from the bedrock of ordinary conversation they are (see, for example, the turn taking practices of debates), the more formalized and ritualized these institutional varieties become (Sacks, Schegloff & Jefferson, 1974).

In ordinary conversation, talk is locally managed, meaning that turn size, content, and type are all free to vary, as is turn taking. Thus, who gets to speak how, when, and about what is not predetermined, and there is a preference for a minimization of turn length (Sacks, Schegloff, & Jefferson, 1974). Ordinary conversation is also characterized by a preference for self-initiated, self-completed repair (Schegloff, Jefferson & Sacks, 1977). In contrast, although institutional talk uses the same basic mechanisms that are available to participants to do ordinary conversation, the distribution of these practices and the purposes for which they are deployed in institutional talk differ markedly from those found in ordinary conversation. For example, teacher-fronted classroom talk is characterized by the preallocation of turns and turn types in favor of teachers (McHoul 1978; Mehan, 1979), who also typically initiate repairs (Gaskill, 1980; McHoul, 1990). This preference organization is directly observable in the recurrent use of Question-Answer-Comment (QAC) sequences in such talk.[2]

This QAC sequential organization is a members' resource for achieving the educational purposes and agendas of classroom talk. More specifically, teachers prototypically do being teachers by asserting in and through their talk the right to select the next speaker, to nominate topics, to ask questions, and to evaluate learners. Conversely, students do being students by orienting to the institutionally specified obligation of answering teachers' questions in a satisfactory manner.

For example, as shown in Fragment 1 (see Appendix 1 for the transcription conventions used here), T initially selects L6[3] through the simultaneous use of a question at line 02 and eye gaze at line 01. However, L1 then looks up and happens to catch T's eye at line 05, which prompts T to reallocate next turn to L1 via two more questions at lines 06 and 09, respectively. L1 duly provides an extended answer in next turn at lines 10–36 (not reproduced here to conserve space). L1 finishes his answering turn at line 37, which is briefly evaluated by T when she says "ok" at line 38. This acknowledgement token constitutes the commenting part of this turn. T then immediately self-selects as next speaker and follows up with another question in the remainder of her turn at lines 38–39, which functions as a follow-up request for more information from the students. More specifically, following the 0.3 second pause at line 40, T opens up the floor to all students at line 41. This last question turn is overlapped by L1's answer turn at line 42, who continues as next speaker:

Fragment 1

```
01 T1:        [X_____
02 T1: →      U::HM (0.6) ARTU̱RO ((L1 turns to look at T))
03 L6         [X
04 L6: →      [yes
05 T1:        [...X____
06 T1: →      [OR GONZA̱LO ((As T reallocates next turn to L1. L6 turns his gaze away
07            from T and turns back to face front))
08 T1:        _____
09 T1: →      ?H WHY: D'YOU THINK GERMAN ...
                  .
                  .
                  .
37 L1: →      AND THEY'RE THE NEI̱GHBORS
38 T1: →      OK:, (0.6) SO WHAT KIND OF PROBLEMS MIGHT GER- GERMAN
39            UNIFICATION BRI̱NG?
40            (0.3)
41 T1: →      > A[NYBODY THINK,]<
42 L1: →         [it would bring] u:h ...
              (Class 1, phase 2)
```

This QAC organizational structure has the concomitant effect of constraining when and how repair may be carried out, and by whom. More specifically, this structure makes Comment turns the sequentially relevant slot from which teachers (and only teachers) may other-initiate repairs in this institutional speech exchange system (McHoul, 1978; 1990). Finally, members' orientation to this sequential organization is collaboratively achieved. If deviations from this sequential organization occur, they become noticeable or even sanctionable.

CONVERSATION ANALYSIS FOR SECOND LANGUAGE ACQUISITION

CA-for-SLA is an emerging approach in applied linguistics and SLA studies that use the transcription procedures and microanalytic techniques of classic CA and apply these resources to the analysis of second language learning or teaching activity (see, for example, Firth & Wagner, 1997; He, 2003; Kasper, 2002, 2003; Markee, 1994, 1995, 2000; 2003a; Mori, 2002, 2003; Seedhouse, 1997, 1999). CA is also used to various degrees by writers who treat it as one of several methodological tools that are available to them, but who do not necessarily claim to be doing CA per se (see, for example, van Lier, 1988, and, more recently, Lazaraton, 2003, 2004, who simply calls her work a microanalytic approach to classroom research). In addition, it is also used by researchers whose a priori theoretical point of departure is a specific learning theory, such as sociocultural theory (Ohta, 2001, Ohta and Nakaone, n.d.), systemic grammar (Young & Nguyen, 2002), or, potentially, a variationist approach to SLA (Tarone & Liu, 1995).

Let us now examine what the central methodological and substantive concerns of CA-for-SLA are. In previous work, I have proposed that a CA-for-SLA methodology should be:

1. Based on empirically motivated, emic accounts of members' interactional competence in different speech exchange systems.
2. Based on collections of relevant data that are themselves excerpted from complete transcriptions of communicative events.

3. Capable of exploiting the analytical potential of fine-grained transcripts.
4. Capable of identifying both successful and unsuccessful learning behaviors, at least in the short term.
5. Capable of showing how meaning is constructed as a socially distributed phenomenon, thereby critiquing and recasting cognitive notions of comprehension and learning. (Markee, 2000, page 45)

For present purposes, I wish to revisit points 3 and 5 in greater detail. Let me begin with point 3. It is a basic methodological tenet of CA that no detail of interaction, however small or seemingly insignificant, may be discounted a priori by analysts as not pertinent or meaningful to the participants who produce this interaction (Heritage, 1988). A natural consequence of this position is that CA transcripts do not just set down the words that are said during a speech event. Rather, they are extremely detailed qualitative records of how talk is co-constructed by members on a moment-by-moment basis.

Minimally, CA transcripts also document how members hesitate, pause, or become silent during talk, how they speed up or slow down their delivery, how they modulate the volume of their speech, how they emphasize certain words or sounds through stress, and how they overlap each other's talk. With the increasing availability and use of video recordings as the primary sources of conversational data, it is now also possible (as illustrated by Fragment 1), indeed, highly preferred, to incorporate a great deal of information about members' gestures, embodied actions, and eye gaze behaviors into transcripts (see, for example, Allen, 1995, 2000; Fox, 1999; Goodwin, 1979, 1981, 1994, 2000; Gullberg, 1998; Heath, 1984, 1986; Kellerman, 1992; Kendon, 1985, 1994; Maynard & Marlaire, 1992; McCafferty, 1998, 2002; McIlvenney, 1995; McNeill, 1992; McNeill & Levy, 1993; Neu, 1990; Ochs, Gonzales, & Jacoby, 1996; Roth & Lawless, 2002; Schegloff, 1984; Streeck, 1994).

For present purposes, I will not dwell on the technical aspects of transcription in any detail (although this is certainly a matter of more than passing interest; see DuBois, 1991; Edwards & Lampert, 1993; Preston, 1982, 1985; Roberts, 1997). Rather, let me now relate these preliminary considerations to the substantive implications of point 5 listed earlier. Following Ochs (1979), I wish to argue that transcription cannot be viewed merely as a laborious, technical chore that has to be completed before the real business of analysis can begin. It is a crucially important, substantive first attempt at describing talk and co-occurring gestures, embodied actions, and eye gaze phenomena as a unified, socially constituted context for second language learning activity.

More specifically, CA transcripts provide an essential platform for respecifying key psycholinguistic concepts in SLA—such as comprehensible input and output (Krashen, 1980; Long 1981, 1996; Swain, 1985, 1995)—as micro moments of socially distributed cognition (Markee, 2000). Indeed, as Lazaraton (in press, a) cogently argues in the conclusion to her paper:

> this article suggests that microanalysis provides unique insights into the complexity of ESL [English as a Second Language] classroom talk and behavior. It is claimed that L2 [Second Language] learners receive considerable input in nonverbal form, which may modify and make verbal input (more) comprehensible. Because the majority of data collection procedures in SLA studies fail to capture nonverbal behavior, its contribution to the language acquisition process remains unspecified. Specifically, classroom input is *not* merely composed of teacher or other learner talk—classrooms are the locus of embodied practice. It is hoped that the empirical, classroom discourse-based research agenda that other SLA researchers are pursuing will take up analyzing, in a systematic and microanalytic fashion, *all* aspects of classroom discourse. And it is not just the lexical and gestural competence required of and displayed by the ESL teacher that deserves

further attention, but the many other fundamental aspects of pedagogical performance which are implicated in the input to and the output from L2 learners in the second language classroom (emphasis in the original).

In the empirical section that follows, I begin by recapitulating the original analysis of a fragment of talk taken from the "Coral" collection (Markee, 2000).[4] Although this first transcript (which is reproduced here as Fragment 2) is considerably more detailed than most transcripts used in the SLA literature, it does not include information about members' gestures, embodied actions, or eye gaze behaviors. It is, therefore, comparatively rough by current CA standards. I then reanalyze the same fragment, using a much more fine-grained retranscription of the same data (see Fragment 3) to show how the inclusion of gestures, embodied actions, and eye gaze behaviors into the transcript results in substantively deeper insights into how learners use talk and kinesic actions as integrated resources for getting comprehensible input and producing comprehensible output.

BACKGROUND INFORMATION

As already noted, Fragment 2 comes from the "Coral" data collection, which consists of eight thematically related excerpts of talk that occurred in an intermediate university ESL class in 1990. The learners were doing a task-based unit in small groups on the theme of the greenhouse effect. One learner, L10, has realized that she does not know the meaning of the word "coral," which occurs in an article from the *New Scientist* that her group was reading. L10 therefore engages her fellow group members, L9 and L11, in multiple attempts to figure out what this word means. In the original data set, Fragment 2 represents L10's fifth attempt at understanding the meaning of this word. It is in this excerpt that L10 experiences a breakthrough in understanding, which, as we will now see, is partly the result of intensive negotiation between L10 and L9. Note also that L10 and L11 orient to the fact that they are both native speakers of Mandarin Chinese, while L9 is not a Mandarin speaker.

ORIGINAL TRANSCRIPT OF THE DATA

Fragment 2

```
001           ((L10 is reading her article to herself)
002 L10:    coral. what is corals
003           (4.0)
004 L9:     ·hh do you know the under the sea, under the sea,
005 L10:    un-
006 L9:     there's uh::
007           (0.2)
008 L9:     [how do we call it]
009 L10:    [have uh some coral]
010 L9:     ah yeah (0.2) coral sometimes
011           (0.2)
012 L10:    eh includ/e/s (0.2) uh includes some uh: somethings uh-
013           (1.0)
014 L10:    [the corals,] is means uh: (0.2) s somethings at bottom of
015 L9:     [((unintelligible))]
016 L10:    [the] sea
```

```
017 L9:    [yeah,]
018 L9:    at the bottom of the sea,
019 L10:   ok uh:m also is a food for is a food for fish uh and uh
020        (0.4)
021 L9:    food?
022        (0.3)
023 L10:   foo-
024 L9:    no it is not a food it is (.)like a stone you know?
025 L10:   oh I see I see I see I see I see I know I know ·hh I see ·h a whi- (0.4) a
026        kind of a (0.2) white stone ·h [very beautiful]
027 L9:                                   [yeah yeah] very big yeah
028        [sometimes very beautiful and] sometimes when the ship moves
029 L10:   [I see I see I ok]
030 L9:    [ship tries ((unintelligible)) I think it was the ((unintelligible; the final
031        part of this turn is overlapped by L10's next turn))
032 L10:   [oh I see (0.2) I see the chinese is uh (0.2)] sanku
033        (0.9)
034 L11:   unh?
035 L10:   sanku
036        (0.6)
037 L9:    what
038 L10:   c[orals]
039 L11:    [corals]
040 L9:    corals oh okay
041 L10:   yeah
           (Class 2, group 3)
```

ORIGINAL ANALYSIS

In the original analysis, I noted that after some preliminary attempts by L9 and L10 to gloss coral as "something that is under the sea,"[5] at lines 004, 012, 014 and 018, which are not particularly productive, we can observe the moment-by-moment, social construction of a breakthrough in understanding in this fragment. More specifically, at line 019, L10 states that coral is food for fish. L9 briefly pauses at line 020, thereby potentially signaling an incipient disagreement, which duly occurs in next turn. At this point, L9 initiates a second position repair at line 021 by repeating the word "food" with a high rising intonation. After another short trouble-relevant pause at line 022, which suggests that L10 is now orienting to L9's previous turns as indicative of potential trouble, L10 begins to repeat the word "food" at line 023. This repetition is presumably done to buttress her claim at line 019 that coral is food for fish.[6] However, at line 024, L9 cuts L10 off with another second position repair. This time, the repair is more direct than the first repair that she initiated at line 021, in that it is not only other-initiated but also other-completed. Furthermore, L9 adds the information that coral is like a stone.

This information is the trigger that promotes a key breakthrough in understanding for L10. At line 025, L10 energetically makes the claim that she has understood what "coral" means. The vehemence with which L10 makes this claim is quite noticeable, in that it strongly suggests that not only is L10 quite confident that she has understood the meaning of this word but that she is also willing to suffer a potential loss of face if she later finds out that she is wrong.

I then claimed that L10 independently provides extra information at lines 025 and 026 that coral is white and very beautiful, which L9 accepts at line 027. At lines 028, 030 and 031, L9 elaborates further on some of the qualities of coral, while L10 overlaps L9's talk by again strongly claiming that she has understood the meaning of this word at lines 029 and 032. Moreover, L10 provides the word "sanku" as the Mandarin translation equivalent of English "coral" in the last part of her turn at line 032 and also at line 035. When L9 indicates at line 037 that she does not understand these translations, L10 translates "sanku" back into English and says "corals" at line 038. Almost simultaneously, L11 overlaps L10 at line 039 by also saying "coral," thereby possibly suggesting that, although she had not participated in any of the interaction in this fragment up to line 034, she too had known throughout all this talk what "coral" meant.

Thus, to conclude, this preliminary analysis used three types of converging cotextual evidence to show that L10 has understood the meaning of the word "coral" by the end of Fragment 2. These include:

1. The vehemence of L10's claims of understanding at lines 025, 029 and 031 is noticeable, in that she would have a hard time retracting her claims of understanding if she were proved wrong.
2. L10 independently providing new information at lines 025 and 026 about the qualities of coral, showing that she is able to relate new information to her already existing store of information about this material.
3. L10 using a two-way translation strategy into and from Chinese to help her fix the meaning of coral.

Finally, from a technical CA perspective, note that the second position repairs that L9, L10, and L11 deploy at lines 021, 023, 034, and 037 constitute the principal practice to which members orient as they seek to achieve (or, in SLA terminology, to negotiate) this breakthrough in understanding. Note that this minutely detailed conversation analysis, which has up until now not been motivated by any extraneous, a priori theoretical concerns (Psathas, 1995), in fact independently converges quite neatly with the current theoretical interest in SLA studies in the role of repair as a catalyst for second language learning (Krashen, 1980; Long, 1981; Swain, 1985, 1995).

Indeed, from an SLA perspective, the turns at lines 019–024 are of particular interest because L9 and L10 coconstruct their talk as a sequence of embedded repairs, during which L9 provides L10 with negative evidence about the semantic scope of the word coral. Thus, to the extent that constructs such as comprehensible input and output, positive and negative evidence, and negotiated interaction all have theoretical value in SLA studies—and there is a great deal of theoretical and empirical research to suggest that they do[7]—the talk reproduced in Fragment 2 can be seen as a rare example of how comprehensible input is coconstructed by participants on a moment-by-moment basis.

RETRANSCRIBED VERSION OF THE DATA

Interesting though this original analysis is, the data on which these findings are based may justifiably be criticized as an inadequate representation of the quality of the communication that actually occurred. The lack of any information about gestures, embodied actions, and eye gaze violates the ethnomethodological principle cited earlier that no detail of interaction may be discounted a priori by analysts as not meaningful to participants (Heritage, 1988). Fortunately, video data are available for this fragment, so that we may compare Fragment 2 with the retranscribed version of the same data, which is reproduced as Fragment 3. This retranscription, in which the talk is reproduced in bold script, and kinesic actions are set off in italic script, allows us to evaluate whether the more detailed transcription shown in Fragment 3 actually makes any substantive difference to our understanding of the structural organization of this talk and also to our understanding of the extent to which kinesic behaviors should be viewed as an intrinsic part of comprehensible input and output.

Fragment 3

((L9, L10 and L11 are all looking down at their class materials, reading an article on global warming. L9, who is facing the camera, is leaning her head on her left hand. L10 has her back turned to the camera, and is facing L9. L11 is in profile, but her hair hides her face))

```
001 L10:    corals. what is corals.
002         (1.3)
003 L9:     ((L9 moves her head slightly to her right to
004         look at the right-hand page of her materials.))
005         (1.3)
006 L?:     hshhh
007         (1.3)
008 L9:     [X_      ((L9 looks up at L10, holding
009         [·hh     her chin in her left hand in
010                  a thinking pose))
011         (1.3)
012 L9:     _____
013 L9:     do you know the under the sea : : ,  ((L9 leans
014                                         forward, and
015                                         drops her left
016                                         hand to her lap))
017 L9:     . . . . . . . ((L9 looks down at L10's article))
018 L9:     under the sea : : ,
019 L10:    un-
020 L9:     there's uh : :
021         (0.2)
022 L9:     [°how do we call it°]
023 L10:    [have uh some co    ]ral
024 L9:                  [X____
025 L9:     ah yeah (0.2)[corals
026 L9:     _____
027         (0.2)  [sometimes]
028                [L9 nods]
029         (0.3)  ((L9 clasps her hands))
030 L9:     [. .   ((L9 moves her hands sideways))]
031 L10:    [gi- uh includ/e/s
032 L9:     [X_____
033 L10:    [(0.2)uh includ/e/s some uh: somethings uh-
034         (1.0)
035 L9:     _____
036 L10:    [some corals.    ]    ((L10 raises her hand as
037 L9:     [((unintelligible))]   she says "corals"))
038 L9:     _____
039 L10:    is means the: (0.2) s [somethings at bottom] of
040                           [((L10 raises her hand and
041                           marks the word "bottom"
042                           with a downward beat of
043                           her right hand))]
```

```
044 L9:    _____
045 L10:   [the  ]   sea.
046 L9:    [yeah.]  ((L9 nods once emphatically))
047 L9:    [at the bottom of the sea,]
048        [((L9 hands briefly unclasps
049        and then clasps her hands again.
050        She points her clasped hands
051        toward L10 and then holds them
052        in front of her face in a thinking gesture,
053        and looks intently at L10.))]
054 L9:    _____
055 L10:   ok uh:m (0.3) also is a food for- is a food for
056 L9:    _____
057 L10:   fish/e/, and uh ((L10 makes a chopping motion
058                         with her right hand, emphasizing
059                         the words "food" and "food for
060                         fish/e/". L10 ends her turn
061                         with her right hand held up
062                         vertically, palm open))
063        (0.4) ((L9 raises her head slightly and withdraws
064              her right hand from her mouth))
065 L9:    food?
066        (0.3)
067 L9:    ____
068 L10:   foo-
069 L9:    no it is not a food.
070        [it is (.) like a: stone. you know,]
071        [((L9 mimics holding an object))]
072 L9:    _____
073 L10:   [oh I see I see I see I see I see]
074        [((L10 throws her hands outward and claps her
075        hands three times, inclining her head downward
076        as she does this))]
077 L9:    _____
078 L10:   I know I know [·hh I see ·h a whi-     ]
079                      [((L10 lifts her head up))]
080        (0.4)
081 L9:    _____
082 L10:   a kind of a (0.2) whi/d/e (.) ⌈ stone              ⌉
083        (((L10 emphasizes the words  |                    |
084        "whi-" and "whi/d/e" with     |                    |
085        her right hand. As she        |                    |
086        says the word "stone"         |                    |
087        L10 raises her right hand      |                    |
088        up to eye level))             |                    |
089 L9:                                  ⌊ ((L9 nods twice)) ⌋
090 L9:    __
091 L10:   [·h]
092 L9:    [yeah] yeah
093 L9:    _____
094 L10:   ve[ry beautiful]
095 L9:      [very big  ] [yeah yeah ]
096                       [L10 brings her right hand
```

```
097                          down to the desk and leans back,
098                            looking at L9))]
099                   [sometimes very beautiful]   ((L9 unclasps and
100 L10:  [oh I see I see I ok          ]       clasps her hands))
101 L9:   _____
102 L10:  oh [I see]
103 L9:      [and som]etimes when the ship moves ((L9 moves
104       her hands back and forth as she says "sometimes",
105       "ship" and "moves"))
106 L9:   _____
107 L10:  oh [I see ]
108 L9:      [ship tries]    [((unintelligible))   ]
109 L10:               [the chinese is uh (0.2)] sanku
110       ((As she says "oh I see" and proceeds to
111       translate "coral" into Chinese, L10 leans over
112       toward L11 and points at L11's reading materials
113       with her pen. Simultaneously, L9 looks down at
114       L11's paper))
115       (0.9) ((L9 raises her eyes to look at L10))
116       [L11 raises her head]
117 L11:  [huh?]
118 L9:   ((L9 raises her gaze to look at L10))
119 L10:  sanku
120       (0.6) ((L10 withdraws her hand from L11's desk
121       and looks down at her own reading materials))
122 L9:   what? ⌐ ((L9 leans back on her chair))
123 L10:        |    c[orals.]
124 L11:        ⌐    [coral]s.
125 L9:   ⌐ ((L9 leans forward and looks down at her desk,
126       |    unclasps her hands and picks up her reading
127       |    materials))
128 L9:   └ corals. oh okay
129       [((L10 leans her head on her right hand))]
130 L10:  [yeah.]
          (Class 2, group 3)
```

It is immediately apparent that this transcript is much longer than the version reproduced in Fragment 2 (130 lines of text, instead of the original 41 required to capture 1 min 3 seconds of interaction). Reproducing this level of detail in the updated transcript is also extremely onerous to transcribe, requiring at least 15 hours of extra transcription for this fragment on top of the time already invested in producing the original transcript. Last but not least, Fragment 3 is also more difficult to read than Fragment 2, particularly for non-CA specialists, whose initial reaction may well be that the level of detail that is included in Fragment 3 is overwhelming. Nonetheless, I will demonstrate that the effort that is required to process this transcript is more than offset by the substantive dividends that accrue to the patient reader.

UPDATED ANALYSIS

The new transcript shown in Fragment 3 allows us to confirm the overall conclusions reached on the basis of the simpler transcript reproduced in Fragment 2, while providing significantly more details that give greater nuance to the original analysis. Let us begin with an analysis of the structural integration of talk and gesture that is observable in the data reproduced in Fragments 3.1–3.3:

Fragment 3.1

```
055 L10:    ok uh:m (0.3) also is a food for- is a food for
056 L9:     _____
057 L10:    fish/e/, and uh ((L10 makes a chopping motion
058                        with her right hand, emphasizing
059                        the words "food" and "food for
060                        fish/e/". L10 ends her turn
061                        with her right hand held up
062                        vertically, palm open))
```

In the gloss at lines 057–062, we can see that emphasis is not only carried out through verbal stress on the words "food" and "food for fish/e/," but that it is visually conveyed by L10's beating out the rhythm of this phrase with her right hand. Similarly, the upward intonation with which the word the word "fish/e/," is marked—a verbal recipient design that suggests that L10 is looking for L9 to confirm her hypothesis at lines 055–057—is confirmed by the way she holds the palm of her right hand open, which visually suggests her openness to further feedback.

This close interaction between talk and hand gestures is also observable in Fragment 3.2:

Fragment 3.2

```
073 L10:    [oh I see I see I see I see I see]
074         [(((L10 throws her hands outward and claps her
075         hands three times, inclining her head downward))
076         as she does this))]
```

More specifically, we can see that L10 claps her hands at lines 074–076 at the same time that she begins to make her first verbal claim of understanding. This clapping motion, which we can interpret as a form of self-congratulation by L10, further confirms the original analysis that it is at this precise moment in the interaction that L10 first understands what "coral" means.

In Fragment 3.3, we may further observe how talk and gesture are again closely coordinated as part of the turn-taking structure to which these participants visibly orient:

Fragment 3.3

```
078 L10:    I know I know [·hh I see ·h a whi-        ]
079                       [(((L10 lifts her head up))]
080         (0.4)
081 L9:     _____
```

```
082 L10:    a kind of a (0.2) whi/d/e (.) ┌ stone                     ┐
083         ((L10 emphasizes the words    │                          │
084         "whi-" and "whi/d/e" with      │                          │
085         her right hand. As she         │                          │
086         says the word "stone"          │                          │
087         L10 raises her right hand       │                          │
088         up to eye level))              │                          │
089 L9:                                     └ ((L9 nods twice))        ┘
090 L9:      ___
091 L10:    [˙h]
092 L9:     [yeah] yeah
093 L9:      _____
094 L10:    ve[ry beautiful]
095 L9:     [very big ]        [yeah yeah                     ]
096                            [L10 brings her right hand
097                             down to the desk and leans back,
098                             looking at L9))]
099         [sometimes very beautiful] ((L9 unclasps and
100 L10:    [oh I see I see I ok    ]        clasps her hands))
```

As in Fragment 3.1, we see L10 using her hand to beat out the rhythm of the stressed words "whi-" and "whi/d/e" at lines 078 and 079. Furthermore, the first response given by L9 that L10 is on the right track is her *nodding* actions at line 089, which collaboratively overlaps L10 saying "stone" at line 082. L9 then adds the second, *verbal*, part of this confirmation when she produces the turn "yeah yeah" at line 092.

Note also that it is L10's hand gesture at lines 087–088 that gives us a clue as to why L9 says "very big" at line 095. L10's gesture seems to project that she is going to say something about the large size of coral reefs. Indeed, this seems to be the understanding of L10's gesture that L9 is pursuing when she responds at lines 103–105 and 108.[8] However, the characteristic that L10 seems to be focusing on from line 094–100 (and briefly acknowledged by L9 at line 099) is the beauty of coral. We can tell this not only from the verbal behavior that occurs at lines 091–095—specifically, L10 draws an in-breath at line 091, suggesting that she is about to say something, and she also overlaps L9's comment about the size of coral reefs with her own characterization of coral as being "very beautiful"—but also from the way she leans back in her seat at lines 096–098. This embodied action visually suggests that L10 has come to some kind of conclusion about what "coral" means and, perhaps, that she is ready to move the talk on to some other activity.

This interpretation is confirmed by L10's translation of the word "coral" into Chinese at line 109. Notice, however, that the extra information about L10's embodied actions given in the gloss at lines 110–114 of Fragment 3.4 provides key information about what L10 is actually achieving through her translation at this particular moment in this particular spate of talk:

Fragment 3.4

```
110    ((As she says "oh I see" and proceeds to
111    translate "coral" into Chinese, L10 leans over
112    toward L11 and points at L11's reading materials
113    with her pen. Simultaneously, L9 looks down at
114    L11's paper))
```

In the original analysis, it was not clear whether L10 was merely remarking to herself (or perhaps thinking aloud) that the Chinese translation of "coral" was "sanku," or whether she was performing another, more focused, action. The gloss at lines 110–114 clarifies beyond doubt that L10 is specifically explaining the meaning of this word to L11, who has demonstrated in prior talk that she does not understand the meaning of this word either. In so doing, L10 further achieves the action of transforming herself from a novice learning from L9 into an expert who is teaching L11 new material.

To conclude this conversation analysis of the structure of participants' verbal practices and embodied actions in Fragments 3.1–3.4, note that in the original analysis, I claimed that L10's identification of coral as a white stone was new information and that this was, therefore, evidence of understanding. In point of fact, this information is contained in the original *New Scientist* article, which states: "When the water is too warm, corals turn white as they expel the algae that live in their tissues and provide them with nutrients" ("How the Heat Trap", p. 22). This reinterpretation of why L10 says that coral is white at lines 078 and 082 does not negate the original conclusion that L10 understands what "coral" means in this fragment. As we have seen, other compelling evidence (both old and new) exists to support this analysis. However, this example of the way that learners integrate written source texts into their talk provides further support for the overall argument that descriptions of comprehensible input and output that limit themselves to oral evidence only are likely to be limited.

Finally, let us look at these data again from an SLA perspective. We have already seen from the original analysis that the catalyst for L10's moment-by-moment breakthrough in understanding in Fragment 3 is L9's use of progressively stronger forms of second position repair, which clarify the meaning of the word "coral" by limiting its semantic scope. Here, I would like to make an observation about the importance of including information about embodied actions and eye gaze behaviors in transcripts. More specifically, I wish to claim that potentially crucial microanalytic information about human cognition and second language learning may be embedded in transcripts that include this type of information.

From a mainstream SLA perspective, it is clear that L10 allocates a considerable amount of attention throughout Fragment 3 (and indeed in the fragments that precede Fragment 3 in the original database) in order to understand the meaning of the word "coral." This noticing behavior is consistent with the findings of the psycholinguistic literature concerning the important role that attention, awareness, and consciousness all play in second language learning (Gass, 1997; Robinson, 1995; Schmidt, 1990, 1993a, 1993b, 1994).

However, for present purposes, it is also noticeable throughout Fragment 3 that L9 too devotes a great deal of attention to helping L10 understand what the word "coral" means. For example, we can observe the "thinking gesture" (holding her chin in her hand) that L9 adopts at lines 008–010 and at lines 052–064, the way she clasps hers hands at key moments in the interaction (see lines 029, 049, and 100), thus projecting an impression of concentration, and the intensity of her gaze throughout Fragment 3. These characteristic gestures are all explicitly noted in the gloss at lines 048–053 of Fragment 3.5:

Fragment 3.5

048   [(((*L9 hands briefly unclasps*
049   *and then clasps her hands again.*
050   *She points her clasped hands*
051   *toward L10 and then holds them*
052   *in front of her face in a thinking gesture,*
053   *and looks intently at L10.*))]

We can also observe how intently L9 gazes at L10 even more precisely by noting the transcription details of L9's eye gaze behaviors throughout the fragment (X__, where X marks the onset of gaze and the continuous line marks the continuation of a participants' gaze). Thus, at line 008, L9 begins to look at L10 and, apart from two momentary breaks at lines 017 and 030, L9 looks almost continuously at L10 until line 113, that is, for 45 out of the 65 seconds of interaction that constitute Fragment 3.

This is an extraordinarily long time for a participant to look at an interlocutor. This practice suggests that L9 is using eye gaze behaviors and the other embodied actions previously described as interactional resources to "do noticing" (Schegloff, 1989) that L10 is experiencing difficulty understanding the word "coral," and that she therefore requires L9's undivided help and attention.

Now, we must be extremely careful to limit any claims about how L9 and L10 do being attentive in this fragment, and even more so about drawing any larger implications about the nature of human cognition and SLA. After all, L10 has her back turned to the video camera, so we cannot directly observe L10's own eye gaze behaviors. Nonetheless, I wish to argue that these data suggest that attention in talk-in-interaction is as much an observable, *socially distributed activity* that is constructed by two or more interlocutors on a moment-by-moment basis as it is an *individual cognitive phenomenon*, whose inner workings are only accessible to researchers through post hoc, personal introspection.

Of course, this is not to say that L10 is not the principal *individual* beneficiary of L9 attending to her comprehension needs (although notice that L11 also incidentally benefits as a result of L9's and L10's joint comprehension work). But the position I am outlining here is significantly different from the one(s) espoused in mainstream, psycholinguistically oriented approaches to SLA, namely, that language learning is a manifestation of human cognition that is located in the mind/brain of individuals. Although this psycholinguistic account should certainly not be dismissed out of hand—after all, CA itself assumes that competent speakers must have some (unspecified) knowledge of clausal structure that enables them to parse the ongoing progress of current turn, so that next speakers can appropriately make a bid for next turn (Sacks, Schegloff, & Jefferson, 1974)—the CA perspective adopted here suggests that language learning may also be productively understood as an interactional achievement that is negotiated in the collective, socially distributed space that constitutes talk-in-interaction.

CONCLUSION

This chapter has briefly reviewed what mainstream CA is and has shown how the transcription procedures and microanalytic techniques of this approach to analyzing talk-in-interaction may be used to describe how second language learning unfolds on a moment-by-moment basis. Following Kasper (2002) and Markee (2003a), I have dubbed this approach CA-for-SLA. As shown by the comparative analyses of Fragments 2 and 3, transcription is not merely an arcane, technical issue that is of interest only to CA specialists. Very fine grained transcripts such as the one reproduced in Fragment 3 lead to important, substantive improvements over analyses that are based on less detailed transcripts. More specifically, as Ochs (1979) suggested, transcripts are preliminary theorizations of members' interactional competence. As such, the minutest details of both verbal *and* kinesic behavior that they contain must be recorded, because they potentially hold vital clues to much larger questions that are of fundamental interest to SLA researchers. Not the least of these is the question: "How are second languages learned through interactional activity?"

This and other issues raised in this chapter are obviously of most direct interest to researchers working within the parameters of broadly sociolinguistic and/or sociocultural approaches to SLA, to classroom researchers, and to applied linguists in general who are interested in understanding how everyday classrooms function. In addition, data such as these also potentially provide useful practical insights into the micro details of classroom talk for teachers and teacher trainers, in that they document what successful language learning activity in small group interaction looks like. It is therefore clear that CA-for-SLA research has a large constituency of potential consumers, who may not themselves be CA specialists. The challenge that now faces CA-for-SLA researchers is to produce a coherent body of research that further develops our understanding of the architecture of interactional activity and that shows how the verbal and kinesic practices described here provide a coherent theoretical and practical respecification of how second language learning in ordinary, everyday communicative contexts actually works.

APPENDIX 1: Transcription Conventions

CA transcription conventions (based on Atkinson & Heritage, 1984).

IDENTITY OF SPEAKERS
T: teacher
L1:   identified learner (Learner 1)
L: unidentified learner
L3?:   probably Learner 3
LL: several or all learners speaking simultaneously

SIMULTANEOUS UTTERANCES
L1: [yes
L2: [yeh   simultaneous, overlapping talk by two speakers
L1: [huh? [oh] I see]
L2:   [what]
L3: [I dont get it   ]   simultaneous, overlapping talk by three (or more) speakers

CONTIGUOUS UTTERANCES
=   a) turn continues at the next identical symbol on the next line
             b) if inserted at the end of one speaker's turn and the beginning of
             the next speaker's adjacent turn, it indicates that there is no gap at
             all between the two turns

INTERVALS WITHIN AND BETWEEN UTTERANCES
(0.3) (1) (0.3) = a pause of between 0.3 second;
            (1.0) = a pause of one second.

CHARACTERISTICS OF SPEECH DELIVERY
?   rising intonation, not necessarily a question
!   strong emphasis, with falling intonation
yes.   a period indicates falling (final) intonation
so,   a comma indicates low-rising intonation suggesting continuation
go:::d   one or more colons indicate lengthening of the preceding sound;
             each additional colon represents a lengthening of one beat
no-   a hyphen indicates an abrupt cut-off, with level pitch

because	underlined type indicates marked stress
SYLVIA	capitals indicate increased volume
°the next thing°	degree sign indicates decreased volume
·hhh	in-drawn breath
hhh	laughter tokens

COMMENTARY IN THE TRANSCRIPT

((coughs))	verbal description of actions noted in the transcript, including non verbal actions
((unintelligible))	indicates a stretch of talk that is unintelligible to the analyst
.... (radio)	single parentheses indicate unclear or probable item

EYE GAZE PHENOMENA

The moment at which eye gaze is coordinated with speech is marked by an X and the duration of the eye gaze is indicated by a continuous line. Thus, in the example below, the moment at which L11's eye gaze falls on L9 in line 412 coincides with the beginning of his turn at line 413.

```
            [X __((L11's eye gaze is now directed at L9)) _____
412 L11: →      ~ [°you can call me and then [ I can say you ] the the address
413 L9:  →                                   [(((L9 nods 4 times]
```

Eye gaze transition is shown by commas

```
            [X _____ , ,
```

The moment at which there ceases to be eye contact (as when a participant looks down or away from his/her interlocutor) is shown by periods

```
            [X _____ ...
```

OTHER TRANSCRIPTION SYMBOLS

co[l]al	brackets indicate phonetic transcription
→	an arrow in the margin of a transcript draws attention to a particular phenomenon the analyst wishes to discuss

NOTES

1. As I have noted elsewhere (Markee, 2000), Schiffrin (1991) suggests that there are at least six other types of CA apart from the ethnomethodological approach discussed here. Within ethnomethodological CA, it is customary to distinguish between conversation analysis that derives from and develops Garfinkel's concerns with developing a theory of social action (Garfinkel 1967, 1974) and other forms of conversational analysis, which are primarily concerned with analyzing the content of talk rather than its observable sequential and other structure (Schegloff, Koshik, & Jacoby Olsher, 2002).
2. See also Mehan (1979) and Sinclair & Coulthard (1975), who call such sequences Initiation-Response-Feedback or Initiation-Response-Evaluation sequences, respectively.
3. The names that appear in this and all other fragments in this paper are pseudonyms.
4. The original transcript in Markee (2000) used slightly different transcription symbols from the ones used here. In order to make the comparison between Fragments 2 and 3 as transparent as possible, I have standardized the transcription symbols used so that they both conform to the standard conventions of CA transcription shown in Appendix 1.
5. This phrase is actually recycled from some previous attempts by L9 in preceding excerpts to explain what coral means to L10.
6. In point of fact, L10 is correct: some types of coral are indeed a source of food for fish. However, the two learners do not pursue this possibility any further. Consequently, this piece of ethnographic information is not utilized in the analysis.
7. See Caroll & Swain (1993); Lightbown & Spada (1990); Long (1996); Long, Inagaki, & Ortega (1998); Lyster (1998); Lyster & Ranta (1997); Nicholas, Lightbown, & Spada (2001); Oliver (1995, 1998).
8. Although most of this talk is unintelligible, L9 is probably talking about the dangers that coral reefs pose to shipping.

REFERENCES

Allen, L. Q. (1995). The effects of emblematic gestures on the development and access of mental representations of French expressions. *Modern Language Journal, 79*, 521–529.

Allen, L. Q. (2000). Nonverbal accommodations in foreign language teacher talk. *Applied Language Learning, 11*, 155–176.

Atkinson, J. M., & Heritage, J. (1984). Transcript notation. In J. M. Atkinson, & J. Heritage (Eds.), *Structures of social action* (pp. ix–xvi). Cambridge, UK: Cambridge University Press.

Caroll, S., & Swain, M. (1993). Explicit and implicit feedback. An empirical study of the learning of linguistic generalizations. *Studies in Second Language Acquisition, 15*, 357–386.

Davidson, J. (1984). Subsequent versions of invitations, offers, requests, and proposals dealing with potential or actual rejection. In J. M. Atkinson & J. Heritage (Eds.), *Structures of social action* (pp. 102–128). Cambridge, UK: Cambridge University Press.

Drew, P. (1984). Speakers' reportings in invitation sequences. In J. M. Atkinson & J. Heritage (Eds.), *Structures of social action* (pp. 129–151). Cambridge, UK: Cambridge University Press.

Du Bois, J. (1991). Transcription design principles for spoken discourse research. *Pragmatics, 1*, 71–106.

Edwards, J. A., & Lampert, M. D. (1993). *Talking data*. Hillsdale, NJ: Lawrence Erlbaum Associates.

Firth, A., & Wagner, J. (1997). On discourse, communication, and (some) fundamental concepts in SLA research. *The Modern Language Journal, 81*, 285–300.

Fox, B. (1999). Directions in research. Language and the body. *Research in Language and Social Interaction, 32*, 51–59.

Garfinkel, H. (1967). *Studies in ethnomethodology*. Englewood Cliffs, NJ: Prentice-Hall.

Garfinkel, H. (1974). The origins of the term ethnomethodology. In R. Turner (Ed.), *Ethnomethodology* (pp. 15–18). Harmondsworth, UK: Penguin.

Gaskill, W. (1980). Correction in native speaker–non-native speaker conversation. In D. Larsen-Freeman (Ed.), *Discourse analysis in second language research* (pp. 125–137). Rowley, MA: Newbury House.

Gass, S. M. (1997). *Input, interaction and the second language learner*. Mahwah, NJ: Lawrence Erlbaum Associates.

Goodwin, C. (1979). The interactive construction of a sentence in natural conversation. In G. Psathas (Ed.), *Everyday language: Studies in ethnomethodology* (pp. 97–121). New York: Irvington.

Goodwin, C. (1981). *Conversational organization: Interaction between speakers and hearers*. New York: Academic Press.

Goodwin, C. (1984). Notes on story structure and the organization of participation. In J. M. Atkinson & J. Heritage (Eds.), *Structures of social action* (pp. 225–246). Cambridge, UK: Cambridge University Press.

Goodwin, C. (1994). Professional vision. *American Anthropologist, 96*, 606–633.

Goodwin, C. (2000). Action and embodiment within situated human interaction. *Journals of Pragmatics, 32*, 1489–1522.

Gullberg, M. (1998). *Gesture as communication strategy in second language discourse*. Lund, Sweden: Lund University Press.

He, A.W. (2003, March 22). *Interactional resources for constructing multiple learning activities in Chinese heritage language classrooms*. Paper presented at the colloquium on Classroom talks: A conversation analytic perspective, American Association of Applied Linguistics, Arlington, VA.

Heath, C. (1984). Talk and recipiency: Sequential organization in speech and body movement. In J. M. Atkinson & J. Heritage (Eds.), *Structures of social action* (pp. 247–265). Cambridge, UK: Cambridge University Press.

Heath, C. (1986). *Body movement and speech in medical interaction*. Cambridge, UK: Cambridge University Press.

Heritage, J. (1988). Current development in conversation analysis. In D. Roger & P. Bull (Eds.), *Conversation* (pp. 21–47). Clevedon, UK: Multilingual Matters.

"How the Heat trap will wreak ecological havoc" from p. 20–34.

How the heat trap will wreak ecological havoc. (1988, October 15). *New Scientist*, pp. 22.

Kasper, G. (2002, March 13). *Conversation Analysis as an approach to Second Language Acquisition: Old wine in new bottles?* Invited talk, SLATE speaker series, University of Illinois at Urbana-Champaign.

Kasper, G. (2003, March 22). *Interactional competence and foreign language learning: The first few weeks*. Paper presented at the colloquium on Classroom talks: A conversation analytic perspective, American Association of Applied Linguistics, Arlington, VA.

Kellerman, S. (1992). "I see what you mean": The role of kinesic behavior in listening, and implications for foreign and second language learning. *Applied Linguistics, 13*, 239–258.

Kendon, A. (1985). Some uses of gesture. In D. Tannen & M. Saville-Troike (Eds.), *Perspectives on silence* (pp. 215–234). Norwood, NJ: Ablex.

Kendon, A. (1994). Do gestures communicate: A review. *Research in Language and Social Interaction, 27*, 175–200.

Krashen, S. D. (1980). The input hypothesis. In J. E. Alatis (Ed.), *Current issues in bilingual education* (pp. 168–180). Washington, DC: Georgetown University Press.

Lazaraton, A. (2003). Incidental displays of cultural knowledge in the NNEST classroom. *TESOL Quarterly, 37*, 213–245.

Lazaraton, A. (2004). Gesture and speech in the vocabulary explanations of one ESL teacher: A microanalytic inquiry. *Language Learning, 54,* 79–118.

Lerner, G. H. (1991). On the syntax of sentences-in-progress. *Language in Society, 20,* 441–458.

Lightbown, P. M., & Spada, N. (1990). Focus-on-form and corrective feedback in communicative language teaching.: Effects on second language learning. *Studies in Second Language Acquisition, 12,* 429–448.

Long, M. H. (1981). Input, interaction and second language acquisition. In H. Winitz (Ed.), *Annals of the New York Academy of Sciences, 379,* 259–278.

Long, M. H. (1996). The role of the linguistic environment in second language acquisition. In W. C. Ritchie & T. K. Bhatia (Eds.), *Handbook of second language acquisition* (pp. 414–468). New York: Academic Press.

Long, M. H., Inagaki, S., & Ortega, L. (1998). The role of implicit negative feedback in SLA: Models and recasts in Japanese and Spanish. *The Modern Language Journal, 82,* 357–371.

Lyster, R. 1998). Negotiation of form, recasts, and explicit correction in relation to error types and learner repair in immersion classrooms. *Language Learning, 48,* 183–218.

Lyster, R., & Ranta, L. (1997). Corrective feedback and learner uptake: Negotiation of form in communicative classrooms. *Studies in Second Language Acquisition, 19,* 37–66.

Markee, N. (1994). Toward an ethnomethodological respecification of second language acquisition studies. In E. Tarone, S. Gass, & A. Cohen (Eds.), *Research methodology in second language acquisition* (pp. 89–116). Hillsdale, NJ: Lawrence Erlbaum Associates.

Markee, N. (1995). Teachers' answers to students' questions: Problematizing the issue of making meaning. *Issues in Applied Linguistics, 6,* 63–92.

Markee, N. (2000). *Conversation analysis.* Mahwah, NJ: Lawrence Erlbaum Associates.

Markee, N. (2003a, March 22). *Zones of interactional transition.* Paper presented at the colloquium on Classroom talks: A conversation analytic perspective. American Association of Applied Linguistics, Arlington, VA.

Markee, N. (2003b). Qualitative research guidelines (Conversation Analysis). *TESOL Quarterly, 37,* 169–172.

Maynard, D., & Marlaire, C. (1992). Good reasons for bad testing performance. The interactional substrate of educational exams. *Qualitative Sociology, 15,* 177–202.

McCafferty, S. G. (1998). Nonverbal expressions and L2 private speech. *Applied Linguistics, 19,* 73–96.

McCafferty, S. G. (2002). Gesture and creating zones of proximal development for second language learning. *Modern Language Journal, 86,* 192–203.

McHoul, A. (1978). The organization of turns at formal talk in the classroom. *Language in Society, 7,* 183–213.

McHoul, A. (1990). The organization of repair in classroom talk. *Language in Society, 19,* 349–377.

McIlvenny, P. (1995). Seeing conversations: Analyzing sign language talk. In P. Ten Have & G. Psathas (Eds.), *Situated order: Studies in the social organization of talk and embodied activities* (pp. 129–150). Washington, DC: International Institute for Ethnomethodology and Conversation Analysis and the University Press of America.

McNeill, D. (1992). *Hand and mind: What the hands reveal about thought.* Chicago: Chicago University Press.

McNeill, D., & Levy, E. T. (1993). Cohesion and gesture. *Discourse Processes, 16,* 363–386.

Mehan, H. (1979). *Learning lessons: Social organization in the classroom.* Cambridge, MA: Harvard University Press.

Mori, J. (2002). Task design, plan, and development of talk-in-interaction: An analysis of a small group activity in a Japanese language classroom. *Applied Linguistics, 23,* 323–347.

Mori, J. (2003, March 22). *Classroom talks, discourse identities, and participation structures.* Paper presented at the colloquium on Classroom talks: A conversation analytic perspective. American Association of Applied Linguistics, Arlington, VA.

Neu, J. (1990). Assessing the role of nonverbal communication in the acquisition of communicative competence in L2. In R. Scarcella, E. S. Andersen & S. D. Krashen (Eds.), *Developmental pragmatics* (pp. 43–72). New York: Academic Press.

Nicholas, H., Lightbown, P., & Spada, N. (2001). Recasts as feedback to language learners. *Language Learning, 51,* 719–758.

Ochs, E. (1979). Transcription as theory. In E. Ochs & B. Schieffelin (Eds.), *Developmental pragmatics* (pp. 43–72). New York: Academic Press.

Ochs, E., Gonzales, P., & Jacoby, S. (1996). "When I come down I'm in the domain state": Grammar and graphic representation in the interpretive activity of physicists. In E. Ochs, E. A. Schegloff, & S. Thompson (Eds.), *Interaction and grammar* (pp. 328–369). Cambridge, UK: Cambridge University Press.

Ohta, A. (2001). *Second language acquisition processes in the classroom.* Mahwah, NJ: Lawrence Erlbaum Associates.

Ohta, A., & Nakaone, T. (n.d). When students ask language-related questions: Student questions and their answers in teacher-fronted and group work classroom interaction. Unpublished manuscript, University of Washington, Seattle.

Oliver, R. (1995). Negative feedback in child NS–NNS conversation. *Studies in Second Language Acquisition, 17,* 459–481.

Oliver, R. (1998). Negotiation of meaning in child interactions. *Modern Language Journal, 82,* 372–386.

Pomerantz, A. (1975). Second assessments: A study of some features of agreements/disagreements. Unpublished doctoral dissertation, University of California, Irvine, CA.

Pomerantz, A. (1978a). Compliment responses: Notes on the cooperation of multiple constraints. In J. N. Schenkein (Ed.), *Studies in the organization of conversational interaction* (pp. 79–112). New York: Academic Press.

Pomerantz, A. (1978b). Attributions of responsibility: Blamings. *Sociology, 12,* 115–121.

Pomerantz, A. (1984a). Agreeing and disagreeing with assessments: Some features of preferred/dispreferred turn shapes. In J. M. Atkinson & J. Heritage (Eds.), *Structures of social action* (pp. 152–163). Cambridge, UK: Cambridge University Press.

Pomerantz, A. (1984b). Pursuing a response. In J. M. Atkinson & J. Heritage (Eds.), *Structures of social action* (pp. 57–101). Cambridge, UK: Cambridge University Press.

Preston, D. (1982). 'Ritin folklower daun 'rong. *Journal of American folklore, 95,* 304–326.

Preston, D. (1985). The Lil' Abner syndrome: Written representations of speech. *American Speech, 60,* 328–336.

Psathas, G. (1986). Some sequential structures in direction-giving. *Human Studies, 9,* 231–246.

Psathas, G. (1995). *Conversation analysis: The study of talk-in-interaction.* Thousand Oaks, CA: Sage.

Roberts, C. (1997). Transcribing talk: Issues of representation. *TESOL Quarterly, 31,* 167–172.

Robinson, P. J. (1995). Attention, memory and the "noticing" hypothesis. *Language Learning, 45,* 283–331.

Roth, W.-M., & Lawless, D. (2002). When up is down and down is up: Body orientation, proximity, and gestures and resources. *Language in Society, 31,* 1–28.

Sacks, H. (1974). An analysis of the course of a joke's telling. In R. Bauman & J. Sherzer (Eds.), *Explorations in the ethnography of speaking* (pp. 337–353). Cambridge, UK: Cambridge University Press.

Sacks, H., & Schegloff, E. A. (1979). Two preferences in the organization of reference to persons and their interaction. In G. Psathas (Ed.), *Everyday language: Studies in ethnomethodology* (pp. 15–21). New York: Irvington.

Sacks, H., Schegloff, E. A, & Jefferson, G. (1974). A simplest systematics for the organization of turn-taking in conversation. *Language, 50,* 696–735.

Schegloff, E. A. (1972). Sequencing in conversational openings. In J. J. Gumperz, & D. Hymes (Eds.), *Directions in sociolinguistics* (pp. 346–380). New York: Holt, Rhinehart & Winston.

Schegloff, E. A. (1979). The relevance of repair to syntax-for-conversation. In T. Givon (Ed.), *Syntax and semantics, Volume 12: Discourse and syntax* (pp. 261–286). New York: Academic Press.

Schegloff, E. A. (1984). On some gestures' relation to talk. In J. M. Atkinson & J. Heritage (Eds.), *Structures of social action* (pp. 266–296). Cambridge, UK: Cambridge University Press.

Schegloff, E. A. (1987). Between macro and micro: Contexts and other connections. In J. Alexander, B. Giesen, R. Munch, & N. Smelser (Eds.), *The micro–macro link* (pp. 207–234). Berkeley: University of California Press.

Schegloff, E. A. (1989). Reflections on language, development, and the interactional character of talk-in-interaction. In M. H. Bornstein & J. Bruner (Eds.), *Interaction in human development* (pp. 139–153). Hillsdale, NJ: Lawrence Erlbaum Associates.

Schegloff, E. A. (1996). Turn organization: One intersection of grammar and interaction. In E. Ochs, E. A. Schegloff, & S. Thompson (Eds.), *Interaction and grammar* (pp. 52–133). Cambridge, UK: Cambridge University Press.

Schegloff, E. A., Jefferson, G., & Sacks, H. (1977). The preference for self-correction in the organization of repair in conversation. *Language, 53,* 361–382.

Schegloff, E. A., Koshik, I., Olsher, D. & Jacoby, S. (2002). Conversation analysis and applied linguistics. In M. McGroarty (Ed.), *ARAL, 22.*

Schiffrin, D. (1991). Conversation analysis. *Annual Review of Applied Linguistics, 11,* 3–16.

Schmidt, R. (1990). The role of consciousness in second language learning. *Applied Linguistics, 11,* 17–46.

Schmidt, R. (1993a). Awareness and second language acquisition. *Annual Review of Applied Linguistics, 13,* 206–226.

Schmidt, R. (1993b). Consciousness, learning and interlanguage pragmatics. In G. Kasper & S. Blum-Kulka (Eds.), *Interlanguage Pragmatics* (pp. 21–42). New York: Oxford University Press.

Schmidt, R. (Ed.). (1994). Deconstructing consciousness in search of useful definitions for applied linguistics. *AILA Review, 11,* 11–26.

Seedhouse, P. (1997). The case of the missing "No": The relationship between pedagogy and interaction. *Language Learning, 47,* 547–583.

Seedhouse, P. (1999). The relationship between context and the organization of repair in the L2 classrooom. *IRAL, XXXVII,* 59–80.

Sinclair, J., & Coulthard, M. (1975). *Towards an analysis of discourse.* Oxford, UK: Oxford University Press

Streeck, J. (1994). Gesture as communication II: The audience as co-author. *Research in Language and Social Interaction, 27,* 239–267.

Stubbs, M. (1983). *Discourse analysis.* Oxford, UK: Basil Blackwell.

Swain, M. (1985). Communicative competence: Some roles of comprehensible input and comprehensible output in its development. In S. Gass & C. Madden (Eds.), *Input in second language acquisition* (pp. 235–253). Rowley, MA: Newbury House.

Swain, M. (1995). Three functions of output in second language learning. In G. Cooke & B. Seidhofer (Eds.), *Principle and practice in applied linguistics: Studies in honour of H. G. Widdowson* (pp. 125–144). Oxford, UK: Oxford University Press.

Tarone E., & Liu, G. (1995). Situational context, variation, and second language acquisition. In G. Cook & B. Seidlhoffer (Eds.), *Principles and practice in applied linguistics: Studies in honour of H. G. Widdowson* (pp. 107–124). Oxford, UK: Oxford University Press.

van Lier, L. (1988). *The classroom and the language learner*. London: Longman.

Young, R., & Nguyen, H. T. (2002). Modes of meaning in high school science. *Applied linguistics, 23*, 348–372.

21

Contrastive Rhetoric

Robert Kaplan
University of Southern California (Emeritus)

WHAT IS CONTRASTIVE RHETORIC?

Languages are multidimensional constructs that should be looked at simultaneously from various perspectives. Autonomous linguists, especially in the United States, have chosen to look at language from a particularly narrow perspective; they have isolated specific problems by excluding from consideration a maximum number of messy variables. Contrastive Rhetoric has, over the past 40 years, tried to look at language from a more multidimensional perspective and also to look across languages.

> If you ask an American composition teacher where contrastive rhetoric begins, you are likely to get the answer "in Kaplan's Doodles Paper of 1966." ... [T]he paper led to a lively discussion which goes on even today ... [W]hether we approve of its specific points or not, its general approach did have a beneficial impact. It compelled students and teachers of rhetoric to look at discoursal macro-patterns in the light of underlying cultural traditions and not only in terms of syntactic features on the linguistic surface. (Enkvist, 1997, p. 190)[1]

Contrastive Rhetoric starts from the assumption that language occurs not in isolated syntactic structures[2] but rather in naturally occurring discourses, whether spoken or written, although admittedly Contrastive Rhetoric has focused almost exclusively on written varieties. The term has been used in two separate contexts—spoken discourse (i.e., multiple-source dialogic) and written discourse (i.e., single-source monologic). Such a distinction, however, oversimplifies the situation; although there are obvious overlaps between the two, to some extent each has evolved in its own direction. That Contrastive Rhetoric should have focused on written discourse seems entirely appropriate because a major real-world problem (a problem of the sort that applied linguists are supposed to recognize and address) lies at the heart of the matter; namely, literacy. Literacy is not constituted of the ability to manipulate grammatical rules and vocabulary, but rather is constituted of the ability to encode and decode discourses (see Grabe & Kaplan, 1996, for further discussion). As the world has become increasingly technologized, literacy has come to be recognized as a global issue.

> Contrastive Rhetoric represents the first serious contemporary study of L2 writing, as well as the only early paradigm where prominence was given to cross cultural research (Poole, 2002, p. 76; see also Connor, 1996; Leki, 1991).

Contrastive Rhetoric has been commonly confronted by three major obstacles. The first of these implicates observation; this obstacle falls squarely into the emit/etic problem in the sense that one cannot observe what one does not recognize as existing. Applied linguists, like any human beings, come at the process of analysis from the point of view of whatever language(s) they happen to speak and recognize the linguistic features evident in that language/those languages. They are impeded from observing obvious features of another language simply because applied linguists do not know the features are there.

The second obstacle lies in the need to categorize features—to systematize them in a manner relevant to the objective. The absence of a convenient metric for such categorization impedes the process. It is possible to say, in English, that Mary is wiser than Jane, and so long as Mary and Jane are the only subjects for categorization, such an observation is quite sufficient. However, as soon as the number of subjects increases, it becomes necessary to devise some sort of metric that will permit comparison not only between Mary and Jane as individuals but rather between two global populations separable along the dimension of wisdom.

Ideally, it would be necessary to devise a "universal" metric capable of providing an apparatus for comparing any and all pertinent features that may be found in human society. Such an exercise would require greater and greater specificity, analyzing wisdom into its essential features. Thus, the third obstacle revolves around the capability to specify the essential features necessary to potential comparison.

This chapter, however, is not concerned with the wisdom of individuals, but rather with text—essentially with written text. The most obvious feature of text lies in its syntactic and lexical dimensions because those features constitute the mechanisms of coherence and cohesion. This implies that sentences are not autonomous; rather they cohere logically and hang together cohesively in their syntactic structure, thus, contributing to the flow of information through the text. If that is the situation, there must be clear relationships between any particular clause and what comes before it and what follows. The problem is to recognize, define, and categorize the various techniques that mark such relationships across languages.

A DEFAULT MODEL FOR ENGLISH

In English, the default model presents **given** information before **new** information, perhaps on the presumption that it is easier for the reader to start with something known.[3] What is **given** can be characterized in several ways:

1. Something may be given because it is simply part of the human condition—for example, all human beings within the normative range have certain body parts in common and certain common relationships among those parts; for example, in English, *Clear as the nose on your face.*
2. Something may be given because it is common to some particular group—a nation, a club, a family; for example, most contemporary residents of the United States are likely to recognize names such as *Abraham Lincoln* and *George Washington.*
3. Something may be given because it is physically present in the context; for example, assuming that there is a door in the environment, one may say, in English, *please open the door* without further specification.
4. Something may be given because it is named/discussed in the discourse; for example, the term *given* in this paragraph.

This English language practice of "old information first" is by no means universal; other languages may employ other practices.

Recognizing and knowing how to use the default model is necessary for users and learners of English, but even for English it is not in itself sufficient. One must also recognize that there are syntactic means for varying the default model. Using structures such as the passive, the cleft sentence, sentence openers like *there is/it is* provides some means of varying the default model. It is not sufficient to know how to construct the syntactic variations from the default model; it is also necessary to understand when it may be appropriate to use such alternative means for example:

There is the door; please open it.
It's warm in here.
That door needs to be opened.
Please wait outside.

All of these sentences may apply to the same physical door and may imply the need to open it; it is pragmatics that determines the conditions under which each may be spoken/written. Sometimes it is rhetorically necessary to put some critical information ahead of given information. It is also necessary to recognize when ellipses are appropriate—when it is permissible to omit what can readily be inferred; for example:

Where are you going next week? To Gallop. [or simply *Gallop.*][4]

In this exchange, the response deletes *I'm going [to]...* because it can readily be inferred from the context. For many residents of the United States, it is safe to omit *New Mexico*, because many know where Gallop is, but the omission is determined by context; if the questioner is a child or a recently arrived immigrant, it may not be possible to omit New Mexico.

The mechanisms for identifying given and new information are language specific. These mechanisms are governed by such language-specific devices as word order (in those languages in which word order is more critical than case endings—English vs. Russian). Articles and demonstratives may serve particular purposes as may such structures as English *there is/there are* when no suitable old-information (or other opener) is readily available. (*There is a rat in the room* is not identical in meaning with *A rat is in the room*.) Causality, using such clause-connectors as *because* or *thus*, must reflect a conceivable causal relationship. The order selected must make sense in terms of the writer's and the reader's perceptions of the phenomenological world. The English song "Oh! Susannah"[5] contains the text:

"...the day I left, it rained all night, the weather it was fine...."

Such description violates normal perceptions of the physical universe—day and night are not interchangeable, and it cannot both rain and be fine simultaneously. Such discontinuities may be used with impunity for literary purposes, but ordinary text is not permitted to violate basic expectations. For example, in the structure:

the horse was sick because it ran slow
            as opposed to
the horse ran slow because it was sick

both structures are syntactically possible but the former structure is unlikely because it violates reader expectations of cause/effect relations based on an understanding of the physical world. Such syntactic markers regulate the form of sentences, adapting them to serve the text strategy. Grammaticality alone is not the answer. So the text is, as Enkvist suggests, "father to the sentence" (1997, p. 199). It is not grammatical rules, but text strategy that determines the choice of syntactic and lexical structures.[6]

Structures are not individually created out of individualized psychological reality or through the application of the rules of a syntactic system. Rather, they are to some extent a matter of appropriating the words of others (Bakhtin, 1981; Norton & Toohey, 2002, p. 117; Odlin, 2002, pp. 254–257).

Beyond the syntactic and lexical dimensions lies the dimension of **discourse pragmatics**—the use of types and patterns of discourse in different communicative situations or the comparison and contrast of types of text within and across languages and social groups. Clearly, this dimension implicates genres. The genres of one language may not occur in another or may occur but may serve an entirely different rhetorical function. For example, the structure called the **counter-factual conditional** constitutes an interesting case; in English the counter-factual condition may be represented by such a sentence as:

If Cleopatra's nose had been longer, the history of the world would have been different.

In this sentence, both parts of the conditional structure are not true; Cleopatra's nose was not longer, and the history of the world is not different. Such structures are not common in all genres in English, but in the genre of sports writing, the structure occurs quite frequently; for example:

If he had just caught the ball, his team would have won.
If he had only not fallen, he would surely have won the gold [medal].

Thus, it occurs in a genre in which it is reasonable to speculate about what might have happened. Such structures are not common in other languages. The counter-factual conditional is rare in written Chinese, although the conventional conditional does occur (Bloom, 1981), for example:

If there were no Communist Party, there would be no New China.

In this "slogan," both clauses imply true conditions; that is, there is a Communist Party, and there is a New China. It has been suggested to me that the counter-factual conditional is rare in Chinese because the practically minded Chinese see no reason to discuss what did not happen, but there is no empirical evidence to support this suggestion. This is not to claim that the counter-factual condition cannot occur in Chinese; in fact, it does occur, although it is used largely for humor, on the grounds, I suppose, that arguing about something that did not happen is ludicrous.

SIX QUESTIONS: WHAT PHENOMENA CONTRASTIVE RHETORIC STUDIES

Discourse pragmatics also includes matters of politeness and hedging (areas that have been extensively studied elsewhere by a number of other scholars—for politeness, see, for example, Brown and Levinson, 1988; Janney and Arndt, 1993; for hedging, see, for example, Crismore and Vande Kopple, 1988; Grabe and Kaplan, 1996) and, in the context of trying to compose text in an L2, it also raises a number of overwhelming questions:

1a. Who has the authority to write?[7]
1b. Who may be addressed?
2a. What may be discussed?
2b. What form may the writing take?

3a. What constitutes evidence?
3b. How can evidence be convincingly arranged?

These questions must be addressed by the incipient writer, because without some sort of answers, it is impossible to construct text; although phrased in a different way, these questions address the central issues of audience, genre, and rhetorical structure:

- Who writes what to whom,
- How,
- Under what circumstances, and
- To what end?

The first two questions—**Who has the authority to write?** and **Who may be addressed?**—are reciprocal, culturally coded, and dependent on the in-culture distribution of power. In any environment, the right to write and the right to be addressed change as the power differential increases—writing to a superior is not always licensed, reading a message from a superior is always sanctioned. (In English, text may be specifically marked "Secret" clearly limiting readership.) Of course, all of the questions listed earlier? assume the existence of a fairly broad distribution of literacy and the use of a common language.[8] Authority to write may be vested in age, relative fame, great attributed wisdom (though the criteria for measuring wisdom are fairly vague), or gender. (See Yoshikawa, 1978, for a discussion of the criteria for licensure to write in Japan.)

This assumption of fairly widespread literacy and of a common language is more complex than it may seem on first thought. There is an additional assumption that the performative ability of the writer and of the reader are reasonably well matched. The writer must make clear (in one way or another) his or her intent, and the reader must have a sufficient performative ability to perceive that intent as well as a willingness to "go along with it" for the purposes of some particular textual event. Further, the writer must have knowledge of his or her subject, and the reader must have at least an interest in that subject, although that interest may be uninformed, and the reader's motivation to read may evolve out of a desire to gain information and/or understanding.

In addition to a reasonably matched performative ability, the writer must be aware of (and must practice) the culturally bound conventions of text presentation—must demonstrate a proper concern for the surface of the text–must practice acceptable spelling, paragraphing, indentation, hyphenation, capitalization, and punctuation. The reader, on the other hand, must be prepared to expect appropriate conventionality in the text or must be made aware that certain conventions will be violated intentionally and purposefully. (See discussion of "ontological difficulty" later in this chapter.)

Given these constraints, the license to write may be exercised. In English, any mother may address her children, and they may address their mother. In English, this general license to write and to be addressed extends through all family members and all close friends. Although this phenomenon is fairly universal, it may be heavily impacted by culturally defined politeness rules (e.g., in some languages, an older relative must be addressed in the subjunctive). Beyond this message level, things get more complicated. One may write to the chief executive of a company, but one will not be distressed if the response (assuming that a response does indeed materialize) originates from some (perhaps unidentified) person in the customer relations department. One may write to one's legislative representative, but one will not be distressed if the response, (assuming that a response does indeed materialize) arrives as a form letter, composed by an anonymous employee but signed by the legislator. The right to address a legislative representative is fairly well restricted to democratic societies in which legislators are elected by popular vote and are perceived to represent and be responsible to their electorate. There are, however, whole sectors of society that are shielded by cultural rules; the greater the power differential between any two individuals, the smaller the probability that writing is licensed and that response may be expected. The power differential may also be marked by politeness rules.

Where the power differential is great, one may employ a surrogate; one may initiate a message through a tax accountant or an attorney, and one may expect a response from the reader's surrogate. In such cases, the originator of the message and the recipient may not be directly involved at all. It is also possible, in cases of wide power differential, that no response will be provided. In other situations, writing may be elicited by an authority figure; for example, at any level of the educational system, a teacher may require written exercises from his or her students such as class exercises, an essay, a written examination paper.[9] In cultures in which the press engages in such activities, one may write a "letter to the editor" with the expectation that it will be published (but not responded to by the editor), thus allowing ordinary persons to address a wider audience, although the editor may refuse to publish or may revise any given contribution prior to publication. Scholars who believe they have a contribution to make to scholarship may write scholarly articles and books addressed to their professional colleagues; in this case, the motivation springs from the author and, to the extent colleagues read the pertinent literature, the readers constitutes a partially captive audience—however, always with the right to refuse to read any given contribution. (Of course, journal editors or editors in publishing houses may refuse to publish.) In each of the illustrations sketched here, the writer is licensed to write; however, in every case, the writer's license is constrained by social forces, by the intended audience, and by the topic. And the reader is licensed to be addressed. In each of these illustrations except the teacher—student relationship, the motivation to write normally arises from the writer; in the teacher–student relationship, the motivation springs from the teacher (who is implicitly the only reader). There are other such cases in which the more powerful member of the communicating group motivates writing; for example, in the event that one receives a message from a governmental agency, that message generally mandates a response.

What may be discussed? and **What form may the writing take?** also constitute a reciprocal pair. What may be discussed is often determined by the membership of the communicating group—writer and readers; one would perhaps discuss personal matters in a letter to a family member, but probably would not do so in a scholarly article or in a letter to a legislator. However, possible topics are also culturally constrained. In societies in which strong religious views are widely held, topics like abortion or alternative life styles are generally not considered appropriate, although abortion may be discussed in the medical literature in such a society; in other societies, such topics may be considered appropriate to political discourse, or to the media in general, or even to personal discourse; for example, it is conceivable that such a topic might occur in correspondence between relatives or close friends. (See, e.g., Kaplan, 2000.)

What may be discussed is also, at least to some extent, constrained by available genres. For example, it is unlikely that an English speaker would present a cooking recipe in the form of a sonnet or that the content of a "romantic" sonnet would be presented in the form of a cooking recipe. Genre restricts possible topic. It is important to note that genres are not universal; sonnets (defined by content as well as by form) do not occur in all cultures, and, where they may occur, they do not necessarily have similar rhetorical purpose. For example, in academic fields:

> . . . genre stability is partially maintained by the "experts" in any disciplinary discourse community, thereby contributing to the community's structuration process. The relatively fully developed nature of the experts' disciplinary selves exerts influence on what can

be said and how, thus contributing to the stability and reproduction of certain systems. These experts are people who, through their publications and research, have reached wide audiences, whose opinions and views serve as authority sources, who have produced some of the key touchstones of the community: [S. B.] Heath's and [E.] Och's work on language socialization..., [W.] Labov's analysis of narratives, [J.] Swales' work on genre, [D.] Tannen's work in discourse analysis, among others... [R. B.] Kaplan's (1966) controversial "doodles" article would not have fueled as much research in contrastive rhetoric if he had written it in the form of a memo, for instance. For one thing, *Language Learning* [the journal in which it first appeared] would not have accepted it for publication. (Ramanathan & Kaplan, 2000, p. 179)

Genres are not arbitrary; they represent communal solutions to discourse problems. "People learn new genres through social contexts. In different communities, ways of representing and presenting knowledge vary. Different communities value different kinds of knowledge and display and package it in ways unfamiliar to those outside the community" (Murray, 2001, p. 284). That being the case, any text exists in a complex relationship with prior text and with co-text; a genre is used to solve a particular communication problem because that genre has been used diachronically, and because it is being used by others synchronically, to solve a similar problem. A text newly brought into existence in a particular genre then becomes part of the textual tradition existing in a vertical continuum from the past to the present and in a horizontal continuum across a discourse community in the present.

The third set of questions—**What constitutes evidence?** and **How can evidence be convincingly arranged?**—also constitutes a reciprocal pair. The arrangement of evidence depends on the selection of evidence, and the selection of evidence depends on the selected arrangement. Berkenkotter and Huckin suggest that research itself " ... is carried out and codified largely through generic forms of writing: Lab reports, working papers, reviews, grant proposals, technical reports, conference papers, journal articles, monographs, and so forth" (1993, p. 476). Each of these genres (and a large number of others conventionally used in the West) define—and are defined by—the nature of evidence acceptable to the discourse communities that use these genres. These genres are common to English (and to Western) scientific and technical discourse communities; discourse communities centered in languages other than English (LOTEs), although they may employ these genres, may employ them in different ways for different purposes, or may not employ them at all. Li, writing about the teaching of writing in the PRC, points out the relative unimportance of data; in China, over long historical time, "[n]atural science, an imported subject, ... was looked down upon as a bunch of 'trivial tricks'" (1996, p. 3). She goes on to say that "definite, specific, concrete language" constitutes a maxim followed with religious zeal by writing teachers in the United States but "[t]he preference for multitudinous specifics ... is at odds with a Chinese literary tradition that prefers a densely selective and suggestive... style " (1996, p. 120).

Earlier, Norton and Toohey (2002, p. 117) were cited in conjunction with the idea that utterances are not uniquely created out of individualized psychological reality or through the application of the rules of a syntactic system. Rather, they are, at least to some extent, a matter of appropriating the words of others. Assuming that to be true, for L2 learners, of course, the "words of others" lie in the first language (L1), not in the L2. Perhaps this may constitute a root cause of plagiarism, but whether or not it implicates plagiarism, it helps to define a difference in the source of evidence. Using evidence derived from the L1 necessarily implicates a set of genres not conventionally perceived to constitute solutions to communication problems in the L2 (i.e., the Western tradition in this discussion).

Thus, three pairs of overwhelming questions interact to frame the context in which writing in an L2 must occur. Beyond that, however, it is not merely the "words of others" that underlie text; the writer working in an L2 brings to the task exactly the linguistic possibilities inherent in the L1. (See Berman & Slobin, 1994 p. 12 for an extended discussion of this matter.)

> ...Most of what falls under "thinking for [writing] in an L2" is usually inaccessible to meta-awareness.... We probably do not "notice" the way the L2 does its filtering, ... and we probably have no awareness of the language specific nature of our own options.... Such knowledge may be very largely "unanalyzed".... In the absence of such awareness, the L2 does not provide loci for (mis)generalization of L1 material.... The blueprint established for the verbal expression of experience continues to function regardless.... Coping with new ways of "thinking for [writing]" ... means attending to features of context that are either not relevant or are defined differently in the native language. (Kellerman, 1995, p. 141)

On a more practical level, Mauranen talks about the fall out of this problem on L2 learners in the context of trying to write text:

> ... [Writers] differ in some of their culturally determined rhetorical practices, and these differences manifest themselves in typical textual features. *The writers seem not to be aware of these textual features, or the underlying rhetorical practices.* This lack of awareness is in part due to the fact that textlinguistic features have not been the concern of traditional language teaching in schools. Sometimes text strategies are taught for the mother tongue, but rarely if ever for foreign languages separately. Such phenomena have therefore not been brought to the attention of [writers] struggling with writing.... Nevertheless, these sometimes subtle differences between writing cultures, often precisely because they are subtle and not commonly observable to the non-linguist, tend to put... [various] native language [writers] at a rhetorical disadvantage in the eyes of [the L2] readers ... This disadvantage is more than a difference in cultural tastes, since it may not only strike readers as lack of rhetorical elegance, but as lack of coherent writing or even [coherent] thinking, which can seriously affect the credibility of non-native writers (1993, pp. 1–2; emphasis added).

Such a consideration seems to lead naturally to a linguistic theory that gives careful attention to awareness and noticing. Chomsky (1981) has advanced a theory of Universal Grammar (UG); it constitutes a mentalist claim that all human beings within the normative range have a biological endowment consisting of an "innate language faculty" permitting children to acquire the grammar of any particular language(s). This faculty is unrelated to other cognitive abilities; it contains awareness of abstract principles that organize language and an awareness of the parameters through which those principles are instantiated in any given language. The trigger for the activity of this faculty arises from minimal exposure to a language, and from only positive evidence of the principles (thus eliminating any sort of error correction). This model has strongly influenced second language acquisition (SLA) research. However, although grammar may indeed be acquired through the "innate language faculty," reading and writing must be taught anew in every generation and seems to respond to negative evidence. Text is not simply the sum of its morphosyntactic components. The UG theory has been challenged and debate rages in the cognitive sciences.[10] On the other hand, a theory that intersects with what is known about literacy acquisition would need to be based in noticing language features apart from grammar. There are a number of competing theories—the competition model, the connectionist model, the emergenist model, the noticing model, and so forth. The noticing model may be closest to what is needed for both contrastive rhetoric and discourse analysis. (See, e.g., Gass, 2002, pp. 178–179; Schmidt, 1990, 1993.)

Among the areas of noticing that a writer may (explicitly or implicitly) bring to attention, and that a reader must struggle to perceive, are those impacted when a writer creates difficulty by choosing to use arcane or technical vocabulary ("contingent difficulty"), or by allowing himself or herself to be understood only up to a point ("tactical difficulty"). The reader may experience difficulty if the writer's representation of the human condition is simply inaccessible or alien ("modal difficulty"). Or the writer may create difficulty by undertaking to bend the language—the text itself—out of its conventional shape ("ontological difficulty"). (Terminology from Steiner, 1978.) Flaunting of the conventions is a perilous exercise, but English-language writers of nonsense verse, for example, have done it successfully (e.g., as in the published verse of e e cummings or Lewis Caroll) as have such English-language novelists as William Faulkner, James Joyce, or Amos Tutuola.[11]

In order for the basic process—the conveyance of ideas, information, and feelings through the text from the generator of text to the receiver of text—to work, there must be an agreement between the generator and the receiver—a compact—to participate in the process. The **generator** (the writer) needs to have a perceivable intent, a perceivable stance toward the text and the content of the text, a perceivable grasp of the text subject, and a perceivable intent to convey something to some group of readers—the receivers of the text. At the same time, the **receiver** of the text must come to the text with an intent, with a stance toward the form and the content of a given text, with some interest in the subject of that text, and with a willingness to "go along" with the text generator at least for the duration that the receiver is in contact with the text. Should the reader not choose to participate in such a compact, the reader has the license to ignore the text—that is, simply NOT to read it.

The writer must be willing to participate in the compact, in part because the writer wishes to have his or her text read but also, and perhaps more important, because the writer is himself or herself a reader, and in that role must anticipate the acceptance of the compact by other readers.

A MODEL OF TEXT-CONDITIONED INTERACTION

A glance at Fig. 21.1 shows how complex the process may be. If all of the conditions implied in the bundles of discourse features in the model suggested in Fig. 21.1 are not met, there will be no (or limited, or misapprehended) transfer of information, etc., from the text generator to the text receiver—from writer to reader—via the text. All of the variables identified in the model will be simultaneously at work in the process when generator and receiver share intimately a common language, but when the text generator has the text language as a second or foreign language, the variables may simply become too numerous to control. If the generator chooses a genre that does not exist in the target language (the L2) or that serves a different unexpected purpose, if the generator does not control the text conventions expected by the receiver, if the generator lacks performative ability, if the generator does not know how to enter into a compact with the receiver, if the generator does not understand the kinds of difficulty she or he can inadvertently introduce, if the shared experience is relatively not in fact shared, there will be no meaningful interaction between generator and receiver through the text. As Schuchalter (in press) writes:

> Our initial response in experiencing texts not belonging to our immediate cultural background is a feeling of strangeness, a lack of comprehension at that which cannot be readily interpreted. . . . Our starting point then in the analysis of any cultural text must be the awareness of a "deep equivocality." Every word, every line, every image may mean something totally different from what we expect.

It is even possible that the inadvertent shortcomings of the generator may annoy the receiver, thereby producing an unexpected and unanticipated discontinuity—for example, a simple refusal to read the text. (See, e.g., Kaplan, 1983.)

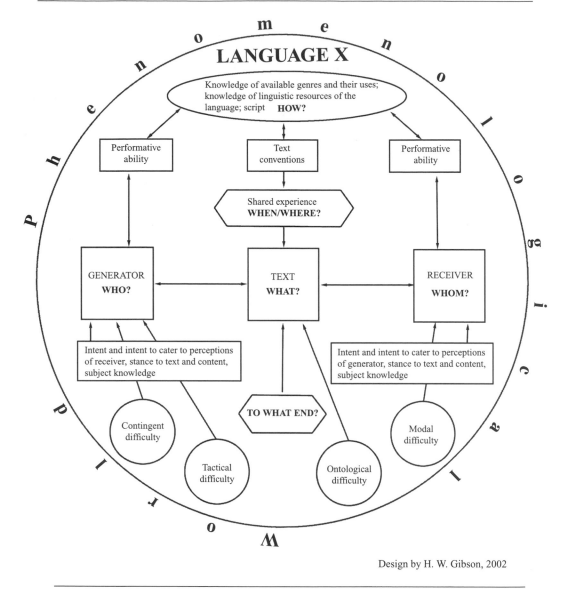

Design by H. W. Gibson, 2002

FIG. 21.1. Model of concerns in Contrastive Rhetoric. (After Grabe & Kaplan 1996, p. 215; Kaplan 2000, p. 90, 1983, p. 147.)

Figure 21.1 attempts to define the features involved in composing in any given language. Obviously, there will be a similar figure for each language one wishes to explore. Non-native speakers of Language A will have in their heads a figure pertinent to their first language (Language B); they will not possess a figure for the language they are trying to learn and in which they are attempting to write. At every point at which the discourse structure of their first language (Language B) conflicts with the discourse structure of the language they are trying to master (Language A), misapprehension will occur. Thus, the genres available in Language A may or may not exist in Language B, or if they do exist in Language B they may serve differing functions. The same problem occurs with respect to each category of features shown in the diagram. Even such matters as the script used may constitute a problem; an individual experienced in dealing with a Roman alphabet will have difficulties with a non-Roman orthography, and vice versa (Red, 2001). This comment assumes that one is dealing with an alphabetic language; if one of the languages in the mix is a language that uses logographic characters (e.g., Japanese Kanji, Chinese characters), the discontinuity increases in scope. Certainly, this problem extends to the conventions of writing—the appearance of the text on the page, as well as to the direction of text flow—left to right/top to bottom; right to left/top to bottom; top to bottom/right to left. Indeed, every feature bundle described in the figure may be the site of discontinuity, confusion, and potential ambiguity. In sum, in order to write in a second language, a level of second-language linguistic ability must first be achieved; such a linguistic ability is necessary but not sufficient. Research in writing has, in this context, fallen somewhat behind research in reading; much of the empirical evidence available derives from reading research (see, e.g., Bernhardt & Kamil, 1995; Grabe, 1991; Kintsch, 1994). The needed level of second-language linguistic ability, often conceived as the primary problem (although such linguistic ability accounts for less than 50% of the variance), leads to the substitution of grammar instruction for writing instruction in real-world classrooms. Such an approach to the teaching of writing constitutes a serious fallacy.

Figure 21.1 represents texts as the negotiated communicative achievements of the participants (the writer and the reader); thus, the entity labeled TEXT appears in the center of the figure. This representation is, in part, indebted to speech-act theory as developed by Austin (1962) and Searle (1969, 1976); i.e., when text is used in specific situational contexts, the writer's intentions and his or her relationship with or to reader must be considered as features of meaning. Such a perspective obviously implicates the use of text genres and the development of specific discourse communities using text for specific purposes (see, e.g., Van Dijk, 1983, 1997).

Several additional points need to be made:

1. Note that a situation like that depicted in Fig. 21.1 will also occur for specific discourse communities—for example, academic chemists, pharmacists, etc.—within any particular language; in other words, discontinuities do not only occur across languages but rather may occur across registers within any given language; such registers may derive from social, economic, political, or historical factors.
2. Note that many of the arrows depicting direction of movement are two headed; that implies that the generator doesn't simply produce the text but rather repeatedly interacts with the text while producing it. By the same token, the receiver does not simply read the text, but rather goes through repeated approaches to the text—perhaps over repeated readings of the entire text, perhaps only through repeated readings of interesting/provocative/difficult portions.
3. Note that both generator and receiver must participate in an informal "compact," agreeing to respect each other's intent to communicate, stance toward the text, and knowledge of the text subject. If the receiver does not wish to take part in the process, he or she can simply lay the text aside. The generator is subject to what is called "tactical difficulty"—when the generator wishes to be understood only up to a point or not at all or wishes to obscure his text through the use of arcane or technical lexicon (i.e., "contingent difficulty"). It is virtually impossible for the receiver to penetrate these difficulties.
4. Note that the two sets of questions—"**Who writes what to whom, when, how, under what circumstances, to what end?**" and "**Who has the authority to write? Who may be addressed?// What may be discussed? What form may the writing take?// What constitutes evidence? How can evidence be convincingly arranged?**"—intersect with the other dimensions of the model. It is the case

that issues of audience, genre, and text conventions are a significant part of the meaning of the text; the text does not exist in a vacuum, but rather is constrained by the genre employed as well as by the performative ability of both text generator and text receiver. In short, the ability of the text generator to exploit the resources of the language (or register) and the ability of the receiver to comprehend the way in which the generator exploits the resources of the language, and the presentation of the text all constitute potential sources of discontinuity—of misunderstanding.

5. Note that text exists in an environment of co-text and pre-text; that is, any text constitutes a continuum with similar texts diachronically and synchronically.

6. Note that some level of more-or-less matched performative ability between generator and receiver, mutually shared, is assumed to exist; that is, knowledge of grammar (one set of the resources of the language), knowledge of genres, of spelling, of the text conventions, and of script are presumed as an essential, necessary but not sufficient pre-condition for participation in the "compact" between generator and receiver.

7. Note that meaning does not reside in the text but rather is a product of the interaction among generator, receiver, and text as constrained by the several variables.

Contrastive Rhetoric undertakes to bring all of these variables into notice, to make both parties to the writing compact aware of the problem sites that may disrupt the message, and to help the learner of an L2 to understand the difficulties he or she may face in undertaking to write in the L2.

WHAT IS THE VALUE OF CONTRASTIVE RHETORIC?

Contrastive Rhetoric had its inception in an attempt to facilitate pedagogy; whatever additional qualities it has achieved are later developments (see, e.g., Kaplan, 1988). It has never been a question whether or not the 1966 doodles were in some sense "correct"; rather the value of the doodles, whatever it may be, arose from the notion that, as Enkvist observed, "[they] compelled students and teachers of rhetoric to look at discoursal macro-patterns in the light of underlying cultural traditions and not only in terms of syntactic features on the linguistic surface" (Enkvist, 1997, p. 190). In that context, it has played a role both in expanding discourse analysis as an academic discipline and in creating change in the teaching of writing in second languages (in the relatively rare instances that writing is actually taught in L2 contexts—see Mauranen earlier in this chapter), in the training of writing teachers, and in the teaching of trainers of teachers.

In short, Contrastive Rhetoric has never been seen as an ivory-tower vision of discourse, either written and spoken. Rather, it has helped to create an environment in which teachers of writing, in both L1 (see, e.g., Panetta, 2001) and L2 (see, e.g., Connor & Kaplan, 1986), have had to take into consideration the structure of discourse above the level of the sentence in given languages as well as the differences in the structure of discourse across languages. As Poole notes, it was "the only early paradigm where prominence was given to cross cultural research" (Poole, 2002, p. 76). It has inspired a very large number of cross-linguistic studies of rhetorical patterns (see, e.g., Kaplan, 2000, especially note pp. 95–96.) As an outgrowth of those many studies, it has played a role in altering the conception of how writing may be taught (although it is fair to say that conventional, grammar-based approaches to teaching writing persist).

Additionally, Contrastive Rhetoric has played a role in other subdomains of research into cross-linguistic discourse and text conventions in English and various other rhetorical traditions, such as Chinese, Japanese, and Korean (Hinds, 1975, 1976, 1983, 1984, 1987), Arabic (Ostler, 1987; Sa'adeddin, 1989), or Thai (Bickner & Peyasantiwong, 1988). As an outgrowth of Contrastive Rhetoric, a large number of ethnographic studies on contrastive discourse traditions have investigated how discourse and text are developed in various cultures and languages. These studies have identified the ways in which rhetorical discourse patterns may differ widely across cultures and languages. In effect, Contrastive Rhetoric has led to an increased cross-cultural knowledge base that sheds light on the influence of L1 rhetorical paradigms on the L2 academic writing of non-native students primarily in English-speaking countries.

Since the 1960s, Contrastive Rhetoric has also come to occupy an important place in seeking a clearer understanding of literacy (and has helped to bring into question the spurious dichotomous designation of literate/illiterate, suggesting that there may be many levels of each). Further, it has helped to displace the notion that literacy constitutes a divine state of grace attributed to those who have received the "right" education in the "right" schools, in the "right" chronological times, in the "right" polities (see, e.g., Clark, 2001) as well as the equally spurious notion that illiteracy is a form of disease that can be stamped out by a sort of educational "magic bullet" similar to those involved in the medical suppression of smallpox and diphtheria. It has even contributed to research in translation (Burrough-Boenisch, 2002), for, as Nawwab, (2002) suggests:

> The translator of any literary text is faced with two immediate problems: rendering the meaning of the original faithfully in language that is idiomatic and in a style that resonates with the unique linguistic traits and flavor of the target language. In the case of translation of Arabic into English the problems are greater because of the vast gap between the different syntactical, *rhetorical*, and linguistic worlds of a Semitic language and an Indo-European tongue. (p. 31; emphasis added).

Contrastive Rhetoric is not an educational cure all. There are problems in language and in language education and in related areas that it does not address at all. But there are problems which it has addressed and in which it has successfully mediated. Its value has been underestimated by some, although its benefits have been exaggerated by others. Its niche lies somewhere between the exaggeration and the underestimation. Perhaps this overview may point to that niche.

APPENDIX A

When the Doodles were first published in 1966 (Kaplan, 1966), they were intended to demonstrate a variety of paragraph movements that exist in writing in different languages, such as English, Semitic (e.g. Arabic), Asian, Romance, or Russian. The purpose of highlighting the various types of paragraph structures and movements was to educate the teachers of L2 writing who have to be aware of the differences in rhetoric in different languages in order to point out differences in English rhetoric to their students.[12]

English   Semitic   Oriental   Romance   Russian

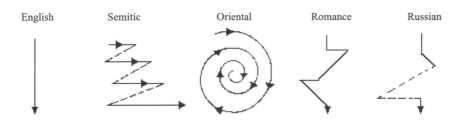

The illustration of paragraph movements was intended to be graphically clear rather than exhaustive, and as I stated then and have repeated on numerous occasions since that time, much more detailed and accurate descriptions would be needed before a meaningful contrastive rhetorical system could be developed. Since its original publication, contrastive rhetoric has acquired both friends and foes, and today much more is known about the movement of information in discourse than was in 1966, when the teaching of English largely focused on grammar and phonology. In the past half a century, a number of studies have been published to show that rhetorical organization of text does indeed differ across various languages. However, the specifics of these differences diverge, depending on who conducted the studies and where they conducted them.

Contrastive rhetoric has consumed much of my thought and much of my time over the past 40 years. I have written about contrastive rhetoric some forty times over these years (in pieces of varying length, but largely with the phrase *contrastive rhetoric* in the title). I hope all that writing and thinking has reflected some growth on my part. I do not deny that my thinking about contrastive rhetoric has become denser, and I do not deny that I have changed my mind about some aspects of the notion but not about the basic conceptualization. In fact, I would still contend that English is more linear than many other languages, as least in the sense that English does not permit the intrusion of quantities of unrelated (or vaguely related) tangential material into a text. The "doodles," however, probably misrepresent reality.

Whenever I have presented the "doodles" to audiences made up of speakers of languages other than English, those speakers have pointed out that it is not English which is linear; rather, their languages, they have claimed, were linear, and English represented some other pattern. The real issue, however, is that there are perceptible differences between languages in rhetorical preference; it hardly matters whether one or another is defined as "linear" or "circular." The perception of linearity represents a classic playing out of the emic/etic variable; every speaker *perceives* his/her language as linear and all others as non-linear. ... Thus, every speaker perceives a difference between what happens in his/her language and what happens in other languages. That fact constitutes the central idea of CR (Kaplan, 2000, pp. 83–84; see also Kaplan, 1991, 2003).[13]

NOTES

1. See Appendix A for information about the Doodles Paper.
2. Isolated sentences rarely occur in human uses of language except in grammar textbooks.
3. Alternative terminology includes *old/new, theme/rheme, topic/comment, focus/presupposition*, and, because subject also normally comes first in the default structure, *subject/predicate*.
4. Note that one may say *I'm going to Gallop, New Mexico*, but *I'm gonna gallop the horse*, so intonation in spoken language is also a key to disambiguating lexical (or syntactic) items.
5. Composed by Stephen Foster and published in his *Songs of the Sable Harmonists* in 1848.
6. If one were asked to conjoin the two clauses *It was/was not raining* and *We did/did not go swimming* into a single sentence, one could construct some 300 alternatives, of which the following are simply examples.
   1. Although it was raining, we went swimming anyway.
   2. Although it was not raining, we did not go swimming.
   3. As it was raining we did not go swimming.
   4. As it was not raining, we went swimming.
   5. Because it was raining, we did not go swimming.
   6. Because it was not raining, we went swimming.
   6. Being that it was raining, we did not go swimming.
   7. Being that it was not raining, we went swimming.
   8. Considering that it was raining, we did not go swimming.
   9. Considering that it was not raining, we did not go swimming.
   10. Despite the fact that it was raining, we went swimming.
   11. Despite the fact that it was not raining, we did not go swimming.

12. Even though it was not raining, we did not go swimming.
13. Even though it was raining, we went swimming.
14. It was raining; consequently, we did not go swimming
16. It was not raining, so we went swimming.
17. It was not raining; Thus, we went swimming.
18. It was not raining; however, we did not go swimming.
19. Since it was raining, we did not go swimming.
20. Since it was not raining, we went swimming.
21. Though it was raining, we went swimming.
22. Though it was not raining, we did not go swimming.
23. We went swimming because it was not raining.
24. We did not go swimming because it was raining.
25. We did not go swimming since it was raining.
26. We did not go swimming as it was raining.
27. We went swimming as it was not raining.
28. We went swimming since it was not raining.

Obviously, these structures are not merely freely interchangeable; they would occur in different contexts and would be addressed to different audiences in different circumstances; for example, the structures beginning with *Being...* are probably more formal than those beginning with *Because....*

7. The term *write* as used here implicates the construction of text, without reference to length. Fill-in-the blank activities—form-filling—is not included in the definition of writing, nor is signing one's name to a preprinted card, e.g., a birthday card, a Christmas card, etc.

8. Both illiteracy and the absence of a common language may be circumvented. In the absence of literacy, correspondents may employ a scribe to write and to read messages. In the absence of a common language, translators may be employed. If one is an English-speaker, for example, and has relatives in, say, Norway, one may write a message in English and give it to a translator to put into Norwegian, and the recipient may write his or her message in Norwegian and have it translated into English.

9. It is relatively unusual for writers to write on command; generally, writers begin from some other motivation.

10. A summary of that debate would be inappropriate in this chapter; for clear reviews, see Elman, 1993, as well as the journal *Bilingualism: Language and Cognition*, since 1998.

11. The mention of Tutuola is not intended to implicate the significant literature written by authors for whom English is a second language (also known as "Contact literature"; e.g., Chinua Achebe, Raja Rao) but rather to illustrate a kind of literature in which the culture-bound conventions are violated.

12. Reprinted from Kaplan, R. B. (1966). Cultural thought patterns in intercultural education, *Language Learning, 16*, 1–20, with permission from Blackwell Publishers, Oxford, U.K.

13. The preceding text should, in any case, be allowed to speak for itself; it is not my intention to provide a detailed history of every twist and turn in my thinking over almost half a century. Rather, the point of this final note is to signal a cessation. This is the last piece on contrastive rhetoric that I will write. This is not an announcement of my retirement from thinking and writing; on the contrary, I hope to continue to think and write about a variety of matters that interest me for some time into the future. Rather, this is an announcement that I firmly believe I have said everything I have to say about contrastive rhetoric. I have nothing more to say on this topic. If the notion has validity, I hope others will pursue it.

REFERENCES

Austin, J. L. (1962). *How to do things with words*. Oxford, UK: Oxford University Press.

Bakhtin, M. (1981). *The dialogic imagination: Four essays by M. M. Bakhtin*. Austin: University of Texas Press.

Bernhardt, E. B., & Kamil, M. L. (1995). Interpreting relationships between L1 and L2 reading: Consolidating the linguistic threshold and the linguistic interdependence hypotheses. *Applied Linguistics, 16*(1), 15–34.

Berkenkotter, C, & Huckin, T. (1993). Rethinking genre for a sociocognitive perspective. *Written Communication, 10*(4), 475–509.

Berman, R. & Slobin, D. (Eds.). (1994). *Relating events in narrative: A crosslinguistic developmental study*. Hillsdale, NJ: Lawrence Erlbaum Associates.

Bickner, R., & Peyasantiwong, P. (1988). Cultural variation in reflective writing. In A. Purves (Ed.), *Writing across languages and cultures* (pp. 160–174). Newbury Park, CA: Sage.

Bloom, A. (1981). *The linguistic shaping of thought*. Hillsdale, NJ: Lawrence Erlbaum Associates.

Brown, P., & Levinson, S. (1988). *Politeness*. Cambridge, UK: Cambridge University Press.

Burrough-Boenisch, J. (2002). *Culture and conventions: Writing and reading Dutch scientific English*. Utrecht, The Netherlands: LOT.

Chomsky, N. (1981). Principles and parameters in syntactic theory. In N. Hornstein & D. Lightfoot (Eds.), *Explanation in linguistics: The logical problem of language acquisition* (pp. 32–75) London: Longman.

Clark, U. (2001). *War words: Language, history and the disciplining of English*. Amsterdam: Elsevier.

Connor, U. (1996). *Contrastive rhetoric: Cross-cultural aspects of second language writing.* Cambridge, UK: Cambridge University Press.

Connor, U., & Kaplan, R. B. (Eds.). (1986). *Writing across languages: Analysis of L2 text.* Reading, MA: Addison-Wesley.

Crismore, A., & Vande Kopple, W. (1988). Readers' learning from prose: The effects of hedges. *Written Communication 5*, 184–202.

Elman, J. L. (1993) Learning and development in neural networks: The importance of starting small. *Cognition, 48*, 71–99.

Enkvist, N. E. (1997). Why we need contrastive rhetoric. *Alternation, 4*(1), 188–206.

Gass, S. (2002). An interactionist perspective on second language acquisition. In R. B. Kaplan (Ed.), *The Oxford handbook of applied linguistics.* (pp. 170–181). New York: Oxford University Press.

Grabe, W. (1991). Current developments in second language reading research. *TESOL Quarterly, 25*(3), 375–406.

Grabe, W., & Kaplan, R. B. (1996). On the writing of science and the science of writing: Hedging in science text and elsewhere. In R. Markkanen & H. Schröder (Eds.), *Hedging and discourse: Approaches to the analysis of a pragmatic phenomenon in academic texts* (pp. 151–167). Berlin: de Gruyter.

Grabe, W., & Kaplan, R. B. (1996). *Theory and practice of writing: An applied linguistic perspective.* London: Longman.

Hinds, J. (1975). Korean discourse types. In H. Sohn (Ed.), *Korean language* (pp. 81–90). Honolulu, HI: University of Hawaii Press.

Hinds, J. (1976). *Aspects of Japanese discourse structure.* Tokoy: Kaitakusha.

Hinds, J. (1983). Contrastive rhetoric. *Text 3*(2), 183–195.

Hinds, J. (1984). Retention of information using a Japanese style of presentation. *Studies in Language, 8*(1), 45–69.

Hinds, J. (1987). Reader versus writer responsibility: A new typology. In U. Connor & R. B. Kaplan (Eds.), *Writing across languages: Analysis of L2 text* (pp. 141–152). Reading, MA: Addison-Wesley.

Janney, R., Arndt, H. (1993). Universality and relativity in cross-cultural politeness research: A historical perspective. *Multilingual, 12*, 13–50.

Kaplan, R. B. (1966). Cultural thought patterns in inter-cultural education. *Language Learning, 16*, 1–20.

Kaplan, R. B. (1983). An introduction to the study of written text: The "discourse compact." In R. B. Kaplan, A. d'Anglejan, J. R. Cowan, B. Kachru, & G. R. Tucker (Eds.), *Annual review of applied linguistics* (pp. 138–151). Rowley, MA: Newbury House.

Kaplan, R. B. (1988). Contrastive rhetoric and second language learning: Notes toward a theory of contrastive rhetoric. In A. C. Purves (Ed.), *Writing across languages and cultures: Issues in contrastive rhetoric.* (pp. 275–304). Beverly Hills, CA: Sage.

Kaplan, R. B. (1991). Contrastive rhetoric. In W. Bright (Ed.), *International encyclopedia of linguistics* (Vol. 1–4; pp. 302–303). New York: Oxford University Press.

Kaplan, R. B. (2000). Contrastive rhetoric and discourse analysis: Who writes what to whom? When? In what circumstances? In S. Sarangi & M. Coulthard (Eds.), *Discourse and social life,* (pp. 82–101). London: Pearson Education.

Kaplan, R. B. (2003). Contrastive rhetoric. In W. Frawley (Ed.), *Oxford, international encyclopedia of linguistics.* (Vol. 4, pp. 236–239) (2nd ed.). New York: Oxford University Press.

Kellerman, E. (1995). Crosslinguistic influence: Transfer to nowhere. In W. Grabe, C. Ferguson, R. B. Kaplan, M. Swain, G. R. Tucker, & H. G. Widdowson (Eds.), *Annual review of applied linguistics, 15: A broad survey of the entire field of applied linguistics* (pp. 125–150). New York: Cambridge University Press.

Kintsch, W. (1994). The role of knowledge in discourse comprehension: A construction–integration model. In R. B. Ruddell, M. R. Ruddell, & H. Singer (Eds.), *Theoretical models and processes of reading* (4th ed.; pp. 951–995). Newark, NJ: International Reading Association.

Leki, I. (1991). Twenty-five years of contrastive rhetoric: Text analysis and writing pedagogies. *TESOL Quarterly 25*, 123–144.

Li, X. (1996). *"Good writing" in cross-cultural context.* Albany, NY: State University of New York Press.

Mauranen, A. (1993). *Cultural differences in academic rhetoric.* Frankfurt am Main, Germany Lang.

Murray, D. E. (2001).Whose "standard"? What Ebonics debate tells us about language, power, and pedagogy. In J. E. Alatis & A.-H. Tan (Eds.), *Language in our time: Bilingual education and official English, Ebonics and Standard English, immigration and the Unz initiative* (pp. 281–291). Washington, DC: Georgetown University Press.

Nawwab, I. I. (2002). Berlin to Makkah: Muhammad Asad's journey into Islam. *Saudi Aramco World 53*(1), 6–32.

Norton, B., & Toohey, K. (2002). Identity and language learning. In R. B. Kaplan (Ed.), *The Oxford handbook of applied linguistics,* (pp. 115–123). New York: Oxford University Press.

Odlin, T. (2002). Language transfer and cross-linguistic studies: Relativism, universalism and the native language. In R. B. Kaplan (Ed.), *The Oxford handbook of applied linguistics* (pp. 253–261). New York: Oxford University Press.

Ostler, S. (1987). English in parallels: A comparison of English and Arabic prose. In U. Connor & R. Kaplan, (Eds.), *Writing across languages: Analysis of L2 text.* Reading, MA: Addison-Wesley.

Panetta, C. G. (Ed.). (2001). *Contrastive rhetoric revisited and redefined.* Mahwah, NJ: Lawrence Erlbaum Associates.

Poole, D. (2002). Discourse analysis and applied linguistics. In R. B. Kaplan (Ed.), *The Oxford handbook of applied linguistics* (pp. 73–84). New York: Oxford University Press.

Ramanathan, V., & Kaplan, R. B. (2000). Genres, authors, discourse communities: Theory and application for (L1 and) L2 writing instructors. *Journal of Second Language Writing, 9*(2), 171–191.

Red, D. L. (2001). Adults learning to read in a second script: What we've learned. In J. E. Alatis & A.-h. Tan (Eds.), *Language in our time: Bilingual education and official English, Ebonics and Standard English, immigration and the Unz initiative* (pp. 2–18). Washington, DC: Georgetown University Press.

Sa'adeddin, M. A. (1989). Text development and Arabic-English negative interference. *Applied Linguistics, 10*(1), 36–51.

Schuchalter, J. (in press). Literature, representation, and the negotiation of cultural lacunae. In H. Schröder (Ed.), *Lacunaology: Studies in intercultural communication.*

Schmidt, R. (1990). The role of consciousness in second language fluency. *Applied Linguistics. 11,* 129–156.

Schmidt, R. (1993). Awareness and second language acquisition. In W. Grabe, C. Ferguson, R. B. Kaplan, G. R. Tucker, H. G. Widdowson, & J. Yalden (Eds.), *Annual review of applied linguistics, 13: Issues in second language teaching and learning.* (pp. 206–226). New York: Cambridge University Press.

Searle, J. R. (1969). *Speech acts.* Cambridge, UK: Cambridge University Press.

Searle, J. R. (1976). A classification of illocutionary acts. *Language and Society, 5,* 1–23.

Steiner, G. (1978). On difficulty. In *On Difficulty and Other Essays* (pp. 18–47). Oxford, UK: Oxford University Press.

Van Dijk, T. A. (1983). *Handbook of discourse analysis* (Vol. 1–4). London: Academic Press.

Van Dijk, T. A. (Ed.). (1997). *Discourse in the language classroom studies: An interdisciplinary approach.* (Vol. 1–2). London Sage.

Yoshikawa, M. (1978). Some Japanese and American cultural characteristics. In M. H. Prosser (Ed.), *The cultural dialogue: An introduction to intercultural communication* (pp. 220–230). Boston: Houghton Mifflin.

22

Corpus Linguistics and L2 Teaching

Susan Conrad
Portland State University

Corpus linguistics is an approach to research and teaching that makes use of computer-assisted analyses of language. The "corpus" is a collection of texts—written, transcribed speech, or both—that is stored in electronic form and analyzed with the help of computer software programs.

Some consider corpus linguistics "essentially a technology" (Simpson & Swales, 2001, p. 1), and the approach clearly *is* dependent on computer technology. However, work within corpus linguistics is also unified by certain philosophical tenets, which make it an identifiable approach, not merely a technology. These tenets follow from a Firthian tradition in language study (Firth, 1957; Palmer, 1968). Central among them is that language study is considered primarily an empirical endeavor, so that descriptions of language and theories about language should be developed from observations of language behavior. As discussed in this chapter, this principle has contributed to some of the controversies surrounding corpus linguistics. (See Stubbs, 1993, for more on the Firthian perspective in contrast to a more cognitive one, and Tognini-Bonelli, 2001, chap. 1, for discussion of the status of corpus linguistics as a theory or methodology.)

The contribution of corpus linguistics to second language (L2) teaching is related to the importance that it puts on the empirical study of large databases of language. The approach has made it possible to conduct studies with more data and more variables than was previously feasible, and to design new kinds of classroom activities that actively engage learners in the analysis of language. In this chapter, I review the contributions of corpus linguistics to L2 teaching with respect to three major areas:

1. Descriptions of language, with applications to pedagogical decisions about what to teach in second language classes.
2. Use of corpus linguistics methods in the classroom with second language learners.
3. Studies of language produced by learners.

Throughout, most discussions and examples focus on English corpus linguistics because the majority of work—and the major controversies—has been with English. The principles apply equally to any second language, however.

In the next section, before covering the three areas, I begin by outlining the defining characteristics of corpus linguistics work. These characteristics apply equally to a study conducted by a team of established language reseachers or to a class activity done by a group of second language learners.

CHARACTERISTICS OF WORK IN CORPUS LINGUISTICS

Four characteristics are shared by work within corpus linguistics. Although I describe each briefly later in this chapter, more details can be found in book-length introductory treatments of corpus linguistics, including Biber, Conrad, and Reppen (1998), Hunston (2002), Kennedy (1998), McEnery and Wilson (1996), Meyer (2002), and Partington (1998).

Use of a Corpus

A corpus is a large, principled collection of naturally occurring texts that is stored in electronic form (on a computer hard drive or server). By "naturally occurring" I mean that the texts were created by users of the language for a communicative purpose, as opposed to being created for the study or teaching of the language. Corpora can include both written and transcribed spoken texts (and see the following for discussion of a new classroom corpus that includes video).

The corpus is meant to represent some variety or varieties of language. The varieties can be very general, such as British English conversation, or quite specific, such as the introduction sections of contemporary medical research articles focused on cancer treatments. The design of the corpus is crucial for reliable and generalizable results, whether the corpus is used on a large scale by researchers or on a smaller scale by learners in a class. A full discussion of issues in corpus design is beyond the scope of this chapter, but it is important to note that good design is not simply a matter of number of words. The types of texts included, the number of different types of texts, the number of different samples of each type of text, the sampling procedure, and the size of each sample are all important considerations. Advances in computer technology have made increasingly large corpora possible. In the 1970s, 1 million-word corpora were considered large (e.g., the London/Oslo-Bergen or LOB corpus, see Johansson, Leech, and Goodluck, 1978); today, the Bank of English contains about 415 million words and is still growing (see current information at www.titania.cobuild.collins.co.uk). Unfortunately, however, our knowledge of the best size and sampling to represent varieties of a language has not kept pace with technological advances. In the early 1990s, Biber (1990, 1993) found 1,000 word samples reliable for representing many grammatical features, and 10 texts reliable for representing the genre categories in the LOB (e.g., press reportage, official documents, academic prose), but since then, little empirical work has been published on corpus design with an eye to finding the most efficient and effective sampling and sizing procedures. Nevertheless, corpus compilation projects seek to make corpora as representative as possible, given what is currently known. Discussions of the principles followed in recent corpus compilation projects can be found in several sources, including Aston and Burnard, 1998; Biber, Johansson, Leech, Conrad, and Finegan, 1999, chap. 1; Granger, 1998; chap. 1; Hennoste, Koit, Roosmaa, and Saluveer, 1998; McCarthy, 1998; Simpson, Lucka, and Ovens, 2000. (See also Kilgarriff, 2001, on the corpus design with reference to word frequencies.)

Use of Computer-Assisted Analysis Techniques

As previously mentioned, corpus linguistics relies on computer-assisted techniques in order to handle the large amount of data in a corpus. The earliest well-known publications (e.g., Sinclair, 1991) and many publications today focus on the use of concordancers. These software programs show all the occurrences of a word with surrounding context, calculate frequencies of words, analyze collocates (words that occur together), and often calculate statistical measures of the strength of word associations (i.e., the likelihood of two words occurring near each other).

Despite the usefulness of concordancers, many areas of interest within language do not lend themselves to analysis with them. For example, Conrad (1999) describes an analysis of linking adverbials (transition words such as *therefore* and *however*) that includes associations among several variables: register (conversation, newspaper writing, and academic prose), semantic category (e.g., result, contrast), position in the clause, grammatical structure (e.g., single adverb, prepositional phrase), and the exact choice of adverbial. Such an analysis requires much more tailoring of the computer processing than is possible with a concordancer. Instead, with knowledge of computer programming, analysts can write specialized programs. For forms that are difficult to analyze automatically, such as adverbials, the programs can be interactive. Similar to a spellchecker in word processing programs, this type of program brings ambiguous forms to the screen, asking the researcher to make judgments about how to code them. Although coding is still a time-consuming process, it is faster and more thorough than finding the forms and coding them by hand because the computer identifies the forms consistently, without its attention wavering. Once the researcher confirms or changes the codes, they are stored and another program can be written to count the codes so that associations between many different characteristics can be analyzed. (For another example of an interactive program, see Biber, Conrad, & Reppen, 1998, chap. 5).

Emphasis on Empirical Analysis of Patterns in Language Use

Corpus linguistic studies often develop from research questions that grow out of intuition or casual observations, and interpretations of analyses often include intuitive impressions about the impact of particular language choices. Nevertheless, the primary focus of corpus linguistics is empirical, based on what is observed in the corpus. Corpus linguists are concerned with the patterns within a language as it is used, determining what is typical and unusual in given circumstances. McCarthy (1998) notes, "The particular strength of computerised corpora is that they offer the researcher the potential to check whether something observed in everyday language is a one-off occurrence or a feature that is widespread across a broad sample of speakers" (p. 151). The implications of this emphasis on empiricism, and the role of intuition in corpus linguistics, is discussed further in the following.

Use of Quantitative and Qualitative/Interpretive Techniques

Work within corpus linguistics varies with respect to how much it emphasizes quantitative analysis and how much it provides descriptions and interpretations without giving counts of features. Highlighting the contrast, a pair of research issue articles in *TESOL Quarterly* addresses quantitative versus qualitative methodologies (Biber & Conrad, 2001; McCarthy & Carter, 2001). However, all studies include both aspects of analysis to some extent. Recognizing patterns of language use necessarily entails making a quantitative assessment because typical patterns must occur more frequently than unusual uses of language. At the same time, numbers alone tell us little about language. Even the most sophisticated quantitative analyses must be tied to functional interpretations of the language patterns.

Corpus linguistics—like all approaches—has particular strengths and weaknesses. The four characteristics noted here account for its primary strength—the capacity for analyzing more variables and data than was previously possible. Corpus linguistics is thus particularly helpful in providing "big picture" perspectives—determining patterns of language behavior across many texts, identifying typical and unusual choices by users, and describing the interactions among multiple variables. It provides a complimentary perspective to (and has never been meant to replace) approaches that give a more intensive analysis of particular situations, such as ethnographies (Harklau, this volume) and case studies (van Lier, this volume) or particular texts, such as text linguistics studies (see Renouf, 1997; Tognini-Bonelli, 2001, chap. 1. However, for emerging techniques in corpus analysis for tracking features in texts, see Conrad, 2002.)

DESCRIPTIONS OF LANGUAGE USE

One of the most notable contributions of corpus linguistics to language teaching thus far has been studies that describe how language features are used. These descriptions are especially important for language teaching because textbooks for second language learners and teachers have commonly been shown to include incomplete or misleading explanations. Tognini-Bonelli (2001, chap. 2), for example, demonstrates that almost 50% of the occurrences of *any* in a corpus do not fit under the descriptions given in pedagogical grammars. Similarly, Biber, Conrad, and Reppen (1998, chap. 3) find that several popular English as a Second Language (ESL) textbooks do not describe the discourse function of subject position *that*-clauses, whereas corpus analysis clearly shows that they are used only in particular circumstances. (See also comparisons of ESL textbooks and corpora by Kennedy, 1987, on quantification and frequency; Holmes, 1988, on doubt and certainty; and Lawson, 2001, on the subjunctive for French as a foreign language.)

Vocabulary

Corpus linguistics has increased our understanding of word use in several ways. The first widespread use of corpus analysis applied to language teaching and learning was with dictionaries for ESL students (see especially descriptions of the Cobuild project in Sinclair, 1987). Numerous publishers in ESL now publish corpus-based dictionaries, which include descriptions of words as they are most commonly used and give examples from corpora to illustrate word use. Some of these dictionaries also give some basic information about the frequency of words in different types of texts and about the most common words or constructions that the words occur with. For example, the entry for *idea* in the *Longman Dictionary of Contemporary English* contains a bar graph that shows the most common words that occur with the noun *idea* in a diverse corpus of English: *good idea* is almost four times more common than the second most common pair, *idea for,* which is followed in frequency by *some idea, new idea, general/rough idea, right/wrong idea,* and *great idea.*

The idea that words tend to appear in the company of other words—collocation— was introduced by Firth, who noted, "You shall know a word by the company it keeps" (cited in Stubbs, 1993, p. 14). However, it has only been with the advent of corpus linguistics that dictionaries have regularly provided collocational information to learners. Furthermore, concordancing software allows all users to analyze the collocates of a selected word for themselves. (See Church & Hanks, 1990; Clear, 1993; and Stubbs, 1995; for more details on how to measure the strength of associations between words.)

Another characteristic of words that has emerged from corpus studies has been called "semantic prosody" (Louw, 1993; Sinclair, 1991): some words are associated with positive news or judgments, others with negative news or judgments. These are not connotations of the word itself, but rather come from the words associated with it. Sinclair (1991), for example, shows that the phrasal verb *set in* is used most often when something bad is beginning—*rot, decay, despair,* and *infection set in.* In terms of L2 teaching, then, the concept of semantic prosody can explain why a learner's construction such as *happiness set in* may sound "odd" even when it is grammatically accurate. (See also Tognini-Bonelli, 2001, chap. 6, for examples of semantic prosody in both English and Italian, and Stubbs, 1996, chap. 7, for further discussion of English.)

A different sort of application of corpus-based vocabulary studies concerns the generation of word lists for vocabulary learning. Building a sufficiently large vocabulary is a daunting task for most learners, and especially for learners wanting to pursue academic studies in their second language. A particularly useful application of corpus linguistics has been in enumerating the words that are common across a variety of academic texts. They are often not as salient as obvious technical vocabulary, but are crucial for comprehension. Coxhead (2000) presents an academic word list analyzed from a corpus that covers 28 subject areas and numerous different types of academic texts. Such an analysis provides a much more principled way of deciding what vocabulary is important to cover in English for Academic Purposes (EAP) textbooks. Corpus-based frequency lists of other types of language—for example, idioms (Moon, 1998) and vague language (Channell, 1994)—have also been useful for L2 teaching.

Finally, corpus-based lexical studies are very useful for disambiguating the uses of related words or multifunctional words. To illustrate with just a few examples, studies include a focus on *actual* and *actually* by Tognini-Bonelli (1993); *between* and *through* (Kennedy, 1991); *such* (Altenberg, 1994); and *get* (Johansson & Oksefjell, 1996).

Descriptions of Grammar

Descriptions of grammar have changed considerably with the incorporation of corpus linguistic techniques, now including much more information about the use of grammatical structures. One way to see the change is to compare the reference grammars of English published by Longman in 1985 and 1999. The first (Quirk, Greenbaum, Leech, & Svartvik, 1985) provided descriptions of structures with occasional mention of corpus analyses of use. The second (Biber et al., 1999) presents results of corpus-based studies for virtually every structure that is described. To take a simple example, consider the presentations of passive constructions using *get*—for example, *He got caught.* Both books describe the structure, discuss its relationship to *get* as a copular verb showing result, explain why the *get* passive rarely includes a *by* prepositional phrase telling the agent, and note that it is most often used with negative circumstances. The difference is that Quirk et al. (1985) give a more theoretical discussion about differentiating the *get*-passives from *get* as a copular verb, whereas Biber et al. (1999) present specific corpus results: for example, the *get* passive is more common in conversation than in fiction, news, or academic prose, but still accounts for only about 0.1% of all the verbs, and the most common verbs in the *get* passive are *get married, get hit, get involved, get left, get stuck* (presumably the first is an exception to the *get*-passive's usual association with negative circumstances!).

Grammatical features of informal spoken language have also received considerable attention in corpus studies. In particular, members of the CANCODE corpus group (Cambridge and Nottingham Corpus of Discourse in English) argue that one weakness of ESL teaching materials has traditionally been their reliance on references and norms that apply to written language, even when they sought to teach spoken language skills (Carter, 1998a; Carter & McCarthy, 1995; Hughes & McCarthy, 1998; McCarthy,

1998; McCarthy & Carter, 1995). Many features of informal spoken language—for example, interruptions, syntactically incomplete utterances, ellipsis, and tails—have been neglected, even though these have important interactional purposes. Biber et al. (1999, chap. 14) also cover numerous features specific to conversational language, such as its linear (rather than hierarchical) syntactic structure and the frequency of nonclausal units.

A host of other corpus-based studies have provided descriptions of the function of specific grammatical features in various kinds of texts. A complete list is beyond the scope of this chapter, but the diversity can be seen by referring to even just a few examples: modals (Coates, 1983), complement clauses (Greenbaum, Nelson, & Weitzman, 1996), certain aspects of existential sentences (Breivik, 1999), vocatives (Leech, 1999), and themes (Gómez-González, 1998).

Lexico-Grammatical Associations

Another aspect of language use that has gained greater prominence through corpus linguistics is the association between vocabulary and grammar. Conrad (2000) provides a simple illustration of this concept with reference to the verbs *know, say,* and *think*. These very common verbs are grammatical with both *that*-complement clauses and *to*-complement clauses. However, a corpus-based analysis of their use in conversation shows very distinct associations between the lexical items and grammatical constructions: all three are common only with *that*-complement clauses. Thus, lexico-grammatical studies address not just what is possible in a language, but what word+structure combinations are favored by users.

The most extensive work in this area has grown out of the Cobuild dictionary project. As it extended into grammar, the Cobuild project focused on the patterns between words and grammatical structures as a useful approach for learners of English (Collins COBUILD English Grammar, 1990). Early work was criticized especially for overwhelming students with lists that were not useful (Owen, 1993). However, later work (Hunston, Francis, & Manning, 1997; Hunston & Francis, 1998, 2000; Hunston & Sinclair, 1999) has emphasized that patterns share aspects of meaning. In other words, the lexico-grammatical associations correspond to functions, so that students can learn functional patterns, not seemingly random lists.

The ability of corpus linguistics to analyze lexico-grammatical and lexical patterns in large corpora is applicable to the growing interest in the importance of formulaic language. Wray (2002) argues that multiword formulaic chunks may play a greater role in language processing and production than formerly believed. Corpus studies show just how common formulaic chunks are. From work with the Cobuild project, in the early 1990s Sinclair was already positing the Idiom Principle—that users have at their disposal "a large number of semi-preconstructed phrases that constitute single choices, even though they might appear to be analyzable into segments" (Sinclair, 1991, p. 110). In addition to the types of patterns previously discussed, further empirical support for the frequency of formulaic language is offered by Biber et al. (1999, chap. 12). They present analyses showing that almost 30% of the words in a corpus of conversation and about 20% in a corpus of academic prose are in three- or four-word recurrent "lexical bundles" (used at least 10 times per million words, spread across at least five different speakers or writers).

Descriptions for Language for Specific Purposes

Perhaps the most accepted contributions of corpus linguistics have been in descriptions of language for specific purposes. Although teachers of more general English may be unclear about the best target language (see the following discussion), teachers and students of a specialized variety want to know the characteristics of that variety and, therefore, analysis of a corpus of that variety is clearly useful.

English for Academic Purposes has received a great deal of attention. Coxhead's (2000) previously mentioned academic word list has important implications for EAP vocabulary materials development. In addition, numerous studies with the Michigan Corpus of Academic Spoken English (MICASE) have investigated a variety of language features—from idiom use (Simpson & Mendis, in press) to the use of *just* (Lindemann & Mauranen, 2001), and markers of discourse management (Swales & Malczewski, 2001) (see also Simpson, Lucka, & Ovens, 2000, and the web site www.hti.umich.edu/m/micase/ for more on MICASE). Biber, Conrad, Reppen, Byrd, & Helt (2002) present an analysis of numerous spoken and written registers that occur at American universities, examining the similarities and differences in groups of linguistic features. One of their surprising findings is that classroom sessions—although meant to provide information—actually have many more of the language features of involved, interactional discourse (such as informal conversation), which usually does not have a primary function of conveying information. It is easy to see how this mix of an informational purpose with more typically conversational language features could present challenges to international students. The work is applicable not only to teaching but also to testing, because it is based on the TOEFL 2000 Spoken and Written Academic Language Corpus, sponsored by Educational Testing Service, for the purpose of making aspects of the Test of English as a Foreign Language (TOEFL) more consistent with the actual language used in universities in the United States.

More specialized varieties have been investigated in a host of other publications. A small sampling includes conditionals in medical discourse (Ferguson, 2001), networks of collocations in plant biology research articles (Williams, 1998), collocations in cancer research article introductions (Gledhill, 2000), and the co-occurrence patterns of a variety of grammatical features in biology and history articles and textbooks (Conrad, 2001). The exact findings for every variety are impossible to cover here, but the contribution of corpus linguistics is clear: Corpus-based studies are allowing more thorough descriptions of these specialized types of discourse.

What Use Are Corpus-Based Descriptions for Language Teaching?

In the previous sections, I have described some of the work in corpus linguistics that has implications for language teaching. However, descriptions of language do not tell us what to teach or how to teach it, and at this juncture it may be useful to review some of the controversies that have arisen concerning how to apply the findings of descriptive corpus-based studies.

Widdowson has argued that corpus linguistics has no guaranteed relevance to pedagogy because corpus-based studies describe use, whereas pedagogy is concerned with "usefulness rather than use" (1991, p. 21). In a number of publications, he stresses that characteristics of usefulness, rather than characteristics of use, should determine what is taught, and that the most important characteristic of usefulness for pedagogy is whether a feature is a catalyst for further learning (Widdowson, 1991, 1993, 2000). He claims that, in contrast to his views, corpus linguists are arguing that only language found in a corpus should be taught in language classrooms, and that frequency of use in a native-speaker corpus can be used to design a syllabus for language teaching.

Despite Widdowson's claims, however, caveats have been expressed by corpus linguists as well. One caution was noted by Aarts in the early 1990s, arguing that not only frequencies but also factors related to users' attitudes toward language need to be taken into account when interpreting corpus work (Aarts, 1991). Even more important, the contribution of corpus linguistics is seen not as replacing other pedagogical considerations, but as adding to them with considerations about language use, including information about lexico-grammatical associations, collocations, and frequency in different contexts. For example, Aston (2000) notes that pedagogy needs to consider difficulty and learnability, interlanguage sequences, and the range of contexts in which a feature is used, as well as other factors. He further argues, though, that findings of corpus studies can now help us to see when language syllabi deserve more consideration or more explicit rationales. For example, if a syllabus includes a language item that is rare, while excluding or delaying a more frequent item, it is reasonable to ask what other pedagogical considerations make this sequencing appropriate (Aston, 2001a; Gavioli & Aston, 2001).

Another question raised about corpus work in English thus far is whether it has focused on language that represents the target for most learners. For learners in the United States or Great Britain, or those studying English with a clear goal of going to one of these countries, analysis of language produced by native speakers of American or British English is likely useful because they will come in contact with this variety. However, for learners who are in an English as a Foreign Language (EFL) situation, who will rarely be around native English speakers, the situation is more controversial. In response to McCarthy and Carter's (1995) call for more attention to the features of informal British conversation, as found in their analysis of the CANCODE corpus, Prodromou (1996a, 1996b) argues that informal British conversation may be both uninteresting and difficult to understand in an EFL setting. Cook (1997, 1998) similarly argues that native speaker language is neither authentic nor natural for foreign language students, and that it is too culture-bound for learners who do not have access to the culture. Widdowson (1991, 1996) argues that the learner community is not the native speaker community, and taken out of the context in which it occurred (even if it remains in the same country), the corpus language is no longer authentic.

Corpus linguists counter these criticisms in a number of ways. Some argue that introducing students to native speaker (NS) language provides them with choices, and it would be patronizing for NS teachers or researchers to decide who can have access to NS language (Carter & McCarthy, 1996). Gavioli and Aston (2001) argue that a corpus is not being offered as a model for learners to imitate, and learners are not expected to be members of the community; rather the learners can learn by being observers and analysts of the native speaker corpora. Yet another approach is to look to the development of other corpora that are more representative of learners' targets. Mauranen (2003) describes the development of ELFA, a corpus of Academic English as a Lingua Franca, collected at the University of Tampere, Finland, in international degree programs and other settings where university activities are regularly carried out in English. The International Corpus of English (Meyer, 2001) will allow analyses with approximately 20 varieties of English from regions of Africa, the South Pacific, Asia, the Caribbean, North America, and Great Britain.

A third controversy over corpus linguistics concerns just what role intuition plays in corpus analysis and how important intuition is to language study and pedagogy generally. Occasionally corpus linguists are accused of claiming that they do not use intuition, that intuition is not important for language teaching, or that corpus observations are privileged over others' insights and interpretations of language (Cook, 1998; Owen, 1993, 1996; Widdowson, 2000). Owen (1996) argues that corpus linguistics has limited use for language teaching because language teaching needs intuitive prescription: Students expect teachers to make decisions of what is correct and incorrect, and "intuitive prescription is fundamental to the psychology of language teaching and learning" (p. 224).

Most corpus linguists, however, acknowledge the important role that intuition and interpretation play in corpus linguistics. In an early edited collection, Leech and Candlin (1986) state that corpus data, like all data, is interpreted subjectively. Stubbs (1995) notes the use of intuition even in measures of word relations—for deciding what is interesting to study, in designing procedures, and in making interpretations. In an introductory text, Biber, Conrad and Reppen (1998, chap. 1) discuss intuition and anecdotal evidence as two ways to develop research questions for corpus studies, and note that any analysis requires human interpretation. Francis and Sinclair (1994) sum up decisions about what information to include and how to include it in the Cobuild Grammar: "Final decisions were made by human beings exercising their judgement" (p. 194). The use of intuition and human interpretation and judgment is not kept hidden in corpus linguistics.

As noted in the description of its characteristics, however, corpus linguistics does give primacy to observed language phenomena over intuition. Those interested in corpus linguistics see this as a strength. de Beaugrande (2001), in response to Widdowson (2000), argues that corpus linguistics has reinstated observation to linguistics, resulting in more methodical and systematic observations and interpretations of language than we get by relying solely on intuition or anecdotal observation. In responding to Cook's (1998) criticisms, Carter (1998b) raises the important point that giving primacy to data analysis actually grants more power to second language speakers. He notes that relying on intuition for interesting language information is actually an elitist enterprise in which native speakers have the power, because learners have less intuition about the use of their second language. Finally, an argument such as Owen's (1996) that students expect teachers to exercise intuitive prescription ignores the major issue that drives corpus linguistics: Many choices in language are made between equally grammatical constructions. Of course teachers are expected to make judgments about clear-cut cases of grammatical versus ungrammatical constructions. But what about constructions that are equally correct and have more subtle differences—the use of *big* versus the use of *large*, or the use of an extraposed versus subject-position *that*-clause? In many cases, the factors used to make such language choices remain subconscious, and teachers would, at best, offer an incomplete guess as an intuitive prescription. The difference in use of seemingly synonymous words, conditions associated with the use of relatively rare features, the association of grammatical structures and certain types of texts, the interactive features of spoken language, semantic prosodies, collocations—all these areas that have been highlighted in corpus studies give information about language choices beyond the accurate/inaccurate divide.

In general, at this point it is too early to assess the impact that descriptive corpus studies will ultimately have on language pedagogy. Although some ESL teachers have commented on the usefulness of ESL corpus-based references for designing materials or reorganizing syllabi (e.g., Scovel, 2000, but see response by Mills, 2001), only a few textbooks that are corpus-informed have thus far been marketed by worldwide publishers (Carter, Hughes, & McCarthy, 2000; McCarthy & O'Dell, 1997). Yet, despite this lack in the commercial market, numerous teachers have written about the effective use of corpus linguistics techniques with their own students. I turn to this area in the next section.

USING CORPUS LINGUISTICS TECHNIQUES IN THE CLASSROOM

One of the ways that corpus linguistics has been applied to L2 teaching is by using corpus-based techniques in language classrooms. When the results of descriptive studies are applied to teaching, the learners are still a step removed from the corpus—teachers and/or researchers do the analyses of the data. When corpus linguistics techniques are used in the classroom, in contrast, the learners are the language researchers. Johns (1994) describes this as "data-driven learning." Unfortunately, there is little empirical research into the effectiveness of corpus-based techniques for language learning, but there are a variety of theoretical reasons for using them and many reports by teachers of student interest and improvement.

Activities that ask learners to analyze corpus data are consistent with a variety of current principles in language learning theory, as has been pointed out by a number of corpus linguists (see, e.g., Aston, 1995; Bernardini, 2001; Gavioli, 2001; Gavioli & Aston, 2001; Johns, 1994; Leech, 1997; Willis, 1998). First, learner autonomy is increased as students are taught how to observe language and make generalizations, rather than depending on a teacher. With the observations and generalizations, the analysis of the corpus promotes hypothesis formation and testing, the pathway by which interlanguage is thought to progress. Furthermore, corpus analysis activities are easily designed to promote noticing and grammatical consciousness-raising (Rutherford, 1987; Schmidt, 1990; Williams, this volume).

One exception to the lack of empirical studies of classroom concordancing activities is work conducted by Cobb (1997, 1999). He examines the vocabulary learning of students when using a concordancer to see words in context compared with using other techniques. Cobb (1997) reports small but consistent gains by students using concordancers for vocabulary learning over students who used the same software without the concordancing feature. Cobb (1999) finds that both definitional knowledge and transfer of comprehension to new texts—in both the short- and long-term—was better for students who used a concordancer in addition to word lists and dictionaries versus those who used only word lists and dictionaries.

There is no lack of publications in which teachers describe concordancing activities that they have found to be effective with students. Useful edited collections include Aston (2001b), Burnard and McEnery (2000) and Wichmann, Fligelstone, McEnery, and Knowles (1997). Here I give just a brief sampling to show the diversity of classroom contexts in which corpus linguistics has been applied.

In ESP applications, Weber (2001) argues that undergraduate writing of formal legal essays improved when the course included the use of concordancing with a corpus of professional essays. Students determined correlations between the generic structure of the essays and the use of certain lexical and grammatical structures. This form-focused activity succeeded in making the essay-writing process "more manageable for the student," Weber reports (p. 15). Similarly, Collins (2000) and Foucou and Kubler (2000) find corpus-based activities useful for business and computer science students, respectively. Donley and Reppen (2001) discuss the use of concordancing with EAP students, to teach general academic vocabulary that is used in many disciplines.

For translation students, classroom uses of corpus linguistics have highlighted the connection between language and culture (see, e.g., Betraccini & Aston, 2001; Botley & Wilson, 2000; and Zanettin, 2001). Other applications have included sensitizing German L2 students to language variation (Jones, 1997); facilitating literary analysis by advanced non-native speakers, such as determining how irony is conveyed in English (Louw, 1997); teaching the use of discourse markers in Italian (Zorzi, 2001); and investigating metaphors (Partington, 1998, chap. 7).

Just as with the application of descriptive corpus-based studies, the use of corpus linguistics techniques in the classroom comes with a number of caveats. The ability to analyze language—as well as to handle computer technology—does not come without training. A number of articles emphasize the need to train students of any level—from low-level learners to in-service teachers. They need to learn a number of technological and research skills: to use the computer, to handle what may at first appear to be an overwhelming amount of data, to make observations, to generalize from observations, and to assess the limitations of the generalizations they derive (e.g., see Bernardini, 2001; Gavioli, 1997; Johns, 1997; Renouf, 1997; Seidlhofer, 2000). Concerned especially with meaningful content and texts whose context is known by students, Seidlhofer

(2000) finds concordancing most useful with her students when they use a corpus made of the students' own papers.

STUDIES OF LEARNER LANGUAGE

The third useful component of corpus linguistics for L2 teaching and learning concerns learner corpora—collections of language produced by L2 learners. These corpora are developed on many scales: large, international projects with texts collected at many sites; projects to develop a large collection of texts from just one site; and smaller corpora compiled by individual researchers for specific research goals. For example, the International Corpus of Learner English (Granger, 1998, 2003) has been coordinated by Granger in Belgium but includes sub-corpora compiled in 17 different countries (see www.fltr.ucl.ac.be/fltr/germ/etan/cecl/Cecl-Projects/Icle/icle.htm). The HKUST Learner Corpus is an example of a large corpus consisting of a particular type of text from one site, the writing of Cantonese-speaking undergraduates at the Hong Kong University of Science and Technology (Milton & Chowdhury, 1994). An example of an individual project is given in Reppen (2001), who describes a collection of writing by fifth grade Navajo first language (L1) students and native speakers, compiled by Reppen and Grabe, used as a component in the analysis of the discourse of fifth-grade students.

Learner corpora are often used for studies that compare learners' language with that of native speakers. These studies can identify areas of difficulty for learners or sources of misunderstandings between learners and native speakers. For example, Cheng and Warren (2000) report preliminary findings comparing non-native speakers and native speakers of English in interactions in Hong Kong. Among their findings is that the non-native speakers and native speakers tend to use tag questions and discourse markers for different pragmatic functions, and that the non-native speakers use vague language in inappropriate ways—inappropriate because the interlocutor shows confusion over the vagueness. They, thus, identify areas contributing to misunderstanding and difficulty in the interactions between non-native and native speakers. This is just one example in an area of study where, again, the variety of analyses is great. For example, Hyland and Milton (1997) compare NS and learners' use of expressions to convey doubt and certainty; Flowerdew (2003) analyzes lexical features of Problem–Solution texts and their rhetorical associations; Virtanen (1998) investigates the use of direct questions in argumentative student writing; and Petch-Tyson (2000) concentrates on demonstrative expressions. The characteristics of the learners studied varies, although most studies cover learners of at least an intermediate proficiency level.

In addition to increasing our understanding of learners' language use, the comparison between a learner corpus and native speaker corpus can also have useful pedagogical applications. Flowerdew (1998) finds that such a comparison helps refine teaching so that courses cover not just the most frequent items in a native-speaker corpus, but those causing the most difficulty for students. She describes such as application for EAP writing and the teaching of cause/effect markers.

Studies of learner corpora also often include comparisons of different learner groups with different first languages, contributing to our ability to distinguish between more universal interlanguage developmental patterns and more L1-influenced development. For example, Ringbom (1998) compares vocabulary use in essays by seven Western European groups included in the International Corpus of Learner English, and in general finds few L1 transfer errors. However, the underuse of multifunctional prepositions by Finns (such as *with, by,* and *at*) may be attributable to the fact that in Finnish these prepositions would be expressed by case endings.

Corpus studies also provide the means for replicating or expanding studies that were done earlier with smaller data collections. An interesting example is a study by Tono (2000). He analyzes morpheme accuracy in a 300,000-word corpus of written texts by Japanese L1 ESL learners, comparing the results to those found in the early morpheme studies with Chinese and Spanish L1 learners, based on the Bilingual Syntax Measure (Dulay & Burt, 1974). He finds that articles and plural -s appear to be later acquired and possessive -s earlier acquired than in the previous study. Certain variables remain to be teased apart—most important, spoken versus written orders of acquisition, in addition to the effect of the L1—but the potential for corpus-based studies and computer-assisted analysis tools is clear: the ability to conduct studies with new, naturalistic data from large numbers of learners and compare the results to previous findings.

Finally, it is also important to note the emergence of what may be the next generation of corpora, which will expand our ability to study learner language in the classroom: a multimedia corpus of language classrooms. The Multimedia Adult ESOL Learner Corpus is a 5-year project videotaping four low-level, adult ESL classes (Reder, Harris, & Setzler, in press). The final corpus will contain approximately 5,000 hours of classroom language, involving roughly 1,000 learners. Video and audio for all the hours of instruction will be stored digitally, with parts of the corpus transcribed and coded for certain pedagogical criteria (for example, the type of participation pattern—teacher-fronted, student-fronted, pairwork, groupwork, free movement, individual). Although still in its early stages, the project will soon offer many opportunities for studies of learner development over time and comparisons of language used during different types of class activities. Unlike previous corpora, the transcribed data will remain linked to the visual recordings of the classroom, making more contextualized analyses possible. Already the corpus has proved useful for professional development activities for teachers (Kurzet, 2000).

CONCLUSION

Corpus linguistics is a young specialization within applied linguistics. Although, as I argue in this chapter, it has already begun to contribute to L2 teaching and our understanding of L2 learning, I see several pressing needs if it is to meet its potential usefulness. I conclude by considering the five most important needs.

First is the need for more empirical studies of the impact of using corpus materials and techniques in the classroom. As noted in the previous description, much of the published work on corpus linguistics has been by teachers describing activities that they thought were helpful for their students. Although teachers' experiences are not to be disregarded, we need principled studies that seek to discover how best to exploit corpus activities, to determine whether currently used activities are a greater aid to acquisition than are more traditional activities, and even simply to describe what learners do as they perform corpus analysis activities. (Many of the issues raised by Chapelle, 2001, for the more general fields of computer-assisted language learning and computer-assisted second language acquisition research also apply to corpus linguistics.)

Second, we need more empirical studies of corpora themselves to determine how to represent varieties of language. Larger and larger corpora are becoming possible with new computer technology, but time and money are still limited even when computer storage space is not. Learning more about the most effective size and sampling techniques will make results from corpus studies not only more generalizable, but will also allow the compilers of corpora to use their time and resources most efficiently.

Third, more corpora—and especially corpora of different varieties—need to be compiled and made available widely. As previously noted, learners in different contexts may well have different targets, and a more diverse collection of corpora from which to choose is more likely to meet the needs of more teachers and learners throughout the world. Because corpus compilation is a lengthy, often expensive process (particularly with spoken and video corpora that must be transcribed and digitized), it is sometimes sponsored by private, commercial companies. Such private ownership can make the corpus inaccessible to those outside the company. This is not to say that the development of privately owned corpora should not be maintained, but widely available corpora are also crucial.

In addition to more corpora, there is a critical need for more computer programmers in corpus linguistics. Most of the work reviewed here relied on concordancing because concordancers are the most widely available software. However, numerous interesting features of language are too complex to analyze with a concordancer. Many descriptions (for example, those in the reference grammar by Biber et al., 1999) required other software, including interactive programs written by the research team. Until more corpus linguists are programming for themselves or more versatile programs are widely available, severe constraints on corpus studies are inevitable. However, few courses in computer programming for applied linguistics are currently offered.

Finally, within corpus linguistics, we need an increase in second language acquisition studies. One of the limitations of many previous SLA studies has been a small number of participants, a small number of language groups represented, or a short time period for the study. Corpus linguistics, if fully exploited, can provide means to get beyond these limitations. An increase in learner corpora and more individualized software programs should facilitate corpus studies and make possible more complex studies than were previously possible with large databases—including analyses such as tracking learners' development of form–function associations or comparing the development of numerous learners over several years, as well as cross-sectional studies with a large number of learners from numerous language groups.

If these developments take place, corpus linguistics will likely have an even greater influence on L2 teaching in the future. Controversies over its applications will no doubt continue as well and continue to serve a useful purpose in forcing corpus linguists to clarify this approach and refine ideas and techniques. It seems likely that corpus linguistics will continue to grow in popularity, given the tremendous increase in publications and presentations over the past 15 years by both researchers and teachers. Already corpus linguistics is providing new perspectives on language in use and new techniques for teaching it.

REFERENCES

Aarts, J. (1991). Intuition-based and observation-based grammars. In K. Aijmer & B. Altenberg (Eds.), *English corpus linguistics* (pp. 44–62). London: Longman.

Altenberg, B. (1994). On the functions of *such* in spoken and written English. In N. Oostdijk & P. de Hann (Eds.), *Corpus-based research into language* (pp. 223–240). Amsterdam: Rodopi.

Aston, G. (1995). Corpora in language pedagogy: Matching theory and practice. In G. Cook & B. Seidlhofer (Eds.), *Principles and practice in applied linguistics* (pp. 257–270). Oxford, UK: Oxford University Press.

Aston, G. (2000). Corpora and language teaching. In L. Burnard & T. McEnery (Eds.), *Rethinking language pedagogy from a corpus perspective* (pp. 7–17). Frankfurt, Germany: Lang.

Aston, G. (2001a). Learning with corpora: An overview. In G. Aston (Ed.), *Learning with corpora* (pp. 7–45). Houston, TX: Athelstan.

Aston, G. (Ed.). (2001b). *Learning with corpora*. Houston, TX: Athelstan.

Aston, G., & Burnard, L. (1998). *The BNC handbook*. Edinburgh, Scotland: Edinburgh University Press.

Bernardini, S. (2001). "Spoilt for choice": A learner explored general language corpora. In G. Aston (Ed.), *Learning with corpora* (pp. 220–249). Houston, TX: Athelstan.

Bertaccini, F., & Aston, G. (2001). Going to the clochemerle: Exploring cultural connotations through ad hoc corpora. In G. Aston (Ed.), *Learning with corpora* (pp. 198–219). Houston, TX: Athelstan.

Biber, D. (1990). Methodological issues regarding corpus-based analyses of linguistic variation. *Literary and Linguistic Computing, 5,* 257–269.

Biber, D. (1993). Representativeness in corpus design. *Literary and Linguistic Computing, 8,* 243–257.

Biber, D., & Conrad, S. (2001). Quantitative corpus-based research: Much more than bean counting. *TESOL Quarterly, 35,* 331–336.

Biber, D., Conrad, S., & Reppen, R. (1998). *Corpus linguistics: Investigating language structure and use.* Cambridge, UK: Cambridge University Press.

Biber, D., Conrad, S., Reppen, R., Byrd, P., & Helt, M. (2002). Speaking and writing in the university: A multi-dimensional comparison. *TESOL Quarterly, 36,* 9–48.

Biber, D., Johansson, S., Leech, G., Conrad, S., & Finegan, E. (1999). *The Longman grammar of spoken and written English.* Harlow, UK: Pearson Education.

Botley, S. P., & Wilson, A. (2000). (Ed.). *Multilingual corpora in teaching and research.* Amsterdam: Rodopi.

Breivik, L. (1999). On the pragmatic function of relative clauses and locative expressions in existential sentences in the LOB corpus. In H. Hasselgård & S. Oksefjell (Eds.), *Out of corpora* (pp. 121–135). Amsterdam: Rodopi.

Burnard, L., & McEnery, T. (Eds.) (2000). *Rethinking language pedagogy from a corpus perspective.* Frankfurt, Germany: Lang.

Carter, R. (1998a). Orders of reality: CANCODE, communication, and culture. *ELT Journal, 52,* 43–56.

Carter, R. (1998b). Reply to Guy Cook. *ELT Journal, 52,* 64.

Carter, R., & McCarthy, M. (1995). Grammar and the spoken language. *Applied Linguistics, 16,* 141–158.

Carter, R., & McCarthy, M. (1996). Correspondence. *ELT Journal, 50,* 369–371.

Carter, R., Hughes, R., & McCarthy, M. (2000). *Exploring grammar in context.* Cambridge, UK: Cambridge University Press.

Channell, J. (1994). *Vague language.* Oxford, UK: Oxford University Press.

Chapelle, C. (2001). *Computer applications in second language acquisition.* Cambridge, UK: Cambridge University Press.

Cheng, W., & Warren, M. (2000). The Hong Kong Corpus of Spoken English: Language learning through language description. In L. Burnard & T. McEnery (Eds.), *Rethinking language pedagogy from a corpus perspective* (pp. 133–144). Frankfurt, Germany: Lang.

Church, K., & Hanks, P. (1990). Word association norms, mutual information, and lexicography. *Computational Linguistics, 16,* 22–29.

Clear, J. (1993). From Firth principles–Computational tools for the study of collocation. In M. Baker, G. Francis, & E. Tognini-Bonelli (Eds.), *Text and technology* (pp. 271–292). Philadelphia: Benjamins.

Coates, J. (1983). The semantics of modal auxiliaries. London: Croon Helm.

Cobb, T. (1997). Is there any measurable learning from hands-on concordancing? *System, 25,* 301–315.

Cobb, T. (1999). Breadth and depth of lexical acquisition with hands-on concordancing. *Computer Assisted Language Learning, 12,* 345–360.

Collins COBUILD English Grammar. (1990). London: Collins.

Collins, H. (2000). Materials design and language corpora: A report in the context of distance education. In L. Burnard & T. McEnery (Eds.), *Rethinking language pedagogy from a corpus perspective* (pp. 51–63). Frankfurt, Germany: Lang.

Conrad, S. (1999). The importance of corpus-based research for language teachers. *System, 27,* 1–18.

Conrad, S. (2000). Will corpus linguistics revolutionize grammar teaching in the 21st century? *TESOL Quarterly, 34,* 548–560.

Conrad, S. (2001). Variation among disciplinary texts: A comparison of textbooks and journal articles in biology and history. In S. Conrad & D. Biber (Eds.), *Variation in English: Multi-dimensional studies* (pp. 94–107). Harlow, UK: Longman.

Conrad, S. (2002). Corpus linguistic approaches for discourse analysis. *Annual Review of Applied Linguistics, 22,* 75–95.

Cook, G. (1997). Language play, language learning. *ELT Journal, 51,* 224–231.

Cook, G. (1998). The uses of reality: A reply to Ronald Carter. *ELT Journal, 52,* 57–63.

Coxhead, A. (2000). A new academic word list. *TESOL Quarterly, 34,* 213–238.

de Beaugrande, R. (2001). Interpreting the discourse of H. G. Widdowson: A corpus-based critical discourse analysis. *Applied Linguistics, 22,* 104–121.

Donley, K., & Reppen, R. (2001). Using corpus tools to highlight academic vocabulary in SCLT. *TESOL Journal, 10,* 7–12.

Dulay, H., & Burt, M. (1974). Natural sequences in child second language acquisition. *Language Learning, 24,* 37–53.

Ferguson, G. (2001). If you pop over there: A corpus-based study of conditionals in medical discourse. *English for Specific Purposes, 20,* 61–82.

Firth, J. R. (1957). Papers in linguistics. Oxford: Oxford University Press.

Flowerdew, L. (1998). Integrating "expert" and "interlanguage" computer corpora findings on causality: Discoveries for teachers and students. *English for Specific Purposes, 17,* 329–345.

Flowerdew, L. (2003). An analysis of the problem–solution pattern in an apprentice and professional corpus of technical writing. *TESOL Quarterly, 37*, 489–511.

Francis, G., & Sinclair, J. (1994). "I bet he drinks Carling Black Label": A riposte to Owen on corpus grammar. *Applied Linguistics, 15*, 190–200.

Foucou, P., & Kübler, N. (2000). In L. Burnard & T. McEnery (Eds.), *Rethinking language pedagogy from a corpus perspective* (pp. 65–73). Frankfurt, Germany: Lang.

Gavioli, L. (1997). Exploring texts through the concordancer: Guiding the learner. In A. Wichmann, S. Fligelstone, T. McEnery, & G. Knowles (Eds.), *Teaching and language corpora* (pp. 83–99). London: Longman.

Gavioli, L. (2001). The learner as researcher: Introducing corpus concordancing in the classroom. In G. Aston (Ed.), *Learning with corpora* (pp. 108–137). Houston, TX: Athelstan.

Gavioli, L., & Aston, G. (2001). Enriching reality: Language corpora in language pedagogy. *ELT Journal, 55*, 238–246.

Gledhill, C. (2000). The discourse function of collocation in research article introductions. *English for Specific Purposes, 19*, 115–135.

Gómez-González, M. A. (1998). A corpus-based analysis of extended multiple themes in PresE. *International Journal of Corpus Linguistics, 3*, 81–113.

Granger, S. (Ed.). (1998). *Learner English on computer*. London: Longman.

Granger, S. (2003). The International Corpus of Learner English: A new resources for foreign language learning and teaching and second language acquisition research. *TESOL Quarterly, 37*, 538–546.

Greenbaum, S., Nelson, G., & Weitzman, M. (1996). Complement clauses in English. In J. Thomas & M. Short (Eds.), *Using corpora for language research* (pp. 76–91). London: Longman.

Hennoste, T., Koit, M., Roosmaa, T., & Saluveer, M. (1998). Structure and usage of the Tartu University corpus of written Estonian. *International Journal of Corpus Linguistics, 3*, 279–304.

Holmes, J. (1988). Doubt and certainty in ESL textbooks. *Applied Linguistics, 9*, 21–43.

Hughes, R., & McCarthy, M. (1998). From sentence to discourse: Discourse grammar and English language teaching. *TESOL Quarterly, 32*, 263–287.

Hunston, S. (2002). *Corpora in applied linguistics*. Cambridge, UK: Cambridge University Press.

Hunston, S., & Francis, G. (1998). Verbs observed: A corpus-driven pedagogic grammar of English. *Applied Linguistics, 19*, 45–72.

Hunston, S., & Francis, G. (2000). *Pattern grammar: A corpus-driven approach to the lexical grammar of English*. Amsterdam: Benjamins.

Hunston, S., Francis, G., & Manning, E. (1997). Grammar and vocabulary: Showing the connections. *ELT Journal, 51*, 208–216.

Hunston, S., & Sinclair, J. (1999). A local grammar of evaluation. In S. Hunston and G. Thompson (Eds.), *Evaluation in text* (pp. 74–101). Oxford, UK: Oxford University Press.

Hyland, K., & Milton, J. (1997). Qualification and certainty in L1 and L2 students' writing. *Journal of Second Language Writing 6*, 183–205.

Johansson, S., & Oksefjell, S. (1996). Towards a unified account of the syntax and semantics of GET. In J. Thomas & M. Short (Eds.), *Using corpora for language research* (pp. 57–75). London: Longman.

Johansson, S., Leech, G., & Goodluck, H. (1978). *Manual of information to accompany the Lancaster-Oslo/Bergen corpus of British English, for use with digital computers*. Oslo, Norway: Department of English, University of Oslo.

Johns, T. (1994). From printout to handout: Grammar and vocabulary teaching in the context of data-driven learning. In T. Odlin (Ed.), *Perspectives on pedagogical grammar* (pp. 293–313). Cambridge, UK: Cambridge University Press.

Johns, T. (1997). Contexts: The background, development and trailing of a concordance-based CALL program. In A. Wichmann, S. Fligelstone, T. McEnery, & G. Knowles (Eds.), *Teaching and language corpora* (pp. 100–115). London: Longman.

Jones, R. (1997). Creating and using a corpus of spoken German. In A. Wichmann, S. Fligelstone, T. McEnery, & G. Knowles (Eds.), *Teaching and language corpora* (pp. 146–156). London: Longman.

Kennedy, G. (1987). Quantification and the use of English: A case study of one aspect of the learner's task. *Applied Linguistics, 8*, 264–286.

Kennedy, G. (1991). *Between* and *through*: The company they keep and the functions they serve. In K. Aijmer & B. Altenberg (Eds.), *English corpus linguistics* (pp. 95–110). London: Longman.

Kennedy, G. (1998). *An introduction to corpus linguistics*. London: Longman.

Kilgarriff, A. (2001). Comparing corpora. *International Journal of Corpus Linguistics, 6*, 1–37.

Kurzet, R. (2002). Teachable moments: Videos of adult ESOL classrooms. *Focus on Basics, 5*(D), 8–11.

Lawson, A. (2001). Rethinking French grammar for pedagogy: The contribution of spoken corpora. In R. Simpson & J. Swales (Eds.), *Corpus linguistics in North America* (pp. 179–194). Ann Arbor: University of Michigan Press.

Leech, G. (1997). Teaching and language corpora: A convergence. In A. Wichmann, S. Fligelstone, T. McEnery, & G. Knowles (Eds.), *Teaching and language corpora* (pp. 1–23). London: Longman.

Leech. G. (1999). The distribution and function of vocatives in American and British English. In H. Hasselgård & S. Oksefjell (Eds.), *Out of corpora* (pp. 107–118). Amsterdam: Rodopi.

Leech, G., & Candlin, C. (1986). Introduction. In G. Leech & C. Candlin (Eds.), *Computers in English language teaching and research*. London: Longman.

Lindemann, S., & Mauranen, A. (2001). It's just real messy: The occurrence and function of "just" in a corpus of academic speech. *English for Specific Purposes, 20,* 459–475.

Longman Dictionary of Contemporary English, 3rd ed. (1995). Harlow, UK: Pearson Education.

Louw, B. (1993). Irony in the text or insincerity in the writer? The diagnostic potential of semantic prosodies. In M. Baker, G. Francis, & E. Tognini-Bonelli (Eds.), *Text and technology* (pp. 157–176). Philadelphia: Benjamins.

Louw, B. (1997). The role of corpora in critical literacy appreciation. In A. Wichmann, S. Fligelstone, T. McEnery, & G. Knowles (Eds.), *Teaching and language corpora* (pp. 240–251). London: Longman.

Mauranen, A. (2003). The corpus of English as lingua franca in academic settings. *TESOL Quarterly, 37,* 513–527.

McCarthy, M. (1998). *Spoken language and applied linguistics.* Cambridge, UK: Cambridge University Press.

McCarthy, M., & Carter, R. (1995). Spoken grammar: What is it and how can we teach it? *ELT Journal, 49,* 207–218.

McCarthy, M., & Carter, R. (2001). Size isn't everything: Spoken English, corpus, and the classroom. *TESOL Quarterly, 35,* 337–340.

McCarthy, M., & O'Dell, F. (1997). *Vocabulary in use, upper intermediate.* New York: Cambridge University Press.

McEnery, T., & Wilson, A. (1996). *Corpus linguistics.* Edinburgh, Scotland: Edinburgh University Press.

Meyer, C. (2001). The International Corpus of English: Progress and prospects. In R. Simpson & J. Swales (Eds.), *Corpus linguistics in North America* (pp. 17–31). Ann Arbor: University of Michigan Press.

Meyer, C. (2002). *English corpus linguistics.* Cambridge, UK: Cambridge University Press.

Mills, D. (2001). Open letter to Tom Scovel. *CATESOL News, 33*(1), 20–21.

Milton, J., & Chowdhury, N. (1994). Tagging the interlanguage of Chinese learners of English. In L. Flowerdew & K. Tong (Eds.), *Entering text* (pp. 127–143). Hong Kong: Language Centre, Hong Kong University of Science and Technology.

Moon, R. (1998). *Fixed expressions and idioms in English: A corpus-based approach.* Oxford, UK: Clarendon.

Owen, C. (1993). Corpus-based grammar and the Heineken effect: Lexico-grammatical description for language learners. *Applied Linguistics, 14,* 167–187.

Owen, C. (1996). Do concordances require to be consulted? *ELT Journal, 50,* 219–224.

Palmer, F. (Ed.) (1968). *Selected papers of J. R. Firth 1952–59.* London: Longman.

Partington, A. (1998). *Patterns and meanings: Using corpora for English language research and teaching.* Amsterdam: Benjamins.

Petch-Tyson, S. (2000). Demonstrative expressions in argumentative discourse—A computer-based comparison of non-native and native English. In S. Botley & A. McEnery (Eds.), *Corpus-based and computational approaches to discourse anaphora.* Amsterdam: Benjamins.

Prodromou, L. (1996a). Correspondence. *ELT Journal, 50,* 88–89.

Prodromou, L. (1996b). From Luke Prodromou. *ELT Journal, 50,* 369–371.

Quirk, R., Greenbaum, S., Leech, G., & Svartvik, J. (1985). *A comprehensive grammar of the English language.* London: Longman.

Renouf, A. (1997). Teaching corpus linguistics to teachers of English. In A. Wichmann, S. Fligelstone, T. McEnery, & G. Knowles (Eds.), *Teaching and language corpora* (pp. 255–266). London: Longman.

Reder, S., Harris, K., & Setzler, K. (2003). A multimedia adult learner corpus. *TESOL Quarterly, 37,* 546–556.

Reppen, R. (2001). Writing development among elementary students: Corpus- based perspectives. In R. Simpson & J. Swales (Eds.), *Corpus linguistics in North America* (pp. 211–225). Ann Arbor: University of Michigan Press.

Ringbom, H. (1998). Vocabulary frequencies in advanced learner English: A cross-linguistic approach. In S. Granger (Ed.), *Learner English on computer* (pp. 41–52). London: Longman.

Rutherford, W. (1987). *Second language grammar: Learning and teaching.* London: Longman.

Schmidt, R. (1990). The role of consciousness in second language learning. *Applied Linguistics, 11,* 129–158.

Scovel, T. (2000). What I learned from the new Longman grammar. *CATESOL News, 32*(3), 12–16.

Seidlhofer, S. (2000). Operationalizing intertextuality: Using learner corpora for learning. In L. Burnard & T. McEnery (Eds.)., *Rethinking language pedagogy from a corpus perspective* (pp. 207–223). Frankfurt, Germany: Lang.

Simpson, R., & Mendis, D. (2003). A corpus-based study of idioms in academic speech. *TESOL Quarterly, 37,* 419–441.

Simpson, R., & Swales, J. (2001). (Eds.). *Corpus linguistics in North America: Selections from the 1999 symposium.* Ann Arbor: University of Michigan Press.

Simpson, R., Lucka, B., & Ovens, J. (2000). Methodological challenges of planning a spoken corpus with pedagogical outcomes. In L. Burnard & T. McEnery (Eds.), *Rethinking language pedagogy from a corpus perspective* (pp. 43–49). Frankfurt, Germany: Lang.

Sinclair, J. (Ed.). (1987). *Looking up.* London: Collins.

Sinclair, J. (1991). *Corpus, concordance, collocation.* Oxford, UK: Oxford University Press.

Stubbs, M. (1993). British traditions in text analysis: From Firth to Sinclair. In M. Baker, G. Francis, & E. Tognini-Bonelli (Eds.), *Text and technology* (pp. 1–33). Philadelphia: Benjamins.

Stubbs, M. (1995). Collocations and semantic profiles: On the cause of the trouble with quantitative studies. *Functions of Language, 2,* 23–55.

Stubbs, M. (1996). *Text and corpus analysis*. Oxford, UK: Blackwell.

Swales, J., & Malczewski, B. (2001). Discourse management and new episode flags in MICASE. In R., Simpson, & J. Swales (Eds.), *Corpus linguistics in North America* (pp. 179–194). Ann Arbor: University of Michigan Press.

Tognini-Bonelli, E. (1993). Interpretative nodes in discourse—*actual* and *actually*. In M. Baker, G. Francis, & E. Tognini-Bonelli (Eds.), *Text and technology* (pp. 193–212). Philadelphia: Benjamins.

Tognini-Bonelli, E. (2001). *Corpus linguistics at work*. Amsterdam: Benjamins.

Tono, Y. (2000). A computer learner corpus-based analysis of the acquisition order of English grammatical morphemes. In L. Burnard & T. McEnery (Eds)., *Rethinking language pedagogy from a corpus perspective* (pp. 123–132). Frankfurt, Germany: Lang.

Virtanen, T. (1998). Direct questions in argumentative student writing. In S. Granger (Ed.), *Learner English on computer* (pp. 94–118). London: Longman.

Weber, J. (2001). A concordance- and genre-informed approach to ESL essay writing. *ELT Journal, 55*, 14–20.

Wichmann, A., Fligelstone, S., McEnery, T., & Knowles, G. (Eds.). (1997). *Teaching and language corpora*. London: Longman.

Widdowson, H. (1991). The description and prescription of language. In J. Alatis (Ed.), *Georgetown University Roundtable on Language and Linguistics, 1991—Linguistics and language pedagogy: The state of the art* (pp. 11–24). Washington, DC: Georgetown University Press.

Widdowson, H. (1993). Perspectives on communicative language teaching: Syllabus design and methodology. In J. Alatis (Ed.), *Georgetown University Roundtable on Language and Linguistics, 1992—Language Communication and social meaning* (pp. 501–507). Washington, DC: Georgetown University Press.

Widdowson, H. (1996). Comment: Authenticity and autonomy in ELT. *ELT Journal, 50*, 67–68.

Widdowson, H. (2000). On the limitations of linguistics applied. *Applied Linguistics, 21*, 3–25.

Williams, G. C. (1998). Collocational networks: Interlocking patterns of lexis in a corpus of plant biology research articles. *International Journal of Corpus Linguistics, 3*, 151–171.

Willis, J. (1998). Concordances in the classroom without a computer: Assembling and exploiting concordances of common words. In B. Tomlinson (Ed.), *Materials development in language teaching* (pp. 44–66). Cambridge, UK: Cambridge University Press.

Wray, A. (2002). *Formulaic language and the lexicon*. Cambridge, UK: Cambridge University Press.

Zanettin, F. (2001). Swimming in words: Corpora, translation, and language learning. In G. Aston (Ed.), *Learning with corpora* (pp. 177–197). Houston, TX: Athelstan.

Zorzi, D. (2001). The pedagogic use of spoken corpora: Learning discourse markers in Italian. In G. Aston (Ed.), *Learning with corpora* (pp. 85–107). Houston, TX: Athelstan.

IV

Second Language Processes and Development

Introduction

In the research on how second and foreign languages (L2/FL) are learned, the systematization of knowledge has resulted in relatively well-defined venues of investigation. Although many, if not most, studies do not exclusively confine themselves to a particular area of L2/FL learning and acquisition, the great advancements in our current understanding of language processes and development have led to increasingly narrowing foci of research areas. For instance, while the study of vocabulary learning has much to contribute to that of learning to read in an L2/FL, increasing knowledge about L2 vocabulary development has resulted in a burgeoning body of research that does not necessarily seek to establish direct connections between L2 vocabulary acquisition and L2 reading. The progressively specialized foci of L2/FL research venues are certainly not unique to the study of language learning processes, but rather, they represent a hallmark of any maturing discipline that has progressed sufficiently to move beyond the frontier.

A number of disadvantages can accompany a dramatic growth in the body of knowledge: (1) If in the early days of L2/FL study it was possible to become well versed in any domain of L2 development within a few years, at the present, the amount of time it takes to attain expertise in L2 knowledge has extended beyond a decade of active engagement in research and publishing. In this regard, the study of L2 processes has merely become similar to other established data-driven disciplines (Simon, 1981/1996). (2) The journals that publish L2/FL research can number in the dozens, and a few dozen publishers in various countries produce over a hundred books each year. The sheer amount of published research has made it work- and time-consuming to stay current in the field. (3) The coverage of important areas in L2/FL research or even making decisions about which domains are important has become a difficult and highly subjective task.

Although the ever-expanding number of publications speaks to the advancements of knowledge about L2/FL development, it is safe to say that at the present time relatively little is known about exactly how second languages are learned. Researchers and teachers alike have come to recognize that the processes of L2/FL learning and acquisition are enormously complex, but it is not possible to say with any degree of certainty what these processes are, how they singly or in combination influence the rate or success of language learning, and what contributing roles particular factors play in language development. The issues that confounded early L2/FL researchers to a great extent have not been resolved, and many questions continue to remain unanswered. For example:

- Why are some individuals better learners than others?
- What factors in effect describe "a good language learner" and what characteristics do "good learners" share?
- What is the role of aptitude in L2 learning and what role does the motivation play?

- What is the role of L1 literacy in L2 learning or in learning to become literate in L2?
- Is explicit teaching more effective than implicit teaching or is it the other way round?
- Does explicit L2 teaching lead to higher language proficiency?
- Why do some learners attain high proficiencies in particular L2/FL skills and others do not?
- What types of learners are more likely to benefit from instruction in what specific L2/FL skills?

In some sense, these and other similar questions cannot be answered independently, and in order to find an answer to any one or two of them, a set of additional puzzles would need to be solved. For instance, some studies have shown that intelligence plays a crucial role in aptitude for language (e.g., Carroll, 1981). However, research conducted in the late 1970s and early 1980s was based on instructed L2 learning that centered on the analytic teaching techniques different from those in the audiolingual or naturalistic methods for L2 teaching. Hence, it was not possible to tell whether it was the learners' intelligence or the teaching method that led to substantial learning gains. Similarly, research has pointed to the connections between extraversion or introversion and language learning aptitude and that extraverts usually make good language learners due to their preferences for interaction (e.g., Chastain, 1975). However, in light of the fact that anywhere between 75% and 83% of the general population are extraverts (Nunnally, 1975; Perkins, 1985), it seems unlikely that such a high proportion of people can have high language learning abilities.

Over the past several decades, L2/FL research has made a large number of claims regarding L2/FL learning processes and development, but most remain vague and to a large extent unsubstantiated. Put simply, the study of L2/FL brings to mind the old truism that the more we know, the more we realize how much we don't know, and at this point in time, we do not know a great deal (although many individual researchers might adamantly dispute this).

A Caveat Emptor. The coverage of L2/FL processes and development in Part IV is incomplete and idiosyncratic, as all similar overviews would be and probably are. The chapters included here consist of two distinct and interconnected clusters: those devoted to mental, cognitive, and learning processes and those that deal with the research on the learning and acquisition of specific L2 skills. As far as the attainment of incremental L2 skills is concerned, it may be difficult to consider, for example, a learner's age, cognitive abilities, and other language learning factors separately from his or her success (or failure) in learning to speak, comprehend, read, and write in L2. In addition, in recent decades many studies of L2/FL learning of what are commonly known as "the four skills" (i.e., speaking, listening, reading, and writing) have become far more cognitively oriented than they used to be in the days of the disciplinary frontier, and research has made important inroads in identifying the role of psychological factors in attaining proficiency in various facets of L2 learning.

The chapters in Part IV cover the following aspects of L2 learning:

- Chapter 23, by **Georgette Ioup**, reviews research that supports or refutes the existence of the critical period in L2 learning and acquisition. This chapter discusses the individual variables that deal with the source of age differences, such as the natural decline in learning ability with normal aging, environmental factors, the motivational/attitudinal disposition of the learner, crosslinguistic factors, and the learner's aptitude for language learning. Although these variables can influence the degree to which late learners reach their full potential, they cannot fully explain why, given the same conditions for L2 acquisition, the amount of variability has been noted among various learners, and why, in the best of circumstances, the full potential of most adult acquisition falls short of nativelike attainment. The explanation may lie in the fact that fundamental differences exist between child and adult language learning.

• Chapter 24, by **Robert DeKeyser** and **Alan Juffs**, reviews research on the role of cognition (i.e., the acquisition and use of knowledge) in L2 learning. The main issues examined in the chapter have to do with how people come to know elements of or about L2 and how they use what they know. DeKeyser and Juffs explain that the multiplicity of answers to both questions can be found in literature and that some learners acquire some specific L2 knowledge explicitly and others implicitly. The distinction between the two types of learners lie in such complex constructs as less structured, formulaic knowledge specific to L2, knowledge transferred from L1, and perhaps access to Universal Grammar (UG). When L2 learners use this knowledge, their actual behavior is even more multifaceted. The discussion focuses on various kinds of knowledge sources and uses in L2 to highlight what seems well established and what remains unknown or controversial.

• Chapter 25, by **ZhaoHong Han** and **Larry Selinker**, examines the phenomenon termed fossilization by Selinker in 1972. Research on fossilization represents an attempt to account for the observation that the vast majority of adult second language learners fail to achieve native-speaker target-language competence. Fossilization implies that both a cognitive mechanism and performance-related structures and forms in L2 production that remain in learner interlanguage over time. Han and Selinker explain that fossilizable structures are persistent, resistant to external influences, and independent of learners' ages, that is, it affects both child and adult L2 learners alike. These factors strongly imply that most L2 learners lack the ability to attain nativelike competence, regardless of their effort. It is for this reason that this strong hypothesis for *all* learners has caused much interest in fossilization and has drawn the attention of many second language researchers and practitioners.

• Chapter 26, by **Merrill Swain**, explores the Output Hypothesis, which stipulates that the act of producing language (speaking or writing) constitutes part of the process of second language learning. In fact, the processes involved in producing language can be quite different than those involved in comprehending language. The input hypothesis has claimed that there was only one necessary and sufficient condition for second language acquisition, and that was the presence of comprehensible input. However, results of many studies of immersion students showed clearly that input alone was insufficient for learners to attain nativelike L2 proficiency. Alternative explanations were sought, and one explanation was the output hypothesis. Swain outlines three functions of output in second language learning: 1) the noticing/triggering function, 2) the hypothesis-testing function, and 3) the metalinguistic/reflective function. The most significant new contribution of studying output and language production is its importance as a cognitive tool in L2 learning and acquisition research.

• Chapter 27, by **Elaine Tarone**, reviews research on speaking in a second language. Learner speech can be analyzed from the point of view of form or function. Formal aspects of the second language that the learner must produce orally are described in terms of the sounds of the language, morphology and syntax of the language, discourse markers of the language, and lexis. However, when the learner speaks, there is a system evidenced in the form of what is spoken: a system with its own formal rules of phonology, morphology, syntax, lexicon, and discourse patterns. This system does not conform exactly to the rules of the target language as spoken by native speakers of the target language, nor does it conform exactly to the rules of the speaker's native language. To communicate effectively, language learners must learn more than just the linguistic form of the second language, but they must also learn how to use those forms to fulfill a variety of functions. Learners' production of oral discourse for functions has identified interactional, transactional, and ludic speech functions reviewed in the chapter.

• Chapter 28, by **Mike Rost**, reviews L2 listening as a complex cognitive process that encompasses receptive, constructive, and interpretive aspects of cognition, which are utilized in both first and second language listening. In L2 development, in many cases, direct intervention is considered necessary because the learner is acquiring a second language after cognitive processing skills in the L1 have been established. L2 listening constitutes not only a skill area in performance, but also a primary means of acquiring a second language. As a goal-oriented activity, listening involves bottom-up processing, in which the listener attends to data in the incoming speech signals as well as top-down processing, in which the listener utilizes prior knowledge and expectations to guide the process of understanding. While L1 and L2 listening utilize the same basic underlying neurological processes that take place in the same parts of the brain, there are important developmental and functional differences between L1 and L2 listening.

• Chapter 29, by **Terence Wiley**, discusses the numerous thorny issues in second language literacy and biliteracy. Wiley foregrounds some of the major points and ideological tensions in the broader field of literacy studies that are directly relevant to the study of second language literacy and biliteracy. In the United States, as well as in many other countries, there is often considerable confusion in popular discourse regarding the extent of literacy and illiteracy among language minorities. Second language literacy and biliteracy may be approached from individual, community, societal, and crossnational perspectives. For language minorities, second language literacy/biliteracy is vital to have access to employment and to the social, political, and economic life of the prevailing society as well as in their local communities. Understanding both the distribution of literacy and access to equitable educational programs are particularly important because many language minorities do not have immediate access to literacy and schooling in their own languages.

• Chapter 30, by **Patricia Byrd**, reviews the teaching of English grammar that often bridges the foundations of theory and data about grammar, second language acquisition (SLA), and classroom teachers' beliefs and practices about teaching grammar. Byrd's broad-based approach shows how much shifting and change in grammar teaching has already occurred and suggests that other more or less continuous shifts can be certainly expected in the future. The two prevalent approaches in grammar instruction remain, in the United States, variations on Chomskyan transformational-generative grammar with its emphasis on underlying psychological processes and systems and the "language-in-use" focus of corpus linguistics and of other approaches to discourse analysis. The chapter discusses the forces that currently influence scholarship and practice in the teaching of grammar and the choices that can be made for effective, principled integration of grammar into curricula and lessons.

• Chapter 31, by **David Eskey**, takes the view that for L2 learners, reading may be both a means to the end of acquiring the language and an end in itself, as an essential skill. While many EFL students may rarely speak the L2 in their day-to-day lives, they may need to read it in order to access the wealth of information recorded exclusively in the language. Eskey explores the differences between learning to read in an L1 or L2 to emphasize that, unlike speaking skills that can be acquired naturally in L2 settings, literacy and reading must be taught because all writing systems are language-based and share some fundamental characteristics. Research suggests that teaching reading strategies can have positive effects on the reading performance of secondlanguage learners. According to Eskey, the issue is not just what strategies can be used and how to use them, but when to use them and for what purpose. In dealing with real texts, the issue is always what problems the text is creating for the reader and what strategies he or she might employ to address and solve these problems.

• Chapter 32, by **Paul Nation**, explores L2 vocabulary learning and points out that the task facing a learner is partly determined by the nature of vocabulary in general, and by the particular nature of English vocabulary. A substantial part of the difficulty of learning a word (its learning burden) depends on whether these aspects of an L2 word are similar to its L1 translation or are regular and predictable from already known L2 words of similar or related meaning. Vocabulary teaching is usually seen as teaching words. A major aim of Nation's chapter is to show that vocabulary teaching should have different foci when learners move from high-frequency to low-frequency vocabulary learning. In addition, vocabulary instruction must ensure that there is a balance of opportunities to learn from meaning-focused input, language-focused learning, meaning-focused output, and fluency development, and that vocabulary learning occurs within a well-planned vocabulary program.

• Chapter 33, by **John Hedgcock**, explores a great deal of research on L2 writing, which entails a spectrum of theoretical, empirical, and pedagogical developments. Hedgcock examines two significant and related influences that are likely to affect the focus of research and pedagogy as the L2 writing community shapes its future agenda. The first of these involves social constructionism, whereas the second concerns an increasingly critical approach to scholarship and pedagogy among the field's experts. Given the increasing influence of socioculturally oriented approaches to L2 literacy, a number of research venues seem to be valuable and profitable, and a few of these include: the L2 writer, the L2 writer's texts, the contexts for L2 writing, and the dynamic interaction among these components in authentic contexts for writing. These primary themes will provide the chapter framework that encompasses theoretical and empirical strands, as well as the central pedagogical issues.

• Chapter 34, by **Eli Hinkel**, takes a look at the analyses of L2 text. Three large domains of research focus on various properties of L2 written text: structuring of the information flow; syntactic, lexical, and rhetorical features of L2 text; and L2 grammar and lexical errors. Numerous studies have examined discoursal, lexical, syntactic, and rhetorical properties of L2 writing of speakers of dozens of languages. Investigations into L2 text have identified the important and significant differences that exist between L1 and L2 writing. Some of these differences stem from divergent written discourse paradigms valued in various rhetorical traditions and often transferred from L1 to L2, for example, discourse organization and information structuring, cohesion, coherence, and clarity. Other crucial factors that confound L2 writing and text have to do with shortfalls of writers' language proficiencies and restricted linguistic repertoire that significantly undermine L2 writers' ability to produce high-quality texts. Many researchers of L2 learning and development have emphasized that even school-age children or highly educated adult L2 learners require years of language training to attain the levels of proficiency necessary to create effective written prose.

REFERENCES

Carroll, J. (1981). Twenty-five years of research on foreign language aptitude. In K. Diller (Ed.), *Individual differences and universals in language learning aptitude* (pp. 83–118). Rowley, MA: Newbury House.

Chastain, K. (1975). Affective and ability factors in second language acquisition. *Language Learning, 25*(1), 153–161.

Nunnally, J. C. (1975). *Introduction to statistics for psychology and education.* New York: McGraw-Hill.

Perkins, D. N. (1985). *General cognitive skills: Why not thinking and learning skills?* Hillsdale, NJ: Lawrence Erlbaum Associates.

Simon, H. 1981/1996. *The science of the artificial.* Cambridge, MA: MIT Press.

23

Age in Second Language Development

Georgette Ioup
University of New Orleans

Consider the members of a hypothetical family that emigrate to a new country, settling in a community where no one speaks their language. Further imagine that this extended family covers an age range from 2 to 50, and that every member becomes fully integrated into the daily life of the new community. Most people when asked the probability that any member of this hypothetical family would become indistinguishable from a native speaker in ten years would give responses that form a descending curve, from 100% for the 2-year-old to 0% for the 50-year-old. Most likely the curve would descend gradually and level off near the age of 20. Do these common assumptions correspond with actual findings on age and second language learning?

In language acquisition theory the concept of a time frame for optimal acquisition of a language is known as the **critical period hypothesis** (CPH). It was first postulated by Lenneberg in 1967 with an onset of 2 years of age and a close at puberty. Lenneberg hypothesized that a decline in ability to acquire a natural language at puberty resulted from the end of neural plasticity and thus the completion of hemispheric lateralization in the human brain. Language learning after the close of the critical period would result in incomplete acquisition. Another way of stating the effect of a critical period is to say that after its close, **ultimate attainment** will be deficient in some way. Lenneberg drew major evidence for his hypothesis from data on recovery from aphasia (language loss) after major brain trauma, as well as acquisition patterns among the congenitally deaf and Down syndrome children. Recovery from aphasia is directly tied to the age at which the trauma occurs. Thus, children whose brain injuries resulted in language loss are likely to regain normal speech while adults are not so fortunate. Furthermore, only deaf individuals who had hearing restored before puberty appeared to achieve normal language acquisition. Lenneberg derived additional support for his position from the observed difficulty in second language learning after the onset of puberty.

Since his initial postulation of the CPH, several questions have plagued researchers. First, has an attested difference in ultimate attainment actually been observed when the acquisition onset (AO) occurs after the close of the critical period? Second, if there is a difference, what causes it? Is it the result of neurobiological maturational factors, or something else? Third, are there any particular aspects of language learning behavior that are affected by late AO? And fourth, how, if at all, does language learning aptitude influence outcomes either before or after the close of the critical period?

In what follows, I will review the studies that attempt to support or refute the critical period, then discuss the individual variables that have been suggested as the source of age differences: the natural decline in learning ability with normal aging, environmental factors such as amount of input available to the learner or access to instruction, the motivational/attitudinal disposition of the learner, crosslinguistic factors, and finally, the learner's aptitude for language learning. I will argue that although these variables can influence the degree to which late learners reach their full potential, they cannot explain why, given the same conditions, there is so much variability, and why, in the best of circumstances, the full potential of most adult acquisition falls short of nativelike attainment. With the exception of aptitude, these individual variables are viewed as necessary but not sufficient to ensure nativelike outcomes. The explanation this chapter puts forth is that there is a *fundamental difference* between child and adult language learning (Bley-Vroman, 1989). Children possess an ability that is lost in most adults—the ability to intuit the rule structure of the language without paying attention to it (Schmidt, 1983, p. 172). Nevertheless, a small number of adults do appear to realize near-native attainment, and only the variable of aptitude can ultimately shed light on how they are different.

THE CRITICAL PERIOD AND FIRST LANGUAGE ACQUISITION

Most researchers agree that there is a critical period for mother tongue or first language (L1) learning. Evidence from feral children who have been reintegrated into society and deaf children after their first exposure to sign language makes it clear that normal first language acquisition does not occur after a fixed age. Such children who have first exposure to language input in early childhood seem to achieve normal language acquisition while those who begin later come nowhere near native ultimate attainment. The most extensively studied case of feral language acquisition is that of Genie (Curtiss, 1977). Genie was discovered after the onset of puberty, having endured an abusive, silent childhood. Even after extensive tutoring by linguistic specialists, she was not able to gain the rule-structured dimensions of language (phonology, morphology, and syntax), although her vocabulary acquisition flourished.

However, since feral children have psychological issues with which to contend that might give rise to learning disabilities, it is more insightful to examine L1 acquisition in the congenitally deaf. Two case studies of language acquisition in deaf adults who had hearing restored upon being fitted with hearing aids after reaching puberty, give results similar to that of Genie. Chelsea (Curtiss, 1994) was fitted with hearing aids in her 30s, and EM (Grimshaw, Adelstein, Bryden, & MacKinnon, 1998) at age 15. Both exhibited severe structural deficits in the little language they were able to acquire. Extensive research comparing onset ages of American Sign Language (ASL) and attained proficiency comes to the same conclusion. Newport (1990) examined three groups of adults who had been using ASL for over 30 years: one group was exposed to ASL in infancy, one group had first exposure between ages 4 and 6, and one group first acquired ASL after age 12. Using morphological criteria, she found a negative correlation with age at first exposure to ASL among the three groups, confirming age constraints on L1 acquisition. (For excellent reviews of this and other evidence supporting a critical period for L1 acquisition, see Long, 1990; Harley & Wang, 1997; Hyltenstam & Abrahamsson, 2000.)

Critical Period Closure

Opinions vary on the age of closure for a critical period. Several large-scale studies of L2 learners note a difference in performance occurring in the teen years. Patkowski (1980) and Johnson and Newport (1989) set the cutoff point in the mid to late teens. However, a study by Mayberry (1993) of L1 learners suggests that the optimal period closes much earlier. Mayberry compared the L1 and L2 acquisition of ASL at different ages. Her subjects fall into four groups—three L1 groups who were congenitally deaf from birth and one L2 group. The three L1 were classified as follows: native signers who were exposed to ASL from their deaf parents, 2) childhood learners whose first exposure occurred between the ages of 5 and 8 when they entered a residential school for the deaf, and late acquirers who began ASL between ages 9 and 13. The L2 group lost hearing after they had already acquired a well-established spoken language, between the ages of 9 and 15. Subjects were tested on their ability to comprehend and reproduce long, complicated sentences. The childhood ASL onset did not perform like the infant learners, but rather were more similar to the late onset L2 signers, sometimes not even as good. These findings suggest that an onset of acquisition beyond the age of 5 is too late to achieve native proficiency in L1, and that the close of the critical period may be much earlier than previously thought. The study by Newport (1990) adds further support to an earlier terminus; her childhood ASL learners did not perform as well as the infant learners.

Additional evidence for an earlier closure comes from studies of child L2 learners. Mack (1998), investigating the perception of English vowels by Korean/English bilinguals, found that nativelike performance correlated with an age earlier than puberty. Subjects were divided into two groups based on their age of arrival in the United States (0-3 and 4-7) and were compared to native speakers. When they were asked to discriminate /i/ from /I/ and /u/ from /U/ (distinctions not made in Korean) in computer-synthesized continua of these pairs, only those who had first exposure to English before age 4 performed as the native speakers did. Additional variables such as length of exposure or degree of Korean proficiency did not strongly correlate with task accuracy. Other large-scale studies discovered slight accents in learners whose first exposure occurred before age 10 (Flege, Frieda, & Nozawa, 1997; Oyama, 1976, 1978; Thompson, 1991; Yeni-Komshian, & Liu, 1997).

Testing in the areas of syntax and semantics also uncovered prepuberty learners who did not match native-speaker performance (Hyltenstam, 1992; Johnson & Newport, 1989). A study by Ioup (1989) documented both syntactic and semantic deficits in university-level subjects who had immigrated between the ages of 6 and 10 and who had 10 years or more of exposure.

Several researchers have proposed the existence of multiple critical periods, each governing a different component of language. One of the first was Seliger (1978) who argued that plasticity in the language portions of the brain terminated according to different schedules, phonology being the first to close. Other researchers who expanded on this idea were Long (1990) and Eubank and Gregg (1999). Long suggested that the critical period for phonology closed at age 6, while those for morphology and syntax terminated near puberty. The acquisition of lexical semantics may remain available throughout an individual's life span.

MULTIPLE DEFINITIONS OF A CRITICAL PERIOD HYPOTHESIS

There is much less agreement on the applicability of the CPH to second language acquisition (L2). Some researchers argue that once a mother tongue is acquired, the cognitive mechanisms that allow for language acquisition are still intact and that from a neurological perspective second language acquisition is just as possible. Johnson and Newport (1989) describe this position as the **exercise hypothesis**. Once the language learning mechanism has been exercised, it remains available. Birdsong (1999) refers to this as the "use it or lose it" approach to the critical period. Others argue that the neurocognitive mechanisms of language acquisition become defective by the close of the critical period so that nativelike attainment in both L1 and L2 cannot occur after that point. Johnson and Newport label this view of the critical period as the **maturational constraint hypothesis.** The language acquisition mechanism deteriorates at a certain point in development causing further language acquisition to be less than optimal. Birdsong refers to this approach as the "use it then lose it" view of the critical period. Only the second definition predicts difficulty in adult L2 acquisition.

There is also disagreement on whether the biological time frame should be labeled a *critical period* since many claim that the term implies an abrupt closure (see Bialystok & Miller, 1999). The term *sensitive period*, which assumes a gradual decline in ability, has been suggested as more appropriate. Oyama (1979) and Long (1990) both point out that the critical period offset in animal species may also be gradual and variable; therefore, the terms *critical* and *sensitive* are often used interchangeably to describe a biologically determined developmental window of opportunity. I will continue to refer to this time frame as the *critical period* since it is the more commonly used term.

Is There Evidence for a Critical Period in L2?

Early support for a critical period in L2 acquisition is found in studies by Asher and Garcia (1969), Oyama (1976, 1978), and Patkowski (1980) comparing L2 acquirers with varying AOs to native speakers. Asher and Garcia assessed the accents of 71 Cuban learners of English and found that those who entered the United States at age 6 or earlier had the highest probability of being judged nativelike. Oyama tested 60 Italian-born immigrants to the United States whose AO was 6 to 20 years and who had a length of residence (LOR) from 5 to 18 years, comparing their performance to native-speaking controls. Subjects were rated by native-speaker judges on perceived accent (1976) then tested on their ability to comprehend sentences through white noise (1978). Only those who began L2 acquisition before age 10 performed in the range of the native-speaking controls.

Patkowski (1980) investigated the acquisition of syntax by assessing 67 immigrants from a variety of language backgrounds who were grouped into those arriving before and after age 15. Results again correlated negatively with age with all but one subject in the younger AO group scoring at a native-speaker level. Subjects in the older AO group produced a normal distribution curve with a few very poor performers, a few scoring very well, but most performing in the midrange. Patkowski concluded that the difference in the distributional function for the two groups provided evidence for a maturationally defined critical period. In the area of pronunciation, since these early studies, other research has documented similar age effects, but not all have been in full agreement as to the source of the age differences.

Until the early 1990s, studies of late arrivals tended to support the critical period hypothesis. Some studies compared adult acquirers to native speakers while others compared child and adult acquirers. One of the most widely cited studies is that of Johnson and Newport (1989). The study examined Korean and Chinese L2 learners of English who had migrated to the United States between the ages of 3 and 39. Half were early arrivals who came before the age of 15; the others were late arrivals who migrated after age 17. Subjects were asked to evaluate the grammaticality of 276 orally presented sentences that exemplified 12 morphological and syntactic constructions, counterbalanced between grammatical and ungrammatical items. Overall results correlated negatively with AO; however, age was relevant only before age 15, as the late learners' scores were randomly dispersed. Performance was within the range of native controls until age 7, declined linearly, but was still high until age 15, and exhibited no well-defined linear age effects in the adult acquirers. The authors concluded, therefore, that there was a maturational constraint on L2 acquisition.

Johnson (1992) replicated the Johnson and Newport (1989) study using an untimed written format. Again, subjects were Korean and Chinese. She found a weaker relationship between age and outcomes, with late arrivals performing in the range of the 8-15 year olds. Johnson attributed the difference to the advantage that time and the written format gave the subjects. Nevertheless, her results still exhibited an overall negative correlation between age of arrival and performance. Liu, Bates, and Li (1992) examined L2 sentence processing by Chinese learners of English. Subjects who began learning English before age 16 utilized the same strategies as the monolingual controls, whereas those who began learning after age 20 employed Chinese-based processing strategies.

Scovel (1988) presented convincing data from several studies to support a terminus at puberty for the ability to lose a foreign accent. Patkowski (1990) tested the same subjects who had participated in his 1980 study, this time on the relationship between age and degree of perceived accent. The results were similar to those found in the 1980 study in that there was a similar negative correlation with age and a discontinuity in the curve.

Several of the studies from this period restricted the investigation to learners who had achieved a near-native level of language competency. One of the first was Coppieters (1987). The study examined 21 very highly proficient second language speakers of French who had begun learning the L2 as adults and who were perceived by native speakers to be nativelike. The study had two parts, a grammaticality judgment test on subtle points of French grammar, and individual interviews with the author where generalizations governing the grammatical points tested were elicited. On the grammaticality judgment portion of the study, near-native speakers differed significantly from native speakers in their assessment of which sentences were correct. More important, the near-native speakers diverged from native speakers on the types of grammatical explanations they offered for the subtle rule-governed contrasts.

Sorace (1993) elicited grammaticality judgments from 20 L1 French and 24 L1 English near-native learners of Italian. Her study was restricted to the acquisition of auxiliary constructions in Italian. Like Coppieters, Sorace found the near-natives' intuitions of grammaticality to be substantially different from native-speaker controls. The French-speaking subjects exhibited divergence while the English-speaking subjects exhibited incompleteness.

Hyltenstam (1992) also limited his investigation to L2 learners who were judged to be nativelike; however, his study differed in that it examined only learners who had begun acquisition before puberty. Subjects were 24 adolescent bilinguals ages 17–18 who were enrolled in Swedish secondary schools. Half had Spanish as their L1 and half were native speakers of Finnish. Only subjects who were identified as nativelike in both phonology and syntax by their teachers were selected for the study. A second criterion was that they should be active bilinguals who used their native language on a regular basis. A demographically matched group of native speakers served as controls. Bilinguals were divided in to two groups, those who arrived on or before age 6 and those who arrived between age 7 and puberty.

Subjects were asked to retell orally four prepared texts and provide a written composition commenting on a silent film. The analysis consisted of counting the number of errors made by each subject. Although the frequency of error was low for all groups, there was a significant difference in the performance of the bilinguals and monolinguals. Hyltenstam found that the late childhood arrivals' performance was in complementary distribution with that of the native speakers. On the other hand, the error totals of early childhood arrivals sometimes matched those of the late arrivals and sometimes those of the native speakers. He also found that certain types of errors were only made by the bilingual subjects. He concluded that late childhood L2 learners do not attain an L1 level of ultimate attainment, even in those cases where the bilingual is perceived to be a native speaker in casual encounters with a monolingual. Whether or not early childhood L2 learners achieved native ultimate attainment may depend on external factors such as the frequency or intensity of L2 use.

MATURATION AND THE ACCESSIBILITY
OF UNIVERSAL GRAMMAR

A further line of inquiry in studies from the pre-1990 period investigated whether the principles and parameters of Universal Grammar (UG) that constrain L1 acquisition (Chomsky, 1981) are available to the second language learner. The question is whether L2 learners still have access to these principles and parameters. Several studies investigated the acquisition of the UG principle of *subjacency*[1] by adult learners whose native language did not manifest this principle. The findings were that adult acquirers did not perform like native speakers. Bley-Vroman, Felix, and Ioup (1988) determined that their adult-onset Korean learners averaged 75% accuracy on a grammaticality judgment measure, while native speakers averaged 95% accuracy. The results imply only partial access to subjacency. On the other hand, Schachter's (1989) study with similar subjects indicated a lack of access to subjacency, as her subjects performed at chance level.

Nevertheless, these results give no information on whether child L2 learners would acquire the principles and parameters of UG. This gap was filled by a study from Johnson and Newport (1991) that compared both early and late acquirers on the principle of subjacency. The study included subjects from four AO groups: 4 to 7, 8 to 13, 14 to 16, and adult, all with Chinese as their L1. Although none of the subjects performed in the range of native speakers, results indicated an effect for age of arrival. The curve declined until early adulthood onsets at which point performance was at chance level, providing further evidence for maturational constraints.

A study by Hilles (1991) testing the UG principle of *Morphological Unity*[2] with a small number of Spanish-speaking learners of English also obtained child/adult differences. Subjects were two children, two adolescents, and two adults in the early stages of L2 acquisition. The study utilized longitudinal data covering a period of 9 months. Only the two children and one of the adolescents followed an acquisition sequence guided by the *Morphological Unity Principle*. This study provides no information on their ultimate attainment, but does give insight into the ability of learners with differing onset ages to utilize the principles of Universal Grammar.

Young-Scholten (1994) examined the ability of adult L2 learners to access UG in the domain of phonology, namely, the ability to reset syllabification parameters when the new language required it. Using data from the L2 acquisition of several L1/L2 language pairs, she concluded that learners may not be able to reset parameters at the phonological level, but must rely on those set for the L1, especially if the settings of the target language were a subset of those in the native language and as a result, they required negative evidence that the L1 settings were not applicable to the L2.

Possible Exceptions to a Critical Period

Until the early 1990s, data-driven research on the critical period gave results that supported maturational constraints. Long's (1990) review article set out a case for a biologically defined period constraining language acquisition. He noted that unless exceptions were found where L2 ultimate attainment after puberty matched native-speaker competence, the critical period hypothesis should be accepted. However, as the 1990s progressed, studies began to question the validity of the CPH. A source of scepticism was the identification of learners who appeared to be exceptions.

Early studies of exceptional learners selected individuals who seemed to have prodigious language learning ability and then tested them in various neurocognitive domains to see how they differed from the norm (Novoa, Fein, & Obler, 1988; Schneiderman & Desmarais, 1988). The aim of these studies was to identify the cognitive correlates of language learning talent. Both studies reported exceptional incidental and verbal memory in their subjects; however, on measures of general intelligence, performance was in the average range. Ioup et al. (1994) did an in-depth analysis of two adult learners of Egyptian Arabic on measures of pronunciation quality, ability to differentiate dialects, grammaticality judgments, and semantic intuitions. The authors found that both subjects were near to or at native performance on all measures, a surprising result given that one of the subjects was untutored and illiterate in the L2.

One of the first to find near-native attainment in an experimental study was Birdsong (1992). He critiqued Coppieters' (1987) study that found gaps in attainment among near-native speakers of French, then conducted his own study using a grammatical judgment test combined with a think-aloud protocol. Fifteen of his subjects fell within the range of native-speaker performance. White and Genesee (1996) assessed the ability to acquire subtle properties of Universal Grammar using francophone near-native speakers of English who began L2 acquisition after puberty. Sixteen of their subjects exhibited nativelike performance on judgment and production measures.

A study by Bongaerts, Van Summeren, Planken, and Schils (1997) assessed the accents of highly proficient Dutch late-onset learners of English who had received extensive instruction in English phonetics. Judges found that many of these learners were indistinguishable from the native controls. The authors suggested that the results might be due to the fact that Dutch and English are typologically similar languages. To see if the results held with typologically dissimilar languages, Bongaerts (1999) evaluated the accents of highly proficient Dutch late-onset learners of French. Three subjects performed in the native-speaker range.

Many other studies assess the accents of learners with different ages of acquisition by using ratings made by native-speaking judges. Accent ratings produce the most variability across and within studies, and provide the least reliable method of establishing nativelike performance. Often learners who are judged comparable to native speakers on the basis of pronunciation are shown to have gaps elsewhere in their internal grammar (cf. Coppieters, 1987; Hyltenstam, 1992). Thompson (1991) rated accents in the spontaneous speech and oral reading of 36 Russian learners of English. She concluded that results on evaluative assessments of pronunciation are influenced by both the nature of the test and the type of judges doing the rating. Linguistically experienced raters were more reliable, but also more lenient than inexperienced raters. Orally read sentences were judged more accented than spontaneous speech. Flege (1999) also discussed variables that may affect rating judgments in studies that evaluate degree of accented speech.

Questioning the Critical Period Hypothesis

Even though studies began to question a biologically ordained critical period, for the most part, they continued to find the same inverse correlation between onset age and test performance, at both the phonological and morphosyntactic levels (Bialystok & Miller, 1999; Birdsong & Molis, 2001; Flege, Frieda & Nozawa, 1997; Flege, Monroe, & Skelton, 1992; Flege, Yeni-Komshian, & Liu, 1999; Stevens, 1999; Thompson, 1991;

Yeni-Komshian, Flege, & Liu, 1997). However, in contrast to the earlier studies, this later research argued that the distribution of the data was better explained by non-maturational factors.

Whether the observed age-related outcomes are the result of neurobiological factors or other variables is an important question that has implications for the theory of language acquisition, specifically the degree to which it is guided by a dedicated modular bioprogram specific to language. As Bialystok and Miller explain, "If the evidence fails to support the existence of such a biological constraint on language acquisition, then the options for language acquisition are more diverse but are based on a much larger role for general cognitive mechanisms and environmental influences throughout all stages of language acquisition" (p. 128).

One of the most frequently made arguments against maturational constraints is that there does not appear to be an identifiable change in the shape of the proficiency function at a point that defines the critical period terminus, something which the definition of a critical period demands. The change does not have to be abrupt, but there should be a period of heightened performance followed by a gradual decline to a plateau near the offset point that continues to show relatively high performance. The function should be discontinuous at this point with no further age-related decline (Newport, 1991). Instead, several studies indicate a steady decay in performance over the life span. A discontinuous nonlinear relationship across age groups would support a (Critical Period), while a linear function that extended from childhood through adulthood and exhibited an overall negative relationship between age and performance is claimed to provide evidence against it (Bialystok & Hakuta, 1999; Bialystok & Miller, 1999; Birdsong, to appear; Flege, 1999). The Johnson and Newport (1989) study exhibits the necessary discontinuous function. The under-15 group displayed a linearly declining learning curve while scores in the over-15 age group were randomly distributed.

Many recent studies, however, do not generate the Johnson and Newport findings. Rather, they document a steadily declining curve from childhood through adulthood. Two such studies examined data from the 1990 U.S. census. Both relied on self-report by immigrants to assess the degree of English fluency.[3] Stevens' (1999) findings led her to conclude that L2 proficiency is strongly related to age of immigration. However, she found no abruptly outlined critical period, but rather a steady decay with those immigrating before age 5 having the highest probability of reporting in adulthood that they spoke "very well." In addition, she determined that factors such as length of residence, higher levels of education, or marriage to a native-born spouse enhanced the probability of greater proficiency. Interestingly, the presence of English-speaking children in the household had little effect on their mother's level of proficiency.

Likewise, using the 1990 census Bialystok and Hakuta (1999) found a continuous age-related declining curve The data came from Chinese- and Spanish-speaking immigrants residing in New York state. Only those with LOR of 10 years or more were included for analysis. The curves for both groups were quite similar, although the Chinese group had lower overall self-reported proficiency. Bialystok and Hakuta concluded that factors other than an innate bioprogram were responsible for the decline. It is important to observe that the fact that performance continues to decline in adulthood as onset age increases does not, in and of itself, argue against a critical period terminus, for adults may become slower learners as they age.

Studies by Flege and his associates ascertained that degree of deviation from an L1 norm increased with age of acquisition onset, but the authors were frequently able to attribute their results to other variables. Non-age factors that affected outcomes were determined to be amount of L1 use (Flege, Frieda, & Nozawa, 1997), amount of L2 use (Flege & Liu, 2001; Flege, Bohn, & Jang, 1997), and amount of input (Flege, Frieda,

& Nozawa, 1997; Flege & Lui, 2001; Flege, Monroe, & Skelton, 1992; Riney & Flege, 1998). However, length of residence was not a significant factor.

Several recent studies administered a variation of the Johnson and Newport (1989) research. Bialystok and Miller (1999) administered a grammaticality judgment task with items similar to those of the Johnson and Newport study. Again, there was an effect for manner of presentation (written versus oral) and a steadily declining linear function across ages. Neither of these results is predicted by a biologically defined critical period. Flege, Yeni-Komshian, and Liu (1999) investigated ultimate attainment in both pronunciation and morphosyntax with 240 native Korean speakers, using for the latter a grammaticality judgment test drawn from Johnson and Newport. Performance in both areas produced an age-related declining function; however, only accent was influenced by AO. Both level of education and self-reported daily amount of English use influenced the morphosyntax results.

Birdsong and Molis (2001) did a replication of Johnson and Newport using the same methods and material, but with subjects from a very different language background, in this case, Spanish. Results were the inverse of Johnson and Newport—the younger group produced no age-related function while the older group did. There appeared to be a ceiling effect on early arrivals; most performed at the native speaker range, making very few errors. Among the late arrivals there was a gradually declining slope exhibiting a strong age effect. The divergent results may be a reflection of the use of different L1s in the two studies, in that the test may be easier for speakers of a language that shares typological similarities with English.

This was the conclusion reached in van Wuijtswinkel's (1994, cited in Kellerman, 1997) study using Dutch subjects in a foreign language environment to replicate Johnson and Newport. Though most had postpubertal initial exposure, performance was extremely high, a result attributed to the typological similarity of the L1 and L2. It appears then that the Johnson and Newport instrument is not as difficult for certain native-language groups.

A replication of Johnson and Newport by DeKeyser (2000) with L1 Hungarian speakers also produced results that diverged from the original study. Like Birdsong and Molis (2001), early arriving subjects exhibited a ceiling effect. However, the late arrivals presented no declining function; rather, their performance was random. Thus, findings for this group were similar to the Johnson and Newport study.

It is important to note that in these post-1990 studies with large subject pools, although variables other than age were able to influence the degree to which late learners attained L2 proficiency, few achieved the level of native speaker. This was true even after a long LOR and with specific variables working in their favor.

Other Explanations for Age Effects

One of the first to develop alternate explanations for any observed child/adult differences was Schumann (1975). He dismissed the biological explanation citing Krashen's (1973) research that argued that hemispheric lateralization was complete by age 5 (although Krashen, himself, did not rule out a different neurobiological explanation for age differences). Instead, Schumann advocated an explanation based on social/psychological factors arising from the social conditions in the environment or the motivational/attitudinal disposition of the learner. Language acquisition will be impeded when learners experience social distance (as part of a dominant, subordinate, or assimilating L2 culture, or from enclosure within a large L2 population confine) and/or psychological distance (when the attitude or motivation of the learner is not optimal). A recent discussion of non-age influences on ultimate attainment in an L2 is found in Marinova-Todd, Marshall, and Snow (2000). These authors also maintain that it is the situation of learning, rather than the potential for learning, that differentiates the attainment of adult and child learners.

Among the situations of learning, amount of L2 input and use figure prominently. Stevens (1999) determined that being married to a native speaker increased the probability of greater proficiency; however, for reasons as yet unknown, living with children who only spoke English did not. Riney and Flege (1998) ascertained that Japanese students who continued their studies in the L2 environment outperformed those who remained in Japan to study. Flege and Liu (2001) found that students enrolled in courses where they interacted with native speakers achieved higher proficiency than nonstudents whose contact was mainly with speakers of their L1. They concluded that it was the input-rich environment the students encountered that was responsible for their higher achievement. Flege, Frieda, and Nozawa (1997) determined that learners who have more contact with native speakers and hence, more input, achieved better accent ratings than learners in L2 contexts that provided less interaction. Since increased input and use correlates with higher attainment, one would expect that length of residence would also be a significant variable; however, few studies have found this to be the case. One is at a loss to explain why longer lengths of residence, which imply greater input and use, do not correlate with increased attainment, as the research would predict.

Several studies established that education impacted level of attainment. Flege, Yeni-Komshian, and Liu (1999) correlated increased proficiency with three variables, one of which was the amount of U.S. education. Whereas degree of foreign accent was related to AO, and performance on lexically based aspects of morphosyntax improved as L2 use increased, achievement on rule-based morphosyntactic portions of the test was a function of the amount of U.S. education the subjects had received. Moyer (1999) found that prior training in pronunciation was related to degree of perceived accent among highly motivated graduate students in German, with those who had received more training achieving the better scores. Likewise, in Bongaerts, van Summeren, Planken, and Schils (1997), more nativelike accents were produced by subjects who had received extensive instruction in phonetics. Stevens' (1999) census survey determined that higher levels of education increased the probability of greater proficiency. The fact that education has some influence on adult attainment actually argues **for** a child/adult difference, since L2 children are cognitively too immature for education to impact their acquisition.

A number of researchers have concluded that L1 influence is responsible for some of the age-related effects. Interestingly, some have found that it produced a positive impact, while others have documented a negative influence. Early on, Wode (1978) noted that similarities between the native and target language could have a debilitating effect. He described the *crucial similarity measure* where learners would assume that similar L1 and L2 structures were identical, thus slowing down their acquisition of those structures. He noted that German-speaking children added an extra step to their acquisition of English negation, one not found in the acquisition patterns of children learning English from typologically dissimilar L1 backgrounds. Since English and German negation pattern so closely, the children assumed a complete overlap and incorporated into their L2 grammars a German rule that does not exist in English.

In a similar vein, Flege (1995, 1999) developed the *speech learning model* to account for age effects in degree of foreign accent. He theorized that the mechanisms needed to produce new sounds remain intact throughout the life span, but that late-onset learners experience difficulty perceiving L2 phones that do not contrast in their L1, since the ability to discern new contrasts decreases with age (1995, p. 239). Thus, sounds that are similar but not quite the same in both languages will be the hardest to master. Conversely, the greater the dissimilarity between the L1 and L2 sounds, the more likely it is that the learner will notice the difference and thus not rely on the L1 to produce the L2 phone.

On the other hand, some have found that similarity between L1 and L2 structures facilitates acquisition. Bialystok (1997), in two small studies, determined that the correspondence between structures in the L1 and L2 was the best predictor of success. The first examined the acquisition of gender marking by English and German speakers learning French. German speakers, who already possessed the concept of gender marking, performed more accurately on French gender across ages of arrival. The second study tested Chinese speakers learning English. Test structures that were similar in the two languages were consistently easier regardless of arrival age. Bialystok and Miller (1999) compared native speakers of Chinese and Spanish who were learning English. Though the two groups were matched on relevant variables, the Spanish speakers outperformed the Chinese speakers. The authors suggested that the typological similarity between Spanish and English allowed the Spanish speakers to progress more rapidly. With the Chinese subjects, any structural similarity that occurred facilitated the acquisition. They concluded that those aspects of the L2 that are structurally different from the L1 are more difficult to master at all acquisition ages. It is important to note, however, that L1 influence only seems to impact adults, since the morpheme studies done in the 1970s using child second language learners do not show any mother tongue influence, either positive or negative.

Some researchers have attributed child/adult differences to the decline in cognitive learning ability that accompanies aging. Bialystok and Hakuta (1999) discuss several studies that documented the deterioration; for example, older learners perform more poorly on paired-associate tasks (Craik, 1986), are more cautious in cognitive tasks (Birkhill & Schaie, 1975), require more trials to learn a list (Rabinowitz & Craik, 1986), and have difficulty remembering details (Hultsch & Dixon, 1990). From these studies they concluded that one explanation for the age-related decline found in most L2 research on age differences is the natural cognitive deterioration that accompanies the aging process. Although Bialystok and Hakuta make no mention of the age at which natural cognitive deterioration begins, one assumes that it would not commence until well past age 35. Schaie and Willis (1996) discussed research that followed subjects, ages 25 to 88, as they performed a range of cognitive tasks. As expected, the data show modest gains in cognitive ability from young adulthood to early middle age, then a gradual decline. Herein lies the problem with attributing the results from studies of age differences in L2 to natural aging. The peak performance in all studies of L2 ultimate attainment is found with learners who began the task before age 6 or 7. Learning started later than that begins to produce the age-related decline. No other area of cognitive learning produces such an advantage for learners younger than age 7. Studies of natural aging do not see a cognitive decline in learning ability until early middle age. Thus, it is hard to see how the natural aging process could be responsible for the critical period age effects found in second language acquisition.

Comparing Child/Adult Acquisition

Several studies document similarities in the manner in which learners with different AOs respond on grammaticality judgment measures. They observe that even though subjects with early AOs exhibit higher performance, they respond with the same error patterns as those with later onsets. Thus, Juffs and Harrington (1995) found the same degree of subjacency transfer in older and younger onset Chinese learners of English. Bialystok and Miller (1999) also found no transfer difference as a function of age with their Chinese learners of English. If a biologically defined critical period is responsible for age effects, one might expect to see differences in the error types made by those within and outside the time frame. The fact that younger and older learners appear to follow the same course of acquisition provides indirect evidence against a critical period. Recently, Schwartz (1998) argued that both child and adult L2 learners have full access to UG. Therefore, in terms of the abstract properties of language, the same acquisition sequences should be followed.

In contrast to Schwartz, Meisel (1997) found that adults do not have full access to UG. He presented L2 data from adults with a number of L1 backgrounds acquiring either German or French negation. Although the various L1/L2 combinations make different predictions for the stages of learning negation, none of the predictions were observed. In contrast to earlier research, Meisel concluded that L2 adults acquiring negation differ from L1 children in that UG does not guide the process.

The same conclusion was reached by Clahsen and Muysken (1986). They compared the acquisition of German word order by L1 children and L2 adults from several L1 backgrounds. The children, through access to UG, quickly realized that German was a verb final language. Adults, in contrast, relied on general learning strategies and therefore, had difficulty, even in late stages, producing the correct word order. Another study that found that child and adult L2 follow different paths with respect to UG is Hilles (1991), discussed earlier.

Non-UG contrasts in child/adult L2 development were observed in Ioup and Tansomboon (1987). The study compared the Thai proficiency of Thai/English bilingual children to that of both beginning and very fluent adults whose L1 was English. Both syntactic and phonological performance were assessed. The authors found that the children were consistently more proficient in phonological aspects of Thai, while both groups of adults were more proficient on the syntactic measures. The child learners outperformed all of the adults on subtle aspects of Thai tone. It appears that what is easiest to acquire is not the same for children and adults.

CASE STUDY SUPPORT FOR A CRITICAL PERIOD

Now let us turn from experimental studies to case studies. Wong-Fillmore (1979) and Schmidt (1983) make for two interesting case study comparisons. Wong-Fillmore observed five Spanish-speaking children, ages 5 to 7, in the early stages of learning English, noting the similarities and differences in their approaches to the task. The study, covering a period of 1 year, allowed for several generalizations that held for all the children. Wong-Fillmore determined that social integration was their main focus; in contrast, they were not particularly concerned with the task of learning a new language. It was more important for them to be socially accepted by the English-speaking children than to learn the language they spoke. Wong-Fillmore predicted that by the end of three years all the children would be fluent English speakers; thus, the individual differences that she described were confined to rate of acquisition only. Interestingly, Nora, the child who progressed far more rapidly than any of the others, was the one who was most socially adept and least concerned with language structure. The one who progressed the least was the child who was most preoccupied with being accurate.

Schmidt (1983) provided a contrasting picture using naturalistic adult acquisition. He detailed the English acquisition of a 33-year-old native speaker of Japanese over the course of three years. The subject, Wes, had made little grammatical progress by the end of the study; thus, his functional grammar remained stabilized. Yet in all respects, Wes seemed to employ the same strategies as Nora, the most successful learner in the Wong-Fillmore study. He was little concerned with grammatical structure, was most interested in making friends with Americans, spent most of his time conversing with English speakers, and was gregarious and outgoing. Clearly, like, Nora, social integration was much more important to him than advancing his knowledge of English.

Schmidt (personal communication) reports that after 20 years of speaking mainly English, Wes's grammatical output had still not improved. One can conclude from a comparison of these two studies that what works naturally for a child to facilitate L2 acquisition does not work at all for an adult. Moreover, one can safely assume that if Wes had been 6 years old instead of 29 in his initial stages of English acquisition, and doing exactly what he was doing as an adult learner, he would have been quite close to nativelike by the end of the 3-year study.

Lardiere (1998) presents a second case study of an adult learner who does "everything right" but still does not advance very far in English. The subject, Patty, is an Indonesian whose home language was Chinese and school language was Indonesian. At age 14, she immigrated from Indonesia to China where she completed her secondary schooling, including a bit of English instruction. At age 22, she moved to the United States and attended a junior college that provided ESL classes.

As stated earlier, most recent age-related research claims that it is the situation of learning, rather than the potential for learning, that is the best predictor of successful ultimate attainment. Factors said to positively enhance the learning situation are daily use of the L2 (Flege, Frieda, & Nozawa, 1997; Flege & Liu, 2001; Riney & Flege, 1998), marriage to a native-speaking spouse (Stevens, 1999), and high levels of education in the L2 (Bialystok & Hakuta, 1994, 1999; Flege, Yeni-Komshian, & Liu, 1999; Stevens, 1999). All these variables characterize Patty.

After attending community college, Patty earned a B.A. and M.A. in accounting at American universities. She subsequently married an American and joined an American company in a senior management position, totally immersing herself in an English-speaking environment. Thus at home, at work, with her family, neighbors, and friends, she spoke English exclusively. Lardiere reports that after living in the United States for almost 18 years, Patty had a fossilized end-state grammar replete with basic errors. This fossilization was determined through observations that were implemented at the end of her tenth and eighteenth year in the United States. During that eight-year interim of total immersion, her grammar did not become more nativelike. We see that although Patty had all the variables necessary to predict successful language acquisition, she did not, in fact, succeed. Her lack of success occurred in spite of the fact that she had an extra advantage that L2 children do not have, one that they are not cognitively mature enough to avail themselves of, that is, formal ESL instruction.

The Role of Aptitude

One case study (Ioup et al., 1994) does not fit the profile described in the previous section. The two subjects in this study tested at close to native speaker performance. Both subjects were English speakers living in Egypt and married to Egyptian nationals. They differed in that one had extensive formal instruction in Arabic, while the other had learned the language through exposure alone. To make her situation more like child language acquisition, the latter subject never learned to read Arabic. Marinova-Todd, Marshall, and Snow (2000), commenting on the success of these two learners, attributed their level of attainment to their high level of motivation, but no such claim can be made because the Ioup et al. study also included similar learners who did not approximate native performance. They were also foreign nationals who had married Egyptians, had long periods of residence in Egypt, had studied Arabic, and had exerted great effort to master the language. At the time of testing, these learners were very fluent, but noticeably non-native. Thus, one has no basis to claim that they were less motivated than the successful learners. Marinova-Todd et al. also attributed the attainment of the two successful learners to the fact that they were language teachers who, therefore, understood linguistic structure. However, the nonsuccessful learners in the study were also professional language teachers. What, then, accounts for the remarkable achievement of the two successful learners? Ioup et al. attributed it to *language-learning aptitude*, asserting that this was the essential variable that distinguished successful from nonsuccessful adult acquisition.

Two data-based studies provide support for the role of aptitude: DeKeyser (2000) and Harley and Hart (1997). Harley and Hart examined 11th grade French immersion students, comparing those who had begun immersion in the first grade with those who had begun it in the seventh grade on proficiency and aptitude measures. There was a difference in how the two groups performed; only the proficiency scores of the late immersion students correlated with analytic language aptitude. The results led the authors to conclude that this type of aptitude is not relevant to child L2 acquisition.

DeKeyser tested 57 Hungarian immigrants to the United States with varying AOs on both grammaticality judgments and language learning aptitude. Results indicated that all but one of the subjects whose acquisition began before the age of 15 performed in the native speaker range. The scores of those arriving after age 15 were randomly distributed with only six performing like the child learners. The correlation between the grammaticality judgment scores and scores on the aptitude test were significant for the adult onset learners only. DeKeyser maintained that the late-onset learners who performed in the near-native range possessed a special talent for language learning. He explained his results by embracing the *fundamental difference hypothesis* (Bley-Vroman, 1989), which contends that children acquire language through an innate language-specific bioprogram while adults must rely on general cognition and knowledge obtained from their first language.

CONCLUSION

This chapter has reviewed the research on age in L2 development and has concluded that child and adult language acquisition are fundamentally different, thus supporting the maturational constraint version of the critical period hypothesis that argues for a modular language acquisition mechanism available to child learners only. Findings indicate that while certain variables significantly advance adult acquisition, they alone do not guarantee nativelike attainment. Subtle, and often not-so-subtle aspects of language appear to allude adults, even when they avail themselves of formal instruction. Only children are able to acquire the subtle properties of a language without paying attention to them. The few adult exceptions to the critical period hypothesis have high language learning aptitude.

One gap has been observed in research on the critical period. There are few studies that provide an in-depth examination of the processes of *child* L2 acquisition, comparing them to both child L1 and adult L2. More information on the availability of UG to child L2 learners is needed, as well as information on the factors that enhance or impede their progress.

NOTES

1. *Subjacency* is the principle of UG that governs when movement can occur across boundaries. It has particular consequences for *wh-* preposing.
2. The *Morphological Unity* principle governs the permissibility of null subjects in a language. It states that null subjects can only exist in languages where either all verb forms are morphologically complex (e.g., Spanish), or none are (e.g., Chinese).
3. Self-report is not always reliable. In recently obtained census data from 1930, which indicated the responses of my father's family, my grandmother claimed to both speak English and be literate. Neither was true. Until her death in 1951, she spoke no English at all, and could neither read nor write in any language.

REFERENCES

Asher, J. & Garcia, R. (1969). The optimal age to learn a foreign language. *Modern Language Journal, 53,* 1219–1227.

Bialystok, E. (1997). The structure of age: In search of barriers to second-language acquisition. *Second Language Research, 13,* 116–137.

Bialystok, E. & Hakuta, K. (1994). *In other words: The psychology and science of second language acquisition.* New York: Basic Books.

Bialystok, E. & Hakuta, K. (1999). Confounded age: Linguistic and cognitive factors in age differences for second language acquisition. In D. Birdsong (Ed.), *Second language acquisition and the critical period hypothesis* (pp. 161–181). Mahwah, NJ: Lawrence Erlbaum Associates.

Bialystok, E. & Miller, B. (1999). The problem of age in second-language acquisition: Influences from language, structure, and task. *Bilingualism: Language and Cognition, 2,* 127–145.

Birdsong, D. (1992). Ultimate attainment in second language acquisition. *Language, 68,* 706–755.

Birdsong, D. (1999). Introduction: Whys and why nots of the critical period hypothesis for second language acquisition. In D. Birdsong (Ed.), *Second language acquisition and the critical period hypothesis* (pp. 1–22). Mahwah, NJ: Lawrence Erlbaum Associates.

Birdsong, D. (to appear). Interpreting age effects in second language acquisition. In J. Kroll & A. de Groot (Eds.), *Handbook of bilingualism: Psycholinguistic perspectives.* Oxford, UK: Oxford University Press.

Birdsong, D. & Molis, M. (2001). On the evidence for maturational constraints on second-language acquisition. *Journal of Memory and Language, 44,* 235–249.

Birkhill, W. & Schaie, K. (1975). The effect of differential reinforcement of cautiousness in the intellectual performance of the elderly. *Journal of Gerontology, 30,* 578–583.

Bley-Vroman, R. (1989). What is the logical problem of second language learning? In S. Gass & J. Schachter (Eds.), *Linguistic perspectives on second language acquisition* (pp. 41–68). Cambridge, UK: Cambridge University Press.

Bley-Vroman, R., Felix, S., & Ioup, G. (1988). The accessibility of universal grammar in adult language learning. *Second Language Research, 4,* 1–32.

Bongaerts, T. (1999). Ultimate attainment in L2 pronunciation: The case of very advanced late L2 learners. In D. Birdsong (Ed.), *Second language acquisition and the critical period hypothesis* (pp. 133–159). Mahwah, NJ: Lawrence Erlbaum Associates.

Bongaerts, T., van Summeren, C., Planken, B., & Schils, E. (1997). Age and ultimate attainment in the pronunciation of a foreign language. *Studies in Second Language Learning, 19,* 447–465.

Chomsky, N. (1981). *Lectures on government and binding.* Dordrecht, The Netherlands: Foris.

Clahsen, H. & Muysken, P. (1986). The availability of universal grammar to adult and child learners: A study of the acquisition of German word order. *Second Language Research, 2,* pp. 93–119.

Coppieters, R. (1987). Competence differences between native and near-native speakers. *Language, 63,* 544–575.

Craik, F. (1986). A functional account of age differences in memory. In F. Klix & H. Hagendorf (Eds.), *Human memory and cognitive capabilities* (pp. 409–422). Amsterdam: Elsevier.

Curtiss, S. (1977). *Genie: A psycholinguistic study of a modern-day 'wild child.'* New York: Academic Press.

Curtiss, S. (1994). Language as a cognitive system: Its independence and selective vulnerability. In C. Otero (Ed.), *Noam Chomsky: Critical assessments* (pp. 211–255). London: Routledge.

DeKeyser, R. (2000). The robustness of critical period effects in second language acquisition. *Studies in Second Language Acquisition, 4,* 499–533.

Eubank, L. & Gregg, K. (1999). Critical periods and (second) language acquisition: Divide and Impera. In D. Birdsong (Ed.), *Second language acquisition and the critical period hypothesis* (pp. 65–99). Mahwah, NJ: Lawrence Erlbaum Associates.

Flege, J. (1995). Second language speech learning theory, findings, and problems. In W. Strange (Ed.), *Speech perception and linguistic experience: Issues in cross-language research* (pp. 233–277). Baltimore: York Press.

Flege, J. (1999). Age of learning and second language speech. In D. Birdsong (Ed.), *Second language acquisition and the critical period hypothesis* (pp. 101–131). Mahwah, NJ: Lawrence Erlbaum Associates.

Flege, J., Bohn, O.-S., & Jang, S. (1997). The effect of experience on non-native subjects' production and perception of English vowels. *Journal of Phonetics, 25,* 169–186.

Flege, J., Frieda, A., & Nozawa, T. (1997). Amount of native-language (L1) use affects the pronunciation of an L2. *Journal of Phonetics, 25,* 169–186.

Flege, J. & Liu, S. (2001). The effect of experience on adults' acquisition of a second language. *Studies in Second Language Acquisition, 23,* 527–552.

Flege, J., Monroe, M., & Skelton, L. (1992). The production of word-final English /t/-/d/ contrast by native speakers of English, Mandarin, and Spanish. *Journal of the Acoustical Society of America, 92,* 128–143.

Flege, J., Yeni-Komshian, G., & Liu, S. (1999). Age constraints on second-language acquisition. *Journal of Phonetics, 25,* 169–186.

Grimshaw, G., Adelstein, A., Bryden, P., & MacKinnon, G. (1998). First language acquisition in adolescence: Evidence for a critical period for verbal language development. *Brain and Language, 63,* 237–255.

Harley, B. & Hart, D. (1997). Language aptitude and second language proficiency in classroom learners of different starting ages. *Studies in Second Language Acquisition, 19*, 379–400.

Harley, B. & Wang, W. (1997). The critical period hypothesis: Where are we now? In A. de Groot & J. Kroll (Eds.), *Tutorials in bilingualism: Psycholinguistic perspectives* (pp. 19–51). Mahwah, NJ: Lawrence Erlbaum Associates.

Hilles, S. (1991). Access to universal grammar in second language acquisition. In L. Eubank (Ed.), *Point counterpoint: Universal grammar in second language acquisition* (pp. 305–338). Philadelphia: Benjamins.

Hultsch, D. & Dixon, R. (1990). Learning and memory and aging. In J. Birren & K. Schaie (Eds.) *Handbook of the psychology of aging* (3rd ed. pp. 258–274). New York: Academic Press.

Hyltenstam, K. (1992). Non-native features of near-native speakers: On the ultimate attainment of childhood L2 learners. In R. J. Harris (Ed.), *Cognitive processing in bilinguals* (pp. 351–368). Amsterdam: Elsevier.

Hyltenstam, K. & Abrahamsson, N. (2000). Who can become nativelike in a second language? All, some, or none? On the maturational constraints controversy in second language acquisition. *Studia Linguistica, 54*, 150–166.

Ioup, G. (1989). Immigrant children who have failed to acquire native English. In S. Gass, C. Madden, D. Preston, & L. Selinker (Eds.), *Variation in second language acquisition: Vol. 2. Psycholinguistic issues* (pp. 160–175). Clevedon, UK: Multilingual Matters.

Ioup, G., Boustagui, E., El Tigi, M., & Moselle, M. (1994). Reexamining the critical period hypothesis: A case study of successful adult SLA in naturalistic environment. *Studies in Second Language Acquisition, 16*, 73–98.

Ioup, G. & Tansomboon, A. (1987). The acquisition of tone: A maturational perspective. In G. Ioup & S. Weinberger (Eds.), *Interlanguage phonology: The acquisition of a second language sound system* (pp. 333–349). Rowley, MA: Newbury House.

Johnson, J. (1992). Critical period effects in second language learning: The effects of written versus auditory materials on the assessment of grammatical competence. *Language Learning, 42*, 217–248.

Johnson, J. & Newport, E. (1989). Critical period effects in second language learning: The influence of maturational state on the acquisition of English as a second language. *Cognitive Psychology, 21*, 60–99.

Johnson, J. & Newport, E. (1991). Critical period effects on universal properties of language: The use of subjacency in the acquisition of a second language. *Cognition, 39*, 215–258.

Juffs, A. & Harrington, M. (1995). Parsing effects in L2 sentence processing: Subject and object asymmetries in *wh*- extraction. *Studies in Second Language Acquisition, 17*, 483–516.

Kellerman, E. (1997). Age before beauty: Johnson and Newport revisited. In L. Eubank, L. Selinker, & M. Sharwood Smith (Eds.), *The current state of interlanguage* (pp. 219–231). Philadelphia: Benjamins.

Krashen, S. (1973). Lateralization, language learning, and the critical period: Some new evidence. *Language Learning, 23*, 63–74.

Lardiere, D. (1998). Case and tense in the 'fossilized' steady state. *Second Language Research, 14*, 1–12.

Lenneberg, E. (1967). *Biological foundations of language.* New York: Wiley.

Liu, H., Bates, E., & Li, P. (1992). Sentence interpretation in bilingual speakers of English and Chinese. *Applied Psycholinguistics, 12*, 251–285.

Long, M. (1990). Maturational constraints on language development. *Studies in Second Language Acquisition, 12*, 251–285.

Mack, M. (1998). English vowel perception in early Korean-English bilinguals and English monolinguals: Is there a difference? Paper presented at the Annual Conference of the American Association for Applied Linguistics, Seattle, WA.

Marinova-Todd, S., Marshall, D., & Snow, C. (2000). Three misconceptions about age and L2 learning. *TESOL Quarterly, 34*, 9–34.

Mayberry, R. (1993). First language acquisition after childhood differs from second language acquisition: The case of American sign language. *Journal of Speech and Hearing Research, 36*, 1258–1270.

Meisel, J. (1997). The acquisition of the syntax of negation in French and German: Contrasting first and second language development. *Second Language Research, 13*, 227–263.

Moyer, A. (1999). Ultimate attainment in L2 phonology. The critical factors of age, motivation, and instruction. *Studies in Second Language Acquisition, 21*, 81–108.

Newport, E. (1990). Maturational constraints on language learning. *Cognitive Science, 14*, 11–28.

Newport, E. (1991). Contrasting conceptions of the critical period for language. In S. Carey & R. Gelman (Eds.), *The epigenesis of mind: Essays on biology and cognition* (pp. 111–130. Hillsdale, NJ: Lawrence Erlbaum Associates.

Novoa, L., Fein, D., & Obler, L. (1988). Talent in foreign languages: A case study. In L. Obler & D. Fein (Eds.), *The exceptional brain: The neuropsychology of talent and special abilities* (pp. 294–302). New York: Guilford.

Oyama, S. (1976). A sensitive period of the acquisition of a nonnative phonological system. *Journal of Psycholinguistic Research, 5*, 261–283.

Oyama, S. (1978). The sensitive period and comprehension of speech. *Working Papers on Bilingualism, 16*, 1–17.

Oyama, S. (1979). The concept of the sensitive period in developmental studies. *Merrill-Palmer Quarterly, 25*, 83–102.

Patkowski, M. (1980). The sensitive period for the acquisition of syntax in a second language. *Language Learning, 30*, 449–472.

Patkowski, M. (1990). Age and accent in a second language: A reply to James Emil Flege. *Applied Linguistics, 11*, 73–89.

Rabinowitz, J. & Craik, F. (1986). Prior retrieval effects in young and old adults. *Journal of Gerontology, 41*, 368–375.

Riney, T., & Flege, J. (1998). Changes over time in global foreign accent and liquid identifiability and accuracy. *Studies in Second Language Acquisition, 20*, 213–244.

Schachter, J. (1989). Testing a proposed universal. In S. Gass & J. Schachter (Eds.), *Linguistic perspectives on second language acquisition* (pp. 73–88). New York: Cambridge University Press.

Schaie, K. & Willis, S. (1996). Psychometric intelligence and aging. In F. Blanchard-Fields & T. Hess (Eds.), *Perspectives on cognitive change in adulthood and aging* (pp. 293–322). New York: McGraw-Hill.

Schmidt, R. (1983). Interaction, acculturation, and the acquisition of communicative competence: A case study of an adult. In N. Wolfson & E. Judd (Eds.), *Sociolinguistics and language acquisition* (pp. 137–174). Rowley, MA: Newbury House.

Schneiderman, E. & Desmarais, C. (1988). The talented language learner: Some preliminary findings. *Second Language Research, 4*, 91–109.

Schumann, J. (1975). Affective factors and the problem of age in second language acquisition. *Language Learning, 25*, 209–235.

Schwartz, B. (1998). The second language instinct. *Lingua, 106*, 133–160.

Scovel, T. (1988). *A time to speak: A psycholinguistic inquiry into the critical period for human speech.* Rowley, MA: Newbury House.

Seliger, H. (1978). Implications of a multiple critical period hypothesis for second language learning. In W. Ritchie (Ed.), *Second language research: Issues and implications* (pp. 11–19). New York: Academic Press.

Sorace, A. (1993). Incomplete vs. divergent representations of unaccusativity in non-native grammars of Italian. *Second Language Research, 9*, 22–47.

Stevens, G. (1999). Age at immigration and second language proficiency among foreign-born adults. *Language in Society, 28*, 555–578.

Thompson, I. (1991). Foreign accents revisited: The English pronunciation of Russian immigrants. *Language Learning, 41*, 177–204.

van. Wuijtswinkel, K. (1994). *Critical period effects on the acquisition of grammatical competence in a second language.* B.A. thesis, Nijmegen University.

White, L. & Genesee, F. (1996). How native is near-native? The issue of ultimate attainment in adult second language acquisition. *Second Language Research, 12*, 233–265.

Wong-Fillmore, L. (1979). Individual differences in second language acquisition. In C. Fillmore (Ed.), *Individual differences in language ability and language behavior* (pp. 203–228). New York: Academic Press.

Wode, H. (1978). Developmental sequences in naturalistic L2 acquisition. In E. Hatch (Ed.), *Second language acquisition: A book of readings* (pp. 101–117). Rowley, MA: Newbury House.

Yeni-Komshian, G., Flege, J., & Liu, H. (1997). Pronunciation of proficiency in L1 and L2 among Korean-English bilinguals: The effect of age of arrival in the U.S. *Journal of the Acoustical Society of America, 102(A)*, 3138.

Young-Scholten, M. (1994). On positive evidence and L2 attainment in L2 phonology. *Second Language Research, 10*, 193–214.

24

Cognitive Considerations in L2 Learning

Robert DeKeyser and Alan Juffs
University of Pittsburgh

INTRODUCTION

Nobody would doubt that language, whether first or second, is an aspect of human cognition. The extent, however, to which language either occupies a separate component of the mind or draws largely on the same mechanisms as other aspects of cognition is hotly debated (see, e.g., Elman et al., 1996; Fodor, 1983, 2000; Jackendoff, 2002; Pinker, 1997 for L1; O'Grady, 1999; Schwartz, 1999; Wolfe-Quintero, 1996 for L2). It is not our intention, of course, to try to resolve this debate here. We have referred to it where necessary, but thought it much more fruitful, given the subject matter of this book, and the shortness of this chapter, to concentrate on what the content of L2 cognition is.

Cognition is really a fancy word for knowledge, its acquisition, and its use. Hence, the main questions we ask in this chapter are simply: How do people come to know elements of/about L2? (Sources of L2 Knowledge), and how do they use what they know of/about L2? (Resources for use in L2). Our main goal will be to show the multiplicity of the answer to both questions. Learners acquire some specific knowledge about the structure of L2 explicitly (with concurrent awareness of what is being learned) and some implicitly (without such awareness). They also have a certain amount of less structured, 'formulaic' knowledge specific to L2, as well as knowledge transferred from L1, and perhaps access to Universal Grammar (UG). On top of this 'real' knowledge, they may have all sorts of misconceptions about what transfers from L1 or L2 or other aspects of L2 structure. This is part of their 'knowledge' too.

When L2 speakers get to use this knowledge, their actual behavior is even more multifaceted. They draw on their knowledge about L2 structure, whether that knowledge be specific to L2, transferred from L1, or part of their biological endowment. They draw variably on universal processing strategies, L1 processing skills, and incipient L2 processing strategies and skills. They put certain structures together from scratch, but often use ready-made chunks. For some structures at some point in time, they consciously access explicit knowledge (knowledge they are aware of); for other structures or at other times they intuitively access implicit knowledge (knowledge they are not aware of). These forms of knowledge may have been acquired implicitly or explicitly, and may or may not have been transformed from explicit to implicit ('proceduralized' and 'automatized') through large amounts of practice, or from implicit to explicit ('analyzed') through reflection.

Just as we have largely sidestepped the issue of whether language is a separate component of human cognition, we have also tried to avoid the terms *competence* and *performance* as much as possible, given that there is a long history of contentious debate about what aspects of language variability fit into *competence* (e.g., R. Ellis, 1990; Gregg, 1990; Tarone, 1990, 2002). Instead, we prefer to speak simply about *knowledge* and *use*. In what follows, then, we will simply discuss (the evidence for) various kinds of knowledge sources and uses in L2, and try to point out what seems well established, and what remains unknown or controversial.

Sources of L2 Knowledge

Universal Grammar

Universal Grammar (UG) is a theory of the linguistic knowledge that human beings bring to the task of acquiring a first language. This knowledge is expressed as a formal grammar that *precisely* describes all categories, and clearly states grammatical relations as operations on those categories (Hall, 1995; Fodor, 2000, p. 11). The precise and detailed nature of such grammars is perhaps their greatest strength.

Most research on UG in the past 20 years has been conducted in the Chomskyan paradigm, known as 'Principles and Parameters' (Chomsky, 1986), which has transformed into 'Minimalism' (Chomsky, 1995). The new theory consists of the lexicon (a learned component), a system of constraints that limit interpretation of combinations of items drawn from the lexicon, as well as a system of constraints on phonology. The constraints provide a system of principles that all languages adhere to; such principles account for similarities among languages. Languages vary in only superficial ways from the point of view of UG, that is, only at phonological form, for example, in their linear order, and of course arbitrary sound-meaning correspondences. This variation is explained by parameters expressed in terms of abstract features, which state where in the derivation abstract features are checked for well-formedness. For example, whether a language puts the *wh-* phrase at the front of the clause or not is a superficial difference—the constraints on interpretation of *wh-* phrases will be much the same. UG is *not* a theory of all language phenomena, but the vital part that constitutes the innate endowment—a blueprint for *any* human language.

Chomskyan theories of UG share some basic properties. The first property is modularity, which can be understood in at least two ways (but perhaps as many as four ways; see Schwartz, 1999). UG is modular in the sense that it is a system of knowledge that is 'encapsulated', or set apart, from other cognitive capacities. This claim remains controversial and continues to be clarified by its proponents (Fodor, 2000; Jackendoff, 2002, p. 71, pp. 90 ff.). Jackendoff points out that while modularity may be plausible, *interfaces* between modules must exist. For example, for the claims of eye-tracking studies of sentence processing to make sense, a link between the visual module of the brain and the syntactic module of the brain must be established and maintained.

UG is modular in a second important sense; namely, it is itself made up of subcomponents. Alone, these subcomponents are relatively simple, but together they can interact to produce systems of great complexity (Gibson & Wexler, 1994; Gold, 1967; but cf. Fodor, 1998).

The claim that UG plays a key but not exclusive role in first language acquisition has won acceptance among most linguists (e.g., Crain & Lillo-Martin, 1999; but cf. MacWhinney, 2001). In contrast, UG as a source of knowledge in adult second language acquisition has been far more controversial (Eubank & Juffs, 2000; Juffs, 2001). Even researchers who accept a role for UG in L1 acquisition do not accept that it plays a role in L2 acquisition (e.g., Bley-Vroman, 1989; Jackendoff, 2002, p. 96, but cf. p. 251; Schachter, 1989). Controversy has arisen because the results obtained from experiments that elicit knowledge of universals among adult second language learners have produced equivocal results, or cannot show that the knowledge could not have come from the first language.

Debate in UG-based L2 research has recently centered on the importance of showing that L2 grammars are underdetermined by input. For example, Schwartz and Sprouse (2000) argue strongly for such a research agenda. In contrast, Hawkins (2001, p. 354) points out that studies that show poverty-of-the-stimulus (POS) effects may be of interest, but tell us little about the *process* of second language acquisition or why there are differences between L1 and L2 acquisition, especially the lack of success in adult SLA. Part of the reason for this conclusion may be that in the 1990s and into the present, attention in linguistic theory has switched to ever more general principles. Much more emphasis has been put into the lexicon, most of which is learned directly from input. It therefore becomes a problem to show that, if an L2 shows evidence of going beyond the input, this L2 knowledge is based not on L1 knowledge already available. For instance, even if Japanese, Korean, and Chinese-speaking learners of English L2 reveal even *some* knowledge of subtle constraints on English *wh-* movement, the UG constraint may be so abstract that it is at work in the L1s of the learners as well, even if those languages do not place *wh-* phrases at the beginning of the clause.

It is therefore important to investigate that parametric variation, especially clustering effects, for example, those contingencies between verb raising, negation, and question formation. A central finding based on formulations of parameters is that second languages appear to permit optionality where L1s do not, particularly in the area of morphosyntax (Sorace, 2000). Another important, and perhaps related, question is why L2 learners' capacity at the morphophonological interface is 'impaired' (Beck, 1998). It is these L1–L2 differences that make SLA expressed in terms of linguistic theory interesting (Hawkins, 2001). If finding evidence for UG principles is difficult, finding influence of first language is easier. Formal grammars are particularly valuable at making precise predictions about such influence, and it is to this issue that we now turn our attention.

The Role of the First Language

Currently, agreement exists that although some developmental phenomena may be shared among learners of different languages, the first language exerts a powerful influence on second language development (Gass & Selinker, 1983, 1992). Language, like the brain, is not an undifferentiated mass, but a complex set of interacting components, many learned, some innate. (If any doubt remains on this point, see Carroll, 2001, on the complex issues facing L2 researchers.) Differential effects of the L1 in different parts of the L2, and at different stages of L2 development, should therefore be expected.

At the level of the lexicon, Kroll and her colleagues (e.g., de Groot & Poot, 1997; Kroll et al., 2002) have shown that, at the first stage of learning, lexical entries in the L2 must access concepts via the L1 lexical entry. Recent brain-imaging studies indicate that fluent bilinguals do not have this problem (Rodriguez-Fornells et al., 2001). In contrast, Juffs (1996, pp. 228–229) and Montrul (1999, p. 216) suggest that in the initial stages of learning argument structure of verbs, the part of lexical knowledge constrained by universal principles, learners resort to a 'universal' template rather than the L1, although the L1 also influences knowledge of this domain.

L1 influence is also claimed to be very strong in morphosyntax. Schwartz and Sprouse (1994) argue that the initial state of second language acquisition is the whole abstract grammar of L1. This transfer includes all the values of parameters that distinguish surface word order, and all of the abstract constraints on interpretation, but of course not the morphophonological entries in the lexicon. Debate now centers around whether second language learners can acquire new abstract features of morphosyntax or whether the acquisition of these components of the grammar is fatally impaired (e.g., Beck, 1998; Hawkins & Chan, 1997; Duffield & White, 1999; Montrul, 2001).

In phonology, Young-Scholten and Archibald (2000) have shown that subtle interactions occur between development of the segmental inventory and constraints on syllable structure in the L2. For example, they have argued that Korean-speaking learners of English L2 use epenthesis in syllable initial clusters because Korean does not distinguish between certain kinds of liquids at the level of feature geometry.

The term crosslinguistic influence is preferred to L1 influence by many researchers (Kellerman & Sharwood-Smith, 1986; Kellerman & Perdue, 1992). One recent example of crosslinguistic influence is reported in Yeni-Komshian, Robbins, and Flege (2001). These researchers note that Korean-speaking learners of English L2 exhibit superior accuracy on the pronunciation of segments in verbs as compared to nouns. They attribute this difference to an increased focus on verbs by Korean speakers due to the verb-final syntax of their L1.

Thus, L1 influence is apparent in all areas of L2 development, although this influence may not be direct.

Formulas

Although universal features of language and the L1 may contribute to L2 knowledge, learners clearly directly memorize pieces of the L2 for use in specific contexts. Formulaic utterances, or chunks, are thus another source of knowledge in the second language (Gass & Selinker, 2001, pp. 207–208). Wray and Perkins (2000) provide an overview of types and functions of formulas and define formulaic utterances as "various types of word string which appear to be stored and retrieved whole from memory."

Although formulas were somewhat neglected by L2 researchers until the later 1990s (Celce-Murcia, 1997), linguists have long been interested in them (e.g., Becker, 1975). With renewed attention to input and frequency effects in L2 learning, interest in formulaic utterances as a source of L2 knowledge has been revived. N. Ellis (2002a) devotes a whole section to formulaic utterances, suggesting that one reason SLA may take so long is that learners have to accumulate a large store of chunks. Ellis does not seem to want to admit a role for any rule-based knowledge, but Wray and Perkins (2000, p. 13) accept the coexistence of both 'rule-based' language and formulas.

L2 researchers such as Myles and her colleagues also accept a role both for formulas and rule-governed utterances in the L2. They are particularly interested in the role of formulaic utterances in the creative construction of underlying rules (Myles, Mitchell, & Hooper, 1999; Myles, Hooper, & Mitchell, 1998). In the 1999 study, they seek to show that learners who are efficient at using formulas go on to develop rule-based systems alongside these formulas, whereas learners who are unable to pick up and use chunks seem to get stuck at a very basic level (Myles et al., 1998, p. 76). The authors relate this difference in success to individual differences in phonological short-term memory (see section on Aptitude): a higher short-term memory permits learners to process and store longer chunks, which in turn leads to better development of rules.

Explicit Learning and Automatization

The acquisition of explicit knowledge can take many forms. The most prototypical is through instruction in metalinguistic rules, but many other ways exist of making learners aware of linguistic structure. Doughty and Williams (1998), for example., provide an extensive discussion of various ways of focusing learners' attention on form, the vast majority of which are likely to lead to increased awareness of linguistic form, and therefore meet our definition of explicit learning: input enhancement, output enhancement, interaction enhancement, negotiation, recasts, consciousness-raising tasks, dictoglosses, input processing instruction, and garden path techniques. While such instruction implies various degrees of awareness, it does not necessarily lead to understanding (cf. Schmidt, 1990, 2001). Activation of the directly resulting knowledge typically involves awareness too; therefore we speak about explicit knowledge. Mere explicit knowledge is of limited direct usefulness for communication (see section on Using Explicit and Implicit Knowledge); therefore the concept of practice has been around for centuries. Practice is meant to make this explicit knowledge more easily accessible, perhaps even to automatize it to such an extent that it becomes functionally equivalent to implicitly acquired knowledge. It can be mechanical, meaningful, or communicative (Paulston & Bruder, 1976).

Few empirical studies on practice and automatization exist in the area of SLA, but a large literature on the acquisition of cognitive skills exists in experimental psychology. That literature has documented how the acquisition of a wide variety of cognitive skills follows a power law, that is, the learning curve takes a very particular shape known in mathematics as a power function (see esp. Newell & Rosenbloom, 1981). While the exact mechanisms underlying this phenomenon remain controversial (see DeKeyser, 2001, and the debate between Rickard, 1997, 1999; Delaney et al., 1998; Palmeri, 1999; and Haider & Frensch, 2002), the phenomenon itself is very robust, and has been documented in the learning of L2 grammar in a study by DeKeyser (1997). Although there are hardly any longitudinal studies of automatization in L2, many studies have investigated the short-term effect of task conditions, especially various amounts and kinds of planning, on the use of (explicit) knowledge for L2 oral production, especially in terms of accuracy, fluency, and complexity (see e.g., Foster & Skehan, 1996, 1999; Mehnert, 1998; Ortega, 1999; Skehan & Foster, 1997, 1999). An urgent need exists for research that combines the longitudinal aspect of DeKeyser (1997) with the ecological validity of these studies with classroom learners. Unless the profession develops a better insight into how explicit knowledge evolves over time as a function of specific types of practice, many will remain skeptical about the usefulness of explicit knowledge (see section on Using Explint and Implicit Knowledge).

Implicit Learning

Although nobody has any doubts about the possibility of explicit learning, only about its usefulness, the situation for implicit learning is the other way around: Nobody doubts that implicitly acquired procedural knowledge would be useful; the main question is to what extent it exists. For about 25 years now, the relationship between implicit and explicit knowledge has been a topic of frequent discussion in the applied linguistics literature (see, e.g., Bialystok, 1979, and Krashen, 1982, for influential early work), and for about the same amount of time, applied linguists have been referring to the ever-growing body of publications on this topic in the experimental psychology literature to justify their theories or to provide the theoretical motivation for their empirical research. Since the early work by Arthur Reber and associates (e.g., 1976; Reber et al., 1980), numerous experiments, mainly with artificial grammar learning and sequence learning tasks, have shown that people can learn to distinguish grammatical from ungrammatical strings of letters without being aware of the underlying rules, at least in a sense that is statistically significant (this usually means that participants in such experiments can make correct grammaticality judgments about 55 to 70% of the time, where 50% would be random). An enormous controversy continues, however, about whether what takes place in such experiments is the implicit learning of abstract rules, with many researchers contending that the knowledge gained is not abstract, not about rules, or neither (e.g., Dulany, Carlson, & Dewey, 1984; Kinder & Assmann,

2000; Perruchet & Pacteau, 1990; Redington & Chater, 1996; Shanks, Johnstone, & Staggs, 1997, among many others). The methodology for this keeps getting more sophisticated; yet the debate is as vigorous as ever, and many new suggestions are being made to get out of the theoretical and methodological quagmire (see esp. Reed & Johnson, 1998, for advice on experimental methodology; and the contributions to French & Cleeremans, 2002, for theoretical innovations).

It should come as no surprise, then, that the debate is also alive and well in applied linguistics, where the learning tasks are much more complex, the experimental methodology much less advanced, and the number of studies comparing (otherwise identical) implicit and explicit treatments much more limited. Only three classroom studies can be said to have made exactly this comparison (according to the stated definition). Von Elek and Oskarsson's final conclusion from the Swedish GUME-project was "The explicit method was almost uniformly superior at all age, proficiency, and aptitude levels" (1973, p. 39), and Scott (1989, 1990) also showed a significant advantage for explicit instruction. Many more classroom studies exist, of course, on the broader concept of focus on form. They tend to lend support to the importance of explicit learning, but it is often hard to pull apart the contributions of explicit instruction, systematic practice, error correction, awareness of form, and so on. For reviews see especially. Doughty and Williams (1998), R. Ellis (2002), Long and Robinson (1998), Norris and Ortega (2000, 2001), and Spada (1997).

A somewhat larger number of studies have investigated the role of implicit and explicit SLA learning in the laboratory. Some of these studies involved miniature linguistic systems learned exclusively for the purpose of the study (Alanen, 1995; de Graaff, 1997; DeKeyser, 1995; N. Ellis, 1993); others dealt with learners who were already studying the target language in question (ESL in Doughty, 1991, and Robinson, 1996, 1997; Spanish in Leow, 1998, and Rosa & O'Neill, 1999). The evidence from all these laboratory experiments is clearly in favor of explicit learning (except for implicit induction of difficult rules in Robinson's 1996 rule-search condition).

Not surprisingly, then, the meta-analysis in Norris and Ortega (2000, 2001) found that the advantage of explicit over implicit instruction is the most clearly documented method effect in the empirical literature on types of instruction. Two important caveats are in order, however. First, the duration of almost all these experiments was very short; this is to the disadvantage of implicit learning, which is known to work through the slow accumulation of instances of massive input. Second, outcome measures allowed for various degrees of monitoring of explicit knowledge (see, e.g., R. Ellis, 2002), which means that it is not always clear to what extent explicit learners would outperform implicit learners under conditions that make it nearly impossible to draw on explicit knowledge. We deal with this issue in more detail in the section on Using explicit and implicit knowledge. The point here, however, is that, where explicit learning yields knowledge that may be of doubtful use without the lengthy automatization processes referred to in the section on Explicit Learning and Automatization, attempts at implicit learning in the classroom or the laboratory do not even seem to yield that. Furthermore, the critical period literature provides ample documentation that, even after many years of constant exposure to L2, implicit learning processes yield knowledge that is far from complete (see DeKeyser & Larson-Hall, in press).

There is now converging evidence from studies in the laboratory, the classroom, and the natural L2 environment (DeKeyser 1997, 1998, 2000, in press; N. Ellis, 2002a, 2002b; R. Ellis, 1993, 1997, 2002) that the best way to develop implicit/procedural/automatized knowledge may not be to try to provide it directly, but instead to foster optimal conditions for its acquisition in the long run, and that means providing an explicit jump start. "Perhaps we do not have to bother with trying to teach implicit knowledge directly" (R. Ellis, 2002, p. 234).

Resources for Use in L2

L1 and Universal Processing Strategies

At the end of the section on the role of the first language, the issue of L1 influence on L2 processing was raised. This area of research in SLA is perhaps one of the least developed in the field (for a review see Harrington, 2001). Much of the early research in this domain was not carried out with formal grammar in mind, because researchers in the formal tradition were focusing on competence knowledge, that is, the property theory part of a theory of SLA rather than the transition part of the theory, or performance issues (Gregg, 1996, p. 51; 2001). However, research into L2 competence often appealed to performance, or processing, as a way of explaining apparent L1–L2 differences, without actually saying what these factors might be (a rare exception is Schachter & Yip, 1990).

In contrast to UG-based research, early studies that seriously addressed processing were carried out in the Competition Model (CM), for example, Harrington, 1987. (See MacWhinney, 1997, 2001, for recent overviews.) In the CM, the first language plays the key role in the process of acquisition and in processing the L2. Therefore, the L1 processing strategy is a source of L2 performance. At the heart of this model is the idea that there are different cues that match semantic roles such as Agent, Patient, and Goal with syntactic positions in the clause. For example, in English, to map a semantic Agent to the grammatical function of Subject, the processor needs to know that a subject is more likely to come before the verb, the verb is more likely to agree with the Subject, that an Agent is more likely to be animate, and so on. Different languages weight these cues in different ways: hence, Animacy for Subject in Japanese has a heavier weighting than in English, and Case marking in German has a heavier weighting than in English. MacWhinney's (2001) summary of studies involving several pairs of language indicate that the L1 influences the processing of the L2. CM is essentially a parallel distributed processing model of language representation and acquisition. The forces driving acquisition are strengths of associations based on distributional properties of the input (MacWhinney, 2001, p. 70). These models deny any role for an innate cognitive architecture *specific* to language.

Two issues arise when one considers the explanatory power of this model. One is that they are based on participants in laboratory studies who process three word strings, for example, NVN, NNV, VNN, and so on. It is not clear that any natural language syntax, or input, is ever so simple. More seriously, the model assumes some hidden connections called additional units (MacWhinney, 2001, p. 72). These additional units are inherently part of the cognitive architecture, but are not described precisely. Recall that the great strength of a formal grammar is the precise statements they make about the target of learning. The units, or features, are characterized by Caplan and Waters (2002, p. 71) as being both too powerful and inadequate to model actual behavior. For example, Caplan and Waters claim that such models fail to capture the fact that object relatives ("the senator who the reporter attacked _ was criticized") are more difficult than subject relatives ("the senator who _ attacked the reporter was criticized"), no matter how many examples a speaker may encounter. Thus, the power of the CM is weakened to the extent that it cannot be shown to account for certain kinds of data (see also Harrington, 2001, p. 114, fn. 9).

L2 sentence processing studies linked to more precisely articulated theories of grammar are less numerous than those in the CM. Most of these studies have assumed a principle-based parser or a parser based on another formal grammar (e.g., Pritchett, 1992; Inoue & Fodor, 1995). They have been more ambitious than CM models in the range of sentence types that they have attempted to investigate in SLA. Juffs and Harrington (1995, 1996) showed that second language learners seem to parse sentences incrementally in much the same way as native speakers. They also sought to show that a processing deficit lay at the heart of difference between Chinese-speaking learners and native speakers of English in processing long-distance *wh-* movement. Williams, Möbius, and Kim (2001) confirmed that non-natives have a filler-gap strategy similar to natives, and that they are less able to recover from misanalysis. Juffs (1998) demonstrated that adult L2 learners seemed as sensitive as native speakers to the interaction of argument structure and plausibility cues in processing, although there were also clear L1 effects.

Formulas

In addition to serving as input for creative construction of competence (Using Explicit and Implicit Knowledge), formulas will also be a source of performance in the L2. Wray and Perkins (2000, p.16, Table 3) point out that although speakers may be able to generate phrases by rule, because of memory constraints it might be easier just to produce stock set-phrases from store. From this point of view, then, a formula is a device for compensating for a performance limitation and not a replacement for rules. In addition to serving a memory function, formulas may also help speakers to make a point through emphasis, help them hold a conversational turn, or retain information. Wood (2001) suggests that formulas could be one way of developing fluency in a second language. Creating a repertoire of formulaic utterances and focusing on automatizing those formulaic utterances in output practice can contribute to learners' fluency.

Using Explicit and Implicit Knowledge

In those cases where implicit learning has led to implicit knowledge of L2 structures, such knowledge should be available for any kind of use, and explicit knowledge is irrelevant. Such may be the happy fate of the L2 speakers who learned the language implicitly as a child, much in the same way they learned their L1. For classroom learners, however, or for adults, implicit learning is very limited; in the former case because of grossly insufficient time/input, for the latter because of restrictions on their implicit learning capacities (and of course, because of both factors for adult classroom learners).

The question arises then, of how and how much learners draw on their explicit knowledge for actual communication. Krashen's (e.g., 1982, 1999) opinion on this point is well known: They don't because they can't, unless they know the rules well, and care to apply them, and have enough time to do so, which means rarely, and that is why the explicit knowledge resulting directly from explicit learning is rather irrelevant. A number of empirical studies could be quoted as evidence for Krashen's point of view, because they are thought to show that learners largely draw on implicit knowledge only, especially for spontaneous speech of course (Macrory & Stone, 2000), but also for meaning-focused writing (Krashen & Pon, 1975), and even for grammaticality judgments and error correction (Bialystok, 1979; Green & Hecht, 1992; Renou, 2000).

The picture, however, is not as bleak as it may seem for explicit knowledge. First of all, a number of these negative findings should probably be attributed to methodological problems (cf. DeKeyser, 2003). Secondly, a number of studies did find positive relationships between (solid) explicit knowledge and use (DeKeyser, 1990a, 1990b; Hulstijn & Hulstijn, 1984). Most important, however, the availability for use of explicitly acquired knowledge is a matter of degree, not of yes or no. As should be clear from the section on explicit learning and automatization, explicitly acquired knowledge can be automatized, but the automatization process takes a long time and does not generalize much beyond the rules and skills practiced, which means that for most structures, most skill uses, and most learners, access to the relevant explicitly learned rules is not fully automatic. This, of course, explains findings like Macrory and Stone's, that students could use past tense morphology in French well on fill-in-the-blank tasks, but not in spontaneous discourse. The less automatized a rule is, the more its application will depend on task characteristics.

Besides the interaction of automaticity and task conditions, however, there are further factors at work. Students with high aptitude, especially with a high working-memory capacity (cf. Age) and perhaps also high degrees of grammatical sensitivity, may be able to juggle explicit knowledge around rather easily during spontaneous communication while others with identical amounts of equally (non)-automatized knowledge may find it much harder to use this knowledge because of bottlenecks in working memory. Finally, the degree of prototypicality of a given use of a given rule (Hu, 2002) will also influence the ease with which the relevant explicit (or implicit) knowledge is triggered. Hu (2002) even argues, on the basis of his empirical findings, that the issue of L2 knowledge use is not so much a matter of implicit versus explicit knowledge, but largely a matter of the extent of explicit knowledge use made possible by the interaction between automaticity, prototypicality, and task conditions (+/- focus on form).

Combining the findings that little implicit learning takes place, that automatization of explicitly learned knowledge is possible but far from automatic, and, that learners can draw on explicit knowledge to the extent that the interaction between the degree of automatization and the degree of task pressure allows, it seems that the focus of the debate in applied linguistics should not be on the usefulness of implicit versus explicit learning or knowledge, but on ways to maximize explicit learning and the automatization of its product.

Individual Differences

Aptitude

It often appears that the word aptitude is almost as unfashionable as grammar. To some extent, this is because of broad political or philosophical concerns, but SLA researchers are especially wary of the concept because it has become strongly identified with a very limited set of tests, such as the Modern Language Aptitude Test (MLAT) and the Pimsleur Language Aptitude Battery (PLAB), which were developed at a time when language teaching was largely audiolingual, and research on naturalistic second language acquisition research was virtually nonexistent. Hence the concern that these instruments may not be the best predictors for learning with more contemporary, communicative methodologies, let alone for untutored acquisition. In our opinion, these concerns are exaggerated. Evidence is accumulating that these traditional tests do predict learning in communicative classrooms (e.g., Ranta, 2002), in immersion classrooms (e.g., Harley & Hart, 1997), among previously instructed students who start functioning in the target community (Harley & Hart, 2002), and among untutored adult immigrants (DeKeyser, 2000).

From the point of view of the cognitive psychologist, there is a different, more serious problem with traditional language aptitude tests, however: They largely treat aptitude and learning as 'black boxes.' The history of research on language learning aptitude since World War II closely parallels the history of research on intelligence since World War I: The first concern was to develop tests with high predictive validity for specific learning contexts; construct validity and understanding the relationship between the building blocks of aptitude and the requirements of different learning contexts came into focus much later (see, e.g., Hunt, 1999; Deary, 2001 for intelligence testing; Carroll, 1981, for language learning aptitude testing).

Research into these building blocks and their interactions with instructional and other environmental factors is still very limited, but is already showing promising results. Strong interactions between aptitude (profiles) and instructional treatments have been documented, for example, by Wesche (1981) in a classroom context, and by Robinson (2002c) in a laboratory context. With more analytic classroom teaching or under conditions of explicit rule learning, aptitude plays a large role; with more holistic teaching methodologies or under conditions of incidental learning in the lab (entirely meaning-oriented) aptitude as traditionally construed plays little or no role. Interactions between aptitude (profiles) and age have been documented, for example, in Harley and Hart (1997) and DeKeyser (2000). For adults and adolescents, aptitude in the traditional sense is a strong predictor of success; for children it is not.

Even more interesting are the research prospects in Segalowitz (1997) and Skehan (2002). Both authors hypothesize a number of interactions between very specific cognitive components of aptitude and different stages of learning; Segalowitz from the point of view of skill acquisition theory within cognitive psychology (following Ackerman, 1987), and Skehan from the point of view of SLA theory. The future of aptitude research in the L2 domain probably lies in the study of these interactions between (components of) aptitude and learning contexts, instructional treatments, age of learning, and stages of acquisition, not only because such research gives a more accurate empirical picture of reality and a better ability to predict success or failure than studies on any of these variables can separately, but also because establishing such interaction effects tells us more about what elementary cognitive mechanisms underlie aptitude, and what cognitive processes take place under various conditions of learning than mere correlational aptitude research or mere experimental research on treatments. Continued success in this area of research, however, will require the development of new fine-grained measures of components of aptitude, such as working memory for language, an area to which we now turn. (For more information on individual differences in SLA, see Dörnyei & Skehan, 2003; Sawyer & Ranta, 2001; for more information on aptitudes and their interaction with educational treatments, see Corno et al., 2002; for more information on constellations of aptitudes of potential relevance to SLA, see Robinson, 2002b; for a collection of recent empirical studies on individual differences in SLA, see Robinson, 2002a.)

Age

In contrast to aptitude research, the role of age in second language acquisition is a popular issue. It is not uncontroversial, however. On the one hand, its practical implications continue to be misunderstood (for a discussion see, e.g., DeKeyser, 2003; DeKeyser & Larson-Hall, in press); on the other hand the very existence of a critical period for second language learning is now being questioned. The very fact that post-puberty learners do not go as far in their second language as children is not disputed; what is at issue is the exact shape of the age-proficiency function, and above all, its cognitive interpretation. While some researchers such as Johnson and Newport (1989) and DeKeyser (2000) have found a strong decline in ultimate attainment for learners whose age of acquisition is around puberty but no significant decline thereafter, others such as Bialystok and Hakuta (1999) or Birdsong (2001) claim to have found a continued decline through adulthood. Furthermore, while Johnson and Newport (1989) and many others see their findings as clear evidence for a maturational phenomenon, rooted deeply in the psychology of cognitive development, and ultimately in developmental cognitive neuropsychology, others such as Birdsong (2001) or Hakuta (2001) argue that the shape of the age function does not correspond to the concept of critical period as it is used in the biological literature, and that the age-proficiency function is merely due to the confusion between age on the one hand and various environmental factors and/or the decline of various aspects of perception and memory throughout adulthood on the other.

Those who do believe that the critical period is real, that is, that the age effects documented are due to maturation in the cognitive domain that takes places roughly between ages 6 and 16, have given various but not incompatible interpretations to this phenomenon. Some hypothesize a shift from implicit or domain-specific to explicit or general-purpose learning processes (Bley-Vroman, 1989; DeKeyser, 2000, in press; Segalowitz, 1997; Skehan, 1998, 2002); others attribute the age effects to changes in the size of working memory (Cochran, McDonald, & Parault, 1999; Elman, 1993; Goldowsky & Newport, 1993; Kersten & Earles, 2001). Increasingly, however, behavioral neurolinguistic as well as neuroimaging studies support the hypothesis that there are fundamental differences in the neurological representation of language between proficient speakers who learned a language as a child and those who learned it as an adult (e.g., Hahne, 2001; Kim et al., 1997; Newman et al., 2002; Weber-Fox & Neville, 1996, 1999), and at least one researcher has linked a variety of neurolinguistic findings with the explicit/declarative versus implicit/procedural distinction (Ullman, 2001). For more information about critical period studies, their interpretation, and the methodological challenges involved in this area, see DeKeyser and Larson-Hall (in press) and Hyltenstam and Ambrahamsson (2003).

Working Memory

Views of working memory in language can be divided into two main types. One is phonological short-term memory (STM), usually measured by the ability to repeat, in the exact order presented, a sequence of digits, words, or nonsense syllables. The second type is a storage and processing capacity, usually measured by the classic reading span task (RST) of Daneman and Carpenter (1980), in which participants must read sentences and then recall individual words that occurred in those sentences. It is possible that the first type of working memory is a component of the second, although many studies have shown no correlation between the two. Furthermore, researchers such as Just and Carpenter (cf. Just, Carpenter, & Keller, 1996) have tried to show that it is only the second kind of capacity that has predictive power where individual differences in language processing and comprehension are concerned.

Working memory (WM) is currently among the most intensively researched and controversial areas of research in first language processing. This intense activity is reflected in the number of edited volumes in recent years (Andrade, 2001; Miyake & Shah, 1999; Tulving & Craik, 2000), as well as numerous journal articles. Disagreements and changes in viewpoints among researchers about the precise nature of working memory itself and the usefulness of tests that claim to measure it outside college-age and intellectual-level participants have naturally arisen (e.g., Baddeley, 2000, pp. 86–87). Moreover, these disagreements reflect differences of opinion about the modular and encapsulated nature of language discussed in the sections on UG and LI and universal processing strategies (e.g., Just & Varma, 2002; MacDonald & Christiansen, 2002; Caplan & Waters, 2002).

Researchers in psychology are already well advanced in the use of brain imaging techniques for investigating working memory, for example, event-related potentials (ERP) (e.g., Fiebach, Schlesewsky, & Friederici, 2002, Vos et al., 2001) and functional magnetic resonance imaging (fMRI) (e.g., Carpenter, Just, & Reichle, 2000). Mainstream SLA researchers are still using basic techniques to measure working memory, for example, the Daneman and Carpenter (1980) reading span test. Early work involving Japanese-speaking EFL learners by Harrington and Sawyer (1992) found correlations between the reading span working memory task (RST) and scores on grammar and reading sections of the TOEFL, but no relationship between scores on the phonological STM task and these proficiency measures. However, for francophone learners of EFL, Berquist (1997) reported both a correlation between the two memory scores and a stronger relationship between STM scores and the TOEIC proficiency measure. Robinson (2002c) reports some reliable correlations between working memory and listening tests in a laboratory study of Japanese-speaking learners acquiring ergativity and constraints on incorporation in Samoan. N. Ellis (1996) reviews a series of studies that suggest that phonological STM is a very strong predictor of L1 and L2 proficiency.

Juffs (2000, 2002) has reported correlations between the two memory measures. However, contrary to many L1 studies, no reliable relationship was found between scores on the working memory measures and online reading times during processing. Using the Waters and Caplan (1996) reading span task, Kroll et al. (2002) also found no reliable relationship between this working memory measure and word naming.

Measures of working memory are typically thought of as measuring individual capacity differences in input processing or comprehension. However, some researchers have begun to investigate whether a role exists for working memory in explaining individual differences in production (Fortkamp, 1999). Robinson (2002c) also reports positive correlation with production tests in his study. Mackey et al., (2002) were interested in a possible relationship between working memory and noticing of interactional feedback, developmental level, and interactionally driven L2 development. Although their conclusions are somewhat tentative, noticing occurred more with high WM learners, phonological STM played a different role depending on the level of the learner, and high WM capacity learners benefited more from interaction. Such conclusions mesh with the advantage noted by Myles, Mitchell, and Hooper (1999) for learners who were better at retaining formulaic utterances.

Further research in this area will need to take into account the following issues: If L2 learning is based on general cognition, WM will be a reliable predictor of attainment and performance only if those tests of WM are also related to general cognitive capacities. If WM is domain specific, and related to domain-specific language processes, we might find a correlation between some measures of WM and online language processing, but fail to find it with WM measures that are more general. Hence, different tests of working memory along with different linguistic tests may help sort out which parts of language learning are served by which parts of the cognitive architecture. Second language researchers are only beginning to take a careful look at these issues and to investigate their relevance for L2 learning. Researchers will need to follow rapid developments in the psychology literature very closely.

CONCLUSION

Thanks to research in a variety of areas, from the experimental psychology of learning and skill acquisition, to the psycholinguistics of sentence processing and lexical retrieval, to more applied research on the effect of learning conditions and individual differences on SLA, we now have much better insights than a couple of decades ago into the complexity of L2 knowledge and use. We understand that L2 knowledge can be acquired implicitly (at least in children) or explicitly, can greatly change in nature over time as a result of practice or reflection, and is drawn on variably depending on the individual and the circumstances.

Many unanswered questions remain, however, about the relationship of L2 knowledge to L1 knowledge and to broader aspects of cognition, and about the interaction between implicit and explicit knowledge at the learning, storage, and retrieval stages. Much work remains to be done to integrate the field of second language acquisition better into cognitive science.

REFERENCES

Ackerman, P. L. (1987). Individual differences in skill learning: An integration of psychometric and information processing perspectives. *Psychological Bulletin, 102*(1), 3–27.

Alanen, R. (1995). Input enhancement and rule presentation in second language acquisition. In R. W. Schmidt (Ed.), *Attention and awareness in foreign language learning* (pp. 259–302). Honolulu: University of Hawai Press.

Andrade, J. (Ed.). (2001). *Working memory in perspective.* New York: Psychology Press.

Baddeley, A. (2000). Short-term and working memory. In E. Tulving & F. Craik (Eds.), *The Oxford handbook of memory* (pp. 77–92). New York: Oxford University Press.

Beck, M.-L. (1998). L2 acquisition and obligatory head movement: English-speaking learners of German and the local impairment hypothesis. *Studies in Second Language Acquisition, 20,* 311–348.

Becker, J. (1975). The phrasal lexicon. In R. C. Schank & B. Nash-Webber (Eds.), *Theoretical issues in natural language processing* (pp. 38–41). Cambridge, UK: ACL Workshop.

Berquist, B. (1997). *Individual differences in working memory span and L2 proficiency: Capacity or processing capacity?* Paper presented at the Proceedings of the GALA '97 Conference on Language Acquisition, Edinburgh, UK.

Bialystok, E. (1979). Explicit and implicit judgements of L2 grammaticality. *Language Learning, 29,* 81–103.

Bialystok, E., & Hakuta, K. (1999). Confounded age: linguistic and cognitive factors in age differences for second language acquisition. In D. Birdsong (Ed.), *Second Language Acquisition and the Critical Period Hypothesis* (pp. 161–181). Mahwah, NJ: Lawrence Erlbaum Associates.

Birdsong, D. (2001). Comprehensive nativelikeness in second language acquisition. Unpublished ms., University of Texas-Austin.

Bley-Vroman, R. (1989). What is the logical problem of foreign language learning? In S. Gass & J. Schachter (Eds.), *Linguistic perspectives on second language acquisition* (pp. 41–68). Cambridge, UK: Cambridge University Press.

Caplan, D., & Waters, G. S. (2002). Working memory and connectionist parsers: A reply. *Psychological Review, 109,* 66–74.

Carpenter, P., Just, M. A., & Reichle, E. D. (2000). Working memory and executive function. *Current Opinion in Neurobiology, 10,* 195–199.

Carroll, J. B. (1981). Twenty-five years of research on foreign language aptitude. In K. C. Diller (Ed.), *Individual differences and universals in language learning aptitude* (pp. 83–118). Rowley, MA: Newbury House.

Carroll, S. E. (2001). *Input and evidence: The raw material of second language acquisition.* Philadelphia: Benjamins.

Celce-Murcia, M. (1997). Direct approaches to L2 instruction: A turning point in communicative language teaching? *TESOL Quarterly, 31,* 141–152.

Chomsky, N. (1986). *Knowledge of language.* New York: Praeger.

Chomsky, N. (1995). *The minimalist program.* Cambridge, MA: MIT Press.

Cochran, B. P., McDonald, J. L., & Parault, S. J. (1999). Too smart for their own good: The disadvantage of a superior processing capacity for adult language learners. *Journal of Memory and Language, 41,* 30–58.

Corno, L., Cronbach, L. J., Kupermintz, H., Lohman, D. F., Mandinach, E. B., Porteus, A. W., & Talbert, J. E. (2002). *Remaking the concept of aptitude. Extending the legacy of Richard E. Snow.* Mahwah, NJ: Lawrence Erlbaum Associates.

Crain, S., & Lillo-Martin, D. (1999). *An introduction to linguistic theory and language acquisition.* Oxford, UK: Basil Blackwell.

Daneman, M., & Carpenter, P. (1980). Individual differences in working memory and reading. *Journal of Verbal Learning and Verbal Behavior, 19,* 450–466.

Deary, I. J. (2001). Human intelligence differences: Towards a combined experimental–differential approach. *Trends in Cognitive Sciences, 5*(4), 164–170.

de Graaff, R. (1997). The eXperanto experiment: Effects of explicit instruction on second language acquisition. *Studies in Second Language Acquisition, 19*(2), 249–276.

de Groot, A. M. B., & Poot, R. (1997). Word translation at three levels of proficiency: The ubiquitous involvement of conceptual memory. *Language Learning, 47,* 215–264.

DeKeyser, R. M. (1990a). From learning to acquisition? Monitoring in the classroom and abroad. *Hispania, 73,* 238–247.

DeKeyser, R. M. (1990b). Foreign language development during a semester abroad. In B. Freed (Ed.), *Foreign language acquisition research and the classroom* (pp. 104–119). Lexington, MA: Heath.

DeKeyser, R. M. (1995). Learning second language grammar rules: An experiment with a miniature linguistic system. *Studies in Second Language Acquisition, 17*(3), 379–410.

DeKeyser, R. M. (1997). Beyond explicit rule learning: Automatizing second language morphosyntax. *Studies in Second Language Acquisition, 19*(2), 195–221.

DeKeyser, R. M. (1998). Beyond focus on form: Cognitive perspectives on learning and practicing second language grammar. In C. Doughty & J. Williams (Eds.), *Focus on form in classroom second language acquisition* (pp. 42–63). New York: Cambridge University Press.

DeKeyser, R. M. (2000). The robustness of critical period effects in second language acquisition. *Studies in Second Language Acquisition, 22*(4), 499–533.

DeKeyser, R. M. (2001). Automaticity and automatization. In P. Robinson (Ed.), *Cognition and second language instruction* (pp. 125–151). New York: Cambridge University Press.

DeKeyser, R. M. (2003). Implicit and explicit learning. In C. Doughty & M. Long (Eds.), *Handbook of second language acquisition.* pp. 313–348. Oxford, UK: Blackwell.

DeKeyser, R. M., & Larson-Hall, J. (in press). What does the critical period really mean? In J. F. Kroll & A. M. B. de Groot (Eds.), *Handbook of bilingualism: Psycholinguistic approaches.* Oxford, UK: Oxford University Press.

Delaney, P. F., Reder, L. M., Staszewski, J. J., & Ritter, F. E. (1998). The strategy-specific nature of improvement: The power law applies by strategy within task. *Psychological Science, 9*(1), 1–7.

Dörnyei, Z., & Skehan, P. (2003). Individual differences in second language learning. In C. Doughty & M. Long (Eds.), *Handbook of second language acquisition.* pp. 589–630. Oxford, UK: Blackwell.

Doughty, C. (1991). Second language instruction does make a difference. Evidence from an empirical study of SL relativization. *Studies in Second Language Acquisition, 13,* 431–469.

Doughty, C., & Williams, J. (1998). Pedagogical choices in focus on form. In C. Doughty & J. Williams (Eds.), *Focus on form in classroom second language acquisition* (pp. 197–261). New York: Cambridge University Press.

Duffield, N., & White, L. (1999). Assessing L2 knowledge of L2 clitic placement. *Second Language Research, 15,* 133–160.

Dulany, D., Carlson, R., & Dewey, G. (1984). A case of syntactical learning and judgment: How conscious and how abstract? *Journal of Experimental Psychology: General, 113,* 541–555.

Ellis, N. C. (1993). Rules and instances in foreign language learning: Interactions of explicit and implicit knowledge. *European Journal of Cognitive Psychology, 5,* 289–318.

Ellis, N. C. (1996). Sequencing in SLA: Phonological memory, chunking, and points of order. *Studies in second language acquisition, 18,* 91–126.

Ellis, N. C. (2002a). Frequency effects in language processing: A review with implications for theories of implicit and explicit language acquisition. *Studies in Second Language Acquisition, 24*(2), 143–188.

Ellis, N. C. (2002b). Reflections on frequency effects in language processing. *Studies in Second Language Acquisition, 24*(2), 297–339.

Ellis, R. (1990). A response to Gregg. *Applied Linguistics, 11*(4), 364–383.

Ellis, R. (1993). The structural syllabus and second language acquisition. *TESOL Quarterly, 27*(1), 91–113.

Ellis, R. (1997). *SLA research and language teaching.* Oxford, UK: Oxford University Press.

Ellis, R. (2002). Does form-focused instruction affect the acquisition of implicit knowledge? *Studies in Second Language Acquisition, 24*(2), 223–236.

Elman, J. L. (1993). Learning and development in neural networks: The importance of starting small. *Cognition, 48,* 71–99.

Elman, J. L., Bates, E. A., Johnson, M. H., Karmiloff-Smith, A., Parisi, D., & Plunkett, K. (1996). Rethinking innateness: A connectionist perspective on development. Cambridge, MA: MIT Press.

Eubank, L., & Juffs, A. (2000). Recent research on the acquisition of L2 competence: Morphosyntax and argument structure. In L. Cheng & R. Sybesma (Eds.), *The first GLOT international state-of-the-art book: The latest in linguistics* (pp. 131–170). Berlin: Mouton de Gruyter.

Fiebach, C. J., Schlesewsky, M., & Friederici, A. D. (2002). Separating syntactic memory costs and syntactic integration costs during parsing: The processing of German *wh*- questions. *Journal of Memory and Language, 47,* 250–272.

Fodor, J. A. (1983). *The modularity of mind.* Cambridge, MA: MIT Press.

Fodor, J. A. (2000). *The mind doesn't work that way: The scope and limits of computational psychology.* Cambridge, MA: MIT Press.

Fodor, J. D. (1998). Unambiguous triggers. *Linguistic Inquiry,* (29), 1–36.

Foster, P., & Skehan, P. (1996). The influence of planning and task type on second language performance. *Studies in Second Language Acquisition, 18*(3), 299–323.

Foster, P., & Skehan, P. (1999). The influence of source of planning and focus of planning on task-based performance. *Language Teaching Research, 3*(3), 215–247.

French, R. M., & Cleeremans, A. (Eds.). (2002). Implicit learning and consciousness: An empirical, philosophical, and computational consensus in the making. Hove, UK: Psychology Press.

Fortkamp, M. B. M. (1999). Working memory capacity and elements of L2 speech production. *Communication and Cognition, 32,* 259–295.

Gass, S., & Selinker, L. (Eds.). (1983). *Language transfer in language learning.* Rowley, MA: Newbury House.

Gass, S., & Selinker, L. (Eds.). (1992). *Language transfer in language learning.* Amsterdam: Benjamins.

Gass, S. M., & Selinker, L. (2001). Second language acquisition : An introductory course. (2nd ed.). Hillsdale, NJ: Lawrence Erlbaum Associates.

Gibson, E., & Wexler, K. (1994). Triggers. *Linguistic Inquiry, 25* (3), 407–454.

Gold, E. M. (1967). Language identification in the limit. *Information and Control, 16,* 447–474.

Goldowsky, B. N., & Newport, E. L. (1993). Modeling the effects of processing limitations on the acquisition of morphology: The less is more hypothesis. In E. Clark (Ed.), *The Proceedings of the 24th Annual Child Language Research Forum* (pp. 124–138). Stanford, CA: CSLI.

Green, P., & Hecht, K. (1992). Implicit and explicit grammar: An empirical study. *Applied Linguistics, 13,* 168–184.

Gregg, K. (1990). The variable competence model of second language acquisition and why it isn't. *Applied Linguistics, 11*(4), 364–383.

Gregg, K. (1996). The logical and developmental problems of second language acquisition. In W. C. Ritchie & T. K. Bhatia (Eds.), *Handbook of second language acquisition* (pp. 50–84). New York: Academic Press.

Hahne, A. (2001). What's different in second language processing? Evidence from event-related brain potentials. *Journal of Psycholinguistic Research, 30*(3), 251–266.

Haider, H., & Frensch, P. A. (2002). Why aggregated learning follows the power law of practice when individual learning does not: Comment on Rickard (1997, 1999), Delaney et al. (1998), and Palmeri (1999). *Journal of Experimental Psychology: Learning, Memory, and Cognition, 28*(2), 392–406.

Hakuta, K. (2001). A critical period for second language acquisition? In D. Bailey, J. Bruer, F. Symons, & J. Lichtman (Eds.), *Critical thinking about critical periods* (pp. 193–205). Baltimore: Paul H. Brookes.

Hall, C. (1995). Formal linguistics and mental representation: Psycholinguistic contributions to the identification and explanation of morphological and syntactic competence. *Language and Cognitive Processes, 10,* 169–187.

Harley, B., & Hart, D. (1997). Language aptitude and second language proficiency in classroom learners of different starting ages. *Studies in Second Language Acquisition, 19*(3), 379–400.

Harley, B., & Hart, D. (2002). Age, aptitude, and second language learning on a bilingual exchange. In P. Robinson (Ed.), *Individual differences and instructed language learning* (pp. 301–330). Philadelphia: Benjamins.

Harrington, M. W. (1987). Processing transfer: Language-specific processing strategies as a source of interlanguage variation. *Applied Psycholinguistics, 8,* 351–377.

Harrington, M. W. , & Sawyer, M. (1992). L2 working memory capacity and L2 reading skills. *Studies in Second Language Acquisition, 14*(1), 25–38.

Harrington, M. W. (2001). Sentence processing. In P. Robinson (Ed.), *Cognition and second language instruction* (pp. 91–124). New York: Cambridge University Press.

Hawkins, R. (2001). The theoretical significance of universal grammar in second language acquisition. *Second Language Research, 21,* 345–367.

Hawkins, R., & Chan, C. Y.-H. (1997). The partial availability of universal grammar in second language acquisition: The 'failed functional features in hypothesis' [sic]. *Second Language Research, 13,* 187–227.

Hu, G. (2002). Psychological constraints on the utility of meta-linguistic knowledge in second language production. *Studies in Second Language Acquisition, 24*(3), 347–386.

Hulstijn, J., & Hulstijn, W. (1984). Grammatical errors as a function of processing constraints and explicit knowledge. *Language Learning, 34,* 23–43.

Hunt, E. (1999). Intelligence and human resources: Past, present, and future. In P. Ackerman, P. Kyllonen, & R. Roberts (Eds.), *Learning and individual differences. Process, trait, and content determinants.* (pp. 3–30). Washington, DC: American Psychological Association.

Hyltenstam, K., & Abrahamsson, N. (2003). Maturational constraints in second language acquisition. In C. Doughty & M. Long (Eds.), *Handbook of second language acquisition* (pp. 539–588). Oxford, UK: Blackwell.

Inoue, A., & Fodor, J. D. (1995). Information-paced parsing of Japanese. In R. Mazuka & N. Nagai (Eds.), *Japanese sentence processing* (pp. 9–64). Hillsdale, NJ: Lawrence Erlbaum Associates.

Jackendoff, R. S. (2002). *Foundations of language.* New York: Oxford University Press.

Johnson, J. S., & Newport, E. L. (1989). Critical period effects in second language learning: The influence of maturational state on the acquisition of English as a second language. *Cognitive Psychology, 21,* 60–99.

Juffs, A. (1996). *Learnability and the lexicon: Theories and second language acquisition research.* Amsterdam: Benjamins.

Juffs, A. (1998). Main verb s.v. reduced relative clause ambiguity resolution in second language sentence processing. *Language Learning, 48,* 107–147.

Juffs, A. (2000, March 11–14). Working memory and L1 influences in ambiguity resolution in L2 English sentence processing. *American Association of Applied Linguistics Annual Meeting.*

Juffs, A. (2001). Formal linguistic perspectives on second language acquisition. In R. Kaplan (Ed.), *The Oxford handbook of applied linguistics* (pp. 87–103). New York: Oxford University Press.

Juffs, A. (2002, April 6–9). Working memory as a variable in accounting for individual differences in second language performance. *American Association of Applied Linguistics Annual Meeting.*

Juffs, A., & Harrington, M. W. (1995). Parsing effects in L2 sentence processing: Subject and object asymmetries in *wh-* extraction. *Studies in Second Language Acquisition, 17*(4), 483–516.

Juffs, A., & Harrington, M. W. (1996). Garden path sentences and error data in second language sentence processing research. *Language Learning, 46,* 286–324.

Just, M. A., Carpenter, P., & Keller, T. (1996). The capacity theory of comprehension: New frontiers of evidence and arguments. *The Psychological Review, 103,* 773–780.

Just, M. A., & Varma, S. (2002). A hybrid architecture for working memory: Reply to MacDonald and Christianson 2002. *Psychological Review, 109,* 55–65.

Kellerman, E., & Perdue, C. (Eds) (1992). Special issue in crosslinguistic influence. *Second Language Research,* *8*(3).

Kellerman, E., & Sharwood-Smith, M. (Eds.). (1986). *Crosslinguistic influence in second language acquisition.* New York: Pergamon.

Kersten, A. W., & Earles, J. L. (2001). Less really is more for adults learning a miniature artificial language. *Journal of Memory and Language, 44,* 250–273.

Kim, K. H. S., Relkin, N. R., Lee, K.-M., & Hirsch, J. (1997). Distinct cortical areas associated with native and second languages. *Nature, 388,* 171–174.

Kinder, A., & Assmann, A. (2000). Learning artificial grammars: No evidence for the acquisition of rules. *Memory and cognition, 28*(8), 1321–1332.

Krashen, S. D. (1982). *Principles and practice in second language acquisition.* Englewood Cliffs, NJ: Prentice-Hall.

Krashen, S. D. (1999). Seeking a role for grammar: A review of some recent studies. *Foreign Language Annals, 32*(2), 245–257.

Krashen, S. D., & Pon, P. (1975). An error analysis of an advanced ESL learner. *Working Papers in Bilingualism, 7,* 125–129.

Kroll, J., Michael, E., Tokowicz, N., & Dufour, R. (2002). The development of lexical fluency in a second language. *Second Language Research, 18,* 137–171.

Leow, R. P. (1998). Toward operationalizing the process of attention in SLA: Evidence for Tomlin and Villa's (1994) fine-grained analysis of attention. *Applied Psycholinguistics, 19*(1), 133–159.

Long, M. H., & Robinson, P. (1998). Focus on form: Theory, research, and practice. In C. Doughty & J. Williams (Eds.), *Focus on form in classroom second language acquisition* (pp. 15–41). New York: Cambridge University Press.

Macrory, G., & Stone, V. (2000). Pupil progress in the acquisition of the perfect tense in French: The relationship between knowledge and use. *Language Teaching Research, 4*(1), 55–82.

MacDonald, M. C., & Christiansen, M. H. (2002). Reassessing working memory: Comment on Just and Carpenter 1992 and Waters and Caplan 1996. *Psychological Review, 109,* 35–54.

Mackey, A., Philip, J., Egi, T., Fuji, A., & Tatsumi, T. (2002). Individual differences in working memory, noticing of interactional feedback and L2 development. In P. Robinson (Ed.), *Individual differences and instructed language learning* (pp. 181–209). Philadelphia: Benjamins.

MacWhinney, B. (1997). Second language acquisition and the competition model. In A. M. B. de Groot & J. Kroll (Eds.), *Tutorials in bilingualism* (pp. 113–144). Mahwah, NJ: Lawrence Erlbaum Associates.

MacWhinney, B. (2001). The competition model: The input, the context, and the brain. In P. Robinson (Ed.), *Cognition and second language instruction.* New York: Cambridge University Press.

Mehnert, U. (1998). The effects of different lengths of time for planning on second language performance. *Studies in Second Language Acquisition, 20*(1), 83–108

Miyake, A., & Shah, P. (Eds.). (1999). *Mechanisms of working memory.* New York: Cambridge University Press.

Montrul, S. (1999). Causative errors with unaccusative verbs in L2 Spanish. *Second Language Research,* (15), 191–219.

Montrul, S. (2001). First language constrained variability in argument structure changing morphology with causative verbs. *Second Language Research, 17,* 144–194.

Myles, F., Hooper, J., & Mitchell, R. (1998). Rote or rule? Exploring the role of formulaic language in the foreign language classroom. *Language Learning, 48,* 323–364.

Myles, F., Mitchell, R., & Hooper, J. (1999). Interrogative chunks in French L2: A basis for creative construction? *Studies in Second Language Acquisition, 21,* 49–80.

Newell, A., & Rosenbloom, P. S. (1981). Mechanisms of skill acquisition and the law of practice. In J. R. Anderson (Ed.), *Cognitive skills and their acquisition* (pp. 1–55). Hillsdale, NJ: Lawrence Erlbaum Associates.

Newman, A. J., Bavelier, D., Corina, D., Jezzard, P., & Neville, H. J. (2002). A critical period for right hemisphere recruitment in American Sign Language processing. *Nature Neuroscience, 5*(1), 76–80.

Norris, J. M., & Ortega, L. (2000). Effectiveness of L2 instruction: A research synthesis and quantitative meta-analysis. *Language Learning, 50*(3), 417–528.

Norris, J. M., & Ortega, L. (2001). Does type of instruction make a difference? Substantive findings from a meta-analytic review. *Language Learning, 51* (Supplement 1), 157–213.

O'Grady, W. (1999). Toward a new nativism. *Studies in Second Language Acquisition, 21*(4), 621–633.

Ortega, L. (1999). Planning and focus on form in L2 oral performance. *Studies in Second Language Acquisition, 21*(1), 109–148.

Palmeri, T. J. (1999). Theories of automaticity and the power law of practice. *Journal of Experimental Psychology: Learning, Memory, and Cognition, 25*(2), 543–551.

Paulston, C. B., & Bruder, M. N. (1976). *Teaching English as a second language: Techniques and procedures.* Cambridge, MA: Winthrop.

Perruchet, P., & Pacteau, C. (1990). Synthetic grammar learning: Implicit rule abstraction or explicit fragmentary knowledge? *Journal of Experimental Psychology: General, 119*(3), 264–275.

Pinker, S. (1997). *How the mind works.* New York: Norton.

Pritchett, B. L. (1992). *Grammatical competence and parsing performance.* Chicago: Chicago University Press.

Ranta, L. (2002). The role of learners' language-analytic ability in the communicative classroom. In P. Robinson (Ed.), *Individual differences and instructed language learning* (pp. 159–179). Amsterdam: Benjamins.

Reber, A. (1976). Implicit learning of synthetic languages: The role of instructional set. *Journal of Experimental Psychology: Human Learning and Memory, 2*, 88–94.

Reber, A., Kassin, S., Lewis, S., & Cantor, G. (1980). On the relationship between implicit and explicit modes in the learning of a complex rule structure. *Journal of Experimental Psychology: Human Learning and Memory, 6*, 492–502.

Redington, M., & Chater, N. (1996). Transfer in artificial grammar learning: A reevaluation. *Journal of Experimental Psychology: General, 125*(2), 123–138.

Reed, J. M., & Johnson, P. J. (1998). Implicit learning. Methodological issues and evidence of unique characteristics. In M. A. Stadler & P. A. Frensch (Eds.), *Handbook of implicit learning* (pp. 261–294). Thousand Oaks, CA: Sage.

Renou, J. M. (2000). Learner accuracy and learner performance: The quest for a link. *Foreign Language Annals, 33*, 168–180.

Rickard, T. C. (1997). Bending the power law: A CMPL theory of strategy shifts and the automatization of cognitive skills. *Journal of Experimental Psychology: General, 126*(3), 288–311.

Rickard, T. C. (1999). A CMPL alternative account of practice effects in numerosity judgments. *Journal of Experimental Psychology: Learning, Memory, and Cognition, 25*(2), 532–542.

Robinson, P. (1996). Learning simple and complex second language rules under implicit, incidental, rule-search, and instructed conditions. *Studies in Second Language Acquisition, 18*(1), 27–67.

Robinson, P. (1997). Generalizability and automaticity of second language learning under implicit, incidental, enhanced, and instructed conditions. *Studies in Second Language Acquisition, 19*(2), 223–247.

Robinson, P. (Ed.). (2002a). *Individual differences and instructed language learning.* Amsterdam: Benjamins.

Robinson, P. (2002b). Learning conditions, aptitude complexes, and SLA. In P. Robinson (Ed.), *Individual differences and instructed language learning* (pp. 113–133). Amsterdam: Benjamins.

Robinson, P. (2002c). Effects of individual differences in intelligence, aptitude, and working memory on adult incidental SLA: A replication and extension of Reber, Walkenfield, and Hernstadt (1991). In P. Robinson (Ed.), *Individual differences and instructed language learning* (pp. 211–265). Amsterdam: Benjamins.

Rodriguez-Fornells, A., Rotte, M., Heinze, H.-J., Nösellt, T., & Münte, T. (2002). Brain potential and functional fRMI evidence for how two languages handle one brain. *Nature, 415*(February), 1026–1029.

Rosa, E., & O'Neill, M. D. (1999). Explicitness, intake, and the issue of awareness: Another piece to the puzzle. *Studies in Second Language Acquisition, 21*(4), 511–556.

Sawyer, M., & Ranta, L. (2001). Aptitude, individual differences, and instructional design. In P. Robinson (Ed.), *Cognition and second language instruction* (pp. 319–353). New York: Cambridge University Press.

Schachter, J. (1989). Testing a proposed universal. In S. Gass & J. Schachter (Eds.), *Linguistic perspectives on second language acquisition* (pp. 73–88). Cambridge, UK: Cambridge University Press.

Schachter, J., & Yip, V. (1990). Grammaticality judgments: Why does anyone object to subject extraction? *Studies in Second Language Acquisition, 12*(4), 379–392.

Schmidt, R. (2001). Attention. In P. Robinson (Ed.), *Cognition and second language instruction* (pp. 3–32). New York: Cambridge University Press.

Schmidt, R. W. (1990). The role of consciousness in second language learning. *Applied Linguistics, 11*(2), 129–158.

Schwartz, B. (1999). Let's make up your mind: Special 'nativist' perspectives on language, modularity of mind, and non-native language acquisition. *Studies in Second Language Acquisition, 21*, 635–656.

Schwartz, B., & Sprouse, R. (1994). Word order and nominative case in non-native language acquisition: A longitudinal study of (L1 Turkish) German interlanguage. In T. Hoekstra & B. D. Schwartz (Eds.), *Language acquisition studies in generative grammar* (pp. 317–368). Amsterdam: Benjamins.

Schwartz, B. D., & Sprouse, R. (2000). When syntactic theories evolve: Consequences for L2 acquisition research. In J. Archibald (Ed.), *Second language acquisition and linguistic theory* (pp. 156–186). Oxford, UK: Blackwell.

Scott, V. M. (1989). An empirical study of explicit and implicit teaching strategies in French. *The Modern Language Journal, 73*(1), 14–22.

Scott, V. M. (1990). Explicit and implicit grammar teaching strategies: New empirical data. *The French Review, 63*(5), 779–789.

Segalowitz, N. (1997). Individual differences in second language acquisition. In A. M. B. de Groot & J. F. Kroll (Eds.), *Tutorials in bilingualism. Psycholinguistic perspectives* (pp. 85–112). Mahwah, NJ: Lawrence Erlbaum Associates.

Shanks, D. R., Johnstone, T., & Staggs, L. (1997). Abstraction processes in artificial grammar learning. *The Quarterly Journal of Experimental Psychology, 50A*(1), 216–252.

Skehan, P. (1998). *A cognitive approach to language learning.* Oxford, UK: Oxford University Press.

Skehan, P. (2002). Theorizing and updating aptitude. In P. Robinson (Ed.), *Individual differences and instructed language learning* (pp. 69–93). Amsterdam: Benjamins.

Skehan, P., & Foster, P. (1997). Task type and task processing conditions as influences on foreign language performance. *Language Teaching Research, 1*(3), 185–211.

Skehan, P., & Foster, P. (1999). The influence of task structure and processing conditions on narrative retellings. *Language Learning, 49*(1), 93–120.

Sorace, A. (2000). Syntactic optionality in L2 acquisition. *Second Language Research, 16*, 93–102.

Spada, N. (1997). Form-focused instruction and second language acquisition: A review of classroom and laboratory research. *Language Teaching, 30*(2), 73–87.

Tarone, E. E. (1990). On variation in interlanguage: A response to Gregg. *Applied Linguistics, 11*(4), 392–400.

Tarone, E. E. (2002). Frequency effects, noticing, and creativity: Factors in a variationist interlanguage framework. *Studies in Second Language Acquisition, 24*(2), 287–296.

Tulving, E., & Craik, F. (Eds.). (2000). *The Oxford handbook of memory.* New York: Oxford University Press.

Ullman, M. T. (2001). The neural basis of lexicon and grammar in first and second language: The declarative/procedural model. *Bilingualism: Language and Cognition, 4,* 105–122.

von Elek, T., & Oskarsson, M. (1973). *A replication study in teaching foreign language grammar to adults* (Research Bulletin No. 16). Gothenburg School of Education.

Vos, S. H., Gunter, T. C., Schriefers, H., & Friederici, A. D. (2001). Syntactic parsing and working memory: The effects of syntactic complexity, reading span, and concurrent load. *Language and Cognitive Processes, 16,* 65–103.

Waters, G. S., & Caplan, D. (1996). Processing resource capacity and the comprehension of garden path sentences. *Memory and Cognition, (24),* 342–355.

Weber-Fox, C. M., & Neville, H. J. (1999). Functional neural subsystems are differentially affected by delays in second language immersion: ERP and behavioral evidence in bilinguals. In D. Birdsong (Ed.), *Second language acquisition and the critical period hypothesis* (pp. 23–38). Mahwah, NJ: Lawrence Erlbaum Associates.

Weber-Fox, C. M., & Neville, H. J. (1996). Maturational constraints on functional specializations for language processing: ERP evidence in bilingual speakers. *Journal of Cognitive Neuroscience, 8,* 231–256.

Wesche, M. (1981). Language aptitude measures in streaming, matching students with methods, and diagnosis of learner problems. In K. C. Diller (Ed.), *Individual differences and universals in language learning aptitude* (pp. 119–154). Rowley, MA: Newbury House.

Williams, J. N., Möbius, P., & Kim, C. (2001). Native and non-native processing of English *wh-* questions: parsing strategies and plausibility constraints. *Applied Psycholinguistics, 22,* 509–540.

Wood, D. (2001). In search of fluency: What is it and how can we teach it? *Canadian Modern Language Review, 57,* 573–589.

Wolfe-Quintero, K. (1996). Nativism does not equal universal grammar. *Second Language Research, 12*(4), 335–373.

Wray, A., & Perkins, M. R. (2000). The functions of formulaic language: An integrated model. *Language and Communication, 20,* 1–28.

Yeni-Komshian, G. H., Robbins, M., & Flege, J. E. (2001). Effects of word class differences on L2 pronunciation accuracy. *Applied Psycholinguistics, 22,* 283–299.

Young-Scholten, M., & Archibald, J. (2000). Second language syllable structure. In J. Archibald (Ed.), *Second language acquisition and linguistic theory* (pp. 64–102). Oxford, UK: Blackwell.

25

Fossilization in L2 Learners

ZhaoHong Han
Teachers College, Columbia University
Larry Selinker
New York University

> "What is essential is often invisible to the eye."
> —Anonymous

This chapter addresses the fundamental issue of why the majority of adult L2 learners are unable to reach the level of competence that they have aspired to, usually native-speaker target-language competence. This problem has been stated most clearly by Kellerman (1995a):

> One of the most enduring and fascinating problems confronting researchers of second language acquisition (SLA) is whether adults can ever acquire native-like competence in a second language (L2), or whether this is an accomplishment reserved for children who start learning at a relatively early age. As a secondary issue, there is the question of whether those rare cases of native-like success reported amongst adult learners are indeed what they seem, and if they are, how it is that such people can be successful when the vast majority are palpably not. (p. 219)

In the history of ideas, the place of this phenomenon is even more important. It has been central to second language acquisition since its founding in the late 1960s and may be the main reason why there is a field of second language acquisition at all. Selinker has long thought that the field of second language acquisition was 'spurred into existence' (discussed in Long [2003] in the text related to his fn. 1) by the idea that no matter what learners do, they will always be stuck in the second language at some distance from expected target-language norms. This idea has led to the hypothesis that being stuck in the L2 occurs with most, if not all, learners even at the most advanced stages. It was this idea that forced early SLA researchers, who believed they were working in a contrastive analysis framework (e.g., Briere, 1968; Nemser, 1971; Selinker, 1966), into positing intermediate linguistic systems that in some serious sense do not seem to change. Nemser, for instance, explicitly had the stabilizing idea, which he attributed to Weinreich (1953) where it is explicitly stated in the preface by Martinet.

These intermediate stable systems were thought to be intermediate between, but more important, different from, the native language as well as from the target language, hence "approximative systems" in Nemser's terms.[1]

One way to address the problem of observed (premature) stabilized forms was inspired by the Interlanguage Hypothesis (Selinker, 1972), which sought to understand the problem in terms of the concept of fossilization, the hypothesized (invisible) interlanguage process whereby interlanguage development in all linguistic domains can cease, and apparently, ceases differentially. The goal of this chapter is to look at and evaluate where the field is with this line of inquiry. This is a complex subject, with much comment over the past 30 years. Therefore, in this chapter only some main ideas will be highlighted. It will first be shown that fossilization can no longer be considered a monolithic concept as it was three decades ago, but rather a concept that is tied up with various manifestations of 'failure,' or "nonprogression of learning," by L2 learners in various contexts. It will then be argued that any attempt to explain fossilization by way of a singular explanation will prove to be inadequate and that contextual concerns of various types will be central. The chapter will end by arguing that in constructing theories of second language acquisition, fossilization remains a central issue to be confronted and explained, hence the need to develop principled approaches to investigating the construct.

The plan of the chapter is to first look at fossilization as a theoretical construct, then to regard the attempts to look at fossilization as an object of empirical study, and finally, to consider implications for theories of second language acquisition.

FOSSILIZATION AS A THEORETICAL CONSTRUCT

In this section an overview is given of a) the various definitions of fossilization that have appeared in the literature over the decades, b) the variables that frequently have been associated with the term, and c) suggested explanations.

Definitions

The term *fossilization* was introduced into the field of second language acquisition by Selinker in 1972 as an attempt to account for the observation that the vast majority of second language learners fail to achieve native-speaker target-language competence. Apparently, this observation, although not necessarily the fossilization idea, is now accepted as fact. Fossilization, as originally conceptualized to account for this fact, implied both a cognitive mechanism known as the *fossilization mechanism* (Selinker, 1972, p. 221) and a performance-related *structural phenomenon*, that is, forms that remain in learner interlanguage over time. As a cognitive mechanism, it was thought to be a constituent of a *latent psychological structure*, one that dictates a learner's acquisition of a second language. This was conceived of as different from the then popular *latent language structure* of Lenneberg (1967) that was widely assumed to be responsible for first language acquisition through a language acquisition device (LAD) that triggered Universal Grammar. This latent psychological structure responsible cognitively for interlanguage and hence, fossilization, has been much commented on over the years (see, e.g., the extended discussion in Ellis [1985]) but has not been directly studied, so that will be left as work for the future. As a performance-based structural notion, fossilization was defined in terms of hypothesized fossilizable structures:

> [F]ossilizable linguistic phenomena are linguistic items, rules, and subsystems which speakers of a particular L1 tend to keep in their interlanguage relative to a particular TL, no matter what the age of the learner or amount of explanation and instruction he receives in the TL.... (Selinker, 1972, p. 215)

This earliest conception suggests several properties of fossilization: fossilizable structures are persistent; they are resistant to external influences; and fossilization affects both child L2 learners and adult L2 learners alike. Behind these factors, it is important to note, is the strong implication that L2 learners lack the ability to attain nativelike competence, no matter what they do. It is precisely this strong hypothesis for *all* learners[2] that accords the construct of fossilization its intrinsic interest; it is what has drawn the attention of many second language researchers and practitioners.

Also, fossilization initially was thought to be shown empirically, primarily through the concept of backsliding, that is, retrogression to an earlier form of interlanguage, and this point is made explicitly in Selinker (1972) and much commented on in the literature. Since 1972, Selinker (working with others) has broadened the referential scope of fossilization: from backsliding to cessation of learning and to ultimate attainment, gradually moving away from the 5% estimate that was made initially concerning the hypothesized successful population of L2 learners, to the claim that no adult L2 learner can hope to achieve nativelike competence in all discourse domains (see, e.g., Selinker, 1996a, 1996b; Selinker & Douglas, 1985; Selinker & Lakshmanan, 1992; Selinker & Lamendella, 1979).

Beyond Selinker's definitions, the second language acquisition literature over the past few decades has also seen numerous interpretations of fossilization. In the eyes of many researchers, fossilization is a product as well as a process.[3] It is also seen to affect the entire interlanguage system as well as its subsystems; it is literally permanent as well as relatively permanent; and it is persistent and resistant. However, there is no unanimity: for some researchers, fossilization happens to every learner and yet to only some learners for other researchers. For some, it is only a stage of interlanguage learning, thereby incorporating the fossilization of correct as well as of incorrect forms (e.g., R. Ellis, 1985; Vigil & Oller, 1976). It can be externally manifested as well as internally determined. Furthermore, it is suggested that fossilization may represent the ultimate outcome of L2 learning (e.g., Tarone, 1994). Clearly, there are many possibilities here, more than we have space to discuss in detail.

One ongoing criticism is that the various definitions of fossilization developed thus far lack sophistication, thereby making the phenomenon unmeasurable (K. Gregg, 1997, SLART-L listserve discussion). In response, Han (1998) suggested a *two-tier* definition, taking into account both the innateness as well as the external manifestations of the phenomenon. Following this criterion, a cognitive and an empirical level with respective definitions are thus obtained:

> COGNITIVE LEVEL: Fossilization involves those cognitive processes,[4] or underlying mechanisms that produce permanently stabilized interlanguage forms.
> EMPIRICAL LEVEL: Fossilization involves those stabilized interlanguage forms that remain in learner speech or writing over time, no matter what the input or what the learner does. (Han, 1998, p. 50)

This two-tier definition solves at least part of the definitional problem by redefining fossilization at two interrelated levels. At the cognitive level, it specifies that fossilization is a cognitive mechanism made up of more than one process; at the empirical level, it ties fossilization with stabilization over time that has manifestations in interlanguage output. The two levels are also tied respectively to fossilization as a process and as a product; that is, the cognitive level pertains to fossilization as a process, whereas the empirical level speaks to its product dimension. The two imply a cause-effect relationship in that it is the cognitive level of fossilization (i.e., fossilization as a process) that gives rise to the empirical level (i.e., fossilization as a product). Moreover, fossilization on the whole is predicated on the condition of "no matter what the input or what the learner does," thus suggesting that fossilization, as a cognitive mechanism, would function regardless of learning conditions, and that fossilization, when showing up in interlanguage output, would be out of the learner's control.

Whether or not this complex definition will work out better in the long run than its predecessors is as yet to be judged by the field. Nevertheless, what does seem clear at this point is that the revised definition, despite getting rid of some problems, still leaves considerable room for interpretation. For example, at the cognitive level, it is still not clear what processes make up the mechanism(s) referred to, and presuming we do know what they are, the questions that ensue are how and when they are activated (this mechanism issue as a problem was discussed as early as Selinker, 1972). At the empirical level, as discussed later, although fossilization is associated with stabilization over time, both the length of the stabilization and its manner remain to be determined.[5] In interpreting cognitive, it also must be recognized that the present intellectual world is quite different from the more behavioral world of the 1960s when the concept was first discussed; now, internal mental processes strictly called cognitive in the past are not really cognitive in this literal earlier sense but also include neural and socio-affective processes.

Denotations and Explanations

Concerning work in fossilization over the years, there is one series of problems that cannot be ignored: The lack of uniformity in the understanding of the notion of fossilization has led researchers to use the term to denote a very wide range of phenomena. A summary of frequently associated variables includes (see also Han, 2003a, 2003b):

- Backsliding (e.g., R. Ellis, 1985; Schachter, 1988; Selinker, 1972).
- Stabilized errors (e.g., Schumann, 1978a).
- Learning plateau (e.g., Flynn & O'Neil, 1988).
- Typical error (Kellerman, 1989).
- Low proficiency (e.g., Thep-Ackrapong, 1990).
- De-acceleration of the learning process (e.g., Washburn, 1991).
- Persistent non-targetlike performance (e.g., Mukattash, 1986).
- Variable outcomes (Perdue, 1993).
- Cessation of learning (e.g., Odlin, 1993).
- Structural persistence (e.g., Schouten, 1996).
- Errors that are impervious to negative evidence (Lin & Hedgcock, 1996).
- Random use of grammatical and ungrammatical structures (Schachter, 1996).
- Ultimate attainment (e.g., Selinker, 1996a, 1996b; passim the SLA literature).
- Habitual errors (SLART-L listserve, 1997).
- Long-lasting free variation (R. Ellis, 1999).
- Persistent difficulty (Hawkins, 2000).

These denotations of potentially relevant variables have, in turn, spawned a myriad of attempted explanations, some of which are based on empirical studies ostensibly devoted to the subject matter of fossilization, and others of which provide speculations without any empirical basis. The major problem, it seems, is assuming fossilization without presenting any longitudinal interlanguage data for the claims made.

As a result, fossilization, in association with the listed variables, is found to be explained in the following plethora of terms, among others (for a comprehensive list, see Han, 2003a, 2003b):

- Multiple factors acting in tandem (e.g., Han & Selinker, 1999; Jain, 1974; Kellerman, 1989; Selinker, 1992; Selinker & Lakshmanan, 1992; Sharwood Smith, 1994).
- Satisfaction of communicative needs (Corder, 1978, 1983; R. Ellis, 1985; Klein, 1986; Klein & Perdue, 1993; Selinker & Lamendella, 1978).
- Absence of corrective feedback (Tomasello & Herron, 1988; Vigil & Oller, 1976).
- Lack of acculturation (e.g., Preston, 1989; Schumann, 1978a, 1978b; Stauble, 1978).
- Lack of input (Schumann, 1978a, 1978b).
- Maturational constraints (e.g., Seliger, 1978).
- L1 influence (e.g., Andersen 1983; Han, 2000; Kellerman, 1989; Schouten, 1996; Selinker & Lakshmanan 1992; Zobl, 1980).
- False automatization (Hulstijn, 1989, 2002a).
- Processing constraints (Schachter, 1996).
- Lack of access to learning principles (White, 1996).
- Lack of verbal analytical skills (DeKeyser, 2000).
- Lack of sensitivity to input (Long, 2003).
- Neural entrenchment (N. Ellis, 2002).

This list reveals multiple, unrelated explanations, presented in a roughly chronologically ordered sequence. Loosely conceived, they fall into the following categories: environmental, cognitive, neurobiological, and socio-affective, which are summed up in Han (2003a, 2003b). Suffice it to say that factors both external and internal to L2 learners contribute to fossilization (though, as argued by Selinker & Lamendella [1978], the so-called 'external' have to be filtered through internal neurofunctional structures and processes). Within the internal factors one can differentiate between cognitive, neurobiological and socio-affective ones. The cognitive factors—in line with more current thinking, as mentioned earlier—now include those that pertain to knowledge-representation, knowledge processing, and psychological processes such as attention, avoidance, and emotion.

Given the multiple dimensions of fossilization (mainly, general and local), any effort to explain the phenomenon through one unitary account will ultimately prove inadequate. Consider, for example, biological maturational constraints as a causal factor. Whereas it may explain away the general failure of the overwhelming majority of adult L2 learners to reach native-speaker competence in an L2, it is incapable of accounting for interlearner as well as intralearner differential success and failure in L2 learning (cf. Pulvermuller & Schumann, 1994). Hence, the biological account cannot serve as a universal ontological account of fossilization (cf. Birdsong, 1999; Scovel, 2000).

Summing up this brief excursion into conceptual issues regarding fossilization, over the years the term has become associated with a wide range of variables, exhibiting divergent interpretations of the construct. The lack of uniformity in the conceptualization and application of the notion, while creating confusion, points to the fact, among other things, that fossilization is no longer a monolithic concept as it was in its initial postulation, but rather a complex construct intricately tied up with varied manifestations of failure (Han, 2002, 2003, 2004). The proliferation of uses of the term *fossilization* is matched in excess by explanatory accounts exhibiting a rich spectrum with almost every perspective on second language acquisition represented: the cognitive, the neural, the environmental, and the socio-affective. Just as each idiosyncratic application of the term adds a new empirical property to the discovery of fossilization, each explanatory account reveals a new underlying factor, and together they weave a large and delicate picture of fossilization. The general understanding of the phenomenon is thus not to be based on a single perspective account but on a yet to be discovered integrative account of the various factors.

FOSSILIZATION AS AN OBJECT OF EMPIRICAL STUDY

Following the first suggestion of the concept of fossilization in the late 1960s, there were repeated attempts to devise a research methodology to successfully discover it empirically. This task has proved to be a difficult one. Historically, the first set of studies on fossilization occurred very early and is exemplified by Watkin (1970). Apparently, he was the first to empirically distinguish with different types of data between what Selinker (1966) called "meaningful performance situations," an early view of the discourse domains view of interlanguage. Watkin, using what is referred to here as *the-typical-error* approach showed that similar errors in article and verb formation occurred in Hindi-English and Japanese-English samples, thereby implicating the target language more than the native language in fossilization, a recurring discussion. With admittedly limited data, he found overgeneralization phenomena where the strategy might be described as reducing the L2 to a simple, functional system similar to that of the L2. In retrospect, though not longitudinal, this study did raise issues of transfer, or lack of it, and the possibility of differential fossilization by structure, issues that are still alive today.

Following Watkin and others from that period, many researchers have attempted to gather various types of data on fossilization, but fossilization is often assumed with the subjects being labeled from the outset as fossilized. The subsequent research effort is then to try to confirm fossilization in learners. One interesting set of studies were the *defossilization studies*. One should revisit the interesting series of case studies done in the 1970s by Schumann's students at UCLA (e.g., Agnello [1977] and Bruzzeze [1977]), since in all these cases, the defossilization attempts were unsuccessful, and this needs to be explained. Even when temporary defossilization seemed to occur, *backsliding* regularly occurred when attention was removed from the target language forms concerned. This lack of defossilization was thought to provide evidence that the subjects were initially fossilized, but a serious discussion about the place of these studies remains to be undertaken.

Another series of studies has relied on *cross-sectional methodology* for establishing what is fossilizable, considered by us as pseudolongitudinal. On the whole, researchers have looked to *persistence* and *resistance* as major indicators of fossilization, even though there is a lack of agreement on what persistent and resistant actually mean. Consequently, these studies have set out to look for different symptoms of fossilization. Some have sought stabilized deviant interlanguage forms; others have looked for typical errors across learners with the same L1, and still others have collected the remaining errors in the interlanguage of the advanced learners in the belief that what remained should be the most persistent and are therefore the most likely candidates for fossilization.

Empirical studies to date thus typically adopted one or a combination of the following methodological approaches: 1) longitudinal, 2) typical-error, 3) advanced-learner, 4) corrective-feedback, and 5) length-of-residence (LOR). Since the literature is vast, a detailed review of these studies is impossible here, so instead one empirical study will be cited to illustrate each of the methodological approaches.

Longitudinal Approach

The *longitudinal approach*, which is highly recommended for studying stabilization leading to fossilization, has few exemplars in the literature, and this is due, primarily, to the amount of energy and time involved. Nonetheless, they are necessary, and one of the best exemplars is Lardiere (1998a).

Lardiere reported on an 8-year longitudinal case study of an adult L2 learner of English. Her subject, Patty, whose L1s were Hokkien and Mandarin Chinese, had lived in the United States for 18 years prior to the study. Out of these 18 years, she was totally immersed in the English-speaking environment for 10 years. Data, admittedly limited, came exclusively from three audio-recorded conversations with Patty. The first and second recordings were 8 years apart; and the second and third recordings were 2 months apart.

One of Lardiere's primary motives for the study was interestingly methodological, namely to question an overreliance, following what is called the 'Weak Continuity Approach', on the criterial production rates of inflectional morphology as evidence for positing underlying syntactic representations in the interlanguage grammar. Lardiere examined Patty's pronominal case marking and past tense inflectional morphology across the three recordings. A quantitative analysis of the subject's past tense marking in finite obligatory contexts showed that Patty had "remained unchanged over the 8 years, despite massive exposure to target-language input by native speakers in a virtually exclusively target-language environment" (p. 17). In contrast, her mastery of pronominal marking is perfect, as evident from a quantitative analysis of the nominative forms that she used as subjects of finite clauses.

This differential result, of both aspects of Patty's interlanguage grammar achieving a steady state, with one successfully meeting the target and the other falling short of it, is interesting and a Universal Grammar explanation is provided with Lardiere (1998b; 2000) subsequently arguing for dissociation between development of inflectional affixation and syntactic knowledge of formal features.

Typical-Error Approach

In studies using *typical-error analysis*, errors that are characteristic of learners with the same L1 background are studied, usually across different proficiency levels. The much quoted studies by Kellerman (e.g., 1989) is a case in point. The major concern here was linguistic features that give rise to the syntactic accent of Dutch-English interlanguage. Two assumptions appear to underlie this study. First, errors that typify a whole community of L2 learners with homogeneous L1 background are the strongest candidates for fossilization; second, errors that are not only common to that community but also stay with its most advanced members are indicative of fossilization.

One well-known example comes from the study conducted by Wekker, Kellerman, and Hermans (1982) of a typical error in Dutch English that involves using 'would' in the protasis of hypothetical conditionals:

If I would be able to live all over again, I would be a gardener. (cited on p. 110)

This study investigated the performance of Dutch learners of English on nonpast and past hypothetical conditional sentences in Dutch and English under experimental conditions. The subjects were first-, second-, and third-year university students and were considered advanced. The study was pseudolongitudinal in that learners at different proficiency levels were used as subjects to provide a pseudodiachronic view of the interlanguage structure under scrutiny. Results obtained showed that all groups of subjects "showed at least some tendency to select $+/+^6$ as the English target, irrespective of their choice in Dutch" and that "even third-year students do not behave like native speakers" (p. 100). The fact that even the most advanced learners persisted in the typical error was, for Kellerman, the evidence of the tendency to fossilize. Looking at relevant evidence in world languages as well as in first language acquisition, he concluded that the fossilized structure was a function of the intersection of multiple tendencies (an early example of the 'Multiple Effects Principle' proposed by Selinker & Lakshmanan [1992]): a) avoidance of directly transferring the modal meaning of

Dutch past tenses to English past tenses intersecting with b) avoidance of structural ambiguity and c) creation of a structural symmetry.

Advanced-Learner Approach

This approach, similar to the previous approach because it uses advanced learners as the major source of information on fossilization, studies very advanced learners, usually calling them *near-native speakers*. The underlying assumption is that "the differences from native speakers are presumably limited, and therefore easier to study" and that "the few deviances from the native norm that do exist should be more certain candidates for inclusion in the category of fossilization" (Hyltenstam, 1988, p.70). Hyltenstam's study was, in fact, the first to deal with lexical fossilization and addressed two questions: Are there any differences between near-native and native speakers in the variation, density, and specificity of their lexicon in literacy-related language use? Are the near-native speakers different from native speakers in the quality and quantity of lexical units that deviate from the native norm? Students at Swedish senior high school level served as subjects. Among them, one half were bilingual in Finnish and Swedish and one half in Spanish and Swedish; these were compared with monolingual Swedish speakers as controls. The bilinguals were considered to be near-natives on the grounds that they could pass as native speakers of Swedish in everyday conversation; that they used their first language on a daily basis; and that they represented the whole range of grade levels. Quantitative measures were used to estimate lexical characteristics of the three groups, and a qualitative lexical error analysis was used to analyze two main error types with results showing insignificant differences between the three groups in the density, variation, and specificity of their lexicon: "the vocabulary, as it is used in the literate tasks in this investigation, seems to be as large, as varied, and as sophisticated in the bilingual groups as in the monolingual group" (p. 79). However, significant differences were found between bilingual subjects and the monolingual subjects in terms of the frequency of errors and the distribution of error types. Hyltenstam concluded that the results had some bearing on fossilization. In his view, the subjects who were near-natives were in an "end state" (Klein, 1986), and that the lexical deviances that remained in their interlanguage must have fossilized. He nevertheless urged that longitudinal studies of near-natives be conducted "to see whether fossilization features really are fossilized, or if they disappear with time, although at a very slow rate" (p. 82).

Corrective-Feedback Approach

A question that appears to confront any fossilization study is how can one establish that for a given learner, fossilization is a permanent condition and not merely a temporary cessation of learning? Selinker and Lamendella (1979) suggest that "the conclusion that a particular learner had indeed fossilized could be drawn only if the cessation of further IL learning persisted in spite of the learner's ability, opportunity, and motivation to learn the target language and acculturate into the target society" (p. 373). Thus, studies of fossilization need to grapple with these two issues: demonstration a) that a certain interlanguage structure has ceased developing, and b) that cessation of progress has occurred (or not) despite the learner being in both an internally and externally favorable position to learn.

To tackle the first issue, researchers have resorted to L2 learner reaction to *corrective feedback* as a means of determining whether or not learning has ceased developing. In Kellerman (1989), for example, it was not only a typical error in Dutch-English interlanguage community but also an error that seemed to be immune to the pedagogical intervention that was made the linguistic focus for investigating fossilization (see also Schouten, 1996). To investigate the second issue, researchers have often chosen to study learners who have lived in the target language environment for some time. The premise here is that the length of residence is correlated with the amount of exposure to the target language, hence a good indicator of the learning environment (see Han [2003c] for a more detailed discussion).

Thep-Ackrapong (1990) used a combination of corrective feedback and length of residence, to study an ethnic Chinese Vietnamese refugee student at an American university for a year and a half. Important from the present point of view, the subject, Lin, was *assumed* to be fossilized from the outset based on the observation that "she made many errors in all aspects of language performance though she had been studying and exposed to English in the United States for over six years" (p. 109). Focusing on infinitival complements and related structures, Thep-Ackrapong tutored the subject for one semester by means of providing explicit rule explanation and corrective feedback, and subsequently observed whether any progress was made. Data collected at three times over a year and a half (i.e., before and after the tutoring session and a year afterwards) indicate that the tutoring had little effect on Lin's use of the linguistic structures. In other words, her errors persisted despite the pedagogical intervention. For the researcher, this result confirmed her conviction that Lin was a fossilized learner, and the lack of progress was, in turn, attributed to Lin's lack of ability to analyze and synthesize linguistic elements.

Length-of-residence (LOR) Approach

Unlike the previous study, in some empirical studies LOR is employed as the singular criterion for determining fossilization, and as such, fossilization is again assumed as opposed to being established through longitudinal study. An example can be found in Washburn (1991), the focus of which was "to identify some characteristics of linguistic behavior that distinguishes fossilized non-native speakers from those who are still learning" (p. v).

Using primarily the well-discussed five years as the cut-off point, Washburn divided her undergraduate subjects into two groups, which she labeled fossilized and nonfossilized respectively. Within a Vygotskian theoretical framework, she devised a number of tasks, including grammaticality judgments, imitations, short-term learning, and picture narration. Data, compiled from several types of recordings, were collected to test several hypotheses, an example of which is that "On the short-term learning task, the nonfossilized subjects will learn (become able to learn) to produce the task utterance more accurately and efficiently than the fossilized subjects, as measured by the number of turns needed and the maintenance of accuracy of form" (p. 78). Subsequent data analyses showed that some of the hypotheses were indeed supported but some were not. For example, the hypothesis just mentioned was strongly supported, but where there was lack of support from the data, attribution was given not to a disbelief in these fossilized learners but to difficulty in accessing the required cognitive processes.

Evaluation of These Various Approaches

This has been a very brief review of a few, hopefully prototypical studies that have attempted to struggle with the difficult task of empirically studying fossilization. Han (1998, 2003a, 2003b, 2003c) and Long (2003) provide more detail on additional studies. What the previous cursory survey shows is that researchers have attempted various means to determine fossilization.

Positively speaking, a *typical error study* shows the pervasiveness of an interlanguage structure within a particular interlanguage group. This way, however, of trying to demonstrate fossilization has the drawback of only producing a general picture of the group at different levels at one point in time and, by definition, cannot show change/nonchange over time in individual interlanguage, where learning takes place. It either reduces the credibility of the typical error as the indicator of fossilization in an L2 learner's interlanguage, or falsely implies that the typical error would fossilize in every learner within the same interlanguage community. This latter assumption cannot be justified since fossilization is understood to be an idiosyncratic process (Nakuma, 1998; Selinker, 1992; Selinker & Lamendella, 1978). The use of such pseudolongitudinal evidence seems effective in revealing the genesis of the interlanguage construction, but weak in revealing individuality and may say nothing about the object of study, fossilization itself.

Turning to *advanced learner studies*, often called *near-native-speaker studies*, one sees a rationale that whatever has remained in the interlanguages of the group studied had been subject to long-term stabilization and changed least. Several types of questions remain here: If these advanced learners have succeeded in moving so close to the target language, why is it not possible for them to move even closer? In the absence of longitudinal evidence, how sure can one be that the deviant features are products of long-term stabilization rather than of more recent restructuring? (See, however, arguments against this rationale in Selinker & Lakshmanan [1992].)

Concerning studies that use *corrective feedback* as the diagnostic of fossilization, there is often the assumption that corrective feedback is a unidimentional rather than a multidimensional interactive process. One consequent problem is that learners' performance following the corrective feedback may be overemphasized, but not the nature of the corrective feedback itself. This can be problematic because in the feedback process, a number of factors—such as the explicitness, the timing, and the learner's interpretation—may interact to determine its effect (for recent studies of learners' response to corrective feedback, see Han, 2001; Mackey, Gass, & McDonough, 2000; Roberts, 1995). It follows, then, that if L2 learners do not respond to corrective feedback in the way the teacher/researcher desires, it is possible that the feedback provided is itself not appropriate and thus the fossilization issue is again not directly attacked (see discussion in Selinker & Lamendella [1978] in response to Vigil & Oller [1976]).

Turning now to the LOR studies, some recent SLA research has seen increased use of LOR in conjunction with age of arrival (AOA) to index L2 ultimate attainment and age effects in SLA (for a most recent collection of studies, see Birdsong, 1999). However, both LOR and AOA may have a limited scope of application here as they confine research to subjects who reside in the target-language environment. Moreover, research based on LOR raises the fundamental question that keeps arising regarding fossilization: In the absence of longitudinal evidence, how can one be sure that an interlanguage form has stabilized or not? LOR presupposes the knowledge of the time it generally takes for acquiring an L2, but this knowledge does not yet exist with regard to L2 acquisition. Time alone, when devoid of any substance, is an uninteresting variable. As Klein (1993) states, "... what matters is the intensity, not the length of interaction" (p. 115). And perhaps, as Selinker and Lamendella (1978) expressed it long ago, what is crucial with fossilization is how the neurofunctional systems engage with stimuli in such environments.

In conclusion, none of the diagnostics mentioned can stand alone as an independent and reliable source of evidence of fossilization. It is clear that empirical research must be preceded by careful consideration of the variety of factors mentioned in previous sections and perhaps others that have yet to be explored. Finally, it has been strongly argued over the years (for recent discussions, see Han, 1998, 2002, 2003a, 2003b; Lardiere, 1998a, 1998b, 2000; Long, 2003) that longitudinal studies are necessary to establishing long-term stabilization in individuals.

UNDERSTANDING FOSSILIZATION AS A PREREQUISITE FOR SLA THEORIES

As previously shown, there have been many attempts to deal with fossilization and each of them involves factors necessary to understanding second language acquisition in general. Thus, it is important for SLA in general that we try to get the logic right to demonstrate fossilization. Given how difficult it is to study fossilization over time and then to extrapolate from controlled experiments to real-life interlanguage interaction, it appears that there must be at least four sets of criteria to demonstrate the existence of fossilization or some form of cessation of learning[7]:

- Empirical studies must be longitudinal.
- There must be abundant positive evidence to the learner.
- The learner must show high motivation.
- The learner must have considerable opportunity for practice.[8]

As Selinker and Mascias (1997) stated, "... only with longitudinal interlanguage data in the context of positive evidence to the learner where there exist motivational criteria are we able to show instances of fossilization" (p. 257).

It is clear that the present state of fossilization research is still characterized by a plurality of unresolved issues, despite the popularity of the term[9]—often in dismaying collocations such as fossilized error or fossilized learner. With great strides made in SLA research over the past three decades, fossilization is no longer a monolithic concept, but rather one tied up with different manifestations of failure or non-learning or getting stuck in L2. Research attempts to examine failure are occurring on both a macroscopic and a microscopic level. On the macroscopic level, researchers (e.g., those who study the critical period effects in SLA) typically look at general failure (i.e., failure across the group of adult L2 learners). On the microscopic level, researchers look at individual learners and focus on the local and differential cessation of learning that takes place in various interlanguage domains such as phonology, morphology, syntax, semantics, lexicon, and pragmatics. Given the widespread use of the concept, it becomes essential that researchers make it clear what they understand by fossilization, at least operationally, in each study.

Research in fossilization, and understanding its etiology, is central to understanding second language acquisition and prerequisite to any SLA theory that purports to be general. This must be so, since, as noted earlier, the recognition that there is something "fundamentally different" (in Bley-Vroman's [1989] terms) about second language acquisition that is intimately related to invisible phenomena underlying fossilization has pushed early researchers into creating the construct of interlanguage in the first place, and thus has provided the impetus for the separate field of second language acquisition.

Over the past decades, significant advances have been made in understanding adult SLA. Several strands of research have come to the fore with great relevance to understanding fossilization. The first is the research on the *critical period* (CP) and *age in general*, long debated issues in SLA. Researchers (see, e.g., Bialystok & Hakuta, 1994; Birdsong & Molis, 2001; Johnson & Newport, 1989; Long, 1990; Marinova,-Todd, Bradford, & Snow, 2000; Patkowski, 1980; Scovel, 1988; Seliger, 1978; Snow, 1987) have vigorously argued for/against the validity of the Critical Period Hypothesis (CPH; Lenneberg, 1967) in the context of SLA. Long's review (1990), examining both the findings and the methodological designs of the past studies on CPH, points to maturational constraints and their potential consequences. Admitting such maturational constraints, Long asserts, allows for a more plausible explanation for reduced ability and failure. Of particular relevance to understanding fossilization is his insight that there exists a cause-and-effect relationship between the timing of the first exposure and ultimate attainment. Adult second language learners appear to begin with some degree of "biological handicap" (Slobin, 1993), and because of this, their learning is doomed to incompleteness. Concerns of fossilization must thus be integrated into the study of the critical period and age concerns in understanding second language acquisition.

A second strand concerns *native language (and 'other' language, interlanguage) transfer*, a perennial issue in any discussion of second language acquisition and where transfer appears to be central to any type of learning. Research on language transfer has taken us afar from an all-or-none view, which prevailed in the early days of SLA research, to a much more qualitative understanding of how prior linguistic knowledge may influence L2 learning. Transfer is now generally recognized to be a cognitive, idiosyncratic, and selective process that to a significant extent determines the quantity and quality of success in an L2. Even though it may consciously be acted upon (Andersen, 1983), L1 influence is largely an invisible implicit force that drives language acquisition (Kellerman, 1995b; Pavlenko & Jarvis, 2001). SLA research has produced a great wealth of evidence showing that this influence, as a psycholinguistic factor, intersects with a host of other factors, external and internal, leading to long-term stabilization (see, e.g., Han, 2000; 2001; Han & Selinker, 1999; Kellerman, 1989; Schachter, 1996; Schumann, 1978a; Selinker & Lakshmanan, 1992) and thus, potentially, to fossilization. So, the transfer concerns must be integrated into the understanding of fossilization in understanding second language acquisition.

A third strand of popular SLA research relates to the extensive work on *form-focused instruction*, which has blossomed in the last 15 years or so (for recent publications on the topic, see Doughty & Williams, 1998; Lightbown, 2000; Norris & Ortega, 2000; Schmidt, 1995). Issues examined along this line include, but are not limited to, the nature of the pedagogical procedures that appear to have an impact on interlanguage development, the role of many variables, such as attention, awareness, noticing, the role of carefully staged instructional interventions, and the role of interaction in leading to the learners' continued restructuring of their interlanguage system. Han and Selinker (2001, 2002, 2003) have tried to show that there is a possible causal relationship between certain pedagogical procedures and fossilization. If this can be demonstrated with systematic evidence, then concerns of fossilization must be integrated into our understanding of form-focused instruction in understanding second language acquisition.

A fourth strand derives from research on *tasks and processing characteristics* of adult L2 learners. Skehan (1998), for example, highlights L2 learners' natural inclination to focus on meaning, not on form. He claims that in the processes of comprehension and production, "meaning takes priority for older learners, and that the form of language has secondary importance" (p. 3). As a result of the meaning priority, learners may tend to employ what he calls a dual-coding approach to L2 learning: rule-based and instance-based, both of which together enable economical, parsimonious, and effective performance. Of particular relevance here is his insight that fossilization—by which he means erroneous exemplar—is the premature product of the rule-based approach, which is then adopted under the instance-based approach in language use, and that "if the underlying system does not so evolve, and if communicative effectiveness is achieved, the erroneous exemplar may survive and stabilize, and becomes a syntactic fossil" (p. 61). So, concerns of fossilization must be integrated into our understanding of social-cognitive demands in understanding second language acquisition.

In conclusion, notwithstanding its yet-to-be-determined nature, the construct of fossilization has enjoyed much popularity in the second language acquisition research literature as well as in the literature and discussions about second language teaching. The view advocated here is that fossilization research of a longitudinal kind must be carried out with care and that while fossilization may not be prevented in any absolute sense, it is possible to discover interventionist procedures to delay its onset, an effort essential and worthwhile in terms of the best learning and teaching traditions.

ACKNOWLEDGMENTS

We thank Mike Long and the anonymous reviewers for their valuable input and suggestions on an earlier version of this chapter, and Paula Korsko and Jung Eun Year for their research assistance. Any errors are ours.

NOTES

1. It is interesting to note that until the late 1960s, none of these researchers knew about the others' work and each discovered the phenomenon independently.
2. In a remark that has caused much discussion over the years, Selinker (1972) made a comment about perhaps 5% of learners possibly being on a different track and maybe being able to achieve nativelike competence. The idea there was not to come up with a precise number, 5% versus 4% or 6% and have to defend that, but to leave the way open to the possibility that some small percentage of people could in principle achieve nativelike status and if this were the case, then these individuals would, by definition, be going along another 'non-interlanguage' path in the learning of a second language. This is still an open question, perhaps unstudyable and ultimately, perhaps, depending upon various definitions of native. This issue is discussed further in the next section.
3. In Kellerman (1989), interestingly, fossilization appears as both a non-countable noun considered as a process and as a countable noun considered as a linguistic product.
4. In this context, cognitive assumes a broader meaning than is traditionally accorded it, encompassing not only aspects of knowledge development and use but also the dimension of emotion (see, e.g., Mandler, 1999; Schumann, 1998; Selinker & Lamendella, 1979). In addition, it is necessary to recognize that cognition results from the interaction between internal mechanisms and external social and cultural environments.
5. Following Selinker's (e.g., 1985, 1993) suggestion, two to five years of stabilization have generally been taken as evidence of fossilization (see, e.g., Han, 1998; Long, 2003). This criterion is, however, arbitrary in nature (for a discussion, see Han, 2003a).
6. + indicates the presence of the periphrastic conditional (would + infinitive) and − indicates the use of a past tense.
7. 'Cessation of learning' can be competence and/or performance related.
8. 'Practice' here does not refer to mechanic drills type of practice, but rather using language under real operating conditions (Johnson, 1996). It includes comprehension and production.
9. As has been pointed out several times, most recently by Long (2003), fossilization may be one of only two or three second language acquisition terms to have made it into a number of popular dictionaries; and it may be unique in being borrowed into other fields such as political discourse.

REFERENCES

Agnello, F. (1977). Exploring the pidginization hypothesis: A study of three fossilized negation systems. In C. Henning (Ed.), *Proceedings of the Los Angeles Second Language Research Forum 1977* (pp. 246–261). Los Angeles: TESL Section, Department of English, University of California.

Andersen, R. (1983). Transfer to somewhere. In S. Gass & L. Selinker (Eds.), *Language Transfer in Language Learning* (pp. 177–201). Rowley, MA: Newbury House.

Bialystok, E. (1978). A theoretical model of second language learning. *Language Learning, 28*(1), 69–83.

Bialystok , E., & Hakuta, K. (1994). *In other words: The science and psychology of second-language acquisition.* New York: Basic Books.

Birdsong, D. (1999). Introduction: Whys and why nots of the critical period hypothesis for second language acquisition. In D. Birdsong (Ed.), *Second language acquisition and the critical period hypothesis* (pp. 1–22). Mahwah, NJ: Lawrence Erlbaum Associates.

Birdsong, D., & Molis, M. (2001). On the evidence for maturational constraints in second language acquisition. *Journal of Memory and Language, 44,* 235–249.

Bley-Vroman, R. (1989). What is the logical problem of foreign language learning? In S. Gass & J. Schachter (Eds.), *Linguistic perspectives on second language acquisition* (pp. 41–68). Cambridge, UK: Cambridge University Press.

Briere, E. (1968). An investigation of phonological interference. *Language 44*, 768–796.

Bruzzeze, G. (1977). English/Italian secondary hybridization: A case study of the pidginization of a second language learner's speech. In C. Henning (Ed.), *Proceedings of the Los Angeles Second Language Research Forum 1977* (pp. 235–245). Los Angeles: TESL Section, Department of English, University of California.

Corder, S. P. (1978). Language-learner language. In J. C. Richards (Ed.), *Understanding second and foreign language learning* (pp. 71–93). Rowley, MA: Newbury House.

Corder, S. P. (1983). A role for the mother tongue. In S. Gass & L. Selinker (Eds.), *Language transfer in language learning* (2nd ed., pp. 85–97). Rowley, MA: Newbury House.

DeKeyser, R. (2000). The robustness of critical period effects in second language acquisition. *Studies in Second Language Acquisition, 22*(4), 499–534.

Doughty, C., & Williams, J. (1998). *Focus on form in classroom second language acquisition.* Cambridge, UK: Cambridge University Press.

Ellis, N. (2002, February). The Processes of Second Language Acquisition. Plenary speech at the Form-Meaning Corrections in Second Language Acquisition Conference, Chicago.

Ellis, R. (1985). Understanding second language acquisition. Oxford, UK: Oxford University Press.

Ellis, R. (1999). Item vs. system learning: Explaining free variation. *Applied Linguistics, 20*(4), 460–480.

Flynn, S., & O'Neil, W. (1988). *Linguistic theory in second language acquisition.* Dordrecht, The Netherlands: Kluwer Academic.

Han, Z-H. (1998). *Fossilization: An investigation into advanced L2 learning of a typologically distant language.* Unpublished doctoral dissertation, University of London.

Han, Z-H. (2000). Persistence of the implicit influence of NL: The case of the pseudo-passive. *Applied Linguistics, 21*(1), 55–82.

Han, Z-H. (2001). Fine-tuning corrective feedback. *Foreign Language Annals, 34*(6), 582–599.

Han, Z-H. (2002, October). *Fossilization: Five central issues.* Paper presented at SLRF 2002, Toronto.

Han, Z-H. (2003a). Fossilization: From simplicity to complexity. *International Journal of Bilingual Education and Bilingualism, 6*(2), 95–128.

Han, Z-H. (2003c, March). *Fossilization: Facts, fancies, fallacies, and methodological problems.* Paper presented at the AAAL 2003 Conference. Arlington, Virginia.

Han, Z-H. (2004). *Fossilization in adult second language acquisition.* Clevedon, UK: Multilingual Matters.

Han, Z-H., & Selinker, L. (1999). Error resistance: Towards an empirical pedagogy. *Language Teaching Research, 3*(3), 248–275.

Han, Z-H., & Selinker, L. (2001). Second language instruction and fossilization. RIS discussion group at the 35th International TESOL Annual Convention, St. Louis, MO.

Han, Z-H., & Selinker, L. (2002). Second language instruction and fossilization. RIS discussion group at the 36th International TESOL Annual Convention, Salt Lake City, UT.

Han, Z-H., & Selinker, L. (2003). Second language instruction and fossilization. RIS discussion group at the 37th International TESOL Annual Convention, Baltimore, MD.

Hawkins, R. (2000). Persistent selective fossilization in second language acquisition and the optimal design of the language faculty. *Essex Research Reports in Linguistics, 34*, 75–90.

Hulstijn, J. (1989). A cognitive view on interlanguage variability. In M. R. Eisenstein (Ed.), *The Dynamic interlanguage: Empirical studies in second language acquisition* (pp. 17–31). New York: Plenum.

Hulstijn, J. (2002a). Towards a unified account of the representation, processing, and acquisition of second language knowledge. In M. Pienemann (Ed.), Special issue of second language research: Language processing and second language acquisition. *Second Language Research, 18*(3), 193–224.

Hyltenstam, K. (1988). Lexical characteristics of near-native second language learners of Swedish. *Journal of Multilingual and Multicultural Development, 9*, 67–84.

Ioup, G., Boustagui, E., Tigi, M., & Moselle, M. (1994). Reexamining the critical period hypothesis: A case study of successful adult SLA in a naturalistic environment. *Studies in Second Language Acquisition, 16*, 73–98.

Jain, M. (1974). Error analysis: Source, cause, and significance. In J. C. Richards. (Eds.), *Error analysis: Perspectives on second language acquisition* (pp. 189–215). New York: Longman.

Johnson, K. (1996). *Language teaching and skill learning.* Oxford: Blackwell.

Johnson, J., & Newport, E. (1989). Critical period effects in second language learning: The influence of maturational state on the acquisition of English as a second language. *Cognitive Psychology, 21*, 60–99.

Kellerman, E. (1989). The imperfect conditional: Fossilization, crosslinguistic influence, and natural tendencies in a foreign language setting. In K. Hyltenstam & L. Obler (Eds.), *Bilingualism across life span* (pp. 87–115). Cambridge, UK: Cambridge University Press.

Kellerman, E. (1995a). Age before beauty. In L. Eubank, L. Selinker, & M. Sharwood Smith (Eds.), *The current state of interlanguage* (pp. 219–232). Amsterdam: Benjamins.

Kellerman, E. (1995b). Crosslinguistic influence: Transfer to nowhere? *Annual Review of Applied Linguistics, 15*, 125–150.

Klein, W. (1986). *Second language acquisition.* Cambridge, UK: Cambridge University Press.

Klein, W. (1993). The acquisition of temporality. In C. Perdue (Ed.), *Adult language acquisition: Crosslinguistic perspectives. Vol II* (pp. 73–118). Cambridge, UK: Cambridge University Press.

Klein, W., & Perdue, C. (1993). Utterance structure. In C. Perdue (Ed.), *Adult language acquisition: crosslinguistic perspectives. Vol II* (pp. 3–40). Cambridge, UK: Cambridge University Press.

Lardiere, D. (1998a). Case and tense in the 'fossilized' steady state. *Second Language Research, 14*(1), 1–26.

Lardiere, D. (1998b). Dissociating syntax from morphology in a divergent L2 end-state grammar. *Second Language Research, 14*, 359–375.

Lardiere, D. (2000). Mapping features to forms in second language acquisition. In J. Archibold (Ed.), *Second language acquisition and linguistic theory* (pp. 102–129). Oxford, UK: Blackwell.

Lenneberg, E. (1967). *Biological foundations of language.* New York: Wiley.

Lightbown, P. (2000). Classroom SLA research and second language teaching. *Applied Linguistics, 21*(4), 431–462.

Lin, Y-H. & Hedgcock, J. (1996). Negative feedback incorporation among high-proficiency and low-proficiency Chinese-speaking learners of Spanish. *Language Learning, 46*(4), 567–611.

Long, M. (1990). Maturational constraints on language development. *Studies in Second Language Acquisition, 12*, 251–285.

Long, M. (2003). Stabilization and fossilization in interlanguage development. To appear in C. Doughty & M. Long (Eds.), *Handbook of Second Language Acquisition* (pp. 487–536). Oxford, UK: Blackwell.

Mackey, A., Gass, S., & McDonough, K. (2000). How do learners perceive interactional feedback? *Studies in Second Language Acquisition, 22*, 471–497.

Mandler, G. (1999). Emotion. In B. Bly & D. Rummelhart (Eds.), *Cognitive science* (pp. 367–384). New York, CA: Academic Press.

Marinova,-Todd, S., Bradford, M., & Snow, C. (2000). Three misconceptions about age and L2 learning. *TESOL Quarterly, 34*(1), 9–34.

Mukattash, L. (1986). Persistence of fossilization. *IRAL, 24*(3), 187–203.

Nakuma, C. (1988). A new theoretical account of 'fossilization': Implications for L2 attrition research. *IRAL 36*(3), 247–56.

Nemser, W. (1971). Approximative systems of foreign language learners. *IRAL, 9*, 115–23.

Norris, J., & Ortega, L. (2000). Effectiveness of L2 instruction: A research synthesis and quantitative meta-analysis. *Language Learning, 50*(3), 417–528.

Odlin, T. (1993). Book review: Rediscovering interlanguage by Selinker, 1992. *Language, 69*(2), 379–383.

Patkowski, M. (1980). The sensitive period for the acquisition of syntax in a second language. *Language Learning, 30*, 449–472.

Pavlenko, A., & Jarvis, S. (2001). Conceptual transfer: New perspectives on the study of crosslinguistic influence. In E. Németh (Ed.), *Cognition in language use: Selected papers from the 7th international pragmatics conference, Volume 1* (pp. 288–301). Antwerp: International Pragmatics Association.

Perdue, C. (1993). *Adult language acquisition: Crosslinguistic perspectives. Volume I: Field methods.* Cambridge, UK: Cambridge University Press.

Preston, D. (1989). *Sociolinguistics and second language acquisition.* Oxford, UK: Blackwell.

Pulvermuller, F. & Schumann, J. (1994). Neurobiological mechanisms of language acquisition. *Language Learning, 44*, 681–734

Roberts, M. (1995). Awareness and the efficacy of error correction. In R. Schmidt (Ed.), *Attention and awareness in foreign language learning* (pp. 163–182). Honolulu, Hawaii: University of Hawaii, Second Language Teaching and Curriculum Center.

Schachter, J. (1988). Second language acquisition and universal grammar. *Applied Linguistics, 9*(3), 219–235.

Schachter, J. (1996). Maturation and the issue of universal grammar in second language acquisition. In W. Ritchie & T. Bhatia (Eds.), *Handbook of second language acquisition* (pp. 159–194). New York: Academic Press.

Schmidt, R. (1995). *Attention and Awareness in foreign language learning.* University of Hawaii at Manoa: Second Language Teaching and Curriculum Center.

Schouten, E. (1996). Crosslinguistic influence and the expression of hypothetical meaning. In E. Kellerman, B. Weltens, & T. Bongaerts (Eds.), *EUROSLA 6: A Selection of Papers. Toegepaste Taalwetenschap in Artikelen* (Applied Linguistics in Article form), *55* (pp. 161–174). Amsterdam: VU Uitgeverij.

Schumann, J. (1978a). *The pidginization process: A model for second language acquisition.* Rowley, MA: Newbury House.

Schumann, J. (1978b). Social and psychological factors in second language acquisition. In J. C. Richards (Ed.), *Understanding second and foreign language learning* (pp. 163–178). Rowley, MA: Newbury House.

Schumann, J. (1998). The neurobiology of affect in language. *Language Learning, 48.*

Scovel, T. (1988). *A time to speak: A psycholinguistic inquiry into the critical period for human speech.* Rowley, MA: Newbury House.

Scovel, T. (2000). A critical review of the critical period research. *Annual Review of Applied Linguistics, 20*, 213–223.

Seliger, H. (1978). Implications of multiple critical periods hypothesis for second language learning. In W. Ritchie (Ed.), *Second language acquisition research* (pp. 11–19). New York: Academic Press.

Selinker, L. (1966). *A psycholinguistic study of language transfer.* Unpublished doctoral dissertation, Georgetown University, Washingtom, DC.

Selinker, L. (1972). Interlanguage. *IRAL, 10*(2), 209–231.

Selinker, L. (1985). Attempting comprehensive and comparative empirical research in second language acquisition: A review of second language acquisition by adult immigrants: A field manual: Part one. *Language Learning, 35*(4), 567–584.

Selinker, L (1992). *Rediscovering interlanguage*. New York: Longman.

Selinker, L. (1993). Fossilization as simplification? In M. Tickoo (Ed.), *Simplification: Theory and application* (pp. 14–28). Anthology series 31. Southeast Asian Ministers of Education Organization, Singapore.

Selinker, L. (1996a). On the notion of 'IL competence' in early SLA research: An aid to understanding some baffling current issues. In G. Brown, K. Malmkjaer, & J. Williams (Eds.), *Performance and competence in second language acquisition* (pp. 92–113). Cambridge, UK: Cambridge University Press.

Selinker, L. (1996b). Research proposal for grant application submitted to the British Library.

Selinker, L., & Lamendella, J. (1978). Two perspectives on fossilization in interlanguage learning. *Interlanguage Studies Bulletin, 3*(2), 143–191.

Selinker, L., & Lamendella, J. (1979). The role of extrinsic feedback in interlanguage fossilization: A discussion of 'rule fossilization.' *Language Learning, 29*(2), 363–375.

Selinker, L., & Douglas, D. (1985). Wrestling with 'context' in interlanguage theory. *Applied Linguistics, 6*(2), 190–204.

Selinker, L., & Lakshmanan, U. (1992). Language transfer and fossilization: The multiple effects principle. In S. Gass & L. Selinker (Eds.), *Language transfer in language learning* (pp. 197–216). Amsterdam: Benjamins.

Selinker, L. & Mascias, R. (1997). Fossilization: Trying to get the logic right. In P. Robinson (Ed.), *Representation and process: Proceedings of the 3rd Pacific Second Language Research Forum, Volume 1* (pp. 257–265). Tokyo: Pacific Second Language Research Forum.

Sharwood Smith, M. (1994). *Second language learning: Theoretical foundations*. London: Longman.

Skehan, P. (1998). *A Cognitive approach to language learning*. Oxford, UK: Oxford University Press.

Slobin, D. (1993). Adult language acquisition: A view from child language study. In C. Perdue (Ed.), *Adult second language acquisition: Crosslinguistic perspectives* (pp. 239–252). Cambridge, UK: Cambridge University Press.

Snow, C. (1987). Relevance of the notion of a critical period to language acquisition. In M. Bornstein (Ed.), *Sensitive periods in development: Interdisciplinary perspectives* (pp. 183–209). Hillsdale, NJ: Lawrence Erlbaum Associates.

Stauble, A. (1978). The process of decreolization: A model for second language development. *Language Learning, 28*, 29–54.

Tarone, E. (1994). Interlanguage. In R.E. Asher (Ed.), *The encyclopedia of language and linguistics 4* (pp. 1715–1719). Elmsford, NY: Pergamon.

Thep-Ackrapong, T. (1990). *Fossilization: A case study of practical and theoretical parameters.* Unpublished doctoral dissertation, Illinois State University.

Tomasello, M. & Herron, C (1988). Down the garden path: Inducing and correcting overgeneralization errors in the foreign language classroom. *Applied Psycholinguistics, 9*, 237–246.

Vigil, N. & Oller, J. (1976). Rule fossilization: A tentative model. *Language Learning, 26*(2), 281–295.

Washburn, G. (1991). *Fossilization in second language acquisition: A Vygotskian perspective.* Unpublished doctoral dissertation, University of Pennsylvania.

Watkin, K. (1970). Fossilization and the interlanguage hypothesis. Unpublished manuscript. University of Washington.

Weinreich, U. (1953). *Languages in contact*. Publication of the Linguistic Circle of New York, No. 1.

Wekker, H., Kellerman, E., & Hermans, R. (1982). Trying to see the 'would' for the trees. *Interlanguage Studies Bulletin, 6*, 22–55.

White, L. (1996). Universal grammar and second language acquisition: Current trends and new directions. In W. Ritchie & T. Bhatia (Eds.), *Handbook of second language acquisition* (pp. 85–120). New York: Academic Press.

Zobl, H. (1980). Developmental and transfer errors: Their common bases and (possibly) differential effects on subsequent learning. *TESOL Quarterly, 14*, 469–479.

26

The Output Hypothesis: Theory and Research

Merrill Swain
The Ontario Institute for Studies in Education
The University of Toronto[1]

INTRODUCTION

In the 1980s, the word "output" was used to indicate the outcome, or *product*, of the language acquisition device. Output was synonymous with "what the learner/system has learned." In the decades that have followed, therefore, it is perhaps not surprising that the second language learning literature has been slow to take on the concept of output as part of the *process* of learning, not simply the product of it. In this chapter, my intent is to provide a description of the "the output hypothesis": the context in which it was proposed, supporting research and theoretical underpinnings, and future directions. This review will show that though an uphill battle, there has been a shift in meaning from output as a noun, a thing, or a product to output as a verb, an action, or a process.

THE OUTPUT HYPOTHESIS

Put most simply, the output hypothesis claims that the act of producing language (speaking or writing) constitutes, under certain circumstances, part of the process of second language learning. Furthermore, the processes involved in producing language can be quite different than those involved in comprehending language (Clark & Clark, 1977). Swain (1995) outlined three functions of output in second language learning: 1) the noticing/triggering function, 2) the hypothesis-testing function, and 3) the metalinguistic (reflective) function. These are discussed further. First, however, it is important to understand the context in which the output hypothesis was formulated.

Context in Which the Output Hypothesis Was Formulated

There are two aspects of the context that are important to mention. One aspect of the context was the dominant theoretical paradigm for second language acquisition

(SLA) research at that time (1980s): information-processing theory. The second was the widespread growth of French immersion programs in Canada, the evaluations of which were showing some rather unexpected findings.

Krashen's writings on the input hypothesis (e.g., 1982, 1985) claimed that there was only one necessary and sufficient condition for second language acquisition, and that was the presence of comprehensible input. Specifically, if learners are at stage "i" in their language development, they can acquire i + 1 if they understand input containing i + 1. Various ways in which input could be made comprehensible to the learner were proposed and investigated. Long (1983, 1985), for example, claimed that certain discourse moves such as clarification requests and comprehension checks served to make input more comprehensible. Considerable research effort was expended on the study of input, and the Xth University of Michigan Conference on Applied Linguistics was devoted entirely to the topic of language input (Gass & Madden, 1985). Pica (this volume) and Long (1996) have since outlined the theoretical developments and findings of this view of SLA. Suffice it to say, that in the early 1980s, the burgeoning field of SLA was dominated by the concept of input.

Indeed, when asked to write about immersion education for a special issue of *Language and Society*, a magazine published by the Office of the Commissioner of Official Languages in Canada, Krashen (1984), after claiming that "no program, to my knowledge, has done as well," stated that "second language acquisition theory provides a very clear explanation as to why immersion works. According to current theory, we acquire language in only one way: when we understand messages in that language, when we receive comprehensible input" (p. 61).

It was certainly the case that the initiation of French immersion programs in Canada in the late 1960s infused parents and teachers with renewed energy and excitement about the teaching and learning of French as a second language (FSL). In these programs, English-speaking children were taught some or all of their curriculum in French beginning with the start of school (early immersion), around grade 4 or 5 (mid immersion), or around grade 6 or 7 (late immersion). Evaluation after evaluation was conducted of these programs (for early summaries, see Lambert & Tucker, 1972; Swain, 1978; Swain & Lapkin, 1982, 1986). The results of these evaluations demonstrated that the French proficiency of the immersion students was more advanced than that of students taking 20 to 30 minutes a day of FSL. Furthermore, on some tests of French listening and reading comprehension, French immersion students obtained scores similar to those obtained by francophone students of the same age. However, to the surprise of some, the speaking and writing abilities of French immersion students were, in many ways, different from those of their francophone peers. It was these latter findings that raised doubts about the validity of the input hypothesis (Swain, 1985), most particularly about the argument that comprehensible input was "the only true cause of second language acquisition" (Krashen, 1984: 61). No one could possibly argue that immersion students did not receive an abundance of comprehensible input.

Alternative explanations were sought. One explanation, based on both informal and formal observations in immersion classrooms, was the output hypothesis (Swain, 1985). Observations revealed that the immersion students did not talk as much in the French portion of the day (in French) as they did in the English portion of the day (in English) (Swain, 1988). More important, the teachers did not "push" the students to do so in a manner that was grammatically accurate or sociolinguistically appropriate.

Thus it was that the initial version of the output hypothesis (Swain, 1985) referred to "comprehensible output." As Swain said, ". . . the meaning of 'negotiating meaning' needs to be extended beyond the usual sense of simply 'getting one's message across.' Simply getting one's message across can and does occur with grammatically deviant forms and sociolinguistically inappropriate language. Negotiating meaning needs to incorporate the notion of being pushed toward the delivery of a message that is not only conveyed, but that is conveyed precisely, coherently, and appropriately. Being 'pushed' in output . . . is a concept parallel to that of the i +1 of comprehensible input. Indeed, one might call this the 'comprehensible output' hypothesis" (pp. 248–9).

Mackey (2002) provides evidence of the reality of the notion of "pushed output." Mackey had adult ESL students watch videotapes of themselves interacting with others and asked the students to recall what they were thinking at the time when the original interaction occurred. Example 1 shows an interaction episode between a learner and a native speaker.

> NNS: And in hand in hand have a bigger glass to see.
> NS: It's err. You mean, something in his hand?
> NNS: Like spectacle. For older person.
> NS: 'Mmm, sorry I don't follow, it's what?
> NNS: In hand have he have has a glass for looking through for make the print
>   bigger to see, to see the print, for magnify.
> NS: He has some glasses?
> NNS: Magnify glasses he has magnifying glass.
> NS: Oh aha I see a magnifying glass, right that's a good one, ok.

The stimulated recall of the learner is provided next as an instantiation of the perception of "being pushed."

> In this example I see I have to manage my err err expression because he does not under-stand me and I cannot think of exact word right then. I am thinking thinking it is nearly in my mind, thinking bigger and magnificate and eventually magnify. I know I see this word before but so I am sort of talking around around this word but he is forcing me to think harder, think harder for the correct word to give him so he can understand and so I was trying, I carry on talking until finally I get it, and when I say it, then he understand it, me. (non-native speaker, excerpt b of example 3 in Mackey, 2002).

Mackey (2002) found a high degree of agreement between learners' perceptions and the researchers' interpretation that an interaction episode involved learners being pushed to make modifications in their output: 81.5% in student–teacher interaction in a classroom setting; 72% in NNS/NS interaction in a laboratory setting; and 64.5% in NNS/NNS interaction, also in a laboratory setting. This suggests that students' perception of being "pushed" is highest when the feedback comes from the teacher and least when it comes from a non-native speaking peer.

Looking back over the research of the late 1980s and 1990s, I think the label "comprehensible output" tended to get in the way of the idea of output as process even though the 1985 formulation was clear that the output hypothesis was about what learners did when "pushed," what processes they engaged in. There were two ways in which the "comprehensible output" label focused research on the product of learning. First, the label was taken literally, and out of context, so that "comprehensible" was taken by some (e.g., Van den Branden 1997) to mean just that—able to be understood— rather than output that was an improved version of an earlier version in terms of its informational content and/or its grammatical, sociolinguistic, or discourse features.

Second, the label (a noun) put the focus on product, rather than on process. Much of the research (e.g., Pica, Holliday, Lewis, & Morgenthaler, 1989; Pornpibul, 2002; Shehadeh, 1999; Van den Branden, 1997) conducted in the late 1980s and 1990s about the output hypothesis was descriptive in nature, and tended to focus more on "oc-currence than acquisition" (Shehadeh, 2002, p. 641). The research demonstrated that learners often responded to negotiation moves such as requests for clarification with modified output. Instances of this modified output were counted and compared according to context and learner variables, for example, the type of task (e.g., Iwashita, 1999) and type of negotiation move (e.g., Pica et al., 1989) that generated it, gender of participants (e.g., Gass & Varonis, 1986; Pica, Holliday, Lewis, Berducci, & Newman, 1991), and proficiency level of participants (e.g., Iwashita, 2001; Shehadeh, 1999).

Three Functions of Output

I turn now to a brief discussion of the roles that output might play in second language learning as proposed by Swain (1995). One function of producing the target language, in the sense of "practicing," is that it enhances fluency. As this seems noncontroversial, particularly if it is not confused with the adage that "practice makes perfect," I will not discuss this role further. We know that fluency and accuracy are different dimensions of language performance, and although practice may enhance fluency, it does not necessarily improve accuracy (Ellis, 1988). In each of the following three sections, I provide examples from the research literature that support the claim being made.

The Noticing/Triggering Function.   The claim here is that *while attempting to produce* the target language (vocally or silently [subvocally]), learners may notice that they do not know how to say (or write) precisely the meaning they wish to convey. In other words, under some circumstances, *the activity of producing the target language* may prompt second language learners to recognize consciously some of their linguistic problems: It may bring their attention to something they need to discover about their second language (possibly directing their attention to relevant input). This awareness triggers cognitive processes that have been implicated in second language learning— ones in which learners generate linguistic knowledge that is new for them, or that consolidate their current existing knowledge (Swain & Lapkin, 1995).

Example 2, taken from a think-aloud session with an eighth grade French immersion student while he is composing, is illustrative.

[2] *La dé. . . truc. . . tion. Et la détruction.* No, that's not a word. *Démolition, démolisson, démolition, démolition, détruction, détruision, détruision, la détruision des arbres au forêt de pluie* (the destruction of the trees in the rain forest).

(from Swain & Lapkin, 1995)

In Example 2, the student has just written *"Il y a trop d'utilisation des chemicaux toxiques qui détruissent l'ozone."* (There's too much use of toxic chemicals which destroy the ozone layer). In his think-aloud, we hear him trying to produce a noun form of the verb he has just used. He tries out various possibilities (hypotheses), seeing how each sounds. His final solution, *"la détruision,"* is not correct, but he has created this new form by making use of his knowledge of French: he used the stem of the verb he has just produced and added a French noun suffix. This example is revealing because it is an incorrect solution. It allows us to conclude that new knowledge has been created through a search of the learner's own existing knowledge, there being no other source. The learner's search was triggered by his own output, which he noticed was incorrect.

Here, as with Schmidt and Frota (1986), noticing means "in the normal sense of the word, that is, consciously" (p. 311). What is noticed is available for verbal report as illustrated in Example 2. Learners may simply notice a form in the target language due to the frequency or salience of the feature (Gass, 1997). Or, as proposed by Schmidt and Frota in their "notice the gap principle," learners may notice that the target language form is different from their own usage. Or, learners may also notice that they cannot say what they want to say in the target language (Swain, 1995). Noticing this "hole" (Doughty & Williams, 1998) may be an important step to noticing the gap.

Izumi (2002), building on previous studies (Izumi & Bigelow, 2000; Izumi, Bigelow, Fujiwara, & Fearnow, 1999), conducted a meticulously designed controlled experiment to examine whether output promotes noticing and learning of English relativization (object-of-preposition [OPREP] type of relative clauses [RCs]) among adult ESL learners. His study addressed two main questions: 1) Does the act of producing the target language promote the noticing of formal elements in it more so than visually enhanced input? 2) Does the act of producing the target language promote the learning of these formal elements more so than does visually enhanced input? There were four treatment groups and a comparison group. The treatment groups differed with respect to output requirements and exposure to enhanced input. Students were given a text to read for purposes of either reconstruction (+O) or comprehension (−O). After either reconstructing the text (in writing) or indicating their comprehension by responding to a set of questions, students read the original text again with the relative clauses either underlined (+EI) or not (−EI). For those who received the enhanced (underlined) input, the head noun, relative pronoun, and preposition in the RC were highlighted by a combination of bolding, shadowing, and font sizes. Then the students again reconstructed the story (+O) or responded to questions (−O). The comparison group was only administered the pre- and posttests. Pre- and posttests were given to assess the students' productive and receptive knowledge of English relativization. Additionally, two measures of noticing were obtained from the notes the students took when they read the text, and the uptake of the form in the output phases of the treatment.

The findings concerning noticing were somewhat mixed. Izumi found that the notes taken by the output groups as they read the text did not include as many head nouns, relative pronouns, and prepositions as those taken by the groups whose input was visually enhanced. However, in terms of immediate uptake of the form as indicated by the number of target-like uses of the OPREP RCs during reconstruction, visually enhancing the input did not add to the effect of output alone.

The findings concerning acquisition were much clearer. The results revealed a significant main effect for output, none for input enhancement, and no interaction effect. In other words, those students who reconstructed the text learned more about relativization than those who engaged in input comprehension activities independently from whether the input was enhanced.

To help explain the puzzle of the apparent greater noticing of the targeted forms by the enhanced input group but the greater learning by the output group, Izumi suggests that the notetaking measure served only to measure a superficial notion of noticing (much like choral repetition). The notetaking measure was a quantitative measure of noticing (attention), and did not take into account qualitative aspects such as the depth (Craik & Lockhart, 1972) or type (e.g., Robinson, 1995; Schmidt, 2001; Tomlin & Villa, 1994) of attention and processing that learners engaged in with the forms in focus.

Depth of processing refers to the degree of analysis and elaboration carried out on input (paraphrasing rather than mere repetition), with greater depth being associated with longer term and stronger memory traces. This implies that quantity of attention is less important than the quality of it, with deeper and elaborate processing being key. Izumi (2002) suggests that within this framework, "input enhancement may have caused mere recirculation or rehearsal at the same, relatively shallow processing level, which led the learners to experience only a short-term retention of the attended form. On the other hand, the greater learning evidenced by the output subjects suggests that output triggered deeper and more elaborate processing of the form, which led them to establish a more durable memory trace" (p. 570).

Although different types of processing (e.g., incidental versus intentional; focal versus peripheral) have been discussed in the SLA literature, Izumi (2002) draws particular attention to the concept of integrative processing as discussed by Graf and colleagues (Graf, 1994; Graf & Schacter, 1989). Graf's point is that not only must one pay attention to the elements but also the relationships among them so as to connect and organize elements into a coherent whole. To cite Izumi (2002) once again, he suggests that "output processing ... pushed ... learners further in their cognitive processing and prompted them to perceive or conceive the unitized structure. This occurs by virtue of the grammatical encoding operations performed during production. As a consequence, the output task served effectively both as the stimulator of integrative processing and as the glue to connect individual form elements, which ... were only vaguely related to one another during the comprehension process" (p. 571). Grammatical encoding is quite different in its effect from grammatical decoding, which does not push learners to reorganize their form-meaning mappings.

The Hypothesis Testing Function.   The claim here is that output may sometimes be, from the learner's perspective, a "trial run" reflecting their hypothesis of how to say (or write) their intent.

Mackey's (2002) study, mentioned earlier, has an excellent example of hypothesis testing from a learner's perspective. The learner is reacting to an interaction episode in which she, another learner, and a teacher are involved. During this episode, among other things, the learner is trying to figure out both the meaning of "suite" and how to say it. Here is what the learner says after seeing the video of the interaction:

> I am thinking at that time why she say "really?" she understands me or does not agree me or does not like my grammar or my pronounce? So I try again with the answer she like to hear but I still try out suit, suit, I cannot get the correct word but I see in my picture, written in the door of the room and I think it is a name, name of this area. I say suit, suit, I was try it to see how I sound and what she will say, and she does not understand me. Sad for teacher ... but I keep trying and here, here, she finally she gets my meaning, and she corrects me, and I see I am not I do not was not saying it in the correct way, it is suite suite and this sound better, sound correct, even to me (non-native speaker, Excerpt b of Example 4 in Mackey, 2002).

If learners were not testing hypotheses, then changes in their output would not be expected following feedback. However, research has shown that learners do modify their output in response to such conversational moves as clarification requests or confirmation checks. For example, in a laboratory setting, Pica et al. (1989) found that over one third of learners' utterances were modified either semantically or morphosyntactically in response to the feedback moves of clarification and confirmation requests. In communicatively oriented second language classroom settings, Loewen (2002) found that almost three quarters of learners' utterances were modified in response to teachers' "on-the-spot" (incidental) feedback (focus on form). The difference between the two settings clearly plays a key role here, a communicative classroom being a context in which learners would more likely feel comfortable to test out their hypotheses than in a test-like situation with a stranger.

Important in this argument is the assumption that the processes in which learners engage to modify their output in response to feedback are part of the second language learning process. However, until recently it has not been shown that modified (reprocessed) output predicted learning, only that output was sometimes modified in response to various feedback moves (see earlier discussion, and Lyster & Ranta, 1997; Lyster, 1998) . Recently, however, research has been directed at establishing whether the production of modified output facilitates L2 learning (e.g., He & Ellis, 1999; Mackey, 1999; Storch, 2000, 2001). In her Ph.D. research, McDonough (2001) found that learners who produced modified output involving the target forms of questions and past tense were more likely to learn them than learners who did not produce modified output. More important, as in Tanaka's Ph.D. research (2000),

McDonough found that output had an effect that was independent from the feedback that triggered it. Additionally, however, McDonough found that the only significant predictor of posttest scores was the production of modified output. This is entirely consistent with Loewen's Ph.D. research (2002) where he found that the best predictor of posttest scores was successful uptake by the students during teacher–student interaction.

As noted earlier, Loewen (2002) examined the occurrence, nature, and effectiveness of incidental focus on form episodes (FFEs) in communicatively oriented classes. Incidental focus on form consisted of instances where teachers reacted to a student's non-targetlike use of linguistic items (grammar, vocabulary, and pronunciation) as they arose in meaning-focused classroom interaction. Broadly speaking, teachers' reactions could be classified into those that provided the student with an answer (e.g., recasts) versus those that pushed the student to produce an answer (e.g., elicitations, clarification requests) (see also Lyster, 1998). Uptake by the students could occur in either case. Loewen observed 32 hours of classroom interaction in 12 different ESL classes of young adults, and found that teacher recasts were the most frequent reactive response, but that both uptake and *successful* uptake were more likely to occur in response to elicitation moves. In other words, students were more likely to modify their output, and do so successfully, when they were pushed to do so.

What is unique about Loewen's study is that, using Swain's (1995) suggestion, he made use of the FFEs that occurred in class to construct test items and then administered them to the particular student who had been directly involved in the FFE. A total of 491 FFEs were used as the basis for these individualized test items. His results showed that the best predictor variable of correct posttest scores was successful uptake, that is, output that was modified successfully during the FFE. This finding suggests that it is important for students to actually produce the targeted linguistic items correctly, supporting the notion that in these cases the learners were actively seeking feedback through hypothesis testing.

Explanations for why there may be a direct relationship between modified output and L2 learning vary—from ways in which producing the output stimulates processes implicated in second language learning (de Bot, 1996; Izumi, 2000; Linnell, 1995; Swain, 1995) to syntactic priming effects of the modified output on subsequent output (Bock, 1986 as cited in McDonough, 2001).

Swain and Lapkin (1995) identified in their learners' think-aloud protocols processes and strategies the learners used to solve language problems they encountered while trying to produce a written text. These strategies included noticing; generating and testing alternatives (generating and testing hypotheses); applying existing knowledge to known or new contexts (increase in control and consolidation); and applying new knowledge (internalization of new heuristics/rules/forms/knowledge). The communicative need engendered by the task pushed learners into thinking about the form of their linguistic output, moving them from semantic to grammatical processing. As Long (1996) says, production is "useful . . . because it elicits negative input and encourages analysis and grammaticization" (p. 448). Likewise, Cumming (1990) observed that the production of written texts particularly elicits these kinds of problem solving in a second language because learners are prompted to treat, while they compose and edit, their emerging texts as an object amenable to metalinguistic analyses and revisions.

De Bot (1996), making use of Levelt's (1989; 1993) language production model, argues that the impact of output in acquisition comes from increasing control over language forms and consolidating what is known (i.e., increasing automaticity of processing), thus releasing attentional resources for higher-level processes. In Levelt's model, the grammatical encoder syntacticizes the preverbal message using the syntactic specifications provided in the lemma in order to derive a surface structure of the message.[2] Consistent with the original formulation of the output hypothesis, Izumi

(2000) suggests that "It is possible that... the very process of grammatical encoding in production sensitizes [the learners] to the possibilities and limitations of what they can or cannot express in the target language. Such sensitization can be heightened by the feedback system available for internal speech and overt speech" (p. 101).

McDonough (2001) argues that modified output can serve as a "prime" for the subsequent production of the structure. She provides an example of syntactic priming involving question forms. In an initial question, the learner omitted an auxiliary verb from the question "What two guys doing?". The NS respondent requested clarification, and the learner modified her question form by adding the auxiliary "are." In the dialogue that followed, the learner produced several other target language (TL) questions with the same structure, suggesting that her modified output primed her subsequent use of the TL structure. McDonough also proposes that because priming results in the repeat production of a syntactic form, over time it will facilitate automatic retrieval of that form.

The Metalinguistic (Reflective) Function.   The claim here is that using language to reflect on language produced by others or the self, mediates second language learning. This idea originates with Vygotsky's sociocultural theory of mind. Sociocultural theory is about people operating with mediating tools (Wertsch, 1980, 1985, 1991). Speaking is one such tool. Swain (2000; 2002) tentatively relabeled "output" as speaking, writing, collaborative dialogue, and/or verbalizing in order to escape the inhibiting effect of the "conduit metaphor" implied in the use of terms such as input and output (Firth & Wagner, 1997; Kramsch, 1995; van Lier, 2000).

Speaking is initially an exterior source of physical and mental regulation for an individual—an individual's physical and cognitive behavior is initially regulated by others. Over time, however, the individual internalizes these regulatory actions—actions such as reasoning and attending. Internalization is an "in growing" (Frawley, 1997) of collective to individual behavior, and this growing inwards is mediated by speaking (and other semiotic tools). As Stetsenko and Arievitch (1997, p. 161) state it: "Psychological processes emerge first in collective behavior, in cooperation with other people, and only subsequently become internalized as the individual's own possessions." This means that the dialogue learners engage in takes on new significance. In it, we can observe learners operating on linguistic data, operations that move inward to become part of the participants' own mental activity. In dialogue with others, we see learning taking place (Donato & Lantolf, 1990; Lantolf, 2000a; Spielman Davidson, 2000; Swain, 2002).

These claims provide a basis for having students work together—eventually students are expected to engage in solo mental functioning, and that solo mental functioning has its source in joint activities. In those joint activities language is used, initially to externally and collaboratively mediate problem solution. Swain and Lapkin (1995; 1998; 2002) have called this joint problem-solving dialogue "collaborative dialogue," which is "taken in," so to speak,—recreated on the intramental plane—by the learner, and serves later to mediate problem solution by him or herself. Collaborative dialogue is thus dialogue in which speakers are engaged in problem solving and knowledge building—in the case of second language learners, solving *linguistic* problems and building knowledge *about language*.[3]

Swain and her colleagues (e.g., Kowal & Swain, 1997; Swain, 1998; Swain & Lapkin, 1998; 2002) have experimented with tasks that encourage students to engage in collaborative dialogue and found that tasks where students are asked to write something together tend to elicit collaborative dialogue as the students discuss how best to represent their intended meaning. Furthermore, they have shown through the use of post test items based on the students' collaborative dialogues that the collaborative dialogues were a source of language learning.

Similarly, Tocalli-Beller's (2002) data provide many examples of collaborative dialogues of pairs of students as they unravel the meaning of puns and riddles. Over time and together, the students work out the meaning of the puns and riddles—learning in action for certain. Later, on their own, the students are able to define the meaning of key words and help their classmates understand the basis of the humor. Data of these sorts, which trace in the learners' dialogue *about* language how they moved from noncomprehension to spontaneous use, provide a pretest/posttest, longitudinal study of learning.

Speaking also completes thought. Vygotsky (1978, 1987), Barnes (1992), Wells (1999), and others have argued that speech can serve as a means of development by reshaping experience. It serves as a vehicle "through which thinking is articulated, transformed into an artifactual form, and [as such] is then available as a source of further reflection" (Smagorinsky, 1998, p. 172), as an object about which questions can be raised and answers can be explored with others or with the self. As Smagorinsky (1998) says, "The process of rendering thinking into speech is not simply a matter of memory retrieval, but a process through which thinking reaches a new level of articulation" (pp. 172–173). Ideas are crystallized and sharpened, and inconsistencies become more obvious.

Swain and Lapkin (in press) provide just such an example of how a student's talk about language crystallizes ideas and, in this case, makes inconsistencies so clear that "unlearning" occurs opening the way for new learning to take place. Sue, a Grade 7 French immersion student, who, as she talks with the researcher during a stimulated recall session, verbalizes her understanding of the meaning of the reflexive pronoun 'se'. She thinks that the reflexive pronoun is in fact a tense marker (a rather remarkable and interesting interpretation of a reflexive pronoun). Key in this example is that through her own verbalization, *Sue talks herself into understanding that she does not understand—a step that must be crucial in her learning process.*

In turn 48, Sue is responding to a question from the researcher about the verb *se lever.* At that point Sue and the researcher are watching a video of Sue where she is noticing the differences between a short story she wrote and a reformulation of it. We can see in Sue's response to the researcher's question about *se lever* that Sue thinks that *se* marks the notion of the progressive aspect as well as the "near future"—*futur proche.*

SR-S. 48: [. . .] because I thought it meant like he was going to. So he was *se lever*, which means like in a moment, not exactly right away.

In turn 58, Sue suggests that *se* marks the progressive aspect ("He's doing it. . . ").

SR-S. 58: He's doing it and then he is doing it again. Instead of just kind of uh he did this and that and that, so it's a better form of saying it by adding the *se*. It's more French.

When asked about the difference between *se brosse les dents* and *brosse les dents* in turn 73, Sue suggests that by removing the *se*, this means that the event happened in the past.

SR-R. 73: Do you see a difference between the two? (*se brosse les dents* and *brosse les dents*)
SR-S. 74: Uh . . . yeah, because when you say *se brosse les dents*, it's kind of like um he is brushing his teeth and then he's gonna comb his hair. But when you take off the *se*, it's like so he brushed his teeth, combed his hair and then kind of left.

In the full data set, there are other examples of Sue's differing interpretations of *se*. Across the excerpts, Sue generates different explanations of the role of the pronoun *se*, and becomes increasingly confused. Finally, she acknowledges that she simply does not understand:

SR-R. 77: [. . .] Why would you need *se*?
SR-S. 78: Um I think . . . I don't know. I don't really get why you do need *se*.

Sue has talked herself into understanding that she doesn't understand the use of *"se"* in French. What Sue's verbalization has accomplished for her is two-fold: She has externalized her thinking, and her externalized thinking provides her with an "object" on which to reflect. Sue's speaking was a tool through which her thinking was articulated and transformed into an artifactual form, and as such became available as a source of further reflection. She recognizes through the inconsistencies in her explanations that she did not understand what this *"se"* is all about—a step that must surely be an important step for her language development to proceed.

From a sociocultural perspective, then, producing language has vital and significant functions in second language learning that need to be explored in the future. Over the last few decades, there's been a shift in meaning from *output as product* to *output as process*—a shift that creates the need for some new metaphors, new research questions, and a new respect for our research tools. If, just for example, verbalization has the impact I am suggesting on second language learning, then research tools such as think-alouds and stimulated recalls, need to be understood as part of the learning process, not just as a medium of data collection (Smagorinsky, 1998; Swain, 2002). Think-alouds and stimulated recalls are not, as some would have it, "brain dumps"; rather, they are a process of comprehending and reshaping experience. They are part of what constitutes learning.

Sociocultural theory, then, puts language production in a "star role," so to speak. Speaking (and writing) are conceived of as cognitive tools—tools that mediate internalization; and that externalize internal psychological activity, resocializing, and recognizing it for the individual; tools that construct and deconstruct knowledge; and tools that regulate and are regulated by human agency.

Information-processing theory and sociocultural theory both provide valuable insights about mind and memory. My view is that we should take full advantage of each theory for the insights each has provided, and for the many each has yet to inspire concerning the role of language production in second language learning. As Lantolf (1996) suggests, different theories afford different insights.

FUTURE DIRECTIONS

There are several directions that research about the output hypothesis could take. Experimental studies within an information-processing framework would seem particularly fruitful. Investigation of the levels and types of processing that output under different conditions engenders seems to me to be a particularly interesting route to pursue. Within a sociocultural theory of mind framework, ethnographic and case study approaches would seem to be more valuable at this point in time, although there is certainly a place for experimental work. Particularly useful to understanding processes and strategies of second language learning will be studies of the dialogue and private speech of learners as they work to solve language-related problems they face in their language production, be they at the level of morphology, syntax, discourse, pragmatics, or conceptualization of ideas. Of considerable sociocultural interest are other broader questions about verbalization; for example, if verbalization is such an important cognitive tool, can it help prevent memory loss? How is cognition distributed through verbalization? In what ways does the environment constrain or enhance learners' opportunities to produce language?

The most significant new understanding for me in studying language production is just how very important it is as a cognitive tool—as a tool that mediates our thinking. Pursuing this idea widens greatly the second language learning and teaching research agenda.

NOTES

1. I would like to thank those who read and commented on an earlier draft of this chapter: Alister Cumming, Huamei Han, David Ishii, Jim Lantolf, Sharon Lapkin, and Harry Swain.
2. Levelt's model assumes that messages are constructed independently of language production. It supports the conduit metaphor of communication.
3. Collaborative dialogue, of course, also serves to mediate solutions to, for example, scientific problems and to construct scientific knowledge, but that is not the focus here.

REFERENCES

Barnes, D. (1992). *From communication to curriculum* (2nd ed.). Portsmouth, NH: Heinemann.

Bock, K. (1986). Syntactic persistence in language production. *Cognitive psychology, 18,* 355–387.

Breen, M. P. (2001). Overt participation and covert acquisition in the language classroom. In M. P. Breen (Ed.), *Learner contributions to language learning: New directions in research* (pp. 112–140). Harlow, UK: Longman.

Clark, H., & Clark, E. (1977). *Psychology and language: An introduction to psycholinguistics.* New York: Harcourt Brace.

Craik, F., & Lockhart, R. (1972). Levels of processing: A framework for memory research. *Journal of Verbal Learning and Verbal Behavior, 11,* 671–684.

Cumming, A. (1990). Metalinguistic and ideational thinking in second language composing. *Written Communication, 7,* 482–511.

de Bot, K. (1996). The psycholinguistics of the output hypothesis. *Language Learning, 46,* 529–555.

Donato, R., & Lantolf, J. P. (1990). The dialogic origins of L2 monitoring. *Pragmatics and Language Learning, 1,* 83–97.

Doughty, C., & Williams, J. (1998). *Focus on form in classroom second language acquisition.* Oxford, UK: Oxford University Press.

Ellis, R. (1988). The role of practice in classroom language learning. *AILA Review, 5,* 20–39.

Firth, A., & Wagner, J. (1997) On discourse, communication, and (some) fundamental concepts in SLA research. *The Modern Language Journal, 81,* 285–300.

Frawley, W. (1997). *Vygotsky and cognitive science, language, and the unification of the social and computational mind.* Cambridge, MA: Harvard University Press.

Gass, S. (1997). *Input, interaction, and the second language learner.* Mahwah, NJ: Lawrence Erlbaum Associates.

Gass, S., & Mackey, A. (2000). *Stimulated recall methodology in second language research.* Mahwah, NJ: Lawrence Erlbaum Associates.

Gass, S., & Madden, C. (Eds.), (1985). *Input in second language acquisition.* Rowley, MA: Newbury House.

Gass, S. M., & Varonis, E. (1986). Sex differences in non-native speaker–non-native speaker interactions. In R. Day (Ed.), *Talking to learn* (pp. 5–25). Rowley, MA: Newbury House.

Graf, P. (1994). Explicit and implicit memory: A decade of research. *Attention and Performance, 15,* 681–696.

Graf, P., & Schacter, D. (1989). Unitization and grouping mediate dissociations in memory for new associations. *Journal of Experimental Psychology: Learning, Memory, and Cognition, 15,* 930–940.

He, X., & Ellis, R. (1999). The roles of modified output and input in the incidental acquisition of word meanings. *Studies in Second Language Acquisition, 21,* 285–301.

Iwashita, N. (1999). Tasks and learners' output in non-native–non-native interaction. In K. Kanno (Ed.), *The acquisition of Japanese as a second language* (pp. 31–52). Amsterdam: Benjamins.

Iwashita, N. (2001). The effect of learner proficiency on interactional moves and modified output in non-native–non-native interaction in Japanese as a foreign language. *System, 29,* 267–287.

Izumi, S. (2000). *Promoting noticing and SLA: An empirical study of the effects of output and input enhancement on ESL relativization.* Unpublished doctoral dissertation, Georgetown University, Washington, DC.

Izumi, S. (2002). Output, input enhancement, and the noticing hypothesis: An experimental study on ESL relativization. *Studies in Second Language Acquisition, 24,* 541–577.

Izumi, S., & Bigelow, M. (2000). Does output promote noticing and second language acquisition? *TESOL Quarterly, 34,* 239–278.

Izumi, S., Bigelow, M., Fujiwara, M., & Fearnow, S. (1999). Testing the output hypothesis: Effects of output on noticing and second language acquisition. *Studies in Second Language Acquisition, 21,* 421–452.

Kowal, M., & Swain, M. (1997). From semantic to syntactic processing: How can we promote it in the immersion classroom? In R. K. Johnson & M. Swain (Eds.), *Immersion education: International perspectives* (pp. 284–309). Cambridge, UK: Cambridge University Press.

Kramsch, C. (1995). The applied linguist and the foreign language teacher: Can they talk to each other? *Australian Review of Applied Linguistics, 18,* 1–16.

Krashen, S. (1982). *Principles and practice in second language acquisition.* Oxford, UK: Pergamon.

Krashen, S. (1984). Immersion: Why it works and what it has taught us. *Language and Society, 12,* 61–64.

Krashen, S. (1985). *The input hypothesis: Issues and implications.* London: Longman.

Lambert, W. E., & Tucker, G. R. (1972). *Bilingual education of children.* Rowley, MA: Newbury House.

Lantolf, J. P. (1996). SLA theory building: "Letting all the flowers bloom!". *Language Learning, 46,* 713–749.

Lantolf, J. P. (2000a). Second language learning as a mediated process. *Language Teaching, 33,* 79–96.

Lantolf, J. P. (Ed.) (2000b) *Sociocultural theory and second language learning.* Oxford, UK: Oxford University Press.

Levelt, W. J. M. (1989). *Speaking: From intention to articulation.* Cambridge, MA: MIT Press.

Levelt, W. J. M. (1993). Language use in normal speakers and its disorders. In G. Blanken, J. Dittmann, H. Grimm, J. Marshall, & C. Wallesch (Eds.), *Linguistic disorders and pathologies: An international handbook* (pp. 1–15). Berlin: de Gruyter.

Linnell, J. (1995). Can negotiation provide a context for learning syntax in a second language? *Working Papers in Educational Linguistics, 11,* 83–103.

Loewen, S. (2002). *The occurrence and effectiveness of incidental focus on form in meaning-focused ESL lessons.* Unpublished doctoral dissertation, University of Auckland, New Zealand.

Long, M. (1983). Native speaker/non-native speaker conversation and the negotiation of comprehensible input. *Applied Linguistics, 4,* 126–141.

Long, M. (1985). Input and second language acquisition theory. In S. Gass & C. Madden (Eds.), *Input in second language acquisition* (pp. 377–393). Rowley, MA: Newbury House.

Long, M. (1996). The role of the linguistic environment in second language acquisition. In W. C. Ritchie & T. K. Bhatia (Eds.), *Handbook of second language acquisition* (pp. 413–468). San Diego: Academic Press.

Lyster, R. (1998). Negotiation of form, recasts, and explicit correction in relation to error types and learner repair in immersion classrooms. *Language Learning, 48,* 183–218.

Lyster, R., & Ranta, L. (1997). Corrective feedback and learner uptake: Negotiation of form in communicative classrooms. *Studies in Second Language Acquisition, 19,* 37–66.

Mackey, A. (1999). Input, interaction, and second language development: An empirical study of question formation in ESL. *Studies in Second Language Acquisition, 21,* 557–587.

Mackey, A. (2002). Beyond production: Learners' perceptions about interactional processes. *International Journal of Educational Research* (Special issue on the role of interaction in instructed language learning). *37,* 379–394.

McDonough, K. (2001). *Exploring the relationship between modified output and L2 learning.* Unpublished doctoral dissertation, Georgetown University, Washington, DC.

Pica, T., Holliday, L., Lewis, N., Berducci, D., & Newman, J. (1991). Language learning through interaction: What role does gender play? *Studies in Second Language Acquisition, 13,* 343–376.

Pica, T., Holliday, L., Lewis, N., & Morgenthaler, L. (1989). Comprehensible output as an outcome of linguistic demands on the learner. *Studies in Second Language Acquisition, 11,* 63–90.

Pornpibul, N. (2002). *The role of writing in EFL students' learning from texts: A case study in a Thai university.* Unpublished doctoral dissertation, University of Toronto (OISE/UT).

Robinson, P. (1995). Attention, memory, and the "noticing" hypothesis. *Language Learning, 45,* 283–331.

Schmidt, R. (2001). Attention. In P. Robinson (Ed.), *Cognition and second language instruction* (pp. 3–32). New York: Cambridge University Press.

Schmidt, R., & Frota, S. (1986). Developing basic conversational ability in a second language: A case study of an adult learner of Portuguese. In R. Day (Ed.), *Talking to learn: Conversation in second language acquisition* (pp. 237–326). Rowley, MA: Newbury House.

Shehadeh, A. (1999). Non-native speakers' production of modified comprehensible output and second language learning. *Language Learning, 49,* 627–675.

Shehadeh, A. (2002). Comprehensible output, from occurrence to acquisition: An agenda for acquisitional research. *Language Learning, 52,* 597–647.

Smagorinsky, P. (1998). Thinking and speech and protocol analysis. *Mind, Culture, and Activity, 5,* 157–177.

Spielman Davidson, S. (2000). *Collaborative dialogues in the zone of proximal development: Grade eight French immersion students learning the conditional tense.* Unpublished doctoral dissertation, University of Toronto (OISE/UT).

Stetsenko, A., & Arievitch, I. (1997). Constructing and deconstructing the self: Comparing post-Vygotskian and discourse-based versions of social constructivism. *Mind, Culture, and Activity, 4,* 159–172.

Storch, N. (2000, December). Is pair work conducive to language learning? The nature of assistance in adult ESL pair work and its effect on language development. Paper presented at the Conference on Scaffolding and Language Learning in Educational Contexts: Sociocultural Approaches to Theory and Practice, University of Technology, Sydney, Australia.

Storch, N. (2001). *An investigation into the nature of pair work in an ESL classroom and its effect on grammatical development.* Unpublished doctoral dissertation, Melbourne University, Australia.

Swain, M. (1978). French immersion: Early, late or partial? *Canadian Modern Language Review, 34,* 577–585.

Swain, M. (1985). Communicative competence: Some roles of comprehensible input and comprehensible output in its development. In S. Gass & C. Madden (Eds.), *Input in second language acquisition* (pp. 235–253). Rowley, MA: Newbury House.

Swain, M. (1988). Manipulating and complementing content teaching to maximize second language learning. *TESL Canada Journal, 6,* 68–83.

Swain, M. (1993). The output hypothesis: Just speaking and writing aren't enough. *The Canadian Modern Language Review, 50,* 158–164.

Swain, M. (1995). Three functions of output in second language learning. In G. Cook & B. Seidlhofer (Eds.), *Principle and practice in applied linguistics: Studies in honour of H.G. Widdowson* (pp. 125–144). Oxford, UK: Oxford University Press.

Swain, M. (1998). Focus on form through conscious reflection. In C. Doughty & J. Williams (Eds.), *Focus on form in classroom second language acquisition* (pp. 64–81). New York: Cambridge University Press.

Swain, M. (2000). The output hypothesis and beyond: Mediating acquisition through collaborative dialogue. In J. P. Lantolf (Ed.), *Sociocultural theory and second language learning* (pp. 97–114). Oxford, UK: Oxford University Press.

Swain, M. (2002, April). Verbal protocols. Paper presented at the joint ILTA/AAAL panel on Drawing the Line: The Generalizability and Limitations of Research in Applied Linguistics. Salt Lake City, UT.

Swain, M., & Lapkin, S. (1982). *Evaluating bilingual education: A Canadian case study.* Clevedon, UK: Multilingual Matters.

Swain, M., & Lapkin, S. (1986). Immersion French at the secondary level: "The goods" and "the bads." *Contact,* 2–9.

Swain, M., & Lapkin, S. (1995). Problems in output and the cognitive processes they generate: A step towards second language learning. *Applied Linguistics, 16,* 371–391.

Swain, M., & Lapkin, S. (1998). Interaction and second language learning: Two adolescent French immersion students working together. *Modern Language Journal, 82,* 320–337.

Swain, M., & Lapkin, S. (2002). Talking it through: Two French immersion learners' response to reformulation. *International Journal of Educational Research* (Special issue on the role of interaction in instructed language learning). *37,* 285–304.

Swain, M., & Lapkin, S. (in press). "Oh, I get it now!" From production to comprehension in second language learning. In D. M. Brinton & O. Kagan (Eds.), *Heritage language acquisition: A new field emerging.* Mahwah, NJ: Lawrence Erlbaum Associates.

Tanaka, J. (2000). *Explicit/implicit learning of focus marking in Japanese as a foreign language: A case of learning through output and negative feedback.* Unpublished doctoral dissertation, University of Toronto (OISE/UT).

Tocalli-Beller, A. (2002, October). Focus on form and meaning through language play. Paper presented at the Second Language Research Forum, Toronto.

Tomlin, R., & Villa, V. (1994). Attention in cognitive science and second language acquisition. *Studies in Second Language Acquisition, 16,* 183–203.

Van den Branden, K. (1997). Effects of negotiation on language learners' output. *Language Learning, 47,* 589–636.

van Lier, L. (2000). From input to affordance: Social-interactive learning from an ecological perspective. In J. P. Lantolf (Ed.), *Sociocultural theory and second language learning* (pp. 245–259). Oxford, UK: Oxford University Press.

Vygotsky, L. S. (1978). *Mind in society: The development of higher psychological processes* (M. Cole, V. John-Steiner, S. Scribner, & E. Souberman, Eds.). Cambridge, MA: Harvard University Press.

Vygotsky, L. S. (1987). *The collected works of L. S. Vygotsky: Volume 1. Thinking and speaking.* New York: Plenum.

Wells, G. (1999). *Dialogic inquiry: Towards a sociocultural practice and theory of education,* Cambridge, UK: Cambridge University Press.

Wertsch, J. V. (1980). The significance of dialogue in Vygotsky's account of social, egocentric, and inner speech. *Contemporary Educational Psychology, 5,* 150–162.

Wertsch, J. V. (1985). *Vygotsky and the social formation of mind.* Cambridge, MA: Harvard University Press.

Wertsch, J. V. (1991). *Voices of the mind: A sociocultural approach to mediated action.* Cambridge, MA: Harvard University Press.

27

Speaking in a Second Language

Elaine Tarone
University of Minnesota

INTRODUCTION

This chapter will consider what is involved when an individual speaks, using a language other than the native language. Speaking is a process of *oral language production*. It is one of the traditional "Four Skills" involved in using a second language, and as such is usually viewed as the most complex and difficult skill to master.

STATEMENT OF PURPOSE

We can analyze speaking from a wide range of perspectives. The chapter will begin with an overview of these perspectives, cross-referenced where possible with other chapters in this book. It will then turn to a consideration of two functions of learner speech: transactional functions (including learners' use of communication strategies) and ludic functions. Following will be a discussion of the form of learner speech, with particular attention paid to characteristics of the pronunciation of adult second language (L2) learners, variation in the forms produced in learner speech, and the sort of knowledge for speaking that learners acquire. Implications and applications for teaching the skill of speaking in a second language will be drawn throughout the chapter.

OVERVIEW OF RESEARCH ON SPEAKING
IN A SECOND LANGUAGE

The scope of research on speaking in a second language is broad, far broader than can be dealt with in a single chapter. Fortunately, at least some of this material is covered in other chapters of this book.

We can analyze learners' speech from the point of view of *form* or *function*. Formal aspects of the second language that the learner must produce orally are described in terms of linguistic system. They include the sounds of the language, morphology and syntax of the language, discourse markers of the language, and lexis: words. Second language learners who attempt to produce second language forms orally do not in fact produce linguistic forms identical to those produced by native speakers; rather they produce interlanguage forms. The interlanguage is the linguistic system evidenced when an adult second language learner attempts to express meanings in the language being learned (Selinker, 1972; Tarone, 1994). When the learner speaks, there is a system evidenced in the form of what is spoken: a system with its own formal rules of phonology, morphology, syntax, lexicon, and discourse patterns. This system does not conform exactly to the rules of the target language as spoken by native speakers of the target language, nor does it conform exactly to the rules of the speaker's native language. The goal of development of the interlanguage is undefined. We can describe this system in its own terms, as an interlanguage system.[1]

The form of learner speech is described in the following chapters:

- Sounds produced orally: phonemic segments, syllables, and prosodic features (this chapter).
- Words and their meanings (Nation, chap. 32).
- Morphemes of the language: affixes and free morphemes like prepositions (Byrd, chap. 30).
- Syntax of the language, including word order (Byrd, chap. 30).
- Discourse markers of the language, including cohesive markers and transition words (Celce-Murcia & Olshtain, chap. 40).
- Variation in the forms produced in learner speech and the implications of this variation for our understanding of learner competence (this chapter).

Learners' progress in producing these forms orally is also described in other chapters of this volume (Lantolf, chap. 19; Pica, chap. 15; Swain, chap. 27; Han & Selinker, chap. 25; Williams, chap. 37).

Of course, second language learners must learn more than just the linguistic form of the second language. They must also learn how to use those forms to fulfill a variety of functions. Scholarship has focused on learners' production of oral discourse for functions that are *interactional* and *transactional* (cf. Brown & Yule, 1983a, 1983b; Yule, 1999) as well as *ludic* (Tarone, 2000). Discourse in its interactional function establishes or maintains social relationships; in its transactional function, it conveys information; in its ludic function, it is used for entertainment. These three functions of learners' speech are covered in this volume:

- Interactional functions of learner language, including politeness and pragmatics (Kasper & Roever, chap. 18), and turn-taking in conversation (Markee, chap. 20).
- Transactional functions of learner language (this chapter).
- Ludic functions of learner language (this chapter).

Taking a top-down approach, in this chapter we will begin with the functions of learner speech. As mentioned earlier, the interactional function is adequately covered in other chapters of this volume, so we will turn to the remaining two of three functions of speaking in a second language: transactional and ludic functions.

FUNCTIONS OF LEARNER SPEECH

Transactional Discourse

Discourse in its transactional function is language used to convey information (Brown & Yule, 1983a, 1983b).

Referential Communication.   Yule (1997) refers to discourse in its transactional function as *referential communication*, defined as

> communicative acts, generally spoken, in which some kind of information is exchanged between two speakers. This information exchange is typically dependent on successful acts of reference, whereby entities (human and nonhuman) are identified (by naming or describing), are located or moved relative to other entities (by giving instructions or directions), or are followed through sequences of locations and events (by recounting an incident or a narrative). (p. 1)

Speakers are not always successful in referential communication even in their native language. This ability is acquired late in the native language, and some native speakers never fully acquire it in their first language (L1). In addition, referential communication in L1 is

> clearly tied to institutional demands, beginning in school, for decontextualized language use, where the participants are not depending on substantially shared experiences or common knowledge. It requires decentering, or the recognition that others typically do not already know or see what the self obviously does. (Yule, 1997, p. 14)

This capacity to imagine the world from the receiver's point of view is central to successful referential communication: In this type of communication, the goal is for the listener to understand in relatively precise terms the information that the speaker is trying to send. For this reason, it is the speaker who can accurately assess both what the listener knows and does not know already, and who will be relatively successful with referential communication (Yule, 1999). Because of the premium placed on precision in encoding information for a possibly unfamiliar listener, referential communication

> . . . is, in spoken language, the necessary transition type of communicative language use that leads to literacy and the ability to cope with written language communication. Just as most written language is transactional in function and designed to be received by nonfamiliars, so too is the kind of talk known as referential communication. (Yule, 1997, p. 14)

Thus, oral transactional discourse appears to be directly related to the development of cognitive academic language proficiency (CALP), which in turn is essential for the development of literacy skills (Cummins, 1984; cf. Wiley, chap. 29).

Yule (1997) describes useful referential communication tasks that teachers can assign students in the second language classroom to encourage the development of transactional competence in the second language. Plentiful illustrations of already-developed tasks are provided, as well as principles to follow in devising new tasks and task formats to use for that purpose as well. Yule's claim that successful referential communication is key to developing the ability to use language in academic contexts suggests a range of potential pedagogical applications. For example, very simple versions of the referential tasks described in Yule (1997) and Tarone and Yule (1989) may be useful to provide undereducated adult English as a Second Language (ESL) students with contexts where they can develop more precision in their ability to use oral language transactionally with unfamiliar interlocutors. In pair-work in such tasks, the speaker has one picture to describe so that a hearer can pick it out from a set of three pictures that are very similar to it. Neither can look at the other's pictures, so the descriptive language must be very clear if the partners are to succeed in successful referential communication.

Communication Strategies. Speakers use communication strategies (CSs) to resolve difficulties they encounter in expressing an intended meaning. In SLA research, CSs have been studied in the context of referential communication[2]. Tarone (1980, p. 420) defines them as "mutual attempts of two interlocutors to agree on a meaning in situations where requisite meaning structures do not seem to be shared." Communication strategies are used both in the native language and the second language (Yule & Tarone, 1990), but they appear to be more common in communication between individuals who do not share proficiency in the same language, probably because there are more referential difficulties in such conversations. For example, second language learners have been shown to encounter difficulties performing referential communication tasks of the sort described in Yule (1997).

Imagine, for example, that a learner in an ESL class is doing a task that requires that he refer to a balloon, but he realizes that he doesn't know how to say "balloon." When this happens the learner may either choose not to refer to the object at all (an avoidance or reduction strategy) or try to find some other linguistic expression that will allow him or her to refer to it (a compensatory strategy). Numerous taxonomies exist for different kinds of compensatory strategies. For example, the learner might use a holistic approximation, referring to a related object (e.g., "something like a ball"); or be more analytic, describing the properties of the referent, as with circumlocution focused on either its physical properties ("a spherical shape, filled with air or gas and tied with a string") or its function ("we use them to decorate at birthday parties"). Code-related strategies may also work, as with code-switching ("globo"), foreignizing ("globe"), or word coinage ("airball"). The speaker may use nonverbal gestures or sound imitation, or appeal for assistance ("How do you say *globo* in English?"). Recall Tarone's (1980) definition of communication strategy use as "mutual": A speaker's selection of one or another of these strategies depends on her assessment of its likelihood of success with her particular interlocutor. For instance, the code-switching or appeal strategies illustrated would work only with listeners who also know Spanish. Similarly, the functional strategy used relies on the speaker's accurate assessment of the listener's cultural knowledge about birthday party decor.

Research on communication strategies has resulted in a number of publications over the years proposing different taxonomies for classifying communication strategies, or documenting L2 learners' communication strategy use on a range of different task types. Two general perspectives have been taken on communication strategy research (Kasper & Kellerman, 1997; Yule & Tarone, 1997). One popular perspective on communication strategies focuses on the cognitive processes involved in selecting one or another strategy, operates with a smaller number of categories, and views learners' ability to use these strategies as something that is innate and cannot be taught to improve performance in using the second language. Although observable linguistic differences exist between communication strategies in using the L1 and in using the L2, proponents of the "psycholinguistic" perspective argue that the underlying cognitive processes are the same, and so do not need to be taught. Examples of this perspective are Bialystok (1990); Bongaerts and Poulisse (1989), Kellerman (1991), and Poulisse (1990). The other common perspective emphasizes the linguistic expressions used as communication strategies, which are extensive and varied, and focuses on the core vocabulary in the L2 that might be useful for communication strategy use. Researchers following this second approach propose that L2 learners can be taught the linguistic expressions needed for effective communication strategy use and given practice to improve their performance in using strategies in speaking in the second language (Yule & Tarone, 1997). Examples of this perspective are Faerch and Kasper (1983), Konishi and Tarone (2004), Paribakht (1985), Tarone (1978b; 1986), and Yule and Tarone (1991).

Unfortunately, research on communication strategies done by researchers in both camps has not maintained the original emphasis on the essential contextuality of communication strategy use. Much effort has been expended to identify different types of communication strategies, classifying them into different taxonomies. This approach means removing the strategies from the interactive context in which they originally occurred, a process that has come under some criticism (V. Cook, 1993; Wagner & Firth, 1997). V. Cook (1993, pp. 131–137) critiques the methodology used in communication strategy research, calling for a wider range of data collection techniques (including introspection), less emphasis on taxonomic description and classification, and more emphasis on looking at the learner's communication strategy choices in the context of situation. These recommendations all make sense, especially if we view the learner's communication strategy use in conversation as an expression of free will and creativity:

> The concept of strategy . . . starts from the learner's choice. The learner is a human being with the free will to opt for one thing or the other; given that the learner is at a particular moment of time in a particular situation, what can the learner choose to do? . . . [there are] possibilities of choice open to the L2 learner in a dynamic situation. (V. Cook, 1993, p. 137)

Recent attempts have been made to examine communication strategy use using more contextualized approaches. Anderson (1998) studied interactions between nonnative speakers of English, and analyzed their use of communication strategies from the perspective of collaborative theory (Wilkes-Gibbs, 1997). Central to collaborative theory is the idea of the "grounding process," the interactive process of presenting and accepting ideas in building common knowledge through communication. Anderson found that the learners' communication strategy use in their interactions could be readily interpreted as serving this kind of grounding process, thus supporting Tarone's (1980) view of communication strategies as tools used in mutual attempts to agree upon a meaning. Wagner and Firth (1997) suggest that conversation analysis might be an appropriate framework for the study of communication strategies. Willey (2001), in fact, successfully uses conversation analysis in just such a study, examining the way the "appeal for assistance" strategy (Tarone, 1978b) is used in the context of discourse between adult ESL students in an intensive English program. He shows, for example, that their use of "direct" versus "indirect" versions of the strategy does not correspond to levels of ambiguity (as claimed by Faerch & Kasper, 1983, in using a more decontextualized approach), but rather to whether the speaker was involved in another course of action (such as telling a story) when they used the strategy. Appeals issued incidentally to the main course of conversational action were indirect, while appeals that were the main focus of the interaction were invariably direct.

These recent papers and studies exemplify a promising recent development in communication strategy research: a research approach that examines the use of these strategies as expressions of a speaker's creativity and choice in the interactional context of problem solving as part of successful referential communication. This approach is very promising, since, as V. Cook (1993) points out, it can also help us to see the relevance of communication strategy use for second language acquisition.

In terms of pedagogical applications, we can again recommend classroom use of tasks described in Yule (1997) and Tarone and Yule (1989) to encourage students' use of communication strategies to build common ground and solve problems that arise in the process of communication. Such activities can help students develop the core vocabulary they need for effective communication, as well as syntactic frames that are useful for that purpose (cf. Konishi & Tarone, 2004). At a deeper level, these activities encourage students to exploit the "possibilities of choice" (V. J. Cook, 1993) they have in dynamic communication situations. Even in pronunciation classes, where we often tend to focus only on getting students to produce standard phonological forms, it is useful to also teach them to use communication strategies when the interlanguage (IL) phonology interferes with comprehensibility. This teaching approach keeps the focus where it should be: on intelligibility (for more on intelligibility and comprehensibility, see The Target of Learning: Nativelike Accent versus Intelligibility).

Ludic Discourse

Ludic discourse involves the use of language for the purpose of amusing and entertaining oneself or others. For most speakers, it is less common than interactional or transactional discourse, and is also much less commonly studied. However, it has been argued that language play is important for second language acquisition (G. Cook, 2000; Tarone, 2000), and some L2 teaching materials provide opportunities for language play (Murphey, 1998). Some studies on language play (at all linguistic levels) are Broner and Tarone (2001), Garvey (1974, 1977), Huizinga (1955), Peck (1978), Rampton (1995), and Weir (1962). In language play, a speaker unpredictably manipulates language forms to provide entertainment and amusement for herself or others. There is no information exchange, and the primary focus is not on establishing or maintaining social relationships. Language play has been defined using Peck's (1978) three conditions, being typically a socially constructed phenomenon which is nonliteral, inherently entertaining, and rule-oriented. One kind of language play involves play with the sounds of language, rhyme, rhythm, song, alliteration, and puns; another type involves semantic play, "play with units of meaning, combining them in ways which create worlds which do not exist: fictions" (G. Cook, 2000, p. 228).

Broner and Tarone (2000) discuss ways that teachers can encourage learners to exercise their creativity in language play in the classroom. Tarone (2000) points out that the IL system could not develop unless the more conservative forces demanding accuracy were counterbalanced with more creative forces favoring innovation. We have seen that communication strategy use may be seen as an expression of choice or free will (V. Cook, 1993), and so, we conclude, as one such force for innovation. Language play is another such force promoting flexibility and innovation in the interlanguage phonological system (Tarone, 2000).

We have seen that there are elements of creativity involved both in the use of communication strategies to negotiate common ground in referential communication, and also in language play with phonological form. We now turn to a discussion of the form itself: interlanguage phonology and research on its development.

FORMAL CHARACTERISTICS OF LEARNER SPEECH

Characteristics of the Pronunciation of L2 Learners

At the time of this writing, it is fair to say that research on pronunciation learning in a second language is less popular than research on interlanguage morphology, syntax, discourse, or pragmatics. It seems that publications in the area of interlanguage phonology often seem to slip under the radar screen of researchers focusing on other aspects of learner language.

It is heartening, therefore, to report that there have been a number of anthologies, monographs, books, or special issues of journals in the last decade that focus on issues related to the acquisition of pronunciation skills in a second language. The reader who is interested in learning more about the findings of research on interlanguage phonology than is possible to report in these few pages should read Archibald (1995, 1998), Ioup and Weinberger (1987), James and Leather (1997), Jenkins (2000), Leather and James (1992, 1997), and Major (1998, 2001). For a particularly thought-provoking proposal for the teaching of pronunciation at a time when English is becoming an international language, and learners use English as a second language with each other more than they do with native speakers of English, Jenkins (2000) offers a stimulating and readable argument for a pedagogy that focuses on "accent addition" and mutual intelligibility as an achievable goal.

Research on interlanguage phonology has characterized the segmental, syllabic, and suprasegmental characteristics of the system, the origins of these characteristics in processes of native language transfer, overgeneralization of target language forms, or language universals of various kinds, and the relative importance of accentedness versus intelligibility as goals of pronunciation teaching.

Segments, Syllables, and Suprasegmentals.   Segments are the individual sounds, or phonemes, of a language. A second language learner needs to master the individual characteristics of the sounds of a new language, as, for example, the fact that in French the /R/ is uvular but in American English the /r/ is a glide. Sometimes there are completely new phonemes to be mastered, as with Xhosa clicks for English L1 speakers. In addition, the learner must master the allophonic rules governing use of segments in the new language: the way sounds change in different contexts. So, for example, in American English the /t/ is aspirated syllable-initially in a word like "tea," but becomes a flap medially in a word like "butter." In Spanish, however, /t/ is neither aspirated syllable-initially (e.g., "ti"), nor flapped medially (e.g., "rato"). Native speakers of English or Spanish learning Spanish or English as a second language will have difficulty mastering such patterns at the segmental level. Research on interlanguage phonology has been extensive at the segmental level (for examples of recent research, see Cichocki et al. (1999), Flege (1991), Flege, Bohn, & Jang (1997), Flege, et al., (1998), and summaries in Leather (1999a) and Major (2001)). Stockman and Pluut (1999) present evidence that segmental characteristics are more influential in many cases than syllable structure in predicting pronunciation errors. Flege's (1995) *Speech Learning Model* predicts the effect of similarity between segments in L1 and L2 on difficulty in acquisition of the L2 segments. Examples of segmental studies are those on Japanese learners' difficulties with English /r/ and /l/ by Sheldon and Strange (1982) and by de Jonge (1995), who also examined certain problematic English segmental contrasts for speakers of Arabic and Spanish.

The syllable, which is composed of consonants and vowels, is a unit of timing in English and other Western languages. The syllable is increasingly seen as more central to processing in second-language acquisition than the phoneme or the distinctive feature (Leather, 1999a, p. 22). Archibald (1998) distinguishes two major approaches to research on the way NL syllable structure affects L2 pronunciation: a structural approach (e.g., Broselow, 1988) and a typological approach (e.g., Eckman, 1991), each adhering to a different sonority principle. Segments can be grouped into sonority types in terms of where they occur in syllable structures; these segment types are, ranging from most to least sonorous: vowels, glides, liquids, nasals, fricatives, and plosives. Tropf (1987) found that degree of sonority of segments correlated well with their acquisition in German L2 by Spanish speakers (see Archibald, 1997, 1998, for a more recent model of sonority). Other research on interlanguage syllable structure includes Broselow, Chen, and Wang (1998), and Hancin-Bhatt and Bhatt (1997).

Though much SLA research has focused on the syllable, other suprasegmental units have also been explored. There has been increasing interest in the mora as a unit of timing in some Asian languages; see, e.g. the discussion in Major, 2001:18–19; Broselow & Park, 1995. In addition, Flege & Munro (1994) suggest that phonologists should also consider the impact of the word on IL phonology, finding that L2 perception responds to phonetic errors distributed over entire word.

Finally, research on suprasegmentals has touched on stress, rhythm, vowel length, tone, intonation, and rhythm in interlanguage phonology. Such suprasegmental (or prosodic) features are often the primary factors affecting judgments of the quality of L2 pronunciation (Anderson-Hsieh, Johnson, & Koehler,1992). Patterns of the placement of stress, or the perceived prominence of a syllable, can vary a good deal from one language to another, and stress patterns tend to be transferred in second language acquisition. See Archibald (1997, 1998) for recent studies of interlanguage stress patterns; Flores (1993) on rhythm in English L2; Kaltenbacher (1997) on German speech rhythm in SLA; Mairs (1989) on Spanish L1 stress patterns in English L2. Tone is pitch at the syllable level, and intonation is pitch patterning at anything from the syllable to the sentence level. There is relatively little SLA research on tone and intonation; some studies of possible interest are de Bot (1994), Holden (1993), and Leather (1997).

Evidence of Phonological Learning Processes: Transfer, Markedness, and Developmental Factors.   The major process influencing the interlanguage sound system is transfer, or the influence of the native language phonology. Learners tend to rely on their native language sound system when they pronounce the L2. This is true of their production of segments, as predicted by the Speech Learning Model (Flege, 1995); their production of syllables (see Eckman & Iverson, 1993); and also in the suprasegmentals they produce (Kaltenbacher, 1997; Mairs, 1989). At one time, *Contrastive Analysis* claimed to be able to predict all pronunciation difficulties by identifying the differences between native language and target language pronunciation patterns; where there were differences, there would be difficulty (Lado, 1957). However, abundant empirical data over the last half century have clearly shown that native language transfer, while it exerts a strong influence on interlanguage phonology, is not the only source of pronunciation errors in SLA. Difficulty in pronouncing L2 sounds is not completely predicted by L1-L2 differences; other factors are involved.

One of those other factors is a kind of language universal called *markedness*. Sounds and types of sounds vary in the frequency with which they occur in world languages; the more frequent sounds (the unmarked ones) appear to be easier to acquire than the less frequent sounds (the marked ones). These markedness relations can be laid out as simple frequencies. Major (2001, p. 42) gives the example of the American English /r/, which is more marked than the American English /l/ because in the languages of the world, the American way of pronouncing /r/ makes up only about 5% of all liquids but the /l/ makes up 42% of them. Markedness relations are often framed as implicational hierarchies that show the relative frequencies of given phonological features. For example, often the presence of Sound Y in any language implies that that language also has Sound X (but not vice versa); thus, Sound X is unmarked (and more frequent) relative to Sound Y. Such implicational hierarchies may be made up of segment types or syllable types; for example, it is a fact that if any language has a CVC syllable structure, it will also have a CV syllable structure. Thus, presence of CVC syllables in any language implies the presence of CV syllables in that language.

Eckman's (1977) *Markedness Differential Hypothesis* (MDH) predicts that, in second language acquisition, native language transfer combines with markedness to shape IL phonology; in general, unmarked phenomena in any implicational hierarchy are acquired before marked phenomena. This influence of markedness on difficulty, order of acquisition, and success in the process of acquisition of interlanguage phonology has been supported by subsequent research (e.g., Eckman & Iverson, 1993). Carlisle has done extensive work validating predictions of the MDH in the consonant clusters of Spanish-speaking learners of English (e.g., Carlisle 1991), and Major (1996) used a VARBRUL analysis of the phonology of Brazilians learning English to show that initial and final consonant clusters conformed to predictions of the MDH. However, because the MDH did not account for all the data, Eckman (1991) subsequently proposed the *Structural Conformity Hypothesis* (SCH), which claims that as natural languages, interlanguages obey all primary language universals (not just markedness universals). Current research supporting the SCH includes Carlisle (1998, 1999).

In addition to NL transfer effects, sometimes there are developmental influences, such as sound substitutions made by second language learners that are the same as, or similar to, those produced by children acquiring the TL as native speakers. Major (1986, 2001) proposed the *Ontogeny Model* (OM) to describe the relationship between the two factors of native language transfer and these universal developmental variants in the acquisition of an IL sound system. The model predicts that at early stages of acquisition of an interlanguage phonology, universal factors (termed "UG") will not play a major role because the influence of transfer is strong and the influence of developmental factors is minimal. According to the model, however, at later stages of acquisition the role of UG will increase because transfer decreases and developmental factors decrease. The Ontogeny Model has received some support from Hancin-Bhatt and Bhatt (1997), who use an Optimality Theory framework to discuss the interaction between NL transfer and the developmental factors described in the OM.

To sum up, then, the interacting factors that influence the pronunciation of a second language include transfer of sound patterns from the native language, and universal influences such as the relative markedness of the particular phonological feature being acquired and developmental features relevant to the particular target language.

Leather (1999a) sums up the pedagogical implications of research on interlanguage phonology this way:

> While the teacher cannot be expected to exert very detailed control on all the phonological environments to which the learner is exposed, the developer of teaching materials can profitably take into account the difficulties that can be predicted—on the basis of markedness, syllable phonotactics, and so on. (p. 37)

More work is needed in the future to find ways to incorporate these research findings into pronunciation textbooks, but all this research assumes that the target of acquisition is known and that learning to pronounce a second language is simply a linguistic matter. It is time to step back and ask a prior question that is also relevant to teaching the pronunciation of a second language: What is the target of pronunciation learning?

The Target of Learning: Nativelike Accent Versus Intelligibility. Brown and Yule (1983b, p. 3) ask, "From the point of view of pronunciation, what is a reasonable model?". The model has often been assumed to be the nebulous "ideal native speaker," and "nativelike pronunciation" has been taken as the goal of L2 pronunciation teaching. It was believed that this was "a proper—if largely unattainable—goal, and that any pronunciation that fell much short of the nativelike could be considered defective and would impair intelligibility" (Leather, 1999a, p. 35). Certainly this has been the assumption of the ubiquitous "Accent Reduction" courses and programs for immigrants that proliferate in U.S. contexts, and is an approach that many, apparently including Pennington (1998), still advocate. In this view, the model is the native speaker of some standard variety of the second language.

Intelligibility can be understood as the degree to which a speaker's utterance is understood by a listener. It is of course an empirical question whether non-nativelike pronunciation impairs intelligibility. Munro and Derwing (2001) undertook an investigation of the relationship between foreign accent and intelligibility. Eighteen native speakers of English judged the pronunciation of ten NSs of Mandarin speaking English as a second language with regard to the amount of global foreign accent, intelligibility, and comprehensibility. Intelligibility was operationalized as the number of deviations between what a speaker said and what listeners could write down (e.g., missing words, wrong words); listeners assigned global comprehensibility scores on a 9-point Likert scale. The study showed that even heavily accented speech was sometimes perfectly intelligible to native speakers. Prosodic errors were much more influential in loss of intelligibility than segmental errors. Other studies replicated their findings and expanded on them; Munro and Derwing (2001), for example, find that L2 speech rates that are somewhat faster than the most common L2 user rates were perceived by native speakers as more comprehensible and less accented, though speeds that were very fast or very slow had low ratings. Interestingly, Derwing, Munro, and Wiebe (1998) show that some pedagogical methods may be effective in improving intelligibility whereas others only affect accentedness.

The goal of "nativelike accent" has always been problematic, and is increasingly being questioned by researchers and educators alike. The goal has been problematic because it has apparently been unattainable for virtually all adult second language learners (see Han & Selinker, chap. 25 on fossilization in SLA). From the very beginning of research on interlanguage, researchers like Scovel (1969) pointed out that second language learners could apparently achieve nativelike proficiency in all areas of the language except pronunciation. Scovel coined the term *Joseph Conrad Phenomenon* to refer to advanced second language learners who apparently sounded like native speakers in their use of syntax, morphology, and discourse, yet retained foreign accents (Henry Kissinger has been offered as a more recent equivalent example of this type of learner). Tarone (1978a) argued that the most likely cause of this retention of native accent is social and affective, since pronunciation is a primary indicator of group membership and identity. Brown and Yule (1983b) pointed out as well the profound sociocultural forces favoring accent retention:

> . . . students are not going to be highly motivated to improve their pronunciation beyond a certain point. Most students identify 'how they speak' with their own personal and cultural identities. Many foreign speakers of English who have lived in Britain for twenty or thirty years understand English just about perfectly, and produce English just about perfectly in every respect, except that they still retain a foreign accent. (p. 22)

V. J. Cook (1993) and Jenkins (2000) among many others in this field, point to the increasing prevalence of English as an International Language (EIL) by non-native speakers of English worldwide (cf. Kachru, chap. 9), and argue that in view of the purposes for which English is now used, mutual intelligibility is a far more sensible target of pronunciation instruction than "nativelike accent."

Jenkins (2000) focuses on the uses of EIL and on intelligibility in conversations between NNSs who do not share the same native language (NL). In her research on such conversations, phonological patterns converged in ways apparently aimed at improving communication. This did not always mean more correct TL-like patterns or more NL-like patterns, and though the learners accommodated toward each other's communicative needs, this didn't always mean adopting one another's phonological features. Jenkins claims that successful communicators gravitated toward an intelligible phonological core. On the basis of this research, Jenkins proposes use of a Lingua Franca Core (LFC) as the learning target in EIL pronunciation teaching. In the LFC, the target is adjusted with a focus on phonemes, cluster simplification patterns, and prosody that are deliberately nonstandard, but masterable and facilitative of intelligibility[3]. The author argues for "accent addition" instead of "accent reduction" (p. 209) and suggests ways accommodation can be practiced in English Language Teaching (ELT) classrooms. Jenkins states that pronunciation teachers and materials writers must be conversant with the sociolinguistic factors involved in the use of

English as an international lingua franca worldwide. Any phonology course designed for teachers of EIL as opposed to English as a Foreign Language (ESL) or English as a Foreign Language (EFL) "is morally obliged to consider L2 accent within a framework of sociolinguistic variation rather than within one of 'NNS' error" (Jenkins, 2000, p. 202).

How then is L2 accent affected by sociolinguistic variation?

Variation in Forms Produced in L2 Learner Speech

Speakers' tendency to vary their production of phonological form in response to a range of social factors has been well attested in the realm of phonological research, not just in second language research but in first language research as well. As a result, the notion of interlanguage variation is far less controversial among phoneticians and phonologists than it is among researchers on interlanguage morphology and syntax. Few if any researchers on IL phonology would argue that variation does not occur or should not be described. Major (2001), for example, states flatly:

> Variation exists and furthermore all language data show variation both in NSs and NNSs... Therefore, any model, theory, or purported explanation that fails to account for variation is not accounting for the data, period. (Major, 2001, p. 69)

Research has documented this systematic variation from the beginning of research on L2 learner language: See Nemser (1971), Dickerson (1975), Dickerson and Dickerson (1977), and Gatbonton (1978), all studies documenting shifts in the accuracy of phonological forms produced on different elicitation tasks. Tarone (1979, 1983) posited that when second language learners pay the most attention to their speech (i.e., are focused on form), their speech in this "careful style" would tend to be more accurate: that is, closer to target language norms. However, in fact, research has shown this view to be too simple.

Both Beebe (1980) and James (1983) tested this claim and although they found systematic shifts in the accuracy of IL phonology, they also found that the "careful" style was not always necessarily closer to TL norms. In both cases, variants from the L1 careful style turned up in the IL careful style, but in Beebe's case, the phonological variants transferred from the Thai L1 careful style actually led to *less* accuracy in English and the Thai informal style variants led to *more* accuracy in English. In other words, the L2 learner's careful style is not objectively more accurate but rather contains forms the learner *believes* to be more accurate. It is the learner's *perception of what is correct* that matters; when learners pay attention to language form, they shift toward that perceived TL norm[4]. Tarone (1988) included these observations in a comprehensive summary of the research studies documenting the existence of interlanguage variation, with substantial evidence in the realm of phonology.

Beebe and Zuengler (1983) and Beebe and Giles (1984) turned for an explanation of IL variation to speech accommodation theory (SAT), (Giles & Byrne, 1982; Giles et al., 1987), which describes convergence and divergence in the speech patterns of interlocutors. Certain phonological features produced by speakers will converge or become more similar to those of interlocutors from whom they desire approval or with whom they wish to express social identity. Similarly, phonological forms will diverge or become dissimilar from those of interlocutors with whom they differ socially. Such accommodation can be short-term, lasting only for the duration of the conversation, or can be long-term—that is, may include the relatively permanent acquisition of phonological forms involved in either convergence or divergence. The claim is that when an L2 learner interacts with a more proficient speaker of the L2 with whom they identify, their phonology will move closer to that of the interlocutor (though see the result of Jenkins (2000), cited earlier). If the learner retains these convergent phonological features in their interlanguage over an extended period of time, we say acquisition has occurred.

Giles, Coupland, and Coupland (1991a, 1991b) later renamed Speech Accommodation Theory (SAT) as Communication Accommodation Theory (CAT) to include a range of nonverbal and discourse dimensions of social interaction such as speech rate, pauses, utterance length, pronunciation, and nonvocal features such as smiling and gaze. Divergence in such a model would mean speakers might emphasize speech and nonverbal differences between themselves and their interlocutors, just as Rampton's (1995) Pakistani students in London did when they deliberately used a "Me no + verb" construction with their teacher. Both convergence and divergence constitute strategies of identification with the communicative norms of some reference group, either present or absent at the time of speaking.

Lybeck's (2002) longitudinal research in Norway supports this model of accommodation and long-term retention for some L2 learners. This longitudinal, naturalistic study shows that pronunciation and cultural identity are closely tied. The degree to which American sojourners used nativelike Norwegian phonological features depended on their acculturation patterns over time, as predicted by Schumann's (1978) model. The more the sojourners acculturated into a tight social network (cf. Milroy, 1980) of Norwegian speakers, the more Norwegian phonological features they used, but when they became alienated from such a network, their use of these features dropped off. Lybeck concludes that those who were members of close-knit target culture groups used linguistic features similar to those of their group members, while learners whose social networks were open and uniplex developed fewer nativelike features.

Competence for Speaking in a Second Language

Given that learner interlanguage *use* is systematically variable, how do we characterize what second language learners *know* at any given point in time?

Gregg (1990) argues that interlanguage variation is merely a performance phenomenon, quite separate from learners' competence, and competence ought to be the only focus of SLA research. Similarly, Long has stated his belief that social contextual factors do not affect the process of second language acquisition to any great degree:

> Few would dispute that SLA takes place in an interactional and sociolinguistic context. A persistent question in the field, however, is the relevance of that context, and of different dimensions of it, to *acquisition*.... The goal of research on SLA, qualitative or quantitative, inside or outside the classroom, in the laboratory or on the street, is to understand how changes in that internal mental representation are achieved, why they sometimes appear to cease (so-called "fossilization"), and which learner, linguistic, and social factors (and where relevant, which instructional practices) affect and effect the process. (Long, 1997, pp. 318–319)

In this view, knowledge of linguistic form is claimed to be a matter of competence, while social factors influence only learners' speech performance; it is taken as a given that competence and performance are completely separate. Variation in performance has nothing to do with learners' knowledge or with possible development of the learner's knowledge of the second language rule system.

In contrast with this position is a collection of papers in Brown, Malmkjaer, and Williams (1996), which addresses the relationship between competence and performance from a range of different perspectives. The scholars in this volume propose different models of learner knowledge that all assume an integral relationship between competence and performance. Brown (1996), for example, posits a kind of cyclical relationship between knowledge and output, each influencing the other.

Interestingly, V. Cook (1996) suggests that in SLA, the target for acquisition is "multi-competence," not a native speaker competence that is impossible by definition.

> But the one thing that L2 learners cannot do *by definition* is become native speakers—fully balanced bilinguals perhaps, natives never. The goal of L2 acquisition should be seen as something other than monolingual native competence. The term 'multi-competence' has been introduced to cover knowledge of more than one language in the same mind (Cook, 1991). There is no assumption that this knowledge corresponds to a monolingual native speaker's in either L1 or L2; this is a matter for empirical research . . . The starting point should be what L2 learners are like in their own right rather than how they fail to reach standards set by people that they are not by definition. Multi-competence is then a necessary basis for second language acquisition research. L2 learners are not failed monolinguals, but people in their own right. (p. 64)

In V. Cook's view, there are different grammars in the mind, but they coexist within the same holistic system, so that the learner can maintain different settings for the same set of parameters.

> The argument is that the description of linguistic competence has been misleadingly based on monolinguals, like a description of juggling based on a person who can throw one ball in the air and catch it, rather than on a description of a person who can handle two or more balls at the same time. Calling the knowledge of a person who knows one language linguistic competence may be as misleading as calling throwing one ball in the air juggling. (V. Cook, 1996, p. 67)

This possibility, proposed early on by Tarone (1983, 1986, 1988, 1990) and R. Ellis (1985), that learner knowledge might itself be variable and probabilistic has been impossible for Gregg—and apparently for others as well—to reconcile with the generative construct of competence. Gregg railed against the idea that variable rule analysis of the sort described by Bayley and Preston (1996) might have psychological reality of any kind, and asked, "Do we really want to claim that a speaker knows, whether consciously or unconsciously, the probabilities for the production of a specific form?" (p. 372). However, new information seems to support this kind of claim. N. Ellis (2002), describing the state of the art in connectionist research on second language acquisition, now claims exactly that "grammatical representations must have variable strengths reflective of their frequency and connections must similarly be variable in weight" (N. Ellis, 2002, p. 372).

This view of learner knowledge itself as inherently variable is an essential claim of Preston's (2000) psycholinguistic model of language variation. Preston's model, although it does not originate in connectionism or in research on language processing, dovetails very nicely with N. Ellis' views on the variable nature of linguistic knowledge. Preston's work is important because it provides the most detailed model available to date showing, in sociolinguistic terms, how interlanguage variability relates to the development of interlanguage knowledge.

In Preston's (2000, 2002) model, the speaker has a choice between two forms within the same competence. In Level I of his model, selection of one or the other construction is achieved via a probabilistic sociocultural selection device, which operates in the way a weighted two-sided coin might operate in a coin toss (Preston, 2000, pp. 10–11). For example, the coin might be weighted one way for utterances directed to one interlocutor and another way for utterances directed to another interlocutor. N. Ellis' (2002) description of language processing gives us a good idea of how those weights might come to be established in the first place, in light of "our incessant unconscious figuring" (p. 146). Level II of the psycholinguistic model describes "not only a grammar whose variable elements are preferred by sociocultural facts but also probabilistically constrained by accompanying grammatical, information status, and other cognitive facts" (Preston, 2000, p. 17). Level III of the model shows longitudinal variation: acquisition over time.

An important claim of Preston's model is that when there is a choice between two linguistic forms, the "vernacular" (in sociolinguistics, the first-learned form of one's language) is stronger in the sense that it is more deeply embedded. We are more fluent in our vernacular. Other language forms (native or nonnative) are postvernacular, less deeply embedded, and weaker. We are always less fluent in the postvernacular. The notion that language constructions internalized in the postvernacular period are always weaker parts of the grammar relates to the traditional notions of style and attention in sociolinguistics. Some items can only be produced by careful monitoring because they are not as firmly embedded, and even then, they may not be retrievable or "correctly" retrievable (Preston, 2000, p. 25).

Preston's concept of weaker interlanguage grammars and weaker parts of grammars requires substantiation from the sort of research on psycholinguistic processes reviewed in N. Ellis (2002). As we know, in light of our earlier discussion of learner creativity and agency (V. J. Cook, 1993, p. 137), the model cannot fully determine the output of either native or interlanguage grammars because the speaker's intention plays a role in activating the sociocultural selection device (Preston, 2000, p. 27). Preston points out, "The 'intention' of a speaker may . . . interact with his or her sociocultural identity. That is, one may choose to 'perform' (or perform to a greater or lesser extent) an available sociocultural identity, and such choices must play a role in the activation of the selection determined by sociocultural selection" (p. 27). Such intentional choices to perform particular sociocultural identities are expressions of speaker creativity, a topic addressed earlier. Preston's model is the most comprehensive to date in integrating linguistic, sociolinguistic, and psycholinguistic data, and allows us to explore the ways in which interlanguage variation may impact second language acquisition in a coherent and theoretically interesting way.

CONCLUSIONS AND FUTURE DIRECTIONS

This brief review of the topic of speaking in a second language has unfortunately had to cover quite a bit of ground. I have tried to refer the interested reader to other recent sources, which can provide more depth and, through references in those sources, a direction for future reading on topics of interest.

A number of future directions for research and development in this area have been mentioned, among them:

- Exploring the usefulness of referential communication tasks for the development of improved language for literacy.
- Examining the use of communication strategies as expressions of a speaker's creativity and choice in interactional context, using such frameworks as Conversation Analysis.
- Studying the role of language play, creativity and agency in the speech of second language learners, and exploring its implications for SLA.
- Exploring the usefulness of Jenkins' Lingua Franca Core as a target for pronunciation teaching English as an International Language.
- Pursuing more research on characteristics of interlanguage phonology, and testing the various theoretical models being proposed.
- Finding more ways to integrate research findings on IL phonology into ESL/EFL/ EIL pronunciation textbooks.
- Developing and testing Preston's (2000, 2002) model of the L2 learner's variable "multi-competence" (V. J. Cook, 1996): identifying the role of sociocultural factors

in the model, the relationship of connectionist psycholinguistic research to the model (N. Ellis, 2002), and tying in insights of Communication Accommodation Theory (Giles, Coupland, & Coupland 1991a, 1991b).

NOTES

1. It does not make sense, in my opinion, to claim as Major (2001, p. 25) does, that "everyone speaks an interlanguage." For one thing, Major does not seem to use Selinker's definition of "interlanguage." The larger point he is trying to make is important: Everyone's native language system (L1) is constantly undergoing change, and is influenced by other language varieties. However, Major's proposal to use the term interlanguage to refer to all spoken language seems counterproductive. Maintaining the original definition of interlanguage makes it possible for us to study L2 learner language as a distinct entity and determine empirically its resemblance to real-world variable and developing L1s.
2. Lazaraton (personal communication) suggests that CSs may also occur in interactional discourse. If we begin to study CSs as they occur in natural conversation, we may be able to empirically validate this claim. At the present time, however, all the CS research of which I am aware has been done in the context of referential communication.
3. Quite possibly a new form of the English language is evolving, as the language is being used as a lingua franca internationally. In 200 years, who knows how English will be pronounced? Perhaps the proposed lingua franca core might in fact become the heart of a new standard English phonology of the future.
4. This insight continues to be validated, most recently by Lin (2001), who examined the production of English syllable onset C clusters by 20 Chinese adult EFL learners in four types of tasks. Systematic style shifting occurred, not in terms of errors, but in terms of syllable simplification strategies. The use of epenthesis increased as the task style became more formal, and the percentage of deletions and replacements become systematically higher in less formal tasks.

REFERENCES

Anderson, M. (1998). *Communication strategies and grounding in NNS-NNS and NS-NS interactions.* Unpublished M.A. qualifying paper, University of Minnesota, Minneapolis.

Anderson-Hsieh, J., Johnson, R., & Koehler, K. (1992). The relationship between native speaker judgments of non-native pronunciation and deviance in segmentals, prosody, and syllable structure. *Language Learning, 42,* 529–555.

Archibald, J. (1994). A formal model of learning L2 prosodic phonology. *Second Language Research, 10,* 215–240.

Archibald, J. (Ed.). (1995). *Phonological acquisition and phonological theory.* Hillsdale, NJ: Lawrence Erlbaum Associates.

Archibald, J. (1997). The acquisition of English stress by speakers of tone languages: Lexical storage vs. computation. *Linguistics, 35,* 167–181.

Archibald, J. (1998). *Second language phonology.* Amsterdam: John Benjamins.

Bayley, R., & Preston, D. (Eds.). (1996). *Second Language Acquisition and Linguistic Variation.* Amsterdam: John Benjamins.

Beebe, L. (1980). Sociolinguistic variation and style-shifting in second language acquisition. *Language Learning, 30*(2), 433–447.

Beebe, L., & Zuengler, J. (1983). Accommodation theory: An explanation for style shifting in second language dialects. In N. Wolfson & E. Judd (Eds.), *Sociolinguistics and language acquisition* (pp. 195–213). Rowley, MA: Newbury House.

Beebe, L., & Giles, H. (1984). Speech accommodation theories: A discussion in terms of second language acquisition. *International Journal of the Sociology of Language, 46,* 5–32.

Bialystok, E. (1990). *Communication strategies: A psychological analysis of second language use.* Oxford, UK: Basil Blackwell.

Bongaerts, T., & Poulisse, N. (1989). Communication strategies in L1 and L2: Same or different? *Applied Linguistics, 10,* 253–268.

Broner, M. & Tarone, M. (2000). Language play in immersion classroom discourse: Some suggestions for language teaching, *Australian Review of Applied Linguistics, 16,* 121–133.

Broner, M., & Tarone, E. (2001). Is it fun? Language play in a fifth grade Spanish immersion classroom. *Modern Language Journal, 85*(3), 363–379.

Broselow, E. (1988). Prosodic phonology and the acquisition of a second language. In S. Flynn & W. O'Neill (Eds.), *Linguistic theory in second language acquisition* (pp. 295–308). Dordrecht, The Netherlands: Kluwer.

Broselow, E., Chen, S.-I., & Wang, C. (1998). The emergence of the unmarked in second language phonology. *Studies in Second Language Acquisition, 20,* 261–280.

Broselow, E., & Park, H.-B. (1995). Mora conservation in second language prosody. In J. Archibald (Ed.), *Phonological acquisition and phonological theory* (pp. 151–168). Hillsdale, NJ: Lawrence Erlbaum Associates.

Brown, G. (1996). Language learning, competence, and performance. In G. Brown, K. Malmkjaer, & J. Williams (Eds.), *Performance and competence in second language acquisition* (pp. 185–203). Cambridge, UK: Cambridge University Press.

Brown, G., Malmkjaer, K., & Williams, J. (Eds.). (1996). *Performance and competence in second language acquisition*. Cambridge, UK: Cambridge University Press.

Brown, G., & Yule, G. (1983a). *Discourse analysis*. Cambridge, UK: Cambridge University Press.

Brown, G., & Yule, G. (1983b). *Teaching the spoken language*. Cambridge, UK: Cambridge University Press.

Carlisle, R. S. (1991). The influence of environment on vowel epenthesis in Spanish/English interphonology. *Applied Linguistics, 12*, 76–95.

Carlisle, R. S. (1998). The acquisition of onsets in a markedness relationship: A longitudinal study. *Studies in Second Language Acquisition, 20*, 245–260.

Carlisle, R. S. (1999). The modification of onsets in a markedness relationship: Testing the interlanguage structural conformity hypothesis. In J. Leather (Ed.), *Phonological issues in language learning (Language Learning 49, Supplement 1)*, (59–93). Malden, MA: Blackwell.

Cichocki, W., House, A. B., Kinloch, A. M., & Lister, A. C. (1999). Cantonese speakers and the acquisition of French consonants. *Language Learning, 49* (Special Issue No. 1), 95–121.

Cook, G. (2000). *Language play, language learning*. Oxford, UK: Oxford University Press.

Cook, V. J. (1991). The poverty-of-the-stimulus argument and multi-competence. *Second Language Research. 7/2*, 103–117.

Cook, V. J. (1993). *Linguistics and second language acquisition*. New York: St. Martin's Press.

Cook, V. J. (1996). Competence and multi-competence. In G. Brown, K. Malmkjaer, & J. Williams (Eds.), *Performance and competence in second language acquisition* (pp. 57–69). Cambridge, UK: Cambridge University Press.

Cummins, J. (1984). *Bilingualism and special education: Issues in assessment and pedagogy*. Clevedon, UK: Multilingual Matters.

de Bot, K. (1994). The transfer of intonation and the missing data base. In E. Kellerman & M. Sharwood-Smith (Eds.), *Crosslinguistic influence in second language acquisition* (pp. 110–119). Elmsford, NY: Pergamon.

de Jonge, C. E. (1995). *Interlanguage phonology: Perception and production*. Unpublished Ph.D. dissertation, Indiana University, Bloomington.

Derwing, T. M., Munro, M. J., & Wiebe, G. (1998). Evidence in favor of a broad framework for pronunciation instruction. *Language Learning, 48*, 393–410.

Dickerson, L. (1975). The learner's interlanguage as a system of variable rules. *TESOL Quarterly, 9*, 401–407.

Dickerson, L., & Dickerson, W. (1977). Interlanguage phonology: Current research and future directions. In S. P. Corder & E. Roulet (Eds.), *The notions: Simplifications, interlanguages, and pidgins and their relation to second language pedagogy. Actes du 5eme Colloque de Linguistique Appliquee* (pp. 18–29). Neufchatel, Switzerland: Libraire Droz.

Eckman, F. (1977). Markedness and the contrastive analysis hypothesis. *Language Learning, 27*, 315–330.

Eckman, F. (1991). The structural conformity hypothesis and the acquisition of consonant clusters in the interlanguage of ESL learners. *Studies in Second Language Acquisition, 13*, 23–41.

Eckman, F., & Iverson, G. (1993). Sonority and markedness among onset clusters in the interlanguage of ESL learners. *Second Language Research, 9*, 234–252.

Ellis, N. (2002). Frequency effects in language processing: A review with implications for theories of implicit and explicit language acquisition. *Studies in Second Language Acquisition, 24*, 143–188.

Ellis, R. (1985). *Understanding second language acquisition*. Oxford, UK: Oxford University Press.

Faerch, C., & Kasper, G. (1983). *Strategies in interlanguage communication*. London: Longman.

Flege, J. E. (1991). Age of learning affects the authenticity of voice onset time (VOT) in stop consonants produced in a second language. *Journal of the Acoustical Society of America, 89*, 395–411.

Flege, J. E. (1995). Second language speech learning: Theory, findings, and problems. In W. Strange (Ed.), *Speech perception and linguistic experience: Issues crosslinguistic research* (pp. 233–277). Timonium, MD: York Press.

Flege, J. E., Bohn, O.-S., & Jang, S. (1997). The production and perception of English vowels by native speakers of German, Korean, Mandarin, and Spanish. *Journal of Phonetics, 25*, 437–470.

Flege, J., Frieda, E. M., Walley, A. C., & Randazza, L. A. (1998). Lexical factors and segmental accuracy in second language speech production. *Studies in Second Language Acquisition, 20*, 155–187.

Flege, J. E., & Munro, M. J. (1994). The word unit in second language speech production and perception. *Studies in Second Language Acquisition, 16*(4), 381–411.

Flores, B. C. (1993). On the acquisition of English rhythm: Theoretical and practical issues. *Lenguas Modernas, 20*, 151–164.

Garvey, G. (1974). Some properties of social play. *Merrill-Palmer Quarterly 20*, 163–180.

Garvey, G. (1977). Play with language and speech. In C. Mitchell-Kernan & S. Ervin-Tripp (Eds.), *Child discourse*. (pp. 27–47) New York: Academic Press.

Gatbonton, E. (1978). Patterned phonetic variability in second language speech: A gradual diffusion model. *Canadian Modern Language Review, 34*, 335–347.

Giles, H., & Byrne, J. (1982). An intergroup approach to second language acquisition. *Journal of Multicultural and Multilingual Development, 3*, 17–40.

Giles, H., Mulac, A., Bradac, J. J., & Johnson, P. (1987). Speech accommodation theory: The first decade and beyond. In M. L. McLaughlin (Ed.), *Communication yearbook 10* (pp. 13–48). Beverly Hills, CA: Sage.

Giles, H., Coupland, N., & Coupland, J. (1991a). *Language contexts and consequences.* Milton Keynes: Open University Press.

Giles, H., Coupland, N., & Coupland, J. (Eds.). (1991b). *Contexts of accommodation. Developments in applied sociolinguistics.* Cambridge, UK: Cambridge University Press.

Gregg, K. (1990). The variable competence model and why it isn't. *Applied Linguistics, 11*(4), 364–383.

Hancin-Bhatt, B., & Bhatt, R. M. (1997). Optimal L2 syllables: Interactions of transfer and developmental effects. *Studies in Second Language Acquisition, 19*, 331–378.

Holden, K. T. (1993). The motive impact of foreign intonation: An experiment in switching English and Russian intonation. *Language and Speech, 36*, 67–88.

Huizinga, Johan. (1955). *Homo ludens.* Boston: Beacon Press.

Ioup, G., & Weinberger, S. (Eds.). (1987). *Interlanguage phonology: The acquisition of a second language sound system.* Rowley, MA: Newbury House.

James, A. R. (1983). Transferability and dialect phonology: Swabian: Swabian English. In A. James & B. Kettemann (Eds.), Dialektphonologie und Fremdsprachenerweb [Dialect phonology and foreign language acquistion] (pp. 162–188). Tubingen, Germany: Narr. Cited in R. C. Major (2001) Foreign Accent: The ontogeny and phylogeny of second language phonology. (p. 73) Mahwah, NJ: Lawrence Erlbaum.

James, A. R., & Leather, J. (Eds.). (1997). *Second language speech: Structure and process.* Berlin: Mouton de Gruyter.

Jenkins, J. (2000). *The phonology of English as an international language.* Oxford, UK: Oxford University Press.

Kaltenbacher, E. (1997). German speech rhythm in L2 acquisition. In J. Leather & A. James (Eds.), *New Sounds 97: Proceedings of the Third International Symposium on the Acquisition of Second Language Speech* (pp. 158–166). Klagenfurt: University of Klagenfurt.

Kasper, G., & Kellerman, E. (Eds.). (1997). *Communication strategies: Psycholinguistic and sociolinguistic perspectives.* Harlow, UK: Longman.

Kellerman, E. (1991). Compensatory strategies in second language research: A critique, a revision, and some (non)implications for the classroom. In R. Phillipson, E. Kellerman, L. Selinker, M. Sharwood-Smith, & M. Swain (Eds.), *Foreign/Second language pedagogy research* (pp. 142–160). Clevedon, UK: Multilingual Matters.

Konishi, K., & Tarone, E. (2004). English constructions used in compensatory strategies: Baseline data for communicative EFL instruction, in D. Boxer & A. D. Cohen (eds.), *Studying speaking to inform second language learning* (pp. 174–198). Clevedon: Multilingual Matters.

Lado, R. (1957). *Linguistics across cultures.* Ann Arbor: University of Michigan.

Leather, J. (1997). Interrelation of perceptual and productive learning in the initial acquisition of second language tone. In A. James & J. Leather (Eds.), *Second language speech: Structure and process* (pp. 75–101). Berlin: Mouton de Gruyter.

Leather, J. (1999a). Second language speech research: An introduction. In Leather, J. (Ed.), *Phonological issues in language learning (Language Learning 49, Supplement 1)* (pp. 1–58). Malden, MA: Blackwell.

Leather, J. (Ed.). (1999b). *Phonological issues in language learning (Language Learning 49, Supplement 1).* Malden, MA: Blackwell.

Leather, J., & James, A. R. (Eds.). (1992). *New Sounds 92: Proceedings of the 1992 Amsterdam Symposium on the Acquisition of Second Language Speech.* Amsterdam: University of Amsterdam.

Leather, J., & James, A. (Eds.). (1997). *New Sounds 97: Proceedings of the Third International Symnposium on the Acquisition of Second Language Speech.* Klagenfurt: University of Klagenfurt.

Lin, Y.-H. (2001). Syllable simplification strategies: A stylistic perspective. *Language Learning, 51*(4), 681–718.

Long, M. (1997). Construct validity in SLA research: A response to Firth and Wagner. *Modern Language Journal, 81*, 318–323.

Lybeck, K. (2002). *The role of acculturation and social networks in the acquisition of second language pronunciation.* Unpublished Ph.D. dissertation, University of Minnesota, Minneapolis.

Mairs, J. L. (1989). Stress assignment in interlanguage phonology: An analysis of the stress system of Spanish speakers learning English. In S. Gass & J. Schachter (Eds.), *Linguistic perspectives on second language acquisition* (pp. 260–283). Cambridge, UK: Cambridge University Press.

Major, R. C. (1986). The ontogeny model: Evidence from L2 acquisition of spanish. *Language Learning, 36*, 453–504.

Major, R. C. (1996). Markedness in second language acquisition of consonant clusters. In R. Bayley & D. Preston (Eds.), *Variation linguistics and second language acquisition* (pp. 75–96). Amsterdam: John Benjamins.

Major, R. C. (Ed.). (1998). *Studies in second language acquisition 20: Special issue on interlanguage phonetics and phonology.* Cambridge, UK: Cambridge University Press.

Major, R. C. (2001). *Foreign accent: The ontogeny and phylogeny of second language phonology.* Mahwah, NJ: Lawrence Erlbaum Associates.

Milroy, L. (1980). *Language and social networks.* Oxford, UK: Basil Blackwell.

Munro, M. J., & Derwing, T. M. (2001). Modeling perceptions of the accentedness and comprehensibility of L2 speech: The role of speaking rate. *Studies in Second Language Acquisition, 23*, 451–468.

Murphey, T. (1998). *Language hungry! An introduction to language learning fun and self-esteem.* Tokyo: Macmillan Language House.

Nemser, W. (1971). Approximative systems of foreign language learners. *International Review of Applied Linguistics, 9*(2), 115–123.

Paribakht, T. (1985). Strategic competence and language proficiency. *Applied Linguistics, 6*, 132–146.

Peck, Sabrina. (1978). Child-child discourse in second language acquisition. In E. Hatch (Ed.), *Second language acquisition: A book of readings* (pp. 383–400). Rowley, MA: Newbury House.

Pennington, M. C. (1998). The teachability of phonology in adulthood: A re-examination. *International Review of Applied Linguistics, 36*(4), 323–341.

Poulisse, N. (1990). *The use of compensatory strategies by Dutch learners of English.* Dordrecht, The Netherlands: Foris.

Preston, D. (2000). Three kinds of sociolinguistics and SLA: A psycholinguistic perspective. In B. Swierzbin, F. Morris, M. Anderson, C. Klee, & E. Tarone (Eds.), *Social and cognitive factors in second language acquisition: Selected proceedings of the 1999 Second Language Research Forum* (pp. 3–30). Somerville, MA: Cascadilla Press.

Preston, D. (2002). A variationist perspective on SLA: Psycholinguistic concerns. In R. Kaplan (Ed.), *Oxford handbook of applied linguistics.* Oxford, UK: Oxford University Press.

Rampton, Ben. (1995). *Crossing: Language and ethnicity among adolescents.* London: Longman.

Schumann, J. (1978). *The pidginization process: A model for second language acquisition.* Rowley, MA: Newbury House.

Scovel, T. (1969). Foreign accents, language acquisition, and cerebral dominance. *Language Learning, 19*, 245–253.

Selinker, L. (1972). Interlanguage. *International Review of Applied Linguistics, 10*, 209–241.

Sheldon, A., & Strange, W. (1982). The acquisition of /r/ and /l/ by Japanese learners of English: Evidence that speech production can precede speech perception. *Applied Psycholinguistics, 3*, 243–261.

Stockman, I. J., & Pluut, E. (1999). Segment composition as a factor in the syllabification errors of second-language speakers. *Language Learning, 49* (Special Issue No. 1), 185–209.

Tarone, E. (1978a). The phonology of interlanguage. In J. Richards (Ed.), *Understanding second and foreign language learning: Issues and approaches* (pp. 15–33). Rowley, MA: Newbury House.

Tarone, E. (1978b). Conscious communication strategies in interlanguage: A progress report. In H. D. Brown, C. Yorio, & R. Crymes (Eds.), *On TESOL '77: Teaching and learning English as a second language* (pp. 194–203). Washington, DC: TESOL.

Tarone, E. (1979). Interlanguage as chameleon, *Language Learning, 29*(1), 181–191.

Tarone, E. (1980). Communication strategies, foreigner talk, and repair in interlanguage, *Language Learning, 30*(2), 417–431.

Tarone, E. (1983). On the variability of interlanguage systems, *Applied Linguistics, 4*(2), 142–163.

Tarone, E. (1986). 'The arm of the chair is when you use for to write': Developing strategic competence in a second language. In P. Meara, (Ed.), *Spoken language* (15–27). London: CILT.

Tarone, E. (1988). *Variation in Interlanguage.* London: Edward Arnold Assoc.

Tarone, E. (1990). On variation in interlanguage: A response to Gregg. *Applied Linguistics, 11*, 392–400.

Tarone, E. (1994). Interlanguage. In R. Asher & S. Simpson (Eds.), *Encyclopedia of language and linguistics* (Vol. 4, pp. 1715–1719). Oxford, UK: Pergamon.

Tarone, E. (2000). Getting serious about language play: Language play, interlanguage variation, and second language acquisition. In B. Swierzbin, F. Morris, M. Anderson, C. Klee, & E. Tarone (Eds.), *Social and cognitive factors in SLA: Proceedings of the 1999 Second Language Research Forum* (pp. 31–54). Somerville, MA: Cascadilla Press.

Tarone, E., & Yule, G. (1989). *Focus on the language learner: Approaches to identifying and meeting the needs of second language learners.* Oxford, UK: Oxford University Press.

Tropf, H. (1987). Sonority as a variability factor in second language phonology. In A. James & J. Leather (Eds.), *Sound patterns in second language acquisition* (pp. 173–191). Dordrecht, The Netherlands: Foris.

Wagner, J., & Firth, A. (1997). Communication strategies at work. In G. Kasper & E. Kellerman (Eds.), *Communication strategies: Psycholinguistic and sociolinguistic perspectives* (pp. 323–344). Harlow, UK: Longman.

Weir, R. (1962). *Language in the crib.* The Hague: Mouton.

Wilkes-Gibbs, D. (1997). Studying language use as collaboration. In G. Kasper & E. Kellerman (Eds.), *Communication strategies: Psycholinguistic and sociolinguistic perspectives* (pp. 238–274). New York: Longman.

Willey, B. (2001, February 25). *Direct and indirect appeals for assistance.* Paper presented at the annual conference of the American Association for Applied Linguistics, St. Louis, Missouri.

Yule, G. (1997). *Referential communication tasks.* Mahwah, NJ: Lawrence Erlbaum Associates.

Yule, G. (1999). *Explaining English grammar.* Oxford, UK: Oxford University Press.

Yule, G. & Tarone, E. (1990). Eliciting the performance of strategic competence, in R. Scarcella, E. Andersen and S. Krashen (eds.), *Developing Communicative Competence in a Second Language* (179–194). Rowley, Mass: Newbury House.

Yule, G., & Tarone, E. (1991). The other side of the page: Integrating the study of communication strategies and negotiated input in SLA. In R. Phillipson, E. Kellerman, L. Selinker, M. Sharwood-Smith, & M. Swain (Eds.), *Foreign language pedagogy: A commemorative volume for Claus Faerch* (pp. 162–171). Clevedon, UK: Multilingual Matters.

Yule, G., & Tarone, E. (1997). Investigating L2 reference: Pros and cons. In G. Kasper & E. Kellerman (Eds.), *Advances in communication strategy research* (pp. 17–30). New York: Longman.

28

L2 Listening

Michael Rost
University of California–Berkeley

Listening refers to a complex cognitive process that allows a person to understand spoken language. Listening encompasses receptive, constructive, and interpretive aspects of cognition, which are utilized in both first language (L1) and second language (L2) listening. In L1 acquisition for children, listening ability and cognition develop interdependently; as such, in normal hearing persons, listening as a specific skill is rarely given direct attention in L1 education. In L2 development, more direct intervention is considered necessary, because in most cases the learner is acquiring a second language after cognitive processing skills and habits in the L1 have been established. In L2 development, listening constitutes not only a skill area in performance, but also a primary means of acquiring a second language. Listening represents the channel through which a learner processes language in *real time*—utilizing pacing, pausing, and units of encoding that are unique to the spoken language.

As a goal-oriented activity, listening involves "bottom-up" processing, in which the listener attends to data in the incoming speech signals as well as "top-down" processing, in which the listener utilizes prior knowledge and expectations to guide the process of understanding. This simultaneous bottom-up and top-down processing takes place at different levels of cognitive organization: phonological, grammatical, lexical, propositional, and discoursal. Because of the multiple levels of organization, every listener utilizes a parallel processing model to find the "best fit" of meaning: Representations at each of these five levels create activation at other levels, while the entire network of interactions serves to produce a "best match" that fits all of the levels. (McClelland et al., 1995).

While L1 and L2 listening utilize the same basic underlying neurological processes that take place in the same parts of the brain, there are important developmental and functional differences between L1 and L2 listening. The pragmatic constraints governing the acquisition of an L1 for a young child and the acquisition of an L2 for an older child or an adult are substantively different. The most significant differences are the needs and motivations of the learner for acquiring the language and the amount and quality of access to speakers of the language over long periods of time. In addition to these pragmatic constraints on L2 acquisition, there is evidence that when the learner passes a "critical period" in early adolescence, some aspects of phonological and grammatical processing and some psychomotor skills (for pronunciation) are no longer sufficiently flexible for complete acquisition and native-like performance in the L2.

This chapter examines research that has characterized the processes of listening, highlighting those areas of particular interest to the development of L2 listening.

PROCESSES IN L2 LISTENING

Listening consists of three basic processing phases that are simultaneous and parallel: *decoding, comprehension,* and *interpretation.* A fourth phase, *listener response,* is often included as well in descriptions of listening competence and performance.

Decoding involves attention, speech perception, word recognition, and grammatical parsing; *comprehension* includes activation of prior knowledge, representing *propositions* in short term memory, and logical inference; *interpretation* encompasses comparison of meanings with prior expectations, *activating participation frames,* and evaluation of discourse meanings. Each of these phases contributes to the larger goal of finding what is relevant to the listener in the input, and what kind of response may be required. The goal of decoding is to feed recognized lexical items and parsed propositions for comprehension. The goal of comprehension is to connect the input with relevant knowledge sources for further interpretation. The goal of interpretation is to present a set of viable *listener response* options to the listener.

Decoding Processes: Attention

In neurological terms, *attention* is a cyclical process requiring three actions: arousal, orientation, and a focus of cognitive resources. These actions occur in various structures within the brain, mainly in the auditory cortex, the auditory brainstem, and the eighth cranial nerve (Hahne & Frederici, 1998). In L2 processing, orientation and focusing involve a suppression of L1 phonological and lexical processing resources (Gernsbacher & Shlesinger, 1997).

Attention is essentially a process of guiding selection of input so that intake of meaning will become more efficient. Because our working memory is quite limited both temporally (the length of time we can process something) and semantically (the number of discrete items we can deal with), a user processing language in real time must decide continuously what to process further. For a proficient listener, in an L1 or an L2, selective attention works well if three conditions are present: the input is presented at a proper speed for processing (neither too slow nor too fast), the number of new items in the input is relatively small compared to the number of already known items, and there are no semantic or syntactic anomalies in the input. If any of these conditions are violated, the listener experiences an "attentional blink" (AB), a detectable disruption in rhythms of the brain which indicates impairment in processing. When too many ABs occur, the listener experiences discomfort with processing and difficulty with input-related tasks (Metsala, 1997; Osterhout & Nicol, 1999).

In L2 acquisition research, the role of attention in long-term learning is a subject of debate. Two main positions have been outlined in this area. Connectionist models (e.g., MacWhinney, 1994) view L2 acquisition in terms of neural connections and interactions, contending that learning takes place in the absence of conscious attention and that learning does not require the intention of the learner to learn. The Noticing Hypothesis (Schmidt, 1995) holds a contrasting viewpoint, namely, that attention is necessary for long-term learning to occur. As Segalowitz and Lightbown (1999) note, part of what fuels the controversy in this area is the lack of agreement on the meaning of such key terms as attentional capacity, conscious awareness, noticing, and intention to learn. For L2 listening, attention is considered to encompass all those aspects of cognition that the listener can control (Shiffrin, 1998).

Decoding Processes: Perception

Auditory perception has the goal of helping the listener make sense of the speech signal. This goal is achieved in three complementary ways: (1) through calculating *articulatory causes* for the sounds that strike the ear (identification of the physical ways the speaker made the sounds, which is enhanced by visual cues when the speaker's face is visible), (2) through experiencing *psychoacoustic effects* (identification of auditory qualities, which may be altered or degraded by competing sounds), (3) through estimating the speaker's *linguistic intentions* (identification of what the speaker is trying to articulate, which is supported by the listener's knowledge of the language). The redundancy of these processes assures that, for competent listeners, most of the continuous speech signal can be broken into segments and categorized for further processing (Massaro, 1994; Best, 1995).

Some speech processing researchers contend that phonetic feature detectors in the auditory cortex, which enable the listener to encode speech into linguistic units, atrophy during development if they are not used. This means that adults eventually retain only the phonetic feature detectors that were stimulated by their native language, and will experience perceptual difficulties in perception of any L2 sounds that are not similar to those in their L1. According to this view, exposure to speech during childhood alters neural organization such that individuals, born capable of learning any language, develop perceptual and cognitive processes that are specialized for their own native language. This means that for adult L2 learners, L2 speech can be difficult to segment into words and phonemes, different phonemes in the second language can sound as if they are the same, and the motor articulations of the second language can be difficult to reproduce (Kuhl, 2000; Iverson et al., 2001).

There is substantial evidence that during the first year of life, the child develops categorical perception for the sounds of its first language, using the "*perceptual magnet effect*" to determine prototypes and variations of all the linguistic sounds it hears. By the end of the first year, the child begins to suppress perception of other non-L1 linguistic sounds, apparently to aid in development of first language acquisition (Kuhl, 1991; Kuhl et al., 1992).

Perception is made possible by coordination of functional neural circuits that integrate across areas of the brain. For aural perception, one such circuit is the phonological rehearsal loop (Gupta & MacWhinney, 1997) which links together the auditory processing in the temporal lobe with attentional and motor processing from prefrontal cortex. We use this loop to store and repeat a series of words that we hear and to speed the perception and learning of new words.

Metrical Cadence and Speech Rate.   Research into speech processing has shown that listeners of any language develop common "preferred strategies" for aural decoding in their L1. These strategies are readily acquired by the L1 child in presence of ample oral input, but apparently are often only partially or imperfectly acquired by the L2 learner because of interference with one's previously acquired L1 aural strategies. At the same time, a similarity of segmentation strategies between the oral properties of one's L1 and L2 may result in *positive transfer,* making speech processing in the L2 easier (Cutler, 1997; Auer et al., 1999).

According to the Optimality Theory (Tesar & Smolensky, 2000; Kager, 1999; Escudero & Boersma, 2001) all L1 listeners acquire a primary *metrical segmentation strategy* to process strings of speech. The strategy acquired is based on the phonolexical system (how content words receive stress) and the phonotactic principles of their "first heard language" (the rhythm of consonantal and vocalic intervals). Together, these allow L1 listeners to segment the words in the speech stream effectively. For most varieties of English, the preferred segmentation strategy utilizes two principles:

(1) a strong syllable marks the onset of a new content word (90% of content words in English have stress on the first syllable; many of course are monosyllabic) and (2) each *pause unit* of speech (most speech is uttered in 2- to –3-second bursts, bounded by pauses) contains one prominent content item (which may be a single word or a phrase). L1 learners also acquire secondary segmentation strategies, but only after the preferred strategies are established (Jusczyk, 1997).

A major factor in comprehensibility of speech for L2 listeners is speech rate. Despite the common belief that slower rates facilitate listening comprehension, empirical studies have yielded contradictory findings. Although in general, listening comprehension improves for L2 listeners when the speech rate is slowed down, this is only one factor in ease of comprehension, and it does not apply universally for all learners nor for all parts of a text (Griffiths, 1992; Cauldwell, 1996). The most consistent finding from speech rate research is that additional pausing at natural pause boundaries, rather than slowed speech itself, seems to aid comprehension (Flowerdew, 1994). This finding suggests that assistance with metrical segmentation is more important than simple speech rate reduction in phonological perception.

Normal speech in English averages from 100 words per minute to 240 words per minute (although some cattle auctioneers have been clocked at 400 words per minute) (Crystal & House, 1990). Nearly all speech styles include some bursts at the high end of this range. As reported by Vandergrift (1999), in live questioning of L2 listeners as they listened to an audio tape, it is most often these fast bursts of speech, especially when they occur at unexpected times, that cause difficulty. One finding from speech rate research is that individual listeners tend to have a "preferred rate" of speaking at which they find listening most comfortable (Brown & Hulme, 1992). This rate does not always correlate with language proficiency, for instance, better listeners do not necessarily prefer a faster rate.

Using a novel approach and developments in audio technology, a study by Zhao (1997) examined the issue of speech rate and listening comprehension from the perspective of listener control. By giving the control of speech rate to the learners and by attending to individuals instead of groups, this study concluded that when given control of the speed of the input, students' listening comprehension improved. This implies that interactive factors, including the listener's perceived role, influence how speed of input affects comprehension. It is known that even in L1 listening, alterations that slow down the input, including disfluencies such as false starts, will aid in comprehension, though there is an obvious ceiling effect to this phenomenon (Brennan & Williams, 1995).

In L2 listening, in addition to aiding comprehension, slower input, along with other simplifications in syntax and rhetorical structure, may aid in acquisition. Some studies indicate that slower speed of input, along with simplification of syntactic structure, aids specifically in short-term L2 vocabulary acquisition (Leow 1993; Ellis, 1994)

In L2 pedagogy, it is clear that a familiarity and comfort level with the L2 phonology is the basis for listening development and language processing. Chun (2002) in reviewing approaches to teaching phonology to L2 learners over the past several decades, argues that four principles need to be observed: (1) pronunciation and intonation must be taught in context; (2) intonational meanings must be generalizable, (3) teaching of pronunciation and intonation must be subordinate to larger communicative purposes, and (4) intonation must be taught with realistic language samples.

The relationship between speech perception and production has been a long-standing issue in L2 acquisition. Many believe that a learner's inability to produce target-like phonology entails a lack of perception ability and that practice with production of target-like pronunciation and intonation will lead to improved perception of L2 phonology. Both of these views have been challenged by research. For example, Yamada & Tokura (1992) have shown that learners can be trained to hear phonetic distinctions (e.g., /r/ vs. /l/), but cannot reliably produce such distinctions in their own speech. Studies like this suggest that L2 learners may come to perceive L2 phonological distinctions accurately, but do not have the pscyhomotor skills to produce them (Flege, 1995).

Decoding Processes: Word Recognition

Word recognition in listening refers to two processes: identification of words and immediate activation of lexical knowledge linked to words that have been recognized. Word recognition achieves two felicitous goals: it locates the onset of the immediately following word and it provides "proactive processing," indicating syntactic and semantic constraints that are used to recognize the immediately following word.

In continuous speech, there is no auditory equivalence to the white spaces in reading continuous text, so the listener does not have reliable cues for marking word boundaries. As such, it is often word recognition that becomes the most salient area of difficulty for L2 listeners. When beginning and intermediate L2 learners are given the opportunity to report what they don't understand in an oral text, it is word recognition problems—identifying but not knowing a word or not recognizing word boundaries—that are most often reported (Rost & Ross, 1991).

Speaking rate influences word recognition. Normal speaking rates are about eight words per every 2- to 3-second burst of speech (Brazil, 1995). The 2- to 3-second burst in natural speech is common across the world's languages, and seems to be a feature adapted to the capacity of our working memories (Chafe, 1994). Because the typical rate of speech is so rapid, word recognition obviously must happen very rapidly as well. The process occurs primarily in a sequential, automized fashion, although listeners must regularly employ "backward recognition" (utilizing the auditory loop in short-term memory) to clarify ambiguities (Massaro & Burke, 1991). Several models of word recognition have been developed: the Cohort Model (Morton, 1969), the TRACE model (Marslen-Wilson, 1987), the Fuzzy Logic Model (Massaro, 1994)) to account for the kinds of psycholinguistic competence that underlies rapid word recognition in speech. All models address the following points. Words are:

(1) Recognized through the interaction of perceived sound and knowledge of the likelihood of a word being uttered in a given context (Luce & Pisoni, 1998).
(2) Recognized essentially in a sequential fashion, but not all words need to be recognized in sequence for speech processing to occur successfully. Unrecognized words can be held in a phonological loop in short term memory while other cues are used to help identify them or, minimally, determine their likely function in the input (Marslen-Wilson, 1990).
(3) Initially accessed by two main clues: the sounds that begin the word and lexical stress.
(4) Recognized when the analysis of the acoustic structure and other available cues eliminates all candidates but one—the most likely candidate. This process need not be complete until an entire "pause unit" or phonological phrase is processed. The phonological loop in short term memory can readily hold about one pause unit, typically 2 to 3 seconds in length.

In essence, this process is aimed at creating lexical effects during perception (see Figure 28.1). Creation of lexical effects is a receptive (bottom-up) process of identifying potential lexical candidates out of known items in the mental lexicon, and deciding upon the most likely candidate strings by invoking contextual constraints, which is an active (top-down) process. For this dual processing to work smoothly, the listener needs to generate multiple candidates as the speech string is processed sequentially.

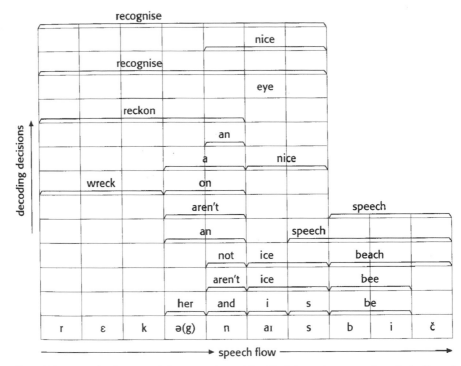

Speech is recognised sequentially as words are identified through progressive elimination of alternate word candidates. Most decoding decisions are required on unstressed parts of the utterance and the listener must often wait until subsequent syllables and words are uttered to complete the decoding of a phrase.

FIG. 28.1. Bottom-up processes in word recognition, from Rost, 2002.

Without a large receptive vocabulary, the listener cannot create lexical effects, and has to rely upon straight matching procedures with known words, a non-dynamic process which is much slower (Marslen-Wilson, 1987).

Vocabulary Size and Listening Comprehension

In principle, listening is facilitated by the size of an individual's mental lexicon and the listeners' facility in spoken word recognition. The activation of background knowledge (*content schemata* and *cultural schemata*) that is needed for comprehension of speech are linked to and launched by word recognition. Speed and breadth in word recognition have been shown to be a consistent predictor of L2 listening ability. (Segalowitz et al., 1998; Laufer & Hulstijn, 2001).

Corpus studies show that a recognition vocabulary of 3,000 word families is necessary for comprehension of "every day" conversations, if we assume that a listener needs to be familiar with—and able to recognize—90% to 95% of content words to understand a conversation satisfactorily (Nation & Waring, 1997; Read, 2001). There is evidence that occurrences of "out of vocabulary" words in a spoken text (i.e., words outside of one's vocabulary knowledge, either nonsense words or unacquired words) create attentional problems that interfere with comprehension of both the immediate and subsequent utterances (Rost & Ross, 1991; Vandergrift, 1997b).

There can be no clear agreement on what a "recognition vocabulary" means because word knowledge involves a number of aspects and continuously expands. Word knowledge includes, on a surface level, recognition of the word's spoken form (including its allophonic variations), its written form, and grammatical functions, and on a deeper level, its collocations, relative frequency in the language, constraints on use, denotations, connotations, association, concepts and referents (N. Schmidt, 2000). There is evidence that depth of knowledge of words influences speed of spoken word recognition, by way of priming effects. Where "neighborhood density" is greater, that is, when semantic connections in the mental lexicon are more complex, word recognition becomes easier. This means that the depth of individual word knowledge determines a given word's degree of integration into the mental lexicon, and therefore the facility with which it is accessed in real time (Luce & Pisoni, 1998).

How one activates vocabulary knowledge while listening has not been widely studied in L2 contexts. Based on L1 research, it is assumed that activation is more readily automized for high frequency (i.e., frequently used) words than for low frequency words. It is also assumed that vocabulary knowledge interacts with other competencies in the process of listening, such as syntactic processing and discourse processing. In L2 contexts, the four major views of the role of vocabulary in language comprehension are as follows:

(1) The instrumentalist view, which sees vocabulary knowledge as being a major prerequisite and causative factor in comprehension.
(2) The aptitude view, which sees vocabulary knowledge as one of many outcomes of having strong general "intelligence" or "feel" for a language.
(3) The knowledge view, which sees vocabulary as an indicator of strong world knowledge. This world knowledge enables listening comprehension.
(4) The access view, which sees vocabulary as having a causal relationship with comprehension provided that the vocabulary can be easily accessed. Access can be improved through practice. This access can involve several factors including fluency of lexical access, speed of coping with affixed forms, and speed of word recognition.

(adapted from Nation, 2001)

Because word recognition and vocabulary knowledge play such an important role in L2 listening and second language acquisition, most approaches to teaching L2 listening involve vocabulary development. Five types of instructional methods are commonly used:

(1) Priming of lexical knowledge through pre-teaching of vocabulary items known to be unfamiliar to L2 learners (Ellis & Heimbach, 1997; VanPatten, 1990);
(2) Concurrent lexical support while listening, either through captioning of videos (Baltova, 1999) or overt signaling and paraphrasing of unfamiliar lexical items in face-to-face delivery (Chaudron, 1988);
(3) Prior simplification of vocabulary in oral texts, including restatements and paraphrases to promote vocabulary learning (Chaudron, 1988)
(4) Emphasis on negotiation of meaning of unknown lexical items during conversational interactions, to promote awareness of lexical gaps in input processing, and on increasing use of contextual strategies for inferring meanings of unknown words (Chaudron, 1988; Pica, Doughty, & Young, 1987)
(5) Group reconstruction activities following listening (sometimes called "dictogloss") to promote awareness of unfamiliar lexical items and attempts to deepen and extend partial vocabulary knowledge (Wajnryb, 1990)

All five methods have demonstrated gains in vocabulary knowledge, as measured through pre- and post-test comparison in comparison to control groups, though part of this gain must be attributed to the additional time of lexical processing that is provided in each method.

Decoding Processes: Syntactic Parsing

As words in speech are recognized, processing the language for meaning requires a partial syntactic mapping of incoming speech onto a grammatical model. A number of syntactic and morphological cues influence how the listener processes meaning: word order, subject-verb (topic-comment) matching, pro-form agreement (e.g., agreement of pronouns with their antecedents), case inflections (e.g., "I" vs. "me"), and contrastive stress. The listener's grammatical knowledge, and ability to utilize that knowledge in real time are used during syntactic processing.

Syntactic processing occurs at two levels, that of the immediate utterance, or sentence, level and that of the extended text, or discourse level. There is some evidence that syntactic processing takes place in two passes. The first pass identifies syntactic categories of units in the speech stream, and the second pass integrates syntax of the immediate utterance with syntax of the larger speech unit that is being processed. (Osterhout & Nicol, 1999).

In the "first pass", syntactic processing, or parsing, accomplishes three basic goals: (1) it speeds up aural processing by use of constraints to assign parts of incoming utterances quickly to inviolable syntactic categories, (2) it allows for prediction of functions of incoming parts of an utterance and for disambiguating partially heard parts of an utterance, (3) and it helps the processor create a *propositional model* of the incoming speech from which *logical inferences* can be calculated for further comprehension.

In fluent listening, the parsing process is known to be highly automatized. Research on "slips of the ear," in which naturally occurring aural errors are studied systematically, have been used as evidence of normal aural syntactic (Garnes & Bone, 1980; Bilmes, 1992). This research illustrates that listeners tend to hear (or mishear) entire functional phrases, rather than single syllables or words. The listener maps out the heard input onto a plausible phonological structure that represents an entire functional phrase, and if a mishearing occurs, it generally produces a syntactically possible (even if pragmatically implausible) "heard utterance." For example, one data entry from Garnes and Bon (1980) cites a listener hearing "go to the car and get the tuna" instead of the speaker's actual utterance "go and get my car tuned up." This mishearing shows how the listener attempts to parse an entire functional unit, here, the verb phrase.

One illustrative study, in which subjects are asked to identify where a "blip" (non-linguistic sound) occurred while they were listening, further demonstrates how normal listeners tend to parse incoming speech as full, functional units, "undisturbed" by disruptions (Bond, 1999a, 1999b). For example, if a "blip" is inserted after the word "somewhere" in an utterance, "I left it somewhere on the porch," most listeners will report hearing the "blip" before "somewhere" because they tend to process "somewhere on the porch" as a single unit, which is resistant to interruption. It is a single unit both in terms of semantic function (i.e., location) and also in terms of syntactic role (i.e., adverbial).

For most fluent listeners, syntactic processing is typically noticed only when an anomaly occurs. Perception of a syntactic anomaly produces a characteristic disruption in L1 listeners. This is called the P-600 effect, in which electrical activity in the auditory cortex, jumps by about 600 microwatts. Interestingly, for most L2 listeners, this syntactic disruption effect typically does *not* occur, suggesting that syntactic processing is not entirely automized.

The "second pass" in syntactic processing involves integrating representations of utterances in the discourse. The most critical syntactic integration processes are (1) determining conjunctions between utterances, including equivalences between text items in adjoined utterances, by calculating cohesion markers for anaphoric (previously mentioned), cataphoric (to be mentioned), and exophoric (external to the text) references, and (2) filling in ellipsis (items that are left out of the utterance because they are assumed to known by the listener, or already "given" in the text), and (3) calculation of logical inferences that link propositions within the discourse, which most often are not explicitly stated.

These integration processes are facilitated by three underlying competencies: (1) A pragmatic knowledge of common discourse functions (e.g., apologies, invitations, complaints) and discourse types (e.g., greeting routines, personal anecdotes). In particular, ability to note episode boundaries or other conventional division points that "bind" sets of utterances together assists in discourse parsing. (Gernsbacher & Foertsch, 1999)

(2) The ability to attend to pitch levels, as episodes in discourse are often "bracketed" intonationally. In English this is achieved through starting a new topic (a set of linked utterances) on a high key and closing the topic, often several turns later, on a low tone.
(3) A knowledge of "discourse markers" that cue speaker intention. Explicit markers may signal an opening of a new episode or topic (e.g., in informal conversation, "Well, anyway, . . ."), a continuation of a current topic or episode ("Right, and another thing. . ."), a reversion to a previous episode or topic ("As I was saying before. . ."), or a redirection of the discourse ("That reminds me of . . .").

There are two similar pedagogic approaches to help L2 learners develop their syntactic processing of oral language, or in effect, to help them learn grammar through listening. The first, "enriched input," provides learners with prerecorded (or scripted) texts that have been "flooded" with exemplars of the target syntactic structure in the context of a meaning-focused task. This approach caters to incidental learning of the target grammar structure through, what Long (1990) first called "focus on form." The second is known by the term first used by VanPatten (1990), "processing instruction." In this approach, learners attend to interpretation tasks that encourage learners to engage in intentional learning by consciously noticing how a target grammar feature (e.g., passive voice) is used in the spoken input, even though the feature is not explicitly called out.

Ellis (2003) reviews a number of studies using these approaches. Concerning the enriched input approach, Ellis concludes that enriched input can help L2 learners acquire new grammatical features and use partially learned features more accurately, and that this form of grammar instruction is at least as effective and often more effective than explicit instruction in grammar. Clear, positive effects, however, seem to be evident only when the treatment provided is prolonged. Concerning input-processing instruction, Ellis concludes that processing instruction in conjunction with explicit grammar instruction leads to the most consistent gains in the ability of learners to comprehend target structures being taught. Furthermore, he concludes that effects of processing instruction on both comprehension and production are more durable than explicit instruction alone.

Paralinguistic Cues in Speech Processing

There is an additional, non-verbal, layer of information in the speech signal that parallels lexical and grammatical cues. This is the paralinguistic layer, which provides meaningful fluctuations in duration (length), pitch (intonation), and intensity (loudness). Crystal (1995) has summarized the six types of information that are typically encoded by the speaker, and available to the listener, through intonation:

(1) Emotional: intonation is used to express the speaker's feelings for the topic;
(2) Grammatical: intonation can be used to mark grammatical structure of an utterance, like punctuation in written language;
(3) Informational: intonation indicates the salient parts of an utterance;
(4) (Textual: intonation is used to help large chunks of discourse contrast or cohere, rather like paragraphs in written language;
(5) Psychological: intonation is used to chunk information into units that are easier to process. For example, lists of words, or telephone or credit card numbers are grouped into units to make them easier to memorize;
(6) Indexical: intonation can indicate membership in specific social or cultural groups. For example, preachers and newscasters often use a recognizable intonation pattern.

Couper-Kuhlen (2001) provides numerous illustrations of how speakers encode these types of information intonationally. In addition, she documents how listeners, in conversational contexts, also respond intonationally to this information, through degrees of signaling understanding, degrees of acceptance of the speaker's perceived meaning, and through attempts to amplify, reduce, or redirect the focus of the discourse.

Integration of Visual and Aural Cues

Speech processing is known to be aided by consistent visual signals from the speaker, in the form of both gestures and articulatory movements (of the mouth, cheeks, chin, throat, or chest) that correspond to production of speech. (Rost (2002) provides a review of gestural signals available in face-to-face communication.) Because of the importance of visual cues, psycholinguists consider speech perception to be bi-modal, involving both auditory and visual senses. (Massaro, 1994). Indeed, it has been shown that children acquire speech perception in their L1 through dependence on visual signals from their caretakers (McGurk & MacDonald, 1976).

When visual and auditory signals do not coincide, there are a great number of incidences of blended mishearings, called the "McGurk Effect," in which part of the signal is taken from visual cues and part from auditory cues. This effect illustrates attempts by the listener to integrate information from multiple channels. (Stork & Hennecke, 1996 provide additional examples and discussion of blended mishearings.) Consistent with the principle of integration, when auditory cues are completely absent (as in listening on the telephone or to the radio), acoustic mishearings and other comprehension problems are significantly higher than in face-to-face delivery of messages (Massaro, 1998).

Comprehension Processes: Identifying Salient Information

Comprehension is essentially a constructive process that takes place in the listener's short-term and long-term memory. It is a process of relating language to references in the real world as well as to concepts and representations in personal memory, and consists of four overlapping sub-processes: identifying salient information, activating appropriate schemata, inferencing, and updating representations.

To comprehend speech, the listener must construct a concept in memory for the lexical items uttered and propositions stated or implied by the speaker. This construction takes place in a state of cognitive uncertainty as there are certain to be mismatches between the speaker's concepts and those of the listener. In other words, what is colloquially referred to as "complete comprehension" takes place without any guarantee of shared concepts, beliefs or knowledge between speaker and listener (Brown, 1995a; Sperber & Wilson, 1986; Krauss & Fussell, 1991).

Because comprehension involves the mapping and updating of references that the speaker uses, the process of comprehending occurs in an ongoing cycle, as the listener is attending to each utterance of the speaker. Each *intonation unit* (often called a *pause unit*) uttered by a speaker includes both *new information* (or focal information) and *given information* (or background information). "New" refers to the assumed status, in the speaker's mind, that the information is *not yet "active"* in the listener's working memory. "New" information then does not necessarily mean that the speaker believes the information itself is novel for the listener. "Given" refers to the status, again in the speaker's mind, that information is already active in the listener's mind. Mutual comprehension is never assured: the speaker may, of course, be mistaken about either assumption. (Allwood, 1995; Chafe, 1994; Keysar et al., 1998; Hinds, 1985).

The interplay of given and new information in spoken discourse is reflected in the prosody of speech: In most varieties of English, utterances with given information tend to end in rising or level intonation and are uttered more quickly, while utterances with new information tend to end in falling intonation (Brazil, 1995). These prosodic elements serve as cues to the listener about how to attend to the information given.

Comprehension Processes: Activating Appropriate Schemata

Understanding what a speaker says depends to a large degree upon shared concepts and shared ways of reacting to the world, or at least the *imagination* of shared concepts. The advantage of shared concepts is that the speaker need not make explicit whatever he or she can assume the listener already knows (Gass & Neu, 1996; Scollon & Scollon, 1995). Although it is impossible that any two persons (even close family members) would share identical concepts for a topic, it is indeed possible that many people who are members of similar communities will share common activation spaces in memory, which allows them to experience "mutual meanings" (Churchland, 1999).

The central component in comprehension is the activation of these concepts, or "modules" of knowledge. Known as *schemas* (often referred to in the plural as *schemata*), these memory structures measure the semantic content of the input for its degree of conformity or variance to knowledge the listener already possesses. The notion of schema as an organizing principle of long-term memory was introduced to explain how listeners created apparent distortions in content when they recalled stories that they heard (Rumelhart, 1980). In a seminal study, Mandler & Johnson (1977) had subjects read a passage involving an unknown cultural ritual ("The War of the Ghosts"). Subjects were tested on their recall at various intervals. The recall protocols revealed a range of distortions of story content, even though the subjects considered their recall to be accurate. This study and many others in the "story grammar" paradigm (e.g., Bransford & Johnson, 1972 ; Kintsch & van Dijk, 1978; Abu-Akel, 1999) and the "reader response" paradigm (e.g., Spiro, 1982; Miall, 1989) demonstrate how background knowledge, expectations, and affect influence the ways we understand and remember what we hear or read. Schemas are in effect "psychological anchors," which create biases in the comprehension process. Unless strong enough evidence is presented to motivate the listener to "move the anchor," the listener will assume that the speaker's meaning is consistent with the schema the listener has (Wilson et al., 1996) and use this schema to initiate and carry forward the comprehension process.

Neurologically, a schema is a set of simultaneously activated "connections" (related nodes) in the frontal cortex of the brain. Each schema may be triggered by activation of any node in the network (Rumelhart, 1997; Rubin, 1996). What defines a schema is its heuristic nature. A set of memory nodes needed to guide one through an activity, such as "withdrawing money from an ATM" or "dealing with phone solicitor," becomes a heuristic when it first works as a "solution" to a comprehension problem (Port & van Gelder, 1995). It is estimated that any adult by age 21 has roughly one million schemas in memory that can be drawn upon in language comprehension. Because these schemas can be interrelated in a variety of ways, the connections among them is nearly infinite (Churchland, 1999). To remain operational as heuristics, new schemas are created every day and existing ones are updated constantly: every time we read, listen to, or observe something new we create a new schema by relating one fact to another through a logical or semiotic link (Altarriba & Forsythe, 1993).

The notions of schemata and particularly culturally-influenced schemata are particularly important in L2 comprehension, because L2 listeners continuously come in contact with assumptions and expectations that are in variance to their own. Comprehension problems arise, not only when schemata are markedly different, but if the listener is unaware of what these schematic differences might be (Lantolf, 1999; Schrauf & Rubin, 1998). L2 pedagogy has taken a significant interest in the notion of schemata and the activation of appropriate background knowledge for listening. Training methods typically incorporate pre-listening activities to raise awareness of cultural schemata that will be needed for comprehension (Long, 1990), and follow up discussion of cultural allusions, cultural preferences, and so on that were included in the listening text (Buck, 2001). Some methods stress the interrelatedness of gaining intercultural competence (awareness of cross-cultural factors in language learning and L2 use) and skill development (Sercu, 2000; Bremer et al. 1996). Methods for teaching academic listening directly incorporate an awareness of cultural and content schemata in extended listening and recall (Flowerdew, 1994). These methods are consistent with general L1 educational methods for promoting use of schematic maps in developing critical thinking and understanding extended texts (e.g., Manzo & Manzo, 1995).

Comprehension Processes: Inferencing

In language comprehension, the process of inferencing is similar to a mathematical inference in that it is a calculation, a problem-solving process, employed when there is sufficient evidence from which some conclusion can be drawn about related propositions (Kintsch, 1998). (For example, if one hears two related propositions, "I brought the ice. It's in the trunk." we can infer that the ice, in the trunk of the speaker's car, might be melting.) Inferencing is involved in comprehension because the conclusions that must be drawn are almost always based on inexplicit evidence. Research on inferencing during comprehension has been carried out in three basic ways: through recall analysis, through test performance, and through introspection protocols.

Recall protocols paired with text analysis has been a primary method of studying inferencing processes for both L1 and L2 listeners (Olson, Duffy, & Mack; 1984; Trabasso & Magaliano, 1996; Golden, 1998; Golden & Rumelhart, 1993; Rost 1994). In this form of comprehension research, the researcher identifies the differences between what is explicitly stated in a text and what the listener "infers" when reconstructing the text or answering questions about the text. This line of research, done primarily in L1 contexts, has shown how listeners utilize *scripts* (sequential patterns of knowledge), *goal hierarchies* (knowledge of organization patterns in a text or discourse type), *conceptual graphs* (idealization of the speaker's assumed meaning), and *causal nets* (cause-effect arcs and conditional logic syllogisms) to remember large stretches of text and to draw inferences as they listen.

Analysis of test performance, which has been extensive in the area of L2 listening, is another way of studying inferencing processes. This type of research outlines the information that is available in the text (or test stem) and projects the presumed cognitive processes that are required to respond to the text (or test stem). These projections are then validated by factor analysis. Using this research paradigm, a study by Freedle & Kostin (1996) analyzed TOEFL (Test of English as a Foreign Language) tests and found the following kinds of inferences being tested: inferring similarities between morphologically similar pairs of words and phrases. (Stem: Her friend was.... Response option: She was friendly...); inferring lexical synonymy. (Stem: He intended to leave... Response option: He wanted to leave...); inferring lexical hierarchies (Stem: She cut her finger. Response option: She injured part of her hand.); inferring case (semantic role) of a noun or noun phrase in a sentence (Stem: He cut the grass. Response option: The grass was cut by him.)

Buck (2001) in an analysis of several listening test formats, found the following types of inferencing questions present in published tests: asking for the main idea of the text or section of the text, asking about anything that is not clearly stated, but that is deliberately indicated by the speaker (e.g., by choice of words or tone of voice or connotations of words); asking about any pragmatic implication or logical entailment.

Introspection research has been particularly fruitful in understanding the problem-solving and inferencing procedures of L2 listeners. Rost & Ross (1991) using text reconstruction and directed questioning, constructed a typology of clarification question types asked by L2 listeners. This typology identified the kinds of inferential questions posed by listeners: global questions (suggesting insufficient information understood on which to base an inference), lexical questions (suggesting insufficient knowledge of word meanings or insufficient context to relate to the word understood), hypothetical questions (suggesting incomplete propositions on which to base inferences), and forward inference questions (suggesting a coherent propositional structure on which to base "normal" inferencing, not based on a perceived deficiency of information).

Vandergrift (1997a, 1999) conducted one-on-one interviews with learners as they listened to L2 audio tapes, stopping periodically to ask the learners what kinds of comprehension problems they were experiencing. The purpose of the research was to discover the types of strategies learners used to infer meaning, and to explore correlations between strategy use and learner proficiency. Based on the work of Vandegrift (1997b, 1999) and O'Malley et al. (1985), there is now a consensus that use of metacognitive strategies—planning for listening, self-monitoring of comprehension processes, and evaluation of one's own performance and problems—are associated with better listeners. As such, pedagogical approaches now incorporate the development of metacognitive strategies for inferring meaning as part of an instructional approach (see Figure 28.2).

Comprehension Processes: Updating Memory

Use of memory during language comprehension is generally discussed as involving two dimensions: long-term memory, associated with the sum of all of a person's knowledge and experience, most of which is inactive at any time, and short-term memory, associated with knowledge that is activated at a particular moment. For purposes of understanding verbal communication, it is preferable to speak in terms of memory activation rather than in terms of memory size. The popular term *short-term memory (STM)*, however, is ambiguous because it is used to refer to either (1) the set of *representations* from long-term memory stores that are currently and temporarily in a state of heightened activation, or (2) the focus of attention or content of awareness that can be held for a limited period of time.

STRATEGY	What the listener does	What the teacher can do to promote this strategy
PLANNING		
Advanced organization	Decide what the objectives of a specific listening task are. Why is it important to attend to this?	Write the topic on the board and ask learners why it might be important to listen to it.
Directed attention	Learners must pay attention to the main points in a listening task to get a general understanding of what is said.	In setting up a listening task ask learners what type of information they are likely to hear.
Selective attention	Learner pay attention to details in the listening task.	Before listeners listen a second time to a recording, set specific types of information for them to listen for.
Self-management	Learners have to manage their own motivation for a listening task.	Before setting up a listening task the teacher talks with the Ss in the L2 so that they become attuned to listening.
MONITORING		
Comprehension monitoring	Learners check their understanding of ideas, through asking confirmation questions.	Teacher sets up a task so that Ss have opportunities to ask for clarification and confirmation.
Auditory monitoring	Learners check their identification of what they hear.	Teacher sets up "bottom up" listening task to check for accurate perception of key words and grammatical structures.
Task monitoring	Learners check their completion of the task.	Teacher sets up task with intermediate steps so that Ss can tell that they are in the process of completing the task.
EVALUATION		
Performance evaluation	Learners judge how well they did on the task	T. sets up task with tangible outcome that can be evaluated by learners.
Problem identification	Learners decide on what problems they still have with the text or task	T. provides follow up to elicit problem areas.

(from Rost, 2002)

FIG. 28.2. Pedagogical approach for developing metacognitive strategies for L2 listeners.

Cowan (1993) argues for a hierarchical conception of STM, with the focus of attention being a subset of the activated neural connections in long-term memory. Consistent with this conception is the notion of *multiple* working memories, modules that are associated with different modalities (e.g., speech vs. writing) and with different kinds of *representations* (e.g., spatial, serial, verbal), any of which is active at any time. Working memory is a "computation space" in which various operations, such as rehearsal, phonological looping of input, information reductions, generalizations, and inferences occur. A computational version of working memory has strict temporal span limitations, namely, a brief sensory component lasting up to three seconds (sometimes called *echoic memory* or a *rehearsal loop*) and a computational "resolution space" lasting up to 30 seconds.

According to Gupta & MacWhinney (1997), there is a strong reason to believe that the rehearsal loop plays a central role in both first and second language listening. By testing the immediate serial recall (ISR) of L2 learners, it is possible to estimate the STM capacity of this rehearsal loop. Differences in the abilities of learners to store items in this loop have been shown to correlate well with differential success in both L1 and L2 learning (MacWhinney, 1996).

Updating of representations, through the use of comprehension and inferencing processes, takes place in the resolution space in short term memory. The ability of the learner to deal with input in real time in this memory space is an essential feature of proficiency in the L2. Three approaches to L2 listening pedagogy have addressed developing this fundamental aspect of proficiency: shadowing, non-reciprocal listening tasks, and note-taking.

Shadowing is a technique using direct or paraphrased repetition, similar to Elicited Imitation (EI) in applied linguistics studies, in which the listener is asked to repeat what the speaker says, in the same language, either verbatim, or in close paraphrase. In training of simultaneous or consecutive translators, verbatim repetition is eventually accompanied by a dual, non-linguistic, task and then by paraphrase.)

The goal of shadowing is to increase the efficiency of working memory, for periods up to 30 seconds, with increasingly complex inputs. By attempting to produce a complete and accurate version of what the speaker has said (including paralinguistic meanings), the listener is exercising the capacity of STM. The underlying cognitive ability for shadowing and paraphrasing is "chunking," the process of using key words to represent whole ideas and then collapsing an extended utterance into a manageable series of key words. Because it has been known for some time that working memory can hold only about seven "items" (Miller, 1956), chunking ability is essential for accurate comprehension of extended texts (Kussmaul, 1995; Robinson, 1991; Mikkelson, 1996).

Non-reciprocal tasks are a type of task involving a one-way delivery of information. In a listening task, the learner hears (or views) input and is given a specific goal, using selected information from the input. Typical tasks used in L2 pedagogy involve filling in grids, completing charts, or selecting or ordering visuals. Listening tasks either use pre-selected "authentic" input (i.e., input that naturally occurs outside of pedagogic settings, such as news programs) or a constructed (pre-modified) input that deliberately employs simplification to assist processing or flooding of certain kinds of text features (as in vocabulary or grammar processing tasks) to facilitate noticing and learning of specific language points. In modern instruction, listening tasks are often in a multimedia environment (Hoven, 1999).

Brown (1995b) studied the effects of pre-modified input on comprehension as measured by task outcomes, and concluded that features of cognitive (processing) load in the input influence task performance (see Figure 28.3).

Tasks which make use of these principles allow listeners to focus their attention on meaning in a continuous fashion, thus increasing the efficiency of working memory when listening to L2 input.

Note-taking, independently and as part of a task sequence (involving preparation, note-taking and reconstruction), has been used as part of listening methodologies to develop comprehension and memory processes in the L2. Note-taking can facilitate comprehension of a lecture in two ways (Di Vesta & Gray 1972): through assistance

Cognitive Load: Principle 1

It is easier to understand any text (narrative, description, instruction, or argument), which involves fewer rather than more individuals and objects.

Cognitive Load: Principle 2

It is easier to understand any text (particularly narrative texts) involving individuals or objects, which are clearly distinct from one another.

Cognitive Load: Principle 3

It is easier to understand texts (particularly description or instruction texts) involving simple spatial relationships.

Cognitive Load: Principle 4

It is easier to understand texts where the order of telling matches the order of events.

Cognitive Load: Principle 5

It is easier to understand a text if relatively few familiar inferences are necessary to relate each sentence to the preceding text.

Cognitive Load: Principle 6

It is easier to understand a text if the information in the text is clear (not ambiguous), self-consistent and fits in readily with information you already have.

(based on Brown et al., 1994)

FIG. 28.3. Cognitive load principles in assessment of difficulty of listening texts.

with *encoding* and through assistance with *retrieval*. As an assistance to encoding, taking notes serves as a way of condensing, evaluating, and organizing lecture content while listening and thus of increasing comprehension. At the very minimum, note-taking seems to help activate the learners' attention and self-monitoring mechanisms (Dunkel 1988; Benson, 1989). As an assistance with retrieval, note-taking results in an accessible, compressed record of the content of a lecture which can be later referred to and which thus promotes long-term retention and recall of the material. Having notes to refer to enables learners to replay the content in STM and also aids reconstruction of long-term representations of the content. Because short term memory is known to be able to handle only about seven items at a time (Miller, 1956), it is essential that any listener learn to chunk complex information into key words or abbreviated propositions that can later be reconstructed.

A number of issues concerning the relationship between note-taking and comprehension and memory have been investigated. One issue is whether taking notes works better for understanding and remembering than just listening. Dunkel, Mishra & Berliner (1989) found no difference in the scores obtained from tests measuring comprehension of main points and specific details between L2 students who took notes and those who just listened. Chaudron, Loschky & Cook (1994) found no difference in the comprehension test scores between those students who were allowed to retain their notes after the lecture and those who were asked to hand them in. Ellis (2003) speculates that one possible reason for these studies failing to find a positive relationship between taking—retaining notes and comprehension may be that the notes were lacking in quality. It is reasonable to assume that notes will only assist comprehension if they are complete, accurate and clear enough to support subsequent reconstruction of key ideas and information.

The key issue, then, is the relationship between note quality and comprehension. Dunkel (1988) used multiple regression analysis to try to identify what specific characteristics of the notes taken by both L1 and L2 students predicted scores on comprehension tests measuring understanding of main concepts and details. She concluded that the key variables were (1) terseness (i.e., the ratio between the number of information units encoded and the number of words used in the notes) and (2) answerability (i.e., the extent to which the notes included information relating to the test items).

Interpretation Processes: Adopting a Pragmatic Perspective

Interpretation is a stage of listening during which the listener orients to the speaker's meaning through adoption of a perspective and an assessment of relevance. Interpreting spoken language is fundamentally based on assuming a *pragmatic perspective*, that is situating oneself in terms of the topic, the setting, the event, the speaker *and* purpose for listening and relationship to the topic, setting, event and speaker. Interpretation can be seen as including *listener response*, both the overt responses and covert responses that a listener makes in response to what a speaker has said. Overt responses include feedback given to the speaker, such as *backchanneling* and *reframing*. Covert responses include *transformative effects*, such as realignments of the relationship with the speaker and affective adjustments of the listener's attitudes and beliefs.

There are numerous ways to portray the listener's pragmatic perspective. Hymes (1972) characterizes seven coordinates, which he called "situation-bound features," that determine the pragmatic perspective of speaker and listener in a communication event:

(1) setting or scene,
(2) participants ("utterers" and "recievers"),
(3) purposes (outcomes, goals),
(4) act sequence (message form and content)
(5) key (formality, politeness, power relations),
(6) instrumentalities (channel, forms of speech),
(7) norms (assumptions or expectations about interaction and interpretation),
(8) genre (text type).

From a pragmatic viewpoint, differences in understanding of discourse will occur because of differences in the participants' perspectives on these coordinates. Misunderstandings abound in all types of discourse, but misunderstandings in cross-cultural communication, in which at least one participant is using an L2, is a particularly fertile ground for studying this phenomenon (e.g., See Gumperz, 1990; 1995; Roberts et al., 1992; Bremer et al., 1996; Sarangi & Roberts,1999; Allwood & Abelar, 1989).

Initially, for interpretation to occur, there must be an engagement by the listener, which entails some level of recognition of each of these coordinates (Verschueren, 1999). The ways and the degree to which the L2 listener comes to recognize these coordinates, comes to gain knowledge about these coordinates, and learns to deal with power relationships with speakers over the negotiation of these coordinates are all critical aspects of development of L2 listening.

Norms in Interpretation. The norms of interpretation that a listener uses are influenced by one's identity in what Fish (1994) calls an interpretive community. All language comprehension is filtered through the norms of the *interpretive community* that one belongs to. An "interpretive community" is defined as any group that shares common contexts and experiences, and the listener is known to draw upon the expectations and norms of the group in language comprehension. Lakoff (2000) points out that this membership is both inclusive and exclusive: people who share the same expectations as the listener will be deemed to "get it," while those who don't share those expectations "just don't get it." Indeed, in order to understand complex genres of discourse (e.g., talk about elements of "pop culture"), it is more essential to be accepted as part of the group you are taking with than to "comprehend" the language used (Duff, 2001).

Interpretation of language by the L2 listener takes place within social frames, real or imagined that influence norms about the ways that the listener acts. The *social frame* for an interaction involves two interwoven aspects: the *activity frame*, which is the activity that the speaker and listener are engaged in, and the *participant frame*, which is the *role* that each person is playing within that activity, or the relative *status* that each participant has (Tyler, 1995).

The determination of the participant frame is a key factor in interpretation by the L2 listener. Carrier (1999) notes that the objective status, or *societal status*, can be predicted from knowledge of existing social mores (e.g., doctors are seen as superior in knowledge to their patients, teachers superior in knowledge to their students), the *situational nature of status* is less predictable. This is because situational status is not socially defined, is co-constructed by both interlocutors in each encounter, and can shift over the course of the encounter. Research on cross-cultural encounters has shown that the way in which interlocutors define their status relative to the other will determine a great deal about how they will communicate with each other, their degree of affective involvement, and what they will understand (Gumperz, 1995; Linell, 1995; Hinnenkamp, 1995).

One aspect of *affective involvement* in an interaction is the raising or lowering of anxiety and self-confidence, and thus the motivation to participate in meaningful, open, and self-revelatory ways. For listeners, greater affective involvement promotes better understanding through better connection with the speaker, while lower affective involvement typically results in less connection, less understanding, and minimal efforts to evaluate and repair any misunderstandings that arise (Pica, 1992). For example, Yang (1993) found in a study of Chinese learners of English a clear negative correlation between learners' levels of anxiety and their listening performance. Aniero (1990) noted that listening anxiety, or *receiver apprehension*, correlated with poor listening performances in pair interactions. One implication is that anxiety about listening is often triggered by social factors, such as perception of roles and status, and the sense that one's interlocutor is not responsive to one's own intentions in the interaction.

Listener anxiety is explained in part by *uncertainty management theory* (Gudykunst et al., 1996). This theory predicts that initial uncertainty and anxiety about another's attitudes and feelings in a conversation are the basic factors influencing communication, and that this uncertainty and anxiety inhibits effective communication. This theory predicts that the amount of information-seeking and "openness" that will take place in an interaction will be determined by the degree of uncertainty. Not all predictions of this theory are realized in practice because of other mitigating social factors. For example, Carrier (1999), researching interactions between L2 students and their professors in a university context, hypothesized that social status would have a negative effect on listening comprehension because opportunities for negotiation of meaning by the L2 speaker would tend be limited. She also hypothesized that comprehension of the NNS (non-native speaker) by an NS (native speaker) interlocutor would also be influenced negatively because the NNS would have fewer opportunities to restate unclear information. Neither hypothesis was supported by her research: She found that the superior party often used politeness strategies, or face-saving strategies (e.g.,

"It's okay, you can ask me a question if you like"). These strategies immediately affect the status relationship between the NS and NNS and to allow for more negotiation of meaning and more attempts at output by the NNS.

Interpretation Processes: Listener Response

Listener response is often considered part of the listening process, as it is interwoven with interpretation and adoption of a pragmatic perspective. Listener response generally involves *display* of *uptake, backchanneling*, and *follow-up acts*.

Though a speaker initiates acts in conversation, the listener has the choice of *uptaking* any initiating move or ignoring it. Typically, the speaker intends the listener to uptake the act in a specific way, in both verbal and non-verbal ways that constitute a normal, or *preferred response*. For example, an invitation leads to a preferred response of an acceptance. A listener response that expresses inability or reluctance to provide completion, or otherwise comply with the speaker's initiating move forms a *challenge*. A *dispreferred response* challenges the presupposition that the addressee has the information or resource the speaker needs and is willing to provide it, or it challenges the speakers right to make the initiating move (e.g., S1: Could you show me some identification, please? S2: What for?)

Challenges are by nature *face-threatening*—they upset the participation frame by demoting one interlocutor's power. Of course, some challenges are less face-threatening than others. Specifically, challenging the presupposition that one is *able* to provide the information is less face-threatening than challenging the presupposition that one is *willing* to provide it. This is why in most cultures it is more "polite" to declare ignorance than to refuse to comply with a request (Tsui, 1994).

Another type of listener response is *backchanneling*. Backchanneling responses are short messages—verbal, semi-verbal, and non-verbal—that the listener sends back during the partner's speaking turn or immediately following the speaking turn. These messages may include brief verbal utterances ("yeah, right"), rhythmic semi-verbal utterances (e.g., "uh-huh", "hmm"), laughs or chuckles, and postural movements, such as nods. Backchanneling, with norms of meaning and use differing from culture to culture and within sub-cultures, is important in conversation for showing a number of listener states: reception of messages, readiness for subsequent messages, agreement on turn-taking, and empathy. Backchanneling occurs more or less constantly during conversations in all languages and settings, though in some languages and in some settings, it seems more prevalent. Maynard (1997) in her analyses of Japanese casual conversation notes clear backchanneling every 2.5 seconds. She terms the interplay between speaker and listener as the "interactional dance." When backchanneling is withheld or disrupted, the interaction becomes perceptibly disordered, and the speaker will usually seek to repair the interaction.

A third class of listener response in discourse is the *follow-up act*. Follow-up acts are responses to a discourse exchange, and can be provided by either the listener or the speaker from the previous exchange. (e.g., S1 [elicit]: I'll see you tomorrow. S2 [response]: Okay, see you. [follow-up act] Could we meet in my office around nine?) Follow-up acts can be endorsements (positive evaluations), concessions (negative evaluations), or acknowledgements (neutral evaluations). A follow-up act may include a move to *reframe* the interaction by adjusting the participation frame or by redirecting the topic (e.g., S1: I'll see you tomorrow. S2: Wait, you can't leave. We haven't finished.).

L2 pedagogy dealing with interpretation in face-to-face encounters has incorporated three approaches: (1) ways of entering *listener roles* and using *interactive procedures* for enhancing listening effectiveness, (2) *two-way (collaborative) tasks*, and (3) *metapragmatic* treatment of speech acts and listener behavior in interactions.

In professional encounters, particularly between native and non-native speakers, (e.g., doctor-patient, manager-employer, mediator-clients), the notions of *listener roles* and *listener response options* have received increasing attention because the acknowledged importance of listening in work settings. For example, in medical encounters, listening is involved in problem assessment (e.g, evaluation of a problem at the initial medical visit), *"gatekeeping"* (e.g., observance of protocols required to see a physican), negotiating forms of treatment, and follow-up visits. Increasingly, education in "responsive listening" has become part of many professional and workplace trainings (e.g., Sarangi & Roberts, 1999; Scollon, 2001).

Similarly, in social settings, the notion of *listener control* in NS-NNS interactions has become an important handle for language training. Using longitudinal studies of NNS in several European settings, Bremer et al. (1996) have documented many of the *social procedures* that L2 listeners must come to use more comfortably and confidently as they become successful listeners and participants in everyday conversations. These procedures include identifying topic shifts, providing backchanneling ("listenership") cues, participating in conversational routines (providing obligatory responses), shifting to topic initiator role, and initiating queries and repair of communication problems.

A proposal by Bremer et al (1996) suggests that a program of instruction might include:

(a) A focus on the use of explicit responses to understanding problems e.g., metalinguistic comments (such as "I'm not sure I understand this") and the use of partial repetition to distinguish the non-understood elements;
(b) A strong encouragement to formulate hypotheses, to develop high inferencing capacities in the struggle for understanding;
(c) Awareness raising of the strategic use of different responses to a problem in understanding that fits the local context;
(d) Awareness of issues of face in conveying problems in understanding and in mitigating face-threats to gate-keepers ;
(e) Encouragement to take initiative in topic nominations as a way of reducing some *frame* and schema difficulties in understanding.

Two-way collaborative tasks are widely used in L2 oral language instruction to promote listening skills. Use of structured communicative tasks involving two-way communication promotes listener control of conversations, including regulating turn-taking, and seeking feedback through clarification, and confirmation checks. (Lynch, 1997). According to Ellis (2003), the key characteristics of an effective two-way collaborative task are (1) a primary focus on meaning (rather than on language form), (2) selection by the learner of linguistic resources needed for completion of task (rather than on all resources all given to the learner), and (3) a tangible outcome (which can be evaluated for its correctness or appropriateness). These features are seen as necessary in promoting learner uptake during the task, rather than mere completion of the task, in that they promote collaborative learning, active listening, negotiation of meaning, and attention to feedback (Pica et al, 1987; Pica, 1994; Lyster & Ranta, 1997; Gass, 1997; Carroll & Swain, 1993).

Metapragmatic treatments are now being employed in listening pedagogy in order to assist learners to become aware of pragmatic forces in interactions. In particular, this style of instruction is aimed at helping learners understand the pragmatic force that decisions by speakers and listeners exert in functional interactions. In explicit metapragmatic instruction, the targeted pragmatic feature (e.g., ways of refusing an invitation) is made the object of treatment through description, explanation, or discussion. In implicit instruction, the pragmatic feature is included in contexts of use and practiced in various activities. A number of researched speech acts (requesting, thanking, apologizing, etc.), discourse features (openings, softenings, etc.) and sociolinguistic factors are now included explicitly in L2 pedagogy. A strong general trend emerging from these studies is a distinct advantage for explicit metapragmatic instruction, for all levels of learners (Kasper & Rose, 1999).

REFERENCES

Abu-Akhel, A. (1999). Episodic boundaries in conversational narratives. *Discourse Studies, 1*, 437–453.

Altarriba, J., & Forsythe, W. J. (1993). The role of cultural schemata in reading comprehension. In J. Altarriba, (Ed.), *Cognition and culture: A cross-cultural approach to cognitive psychology.* Amsterdam: Elsevier.

Allwood, J. (1993). Feedback in Second Language Acquisition. In C. Perdue (Ed.), *Adult Language Acquisition. Cross Linguistic Perspectives, Vol. II.* (pp. 196–235). Cambridge, UK: Cambridge University Press.

Allwood, J., & Abelar, Y. (1989). Lack of understanding, misunderstanding and language acquisition. In G. Extra & M. Mittner (Eds.), Proceedings of the AILA-conference, Brussels.

Allwood, J. (1995). Mutual inferencing in conversation. In I. Marková, C. Graumann, & K. Foppa (Eds.), *Mutualities in dialogue* (pp. 101–123). Cambridge, UK: Cambridge University Press.

Aniero, S. (1990). The influence of receiver apprehension among Puerto Rican college students. Doctoral Dissertation. New York University. *Dissertation Abstracts International, 50*, 2300A.

Auer, P., Couper-Kuhlen, E., & Muller, F. (1999). *Language in Time: The rhythm and tempo of spoken interaction.* Oxford, UK: Oxford University Press.

Baddeley, A. (1986). *Working memory.* Oxford, UK: Oxford University Press.

Baltova, I. (1999). Multisensory Language Teaching in a Multidimensional Curriculum: The Use of Authentic Bimodal Video in Core French. *Canadian Modern Language Review, 56*, 31–48.

Benson, M. (1989). The academic listening task: A case study. *TESOL Quarterly 23*(3), 421–445.

Best, C. (1995). A direct realist view of cross-language speech perception. In W. Strange (Ed.), *Speech perception and linguistic experience: Theoretical and methodological issues.* Timonium, MD: York Press.

Bilmes, J. (1992). Mishearings. In G. Watson and R. Seiler (Eds.), *Text in Context: Contributions to ethnomethodology* (pp. 79–98). London: Sage.

Bond, Z. (1999a). *Slips of the ear: Errors in the perception of casual conversation.* San Diego, CA: Academic Press.

Bond, Z. (1999b). Morphological errors in casual conversation. *Brain and Language, 68*, 144–150.

Bransford, J., & Johnson, M. (1972). Contextual prerequisites for understanding: Some investigations of comprehension and recall. *Journal of Verbal Learning and Verbal Behavior, 11*, 717–726.

Brazil, D. (1995). *A grammar of speech.* Oxford, UK: Oxford University Press.

Bremer, K., Roberts, C., Vasseur, M. Simonot, & Broeder, P. (1996). *Achieving understanding: Discourse in intercultural encounters.* London: Longman.

Brennan, S. E., & Williams, M. (1995). The feeling of another's knowing: prosody and filled pauses as cues to listeners about the metacognitive states of speakers. *Journal of Memory and Language, 34*, 383–398.

Brown, Gillian, Malmkjaer, K., Pollitt, A., & Williams, J. (1994). *Language and understanding.* Oxford, UK: Oxford University Press.

Brown, Gillian (1995a). *Speakers, listeners and communication: Explorations in discourse analysis.* Cambridge, UK: Cambridge University Press.

Brown, Gillain (1995b). Dimensions of difficulty in listening comprehension. In D. Mendelsohn & J. Rubin (Eds.), *A guide for the teaching of second language listening* (pp. 59–73). San Diego, CA: Dominie Press.

Brown, G. D., & Hulme, C. (1992). Cognitive processing and second language processing: the role of short-term memory. In R. Harris (Ed.), *Cognitive Processing in Bilinguals* (pp. 105–121) Amsterdam: Elsevier.

Buck, G. 2001. *Assessing listening.* Cambridge, UK: Cambridge University Press.

Carrier, K. (1999). The social environment of second language listening: Does status play a role in comprehension? *Modern Language Journal, 83*, 65–79.

Carroll, S., & Swain, M. (1993). Explicit and implicit feedback. *Studies in Second Language Acquisition, 15*, 357–386.

Cauldwell, R. (1996). Direct encounters with fast speech on CD-audio to teach listening. *System, 24*, 521–528.

Chafe, W. (1994). *Discourse, consciousness, and time: The flow and displacement of consciousness in speaking and writing.* Chicago: University of Chicago Press.

Chaudron, C., Loschky, L., & Cook, J. (1994). Second language listening comprehension. In J. Flowerdew (Ed.), *Academic listening: Research perspectives* (pp. 75–92). Cambridge, UK: Cambridge University Press.

Chaudron, C. (1988). *Second language classrooms.* Cambridge, UK: Cambridge University Press.

Chun, D. (2002). Discourse and intonation in L2: From theory and research to practice. Amsterdam: Benjamins.

Chun, D., & Plass, J. L. (1996). Effects of multimedia annotations on vocabulary acquisition. *The Modern Language Journal, 80*(2), 183–198.

Chun, D., & Plass, J. L. (1997). Research on text comprehension in multimedia environments. *Language Learning & Technology, 1*(1), 60–81.

Churchland, P. (1999). Learning and conceptual change: The view from the neurons. In A. Clark and P. Millican. *Connectionism, concepts, and folk psychology* (pp. 7–43). Oxford, UK: Oxford University Press.

Couper-Kuhlen, E. (2001). Intonation and discourse: current views from within. In D. Schiffrin, D. Tannen, & H. Hamilton (Eds.), *Handbook of Discourse Analysis*. Oxford, UK: Blackwell.

Cowan, N. (1993). Activation, attention and short-term memory. *Memory and Cognition, 21*, 162–167.

Crystal, T., & House, A. (1990). Articulation rate and the duration of syllables and stress groups in connected speech. *Journal of Acoustic Society of America, 88*, 101–112.

Crystal, D. (Ed.), (1995). *The Cambridge encyclopedia of the English language*. Cambridge, UK: Cambridge University Press.

Cutler, A. (1997). The comparative perspective on spoken language processing. *Speech Communication, 21*, 3–15.

Di Vesta, F., & Gray, S. (1972). Listening and note-taking. *Journal of Educational Psychology, 63*, 8–14.

Duff, P. A. (2001). Language, literacy, content, and (pop) culture: Challenges for ESL students in mainstream courses. *The Canadian Modern Language Review, 59*, 103–132.

Dunkel, P., Mishra. S., & Berliner, D. (1989) Effects of notetaking, memory, and language proficiency on lecture learning for native and non-native speakers of English. *TESOL Quarterly, 23*, 543–549.

Dunkel, P. (1988). The content of L1 and L2 students' lecture notes and its relation to test performance. *TESOL Quarterly, 22*, 259–281.

Ellis, N. (1994). Consciousness in second language learning: Psychological perspectives on the role of conscious processes in vocabulary acquisition. *AILA Review, 11*, 37–56.

Ellis, R. (2003). *Task-based language learning and teaching*. Oxford, UK: Oxford University Press.

Ellis, R. & Heimbach, R. (1997). Bugs and birds: Children's acquisition of second language vocabulary through interaction. *System 25*, 247–259.

Escudero, P., & Boersma, P. (2001). Modelling the perceptual development of phonological contrasts with Optimality Theory and the Gradual Learning Algorithm, Proceedings of the 25th Penn Linguistics Colloquium. Penn Working Papers in Linguistics.

Fish, S. (1994). *There's no such thing as free speech and it's a good thing, too*. New York: Oxford University Press.

Flege, J. (1995). Second-language speech learning: Theory, findings, and problems. In W. Strange, (Ed.), *Speech perception and linguistic experience: Theoretical and methodological issues*. Timonium, MD: York Press.

Flowerdew, J. (1994). *Academic listening: Research perspectives*. Cambridge, UK: Cambridge University Press.

Freedle, R., & Kostin, I. (1996). The prediction of TOEFL listening comprehension item difficulty for minitalk passages: Implications for construct validity. TOEFL Research Report, No. RR-96-20. Princeton, NJ: Educational Testing Service.

Garnes, S., & Bond, Z. (1980). A slip of the ear: A snip of the ear? A slip of the year? In V. Fromkin (Ed.), *Errors in linguistic performance*. New York: Academic Press.

Gass, S. (1997). *Input, interaction, and the second language learner*. Mawah, NJ: Lawrence Erlbaum Associates.

Gass, S., & Neu, J. (Eds.). (1996). *Speech acts across cultures. Challenges to communication in a second language*. Berlin: Mouton.

Gernsbacher, M., & Foertsch, J. (1999). Three models of discourse comprehension. In S. Garrod, & M. Pickering. (Eds.), *Human language processing*. East Sussex, UK: Psychology Press.

Gernsbacher, M., & Shlesinger, M. (1997). The proposed role of suppression in simultaneous interpretation. *Interpreting, 2*, 119–140.

Gernsbacher, M. (1990). *Language Comprehension as Structure Building*. Hillsdale, NJ: Lawrence Erlbaum Associates.

Golden, R. (1994). Analysis of categorical time-series text recall data using a connectionist model. *Journal of Biological Systems, 2*, 283–305.

Golden, R. (1998). Knowledge digraph contribution analysis of protocol data. *Discourse Processes, 25*, 179–210.

Golden, R., & Rumelhart, D. (1993). A parallel distributed processing model of story comprehension and recall, *Discourse Processes, 16*, 203–237.

Griffiths, R. (1992). Speech rate and listening comprehension: Further evidence of the relationship. *TESOL Quarterly, 26*, 385–390.

Grosjean, F., & Frauenfelder, U. (Eds.). (1996). Spoken word recognition paradigms. Special issue of *Language and Cognitive Processes, 11*, 553–699.

Gudykunst, W., Ting-Toomey, S., & Nishida, T. (Eds.). (1996). *Communication in personal relationships across cultures*. Thousand Oaks, CA: Sage.

Gumperz, J. (1990). The conversational analysis of interethnic communication. In R. Scarcella, R. E. Anderson, & S. Krashen (Eds.), *Developing communicative competence in a second language*. Boston: Heinle and Heinle.

Gumperz, J. (1995). Mutual inferencing in conversation In I. Markova, C. Graumann, & I. Foppa (Eds.), *Mutualities in Dialogue*. Cambridge, UK: Cambridge University Press.

Gupta, P., & MacWhinney, B. (1997). Vocabulary acquisition and verbal short-term memory: Computational and neural bases. *Brain and Language, 59*, 267–333.

Hahne, A., & Frederici, A. (1998). ERP-evidence of for autonomous first-pass parsing processes in auditory language comprehension. *Journal of Cognitive Neuroscience*, supplement, p. 125.

Harris, R., Lee, D., Hensley, D., & Schoen, L. (1988). The effect of cultural script on memory for stories over time. *Discourse Processes 11*, 413–431. 1988.

Hinds, J. (1985). Misinterpretations and common knowledge in Japanese. *Journal of Pragmatics 9*, 7–19.

Hinnenkamp, Volker (1995). Intercultural Communication. In J. Verschueren, J. Ostman, & J. Blommaert (Eds.), *Handbook of Pragmatics*. Amsterdam: Benjamins.

Hoven, D. (1999). A model for listening and viewing comprehension in multimedia environments. *Language Learning and Technology, 3*, 89–103

Hymes, D. (1972). *Towards communicative competence*. Philadelphia: University of Pennsylvania Press.

Iverson, P., Kuhl, P., Akahane-Yamada, R., Diesch, E., Tokura, Y., Ketterman, A., & Siebert, C. (2001). *Speech, Hearing and Language: work in progress, 13*, 106–118

Jusczyk, P. (1997). *The discovery of spoken language*. Cambridge MA: MIT Press.

Kager, R. (1999). Optimality Theory. Cambridge: Cambridge University Press.

Kasper, G., & Rose, K. (1999). Pragmatics and SLA. *Annual Review of Applied Linguistics, 19*, 81–104.

Keysar, B., Barr, D., Balin, J., & Paek, T. (1998). Definite reference and mutual knowledge: Process models of common ground in comprehension. *Journal of Memory and Language, 39*, 1–20.

Kintsch, W., & van Dijk, T. (1978). Toward a model of text comprehension and production. *Psychological Review, 85*, 363–394.

Kintsch, W. (1998). *Comprehension*. Cambridge, NY: Cambridge University Press.

Kohonen, T. (1984). *Self-organization and associative memory*. Berlin: Springer-Verlag.

Kramsch, C. (1997). Rhetorical models of understanding. In T. Miller (Ed.), *Functional approaches to written text: classroom applications*. Washington, DC: USIA.

Krauss, R., & Fussell, S. (1991). Constructing shared communicative environments. In L. Resnick, J. Levine, & S. Teasley (Eds.), *Perspectives on socially shared cognition* (pp. 172–200). Washington, DC: American Psychological Association.

Kuhl, P. K. (2000). A new view of language acquisition. *Proceedings of the National Academy of Science, 97*, 11850–11857.

Kuhl, P. (1991). Perception, cognition, and the ontogenetic and phylogenetic emergence of human speech. In S. Brauth, W. Hall, & R. Dooling (Eds.), *Plasticity of Development*. Cambridge, MA: MIT Press.

Kuhl, P., Williams, K., Lacerda, F., Stevens, K., & Lindblom, B. (1992). Linguistic experience alters phonetic perception in infants by 6 months of age. *Science, 255*, 606–608.

Kussmaul, P. (1995). *Training the translator*. Amsterdam: Benjamins.

Lakoff, R. (2000). *The language war*. Berkeley CA: University of California Press.

Lantolf, J. (1999). Second culture acquisition: cognitive considerations. In E. Hinkel (Ed.), *Culture in second language teaching and learning*. Oxford, UK: Oxford University Press.

Laufer, B., & Hulstijn, J. (2001). Incidental vocabulary acquisition in a second language: The construct of task-induced involvement. *Applied Linguistics, 22*, 1–26.

Leow, R. (1993). To simplify or not to simplify: A look at intake. *Studies in Second Language Acquisition, 15*, 333–355.

Leow, R. (2000). A Study of the Role of Awareness in Foreign Language Behavior, *Studies in Second Language Acquisition, 22*, 557–584.

Lewis, R. L. (1999). Specifying architectures for language processing: Process, control, and memory in parsing and interpretation. In M. Crocker, M. Pickering, & C. Clifton (Eds.), *Architectures and Mechanisms for Language Processing*. Cambridge, UK: Cambridge University Press.

Linell, P. (1995). Troubles with mutualities: towards a dialogical theory of misunderstanding and mis-communication. In I. Marková, C. Graumann, & K. Foppa (Eds.), *Mutualities in dialogue*. (pp. 176–213). Cambridge, UK: Cambridge University Press.

Long, D. (1990). What you don't know can't help you: An exploratory study of background knowledge and second language listening comprehension. *Studies in Second Language Listening, 12*, 65–80.

Luce, P. A., & Pisoni, D. B. (1998). Recognizing spoken words: The neighborhood activation model. *Ear and Hearing, 19*, 1–36.

Lynch, T. (1997). Life in the slow lane: observations of a limited L2 listener. *System, 25*, 385–98.

Lyster, R., & Ranta, L. (1997). Corrective feedback and leaner uptake: Negotiation of form in communicative classrooms. *Studies in Second Language Listening, 19*, 37–66.

Mandler, J., & Johnson, N. (1977). Remembrance of things parsed: story structure and recall. *Cognitive Psychology, 9*, 111–51.

Manzo, A, & Manzo, U. (1995). *Teaching children to be literate: a reflective approach*. New York: Harcourt Brace Jovanovich College.

Marslen-Wilson, W. (1990). Activation, competition, and frequency in lexical access. In G. Altmann (Ed.), *Cognitive Models of Speech Processing: Psycholinguistic and Computational Perspectives* (pp. 148–172) Cambridge, MA: MIT Press.

Marslen-Wilson, W. (1987). Parallel processing in spoken word recognition. *Cognition, 25*, 71–102.

Massaro, D. W. (1998). *Perceiving talking faces: from speech perception to a behavioral principle*. Cambridge, MA: MIT Press.

Massaro, D. (1994). Psychological aspects of speech perception. *Handbook of psycholinguistics*. New York: Academic Press.

Massaro, D., & Burke, D. (1991). Perceptual development and Auditory Backward Recognition Masking. *Developmental Psychology, 27*, 85–96.

Massaro, D. (1987). Speech perception by eye and ear: a paradigm for psychological inquiry. Hillsdale, NJ: Lawrence Erlbaum Associates.

Maynard, S. (1997). *Japanese communication: Language and thought in context*. Honolulu: University of Hawaii Press.

MacWhinney, B. (1996). Language Specific Prediction in Foreign Language Learning. *Language Testing, 12*, 292–320.

MacWhinney, B. (1994). Implicit and Explicit Processes. *Studies in Second Language Acquisition, 19*, 277–281.

McGurk, H., & MacDonald, J. W. (1976). Hearing lips and seeing voices. *Nature, 264*, 746–748.

McClelland, J., McNaughton, B., & O'Reilly, R. (1995). Why there are complementary learning systems in hippocampus and neocortex: Insights from the successes and failures of connectionist models of learning and memory. *Psychological Review, 102*, 419–457.

McQueen, J., Cutler, A, Briscoe, T., & Norris, D. (1995). Models of continuous speech recognition and the contents of the vocabulary. *Language and Cognitive Processes, 10*, 309–331.

Metsala, J. (1997). An examination of word frequency and neighborhood density in the development of spoken word recognition, *Memory and Cognition, 25*, 47–56.

Miall, D. (1989). Beyond the schema given: Affective comprehension of literary narratives. *Cognition and Emotion, 3*, 55–78.

Mikkelson, H. (1996). Community interpreting. *Interpreting, 1/1*, 125–129.

Miller. G. (1956). The magical number seven, plus or minus two: some limits on our capacity for processing information, *The Psychological Review, 63*, 81–97 (republished in *Memory and Cognition, 13*, 202–207).

Morton, J. (1969). Interaction of information in word recognition. *Psychological Review, 76*, 165–78.

Nation, P. (2001). *Learning Vocabulary in Another Language*. Cambridge, UK: Cambridge University Press.

Nation, P., & Waring, R. (1997). Vocabulary size, text coverage, and word lists. In N. Schmitt and M. McCarthy (Eds.), *Vocabulary: Description, Acquisition and Pedagogy* (pp. 6–19). Cambridge, UK: Cambridge University Press.

O'Malley, J., Chamot, A., Stewner-Manzanares, G., Kupper, L., & Russo, R. (1985). Learning strategies used by beginning and intermediate ESL students. *Language Learning, 35*, 21–46.

Olson, D. H., Duffy, S. A., & Mack, R. (1984). Thinking-out-loud as a method for studying real-time comprehension processes. In D. Kieras & M. Just (Eds.), *New methods in reading comprehension research* (pp. 253–286). Hillsdale, NJ: Lawrence Erlbaum Associates.

Osterhout, L., McLaughlin, J., & Bersick, M. (1997). Event related potentials and human language. *Trends in Cognitive Sciences, 1*, 203–209.

Osterhout, L., & Nicol, J. (1999). On the distinctiveness, independence, and time course of the brain responses to syntactic and semantic anomalies. *Language and Cognitive Processes, 14*, 283–317.

Pica, T., Young, R., & Doughty, C. (1987). The impact of interaction on comprehension. *TESOL Quarterly, 21*, 737–58.

Pica, T. (1992). The textual outcomes of native speaker-non-native speaker negotiation: What do they reveal about second language learning? In C. Kramsch & S. McConnell-Ginet (Eds.), *Text and context: Cross-disciplinary perspectives on language study*. Lexington, MA: Heath.

Pica, T. (1994). Research on negotiation: what does it reveal about second language learning conditions, processes, and outcomes? *Language Learning, 44*, 493–527.

Port, R., & Gelder, T. V. (Eds.). (1995). *Mind as motion: Explorations in the dynamics of cognition*. Cambridge, MA: MIT Press.

Read, J. 2001. *Assessing vocabulary*. Cambridge, UK: Cambridge University Press.

Roberts, C., Davies, E., & Jupp, T. (1992). *Language and discrimination: A study of communication in multiethnic workplaces*. London: Longman.

Robinson, D. (1991). *The translator's turn*. Baltimore: John Hopkins University Press.

Rost, M. (2002). *Teaching and researching listening*. London: Longman.

Rost, M. (1994). On-line summaries as measures of lecture understanding. In J. Flowerdew (Ed.), *Academic listening: research perspectives*. Cambridge, UK: Cambridge University Press.

Rost, M., & Ross, S. (1991). Learner use of strategies in interaction: typology and teachability. *Language Learning, 41*, 235–73.

Rost, M. (1990). *Listening in language learning*. London: Longman.

Rubin, D. (Ed.). (1996). *Remembering our past: Studies in autobiographical memory*. Cambridge, UK: Cambridge University Press.

Rumelhart, D. (1980). Schemata: The building blocks of cognition. In R. Spiro, B. Bruce, & W. Brewer (eds.). *Theoretical issues in reading comprehension* (pp. 33–58). Hillsdale, N.J.: Lawrence Erlbaum Associates.

Rumelhart, D. (1997). The architecture of mind: A connectionist approach. In J. Haugeland (Ed.), *Mind Design II*. Cambridge, MA: MIT Press.

Sarangi, S., & Roberts, C. (Eds.). (1999). *Talk, work and institutional order: Discourse in medical, mediation and management settings*. Berlin: Mouton de Gruyter.

Schmitt, N. (2000). *Vocabulary in language teaching*. Cambridge, UK: Cambridge University Press.

Schmidt, R. (2001). Attention. In P. Robinson (Ed.), *Cognition and second language instruction* (pp. 3–32) Cambridge, UK: Cambridge University Press.

Schmidt, R. (1995). *Attention and awareness in foreign language learning*. Honolulu: University of Hawaii Press.

Schrauf, R., & Rubin, D. (1998). Bilingual autobiographical memory in older adult immigrants: a test of cognitive explanations of the reminiscence bump and the linguistic encoding of memories. *Journal of Memory and Language, 39*, 437–457.

Scollon, R., & Scollon, S. (1995). *Intercultural communication: A discourse approach*. Oxford, UK: Blackwell.

Scollon, R. (2001). Action and text. toward an integrated understanding of the place of text in social (inter).action. In R. Wodak & M. Meyer (Eds.). *Methods of critical discourse analysis*. London: Sage.

Segalowitz, N., Segalowitz, A., & Wood, A. (1998) Assessing the devleopmneet of automaticity in second language word recognition. *Applied Psycholinguistics, 19*, 53–67.

Segalowitz, N., & Lightbown, P. (1999). Psycholinguistic approaches to SLA. In *Annual Review of Applied Linguistics*. Cambridge, UK: Cambridge University Press.

Sercu, L. (2000). The acquisition of intercultural competence. In L. Sercu (Ed.), *Intercultural competence: a new challenge for language teachers and trainers*. Center of Language and Intercultural Studies. Allborg, Denmark: Allborg University.

Shiffrin, R. (1988). Attention. In R. Atkinson, G. Herrnstein, G. Liddzey, & R. Luce (Eds.), *Handbook of experimental psychology* (2nd edition, Vol. 2). New York: Wiley.

Sperber, D., & Wilson, D. (1986). *Relevance: Communication and cognition*. Oxford, UK: Basil Blackwell.

Spiro, R. J. (1982). Long-term comprehension: Schema-based versus experiential and evaluative understanding. *Poetics, 11*, 77–86.

Stork, D. G., & Hennecke, M. E. (Eds.). (1996). *Speechreading by Humans and Machines*. Springer-Verlag: Berlin.

Strange, W. (1995). Cross-language studies of speech perception: A historical review. In W. Strange (Ed.), *Speech perception and linguistic experience: Issues in cross-language speech research*. (pp 3–45). Timonium, MD: York Press

Tesar, B., & Smolensky, P. (2000). Learnability in Optimality Theory. Cambridge, MA: MIT Press.

Trabasso, T., & Magliano, J. (1996). Conscious understanding during comprehension. *Discourse Processes, 21*(3), 255–287.

Tsui, A. (1994). *English conversation*. Oxford, UK: Oxford University Press.

Tyler, A. (1995). Co-constructing miscommunication: the role of participant frame and schema in cross-cultural miscommunication. *Studies in Second Language Acquisition, 17*, 129–152.

Vandergrift, L. (1999). Facilitating second language listening comprehension: acquiring successful strategies. *English Language Teaching Journal, 53*, 168–176.

Vandergrift, L. (1997a). The Cinderella of communication strategies: reception strategies in interactive listening". *The Modern Language Journal, 81*, 494–505.

Vandergrift, L. (1997b). The strategies of second language listeners: a descriptive study. *Foreign Language Annals, 30*, 387–409.

VanPatten, B. (1990). Attending to form and content in input: an experiment in consciousness. *Studies in Second Language Acquisition, 12*, 287–301.

Verschueren, J. (1999). *Understanding pragmatics*. London: Arnold.

Wajnryb, R. (1990). *Grammar Dictation*. Oxford, UK: Oxford University Press.

Wilson, T., Houston, C., Etling, K., & Brekke, N. (1996). A new look at anchoring effects: Basic anchoring and its antecedents. *Journal of Experimental Psychology, 4*, 387–402.

Yamada, R., & Tohkura, Y. (1992). Perception of American English/r/and/l/by native speakers of Japanese. In E. Tohkura, E. Vatikiotis-Bateson, & Y. Sagisaka (Eds.), *Speech perception, production, and linguistic structure*. (pp. 155–74). Tokyo: Ohmsha.

Yang, R-L. (1993). A study of the communicative anxiety and self-esteem of Chinese students in relation to their oral and listening proficiency in English. Doctoral dissertation, University of Georgia. *Dissertation Abstracts International, 54*, 2132A.

Zhao, Y. (1997). The effects of listener's control of speech rate on second language comprehension. *Applied Linguistics, 18*, 49–68.

Zwann, R., & Brown, C. (1996). The influence of language proficiency and comprehension skill on situation model processing. *Discourse Processes, 21*, 289–327.

29

Second Language Literacy and Biliteracy

Terrence G. Wiley
Arizona State University

INTRODUCTION AND OVERVIEW

Embarking on any discussion of literacy with those who are literate is problematic, not only because the topic can become technical but also because literacy is so ever-present and familiar. Probing the subject in any depth reveals that it is often laden with tacit assumptions that impact theory, policy, and practice. Second language literacy and biliteracy studies are potentially even thornier because all the assumptions and debates within literacy studies broadly remain despite any attempt to narrow the focus. Thus, it is necessary to foreground some of the major issues and ideological tensions in the broader field of literacy studies that necessarily intrude on the study of second language literacy and biliteracy.

BACKGROUND

Nomenclature

Critically reflecting on nomenclature used in discussions related to literacy is important, particularly in the United States where there is often considerable confusion in popular discourse regarding the extent of literacy and illiteracy among language minorities. In recent years, there has been increasing sensitivity concerning the need to use non-stigmatizing nomenclature when referring to language minorities. For some, the expression "language minority" itself may seem negatively ascriptive. Nevertheless, the expression will be used in this chapter, referring to those who speak languages other than English or so-called "nonstandard" varieties of English as their initial household or community language(s). They may be considered "minorities" either in a strict numerical sense and/or in the sociopolitical sense of being members of "non-dominant" language groups. "Language minority" is preferred herein because it provides a basis for appealing to legal rights and protections that other more euphemistically motivated labels lack (see Skutnabb-Kangas, 2000; Wiley, 1996, particularly chap. 6; and Wiley, 2001, 2002b).

Nomenclature is also important because it reveals implicit assumptions and biases that are not without social consequences. *Non*literacy merely notes the absence of literacy without specifying any expectations, but *il*literacy implies a failure to become literate and educated amidst societal expectations to do so. *Pre*literacy assumes the inevitability of literacy. Thus, when a person is called illiterate it implies a social failing, often a personal failing. If a group is called preliterate, the assumption is that they are somewhere on a developmental path toward the inevitable. Historical and anthropological discussions relating to the rise of literacy in human societies have often treated literacy as a technological advance resulting in a qualitative cognitive divide separating the literate from the nonliterates. Gee (1986) concluded this alleged divide represents "a new, more subtle version of the savage-versus-civilized dichotomy.... [nonliterates] were sometimes said to be 'mystical and prelogical' incapable of abstract thought, irrational, childlike,... and inferior" (pp. 720–721; text in brackets added).

The Importance and Functions of Second Language Literacy and Biliteracy

Biliteracy is common around the world. It is promoted in the European Economic Union. India has two national official languages—Hindi and English—along with 15 regional languages that coexist with them. Switzerland has four official national languages: German, French, and Italian have federal status, along with Romansh, which has local status. Canada is officially bilingual and uses French and English as languages of literacy. In the United Kingdom, Wales has a dual language policy that now promotes biliteracy in Welsh along with English (Baker & Jones, 2000). Language minorities are well positioned to become biliterate if they can develop literacy and have access to quality education in the majority or dominant language (Wiley, 2002a). Unfortunately, all too often this is not the case.

Second language literacy and biliteracy may be approached from individual, community, societal, and cross-national perspectives. Individuals become biliterate for many reasons. Literacy in more than one language has both pragmatic and status significance. Second language literacy/biliteracy is vital for language minorities to have access to employment and to access the social, political, and economic life of the prevailing society as well as in their local communities (Spener, 1994). Those migrating from one country to another seeking better economic or educational opportunities, or fleeing hardships or discrimination in their countries of origin, may need to acquire literacy in a second language (Skutnabb-Kangas, 2000). Given the importance of literacy and educational achievement in the contemporary world for economic access, social participation, and political participation, understanding both the distribution of literacy and access to equitable educational programs are particularly important because many language minorities do not have immediate access to literacy and schooling in their own languages.

Biliteracy serves many social and personal uses around the world and in the United States. It has pragmatic functions in facilitating international travel and trade. At the community level in the United States, for example, native language newspapers assist immigrants and other language minorities by providing a means by which they can use their stronger language of literacy while they acquire English literacy. They can also keep abreast of local news and news from their country of origin not dealt with in English language newspapers. In this regard, recent alternative language newspapers function similarly to those of the past. In 1910, for example, there were 540 German language newspapers in the United States (Wiley, 1998). Presently, Spanish, Chinese, and Vietnamese newspapers, to name a few, serve similar functions in biliterate communities. Many around the world also acquire biliteracy to sustain their religious identities. Sacred texts may exist in classical languages or languages not commonly used for other purposes: Muslims study classical Arabic to read the *Koran*, orthodox Jews learn Hebrew to read the *Torah* (Baker & Jones, 2000).

There has always been an elitist tendency to treat literacy as social capital and the same has been true for biliteracy. Historically, biliteracy was an expectation for the literati, who were not even considered fully literate unless they could read Latin or Greek, even if they could read and write their vernacular language (Wiley, 1996). French became the prestige language of literacy and "reason" during the European Enlightenment, and many, including American revolutionary leaders, were biliterate in English and French. English second language literacy has assumed a similar world-wide prestige today. Native English speakers who are biliterate are commonly held in admiration in the United States if they acquire competence and literacy in languages other than English. In contrast, language minorities who achieve functional literacy in English are generally not similarly admired by English-speaking monolinguals for their biliterate abilities (Wiley, 2002a). The distribution of literacy within a society is often taken to be a barometer of societal well-being and, between nations, is seen as a sign of national strength and competitiveness.

Common Misperceptions about Literacy and Language Diversity

A number of misperceptions underlie the popular understandings about literacy and language diversity in the United States. These misperceptions are based on what various scholars have identified as the dominant monolingual English language ideology (cf. Kloss, 1971; Krashen 1997, 1999; Macías, 1985; Ovando & McLaren, 2000; Schmidt, 2000; Wiley, 1999, 2000). Some of the most common misperceptions are: (a) illiteracy in the United States is primarily attributable to the presence of languages other than English; (b) social and regional varieties, or "dialects," of English are "illiterate" and weaken the purity of "standard" English; (c) lack of English oral facility indicates a lack of English literacy; and (d) bilingual education has failed because it keeps language minorities from learning English and becoming highly literate. Although these misperceptions have no authority among applied linguists, they are widely believed and often influence policymaking. Some examples of works that help to refute them are Baugh (1999), Crawford (2000), Hakuta (1986), Krashen (1997, 1999), Lippi-Green, (1997); Tse (2001), Wiley (1996); Wiley & Lukes (1996).

DEFINING LITERACY AND BILITERACY

There is no universally accepted definition of literacy. In fact, in recent years it has become common for many scholars to challenge the singular construct of literacy with "literac*ies*/multiliterac*ies*," even though our spellcheckers have not been programmed to accept the pluralization. Defining literacy is also complicated because notions of literacy are not static. Expectations regarding literacy skills inflate over time, giving the false impression that literacy standards and performance of recent generations are falling (Berliner & Biddle, 1995; Bracey, 1997; Resnick & Resnick, 1977).

The following basic distinctions are important in constructing a typology of literacy: *native language* literacy, *second dialect* literacy, *second language* literacy, and *biliteracy/multiliteracy* (cf. Macías, 1990). It is also worth noting that typologies of second language literacy are generally framed with implicit reference to a standard oral language of literacy. Given that one may be deaf from birth and acquire literacy in a print language, to extend the notion of language beyond oral languages is important. Similarly, since the blind may acquire literacy in Braille, the notion of print needs to be extended beyond visual systems.

Traditional Definitions

Ever since the rise of mass education, there has been widespread concern regarding the extent of literacy, the effectiveness of literacy instruction, and low performance. Contemporaneous with the rise of social efficiency and technologist orientations in education, there has been alarm over underachievement and "laggards" in the schools (see Kliebard, 1996) as well as very legitimate concerns about disproportionate school failure and underachievement among some language minority groups. Any attempt to assess the distribution of literacy in society, performance in schools, or the knowledge and skills necessary to function in a literate society involves either implicit or explicit notions of what it means to be literate. In this context, examination of some of the more common definitions is helpful, with the qualification that additional definitions are plentiful (see Wiley, 1996 for elaboration).

Minimal literacy refers to the ability to read or write something, at some level, in some context(s). In the past, even the ability to write one's own name or read a simple passage out loud were taken as an adequate display of literacy (Resnick & Resnick, 1977). During World War I, language minority immigrants trying to enter the United States were required to show that they had minimal literacy abilities by reading short passages from the *Bible* in their native language (see Wiley, 1996, chap. 4). Even this simple test, which was sensitive to language background, was not without bias given the diversity of religious orientations of the immigrants.

Conventional literacy refers to the ability to use print by reading, writing, and comprehending "texts on familiar subjects and to understand" print within one's environment (Hunter & Harman, 1979, p. 7). This definition begs the question somewhat because there are no consensus definitions of reading and writing. Consider that "familiar" texts could include a wide range of reading levels (from a skills-based point of view) and a wide variety of materials (from a social practices perspective). Language minorities asked to demonstrate their conventional literacy rarely are assessed on texts in their native language.

Basic literacy presumes a foundational level of skills from which *continued* literacy development is sustained through individual effort (Macías, 1990; Venezky, Wagner, & Ciliberti, 1990). Mikulecky (1990) has warned, "there is little evidence that basic literacy in itself wields a magical transforming power for learning" (p. 26).

Functional literacy refers to the ability to use print in order to achieve individual goals as well as the print-related obligations of employment, citizenship, daily problem solving, *and* participation in the community. It includes the notion of conventional literacy while locating it in economic and social contexts. Functional literacy has dominated popular and policy discussions about literacy, but the notion has been criticized for imposing a middle-class bias in notions of functional competence (see Hunter & Harman, 1979). Given these criticisms, Kirsch and Jungeblut (1986) devised three broad domains of literacy assessment—*prose, document,* and *quantitative*— subsequently used in the National Adult Literacy Survey (see the following discussion).

Elite and Unconventional Definitions

Elite literacy evokes the notion of literacy as a "possession" of knowledge and skills acquired in school and legitimized by the academic credentials one "holds," which constitute a sociocultural capital for *strategic power* (Erickson, 1984). Elite literacy is sanctioned and accredited by official endorsement and certified with diplomas from universities, which function as surrogates for mastery and high levels of attainment in culturally approved knowledge, expressed in standard language and institutionally approved genres. Elite education may include literary instruction in foreign languages, usually with a focus on "high" culture and "great" literature rather than on functional or vernacular literacy. "Cultural literacy," the creation of E. D. Hirsch (1987; see also Hirsch, Kett, & Trefil, 1988) may be seen as an attempt to define a monocultural elite version of literacy as the basis for mass acquisition.

Analogical literacies pertain to knowledge and skills related to particular types of content, knowledge, technologies, and methodologies. They extend traditional notions of literacy with other technologies and specialized areas of knowledge. There has been much ado about computer literacy, numeracy, historical literacy, and graphicacy (used by geographers; Graff, 1994). Macías (1990) has cautioned that the analogical literacies can become "secondary aspects of literacy study, not parts of the definition of literacy" (p. 19), thus confusing or confounding the definition of literacy with the analogical or secondary aspects of literacy. Kress (2003) focuses on the relationship between literacy and various new technological modalities of literacy in the new media age.

Ethnographically Informed Definitions of Literacy

Restricted literacy refers to "participation in script activities" that remain "restricted to a minority of self-selected" people (Scribner & Cole, 1981, p. 238). It differs from functional literacy because "those who do not know it can get along quite well" without it (p. 238) and because it fails to "fulfill the expectations of those social scientists who consider literacy a prime mover in social change" (p. 239). Restricted literacies are usually learned informally for specific purposes within a self-contained community rather than in school or wider societal contexts.

Similarly, *vernacular literacies* pertain to "unofficial" or "local" practices rather than to conventional or academic standards wherein the defining group may be in opposition to academic or institutionally sanctioned genres or channels of communication. They may be designed to challenge formal rules of what can be written. Shuman (1993) contends that vernacular literacies are intended to confront privileged channels and genres of communication. Vernacular literacies intentionally use "oral" styles in writing and also include so-called nonstandard and nonacademic varieties of language.

Situated literacies (Barton, Hamilton, & Ivanic, 2000) reorient the focus of attention to the role of literacy in social practices, wherein literacies are "the link between the activities of reading and writing and the social structures in which they are embedded and which they shape" (p. 7). As Gee (2000) notes, "there are as many literacies as there are ways in which written language is recruited within specific social practices to allow people to enact and recognize specific social identities . . . and specifically situated social activities. . . . That's why the New Literacy Studies often uses the literacy in the plural, literacies" (p. iii). *Multiliteracies* (Cope & Kalantzis, 2000) provide a similar way of referring to situated literacies. The notion is likewise derived from the social practices perspective and ideological orientation (discussed next) identified by Street (1984, 1993, 1995, 1999). Barton et al. (2000) note that a fundamental unit of social theory is *literacy practices*, which is simply "what people do with literacy" (p. 7). Following Street (1993), they contend "practices are not observable units of behavior since they also involve values, attitudes, feelings, and social relationships" (p. 7).

SCHOLARLY ORIENTATIONS TOWARD LITERACY AND BILITERACY

The study of literacy, second language literacy, and biliteracy are interdisciplinary, drawing from linguistics (particularly applied linguistics), education, sociology, psychology, history, and anthropology (cf. Baynham, 1995, p. 21). Nevertheless, there are some common areas of emphasis and difference across, and sometimes within, these disciplines. In an effort to analyze how different scholars approach literacy, Street (1984, 1993, 1995, 1999) identifies two broad approaches or "models": *autonomous* and *ideological.*

The Autonomous Orientation

The autonomous orientation focuses on formal mental properties of decoding and encoding text, and comprehending vocabulary without any in-depth analyses of how these processes are used within sociocultural contexts. The achievement of the learner in obtaining literacy is characterized in terms of how it correlates with individual psychological development. Cognitive consequences are considered to result from the ability to master print and characteristics associated with particular types of texts, often in the essayist tradition (Street, 1984). Even if the social practices in which they are used are alluded to, there is little attention to their sociocultural and institutional embeddedness. Major proponents of this orientation are Goody and Watt (1988), Havelock (1963, 1988), Olson (1977, 1984, 1988), and Ong (1982, 1988, 1992). In subsequent work, Goody (1988, 1999), Ong (1992), and Olson (1994, 1999), have moderated their earlier positions somewhat (see Street's, 1999, commentary).

Social Practices and Ideological Orientations

The social practices view of literacy has its origins in a variety of sources. Scribner and Cole (1978, 1981) went in search of cognitive effects of literacy and schooling and ended up endorsing a strong social practices view of literacy. Heath's (1983) *Ways with Words* provided a significant example of an in-depth, ethnographic analysis of three communities' oral and literate practices. Street (1984) helped to demonstrate commonalities in his work and that of others focusing on social practices. Gee (1986) and Cook-Gumperz (1986) complemented this general direction. Other noteworthy works followed (e.g., Baynham, 1995; Street, 1993). In the early and mid-1990s, a consensus was forming around the social practices view and what was more broadly being referred to as the *New Literacy Studies* (Willinsky, 1990). According to Gee (2001), there are two major claims of this orientation:

> [First,] if you want to know how reading and writing work, don't look at them directly and in and of themselves. Rather, look directly at specific social practices in which specific ways of writing and reading are embedded. Furthermore, look at how specific ways of reading and writing, within these social practices are always integrally connected to specific ways of using oral language.... (p. iii)

> [Second,] literacy is not first and foremost a mental possession of individuals. Rather, it is first and foremost a social relationship among people, their ways with words, deeds, and things, and institutions. Literacy is primarily and fundamentally out in the social, historical, cultural, and political world. It is only secondarily a set of cognitive skills, which subserve literacies as social acts in quite diverse ways in different contexts (p. iv).

Gee's second point identifies where the social practices orientation differs with the autonomous view, which is largely one of emphasis and directionality. The issue is not that social practices scholars are disinterested in cognitive development, but that they maintain language and literacy skills or proficiencies are better understood and analyzed in social context, rather than as independent, autonomous skills, whether they are *in* or *out* of school (e.g., Hull & Schultz, 2002; Kalmar, 2001; Scribner, 1981; and Taylor, 1997).

Heath's (1983, 1988) and Street's (1984) work in particular has strong implications for studies of second language literacy and biliteracy, even though they are not directly focused on them. Heath's study includes a focus on speech and literate activities in "literacy events" among three speech communities that had different "ways with words," and most significantly different practices of language and literacy socialization, which are not always understood or appreciated by schools. Street's (1984) study includes a focus on rural literacy practices in Iran. Both studies emphasize how literacy practices are socially embedded and constructed across various language communities. Taylor (1997) and Weinstein-Shr (1993), to name only a few, have provided useful studies of immigrant language minority communities consistent with the social practices perspective.

The ideological orientation emphasizes that literacy practices "are aspects not only of 'culture' but also of power structures" (Street, 1993, p. 7). Similarly, Levine (1982) saw these literacy practices as being embedded in historical contexts and as including activities in which an individual both wishes to engage and may be *compelled* to engage (p. 264). Other works that are relevant to this perspective are Auerbach (1989, 1992a, 1992b), Delgado-Gaitán and Trueba (1991), Edelsky (1996), Freire and Macedo (1987), Lankshear (1997), Luke (1988), Stuckey (1991), and Walsh (1991). The viewpoints of these writers are hardly uniform, but generally illustrate the embeddedness of literacy in social practices; institutions; sociocultural, economic, and political practices; and ideologies "that guide the processes of communicative production; the outcomes of utterances and texts produced in these practices" (Grillo, 1989, p. 15).

Again, from the ideological orientation, literacy practices are viewed as neither a neutral nor autonomous process, nor as mere individual achievements. Rather, they are seen as being shaped by the dominant social, economic, and political institutions in which they are socially, culturally, and politically embedded. Given that some groups succeed in school whereas others fail, the ideological approach seeks to interrogate the way in which literacy development is undertaken by scrutinizing implicit biases and the hidden curriculum in schools that can privilege some groups to the exclusion of others. From this perspective, differential literacy outcomes across groups generally, and for language minorities specifically, represent structural, systematic, or institutional bias (Wiley 1996; cf. Haas, 1992). Thus, from an ideological orientation, it is important to explore how differences in literacy and educational achievement function across groups, including language minority groups.

Deschooling Literacy

One is the relationship between literacy and schooling. In a landmark study, Scribner and Cole (1978, 1981, 1988) attempted to unravel the purported cognitive effects of literacy per se, from those specific to school practices by studying a West African people—the Vai of Liberia—who acquired literacy without going to school. Scribner and Cole sought "a practice account of literacy" (1981, p. 235). Heath's (1980, 1983, 1986, 1988) work overlapped in timeframe with Scribner and Cole's study. One of her contributions was to avoid dichotomizing literacy and orality by studying their interaction in social contexts. Heath helped to *deschool* the notion of literacy by focusing on *literacy functions* in broader community and social contexts such as daily business, social, and news-related functions, as well as memory supportive and record-keeping functions. This provided an alternative to oral communication through notes, and authoritative functions used to confirm, validate, or support beliefs by appealing to the authority of texts, both religious and secular. Deschooling the notion of literacy allows us to move beyond confounding literacy with school-based notions and practices, and may even enrich classroom literacy practices (Cook-Gumperz & Keller-Cohen, 1993; Hull, 1997; Hull & Schultz, 2000; Street, 1993, 1995, especially chap. 5; Weinstein-Shr, 1993).

ASSESSING AND MEASURING SOCIETAL
LITERACY AND BILITERACY

Many among the speakers of the world's estimated 5,000 or so spoken languages may achieve literacy in a second language rather than in the language(s) of the households into which they are born. Similarly, to become literate, many must acquire literacy in a standardized variety of language that diverges from their own social or regional variety. In the United States, this challenge is faced by speakers of Appalachian English, Ebonics or African American vernacular English, and Hawaiian English Creole, among others. These second "dialect" issues in literacy acquisition are also of major importance when studying literacy among *language minorities* and other second language learners, such as international students studying English as a foreign language and native speakers of English studying foreign languages. Second language literacy research must deal with all three populations, if it is to inform educational practice and policy in any meaningful way (cf. Verhoeven, 1994).

Unfortunately, much of what constitutes second language acquisition research is drawn from populations or samples of convenience, that is, from populations that the researchers can easily access. Thus, findings are often very population- and context-specific, but may be reported as if they are broadly applicable beyond the target group. For university second language learners, studies generally assume literacy in a first language, but often fail to probe it, as the focus of the research is the second language. The notion of second language itself often presumes literacy wherein reading and writing are two of four traditional skills (e.g., Kaplan, 2002, part 2). Yet, when dealing with adult education populations, first language literacy or extensive training in school-based literacy skills or practices cannot be assumed. Among language minority immigrant children and adults in the United States who have migrated from Mexico or Central or South America; though labeled as native Spanish speakers, they may in fact be native speakers of indigenous languages. In Mexico alone, 53 minority languages of instruction are recognized in addition to Spanish. Thus, when children or adults from these language backgrounds immigrate to the United States, English literacy may not even represent a second language of literacy, but rather a third, and they may or may not have only had access to prior literacy training in Spanish as a second language.

The current educational standards movement and the widespread enthrallment with accountability measures are not new, but they are nuanced by new twists of particular relevance for language minority students attempting to acquire English literacy at school. The 20th century began with a pervasive fascination with efficiency and standardized testing. The goal then was to predict the "probable destinies" of children and to relegate them to differing educational tracks (Kliebard, 1996). Widespread testing of children and adults was insensitive to the fact that many of those tested lacked sufficient proficiency in English to be tested. When adult language minority immigrants were tested by the military, testing was only conducted in English. The results of such assessments were often used to "prove" that minorities were inferior (see Gould, 1981; Weinberg, 1995; Wiley, 1996).

Today, as in the past, particularly where there have been efforts to restrict opportunities for language minority students to develop bilingualism and biliteracy, such as in Arizona and California, the drive for accountability and one-size-fits-all standards has resulted in many language minority children being assessed on standardized tests in English before they have developed sufficient proficiency in English. Today, unlike the past, the push to test incipient learners of English is rationalized as ensuring that quality education will be maintained for all. The efficacy and appropriateness of testing language minority children with commercial standardized tests has become a major area of controversy (Quezada, Wiley, & Ramírez, 2002; Wright, 2002).

One of the dangers of making between-group comparisons among language minority groups or between them and the general population as a whole is that differential performances tend to be reported in the popular media much like basketball scores with some groups always being the winners and other the losers. Socioeconomic conditions and opportunities, differential power relations, and discriminatory practices must be considered when differential results are interpreted to avoid reinforcing stigmatized notions prevalent in society. Literacy measurement can have a constructive role if it is used to determine the kinds of literacy necessary for equitable participation in society as well those desired by individuals within their own communities.

Approaches to National and Large Data Set Literacy Assessments

There have been three types of literacy assessment measures: (a) *direct measures* or tests; (b) *educational equivalencies* or *surrogate measures*, which use a certain number of years of schooling as an indicator of literacy; and (c) *self-reported* measures. There are drawbacks to all three approaches, but, if used cautiously these data provide a gauge for evaluating needs and designing programs that provide opportunities for access and equity. Unfortunately, what typically has been and still is missing in nearly all large data sets and national surveys is a concentration on literacy in languages other than English. This lapse reinforces the common perception that English literacy is the only language of literacy worth measuring or assessing (see Wiley, 1996, chap. 4).

A major criticism of direct measures is that they represent inauthentic assessments of an individual's actual ability to function in the real world (Erickson, 1984). Specifically, they are tests of "explicitness" (Gee, 1986, p. 732), that is, the ability to make things precise or obvious. Such tests are those of the type that we find in schools. The critical issue from the standpoint of assessing literacy outside of school contexts is that just because one performs well on school-based exams does not mean he or she can function in real-world contexts. Competency-based tests of functional literacy are all exposed to concerns about ecological validity because they often lack an ethnographic grounding and because the standards and skills selected are imposed. In addition to these concerns, the issue of test bias is particularly troublesome for language minorities, including speakers of so-called nonstandard varieties. The test itself as a literacy event possesses a particular problem considering that "while procedures for taking standardized tests are presumably the same everywhere, test takers may respond quite differently to those procedures" (Wolfram & Christian, 1980, p. 180). More important, however, speakers of stigmatized social and regional varieties of language can become acutely aware of the imposition of standards that by design subordinate the language of their homes and communities, because they may have had their language varieties corrected by teachers or have been mocked or ridiculed. Thus, in a formal examination they may "perceive a test on language abilities as an instrument designed to measure them according to someone else's standards, not their own" (Wolfram & Christian, 1980, p. 181).

Educational equivalencies or surrogate measures of literacy provide an easy, economical way of assessing literacy, but concerns persist that grade-level equivalencies are arbitrary, there is no assurance that literacy in school is retained (Hunter & Harman, 1979), and no guarantee that the quality of instruction from one school to the next is equivalent (Wiley, 1996).

Self-reported data remain the easiest and least expensive way to assess national literacy, or the literacy of large, selected groups, or members of a specific language background group. The U.S. Census has collected national literacy data since 1850 (Venezky, Kaestle, & Sum, 1987). However, self-reported data is not as reliable as direct measures because individuals can report an inflated or deflated assessment of their abilities. On the positive side, however, there is evidence indicating a strong correlation between self-reported census data and direct measures of the English Proficiency Survey (McArthur, 1993).

Conceptual Issues Related to National Assessment

The recent approach in U.S. national assessments of literacy has been to conceptualize literacy in three domains (Greenberg et al., 2001):

- *Prose literacy*–the knowledge and skills needed to understand and use information from texts, including editorials, news stories, poems, and fiction.
- *Document literacy*–the knowledge and skills required to locate and use information contained in materials, including job applications, payroll forms, transportation schedules, maps, tables, and graphs.
- *Quantitative literacy*–the knowledge and skills required to apply arithmetic operations, either alone or sequentially, using numbers embedded in printed materials (p. 8).

This schema has advantages over prior efforts to measure functional literacy, although the basic approach retains a conceptualization of literacy as individual knowledge and skills. Conceptualizing literacy within these three domains breaks with the older practice of dichotomizing literacy/illiteracy. Nevertheless, a number of issues remain:

> Are all tasks involving documents distinct from those involving quantitative tasks? For example, tax forms would seem to involve both document-related skills and quantitative skills. Are skills that are identified as being specific to one domain (e.g., prose skills) all confined to that domain? How well do simulated tasks represent real-world tasks? How many of the skills assessed have been learned but forgotten due to lack of need or practice? Do these thresholds become functionally equivalent to the former dichotomization of literacy/illiteracy? In other words, have we merely exchanged the long-term concern about illiteracy for one over low levels of literacy? What happens when these literacy domains are superimposed on a multilingual population? Furthermore, does the notion of continuum hold up across languages or only within them? If literacy is embedded within social practices, is there a continuum that reflects these various social practices? (Wiley, 1996, pp. 76–77, see chap. 4 for elaboration.)

Limitations of National Measures of Literacy for Language Minority Students

Most national and large data set surveys of literacy primarily assess only English literacy. Macías (1994) identified four types of limitations that are particularly noteworthy when attempting to assess literacy among language minorities. These are: (a) ignoring literacy in languages other than English; (b) overemphasizing English oral language proficiency; (c) sampling biases; and (d) ambiguity in linguistic, ethnic, and racial identification. For the past three decades, the United States has experienced its second highest period of foreign immigration and has one of the largest Spanish-speaking populations in the world. By failing to survey literacy in Spanish and other languages, literacy is by default equated with English literacy, and the literacy picture of the United States remains both incomplete and distorted. By failing to assess other languages of literacy, results inflate the perception of a "literacy crisis" (Graff, 1994), which stigmatizes those only literate in other languages and underinforms educational policymaking by failing to distinguish nonliterates from those who are literate (Wiley, 1996).

Findings from National Adult Literacy Survey

The 1992 National Adult Literacy Survey (NALS) was touted as providing the most current comprehensive data on English literacy in the United States. Mandated by Congress, the NALS survey built on the conceptual model developed for the Young Adult Literacy Survey (YALS) that conceptualizes literacy along a continuum within three domains (prose, document, and quantitative literacy). Each of these domains used items that simulated real-world literacy tasks and seeks to determine five levels of literacy (Wiley, 1996). NALS was more sensitive to issues of ethnic diversity than most prior studies and included self-reported demographic questions related to language diversity, which were later used for a biliteracy analysis. The NALS also provided English and Spanish versions of the background questionnaire (Macías, 1994, p. 33).

The preface to the report (Kirsch et al., 1993) noted a demographic increase of those who speak languages other than English. However, the NALS only assessed English literacy through direct assessment. The initial findings of the NALS made for sensational headlines in the nation's leading newspapers and magazines. Among some of the more far-fetched claims reported were that an astonishing 90 million people were allegedly literacy deficient. A careful reading of the initial report should have lent itself to a less reckless interpretation. Kirsch et al. (1993) note that, "The approximately 90 million adults who performed in Levels 1 and 2 did not necessarily perceive themselves as being "at risk." ... It is therefore possible that their skills, while limited, allow them to meet some or most of their personal and occupational literacy needs" (p. xv). Although it makes for smaller headlines and probably sells fewer newspapers, more recent reports have now become newsworthy by correcting the original claims. Now only 5% of those surveyed are considered not literate on the basis of not having answered any questions (see Mathews, 2001). Other problems have related to the five-level scale for each of the three domains. This scale is supposed to increase in difficulty. Ideally, as an implicational scale, Level 1 tasks should be easier than Level 2 tasks. However, some items do not appear to have scaled as predicted (see also Berliner, 1996).

Of more relevance to the issue of biliteracy is the self-reported data. Additional analyses of the NALS have recently been completed in which special attention has been given to language minorities based on self-reported information such that it is possible to construct a biliteracy variable. Participants in the NALS also completed a background survey in English or Spanish. Those who spoke a language other than English before beginning their formal schooling completed a self-reported survey regarding their fluency and literacy in their native language. Unfortunately, by limiting the survey only to this group, native English speakers who later became biliterate were not included (Greenberg et al., 2001). Findings indicated:

> Bilingual and biliterate individuals tended to have received a substantial level of formal education in their native country before immigrating to the United States. ... The age of arrival in the United States was the primary predictor of which language through the formal education they received in the United States. Those who arrived later in life, without the benefit of a substantial amount of education received in the native country, were the least likely to develop English literacy skills. ... Social policy efforts to address these concerns face the challenge that many in need of ESL and basic skills training have had little or no formal education in any language. (pp. 89–90)

Based on Greenberg et al.'s (2001) analysis of the NALS self-reported data for language minorities only, approximately 70% of that group reported being biliterate at the time of the survey. When correlated with race, the biliteracy rate among Whites was only 3%, and only 2% for African Americans. Biliteracy rates were much higher for

Hispanics, with 35% being biliterate, 33% literate only in English, and 27% literate only in Spanish. Biliteracy was highest among Asians and Pacific Islanders, of whom nearly half (47%) were biliterate. Higher biliteracy rates among Hispanics and Asians were to be expected, as recent immigration rates have been higher for these groups. Based on NALS data, biliterates tended to have higher levels of education than monoliterates. Among biliterates, 48% acquired some postsecondary education, compared to only 43% for those literate only in English. Most bilinguals and biliterates do not have *balanced* abilities in two or more languages, given that their language and literacy experiences and contexts for learning are rarely parallel across languages (Valdés, 2001).

Despite the many limitations of NALS data, the findings are important because in the United States most national literacy estimations focus solely on English. Their failure to acknowledge literacy among those who are literate in languages other than English inflates the magnitude of a perceived "literacy crisis" (Wiley, 1996). However, even as such data are useful in informing national educational policies, findings need to be weighed against ethnographic studies that probe the functions and meanings of literacy in social contexts. A number of ethnographic studies of learners of English as a second language (e.g., Klassen & Burnaby, 1993; Weinstein-Shr, 1993) indicate that many immigrants can function successfully within their daily lives without competencies in English literacy. Thus, they need not be stigmatized as being cognitively deficient. Similar studies (e.g., Cushman, 1998; Taylor & Dorsey-Gaines, 1988) indicate that marginalized families living in poverty often have more literacy skills than they are usually given credit for and are not necessarily liberated from their poverty by their literacy. They are blocked from economic mobility because they lack formal schooling.

PROMOTING BILITERACY

In recent decades, bilingual education policy in the United States has allowed *transitional* bilingual education. Contrary to popular perceptions, the United States has never endorsed the kind of *maintenance* programs that would ensure that language minority students could attain biliteracy. Federal policies have not been the most effective in promoting biliteracy, although they have eased the pain of transition for those language minority students who have been allowed to participate in transitional bilingual programs. Bilingual policies have also been targeted by English-only activists who have restricted transitional bilingual education in several states (e.g., California, Arizona, and Massachusetts).

There are other models that are more effective than transitional bilingual programs. For example, there are *immersion programs* for monolingual English-speaking students. Although there are different configurations, immersion programs typically begin with instruction in the target foreign language and gradually introduce literacy in the dominant language. For language minority students, *maintenance* programs are more effective than transitional programs in promoting the retention of the native language while developing English literacy (Baker & Jones, 2000). *Dual immersion*, or *two-way bilingual* programs, have proven successful when English-speaking language majority and language minority children are brought together in the same program (Christian, Howard, & Loeb, 2000). However, in these programs special consideration needs to be given to language minority students, because some evidence suggests that these programs advantage English speakers more than language minority students (Valdés, 1997).

A pressing issue is the need to preserve threatened languages because the majority of the world's estimated 5,000–6,000 languages are endangered (Skutnabb-Kangas, 2000). Literacy can have a role in helping to preserve and promote these languages, assuming that their speakers want to have their languages written down, which is occasionally not the case, if literacy is seen as antithetical to the ecology of language in the community (see Hinton & Hale, 2001).

Foreign language education provides another path by which biliteracy can be attained. Unfortunately, in the United States, opportunities for foreign language instruction are far less favorable than they are in many other countries. Instruction is usually delayed until middle school or high school, and program goals do not always include the goal of biliteracy. Consequently, many who study foreign languages fail to acquire more than a very rudimentary knowledge of them (Ovando & Wiley, 2003).

One positive trend in the United States since 1999, is that there has been national attention accorded to developing students' heritage languages (see Peyton, Ranard, & McGinnis, 2001). Although not all are pleased with the *heritage language* (HL) label (see Wiley, 2001), HL learners have been defined as those who grow up in a home where a language(s) other than English is used. They may either have a passive understanding of the language or be partially bilingual in the language and participate in a variety of program types (see Wiley & Valdés, 2001). Many universities have recently been moving to make HL literacy the primary goal of their programs. Spanish, Chinese (Mandarin), Japanese, Korean, Russian, and Khmer (Cambodian) are just a few of the languages now being offered for HL learners. Asian languages are also currently taught in Asian American immigrant communities.

Promoting heritage language literacies offers a promising opportunity for increasing the number of biliterate individuals in the United States, but the major challenge remains working to change popular misconceptions and attitudes toward multilingualism and biliteracy.

REFERENCES

Auerbach, E. (1989). Toward a social-contextual approach to family literacy. *Harvard Educational Review, 59*(2), 165–182.

Auerbach, E. (1992a). Literacy and ideology. In W. Grabe & R. B. Kaplan (Eds.), *Annual Review of Applied Linguistics, 1991, Vol. 12* (pp. 71–86). New York: Cambridge University Press.

Auerbach, E. R. (1992b). *Making meaning, making change: Participatory curriculum development for adult ESL literacy.* McHenry, IL: Center for Applied Linguistics and Delta Systems.

Baker, C., & Jones, S. P. (2000). *Encyclopedia of bilingual education and bilingualism.* Clevedon, UK: Multilingual Matters.

Barton, D., Hamilton, M., & Ivanic, R. (Eds.). (2000). *Situated literacies: Reading and writing in context.* London: Routledge & Kegan Paul.

Baugh, J. (1999). *Beyond Ebonics: Linguistic pride and racial prejudice.* Austin: University of Texas Press.

Baynham, M. (1995). *Literacy practices: Investigating literacy in social contexts.* London: Longman.

Berliner, D. (1996). Nowadays, even the illiterates read and write. *Research in the Teaching of English 30*(3), 334–351.

Berliner, D. C., & Biddle, B. J. (1995). *The manufactured crisis: Myths, fraud, and the attack on America's public schools.* Reading, MA: Addison-Wesley.

Bracey, G. W. (1997). *Setting the record straight: Misconceptions about public education.* Alexandria, VA: Association for Supervision and Curriculum Development.

Brighman, C. C. (1923). *A study in American intelligence.* Princeton, NJ: Princeton University Press.

Christian, D., Howard, E. R., & Loeb, M. I. (2000). Bilingualism for all: Two-way immersion education in the United States. *Theory into Practice, 39*(4), 258–266.

Cook-Gumperz, J. (Ed.). (1986). *The social construction of literacy.* Cambridge, UK: Cambridge University Press.

Cook-Gumperz, J., & Keller-Cohen, D. (Eds.). (1993). Alternative literacies: In school and beyond [Theme issue]. *Anthropology & Education Quarterly, 24*(4).

Cope, B., & Kalantzis, M. (Eds.). (2000). *Multiliteracies: Literacy learning and the design of social futures.* London: Routledge & Kegan Paul.

Crawford, J. (2000). *At war with diversity: U.S. language policy in an age of anxiety.* Clevedon, UK: Multilingual Matters.

Cushman, E. (1998). *The struggle and the tools: Oral and literate strategies in an inner city community.* Albany, NY: State University Press of New York Press.

Delgado-Gaitán, C. & Trueba, H.T. (1991). *Crossing cultural borders: Education for immigrant families in America*. New York: Falmer Press.

Edelsky, C. (1996). *With literacy and justice for all: Rethinking the social in language and education*, 2nd ed. London: Falmer Press.

Erickson, F. (1984). School literacy, reasoning, and civility: An anthropologist's perspective. *Review of Educational Research, 54*, 525–546.

Freire, P., & Macedo, D. (1987). Literacy and critical pedagogy. In P. Freire & D. Macedo (Eds.), *Literacy: Reading the word and the world* (pp. 141–159). Amherst, MA: Bergin & Garvey.

Gee, J. P. (1986). Orality and literacy: From the savage mind to ways with words. *TESOL Quarterly, 20*(4), 719–746.

Gee, J. P. (2000). New people in new worlds: Networks, the new capitalism, and schools. In B. Cope & M. Kalantzis (Eds.), *Multiliteries: Literacy learning and the design of social futures* (pp. 43–68). London: Routledge & Kegan Paul.

Gee, J. P. (2001). Forword. In T. M. Kalmar (Ed.), *Illegal alphabets: Latino migrants crossing the linguistic border* (pp. i–iv). Mahwah, NJ: Lawrence Erlbaum Associates.

Goody, J. (1987). *The interface between the written and the oral*. Cambridge, UK: Cambridge University Press.

Goody, J., & Watt, I. (1988). The consequences of literacy. In E. R. Kintgen, B. M. Kroll, & M. Rose (Eds.), *Perspectives on literacy* (pp. 3–27). Carbondale, IL: Southern Illinois University Press. Reprinted from The consequences of literacy. *Comparative Studies in Society and History, 5*, 304–326.

Goody, J. (1999). The implications of literacy. In D. A. Wagner, R. L. Venezky, & B. V. Street (Eds.), *Literacy: An international handbook* (pp. 29–33). Boulder, CO: Westview Press.

Gough, K. (1988). Implications of literacy in traditional China and India. In E. R. Kintgen, B. M. Kroll, & M. Rose (Eds.), *Perspectives on literacy* (pp. 44–56). Carbondale, IL: Southern Illinois University Press.

Gould, S. J. (1981). *The mismeasure of man*. New York: Norton.

Graff, H. J. (1994). Literacy, myths, and legacies. In L. Verhoeven (Ed.), *Functional literacy: Theoretical issues and educational implications* (pp. 37–60). Amsterdam: John Benjamins.

Greenberg, E., Macías, R. F., Rhodes, D., & Chan, T. (2001). *English literacy and language minorities in the United States*. Washington, DC: National Center for Educational Statistics, U.S. Department of Education. NCES 20014–464.

Grillo, R. D. (1989). *Dominant languages*. Cambridge, UK: Cambridge University Press.

Haas, M. (1992). *Institutional racism: The case of Hawaii*. Westport, CT: Praeger.

Hakuta, K. (1986). *Mirror of language: The debate on bilingualism*. New York: Basic Books.

Harris, R. (1986). *The origins of writing*. La Salle, IL: Open Court.

Havelock, E. A. (1963). *Preface to Plato*. Cambridge, MA: Belknap Press of Harvard University Press.

Havelock, E. A. (1988). The coming of literate communication to western culture in Kintgen et al. (Eds.) (1988), *Perspectives on literacy*. In E. R. Kintgen, B. M. Kroll, & M. Rose (Eds.), *Perspectives on literacy* (pp. 127–134). Carbondale, IL: Southern Illinois University Press.

Heath, S. B. (1980). The functions and uses of literacy. *Journal of Communication, 30*(1), 123–133.

Heath, S. B. (1983). *Ways with words: Language, life, and work in communities and classrooms*. Cambridge, UK: Cambridge University Press.

Heath, S. B. (1986). Social contexts of language development. In D. Holt (Ed.), *Beyond language: Social and cultural factors in schooling language minority students* (pp. 143–186). Los Angeles: California State University, Evaluation, Dissemination, and Assessment Center.

Heath, S. B. (1988). Protean shapes in literacy events: Ever-shifting oral and literate traditions. In E. R. Kintgen, B. M. Kroll, & M. Rose (Eds.), *Perspectives on literacy* (pp. 348–370). Carbondale, IL: Southern Illinois University Press.

Hinton, L. & Hale, K. (Eds.) (2001). *The green book of language revitalization*. New York: Academic Press.

Hirsch, E. D. (1987). *Cultural literacy: What every American needs to know*. Boston: Houghton Mifflin.

Hirsch, E. D., Kett, J. F., & Trefil, J. (1988). *The dictionary of cultural literacy. What every American needs to know*. Boston: Houghton Mifflin.

Hull, G. (1997). *Changing work: Critical perspectives on language, literacy, and skills*. Albany, NY: State University of New York Press.

Hull, G., & Schultz, K. (Eds.). (2002). *School's out: Out-of-school literacies with classroom practice*. New York: Teachers College Press.

Hunter, C., & Harman, D. (1979). *Adult illiteracy in the United States*. New York: McGraw-Hill.

Kalmar, T. M. (2001). *Illegal alphabets: Latino migrants crossing the linguistic border*. Mahwah, NJ: Lawrence Erlbaum Associates.

Kaplan, R. B. (2002). *The Oxford handbook of applied linguistics*. Oxford, UK: Oxford University Press.

Kirsch, I. S., & Jungeblut, A. (1986). *Literacy: Profiles of America's young adults*. (Report No. 16-PL-02). Princeton, NJ: Educational Testing Service. (ERIC Document Reproduction Service No. ED 275 701)

Kirsch, I. S., Jungeblut, A., Jenkins, L., & Kolstad, A. (1993). *Adult literacy in America: A first look at the results of the national adult literacy survey*. Washington, DC: U.S. Department of Education, Office of Educational Research and Improvement, Educational Information Branch.

Klassen, C., & Burnaby, B. (1993). "Those who know": Views on literacy among adult immigrants in Canada. *TESOL Quarterly, 27*, 377–397.

Kliebard, H. M. (1996). *The struggle for the American curriculum*, (2nd ed.). New York: Routledge & Kegan Paul.

Kloss, H. (1971). Language rights of immigrant groups. *International Migration Review, 5*, 250–268.

Krashen, S. D. (1997). *Under attack: The case against bilingual education*. Culver City, CA: Language Education Associates.

Krashen, S. D. (1999). *Condemned without a trial: Bogus arguments against bilingual education*. Portsmouth, NH: Heinemann.

Kress, G. (2003). *Literacy in the new media age*. London: Routledge & Kegan Paul.

Lankshear, C., with Gee, J. P., Knoble, M., & Searle, C. (1997). *Changing literacies*. Buckingham: Open University Press.

Levine, K. (1982). Functional literacy: Fond illusions and false economies. *Harvard Educational Review, 52*(3), 249–267.

Lippi-Green, R. (1997). *English with an accent: Language, ideology, and discrimination in the United States*. New York: Routledge & Kegan Paul.

Luke, A. (1998). *Literacy, textbooks, and ideology: Postwar literacy instruction and the mythology of Dick and Jane*. London: Falmar.

Macías, R. F. (1985). Language and ideology in the United States. *Social Education* (February), 97–100.

Macías, R. F. (1990). Definitions of literacy: A response. In R. L. Venezky, D. A. Wagner, & B. S. Ciliberti (Eds.), *Toward defining literacy* (pp. 17–23). Newark, DE: International Reading Association.

Macías, R. F. (1994). Inheriting sins while seeking absolution: Language diversity and national statistical data sets. In D. Spener (Ed.), *Adult biliteracy in the United States* (pp. 15–45). Washington: Center for Applied Linguistics.

Mathews, J. (2001, July 22). Landmark illiteracy analysis is flawed, statistics faulty, study director says. *Washington Post*. Reprinted in the *Arizona Republic*.

McArthr, E. K. (1993). *Language characteristics and schooling in the United States: A changing picture*. Washington, DC: National Center for Educational Statistics. (NCES Report No. 93–699)

Mikulecky, L. J. (1990). *Literacy for what purpose?* (Report No.). In R. L. Venezky, D. A. Wagner, & D. S. Ciliberi (Eds.), *Toward defining literacy* (pp. 24–34). Newark, DE: International Reading Association. (ERIC Document Reproduction Service No. ED 313 677)

Olson, D. R. (1977). From utterance to text: The bias of language in speech and writing. *Harvard Educational Review, 47*, 257–281.

Olson, D. R. (1984). See! Jumping! Some oral language antecedents of literacy. In H. Goelman, A. A. Oberg, & F. Smith (Eds.), *Awakening to literacy* (pp. 185–192). Portsmouth, NH: Heinemann.

Olson, D.R. (1988). The bias of language in speech and writing. In E. R. Kintgen, B. M. Kroll, & M. Rose (Eds.), *Perspectives on literacy* (pp. 175–189). Carbondale, IL: Southern Illinois University Press.

Olson, D. R. (1994). *The world on paper: The conceptual and cognitive implications of reading and writing*. Cambridge, UK: Cambridge University Press.

Olson, D. R. (1999). Literacy and language development. In D. A. Wagner, R. L. Venezky, & B. V. Street (Eds.), *Literacy: An international handbook* (pp. 132–136). Boulder CO: Westview Press.

Ong, W. J. (1982). *Orality and literacy: The technologizing of the word*. London: Methuen.

Ong, W. J. (1988). Some psychodynamics of orality. In E. R. Kintgen, B. M. Kroll, & M. Rose (Eds.), *Perspectives on literacy* (pp. 28–43). Carbondale, IL: Southern Illinois University Press.

Ong, W. J. (1992). Writing is a technology that restructures thought, in Downing et al. (Eds.), *The linguistics of literacy* (pp. 293–319). Amsterdam: John Benjamins.

Ovando, C. J., & McLaren, P. (Eds.). (2000). *The politics of multiculturalism and bilingual education: Students and teachers caught in the crossfire*. Boston: McGraw-Hill.

Ovando, C. J., & Wiley, T. G. (2003). Language education in the conflicted United States. J. Bourne & E. E. Reid (Eds.), *World yearbook of education 2003: Language education* (pp. 141–155). London: Kogan Page.

Peyton, J., Ranard, D. A., & McGinnis, S. (Eds.). (2001). *Heritage languages in America: Blueprint for the future*. Washington, DC/McHenry, IL: Center for Applied Linguistics and Delta Systems.

Quezada, M. S., Wiley, T. G., Ramírez, D. (2002). How the reform agenda shortchanges English learners. In E. W. Stevens & G. H. Wood (Eds.), *Justice, ideology, and education: An introduction to the social foundations of education* (4th ed.), (pp. 104–109). New York: McGraw-Hill.

Resnick, D. P., & Resnick, L. B. (1977). The nature of literacy: An historical exploration. *Harvard Educational Review, 47*(3), 370–385.

Schmidt, R. (2000). *Language policy and identity politics in the United States*. Philadelphia, PA: Temple University Press.

Scribner, S. (1981). Studying working intelligence. In B. Rogoff & J. Lave (Eds.), *Everyday cognition: Development in social context*. Cambridge, MA: Harvard University Press.

Scribner, S., & Cole, M. (1978). Literacy without schooling: Testing for intellectual effects. *Harvard Educational Review, 48*, 448–461.

Scribner, S., & Cole, M. (1981). *The psychology of literacy*. Cambridge, MA: Harvard University Press.

Scribner, S., & Cole, M. (1988). Unpacking literacy. In E. R. Kintgen, B. M. Kroll, & M. Rose (Eds.), *Perspectives on literacy* (pp. 57–70). Carbondale, IL: Southern Illinois University Press.

Shuman, A. (1993). Collaborative writing. In B. Street (Ed.), *Crosscultural approaches to literacy* (pp. 247–271). Cambridge, UK: Cambridge University Press.

Skutnabb-Kangas, T. (2000). *Linguistic genocide in education or worldwide diversity and human rights?* Mahwah, NJ: Lawrence Erlbaum Associates.

Spener, D. (Ed.). (1994). *Adult biliteracy in the United States.* Washington, DC: Center for Applied Linguistics.

Street, B. V. (1984). *Literacy in theory and practice.* Cambridge, UK: Cambridge University Press.

Street, B. V. (Ed.). (1993). *Crosscultural approaches to literacy.* Cambridge, UK: Cambridge University Press.

Street, B. V. (1995). *Social literacies: Critical approaches to literacy in development, ethnography, and education.* London: Longman.

Street, B. V. (1999). The meanings of literacy. In D. A. Wagner, R. L. Venezky, & B. V. Street (Eds.), *Literacy: An international handbook* (pp. 34–40). Boulder, CO: Westview Press.

Stuckey, J. E. (1991). *The violence of literacy.* Portsmouth, NH: Heinemann.

Taylor, D. (Ed.). (1997). *Many families, many literacies: An international declaration of principles.* Portsmouth, NH: Heinemann.

Taylor, D. M., & Dorsey-Gaines, C. (1988). *Growing up literate: Learning from inner-city families.* Portsmouth, NH: Heinemann.

Tse, L. (2001). *"Why don't they learn English?" Separating fact from fallacy in the U.S. language debate.* New York: Teachers College Press.

Valdés, G. (1997). Dual language immersion programs: A cautionary note concerning the education of language minority students. *Harvard Educational Review, 67*(3), 391–429.

Valdés, G. (2001). Heritage language students: Profiles and possibilities. In J. Payton, D. A. Ranard, & S. McGinnis, (Eds.), *Heritage languages in America: Blueprint for the future* (pp. 37–77). Washington, DC/McHenry, IL: Center for Applied Linguistics and Delta Systems.

Venezky, R. L., Kaestle, C., & Sum, A. (1987). *The subtle danger: Reflections on the literacy abilities of America's young adults.* (Report No. 16-CAEP-01). Princeton, NJ: Educational Testing Service, Center for the Assessment of Educational Progress.

Venezky, R. L., Wagner, D. A., & Ciliberti, B. S. (Eds.). (1990). *Toward defining literacy.* Newark, DE: International Reading Association.

Verhoeven, L. (1994). Linguistic diversity and literacy development. In L. Verhoeven (Ed.), *Functional literacy: Theoretical issues and educational implications* (pp. 199–220). Amsterdam: John Benjamins.

Walsh, C. E. (Ed.) (1991). *Literacy as praxis: Culture, language, and pedagogy.* Norwood, NJ: Ablex.

Weinberg, M. (1995). *A chance to learn: A history of race and education in the United States,* (2nd ed.). Long Beach, CA: California State University Press.

Weinstein-Shr, G. (1993). Literacy and social process: A community in transition. In B. Street (Ed.), *Crosscultural approaches to literacy* (pp. 272–293). Cambridge, UK: Cambridge University Press.

Wiley, T. G. (1996). *Literacy and language diversity in the United States.* Washington, DC: Center for Applied Linguistics.

Wiley, T. G. (1998). The imposition of World War I era English-only policies and the fate of Germans in North America. In T. Ricento & B. Burnaby (Eds.), *Language and politics in the United States and Canada* (pp. 211–241). Mahwah, NJ: Lawrence Erlbaum Associates.

Wiley, T. G. (1999). Comparative historical perspectives in the analysis of U.S. language policies. In T. Heubner, & C. Davis (Eds.), *Political perspectives on language planning and language policy,* pp. 17–37. Amsterdam: John Benjamins.

Wiley, T. G. (2000). Continuity and change in the function of language ideologies in the United States. In T. Ricento (Ed.), *Ideology, politics, and language policies: Focus on English* (pp. 67–85). Mahwah, NJ: Lawrence Erlbaum Associates.

Wiley, T. G. (2001). On defining heritage languages and their speakers. In J. Payton, D. A. Ranard, & S. McGinnis, (Ed.), *Heritage languages in America: Blueprint for the future* (pp. 29–36). Washington, DC/McHenry, IL: Center for Applied Linguistics and Delta Systems.

Wiley, T. G. (2002a). Biliteracy. In B. Guzzetti (Ed.), *Literacy in America: An encyclopedia: An encyclopedia of history, theory, and practice* (pp. 57–60). ABC-CLIO Publishers.

Wiley, T. G. (2002b). Accessing language rights in education: A brief history of the U.S. context. In J. Tollefson (Ed.), *Language policies in education: Critical readings* (pp. 39–64). Mahwah, NJ: Lawrence Erlbaum Associates.

Wiley, T. G., & Lukes, M. (1996). English-only and standard English ideologies in the United States. *TESOL Quarterly, 30*(3), 511–535.

Wiley, T. G., & Valdés, G. (2001, July). Heritage language instruction in the United States: A time for renewal. *Bilingual Research Journal, 24*(4), iii–vii. Retrieved July 3, 2003, from http://brj.asu.edu/v244/indexg.html

Willinsky, J. (1990). *The new literacy studies: Redefining reading and writing in the schools.* New York: Routledge.

Wolfram, W., & Christian, D. (1980). On the application of sociolinguistic information: Test evaluation and dialect differences in Appalachian English. In T. Shopen & J. M. Williams (Eds.), *Standards and dialects in English* (pp. 177–204). Cambridge, MA: Winthrop.

Wright, W. (2002). The effects of high stakes testing in an inner-city elementary school: The curriculum, the teachers, and the English language learners. *Current Issues in Education* [Online], 5(5). Retrieved *February* 1, 2003, from http://cie.asu.edu/volume5/number5/index.html

30

Instructed Grammar

Patricia Byrd
Georgia State University

INTRODUCTION

The teaching of English grammar rests on an ever-shifting foundation of theory and data about (a) grammar, (b) second language acquisition (SLA), and (c) classroom teachers' beliefs and practices about teaching grammar. At any point in time, we may write and talk as if the foundation were firm, but the long view shows how much shifting and change has already occurred and suggests that we can expect other shifts more or less continuously. In this chapter, I review forces currently influencing scholarship and practice in the teaching of grammar to suggest the choices that can be made by scholars and teachers for effective, principled integration of grammar into curricula and lessons.

GRAMMAR IN USE

The dominant approach to linguistics, at least in the United States, continues to be variations on Chomskyan transformational-generative grammar (see Joseph, Love, & Taylor, 2001, for a summary of Chomsky's work). With its emphasis on underlying psychological processes and systems, that approach to linguistics has had substantial influence on SLA theories and research, especially in the form of Universal Grammar (see Mitchell & Myles, 1998, for an overview of UG in SLA) and has not, because of this interest in "language" rather than in a particular language, been a source of equally substantive data or insight about the English language.

In contrast, the "language-in-use" focus of corpus linguistics and of other approaches to discourse analysis has led to major new tools and information for grammar instruction (see Joseph, Love, & Taylor, 2001, on the British linguist John Firth; also see, Conrad, chap. 22, this volume; Celce-Murcia & Olshtain, chap. 40, this volume; Hinkel, chap. 34, this volume; Stubbs, 1993). Corpus linguistics involves the development and use of collections of spoken or written texts in computer readable format. These corpora are then analyzed to reveal patterns of usage, for example, words that are used together frequently, grammatical patterns in particular types of writing or speech, and other unifying patterns observed in the corpus. The analysis of large samples of various types of English, both spoken and written, and in numerous genres is revolutionizing our understanding of how the resources of English (its vocabulary and grammar) are distributed among different discourse types.

Organization and Conceptualization of Relationships Among Grammatical Units

In the United States, both theoretical linguistics and pedagogical grammar generally build from a syntactic and sentence-level analysis that includes both functional units such as "subject" and "predicate" and word class units such as "noun" and "preposition." The results of this approach with its focus on grammatical forms can most easily be seen in two widely influential types of publications: (a) the large-scale English grammar reference books (e.g., Quirk et al., 1985) and (b) ESL/EFL (English as a Second Language/English as a Foreign Language) grammar textbooks with their chapters on nouns, on verbs, on prepositions, on adverbs, on clauses, and so forth (e.g., Azar, 1999). Within the noun chapter, nouns are presented in terms of forms (singular, plural, irregular), syntax (subject, object), and meaning (abstract nouns, concrete nouns) but the focus is on nouns as nouns.

There are other ways to organize grammar. When grammar is studied as arising FROM context, then a variety of forms emerge as essential to the expression of particular meanings in particular discourse contexts (Byrd, 1998). In terms that Larsen-Freeman (2001) has made familiar in TESL/TEFL, "forms" get their "meanings" when used in particular "contexts." But more than that, it's not just that different types of verbs are related to each other but that in particular kinds of discourse the idea of relationship must be expanded to include the bond among verbs, nouns, adverbs, textual order, and even particular vocabulary.

Studies using the multidimensional approach developed by Biber (e.g., Biber, 1988, 1999; Biber & Conrad, 2001; Conrad, 2000, 2001, 2002) and other studies of grammar in various discourse settings (e.g., Bardovi-Harlig, 1994; Halliday, 1994; Schiffrin, 1981) demonstrate the organization of the underlying grammatical patterns that characterize various types of discourse. For example, "involved" is the term used by Biber (1988) for conversational interactions with speakers talking back and forth in real time. His analysis shows that spoken conversations in English tend to use a particular range of grammatical features. Table 30.1 provides the list of lexical and grammatical features listed for "involved" communication, with those features given in the original statistical order in the left column and then reorganized in the right column to show the larger patterns that need to be considered for materials and for curricular design.

That is, to participate in a conversation in English, an ESL/EFL student needs to know how to ask and answer questions, to talk about *you* and *me*, to reduce sentences and clauses to shorter versions, and to use a specific set of vocabulary. Notice particularly that the verbs tend to be present tense versions of *be* and *do* along with a subset of the modal auxiliaries for possibility meanings. To learn to have a conversation in English is not to learn first about verb tenses and then about nouns and then about questions as separate entities only vaguely related to each other. In conversation, these forms are strongly related to each other.

This clustering of grammatical features is true not just of conversational English but of other discourse types, including narrative. Using multidimensional analysis, Biber (1988) and Conrad (2001) delineate the features of communication that involve some type of narrative (fiction, history, and other uses of narrative or recasting of past events in a narrative format). As with conversational discourse, narrative joins together grammatical features that include not only past tense verbs but also perfect aspect verbs, third person pronouns, public verbs such as *say* or *mention*, synthetic negation (using *no* rather than *not*), and participial clauses. While her focus is on stages in second language (L2) development, Bardovi-Harlig (2000, 1998, 1994) provides details useful for other purposes in her discussion of the lexical and grammatical features of

TABLE 30.1

Grammatical Features of "Involved" Communication

In the original order based on numerical strength from highest to lowest	*Reorganized to put forms into categories characteristic of conversational spoken English*
private verbs: *believe, doubt, know,* etc.	**Verbs**
THAT deletion [*the book I bought*]*	present tense verbs
contractions	DO as pro-verb
present tense verbs	BE as main verb
2nd person pronouns	possibility modals
DO as pro-verb [*Who needs a pen? I do.*]*	
analytic negation [*I don't need a pen.*]*	**Nouns and Pronouns**
demonstrative pronouns	2nd person pronouns
general emphatics	demonstrative pronouns
1st person pronouns	1st person pronouns
pronoun IT	indefinite pronouns
BE as main verb	pronoun IT
causative subordination	
discourse participles	**Phrases and Clauses**
indefinite pronouns	THAT deletion
general hedges	contractions
amplifiers	analytic negation
sentence relatives: [*She gave me a pen, which I appreciated very much.*]	causative subordination
	sentence relatives
WH questions	WH questions
possibility modals	final prepositions
non-phrasal coordination [*What do you need? Pen, pencil, whatever.*]*	conditional subordination
	Vocabulary
final prepositions [*Who'd you get the pen from?*]"	private verbs
adverbs	general emphatics
conditional subordination	discourse participles
	general hedges
	adverbs

Note. Data adapted from Biber, 1988 (p. 102).

* Examples added.

narrative discourse. Working in the tradition of linguistic rather than literary analysis of narrative (e.g., Dry, 1992; Labov & Waletsky, 1967), she analyzes L2 learner narratives in terms of two intertwined elements: the foreground that tells the basic past time story and the background that gives the reader additional information needed to understand the story. The foreground is told in chronological order and, while other choices are possible, uses primarily simple past tense verbs. The background can be considerably more complicated as the writer/speaker gives the reader/listener information needed to understand the story, including events that happened before, cultural background, personalities of characters and their relationships, and more. Thus, the background can include a wide range of verbs including past perfect for events that happened before the core story, present tense for generalizations that are still true, past tense for generalizations that are still true but that are presented in past tense because of verb harmony, and others.

For scholars and teachers interested in grammar instruction, these studies of the linguistic features of different discourse types suggest that the grammar element in language study can be organized in a coherent, meaningful way. In contrast to the list of grammar traditionally used to organize materials and courses, a discourse-based approach puts meaning and communication at the forefront and pulls grammar from the types of communication needed by students.

Grammatical Subsets

We are accustomed to thinking about languages in terms of traditional subsets such as inflectional groups or closed sets such as determiners or open sets such as verbs or structural units such as subject, verb phrases, and predicates. Because we are so accustomed to these groupings, we naturally turn to them in our designs of studies, courses, and materials in general linguistics and in English grammar (whether for teacher training courses or ESL/EFL courses). In addition to showing us that other organizations of grammatical units are possible for teaching purposes, corpus and discourse studies help to clarify the often surprising ways that these abstract linguistic structures are used in real communication.

Frequency studies show that members of the same inflectional group do not always have equal frequency of use or comparable range of use. For example, consider the data in Table 30.2 in the British National Corpus for these everyday words (Leech, Rayson, & Wilson, 2001)–nouns *door/doors* and the verbs *walk/walks/walked/walking*.

TABLE 30.2

Frequency and Range of Use for Selected Nouns and Verbs

Word	Frequency per million words	Range (use in the subsets of the corpus out of a maximum of 100)	Dispersion value from 0 to 100 (to show how evenly the word is used across the whole corpus)
door	254	100	87
doors	48	100	93
walk	66	100	92
walks	7	97	92
walked	94	100	87
walking	48	100	92

Such data could not mean, I don't imagine, that we would teach students to use *door* rather than *doors*. Learning the morphological relationship between singular and plural regular nouns would remain a learning goal. However, we need to explore the differences between the usage of the words to learn more about how English is actually used in context, seeking information to make materials and lessons more authentically accurate as well as meaningful (e.g., Biber & Reppen, 2002).

In addition to the unbalanced use of members of inflectional groups, members of other grammatical sets do not necessarily have the same frequency or range of uses. Biber et al. (1999) report that in the corpus they developed for the *Longman Grammar of Spoken and Written English*, the demonstrative pronoun *that* is heavily used in conversational English. In the WordbanksOnline subcorpus of spoken English collected in the United Kingdom, *that* is used 173,191 times; *this*, 39,930; *these*, 9,136; and *those* 7,355. The demonstratives *this/that/these/those* are, of course, related to each other in form and function, but they are not used in communication in exactly the same ways or proportions. This insight into the demonstrative-in-use is contrary to the traditional way of presenting these words as a set with meanings that are related to physical (and sometimes emotional) closeness or distance from the speaker and that are chosen based on the singular/plural form of the noun in conjunction with that near/far meaning. In Larsen-Freeman's terms (2001), the traditional approach works with form and meaning but neglects context. The instructional challenge is to place these words in appropriate contexts so that students learn how to use them effectively rather than just knowing their definitions.

Grammar and Vocabulary Connections

In the past few years, the learning and teaching of second language vocabulary has become a major area of research and scholarship (see Nation, chap. 32, this volume). Research on English grammar provided in corpus linguistics supports that change by showing how closely vocabulary and grammar are connected. The study of what is termed *lexicogrammatical* features of English shows how particular words are frequently used in particular grammatical settings. A lexicogrammar of English includes information about connections between words and grammar such as that found with prepositional verbs, for example, like *approve of* or *marry to*, that generally require the use of a particular prepositional phrase when a complement is given. Other intersections between words and grammar include observations such as that reported by Biber et al. (1999, p. 459) that "many verbs have a strong association with either present or past tense." In their corpus, *bet, doubt, know, matter, mean, mind, recon, suppose*, and *thank* occur over 80% of the time in present tense; *care, differ, fancy, imply, tend*, and *want* occur over 70% of the time in present tense; *exclaim, eye, glance, grin, nod, pause, remark, reply, shrug, sigh, smile*, and *whisper* are used over 80% of the time in past tense; *bend, bow, lean, light, park, seat, set off, shake, stare, turn away, wave*, and *wrap* are used over 70% of the time in past tense.

Conrad (2000) predicted that in the 21st century the teaching of vocabulary and grammar would be closely integrated. Her example of the strong ties between particular words and particular grammar is the relationship between the verbs such as *know, say*, and *think* and particular verb complement types—*that*-complements or the infinitive complement. She makes two points about these connections. First, grammatical analysis can abstract from the data a system that shows the possibilities for complements with particular verbs. The possibilities are that *know, say*, and *think* can take either complement type. However, what is possible is not always what is actually done when the forms are used for communication. In use, only the *that*-complement is frequently used with these verbs. Second, words like these verbs need to be taught along with their complement types, echoing a point made by Nation (2001) that knowledge of a word includes knowledge of the grammar associated with the use of that word.

Challenges to Widely Held Beliefs

The new data we are getting about English grammar provide various types of challenges for those involved with instructed grammar. First, we must think about how to integrate all of the new information about English grammar into our work. What do we do with frequency data? How do we handle the lexicogrammatical relationships? How do we modify our sense of what English grammar is to account for the new insights into forms-in-use? We also have to face information that disproves some of our traditional beliefs about English grammar.

Teachers have long taught lessons based on the belief that the most common verb tense in present time communication is the present progressive. Unfortunately, the belief is wrong. Biber and Conrad (2001) demonstrate that the most common verb form in conversational, interactive English is the simple present tense. Here is a short sample from a conversation around the supper table from Wordbanks*Online* to illustrate this point. Bold has been added.

Speaker 1: What **is** it **is** it guacamole?
Speaker 2: No **it's** erm spinach actually
Speaker 1: Spinach? Oh yum.
Speaker 2: and double cream and garlic.
Speaker 1: New to me so.

Speaker 2: Parsley.
Speaker 1: Oh thank you very much.
Speaker 2: You**'re** welcome.
Speaker 2: **Do** you want me to remove the dog?
Speaker 1: No he**'s** all right. Interesting. Mm. Mm.
Speaker 2: Go away.
Speaker 1: Interesting. Mm. Tabasco. **Did** you make make it up or **was** it a recipe.
Speaker 2: I **made** it up from what **was** on the shelves.
Speaker 1: Yeah I really **love** spinach.

Another challenge to strongly held beliefs about grammar has to do with the notion of grammatical "creativity" that comes from Chomskyan linguistics: A language has an almost infinite vocabulary that can be plugged into syntactic slots to create any possible message in sentences that have never been used before. Reports on language-in-use suggest a more complicated system that includes a significant role for set phrases such as (a) **idioms** (*I'm not cut out for this type of work*), (b) **collocations** (where two words occur in the same range of words more often than could be by accident) such as the strong relationships between the prepositions *before, at, for, on, over,* and *after* in front of the noun *Christmas* in WordbanksOnline data, and (c) **lexical bundles** of three or more words that recur together in many different types of discourse such as the phrase *I don't want to . . .* in conversational English (Biber & Conrad, 1999). At first glance, these might appear to be topics for the vocabulary rather than the grammar portion of a course or set of materials. However, idioms, collocations, and lexical bundles point to important issues in the organization, presentation, teaching, and learning of English grammar. To put the grammar teacher's problem in context, consider the following data about fixed phrases in English.

In Wordbanks*Online*, the adverb *always* occurs 6,058 times (out of its 56,000,000 words). One of the top collocates for *always* is *I*, suggesting that we often use this emphatic pronoun while expressing our own opinions or habits. Of the 6,058 uses of *always*, 1,718 (28%) involve the combination of *I always. . . .* In that setting, the lexical verbs most likely to be used are *thought, wanted, felt, say, think, feel, used, knew, remember, get, said, try, find, look, believed, make, like, got, tell, want, put, seem, liked, found, took, buy, loved, take, wondered, watch, told, keep, wear, use, tried, enjoy, end, play, believe, expect, come, love, carry, see.* That is, users of English are very likely to use *always* in a set of words that runs across several syntactic slots and that includes both function words and lexical words: (a) *I always thought (that) . . . ,* (b) *I've always thought (that) . . . ,* (c) *I have always thought of. . . . ,* and so forth. In their study of similar patterns in conversational English and English academic prose, Biber and Conrad (1999, p. 183) find numerous recurring sets of words that are "not complete structural units and not fixed expressions." Their investigation shows the wide range of lexical bundles characteristic of conversation and of academic prose. Examples from conversation include phrases such as the following (p. 185): *I don't know what . . . , I don't want to . . . ,* and *You don't have to. . . .* Academic prose includes numerous lexical bundles that build from various types of prepositional structures (pp. 186–187): *one of the most . . . , percent of the . . . , the nature of the . . . , the ways in which . . . , as a function of . . . ,* and *on the other hand. . . .*

As for our "creativity" in language use: Yes, we can be; no, we often aren't. When we use English to communicate, research demonstrates that we often use set pieces of language. Stubbs (2001) discusses the contrast in terms of "creativity" and "routine." Sinclair (1991) proposes two connected principles: (a) the idiom principle and (b) the open-choice principle—a contrast also discussed in detail in Hunston (2002). For language teaching, this insight provides two challenges: (a) collecting accurate, usable information about those set pieces and the particular contexts where they are used and (b) providing instruction and instructional materials that are both accurate about the grammar and effective in helping students learn how to be creative users of the many set pieces that make up language as it is really used.

SECOND LANGUAGE ACQUISITION AND INSTRUCTED GRAMMAR

Starting in the late 1970s and perhaps peaking in the late 1980s, the work of Krashen (1977, 1982) combined with the influence of the concepts of communicative competence and communicative language teaching (CLT) led many SLA specialists, teaching methodologists, and even classroom teachers into a rejection not just of instructed grammar but of many other aspects of second language instruction (for historical background see e.g., Celce-Murcia, 1991; Ellis, 2002). SLA specialists have managed to correct course to less extreme positions about the second language learning process and the role of the second language teaching (and grammar instruction) in that process (Doughty & Williams, 1998c; Ellis, 2002; Lightbown, 1998, 2000; Long, 1988; Long & Robinson, 1998; Norris & Ortega, 2000; Richards, 2002). Research into teaching and learning of grammatical forms is widely practiced as a fundamental area of interest for the discipline. In some instances, research uses grammar as a tool to gain insights into second language learning processes (e.g., Bardovi-Harlig, 2000; Leeman, 2003); in other instances, the research focuses on grammar in the classroom in "classroom-based SLA" (e.g., Doughty & Williams, 1998b).

DICHOTOMIES

Numerous SLA publications structure their observations and reports about the learning and teaching of English grammar around a selection of dichotomies: accuracy versus fluency, focus on form versus focus on forms, direct versus indirect (grammar) instruction. These important topics are also basic to decision making for principled teaching of grammar.

Accuracy Versus Fluency

In most uses, *accuracy* refers to "grammatical accuracy" but other areas of language use can be involved, too: spelling and/or pronunciation. *Fluency* implies the ability to easily understand and participate in communication, generally spoken, in the person's second language. (See Richards, 2002, for an overview of fluency-accuracy connections.) As with many dichotomies, this one all too quickly can lead to false distinctions—after all, fluency requires some grammatical accuracy for comprehension and grammatical accuracy without fluency probably leads to silence. However, different learners do have different needs for accurate fluency: (a) a tourist can have a wonderful vacation while using her second language with limited accuracy and limited fluency; (b) a "guest worker" can succeed in many types of jobs with fluent but quite inaccurate spoken language; (c) a student learning English to pass a college-entrance exam focused on grammatical accuracy needs (and seeks) little in the way of fluent communicative skill in that language; (d) a student studying in a university where a second language is used needs quite a different capacity in the language. The goals for grammatical accuracy and communicative fluency necessarily change based on the purposes of the learners as well as the purposes of the families, societies, and governments that have an interest in the second language development of particular groups of learners.

Current interest in grammatical accuracy for some SLA researchers has to do with recognition that accuracy has not automatically developed in the second language of students who have participated in long-term study focused on fluency. The French language skills of students in the immersion programs in Canada have led to concerns such as that expressed by Long and Robinson (1998):

> Evaluations of French immersion programs in Canada, moreover, have found that although many child starters are successful in other subjects, eventually comprehend the L2 statistically indistinguishably from native speakers, and speak fluently, "their productive skills remain far from nativelike, particularly with respect to grammatical competence" (Swain, 1991), even after more than 12 years of immersion at school and university in some cases. Some errors, such as failure to use the *vous* form appropriately, can be traced to infrequent exposure in classroom input (Harley & Swain, 1984), but others, such as failure to mark gender on articles correctly, cannot. Given that almost every utterance and sentence to which the students have been exposed throughout their schooling will have contained examples of gender-marked articles, it is unlikely that more exposure is all the students need. Rather, additional salience for the problematic features seems to be required, achieved either through enhancement of positive evidence or through provision of negative evidence of some kind. (pp. 20–21)

Swain (1998) summarizes the research on the language development of students in the French immersion program:

> More than two decades of research in French immersion classes suggests that immersion students are able to understand much of what they hear and read even at early grade levels. And, although they are well able to get their meaning across in their second language, even at intermediate and higher grade levels they often do so with non-targetlike morphology and syntax. (For overviews of this research, see, e.g., Genesee, 1987; Swain, 1984; Swain & Lapkin, 1986. For detailed accounts, see, e.g., Harley, 1986, 1992; Harley & Swain, 1984; Vignola & Wesche, 1991.) This research, related to the French proficiency of immersion students, makes clear that an input-rich, communicatively oriented classroom does not provide all that is needed for the development of targetlike proficiency (Swain, 1985). It also makes clear that teaching grammar lessons out of context, as paradigms to be rehearsed and memorized, is also insufficient. (p. 65)

The problem, then, is how to add instruction in grammar to the curriculum in ways that will be effective to achieve the goals of the Canadian educational system for these learners of having bilingual citizens who are accurate and fluent in both of their languages. Attempts by SLA researchers to deal with the challenge of including the teaching of grammar in a communicative language teaching context often now turn to two related topics: focus on form(s) and direct versus indirect grammar instruction.

Focus on Form Versus Focus on Forms

Starting with publications in the late 1980s, Long's formulation of "focus on form" has been widely influential, if variously interpreted, in second language acquisition research, especially for studies of instructed SLA (e.g., Long & Robinson, 1998; Doughty & Williams, 1998b). Doughty and Williams (1998a) provide the following definition of the phrase *focus on form*:

> Most researchers currently investigating the role of attention to form attribute the reawakening of interest in this issue to Michael Long (1988, 1991). In that seminal work, Long distinguished between a *focus on formS*, which characterizes earlier, synthetic approaches to language teaching that have as their primary organizing principle for course design the accumulation of individual language elements (e.g., forms such as verb endings or agreement features, or even functions such as greetings or apologies) from what he (and now we) call *focus on form*. The crucial distinction . . . is that focus on form entails a prerequisite engagement in meaning before attention to linguistics features can be expected to be effective. (p. 3)

For researchers and teachers who (a) worked from a belief that direct instruction in grammar was wrong but (b) who observed students becoming fluent without becoming equally accurate, this approach provided permission to reexamine ways in which grammatical accuracy might be included in the curricular goals for L2 courses and programs within the CLT framework.

Explicit Versus Implicit (Grammar) Learning and Teaching

Explicit (and overt) versus implicit (and deductive) learning is a complex area of SLA research, theory building, and belief (see e.g., Doughty & Williams, 1998b; Leeman, 2003). While research led Long and others to reconsider the place of explicit, overt attention to grammar, focus on form has been variously interpreted with some versions including highly explicit instruction and others seeking ways to integrate grammar in as indirect, unobtrusive a manner as possible (see Doughty & Williams, 1998a for an overview of these variables).

The Appeal of Recasting Versus Other Possible Teaching Techniques

The reintroduction of (somewhat) explicit grammar instruction into the CLT framework naturally led to discussion and study of the most effective ways to have *focus on form* in the classroom. Because the impetus for the reintroduction of explicit grammar teaching was concern over the lack of accuracy (that is, the continuing grammar errors in the spoken and written production of learners), the initial emphasis has been on error correction strategies. In addition, because of the desire to have that error-focused instruction be as indirect as possible, numerous researchers and teachers have turned to a teaching strategy called *recasting* (e.g., Doughty & Varela, 1998; Leeman, 2003; Lightbown & Spada, 1999). A recast provides implicit negative feedback along with implicit positive feedback: A student says something that contains an error; the teacher repeats what was said but with the error corrected; the student (if he or she realizes what is going on and attends to the teacher's words) hears the difference and recognizes that he or she needs to do/learn something differently. While recasts are clearly favored by Long and his colleagues, other work in the focus on form universe employs a wider range of activity types that include explicit (as well as implicit) study and practice as long as these are done with communicative goals at the fore (e.g., Lightbown & Spada, 1999). While descriptions of teaching materials (e.g., Skierso, 1991) often classify activities on a continuum from "non-communicative" to "communicative," my experience as a teacher, a materials writer, and a teacher educator is that just about any activity can be used for communication and that just about any activity can be turned into a deadly, dull, teacher-focused, non-student-involved non-communicative event. The old *TESOL Newsletter* had for many years a column called "It Works!" with activities contributed by various teachers. A colleague used to say that he bet that he could "make it not work." That is, activities in and of themselves are neutral to communication and learning. How they are used by teachers turns them into communicative or non-communicative events.

TASKS AND TASK-BASED INSTRUCTION

In addition to focus on form, SLA research has provided instructed grammar with another tool in the form of task-based instruction (Ellis, 2003, chap. 39, this volume; Bygate, Skehan, & Swain, 2001; Long & Crookes, 1992). Language teaching as a profession always struggles under the burden of not having a natural content. While biologists teach biology and psychologists teach psychology, language teachers cannot directly teach English or Spanish but have to clothe the language in some topic selected from the universe of possible content. The result has often been a random assortment of topics selected on the basis of vaguely conceptualized notions of "things interesting to learners." Even content-based approaches that put meaning and communication and coherent sets of content at the center of the curriculum (e.g., Snow & Brinton, 1997) have problems justifying the selection of any particular content area. Much of the classroom-based SLA literature on tasks involves attempts to specify the nature of a task as a teaching strategy or event, especially in opposition to "exercises" or "activities" (see Ellis, 2003, for an overview). For syllabus design, however, the most useful formulations start with student needs analysis and specification of the real world communication "tasks" required as the goal of instruction and learning (see Long & Crookes, 1992; Doughty & Varela, 1998). By putting student needs analysis into the form of "real world" tasks as the source for "language-learning tasks," we can make rational, principled decisions about the focus of instruction. Knowing the real world tasks to be handled by learners means that we can reasonably expect to be able to analyze those tasks for the language (vocabulary as well as grammar) and communication tasks that will be required of learners—and that can be the focus for instruction.

KNOWLEDGE, BELIEFS, AND BEHAVIORS
OF CLASSROOM TEACHERS

For the 25th anniversary issue of the *TESOL Quarterly*, Celce-Murcia (1991) traced the history of the teaching of grammar in the period between 1967 and 1991, providing overviews of the audiolingual approach, the cognitive code approach, the comprehension approach, and the communicative approach. Now, over a decade later, the teaching of grammar by classroom teachers seems to fall on a continuum between (a) continued use of teacher-fronted presentation and drill of grammar items and (b) complete rejection of the teaching of grammar at all. In an article about the pressure from the U.S. federal government on elementary and secondary schools to move ESL students rapidly into mainstream courses, *The New York Times* reported the following scene in a Colorado high school (Dillon, 2003):

> Earlier this month, an 18-year-old born in Veracruz, Mexico, who has studied English at Fort Lupton High for four years, stumbled repeatedly in a classroom drill on the idiomatic uses of "the."
> "Where are you going?" the teenager's teacher asked, pointing at the word "store" on the blackboard.
> He said, "I'm going to store."
> The teacher corrected, "No, you need to use 'the' before store," and pointed to the word "beach."
> He said, "I'm going to beach." Again, she corrected him.

That is, decontextualized drill of grammar using random content, some of which is inappropriate to the setting ("beach" in Colorado?), remains a feature of many ESL classrooms. At an extreme away from that classroom and that teacher is the context reported in Doughty and Varela (1998):

> The subjects in the experiment were 34 middle school students from two different intact classes studying science at an intermediate ESL level in a suburban east coast school district.... Prior to the study, both teachers of these students admitted to spending little if any time on grammar instruction or correction in their science classes, either orally or in writing. However, students received some focus on formS in their language arts classes, although even that portion of the curriculum embraces a "whole language" approach in which instruction emphasizes integrating reading and writing skills for communication, and grammar instruction is minimal.... At the time of the study, [the students] remained non-targetlike in their use of many features of English despite their language arts teachers'

attempts to focus on forms, which, as noted by Varela, was unfortunate given that their achievement in mainstream classes could be hindered until they were able to reach a level of precision in their oral and written grammar that would be acceptable to main-stream teachers. Nonetheless, prior to their participation in this study, both of the ESL science teachers routinely rejected the inclusion of explicit grammatical instruction in their lessons for fear that it might manipulate, take away from, or hinder science learning or communication about science. (p. 119)

Fortunately, the project described by Doughty and Varela did lead students to improve their use of past tense verbs in the lab reports that they gave orally and wrote for their ESL science course. Otherwise, practice based on belief in CLT is just as surely failing ESL students as the older belief system in rote drill of a random collection of grammar items.

The teaching of grammar in many ESL/EFL settings (at least in the United States) presents a number of challenges for those who want to influence classroom instruction in grammar because of various aspects of teacher knowledge, belief, and behavior along with pressures on many teachers that result from class size and lack of job stability and support for professional growth. While those teachers with advanced degrees in the field sometimes have had some instruction in English grammar and the teaching of English grammar (see the various ways that English grammar is handled in M.A. programs in TESL/EFL in Liu & Master, 2003; Ferris, 2002), many other teachers do not have degrees in the field and have limited knowledge of either English grammar or issues in effective teaching of grammar. Even teachers with M.A. degrees in the field have often only taken general courses in theoretical linguistics rather than courses that delve into English grammar in detail. Additionally, many classroom teachers have little or no connection with the larger profession and seldom attend professional meetings where they might find out about alternative ways of handling grammar instruction.

Because they have never taken a course in English grammar or because they were minimally interested in that course when they were in their degree programs, many teachers learn their grammar from the ESL/EFL grammar textbooks that they use in their classes. The best-selling textbooks in ESL/EFL remain drill-based grammar books. Thus, many teachers learn to think about grammar as a set of grammatical forms that are organized in form sets (types of verb tenses, types of clauses, etc.) but not connected to any communication patterns.

ESL teachers in U.S. college programs have a reputation (within their institutions and with publishers) for being ruthless users of copy machines to violate copyright law by making class sets of materials to supplement (or replace) the required textbooks for their courses. The chair of a large ESL program at a U.S. college kept records of the kinds of materials copied by teachers: She found that no matter what the course that the teacher was supposed to be teaching—reading or writing or oral communication—the great bulk of the handouts being copied were taken directly from grammar textbooks, especially from the grammar textbooks and resource books by Azar (1999).

While many teachers still work from beliefs in grammar drill, others have adopted what Lightbown (1998) terms the "new orthodoxy":

The impact of new approaches to language teaching is often brought home to me when classroom teachers give me minilectures on the value of unfettered communication in the classroom, the power of comprehensible input, and perhaps, above all, the danger of raising the affective filter by correcting learners' errors when they are in the midst of a communicative act (Krashen, 1982)! If language is to be the focus of the learner's attention at any time, they argue, it should be in their home study materials or in a separate lesson. Sometimes these separate lessons may be motivated by consistent errors that the teacher is aware of, but errors should not be pointed out in the midst of a task or other communicative activity. Such a view is explicit, of course, in the "natural approach" of Krashen and Terrell (1983), but I am fascinated by how this has—at least among many teachers—become the new orthodoxy, embraced by many teachers who would not be able to trace its origins. (p. 191)

As a result of these factors, teachers are a difficult audience to reach with messages about changes in the ways that they teach English grammar in their ESL/EFL classes. Even those who find time and energy to seek professional development are reasonably suspicious of the latest new theory after all the changes in advice over the years. Teachers are reasonably suspicious of advice from academics who have little (or little recent) experience in L2 classrooms. Change is more likely to occur when researchers work cooperatively and consistently within classroom settings (for examples of such cooperation see, e.g., Doughty & Varela, 1998; Burns & McPherson, 2001; Williams & Evans, 1998).

INTERSECTIONS

Connections need to be made that bring together (a) grammar as revealed by studies of language in use, (b) SLA research on effective form-focused task-based instruction, and (c) teacher support to evaluate new information and to integrate it into their belief systems and into their teaching practices. I conclude by delineating five such intersections.

Learner Corpora

Many, and perhaps most, studies of second language acquisition use collections of learner language as the basis for study. These collections are not necessarily in computer format or analyzed using software or corpus linguistics methods. The creation and analysis of these corpora is a natural intersection of teachers, linguists, and SLA specialists. Examples of effective collection and use of learner English that have led to publications illustrate many different methodologies for data collection and analysis along with the wide variety of research topics being studied: Bardovi-Harlig (1992, 2000) collected samples of adult ESL student writing and interview materials over a period of months. Doughty and Varela (1998) planned an intervention strategy to teach past tense in writing and talking about science by middle school students and collected written and spoken data about the effects of that intervention. Ellis (1992, 1997) observed two children in ESL class to collect data on how they made requests and how the language they used to make requests changed over time. Hinkel (2002) used a collection of student essays to study language and rhetoric in learners' prose. A continuing problem for SLA research is the limited access to the corpus used in a particular scholar's work, making replication and extension of that work by other scholars impossible. Thus, the development of widely available collections such as the CHiLDES (Child Language Data Exchange System) is a valuable tool for second language acquisition research. Also, while teachers are required to provide access to learners and classrooms, they are not necessarily pulled into the projects or given access to the results of the studies. For this intersection to be successful, more collaborative work is needed but we also need wider dissemination of the research results in formats accessible to nonspecialist audiences.

The Acquisition of Grammar Clusters

Most published SLA studies of English grammar focus on a single grammar form or on a random assortment of forms that have been studied by other SLA researchers or that are known to be problems for learners. Studies of grammar in use have shown how grammatical forms tend to cluster in particular settings, with the implication that fluent, accurate performance in that discourse setting will require control over a whole set of features. Past tense alone does not a narrative make. More work at the intersection of SLA and discourse-based studies of English grammar is needed to help us understand how the whole set of grammar (and vocabulary) develop over time. The power of such work is illustrated by studies such as Bardovi-Harlig (1994, 1998, 2000) where she studies the interrelationships among three features of L2 learner narratives: (1) chronological order, (2) time adverbials, and (3) past tense verbs. Her work shows that learners go through a developmental process that begins with use of chronological order so that sequencing is used to tell the story by learners who have limited vocabulary or grammar. As their language develops over time, learners then add time adverbials to their stories and start to be able to add background information to the narrative foreground. At this stage they continue to use chronological order but are not totally dependent on it because they have new vocabulary to indicate time. The next stage involves the addition of past tense verbs to go along with chronological order and adverbs with some reduction in the use of adverbials because they are no longer totally dependent on them. At a later stage when use of past tense has stabilized, learners can add the use of past perfect forms to talk about things that happened before the main events of the narrative. However, past perfect is seldom required since simple past tense and adverbials can carry the same meaning (and since past perfect is not commonly used by native speakers and so is not much in evidence in the input received by learners)—so this next stage is not one that all learners reach even when given instruction in the past perfect. At the final stage, students are still combining chronological order, adverbials, and verb tense to create narratives that effectively combine both foreground and background information. In addition to that very useful information about the learning of those three aspects of narrative discourse, information about the parallel development of the ability to use noun phrases and pronoun reference would be helpful for understanding how learner language develops over time. Bardovi-Harlig (2000) quotes Schumann (1987, p. 38): "In standard language, verb morphology interacts with, supports, and often duplicates the work done by pragmatic devices in expressing temporality." Teachers of English grammar need that information on those connections and about how students learn to use the various forms in integrated sets.

The Acquisition of Set Phrases

According to SLA research and to the common experience of teachers and learners, beginners and lower proficiency students often depend on chunks of language that have been learned as chunks. The next stage of learning involves sorting out the words and grammatical processes involved in the creation of those chunks. Both of those insights into language learning and language use are widely reported and generally accepted by teachers as well as scholars (Ellis, 1997; Lightbown & Spada, 1999). What we do not know is how to help students at more advanced levels to recognize, learn, and use the set phrases that corpus linguistics research has shown to underlie native speaker versions of English in many different discourse settings. ESL/EFL teachers and materials writers (and students) have long worked with idioms, but the studies on collocations and on lexical bundles reviewed earlier in this chapter are a special challenge for SLA and for pedagogical grammar.

Planning Ahead for Focus on Form

Long's formulation of focus on form has been highly influential and is often quoted by SLA researchers who are attempting to implement the system in classrooms. Doughty and Williams (1998a, p. 3) quote two versions of Long's requirements for focus on form:

[version 1] focus on form ... overtly draws students' attention to linguistic elements as they arise incidentally in lessons whose overriding focus is on meaning or communication. (Long, 1991, pp. 45–46)

[version 2] focus on form often consists of an occasional shift of attention to linguistic code features—by the teacher and/or one or more students—triggered by perceived problems with comprehension or production. (Long & Robinson, 1998)

Communication is the goal; linguistic elements such as grammar and vocabulary are used only when there are problems in the communication. When the statements are read from the point of view of classroom and teacher realities and also of language in use, new interpretations are possible for potentially puzzling elements in the formulation. The statement is often interpreted to mean that selection of the linguistic element is made in real time based solely on student error in speech. Lightbown (1998) points out the difficulty for classroom teachers of handling this task in the midst of complicated, fast-moving communication involved in classes with large numbers of students. Additionally, the interpretation that the recasting is strictly a spontaneous event does not seem to include recognition that students can usually be sorted (roughly enough) into proficiency levels based both on what they can do and know and on what they still struggle to do consistently and what they haven't learned to do yet. A teacher does not need long experience of particular groups of students to be able to predict the kinds of errors that the students are going to make and that are going to impede communication. Additionally, teacher analysis of the real world tasks for which students are preparing should lead to the selection of particular discourse types that involve particular grammar and vocabulary. Planning ahead is possible based on knowledge of students as well as knowledge of the difficulties that the language required by certain tasks gives students.

Effective Use of Recasts

Leeman (2003) reports on a study of her use of recasts with English-speaking students of Spanish in a research project aimed at understanding negative and positive feedback. That is, her purposes have to do with understanding SLA processes rather than with investigating classroom-based SLA. To achieve her goals, "it was decided that the ideal structure would have low perceptual salience and limited communicative value and be likely to go unacquired by classroom learners despite its frequency in the L2 input. . . ." (p. 46). Her methods involved one-on-one interactions with the students. This use of recasts is at the extreme end of a continuum from the requirements for use of that technique in classroom settings.

Recasts are difficult to do well in typical classrooms for at least two reasons: (a) the teacher's attention is both focused and scattered as he or she works with the individual but it also involves awareness of the whole group and (b) students are likely to misunderstand the recast if they are focused on communication (Lightbown, 1998; Lyster & Ranta, 1997). That is, a teacher may not notice in accurate detail what a student says and the student may not get the point of the repetition of her or his statement. Additionally, some learners may not be good at learning through spoken input. Also, many teachers are not well informed about English grammar and could easily make inappropriate choices about which elements in a student's production to focus on. Thus, recasts are easy to do ineffectively and require substantial prior decision making and even training for a teacher (Doughty & Varela, 1998). In the process followed by Doughty and Varela, selection of the grammar form for recasting was made based on two weeks of observation of the work of the students to select a form that was problematic for them and that was central to their success in their academic task of carrying out scientific demonstrations and preparing oral and written lab reports about their work. This approach to recasting suggests an intersection with language in use research and methods along with implementation of a task-based curriculum. When a teacher knows the kind of communication that her students must control, then analysis of the grammatical and lexical patterns of samples of that discourse can lead to principled decisions about the language that needs to be the focus of her classes. Thus, other areas of grammar can reasonably be put aside to focus on the centrally important forms and words whether the teacher decides to limit grammar to recasts or explores a wider range of instructional activity types.

Grammar FROM Context

When task-based curricular approaches are combined with information from discourse studies, teachers, curriculum designers, and materials writers are given a powerful tool to provide students with useful preparation for their lives outside the language classroom. Doughty and Varela (1998) model that combination for us. The students are learning English and science in a science class. They need to know how to carry out certain procedures required by the science curriculum set up by the government and implemented in the school system. The spoken and written products required for success in that curriculum are important real world tasks. Those tasks are carried out with particular combinations of grammar and vocabulary. Certain of the grammatical forms give the students more trouble than others. By analyzing the tasks and the students, the teacher is able to reach principled decisions about what the students need to know how to do. Working with a researcher who contributes to their partnership knowledge about effective use of recasting and analysis of discourse for grammatical features, the teacher helps to create a program of communicative tasks along with grammar instruction that gives students information about past tense verbs in scientific communication and that trains the students to be aware of that use and to learn to incorporate it in their own scientific communication. Using this jointly planned approach, the teacher begins the hard work of motivating, challenging, interesting, and pushing as many of the students as possible to become accurate and fluent in handling those important tasks—while her researcher-colleague helps to collect and analyze data about the success of the program. The grammar isn't random but is selected based on the central features of the discourse to be learned and on student problems with the language of that discourse. The grammar isn't the purpose for the lesson but is required for the students to successfully carry out their academic task. The teaching and learning of the grammar isn't separated off from the learning of scientific writing and speaking; students learn that certain language—vocabulary and the grammatically required forms to go along with the vocabulary—is expected by this teacher and by the larger community of people who read and write about scientific demonstrations and experiments.

REFERENCES

Azar, B. S. (1999). *Understanding and using English grammar* (3rd ed.). White Plains, NY: Pearson Education.

Bardovi-Harlig, K. (1992). The use of adverbials and natural order in the development of temporal expression. *International Review of Applied Linguistics in Language Teaching, 3*(4), 299–315.

Bardovi-Harlig, K. (1994). Reverse-order reports and the acquisition of tense: Beyond the principle of chronological order. *Language Learning, 44*(2), 243–282.

Bardovi-Harlig, K. (1995). A narrative perspective on the development of the tense/aspect system in second language acquisition. *Studies in Second Language Acquisition, 17* (2), 263–291.

Bardovi-Harlig, K. (1998). Narrative structure and lexical aspect. *Studies in Second Language Acquisition, 20,* 471–508.

Bardovi-Harlig, K. (2000). *Tense and aspect in second language acquisition: Form, meaning, and use.* Malden, MA: Blackwell.

Biber, D. (1988). *Variation across speech and writing.* Cambridge, UK: Cambridge University Press.

Biber, D. (1999). A Register Perspective on Grammar and Discourse: Variability in the Form and Use of English Complement Clauses. *Discourse Studies, 1*(2), 131–150.

Biber, D., & Conrad, S. (2001). Corpus-based research in TESOL: Quantitative corpus-based research: Much more than bean counting. *TESOL Quarterly, 35*(2), 331–336.

Biber, D., & Conrad, S. (1999). Lexical bundles in conversation and academic prose. In H. Hasselgard & S. Oksefjell (Eds.), *Out of corpora: Studies in honour of Stig Johansson* (pp. 181–190). Amsterdam: Rodopi.

Biber, D., Johansson, S., Leech, G., Conrad, S., & Finegan, E. (1999). *Longman grammar of spoken and written English.* Harlow, UK: Pearson Education Limited.

Biber, D., & Reppen, R. (2002). What does frequency have to do with grammar teaching? *Studies in Second Language Acquisition, 24*(2), 199–208.

Burns, A., & McPherson, P. (2001). An Australian adult ESL settlement classroom. In J. Murphy & P. Byrd (Eds.), *Understanding the courses we teach: Local perspectives on English language teaching.* Ann Arbor: University of Michigan Press.

Bygate, M., Skehan, P., & Swain, M. (2001). *Researching pedagogic tasks: Second language learning, teaching and testing.* Harlow, UK: Longman.

Byrd, P. (1998). Grammar FROM context. In P. Byrd & J. Reid (Eds.), *Grammar in the composition classroom: Essays on teaching ESL for college-bound students* (pp. 54–68). Boston: Heinle & Heinle.

Celce-Murcia, M. (1991). Grammar pedagogy in second and foreign language teaching. *TESOL Quarterly, 25*(3), 459–480.

Child Language Data Exchange System. A collection of child learner corpora at http://childes.psy.cmu.edu/

Conrad, S. (2000). Will corpus linguistics revolutionize grammar teaching in the 21st century? *TESOL Quarterly, 34*(3), 548–559.

Conrad, S. (2001). Variation among disciplinary texts: A comparison of textbooks and journal articles in biology and history. In S. Conrad & D. Biber (Eds.), *Variation in English: Multidimensional studies.* Harlow, UK: Longman.

Conrad, S. (2002). Corpus linguistics approaches for discourse analysis. *Annual Review of Applied Linguistics, 22* (Discourse and Dialogue), 75–95.

Dillon, S. (2003, November 5). School districts struggle with English fluency mandate. *The New York Times.* Retrieved November 5, 2003, from www.nytimes.com.

Doughty, C., & Varela, E. (1998). Communicative focus on form. In C. Doughty & J. Williams (Eds.), *Focus on form in classroom second language acquisition* (pp. 114–138). Cambridge, UK: Cambridge University Press.

Doughty, C., & Williams, J. (1998a). Issues and terminology. In C. Doughty & J. Williams (Eds.), *Focus on form in classroom second language acquisition* (pp. 1–11). Cambridge, UK: Cambridge University Press.

Doughty, C., & Williams, J. (1998b). *Focus on form in classroom second language acquisition.* Cambridge, UK: Cambridge University Press.

Doughty, C., & Williams, J. (1998c). Pedagogical choices in focus on form. In C. Doughty & J. Williams (Eds.), *Focus on form in classroom second language acquisition* (pp. 197–261). Cambridge, UK: Cambridge University Press.

Dry, H. A. (1992). Foregrounding: An assessment. In S. J. J. Hwang & W. R. Merrifield (Eds.), *Language in context: Essays for Robert E. Longacre* (pp. 435–450). Dallas, TX: Summer Institute of Linguistics and the University of Texas at Arlington.

Ellis, R. (1992). Learning to communicate in the classroom: A study of two language learners' requests. *Studies in Second Language Acquisition, 14,* 20.

Ellis, R. (1997). *Second language acquisition.* Oxford, UK: Oxford University Press.

Ellis, R. (2002). The place of grammar instruction in the second/foreign language curriculum. In E. Hinkel & S. Fotos (Eds.), *New perspectives on grammar teaching in second language classrooms* (pp. 17–34). Mahwah, NJ: Lawrence Erlbaum Associates.

Ellis, R. (2003). *Task-based language learning and teaching.* Oxford, UK: Oxford University Press.

Ferris, D. R. (2002). *Treatment of error in second language student writing.* Ann Arbor: University of Michigan Press.

Genesee, F. (1987). *Learning through two languages.* New York: Newbury House.

Halliday, M. A. K. (1994). *An introduction to functional grammar* (2nd ed.). London: Edward Arnold.

Harley, B. (1986). *Age in second language acquisition.* Clevedon, UK: Multilingual Matters.

Harley, B. (1992). Patterns of second language development in French immersion. *Journal of French Language Studies, 2*(2), 159–183.

Harley, B., & Swain, M. (1984). The interlanguage of immersion students and its implications for second language teaching. In A. Davies, C. Criper, & A. Howatt (Eds.), *Interlanguage* (pp. 291–311). Edinburgh: Edinburgh University Press.

Hinkel, E. (2002). *Second language writers' text: Linguistic and rhetorical features.* Mahwah, NJ: Lawrence Erlbaum Associates.

Hunston, S. (2002). *Corpora in applied linguistics.* Cambridge, UK: Cambridge University Press.

Joseph, J. E., Love, N., & Taylor, T. J. (2001). *Landmarks in linguistic thought II.* London: Routledge & Kegan Paul.

Krashen, S. (1977). The monitor model for adult second language performance. In M. Burt, H. Dulay, & M. Finocchiaro (Eds.), *Viewpoints on English as a second language* (pp. 152–161). New York: Regents.

Krashen, S. (1982). *Principles and practice in second language acquisition.* Oxford: Pergamon.

Krashen, S., & Terrell, T. (1983). *The natural approach.* New York: Pergamon.

Labov, W., & Waletsky, J. (1967). Narrative analysis: Oral versions of personal experience. In J. Helms (Ed.), *Essays on the verbal and visual arts* (pp. 12–44). Seattle, WA: University of Washington Press.

Larson-Freeman, D. (2001). Teaching grammar. In M. Celce-Murcia (Ed.), *Teaching English as a second or foreign langugage* (3rd ed.). Boston: Heinle & Heinle.

Leech, G., Rayson, P., & Wilson, A. (2001). *Word frequencies in written and spoken English based on the British National Corpus.* Harlow, UK: Longman.

Leeman, J. (2003). Recasts and second language development. *Studies in Second Language Acquisition, 25,* 37–63.

Lightbown, P. (1998). The importance of timing in focus on form. In C. Doughty & J. Williams (Eds.), *Focus on form in classroom second language acquisition* (pp. 177–196). Cambridge, UK: Cambridge University Press.

Lightbown, P. (2000). Anniversary article: Classroom SLA research and second language teaching. *Applied Linguistics, 21*(4), 431–462.

Lightbown, P., & Spada, N. (1999). *How languages are learned* (2nd ed.). Oxford, UK: Oxford University Press.

Liu, D., & Master, P. (Eds.). (2003). *Grammar teaching in teacher education.* Alexandria, VA: TESOL.

Long, M. (1988). Does second language instruction make a difference? A review of the research. *TESOL Quarterly, 17*(3), 8–31.

Long, M. (1991). Focus on form: A design feature in language teaching methodology. In K. d. Bot, R. Ginsberg, & C. Kramsch (Eds.), *Foreign language research in cross-cultural perspective* (pp. 39–52). Amsterdam: John Benjamins.

Long, M., & Crookes, G. (1992). Three approaches to task-based syllabus design. *TESOL Quarterly, 26*(1), 27–55.

Long, M. H., & Robinson, P. (1998). Focus on form: Theory, research, and practice. In C. Doughty & J. Williams (Eds.), *Focus on form in classroom second language acquisition* (pp. 15–41). Cambridge, UK: Cambridge University Press.

Lyster, R., & Ranta, L. (1997). Corrective feedback and learner uptake: Negotiation of form in communicative classrooms. *Studies in Second Language Acquisition, 19*(1), 37–66.

Mitchell, R., & Myles, F. (1998). *Second language learning theories.* London: Arnold Publishers.

Nation, I. S. P. (2001). *Learning vocabulary in another language.* Cambridge, UK: Cambridge University Press.

Norris, J., & Ortega, L. (2000). Effectiveness of L2 instruction: Research synthesis and quantitative meta-analysis. *Language Learning, 50*(3), 417–528.

Quirk, R., Greenbaum, S., Leech, G., & Svartvik, J. (1985). *A comprehensive grammar of the English language.* London: Longman.

Richards, J. C. (2002). Accuracy and fluency revisited. In E. Hinkel & S. Fotos (Eds.), *New perspectives on grammar teaching in second language classrooms* (pp. 35–50). Mahwah, NJ: Lawrence Erlbaum Associates.

Schiffrin, D. (1981). Tense variation in narrative. *Language, 57*(1), 45–62.

Schumann, J. H. (1987). The expression of temporality in basilang speech. *Studies in Second Language Acquisition, 21,* 21–41.

Sinclair, J. (1991). *Corpus concordance collocation.* Oxford: Oxford University Press.

Skierso, A. (1991). Textbook selection and evaluation. In M. Celce-Murcia (Ed.), Teaching English as a second or foreign language (pp. 432–453). Boston: Heinle and Heinle.

Snow, M. A., & Brinton, D. (1997). *The content-based classroom: Perspectives on integrating language and content.* New York: Longman.

Stubbs, M. (1993). British traditions in text analysis: From Firth to Sinclair. In M. Baker, G. Francis, & E. Tognini-Bonelli (Eds.), *Text and technology: In honor of John Sinclair* (pp. 1–33). Amsterdam: John Benjamins.

Stubbs, M. (2001). *Words and phrases: Corpus studies of lexical semantics.* Oxford, UK: Blackwell.

Swain, M. (1984). A review of immersion education in Canada: Research and evaluation studies. In J. Lundin and D. P. Dolson (Eds.), Studies on immersion education: A collection for U.S. educators. Sacramento, CA: California State Department of Education. (ERIC No. ED 239 509).

Swain, M. (1985). Communicative competence: Some roles of comprehensible input and comprehensible output in its development. In S. Gass & C. Madden (Eds.), *Input in second language acquisition* (pp. 235–253). Rowley, MA: Newbury House.

Swain, M. (1991). French immersion and its offshoots: Getting two for one. In B. Freed (Ed.), *French language acquisition: Research and the classroom* (pp. 91–103). Lexington, MA: Heath.

Swain, M. (1998). Focus on form through conscious reflection. In C. Doughty & J. Williams (Eds.), *Focus on form in classroom second language acquisition* (pp. 64–81). Cambridge, UK: Cambridge University Press.

Swain, M., & Lapkin, S. (1986). Immersion French at the secondary level: The "goods" and the "bads." *Contact, 5,* 2–9.

Vignola, M.-J., & Wesche, M. (1991). Le savoir ecrire en langue maternelle et en langue second chez les diplomes d'immersion francaise. *Etudes de linguistique appliquee, 82,* 94–115.

Williams, J., & Evans, J. (1998). What kind of focus and on which forms? In C. Doughty & J. Williams (Eds.), *Focus on form in classroom second language acquisition* (pp. 139–155). Cambridge, UK: Cambridge University Press.

WordbanksOnline. A corpus of English based on the Bank of English. London: HarperCollins Publishers, UK. Retrieved June 1, 2003, from http://www.collinswordbanks.co.uk/default.asp

31

Reading in a Second Language

David E. Eskey[1]
University of Southern California

INTRODUCTION

Reading and Second Language Acquisition

For second language learners, reading may be both a means to the end of acquiring the language, as a major source of comprehensible input, and an end in itself, as the skill that many serious learners most need to employ. Many students of English as a Foreign Language (EFL), for example, rarely speak the language in their day-to-day lives but may need to read it in order to access the wealth of information recorded exclusively in the language. In complementary fashion, this reading can serve as an excellent source of the authentic language students need to interact with in quantity—language that is always meaningful, often in fully grammatical form, and that includes every feature of the target language but pronunciation. Krashen (1993) claims that students who read frequently

> acquire, involuntarily and without conscious effort, nearly all of the so-called "language skills" many people are so concerned about. They will become adequate readers, acquire a large vocabulary, develop the ability to understand and use complex grammatical constructions, develop a good writing style, and become good (but not necessarily perfect) spellers. (p. 84)

In recognizing the truth of this claim (what Krashen sums up as "the power of reading"), the field has come a long way since the audiolingual era when reading and writing were marginalized as "secondary reinforcement" for learning the spoken language (Fries, 1945).

RESEARCH ON READING

L1 Research Applied to L2

Specialists in second language (L2) reading are often criticized for depending too heavily on research in first language (L1) reading, instead of focusing more narrowly on studies of reading in a second language. There is some truth to this—especially in respect to language issues, which create far more problems for L2 readers than for L1 readers—but research on L1 reading provides a foundation for exploring both the similarities and differences between L1 and L2 reading. Just as in language acquisition research, where for years L2 specialists paid no attention to research in L1 language acquisition, despite its obvious relevance, similarities between these two kinds of reading far outweigh the differences. The differences are important and must be addressed, but reading is reading in any context, just as language acquisition is language acquisition. If human beings are the only living creatures who speak, they are also the only living creatures who read, and they do so in much the same way throughout the world. Children acquire language instinctively (Pinker, 1994). They must be taught literacy, but all writing systems are language based and share some fundamental characteristics.

An Overview of Research on Reading

In the 1960s before the advent of what has come to be known as "cognitive psychology," most research on reading was hardly worth—well, reading—because the then dominant behaviorist models in psychology could not accommodate discussion of mental events, and reading is, almost purely, a mental event. One major exception was Edmund Burke Huey's (1908) *The Psychology and Pedagogy of Reading*, but this sank without a trace in the behaviorist sea before being rediscovered in more recent times. Comparisons with linguistics (which Chomsky has always characterized as a branch of cognitive psychology) come to mind; but language behavior, in the form of spoken and written discourse, has always been accessible to direct empirical investigation, whereas reading produces almost no physical data for investigation, with the minor exception of eye movements.

By the late 1970s, however, reading specialists like Kenneth Goodman (e.g, Goodman, 1975) and linguists like Ronald Wardhaugh (1977) were disputing the notion that reading is merely the passive side—complementing the active skill of writing—of being literate. Like the other receptive skill listening (with which it has much in common as a psycholinguistic processing skill), reading is now generally understood to be an active, purposeful, and creative mental process in which the reader engages in the construction of meaning from a text, partly on the basis of new information provided by that text but also partly on the basis of whatever relevant prior knowledge, feelings, and opinions that reader brings to the task of making sense of the words on the page.

Research in the 1970s and 1980s was characterized by a search for more accurate and more revealing models of the reading process. Major advances in our understanding of what readers actually do when they read followed from a shift in orientation from commonsense *bottom-up* (from text to brain) models of the process—in which the reader is assumed to decode precisely (in the case of English) from left to right, from letters into words, and from words into larger grammatical units in retrieving the writer's meaning, step by step, from the text—to a totally different kind of model, the so-called *top-down* (from brain to text) model of the reading process. This shift, sometimes referred to as the top-down revolution—a movement in which Goodman and, later, Frank Smith (e.g., Smith, 1973) were especially prominent—generated massive research support and was widely accepted, in one form or another, by reading specialists everywhere. Top-down descriptions of the reading process characterize it as what Goodman (1967) once called, in a famous remark, "a psycholinguistic guessing game." The notion is that readers do not decode in precise or sequential fashion but instead attack the text with expectations of meaning developed before and during the process, take in whole chunks of text (in short, jerky eye movements called *saccades*) making use of just as much of the visual information on the page as they need to confirm and extend their expectations—a process of predicting, sampling, and confirming in which readers interact with texts by combining information they discover there with the knowledge they bring to it in constructing a comprehensive meaning for the text as coherent discourse. Since prior knowledge plays such a major role in this conception of reading, reading specialists also devoted considerable attention to research on *schema theory*, research that attempted to account for the way in which human beings store and organize information in networks of related notions called *schemata* (or, more rarely, *plans*, *scripts*, or *scenarios*). In this area, the work of Rumelhart and his associates was especially influential (e.g., Rumelhart, 1980).

During the latter part of the 1980s, top-down models were increasingly challenged by proponents of *interactive* models of the process, who point out that strictly top-down models cannot fully account for the results of much empirical research (Stanovich, 1980, provides an excellent summary)—research that, for example, shows that skillful readers can process linguistic forms in print both more accurately and more rapidly than less skillful readers can even in context-free situations where no prediction is possible, and that weaker readers are as likely as strong ones to guess at meaning on the basis of prior knowledge—both results that run counter to top-down assumptions. From such research results, advocates for these interactive models (which should not be confused with the interactive reader/text process described earlier) infer that successful reading entails a balanced interaction between bottom-up and top-down processing skills, thus restoring the simple decoding of text to a more central role and raising doubts about the guessing game metaphor. Although it might be argued that these interactive models are simply modifications of the topdown approach, which do not involve the kind of radical new conception of the reading process that the movement from bottomup to top-down models entailed, they have become the standard for discussions of the psycholinguistics of reading.

After this period of relative coherence during which most researchers focused on reading as a psycholinguistic process, reading research in the 1990s splintered into a number of incommensurate perspectives. By the late 1980s, reading research had, as noted, coalesced around interactive models, which give equal weight to bottom-up processing of texts (i.e., decoding) and top-down construction of meanings for those texts (i.e., comprehension). Stanovich (1992) provides an excellent example of this balanced view. Today, however, the field is very much engaged in what Kamil, Intrator, & Kim (2000) describe as both "broadening the definition of reading" and "broadening the reading research agenda" to include a wide variety of social, cultural, neurobiological, and even political perspectives on reading.

Recently, for example, many prominent researchers have moved beyond the study of reading as a psycholinguistic process to consider reading as a form of sociocultural practice. These researchers are concerned with such questions as how much, what, and why—as opposed to merely how—people read, if and when they do, with special reference to the reading behaviors of particular socioeconomic groups. Building on works on literacy by sociolinguists like Heath (1983) and Street (1984), such scholars as Gee (2000) have begun to explore this sociocultural dimension of reading. Others, like Friere (Friere & Macedo, 1987) and Shannon (1996), have taken this perspective to the level of "critical literacy" in which reading behavior is regarded as a form of political behavior.

At the same time researchers in cognitive science have moved beyond psycholinguistic models toward work in neurobiology, and some studies have been done on the neurobiology of reading, especially in relation to dyslexia (Shaywitz et al., 2000). Still another direction is represented by studies of new technologies in reading that focus on the nature of reading in the rapidly expanding electronic media (Kamil & Lane, 1998).

These many new perspectives on reading research have been accompanied by related changes in research methodology. Experimental research has largely given way to classroom-centered action research (McFarland & Stansell, 1993) and narrative (Gilbert, 1993) and ethnographic approaches (e.g., Heath, 1983). There is less emphasis on the typical reader and more on targeted groups or individuals. Thus, protocol analyses (Pressley & Afflerbach, 1995) and case studies of single readers (Neuman & McCormick, 1995) have become increasingly popular.

In contrast to information-processing models, these newer perspectives have given reading research a more human face but have also reduced the generalizability of its results and raised doubts about the internal coherence of a subject as broad and complex as reading.

Since reading is a kind of experience (albeit in purely symbolic form), potentially involving the entire range of any reader's thought processes, feelings, imagination, and beliefs, as shaped by his or her genes and real-world experience, it is hardly surprising that no single model of reading behavior can dominate reading research for long. Even the boundaries of the topic are fluid, reading being just one instantiation of the larger concept of literacy. In the latest *Handbook of Reading Research* (Kamil et al., 2000), essentially the bible of reading researchers, all seven of the book's subheadings are labeled as discussions of literacy, not reading. As the editors of that volume suggest, the remarkable diversity of perspectives on reading characteristic of reading research today may either be described, optimistically, as "creating new frontiers of thought" or, more skeptically, as "creating confusion" about a subject that probably cannot be captured in a unified model.

Research on Second Language Reading: Specific Issues

Whether in a first or a second language context, most reading research can be subsumed under three major headings, all of which have been mentioned in passing—reading as a psycholinguistic process, reading as sociocultural practice, and reading as individual behavior—because every human reader is, simultaneously, (1) a member of the species (a human reader who reads as humans do, as opposed to some other kind of reader—a computer, for example), (2) a member of a network of sociocultural groups (possibly, in relation to the writer, a member of a radically different culture), and (3) an individual (and thus, within the limits established in (1) and (2), cognitively and affectively unique to some extent). Within this general framework, research in the following specific areas seems especially pertinent to major issues in the field of second language reading.

Reading as a Psycholinguistic Process

Reading and Language Proficiency.   Not surprisingly, the variable that correlates best with success in second language reading is proficiency in the language. Motivation and background knowledge (of content) are also important, but reading begins with decoding of language; and reading comprehension, although it involves both bottom-up and top-down processing, begins with, and so depends on, rapid and accurate decoding of the text (Birch, 2002). In any discussion of second language reading, the place to begin is thus proficiency in the language. Serious discussion of this issue can be traced to Clarke's (1980) "short-circuit" hypothesis, which challenged the notion that skillful readers in one language could simply transfer their skills to reading in a second language (the so-called "language interdependence" hypothesis; see, e.g., Cummins, 1984). Clarke argued for a language proficiency "threshold"; readers whose knowledge of the target language fell below that threshold, no matter how proficient in their first language reading, could not transfer their skills to their second language reading until they had mastered more of the language. Hudson (1982) demonstrated that this threshold cannot be identified in absolute terms but varies with the reader's motivation and knowledge. Clarke's basic premise however has stood the test of time and was addressed most extensively in Alderson's (2000) book-length treatment of the subject. With reference to the competing hypotheses, Carrell (2001) observes, in relation to a more recent study:

> It may be more profitable to think of these two hypotheses in terms of Bernhardt and Kamil's restatements of them: *"How first language (L1) literate does a second language reader have to be to make the second language knowledge work?"* and *"How much second language (L2) knowledge does a second language reader have to have in order to make the first language (L1) reading knowledge work?"* (Bernhardt & Kamil, 1995, p. 32)

Reading and Vocabulary.   The relationship between reading and knowledge of vocabulary is well-documented and reciprocal. It is now well understood that the best (some would argue the only) way to acquire the extensive vocabulary required for reading widely in a second language is reading itself, and it is equally well understood that a prerequisite for such reading is an extensive vocabulary—a classic chicken and egg situation. Edward Fry (1981) has claimed that readers who encounter more than one unknown word in twenty in a text will be reading at what he calls "frustration level" and will thus be unlikely to continue reading—a sobering thought for teachers of adult second language readers who want to read adult material but often lack the vocabulary required to do so successfully. Huckin, Haynes, and Coady (1993) provide a good summary of research for second language readers, addressing most of the major issues, starting with automatic word recognition, a "necessary but not sufficient" condition (Stanovich, 1991) for successful reading comprehension. For second language readers, the issues are obviously more complex. Such readers are often slower and less automatic in recognizing words in the target language than first language readers are (Favreau & Segalowitz, 1983). In subsequent studies, Segalowitz, Segalowitz, and Wood (1998) have shown that extended experience in reading a second language has positive effects on word recognition for adult subjects, and Geva, Wade-Woolley, and Shaney (1993) have explored this issue with younger learners learning to read in two languages. Both studies show that the development of fast and accurate word-recognition skills is a complex process for second language readers that involves a wide range of knowledge and skills.

Many texts for the teaching of second language reading promote guessing from context as a major means of decoding unknown words, but research suggests that this strategy is overrated and often leads to misidentifications (Bensoussan & Laufer, 1984). Similarly, research demonstrates that second language readers, whether guessing or not, frequently misidentify words (Bernhardt, 1991). Thus, although reading remains the best means of acquiring a larger vocabulary, care must be taken not to immerse readers in texts that are lexically beyond them, which does in fact reduce reading to a kind of guessing game. The reciprocal relationship mentioned earlier between reading and vocabulary must, in practice, be handled with care: Second language readers should be lexically prepared for any texts assigned and the texts should meet, or be taught in such a way as to meet, Krashen's $i + 1$ standard for comprehensibility. Vocabulary cannot be force-fed through reading, and second language readers cannot read texts that are lexically beyond their proficiency.

Reading and Grammar.   Although a firm grasp of syntax is obviously required for successful decoding, researchers in this area have not been successful in disentangling knowledge of sentence structure from other kinds of knowledge—especially knowledge of vocabulary—to determine its particular contribution to reading comprehension. Some work has been done on syntactic simplification and elaboration, but the results are inconclusive. Carrell (2001) summarizes:

> ...the research on syntactic simplification and elaboration shows that while syntactic simplification can enhance foreign or second language reading comprehension, the picture is a complex one, with linguistic complexity interacting with such other factors as age, proficiency level, cultural background knowledge, and, possibly, item type.

Reading and Text Structure.   At the level of discourse, research suggests that knowledge of text structure contributes to reading comprehension (Carrell, 1992; Riley, 1993). That is, a reader who understands the way in which the kind of discourse he or she is reading is typically organized and will find it easier to comprehend such texts. Like knowledge of the lexis and grammar of a language, this kind of knowledge is part of what readers need to know to read successfully in a second language.

Reading Rate

Fluent decoding depends on the reader having achieved what reading specialists call "automaticity," that is, the ability to convert most written language into meaningful information so automatically that the reader does not have to think about the language and can concentrate on combining the information obtained with background knowledge to construct a meaning for the text. This requires the kinds of knowledge reviewed earlier—knowledge of the real world and knowledge of lexis, grammar, and text structure—but it also requires the skill of reading in meaningful groups of words, sometimes called "chunking" and often described in terms of *reading rate*, the ability to decode so many words per minute. Fluent decoding is thus both rapid and accurate decoding, because the human brain cannot acquire information from language that it does not understand or from language that is being processed too slowly. In practice, the two are interrelated, given the way in which the human memory system works. The system has three parts: sensory store, short-term memory, and long-term memory (Stevick, 1976). Sensory store merely records the visual image of the script or print the reader is reading. Short-term memory converts this image into meaningful information. Since it holds only 5 to 7 units at a time, for efficient reading these units must be reasonably large and meaningful. The units cannot be individual words, that, similarly, have little meaning by themselves. Words do not, as common sense suggests, give meaning to sentences so much as sentences give meaning to words. Consider these sentences:

> There is water in the *well*.
> He was sick but he is *well* now.
> He plays football *well*.
> He saw tears *well* up in her eyes.
> "*Well*, I don't know," he said.

By itself, the word *well* has many possible meanings—and therefore no clear meaning—but when combined with other words, it takes on clear meanings. To read for meaning, then, a reader must bring meaningful groups of words into short-term memory. Letter-by-letter or word-by-word reading fill short-term memory with meaningless units; no meaningful information gets through to combine with the reader's background knowledge for placement in long-term memory (where knowledge is stored in the form of concepts or ideas, not words). Automaticity is thus a product of both knowledge of language and skill in processing language in written form.

Reading and Background Knowledge (Content Discourses)

Successful reading begins with fluent decoding, but this must be accompanied by the reader's construction of a meaning for the text (commonly referred to as reading comprehension), which goes well beyond decoding. Every written text provides information for the reader, but the meaning of the text must be determined by a reader who can relate that information to some relevant body of knowledge. To make sense of the new information provided by a text, or written discourse, a reader must have some knowledge of what the discourse is about—its content—to which to relate that new information. The reader's brain is not an empty container to be filled with meaning from the text. The brain is full of knowledge in the form of schemata, which collectively add up to "a picture of the world," according to Frank Smith (1975), that readers carry around in their heads. Therefore the brain relates new information taken from the text to the much larger body of knowledge it already has to make sense of or give a meaning to the text as a whole. As Smith says "what the brain tells the eyes" is much more important that "what the eyes tell the brain."

If a reader cannot determine what a text is about, that reader cannot comprehend the discourse it contains even if he or she can decode the text perfectly. For example, many people can decode each of the sentences in the following "opaque" text but cannot even say what the text is about, let alone what it means:

> The procedure is quite simple. First, you arrange the items in separate piles. Of course, one pile may be sufficient depending on how much there is to do. If you have to go somewhere else due to lack of facilities, that is the next step; otherwise, you are pretty well set. It is important not to overdo things. That is, it is better to do too few things at once than too many. In the short run, this may not seem important but complications can easily arise. A mistake can be expensive as well. At first, the whole procedure will seem complicated. Soon, however, it will become just another facet of life. It is difficult to foresee any end to the necessity for this task in the immediate future, but then, one never can tell. After the procedure is completed, one arranges the materials into different groups again. Then they can be put into their appropriate places. Eventually they will be used once more and the whole cycle will then have to be repeated. However, that is part of life.

When told that the subject is washing clothes, however, most readers can apply that knowledge to a second reading of the text and suddenly understand it perfectly.

By contrast, most American readers have no trouble comprehending the following (relatively) normal text and answering the comprehension questions that follow:

> It was the day of the big party. Mary wondered if Johnny would like a kite. She ran to her bedroom, picked up her piggy bankand shook it. There was no sound!
>
> 1. Does this story take place in the past, present, or future?
> 2. What did Mary wonder?
> 3. What does the word *would* signal?
> 4. What is a *kite*?
> 5. What is a *piggy bank*?
> 6. What kind of party is this text about?
> 7. Are Mary and Johnny adults or children?
> 8. How is the kite related to the party?
> 9. Why did Mary shake her piggy bank?
> 10. Mary has a big problem; what is it?

The first five questions can be answered by decoding alone: The text provides the relevant information (as long as the reader knows the meaning of the words and structures in English and recognizes the text as a story); but to answer the second five questions (simple enough for most native speakers but more problematical for non-native speakers who may not have a Western *kids' birthday party* schema), the reader must bring cultural knowledge to the text, which provides no direct information on these topics. In other words, to comprehend even this simple story, a reader must, simultaneously, engage in bottom-up decoding and top-down interpretation of the text to construct a plausible meaning for it, a process called *parallel processing*.

Thus, reading as a psycholinguistic process, when performed successfully, entails both rapid and accurate decoding and the construction of meaning based on prior knowledge. Second language readers often have problems with both processes.

Reading as Sociocultural Practice

It is now generally understood that literacy varies from culture to culture. That is, the members of different cultures do different kinds of reading (and writing) for different purposes. Most human beings learn to speak at least one language and therefore use language to communicate with others, but people must be taught to read and may never learn to do so. As human beings we have what could fairly be called a biological instinct to learn to speak, but we must be taught to read in some particular culture that employs written language for some particular purposes. Thus becoming literate means not only acquiring the kinds of skills and knowledge already discussed; it also means being enculturated (to the reader's own culture) or acculturated (to another culture) in a kind of apprenticeship, which Smith (1988) has compared to joining a club—the *literacy club*—composed of those who read and write in some particular culture.

L1/L2: Phonology and Orthography.   Given the variety of writing systems, even decoding may differ crosslinguistically. Among others, Koda (1989) and Haynes and Carr (1990) have determined, for example, that students of English as a Second Language (ESL) who have learned to read in a language that does not employ an alphabetic writing system often have problems in decoding English texts.

Reading and Background Knowledge (Cultural Discourses).   At higher levels, most writers write for a culturally similar audience of readers and thus assume that these readers share a common knowledge base and a common value system, but common knowledge and values vary across groups (e.g., across cultures and across classes and ethnic enclaves even within a single complex culture). Writers also produce the kinds of discourse that have evolved naturally within their cultures (e.g., sonnets or haiku, personal essays or research papers), which may not be familiar to the second language reader. Although certain kinds of disciplinary knowledge (like scientific knowledge) can reasonably be described as universal, second language readers frequently encounter topics and attitudes in their reading (as in the birthday party story) that are new or strange to them and interfere with comprehension.

Thus learning to read in a second language not only entails mastering a new language in its written form, but also learning to engage in a new set of social practices that may conflict with those the reader is used to.

Critical Literacy.   During the past 10 or 15 years, a body of work has emerged in the field dealing with what is sometimes called "the politics of literacy," or, more grandly, "critical literacy," which addresses language teaching in relation to various sociopolitical concerns. The patron saint of this work is Paolo Freire who, in his earliest writings, made the valid point that in teaching so-called world languages to oppressed peoples, second language teachers should teach these languages as useful tools to be used in overcoming their oppression. Although some of this work is thought-provoking and a useful reminder that language teaching, like other kinds of teaching, does involve sociopolitical issues (Benesch, 1993; Gee, 1990), much of it grossly exaggerates the political dimension of language teaching. Much of it also, unfortunately, reflects the kind of political correctness that has made a laughingstock of many English departments at U.S. universities. Based on post-everything analyses that have largely been laughed out of the hard sciences as a result of physicist Alan Sokal's famous hoax (in which he submitted a transparent parody of postmodern discourse, "Transgressing the Boundaries—Toward a Transformative Hermeneutics of Quantum Gravity," to a major postmodern journal that promptly published the piece as a serious contribution to scholarship (Sokal, 1996; see Weinberg, 1996, for a lively discussion of this event), this work attempts to place language teaching in the van of a crusade for social justice. As Kaplan and Baldauf observe, however,

> ... one must be careful not to replace one kind of exploitation of minorities with another kind, or to replace one existing minority with a new minority created by the process intended to redress injustice ... This is in fact what Friere seems to recommend in his approach to the empowerment of minorities; he suggests turning the minority into a majority and creating a new minority out of the present majority so that the new minority may be exploited by the old minority. (Kaplan & Baldauf Jr., 1997, p. 81)

Such recommendations are, in any case, rarely feasible or in any danger of being implemented by people with real political power, and this work is full of Canute-like proposals for turning back the sea of history. The teaching of English as a second or foreign language is a favorite target, English being guilty of having acquired "hegemonic" status, and ESL teachers are frequently accused of aiding and abetting an imperialist plot by the United States and United Kingdom to take over the world by linguistic means, destroying other languages in the process (Phillipson, 1992). Since many in the language teaching profession seem committed to the simplistic credo "the more cultures and languages, the better" (as opposed to recognizing the obvious—that multilingualism and multiculturalism can be either a blessing or a curse, or a little of both), this work will always find an avid readership, but it seems to have little to contribute to the improvement of second language teaching.

Reading as Individual Behavior

Of course, no human reader is ever just a generic text processor or a simple clone of all the other members of some literacy club (or even a combination of the two), though every kind of reading is strongly constrained by the nature of the reader's brain as a linguistic processing device and by the reader's social and cultural experience. Within these constraints, however, readers differ in what they read, how much they read, how well they read, and how much they depend on or care about reading. Every reader is, in short, an individual whose attitudes toward reading and reading behavior are, to a considerable extent, idiosyncratic and unpredictable. Moreover, to become a skillful reader, a reader must read a lot (just as a swimmer must swim a lot to become a skillful swimmer). Thus engaging in extensive reading behavior is a prerequisite for developing reading skills, especially at the level required for most kinds of formal education, and readers are most likely to engage in such behavior if they have access to texts that are interesting to them as individuals and relevant to their particular needs. Reading from this point of view consists of every individual reader developing a reading habit over time by reading texts of interest and value to him or herself and reading those texts extensively.

Case Studies and Reading Protocols.   Case studies are one means of investigating readers as individuals, and the arguments that Neuman and McCormick (1995) advance for this kind of single subject research appear to apply with equal force to first and second language reading. Cho and Krashen's (1994) study of a Korean girl who became enamored of the series of books about Sweet Valley High provides a well-known example of such work. A second means of investigating readers as individuals is protocol analyses, which requires direct interaction with readers. Bernhardt (1991) makes a strong case for the use of protocols in researching, teaching, and testing L2 reading on the grounds that there is no way of predicting what specific problems a given group of second language readers will have in comprehending particular texts.

Extensive Reading.   A major topic in the field of teaching L2 reading is extensive reading, many versions of which allow individual readers to select their own texts. Day and Bamford (1998) is an excellent overview; Krashen (1993) makes the case for this approach to instruction; and Elley and Mangubhai (1983) and Robb and Susser (1989) provide reviews of successful extensive reading programs. Since this is an approach to the teaching of reading, it will be discussed in more detail next.

Evaluation of Reading

Reading is the hardest language skill to assess because so much depends on what is being read by whom. Beyond a certain minimal competence, there is no general proficiency in reading, every reader being more proficient at reading some texts than others. Thus any passage selected for testing will favor some readers and disadvantage others, since no two readers have exactly the same proficiency in language or exactly the same funds of knowledge. In testing reading comprehension, it is also difficult to determine what kinds of questions any reader who understands a text should be able to answer—that is, what constitutes reading comprehension for particular texts. In practice, of course, educators do attempt to assess reading skills, and Alderson (2000) provides a recent and comprehensive review of the most compelling work in this area. Significant variables identified include question types (e.g., multiple-choice versus open-ended); language effects (e.g., the language of assessment—L1 or L2); and second language proficiency (e.g., more proficient, experienced versus less experienced, beginning) (Wolf, 1993). In summarizing this literature, Carrell (2001) observes:

> What can safely be concluded from the results of research on the assessment of second language reading is caution in the interpretation of findings utilizing reading tests.... Performance on reading assessment measures is dependent upon many factors, including the assessment task type, the language of the assessment, the reading texts, and so on. Therefore, researchers often recommend multiple measures for testing reading comprehension. (Shohamy, 1984)

IMPLICATIONS FOR TEACHING

Reading Research and the Teaching of Reading

A major issue in the field of L2 teaching is the relationship between such teaching and research on language acquisition. Currently, many teachers, and many more researchers, seem to take it for granted that good teaching practices can and should be derived directly from research. The only problems with this notion that they recognize are identifying which research is best and filling in whatever gaps may exist. The road from research to practice is assumed to be a one-way thoroughfare with no detours, and teachers, who often take other routes, are frequently condemned for not basing their teaching on "scientific" research results. These are dangerously simplistic beliefs, because teaching and research call for very different kinds of knowledge and skills. As Ellis (1998) observes:

> Teachers operate in classrooms where they need to make instantaneous decisions regarding what and how to teach. Researchers, more often than not, work in universities, where a system of rewards prizes rigorous contributions to a theoretical understanding of issues. Teachers require and seek to develop practical knowledge; researchers endeavor to advance technical knowledge....
>
> Technical knowledge is acquired deliberately either by reflecting deeply about the object of inquiry or by investigating it empirically, involving the use of a well-defined set of procedures for ensuring the validity and reliability of the knowledge obtained. Technical knowledge is general in nature; that is, it takes the form of statements that can be applied to many particular cases. For this reason, it cannot easily be applied off-the-shelf in the kind of rapid decision making needed in day-to-day living....
>
> In contrast, practical knowledge is implicit and intuitive. Individuals are generally not aware of what they practically know.... [It] is acquired through actual experience by means of procedures that are only poorly understood. Similarly, it is fully expressible only in practice, although it may be possible, through reflection, to codify aspects of it. The great advantage of practical knowledge is that it is proceduralized and thus can be drawn on rapidly and efficiently to handle particular cases. (pp. 39–40).

As a major case in point, in the United States reading policy makers have recently adopted a very strong version of this teaching-derived-directly-from-research fallacy. In 1999, a committee of researchers dubbed "The National Reading Panel," convened by the director of The National Institute of Child Health and Human Development (NICHD) at the behest of Congress, submitted a report intended to assess the validity of current reading research and the implications of that research for the teaching of reading. This report attempted to establish (1) what constitutes valid reading research, (2) what research is most relevant to teaching, and (3) what the implications are of the research selected for "best practices" in the teaching of reading. As noted in the appended "Minority View," the findings of the panel are (not surprisingly, given the magnitude of the charge and the few months the panel had to complete it) suspect on all counts but especially on the question of teaching:

> As a body made up mostly of university professors. . . its members were not qualified to be the sole judges of the "readiness for implementation in the classroom" of their findings or whether the findings could be "used immediately by parents, teachers, and other educational audiences." Their concern, as scientists, was whether or not a particular line of instruction was clearly enough defined and whether the evidence of its experimental success was strong. (Minority View, p. 2)

This has not, however, prevented the widespread adoption of the report by U.S. school districts as the last word on reading and the teaching of reading, much to the detriment of reading teachers whose experience has led them to different conclusions from those of the report.

The real issue here is not whether teachers or researchers know best, but what contributes most to success in the teaching of reading—or any other subject. The answer is neither research-based practices nor particular approaches, methods, and materials. The answer is good teaching. Speaking for himself and his associates, Richard Allington (2000) writes:

A series of studies have confirmed what was probably obvious from the beginning. Good teachers, effective teachers, matter much more than particular curriculum materials, pedagogical approaches, or "proven programs." It has become clear that investing in good teaching—whether through making sound hiring decisions or planning effective professional development—is the most "research-based" strategy available. If we truly hope to attain the goal of "no child left behind," we must focus on creating a substantially large number of effective, expert teachers. . . . Effective teachers manage to produce better achievement regardless of which curriculum materials, pedagogical approach, or reading program they use. (pp. 742–743)

Thus the suggestions for teaching that follow are not offered as magic formulas guaranteed to produce success, but as guidelines that might be helpful to good teachers, who will know how to adapt them in practice for the particular students in their particular classrooms.

Classroom Procedures

The problem for most teachers of reading in any language is that reading does not generate any product that a teacher can see or hear. Reading is an invisible process. (It is therefore much like listening, but a teacher can ask students to perform tasks while listening—for example, giving students a dictation). Most teachers take the process for granted and go directly to the creation of a related product—for example, asking students to answer comprehension questions orally or in writing. These activities test reading but do not teach it, and this contributes little to improving any student's reading performance.

Intensive/Extensive Reading

Historically, procedures for teaching reading have often been divided into procedures for teaching *intensive* reading (working with small amounts of text in class to make various points about the nature of texts and the reading process) and procedures for teaching *extensive* reading (assigning whole texts to be read outside of class or in a reading lab setting). These are useful categories for structuring programs, but they do not shed much light on the purpose of asking students to engage in either kind of activity—that is, on how engaging in such activities can help them to become better readers.

One good way of addressing this question is to turn the question upside down: How do people learn to read a language? And, once they have learned to do it, how do they learn to read better? The answer to both questions is surprisingly simple. People learn to read, and to read better, by reading. No one can teach someone else to read: The process is largely invisible and thus cannot be demonstrated, and it mainly occurs at the subconscious level and thus cannot be explained in any way that a reader could make conscious use of.[2] However, anyone can learn to do it, just as anyone can learn to draw or to sing at some minimal level of competence. Every normal human being is capable of learning to read, given the right opportunity and guidance.

The reading teacher's job is thus not so much to teach a specific skill or content as to get students reading and to keep them reading—that is, to find a way to motivate them to read, and to facilitate their reading of whatever texts they have chosen to read or been asked to read.

Motivation

Procedures for motivating students to read tend to focus on students as individuals or as members of particular groups. To engage in something as challenging as reading regularly in a second or foreign language, learners must be highly motivated, and what motivates one reader or group of readers might not motivate another.

Matching Readers and Texts

The solution to this problem begins with locating appropriate texts, that is, texts that the reader wants or needs to read. Since people learn to read, and to read better, by reading, a major part of the reading teacher's job is to introduce students to appropriate texts—texts at the right level linguistically and texts that are both interesting to them and relevant to their particular needs—and to induce them to read such texts in quantity. For some students, it may be enough to make appropriate texts available, but for others, more guidance may be required. For the full range of students, the teacher must create his or her version of the literacy club and find ways to persuade as many students as possible to join and to become literate—that is, to read texts and to respond to those texts in the ways that typical club members do.

Extensive Reading Programs

As noted earlier, extensive reading programs have recently emerged as a major pedagogical response to the problem of finding appropriate texts for particular groups of readers or for individuals, and for inducing them to read such texts in quantity. Unlike earlier attempts to incorporate extensive reading in curricula, these programs are not mere components in a larger program that also involves intensive reading: The extensive reading *is* the program.

Often called Sustained Silent Reading (SSR) today, these programs come in various forms. Under such additional acronyms as FVR (Free Voluntary Reading), DEAR (Drop Everything and Read), and many others, all of them require L2 students to read substantial amounts of L2 text. They differ with respect to degree of student choice: Some allow students to choose their own materials; some allow students to make choices from prescribed reading lists; some assign readings; and various combinations are possible. They also differ with respect to what is expected of participating students: Some require nothing more than the reading; some require summaries or book reports; and some require, more traditionally, exams or writing assignments based on the readings.

Facilitation

Procedures for facilitating L2 reading tend to focus on teaching the reader (any reader) how to manage reading as a cognitive process more painlessly and efficiently—that is, on making L2 reading as easy as possible for the learner. Most current work on the teaching of such reading takes this general approach, possibly because this is the one area in which reading teachers can justify doing some direct teaching. It also gives publishers something to publish, that is, materials for teaching strategies for reading.

Teaching Cognitive Strategies

Thus in addition to providing—or providing access to—appropriate materials, reading teachers often teach cognitive strategies for reading, both for bottom-up processing (e.g., reading at a reasonable rate—which, as noted, really means reading in meaningful groups of words—and reading without stopping to look up words in the dictionary) and for top-down processing (e.g., skimming a text before reading and formulating specific questions that the text might be expected to answer). The following checklist provides an overview of the kind of strategies reading teachers often teach:

A CHECKLIST OF READING STRATEGIES:
1. Prereading.
   A. Bottom up, e.g., vocabulary building
   B. Top down, e.g., schema bulding
   C. Text attack, e.g., skimming
2. While reading.
   A. Bottom up, e.g., employing knowledge of morphology (any word with *tempor* in it has something to do with time)
   B. Top down, e.g., reading to find the answers to questions (SQ3R)
3. Post reading
   For example, asking questions based on purpose of text or asking questions that call for critical reading
4. Follow-up
   For example, moving on to other texts on the same topic or to other language modes (listening, speaking, writing)

There is a substantial literature on the teaching of such strategies, both in the form of resources for teachers and text materials for students. In one of the better texts for teachers, Anderson (1999), for example, identifies, discusses, and promotes eight useful teaching strategies—activating background knowledge, cultivating vocabulary, teaching for comprehension, increasing reading rate, verifying reading strategies, evaluating progress, building motivation, and selecting appropriate materials—many of which entail teaching students to employ specific cognitive strategies for successfully decoding and interpreting texts. In fact, most of the current literature on the teaching of second language reading is largely devoted to the teaching of such strategies (e.g., Aebersold & Field, 1997; Nuttall, 1996; Urquhart & Weir, 1998; Day, 1993). So, for that matter, is much of the literature on the teaching of first language reading (e.g., Mikulecky, 1990). The first L2 textbook based on a psycholinguistic model and the first to incorporate this approach was *Reader's Choice* by Silberstein, Dobson, and Clarke (2002), which is now in its fourth edition, but many others have appeared during the past 20 years (e.g., Zukowski-Faust, Johnson, & Templin, 2002; Rosen & Stoller, 1994; and Mikulecky, 1990).

Teaching Metacognitive Strategies

As interest in the teaching of strategies developed, many reading specialists and teachers discovered that simply teaching students a list of cognitive strategies for reading did not help every student to become a better reader. As it happens, successful cognition, or thinking, must be directed and monitored by higher levels of cognition called *metacognition*, or thinking about thinking. The issue is not just what strategies can be used and how to use them, but when to use them and for what purpose. In dealing with real texts, the issue is always what problems the text is creating for the reader and what strategies he or she might employ to address and hopefully solve these problems. More recent work on reading incorporates these insights.

In support of this approach, a number of research studies suggest that teaching reading strategies can have positive effects on the reading performance of second language learners. Carrell, Gajdusek, and Wise (1998) attempted to determine which of these studies met the criterion of teaching both cognitive and metacognitive strategies; they cite Carrell (1985) and Raymond (1993) as having fully met this criterion. Other studies of note include Carrell, Devine, and Eskey (1988), Kern (1989), and Zimmerman (1997) for the teaching of vocabulary.

Classroom Procedures: A Final Note

In addition to motivating students, successful L2 reading teachers do their best to facilitate reading for them. These two kinds of procedures are, it should be noted, complementary, since students who enjoy reading are more likely to read successfully, and students who read successfully are more likely to enjoy it.

Because no two classes are alike, however, it cannot be assumed that any reading teacher can know in advance what his or her students' major problems will be. That must be determined by interacting directly with a given group of readers as they read. Good second language reading teachers create, as noted, a new kind of literacy club for their students, sharing their own reading and responding to it as native speakers normally do. They also read with their students, making use of such simple protocols as asking students to paraphrase what they are reading or to speculate on where the text might be going in order to determine what their real problems are. Bernhardt (1998) makes a compelling case for this, and reminds the profession that teaching any kind of reading successfully most often requires a skillful and dedicated teacher as well as motivated and competent students. There are no magic approaches or methods for the teaching or learning of second language reading, but good teachers and students, working together, sometimes get the job done successfully.

NOTES

1. To the great loss of the applied linguistics community, David Eskey passed away in October 2002 after completing the first draft of this chapter. Thanks to Eleanor Black Eskey for materials used in the final revisions of the manuscript.
2. It has been noted, however, by Birch (2002) and others that L2 readers whose L1 does not have a Romanized alphabet can experience difficulties with orthographic and phonological correlations that can be taught.

REFERENCES

Aebersold, J., & Field, M. (1997). *From reader to reading teacher.* New York: Cambridge University Press.
Alderson, J. C. (2000). *Assessing reading.* Cambridge, UK: Cambridge University Press.
Allington, R. (2000). *What really matters for struggling reader.* London: Longman.
Anderson, N. J. (1999). *Exploring second language reading: Issues and strategies.* Boston, MA: Heinle & Heinle.
Benesch, S. (1993). ESL, ideology, and the politics of pragmatism. *TESOL Quarterly, 27*(4), 705–717.
Bensoussan, M., & Laufer, B. (1984). Lexical guessing in context in EFL reading comprehension. *Journal of Research in Reading, 7,* 15–32.
Bernhardt, E. (1991). *Reading development in a second language: Theoretical, empirical, and classroom perspectives.* Norwood, NJ: Ablex.
Bernhardt, E. B. (1998). Sociohistorical perspectives on language teaching in modern America. In H. Byrnes (Ed.), *Perspectives in research and scholarship in second language learning* (pp. 39–57). New York: Modern Language Association.
Bernhardt, E. B., & Kamil, M. L. (1995). Interpreting relationships between L1 and L2 reading: Consolidating the linguistic threshold and the linguistic interdependence hypotheses. *Applied Linguistics, 16* (1), 15–34.
Birch, B. (2002). *English L2 reading: Getting to the bottom.* Mahwah, NJ: Lawrence Erlbaum Associates.
Carrell, P. (1992). Awareness of text structure: Effects on recall. *Language Learning, 42,* 1–20.
Carrell, P. L. (1985). Facilitating ESL reading by teaching text structure. *TESOL Quarterly, 19*(4), 727–752.
Carrell, P. L. (2001). The influence of purpose for reading on second language reading: Reading procedural texts in ESL. *Reading in a Foreign Language, 13*(2), 220–251.
Carrell, P. L., Gajdusek, L., & Wise, T. (1998). Metacognition and EFL/ESL reading. *Instructional Science, 26,* 97–112.
Carrell, P., Devine, J., & Eskey, D. (1988). *Interactive approaches to second language reading.* New York: Cambridge University Press.
Cho, K.-S., & Krashen, S. (1994). Acquisition of vocabulary from the Sweet Valley Kids series: Adult ESL acquisition. *Journal of Reading, 37,* 662–667.
Clarke, M. (1980). The short circuit hypothesis of ESL reading: When language competence interferes with reading performance. *The Modern Language Journal, 64,* 114–124.

Cummins, J. (1984). *Bilingualism and special education: Issues in assessment and pedagogy.* Clevedon, UK: Multilingual Matters.

Day, R., & Bamford, J. (1998). *Extensive reading in the second language classroom.* New York: Cambridge University Press.

Day, R. (Ed.). (1993). *New ways in teaching reading.* Alexandria, VA: TESOL.

Elley, W., & Mangubhai, F. (1983). The impact of reading on second language learning. *Reading Research Quarterly 19,* 53–67.

Ellis, N. (1998). Emergentism: Connectionism and language learning. *Language Learning 48,* 31–64.

Favreau, M., & Segalowitz, N. S. (1983). Automatic and controlled processes in the first and second language reading of fluent bilinguals. *Memory and Cognition, 11*(6), 565–574.

Friere, P., & Macedo, D. (1987). *Literacy: Reading the word and the world.* South Hadley, MA: Bergin & Garvey.

Fries, C. (1945). *Teaching and learning English as a foreign language.* Ann Arbor: University of Michigan Press.

Fry, E. (1981). Graphical literacy. *Journal of Reading, 24,* 383–389.

Gee, J. (1990). *Social linguistics and literacies.* Bristol, PA: Falmer Press.

Gee, J. (2000). Discourse and sociocultural studies in reading. In M. L. Kamil, P. B. Mosenthal, P. D. Pearson, & R. Barr (Eds.), *Handbook of reading research, Vol III* (pp. 195–208). Mahwah, NJ: Lawrence Erlbaum Associates.

Geva, E., Wade-Woolley, L., & Shaney, M. (1993). The concurrent development of spelling and decoding in two different orthographies. *Journal of Reading Behavior, 25,* 383–406.

Gilbert, P. (1993). Narrative as gendered social practice: In search of different story lines for language research. *Linguistics and Education, 5,* 211–218.

Goodman, K. S. (1967). Reading as a psycholinguistic guessing game. *Journal of the Reading Specialist, 4,* 126–135.

Goodman, K. S. (1975). The reading process. In F. W. Gollash (Ed.), *Language and literacy: The selected writings of Kenneth Goodman* (pp. 5–16). London: Routledge & Kegan Paul.

Haynes, M., & Carr, T. (1990). Writing system background and second language reading: A component skills analysis of English reading by native speaker-readers of Chinese. In J. C. Alderson & A. H. Urquhart (Eds.), *Reading and its development: Component skills approaches* (pp. 375–421). New York: Academic Press.

Heath, S. B. (1983). *Ways with words: Language, life, and work in communities and classrooms.* New York: Cambridge University Press.

Huckin, T., Haynes, M., & Coady, J., (Eds.). (1993). *Second language reading and vocabulary learning.* Norwood, NJ: Ablex.

Hudson, T. (1982). The effects of induced schemata on the short circuit in L2 reading: Non-decoding factors in L2 reading performance. *Language Learning, 32,* 1–31.

Huey, E. B. (1908). *The psychology and pedagogy of reading. With a review of the history of reading and writing and of methods, texts, and hygiene in reading.* New York: Macmillan.

Kamil, M. L., & Lane, D. M. (1998). Researching the relationship between technology and literacy: An agenda for the 21st century. In D. Reinking, M. McKenna, L. D. Labbo, & R. Kieffer (Eds.), *Handbook of literacy and technology: Transformations in a post-typographic world* (pp. 323–342). Mahwah, NJ: Lawrence Erlbaum Associates.

Kamil, M. L., Intrator, S. M., & Kim, H. S. (2000). The effects of other technologies on literacy and literacy learning. In M. L. Kamil, P. B. Mosenthal, P. D. Pearson, & R. Barr (Eds.), *Handbook of reading research, Vol III* (pp. 771–788). Mahwah, NJ: Lawrence Erlbaum Associates.

Kamil, M., Mosenthal, P., Pearson, P. & Barr, R. (2000). *Handbook of reading research: Volume III.* Mahwah, NJ: Lawrence Erlbaum Associates.

Kaplan, R. B., & Baldauf Jr., R. B. (1997). *Language planning: From practice to theory.* Clevedon, UK: Multilingual Matters.

Kern, R. G. (1989). Second language reading strategy instruction: Its effects on comprehension and word inference ability. *The Modern Language Journal, 73,* 135–149.

Koda, K. (1989). The effects of transferred vocabulary knowledge on the development of L2 reading proficiency. *Foreign Language Annals, 22,* 529–540.

Krashen, S. (1993). *The power of reading.* Englewood, CO: Libraries Unlimited.

McFarland, K. P., & Stansell, J. C. (1993). Historical perspectives. In L. Patterson, C. M. Santa, K. G. Short, & K. Smith (Eds.), *Teachers are researchers: Reflection and action* (pp. 12–18). Portsmouth, NH: Heinemann.

Mikulecky, B. (1990). *A short course in teaching reading skills.* Reading, MA: Addison-Wesley.

Neuman, S. B., & McCormick, S. (Eds.). (1995). *Single subject experimental research: Applications for literacy.* Newark, DE: International Reading Association.

Nuttall, C. (1996). *Teaching reading skills in a foreign language.* Oxford: Heinemann.

Phillipson, R. (1992). *Linguistic imperialism.* Oxford, UK: Oxford University Press.

Pinker, S. (1994). *The language instinct.* New York: HarperCollins.

Pressley, M., & Afflerbach, P. (1995). *Verbal protocols of reading: The nature of constructively responsive reading.* Hillsdale, NJ: Lawrence Erlbaum Associates.

Raymond, P. M. (1993). The effects of structure strategy training on the recall of expository prose for university students reading French as a second language. *The Modern Language Journal, 77*(4), 445–458.

Riley, G. (1993). A story structure approach to narrative text comprehension. *Modern Language Journal, 77,* 417–430.

Robb, T. N., & Susser, B. (1989). Extensive reading versus skills building in an EFL context. *Reading in a Foreign Language, 5*, 239–251.

Rosen, N., & Stoller, F. (1994). *Javier arrives in the U.S.* Englewood Cliffs, NJ: Prentice-Hall.

Rumelhart, D. E. (1980). Schemata: The building blocks of cognition. In R. J. Spiro, B. C. Bruce, & W. F. Brewer (Eds.), *Theoretical issues in reading comprehension* (pp. 33–35). Hillsdale, NJ: Lawrence Erlbaum Associates.

Segalowitz, S., Segalowitz, N., & Wood, A. (1998). Assessing the development of automaticity in second language word recognition. *Applied Psycholinguistics, 19*, 53–67.

Shannon, P. (1996). Poverty, literacy, and politics: Living in the USA. *Journal of Literacy Research, 28*, 430–439.

Shaywitz, B. A., Pugh, K. R., Jenner, A. R., Fulbright, R. K., Fletcher, J. M., Gore, J. C., & Shaywitz, S. E. (2000). The neurobiology of reading and reading disability (dyslexia). In M. L. Kamil, P. B. Mosenthal, P. D. Pearson, & R. Barr (Eds.), *Handbook of reading research* (Vol. 3, pp. 229–249). Mahwah, NJ: Lawrence Erlbaum Associates.

Shohamy, E. (1984). Does the testing method make a difference? The case of reading comprehension. *Language Testing, 1*, 147–170.

Silberstein, S., Dobson, B., & Clarke, M. (2002). *Reader's choice* (4th ed.). Ann Arbor: University of Michigan Press.

Smith, F. (1973). *Psycholinguistics and reading.* New York: Holt, Rinehart & Winston.

Smith, F. (1975). *Comprehension and learning.* New York: Holt, Rinehart & Winston.

Smith, F. (1988). *Joining the literacy club.* Portsmouth, NH: Heinneman.

Sokal, A. (1996). Transgressing the boundaries: Toward a transformative hermeneutics of quantum gravity. *Social Text, 14*, 217–252.

Stanovich, K. E. (1980). Toward an interactive-compensatory model of individual differences in the development of reading fluency. *Reading Research Quarterly, 16*, 32–71.

Stanovich, K. E. (1991). Word recognition: Changing perspectives. In R. Barr, M. L. Kamil, P. Mosenthal, & P. D. Pearsen (Eds.), *Handbook of reading research,* (Vol. 2, pp. 418–452). New York: Longman.

Stanovich, K. E. (1992). Speculations on the causes and consequences of individual differences in early reading acquisition. In P. Gough, L. Ehri, & R. Treiman (Eds.), *Reading acquisition* (pp. 307–342). Hillsdale, NJ: Lawrence Erlbaum Associates.

Stevick, E. (1976). *Memory, meaning, and method.* Rowley, MA: Newbury House.

Street, B. (1984). *Literacy in theory and practice.* Cambridge, UK: Cambridge University Press.

Urquhart, A. H., & Weir, C. J. (1998). *Reading in a second language: Process, product, and practice.* New York: Longman.

Wardhaugh, R. (1977). *The contexts of language.* Cambridge, MA: Newbury House.

Weinberg, S. (1996). Sokal's hoax. *The New York Review of Books, Vol. XLIII, number 13* (August 8, 1996), 11–15.

Wolf, D. (1993). A comparison of assessment tasks used to measure FL reading comprehension. *Modern Language Journal, 77*, 473–489.

Zimmerman, C. B. (1997). Do reading and interactive vocabulary instruction make a difference?: An empirical study. *TESOL Quarterly, 31*, 121–140.

Zukowski-Faust, J., Johnston, S., & Templin, E. (2002). *Steps to academic reading* (3rd ed.). Boston, MA: Heinle & Heinle.

32

Teaching and Learning Vocabulary

I.S.P. Nation
Victoria University of Wellington, New Zealand

THE STATISTICAL NATURE OF ENGLISH VOCABULARY

The vocabulary learning task facing a learner of English is partly determined by the nature of vocabulary in general, and by the particular nature of English vocabulary. For well over 100 years, researchers into the frequency distribution of vocabulary have been aware that some words occur more frequently than others. If we take a long coherent written text and count the different words it contains and how often each one occurs, we see a pattern that is repeated in other kinds of texts. The following observations are typical.

- The most frequent word in a text, usually *the*, will account for about 6%–7% of the running words in the text.
- The ten most frequent words will account for about 25% of the running words in a text.
- The 100 most frequent words will account for about 50% of the running words in the text.
- The 1,000 most frequent words will account for at least 70%–80% of the running words in the text.

This pattern of initially very high coverage for the most frequent words and then a rapidly decreasing coverage for subsequent words is a very striking one. The perceptive scholar George Zipf (1949) attempted to explain this in one of his laws. In essence, Zipf's law says, "If we multiply the frequency of an item in a ranked frequency list of vocabulary by its rank on the frequency list, the result is a constant figure." This constant figure is typically around 10% of the total length of the corpus. Table 32.1 shows these figures for the most frequent lemmas in the 1,000,000 token Brown corpus (Francis & Kucera, 1982) at rank intervals of 10. The match is not perfect and there is clearly a decrease in the frequency times rank figure as we move to lower frequency items. Nevertheless, there is a pattern here. It is possible to make some observations based on this pattern.

TABLE 32.1

Ranked Frequency Figures and the Product of Rank Times Frequency from
the Francis & Kucera Count (1982)

Word	Rank	Frequency	Frequency × Rank
to	10	11,165	111,650
as	20	6,029	120,580
an	30	3,727	111,810
make	40	2,312	92,480
could	50	1,782	89,100
come	60	1,561	93,660
may	70	1,307	91,490
must	80	1,017	81,360
so	90	932	83,880
just	100	795	79,500

- Some words occur much more frequently than other words.
- In a ranked list, the frequency of items initially drops very quickly and then drops gradually.
- There is a small number of very frequent words and a very large number of low frequency words.
- If we want to separate high frequency from low frequency words, the dividing line will be arbitrary.

These observations have direct implications for course design for the teaching and learning of vocabulary.

- There is a group of between 1,500 and 2,000 high frequency words that are the most important vocabulary learning goal (West, 1953). These words are so frequently and widely used that they need to be well learned as quickly as possible. Because of their usefulness, they deserve all kinds of attention from teachers and learners.
- The low frequency words, of which there are thousands, do not deserve teaching time, but gradually need to be learned. The most effective way of dealing with them is for the learners to work on strategies for learning and coping with them. These strategies can be the focus of the teacher's efforts.

We have looked briefly at the statistical nature of English vocabulary and the broad implications of this for vocabulary learning. Now let us look at the origins and structure of English vocabulary with the same purpose of drawing implications for teaching and learning.

THE ETYMOLOGICAL NATURE OF ENGLISH VOCABULARY

The vocabulary of modern English largely comes from two major sources and this has a direct effect on the task facing a learner of English both as a first language or as a second language. Germanic languages, particularly Anglo-Saxon, are the main source of the high frequency words of English. According to Bird (1987), Germanic words make up 97% of the most frequent 100 words of English (for example, *the*, *all*, *have*, *time*, *say*), 57% of the first 1,000, 39% of the second 1,000, and around 36% of the remaining vocabulary. These words are the oldest words of English, are typically short, and combine with other words rather than prefixes or suffixes to refer to related ideas (lunch time, horse flesh, head of the school, back door). The other major source is Latin either directly through the influence of the church or indirectly through French. The single major historical event that established the influence of Latin through French was the Norman invasion of England in 1066. Latin-based words make up 3% of the first 100, 36% of the first 1,000 (for example, *research*, *company*, *information*, *social*, *important*), and 51% from the second 1,000 on. Typically these words are multisyllabic, have prefixes and suffixes and can make related words by adding prefixes and suffixes, and have some degree of formality about them. Often there are less formal Anglo-Saxon words that convey roughly the same idea, but with less formality or status (get–obtain; make–construct; be–exist; see–perceive). This type of contrast is well illustrated by the Academic Word List (Coxhead, 2000). The AWL is a list of 570 word families that occur reasonably frequently across a wide range of academic disciplines and that are not in the most frequent 2,000 words of English. The AWL covers about 10% of the words in academic texts. Over 90% of the words in the AWL come from French, Latin, or Greek. In academic texts a large number of these words can be replaced by Anglo-Saxon words. What is partly lost by this replacement is the air of precision and seriousness that the academic vocabulary conveys.

Having vocabulary from both Germanic and Latinate sources (and also Greek, although this makes up at most 6% of English vocabulary) complicates the learning of English. First, there is more vocabulary to learn. Second, words referring to the same general concept are not visibly related to each other. The classic examples are:

    sheep - mutton
    cows - beef
    pigs - pork.

Third, although Anglo-Saxon and Latinate words may refer to roughly the same ideas, they carry different status messages. Corson (1985, 1997) describes the Greco-Latin vocabulary of English as being a lexical bar (or barrier). In order to achieve in academic study, learners must cross this lexical bar by gaining control, both receptively and productively, of the Greco-Latin vocabulary of English. If they do not cross this bar they will be unlikely to succeed in academic study. According to Corson, this bar is difficult to cross because the Greco-Latin vocabulary is more difficult to process because the words are long and made up of prefixes, stems, and suffixes, because some native speakers feel that using this vocabulary is like "putting on airs," and because there needs to be considerable reading of formal language to meet and acquire this vocabulary.

Now that we have seen what English vocabulary is like, let us now look at what needs to be learned about it.

KNOWING A WORD

Table 32.2 lists various aspects of knowledge that are involved in knowing a word.

These aspects of knowledge fit into three groups: knowing the form of a word (its spelling, sound, and word parts); knowing the meaning of a word (linking its form and meaning, knowing a concept for the word and what it can refer to, and knowing what other words of related meaning it can be associated with); and knowing how a word is used (the grammar of the word including part of speech and the sentence patterns it fits into, collocates of the words, and whether the word is formal or

TABLE 32.2

What Is Involved in Knowing a Word

Form	spoken	R	What does the word sound like?
		P	How is the word pronounced?
	written	R	What does the word look like?
		P	How is the word written and spelled?
	word parts	R	What parts are recognizable in this word?
		P	What word parts are needed to express the meaning?
Meaning	form and meaning	R	What meaning does this word form signal?
		P	What word form can be used to express this meaning?
	concept and referents	R	What is included in the concept?
		P	What items can the concept refer to?
	associations	R	What other words does this make us think of?
		P	What other words could we use instead of this one?
Use	grammatical functions	R	In what patterns does the word occur?
		P	In what patterns must we use this word?
	collocations	R	What words or types of words occur with this one?
		P	What words or types of words must we use with this one?
	constraints on use	R	Where, when, and how often would we expect to meet this word?
	(register, frequency, etc.)	P	Where, when, and how often can we use this word?

Note. In column 3, R = receptive knowledge. P = productive knowledge. Adapted from Nation, 2001, p. 27.

informal, polite or rude, used mainly by children and so on, or has no restrictions on its use).

A substantial part of the difficulty of learning a word (its learning burden) depends on whether these aspects of an L2 word are similar for its L1 translation or are regular and predictable from already known L2 words of similar or related meaning (Nation, 1990, 1994). For example, a Japanese learner of English learning the term *ice cream* does not have a lot to learn because the concept is already familiar from first language experience; the form is very similar "aisu kurimu" because the Japanese word is a loan word from English, it is the same part of speech, and has no restrictions on its use. The differences in pronunciation may be a little interfering but are typical of changes that need to be made to loan words. Learning a word like *yacht* is more difficult. The spelling does not relate to L1 patterns and in English it is an irregularly spelled word. It is not difficult to pronounce and does not contain any prefixes or suffixes. Linking its meaning and form will require some effort unless it is a loan word, and learning its precise meaning may require learning a new concept. It is a regular countable noun and, if learners are familiar with the behavior of countable nouns in English, should not be difficult to learn.

Teachers can use an analysis of the learning burden of a word to guide their teaching of high frequency words. Such an analysis can help them focus on difficult aspects and help them draw attention to regular features of the word so that learners can see useful patterns.

Notice that each part of Table 32.2 is divided into receptive and productive knowledge. Receptive knowledge is sometimes called passive knowledge and is the kind of knowledge needed to deal with a word in listening and reading. Productive knowledge is sometimes called active knowledge and is the kind of knowledge needed to use a word in speaking and writing. Productive knowledge requires more learning than receptive knowledge (Ellis & Beaton, 1993).

These different kinds of knowledge require different kinds of teaching and learning, which we will now look at by seeing how vocabulary can be learned through listening, speaking, reading, and writing.

Vocabulary and Listening

The research on learning vocabulary through listening reveals a principle that holds true for all kinds of vocabulary learning—the more the teacher can help the learners give deliberate attention to particular words, the more likely these words are to be learned (Hulstijn, 2001). Although it has often been stated that learning best occurs through meaning-focused use—meeting words in context—this statement is not supported by research. In fact, the opposite is true. The more deliberate, de-contextualized attention a learner gives a word, the more likely it is to be learned. This research finding should not be interpreted as saying that words should not be learned in context. It is more usefully interpreted as saying that every course should involve some deliberate attention to vocabulary as well as opportunities to meet the words in meaning-focused use. Target vocabulary should be met in the four strands of learning through meaning-focused input, learning through meaning-focused output, learning through deliberate study, and learning through fluency-focused activities.

Elley (1989) found that vocabulary learning from listening to stories was positively affected if the story was interesting, comprehensible, and involved repetition, and if the teacher drew attention to some words by quickly providing a definition. There are several studies where learners have the opportunity to negotiate the meaning of unknown vocabulary either with the teacher (Ellis, Tanaka, & Yamazaki, 1994; Ellis, 1994, 1995; Ellis & Heimbach, 1997; Ellis & He, 1999), or with each other (Newton, 1995). Negotiation provides favorable conditions for learning, greatly increasing the likelihood that a word will be learned. Negotiation, which involves working out the meaning of a word through discussion, sets up all the conditions needed for effective learning: interest, understanding, repetition, deliberate attention, and generative use (the use of a word in a new context). Negotiation, however, takes time and takes time away from focus on the message of the text. Thus it is not possible for learners to negotiate every unfamiliar or partly unfamiliar item. Newton (1995) found that although negotiation usually resulted in learning, most learning occurred through the less certain procedure of simply putting the word in context without negotiation. This kind of meeting is less likely to result in learning but, because it is the more common default procedure with more likelihood of occurring, accounted for the bulk of the vocabulary learning. Thus, teachers should feel happy when they observe learners orally negotiating unknown words, but they should also realize that there will be a lot of other nonobservable learning taking place. The negotiation studies also show that a learner need not be an active negotiator in order to learn. Those who quietly observe negotiation and have a stake in the task seem to learn equally well (Stahl & Clark, 1987).

Although there is no clear research on this for listening, it is likely that there should not be more than one or two unknown words per 100 running words in order for unassisted learning from context to occur. To learn from listening, the unknown words need to occur in easily understood texts with a great amount of supportive context.

If the goal is listening fluency that will develop fluent access of known vocabulary, then the listening input should contain no unknown words and there should be some pressure to perform faster than usual. This can be done by hearing the same story several times with each retelling done at a slightly faster speed, and by listening to graded readers at levels below the level for learning from meaning-focused input. That is, learners who would usually read at Stage 4 in a graded reading series should be listening to develop fluency with stories read to them from readers at Stages 2 or 3.

When presenting listening material for learning through meaning-focused input, teachers should draw on a range of procedures for getting the learners to give deliberate attention to vocabulary. These include quickly giving definitions or translations of unknown words, encouraging learners to signal when they don't understand a word or part of the story, questioning learners on parts of the story as it is told, quickly noting words on the blackboard and indicating their related derived or inflected forms, and putting up a list of target vocabulary before the reading.

Vocabulary and Speaking

The vocabulary needed for listening and speaking tends to be smaller than the vocabulary needed for reading and writing. Part of the reason for this is that listening and speaking tend to be informal activities using colloquial language. This colloquial language consists largely of words within the first 2,000 words of English. A few of these words, like *hello, yeah, please, good-day* are largely limited to spoken language. In his study of text types, Biber (1989) found that in the text types of intimate interpersonal interaction and informational interpersonal interaction, the only written text was friendly letters; all the rest were spoken. Schonell, Meddleton, and Shaw's (1956) study of the oral vocabulary of the Australian worker found that the most frequent 1,000 words covered 94% of the running words, and the most frequent 2,000 words almost 99%. This contrasts with the most frequent 2000 words covering barely 80% of the running words in academic text (Coxhead, 2000).

We have seen how negotiation can be a means of setting up conditions for vocabulary learning in spoken activities. Newton's (1995) research showed that all the negotiated vocabulary occurred in the written input to the task, that is, the handout setting out the background, task, and procedure for the speaking activity. Observing learners doing speaking activities and noting what vocabulary is used and how it is used can help teachers get a good feel about how to design such tasks. The careful design of the input sheets can be a major factor influencing vocabulary learning from spoken activities.

Vocabulary learning can be made more deliberate, and thus more likely to occur if the focus of the activity is on a particular word. The following example, focusing on *registration*, comes from Nation and Hamilton-Jenkins (2000).

Group these jobs into those that you think require registration (like nursing) and those that do not.

teacher   doctor   shop assistant
lawyer   plumber   bus driver
cleaner   engineer   computer programmer

There are several activities for developing spoken fluency with vocabulary. The simplest of these involve hearing words like numbers, days of the week, months of the year, and names of objects and quickly responding by pointing to first language translations or representations of the words. For example, to practice fluency in listening to numbers, the learners can listen to numbers and quickly write or point to them in figures as in the following list.

1 2 3 4 5 6 7 8 9 10

Considerable repetition with increasing speed is needed to get real fluency. When listening fluency is good, then the learners act as the teacher and say the items while the teacher responds by pointing or writing.

The classic activity for developing spoken fluency is the 4/3/2 activity, which sets up the conditions typically needed to develop fluency of access to vocabulary. In the 4/3/2 activity the learners work in pairs. One member of each pair, A, is the speaker and the other, B, is the listener. A talks on a topic for 4 minutes while B listens and says nothing. Then the learners change partners and A gives exactly the same talk again to a new B but in only 3 minutes. Once again B simply listens and says nothing. Finally, the learners change partners again. A gives the same talk for the third time to a new partner B but in only 2 minutes. Thus, A has to give the same talk three times in a decreasing amount of time. After this, all the Bs become speakers and the As listeners and the same procedure is followed. Research on 4/3/2 shows that not only does speed of speaking increase from the 4-minute talk to the 2-minute talk, but there is also a decrease in errors and an increase in grammatical complexity (Arevart & Nation, 1991).

Vocabulary and Reading

As with the skills of listening and speaking, reading can be an opportunity for learning through meaning-focused use, deliberate vocabulary learning, and fluency development. A distinction is often made between extensive reading and intensive reading. Extensive reading involves reading for pleasure and reading large quantities of material. From a vocabulary perspective, extensive reading can be a way to learn new vocabulary through meaning-focused input, and to establish, enrich, and develop fluency with known vocabulary. Where the goal is to learn new vocabulary, this unknown vocabulary should appear at a density not more than 1 unknown word in every 50 running words (Hu & Nation, 2000). It should also be repeated with an optimal space between the repetitions so that previous knowledge is still retained and yet there is some degree of novelty to the repetition. Ideally, many of the repetitions should involve some degree of generative use, that is, the word occurs in a new context. For most learners of English, these conditions are most likely to occur in the numerous series of graded or simplified readers, where books are written within a limited vocabulary usually with about six vocabulary stages such as 300 words, 700 words, 1,000 words, 1,500 words, 2,000 words, and 2,500 words. Thus at Stage 1, learners at an elementary level (learners with a vocabulary of around 300 words) can read substantial texts and be familiar with most of the words used in these texts. Descriptions and evaluations of the books and the various series can be found in Day and Bamford (1998) and Hill (1997). Nation and Wang's (1999) research suggests that learners should be reading at least 1 graded reader every 1-2 weeks, and be reading at least 20 graded readers a year.

There is some prejudice against graded readers, largely by teachers, because they feel that graded readers are not authentic in that they involve controlled or adapted text rather than text intended for native speakers. However, these texts should be seen as authentic in that they provide conditions under which learners at all levels of proficiency can read with a degree of comprehension, ease, and enjoyment that is near that of a native speaker reading unsimplified text. Without graded readers, reading for a second language learner would be one continuous struggle against an overwhelming vocabulary level (Nation & Deweerdt, 2001). Teachers need to be familiar with the various series of graded readers and the procedures for setting up and running an effective extensive reading program.

Intensive reading usually involves the interactive reading of a text that contains a fairly heavy vocabulary load. That is, learners are familiar with less than 95% of the running words in the text. Traditionally, intensive reading involves the teacher explaining a text to the learners often using the first language for the explanation. There are other types of intensive reading including Palincsar and Brown's (1986) reciprocal reading, Scott et al.'s (1984) standard reading exercise, and learners reading individually with the help of a dictionary. Vocabulary learning during intensive reading fits into the strand of language-focused learning (Nation, 2001) where learners pay deliberate attention to vocabulary. There are various vocabulary aids and exercise types that are used in intensive reading. These include preteaching of vocabulary, glossing, matching words in the text with definitions provided at the end of the text, word part building and analysis, and finding collocations. Nation (2001, pp. 98–108) has an extensive list of these.

There are important vocabulary coping and learning strategies that can be first approached through reading. These are guessing the meaning of unknown words from context clues, using word cards to learn new vocabulary met in reading, using word parts to help words stick in memory, and using dictionaries to find the meanings of new words and to enrich knowledge of previously met words. We will look at these strategies in detail later.

Developing fluency in reading can be done very effectively through the use of speed reading texts. Typically, these are texts around 500–1,000 words long that contain no unknown vocabulary and which are accompanied by comprehension questions. These texts are read under timed conditions and the speed of reading in words per minute and the comprehension score are noted on charts. Most learners are expected to double their reading speed after 3–4 weeks' practice, reading four or five texts a week. It is usually not difficult for learners to increase their reading speed because initially they tend to read very slowly at speeds around 100 words per minute. Untrained native speakers can read at 250 words per minute and it is possible with practice to reach speeds around 500 words per minute. Speed reading courses encourage fluent access to vocabulary. The conditions needed for fluency development are (1) no unfamiliar language features including no unknown vocabulary in the text, (2) a focus on the message of the text, (3) some pressure to perform at a higher than normal speed, and (4) quantity of such practice. These conditions may also be met by getting learners to read graded readers that are below their normal level. That is, a learner who is reading a Stage 4 graded reader for meaning-focused vocabulary growth where 98% of the running words are already known, should be reading a Stage 2 or 3 reader for fluency development where 100% of the running words are known.

Vocabulary and Writing

Studies have shown that there is a relationship between richness of vocabulary in writing, the learners' level of proficiency, and raters' assessment of the quality of the writing. There does however seem to be a considerable lapse of time before items that are learned receptively become a part of learners' productive use in writing. Corson's

(1995) work on the lexical bar suggests that it is important for learners to be able to display their knowledge of academic vocabulary in writing to show that they are members of the academic community.

Just as it is possible to design speaking activities to help learners focus on and use target vocabulary, so it is possible to design writing activities that help items in the input to the writing task become a part of the written output. This is likely to be most effective if the items focused on are already part of the learners' receptive vocabulary. Linked skills activities can be a major means of bringing receptive vocabulary into productive use.

A linked skills activity consists of about three activities that build on each other in a sequence and involve a mixture of listening, speaking, reading or writing. In linked skills activities aimed at writing, the writing activity will be the final part of the sequence. For example, a reading, speaking, and writing linked skill sequence could be arranged in the following way: (1) The learners read a text on a topic like family violence, (2) they then form small groups and discuss what they have read, guided by some discussion questions prepared by the teacher or by following a set format of questions, and (3) after discussing, they then work together to produce a written report of the results of their discussion. If the topic is a difficult one, or if learners' proficiency is low, step 2, the discussion, could be carried out in the first language. Research (Lameta-Tufuga, 1994) has shown that discussion in the first language can result in better performance in the final task in the second language, partly because learners truly get to grip with the ideas, and the necessary second language vocabulary gets clarified and set in a helpful context during the first language discussion.

The Dictogloss activity (Wajnryb, 1988) is a linked skills activity where learners listen to a text, take notes while they listen, work together in small groups to reconstruct the text, and then compare their text with the original.

Activities that directly focus on vocabulary can encourage the use of the vocabulary in later writing, but research indicates that preteaching has to be substantial before it affects the following task (Graves, 1986).

Linked skills tasks encourage the development of writing fluency, largely because by the time the learners do the final writing task, they are well in control of the language and ideas that they have to deal with. They are thus able to perform at a higher level than normal because of this preparation, and this is one of the conditions necessary for fluency development.

Vocabulary Strategies

There are four major vocabulary learning and coping strategies that need to be worked on until learners are able to use them with confidence and ease. This means that each strategy needs to be studied, practiced with feedback, and developed to a high level of fluency. Typically this will involve working on the strategy for several weeks for a few minutes several times a week. The strategies deserve such time and effort because they enable learners to deal with the thousands of low frequency words that they will meet in their use of English. After learners know the high frequency words of the language, the teacher's main focus should be on strategy development. Strategy development, however, should start while the learners are working on high frequency vocabulary.

Guessing from Context.   The most important strategy is guessing the meaning of unknown words from context clues. Some researchers do not like to use the term "guessing" and prefer a term like "inferring" because the process should be systematic and focused on a range of available clues. It is most convenient to develop the strategy through reading and there are several important prerequisites if guessing is going to be successful. The learners must have developed some skill in reading and should read a lot. Ninety-eight percent of the running words in the texts that are used for guessing should be already familiar to the learners. This means that there will be a substantial amount of comprehensible supportive context for each unfamiliar word, on average about 50 familiar words. If these prerequisites are satisfied, then training in guessing can have useful effects. Training can focus on the linguistic clues available for guessing—the part of speech of the word, its immediate context, and its wider context of conjunction relationships—and on the background knowledge clues. Because the linguistic clues are more generalizable, these should get more attention, but successful guessing depends on a combination of a language item and a message focus. Initially guessing may be slow, but the aim is to reach a level of skill where guessing does not disrupt the flow of reading.

Learning from Word Cards.   Rote learning of second language words and their first language translations has long been out of favor in language teaching. However, there is a very substantial amount of research to show that such learning is very efficient and effective and that there are useful guidelines to follow to optimize such learning. It is important that this direct learning supports and is supported by opportunities to meet and use words in context and to develop fluency in using the words. The four strands of learning from meaning-focused input, deliberate study (of which learning from word cards is a part), learning from meaning-focused output, and fluency development should be equally present in a course, each occupying about the same amount of course time.

The learning from word card strategy involves learners in making small cards about 1.5 inches (4 cm) by 1.2 inches (3 cm) and writing useful vocabulary taken from lists, reading, or lessons on one side and the first language translation on the other side of the card. Phrases may be written as well as words. Other information can be added to the card, but in general it is best to keep the cards simple. Some dictionaries, the COBUILD dictionary and the *Longman Dictionary of Contemporary English*, mark high frequency words in the dictionary and learners should initially focus on these. The learners should carry a pack of about 50 cards around with them held together by a rubber band and when they have a free moment, for example while traveling on the bus or train or waiting for someone, they quickly go through the cards trying to recall the meaning of each word and turning the card over when they cannot in order to see the meaning. Learning is most effective if the following guidelines are followed.

1. Try to retrieve the meaning of the word before turning the card over to look at the translation. This retrieval is the factor that is important for learning.
2. Space the repetitions so that going through the cards is not concentrated in an hour of study, but is spread a few minutes at a time across the day and week. Ideally the repetitions should become increasingly spaced, eventually with intervals of a month or more between repetitions.
3. Keep changing the order of the cards in the pack. This avoids serial learning where one word becomes the cue for the following word. It also allows words requiring more attention to be placed at the beginning of the pack and others that are easily learned to be placed in other packs or later in the pack.
4. Say the word to yourself when looking at the card. This helps words enter long-term memory.

5. Use L1 translations when making the cards. These are preferable to L2 definitions because they are easier to understand. Several pieces of research have shown the superiority of L1 translations over L2 definitions (Nation, 2001, p. 304).
6. Where a word is difficult to learn, make sure you have a clear idea of its pronunciation, and use mnemonic tricks like the keyword technique (Nation, 2001, pp. 311–314) or breaking the word into prefix, stem, and suffix to see related forms and the meaning of the parts. Putting the word in an illustrative sentence may also make it easier to learn.
7. Avoid putting related words together in the same pack of cards. Opposites, synonyms, and members of the same lexical set like names of fruit, months of the year, or things in the kitchen should not be learned at the same time because they tend to interfere with each other and make learning more difficult (Nation, 2000).
8. When the words have been learned receptively (see the L2 word recall the L1 translation) they should then be learned productively (see the L1 translation and recall the L2 word). Productive learning is more difficult than receptive learning. If time is short and there is a need to choose between receptive and productive learning, it is more effective to do productive learning because this includes the knowledge needed for receptive use as well as for productive use.

Learning from word cards is a very effective way to quickly boost vocabulary size. Learners should make their own cards because making the cards is the first important meeting with the words that allows later retrieval. It is not unusual to be able to correctly retrieve the meaning of about 70% of the words in a pack after one run through the pack.

Word cards are much more preferable than vocabulary notebooks. Vocabulary notebooks have the disadvantages of presenting the word and its meaning together and thus not providing an opportunity for retrieval. The words are in a fixed sequence and thus flexibility of attention is lost.

Learners need training and encouragement in the use of word cards and this can take the form of rules to learn, demonstrations of learning, display of cards, and reports on successes and problems in learning.

Using Word Parts.   As we have seen, a large proportion of English words come from French, Latin, or Greek. As a result many English words have prefixes and suffixes, and have stems that appear in other words, for example, *transport, porter, importation, deportation, important, reporter, supportive, export.* In general, the suffixes mostly signal the part of speech of the word, although some like *-less, -ful,* and *-able* have strong lexical meanings. The prefixes often add a strong lexical meaning to the word, sometimes more than the stems do.

There have been several frequency counts of prefixes that show that a small number of prefixes occur very frequently while the remainder are of rather low frequency. Bauer and Nation (1993) created a graded list of affixes based on the criteria of frequency (the number of different words containing the affix), regularity (how much the spoken or written form of the stem or affix changes when they are joined), productivity (how much the affix is still used to create new words), and predictability (the number and relative frequency of different meanings of the affix i.e., how easy it is to predict that a particular form will have a particular meaning). This list can be used as a rough syllabus for dealing with affixes.

Level 1
A different form is a different word. Capitalization is ignored.

Level 2
Regularly inflected words are part of the same family. The inflectional categories are: plural; third person singular present tense; past tense; past participle; *-ing*; comparative; superlative; possessive.

Level 3
-able, -er, -ish, -less, -ly, -ness, -th, -y, non-, un-, all with restricted uses.

Level 4
-al, -ation, -ess, -ful, -ism, -ist, -ity, -ize, -ment, -ous, in-, all with restricted uses.

Level 5
-age (leakage), -al (arrival), -ally (idiotically), -an (American), -ance (clearance), -ant (consultant), -ary (revolutionary), -atory (confirmatory), -dom (kingdom; officialdom), -eer (black marketeer), -en (wooden), -en (widen), -ence (emergence), -ent (absorbent), -ery (bakery; trickery), -ese (Japanese; officialese), -esque (picturesque), -ette (usherette; roomette), -hood (childhood), -i (Israeli), -ian (phonetician; Johnsonian), -ite (Paisleyite; also chemical meaning), -let (coverlet), -ling (duckling), -ly (leisurely), -most (topmost), -ory (contradictory), -ship (studentship), -ward (homeward), -ways (crossways), -wise (endwise; discussion-wise), anti- (anti-inflation), ante- (anteroom), arch- (archbishop), bi- (biplane), circum- (circumnavigate), counter- (counter attack), en- (encage; enslave), ex- (ex-president), fore- (forename), hyper- (hyperactive), inter- (inter-African, interweave), mid- (midweek), mis- (misfit), neo- (neo-colonialism), post- (post-date), pro- (pro-British), semi- (semi-automatic), sub- (subclassify; subterranean), un- (untie; unburden).

Level 6
-able, -ee, -ic, -ify, -ion, -ist, -ition, -ive, -th, -y, pre-, re-.

Level 7
Classical roots and affixes

The main value in learning word parts is to use them as a kind of mnemonic for new vocabulary. This works in a way similar to the keyword technique in that the new word is broken into parts, then its meaning is rephrased to contain the meaning of the parts. This then relates the new knowledge of the word form and its meaning to the old knowledge of the word parts and their meaning. So, the word *progression* would be broken into *pro-* (forward), *-gress-* (to move), *-ion* (noun) and have its meaning phrased as "a movement forward."

Using this word part strategy involves learning a relatively small number of prefixes and suffixes (about 20–40), being able to recognize them in words, and being able to relate their meanings to the meaning of the word with the help of a dictionary. Like all the vocabulary strategies we have looked at, this strategy deserves teaching time because of the large number of words it can be applied to.

Using a Dictionary. The guessing from context strategy can provide access to the meaning of a word in a given context. One of the steps in such a strategy can be checking that a guess is correct by looking up the word in a dictionary. The guessing from context strategy can also be a way of acquiring new vocabulary. Dictionary use may also have this goal, especially if the learner is able to make use of the various kinds of information in a dictionary. Learners' dictionaries like the (COBUILD English dictionary, like the *Longman Dictionary of Contemporary English*, and the *Oxford Advanced Learner's Dictionary*) contain a wealth of information on the range of aspects of what is involved in knowing a word. In addition, they attempt to present this information in as clear and as accessible a way as possible, through the use of controlled defining vocabularies, numerous examples of words in use, and information about related words.

Research on dictionary use, however, shows that most learners make limited use of this information and are largely unfamiliar with how to make use of the information provided. Training in the use of dictionaries can have benefits both for receptive and productive vocabulary knowledge.

Because most defining vocabularies are around 2,000 words, learners will need to have control of the high frequency words of English before making use of monolingual dictionaries. Before this, bilingual and bilingualized dictionaries need to be used, and training in dictionary use can begin with these.

Vocabulary Testing

The need to focus on the high frequency vocabulary has often been mentioned in this survey of vocabulary learning and teaching. There are now several tests that help teachers discover whether their learners know the high frequency words of English and to what extent the low frequency vocabulary is known.

The Vocabulary Levels Test (Schmitt, Schmitt, & Clapham, 2001: Schmitt, 2000; Nation, 2001) uses the following format:

1   business
2   clock   ____part of a house
3   horse   ____animal with four legs
4   pencil   ____something used for writing
5   shoe
6   wall

It is divided into five levels: the 2,000 word level (high frequency words), the 3,000 word level (low frequency), the 5,000 word level (low frequency), the AWL level (high frequency for learners with academic purposes), and the 10,000 word level (low frequency). Each level contains ten blocks of items like the one illustrated here and thus tests 30 words. It tests receptive knowledge and does not require the learners to have a precise knowledge of the meaning of each word because the distractors are not related in meaning. It measures whether there is some knowledge of the word to build on. There is also a productive levels test (Laufer & Nation, 1999) that uses items like those shown next. It is also divided into the same five levels as the Vocabulary Levels Test.

They need to spend less on <u>adminis</u>____ and more on production.
He saw an ang____ from Heaven.
The entire <u>he</u>____ of goats was killed.
Two old men were sitting on a park <u>ben</u>____ and talking.
She always showed <u>char</u>____ toward those who needed help.

The tests are diagnostic tests intended to help teachers find out whether their learners know the high frequency words, and how many low frequency words they know. This is important because the way teachers deal with high frequency and low frequency words should differ considerably.

There is now a growing body of research on vocabulary testing and an excellent book (Read, 2000) devoted solely to this topic. A common finding in vocabulary testing research is that if learners are tested on the same words using different test formats, the results correlate at .7. This indicates that while there is a substantial amount of shared variance, there are also substantial differences between the tests. Different formats tap different aspects of vocabulary knowledge with different degrees of sensitivity. This has implications for choosing vocabulary tests and for measuring vocabulary learning in experimental research.

When choosing a test to use with learners, it is important to think clearly about what aspects of knowledge need to be measured (see Table 32.2) and what kind of knowledge (receptive/productive, precise knowledge/partial knowledge) is most suitable and fair to measure (Joe, Nation, & Newton, 1996).

For example, when designing a weekly test to encourage vocabulary learning and to see what is remembered of the new words met during the week, the teacher should be aware that learning a word is a long-term cumulative process and only partial knowledge could be expected after one or two meetings. This partial knowledge, however, is a very important first step toward gaining full control of the word. The most appropriate kind of test in these circumstances is one that focuses on a very central aspect of word knowledge, knowing the meaning of a word, and that allows the learners to make use of partial knowledge. A receptive multiple-choice test using first language synonyms, or a matching test with three or four words and six or seven simply expressed definitions, could be a sensible choice.

When measuring vocabulary learning in experimental research, it is very useful to test the same words in several different ways. For example, in an experiment investigating the amount of vocabulary learning from graded reading, if there were three tests of the same words, say a multiple-choice test, an interview test, and a collocation test, then the strength of knowledge of each word could be determined and different types and strengths of knowledge could be related to the different ways the words occurred in the texts.

Vocabulary teaching is usually seen as teaching words. A major aim of this review has been to show that there is much more to it than this. Vocabulary teaching should have different focuses when learners move from high frequency to low frequency vocabulary learning. For the teacher this means a move from a focus on particular high frequency words to a focus on strategies. For the learners, the change will not be so noticeable as learners should continue to expand their vocabulary. Vocabulary teaching must also be seen as ensuring that there is a balance of opportunities to learn from each of the strands of meaning-focused input, language-focused learning, meaning-focused output, and fluency development. Neglect of one or more of these strands will mean that learning is not efficiently done and that vocabulary is unlikely to be ready for use. Vocabulary learning needs to occur within a well-planned vocabulary program.

REFERENCES

Arevart, S., & Nation, I.S.P. (1991). Fluency improvement in a second language. *RELC Journal, 22*, 84–94.

Bauer, L., & Nation, I.S.P. (1993). Word families. *International Journal of Lexicography, 6*, 253–279.

Biber, D. (1989). A typology of English texts. *Linguistics, 27*, 3–43.

Bird, N. (1987). Words, lemmas, and frequency lists: old problems and new challenges (Parts 1 & 2). *Almanakh, 6*, 42–50.

Corson, D. J. (1985). *The Lexical Bar*. Oxford: Pergamon.

Corson, D. J. (1995). *Using English Words*. Dordrecht, The Netherlands: Kluwer.

Corson, D. J. (1997). The learning and use of academic English words. *Language Learning, 47*, 671–718.

Coxhead, A. (2000). A new academic word list. *TESOL Quarterly 34*, 2, 213–238.

Day, R. R., & Bamford, J. (1998). *Extensive reading in the second language classroom*. Cambridge, UK: Cambridge University Press.

Elley, W. B. (1989). Vocabulary acquisition from listening to stories. *Reading Research Quarterly, 24*, 174–187.

Ellis, N. C., & Beaton, A. (1993). Factors affecting foreign language vocabulary: Imagery keyword mediators and phonological short-term memory. *Quarterly Journal of Experimental Psychology, 46A*, 533–558.

Ellis, R. (1994). Factors in the incidental acquisition of second language vocabulary from oral input: A review essay. *Applied Language Learning, 5*, 1–32.

Ellis, R. (1995). Modified oral input and the acquisition of word meanings. *Applied Linguistics, 16*, 409–441.

Ellis, R., & He X. (1999). The roles of modified input and output in the incidental acquisition of word meanings. *Studies in Second Language Acquisition, 21*, 285–301.

Ellis, R., & Heimbach, R. (1997). Bugs and birds: Children's acquisition of second language vocabulary through interaction. *System, 25*, 247–259.

Ellis, R., Tanaka, Y., & Yamazaki, A. (1994). Classroom interaction, comprehension, and the acquisition of L2 word meanings. *Language Learning, 44*, 449–491.

Francis, W. N., & Kucera, H. (1982). *Frequency analysis of English usage*. Boston: Houghton Mifflin.

Graves, M. F. (1986). Vocabulary learning and instruction. *Review of Research in Education, 13*, 49–89.

Hill, D. R. (1997). Survey review: Graded readers. *ELT Journal, 51*, 57–81.

Hu, M., & Nation, I.S.P. (2000). Vocabulary density and reading comprehension. *Reading in a Foreign Language, 13*(1), 403–430.

Hulstijn, J. H. (2001). Intentional and incidental second language vocabulary learning: A reappraisal of elaboration, rehearsal, and automaticity. In P. Robinson (Ed.), *Cognition and second language instruction* (pp. 258–286). Cambridge, UK: Cambridge University Press.

Joe, A., Nation, P., & Newton, J. (1996). Vocabulary learning and speaking activities. *English Teaching Forum, 34*(1), 2–7.

Lameta-Tufuga, E. U. (1994). *Using the Samoan language for academic learning tasks*. Unpublished MA thesis, Victoria University of Wellington.

Laufer, B., & Nation, P. (1999). A vocabulary size test of controlled productive ability. *Language Testing, 16*, 36–55.

Nation, I. S. P. (1990). *Teaching and learning vocabulary*. Rowley, MA: *Newbury House*.

Nation, I. S. P. (Ed.), (1994). *New ways in teaching vocabulary*. Alexandria, VA: TESOL.

Nation, I. S. P. (2000). Learning vocabulary in lexical sets: Dangers and guidelines. *TESOL Journal, 9*(2), 6–10.

Nation, I. S. P. (2001). *Learning vocabulary in another language*. Cambridge, UK: Cambridge University Press.

Nation, I. S. P. & Deweerdt, J. (2001). A defence of simplification. *Prospect, 16*(3), 55–67.

Nation, P., & Hamilton-Jenkins, A. (2000). Using communicative tasks to teach vocabulary. *Guidelines, 22*(2), 15–19.

Nation, P., & Wang, K. (1999). Graded readers and vocabulary. *Reading in Foreign Language, 12*, 355–380.

Newton, J. (1995). Task-based interaction and incidental vocabulary learning: A case study. *Second Language Research, 11*, 159–177.

Palincsar, A. S., & Brown, A. L. (1986). Interactive teaching to promote independent learning from text. *The Reading Teacher, 40*, 771–777.

Read, J. (2000). *Assessing vocabulary*. Cambridge, UK: Cambridge University Press.

Schmitt, N. (2000). *Vocabulary in language teaching*. Cambridge, UK: Cambridge University Press.

Schmitt, N., Schmitt, D., & Clapham, C. (2001). Developing and exploring the behavior of two new versions of the vocabulary levels test. *Language Testing, 18*(1), 55–88.

Schonell, F. J., Meddleton, I. G., & Shaw, B. A. (1956). *A study of the oral vocabulary of adults*. Brisbane: University of Queensland Press.

Scott, M., Carioni, L., Zanatta, M., Bayer, E., & Quintanilha, T. (1984). Using a 'standard exercise' in teaching reading comprehension. *English Language Teaching Journal, 38*(2), 114–120.

Stahl, S. A., & Clark, C. H. (1987). The effects of participatory expectations in classroom discussion on the learning of science vocabulary. *American Educational Research Journal, 24*, 541–545.

Wajnryb, R. (1988). The dicto-gloss method of language teaching: A text-based communications approach to grammar. *English Teaching Forum, 26*(3), 35–38.

West, M. (1953). *A general service list of English words*. London: Longman.

Zipf, G. (1949). *Human behavior and the principle of least effort: An introduction to human ecology*. New York: Hafner.

33

Taking Stock of Research and Pedagogy in L2 Writing

John S. Hedgcock
Monterey Institute of International Studies

Like facets of second language (L2) learning examined elsewhere in this volume, L2 writing entails a spectrum of theoretical, empirical, and pedagogical developments that are difficult to synthesize in a single, coherent survey. Silva (1993) noted that, even as recently as the early 1990s, the discipline lacked a "comprehensive theory" (p. 668). L2 writing has nonetheless come into its own as a field of inquiry, generating diverse research and scholarship. This chapter examines several of the field's central underpinnings, drawing on developments in applied linguistics, TESL/TEFL, cognitive psychology, and composition studies that have led to the dynamic, interdisciplinary nature of L2 writing studies. The discussion likewise explores trends that have engaged L2 writing experts in recent decades, among them the conceptualization of L2 writing as a specialized literacy, the interplay among literate skills, advances in pedagogy, studies of expert and peer response, and the reshaping of assessment practices.

Through this review, I hope to highlight ways in which L2 writing, as a community of practice (Lave & Wenger, 1991), has become diversified in terms of its goals, knowledge sources, and methods of inquiry. As in many emergent disciplines, the growing pains experienced by the field have been characterized by no shortage of self-conscious questioning and polemics (Benesch, 1993, 2001; Leki, 2000; Pennycook, 2001). Two significant and related influences are sure to affect the focus of research and pedagogy as the L2 writing community shapes its future agenda. The first of these involves social constructionism, whereas the second concerns an increasingly critical approach to scholarship and pedagogy among the field's experts.

SURVEYING THE DISCIPLINARY LANDSCAPE IN L2 WRITING RESEARCH AND PEDAGOGY

Unlike research in L1 composition and literacy, with its long and well-documented history (Berlin, 1987), L2 writing research has a comparatively short biography. With the exception of research in contrastive rhetoric and ESL, scant findings were reported in the literature prior to 1980. Leki (2000) echoed this assessment, noting that "relatively little writing research appears in the main applied linguistics periodicals" (p. 101). Despite its embryonic nature, L2 writing research merits serious attention as a vital area of inquiry in L2 learning and teaching. To establish principles for formulating a coherent research agenda and instructional paradigm, Silva (1990) proposed that the following "basic elements" needed to be featured prominently in the research agenda: (1) the writer, (2) the L1 reader, (3) the L2 text, (4) the contexts for L2 writing, and (5) the interaction of these elements (pp. 18–19).

Given the increasing influence of socioculturally oriented approaches to L2 literacy, I propose merging Silva's (1990) second and fourth elements and expanding the scope of several others, as follows:

- The L2 writer (including his or her personal knowledge, language proficiency, academic skills, attitudes, motivation, cultural orientation, educational needs, and so on).
- The L2 writer's texts (as described in terms of genre, purpose, rhetorical mode, discourse structure, morphosyntactic patterns, lexical features, and so forth).
- The contexts for L2 writing (educational, social, cultural, political, economic, situational, and physical), including the L2 writer's audience (e.g., L2 teachers, instructors in academic disciplines, peer readers, disciplinary peers, correspondents, employers, and so on).
- The dynamic interaction among these components in authentic contexts for writing (including classrooms, the academic community, the workplace, and so forth).

These primary themes will provide a framework for the major sections of this chapter, which will examine theoretical and empirical strands, as well as pedagogical issues that have taken center stage in the professional dialogue in recent years.

Focus on the L2 Writer

With increasing systematicity, L2 writing researchers and educators have focused more squarely on L2 writers as complex individuals who approach writing in unique ways. Appropriately, the unique features of L2 writers and their relationships with their target communities have been examined by a number of authorities (e.g., Bräuer, 2000; Ferris & Hedgcock, 1998; Leki, 1992; Raimes, 1998; Silva, 1993). L2 professionals have long recognized the sometimes extraordinary literacy demands placed on L2 writers. L1 compositionists have likewise begun to recognize individual and collective variation among L2 writers, whose needs as language learners and novice writers set them apart in terms of their linguistic, sociocultural, and educational needs (Cooper & Odell, 1999). In line with trends in language socialization research (e.g., Norton, 2000), the issue of the writer's identity has become an influential theme in L2 writing, focusing researchers' attention on individual and collective factors such as L1 and L2 development, ethnicity, race, class, gender, power, and social affiliation patterns (Benesch, 2001; Clark & Ivanic, 1997; Ivanic, 1998).

A significant implication of writer-based research is that L2 writers represent a distinct population from monolingual writers. Scholarship has likewise suggested that L1-based methods should not be applied uncritically to L2 writing research and pedagogy (Cumming, 1998; Silva, 1993). L2 writers' implicit and explicit linguistic knowledge, educational backgrounds, multilingual literacy skills, and strategic abilities may necessitate instructional practices geared sensitively to the needs of L2 populations (Leki, 1995a, 2000). Raimes (1985) argued that L2 writers might need "more of everything" in terms of heuristics, content, writing practice, and feedback than their mother tongue counterparts (p. 250). Moreover, some authorities have proposed that L2 writers should be taught by professionals who have expertise in L2 learning and who are equipped to devote "time and attention across the board to strategic, rhetorical, and linguistic concerns" (Silva, 1993, p. 670). Although the pedagogical imperative in L2 writing is certainly more complex than it was in the mid-1980s, Raimes' appeal for the profession's recognition of the unique needs of L2 writers is more prescient than ever.

Focus on Text: Contrastive Rhetoric and L2 Writing

L2 writers' texts are likewise inherently distinct from texts produced by mother tongue writers (Leki, 1991). Following on Kaplan's (1966) pioneering study, contrastive rhetoricians have carefully investigated "the organization of discourse paradigms and rhetorical structure of text in languages other than English" (Hinkel, 2002, p. 5). Contrastive rhetoric (CR) similarly examines "the effects of NNSs' L1 rhetorical construction of textual frameworks on the texts that NNSs produce in ESL" (p. 5). With its primary focus on writers' *products*, CR research has ignited lively discussions of the putative influences of L2 writers' mother tongues, L1 rhetorical patterns, and educational traditions on the construction of their written products. Arguably one of the more controversial strands of L2 writing research, CR has contributed markedly to our understanding of rhetorical patterns in written text, the frequency of rhetorical features across genres, and patterns of text construction across languages. CR has similarly informed comparative descriptions of the interactions among L1 and L2 written genres, morphosyntactic properties, lexical range, textual devices for building coherence and cohesion, and the role of audience in diverse rhetorical traditions (Connor & Kaplan, 1987; Panetta, 2001).

In her detailed synthesis of the CR literature, Connor (1996) described ways in which CR has shaped current knowledge about discursive paradigms in non-anglophone rhetorical traditions. Connor situated CR as a domain of applied linguistics that has "expanded across interdisciplinary boundaries" to encompass theories of linguistic relativity, rhetoric, text linguistics, discourse types and genres, literacy, and translation (p. 7). Connor characterized written discourse as embedded in culture and inextricably linked with conceptions of literacy. However, lacking a truly unified theory, CR continues to rely on divergent research methods and sometimes disparate data sources (Connor, 1996; Hinkel, 2002; Leki, 1991; Panetta, 2001).

Consequently, CR findings can be difficult to compare, and their interpretation has been subject to serious criticism. Some, for example, have asserted that CR research is ethnocentric (if not anglocentric) and culturally deterministic (Leki, 1997, 2000; Raimes, 1998). Others have charged that CR represents L2 texts as static, essentializes L2 writers and their home cultures, and neglects to address the importance of audience in L2 writing (Kubota, 1999; Scollon, 1997). Nonetheless, CR research has not only expanded the knowledge base about the nature of text and written discourse but also informed L2 instruction by suggesting principles for guiding L2 writers toward structuring their texts to meet the expectations of L2 readers (Kirkpatrick, 1997).

Socioeducational Contexts for L2 Writing

A key premise of CR and related disciplines such as text linguistics and corpus analysis holds that all written communication is embedded in communities of readers and writers (Connor, 1996; Panetta, 2001). These fields have generated quantitative and qualitative studies of particular groups of novice writers and their unique needs. This research has effectively demonstrated that all texts, text types, and genres transacted within communities of writers reflect the purposes and values of those communities (Berkenkotter & Huckin, 1995; Johns, 1997, 2002b; Swales, 1990, 1998). Although much exploration of context remains to be done, contextually oriented inquiry has, in fact, profoundly influenced the character, content, and practices of L2 writing research and instruction.

Social Constructionism, Genre Studies, and ESP/EAP.   Current-traditional approaches to composition pedagogy entailed the imitation and reproduction of rhetorical patterns or modes (e.g., exposition, illustration, comparison, classification, argumentation, and so on) based on literary models and student-generated samples. L2 writing instruction designed along these lines was also characterized by a focus on morphosyntactic and lexical accuracy (Kroll, 2001; Silva, 1990). In the 1970s, however, ESL writing instruction at the postsecondary level "began to turn away from a linguistic approach and look to L1 perspectives for insights" (Leki, 2000, p. 100). Although traditional, product-oriented approaches have hardly become extinct in L1 and L2 composition classrooms, L2 writing researchers and scholars have developed an understanding of the inherently social nature of literacy development—writing skills, in particular.

The acceptance of social constructionist, or socioliterate, views of L1 and L2 literacy development has precipitated considerable progress in theory building and classroom instruction. Johns (1997) defined and synthesized approaches to the social construction of discourses, maintaining that, according to socioliterate principles, "literacies are acquired through exposure to discourses from a variety of social contexts" (p. 14). By means of this exposure, which may entail an array of locally designed instructional practices, learners construct their own genre theories: "In this view, the role of learners is an active one: Students are constantly involved in research into texts, roles, and contexts and into the strategies that they employ in completing literacy tasks within specific situations" (Johns, 1997, p. 15). By acknowledging this socially-informed, discursively-based perspective on writing instruction, L2 professionals have realized that effective writing instruction must enable students to become readers and writers of the genres and text types associated with the Discourses (Gee, 1996, 1999), communities of practice (Lave & Wenger, 1991), and literacy clubs (Smith, 1988) that they aspire to join. These Discourses include educational, professional, and vocational communities comprising all manner of expert and novice practitioners.

As L2 writing and literacy studies have "become more interested in literacy as social practice" (Leki, 2000, p. 101), inquiry and instructional practice over the last two decades have identified L1 and L2 writing activities as components of a complex process of literacy development. The cultures and social contexts in which various literacies emerge inevitably influence these developmental processes (Berkenkotter & Huckin, 1995; Cook-Gumperz, 1986; K. Hyland, 2000, 2002; Schleppegrell & Columbi, 2002; Spack, 1997). Thus, literacy experts no longer view the emergence of literacy as a unitary psychocognitive process that unfolds independent of sociocultural context: "Different sorts of literacy skills . . . develop to serve the needs of each social/cultural group" (Grabe & Kaplan, 1996, p. 14).

Against the backdrop of social constructionist and socioliterate views, some L2 writing experts have suggested that L2 writing instruction may produce optimal results when it focuses on genre-specific rhetorical features, audience expectations, and tools for improving lexicogrammatical variety and accuracy (Byrd & Reid, 1998; Ferris, 2002; Ferris & Hedgcock, 1998). As a construct and a practical instrument, genre has achieved a prominent position in the field of L2 writing. In her appraisal of the uses and misuses of genre analysis, Hyon (1996) referred to genre as "a popular framework for analyzing the form and function of nonliterary discourse" and "a tool for developing educational practices in fields such as rhetoric, composition studies, professional writing, linguistics, and English for specific purposes (ESP)" (p. 693). Echoing Hyon's (1996) portrayal of the value of genre studies in the ESL/EFL context, Johns (2002c) identified eight principles that suggest directions for L2 writing theory, research, and educational practice:

- "Texts are socially constructed" (p. 12). Community and culture strongly influence text processing and production.
- Texts are purposeful, their functions being determined by the context and community.
- Some genres enjoy more prestige than others.
- Community constraints may govern textual conventions, and novice writers may need to work within these boundaries.
- The grammar of expository texts and the associated metadiscourse serve collective and individual purposes within a genre and context.
- Communities and contexts regulate the features of texts (e.g., content, argumentation style, and so on).
- "Genres are ideologically driven" (p. 13). All texts reflect the values and purposes of those who produce and process them.
- The linguistic features of texts and the associated metadiscourse "should never be taught separately from rhetorical considerations," as expert writers select and use language purposefully (p. 13).

In this socially grounded framework, genre serves as a vehicle for understanding the formal properties of L1 and L2 texts, as well as the value systems and "ways of being" (Geertz, 1983) aligned with them (Paltridge, 1997, 2001). Genres "provide ways for getting things done among readers and writers whose cultures and communities mold their literacy practices" (Johns, 1997, p. 15). Consequently, L2 writing professionals who work in English for Special Purposes (ESP) and English for Academic Purposes (EAP) have embraced the commonsense precept that, in order to become proficient in using and producing particular genres, one must learn to understand, analyze, reproduce, and even critique those genres.

ESP, originally a pedagogical approach designed for ESL and EFL learners seeking to develop English language skills rather quickly, had pragmatic aims. ESP professionals emphasized registers, morphosyntactic features, and rhetorical patterns in particular disciplines, as in the English for Science and Technology (EST) tradition (Johns & Dudley-Evans, 1991; Robinson, 1992; Swales, 1985). Investigators embracing a functional-systemic approach gradually shifted their research focus from discrete features of register (e.g., lexical repetition, pronoun anaphora, prepositional phrases, and so on) to more global discursive patterns, including the arrangement of information in texts and rhetorical variation across text domains (Bhatia, 1993; Halliday & Martin, 1993; Martin, 1992).

EAP has taken a somewhat different direction, given its mission to equip ESL and EFL writers with more broadly defined academic literacy skills necessary for undergraduate and graduate study in English-medium institutions. For example, EAP curricula in North American universities are often designed to prepare students for required composition courses (Harklau, Losey, & Siegel, 1999). Accordingly, EAP courses aim to guide students through the instructional challenges that English-speaking students confront (Dudley-Evans & St. John, 1998). The usual purpose of EAP instruction "is to enable students to write better not for EAP writing classes but for academic purposes" (Leki & Carson, 1997, p. 39). Nonetheless, critics have identified disjunctions between the tasks and texts required in EAP courses and those required in academic disciplines. EAP writing courses may not, in fact, demand the same genres and text types required in the sciences, social sciences, and humanities. Leki and Carson (1994, 1997) reported that EAP writing prompts largely involved personal topics leading to self-expressive text forms. Meanwhile, assignments in academic disciplines primarily demanded writing about source texts, with expressive writing representing but a small fraction of the total.

Genre knowledge, of course, is not an instructional aim in itself; rather, it serves as a vehicle for engaging with core content. Early ESP and EAP models focused on rhetorical and grammatical descriptions of discipline-specific texts (e.g., laboratory reports, bibliographic summaries, political briefs, memos, analytic essays, and so forth), with a view toward enabling writers to imitate textual prototypes. In contrast, socioliterate and genre-based instructional models aim to represent texts and genres as socially constructed artifacts exemplifying dynamic interactions among participants within (and across) disciplinary communities (Berkenkotter & Huckin, 1995; Johns, 1997; Swales, 1990). Rather than training novice writers simply to reproduce "recognisable genres," genuine genre-based literacy instruction views writing "as an act of communication" in which literacy constitutes "a joint journey through ideas" (Littlewood, 1995, p. 433). Those who have successfully investigated and experimented with socioliterate and genre-based writing pedagogies likewise stress the instability and fluidity of genres, which can only be fully understood when linked to the social practices of experts and novices who write in them (Freedman & Medway, 1994; Johns, 2002a, 2002c; Ramanathan & Kaplan, 2000).

Critical Pedagogy and L2 Writing. With a number of scholars appealing to "Freirean notions of liberatory literacy practices" (Grabe & Kaplan, 1996, p. 32), the ethical and political dimensions of L2 writing instruction, including socioliterate models and ESP/EAP, have come under careful scrutiny in recent years (cf. Freire, 1970, 1985, 1994; Freire & Macedo, 1987). Zamel (1993) argued that academic literacy instruction should enable writers to comprehend, analyze, and negotiate the demands of academic disciplines. Because academic writing varies widely across disciplines, L2 writers may find themselves underequipped to investigate this variation and to produce writing deemed successful by disciplinary faculty. Zamel thus recommended the adoption of a critical view of "academic" genres as presented in writing courses and the disciplines, encouraging professionals and students to question the discourse and its power relations. Benesch (2001) and others have similarly challenged assumptions about the genuine educational "needs" of L2 writers—and how they are served by teachers and institutions—in the context of economic and political influences on literacy education at the tertiary level.

In line with a growing number of L2 writing experts, Belcher and Braine (1995) pointed out that we should no longer understand academic literacy instruction as "neutral, value-free, and nonexclusionary" (p. xiii). L2 writing scholarship has thus begun to address issues of critical pedagogy, including critical needs analysis (Benesch, 1993, 1996; Leki, 2000), critical discourse analysis (Fairclough, 1995), critical writing about academic genres (Benesch, 2001; K. Hyland, 2002), the complexity of text appropriation and plagiarism (F. Hyland, 2000; Pennycook, 1996), race and class issues (Canagarajah, 1993; Vandrick, 1995), gender (in)equality (Belcher, 1997), and identity (Norton, 1997). A major thread in applications of critical pedagogy to L2 literacy education stems from the charge that social constructionist approaches overlook "sociopolitical issues affecting life in and outside of academic settings" (Benesch, 2001, p. xv). Whereas ESP/EAP and socioliterate approaches maintain that writing instruction always has social purposes, critical pedagogy challenges the precept that those purposes are necessarily beneficial to novice writers.

Toward Multidimensionality and Interdisciplinarity

The L2 writing literature reveals progress toward developing a comprehensive framework for understanding L2 writers, L2 texts, and the socioeducational contexts of L2 writing (see Silva, Brice, & Reichelt, 1999). The field unquestionably needs extensive, in-depth research on writers, their strategies, their processes, their perceptions of discourse communities, and the influences of writing instruction. The preceding review nonetheless implies progress, albeit uneven, toward a broadly based portrayal of the complexity of L2 writing processes, a situation that Pennycook (1997) described as a positive "pluralisation of knowledge" (p. 263).

An imperative of L2 research and instructional practice should entail promoting a deeper, broader appreciation of the complex, multilayered relationships among the variables that drive L2 writers, L2 teachers, literate communities, and educational institutions. Grabe and Kaplan (1996) formulated three generalizations to summarize the state of the art in L2 writing as of the mid-1990s: (1) Research findings are often contradictory; (2) Numerous outcomes and interpretations reflect anticipated findings and coincide with L1 findings; (3) Advances in L2 writing research will partly depend on "carefully developed studies and research designs" and "more carefully controlled research situations" (p. 143). I would argue that these global assessments aptly characterize the state of the art at the beginning of the 21st century.

Conscious of its role in shaping theory and practice, the discipline has identified salient issues of concern to researchers, policymakers, practitioners, and students (Leki, 2000; Smoke, 1998; Tannacito, 1995). The preceding discussion surveys themes of interest and urgency in L2 writing; the following section touches on empirical and practical issues that have gained prominence in the field's professional agenda. Before shifting to a treatment of pedagogical praxis and innovation, I would like to suggest that L2 writing professionals stand to benefit from establishing inter- and crossdisciplinary alliances as a means of invigorating dialogue and deepening awareness of how much we have yet to learn about L2 writers, their struggles, and the complexity of their written products. The divergent directions taken by applied linguists and compositionists (cf. Leki, 2000) could possibly lead the field's participants back toward converging interests. L2 writing may, indeed, lack a unified set of purposes. However, singleness of mind and unity of mission are perhaps neither likely nor desirable (Hedgcock, 2002).

Silva, Leki, and Carson (1997) maintained that L2 writing could be fixed somewhere near "the intersection of second language studies and composition studies" (p. 399). In a similar appraisal of disciplinary boundaries, Matsuda (1999) called for enhanced interaction among TESL/TEFL professionals and composition specialists, noting that "until fairly recently, discussions of [ESL] issues in composition studies have been few and far between " (p. 699). I would tentatively concur with Matsuda in disfavoring a merger. Such an alliance would be impractical, given the vast differences in orientation and agenda between the applied linguistics/TESL/TEFL/FL constituencies on the one hand and L1 composition communities on the other. Furthermore, as a community of practice, L2 writing stands to gain from a plurality of voices and the insights of diverse empirical and pedagogical traditions.

L2 WRITING INSTRUCTION: INNOVATIONS AND FUTURE DIRECTIONS

In light of socially and contextually grounded views that recognize multiple literacies, L2 writing research and pedagogy have extended their boundaries to include cognitive and linguistic skills previously viewed as only marginally relevant to composition instruction. Among the proficiencies now associated with developing academic, professional, and vocational literacies, reading represents perhaps the most important skill area to have been systematically examined by researchers concerned with the acquisition of L2 literacy. Ferris and Hedgcock (1998) observed that empirical findings supporting "strong connections between reading ability and writing performance have led . . . researchers to infer that efficient reading skills lay a foundation for the growth of writing proficiency . . . " (p. 34). Belcher and Hirvela's (2001) volume brought together studies of reading-writing links in L2 literacy, at the same time addressing the influences of L1 literacy skills on the development of L2 abilities. In his state-of-the-art review of L2 reading-writing connections, Grabe (2001) addressed five literacy interactions: "reading to learn, writing to learn, reading to improve writing, writing to improve reading, and reading and writing together for better learning" (p. 15). Thus grounded in the view that L2 writing must be situated with respect to models of literacy, the discussion will now address instructional issues that have gained prominence in the recent professional dialogue and that are likely to inform L2 composition instruction and teacher education in the near future: process-oriented pedagogies, peer response, expert (teacher) feedback, error treatment, and L2 writing assessment.

Process-Oriented Writing Instruction

Instructional approaches in L2 composition have in some respects paralleled developments in L1 composition. In its early days (roughly the mid-1960s), L2 writing instruction emphasized the production of well-formed sentences. Influenced largely by audiolingualism, composition pedagogy served mainly to reinforce oral patterns and to test grammatical knowledge. The writing curriculum typically included controlled compositions designed to give writers practice with selected morphosyntactic patterns. Also product-oriented, the current-traditional model featured the production of connected discourse and the arrangement of sentences into paragraphs based on prescribed templates. Writing tasks included the imitation of selected rhetorical patterns (e.g., exposition, classification, comparison, argumentation, and so forth) based on models (Berlin, 1987).

Still "alive and well in L1 writing instruction" (Grabe & Kaplan, 1996, p. 31), current-traditional approaches frequently characterize the teaching of writing in many L2 settings. However, process-oriented pedagogies are increasingly pervasive in the North American educational milieu, including ESL settings, though they are certainly not widespread in EFL environments. Emig's (1971) pioneering study of Grade 12 students' composing procedures is often cited as the first to reveal that text construction processes did not correspond to the linearity of traditional and current-traditional models. Emig discovered that successful writers seldom followed a straightforward, cumulative path in creating texts, an observation that led to significant changes in how L1 composition was taught and eventually to innovations in L2 writing instruction. Whereas insights into writing processes have had a profound impact on L1 and L2 composition theory and practice, no singular "process pedagogy" resulted from this paradigm shift. I have thus deliberately selected the term "process-oriented" to describe current instructional models. Expressionist views (e.g., Elbow, 1981, 1994; Zamel, 1982, 1983) and cognitivist models in composition theory (e.g., Bereiter & Scardamalia, 1987; Flower, 1989; Manchón-Ruiz, 1997), for example, have led to the formulation of a range of methods, procedures, and practices that can all be characterized as promoting "process writing" (Ferris & Hedgcock, 1998; Kroll, 2001).

We can nonetheless identify core characteristics of process-oriented pedagogies, which reflect the premise that composing involves the management of numerous structural and rhetorical systems, with expository and argumentative prose requiring the greatest complexity (Grabe & Kaplan, 1996). In contrast to the current-traditional approach, process-oriented pedagogies are marked by the following features, among others:

- Discovery and articulation of writers' authorial voices.
- Free writing, journaling, and private writing activities designed to enhance writers' fluency, creativity, and exploration of source texts.

- Localization of writing processes and texts in authentic contexts to develop writers' sense of audience and reader expectations.
- Constructing purposeful tasks that engage writers and promote their investment in creating meaningful texts.
- Modeling and monitoring of invention, prewriting, and revision strategies.
- Recursive practices such as multidrafting, which demonstrate that writing for an authentic audience is often a nonlinear, multidimensional process.
- Formative feedback from real readers in peer response workshops, student-teacher conferences, collaborative writing projects, and so on.
- Provision of meaningful content for writing tasks, with a corresponding emphasis on representing ideas, rather than solely on producing grammatically accurate prose.

It has become almost axiomatic that L2 writing instruction should be solidly grounded in what writers "actually do as they write" (Raimes, 1991, p. 409). In addition to pointing toward the legitimacy of cognitively and socially informed instructional options, "the writing process perspective has captured certain important truths about language" (Grabe & Kaplan, 1996, p. 87). At the same time, we should avoid the presupposition that process approaches represent "a wholly positive innovation" (p. 87). That is, the principles and practices of process writing are not always compatible with the cultural, philosophical, and educational orientations of all educational settings or institutions.

Peer Response

A prevalent practice in process-oriented writing instruction, peer response is embraced by many L1 and L2 practitioners and theorists. In their theoretically oriented yet practical guide on peer response, Liu and Hansen (2002) characterized peer response as "the use of learners as sources of information and interactants" for one another, with the purpose of guiding learners to "assume roles and responsibilities normally taken on by a . . . trained teacher, tutor, or editor in commenting on and critiquing . . . drafts in both written and oral formats" (p. 1). In peer groups, novice writers collaborate to generate ideas, exchange texts, and construct feedback on the content and form of written drafts. Peer response proponents emphasize the importance of valuing diversity and cooperative inquiry, as well as the positive affect and learner-centeredness associated with peer interaction. Nonetheless, classroom practitioners sometimes report that student writers (particularly novices for whom L2 writing essentially constitutes a form of language practice) resist peer review, strongly preferring "expert," teacher feedback (Ferris, 1995, 1997; Hedgcock & Lefkowitz, 1996). Empirical findings now strongly suggest that, to produce pedagogically valuable results, peer response processes "must be modeled, taught, and controlled if it is to be valuable" (Kroll, 2001, p. 228).

Expert Response

Along with peer response, expert teacher feedback processes and their effectiveness have ignited interesting and spirited exchanges among L2 writing experts, particularly in the last decade. L2 writing research has consequently produced a growing corpus of quantitative and qualitative studies of teacher response behaviors, teacher-written comments and corrections, novice writers' perceptions of teacher feedback, writers' feedback incorporation processes, and the formal development of writers' texts as a result of teacher intervention. We can divide the theme of expert response into two broad categories: formative feedback and error feedback.

A complement to error feedback and grammatical correction, formative feedback primarily aims to provide writers with between-draft written or oral commentary to promote subsequent revisions. The role of expert intervention in L2 writing has become extremely important because process-oriented pedagogies feature multidrafting as a fundamental aspect of syllabus design and classroom practice and thus rely on this important form of input. Like peer feedback, teacher intervention can have a strong impact on the quality of revised texts (Conrad & Goldstein, 1999; Ferris, 2003). However, studies have shown that expert feedback may not convert to intake or long-term uptake. Furthermore, expert feedback may not necessarily improve text quality or develop writers' autonomous revision skills (F. Hyland, 2000). Ferris et al. (1997), for example, claimed that reliable and comparable investigations of L2 teacher response were "surprisingly rare" (p. 157). A global insight offered by this research is that the effects of expert feedback depend on writers' proficiency levels, their educational needs and expectations, curricular and institutional constraints, the nature of writing tasks, the focus of teacher commentary, and learner training (Ferris, 2002, 2003; Ferris & Hedgcock, 1998).

The common wisdom that teachers' marks and corrections are noticed and processed by student writers has come under careful scrutiny among experts on both sides of the error feedback/correction debate. In his critical review of L2 error treatment research, Truscott (1996) proposed that there was "no evidence" favoring grammar correction in L2 writing instruction, boldly asserting that "correction is harmful rather than simply ineffective" and that "grammar correction should be abandoned," in light of the putative absence of "valid reasons" for continuing the practice (p. 360). Ferris (1999) responded to Truscott's controversial thesis by acknowledging the latter's informed reservations concerning the inadequacy and impracticality of conventional correction systems. However, Ferris described Truscott's (1996) appeals as "premature and overly strong" (p. 1), taking him to task for presenting "limited, dated, incomplete, and inconclusive evidence" to attack a "pedagogical practice that is. . . highly valued by students" and on which "many thoughtful teachers spend a great deal of time and mental energy" (p. 9). In his riposte, Truscott (1999) held his ground by reasserting that correction is "in general, a bad idea" (p. 121), while supporting Ferris' (1999) call for strengthening the error treatment research agenda. Given the state of the error treatment controversy, conclusions regarding the impact of form-focused feedback in L2 writing may be a long way off. Nonetheless, Ferris (2002, 2003) summarized and evaluated numerous studies of teacher intervention, observing that the expressiveness and formal accuracy of L2 writers' texts can, indeed, be improved through well-constructed teacher commentary.

L2 Writing Assessment

The quality, quantity, frequency, and timing of expert feedback in L2 writing exemplify several of the evaluative purposes of formative feedback and error treatment, issues that are connected to performance and proficiency assessment. As an instructional procedure at the core of an important research effort, summative writing assessment should perhaps be distinguished from formative feedback, as summative appraisals are often used by educational agencies and institutions for purposes such as admissions, placement, and exit screening. Because L2 writing represents a "worthwhile enterprise in and of itself," practitioners and researchers now recognize the "ever greater demand for valid and reliable ways to test writing ability, both for classroom use and as a predictor of future professional or academic success" (Weigle, 2002, p. 1). The expanding body of books and articles related to writing assessment, as well as the 1994 debut of the journal, *Assessing Writing*, attest to the prominent role played by assessment in the field.

Research on the construction, deployment, scoring, validation, and revision of large-scale instruments such as the Test of English as a Foreign Language (TOEFL) writing component (formerly the Test of Written English, or TWE) has demonstrated that measuring student writers' performance fairly and meaningfully requires meticulous attention to an array of linguistic, rhetorical, and psychocognitive operations (Cumming, Kantor, & Powers, 2002; Hamp-Lyons & Kroll, 1997). In addition to identifying principles underlying equitable measurement tools, experts have emphasized that informative writing assessments must be situated with respect to their contexts and functions. Weigle's (2002) review of recent advances in L2 writing research identified seven key questions concerning the design and implementation of assessment tools:

- What are we trying to test?
- Why do we want to test writing ability?
- Who are our test takers?
- Who will score the tests, and what criteria ... will be used?
- Who will use the information that our test provides?
- What are the constraints ... that limit the amount and kind of information we can collect about test takers' writing ability?
- What do we need to know about testing to make our test valid and reliable? (p. 2)

In response to inquiry into large-scale and classroom assessment practices, the perils and pitfalls of evaluating students' texts have become increasingly apparent (Cumming, 1990; Hamp-Lyons, 1991). Kroll (1998), for example, underscored the complexity of assessing the writing performance and proficiency of ESL and EFL writers, stressing the overwhelming evidence that "writing abilities develop in interaction with other language skills" (p. 219). Linguistic accuracy serves as an influential, and therefore problematic, formal dimension known to influence raters' perceptions of writing quality (Chiang, 1999; Wolfe-Quintero, Inagaki, & Kim, 1998). Further complicating the task of appraising student writing is the variation seen across tasks and texts (Connor & Mbaye, 2002; Reid & Kroll, 1995; Way, Joiner, & Seaman, 2000), as well as reader expectations and raters' complex (and often biased) decision-making processes (Cumming, Kantor, & Powers, 2002; Hamp-Lyons & Mathias, 1994; Weigle, 1999). Leki (1995b) observed that a text judged as "good" in one situation may not be "successful for all circumstances." In fact, "different contexts impose different, even contradictory, constraints on writers" (p. 24). Furthermore, a single writing sample (e.g., a timed in-class essay or a research paper) can only represent a single performance; thus, it may not fairly or fully reflect a writer's progress or range of abilities. Purves (1992) brought this point home in his comparison of traditional writing assessments to sporting competitions: Like a novice writer undertaking a summative writing assessment (e.g., a placement test or the TOEFL writing component), an athlete succeeds or fails based on an evaluation of a single performance on a single occasion—not on a longitudinal appraisal of his or her record over time on an array of tasks (Hamp-Lyons & Condon, 2000; White, 1994, 1995).

Such commonsense insights and criticisms, coupled with scrupulous empirical studies of numerous assessment variables, have led practitioners and researchers to raise serious concerns about both reliability and validity—particularly construct validity—in measuring L2 writing performance. According to Hamp-Lyons and Kroll (1996), conventional wisdom holds that "no test can be more valid than it is reliable; if scores are not stable and consistent then they are essentially meaningless and cannot be valid" (p. 65). Nonetheless, they also noted that "the knife cuts both ways: If a test is not valid, there is no point in its being reliable since it is not testing any behavior of interest" (p. 65). The complex synergy between reliability and validity has generated intense discussion and inquiry in the writing assessment community, where experts continually express reservations regarding the stability and consistency of scoring procedures, particularly those deployed by raters using holistic scales (Connor & Mbaye, 2002; Cumming, 1990). Yet, as Cumming, Kantor, and Powers (2002) pointed out, little research has precisely described what evaluators "attend to when they score compositions and, in particular, how such assessments correspond to students' actual proficiency in writing in a second language." As a result, "most holistic and other analytic rating scales lack firm empirical substantiation" (p. 68).

Systematic inquiry into these crucial relationships is well under way; meanwhile, methodologists and curriculum specialists have situated assessment as fundamental to the instructional process (e.g., Alderson, Clapham, & Wall, 1995; Bailey, 1998). Ferris and Hedgcock (1998) maintained that "writing assessment is pedagogical in the sense that, when reliable and valid, its outcomes inform writers in ways that will directly and indirectly promote their progress" (p. 227). In the context of process pedagogies and the increased emphasis on authenticity in L2 literacy instruction, Cohen (2001) effectively summed up the assessor's dilemma: "Perhaps the main thing to be said about the testing of written expression is that it is a poor substitute for repeated samplings of a learner's writing ability while not under the pressure of an exam situation." Indeed, he wrote, process approaches to L2 composition suggest that "it is unnatural for a learner to write a draft of a composition and submit it for a grade" (p. 534).

In view of these contradictions, assessment experts have recognized the lack of face and construct validity in traditional forms of direct writing assessment. One can find consensus that instruments must be situated in their contexts before their effectiveness can be measured: "Only when we know what we are seeking to discover can we claim that a particular kind of assessment is appropriate..." (White, 1995, p. 34). In addition to constructing suitable instruments that coincide with their contexts and functions, valid instruments must reflect fundamental measurement precepts. To remedy the problems identified by Cohen (2001), to promote the interdependence between valid assessment and meaningful writing instruction, and to match assessment practices with genuine purposes, the field has moved toward "changing the assessment paradigm" through alternative assessment (Hamp-Lyons & Condon, 2000, p. 7).

The writing portfolio is perhaps the standard-bearing alternative instrument in L2 composition assessment (Ferris & Hedgcock, 1998; Kroll, 1998; Weigle, 2002). A writing portfolio consists of multiple samples of student writing that demonstrate performance on multiple tasks. A portfolio presents a collection "that is a subset of a larger archive. Theoretically, the archive is the whole of a student's work, but more practically and more frequently, it is a subset of writing completed in a class, a program, a school" (Yancey, 1992, p. 86). Although U.S. educators introduced portfolios in the 1970s, the "current explosion in portfolio-based writing assessment" can be traced to the mid-1980s (Hamp-Lyons & Condon, 2000, p. 15). Because portfolios "have spread like wildfire" and so many K-12 and tertiary institutions have created and adapted portfolio systems, "an incredibly broad range is found" (Hamp-Lyons & Condon, 2000, p. 15).

Due in part to this variation, assessment experts have discouraged instructors from embracing portfolio assessment uncritically. Although referring primarily to trends in L1 composition, Elbow's (1996) observation concerning alternative assessment applies equally well to L2 writing instruction: "Portfolios are not perfect: They suffer from being a fad and thus are sometimes used in ill-considered or degraded ways. But they represent a huge improvement over assessment based on single samples of writing" (p. 120). To rectify flaws in portfolio designs and assessment procedures, the L1 and L2 composition communities have produced a considerable body of empirical and critical work aimed at strengthening portfolio assessment (Calfee & Perfumo, 1996; Hamp-Lyons, 1991; Hamp-Lyons & Condon, 2000; Weigle, 2002; White, Lutz, & Kamusikiri, 1996). A significant outcome of this work has been the formulation of clear, useful criteria for developing portfolio systems and for specifying the actual substance of a portfolio document. In their comprehensive book, Hamp-Lyons and Condon (2000) identified the following characteristics as crucial to constructing and implementing an effective portfolio instrument: context, range, context richness, delayed evaluation, selection, student-centered control, reflection and self-assessment, growth along specific parameters, and development over time. These principles in some respects distill the best practices of portfolio-based assessment of L2 writing as now reflected in the impressive body of theoretical and practical resources on the topic. Of course, considerable progress remains to be made in perfecting portfolio assessment before it becomes widely adopted in foreign and second language education.

SUMMARY AND FUTURE DIRECTIONS

As suggested in my prefatory comments, a chief purpose of this chapter was to trace dimensions of L2 writing that reflect the discipline's diversification and growth as a community of practice. With a research agenda that explicitly features the L2 writer, L2 texts, contexts for L2 writing, L2 writers' disciplines, and the dynamic interaction of these components in authentic contexts, the field has achieved a fuller understanding of the diverse population of learners and the written products they generate. Cognitively, socially, and culturally based research strands have in numerous respects complemented formal traditions in empirical writing research. Social constructionism and genre analysis have demonstrated that texts and their forms are most meaningfully described with reference to the sociocultural contexts in which they emerge and evolve. This productive interplay between research paradigms has led to a realization that researchers and practitioners need to understand the value systems driving writers and their texts.

Notwithstanding these promising developments, a curious gap in the L2 writing literature is worth examining and addressing. It is perplexing that the procedural dimensions of day-to-day classroom writing instruction are so rarely examined in a profession dedicated to teaching. With a number of exceptions (e.g., Ferris & Hedgcock, 1998; Kroll, 2001; Leki, 1992; Raimes, 1985, 1998), the L2 literature offers a dearth of extensive discussion of, and explicit guidelines for, the practices and processes of *teaching* L2 writing. Instructional activities such as feedback techniques, needs analysis, and assessment have received welcome and appreciated treatment. Nonetheless, the nuts-and-bolts aspects of planning and delivering instruction are topics worthy of more extensive discussion and scrutiny. Few sources are available to assist classroom teachers in developing curricula, constructing syllabi, designing lessons, devising assignments, creating effective teaching materials, and perfecting classroom techniques such as presenting information, facilitating student interaction, and managing student activities. Given the inevitable growth of the L2 writer population and the consequent need to prepare teachers who can serve their needs, it is incumbent upon the profession to develop practical tools for guiding effective instruction.

As empirical inquiry in L2 writing has broadened and become more self-aware, critical, and socioculturally grounded, pedagogical practices have similarly gravitated toward a more sociocognitive orientation in how instruction is planned, delivered, and evaluated. That is not to suggest that the L2 writing profession will not continue to suffer from an identity crisis due to its sometimes awkward positionality vis-à-vis applied linguistics, TESOL/TEFL, foreign language education, and the L1 composition/rhetoric community. However, leaders in the field seem to have taken discernible steps toward establishing the discipline's role and purposes with more confidence by drawing systematically and reflexively on educational, intellectual, and empirical traditions that can (and should) inform our practices (Ramanathan & Atkinson, 1999). Process-oriented approaches to L2 writing instruction, for example, have been widely (though not universally) embraced in many educational settings. To evaluate the outcomes and desirability of this influential paradigm shift, researchers and practitioners have engaged in grounded inquiry, to say nothing of sometimes painful soul-searching.

No unitary theory or model of L2 writing has yet emerged as a foundation on which to build a coherent disciplinary identity. In the current, relativist climate of scholarly inquiry, perhaps a singular theory is neither necessary nor desirable. Be that as it may, an influential trend that is sure to shape the profession in the 21st century involves intensified reflexivity between research and pedagogy. Raimes (1998) suggested that L2 writing teachers, researchers, and theorists should promote the field's progress by pursuing multiple types of inquiry. The pursuit of these objectives is perhaps well under way. Furthermore, no single thematic area within the profession's realm of expertise can easily move forward without availing itself of the accumulated knowledge of allied disciplines. The disciplinary conversation on issues such as instructional processes, peer and expert response, and assessment, for instance, can no longer rely solely on applied linguistics, TESOL/TEFL, and L1 composition studies. L2 writing professionals will inevitably be required to call on discoveries in second language acquisition, computational linguistics, cognitive and educational psychology, critical studies, semiotics, and so on. In the same way that the boundaries of expertise in L2 writing instruction have broadened to include the social contexts and purposes for which writers write, research on L2 writers, texts, and contexts now more intentionally avails itself of a wide sphere of knowledge.

REFERENCES

Alderson, J. C., Clapham, C., & Wall, D. (1995). *Language test construction and evaluation.* Cambridge, UK: Cambridge University Press.

Bailey, K. M. (1998). *Learning about language assessment: Dilemmas, decisions, and directions.* Boston: Heinle & Heinle.

Belcher, D. (1997). An argument for nonadversarial argumentation: On the relevance of the feminist critique of academic discourse to L2 writing pedagogy. *Journal of Second Language Writing, 5,* 1–21.

Belcher, D., & Braine, G. (Eds.). (1995). *Academic writing in a second language.* Norwood, NJ: Ablex.

Belcher, D., & Hirvela, A. (Eds.). (2001). *Linking literacies: Perspectives on L2 reading-writing connections.* Ann Arbor: University of Michigan Press.

Benesch, S. (1993). ESL, ideology, and the politics of pragmatism. *TESOL Quarterly, 27,* 705–717.

Benesch, S. (1996). Needs analysis and curriculum development in EAP: An example of a critical approach. *TESOL Quarterly, 30,* 723–738.

Benesch, S. (2001). *Critical English for academic purposes: Theory, politics, and practice.* Mahwah, NJ: Lawrence Erlbaum Associates.

Bereiter, C., & Scardamalia, M. (1987). *The psychology of written composition.* Hillsdale, NJ: Lawrence Erlbaum Associates.

Berkenkotter, C., & Huckin, T. (1995). *Genre knowledge in disciplinary communication.* Hillsdale, NJ: Lawrence Erlbaum Associates.

Berlin, J. (1987). *Rhetoric and reality: Writing instruction in American colleges, 1900–1985.* Carbondale: Southern Illinois University Press.

Bhatia, V. J. (1993). *Analyzing genre: Language use in professional settings.* London: Longman.

Bräuer, G. (Ed.). (2000). *Writing across languages.* Stamford, CT: Ablex.

Byrd, P., & Reid, J. (1998). *Grammar in the composition classroom: Essays on teaching ESL for college-bound students.* Boston: Heinle & Heinle.

Calfee, R., & Perfumo, P. (Eds.). (1996). *Writing portfolios in the classroom: Policy and practice, promise, and peril.* Hillsdale, NJ: Lawrence Erlbaum Associates.

Canagarajah, S. (1993). Comment on Ann Raimes's "Out of the woods: Emerging traditions in the teaching of writing": Up the garden path: Second language writing approaches, local knowledge, and pluralism. *TESOL Quarterly, 27,* 301–306.

Chiang, S. Y. (1999). Assessing grammatical and textual features in L2 writing samples: The case of French as a foreign language. *Modern Language Journal, 83*, 219–232.

Clark, R., & Ivanic, R. (1997). *The politics of writing.* London: Routledge & Kegan Paul.

Cohen, A. D. (2001). Second language assessment. In M. Celce-Murcia (Ed.), *Teaching English as a second or foreign language* (3rd ed.) (pp. 515–534). Boston: Heinle & Heinle.

Connor, U. (1996). *Contrastive rhetoric: Crosscultural aspects of second language writing.* Cambridge, UK: Cambridge University Press.

Connor, U., & Kaplan, R. (Eds.). (1987). *Writing across languages: Analysis of L2 text.* Reading, MA: Addison-Wesley.

Connor, U., & Mbaye, A. (2002). Discourse approaches to writing assessment. *Annual Review of Applied Linguistics, 22*, 263–278.

Conrad, S. M., & Goldstein, L. M. (1999). ESL student revision after teacher-written comments: Text, contexts, and individuals. *Journal of Second Language Writing, 8*, 147–179.

Cook-Gumperz, J. (Ed.). (1986). *The social construction of literacy.* Cambridge, UK: Cambridge University Press.

Cooper, C. R., & Odell, L. (Eds.). (1999). *Evaluating writing: The role of teachers' knowledge about text, learning, and culture.* Urbana, IL: National Council of Teachers of English.

Cumming, A. (1990). Expertise in evaluating second language compositions. *Language Testing, 7*, 31–51.

Cumming, A. (1998). Theoretical perspectives on writing. *Annual Review of Applied Linguistics, 18*, 61–78.

Cumming, A., Kantor, R., & Powers, D. E. (2002). Decision making while rating ESL/EFL writing tasks: A descriptive framework. *Modern Language Journal, 86*, 67–96.

Dudley-Evans, T., & St. John, M. J. (1998). *Developments in English for specific purposes: A multidisciplinary approach.* Cambridge, UK: Cambridge University Press.

Elbow, P. (1981). *Writing with power: Techniques for mastering the writing process.* New York: Oxford University Press.

Elbow, P. (1994). *Voice and writing.* Davis, CA: Hermagoras Press.

Elbow, P. (1996). Writing assessment: Do it better, do it less. In E. M. White, W. D. Lutz, & S. Kamusikiri (Eds.), *Assessment of writing: Politics, policies, practices* (pp. 120–134). New York: Modern Language Association.

Emig, J. (1971). *The composing process of twelfth graders.* Urbana, IL: National Council of Teachers of English.

Fairclough, N. (1995). *Critical discourse analysis.* London: Longman.

Ferris, D. (1995). Student reactions to teacher response in multiple-draft composition classrooms. *TESOL Quarterly, 29*, 33–53.

Ferris, D. (1997). The influence of teacher commentary on student revision. *TESOL Quarterly, 31*, 315–339.

Ferris, D. (1999). The case for grammar correction in L2 writing classes: A response to Truscott (1996). *Journal of Second Language Writing, 8*, 1–11.

Ferris, D. (2002). *Treatment of error in L2 student writing.* Ann Arbor: University of Michigan Press.

Ferris, D. (2003). *Response to student writing: Implications for second language students.* Mahwah, NJ: Lawrence Erlbaum Associates.

Ferris, D., & Hedgcock, J. (1998). *Teaching ESL composition: Purpose, process, and practice.* Mahwah, NJ: Lawrence Erlbaum Associates.

Ferris, D., Pezone, S., Tade, C., & Tinti, S. (1997). Teacher commentary on student writing: Descriptions and implications. *Journal of Second Language Writing, 6*, 155–182.

Flower, L. (1989). Cognition, context, and theory building. *College Composition and Communication, 40*, 449–461.

Freedman, A., & Medway, P. (Eds.). (1994). *Learning and teaching genre.* Portsmouth, NH: Boynton/Cook.

Freire, P. (1970). *Pedagogy of the oppressed.* New York: Continuum.

Freire, P. (1985). *The politics of education.* South Hadley, MA: Bergin & Garvey.

Freire, P. (1994). *Pedagogy of hope.* New York: Continuum.

Freire, P., & Macedo, D. (1987). *Literacy: Reading the word and the world.* South Hadley, MA: Bergin & Garvey.

Gee, J. P. (1996). *Social linguistics and literacies: Ideology in discourses* (2nd ed.). London: Taylor & Francis.

Gee, J. P. (1999). *An introduction to discourse analysis: Theory and method.* New York: Routledge & Kegan Paul.

Geertz, C. (1983). *Local knowledge: Further essays in interpretive anthropology.* New York: Basic Books.

Grabe, W. (2001). Reading-writing relations: Theoretical perspectives and instructional practices. In D. Belcher & A. Hirvela (Eds.), *Linking literacies: Perspectives on L2 reading-writing connections* (pp. 15–47). Ann Arbor: University of Michigan Press.

Grabe, W., & Kaplan, R. B. (1996). *Theory and practice of writing.* London: Longman.

Halliday, M. A. K., & Martin, J. (1993). *Writing science: Literacy and discursive power.* Pittsburgh, PA: University of Pittsburgh Press.

Hamp-Lyons, L. (Ed.). (1991). *Assessing second language writing in academic contexts.* Norwood, NJ: Ablex.

Hamp-Lyons, L., & Condon, W. (2000). *Assessing the portfolio: Principles for practice, theory, and research.* Cresskill, NJ: Hampton Press.

Hamp-Lyons, L., & Kroll, B. (1996). Issues in ESL writing assessment. *College ESL, 6* (1), 52–72.

Hamp-Lyons, L., & Kroll, B. (1997). *TOEFL 2000—Writing: Composition, community, and assessment.* Princeton, NJ: Educational Testing Service.

Hamp-Lyons, L., & Mathias, S. P. (1994). Examining expert judgments of task difficulty on essay tests. *Journal of Second Language Writing, 3*, 49–68.

Harklau, L., Losey, K. M., & Siegel, M. (Eds.). (1999). *Generation 1.5 meets college composition.* Mahwah, NJ: Lawrence Erlbaum Associates.

Hedgcock, J. (2002). Toward a socioliterate approach to language teacher education. *Modern Language Journal, 86,* 299–317.

Hedgcock, J., & Lefkowitz, N. (1996). Some input on input: Two analyses of student response to expert feedback in L2 writing. *The Modern Language Journal, 80,* 287–308.

Hinkel, E. (2002). *Second language writers' text: Linguistic and rhetorical features.* Mahwah, NJ: Lawrence Erlbaum Associates.

Hyland, F. (2000). ESL writers and feedback: Giving more autonomy to students. *Language Teaching Research, 4,* 33–54.

Hyland, K. (2000). *Disciplinary discourses: Social interactions in academic writing.* London: Longman.

Hyland, K. (2002). Genre: Language, context, and literacy. *Annual Review of Applied Linguistics, 22,* 113–135.

Hyon, S. (1996). Genre in three traditions: Implications for ESL. *TESOL Quarterly, 30,* 693–722.

Ivanic, R. (1998). *Writing and identity: The discoursal construction of identity in academic writing.* Amsterdam: John Benjamins.

Johns, A. M. (1997). *Text, role, and context: Developing academic literacies.* New York: Cambridge University Press.

Johns, A. M. (2002a). Destabilizing and enriching novice students' genre theories. In A. Johns (Ed.), *Genre in the classroom: Multiple perspectives* (pp. 237–246). Mahwah, NJ: Lawrence Erlbaum Associates.

Johns, A. M. (Ed.). (2002b). *Genre in the classroom: Multiple perspectives.* Mahwah, NJ: Lawrence Erlbaum Associates.

Johns, A. M. (2002c). Introduction. In A. Johns (Ed.), *Genre in the classroom: Multiple perspectives* (pp. 3–13). Mahwah, NJ: Lawrence Erlbaum Associates.

Johns, A. M., & Dudley-Evans, T. (1991). English for specific purposes: International in scope, specific in purpose. *TESOL Quarterly, 25,* 297–314.

Kaplan, R. B. (1966). Cultural thought patterns in intercultural education. *Language Learning, 16,* 1–20.

Kirkpatrick, A. (1997). Using contrastive rhetoric to teach writing: Seven principles. *Australian Review of Applied Linguistics, 14,* 89–102.

Kroll, B. (1998). Assessing writing abilities. *Annual Review of Applied Linguistics, 18,* 219–240.

Kroll, B. (2001). Considerations for teaching an ESL/EFL writing course. In M. Celce-Murcia (Ed.), *Teaching English as a second or foreign language* (3rd ed.), (pp. 219–232). Boston: Heinle & Heinle.

Kubota, R. (1999). Japanese culture constructed by discourses: Implications for applied linguistics research and ELT. *TESOL Quarterly, 33,* 9–35.

Lave, J., & Wenger, E. (1991). *Situated learning: Legitimate peripheral participation.* Cambridge, UK: Cambridge University Press.

Leki, I. (1991). Twenty-five years of contrastive rhetoric: Text analysis and writing pedagogies. *TESOL Quarterly, 25,* 123–143.

Leki, I. (1992). *Understanding ESL writers: A guide for teachers.* Portsmouth, NH: Boynton/Cook.

Leki, I. (1995a). Coping strategies of ESL students in writing tasks across the curriculum. *TESOL Quarterly, 29,* 235–260.

Leki, I. (1995b). Good writing: I know it when I see it. In D. Belcher & G. Braine (Eds.), *Academic writing in a second language* (pp. 23–46). Norwood, NJ: Ablex.

Leki, I. (1997). Cross-talk: ESL issues and contrastive rhetoric. In C. Severino, J. C. Guerra, & J. E. Butler (Eds.), *Writing in multicultural settings* (pp. 234–244). New York: Modern Language Association.

Leki, I. (2000). Writing, literacy, and applied linguistics. *Annual Review of Applied Linguistics, 20,* 99–115.

Leki, I., & Carson, J. (1994). Students' perceptions of EAP writing instruction and writing needs across the disciplines. *TESOL Quarterly, 28,* 81–101.

Leki, I., & Carson, J. (1997). "Completely different worlds": EAP and the writing experiences of ESL students in university courses. *TESOL Quarterly, 31,* 39–69.

Littlewood, W. (1995). Writing and reading as a joint journey through ideas. In M. L. Tickoo (Ed.), *Reading and writing: Theory into practice* (pp. 421–437). Singapore: SEAMEO Regional Language Centre.

Liu, J., & Hansen, J. G. (2002). *Peer response in second language writing classrooms.* Ann Arbor: University of Michigan Press.

Manchón-Ruiz, R. (1997). Learners' strategies in L2 composing. *Communication and Cognition, 30,* 91–114.

Martin, J. (1992). *English text: System and structure.* Philadelphia: John Benjamins.

Matsuda, P. K. (1999). Composition studies and ESL writing: A disciplinary division of labor. *College Composition and Communication, 50,* 699–721.

Norton, B. (Ed.). (1997). Language and identity (Special issue). *TESOL Quarterly, 31*(3),

Norton, B. (2000). *Identity and language learning: Gender, ethnicity, and educational change.* Harlow, UK: Pearson Education.

Paltridge, B. (1997). *Genre, frames, and writing in research settings.* Amsterdam: John Benjamins.

Paltridge, B. (2001). *Genre and the language learning classroom.* Ann Arbor: University of Michigan Press.

Panetta, C. G. (2001). *Contrastive rhetoric revisited and redefined.* Mahwah, NJ: Lawrence Erlbaum Associates.

Pennycook, A. (1996). Borrowing others' words: Text, ownership, memory, and plagiarism. *TESOL Quarterly, 30,* 201–230.

Pennycook, A. (1997). Vulgar pragmatism, critical pragmatism, and EAP. *English for Specific Purposes, 16,* 253–269.

Pennycook, A. (2001). *Critical applied linguistics: A critical introduction.* Mahwah, NJ: Lawrence Erlbaum Associates.

Purves, A. (1992). Reflections on research and assessment in written composition. *Research in the Teaching of English, 26,* 108–122.

Raimes, A. (1985). What unskilled ESL students do as they write: A classroom study of ESL college student writers. *TESOL Quarterly, 18,* 229–258.

Raimes, A. (1991). Out of the woods: Emerging traditions in the teaching of writing. *TESOL Quarterly, 25,* 407–430.

Raimes, A. (1998). Teaching writing. *Annual Review of Applied Linguistics, 18,* 142–167.

Ramanathan, V., & Atkinson, D. (1999). Ethnographic approaches and methods in L2 writing research: A critical guide and review. *Applied Linguistics, 20,* 44–70.

Ramanathan, V., & Kaplan, R. B. (2000). Genres, authors, discourse communities: Theory and application for (L1 and) L2 writing instructors. *Journal of Second Language Writing, 9,* 171–191.

Reid, J., & Kroll, B. (1995). Designing and assessing effective classroom writing assignments for NNS and ESL students. *Journal of Second Language Writing, 4,* 17–42.

Robinson, G. (1992). *ESP today.* Hemel Hempsted, UK: Prentice-Hall.

Schleppegrell, M. J., & Columbi, M. C. (2002). *Developing advanced literacy in first and second languages: Meaning with power.* Mahwah, NJ: Lawrence Erlbaum Associates.

Scollon, R. (1997). Contrastive rhetoric, contrastive poetics, or perhaps something else? *TESOL Quarterly, 31,* 352–358.

Silva, T. (1990). Second language composition instruction: Developments, issues, and directions in ESL. In B. Kroll (Ed.), *Second language writing* (pp. 11–23). New York: Cambridge University Press.

Silva, T. (1993). Toward an understanding of the distinct nature of L2 writing: The ESL research and its implications. *TESOL Quarterly, 27,* 657–671.

Silva, T., Brice, C., & Reichelt, M. (Eds.). (1999). *An annotated bibliography of scholarship in second language writing: 1993–1997.* Stamford, CT: Ablex.

Silva, T., Leki, I., & Carson, J. (1997). Broadening the perspective of mainstream composition studies. *Written Communication, 14,* 398–428.

Smith, F. (1988). *Joining the literacy club: Further essays into education.* Portsmouth, NH: Heinemann.

Smoke, T. (Ed.). (1998). *Adult ESL: Politics, pedagogy, and participation in classroom and community program.* Mahwah, NJ: Lawrence Erlbaum Associates.

Spack, R. (1997). The acquisition of academic literacy in a second language. *Written Communication, 14,* 3–62.

Swales, J. (Ed.). (1985). *Episodes in ESP.* Oxford, UK: Pergamon.

Swales, J. (1990). *Genre analysis: English in academic and research settings.* Cambridge, UK: Cambridge University Press.

Swales, J. (1998). *Other floors, other voices: A textography of a small university building.* Mahwah, NJ: Lawrence Erlbaum Associates.

Tannacito, D. J. (1995). *A guide to writing in English as a second or foreign language: An annotated bibliography of research and pedagogy.* Alexandria, VA: TESOL.

Truscott, J. (1996). The case against grammar correction in L2 writing classes. *Language Learning, 46,* 327–369.

Truscott, J. (1999). The case for 'The case against grammar correction in L2 writing classes': A response to Ferris. *Journal of Second Language Writing, 8,* 111–122.

Vandrick, S. (1995). Privileged ESL university students. *TESOL Quarterly, 29,* 375–380.

Way, D., Joiner, E., & Seaman, M. (2000). Writing in the secondary foreign language classroom: The effects of prompts and tasks on novice learners of French. *Modern Language Journal, 84,* 171–184.

Weigle, S. C. (1999). Investigating rater/prompt interactions in writing assessment: Quantitative and qualitative approaches. *Assessing Writing, 6,* 145–178.

Weigle, S. C. (2002). *Assessing writing.* Cambridge, UK: Cambridge University Press.

White, E. M. (1994). *Teaching and assessing writing* (2nd ed.). San Francisco: Jossey-Bass.

White, E. M. (1995). An apologia for the timed impromptu essay test. *College Composition and Communication, 46,* 30–45.

White, E. M., Lutz, W. D., & Kamusikiri, S. (Eds.). (1996). *Assessment of writing: Politics, policies, practices.* New York: Modern Language Association.

Wolfe-Quintero, K., Inagaki, S., & Kim, Y.-Y. (1998). *Second language development in writing: Measures of fluency, accuracy, and complexity.* Honolulu: University of Hawaii Press.

Yancey, K. B. (Ed.). (1992). *Portfolios in the writing classroom.* Urbana, IL: National Council of Teachers of English.

Zamel, V. (1982). Writing: The process of discovering meaning. *TESOL Quarterly, 16,* 195–209.

Zamel, V. (1983). The composing processes of advanced ESL students: Six case studies. *TESOL Quarterly, 17,* 165–187.

Zamel, V. (1993). Questioning academic discourse. *College ESL, 3*(1), 28–39.

34

Analyses of Second Language Text and What Can Be Learned From Them

Eli Hinkel
Seattle University

INTRODUCTION

Analyses of second language (L2) text largely examine L2 writing, while L2 spoken production is usually investigated in the field of conversational analysis (see Markee, chap. 20, this volume). Since the emergence of applied linguistics as a discipline in the 1950s and 1960s, three large domains of research have focused on various properties of L2 written text: structuring of the information flow in discourse, syntactic, lexical, and rhetorical features employed in L2 text, and to a smaller extent, L2 grammar, and lexical errors.

In general terms, the analysis of grammatical and lexical errors in L2 written text is derived from the contrastive (error) analysis that predominated in L2 learning research between the 1950s and 1970s. Error analysis was based on an assumption that many (if not most) L2 errors are an outcome of L1 to L2 transfer of syntactic and lexical regularities and language properties.

Discourse analysis accounts for global features of text and the organization of ideas in writing. Contrastive rhetoric, as a subdomain of applied linguistics (Kaplan, 1966), gave rise to and continues to promote an examination of discourse features in the L2 writing of non-native speakers of English (NNSs) (see also chap. 33). It is important to keep in mind, however, that relatively little research on L2 writing had been carried out prior to the 1980s, when the numbers of NNSs in U.S. colleges and universities began to climb dramatically.

Historically, important advancements in contrastive rhetoric were reflected in a growing body of knowledge about the order and ideational structure of discourse and discourse moves, also called Discourse Blocs (Kaplan, 1983), in L2 writing. The innovations in contrastive rhetoric studies coincided with rapid advances in text linguistics. Speaking broadly, text analysis had the goal of identifying global discourse features that can be marked by means of syntactic and lexical elements, such as verb tenses or sentence transitions (Coulthard, 1985; de Beaugrande & Dressler, 1972; Halliday & Hasan, 1976, 1989; van Dijk, 1985).

In a distinct domain of applied linguistics, investigations in contrastive rhetoric and discourse structuring in various rhetorical traditions and across different cultures have also been extended to studies of comparative uses of textual features in L2 written prose. Analyzing written discourse paradigms and text attributes became the objective of many studies that worked with L1 writing of native speakers of English (NSs) in, for example, Australia, Canada, the United States, United Kingdom, and New Zealand, and those in the English L2 writing of speakers of many other languages. A vast body of research has thus far compared discourse and textual features employed in L2 writing of speakers of such languages as (in alphabetical order) Arabic, Chinese, Czech, Dutch, Farsi, Finnish, French, Hebrew, Hindi, German, Indonesian, Japanese, Korean, Malay, Russian, Spanish, Swedish, Thai, and Vietnamese, as well as several varieties of English.

Most studies of various features of L2 discourse and text have been motivated by immediate and long-term research and curriculum development goals, as well as pedagogically driven needs of particular groups of L2 students and learners in various locations, specific interests of individual researchers, available sources of text data, and/or attempts to apply the findings of predominantly English language-based text linguistics to L2 text (e.g., Al-Khatib, 2001; Carlson, 1988; Clyne, 1987; Grabe, 1987; Hinkel, 1994; Johnson, 1992; Taylor & Chen, 1991). To date, a coherent picture of syntactic, lexical, rhetorical, or discoursal features of L2 text has yet to emerge. However, in sum total, much has been learned about features of text produced by L2 writers in different contexts and for divergent academic, social, and communication purposes.

This chapter provides an overview of the methods widely used for analyzing L2 discourse and text, and the findings of research on macro and micro features of text. Additionally, computerized databases of L2 writing and the constraints that seem to confound analyses of L2 written corpora are briefly discussed.

QUALITATIVE AND QUANTITATIVE METHODS OF L2 TEXT ANALYSIS

Analyzing L2 writing is a time-consuming and laborious process. Investigations of L2 text have varied dramatically in the size of their data samples and types of writing. Most analyses have consisted of small-scale studies that utilized written texts produced by one to a half dozen writers (e.g., Arndt, 1993; Choi, 1988; Mauranen, 1996), and only a few had access to (or resources to work on) larger numbers of texts written by dozens or hundreds of L2 writers. On the other hand, studies that focused on specific excerpts of discourse or narrowly defined textual features, such as introductions to research papers or hedges and modal verbs, include larger samples written by 10 to 25 NNSs (e.g., Basham & Kwachka, 1991; Swales, 1990).

To a great extent, the theoretical frameworks and research methodologies for analyses of L2 discourse and text rely on those developed and formulated in such domains of applied linguistics as text linguistics, discourse analysis, ethnography, and cognitive psychology. Although much research on L1 English-language writing has been carried out in such disciplines as rhetoric and composition, on the whole, the study of rhetoric has had a minimal impact on analyses of L2 text. The philosophical underpinnings of the Anglo-American and other western rhetorical traditions draw on the classical Aristotelian and Greco-Roman foundational premises (e.g., invention, organization, and language and stylistics) not easily applicable to L2 discourse and text. On the other hand, quantitative and qualitative research methods designed for applied linguistics analyses of texts, written primarily in English, have been a great deal more useful in studies of L2 discourse moves and markers, text construction, and lexicogrammatical features (Halliday, 1994; Hoey, 1991; Grabe & Kaplan, 1996; Kaplan, 1988; Nattinger & DeCarrico, 1992).

To date, the majority of investigations into L2 writing have focused on the organizational and ideational structure of L2 discourse and the features of L2 text. Comparative studies have sought to account for differences and similarities between the properties of L2 discourse and text and those identified in the L1 writing of native English speakers who can be, for example, university students or authors of published research articles. In such examinations, comparisons can be made in regard to L1 and L2 global (macro) discourse construction, arrangements of ideas, cohesion, and coherence. Additionally, researchers can scrutinize textual (micro) features that have the function of marking discourse organization and aiding in the development of cohesive and coherent prose. As with the research on L2 discourse, the primary objectives of practically all L2 text analyses and comparative studies have stemmed from the pedagogical needs of L2 writing instruction for university students and academically bound language learners and professionals.

L2 DISCOURSE AND MACRO FEATURES OF TEXT IN BROAD STROKES

The contrastive rhetoric hypothesis (Kaplan, 1966) is largely concerned with discourse structuring and logical organization of information in various rhetorical traditions. The crosscultural analysis of discourse postulates that systematic differences exist in how topic continuity is established and coherence is developed in rhetorical traditions and writing in different languages and cultures. In the case of literate and educated speakers of various languages, L1-specific ways of organizing discourse and information may be transferred to the discourse organization in L2 writing. Thus, the overarching goal of the contrastive rhetoric hypothesis was to assist teachers and academically bound ESL students who needed to learn to write in L2 by identifying the differences among patterns in written discourse.

Global features of L2 written discourse, such as discourse moves, organization, structuring, as well as attendant issues of clarity, explicitness, fluidity, and contents of writing, represent broader and more abstract constructs than those commonly examined in analyses of text (Grabe & Kaplan, 1996; Hinkel, 1997, 1999; Indrasuta, 1988; Johns, 1997; Kaplan, 2000). For example, a number of studies has been devoted to stylistic properties of various types of L2 writing, such as textual indirectness in academic essays or narrative personalization.

In the 1980s and 1990s, research on the L2 writing of university students in a number of English-speaking countries established that discourse construction and rhetorical paradigms differ in consistent and important ways in the L1 writing of NSs and L2 written prose. Additionally, investigations devoted to discourse construction across languages and cultures have been able to determine that, for instance, marked similarities exist in the rhetorical development of text written in some European languages, such as Czech and German, or Asian languages, such as Chinese, Japanese, and Korean. For example, in German and Czech academic writing, as well as in the L2 prose of German learners of English and scholars, digressions and deviations from the main topic are considered to be acceptable, as are repetitions, recapitulations, and restatements, abstract argumentation, and broad generalizations (e.g., Clyne, 1987; Cmejrkova, 1996).

On the other hand, classical rhetoric and discourse construction in Chinese, Japanese, and Korean writing, as well as in the L2 prose of speakers of these languages, have been shown to include predictable organizational paradigms with the main idea at the end, indirect argumentation, allusions, and references to history and authority as evidence (Hinds, 1983, 1987, 1990; Matalene, 1985; Park, 1988; Scollon, 1991). Cai (1999, p. 294) points out that classical Chinese rhetoric and style has an indelible effect on the academic writing of L2 students in U.S. colleges and universities. According to the author, in L2 writing instruction, Anglo-American discourse strategies, topic development, rhetorical and linguistic norms, as well as the "sociocultural contexts in which these norms are embedded" should be explicitly taught because these "are essential in English academic writing."

The division of discourse organization paradigms into what has become known as "reader-responsible" or "writer-responsible" text was originally proposed by Hinds (1987, 1990), based on his research on Japanese, Korean, and Chinese writing. Hinds noticed that in the written discourse in these languages, the main point or the thesis is not necessarily presented to the reader at the beginning or, alternatively, can remain implicit throughout the text. In such texts, the responsibility for determining the writer's main idea is left to the reader, who then needs to deduce the writer's position and the central argument from context. On the other hand, in writer-responsible prose, explicitness, clarity, and lexical precision are considered to be requisite. Hence, it is the writer's job to construct discourse and text in which the purpose of writing is directly stated at the outset, and the writer's discourse and argument is expected to be clear and easy to follow. At present, in L2 writing instruction, the concepts of reader- or writer-responsible texts have become commonplace. Today, it would be difficult to find an ESL writing textbook that does not mention that in Anglo-American writing, it is the writer who is responsible for making the text transparent and explicit to the reader.

Other studies examined discourse construction and rhetorical organization in such diverse languages as Arabic and Spanish. Specifically, Ostler (1987) found that the L2 writing of Arabic speakers included a significantly higher rates of parallel and coordinate constructions, as well as greater numbers of discourse moves and rhetorical support elements than were found in the writing of NSs. Sa'adeddin (1989) further explains that in argumentation and rhetorical persuasion, colloquial Arabic discourse relies on parallelism, repetition, and broad generalizations, as well as ornate and elaborate vocabulary. Thus, according to Sa'adeddin, when writing in English, Arabic speakers may simply transfer from L1 the usage of coordinate and parallel constructions prevalent in interactive rhetorical style and persuasion. In his study of modern Arabic writing, Hatim (1991) similarly found that considerations of audience and interaction with audience play an important role in how Arabic written discourse, persuasion, and rhetorical moves are constructed.

In regard to the L2 writing of Spanish speakers, research has consistently demonstrated that they write longer essays and longer, more complex, and elaborated sentences than NSs do (e.g., Carlson, 1988; Montano-Harmon, 1991). In addition, Spanish speakers use significantly higher rates of coordinate clauses and phrases, long abstract words, and broad generalizations when compared to those in the writing of NSs of similar age and educational levels. In fact, Reid's (1992) study of writing of English, Spanish, and Arabic speakers demonstrated that the prose of Spanish L1 writers exhibits coordination patterns similar to those that Ostler (1987) identified in the L2 writing of Arabic-speaking university students.

According to some researchers, however, the divergences between L1 and L2 discourse structuring can also be attributed to L2 writers' developmental constraints and inexperience rather than the transfer of L1 rhetorical paradigms (Mohan & Lo, 1985). Additionally, the studies of published articles written by Chinese and English speakers (Taylor & Chen, 1991), and essays written by Korean students in a U.S. university (Choi, 1988) demonstrated that discourse structuring in L1 and L2 writing can show both differences and similarities. In both cases, the authors note that due to the internalization of scientific discourse and the effects of English writing instruction in many countries, the structural divergences between the Anglo-American discourse organization patterns and those in other rhetorical traditions have been continuously diminished over time and are likely to become even less pronounced in the future.

On the whole, however, the influence of L1 discourse and rhetorical paradigms in organizing information represents an established venue in numerous investigations on writing and text across cultures and languages. To a great extent, a large body of research on discourse construction patterns in writing in various rhetorical traditions has led to a greater understanding of many issues that confound ESL writing and its teaching and learning.

In particular, Silva (1993) highlights the most pronounced differences between practically all facets of writing in L1 and L2. In his synthesis of 72 published research reports and empirical studies, Silva points out that L2 writing is crucially distinct from L1 writing in regard to the writing process, such as composing and revision, and macro features of discourse organization. Based on the findings of dozens of studies carried out prior to 1993, Silva emphasizes that the processes of writing in L2 are fundamentally different from those entailed in writing in L1, L2 writers engage in less discourse and text planning, reviewing, and revising than L1 basic writers, while producing L2 text is far more work- and time-consuming, and revision is demonstrably more difficult.

To summarize Silva's conclusions, compared to the discourse structuring and development in L1 basic and student writing, L2 writers:

- Organize and structure discourse moves differently.
- Take a logically and conceptually different approach to rhetorical argumentation, persuasion, and exposition/narration.
- Over- or underestimate the amount of readers' background knowledge and the need for textual clarity, explicitness, and specificity.
- Differently orient the reader, and introduce and develop topics.
- Employ different strategies for extracting/citing information from sources, as well as paraphrasing, quoting, and including source material in their writing.
- Develop text cohesion differently, with weak lexical/semantic ties and theme connections, and a preponderance of overt conjunctive markers.

Silva concludes his overview of research by saying that "L2 writing is strategically, rhetorically, and linguistically different in important ways from L1 writing" (p. 669). In light of these fundamental differences, Silva points out that the learning needs of L2 writers are distinct from those of L1 writers, whether basic or skilled, and that teachers who work with L2 writers require special and focused training to deal with cultural, rhetorical, and linguistic differences of their students.

To this end, research into how L2 discourse and text are constructed, as well as contrastive analyses of discourse, have proven to be very useful in the teaching of L2 writing and creating more appropriate curricula (e.g., Leki, 1992; Reid, 1993). In particular, an important outcome of research into L2 written discourse is the increased knowledge about discourse and text in writing traditions other than Anglo-American, including such written genres as news reports, academic publications, student writing, e-mail messages, and business correspondence.

ANALYSES OF MICRO FEATURES OF L2 TEXT

In addition to the analysis of discourse in L2 writing, a large number of studies have been devoted to the comparative analyses of lexical, syntactic, and rhetorical features of L1 and L2 texts, usually produced in the contexts of their academic endeavors. Much research, for example, investigated the uses of discourse markers, cohesion and coherence devices, modal verbs, hedges, and modifiers in L1 and L2 prose (Connor & Johns, 1990; Field & Oi, 1992; Flowerdew, 2000; Hinkel, 1995, 2001a; Johns, 1984, 1990; Johnson, 1992; Khalil, 1989; Mauranen, 1996; Reid, 1992; Swales, 1990).

A typical study of L2 text features may undertake to determine, for example, how explicit cohesive devices are used in L1 and L2 academic essays. For this purpose, researchers may compare the frequencies and contexts of sentence conjunctions (e.g., *furthermore, however,* and *thus),* coordinating conjunctions (e.g., *and, but, yet,* and *so),* and/or summary markers (e.g., *in short* and *in sum)* (e.g., Field & Oi, 1992; Hinkel, 2001b; Johns, 1984; Khalil, 1989; Schleppegrell, 1996). Similarly, to analyze the uses of modal verbs, usage measurements can be computed separately or together for possibility and ability modals (e.g., *can, may, might, could)* or obligation and necessity modals (e.g., *must, should, need).*

A study methodology can entail counting the number of conjunctions or modal verbs by type in each essay, followed by obtaining a mean (or median) value of occurrences of a particular conjunction in all essays in a sample of texts or in a single essay. In quantitative analyses, for instance, descriptive values for uses of similar features can be obtained for NS and NNS texts. Then these are usually compared and analyzed statistically to determine whether they are used similarly or significantly differently in the two samples.

For example, a short excerpt from an L2 text on the topic of international sports events and competitions is presented here. In this 94-word passage, the writer employs the ability modal *can* six times and the obligation modal *should* twice, and it is easy to notice that the text probably relies on the usage of *can* to excess.

> We *can* see that sports make people show their love of their own country. You *can* hear special team songs in every game. This is not just about individuals, but nations. We *can* see passion, happy or sad around audiences and players because sports bring us energy and living. In the sports world, everyone is equal, every player *can* have the same condition to do what he or she *should* do the best. Also, we *can* understand every country is equal. So, we *should* be proud of our country, and we *can* enjoy the success together.

In this case, a computation of the frequency rate of *can* is approximately 6.4% (6/94) and *should* is 2.1% (2/94). Of course, no generalizations about the writer's uses of these two modals or their frequency rates can be made based on such a short excerpt. However, in larger and representative samples of L1 and L2 writing, comparisons of descriptive measurement values by means of appropriate statistical tests can allow researchers to gauge whether in an L2 writing sample of, say, 15,000–20,000 words, the overall usage of specific syntactic and lexical features approximates that in a parallel L1 writing sample. In L2 writing instruction, such comparisons can (and often do) lead to fine-tuning course curricula, added attention to specific areas of teaching, or individualized assistance for L2 learners.

In analyses of L2 text, the degrees of fluency, for example, can be assessed by means of measuring relative text lengths, as well as lengths of sentences, clauses, or words, in combinations with supplemental measures of accuracy, and lexical and syntactic complexity (e.g., Carlson, 1988; Hinkel, 2003a; Park, 1988; Schleppegrell, 2002). In large-scale assessments that involve hundreds or thousands of writers, developmental indexes have also been driven by research into specific attributes of L2 writing and text (e.g., Basham & Kwachka, 1991, Hamp-Lyons, 1991a; Hamp-Lyons & Kroll, 1996; Reid, 1993; Weigle, 2002).

Analyses of L2 text have further delved into various textual genres commonly associated with various L2 writing tasks. These include formal essays, university term and diploma projects, business letters, recommendations letters, e-mail messages, and journals produced by L2 writers (Al-Khatib, 2001; Bouton, 1995; Choi, 1988; Hinkel, 2001b; Jenkins & Hinds, 1987). Furthermore, research has examined the properties of L2 text produced by adult L2 writers in colleges and universities with an English medium of instruction (e.g., in Hong Kong, India, or Singapore), as well as the writing of young language learners in the course of their schooling.

Among the investigations of ESL children's writing, Edelsky (1986) and Hudelson (1988) found that texts produced by young ESL writers are very similar to those of young native speakers, although L1 culture has a definitive influence on L2 children's view of writing and its functions and purposes. On the other hand, Maguire and Graves (2001, p. 588) reported that school-age L2 learners "use different genres, rhetorical styles, modalities, and semantic and syntactic structures" and that their writing should be viewed as a means of facilitating the development of children's language proficiency. Other researchers who carried out empirical investigations of writing development indicate that it takes years of persistent, knowledgeable, and attentive teaching for L2 school-age learners to attain sufficient language control to produce academic writing effectively similar to that of L1 children of matching ages (Hakuta, Butler, &Witt, 2000; Scarcella & Chunok, 1989; Valdes & Sanders, 1999).

It is important to note, however, that relatively little research has been specifically devoted to the proficiency, development, and text features in the L2 writing of school-age children. A great majority of published reports deal with the discourse and linguistic features of text produced by adults in academic, professional, language learning, or literacy contexts.

FINDINGS OF L2 TEXT ANALYSES

As was mentioned earlier, Silva's (1993) synthesis of research on L2 writing processes and discourse also addresses the research findings that deal with morphosyntactic and lexical features of L2 text. Specifically, according to Silva's summary, L2 writers employ simpler sentences with more authoritative warnings, admonitions, personal references and narratives, and repetitions of ideas and vocabulary. In regard to its linguistic features, NNS prose contains fewer syntactically complex constructions, such as subordinate clauses, descriptive adjective phrases, hedges, modifiers of most types, compound noun phrases, and possessives, but more coordinators, sentence transitions, and pronouns[1]. To summarize, compared to L1 writers, L2 writers have a restricted syntactic and stylistic repertoire, as well as severely limited range of accessible lexis that can be used in writing. In all, Silva points out that "L2 writers' texts were less fluent . . . , less accurate . . . , and less effective" (p. 668) than those of NSs, and "in terms of lower level linguistic concerns, L2 writers' texts were stylistically distinct and simpler in structure."

Based on earlier research, Silva (1993, p. 669) calls for a reconceptualization of how L2 writing and text production are taught in U.S. colleges and universities: "The prevalent assumption that L1 and L2 writing are, for all intents and purposes, the same" is unexamined and has remained largely unvalidated, and the many findings of research "make this assumption untenable." Silva emphasizes that L1 "composition theories, which are, incidentally, largely monolingual, monocultural, ethnocentric, and fixated on the writing of NES [native English speaker] undergraduates in North American colleges and universities" are inapplicable to teaching L2 writing, do L2 writers a great disservice, and are, quite possibly, counterproductive.

Almost a decade later, a large scale empirical analysis of 68 lexical, syntactic, and rhetorical features of L2 text was carried out by Hinkel (2002), who examined 1,457 (around 435,000 words) NS and NNS placement essays written in several universities across the United States. The L2 text corpus included texts written by speakers of six languages: Arabic, Chinese, Indonesian, Japanese, Korean, and Vietnamese. All NNS students (1,215) were advanced and trained L2 writers, a large majority of whom were holders of U.S. academic degrees. Hinkel reports that, even after years of ESL and composition training, L2 writers' text continues to differ significantly from that of novice (first-year) NS students in regard to most features examined in her study. The results of her analysis indicate that even advanced and trained L2 writers have a severely limited lexical and syntactic repertoire that enables them to produce simple texts restricted to the most common language features that occur predominantly in conversational discourse. Hinkel concluded that L2 texts do not approximate those in L1 basic academic writing because NSs of English already have a highly developed (native) language proficiency that a majority of NNSs require years to develop, in most cases as adults. Like Silva (1993), Hinkel calls for changes in the methodologies for teaching L2 writing that are based on the pedagogy intended for teaching composition to NSs.

COMPUTER TEXT BASES AND ANALYSES OF L2 WRITTEN CORPORA

Beginning in the late 1980s, due to the advancements in computer technology that permitted analyses of large amounts of printed or typed text, corpus-based studies dramatically altered the methodologies for analyzing syntactic, lexical, and collocational features employed in various written genre in English (e.g., Biber, 1988; Leech, Rayson, & Wilson, 2001; Renouf & Sinclair, 1991; Sinclair, 1991; Stubbs, 1996). The rapid changes in text linguistics and the new knowledge obtained from the analyses of large text corpora have also influenced the methods and scope of research in L2 writing.

As an outcome, the studies of the syntactic, lexical, and other micro features of L2 text have similarly changed their methodological approaches, as well as the sizes and types of L2 written corpora. To illustrate, the new genres of L2 text that lend themselves to computerized investigations, NS and NNS e-mail messages can be examined in regard to their grammar structures, syntactic accuracy, lexical ranges and complexity, and common politeness formulae (Chang & Hsu, 1998; Gonzalez-Bueno & Perez, 2000; Li, 2000).

Other research projects investigate L2 academic writing in corpora that range from 50,000 to 500,000 words and include texts produced by tens or hundreds of students (Flowerdew, 2001; Granger, 1998; Hyland & Milton, 1997). In L2 writing assessment, the size and scope of analyses evolved from exclusive reliance on impressionistic ratings of essays by specially trained readers to computations of frequency and percentage rates with which particular syntactic, lexical, and discourse features are employed in learner prose (Frase et al., 1999; Hamp-Lyons, 1991b; Reid, 1993; Weigle, 2002).

It is important to note, however, that despite the increase in the size of L2 written corpora, the investigations of discoursal, syntactic, and lexical features largely remained focused on the attributes of text similar to those examined in the numerous studies carried out prior to the technological and methodological innovations in text linguistics (e.g., Choi, 1988; Field & Oi, 1992; Hinkel, 2001a, 2002, 2003a; Johns, 1984; Ostler, 1987). In particular, language errors, coherence and cohesion markers (such as coordinating conjunctions and demonstrative pronouns), clause subordinators, modal verbs, personal pronouns, prepositions, adjectives, hedges, and intensifiers remained among the mainstays of research on computerized textual databases (Flowerdew, 1998, 2000; Granger, 1998, 2002; Granger & Tribble, 1998; Green, Christopher & Lam, 2000; Hyland & Milton, 1997; Lorenz, 1998; Reid, 1992; Ringbom, 1998; Tribble, 2001).

To some extent, the reason that computer analyses of written learner corpora have continued to focus on syntactic, lexical, and rhetorical features very similar to those extensively examined in a large number of earlier studies is that, compared to published English-language texts, most L2 writing includes a limited range of linguistic constructions (Granger, 2002; Hinkel, 2001b, 2002, 2003b). Another issue with the current L2 learner corpora is that such databases as International Corpus of Learner English consist exclusively of L2 texts written by speakers of European languages, such as Dutch[2], Finnish, French, German, Spanish, and Swedish.

On the other hand, the innovations brought about by the advances in computerized L2 text analyses permit insights into the characteristics of L2 text that cannot be attained by means of manual studies (Granger, 2002; Granger & Rayson, 1998), for example:

- Frequent co-occurrences of words in different genres of L2 text.
- Overuse or underuse of particular lexis or grammar constructions, for example, *find*, *want*, and *know* are by far the most common verbs in the L2 writing of Swedish speakers (Ringbom, 1998).
- L1 to L2 transfer of specific lexical and syntactic patterns, for example, distinctive phrases and patterns can be found, for example, in the writing of the speakers of French but not Dutch and German (Granger, 2002).
- Classification of errors by types (e.g., grammatical, collocational, or stylistic) and frequencies of their occurrence.

Meunier (1998) points out, however, that the typical computations of type/token ratio of words in a text used to measure the amount of lexical variation do not seem to reflect a relative quality of L2 texts because lexically varied prose is not necessarily of good quality. For example, if some NNS writers have a good vocabulary range but poor discourse organization or grammar skills, their text would not be of high quality, even when it is lexically rich. To be specific, Lorenz (1998) found that in the case of advanced German speakers with substantial and developed L2 English vocabulary repertoires, it was not so much a lack of accessible lexis that made their L2 writing appear non-native, but the ways in which particular lexical items were used (see also Lewis, 1993, 1997, and Nattinger & DeCarrico, 1992, for additional discussion on idiomaticity, collocations, and formulaic lexical phrases in written text).

Similar to the findings of studies carried out earlier based on smaller samples of various genres in L2 writing, the results of the computerized analyses of L2 writing have also clearly demonstrated that L2 written discourse and text are crucially and significantly distinct from those produced by L1 writers in English.

ISSUES AND COMPLEXITIES IN L2 TEXT RESEARCH

Technological advances in computerized text analyses of English-language corpora have allowed researchers to shed light on the real-life uses of syntactic, lexical, and collocational features in native speaker language production. In the past several decades, some of the large native English corpora have worked with spoken and written text bases as large as 30 million words (Biber et al., 1999; Leech, Rayson, & Wilson, 2001; Stubbs, 2001) (see also Collins COBUILD corpus-based learner dictionaries developed by researchers at the University of Birmingham).

One of the key differences between analyses of corpora of L1 English-language corpora and L2 text analyses lies in the fact that, for instance, the corpora of written English include large amounts of published (i.e., polished and edited) texts. On the other hand, L2 texts are either handwritten or typed by NNSs, whose language usage (e.g., spelling, word formation, or phrasing) is distinct from that in practically any type of native speaker prose.

One of the stumbling blocks in investigations of L2 handwritten texts is that current software for converting handwriting into typed text is highly unreliable, and to overcome software problems, L2 texts are keyed after they are written (e.g., Meunier, 1998; Shaw & Liu, 1998). However, to allow computer programs to count a number of occurrences of, for example, particular words or constructions, decisions need to be made whether to correct spelling, grammar, or lexis to make them uniform or leave the original text intact.

Although studies of L2 text have mainly been driven by the growing body of findings and publications in computerized analyses of English language corpora, to date a consistent methodology for L2 corpus research has not yet emerged. Some researchers, such as Ferris (1993), claimed that computer analyses of L2 text may not be possible in the near future. Computerized analyses of typed L2 essays obtained in large scale assessments (e.g., the Test of Written English) reported significant proportions (up to 21%) of misidentified L2 textual features (Frase et al., 1999).

Developers of L2 written corpora also reported additional confounding complexities associated with building and analyzing text bases (Granger, 2002; Meunier, 1998):

- When L2 text is keyed or scanned, a number of errors are routinely introduced (e.g., omissions, additions, and misrepresentations), and proofreading typed L2 texts against the originals is an extremely laborious, time-consuming, and iterative process.
- Computerized analyses of L2 corpora do not permit analyses of global and abstract discourse features (e.g., sufficient/explicit rhetorical support), many grammar features (e.g., referential/nonreferential pronouns, as in *they tell me* . . .), sentence or T-unit counts, or measurements of lexical density; these have to be carried out manually.
- In analyses of L2 errors, error tagging is a manual and time-consuming process, and the classification of errors is often subjective.
- Word counts of the same texts can diverge significantly (up to 10%), when different types of software are used (e.g., hyphenated words or contractions can be counted as either one or two words). In such cases, statistical analyses, fundamentally dependent on baseline word counts, can be invalidated.

The following example is excerpted from a L2 university essay on taking risks in order to succeed to illustrate the difficulties of computerized parsing and tagging of L2 text.

> I think that the adecatte combination between this aditudes in life is the key for open the succed's door. In one way, take a risk can be important to rich some relevant chance, for example, "shakira", who is a very important pop singer, take a risks when she and her family recordered her first Long play. They spend all the money that they had in the bank and now they are rich and she is a important artist. but in and other way, people have lost all them fortune for a bat business so many people preffer work hard and work for sure. In conclusion. In all the success cases we will discoves that the combination between take risk and take care is the key.

In many cases, even if the writer's spelling is corrected, computer tagging of syntactic and lexical features, as in this example, would be very difficult. In fact, this particular text may need to be sounded out at least to understand what it says.

In light of the fact that reliable automatic analyses of L2 text still lag behind those of published or transcribed L1 English language corpora, most L2 text studies published to date have relied on manual analyses of discourse, syntactic, lexicalized, and rhetorical features. Tagging and hand-counting features are extremely work- and time-consuming processes that impose limitations on the amounts of text that can be analyzed by a single researcher or even a group of researchers.

SUMMARY AND CONCLUSION

In the past half century, numerous studies have examined discoursal, lexical, syntactic, and rhetorical properties of L2 writing. Practically all research on L2 written prose has focused on the features of discourse and text identified in research in text linguistics that accounts for how lexical, syntactic, stylistic, and rhetorical elements combine to create particular types of prose and genres. Investigations into L2 text have identified the important and significant differences that exist between L1 and L2 writing. In part, these differences stem from divergent written discourse paradigms valued in various rhetorical traditions and often transferred from L1 to L2. Such global features of L2 discourse as organization and information structuring, topic development and continuity, as well as text cohesion, coherence, and clarity appear to be greatly influenced by the rhetorical and text construction norms that differ widely across languages and cultures.

Research has also demonstrated that other crucial factors that confound L2 writing and text have to do with shortfalls of writers' language proficiencies and restricted linguistic repertoire that significantly undermine L2 writers' ability to produce high quality texts. Based on the results of their studies, many researchers of L2 learning and development have emphasized that even school-age children or highly educated adult L2 learners require years of language training to attain the levels of proficiency necessary to create effective written prose.

ACKNOWLEDGMENTS

My sincere thanks to Robert B. Kaplan and Rodney Hill for their insightful comments and suggestions on an earlier draft of this chapter. Through the years, their unfailing help and support have become indispensable.

NOTES

1. For similar findings of large-scale empirical investigations, see also, Carlson (1988), Flowerdew (2000, 2001), Hinkel (2001a, 2001b, 2002, 2003a, 2003b), Johns (1997), Reid (1992), Ringbom (1998), Schleppegrell (1996, 2002), and Shaw and Liu (1998), to mention just a few.
2. Other L2 corpora, e.g., Longman's Learner Corpus and Hong Kong University of Science and Technology Learner Corpus, are proprietary and accessible only to the researchers affiliated with these institutions.

REFERENCES

Al-Khatib, M. (2001). The pragmatics of letter-writing. *World Englishes, 20*(2), 170–200.
Arndt, V. (1993). Response to writing: Using feedback to inform the writing process. In M. Brock & L. Walters (Eds.), *Teaching composition around the Pacific Rim: Politics and pedagogy* (pp. 90–116). Clevedon, UK: Multilingual Matters.
Basham, C., & Kwachka, P. (1991). Reading the world differently: A crosscultural approach to writing assessment. In L. Hamp-Lyons (Ed.), *Assessing second language writing in academic contexts* (pp. 37–49). Norwood, NJ: Ablex.
Biber, D. (1988). *Variation across speech and writing.* Cambridge, UK: Cambridge University Press.
Biber, D., Johansson, S., Leech, G., Conrad, S., & Finegan, E. (1999). *Longman grammar of spoken and written English.* Harlow, Essex: Pearson.

Bouton, L. (1995). A crosscultural analysis of the structure and content of letters of reference. *Studies in Second Language Acquisition, 17*(2), 211–244.

Cai, G. (1999). Texts in contexts: Understanding Chinese students' English compositions. In C. Cooper & L. Odell (Eds.), *Evaluating writing: The role of teachers' knowledge about text, learning, and culture* (pp. 279–299). Urbana, IL: NCTE.

Carlson, S. (1988). Cultural differences in writing and reasoning skills. In A. Purves (Ed.), *Writing across languages and cultures: Issues in contrastive rhetoric* (pp. 109–137). Newbury Park, CA: Sage.

Chang, Y.-Y. & Hsu, Y. P. (1998). Requests on e-mail: A crosscultural comparison. *RELC Journal, 29*(2), 121–151.

Choi, Y. (1988). Text structure of Korean speakers' argumentative essays in English. *World Englishes, 7*(2), 129–142.

Clyne, M. (1987). Cultural differences in the organization of academic texts. *Journal of Pragmatics, 11*(1), 211–247.

Cmejrkova, S. (1996). Academic writing in Czech and English. In E. Ventola & A. Mauranen (Eds.), *Academic writing: Intercultural and textual issues* (pp. 137–152). Amsterdam: John Benjamins.

Connor, U., & Johns, A.M. (Eds.). (1990). *Coherence in writing: Research and pedagogical perspectives.* Alexandria, VA: TESOL.

Coulthard, M. (1985). *An introduction to discourse analysis* (2nd ed.). London: Longman.

de Beaugrande, R. & Dressler, W. (1972). *Introduction to text linguistics.* London: Longman.

Edelsky, C. (1986). *Writing in a bilingual program: Habia una vez.* Norwood, NJ: Ablex.

Ferris, D. (1993). The design of an automatic analysis program for L2 text research: Necessity and feasibility. *Journal of Second Language Writing, 2*(2), 119–129.

Field, Y., & Oi, Y. L. M. (1992). A comparison of internal conjunctive cohesion in the English essay writing of Cantonese speakers and native speakers. *RELC Journal, 23*(1), 15–28.

Flowerdew, L. (1998). Integrating expert and interlanguage computer corpora findings on causality: Discoveries for teachers and students. *English for Specific Purposes, 17*(4), 329–345.

Flowerdew, L. (2000). Investigating errors in a learner corpus. In L. Burnard & T. McEnery (Eds.), *Proceedings in the teaching and language corpora conference* (pp. 145–154). Frankfurt: Peter Lang.

Flowerdew, L. (2001). The exploitation of small learner corpora in EAP material design. In M. Ghadessy, A. Henry, & R. Roseberry (Eds.), *Small corpus studies and ELT* (pp. 363–380). Amsterdam: John Benjamins.

Frase, L., Faletti, J., Ginther, A., & Grant, L. (1999). *Computer analysis of the TOEFL Test of Written English* (Research report 64). Princeton, NJ: Educational Testing Service.

Gonzalez-Bueno, M., & Perez, L. C. (2000). Electronic mail in foreign language writing: A study of grammatical and lexical accuracy, and quantity of language. *Foreign Language Annals, 33*(2), 189–198.

Grabe, W. & Kaplan, R. B. (1996). *Theory and practice of writing.* London: Longman.

Grabe, W. (1987). Contrastive rhetoric and text-type research. In U. M. Connor & R. B. Kaplan (Eds.), *Writing across languages: Analysis of L2 text* (pp. 115–137). Reading, MA: Addison-Wesley.

Granger, S. (1998). *Learner English on computer.* London: Longman.

Granger, S. (2002). A bird's-eye view of computer learner corpus research. In S. Granger, J. Hung, & S. Petch-Tyson, (Eds.), *Computer learner corpora, second language acquisition, and foreign language teaching.* (pp. 3–36). Amsterdam: John Benjamins.

Granger, S., & Rayson, P. (1998). Automatic lexical profiling of learner texts. In Granger, S. (Ed.), *Learner English on computer* (pp. 119–131). London: Longman.

Granger, S., & Tribble, C. (1998). Learner corpus data in the foreign language classroom: Form-focused instruction and data-driven learning. In Granger, S. (Ed.), *Learner English on computer* (pp. 199–209). London: Longman.

Green, C., Christopher, E., & Lam, J. (2000). The incidence and defects on coherence of marked themes in interlanguage texts: A corpus-based enquiry. *English for Specific Purposes, 19*(2), 99–113.

Hakuta, K., Butler, Y., & Witt, D. (2000). *How long does it take English learners to attain proficiency?* Retrieved July 3, 2003 from http://www.stanford.edu/~hakuta/Docs/HowLong.pdf

Halliday, M. A. K. (1994). The construction of knowledge and the grammar of scientific discourse, with reference to Charles Darwin's *The Origin of Species.* In M. Coulthard (Ed.), *Advances in written text analysis,* (pp. 136–156). New York: Routledge & Kegan Paul.

Halliday, M. A. K., & Hasan, R. (1976). *Cohesion in English.* London: Longman.

Halliday, M. A. K., & Hasan, R. (1989). *Spoken and written language.* Oxford, UK: Oxford University Press.

Hamp-Lyons, L. (1991a). Issues and directions in assessing second language writing in academic contexts. In L. Hamp-Lyons (Ed.), *Assessing second language writing in academic contexts* (pp. 323–329). Norwood, NJ: Ablex.

Hamp-Lyons, L. (1991b). Reconstructing "academic writing proficiency." In L. Hamp-Lyons (Ed.), *Assessing second language writing in academic contexts* (pp. 127–153). Norwood, NJ: Ablex.

Hamp-Lyons, L., & Kroll, B. (1996). Issues in ESL writing assessment: An overview. *College ESL,* 52–72.

Hatim, B. (1991). The pragmatics of argumentation in Arabic: The rise and fall of text type. *Text, 11*(1), 189–199.

Hinds, J. (1983). Contrastive rhetoric. *Text 3*(2), 183–195.

Hinds, J. (1987). Reader versus writer responsibility: A new typology. In U. Connor & R. B. Kaplan (Eds.), *Writing across languages: Analysis of L2 text.* (pp. 141–152). Reading, MA: Addison-Wesley.

Hinds, J. (1990). Inductive, deductive, quasi-inductive: Expository writing in Japanese, Korean, Chinese, and Thai. In U. Connor & A. Johns (Eds.), *Coherence in writing* (pp. 87–110). Alexandria, VA: TESOL.

Hinkel, E. (1994). Native and non-native speakers' pragmatic interpretation of English text. *TESOL Quarterly, 28*(2), 353–376.

Hinkel, E. (1995). The use of modal verbs as a reflection of cultural values. *TESOL Quarterly, 29*, 325–343.

Hinkel, E. (1997). Indirectness in L1 and L2 academic writing. *Journal of Pragmatics, 27*(3), 360–386.

Hinkel, E. (1999). Objectivity and credibility in L1 and L2 academic writing. In E. Hinkel (Ed.), *Culture in second language teaching and learning.* (pp. 90–108). Cambridge, UK: Cambridge University Press.

Hinkel, E. (2001a). Matters of cohesion in L1 and L2 academic texts. *Applied Language Learning, 12*(2), 111–132.

Hinkel, E. (2001b). Giving examples and telling stories in academic essays. *Issues in Applied Linguistics, 12/2*, 149–170.

Hinkel, E. (2002). *Second language writers' text.* Mahwah, NJ: Lawrence Erlbaum Associates.

Hinkel, E. (2003a). Simplicity without elegance: Features of sentences in L2 and L1 academic texts. *TESOL Quarterly, 37*(2), 275–301.

Hinkel, E. (2003b). Adverbial markers and tone in L1 and L2 students' writing. *Journal of Pragmatics, 35*(7), 1049–1068.

Hoey, M. (1991). *Patterns of lexis in text.* Oxford, UK: Oxford University Press.

Hudelson, S. (1988). *Write on: Children's writing in ESL.* Englewood Cliffs, NJ: Prentice-Hall.

Hyland, K., & Milton, J. (1997). Qualification and certainty in L1 and L2 students' writing. *Journal of Second Language Writing 6*(2), 183–205.

Indrasuta, C. (1988). Narrative styles in the writing of Thai and American students. In A. Purves (Ed.), *Writing across languages and cultures: Issues in contrastive rhetoric* (pp. 206–227). Newbury Park, CA: Sage.

Jenkins, S., & Hinds, J. (1987). Business letter writing: English, French, and Japanese. *TESOL Quarterly, 21*(2), 327–349.

Johns, A. (1984). Textual cohesion and the Chinese speaker of English. *Language Learning and Communication, 3*, 69–74.

Johns, A. (1990). Coherence as a cultural phenomenon: Employing ethnographic principles in the academic milieu. In U. Connor & A. Johns (Eds.), *Coherence in writing* (pp. 211–225). Alexandria, VA: TESOL.

Johns, A. (1997). *Text, role, and context: Developing academic literacies.* Cambridge, UK: Cambridge University Press.

Johnson, P. (1992). Cohesion and coherence in compositions in Malay and English. *RELC Journal, 23*(2), 1–17.

Kaplan, R. B. (1966). Cultural thought patterns in intercultural education. *Language Learning, 16*(1), 1–20.

Kaplan, R. B. (1983). Contrastive rhetorics: Some implications for the writing process. In A. Freedman, I. Pringle, & J. Yalden (Eds.), *Learning to write: First language/second language* (pp. 139–161). London: Longman.

Kaplan, R. B. (1988). Contrastive rhetoric and second language learning: Notes towards a theory of contrastive rhetoric. In A. Purves (Ed.), *Writing across languages and cultures: Issues in contrastive thetoric* (pp. 275–304). Newbury Park, CA: Sage.

Kaplan, R. B. (2000). Contrastive rhetoric and discourse analysis: Who writes what to whom? When? In what circumstances? In S. Sarangi & M. Coulthard (Eds.), *Discourse and social life* (pp. 82–102). Harlow, UK: Longman.

Khalil, A. (1989). A study of cohesion and coherence in Arab EFL college students' writing. *System 17*(3), 359–371.

Leech, G., Rayson, P., & Wilson, A. (2001). *Word frequencies in written and spoken English.* London: Longman.

Leki, I. (1992). *Understanding ESL writers.* Portsmouth, NH: Boyton/Cook.

Lewis, M. (1993). *The lexical approach.* Hove, UK: LTP.

Lewis, M. (1997). Pedagogical implications of the lexical approach. In J. Coady & T. Huckin (Eds.), *Second language vocabulary acquisition: A rationale for pedagogy* (pp. 255–270). Cambridge: Cambridge University Press.

Li, Y. (2000). Linguistic characteristics of ESL writing in task-based e-mail activities. *System, 28*, 229–245.

Lorenz, G. (1998). Overstatement in advanced learners' writing: Stylistic aspects of adjective intensification. In S. Granger (Ed.), *Learner English on computer* (pp. 53–66). London: Longman.

Maguire, M., & Graves, B. (2001). Speaking personalities in primary school children's writing. *TESOL Quarterly, 35*(4), 561–593.

Matalene, C. (1985). Contrastive rhetoric: An American writing teacher in China. *College English, 47*, 789–807.

Mauranen, A. (1996). Discourse competence: Evidence from thematic development in native and non-native texts. In E. Ventola & A. Mauranen (Eds.), *Academic writing: Intercultural and textual issues* (pp. 195–230). Amsterdam: John Benjamins.

Meunier, F. (1998). Computer tools for the analysis of learner corpora. In S. Granger (Ed.), *Learner English on computer* (pp. 19–37). London: Longman.

Mohan, B., & Lo, W. A. (1985). Academic writing and Chinese students: Transfer and developmental factors. *TESOL Quarterly, 19*(3), 515–534.

Montano-Harmon, M. (1991). Discourse features of written Mexican Spanish: Current research in contrastive rhetoric and its implications. *Hispania, 74*(3), 417–425.

Nattinger, J. & DeCarrico, J. (1992). *Lexical phrases and language teaching.* Oxford, UK: Oxford University Press.

Ostler, S. (1987). English in parallels: A comparison of English and Arabic prose. In U. Connor & R. Kaplan (Eds.), *Writing across languages: Analysis of L2 text* (pp. 169–185). Reading, MA: Addison-Wesley.

Park, Y. M. (1988). Academic and ethnic background as factors affecting writing performance. In A. Purves (Ed.), *Writing across language and cultures* (pp. 261–273). Newbury Park, CA: Sage.

Reid, J. (1992). A computer text analysis of four cohesion devices in English discourse by native and non-native writers. *Journal of Second Language Writing, 1*(2), 79–107.

Reid, J. (1993). *Teaching ESL writing.* Englewood Cliffs, NJ: Prentice-Hall.

Renouf, A., & Sinclair, J. (1991). Collocational frameworks in English. In K. Aijmer & B. Altenberg (Eds.), *English corpus linguistics* (pp. 128–143). New York: Longman.

Ringbom, H. (1998). Vocabulary frequencies in advanced learner English. In S. Granger (Ed.), *Learner English on computer* (pp. 41–52). London: Longman.

Sa'adeddin, M. A. (1989). Text development and Arabic-English negative interference. *Applied Linguistics, 10*(1), 36–51.

Scarcella, R., & Chunok, L. (1989). Different paths to writing proficiency in a second language? A preliminary investigation of ESL writers of short-term and long-term residence in the United States. In M. Eisenstein (Ed.), *The dynamic interlanguage: Empirical studies in second language variation* (pp. 137–154). New York: Plenum.

Schleppegrell, M. (1996). Conjunction in spoken English and ESL writing. *Applied Linguistics, 17*(3), 271–285.

Schleppegrell, M. (2002). Challenges of the science register for ESL students: Errors and meaning-making. In M. Schleppegrell & M. Colombi (Eds.), *Developing advanced literacy in first and second languages* (pp. 119–142). Mahwah, NJ: Lawrence Erlbaum Associates.

Scollon, R. (1991). Eight legs and one elbow: Stance and structure in Chinese English compositions. In (Ed.), *Proceedings of the 2nd North American Conference on Adult and Adolescent Literacy* (pp. 26–41). Ottawa: International Reading Association.

Shaw, P. & Liu, E. T. K. (1998). What develops in the development of second language writing. *Applied Linguistics, 19*(2), 225–254.

Silva, T. (1993). Toward an understanding of the distinct nature of L2 writing: The ESL research and its implications. *TESOL Quarterly, 27*(4), 657–677.

Sinclair, J. (1991). *Corpus, concordance, collocation.* Oxford, UK: Oxford University Press.

Stubbs, M. (1996). *Text and corpus analysis.* Oxford, UK: Blackwell.

Stubbs, M. (2001). *Words and phrases: Corpus studies of lexical semantics.* Oxford, UK: Blackwell.

Swales, J. (1990). Non-native speaker graduate engineering students and their introductions: Global coherence and local management. In U. Connor & A. Johns (Eds.), *Coherence in writing* (pp. 189–207). Alexandria, VA: TESOL.

Taylor, G., & Chen, T. (1991). Linguistic, cultural, and subcultural issues in contrastive discourse analysis: Anglo-American and Chinese scientific texts. *Applied Linguistics, 12*, 319–336.

Tribble, C. (2001). Small corpora and teaching writing. In M. Ghadessy, A. Henry, & R. Roseberry (Eds.), *Small corpus studies and ELT* (pp. 381–408). Amsterdam: John Benjamins.

Valdes, G., & Sanders, P. (1999). Latino ESL students and the development of writing abilities. In C. Cooper & L. Odell (Eds.), *Evaluating writing: The role of teachers' knowledge about text, learning, and culture* (pp. 249–278). Urbana, IL: National Council for Teachers of English.

van Dijk, T. (Ed.). (1985). *Handbook of discourse analysis.* (4 vols) London: Academic Press.

Weigle, S. (2002). *Assessing writing.* Cambridge, UK: Cambridge University Press.

V

Methods and Curricula in Second Language Teaching

Introduction

Ideally, the purpose of a method for second language (L2) teaching is to connect the theories or research findings on how second languages are learned with how they can be taught. Thus, in real terms, teaching methods are theories translated into practical classroom applications. Various methods can emphasize different facets of L2 learning and teaching. For example, the communicative method that today represents a prevalent approach to teaching L2 and foreign language (FL) in many English-speaking countries aims to improve learners' oral communication skills and spoken fluency. On the other hand, the grammar translation method widely popular in the countries where FL is learned in the classroom is geared toward developing and enhancing the knowledge of formal grammar and vocabulary.

The concept of an L2 teaching method has traditionally occupied a central role in teacher training and curriculum development. Usually, divergent L2 teaching methods are accompanied by specific syllabuses (not to be confused with class syllabi) or curricula that in effect constitute rather well-delineated guidelines for teaching. Although many methodologists of L2/FL teaching believe that syllabuses are distinct from curricula, equally many see them as different terms for largely the same thing, that is, the specifications of what is to be taught and learned with reasoned explanations of why these facts of language are to be taught and learned. The syllabus specifications or curriculum guidelines, together with other aspects of ascribed classroom instruction, in effect represent what is referred to as teaching method.

A Side Note: Syllabuses should not be confused with teaching methods, even though each method includes a particular type of syllabus (otherwise known as curricular guidelines). Depending on a point of view, two major varieties of syllabuses can be identified: synthetic and analytic. Among the synthetic syllabuses, one can count five or six main varieties: structural, lexical, notional, functional, and situational/topical. Additionally, analytic syllabuses include such exemplars as procedural, process, and task-based. Depending on one's interpretation, though, at some juncture teaching methods and syllabuses can merge and/or be grouped into, for example, process methods with learner/learning-focused syllabi or procedural methods with cognitive-focused/task-based syllabi.

The methods for teaching practically always include such requisite features as learning objectives and techniques for L2/FL teaching in order to accomplish these objectives, as well as types of suitable classroom activities and the roles of teachers (e.g., student-centered/teacher-centered methods or the teacher as enabler or facilitator), teaching materials, and learning tasks. In most cases, the teachers are expected to connect the characteristics of specific methods and curricula to the daily practice of teaching and student learning.

Teaching methods have evolved rapidly during the past several decades, although the creation of new methods for L2 teaching had been dramatically slower in the previous millennia. For instance, between the 1940s and the 1970s, L2 practitioners saw a number of methods wax and wane:

- The Audiolingual method (also called Situational Language Teaching in some English-speaking countries) was the coin of the L2 realm for almost four decades until the 1960s.
- With the fall of audiolingualism, the Silent Way, Suggestopedia, and Total Physical Response arrived on the scene. Another method, sometimes called Community Language Learning, was also popular in some locations and contexts.

These L2 teaching methods that have since fallen out of favor are not included in the overview of methods in Part V.

The chapters in Part V discuss **the two main L2 and FL teaching methods** that are widely adopted today, although in divergent contexts and for different types of learners.

1. The humanistic and interactive/interactional methods became predominant in L2 teaching in the 1980s and 1990s with the arrival of the Communicative Language Teaching (CLT). One of the fundamental principles of CLT is that learners need to engage in meaningful communication to attain communicative fluency and thus become enabled to carry out authentic communication, predominantly in ESL/L2 settings. Chapter 35 by **Sandra Savignon** presents a thorough discussion of CLT goals and evolution over time.
2. Many researchers claim, however, that in EFL contexts, where learners do not use FL outside the classroom, the need for authentic communication is dramatically reduced. In the case of FL learners, the primary objective of FL teaching and learning is to prepare learners to pass exams that crucially determine a learner's future careers. Thus, for such learners who represent a great statistical majority of all students of English, the Grammar Translation Method (GMT) is far more appropriate. In Chapter 36, **Sandra Fotos** discusses the origins and the current developments in GMT.

While the instructional objectives of these (and other) broad-based methodologies for L2/FL teaching can be relatively well defined, an immense amount of controversy has accompanied the ways in which they can be achieved. Although the main thrust of the prevalent teaching methods largely adhere to the fundamental and distinct methodological principles, the curricula for achieving teaching and learning objectives can differ greatly across a large number of variations of the popular methods. Many of these are rooted in CLT and advocate communicative fluency, meaningful and authentic communication, and minimal explicit teaching and error correction.

The following important **variations of CLT** are also covered in Part V:

- Chapter 37, by **Jessica Williams**, reviews the many incarnations of Focus-on-Form Instruction that have emerged in the past few decades since its origination in the early 1980s.
- Chapter 38, by **Ann Snow**, takes a close look at the Content-based Instruction that has proven to be highly influential in the schooling of learners of various ages.
- Chapter 39, by **Rod Ellis**, examines the benefits of instructed (versus purely naturalistic) language learning and teaching and emphasizes the benefits of Task-based Teaching.

In addition to the development of communicative fluency, however, researchers on L2 teaching and learning have underscored the need for accuracy in L2 production and use. The CLT emphasis on fluency without great regard for accuracy and quality in L2 production has led to dissatisfaction among large numbers of methodologists and practitioners alike. Thus, without completely and explicitly rejecting CLT, which is probably the dominant methodology in L2 teaching in most English-speaking countries, recognized experts have proposed a variety of methods and curricula to improve the quality of L2 learning and learner language. These teaching methods have the goal of combining **L2/FL communicative fluency** with an important emphasis on **linguistic accuracy**:

- Chapter 40, by **Marianne Celce-Murcia** and **Elite Olshtain**, discusses Discourse-based teaching that seeks to explicitly address the issues of accuracy and the uses of linguistic features in L2.
- Chapter 41, by **Carol Chapelle**, explains how Computer-Assisted Language Learning can lead to enhancements in terms of both fluency and accuracy of L2/FL learner production and teaching.

A number of other methods have also been created, but with diferent degrees of popularity. Many of these represent derivatives of CLT with added ingredients frequently borrowed from teaching and disciplines other than those developed specifically for L2/FL instruction, such as educational theories for teaching in urban schools or adult education.

As has been mentioned, large numbers of L2/FL teaching methods, often found under different names, are likely to be found in many textbooks for teachers and teaching, the work of many L2 theoreticians, various L2/FL contexts, settings, and geographical locations. Many of these were originally designed to imitate how children learn their first language, even though research has demonstrated that adult learners have entirely different language learning constraints and learn the language in completely different ways.

The following and often overlapping CLT-based teaching methods and curricula are not included in Part V due to their reduced or waning popularity. The list is not exhaustive but consists merely of examples:

- Whole-Language Teaching.
- The Natural Approach.
- Cooperative Language Learning.
- Collaborative Teaching/Learning.
- Community-based Learning.

In addition, the chapters in Part V do not include an overview of the Lexical Approach, as well as a large number of syllabus-based methods, such as those mentioned earlier, for example, the Notional-Functional Syllabus, the Structural Syllabus, the Functional Syllabus, or the Situational/Topical Syllabus (see The Side Note).

A Caveat Emptor

A number of key issues with the view of L2 instruction that pivots on particular methods have emerged to highlight the fact that teaching methods find themselves in a perpetual state of flux.

1. No single method can be useful or even beneficial to all learners in all teaching contexts.

2. Methods often become subject to changing points of view on what is best for whom at a particular time.
3. The continual shifts in the development of "best," the "most effective," or "the most appropriate" method have led to what is occasionally termed "band-wagon-ism" when fleeting fashions in teaching come to dominate instructional objectives, curricula, mind-sets, and materials.

• Part V concludes with Chapter 42, by **Neil Anderson**, on L2 Learning Strategies and learner strategy training. The goal of learning strategies is to improve language learning and performance in the use of a second language. To this end, the use of effective learning strategies can represent an advantage when employed in conjunction with any L2 teaching method or in the context of practically any type of language learning. Although many productive language learning strategies can and have been identified, as with language teaching methods, relying on any one strategy can rarely be effective in isolation. Most learning strategies are interconnected and should be used in process and in combination, similar to L2 learning processes overall.

35

Communicative Language Teaching: Strategies and Goals

Sandra J. Savignon
Pennsylvania State University

On the threshold of the 21st century, communicative language teaching (CLT) has become as familiar to discussions about the practice and theory of second and foreign language teaching as the Big Mac is to fast food. The appeal is worldwide. And while the particular characteristics may vary from one context to another, the identifiable features remain the same. Or do they? Just what is CLT? Is it a method of teaching? Does it have characteristics that are universally understood and implemented? If so, what are they? Most important, is CLT a meaningful and lasting reorientation of classroom language teaching, or does it represent but one more swing of the pedagogy pendulum?

This chapter considers CLT within the broader historical spectrum of methods or approaches to language teaching, the theoretical grounding for the epistemology of practice offered by CLT, and the interpretation or implementation of that practice in language teaching contexts around the world. In conclusion, we will consider the implications of CLT for teaching training or education, both preservice and inservice.

LINGUISTIC THEORY AND CLASSROOM PRACTICE

The essence of CLT is the engagement of learners in communication to allow them to develop their communicative competence. Use of the term *communicative* in reference to language teaching refers to both processes and goals in classroom learning. A central theoretical concept in CLT is *communicative competence*, a term introduced in the early 1970s in discussions of language (Habermas, 1970; Hymes, 1971) and second or foreign language learning (Jakobovits, 1970; Savignon, 1971). Competence is defined in terms of the expression, interpretation, and negotiation of meaning and looks to second language acquisition research to account for its development (Savignon, 1972, 1983, 1997). The identification of learner communicative needs provides a basis for curriculum design. Terms sometimes used to refer to features of CLT include process oriented, task based, and inductive, or discovery oriented.

The elaboration of what has come to be called CLT can be traced to concurrent 20th century developments in linguistic theory and language learning curriculum design both in Europe and in North America. In Europe, the language needs of a rapidly increasing group of immigrants and guest workers along with a rich British linguistic tradition, which included social as well as linguistic context in the description of language behavior, led to development of a syllabus for learners based on notional-functional concepts of language use. This notional-functional approach to curriculum design is derived from neo-Firthian systemic or functional linguistics, which views language as meaning potential and maintains the centrality of context of situation in understanding language systems and how they work (Firth, 1930; Halliday, 1978). With sponsorship from the Council of Europe, a Threshold Level of language ability was proposed for each of the languages of Europe in terms of what learners should be able to do with the language (van Ek, 1975). Functions were based on the assessment of learner needs and specified the end result or goal of an instructional program. The term *communicative* was used to describe programs that followed a notional-functional syllabus based on needs assessment, and the Language for Specific Purposes (LSP) movement was launched.

Concurrent development within Europe focused on the process of classroom language learning. In Germany, against a backdrop of social democratic concerns for individual empowerment articulated in the writings of the philosopher Jürgen Habermas (1970), language teaching methodologists took the lead in the development of classroom materials that encouraged learner choice (Candlin, 1978). Their systematic collection of exercise types for communicatively oriented English language teaching was used in teacher in-service courses and workshops to guide curriculum change. Exercises were designed to exploit the variety of social meanings contained within particular grammatical structures. A system of "chains" encouraged teachers and learners to define their own learning path through principled selection of relevant exercises (Piepho, 1974; Piepho & Bredella, 1976). Similar exploratory projects were also initiated by Candlin at his academic home, the University of Lancaster, England, and by Holec (1979) and his colleagues at the University of Nancy, France. Supplementary teacher resource materials promoting classroom CLT became increasingly popular (e.g., Maley & Duff, 1978). There was also a renewed interest in learner vocabulary building. The widespread promotion of audiolingual methodology with a focus on accuracy in terms of so-called "native" grammatical or syntactic form had resulted in the neglect of learner lexical resources (Coady & Huckin, 1997).

At about this same time, pioneering research on adult classroom second language acquisition at the University of Illinois (Savignon, 1971, 1972) used the term communicative competence to characterize the ability of classroom language learners to interact with other speakers, to make meaning, as distinguished from their ability to recite dialogues or to perform on discrete-point tests of grammatical knowledge. At a time when pattern practice and error avoidance were the rule in language teaching, this study of adult classroom acquisition of French looked at the effect of practice in the use of coping strategies as part of an instructional program. By encouraging them to ask for information, to seek clarification, to use circumlocution and whatever other linguistic and nonlinguistic resources they could muster to negotiate meaning, to stick to the communicative task at hand, teachers were invariably leading learners to take risks and to speak in other than memorized patterns.

Test results at the end of the instructional period showed conclusively that learners who had engaged in communication in lieu of doing laboratory pattern drills performed with no less accuracy on discrete-point tests of grammatical structure. On the other hand, their communicative competence as measured in terms of fluency, comprehensibility, effort, and amount of communication in unrehearsed communicative tasks significantly surpassed that of learners who had had no such practice. Learner reactions to the test formats lent further support to the view that even beginners re-spond well to activities that let them focus on meaning as opposed to formal features.

A collection of role-plays, games, and other communicative classroom activities was developed subsequently for inclusion in the adaptation of the French CREDIF materials, *Voix et Visages de la France*. The accompanying guide (Savignon, 1974/1978) described their purpose as that of involving learners in the experience of communi-cation. Teachers were encouraged to provide learners with the French equivalent of expressions like "What's the word for . . . ?", "Please repeat," "I don't understand," expressions that would help them to participate in the negotiation of meaning. Not unlike the efforts of Candlin and colleagues working in Europe, the focus was on classroom process and learner autonomy. The use of games, role-play, pair and other small group activities gained acceptance and was subsequently recommended for inclusion in language teaching programs generally.

The coping strategies identified in the Savignon (1971, 1972) study became the basis for the subsequent identification by Canale and Swain (1980) of strategic com-petence in their three-component framework for communicative competence, along with grammatical competence and sociolinguistic competence. Grammatical compe-tence represented sentence-level syntax, forms that were the focus of Chomskyan theoretical linguistic inquiry and a primary goal of both grammar-translation and audiolingual methodologies. Consistent with a view of language as social behavior, sociolinguistic competence represented a concern for the relevance or appropriacy of those forms in a particular social setting or context.

Inclusion of sociolinguistic competence in the Canale and Swain framework re-flected the challenge within American linguistic theory to the prevailing focus on syntactic features. Dell Hymes (1971) had reacted to Noam Chomsky's (1965) charac-terization of the linguistic competence of the "ideal native speaker" and had used the term *communicative competence* to represent the use of language in social context, the observance of sociolinguistic norms of appropriacy. His concern with speech commu-nities and the integration of language, communication, and culture was not unlike that of Firth and Halliday in the British linguistic tradition. Hyme's communicative competence may be seen as the equivalent of Halliday's meaning potential. Social interaction rather than the abstract psycholinguistic functioning of the human brain would become an identifying feature of CLT.

In subsequent interpretations of the significance of Hymes' perspective for lan-guage learners, methodologists working in the United States tended to focus on na-tive speaker cultural norms or accepted ways of behaving and the difficulty if not the impossibility of authentically representing these norms in a classroom of nonnatives. In light of this difficulty, the appropriateness of communicative competence as an in-structional goal for classroom learners was questioned (Paulston, 1974). CLT thus can be seen to derive from a multidisciplinary perspective that includes, at least, linguis-tics, psychology, philosophy, sociology, and educational research. The focus has been the elaboration and implementation of programs and methodologies that promote the development of functional language ability through learner participation in commu-nicative events. Central to CLT is the understanding of language learning as both an educational and a political issue. Language teaching is inextricably tied to language policy. Viewed from a multicultural intranational as well as international perspective, diverse sociopolitical contexts mandate not only a diverse set of language learning goals, but a diverse set of teaching strategies. Program design and implementation de-pend on negotiation between policy makers, linguists, researchers, and teachers, and evaluation of program success requires a similar collaborative effort. The selection of methods and materials appropriate to both the goals and context of teaching begins with an analysis of socially defined language learner needs as well as the customary styles of learning in a given educational setting.

DISCOURSE COMPETENCE AND THE EMERGENCE OF ENGLISH AS A GLOBAL LANGUAGE

Along with a better understanding of the second language acquisition process itself, the emergence of English as a global or international language has had a profound influence on language teaching, confronting language teacher education with new demands worldwide.

With specific reference to English, CLT includes recognition that the norms followed by those in the "inner circle" of English language users, to adopt the terminology proposed by Kachru (1992), may not be an appropriate goal for learners (Pennycook, 2001; Savignon, 2001, 2002). School programs typically have identified as an instructional goal one variety of English or another. British English has long been a preferred model in many contexts, and American English has become increasingly popular, particularly in Asia (Wang, 2002). Recruitment of "native" speakers from Britain, the United States, and other English-speaking nations is often seen to enhance an instructional program. Whether or not they are qualified teachers, such recruits may benefit from a prestige and privileges not shared by local teachers. When this happens a program may in fact be harmed more than it is helped by their participation.

In a postcolonial, multicultural world where users of English in the "outer" and "expanding circles" outnumber those in the inner circle by a ratio of more than two to one, reference to the terms "native" or "nativelike" in the evaluation of communicative competence seems in some settings simply inappropriate. Even the decision as to what is or is not one's "native" language is arbitrary and seems best left to the individual concerned. Teachers need also to remember that learners differ markedly in their reactions to learning a language for communication. Some may welcome apprenticeship in a new language and view it as an opportunity. For others however the need to find new ways of self-expression may be accompanied by feelings of alienation and estrangement.

These phenomena may be individual or generalizable to an entire community of learners. In Spanish-speaking Puerto Rico, for example, a long-standing general resentment of U.S. domination exerts a powerful negative influence on English language instruction. Not only learners but sometimes teachers may consciously or subconsciously equate communicative English language learning with disloyalty to the history and culture of the island. Studying the rules of grammar and memorizing vocabulary lists are one thing. Using English for communication in other than stereotypical classroom exercises is quite another. Where they exist, such feelings are a strong deterrent to second or foreign language use, even after 10 or more years of instruction.

The influence of community values and attitudes on instructional programs can be found in language programs worldwide and is often precipitated by economic or political events. At the turn of the 20th century, for example, German was the most popular modern foreign language in U.S. school curricula. These programs in turn supported numerous departments of German literary and linguistic studies at U.S. colleges and universities. With the entry of the United States into World War I, enrollments in German plummeted and teachers of German were viewed with suspicion. Many lost their jobs. This enrollment pattern persisted throughout World War II, and today many higher education programs have been merged or deleted.

Attitudes toward a new language can of course be highly individual. They find expression in many different forms. For example, when she was asked what it was like to write in English, Korean novelist Mia Yun (1998) replied that it was "like putting on a new dress." Writing in English makes her feel fresh, lets her see herself in a new way, offers her freedom to experiment. Note the sharp constrast of her sentiments with those of the protagonist in a short story by novelist Salomon Rushdie.

Give me a name, America, make of me a Buzz or Chip or Spike. . . . No longer a historian but a man without histories let me be. I'll rip my lying mother tongue out of my throat and speak your broken English instead. (Rushdie, 2001, p. 75).

With respect to the documentation of crossvarietal differences of English, research to date has focused most often on sentence-level lexical and syntactic features. Consequently, attempts such as the Educational Testing Service (ETS) Test of English for International Communication (TOEIC) to represent norms for a standard English for international communication reflect a primarily lexical and syntactic emphasis (Lowenberg, 1992). The hegemony of essentially Western conventions at the levels of discourse and genre is less easily represented or challenged. Pressures for a "democratization" of discursive practices (Fairclough, 1992) have in some settings resulted in genre mixing and the creation of new genres. In professional communities, however, conformity to the practices of an established membership continues to serve an important gatekeeping function (Foucault, 1981). The privilege of exploiting generic conventions becomes available only to those who enjoy a certain stature or visibility. With particular reference to the academic community, Bhatia (1997) summarizes the situation as follows:

> Much of the academic discourse still fails to acknowledge the sources of variations, especially those of marginality and exclusion, giving the impression that there is, or should be, no variation in the way genres are constructed, interpreted, and used. (p. 369)

Differences in the way genres are constructed, interpreted, and used clearly extend beyond lexical and syntactic variation. Such differences are currently thought of as discursive in nature and included in discourse competence, a fourth component of communicative competence identified subsequently by Canale (1983).

SOCIOCULTURAL CONTEXTS OF COMPETENCE

In her discussion of the contexts of competence, sociolinguist Margie Berns (1990) stresses that the definition of a communicative competence appropriate for learners requires an understanding of the sociocultural contexts of language use. In addition, and as we discussed earlier, the selection of a methodology appropriate to the attainment of communicative competence requires an understanding of sociocultural differences in styles of learning. Curricular innovation is best advanced by the development of local materials, which, in turn, rests on the involvement of local classroom teachers.

Perhaps the best summary of the core tenets of CLT is that offered by Berns (1990; see Savignon, 2002, p. 6):

1. Language teaching is based on a view of language as communication. That is, language is seen as a social tool that speakers and writers use to make meaning; we communicate about something to someone for some purpose, either orally or in writing.
2. Diversity is recognized and accepted as part of language development and use in second language learners and users as it is with first language users.
3. A learner's competence is considered in relative, not absolute, terms of correctness.
4. More than one variety of a language is recognized as a model for learning and teaching.
5. Culture is seen to play an instrumental role in shaping speakers' communicative competence, both in their first and subsequent languages.

6. No single methodology or fixed set of techniques is prescribed.
7. Language use is recognized as serving the ideational, the interpersonal, and the textual functions and is related to the development of learners' competence in each.
8. It is essential that learners be engaged in doing things with language, that is, that they use language for a variety of purposes, in all phases of learning. Learner expectations and attitudes have increasingly come to be recognized for their role in advancing or impeding curricular change.

What About Grammar?

Discussions of CLT not infrequently lead to questions of grammatical or formal accuracy. The perceived displacement of attention to morphosyntactic features in learner expression in favor of a focus on meaning has led in some cases to the impression that grammar is not important, or that proponents of CLT favor learner self-expression without regard to form.

While involvement in communicative events is seen as central to language development, this involvement necessarily requires attention to form. Communication cannot take place in the absence of structure, or grammar, a set of shared assumptions about how language works, along with a willingness of participants to cooperate in the negotiation of meaning. In their carefully researched and widely cited paper proposing components of communicative competence, Canale and Swain (1980) did not suggest that grammar was unimportant. They sought rather to situate grammatical competence within a more broadly defined communicative competence. Similarly, the findings of the Savignon (1971, 1972) study did not suggest that teachers forsake the teaching of grammar. Rather, the replacement of language laboratory structure drills with meaning-focused self-expression was found to be a more effective way to develop communicative ability with no apparent decrease in morphosyntactic accuracy. Learner performance on tests of discrete morphosyntactic features also was not a good predictor of their performance on a series of integrative communicative tasks.

The nature of the contribution to language development of both form-focused and meaning-focused classroom activity remains a question in ongoing research. The optimum combination of these activities in any given instructional setting depends no doubt on learner age, nature and length of instructional sequence, opportunities for language contact outside the classroom, teacher preparation, and other factors (Lightbown & Spada, 2000). Regardless of such differences, however, research findings overwhelmingly support the integration of form-focused exercises with meaning-focused experience. Grammar is important; learners seem to focus best on grammar when it relates to their communicative needs and experiences. Nor is explicit attention to form to be perceived as limited to sentence-level morphosyntactic features. Broader features of discourse, sociolinguistic rules of appropriacy, and communication strategies themselves may be included.

TEACHERS AND TESTS

By definition CLT puts the focus on the learner. As we have seen, learner communicative needs provide a framework for elaborating program goals in terms of functional competence. This implies global, qualitative evaluation of learner achievement as opposed to quantitative assessment of discrete linguistic features.

Debate on appropriate language testing persists, however, and curricular innovation is often doomed in advance by a failure to make corresponding changes in learner evaluation. Current efforts at educational reform favor such things as essay writing, in-class presentations, and other more holistic assessments of learner competence. Some programs have initiated portfolio assessment, the collection and evaluation of learner poems, reports, stories, videotapes, and similar projects in an effort to better represent and encourage learner achievement in terms of their communicative competence. Such efforts are not without problems and often encounter resistance from teachers, administrators, parents, and learners themselves. Current controversy surrounding U.S. education policy that seeks to establish national standards of proficiency for all learners is but one illustration of the continuing debate as to the best ways to assess learner achievement and, ultimately, program effectiveness (Schwartz, 2002). As we will see next, the elaboration and acceptance of appropriate assessment procedures remains a central issue in the implementation of CLT worldwide.

Depending on their own preparation and experience, teachers clearly differ in their reactions to CLT. Some feel understandable frustration at the seeming ambiguity in discussions of communicative ability. Negotiation of meaning may be a lofty goal, but this view of language behavior lacks precision and does not provide a universal scale for the assessment of individual learners. Ability is viewed, rather, as variable and highly dependent on context and purpose as well as the roles and attitudes of all involved. Other teachers welcome the opportunity to select and/or develop their own materials, providing learners with a range of communicative tasks. And they are comfortable relying on more global, integrative judgments of learner progress.

An additional source of frustration for some teachers are second language acquisition research findings that show the route, if not the rate, of language acquisition to be largely unaffected by classroom instruction (see Ellis, 1985, 1997). Crosslinguistic studies of developmental universals in first language acquisition initiated in the 1970s were soon followed by second language acquisition studies. Acquisition, assessed on the basis of expression in unrehearsed, oral communicative contexts, seemed to follow a similar morphosyntactic sequence regardless of learner age or context of learning. Although they served to bear out the informal observations of teachers, namely that textbook presentation and drill do not ensure learner use of these same structures in their own spontaneous expression, the findings were nonetheless disconcerting. They contradicted both grammar-translation and audiolingual precepts that placed the burden of acquisition on teacher explanation of grammar and controlled practice with insistence on learner accuracy. They were further at odds with textbooks that promise "mastery" of "basic" French, English, Spanish, and so forth. Teacher rejection of research findings, renewed insistence on tests of discrete grammatical structures, and even exclusive reliance in the classroom on the learners' native or first language, where possible, to be sure they "get the grammar," have been in some cases reactions to the frustration of teaching for communication.

VARIATION AND OTHER SOCIOLINGUISTIC ISSUES

Numerous sociolinguistic issues await attention. Variation in the speech community and its relationship to language change are central to sociolinguistic inquiry. Sociolinguistic perspectives on variability and change highlight the folly of describing native speaker competence, let alone non-native speaker competence, in terms of "mastery" or "command" of a system. If the "ideal non-native speaker" is nonexistent, a creature who exists only in our imagination, what does this tell us about the "ideal *non-native* speaker"? Is she someone who has attained an imagined native speaker competence? Or is she rather someone who is eager to develop communicative competence in a new language and looks to native speaker "experts" for instruction and advice? The professional stance adopted by some linguists and methodologists suggests that they would consider her to be the latter.

The point is that all language systems show instability and variation. Learner language systems show even greater instability and variability in terms of both the amount and the rate of change. Sociolinguistic concerns with identity and accommodation help to explain the construction by bilinguals of a "variation space" that is different from that of a native speaker. It may include retention of any number of features of a previously acquired system of phonology, syntax, discourse, or communication strategies. As is the case with learner attitudes, the phenomenon may be individual or, in those settings where there is a community of learners, general.

Such sociolinguistic perspectives have been important in understanding the implications of norm, appropriacy, and variability for CLT. They continue to suggest avenues of inquiry for further research and materials development. Use of authentic language data has underscored the importance of context—setting, roles, genre, and so forth—in interpreting the meaning of a text. A range of both oral and written texts in context provides learners with a variety of language experiences, experiences they need to construct their own variation space, to make determinations of appropriacy in their own expression of meaning. "Competent" in this instance is not necessarily synonymous with "nativelike." Negotiation in CLT highlights the need for interlinguistic, that is, intercultural awareness on the part of all involved (Byram, 1997). Better understanding of the strategies used in the negotiation of meaning offers a potential for improving classroom practice of the needed skills.

Although we have become accustomed to thinking of communication in terms of two channels, oral and written, such distinction is far from neat and is becoming increasingly blurred. The rapid adoption of electronic messages, or e-mail, has led to the development of styles that appear at once to be both written and oral. Norms of appropriacy in this new medium continue to evolve and will undoubtedly show considerable fluctuation before they achieve some semblance of stability. To be sure, language use is governed by norms. However, as we have observed earlier in reference to discourse style and genre, language practice is also creative and evolves with time in response to changes in communicative needs and opportunities. Established norms are forever susceptible to challenge.

Along with other sociolinguistic issues in language acquisition, the classroom itself as a social context has been neglected. Classroom language learning was the focus of a number of research studies in the 1960s and early 1970s. However, language classrooms were not a major interest of the second language acquisition research that rapidly gathered momentum in the years that followed. The full range of variables present in educational settings was an obvious deterrent. Other difficulties included the lack of well-defined classroom processes to serve as variables and lack of agreement as to what constituted learning success. Confusion of form-focused drill with meaning-focused communication persisted in many of the textbook exercises and language test prototypes that influenced curricula. Not surprisingly, researchers eager to establish second language acquisition as a worthy field of inquiry turned their attention to more narrow, quantitative studies of the acquisition of selected morphosyntactic features.

SOCIOCULTURAL COMPETENCE FOR A DIALOGUE OF CULTURES

Consistent with a view of language as social behavior, sociolinguistic competence is, as we have seen, integral to overall communicative competence. Second or foreign language culture and its teaching have of course long been a concern of language teachers. If early research addressed the possibility of including some aspects of culture in a foreign language curriculum (e.g., Lado, 1957), most recent discussion has

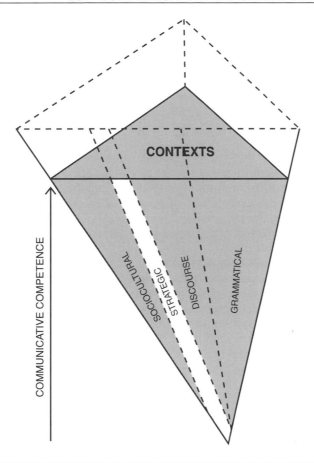

FIG. 35.1. Components of communicative competence. (Reprinted with permission from Sandra J. Savignon (2002), *Interpreting Communicative Language Teaching: Contexts and Concerns in Teacher Education.* New Haven, CT: Yale University Press.

underscored the strong links between language and culture and their relevance for teaching and curriculum design (Valdes, 1986; Byram, 1989; Damen, 1990; Kramsch, 1993, 1995, 1998). So dominant has become the view of culture and language as integral, one to the other, that the term *sociocultural* has come to be substituted for the term *sociolinguistic* in representing the components of communicative competence (Byram, 1997; Savignon, 2002; Savignon & Sysoyev, 2002) (see Fig. 35.1).

Inadequate attention to stereotypes and overgeneralizations in relation to culture have often served to perpetuate one of two widespread myths: 1) people are all the same, or 2) everyone is different. To be sure, all myths can be seen to contain some element of truth. In the comparison of representatives from different contexts and cultures, psychologists have identified traits that appear to differentiate one culture from another (Hofstede, 1980). On the other hand, each individual is unique and may not conform to a more general norm. In the final analysis, efforts to identify similarities and differences between cultures have sometimes served to raise more questions than they have provided answers.

Interest in teaching culture along with language has led to the emergence of various integrative approaches. The Russian scholar Victoria Saphonova (1991, 1992, 1996) has introduced a sociocultural approach to teaching modern languages that she has described as "teaching for intercultural L2 communication in a spirit of peace and a dialogue of cultures" (Saphonova, 1996, p. 62). In addition to the grammatical, discoursal, and strategic features of language use in the L2 curriculum (see Savignon, 1983, 1997), Saphonova and her German colleague Gerhard Neuner (1994) place particular emphasis on the development of sociocultural competence.

Dialogue of cultures is a term introduced by Bakhtin (1981, 1986) and Bibler (1991). For these philosophers, dialogue is the very essence of humanity and mutual understanding. As for culture, it is said to be a "concentration of all other meanings (social, spiritual, logical, emotional, moral, aesthetic) of human existence" (Bibler, 1991, p. 38). Elaborating on these two concepts, scholars have suggested that culture can be seen as a special form or link of interaction between civilizations and epochs. Seen in this way, culture can exist only in the special relationships between past, present, and future in the history of humankind. For example, inasmuch as it provides a link of the present with both the past and the future, the 20th century can be seen as a period of interaction between the cultures of the 19th and 21st centuries. Given the dialogic nature of culture, we cannot fully understand one culture in the absence of contact with other cultures. Thus, dialogue can be seen to be at the very core of culture, where culture is understood as a dialogical self-consciousness of every civilization.

For Saphonova (1996), learning a foreign culture does not start from an absolute zero. By the time most learners begin the study of a foreign or second language and culture they have already formed certain concepts, stereotypes, and expectations about this culture. These expectations are by no means fixed, but they will influence the way learners comprehend and interpret a given culture. In addition, the learner's own sociocultural environment will also considerably impact learning. Neuner (1994) identifies three groups of factors that influence learner interpretation of a second culture (C2).

1. *Dominant social and political factors*. The sociopolitical nature of the learner's home context, including the ideological attitude toward the foreign or second language and the historical, cultural, and socioeconomic contexts in which it is used.
2. *Factors of socialization* including family, school, neighborhood, work, and friends through interpersonal relations, education, and mass media.
3. *Individual factors* such as age, personal experience, specific knowledge of second or foreign language context and its representatives, cognitive development, interests, and needs.

Immersion into a dialogue of cultures begins with a *text*. A text can take one of three forms: (1) the written representation of speech, (2) an individual oral utterance in a communicative event or, and (3) any sign or symbol (a drawing, a thing, or activity). Numerous scholars have argued that text extends far beyond the borders of the semiotic meaning of the term (Bakhtin, 1986; Bibler, 1991; Kramsch, 1993; Shannon, 1995). Actual physical presence in a second or foreign language context can of course offer a particularly rich context for the interpretation of texts. However, immersion in itself does not guarantee readiness for intercultural communication. Conversely, preparation for dialogue can begin well ahead of such immersion. The challenge lies in selecting an appropriate text as well as devising ways for learners to produce their own texts as subjects in a dialogue of cultures (Savignon & Sysoyev, 2002).

The emergence of a focus on sociocultural competence can be seen in other European nations as well. The free flow of people and knowledge within the European Union has increased both the need and the opportunity for language learning and intercultural understanding. To meet this need, increased learner autonomy is essential to language education (Schalkwijk, van Esch, Elsen, & Setz, 2002).

Network-based computer-mediated communication (CMC) is currently being used to create discourse communities. Brammerts (1996), for example, describes the creation of the International E-Mail Tandem Network, a project funded by the European Union that involves universities from more than ten countries. Developed to promote "autonomous, cooperative, and intercultural learning" (p. 121), the project is an extension of the tandem learning that was initiated in the 1970s in an effort to unite many states in a multicultural, multilingual Europe. Pairs of learners from different language backgrounds create a "learning partnership" in the pursuit of the mutual development of both communicative and intercultural competence. The network has expanded to include a number of bilingual subnets, for example, Danish-German, French-English, German-Arabic, each with a bilingual forum to provide an opportunity for questions and discussion (see also Wolff, 1994). A more elaborate telecollaboration between entire classrooms of learners is a focus of ongoing research in the development of communicative proficiency (Kinginger, 2004).

WHAT CLT IS NOT

Disappointment with both grammar-translation and audiolingual methods for their inability to prepare learners for the interpretation, expression, and negotiation of meaning, along with enthusiasm for an array of alternative methods increasingly labeled communicative, has resulted in no small amount of uncertainty as to what are and are not essential features of CLT. Thus, a summary description would be incomplete without brief mention of what CLT is not.

CLT is not concerned exclusively with face-to-face oral communication. The principles of CLT apply equally to reading and writing activities that involve readers and writers engaged in the interpretation, expression, and negotiation of meaning; the goals of CLT depend on learner needs in a given context. CLT does not require small group or pair work; group tasks have been found helpful in many contexts as a way of providing increased opportunity and motivation for communication. However, classroom group or pair work should not be considered an essential feature and may well be inappropriate in some contexts. Although it may be recognized worldwide, CLT has not gained acceptance in all settings (for examples, see Richards & Rogers, 2001; Rao, 2002; and Fotos, chap. 36, in this volume). Applied linguists who are more theoretically inclined may consider discussion of CLT to be passé (Bhatia, 2002; Savignon, 2003). Finally, CLT does not exclude a focus on metalinguistic awareness or knowledge of rules of syntax, discourse, and social appropriateness.

CLT cannot be found in any one textbook or set of curricular materials inasmuch as strict adherence to a given text is not likely to be true to the processes and goals of CLT. In keeping with the notion of context of situation, CLT is properly seen as an approach or theory of intercultural communicative competence to be used in developing materials and methods appropriate to a given context of learning. No less than the means and norms of communication they are designed to reflect, communicative teaching methods will continue to be explored and adapted.

CLT AND TEACHER EDUCATION

Considerable resources, both human and monetary, are being deployed around the world to respond to the need for language teaching that is appropriate for the communicative needs of learners. In the literature on CLT, teacher education has not received adequate attention. What happens when teachers try to make changes in their teaching in accordance with various types of reform initiatives, whether top-down ministry of education policy directives or teacher-generated responses to social and technological change. A number of recent reports of reform efforts in different nations provide a thought-provoking look at language teaching today as the collaborative and context-specific human activity that it is. Themes appear and reappear, voices are heard in one setting to be echoed in yet another. Such first-hand observation provides valuable insights for researchers, program administrators, and prospective or practicing teachers who work or expect to work in these and other international settings.

Curricular Reform in Japan

Several recent studies have focused on curricular reform in Japan. Redirection of English language education by Mombusho, the Japan Ministry of Education, includes the introduction of a communicative syllabus, the Japan Exchange and Teaching (JET) Program, and overseas in-service training for teachers. Previous encouragement to make classrooms more "communicative" through the addition of "communicative activities" led to the realization by Mombusho that teachers felt constrained by a structural syllabus that continued to control the introduction and sequence of grammatical features. With the introduction of a new national syllabus, structural controls were relaxed and teachers found more freedom in the introduction of syntactic features. The theoretical rationale underlying the curriculum change in Japan includes both the well-known Canale and Swain (1980) model of communicative competence and the hypothetical classroom model of communicative competence, or "inverted pyramid," proposed by Savignon (1983).

Minoru Wada (1994, p. 1), a university professor and senior advisor to Mombusho in promoting English language teaching reform in Japan, explains the significance of these efforts:

> The Mombusho Guidelines, or course of study, is one of the most important legal precepts in the Japanese educational system. It establishes national standards for elementary and secondary schools. It also regulates content, the standard number of annual teaching hours at lower level secondary (junior high) schools, subject areas, subjects, and the standard number of required credits at upper level secondary (senior high) schools. The course of study for the teaching of English as a foreign language announced by the Ministry of Education, Science, and Culture in 1989 stands as a landmark in the history of English education in Japan. For the first time it introduced into English education at both secondary school levels the concept of communicative competence. [.....] The basic goal of the revision was to prepare students to cope with the rapidly occurring changes toward a more global society. The report urged Japanese teachers to place much more emphasis on the development of communicative competence in English.

Following the educational research model for classroom language teaching adapted by Kleinsasser (1993) in considering language teachers' beliefs and practices, Sato (2000) reports on a year-long study of teachers of English in a private Japanese senior high school. Multiple data sources, including interviews, observations, surveys, and documents, offer insight into how EFL teachers learn to teach in this particular context. Among the major findings was the context-specific nature of teacher beliefs that placed an emphasis on managing students, often to the exclusion of opportunities for English language learning.

High Stakes Public Examinations in Hong Kong and Costa Rica

Using both qualitative and quantitative methods, Cheng (1997) has documented the influence of a new, more communicative English language test on the classroom teaching of English in Hong Kong, a region that boasts a strong contingent of applied linguists and language teaching methodologists and has known considerable political and social transformation in recent years. In keeping with curricular redesign to reflect a more task-based model of learning, alternative public examinations were developed to measure learners' ability to make use of what they have learned, to solve problems, and complete tasks. At the time curricular changes were introduced, English language teaching was characterized as "test-centered, teacher-centered, and textbook-centered" (Morris et al., 1996). Cheng's ambitious multi-year study found the effect of washback of the new examination on classroom teaching to be limited. There was a change in classroom teaching at the content level but not at the methodological level.

The role of washback in Costa Rica, a small nation with a long democratic tradition of public education, contrasts with the findings of the Hong Kong study. Quesada-Inces (2001), a teacher educator of many years experience, reports the findings of a multi-case study to explore the relationship between teaching practice and the Bachillerato test of English, a national standardized reading comprehension test administered at the end of secondary school. Although teachers expressed a strong interest in developing learner communicative ability in speaking and writing English, the reading comprehension test was seen to dominate classroom emphasis, particularly in the last two years of secondary school. The findings match what Messick (1996) has called "negative washback," produced by construct underrepresentation and construct irrelevance. The Bachillerato test of English does not cover all the content of the curriculum; ultimately it assesses skills less relevant than those skills that go unmeasured. The English testing situation in Costa Rica is not unlike that described by Shohamy (1998) in Israel where two parallel systems can be seen to exist, one the official national educational policy and syllabus, the other reflected in the national tests of learner achievement. Quesada-Inces concludes his report on a personal note:

> I cannot understand that so much effort is lost in pretending to have quality education when all we care about is a percentage that tells us that things are right on the surface . . . [ ] . . the Ministry of Education division that is concerned with national tests is the Quality Control Division, a denomination which suggests mass production of merchandise in a factory. I hope this project can help so that my children, my children's children, and all Costa Rican children are treated more like human beings in schools than as mere production merchandise. (p. 249–250)

English in Taiwan

In another Asian setting, Wang (2000; see also Savignon & Wang, 2003) looks at the use and teaching of English in Taiwan. Adopting a sociocultural perspective on language use and language learning prerequisite to pedagogical innovation, Wang considers attitude, function, pedagogy (Berns, 1990), and learner beliefs with respect to classroom teaching practice. A national initiative to promote CLT in schools has led to the introduction of English at the fifth grade level. On a visit in the spring of 2001 to address an islandwide meeting of university professors of English, I had occasion to hear the newly elected mayor of Taipei affirm (in English) his ambitious goals for the city. He wants to make Taipei a bilingual environment, with all signs in English as well as in Chinese. He emphasized the need for English if Taiwan is to remain economically competitive and made specific reference to the TOEFL scores of students in mainland China, Hong Kong, and Singapore. The very presence of the mayor at a professional meeting of English teachers signals a recognition of the need for cooperation in attaining goals of communicative competence.

> Much has been done to meet the demand for competent English users and effective teaching in Taiwan. Current improvements, according to the teacher experts, include the change in entrance examinations, the new curriculum with a goal of teaching for

communicative competence, and the islandwide implementation in 2001 of English education in the elementary schools. However, more has to be done to ensure quality teaching
and learning in the classrooms. Based on the teacher experts' accounts, further improvements can be stratified into three interrelated levels related to teachers, school authorities,
and the government. Each is essential to the success of the other efforts. (Wang, 2002)

DIRECTIONS FOR FUTURE RESEARCH

In each of the studies included in this brief overview, the research was both initiated
and conducted by local educators in response to local issues. While each study is
significant in its own right, they are by no means comprehensive and can only suggest
the dynamic and contextualized nature of English language teaching in the world
today. Nonetheless, the settings that have been documented constitute a valuable
resource for understanding the current global status of CLT. Viewed in kaleidoscopic
fashion, they appear as brilliant multi-layered bits of glass, tumbling about to form
different yet always intriguing configurations. From these data-rich records of English
language teaching reform on the threshold of the 21st century four major themes
emerge, suggestive of the road ahead:

1. The highly contextualized nature of CLT is underscored again and again. It
would be inappropriate to speak of CLT as a teaching 'method' in any sense of that
term as it was used in the 20th century. Rather, CLT is an approach that understands
language to be inseparable from individual identity and social behavior. Not only
does language define a community; a community, in turn, defines the forms and uses
of language. The norms and goals appropriate for learners in a given setting, and the
means for attaining these goals, are the concern of those directly involved.

The challenge for teacher education is considerable. From the perspective of postmodern critical theory, Kinginger (2002) provides a potentially useful overarching
discussion of both theoretical and practical issues in meeting the challenge. Using the
notion of "error" in language learning/teaching, Kinginger illustrates how teachers
can be helped to develop interpretive skills for evaluating and using competing expert
discourses in making decisions concerning their own teaching practice. The development of interpretive and reflective skills offers a very practical and fruitful alternative
for language teacher education that currently seems compelled to choose between a
single methodological stance or a bewildering smorgasbord of options from which
teachers are invited to make their selection.

2. Directly related both to the concept of language as culture in motion and to the
multilingual reality in which most of the world population finds itself is the futility
of any definition of a native speaker. The term came to prominence in descriptive
structural linguistics in the mid 20th century and was adopted by language teaching
methodologists to define an ideal for language learners. Currently, sales by British
and American presses of profitable publications for learners and teachers of English
as a global language are aided by lingering notions that "authentic" use of English
somehow requires the involvement of a "native" speaker.

3. One cannot help but be struck by the richness of the data found in many of
the texts, including surveys and interviews with teachers. As is true within the social
sciences more generally, we are increasingly aware that in our attempts to discern
system or rationality, we have been led to focus on certain observable patterns while at
the same time disregarding all that defies classification. Just as the implementation of
CLT is itself highly contextualized, so, too, are the means of gathering and interpreting
data on these implementations. When I shared these and other reports with a group
of graduate students in applied linguistics, I was pleased by their response to one

text in particular. They liked the account by a Japanese teacher of how she relates the communicative teaching of English to precepts of Zen Buddhism (Kusano Hubbell, 2002). Many found her narrative to be "novel," and "refreshing," For an Argentinean woman it "represented CLT not only as a theoretical ideal but also as something highly adaptable to the realities of many different settings." She found it annoying that "CLT has primarily been depicted from a Eurocentric or North American point of view" (Savignon, 2002, p. 210).

4.   Time and again, assessment appears to be the driving force behind curricular innovations. In many settings, demands for accountability along with a positivistic stance that one cannot teach that which cannot be described and measured by a common yardstick continue to influence program content and goals. Irrespective of their own needs or interests, learners prepare for the tests they will be required to pass. High stakes language tests often determine future access to education and opportunity. They may also serve to gauge teaching effectiveness. And yet, tests are seldom able to adequately capture the context-embedded collaboration that is the stuff of human communicative activity. A critical reflexive analysis of the impact of tests on language teaching practice, then, would seem a good place to enter into a consideration of how language teaching practices in a given context might be adapted to better meet the communicative needs of the next generation of learners.

REFERENCES

Berns, M. (1990). *Contexts of competence: Social and cultural considerations in communicative language teaching.* New York: Plenum.

Bakhtin, M. (1981). *The dialogic imagination.* (M. Holquist & C. Emerson, Trans.). Austin, TX: University of Texas Press.

Bakhtin, M. (1986). *Speech genres and other late essays.* (C. Emerson, M. Holquist, & W. V. McGee, Trans.). Austin, TX: University of Texas Press.

Bhatia, V. (1997). The power and politics of genre. *World Englishes, 16,* 359–371.

Bhatia, V. (2002). Response to S. J. Savignon, teaching English as communication: A global perspective. *World Englishes, 22,* 69–71.

Bibler, V. (1991). *M. M. Bakhtin, or the poetics of culture.* Moscow: Politizdat Press.

Brammerts, H. (1996). Language learning in tandem using the internet. In Mark, Warschauer (Ed.), *Telecollaboration in foreign language learning.* Manoa: Second Language Teaching and Curriculum center, University of Hawaii.

Byram, M. (1989). *Cultural studies in foreign language education.* Clevedon, UK: Multilingual Matters.

Byram, M. (1997). *Teaching and assessing intercultural communicative competence.* Clevedon, UK: Multilingual Matters.

Canale, M. (1983). From communicative competence to communicative language pedagogy. In J. Richards & R. Schmidt (Eds.), *Language and communication* (pp. 2–27). London: Longman.

Canale, M., & Swain, M. (1980). Theoretical bases of communicative approaches to second language teaching and testing. *Applied Linguistics* 1:1–47.

Candlin, C. (1978). *Teaching of english: Principles and an exercise typology.* London: Langenscheidt-Longman.

Cheng, L. (1997). *The washback effect of public examination change on classroom teaching: An impact study of the 1996 Hong Kong certificate of education in English on the classroom teaching of English in Hong Kong secondary schools.* Unpublished doctoral dissertation, University of Hong Kong.

Chomsky, N. (1965). *Aspects of the theory of syntax.* Cambridge, MA: MIT Press.

Coady, J., & Huckin, T. (Eds.). (1997). *Second language vocabulary acquisition.* Cambridge, UK: Cambridge University Press.

Damen, L. (1990). *Culture learning: The fifth dimension in the language classroom.* Reading, MA: Addison-Wesley.

Ellis, R. (1985). *Understanding second language acquisition.* Oxford, UK: Oxford University Press.

Ellis, R. (1997). *SLA research and language teaching.* Oxford, UK: Oxford University Press.

Fairclough, N. (1992). *Discourse and social change.* Cambridge, UK: Polity Press.

Firth, J. R. (1930). *Tongues of men.* London: Watts & Co.

Foucault, M. (1981). *The archeology of knowledge.* New York: Pantheon.

Habermas, J. (1970). Toward a theory of communicative competence. *Inquiry 13,* 360–375.

Halliday, M. A. K. (1978). *Language as social semiotic: The social interpretation of language and meaning.* Baltimore, MO: University Park Press.

Hofstede, G. (1980). *Culture's consequences: International differences in work-related values*. London: Sage.

Holec, H. (1979). *Autonomy and foreign language learning*. Strasbourg: Council of Europe.

Hymes, D. (1971). Competence and performance In linguistic theory. In R. Huxley & E. Ingram (Eds.), *Language acquisition: Models and methods* (pp. 3–28). London: Academic Press.

Jakobovits, L. (1970). *Foreign language learning: A psycholinguistic analysis of the issues*. Rowley, MA: Newbury House.

Kachru, B. (1992). World Englishes: Approaches, issues, and resources. *Language Teaching, 25*, 1–14.

Kinginger, C. (2002). Genres of power in language teacher education: Interpreting the 'experts.' In S. J. Savignon (Ed.), *Interpreting communicative language teaching: Contexts and concerns in teacher education* (pp. 193–207). New Haven, CT: Yale University Press.

Kinginger, C. (2004). Communicative foreign language teaching through telecollaboration. In C. Van Esch & O. Saint John (Eds.), *New insights in foreign language learning and teaching* (pp. 63–98). Frankfurt Am Main: Peter Lang Verlag.

Kleinsasser, R. (1993.) A tale of two technical cultures: Foreign language teaching. *Teaching and Teacher Education, 9*, 373–383.

Kramsch, C. (1993). *Context and culture in language teaching*. Oxford: Oxford University Press.

Kramsch, C. (1995). The cultural component of language teaching. *Language, Culture and Curriculum, 8*, 83–92.

Kramsch, C. (1998). *Language and culture*. Oxford: Oxford University Press.

Kusano Hubbell, K. (2002). Zen and the art of English language teaching. In S. J. Savignon (Ed.), *Interpreting communicative language teaching: Contexts and concerns in teacher education* (pp. 82–88). New Haven: Yale University Press.

Lado, R. (1957). *Linguistics across cultures*. Ann Arbor: University of Michigan Press.

Lightbown, P., & Spada, N. (2000). *How languages are learned* (2nd ed.). Oxford, UK: Oxford University Press.

Lowenberg, P. (1992). Testing English as a world language: Issues in assessing non-native proficiency. In Braj. B. Kachru (Ed.), *The other tongue: English across cultures* (pp. 108–121), (2nd ed.). Urbana: University of Illinois Press.

Messick, S. (1996). Validity and washback in language testing. *Language Testing 13*(3), 241–256.

Maley, A., & Duff, A. (1978). *Drama techniques in language learning*. Cambridge, UK: Cambridge University Press.

Morris, P. (1996). *Target Oriented Curriculum Evaluation Project: Interim Report*. Instep, Hong Kong: University of Hong Kong Faculty of Education.

Neuner, G. (1994). *The role of sociocultural competence in foreign language teaching and learning*. Strasbourg: Council of Europe.

Paulston, C. (1974). Linguistic and communicative competence. *TESOL Quarterly, 8*, 347–362.

Piepho, H. E. (1974). *Kommuicative kompetence als übergeordnete lernziel des Englischunterrichts*. Dornburg-Frickhofen, West Germany: Frankonius.

Piepho, H. E., & Bredella, L. (Eds.). (1976). *Contacts: Integriertes Englischlehrwerk für klassen 5-10*. Bochum, West Germany: Kamp.

Pennycook, A. (2001). *Critical applied linguistics*. Mahwah, NJ: Lawrence Erlbaum Associates.

Quesada-Inces, R. (2001). *Washback overrides the curriculum: An exploratory study on the washback effect of a high-stakes standardized test in the Costa Rican EFL high school context*. Unpublished doctoral dissertation, Pennsylvania State University.

Rao, Z. (2002). Bridging the gap between teaching and learning styles in East Asian contexts. *TESOL Journal, 11*(2), 5–11.

Richards, J., & Rogers, T. (2001). *Approaches and methods in language teaching* (2nd ed). Cambridge, UK: Cambridge University Press.

Rushdie, S. (2001, July 16). Summer of Solanka. *The New Yorker Magazine*, July 16.

Saphonova, V. (1991). *Sociocultural approach in teaching modern languages*. Moscow: Vysshaya Shkola.

Saphonova, V. (1992). *Cultural studies and sociology in language pedagogy*. Voronezh, Russia: Voronezh University Press.

Saphonova, V. (1996). *Teaching languages of international communication in the context of dialogue of cultures and civilizations*. Voronezh: Istoki.

Sato, K. (2000). EFL teachers in context: Beliefs, practices, and interactions. Unpublished doctoral Dissertation, University of Queensland, Australia.

Savignon, S. J. (1971). *A study of the effect of training in communicative skills as part of a beginning college French course on student attitude and achievement in linguistic and communicative competence*. Unpublished doctoral dissertation, University of Illinois, Urbana-Champaign.

Savignon, S. J. (1972). *Communicative competence: An experiment in foreign language teaching*. Philadelphia, PA: Center for Curriculum Development.

Savignon, S. J. (1974). Teaching for communication. In R. Coulombe, R. J. Barré, C. Fostle, N. Poulin, & S. Savignon (Eds.), *Voix et visages de la France: Level 1 teachers' guide*. Chicago: Rand McNally. (Reprinted in *English Teaching Forum, 16*, 2–5: 9, 1978.

Savignon, S. J. (1983). *Communicative competence: Theory and classroom practice*. Reading, MA: Addison-Wesley.

Savignon, S. J. (1997). *Communicative competence: Theory and classroom practice* (2nd ed.). New York: McGraw-Hill.

Savignon, S. J. (2001). Communicative language teaching for the twenty-first century. In M. Celce-Murcia, (Ed.), *Teaching English as a second or foreign language* (pp. 13–28). Boston: Heinle & Heinle.

Savignon, S. J. (Ed.). (2002). *Interpreting communicative language teaching: Contexts and concerns in teacher education.* New Haven, CT: Yale University Press.

Savignon, S. J. (2003). Teaching English as communication: A global perspective. *World Englishes, 22,* 55–66.

Savignon, S. J., & Sysoyev, P. (2002). Sociocultural strategies for a dialogue of cultures. *Modern Language Journal, 86,* 508–524.

Savignon, S. J., & Roithmeier, W. (in press). Computer-mediated communication: Texts and strategies. *CALICO Journal, 21,* 265–290.

Savignon, S. J., & Wang, W. (2003). Communicative language teaching in EFL contexts: Learner attitudes and perceptions. *International Review of Applied Linguistics, 41,* 223–249.

Schalkwijk, E., van Esch, K., Elsen, A., & Setz, W. (2002). Learner autonomy and language teacher education. In Savignon, S. J. (Ed.). *Interpreting communicative language teaching: Contexts and concerns in the teacher education* (pp. 165–190). New Haven: Yale University Press.

Schwartz, A. (2002). National standards and the diffusion of innovation: Language teaching in the U.S.A. In S. J. Savignon. (Ed.), *Interpreting communicative language teaching: Contexts and concerns in teacher education,* (pp. 112–130). New Haven, CT: Yale University Press.

Shannon, P. (1995). *Text, lies, and videotape: Stories about life, literacy, and learning.* Portsmouth, NA: Heinemann.

Shohamy, E. (1998). Testing methods, testing consequences: Are they ethical? Are they fair? *Language Testing,* 14–15.

Valdes, J. (Ed.). (1986). *Culture bound: Bridging the culture gap in language teaching.* Cambridge: Cambridge University Press.

Van Ek, J. (1975). *Systems development in adult language learning: The threshold level in a European unit credit system for modern language learning by adults.* Strasbourg: Council of Europe.

Wada, M. (Ed.). (1994). The course of study for senior high school: Foreign languages (English Version). Tokyo: Kairyudo.

Wang, C. (2000). A sociolinguistic profile of English in Taiwan: social context and learner needs. Unpublished doctoral dissertation, Pennsylvania State University.

Wang, C. (2002). Innovative teaching in EFL contexts: The case of Taiwan. In S. J. Savignon (Ed.), *Interpreting communicative language teaching: Contexts and concerns in teacher education.* New Haven, CT: Yale University Press.

Wolff, J. (1994). *Ein TANDEM für jede Gelegenheit?* Sprachlernen in verschiedenen Begegnungssitutationen. [*A tandem for everyone?: Language learning in different contexts.*] *Die Neueren Sprache, 93,* 374–385.

Yun, M. (1998). Interview on National Public Radio, Weekend Edition, Sunday, Nov. 15, 1998.

Traditional and Grammar Translation Methods for Second Language Teaching

Sandra Fotos
Senshu University

It is a time-honored adage that there is "nothing new under the sun" and this statement certainly applies to second language instruction. One historian reviewing language teaching pedagogy in Europe and different English-speaking countries observed, "[M]uch that is being claimed as revolutionary in this century is merely a rethinking and renaming of early ideas and procedures . . . the total corpus of ideas accessible to language teachers has not changed basically in 2,000 years" (Kelly, 1969, p. ix; p. 363). The same methods have come in and out of fashion, and the same arguments for and against a particular approach presented today have been made many times in the past.

This chapter discusses traditional approaches to second language instruction, in particular the Grammar Translation approach, although communicative approaches must also be considered traditional because they were repeatedly introduced over the centuries. The history of language teaching in Europe is considered in order to appreciate the historical basis of the various approaches and methods used in teaching English as a Second Language (ESL) today, and aspects of current grammar pedagogy are discussed, especially in the English as a Foreign Language (EFL) context, where accuracy concerns are often paramount.

SOURCES

Many works on second language (L2) instruction begin with a simplified survey of the history of language teaching (e.g., Celce-Murcia, 2001; Larsen-Freeman, 2000; Hymes, 1980; Mackey, 1965; Hinkel & Fotos, 2002; Richards & Rodgers, 2001; Rutherford, 1987; Stern, 1983), usually drawing on information published in two seminal works, Howatt's *A History of English Language Teaching* (1984; also see Howatt's recent update, 1997), and Kelly's *25 Centuries of Language Teaching* (1969). The former chronologically examines L2 learning pedagogy in Europe from the Middle Ages (during and after the fall of the Roman Empire in the third to fifth century to 1400), the period considered to mark the transition from classical Greco-Roman cultures to the modern era. The latter work, as its title suggests, treats language teaching practices from 500 BC to 1969 from a pedagogical rather than chronological perspective, and is organized by sections such as "Teaching Meaning," "Teaching Grammar," and "How is the Course Ordered." Other often-cited summaries of linguistic and grammatical development and pedagogy are Titone's (1968) *Teaching Foreign Languages: An Historical Sketch* and Robin's early *Ancient and Mediaeval Grammatical Theory in Europe* (1951) and his widely known *A Short History of Linguistics* (1997), which is now in its fourth edition. An examination of Latin reading pedagogy in the Middle Ages, *Reynolds' Medieval Reading: Grammar, Rhetoric and the Classical Text* (1996), discusses the role of grammar instruction in reading, and a recent volume on Middle Age language teaching, Law's *Grammar and Grammarians in the Early Middle Ages* (1997), reviews linguistic thought from 600 to 1100, and traces the changes in Latin grammar teaching pedagogy, especially the shift in focus from second language to foreign language teaching methodology. A late 19th century work, Sweet's *The Practical Study of Languages* (1899/1964) is often cited, as is his *New English Grammar* (1892). Critical summaries of historical trends appear in Mackey's *Language Teaching Analysis* (1965), Richards and Rodgers' *Approaches and Methods in Language Teaching* (2001), and Stern's *Fundamental Concepts of Language Teaching* (1983). The history of linguistics, as distinct from grammar, is overviewed in the final chapter of Hudson's textbook, *Essential Introductory Linguistics* (2000).

These works inform the following discussion of L2 teaching pedagogy in Europe and North America from the Classical Period to the present. The teaching of English as a second and foreign language is a special focus.

GRAMMAR AND LANGUAGE TEACHING DURING THE CLASSICAL PERIOD (500 BC TO 300 AD)

The Origin of Grammar in Greece

It has been suggested that interest in grammar is a natural outcome of contact with people speaking a language other than their own (Robins, 1997, pp. 14–15). Thus, the systematic treatment of grammar in language teaching and learning is considered to have begun 4,000 years ago as a result of the large-scale expansion of the Greek sphere of influence. Records indicate that non-Greek speaking subjects of city–states studied Greek as an L2 with home tutors or slaves in order to develop both oral and literacy skills. Phonology was taught using letters, syllables, words, and phrases, with emphasis on correct pronunciation. Texts were studied by reading aloud and by paraphrase, defined as rewriting the text into an easier form with simplified vocabulary and grammar. The rhetorical style of the text was also studied. Dialogues were used to teach the spoken language, and memorization of texts was encouraged. The earliest records of linguistic study date to the sixth and fifth centuries, the start of the Classical Age. Grammar and rhetoric were therefore closely related from the beginning of language studies.

The Greek philosopher Plato (circa 429–347 BC) is considered to be the first to have examined the relationship between the form and meaning of words and to have distinguished between the grammatical categories of nouns and verbs. During Plato's time the term *grammatikos* referred to someone who could read and write. *Gramma*—the root of the word "grammar"—meant "letter" (Robins, 1997, p. 17). In *Poetics* Book 20, Plato's pupil Aristotle (384–322 BC) added the concept of conjunctions (the construct at that time including considerably more than current usage since it referred to anything that was not a noun or a verb), articles, adjectives, and the idea of the word as the smallest meaningful unit. Aristotle also identified verb tenses, noting that they expressed time.

In the third century BC, pronouns, active and passive voice, intransitive verbs, and the concepts of case and mood were described in the first Greek grammars developed by the Stoic philosophers of Athens, a group who considered grammar to be part of philosophy and rhetoric. The Stoics also combined proper and common nouns, previously treated separately, into a single grammatical category, creating an early linguistic theory and developing a term for linguistics, *grammatiké*. Robins considers that modern grammar began with the work of the Stoics (1997, p. 34).

Formal study of grammar as a field commenced in the third century BC when scholars at the great library in the Greek colony of Alexandria, Egypt, began to collect and compare different versions of Greek literary texts, especially the works of Homer (Hudson, 2000). This process required the ability to identify the "correct" version of a given text, and resulted in the development of grammatical rules as the standard for determining text correctness. One of the oldest western grammar books was written in the second century BC and presented rules based on the six parts of classical Greek grammar: prosody (rules for reading aloud), exegesis (critical interpretation) of tropes (figurative usages), study of diction and content, study of etymologies, study of criticism, and study of analogies, the final category corresponding to formal grammar and consisting of rules for inflection, declension, and other regularities (Reynolds, 1996, p. 20). Grammar was thus considered to be the basis of both language and rhetoric, which was defined as the letter, the syllable, the word, and the phrase. Learning correct grammar, therefore, began with study of penmanship and letters, followed by study of the correct combination of letters into syllables, syllables into words, and words into phrases (Reynolds, 1996, p. 18), recognized as a bottom-up approach today.

Dionysius Thrax, a scholar in Alexandria in the first century BC, produced a short treatise on Greek grammar that became the standard textbook of that time, continuing to be used until well into the 18th century. Defining grammar as "empirical knowledge of the language of poets and prose-writer" (Dionysius, as quoted in Robins, 1997, p. 38), Dionysius emphasized the link between grammar and literature, identifying and defining Greek's eight parts of speech: noun, verb, participle, article, pronoun, preposition, adverb, and conjunction. These, he suggested, were determined by morphology (inflection) and syntax (referring to function and position in the sentence matrix). Tenses were divided into past, present, and future, with past divided into the imperfect, perfect, pluperfect, and indeterminate, and he also identified three voices, active, middle, and passive. He recommended that instruction of grammar should consist of six steps: (1) Reading a work aloud, "with due regard to the prosodies," (2) Explanation of the literary expressions used in the work, (3) Provision of notes on phraseology and subject matter, (4) Discovery of etymologies, (5) Working out the regularities of the language, or the analogies, and (6) "Appreciation of literary compositions, which is the noblest part of grammar" (Robins, 1997, p. 38–39). Indeed, this pedagogy survives energetically into the present!

Dionysius' work is considered to be one of the first pedagogical grammars (Odlin, 1994, p. 7), as well as a model for both Latin grammars and the grammars of vernacular languages of Western Europe and other regions. Thus, by the first century BC the grammatical framework was developed that has remained the foundation of grammar pedagogy to the present. As Robins noted, such Alexandrian scholars brought grammar to "the state in which the later Latin grammarians, and through them the European tradition, took it over" (1997, p. 36).

Although a treatment of syntax is missing from Dionysius' work, this was later provided by Appolonius Dyscolus, a scholar living during the Roman Empire who studied Greek grammar and suggested that conjunctions function to join other parts of speech. Appolonius also noted that definite articles could be anaphoric (referring to previous mention of the noun) and he clarified the grammatical and semantic functions of Greek case inflections (Robins, 1951, p. 43). Apollonius' work was later used as a framework by a major Latin grammarian, Priscian.

It should be noted, however, that the Greek grammar system was derived from literature, not from colloquial speech. Thus, no distinction was made between descriptive grammar (the structure and function of language within a community) and normative or prescriptive grammar (defining correct usage).

Grammar and Language Teaching Pedagogy During the Roman Empire

After Greece was conquered by the Roman Empire around 146 BC, Latin became the major language of the Western world, with a concomitant rise of Latin grammars based on the eight Greek grammatical categories. Since the two languages were not dissimilar, Greek grammatical categories fit Latin fairly well despite the fact that Latin had six case endings for nouns (Greek had five) and also had no article system. This situation is entirely different from using the eight Greek grammatical categories with substantially dissimilar language such as English (e.g., see the beginning of Curme's 1947 textbook for a treatment of English grammar organized according to the eight parts of speech). Instructional pedagogy also followed the Greek emphasis on reading sentences aloud, paraphrasing passages, and studying rhetoric. During this period, grammar was defined as "the art in which the skills and structures of reading the [classical] authors are learned" (Reynolds, 1996, p. 2).

As before, the letter was considered the basis of grammar, followed by the syllable, the word, and the phrase, grammar being seen as the means for teaching the correct combination of these components. Correctness was the core of the classical view—a position still found in many foreign language classrooms today—and Latin was the only medium of instruction in schools (Mackey, 1965). Regardless of the student's first language, education was conducted in Latin, and grammar was viewed as the way to read classical texts, regarded as important vehicles of moral education. Word by word, heavily supported by interlinear and/or marginal glosses in the vernacular, and parallel translation (placing the vernacular text next to the target language text on the page), students read edifying passages and single sentences from classical literature and the Bible, and memorized sayings, metaphors, and adages intended to build a worthy character. Education was appreciated not only for the acquisition of literacy and rhetorical skills, but was also conceived as important for the development of morality[2].

During this period, there was no use of visual aids for grammar study. Papyrus records from the first to the third centuries AD, the earliest written copies of grammatical texts from a European civilization, did not used columns, tables, or diagrams (Law, 2003, p. 249). However students performed grammar drills and read dialogues, often in question-and-answer format.

During the late Latin period (from the third century AD), noted grammarians such as Donatus (c. AD 400) and Priscian (c. AD 500), followed Greek grammarians, particularly Appolonius, closely to produce Latin grammar textbooks. These works, particularly the *Ars Minor* of Donato, which was based on a question-and-answer format and is considered to be the most successful textbook in Western history (Reynolds, 1996, p. 10), were the major Latin texts during the Middle Ages and Renaissance, even surviving into the 20th century.[3] The rise of Christianity and the subsequent conversion of European tribes to Roman Christianity during the Late Latin period resulted in the spread of Latin into Irish, Celtic, Anglo-Saxon, Germanic, and other populations, necessitating the development of form-oriented, descriptive grammars (Law, 2001) and the development of methodology for the widespread teaching of Latin as a second language.

Regarding the notional/functional, oral, situational and Audio-Lingual approaches (see discussions in Richards & Rodgers, 2001 and Howatt, 1997) of the early to middle 20th century—pedagogy which linked target language structures to situations and functions through oral practice and taught grammar inductively through input—and contemporary communicative pedagogy today, it is interesting to note that as early as 398 AD St. Augustine of Hippo (354–430) advocated linking form and meaning within the context of the speech act by introducing new material through dialogues set within the social situation requiring its use, a basic principle of functional, situational and communicative approaches (e.g., see Breen, 1986; Brumfit & Johnson, 1979; Canale & Swain, 1980; Howatt, 1997; Krashen, 1981; Krashen & Terrell, 1983, Savignon 1991).

GRAMMAR AND LANGUAGE TEACHING DURING THE MIDDLE AGES (ca.300 AD THROUGH THE LATE 1400s)

The civilization of this period was a combination of institutions from the Roman Empire, Christianity, and the cultures of other European peoples. Strongly relying on theories, approaches, and pedagogy from the Classical period, grammar study during the early Middle Ages (from the 8th to the 12th century) was based on the works of Priscian and Donatus, particularly the *Ars Minor* of the latter, and was characterized by continuity with the past despite the fact that classical Latin differed from the language of the Bible, composed in fourth and fifth century Latin, the *Vulgate*. Latin was the only language studied at school, although students spoke French or English as the vernacular (the first language, or the L1, as compared with the second/foreign language, the L2 or FL). Thus, as noted by Reynolds, during this period, learning to read meant learning to read a foreign language (1996, p. 8). Law sums up the contribution of this period:

> Perhaps the greatest achievement of the early Middle Ages was the descriptive grammars— the transformation of the language-centered grammars of Antiquity into the Latin-centered textbooks of the Insular grammarians. These were the first comprehensive, formally based descriptions of Latin—the first Western foreign language grammars. (1997, p. 85)

The early Middle Ages, especially from the seventh and eighth centuries, was also characterized by content-based instruction, the use of Latin to instruct students in other, nonliterary subjects. In fact, during the Middle Ages and the Renaissance, it was assumed that all classes, not only language classes, would be conducted in Latin, although the use of spoken Latin began to die out from the 1700s, being replaced by the L1 as the medium of education.

During the later part of the Middle Ages, from the twelfth century to the Renaissance, interest in grammar grew due to translations into Latin and commentaries on Greek literature. As noted, the L1 of students at the time was not Latin, so there was increasing need for grammar teaching texts as distinct from scholarly works on grammar rules and the philosophy of grammar. One widely used L2 textbook, the *Doctrinale* of Alexander of Villedieu (c. 1200), followed the grammatical works of Priscian but did not include rules; rather verse was used to model grammar forms (Robins, 1997), resembling the current emphasis on meaning-focused instruction where students inductively acquire knowledge of grammar rules through exposure to large amounts of communicative input containing target grammar structures (Fotos, 1998, 2002).

During this period philosophers speculated on the nature of grammar and its relationship to language and philosophy, developing theories about the structure of language. This approach was called Speculative Grammar and its adherents, the

Modistae, believed that grammar rules existed outside of language—a universal grammar structure that was independent of any particular language. The Modistae held that, "There is one grammatical system fixed and valid for all language which the philosopher alone is able to discover and justify; the observed differences between languages must be treated...as a matter of vocabulary not of structure" (Robins, 1951, p. 79). This concept of grammar as a universal property of the human mind has emerged several times, most recently in the 20th century work of Chomsky (1957) and his successors.

Reynolds characterizes Middle Age Latin teaching (1996, pp. 20–21) as closely derived from classical pedagogy and consisting of: (1) prosody, or reading the text out loud correctly; (2) exegesis of tropes; (3) study of diction and content—the rhetorical analysis of texts; (4) study of words; (5) study of analogies, this constituting the formal study of grammar; and (6) criticism. Reading took place word by word, and was accompanied by glosses, L1 comments written between the lines or in the margins. Such glosses translated the text into the L1 and explained or elaborated the meaning. Thus, "the mother tongue of the students was an essential explanatory mode in the learning of Latin vocabulary" (Reynolds, 1996, p. 71), and determined the pedagogical approach for understanding the words of the text. It is noteworthy that the use of L1 to study the L2 remains a feature of many foreign language classrooms today.

Dictation was used, as well as paraphrase, to determine whether the text was understood correctly. Rhetorical analysis examined the style of the text and was especially focused developing students' ability to speak well. Rhetoric at this time consisted of five parts: finding a subject, arrangement, diction and style, memorization, and delivery (Reynolds, 1996, p. 26–27). The texts themselves were either isolated sentences, dialogues, or passages and often contained moral lessons intended to build character. As mentioned, notable quotations, phrases, and adages were used frequently and the students were expected to memorize these to acquire a high level of culture and a moral character.

Although grammatical correctness was heavily emphasized during this period, use of the classical eight parts of speech as an approach to grammar instruction became problematic since English expresses syntactic relations by word order, whereas Latin inflections indicate word relationships.[4] This incongruity led to a teaching technique whereby students were given parallel sentences in English and Latin, with deliberate mistakes in the Latin sentences, and were told to correct them. Thus, the tradition of reading and writing sample sentence based on models continued strongly through this period. Another problem was syntax. In Middle English, relationships among sentence components were expressed by word order but in Latin, word relationships were expressed by inflections; so learners had to memorize inflections and rely on glosses indicating parts of speech to learn Latin syntax from the reading passages.

By the eighth century, visual aids such as column layout, diagrams, pictures, and charts had become common (Law, 1997), resulting in "double translation" books that presented the target language in one column and a vernacular translation in the other, the first published about 1483 (Howatt, 1984). In addition, foreign language textbooks teaching English, French, and other languages made their first appearance as a result of trade among European nations and immigration (Law, 1997). For example, an early EFL teacher, the Frenchman Gabriel Meurier, wrote a widely used double manual, *A Treatise for to Learn to Speak French and English*, in Antwerp in 1553 particularly aimed at merchants. Such bilingual texts contained no grammatical explanation and were usually organized according to situation and function: for example, greetings, household conversations, shopping, and so forth (Kelly, 1969).

The dictionaries and phrasebooks that appeared in the early 1500s followed this double manual format, with the target language and a vernacular translation side by side. By the mid-1500s situational and functional dialogues were common, especially concerning commercial affairs, and were used by the many Protestant European refugee teachers fleeing religious persecution who taught English and other languages to their fellow refugees in England. In a chapter titled "'Refugiate in a Strange Country:' The Refugee Language Teachers in Elizabethan London," discussing the impact of these religious refugees on the teaching of English, Howatt (1984) presents sample dialogues from such early textbooks as *Familiar Dialogues*, a bilingual, dialogue-based EFL textbook published in 1586. This book was arranged in three columns with English in the left column, a semiphonetic transcription in the middle, and French in the right. Penmanship and dictation were used, and grammar drills were common.

These functional/situational works are strikingly similar to those multidimensional second/foreign language teaching textbooks used from the middle 20th century up to the present characterized by both situational and function dialogues on topics such as "Apologizing" or "At the Post Office."

THE RENAISSANCE

Based on the intellectual and artistic progress in the early 1400s in Italy that had spread to other parts of Europe by the 1500s, the Renaissance was characterized by exploration, advances in geography and map making, and the colonization of new lands, the latter resulting in considerable language contact as well as the rise of humanist philosophies. The printing press was also developed during this period. An immediate use of the printing press was production and distribution of Greek and Latin classics throughout Europe (Mackey, 1965) and it was during this period that grammar teaching was separated from the study of literature.

A typical grammar teaching plan was presented in 1627 by Brinsley (quoted in Kelly, 1969, p. 50):

Thus to goe forward in every rule:
1. Reading it over to the children;
2. Shewing the plaine meaning in as few words as you can;
3. Propounding every piece of it in a short question, following the words of the booke, & answering it yourself out of the words of the book;
4. Asking the same questions of them & trying how themselves can answer them, still looking upon their books. Then let them goe in hand with getting it amongst themselves.

It is interesting to compare this question-based procedure, which continued until the 19th century, with Dionysius Thrax's recommendations for grammar instruction in the first century BC, with examples of EFL lessons described in the subsequent section on contemporary pedagogy, and with current debates about the place of grammar instruction in the writing curriculum for native speakers of English (e.g., see the arguments in Hunter & Wallace, 1995).

According to Howatt (1984, p. 33), there were two alternative approaches to traditional translation and rule memorization methods of language education in the late 16th and early 17th century. The first was the humanist tradition derived from Erasmus and Vives, and the second was an antigrammar tradition, represented by the works of Francis Bacon and the Czech educator, Jan Comenius (1592–1670)[5]. This reformist approach stressed the use of literacy for moral education (see end note 2), double translation, and inductive rule learning rather than formal grammatical instruction on rules followed by practice. Publishing the major textbook *Ianua Linguarum Reserata*, in 1331, which taught vocabulary through key sentences, Comenius later published the *Orbis Sensualium Pictus* in 1654, an innovative text using pictures to teach vocabulary. He recommended that the teachers also show the students real examples of the pictured objects and involve all the senses in experiencing them. Although this approach did not become widely accepted, the book was reissued several times in the early 1700s and again in 1887. Other educators, such as Vives (1500), who taught Latin by inductive principles, G. H. Cominius (1520), Erasmus (1520), and Lubinus (1550) recommended that grammar teaching be discontinued or be limited to beginners, more advanced students inductively generating rules by exposure to texts. Kelly comments:

> Lubinus's attack had a surprisingly modern touch: for him grammar repels the pupils and bores the master; its emphasis on rules encourages, rather than presents, bad stylistic habits; it clutters the mind with reasons and connections before the facts to be reasoned out are known (1969, p. 37–38).

Lamy (1645–1751) recommended an approach that was the basis of the 19th century natural methodology: the idea that languages could be learned in the same way that first languages are learned. This theory reappeared in the early 1980s in the work of researchers such as Krashen (1981, Krashen & Terrell, 1983), and these early works also evoke comparison with contemporary approaches advocating use of material appealing to different learning styles and strategies (Oxford, 2001; Reid, 1998).

Polyglot dictionaries also appeared in the Renaissance and were often multilingual, with as many as seven languages (Kelly, 1969, p. 25).

THE 1600s AND 1700s: PEDAGOGICAL GRAMMARS, DICTIONARIES, AND GRAMMAR TRANSLATION

As noted in a preceding section, the distinction between grammar usage (prescription) and grammar description was lacking in Classical and early Middle Age treatments. However, by the 1500s, the role of common usage in the formulation of grammatical rules was increasingly accepted. Defining pedagogical grammars as "the types of grammatical analysis and instruction designed for the needs of second language students," Odlin (1994, p. 1) discusses grammar as prescription, description, an internalized system, and as an axiomatic system—this latter being pedagogical grammar. As an example of usage change driving grammar rules, Odlin notes the replacement of *thou* by *you* during the 1600s (1994, p. 2).

This distinction is extended by Corder (1988), who notes that pedagogical grammars are basically "textbooks in the methodology of grammatical presentation" (p. 127) and are distinct from expositions of grammatical theory. In his treatment of pedagogical grammar, Corder identifies four parts of grammar instruction: (1) data on and examples of the target language, (2) descriptions and explanations, (3) induction exercises, and (4) hypothesis testing exercises (1988, p. 134). These sections are clearly present in Johnson's 1640 pedagogical grammar, *English Grammar*. Johnson used both the Classical grammatical theory of Donatus, Priscian, and the Middle Age grammarians, the post-Renaissance "standard theory" represented by "Lily's Grammar"[6] (Howatt, 1984, p. 95), as well as a new theory following a "reasoned approach" pioneered by the French scholar Petrus Ramus.

The *Grammatica Linguae Anglicanae* by John Wallis (1616–1703) was a second pedagogical grammar appearing during this period. It used a contrastive approach to focus on pronunciation, concentrating on " those features of English which are most likely to strike the foreign learner as especially characteristic of English" (Howatt, 1984, p. 98). This approach resembles the Contrastive Analysis approach of the early and mid 20th century, in which linguists conducted contrastive analyses of the L1 and target languages to predict where learners might be expected to experience difficulties, (see Ellis, 1994, for a full discussion). This work is also considered notable because of its efforts to separate English from Latin. As Howatt notes:

It is not, perhaps, entirely inappropriate that the best grammars of English in the seventeenth century should have been written with foreigners in mind, or that the best grammars of the twentieth century . . . should be rooted in the same soil. (1984, p. 100)

During this period there was a growing distinction between the grammar teaching practices of traditional Latin-based curriculums and innovative educators who opened progressive schools offering instruction in English. Thus, literacy in the L1 moved to the fore as Latin was gradually replaced by the use of English and French as mediums of instruction. Also during this period English orthography, pronunciation, and usage were standardized through the publication of dictionaries by Johnson, Walker, and Webster (Kelly, 1969).

THE RISE OF THE GRAMMAR-TRANSLATION METHOD

Although translation has always been a part of language learning, the beginnings of the modern Grammar-Translation method (GTM) are found in Renaissance lessons aimed at teaching both style and grammar. Formal use of translation to teach languages was common from the Classical period through the third century AD, but was not officially used—in the sense of appearing in textbooks—after that until the late Middle Ages, with the development of parallel translations or double texts. However, it must be recalled that glosses (translations and notes in the L1 made in between lines of Latin text or in the margins) were common throughout the Middle Ages and thus provided essential but unofficial translations and support in the learners' L1.

As mentioned, at first grammar structures and rules were taught in Latin, the target language, regardless of the learners' L1, but by the end of the 1700s, the teaching of Latin grammar had become separated from the study of literature. Grammar was thus studied independently, with explanations of rules provided in the L1. The basic concept of the developing GTM was that students had to know the grammar of their own language in order to learn an L2 through translation, paraphrase, and dictation. Since the GMT was developed to teach Greek and Latin through the L1 it focused heavily on learning vocabulary and rote memorization of syntax, morphology, and grammar rules. Until the end of the 18th century it was customary to translate from the students' L1 into the target language. However, by the end of the 1700s, the direction was often reversed, with translation from the L2 into the L1, using memorized grammar rules as a guide. This trend continued into the 19th century and remains a feature of the strong position of the GTM in many foreign language classrooms. For example, a grammar text in the 1840s described the following three-part lesson plan: (1) a statement of the grammar rule; (2) presentation of new vocabulary; (3) and translation of a text into the target language.

The best-known GTM texts of the 1800s were based on German scholarship (Richards & Rodgers, 2001) such as Ollendorf's textbook, *A New Method of Learning to Read, Write, and Speak a Language in Six Months* teaching German to speakers of English and French, these following grammar textbooks written by Meidinger at the end of the 1700s. Ollendorf (1803–1865) used a structural syllabus with grammar points graded from easy to difficult, and introduced grammar structures one at a time. Lessons followed a set format (Kelly, 1969, p. 52): (1) statement of the grammar rule; (2) study of new vocabulary; (3) translation of sentences from the L1 to the L2; (4) some translation of sentences from the L2 into the L1; and, later in the course, when the students had gained proficiency, (5) translation of a L1 prose passage into the L2.

In the later part of the 1800s, another German language teacher, Karl Plötz (1819–1881), continued the trend toward an exclusive focus on rules and exactness by his method based on memorization of rules and paradigms and translation of disconnected, artificial sentences exemplifying rules to and from the L1 (Mackey, 1965). Regarding this period, Kelly notes that through the strict application of the GTM:

> Language teaching drifted further from the languages taught by reason of the abandonment of authentic specimens of literature for synthetic passages that were built around rules, exceptions, and restricted vocabulary selected for its congruence with grammatical rules. Language skill was equated with ability to conjugate and decline. (1969, p. 53)

THE REFORM MOVEMENT: A REACTION AGAINST THE GTM

The GTM became the major language teaching pedagogy in Europe and North America for a 100-year period from the 1840s to the 1940s, and continues to be used today, primarily in the foreign language or EFL teaching situation. Although, as seen in the preceding sections, there were continual movements against formal grammar teaching throughout the Medieval Period and the Renaissance—many inspired by the work of Comenius—the 19th century witnessed a particularly strong reaction against the GMT, especially during the last half of the century. In 1867 the Frenchman Claude Marcel (1793–1876) used a "rational method" recommending abolishment of rule memorization and translation in favor of communicative comprehension of texts, listening materials, and extensive reading of simple material, this followed by speaking and writing activities (Mackey, 1965, p. 143). Similar natural methods were proposed by other authors, for example, in *The Art of Teaching and Studying Languages* published in Paris 1880 by Francois Gouin (1831–1896). This method recommended physically acting out sentences (similar to Asher's Total Physical Response approach of the late 1970s [1977]), visualization, linking new material with previously learned material, and relating new vocabulary to previous activities, all of which were related to the interests of the learner. Again, it should be noted that such activities remain common today as a means of assisting processing and subsumption of newly learned material. Mackey comments on this approach: "The language was first introduced through the ear, then reinforced through the eye and hand by reading and writing (1969, p. 144).

Harkening back to Middle Age and Renaissance educators who criticized study of grammar, memorization of rules, and practice with isolated sentences designed to exemplify the rule or structure studied—and foreshadowing the focus on communicative competence in the final quarter of the 20 century (see, Brumfit & Johnson, 1979; Canale & Swain, 1980; Hymes, 1971; Krashen, 1981; Krashen & Terrell, 1983; Savignon, 1972, 1991)—such concepts became the basis of reform movements at the end of the 19th century based on the primacy of oral methods and discourse level input. Strongly resembling communicative approaches of the 1980s such as the Natural Approach (Krashen & Terrell, 1983),[7] the 19th century reform approaches held that the best way to learn languages was through conversation, with no formal study of grammar rules, and no comparison of the L1 and the target language. By the end of the century, these approaches had developed into the Direct Method, which used conversation and cultural content to teach grammar inductively.

METHODS OF THE EARLY 1900s

The Direct Method, Natural Method, Conversation Method

Regarding the relationship of these oral-based approaches of the late 1800s and early 1900s to the rise of communicative and humanistic approaches in the 1970s and 1980s, Howatt observes:

The communicative language teaching methods which have attracted a good deal of interest over the last ten years [the 1980s] are the most recent manifestation of ideas which were last revived about a hundred and twenty years ago by... immigrant teachers in America. (1984, p. 192)

According to Mackey (1965, p. 146), the term "direct method" was first formalized in 1901, and the approach was officially adopted by France and German shortly after. Based on the work of Montaigne in the 16th century, languages were taught following a situational approach that emphasized politeness, behavior at home and at work, and eschewed formal grammar teaching entirely. Writing about GTM, in particular the isolated sentence of Ollendorff and Plötz, the English linguist Henry Sweet (1845–1912) identified an "arithmetical fallacy." This was the tendency for word-by-word translations, built up like an arithmetic progression, resulting in contrived and artificial sentences such as *The philosopher pulled the lower jaw of the hen* (Sweet, 1899, 1964, p. 73), the famous sentence often cited to illustrate the futility of a word-based approach to syntax. Although the isolated words make sense, the sentence as a whole is strange and unnatural and would never be spoken in normal discourse. To overcome this, the Direct Method did not allow translation but presented the target language in meaningful contexts, using visual aids and pantomime to introduce new vocabulary. Students were required to only speak target language, and grammar rules were presented inductively. Reading and writing were based on oral practice and correct pronunciation was emphasized.

The Direct Method was introduced to the United States under the name of the Natural Method in 1869, when the Frenchman Lambert Sauveur (1826–1907) moved to Boston, met the German Gottlieb Heness, and opened the Sauveur-Heness School of Modern Languages, later publishing textbooks teaching French and German based on dialogues. In 1878 Maximilian Berlitz (1852–1921) opened a language school in Rhode Island and subsequently published dialogue and question-and-answer based textbooks using the Direct Method and a structural syllabus. By 1914, there were more than 200 Berlitz schools in Europe and the United States (Howatt, 1984, p. 203). The chain is now worldwide and continues to be successful, particularly with adult learners, and still uses Direct Method pedagogy. Richards and Rodgers summarize the features of the Direct Method and other Natural Methods of the period (2001, p. 8): (1) An oral methodology is used, with attention to pronunciation; (2) students listen to the target language before reading or writing it; (3) vocabulary is presented in communicative contexts and is not taught as an isolated list of terms; (4) grammar is presented inductively and practiced in communicative contexts; (5) translation is avoided, and (6) the L1 is used as little as possible.

The Rise of EFL Teaching in the 20th Century

Similar methods were used by the British linguist Harold Palmer (1877–1949), a follower of the Direct Method who is considered to have developed the profession of teaching EFL in modern times. During the 1920s Palmer was linguistic advisor to the Japanese Ministry of Education and conducted research in Tokyo. Although he advocated an Oral Method using vocabulary study and actions, this approach did not find wide acceptance among Japanese educators for reasons discussed in a subsequent section. A colleague and collaborator of Palmer's, Michael West (1888–1973), who was involved in EFL teaching in India, emphasized vocabulary study and the need to read simplified materials as the first step in language learning. In the United States, EFL teaching benefited from the work of linguists such as Leonard Bloomfield and Charles Fries[8], first through their involvement in war-time language training, then through their work on teaching English as a second and foreign language—work that followed a structural approach and led to the establishment of the U.S. Army's Monterey Language School and the development of the Audiolingual Approach using a structured oral practice approach. Like Palmer, Fries also went to Japan as a consultant for development of that nation's EFL program. In the mid 1950s, the British Council began its own activities in EFL education, often using the works of the British linguist M.A. K. Halliday, whose work relates "elements of grammatical structure to their use in discourse" (Howatt, 1984, p. 276).

The Grammar-Translation Method

Discussing his own use of the GTM for learning Latin, Cordor (1988) observes that this method typically required three books—a dictionary, a grammar, and a reader—since the main activities were oral translations from Latin into English using the reader, drill and practice on grammatical forms such as conjugations of verbs and declensions of nouns, and written translations from Latin into English. He notes that formal instruction on grammatical rules and categories was lacking: "The teaching and learning of the theoretical foundations on which the description of the language was based were largely inductive ... very little was said about syntax" (p. 128). In contrast, he continues, the late 20ᵗʰ century GTM is characterized by grammatical instruction based on pedagogical grammar—grammar designed to promote communicative competence in the second/foreign language learner, not grammar designed for the native speaker. Richards and Rodgers summarize the main features of the contemporary GTM:

> The goal of foreign language study is to learn a language in order to read the literature or in order to benefit from the mental discipline and intellectual development that result from foreign language study. Grammar Translation is a way of studying a language ... first through detailed analysis of its grammar rules, followed by application of this knowledge to the task of translating sentences and texts into and out of the target language. It hence views language learning as consisting of little more than memorizing rules and facts .... (2001, pp. 3–4)

The authors also note that the L1 is the medium of instruction, a structural syllabus is generally used, accuracy is emphasized, grammar is taught deductively through rule learning, speaking and listening are generally neglected, vocabulary is drawn from the reading texts, and the sentence is the unit of teaching and practice. As a subsequent section will show, this approach differs in several important areas from contemporary GTM as used in many EFL settings.

In a discussion of assessing language proficiency, Sharwood Smith makes the interesting observation that translation is now considered to be a special skill, without a direct link to proficiency in the target language (Sharwood Smith, 1994). If this is so, one may well ask why it has survived for thousands of years as a pedagogical tool. Kelly suggests that translation has been remarkably robust in modern times because of its importance in examination syllabuses (1969, p. 176), a situation continuing to the present in many EFL contexts.

METHODS OF THE MIDDLE TO LATE 20ᵗʰ CENTURY

In her overview of pedagogical trends in the past 100 years, Celce-Murcia (2001, p. 5) discusses the terms *approach, method,* and *technique,* suggesting that the first is the broadest concept, intended to operationalize a particular theory, whereas the second is a set of procedures, and the third is a specific activity.

There are a number of reviews of the various approaches and methods of the mid to end of the 20ᵗʰ century (see Celce-Murcia, 2001; Howatt, 1997; Larsen-Freeman,

2000; Richards & Rodgers, 2001; Stern, 1983). These include the Oral-Situational Approach in England from the 1920s; various structural/behavioral approaches such as the Audiolingual Approach in the United States from World War II; the functional approaches of the 1970s in Europe—continued in the text-based work of Halliday; the impact of Chomsky's argument for Universal Grammar (1957)—an idea that has emerged several times during the history of language teaching; cognitive approaches that have developed since the mid 1980s through the impact of cognitive psychology and psycholinguistics (see Skehan, 1998); communicative pedagogy (Savignon, 1972) developing into various affective-humanistic approaches such as Krashen and Terrell's Natural Approach (1983); lexical-based approaches built on corpora; and—based on the failure of purely communicative approaches to produce high levels of learner accuracy, thus indicating the need for instructed L2 learning (see Norris & Ortega, 2000)—the recent interaction-based (Gass, 1997) and focus-on-form (Long, 1991) approaches that allow for explicit or implicit grammar instruction during meaning-focused interaction and input (for example, see Ellis, 2002; Fotos, 1998, 2001, 2002; Samuda, 2001). These posit an interface between formal instruction and language acquisition, and represent a middle position between a structure-based presentation of grammar points and a purely communicative approach that holds that formal instruction does not impact upon L2 acquisition (e.g., Krashen, 1981). This is basically the *langue/parole* distinction (language as a system/language in use) posited by Saussure (1916) at the beginning of the 20th century (see Stern, 1983, pp. 126–129 for a discussion). Other chapters in this volume treat these diverse approaches in more detail.

Regarding such pendulum swings in language teaching methodology, Mackey's 1965 observation that many of the methods developed in the past are still in use remains true today. He summarizes a basic pedagogical tension that endured through the centuries and continues to the present:

> If we now glance back at the development of language-teaching method we see that it first swings from the active oral use of Latin in ancient and medieval times to the learning by rules of the Renaissance grammars, back to oral activity with Comenius, back to grammar rules with Plötz, and back again to the primacy of speech in the Direct Method. (1965, p. 151)

Thus, from this perspective, the term "traditional approaches" not only refers to grammar-based instruction, translation, rule memorization, pattern practice, and other methods associated with the GTM, but also to the use of meaning-focused situational and functional dialogues, content-based instruction using the L2, oral-based inductive approaches, and the interactive communicative approaches developed since the 1970s, since they, too, have been used since antiquity.

GRAMMAR TRANSLATION VERSUS COMMUNICATIVE LANGUAGE TEACHING IN THE EFL CONTEXT

This section uses the teaching of English as an example of foreign language instruction since one third of the world's population either speaks English as a first or second language, or is studying it as a foreign language (Crystal, 1985). In addition, it is widely recognized that most English language instruction in the world occurs in the foreign language situation, generally with teachers who are non-native speakers of English themselves (Braine, 1999). It has also been noted (Fotos, 2001, p. 142) that many EFL situations have a centrally controlled education system with a set curriculum, prescribed textbooks, and highly competitive nationwide examinations determining admission to middle, secondary, and tertiary institutions. Such examinations usually have an English component requiring reading comprehension, knowledge of grammar rules, vocabulary, and translation skills. As a result, English language teaching is often aimed at mastery of the points tested on such examinations. Therefore, it is not surprising that traditional EFL instruction usually emphasizes the development of knowledge about English, including grammar rules, and the development of vocabulary and translation skills, rather than the development of communicative ability (e.g., see Bright, 1968, on teaching English in Africa and Robinson, 1960, in teaching English in Southeast Asia).

For example, in a typical EFL reading class, the teacher presents an L2 reading passage and explains L2 grammar points and new vocabulary in the L1. This is often followed by student repetition of the new words. The teacher then reads the L2 passage aloud, sentence by sentence, as a model for the students' repetition. The teacher translates the L2 text into the L1, usually word by word, and discusses the grammar, rhetorical, and stylistic features in detail. Students take notes, frequently writing the L1 translation above the word or sentence, in a manner reminiscent of medieval glosses. This is followed by grammar practice drills in the L2, sentence and text level translation exercises into the L1, and occasionally, L2 sentence production using the newly introduced target structures and/or vocabulary words (Anderson, 1993; Fotos, 2001; Gorsuch, 1998; Li, 1998; Shih, 1999), although both Shih (1999) and Gorsuch (1998) note that students often do not write in the target language at all since translation generally takes place from the L2 into the L1. Thus, there is no output, a component that, together with target language input, is suggested to be necessary for second language learning (Swain, 1985) (see Swain, chap. 26 this volume).

In a typical EFL grammar or general English classes, the teacher presents the new structure, explaining it in the L1, and introducing new vocabulary. Perhaps a tape of a dialogue containing the structure and vocabulary is played, and the students repeat the sentences, later practicing them again in pairs. After this, the students usually translate the L2 dialogue into the L1, often word by word, again supported by L1 glosses for meaning and usage written in the lines of the L2 passage, and as a final activity, listening and L2 grammar practice exercises are given (Fotos, 2001; Li, 1998; Shih, 1999).

In the strongest use of the GTM, students are presented with a difficult target language text and are required to make a word-by-word translation into the L1. Then the translation is reordered to match L1 syntax and finally, the rough translation is improved (Gorsuch, 1998, pp. 8–9). The result is that students are more focused on the L1 end-product than on the grammar, vocabulary, and meaning of the L2, a practice that has been suggested to produce washback effects on the English section of secondary and tertiary entrance examinations (Gorsuch, 1998). Since no production of the L2 is required, L2 communicative gains are minimal.

Characterizing the GTM in the 19th century as driven by the Oxford and Cambridge Local Examinations initiated in 1858, which increased the status of modern languages, including English, Howatt (1984, pp. 133–134) notes its "stress on accuracy, obsession with 'completeness,' and neglect of spoken language," a situation continuing in many EFL situations to this day. It is therefore no surprise that, similar to protests in the past, the GTM has been widely criticized over the past decades for its focus on word/sentence level meanings, its extensive use of the L1, and its failure to provide opportunities for the development of the English communicative skills increasingly needed in a global society (e.g., see Anderson, 1993; Canagarajah, 1999; Gorsuch, 1998; Lamie, 2000; Li, 1998; Shih, 1999; Yu, 2001). Furthermore, L2 grammar rules are not presented in ways that allow the development of form-meaning relationships, encouraging processing and proceduralization. Consequently many of the centralized educational agencies, particularly in Asian EFL contexts, have recently adopted plans for the introduction of communicative approaches based on the model of Canale and Swain (1980), which holds that communicative competence includes both linguistic knowledge and the ability to use this knowledge for meaning-focused communication. In many EFL situations, communicative language teaching (CTL) is considered to have the following general features (Sato & Kleinsasser, 1999): (1) provision of meaning-focused input and opportunities for meaningful output in the form of tasks, dialogues, and activities rather than the explicit study of grammar and translation; (2) use of real-life content for material that is relevant to the needs of the learners; (4) use of pair/group activities; (5) a nonthreatening classroom atmosphere, with learner independence promoted and the teacher as facilitator.

However, there are severe problems operating against success of this model of CLT in many EFL situations (see Anderson, 1993; Canagarajah, 1999; Lamie, 2000; Li, 1998; Liu & Littlewood, 1997; Rao, 2002; Yu, 2001). First, the difficulty of obtaining adequate access to communicative use of the target language is paramount since CLT requires large amounts of input and opportunities for output so that the students can acquire grammatical and vocabulary knowledge indirectly. Target language use within the classroom is often quite limited, particularly if the teacher discusses grammar, vocabulary, and stylistic concerns in the students' L1—a common feature of the current GTM—and, outside the classroom, there is usually no access to the target language. Second, many non-native speaking EFL teachers lack adequate preparation in using Western style CLT methodology and feel that their spoken English ability as well as their pragmatic and cultural knowledge is not adequate (Canagarajah, 1999; Lamie, 2000; Li, 1998; Yu, 2001). In addition, in many areas there are few opportunities for professional development in use of CLT pedagogy. A survey of Japanese high school teachers' professional development (Lamie, 2000) indicates this clearly, and points out the difficulty of expecting teachers to embrace CTL without adequate in-service preparation. Furthermore, since teachers are often required to use official textbooks—these usually based on a structural approach—it is necessary to convert these materials to communicative activities. Many teachers report a lack of both time and expertise for such conversion (Lamie, 2000; Li, 1998, Sato & Kleinsasser, 1999). Finally, the presence of grammar-and translation-based examinations in English requires that a major part of each English lesson be spent teaching grammar, vocabulary, translation, and test-taking skills. As Savignon notes (1991), failure to change evaluative procedures has often rendered curricular innovations useless.

Thus, many attempts to introduce CTL in EFL contexts have only had limited success (Brindley & Hood, 1990; Li, 1998; Liu & Littlewood, 1997; Rao, 2002; Sato & Kleinsasser, 1999, Yu, 2001). Access to the target language remains a problem, and the need for students to develop sufficient accuracy to pass proficiency examinations in English remains a paramount teaching objective.

A final consideration is whether CLT is always appropriate for specific EFL cultural contexts—although this should perhaps be the first consideration. Researchers such as Braine (1999), Canagarajah (1999), Li (1998), Liu and Littlewood (1997), Pennycook (2000), and Rao (2002) have discussed the cultural politics and critical pedagogy of English language teaching in the light of imposing CLT and other Western pedagogies on teachers and students who may not welcome it because of their lack of familiarity with the activities, their need to spend time on grammar, vocabulary, and translation activities because of examinations, and the existence of cultural factors mitigating against CLT practices of oral production, including question asking and active participation in groups. Thus, CLT pedagogy may not match the traditional teaching and learning styles of the culture (see Li, 1998; Liu & Littlewood, 1997; Rao, 2002). These points and the previous considerations often lead teachers to employ CLT sparingly in their classrooms, even though it is generally believed to be valuable, and weak or strong versions of the GTM continue to prevail.

COMBINING GRAMMAR TRANSLATION AND COMMUNICATIVE LANGUAGE TEACHING

An obvious solution to the tensions between GTM and CLT in the EFL context is an eclectic combination of methods and activities, with grammar, vocabulary, and translation activities retained and communicative activities added that contain abundant uses of target L2 structures and vocabulary, thus permitting exposure to target structures and providing opportunities for negotiated output in the target language. Considerable research has been done recently (see the review in Ellis, 2003) on the benefits of task-based learning for providing input and opportunities for students to negotiate meaning, this producing "pushed output" where the students improve their target language communication when responding to questions from their partners (Long & Porter, 1985; Pica, Young, & Doughty, 1987; Swain, 1985), and the use of interactive tasks has been proposed as a communicative method of grammar study. Researchers such Celce-Murcia, Dörnyei, and Thurrell (1998), and Ellis (2002, 2003) suggest that both grammar explanation and communicative activities are necessary to promote comprehension of the target structure and to allow for practice of grammar structures and vocabulary, and task-based activities offer the means to combine traditional and communicative pedagogies.

Thus, rather than advocating the either/or positions regarding the GTM and CTL that have characterized the past, it is time to take the position that a combination of grammar instruction and the use of communicative activities provide an optimum situation for effective L2 learning.

NOTES

1. Regarding such reviews Stern cautions, "But because books of this kind are mainly concerned with modern thought, the historical antecedents are often no more than a backdrop to set off with bold strokes those aspects the writer wishes to emphasize, and the historical treatment is necessarily brief and often reveals a definite bias" (1983, p. 77). He also notes the lack of "comprehensive and authoritative general histories of language teaching" (ibid), a situation continuing to the present.
2. It is interesting to observe that even today literacy is still strongly linked to morality. This derives from the fact that literacy was historically associated with the Bible since the Middle Ages in the West, and to Buddhist, Hindu, and Islamic religious scripture as well.
3. Robins (1951, p. 63) notes a striking similarity between the organization of grammatical categories and the presentation of material in the standard Latin textbook used in the 1940s and 1950s, Kennedy's *Latin Primer*, and ancient texts by Donatus and Priscian.
4. Since Latin did not have articles, Latin demonstrative pronouns such as *hic, hec,* and *hoc* were sometimes glossed as articles in French or English. Reynolds speculates that the "Latin of the text is being made to conform to the structures of the mother tongue of the students . . ." (1996, p. 68).
5. See Howatt's Chapter 3, "Towards 'The great and common world'" (1984, pp. 32–51) for a discussion of Comenius.
6. *A Short Introduction of Grammar*, a Latin textbook written by William Lily (1468–1522) and reissued by a committee established by Henry VIII in the 1530s, was the accepted method for grammar teaching in English schools, remaining in use until the 19th century. Called "Lily's Grammar" or the "Royal Grammar" it was written in two parts, the first titled "A Short Introduction to the Parts of Speech" and the second *Brevissima Institutio,* a long description of Latin rules written in Latin (Howatt, 1984, p. 32–33).
7. Commenting on the similarities over the centuries of the GTM and repeated communicatively oriented opposition to memorization of rules and translation, Howatt observes, "In writing a history of language teaching, and, possibly, of many other human activities, it is always tempting to prick the balloon of contemporary self-satisfaction by demonstrating that what has been taken as evidence of progress in our time has, in fact, 'all been done before'"(1984, p. 152).
8. Howatt (1984, p. 265) notes that Bloomfield and Fries, especially the latter's work at the English Language Institute at the University of Michigan, are considered to have developed the field of applied linguistics.

REFERENCES

Anderson, J. (1993). Is a communicative approach practical for teaching English in China?: Pros and cons. *System*, 21(4), 471–480.

Asher, J. (1977). *Learning another language through actions: The complete teacher's guidebook.* Los Gatos, CA: Sky Oak Productions.

Braine, G. (1999). Introduction. In G. Braine (Ed), *Non-native educators in English language teaching* (pp. xiii–xx). Mahwah, NJ: Lawrence Erlbaum Associates.

Braine, G. (Ed.). (1999). *Non-native educators in English language teaching.* Mahwah, NJ: Lawrence Erlbaum.

Breen, M. (1986). Process syllabus design. In C. Brumfit (Ed.), *General English syllabus design: ELT document 117.* (pp. 47–60). Oxford: Pergamon.

Bright, J. (1968). The training of teachers of English as a second language in Africa. In G. Perrin (Ed.), *Teachers of English as a second language* (pp. 14–43). Cambridge, UK: Cambridge University Press.

Brindley, G., & Hood, S. (1990). Curriculum innovation in adult ESL. In G. Brindley (Ed.), *The second language curriculum in action* (pp. 232–248). Sydney, Australia: National Center for English Language Teaching and Research.

Brumfit, C., & Johnson, K. (Eds.) (1979). *The communicative approach to language teaching.* Oxford, UK: Oxford University Press.

Canagarajah, A. S. (1999). *Resisting linguistic imperialism in English language teaching.* Oxford, UK: Oxford University Press.

Canale, M., & Swain, M. (1980). Theoretical bases of communicative approaches to second language teaching and testing. *Applied Linguistics*, 1, 1–47.

Celce-Murcia, M., Dörnyei, Z., & Thurrell, S. (1998). On directness in communicative language teaching. *TESOL Quarterly*, 32, 116–119.

Celce-Murcia, M. (2001). Language teaching approaches: An overview. In M. Celce-Murcia (Ed.), *Teaching English as a second or foreign language* (3rd ed.) (pp. 1–3). Boston: Heinle & Heinle.

Chomsky, N. (1957). *Syntactic structures.* The Hague, Netherlands: Mouton.

Corder, S. P. (1988). Pedagogical grammars. In W. Rutherford & M. Sharwood Smith (Eds.), *Grammar and second language teaching* (pp. 123–145). New York: Newbury House.

Crystal, D. (1985). How many millions? The statistics of English today, *English Today*, 1, 7–9.

Curme, G. (1947). *English grammar.* New York: Barnes & Noble.

Ellis, R. (1994). *The study of second language acquisition.* Oxford, UK: Oxford University Press.

Ellis, R. (2002). The place of grammar instruction in the second/foreign language curriculum. In E. Hinkel & S. Fotos (Eds.), *New perspectives on grammar teaching in second language classrooms* (pp. 17–34). Mahwah, NJ: Lawrence Erlbaum Associates.

Ellis, R. (2003). *Task-based language learning and teaching.* Oxford, UK: Oxford University Press.

Fotos, S. (1998). Shifting the focus from forms to form in the EFL classroom. *ELT Journal*, 52(4), 301–307.

Fotos, (2001). Cognitive approaches to grammar instruction. In M. Celce-Murcia (Ed.), *Teaching English as a second or foreign language* (3rd ed.) (pp. 276–285). Boston: Heinle & Heinle.

Fotos, S. (2002). Structure-based interactive tasks for the EFL grammar learner. In E. Hinkel & S. Fotos (Eds.), *New perspective on grammar teaching in second language classrooms* (pp. 135–155). Mahwah, NJ: Lawrence Erlbaum Associates.

Gass, S. (1997). *Input, interaction, and the second language learner.* Mahwah, NJ: Lawrence Erlbaum Associates.

Gorsuch, G. (1998). *Yakudoku* EFL instruction in two Japanese high school classrooms: An exploratory study. *JALT Journal*, 20(1), 6–32.

Hinkel, E., & Fotos, S. (2002). From theory to practice: A teacher's view. In E. Hinkel & S. Fotos (Eds.), *New perspectives on grammar teaching in second language classrooms* (pp. 1–12). Mahwah, NJ: Lawrence Erlbaum Associates.

Howatt, A. (1984). *A history of English language teaching.* Oxford, UK: Oxford University Press.

Howatt, A. (1997). Talking shop: Transformation and change in ELT. *ELT Journal*, 51(3), 263–268.

Hudson, G. (2000). *Essential introductory linguistics.* Oxford, UK: Blackwell.

Hunter, S., & Wallace, R. (1995). *The place of grammar in writing instruction: Past, present, and future.* Portsmouth, NH: Heinemann.

Hymes, D. (1971). Competence and performance in linguistic theory. In R. Huxley & E. Ingram (Eds.), *Language acquisition: Models and methods* (pp. 3–28). London: Academic Press.

Hymes, D. (1980). *Language in education: Ethnolinguistic essays.* Washington, D.C: Center for Applied Linguistics.

Kelly, L. (1969). *25 centuries of language teaching.* Rowley, MA: Newbury House.

Krashen, S. (1981). *Second language acquisition and second language learning.* Oxford, UK: Oxford University Press.

Krashen, S., & Terrell, T. (1983). *The natural approach: Language acquisition in the classroom.* New York: Pergamon.

Lamie, J. (2000). Teachers of English in Japan: Professional development and training at a crossroads. *JALT Journal* 22(1), 27–45.

Larsen-Freeman, D. (2000). *Techniques and principles in language teaching* (2nd ed). Oxford, UK: Oxford University Press.

Law, V. (1997). *Grammar and the grammarians in the early Middle Ages*. New York: Longman.

Law, V. (2003). *The history of linguistics in Europe from Plato to 1600*. Cambridge, UK: Cambridge University Press.

Li, Defeng. (1998). "It's always more difficult than you plan and imagine": Teachers' perceived difficulties in introducing the Communicative Approach in South Korea. *TESOL Quarterly, 32*, 677–703.

Liu, N.F., & Littlewood, W. (1997). Why do many students appear reluctant to participate in classroom learning discourse? *System, 25*(3), 371–384.

Long, M. (1991). Focus on form: A design feature in language teaching methodology. In K. de Bot, D. Coste, R. Ginsberg & C. Kramsch (Eds.), *Foreign language research in crosscultural perspective* (pp. 39–52). Amsterdam: Benjamins

Long, M., & Porter, P. (1985). Group work, interlanguage talk, and second language acquisition. *TESOL Quarterly, 19*, 207–228.

Mackey, W. (1965). *Language teaching analysis*. London: Longman.

Norris, J., & Ortega, L. (2000). Effectiveness of L2 instruction: A research synthesis and quantitative meta-analysis. *Language Learning, 50*(3), 417–428.

Odlin, T. (1994). Introduction. In T. Odlin (Ed.), *Perspectives on pedagogical grammar*. Cambridge, UK: Cambridge University Press.

Oxford, R. (2001). Language learning styles and strategies. In M. Celce-Murcia (Ed.), *Teaching English as a second or foreign language* (3rd ed.) (pp. 359–366). Boston: Heinle & Heinle.

Pennycook, A. (2000). The social politics and the cultural politics of language classrooms. In J. Kelly & W. Eggington (Eds.), *The sociopolitics of English language teaching* (pp. 89–103). Clevedon, UK: Multilingual Matters.

Pica, T., Young, R., & Doughty, C. (1987). The impact of interaction on comprehension. *TESOL Quarterly, 21*, 737–757.

Rao, Z. (2002). Bridging the gap between teaching and learning styles in East Asian contexts. *TESOL Journal, 11*(2), 5–11.

Reynolds, S. (1996). *Medieval reading: Grammar, rhetoric, and the classical text*. Cambridge, UK: Cambridge University Press.

Richards, J., & Rodgers, T. (2001). *Approaches and methods in language teaching: A description and analysis* (2nd ed.). Cambridge, UK: Cambridge University Press.

Reid, J. (Ed.) (1998). *Understanding learning styles in the second language classroom*. Upper Saddle River, NJ: Prentice-Hall.

Robins, R. (1951). *Ancient and mediaeval grammatical theory in Europe*. London: Kennikat Press.

Robins, R. (1997). *A short history of linguistics* (4th ed.). New York: Longman.

Robinson, K. (1960). *English teaching in South-East Asia*. Bungay, Suffolk: Richard Clay.

Rutherford, W. (1987). *Second language grammar learning and teaching*. New York: Longman.

Rutherford, W. (1988). Grammatical consciousness raising in brief historical perspective. In W. Rutherford & M. Sharwood Smith (Eds.), *Grammar and second language teaching* (pp. 15–19). New York: Newbury House.

Samuda, V. (2001). Guiding the relationship between form and meaning during performance: The role of the teacher. In M. Bygate, P. Skehan, & M. Swain (Eds.), *Researching pedagogical tasks: Second language learning, teaching, and testing*. London: Pearson.

Sato, K., & Kleinsasser, R. (1999). Communicative language teaching (CLT): Practical understandings. *The Modern Language Journal, 83*, 494–517.

Saussure, F. (1916). *Cours de linguistique générale*. Translated (1959) as Course in general linguistics by W. Baskin. New York: McGraw-Hill.

Savignon, S. (1972). *Communicative competence: An experiment in foreign language teaching*. Reading, MA: Addison-Wesley.

Savignon, S. (1991). Communicative language teaching: State of the art. *TESOL Quarterly, 25*(2), 261–277.

Sharwood Smith, M. (1994). *Second language learning: Theoretical foundations*. New York: Longman.

Shih, M. (1999). More than practicing language: Communicative reading and writing for Asian settings. *TESOL Journal, 8*, 20–25.

Skehan, P. (1998). *A cognitive approach to language learning*. Oxford, UK: Oxford University Press.

Stern, H. (1983). *Fundamental concepts of language teaching*. Oxford, UK: Oxford University Press.

Swain, M (1985). Communicative competence: Some roles of comprehensible input and comprehensible output in its development. In S. Gass & C. Madden (Eds.), *Input in second language acquisition* (pp. 235–253). Rowley, MA: Newbury House.

Sweet, H. (1892). *A new English grammar*. Oxford, UK: Clarendon.

Sweet, H. (1964). *The practical study of languages*. Oxford, UK: Oxford University Press. (Original work published 1899. London: J.M. Dent & Sons).

Titone, R. (1968). *Teaching foreign languages: An historical sketch*. Washington, DC: Georgetown University Press.

Yu, Liming. (2001). Communicative language teaching in China: Progress and promise. *TESOL Quarterly, 35*, 194–197.

Form-Focused Instruction

Jessica Williams
University of Illinois at Chicago

Focus on Form (FonF), a term first coined by Long (1988, 1991; Long & Crookes, 1992) to describe a brief, often instructional focus on linguistic features embedded in meaningful communication, has come to mean different things to those who have adopted the term. The widespread embrace of the term in all of its interpretations is perhaps an effect of the inevitable swing of the pendulum: In the early days of communicative language teaching, during which some meaning-focused approaches eschewed any attention to form at all, many researchers and teachers, who had perhaps always been skeptical, now saw FonF as permission to reintroduce grammar into their classrooms, where it had long been taboo or taught surreptitiously. It is also likely that many teachers, especially those outside of the United States, never abandoned the teaching of grammar in spite of this trend (Skehan, 1998; Thornbury, 1998).

MULTIPLE TERMS AND DEFINITIONS

Whatever the reason, the notion of focus on form seems to have struck a chord among many teachers. However, the varied interpretations and plethora of rather similar terms have resulted in some inevitable confusion with regard to definitions. R. Ellis (2001) uses *form-focused instruction* (FFI) as an umbrella term for all approaches that draw learner attention to formal aspects of language. This definition, "any planned or incidental instructional activity that is intended to induce learners to pay attention to linguistic form," (pp. 1–2) includes FonF but potentially also decontextualized, highly metalinguistic, teacher-centered grammar instruction, characteristic of what Long calls *focus on formS*. He reserves the more specific term *incidental focus on form* to refer to the type of instruction described by Long and Robinson (1998). Spada (1997) also uses the term FFI but her use appears to be quite similar to the term FonF as used by Doughty and Williams (1998a).

This chapter is an attempt to clarify what has been written about FonF and to explore some of the important features of such an approach. Long and Robinson operationalize FonF in terms of the allocation of the learner's focal attention, explicitly tying it to Schmidt's "noticing" hypothesis (1994, 1995).

... during an otherwise meaning-focused classroom lesson, focus on form often consists of an occasional shift of attention to linguistic code features—by the teacher and/or one or more students—triggered by perceived problems with comprehension or production. (p. 23)

This definition includes minimally the following features:

- An overall emphasis on the communication of meaning.
- A brief diversion from that emphasis on communication to focus on language as object.
- A problem-based trigger for the diversion.

The problem-oriented trigger, with the focus of attention on a particular item, is brought about incidentally by a breakdown or error of some sort, or perhaps some difficulty in either production or comprehension. From a pedagogical perspective, this means that teachers should wait for issues to emerge and respond to them as needed. Doughty and Williams (1998a) and many of the authors in that volume (e.g., Harley, 1998; Swain, 1998) broaden this definition somewhat, allowing for a planned, and even separated, instructional focus on form that need not begin with a real-time problem-trigger. R. Ellis (2001) suggests that this is an abandonment of the incidental nature of FonF central to its definition and that this change is likely to have important consequences for instruction. Doughty and Williams (1998b) clearly suggest that an optimal FonF technique would be one in which meaning and form are processed simultaneously, but offer alternatives as well (see also Doughty, 2001). Given the strict definition offered by Long and Robinson and the varying interpretations offered in the literature, it is important to explore what is meant by the various understandings of the term FonF. Table 37.1 offers a comparative view of how these terms have been defined[1]. The one thing that all of these share is the feature *focus on*

TABLE 37.1

Definitions of Focus on Form

	Long & Robinson (1998) FonF	*Doughty & Williams (1998) FonF (including others in volume)*	*Spada (1997) FFI*	*Ellis (2001) FFI*	*Ellis (2001) Incidental FonF*
Overall and primary focus on meaning	++	++	++	+	++
Attention to language as object	++	++	++	++	++
Brief	++	+	+	+	++
Proactive	−	+	+	+	−
Explicit	−	+	+	+	+
Separate from meaning focus	−	+	+	+	−
Problem-oriented trigger for attention to form:					
Real-time problem	++	+	+	+	+
IL-based problem	++	++	?	+	+

Note. ++ required feature; + possible feature; − prohibited feature; ? not specified

[1] I am indebted to Charlene Polio for her contributions to this table.

language as object. Some of the features will be discussed a greater length later in this chapter.

I will now explore these definitions in more detail, beginning with the one used in Doughty and Williams. The term FonF consists of two parts: the *focus* and the *form*. The first F is perhaps the more crucial in that it points to cognitive engagement and learning processes. In Doughty and Williams (1998b), *focus* is taken to mean any brief turning or dividing of learner attention during an act of communication, such as reading, conversing, listening, and so forth, toward some feature of language. The essential characteristic is that although there is a brief or simultaneous focus on code features: pronunciation, inflectional morphology, word form, word definition, and the like, the overriding focus is on the processing of meaning as part of an act of communication, and furthermore, that the diversion to form is in service of communication of meaning.

In most studies, *form* is assumed to be a structural feature. In fact, though, it need not be limited to these kinds of items. It can and should be viewed more broadly. FonF could equally involve the drawing of learner attention to a second language pragmatic convention (Bardovi-Harlig & Dörnyei, 1998; Celce-Murcia, Dörnyei, & Thurrell, 1997; Takahashi, 2001; see Kasper, 2001, for a general discussion). For example, Cook (2001) describes the morphological contextualization cues that are crucial to pragmatically appropriate discourse in Japanese. Learners often will not notice these morphemes because they are not salient and because they have no referential meaning. If they are not noticed, they are unlikely to be learned. Such features might be a candidate for FonF.

Indeed, Long (1996) himself offers an example of using FonF to call attention to problematic words. In this case, the *form* would be lexical. FonF might include the use of a typographic enhancement or glossing of words in a reading, to heighten learner attention to a word's meaning, not just its structural features. This flagging of lexical items and in particular, their meaning rather than a grammatical form, is a broader view of FonF; in that, instead of processing form along with meaning, the learner is processing word meaning in the context of comprehending spoken or written text (see Hulstijn, 2001). This falls within the general perspective of simultaneous or dual processing, which is at the heart of FonF. An example of this can be found in Rott, Williams, and Cameron (2002), a study that applies FonF techniques to lexical acquisition, in a treatment that combines the possibilities of structured input, guided output, and subsequent access to input to encourage learners to notice new lexical items. The defining characteristic of *form* in all of these examples of FonF is that, however briefly, language is treated as an object rather than exclusively as a tool for communication (see R. Ellis, Basturkmen, & Loewen, 2001b).

A FonF TAXONOMY

There are variety of techniques and activities that have been suggested to promote FonF, many of which have been discussed in the literature (Doughty & Williams, 1998b; R. Ellis, 2001; Nassaji, 1999; Spada, 1997). Because of the diversity of these ideas, it is useful to situate them within some sort of taxonomy. It seems evident that some level of attention to form makes pedagogical sense, yet it is not always clear which are aspects of various FonF activities and techniques that make them effective, or more likely, sometimes effective and sometimes not. A taxonomy can help isolate the features of the various instructional techniques in order to analyze them separately, and ultimately, manipulate them for more effective instruction. Doughty and Williams (1998b) made a first attempt at this. In this paper, I reevaluate several of these features, and consider new ones, shown here in Figure 37.1.

Problematicity

- Planning
  - proactive ⟵⟶ reactive*
  - targeted ⟵⟶ general
- Obtrusive ⟵⟶ unobtrusive* (interrupts processing)
- Teacher ⟵⟶ learner responsibility

FIG. 37.1. Some features of FonF for (re)consideration
*from Doughty and Williams (1998b)

Problematicity

One of the central features of FonF is that it revolves around a learner problem or difficulty. Ellis et al. (2001b; R. Ellis, 2001) stress this point in particular. They take us back to Long and Robinson's original definition—that FonF arises out of a (perceived) problem in communication and thus should perhaps be limited to incidental treatment, that is, responses to problems as they emerge during a lesson. This is what is referred to as a *real-time* problem in Table 37.1. They make the further claim that this is likely to lead to what they call *extensive* FonF, that is, a scattershot treatment in which various forms come into instructional focus as errors or communicative breakdown occur. They contrast this with *intensive* FonF, in which a limited number of forms are selected in advance for repeated emphasis. Clearly, such treatment is only likely to occur if the focus is preplanned rather than incidental. For example, the forms in Doughty and Varela (1998) were selected on the basis of an earlier analysis of the learners' interlanguages (ILs). This type of problem trigger is referred to an *IL-based* problem in Table 37.1. This is an important distinction, given the divergent results from studies of recasting, a technique that is often cited as useful in FonF instruction (see Nicholas, Lightbown, & Spada, 2001). A recast is defined by Long (to appear) as an immediate reformulation of a learner's nontargetlike utterance as a targetlike utterance, with as little change in meaning as possible. Research by Lyster (1998; Lyster & Ranta, 1997) suggests that recasting is not terribly effective, whereas Ayoun (2001), Braidi (2002), Doughty and Varela (1998), and Long, Inagaki, and Ortega (1998) report the opposite. Lyster's findings may stem from the fact that the teachers in these studies provided extensive recasting. That is, a variety of forms were recast, others were ignored, and few forms came into focus more than once, resulting in their potential ambiguity for learners. Learners were unsure whether the recasts were corrections or simply affective or meaning-based feedback. In the second set of studies, in contrast, forms were preselected for narrow and intensive focus, based on an earlier analysis of the learners' ILs.

There is one other implication of Ellis' emphasis on perceived communication problems in the definition of FonF. In addition to the proactive (preplanned)-reactive distinction, Ellis, Basturkmen, and Loewen (2001b) use the term *preemptive* FonF. In this case, the trigger may not be an actual or perceived problem; instead, it may simply be a problem that is anticipated. In other words, no problem-based trigger is required. For instance, if the teacher thinks learners might encounter difficulty with a form or structure, she may preempt this possibility by initiating a brief sequence focusing on form and providing learners with positive evidence about the form in question. Because the sequence was not planned, but rather, Ellis et al. maintain, initiated on the spur of the moment, they classify it as incidental. Although such moves are inevitably represented in communicative classrooms and may be an important instructional move to investigate further, the question is: Is it FonF? The question brings us back to *problematicity*, which is a central and essential feature of FonF. Broadly speaking, all manifestations of FonF are in response to problems that learners have with form.

In some cases, the problem is noted by the teacher or researcher, resulting in planned and specifically targeted FonF instruction (e.g., Doughty & Varela, 1998; Izumi & Bigelow, 2000; Swain, 1998; Williams & Evans, 1998); in other cases, the teacher response is spontaneous feedback on error (Lyster & Ranta, 1997; Williams, 2001), or attention to form may be initiated by the learners themselves in requests for assistance (R. Ellis, Basturkmen, & Loewen, 2001a; Williams, 1999) or as an outcome of negotiation (de la Fuente, 2002; R. Ellis, 1999; Mackey, 1999; Oliver, 1995, 2000; Pica, 1994, 1997, 2002; Pica et al., 1989; Shehadeh, 1999, 2001).

In the case of learner requests for assistance, it is important to note that the problem trigger need not be an error. The learners may encounter a word they do not understand, a form they do not know how to use, or find that they are unable to express their intended meaning because of a "hole" in their interlanguage (de la Fuente, 2002; Izumi & Bigelow, 2000; Rott, Williams, & Cameron, 2002; Shehadeh, 2001; Swain & Lapkin, 1995; Swain, 1998; Williams, 1999). This need may prompt them to ask the teacher for assistance. Need is an important element in successful learning, at least of vocabulary, according to Laufer and Hulstijn (2001). In all of these cases, as well as in the much-explored case of negotiation, there is an actual problem. In this light, it seems questionable whether this learner-initiated focus on form, as described by R. Ellis, Basturkmen, and Loewen (2001a) and Williams (1999), can actually be called preemptive.

In Ellis' teacher-initiated preemptive focus on form, the claim is that this focus is purely incidental, that the teacher decides on the spur of the moment that learners might encounter difficulty processing a word or form that is part of the lesson, and that he or she therefore launches into a brief, (explicit) instructional sequence. However, in contrast to learner-initiated FonF, the "problem" here is only anticipated and, as Ellis et al. demonstrate, the guess is not always accurate. Because these kinds of sequences potentially do away with a central feature of FonF, problematicity, one may question whether this is FonF at all, at least as defined here. This is an example of how the term has been stretched to fit our need to describe various kinds of communicative interaction and instruction in which learners and teachers treat language as object.

Planning

Doughty and Williams offered proactive versus reactive as a fundamental distinction in making FonF decisions. However basic, this distinction may be too broad and has been subject to varied interpretation, probably due to confusion with the more general term, planning. It may be more useful to consider several related features, in particular, to distinguish among the following: (a) overall lesson planning, (b) whether a technique or approach is proactive or reactive, and (c) the degree to which a technique or an activity has a specific instructional target (i.e., a form that will be focused on).

Overall planning (a) simply means that the use of specific techniques and activities can (should) be planned. For example, recasting is clearly a reactive technique (b), yet the decision to recast, as well as the target of the recasting (c) may be made in advance (a). Reactive FonF techniques, such as recasting, may be either targeted in order to provide intensive treatment or may be general, resulting in extensive treatment. Within our definition of FonF, targeted recasting (c) would be based on a previously established IL profile, rather than a real-time communication problem, although the individual recasts would be in response to real-time errors (b).

This targeted-general distinction can also be applied to proactive FonF. If a specific form is to be in focus, a teacher might opt for a proactive technique such as some form of input enhancement, perhaps textual highlighting or input flooding (see Wong & Simard, 1999, for examples and discussion). Another possibility for planned and specifically targeted FonF is a focused communication task, during which, it is hoped, learners will use the preselected form while performing some meaning-centered task (Loschky & Bley-Vroman, 1993; Samuda, 2000; Spada & Lightbown, 1999).

Alternatively, general (nontargeted) accuracy might be promoted without specifying any particular form by increasing learner planning time, and/or giving instructions to attend to accuracy. Mehnert (1998), Ortega (1999) and Foster and Skehan (1999) all report ways in which opportunities to plan production allow learners to focus on form spontaneously and increase accuracy, as well as try out more complex forms at the forward edge of their ILs.

Attention to form can also be encouraged with the use of two-way convergent tasks, which can promote negotiation (Pica, Kanagy, & Faludon, 1993; Pica, 2002). Some of these have been shown to increase learners' attention to some forms (Mackey, 1999; Pica, 1994; Shehadeh, 2001). However, in most sequences involving morphosyntax, it is difficult to predict what the locus of negotiation will be, and thus these must be considered nontargeted FonF activities. Task repetition can also increase learner attention to form, though in this case, the changes documented in empirical studies are mainly in complexity and sophistication rather than accuracy (Bygate, 2000; Gass et al., 1999). Again, the effect is general improvement in language use rather than on specified forms. These nontargeted proactive choices do present a potential problem for our definition of FonF, however. Do they conform to the problematicity criterion? In fact, they probably do, simply more indirectly. Learners with more planning time and opportunity to repeat activities may be better able to identify their difficulties and address them more autonomously in these activities.

Thus, the proactive-reactive feature is related to, but separate from, the targeted-general feature, and both can be related to advance planning. In summary, planning can be seen in three levels of instructional design:

- Planned choice of techniques and activities.
- Reactive versus proactive techniques.
- Specification of instructional target.

Some examples of instructional activities as they reflect these features may be helpful. Figure 37.2 illustrates these graphically.

So far, we have discussed the planned side of Figure 37.2. It is also possible to focus on form without having made a decision to do so in advance. It is common for a teacher to notice a general problem that students are having and to address it in some way, with a brief mini-lesson on form or by calling learner attention to the issue more implicitly (Lightbown, 1991; Lightbown & Spada, 1994; Long & Robinson, 1998; VanPatten, 1993). This would be unplanned, reactive FonF. Another quite different example of unplanned FonF would be the case of learners independently choosing to focus on form as a result of individual difficulties in production or comprehension (e.g., Ellis, Basturkmen, & Loewen, 2001b; Williams, 1999). The final possibility, in parentheses in Figure 37.2, is teacher-initiated preemptive FonF, as described by Ellis, Basturkmen, and Loewen (2001b), in which a teacher anticipates learner difficulty. This falls outside of FonF as defined here, because it does not involve the crucial feature of problematicity.

Obtrusiveness

A second basic feature discussed in Doughty and Williams is obtrusiveness. In Doughty and Williams, obtrusiveness simply refers to the degree to which an activity or technique interrupts the flow of communication. A more crucial issue for acquisition, perhaps, is whether it interrupts the processing of meaning. This is a cognitive rather than communicative perspective. Whether this interruption of processing is even possible,

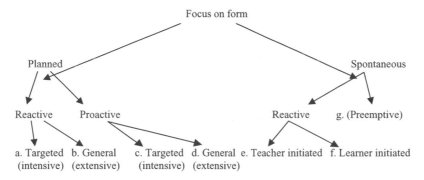

Examples of activities/instructional sequences with these features:
a.   Narrow recasting of preselected form(s)
b.   General recasting of learner error
c.   Enhanced input, focused communicative tasks
d.   Increased planning time for task; negotiation tasks
e.   Scattershot response to learner error, e.g., "mini-lessons" in response to learner problems
f.   Learner-initiated FonF, e.g., learner requests for assistance
g.   (mini-lessons in anticipation of learner problems)

FIG. 37.2. Planning in FonF activities and techniques

and if so, what its effect on second language learning might be, is not yet clear. De Bot (2000) argues that processing, and in particular, retrieval, cannot be interrupted. However, many pedagogical techniques appear to be predicated on the assumption that some interruption is required in order to actively direct learners' attention to a form, or to engage learners in the deeper processing that some claim is necessary for transfer to long-term memory (see R. Ellis, 1999, for discussion). At the other end of the spectrum is the prospect of simultaneous processing of form and meaning. Unfortunately, it is not certain whether this is possible either (Robinson, 1995; see Doughty, 2001, for relevant research on this topic from the psychology literature).

In part, any determination regarding these debates will depend on whether (and what level of) awareness is considered a requirement for the conversion of input to intake, a question that remains controversial (Leow, 1997b, 2000; Rosa & O'Neill, 1999, Schmidt, 2001, in press; Simard & Wong, 2001). If higher levels of awareness are required, this could limit the possibilities for simultaneous processing of form and meaning. VanPatten (1990, 1996) has long maintained, based on a limited capacity model, that the simultaneous processing of form and meaning is unlikely, at least in the initial stages of acquisition. His claim is that form will only be processed when meaning is already clear to the learner (and therefore is processed at little or no cost). There is some evidence that even supposedly unobtrusive interventions can result in a diminution of performance in the processing of meaning, even as the enhancement may increase noticing of form. Overstreet (1998), for instance, reports lower comprehension scores for texts with multiple kinds of typographic enhancement than for unenhanced texts. A number of other studies of textual enhancement report only its effect on the noticing or use of form, without controlling for an effect on comprehension, making it difficult to determine its overall impact (Alanen, 1995; Jourdenais et al., 1995; Leeman et al., 1995).

On the other hand, it has been argued that greater awareness allows for more elaborate forms of learning (see Rosa & O'Neill, 1999; Simard & Wong, 2001; Schmidt, 1995, for discussion) and a variety of experimental studies have suggested an advantage for explicit instruction for the noticing and/or learning of at least *some* rules or structures and under *some* conditions (e.g., Carroll & Swain, 1993; DeKeyser, 1995; N. Ellis, 1993; R. Ellis, 2002; Kupferberg & Olshtain, 1996; Nassaji & Swain, 2000; Robinson, 1996, 1997; Rosa & O'Neill, 1999; Spada & Lightbown, 1993, 1999; Takahashi, 2001; L. White, 1991; see N. Ellis & Laporte, 1997, for a discussion). Norris and Ortega (2000), in their meta-analysis of effect-of-instruction studies, conclude that more explicit forms of intervention lead to greater gains than implicit instruction (though see Doughty, in press, for an alternate interpretation).

R. Ellis (1998) refers to most of these pedagogical options as "explicit instruction" and some would be considered obtrusive in that communication is interrupted in order to direct learner attention to language form. Indeed, some may not qualify as FonF. For instance, although they are included on the FonF continuum in Doughty and Williams (1998b), there is some question as to whether the consciousness-raising tasks in studies by Fotos (1993, 1994, 2002) should actually be called FonF at all, as defined by the criteria of meaning focus, brief diversion, and problematicity. Fotos (2002) argues that an explicit focus is required in foreign language settings, in which copious target language input is absent. Some of these tasks have as their content focus the grammatical rules themselves. Although the learners are indeed interacting, they are simply communicating about grammar. The entire activity treats language as an object rather than as a tool for communication. This constitutes an important difference between these activities and others that are aimed at increasing metalinguistic awareness, such as the tasks used by Swain and her colleagues, in collaborative writing (1998, 2000; Swain & Lapkin, 1995) or in feedback on writing errors (Nassaji & Swain, 2000). In these tasks, too, the interaction may focus on formal features of the language, but the discussion is in service of a wider communicative purpose. That said, such tasks, for example, the dictogloss reconstruction, stand at the outer edge of the FonF continuum.

A less obtrusive possibility, mentioned earlier, is to expose learners to a new form in the input (for which they are developmentally ready), or a Target Language (TL) alternative to an IL form, with that form highlighted or flagged in some way, what R. Ellis (2001) calls *enriched input*. The input may also be enriched by increasing the frequency of a preselected form in a text in order to direct the learner's attention to it. De Bot (2000) suggests that for learning to be facilitated, instructional tasks must make TL candidates in the input more attractive for selection than non-TL candidates. Textual enhancement and flooding may serve this goal. Various forms of typographic and other textual enhancement of written input have been discussed at length in the literature (e.g., Alanen, 1995; Jourdenais et al., 1995; Leow, 1997a; Takahashi, 2001; J. White, 1998). According to a review of these studies by Wong and Simard (1999), the results for this type of intervention are mixed. Although the bulk of the studies on which they report do demonstrate some positive effect for such enhancement, the authors make the point that the results are often difficult to interpret because of inconsistencies in research design. Specifically, the enhancements have often been mixed with other interventions, and other effects, such as on comprehension, may not be reported. In addition, the positive effects varied: Some only reported an improvement on noticing measures, some on use, and rather fewer, on measures of accuracy or acquisition.

A more explicit and obtrusive approach can be found in the processing instruction procedures of VanPatten (1996, in press). R. Ellis uses the term, *structured input* (1998, 2001) and argues that this is focus on formS because it gives primary attention the forms to be learned. VanPatten argues that it is precisely because these activities require learners to attend to form in order to process meaning that they are effective (VanPatten, 1996; VanPatten & Lee, 1995). In this approach, learners are exposed to input containing relevant problematic structures, but they are also explicitly instructed as to how the structures should be processed. Most studies of input processing have examined the effect of this technique on forms known to cause learners difficulty, either because they carry little meaning (e.g., redundant inflectional morphology) or because they violate learner expectations (e.g., declarative sentences in which the first noun is not the subject). This would meet the problematicity criterion of FonF. Whether input processing qualifies as a brief diversion and meaning focused is open to question, but results suggest that it is an effective technique for learning these forms (VanPatten, in press). One reason for this may be that the aim of this technique is to guide learner processing of input, perhaps a more realistic goal compared to explicit techniques that are aimed at immediate acquisition and use. Doughty (in press) argues that it is these units of processing, rather than units of language, which should be the target of instruction. Other approaches combine input-based techniques, such as floods/typographic enhancement with feedback and production practice, with positive effects generally reported (e.g., Alanen, 1995; Leeman et al., 1995; Spada & Lightbown, 1999; Williams & Evans, 1998).

Locus of Responsibility

FonF activities have thus far been described in terms of four features: problematicity, proactive-reactive, targetedness, and obtrusiveness. The first is a required feature; the last three are continua along which activities may range. However, consideration of these three features neglects one crucial element in the learning process: who is doing the planning, reacting, targeting, and interrupting. For the most part, the features described so far refer to choices that the teacher makes. Since only the leaner can do the learning, it seems appropriate to turn our focus to the role of the learner. In Doughty and Williams (1998b, p. 259), this aspect of FonF was described in either/or terms: Is the learner's attention *attracted* (implicitly) or *directed* (more forcefully and directly)? Does the learner or teacher manipulate the forms? Both of these point to the locus of responsibility as another essential feature of FonF: Is it the teacher/materials or the learner who takes responsibility for initiating the cognitive processes involved in acquisition? (Always keeping in mind, of course, that ultimately, it is always up to the learner.)

Again, there is a wide range, starting from traditional activities, in which the teacher or materials take primary responsibility for focusing on formS. Those techniques, in which the teacher controls the process, such as the provision of explicit explanations, and present-and-practice activities, also tend to be the most obtrusive; indeed, most could not be considered FonF. Thus, the extreme—teacher responsible—end over-laps with a high level of obtrusiveness, that is, such activities tend to interrupt the processing of meaning.

A second, intermediate position would include those techniques that, though still teacher/materials-directed, place more responsibility with the learner in that they provide learners with a guided *opportunity* to engage in cognitive processes that are thought to facilitate acquisition of a targeted form. This would include many of the techniques and activities already mentioned. Processing instruction (VanPatten & Cadierno, 1993; VanPatten & Sanz, 1995; Wong, 2001) would be one example. Other activities in this category, such as recasting and structured input activities, are those that encourage learners to notice the gap, that is, to see where their IL falls short of the target. Cognitive processes involved in intake might also be triggered by learners' simply not knowing, but needing, the TL form, resulting in their noticing a so-called hole in their IL. This in turn may increase the salience, and consequently, learner noticing of forms in the TL that they need. This noticing may be occasioned by an output task, as when learners became aware of holes in their ILs while reconstructing a text. This is particularly evident in dialogic activities, as reported in Swain's work (Swain, 1998, 2000; Swain & Lapkin, 1998; see also de la Fuente, 2002; Izumi & Bigelow, 2000; Laufer & Hulstijn, 2001; Rott, Williams, & Cameron, 2002; Thornbury, 1997).

In their analysis of FonF features of various tasks and techniques, Doughty and Williams (1998b) list almost no tasks in which the focus on form is NOT orchestrated by the teacher. The tasks and activities just discussed are no exception. It is possible to give somewhat more responsibility to the learner for focusing on language form. However, this would most likely require that any specific target for the focus on form be relinquished. One promising possibility already mentioned is allowing learners to plan their production. A widely held assumption is that the human mind is a limited capacity processor (see Schmidt, 2001). VanPatten (1996) has argued that learners have a natural tendency to process meaning before form. One way of helping learners to manage the cognitive load of simultaneous processing is to give them more time to plan their production.

Mehnert (1998), Ortega (1999), and Foster and Skehan (1999) all report ways in which opportunities to plan production allow learners to focus on form spontaneously and increase accuracy, as well as try out more complex forms at the forward edge of their ILs. Specifically, Mehnert (1998) found that, with even a minute of planning time, accuracy increased significantly on an exposition task, with a longer period needed for an instructional task. Some research has shown that the effect of planning extends beyond increasing formal accuracy. Increased pretask planning time may also affect fluency and complexity, depending on the task, the amount of time, and the proficiency of the learners. In her review of planning studies, Ortega proposes that "an increased focus on form during pretask planning... (provides) the space for the learner to devote conscious attention to formal and systematic aspects of the language needed for a particular task" (1999, p. 120). She notes that, in many studies, it is not clear whether planning time results in planning of actual language use or whether it eases the cognitive load by allowing learners to manage more global task demands initially, freeing up attention to devote to accuracy during execution of the task. In her own study of the effect of planning time, she included retrospective interviews and found that, in fact, learners do both, often planning at the sentence level. However, she found no significant effect for planning time on accuracy in a story retell task. Overall, the results for effect of planning time on accuracy are mixed and difficult to compare because they involve different tasks, planning conditions, and proficiency levels. However, Ortega notes that there is enough evidence of increased focus on form with additional planning time to make it a promising avenue for further research. Although in some studies, the task has included instructions to pay attention to accuracy, the decision for how planning time should be used rests with the learner. We can therefore classify such activities as learner-responsible.

Manipulation of Task Features to Encourage Cognitive Processing

Beyond planning time, one can speak more broadly of the manipulation of task features, which can help free up learners' attention so that they can focus on form independently and as needed (Robinson, 2001; Skehan & Foster, 2001). Skehan (1996) suggests, for instance, that if task familiarity is increased or complexity is decreased, learners may be more able to focus on accuracy. In fact, however, Skehan and Foster (1999) found that fluency was more likely to be influenced by the predictability of a task than accuracy. Skehan and Foster (2001) now see these two performance demands in competition with each other. Robinson (2001) argues that a reduction in the cognitive task demands may actually work against IL development. He proposes that increased cognitive demands will result in greater learner noticing and rehearsal in memory, which in turn, will lead to more incorporation of input and greater modification of output. Only empirical studies will reveal the effects of the manipulation of these task features.

One such study, Gass et al. (1999), examined the effect of task repetition on accuracy, with the underlying assumption that with the increased content familiarity that accompanied the repeated task, more attention might be available to improve accuracy. During the execution of a task with familiar content and structure, learners had opportunity to draw on their knowledge of the TL and consequently, modify their output in the direction of the target. They were able to compare their IL production, not to the target input, but to an aspect of their IL knowledge that they did not yet fully control but could access when they devoted more attention to retrieving it. Gass et al. found some modest improvements, although they found that they did not carry over to new tasks. Izumi et al. (1999) report similar effects for task repetition, in this case, on noticing. This manipulation of task features may prove a useful pedagogical tool, particularly for nontargeted proactive FonF, which is both unobtrusive and places a large degree of the responsibility on the learner.

Focus on Form and Stages of IL Acquisition

Many models have been suggested for second language learning (e.g., Gass, 1997; N. Ellis, 2001; R. Ellis, 1997; Johnson, 1996; VanPatten, 1996). They differ on fundamental points, such as the role of noticing, explicit knowledge, and output, and on many details. An analysis and evaluation of these models are beyond the scope of this chapter. What we can take from them is the notion that learner interaction with language data changes at different stages of development, and that instruction may impact the acquisition process differently at these various points. Instruction should therefore be targeted thoughtfully, based on where learners are in this process. In fact, very little work has explicitly addressed the need to differentiate the effect of FonF at points of IL development although some have examined the differential effect of drawing/attracting attention to form at different levels of proficiency or developmental readiness (Mackey, 1999; Mackey & Philp, 1998; Nassaji & Swain, 2000; Spada & Lightbown, 1999; Williams & Evans, 1998).

The process begins with input. No matter what model one subscribes to, input is necessary for the process to begin. It is not sufficient for input to be available however; learners must somehow take in this data and process it. One widely held belief is that in order for this to take place, the learner must attend to input (Schmidt, 1990, 1994, 1995). Attention, and its "subjective correlate" (Schmidt, 2001, p. 5), noticing, is a construct that has been variously defined and subject to some controversy. Several different kinds of noticing have been suggested in the literature. At the most general level, we may think of noticing as simply the registration of a form or word that has not been attended to before. What gets noticed may be influenced by a number of factors, including frequency, salience, affect, and situational factors such as time pressure. VanPatten has also argued that less salient or meaningful forms are unlikely to be noticed until the message in which they are embedded is understood. These are all features of materials and activities that can be manipulated in order to encourage initial learner noticing.

Several studies have attempted to measure noticing or in some cases, simply memory, assuming that this is the first step on the way to acquisition. In other words, do learners remember a word or form from a previous activity, text, or the like? As yet though, we do not have a clear idea of how directly this relates to their acquisition. One problem with most SLA research on noticing has to do with measurement. Most measurements (Fotos, 1994; Izumi et al., 1999; Jourdenais et al., 1995; Leow, 1997b; VanPatten, 1990; Wong, 2001, interalia) are quite demanding, requiring that learners do something—circle, underline, make checkmarks—or even verbalize their awareness. As Schmidt (2001 and elsewhere) has repeatedly noted, registration does not require the level of awareness that the measures used in these studies may require. Fewer studies have used less direct techniques for measuring registration more common in psychological research, such as reaction time or fixation time in eye-tracking.

At least two other types of noticing have been explored: *noticing the gap* and *noticing the hole* (Swain, 1995, 1998). They appear to be related, but differ in crucial ways. *Noticing the gap* occurs when learners notice that their IL differs from the target. This is another way of saying that they figure out that they are making an error, perhaps that they are using a stabilized IL form. It necessarily involves noticing both the IL and TL forms, presumably input and output forms, a process sometimes referred to as *cognitive comparison* (Doughty, 2001). Noticing the gap may require restructuring of IL knowledge and the formation of new form-meaning connections. The second, *noticing the hole*, takes place at the point at which learners realize that they do not have the means to say something that they want to say. This differs from *noticing the gap*, in that learners may not yet have developed an IL form to express what they want. Activities that promote *noticing the hole* seek to intervene at the point at which input becomes intake, an earlier stage in the acquisition process. There is no guarantee that the hole will be filled by a TL form (although this would clearly be the pedagogical goal). In addition, ideally, following the learner's realization of need, input data will be available to provide him or her with positive evidence about the IL.

In contrast, activities that facilitate *noticing the gap* attempt to destabilize the IL and move it toward more targetlike accuracy, a later stage in acquisition, with a combination of positive and negative evidence. By definition, *noticing the gap* suggests the presence of an IL form to which the TL form can be compared. Learners may believe they already "know" the word or form and they must now notice that they do not, at least not exactly or completely. From a pedagogical perspective, this may a significantly more difficult goal than getting learners to notice an IL hole. Some have argued (Long & Robinson, 1998; L. White, 1991) that it is in these cases that the provision of negative evidence is necessary or at least helpful.

It is important to be precise about this issue since in many cases, techniques are presented as "useful" or "effective" without specification of when they might best be used. Some techniques involving explicit instruction and structured input are attempts to modify IL in the early stages of acquisition. In other words, they are attempts to impact the course of acquisition at the initial point of intake, either to ensure that input becomes intake, or that intake is targetlike by structuring input appropriately. This is one of the central claims of VanPatten's input processing: that, in fact, this is the only point at which classroom activities can have an impact on the developing IL. He argues that output practice only impacts control; it can speed up access to IL forms, increasing fluency, but will have no effect on the developing system. Only input available during the process of comprehending meaning can do that. It is, of course, possible for these pedagogical activities to take place prior to the learner developing any IL form and this seems to be the intention, based on VanPatten's model (1996). However, in practical terms, it also seems likely that much of the input processing work done in real classrooms occurs when learners have already developed somewhat stabilized IL forms, which the teacher hopes can be destabilized with processing instruction. An important research goal for processing instruction is to investigate whether it is equally effective in destabilizing non-TL forms as it is at establishing new form-meaning connections in the IL.

Opportunities for noticing the hole occur in activities in which learners feel the need to use a form that they lack, presumably a task-useful or, better still, the ever-elusive task-essential activity (Loschky & Bley-Vroman, 1993). Possibilities for noticing holes in IL morphosyntax can be found in a number of studies (e.g., Day & Shapson, 1991; Harley, 1998; Loschky & Bley-Vroman, 1993). Another familiar example is Swain's use of the dictogloss or other types of text recreation (1998, 2000; Thornbury, 1997). The important difference between some of these activities and those using structured input is that the noticing process is triggered by an output activity. Learners are asked to reconstruct a passage that is fairly easily understood. However, actually recreating it requires that they do so with a good deal of precision. The need to do this prompts them to focus on forms they may not have in their IL. In other instances, it could trigger a discussion among learners who may have contrasting forms in the ILs. The discussion could begin a restructuring process, although it is not clear what the long-term effect of these activities might be.

Izumi et al. (1999) describe a variation on this method of using output to encourage noticing the gap or hole. In their study, learners were also required to reconstruct a text, but had a subsequent opportunity to study relevant input. The intention here was to focus the learners' attention more narrowly on the subsequent input that they would need for the next output task. In contrast, in Swain's tasks, learners consulted one another in dialogic reconstructions of meaning, but had no recourse to the original input, thus allowing for the possibility that the target forms would be reconstructed incorrectly. Indeed this did happen, though rarely. In the Izumi et al. study, learners were allowed to recheck their hypotheses against the target before reattempting output and this treatment did seem to increase noticing. Activities that draw learner attention to holes in the lexicon are considerably easier to construct (e.g., de la Fuente, 2002; R. Ellis & He, 1999; R. Ellis et al., 1999; R. Ellis, Tanaka, & Yamakazi, 1994; He & R. Ellis, 1999; Loschky, 1994).

The difference between noticing the hole and noticing the gap may be crucial in terms of these storage requirements and the cognitive processes involved. Noticing the gap requires cognitive comparison. This means incoming input would have to be compared either to representations stored in long-term memory or to traces left in short-term memory. Precisely how this works is not clear (though see Doughty, 2001). De Bot (2000) maintains that direct comparison is unlikely, in that incoming input is always processed before it is stored and any comparison to it can be made. Noticing the hole, on the other hand, would seem to be a simpler process in that it does not require comparison to representations that have been previously stored (except possibly L1 representations).

The foregoing discussion has focused on noticing TL forms in the input. Clearly, however, if this input never makes it to long-term memory, the activities that prompt this noticing are of limited effectiveness. It is therefore necessary also to explore tasks and techniques that encourage the incorporation of new input into the developing IL system. One promising avenue is to encourage deeper processing of new forms. Although the depth of processing theory (Wittrock, 1974; Craik & Tulving, 1975) has been subject to much revision and criticism, psychologists seem to be in general agreement that new knowledge that is processed more elaborately is more likely to be retained than that which is processed less elaborately (R. Ellis, 1999; Hulstijn, 2001). Generative models claim that learning and retention are improved when learners use, reformulate, or elaborate the new information, thereby creating connections between old and new knowledge. In second language acquisition research, work in this area has primarily focused on lexical acquisition and results have been mixed (Joe, 1998; Rott, Williams, & Cameron, 2002; Zaki & R. Ellis, 1999).

NEGOTIATION AND FEEDBACK

Two of the most widely researched ways to encourage learner noticing occur (1) implicitly, in the breakdown of communication followed by negotiation, and (2) more directly, through feedback on error. Negotiation has traditionally been understood as resulting from problems of message comprehensibility, that is, when interlocutors restructure their utterances in an effort to understand or to be understood (e.g., de la

Fuente, 2002; R. Ellis, 1999; Mackey, 1999; Oliver, 1995, 2000; Pica, 1994, 1997; Pica et al., 1989; Polio & Gass, 1998; Shehadeh, 1999; Van den Branden, 1997). Gass and Varonis (1991) distinguish among several types of problems with message comprehensibility, only some of which generally result in negotiation. Only what they call *incomplete understanding* is likely to lead to negotiation because it is only in these circumstances that a problem in comprehensibility is recognized. This incorporates the problematicity that is central to Long and Robinson's original definition of FonF. Although most early research demonstrated the importance of negotiation for increasing the comprehensibility of input, Pica claims that negotiation also can focus learner attention on language form: by making target input more noticeable and by providing feedback on output, and in the process, calling attention to discrepancies between the IL and the TL. What is not clear, however, is exactly what the cognitive consequences of breakdown followed by negotiation might be. To what degree does it constitute an interruption in the processing of meaning? On the one hand, the main virtue of negotiation, it is said, is that it can offer a simultaneous focus on form and meaning, thus establishing or strengthening the form-meaning connection. On the other hand, a breakdown does imply some sort of interruption of communication and therefore, perhaps, also of processing. Again, it is not apparent whether this interruption provides a favorable condition for acquisition.

The benefits of negotiation as a FonF activity are not immediately obvious. First, it is clear from many studies that most negotiation revolves around meaning, especially in authentic communication. It is possible to negotiate a satisfactory outcome in which communication is restored without ever focusing on form. Even if the negotiation does involve form, the resolution may be ambiguous to the learner. Second, it is likely that benefits of negotiation, whatever they might be, are not uniform. Two types, corresponding, once again, to the two types of noticing described (of gaps and holes), are generally claimed in experimental studies. Studies by R. Ellis and colleagues, primarily of targeted lexical acquisition, demonstrate the facilitating effect on noticing or recognition of unknown items (R. Ellis & He, 1999; R. Ellis et al., 1999; R. Ellis, Tanaka, & Yamazaki, 1994; He & R. Ellis, 1999). The effect of negotiation in these studies is to highlight for learners what they do not know and increase the salience of the relevant data in the input.

Other studies have focused on modification of output, that is, changes in non-TL forms in the direction of target accuracy. This comes either as a result of communicative breakdown, usually among learners, or in the form of *negotiation of form* (Lyster & Ranta, 1997) by a teacher or researcher. The latter will be taken up next. The former has been explored extensively, primarily in experimental studies (e.g., de la Fuente, 2002; Pica, 1994, 2002; Pica et al., 1989; Mackey, 1999). These studies have demonstrated positive effects for negotiation in situations where learners were required to address problems in their own production and frequently, notice the difference between their own production and the forms in the TL input.

Although the negotiation may provide for many of the acquisitional needs of learners, it is not a particularly dependable pedagogical technique. Pica (1997, 2002) and others (Foster, 1998; Musumeci, 1996; Williams, 1999) have claimed that negotiation in the classroom, either among learners or between learners and the teacher, are not as frequent as might be wished. Nor can transfer-of-information tasks guarantee that learners will negotiate (Foster, 1998), and certainly not on preselected forms if the primary focus is to remain on the communication of meaning. With reference to the FonF features already described, the advantages conferred by the interactional modifications resulting from negotiation would presumably be rather broad. It would be difficult to provide targeted instruction through negotiation, at least with the tools we have now. Because it most often revolves around message (in)comprehensibility, it comes as no surprise that negotiation generally focuses on the lexicon and not morphosyntactic features (e.g., Mackey, Gass, & McDonough, 2000; Pica, 1994; Pica, Kanagy, & Faludon, 1993; Van den Branden, 1997; Williams, 1999). Skehan and Foster (2001) maintain that this has little to do with limitations on attentional capacity. Rather, the built-in redundancy of language allows learners to communicate effectively without the need for TL accuracy. Pica (1997) notes, however, that the fact that learners rarely negotiate morphosyntactic and other less salient features is not because it is not possible to do so, but because the kinds of activities typical of communicative classrooms rarely require them. This would be an important avenue to pursue: to get learners to focus their negotiations on a wider variety of predetermined features.

Lyster (1998; Lyster & Ranta 1997) has distinguished between the negotiation of meaning just described, and the negotiation of form, which has the more pedagogical purpose of increasing accuracy and precision of message form, and is usually initiated by the teacher or a researcher. In this case, message comprehensibility is not usually at issue; rather, it includes various forms of feedback on error in message form. There is a continuing controversy over the effectiveness of this technique since it is not always certain that what the teacher (or other interlocutor) points out as an error will actually be noticed as an error. Even if this does happen, it is not certain that the learner will be able to do anything about it (see Nicholas, Lightbown, & Spada, 2001, for a review of this issue).

Lyster and Ranta distinguish among various types of feedback and indeed, there has been a proliferation of terms in the literature. Muranoi (2000) uses the term *interaction enhancement* to describe a pedagogical technique that interweaves input and output enhancement. In his study, in response to TL use, the teacher repeated learners' output, helping to confirm learners' hypotheses. In response to nontargetlike output, the teacher requested repetition, and if necessary, recast learner output. Muranoi found this technique effective in increasing accuracy in article use. Similar results can be found in Noboyoshi and R. Ellis (1993) and Takashima and R. Ellis (1999).

Recasts are a subset of feedback on error. These have been defined as modifications of learner output toward the target by an interlocutor/teacher, and have been found effective as a method of providing focused feedback on errors in form, both in experimental (Braidi, 2002; Mackey & Philp, 1998; Long, Inagaki, & Ortega, 1998) and classroom studies (Ayoun, 2001; Doughty & Varela, 1998). However, Lyster (1998) argues that only those forms of feedback that push learners to use their own resources in reformulating output are effective in destabilizing IL, and thus he doubts the value of recasts as a classroom technique. He claims that learners may not know that their nontargetlike output is being corrected, making it difficult for them to detect any changes made in the teacher's recast. Indeed, Seedhouse (1997) has shown that teachers are exceedingly reluctant to tell learners explicitly that they are wrong, and they are far more likely to affirm content or positive effort than point out learners' errors.

There may be several reasons that Lyster found little effect for recasts in his classroom study. First, it is clear from his results that the feedback to the learners was extensive: Learners received feedback on many different errors, but feedback on any one specific error was infrequent. This stands in contrast to the Doughty and Varela study, in which the teacher targeted just two forms on which to provide feedback, and they did so intensively. In addition, in their study, the errors were always recast in the same way, by rising intonation to signal the error clearly, followed by a targetlike recast of the error if the learner could not provide the TL form. This is perhaps another reason for the effectiveness of the treatment in the Doughty and Varela study, as well as the experimental studies on recasts and interaction enhancement. The teachers in that study did not simply reformulate the utterance; rather, they first used emphatic and rising intonation in their repetition of the learner error and only then provided the TL form, perhaps reducing the ambiguity of the feedback.

If learners do not realize the teacher's response is corrective, they may not notice the gap between the production and the TL form offered in the recast. Mackey, Gass, and McDonough (2000) report that learners are especially unlikely to notice the corrective nature of recasts if the error is in morphosyntax. Nicholas, Lightbown, and Spada (2001) point out that in first language learning, there is a difference in the rate of recasts that caregivers provide, depending on whether the child's utterance is ill-formed or well-formed. They receive hundreds of such responses, yielding a very real computational difference between those responses that get recast and those that do not. No such rate difference has been observed in SL classrooms, perhaps increasing the need for a clearly signaled negative evidence for these learners. Finally, Lyster's use of *uptake*, or immediate repetition of the reformulated learner utterance, as a measure may unnecessarily limit our view of the effectiveness of recasts. Oliver (1995) noted that often, the structure of turn-taking in classrooms may not provide learners with an opportunity for uptake. Also, the delayed effects of attention to form, while difficult to document in the classroom, have been documented experimentally (e.g., de la Fuente, 2002; Gass &Varonis, 1989; Mackey, 1999; Van den Branden, 1997). Ohta (2000, 2001) has also shown that even when learners do not respond immediately to a teacher's or other learner's recast, they may make use of them later, especially in *private speech*, barely audible rehearsals that are not ordinarily picked up in studies of entire classes. She also found that learners in teacher-fronted Japanese foreign language classes would engage in silent rehearsal of recast utterances that were directed at other learners, suggesting that the benefit of recasts may not be restricted to the learners whose utterances are recast, but may extend to other listeners as well. Pica (1992) found similar "observer" benefits for negotiation.

There is, of course, a voluminous literature on the effect of error correction more generally, beyond the narrow considerations of recasting. Despite continuing heated arguments on the subject, there appears to be a growing body of evidence from studies in and out of the classroom that suggests that negative feedback of various kinds can make input data more salient and help learners notice the gap between their own production and the target.

Conclusion

In summary, a major role for FonF appears to be in the area of (1) noticing a form/word for the first time in the input, potentially leading to a conversion to intake, (2) noticing that an IL form is at odds with the TL input ("the gap"), leading to destabilization of that form, or (3) incorporation of a new form into the developing IL. In addition, in our consideration of the effectiveness of FonF at various points in IL development, the possibility of FonF activities' increasing learner control over IL knowledge has not even been considered. Can the speed and efficiency with which learners can access their knowledge be increased with the use of FonF activities? This possibility is discussed by Gass et al. (1999), specifically regarding the use of task repetition to free up learner attention. Indeed, any of the possibilities discussed here that involve manipulation of task features to adjust attention levels would also be promising candidates for increasing learner access to knowledge. Thus, it is at least theoretically possible to find suitable activities to facilitate language acquisition and increasing control at many stages of development.

Along with all the supportive evidence, however, there is enough counterevidence, both experimental and anecdotal, to warrant continuing careful and skeptical consideration of the effect of FonF. Some suggest the FonF is more useful in later stages of development (VanPatten, 1996; Williams, 1999) because in the early stages, learners concentrate almost entirely on decoding and expressing meaning. However, further critical discussion of the effectiveness of FonF even at later stages is also indicated, specifically, on the destabilization of IL forms that have been used by the learner for an extended period. Obviously, sometimes FonF works; sometimes it does not. The more we know about the factors involved in the activities described here and about the cognitive processes they engage, the more likely we will be to find the reasons for the variable results for FonF reported in the literature, knowledge that can be turned to increasing pedagogical effectiveness.

REFERENCES

Alanen, R. (1995). Input enhancement and rule presentation in second language acquisition. In R. Schmidt (Ed.), *Attention and awareness in foreign language learning and teaching* (pp. 259–302). Honolulu: University of Hawaii Press.

Ayoun, D. (2001). The role of positive and negative feedback in the second language acquisition of the *passé composé* and *imparfait*. *Modern Language Journal, 85,* 226–243.

Bardovi-Harlig, K., & Dörnyei, Z. (1998). Do learners recognize pragmatic violations? *TESOL Quarterly, 32,* 233–262.

Braidi, S. (2002). Reexamining the role of recasts in native-speaker nonnative-speaker interactions. *Language Learning, 52,* 1–42.

Bygate, M. (2000). The effects of task repetition on the structure and control of oral language. In M. Bygate, P. Skehan, & M. Swain (Eds.), *Researching pedagogic tasks* (pp. 23–48). Harlow, UK: Pearson.

Carroll, S., & Swain, M. (1993). Explicit and implicit negative feedback: An empirical study of the learning of linguistic generalizations. *Studies in Second Language Acquisition, 15,* 357–386.

Celce-Murcia, M., Dörnyei, Z., & Thurrell, S. (1997). Direct approaches in L2 instruction: A turning point in communicative language teaching? *TESOL Quarterly, 31,* 141–152.

Cook, H. (2001). Why can't learners of JFL distinguish polite from impolite speech styles? In K. Rose & G. Kasper (Eds.), *Pragmatics in language teaching* (pp. 80–102). Cambridge, UK: Cambridge University Press.

Craik, F., & Tulving, E. (1975). Depth of processing and the retention of words in episodic memory. *Journal of Experimental Psychology, 104,* 268–294.

Day, E., & Shapson, S. (1991). Integrating formal and functional approaches in language teaching in French immersion: An experimental study. *Language Learning, 41,* 25–58.

De Bot, K. (2000). Psycholinguistics in applied linguistics: Trends and perspectives. *Annual Review of Applied Linguistics, 20,* 224–237.

DeKeyser, R. (1995). Learning second language grammar rules: An experiment with a miniature linguistic system. *Studies in Second Language Acquisition, 17,* 379–410.

de la Fuente, M. J. (2002). Negotiation and oral acquisition of L2 vocabulary: The roles of input and output in receptive and productive acquisition of words. *Studies in Second Language Acquisition, 24,* 81–112.

Doughty, C. (2001). Cognitive underpinnings of focus on form. In P. Robinson (Ed.), *Cognition and second language instruction* (pp. 206–257). Cambridge, UK: Cambridge University Press.

Doughty, C. (2003). Instructed SLA: Constraints, compensation, and enhancement. In C. Doughty & M. Long, (Eds.), *Handbook of second language acquisition* (pp. 256–310). New York: Blackwell.

Doughty, C., & Varela, E. (1998). Communicative focus on form. In C. Doughty & J. Williams (Eds.), *Focus on form in classroom second language acquisition* (pp. 114–138). Cambridge: Cambridge University Press.

Doughty, C., & Williams, J. (Eds.), (1998a). *Focus on form in classroom second language acquisition.* Cambridge, UK: Cambridge University Press.

Doughty, C., & Williams, J. (1998b). Pedagogical choices in focus on form. In C. Doughty & J. Williams (Eds.), *Focus on form in classroom second language acquisition* (pp. 197–261). Cambridge, UK: Cambridge University Press.

Ellis, N. (1993). Rules and instances in foreign language learning: Interactions of implicit and explicit knowledge. *European Journal of Cognitive Psychology, 5,* 289–319.

Ellis, N. (2001). Memory for language. In. P. Robinson (Ed.), *Cognition and second language instruction* (pp. 33–68). Cambridge, UK: Cambridge University Press.

Ellis, N., & Laporte, N. (1997). Contexts of acquisition: Effects of formal and naturalistic exposure on second language acquisition. In A. de Groot & J. Kroll (Eds.), *Tutorials in bilingualism* (pp. 53–83). Mahwah, NJ: Lawrence Erlbaum Associates.

Ellis, R. (1993). The structural syllabus and second language acquisition. *TESOL Quarterly, 27,* 91–113.

Ellis, R. (1997). A theory of instructed second language acquisition. In R. Ellis (Ed.), *SLA research and language teaching* (pp. 107–133). Oxford, UK: Oxford University Press.

Ellis, R. (1998). Teaching and research: Options in grammar teaching. *TESOL Quarterly, 32,* 39–60.

Ellis, R. (1999). Theoretical perspectives on interaction and language learning. In R. Ellis (Ed.), *Learning a second language through interaction* (pp. 3–31). Amsterdam: Benjamins.

Ellis, R. (2001). Investigating form-focused instruction. *Language Learning, 51,* Supplement 1, 1–46.

Ellis, R. (2002). Methodological options in grammar teaching. In E. Hinkel & S. Fotos (Eds.), *New perspectives on grammar teaching in second language classrooms* (pp. 155–179). Mahwah, NJ: Lawrence Erlbaum Associates.

Ellis, R., Basturkmen, H., & Loewen, S. (2001a). Learner uptake in communicative ESL lessons. *Language Learning, 51*, 281–318.

Ellis, R., Basturkmen, H., & Loewen, S. (2001b). Preemptive focus on form in the ESL classroom. *TESOL Quarterly, 35*, 407–432.

Ellis, R., & He, X. (1999). The roles of modified input and output in the incidental acquisition of word meanings. *Studies in Second Language Acquisition, 21*, 285–301.

Ellis, R., Heimbach, R., Tanaka, Y., & Yamazaki, A. (1999). Modified input and the acquisition of word meanings by children and adults. In R. Ellis (Ed.), *Learning a second language through interaction* (pp. 63–114). Amsterdam: Benjamins.

Ellis, R., Tanaka, Y., & Yamazaki, A. (1994). Classroom interaction, comprehension, and the acquisition of L2 word meanings. *Language Learning, 43*, 449–491.

Foster, P. (1998). A classroom perspective on the negotiation of meaning. *Applied Linguistics, 19*, 1–23.

Foster, P., & Skehan, P. (1999). The influence of source of planning and focus of planning on task-based performance. *Language Teaching Research, 3*, 215–245.

Fotos, S. (1993). Consciousness-raising and noticing through focus on form: Grammar task performance versus formal instruction. *Applied Linguistics, 14*, 385–407.

Fotos, S. (1994). Integrating grammar instruction and communicative language use through grammar consciousness-raising tasks. *TESOL Quarterly, 28*, 323–351.

Fotos, S. (2002). Structure-based interactive tasks for the EFL grammar learner. In E. Hinkel & S. Fotos (Eds.), *New perspectives on grammar teaching in second language classrooms* (pp. 135–154). Mahwah, NJ: Lawrence Erlbaum Associates.

Gass, S. (1997). *Input, interaction, and the second language learner.* Mahwah, NJ: Lawrence Erlbaum Associates.

Gass, S., & Varonis, E. (1989). Incorporated repairs in NNS discourse. In M. Eisenstein (Ed.), *Variation and second language acquisition* (pp. 71–96). New York: Plenum.

Gass, S., & Varonis, E. (1991). Miscommunication in nonnative speaker discourse. In N. Coupland, H. Giles, & J. Weimann (Eds.), *Miscommunication and problematic talk* (pp. 121–145). Newbury Park, CA: Sage.

Gass, S., Mackey, A., Alvarez-Torres, M. J., & Fernandez-García, M. (1999). The effects of task repetition on linguistic output. *Language Learning, 49*, 549–581.

Harley, B. (1998). The role of focus-on-form tasks in promoting child L2 acquisition. In C. Doughty & J. Williams (Eds.), *Focus on form in classroom second language acquisition* (pp. 156–174). Cambridge, UK: Cambridge University Press.

He, X., & Ellis, R. (1999). Modified output and the acquisition of word meaning. In R. Ellis (Ed.), *Learning a second language through interaction* (pp. 113–132). Amsterdam: Benjamins.

Hulstijn, J. (2001). Intentional and incidental second language vocabulary learning: A reappraisal of elaboration, rehearsal, and automaticity. In P. Robinson (Ed.), *Cognition and second language instruction* (pp. 258–286). Cambridge, UK: Cambridge University Press.

Izumi, S., Bigelow, M., Fujiwara, M., & Fearnow, S. (1999). Testing the output hypothesis: Effects of output on noticing and second language acquisition. *Studies in Second Language Acquisition, 21*, 421–452.

Izumi, S., & Bigelow, M. (2000). Does output promote noticing and second language acquisition? *TESOL Quarterly, 34*, 239–278.

Joe, A. (1998). What effects do text-based tasks promoting generation have on incidental vocabulary acquisition? *Applied Linguistics, 19*, 357–377.

Johnson, K. (1996). *Language teaching and skill learning.* Oxford, UK: Blackwell.

Jourdenais, R., Ota, M., Stauffer, S., Boyson, B., & Doughty, C. (1995). Does textual enhancement promote noticing? A think-aloud protocol analysis. In R. Schmidt (Ed.), *Attention and awareness in foreign language learning* (pp. 183–216). Honolulu: University of Hawaii Press.

Kasper, G. (2001). Classroom research on interlanguage pragmatics. In K. Rose & G. Kasper (Eds.), *Pragmatics in language teaching* (pp. 33–60). Cambridge, UK: Cambridge University Press.

Kupferberg, I., & Olshtain, E. (1996). Explicit contrastive instruction facilitates the acquisition of difficult L2 forms. *Language Awareness, 3*, 149–165.

Laufer, B., & Hulstijn, J. (2001). Incidental vocabulary acquisition in a second language: The construct of task-induced involvement. *Applied Linguistics, 22*, 1–26.

Leeman, J., Arteagoitia, I., Fridman, B., & Doughty, C. (1995). Integrating attention to form with meaning: focus on form in content-based Spanish instruction. In R. Schmidt (Ed.), *Attention and awareness in foreign language learning* (pp. 217–258). Honolulu: University of Hawaii Press.

Leow, R. (1997a). The effects of input enhancement and text length on adult readers' comprehension and intake in second language acquisition. *Applied Language Learning, 8*, 151–182.

Leow, R. (1997b). Attention, awareness, and foreign language behavior. *Language Learning, 47*, 467–505.

Leow, R. (2000). A study of the role of awareness in foreign language behavior: Aware versus unaware learners. *Studies in Second Language Acquisition, 22*, 557–582.

Lightbown, P. (1991). What have we here? Some observations on the influence of instruction on L2 learning. In R. Phillipson, E. Kellerman, L. Selinker, M. Sharwood Smith, & M. Swain (Eds.), *Foreign/second language pedagogy research* (pp. 197–212). Clevedon, UK: Multilingual Matters.

Lightbown, P., & Spada, N. (1994). An innovative program for primary ESL in Quebec. *TESOL Quarterly, 28*, 563–579.

Long, M. H. (1988). Instructed interlanguage development. In L. Beebe (Ed.), *Issues in second language acquisition* (pp. 113–141). New York: Newbury House.

Long, M. H. (1991). Focus on form: A design feature in language teaching methodology. In K. de Bot, R. Ginsberg, & C. Kramsch (Eds.), *Foreign language research in crosscultural perspective* (pp. 39–52). Amsterdam: John Benjamins.

Long, M. H. (1996). The role of the linguistic environment in second language acquisition. In W. Ritchie & T. Bhatia (Eds.), *Handbook of research on second language acquisition* (pp. 413–468). New York: Academic Press.

Long, M. H. (to appear). Recasts in SLA: The story so far. *Problems in SLA*. Mahwah, NJ: Lawrence Erlbaum Associates.

Long, M. H., & Crookes, G. (1992). Three approaches to task-based syllabus design. *TESOL Quarterly, 26*, 27–56.

Long, M. H., Inagaki, S., & Ortega, L. (1998). The role of implicit negative feedback in SLA: Models and recasts in Japanese and Spanish. *Modern Language Journal, 82*, 357–371.

Long, M., & Robinson, P. (1998). Theory, research, and practice. In C. Doughty & J. Williams (Eds.), *Focus on form in classroom second language acquisition* (pp. 15–41). Cambridge, UK: Cambridge University Press.

Loschky, L. (1994). Comprehensible input and second language acquisition: What is the relationship? *Studies in Second Language Acquisition, 16*, 303–324.

Loschky, L., & Bley-Vroman, R. (1993). Grammar and task-based methodology. In G. Crookes & S. Gass (Eds.), *Tasks and language learning* (pp. 123–67). Clevedon, UK: Multilingual Matters.

Lyster, R. (1998). Recasts, repetition, and ambiguity in L2 classroom discourse. *Studies in Second Language Acquisition, 20*, 51–80.

Lyster, R., & Ranta, L. (1997). Corrective feedback and learner uptake: Negotiation of form in communicative classrooms. *Studies in Second Language Acquisition, 19*, 37–66.

Mackey, A. (1999). Input, interaction, and second language development: An empirical study of question formation in ESL. *Studies in Second Language Acquisition, 21*, 557–587.

Mackey, A., Gass, S., & McDonough, K. (2000). How do learners perceive interactional feedback? *Studies in Second Language Acquisition, 22*, 471–497.

Mackey, A., & Philp, J. (1998). Recasts, interaction, and interlanguage development: Are responses red herrings? *Modern Language Journal, 82*, 338–356.

Mehnert, U. (1998). The effects of different lengths of time for planning on second language performance. *Studies in Second Language Acquisition, 20*, 83–108.

Muranoi, H. (2000). Focus on form through interaction enhancement: Integrating formal instruction into a communicative task in EFL classrooms. *Language Learning, 50*, 617–673.

Musumeci, D. (1996). Teacher-learner negotiation in content-based instruction: Communication at cross-purposes? *Applied Linguistics, 17*, 286–325.

Nassaji, H. (1999). Toward integrating form-focused instruction and communicative interaction in the second language classroom: Some pedagogical possibilities. *Canadian Modern Language Review, 55*, 385–402.

Nassaji, H., & Swain, M. (2000). A Vygotskian perspective on corrective feedback in L2: The effect of random versus negotiated help on the learning of English articles. *Language Awareness, 9*, 35–51.

Nicholas, H., Lightbown, P., & Spada, N. (2001). Recasts as feedback to language learners. *Language Learning, 51*, 719–758.

Nobuyoshi, J., & Ellis, R. (1993). Focused communication tasks and second language acquisition. *ELT Journal, 47*, 203–210.

Norris, J., & Ortega, L. (2000). Effectiveness of L2 Instruction: A research synthesis and quantitative meta-analysis. *Language Learning, 50*, 417–528.

Ohta, A. (2000). Rethinking recasts: A learner-centered examination of corrective feedback in the Japanese language classroom. In J. K. Hall & L. Verplaetse (Eds.), *Second and foreign language learning through classroom interaction* (pp. 47–71). Mahwah, NJ: Lawrence Erlbaum Associates.

Ohta, A. (2001). *Second language acquisition processes in the classroom*. Mahwah, NJ: Lawrence Erlbaum Associates.

Oliver, R. (1995). Negative feedback in child NS-NNS conversation. *Studies in Second Language Acquisition, 17*, 459–482.

Oliver, R. (2000). Age differences in negotiation and feedback in classroom and pairwork. *Language Learning, 50*, 119–151.

Ortega, L. (1999). Planning and focus on form in L2 oral performance. *Studies in Second Language Acquisition, 21*, 109–145.

Overstreet, M. (1998). Text enhancement and content familiarity: The focus of learner attention. *Spanish Applied Linguistics, 2*, 229–258.

Pica, T. (1992). The textual outcomes of native speaker–non-native speaker negotiation: What do they reveal about second language learning? In C. Kramsch & S. McConnell-Ginet (Eds.), *Text and context* (pp. 198–237). Cambridge, MA: Heath.

Pica, T. (1994). Research on negotiation: What does it reveal about second language acquisition? *Language Learning, 44*, 493–527.

Pica, T. (1997). Second language teaching and research relationships: A North American view. *Language Teaching Research, 1*, 48–72.

Pica, T. (2002). Subject-matter content: How does it assist the interactional and linguistic needs of classroom language learners? *Modern Language Journal, 86*, 1–19.

Pica, T., Holliday, L., Lewis, N., & Morgenthaler, L. (1989). Comprehensible input as an outcome of linguistic demands on the learner. *Studies in Second Language Acquisition, 11*, 63–90.

Pica, T., Kanagy, R., & Faludon, J. (1993). Choosing and using communicative tasks for second language research and instruction. In S. Gass & G. Crookes (Eds.), *Tasks and language learning: Integrating theory and practice* (pp. 9–34). Clevedon, UK: Multilingual Matters.

Polio, C., & Gass, S. (1998). The role of interaction in native speaker comprehension of non-native speaker speech. *Modern Language Journal, 82*, 308–319.

Robinson, P. (1995). Review article: Attention, memory, and the noticing hypothesis. *Language Learning, 45*, 283–331.

Robinson, P. (1996). Learning simple and complex second language rules under implicit, incidental, rule-search, and instructed conditions. *Studies in Second Language Acquisition, 18*, 27–68.

Robinson, P. (1997). Automaticity and generalizability of second language learning under implicit, incidental, enhanced, and instructed conditions. *Studies in Second Language Acquisition, 19*, 233–247.

Robinson, R. (2001). Task complexity, cognitive resources, and syllabus design: A triadic framework for examining task influences on SLA. In P. Robinson (Ed.), *Cognition and second language instruction* (pp. 287–318). Cambridge, UK: Cambridge University Press.

Rosa, E., & O'Neill, M. (1999). Explicitness, intake, and the issue of awareness: Another piece of the puzzle. *Studies in Second Language Acquisition, 21*, 511–553.

Rott, S., Williams, J., & Cameron, R. (2002). The effect of multiple-choice L1 glosses and input-output cycles on lexical acquisition and retention. *Language Teaching Research, 6*, 183–222.

Samuda, V. (2000). Guiding relationships between form and meaning during task performance: The role of the teacher. In M. Bygate, P. Skehan, & M. Swain (Eds.), *Researching pedagogic tasks* (pp. 119–140). Harlow, UK: Pearson.

Schmidt, R. (1990). The role of consciousness in second language learning. *Applied Linguistics, 11*, 17–46.

Schmidt, R. (1994). Deconstructing consciousness in search of useful definitions for applied linguistics. In J. Hulstijn & R. Schmidt (Eds.), *Consciousness in second language learning* (pp. 11–26): AILA Review. Vol. 11.

Schmidt, R. (1995). Consciousness and foreign language learning. In R. Schmidt (Ed.), *Attention and awareness in foreign language learning* (pp. 1–63). Honolulu: University of Hawaii Press.

Schmidt, R. (2001). Attention. In P. Robinson (Ed.), *Cognition and second language instruction* (pp. 3–32). Cambridge, UK: Cambridge University Press.

Schmidt, R. (in press). *The centrality of attention in SLA*. Cambridge, UK: Cambridge University Press.

Simard, D., & Wong, W. (2001). Alertness, orientation, and detection: The conceptualization of attentional functions in SLA. *Studies in Second Language Acquisition, 23*, 103–124.

Seedhouse, P. (1997). The case of the missing "no": The relationship between pedagogy and interaction. *Language Learning, 47*, 547–583.

Shehadeh, A. (1999). Non-native speakers' production of modified comprehensible output and second language learning. *Language Learning, 49*, 627–675.

Shehadeh, A. (2001). Self- and other-initiated modified output during task-based interaction. *TESOL Quarterly, 35*, 433–457.

Skehan, P. (1998). *A cognitive approach to language learning*. Oxford, UK: Oxford University Press.

Skehan, P. (1996). A framework for the implementation of task-based instruction. *Applied Linguistics, 17*, 38–62.

Skehan, P., & Foster, P. (1999). The influence of task structure and processing conditions on narrative retellings. *Language Learning, 49*, 93–120.

Skehan, P., & Foster, P. (2001). Cognition and tasks. In P. Robinson (Ed.), *Cognition and second language instruction* (pp. 183–205). Cambridge, UK: Cambridge University Press.

Spada, N. (1997). Form-focused instruction and second language acquisition: A review of classroom and laboratory research. *Language Teaching Abstracts, 30*, 73–87.

Spada, N., & Lightbown, P. (1993). Instruction and the development of questions in the L2 classroom. *Studies in Second Language Acquisition, 15*, 205–221.

Spada, N., & Lightbown, P. (1999). Instruction, first language influence, and developmental readiness in second language acquisition. *Modern Language Journal, 83*, 1–22.

Swain, M. (1995). Three functions of output in second language learning. In G. Cook & B. Seidlhofer (Eds.), *Principle and practice in applied linguistics* (pp. 125–44). Oxford, UK: Oxford University Press.

Swain, M. (1998). Focus on form through conscious reflection. In C. Doughty & J. Williams (Eds.), *Focus on form in classroom second language acquisition* (pp. 64–81). Cambridge, UK: Cambridge University Press.

Swain, M. (2000). The output hypothesis and beyond: Mediating acquisition through collaborative dialogue. In J. Lantolf (Ed.), *Sociocultural theory and second language learning* (pp. 97–114). Oxford, UK: Oxford University Press.

Swain, M., & Lapkin, S. (1995). Problems in output and the cognitive processes they generate: A step towards second language learning. *Applied Linguistics, 16*, 371–391.

Swain, M., & Lapkin, S. (1998). Interaction and second language learning: Two adolescent French immersion students working together. *Modern Language Journal, 82*, 320–337.

Takahashi, S. (2001). The role of input enhancement in developing pragmatic competence. In K. Rose & G. Kasper (Eds.), *Pragmatics in language teaching* (pp. 171–199). Cambridge, UK: Cambridge University Press.

Takashima, H., & Ellis, R. (1999). Output enhancement and the acquisition of past tense. In R. Ellis (Ed.), *Learning a second language through interaction* (pp. 173–188). Amsterdam: Benjamins.

Thornbury, S. (1998). Comments on "Direct approaches in L2 instruction." *TESOL Quarterly, 32*, 109–115.

Thornbury, S. (1997). Reformulation and reconstruction: Tasks that promote noticing. *ELT Journal, 51*, 326–335.

Van den Branden, K. (1997). Effects of negotiation on language learners' output. *Language Learning, 47*, 589–636.

VanPatten, B. (1990). Attending to form and content in the input: An experiment in consciousness. *Studies in Second Language Acquisition, 12*, 287–301.

VanPatten, B. (1993). Grammar teaching for the acquisition-rich classroom. *Foreign Language Annals, 26*, 435–450.

VanPatten, B. (1996). *Input processing and grammar instruction.* New York: Ablex.

VanPatten, B. (2002). Processing instruction: An update. *Language Learning, 52*, 755–803.

VanPatten, B., & Cadierno, T. (1993). Explicit instruction and input processing. *Studies in Second Language Acquisition, 15*, 225–243.

VanPatten, B., & Lee, J. (1995). *Making communicative language happen.* New York: McGraw-Hill.

VanPatten, B., & Sanz, C. (1995). From input to output: Processing instruction and communicative tasks. In F. Eckman, D. Highland, P. Lee, J. Mileham, & R. Weber (Eds.), *Second language acquisition theory and pedagogy* (pp. 169–185). Mahwah, NJ: Lawrence Erlbaum Associates.

White, J. (1998). Getting the learners' attention: A typographical input enhancement study. In C. Doughty & J. Williams (Eds.), *Focus on form in classroom second language acquisition* (pp. 85–113). Cambridge, UK: Cambridge University Press.

White, L. (1991). Adverb placement in second language acquisition: Some positive and negative evidence in the classroom. *Second Language Research, 7*, 133–161.

Williams, J. (1999). Learner-generated attention to form. *Language Learning, 49*, 583–625.

Williams, J. (2001). The effectiveness of spontaneous attention to form. *System, 29*, 325–340.

Williams, J., & Evans, J. (1998). What kind of focus on which forms? In C. Doughty & J. Williams (Eds.), *Focus on form in classroom second language acquisition* (pp. 139–155). Cambridge, UK: Cambridge University Press.

Wittrock, M. (1974). Learning as a generative process. *Educational Psychologist, 11*, 87–95.

Wong, W. (2001). Modality and attention to form and meaning in the input. *Studies in Second Language Acquisition, 23*, 345–388.

Wong, W., & Simard, D. (1999). *Textual enhancement as input enhancement: A state of the art review.* Unpublished manuscript.

Zaki, H., & Ellis, R. (1999). Learning vocabulary through interacting with a written text. In R. Ellis (Ed.), *Learning a second language through interaction* (pp. 153–169). Amsterdam: Benjamins.

38

A Model of Academic Literacy for Integrated Language and Content Instruction

Marguerite Ann Snow
California State University, Los Angeles

Mohan (1986) was the first to explicitly state the challenge of content-based instruction (CBI): "What is needed is an integrative approach which relates language learning and content learning, considers language as a medium of learning, and acknowledges the role of context in communication" (p. 1). What this "integrative approach" entails has been the subject of much discussion in the literature over the past 15 or so years. Brinton and Holten (2001), for example, compared three definitions of CBI from Bycina (1986), Brinton, Snow, and Wesche (1989), and Wesche (1993) noting five similarities that can be summarized as follows:

- The goal of CBI is to provide a meaningful context for language teaching to occur.
- The organization of a CBI course centers on content.
- Content drives the curriculum, that is, it is the starting point for decisions about what is taught.
- Language and content are taught concurrently.
- Comprehensible input, provided through the content materials leads to language acquisition. (p. 240)

More recently, Davison and Williams (in Mohan, Leung, & Davison, 2001) defined integrated language and content teaching as a "heuristic label for a diverse group of curriculum approaches which share a concern for facilitating language learning, broadly defined, through varied but systematic linking of particular subject matter and language in the context of learning activities" (p. 57). In their review of current approaches to communicative language teaching (CLT), Wesche and Skehan (2002) singled out content-based instruction and task-based instruction as two trends in curricular design that conform to CLT principles, noting that contextual and pedagogical features shared by different forms of CBI include:

- The premise that learners in some sense receive 'two for one,' that is, content knowledge and increased language proficiency.
- A language curriculum in which expository texts and discourse are central.
- Orientation into a new culture or 'discourse community'.
- Adaptation of language input, interactional moves, and context to accommodate learners' limited language proficiency.
- Focus on academic language proficiency. (p. 221)

Finally, Pally (2000) added to the CBI terminology by introducing the term *sustained CBI*, defined as "classes in which students practice English language skills—reading, writing, speaking, listening, and grammatical forms—in the process of studying one subject area, usually for a semester" (p. vii). Murphy and Stoller (2001) went a step further, expanding on Pally's term and offering a new acronym, *sustained-content and language teaching* (SCLT). In their view, SCLT has two major components. The first is a focus on the exploration of a single content area or what Murphy and Stoller call a *carrier topic*. The second component is a complementary focus on second language learning and teaching (which includes the teaching of the four skills; cognitive and metacognitive strategies; study skills; vocabulary, grammar, and pronunciation, etc.).

STATEMENT OF PURPOSE

While discussion of the parameters of CBI is clearly ongoing, the viability of CBI as an approach to second and foreign language teaching is generally unquestioned, or, as Davison and Williams have pointed out, "A common rationale has developed for such programs, despite . . . different theoretical origins and orientations" (p. 52). As content-based instruction enters its third decade, its place among language teaching approaches is seemingly secure. Starting with Mohan (1986), the chronology of book-length treatments reveals sustained growth of the approach (c.f. Brinton, Snow, & Wesche, 1989, 2003; Crandall, 1987; Krueger & Ryan, 1993; Snow & Brinton, 1997; Stryker & Leaver, 1997; Kasper, 2000; Pally, 2000) and subsequent editions of several widely used methodology textbooks have either added CBI to the list of methods described or expanded its coverage (c.f. Larsen-Freeman, 2000; Celce-Murcia, 2001; Richards & Rodgers, 2001; Richard-Amato, 2003). With this growth, new trends in CBI have arisen while implementation issues persist. This chapter looks at key trends and issues in CBI from two vantage points: 1) the necessary conditions for CBI, and 2) the blending of CBI and approaches to English for Academic Purposes (EAP).

THE NECESSARY CONDITIONS FOR CONTENT-BASED INSTRUCTION

Wesche and Skehan (2002) noted that "CBI can be very effective for both language and content learning. However, ensuring the necessary conditions to achieve this presents an ongoing challenge" (p. 220). Indeed, the literature is rich with discussions of these challenges. Some have taken on the discussion from the point of view of models or curricular implementation. Others have focused on the roles of teachers the language teacher or the content teacher, or both. Still others have approached the issue from the point of view of teacher training.

Models

Brinton, Snow, and Wesche's (1989) classification of CBI into three prototype models—theme-based, sheltered, and adjunct—provided useful exemplars for program development in the early days of CBI and may have served as a catalyst for many published reports over the years about factors involved in both the successes and failures of CBI programs. In the theme-based model, the language instructor builds the teaching language skills around selected topics or themes. The literature contains many reports of successful theme-based initiatives across a wide variety of topics and levels. Gianelli (1997), for example, described "dramatic" results in a Texas middle school when teachers implemented a thematic curriculum and Rosser (1995) reported on an academic writing and research class at the university level developed around the theme of the life of Anne Frank in which students' writing reflected a deepening intellectual engagement with the topic over the course of the term. Concerns, however, about the need to improve coherence in content-based curricula have been expressed. Stoller and Grabe's (1997) "6 T's" framework developed out of the need to offer guidelines to CBI teachers.[1]

Other accounts over the years have focused on implementation of the adjunct model—where a language course and a content course are linked for purposes of instruction—and have reported many positive findings (see Brinton, Snow, & Wesche, 1989, 2003; Snow & Brinton, 1988; Benesch, 1988 for early examples). Others have underscored the challenges of adjunct instruction. Iancu (1997), for instance, chronicled the struggles of integrating separate ESL courses (writing and grammar, speech, reading, listening, and note taking) with content courses in history and sociology. Goldstein, Campbell, and Cummings (1997) described how issues of authority led ESL adjunct writing instructors to compare themselves to "flight attendants" at the service of the content professors "in the cockpit" and how issues of trust led students to question the ESL instructors' control of the content.

In the sheltered model, the instructor (usually a content specialist) teaches a content-area course (e.g., social studies, science) using special strategies aimed at making subject matter more comprehensible. In the original sheltered experiment at the University of Ottawa, second language students (both English as a second language and French as a second language) enrolled in sections of sheltered psychology taught in their second language. Results revealed that students in the sheltered psychology classes significantly improved their language skills while mastering the course content, indicating that subject matter teaching can be language teaching under the right conditions. With the expansion of the sheltered model into middle and high school programs for ESL students, Kinsella (1997), however, decries the fact that sheltered instruction has become too "teacher-driven" and "curriculum-centered." Her solution is for teachers to shift the focus to the learner by designing "learning to learn" activities so that students can become self-directed, independent learners when they leave sheltered classes. More recently, Short (2002), in a study of sheltered social studies classes at the middle school level, found that teachers, even those trained in sheltered instructional techniques, continued to place greater emphasis on content than language, missing many "teachable moments" for explicit focus on language.

Another outgrowth of the focus on models has led to the adaptation of the three prototype models to the specialized conditions of particular settings. Adamson (1993), for instance, discussed the *precourse*, which combines elements of an adjunct course and theme-based course. Students enrolled in a theme-based ESL course joined a regular undergraduate course "Introduction to Linguistics" for three weeks. They attended lectures, participated in discussions, wrote a research paper, and took an exam on the content material covered during the three-week unit. In another variation, Brinton and Holten (2001) described the *simulated adjunct program* in which "content is imported into an ESL class via authentic video lectures from undergraduate content-area classes" (p. 243). In a variation of the well-known writing fellows model, Blakely (1997) designed a CBI model in which specially trained native-speaking undergraduates paired up with non-native classmates to study the content of courses that both were taking. In another variation of the adjunct model, Snow and Kamhi-Stein (1997, 2002) designed a faculty development program in which content-area faculty paired with language specialists and redesigned their courses to focus on the teaching of academic literacy skills. Using an ESP-type format, Schramm (personal communication), described the "language specialist" model used in the Mechanical Engineering Department at the University of Minnesota where he developed language resources for ESL students that were independent of any particular courses. And in the EFL setting, Murphey (1997) adapted theme-based instruction to a very traditional language teaching context in Japan and described practical ways to integrate content with English through a *workshop* model. *Content-Based Instruction in Higher Education Settings* (Crandall & Kaufman, 2002) provides further examples of recent adaptations of the three prototype models.

As an alternative to classifying CBI in terms of models, Davison and Williams (in Mohan, Leung, & Davison, 2001) have proposed a comprehensive framework for language and content integration that describes the focus of teaching at the level of program, syllabus, unit of work, lesson, or activities within a lesson. The advantage, they note, is that unlike Brinton, Snow, and Wesche's (1989) prototype models, their framework distinguishes between curriculum focus, theoretical model or approach, teaching materials, organizational arrangements, and teacher roles. Onto this framework, Davison and Williams map the many different initiatives in integrated language and content teaching, including the prototype models discussed earlier as well as many other types of instruction, for both native and non-native English-speaking students, including the Cognitive Academic Language Learning Approach (CALLA), genre-based approaches, and language across the curriculum as well as approaches that do not typically aim to integrate language and content instruction such as functional-notional approaches.

In justifying the framework, Davison and Williams reject the term "content-based language teaching" as "...conflating a number of different models and approaches with different emphases" (Mohan, Leung, & Davison, 2001, p. 60). Their framework instead presents language and content integration as a "cline" ranging from "contextualized" language teaching to "language-conscious" content teaching. Given the range of definitions and approaches, the benefit of such a descriptive framework, according to Davison and Williams, is to elucidate the important distinctions between approaches and provide a common language to talk about language and content teaching.

This framework may indeed advance the discussion of language teaching in general by highlighting key components of widely used approaches. It may also plot the location of integrated approaches specifically within the array of approaches to second and foreign language teaching; however, the conceptualization proposed by Met (1998) may yet provide the most straightforward representation in the content-based literature. Met (1998), envisioning a continuum, places "content-driven" approaches like total immersion on one extreme; on the other extreme are "language-driven" approaches such as language classes that make frequent use of content for language practice. Along the continuum are other approaches (e.g., partial immersion, sheltered, etc.). Classification along the continuum depends on the objectives of the program, the target student population, and the requirements of the instructional setting. The continuum includes a mixture of models, those typically used to teach second and foreign languages and those that are typically implemented at different educational levels (i.e., adjunct programs at secondary or postsecondary levels with adolescents or adults or theme-based courses across all educational and age levels).

Curricular Implementation

Davison and Williams (in Mohan, Leung, & Davison, 2001) also identified two main theoretical problems in relation to planning an integrated language and content curriculum: 1) the selection of the sequencing of language; and 2) the content and scope of the curriculum. Snow, Met, and Genesee (1989) developed a framework to address problems of selection and scope. In their framework, language and content teachers work collaboratively to define two types of language teaching objectives. The first type is "content-obligatory" language, defined as the types of language (i.e., grammar items, specialized vocabulary, rhetorical structures, etc.) that are necessary for students to understand and master the subject matter of any given content. The second objective is "content-compatible" language, which includes selection of language forms and structures that pair naturally with a given content material. This kind of objective allows teachers to provide extended practice, for example, with troublesome grammar points.

The Snow, Met, and Genesee framework has been implemented extensively in various projects at the University of Minnesota's Center for Advanced Research on Language Acquisition (CARLA). A sample science lesson plan, *"Plantas: Las Partes y el Ciclo de Vida"* ("Plants: Their Parts and Life Cycle") designed for a Grade 2 Spanish immersion class utilizes the framework (Tedick, Jorgensen, & Gellert, 2001). In the lesson, students learn about the parts of plants and their functions. The content-obligatory language components included: 1) appropriate words to describe plant parts and functions (e.g., *semilla* (seed), *tallo* (stem); 2) the phrase *"Es la/el"* ("It is the") to identify and classify plant parts; 3) the phrase "Es como un/una" ("It is like a/an") to write similes to describe the plant parts; 4) use of descriptive words to write similes; and 5) terms to identify plants and their parts that we eat (e.g., *zanahoria-raiz* (carrot-root), *lechuga-hoja* (lettuce- leaf), *fresa-fruta* (strawberry-fruit)). Content-compatible language objectives such as using the phrase *"Yo creo es"* ("I think it is") to classify plant parts, and writing similes with accurate gender agreement were also included in the lesson to provide further language practice. The teacher and students checked their work using a holistic rubric that described the range of features of similes.

Stoller and Grabe (1997) developed the "6 T's Approach" as a systematic framework for dealing with issues of selection and scope of content in CBI. *Theme* is the first "T"—the central ideas that organize major curricular units. Themes are selected for their match with students' interests and needs, institutional expectations, program resources, and teachers' abilities and interests. The second "T" is *topics,* the subunits of content that explore a more specific aspect of the theme. *Texts,* the third "T," are defined by Stoller and Grabe as the content resources that drive planning of the theme units. These might include readings, audio and video tapes, maps, software, Internet sites, graphic representations, guest speakers, and field trips. The fourth "T," *threads,* creates linkages across units. They are generally abstract concepts such as *responsibility,* which are used as the thread to link thematic units on civil rights, pollution, and Native Americans. The fifth "T," *tasks,* are the instructional activities designed by teachers to fulfill language, content, and strategy training objectives. These are the everyday activities of the class. *Transitions,* the sixth "T," are specifically planned actions that provide coherence across topics in a thematic unit and across tasks within topics. These can include both topical transitions such as shifts in emphasis from global population trends in a thematic unit on demography, to trends in developing countries, to trends in students' home countries. Task transitions might require students to interpret a graph illustrating population trends, create a graph with new data, or write the information contained in the graph into paragraph form.

In a more recent view, Stoller (2002) takes the position that the success of CBI depends on the details of its implementation. She advocates adding "positive tension" by selecting input with multiple perspectives, different but complementary views, and opposing viewpoints. She also suggests employing techniques that incorporate "positive complexity" by devising tasks that require students to reinvest their language skills, cognitive skills, and content knowledge to negotiate new information and to incorporate problem-solving tasks into instruction that becomes progressively more complex. Stoller emphasizes that educators, outside public school contexts where there is an inherent demand for sustained content, must aim for the systematic buildup of content knowledge from multiple sources and from different perspectives, rather than be satisfied with the superficial examination of limited content, in order to nurture improvement of language skills and the acquisition of knowledge.

Frameworks such as the 6 T's and the movement toward SCLT are a backlash against the "potpourri" (Jacobs, 1990) problem that often plagues theme-based courses where content is often parceled out in bits and pieces with little regard to maintaining its integrity. Pally (2000) noted that the notion of sustained content evolved from thinking about how native English-speaking students acquire expertise, namely by learning subject matter and critical thinking skills required for academic study in content classes. Sustained CBI mirrors how native speakers learn higher-level reading and writing skills by studying one subject over time, the kind of study to which many non-native students are exposed once they finish ESL classes. The special issue of the *TESOL Journal* (Autumn, 2001), guest-edited by Murphy and Stoller, provides an interesting glimpse into six settings where teachers have operationalized the notion of sustained content teaching in both ESL and EFL settings and at a variety of educational levels (middle school through university) for purposes such as teaching academic vocabulary with the support of corpus linguistics tools (Donley & Reppen, 2001), to assisting health science majors improve their "listening-to-learn" skills in Barcelona, Spain (Kerans, 2001). Others such as Heyden (2001) provided recent accounts of the application of sustained content. In this example, Heyden, concerned that the content of the typical ESL freshman composition class is "confusingly disjointed," replaced the typical essay anthology with a novel that his students read over a 14-week semester. For each reading assignment, students wrote double-entry journals, which helped them keep up with the reading and make sense in writing of what they were reading. They also developed a selected topic from the novel into a research paper that included a proposal, site visit, research report, synthesis, reflection, and bibliography. In summing up the results of the experiment in sustained content, Heyden (2001) referred to a student's comment: "I felt like I was inside a world I like learning about" (p. 20).

Instructional Interventions

In 1988, Swain remarked that in the immersion context, "... not all content teaching is necessarily good language teaching" (p. 68) and more recently, Lyster and Ranta (1997) reiterated the same point: "Subject-matter teaching does not on its own provide adequate language teaching: Language used to convey subject matter needs to be highlighted in ways that make certain features more salient to L2 learners" (p. 41). A large-scale project being conducted in Holland by a team of researchers interested in CBI provides a classroom-based illustration of this ongoing concern (Hajer & Koole, 2001; van Eerde et al., 2001). The project, motivated by statistics that show that students from large immigrant groups in Holland such as Turks and Moroccans perform less well than their Dutch peers, focuses on the first year of secondary education, specifically mathematics classes, where these same students are also overrepresented in groups that quit subjects like math. Research questions being investigated ask: To what extent do the teachers create opportunities to learn the language of mathematics? To what extent do teachers give the students possibilities to verbalize their solutions through language production? To what extent do teachers give feedback on content and form?

In one of their studies, two teachers were followed extensively in multilingual math classes in the course of instruction; research methods included classroom observation, think-aloud protocols, and interviews (van Eerde et al., 2001). Both teachers used a methodology for teaching math called Realistic Mathematics Education, which assumes that mathematics has its roots in real-life and students should be guided to transform a context problem from daily life into a representation that can be manipulated mathematically. Despite this purported instructional focus on real-life contexts, the classroom observation data indicated that neither teacher paid much attention to the introduction of contexts. In one example, think-aloud tasks revealed that second language students frequently did not understand terms from daily life contexts that were essential to solving the math problem (e.g., the word "stopper" in a problem dealing with the volume of water in a bathtub). In other observations, researchers found that sociomathematical norms such as the quality of mathematical solutions remained implicit. In one math class, for instance, the teacher asked for a "more simple" solution than one provided by a student without ever explaining or exemplifying the meaning of a "simple" solution in the context of math. Even though one of the teachers deliberately promoted active participation and showed a wide repertoire of strategies for stimulating thinking and meaning construction, both teachers missed opportunities to "put the symbiosis of math and language learning theory into practice" (p. 26). The researchers concluded that in order to combine content and language teaching into language sensitive content instruction, the teachers needed to pay more attention to the selection of contexts that were familiar to all students and to better introduce and orient students to the contexts and the mathematics textbook.

A series of investigations in immersion classes by Swain and Lapkin (Lapkin, 2002; Swain, 2001; Swain & Lapkin, 1998) aimed to show how language instruction can be integrated into content instruction through systematic intervention. They also sought to extend the output hypothesis, results of which may have relevance for all kinds of CBI. In these studies, collaborative tasks with the goal of linguistic accuracy were designed to assist students to extend their language output. Three functions of output underlie the collaborative tasks: 1) getting language learners to notice the target language while attempting to produce it, 2) getting learners to use their output as a means of hypothesis formulating and testing, and 3) getting learners to engage in metatalk—to use language to reflect on language use. Collaborative tasks such as a dictogloss, jigsaw, and reformulation were used in the studies to get students to produce language-related episodes (LREs). Results of the research to date indicate that the collaborative tasks increased the amount of output, helped students focus attention on language as they formulated and tested hypotheses about their language, and provided opportunities for output to function as a metalinguistic tool. Interventions such as those used by Swain and Lapkin may indeed be one means to systematically integrate language and content instruction by getting students to reflect on their own language production as they attempt to create meaning.

Teacher Preparation

Another perspective on the necessary conditions for effective CBI is the role of teacher preparation and training. Lorenz and Met (1988) were among the first to recognize, in their case for immersion, that integrating language and content instruction may require specialized skills. Kaufman (1997), however, almost 10 years later noted that "...documentation on new ways to prepare teachers for operating within interdisciplinary paradigms is sparse" (p. 175). Kaufman described a preservice training program that used a constructivist approach to create collaborative experiences for ESL, science, and social studies teacher candidates to learn language and disciplinary content for linguistically diverse classrooms. Peterson (1997) asked, "What type of teacher preparation program is capable of empowering teachers to perform capably in such demanding [CBI] contexts?" (p. 161). To answer this question, Peterson developed an inventory of the target competencies—beyond those of a general language teacher—that enable teachers to plan and implement CBI; she also provided sample scenarios reflecting the knowledge, skills, and attitudes they need for effective integration of language and content teaching.

Promising work by Bigelow and Ranney (2001) goes a step forward. In a study that focused on assisting preservice teachers to address learners' language needs when teaching content, Bigelow and Ranney collected the lesson plan assignments of preservice teachers, asked the teachers-to-be to reflect on their lesson planning processes in the fall and spring, and conducted in-depth interviews with the student teachers. Among many interesting findings, the researchers found that the difficulty of integrating language and content went beyond the preservice teachers' abilities to write good objectives. Early on in the process, the preservice teachers' conceptualization of language aims focused mainly on vocabulary and what the researcher called "macro-level" skills (e.g., "Students will read a text."); the preservice teachers, however, had trouble anticipating the forms and functions that ESL students needed to complete such macro-level tasks. Over the course of their training, the preservice teachers became more adept at articulating language objectives and they became more skillful at linking the objectives to both instructional activities and assessment measures. In addition, lesson plans began to show a better balance between vocabulary and form. Furthermore, the overall quantity of micro-level language objectives increased. However, macro-level objectives for the productive skills of speaking and writing remained steady, suggesting that the preservice teachers had more difficulty breaking down these skills in their lesson plans, prompting the researchers to note that the preservice teachers in the study may have been limited by their lack of metalinguistic knowledge.

Crandall (1998) pointed to the difficulty of crossing over disciplinary boundaries: "It is not surprising that . . . both language and content area teachers may be frightened at the prospect of integrating language and content instruction, since there is limited attention to language needs in the preparation of content teachers, and limited attention to either the specific discourse of academic disciplines or the practical concerns of needs analysis, text adaptation, curriculum development, or collaborative teaching in most language teacher education programs" (p. 2). Wong, Fillmore, and Snow (2002) concur, arguing that teachers need a thorough understanding of how languages figure into education—or educational linguistics—a perspective that few teacher education programs provide. Teachers should, they maintain, know about characteristics of oral and written language and be offered such courses as "Language and Linguistics," "Sociolinguistics for Educators in a Linguistically Diverse Society," and "Second Language Learning and Teaching."[2]

Wong, Fillmore, and Snow (2002), in fact, contend that all teachers, not only those serving bilingual and second language students, should have a thorough grounding in language and it role in education. Prospective educators need to know more about language in order to take on five functions as teachers: 1) teacher as communicator—how teachers can structure their own language output for maximum clarity to work effectively with students from many different cultural, social, and linguistic backgrounds; 2) teacher as educator—how teachers can help students learn and use aspects of language associated with the academic discourse of the various school subjects; 3) teacher as evaluator—how teachers can make valid judgments about students' abilities by understanding variation in language use such as vernacular varieties of English, normal progress for second language learners, or developmental delays or disorders; 4) teacher as educated human being—how teachers can understand basic concepts about language and literacy to engage in public discussions and make informed decisions about issues underlying second language learning and bilingual education; and 5) teacher as agent of socialization—how teachers can help students learn the everyday practices, the system of values and beliefs, and the means and manners of communication of their cultural communities and, at the same time, how they can help students make the transition in ways that do not undermine the role played by parents and family members in their communities.

THE BLENDING OF CBI AND EAP

In comparing CBI and English for Specific Purposes (ESP), Johns (1997a) notes that both movements stem from unease about the separation of language instruction from the context and demands of real language use, or what Johns calls "TENOR" (Teaching English for No Obvious Reason) (p. 364). Both CBI and ESP, according to Johns, "encourage the transfer of language skills and content to real life by bringing genuine language and authentic classroom activities to students" (p. 364). Johns notes, however, that the movements differ in scope and focus. CBI has generally been implemented in ESL settings, while ESP has primarily been applied to EFL settings. ESP courses have mainly been designed for adult students and have traditionally focused on reading since, at least, historically, learners have needed English to access science and technology texts written in English. In contrast, CBI courses have typically been developed for English learners across age groups and educational levels, typically in classes with a multiskills focus.

EAP, coming out of the ESP tradition, has also primarily focused on adult learners of English, namely, international students preparing to study in English-medium postsecondary settings or ESL students currently enrolled in English-medium tertiary institutions. Over the years, CBI and EAP have essentially existed as separate traditions with different literatures with researchers and practitioners tending to identify with one or the other traditions. Work in EAP has focused on genre analysis, for example, of research papers or literature reviews (e.g., Swales, 1990; Swales & Lindemann, 2002), instructional strategies for teaching EAP (e.g., Jordan, 1997), and writing in the disciplines such as engineering and business management (e.g., Belcher & Braine, 1995). EAP has also developed a healthy research tradition. Flowerdew and Peacock (2001), for instance, offer a comprehensive survey of research in EAP in such areas as needs assessment, academic vocabulary, and the skill areas of lecture comprehension, academic reading, and oral discussion. Work in CBI, on the other hand, has tended to focus more on models and curricula, but it also benefits from a solid research base, provided mainly from nearly four decades of immersion research, but gradually being informed by a wider cross-section of research (see Grabe & Stoller; 1997, Snow, 1998; and the special issue of the *Canadian Modern Language Review* (Wesche, 2001) for recent reviews of immersion and content-based research).

Underlying the EAP tradition is the notion of academic literacy, conceptualizations of which have been influenced by various epistemologies, including composition and rhetoric. Zamel and Spack (1998) noted the evolving definition:

> Academic literacy, which once denoted simply the ability to read and write college-level texts, now must embrace multiple approaches to knowledge. Hence, our use of the term *literacies*. College classrooms have become sites where different languages and cultures intersect, including the various discourses of students, teachers, and researchers. In our experience, the result of this interaction, even when (perhaps because) it involves struggle and conflict, is most often intellectual growth, for these different languages and cultures build on and give shape to one another. (p. ix)

Academic literacy in Johns' (1997b) view must have at its core social factors in literacy development. In "socioliterate" views, students acquire literacies primarily through exposure to discourses from a variety of social contexts. Johns advocates an approach in which ". . . literacy classes become laboratories for the study of text, roles, and contexts, for research into evolving student literacies and developing awareness and critique of communities and their textual contracts" (p. 19).

Indeed Cummins (1981, 1984, 2000a) must be credited with starting the dialogue about academic language proficiency as it relates to younger learners. Drawing on the work of Skutnabb-Kangas and Toukomaa (1976) in Finland, his well-known theoretical framework for conceptualizing language proficiency makes the distinction between social language, or Basic Interpersonal Communication Skills (BICS), and academic language, or cognitive academic language proficiency (CALP)—notions that have heavily influenced the field and perhaps, more important, started bridging the gap between EAP focused on postsecondary learners and settings and CBI concerned with second language learners in K-12 contexts.

More recently, other conceptualizations of academic literacy have emerged. Adamson (1993) was one of the first to suggest a model of second language academic competence. In his view, academic competence consists of at least three abilities: 1) the ability to use a combination of linguistic, pragmatic, and background knowledge to reach a basic understanding of content material; 2) the ability to use appropriate strategies to enhance knowledge of content material; and 3) the ability to use appropriate strategies to complete academic assignments with less than a full understanding of the content material. When understanding falls below a certain level, the process of learning fails and the student's only alternative is to apply coping strategies such as copying and memorization.

Short (1998, 2002) developed the Language-Content-Task (LCT) framework, a model of academic literacy that can guide teachers as they organize language and content instruction. Using the example of social studies, the framework is depicted graphically as three intersecting rings: Task, Content, and Language. Within the Task ring is *procedural knowledge,* within the Content ring are *content topics* for social studies, and within the Language ring are *semantics, syntax, pragmatics,* and *functions.* The Task and Content rings share tasks related to the habits of the minds of historians (i.e., the approach a given discipline might take to exploring a problem or performing a task); the Content and Language rings overlap in the area of social studies register and the Task and Language rings share explanations of the task and the language needed to perform the task. In the center, the three rings have *interaction* in common. Interaction, in Short's framework, implies the ability to understand and participate in the co-construction of knowledge in the classroom.

Solomon and Rhodes (1996) went to the field to determine how ESL educators define academic language. Respondents to their survey were elementary, middle, and high school ESL teachers, graduate students in training to become ESL professionals, ESL teacher trainers, and administrators. Most of the respondents identified vocabulary as a key feature of academic language and gave examples of terms like "circle," "community," and "carbohydrate" from content areas such as math, social studies, and science. Others contrasted academic language with social language, noting that use of the word "show" may be appropriate in social conversation, but "indicate" would be more typical in an academic context. One K-12 program coordinator emphasized that academic language can only be acquired at school: "Academic language is the language of lecture and textbooks. It is filled with expectations of prior knowledge and background and cultural uniformity" (p. 6).

More recently, Bailey and Butler (2002) have developed an evidentiary framework for operationalizing academic language proficiency. Targeting K-12 education, the framework is motivated in part by the U.S. government's No Child Left Behind Act (2001), which requires states to assess the English language development of all English language learners despite the fact that available assessments generally do not reflect the requisite academic language needed for demonstrating content knowledge and participating in mainstream classes. The framework, which is based on multiple data points including classroom observation and course textbook analyses, will lead to the development of test specifications and prototype tasks that can be used by test developers to design tests of academic language proficiency.

In Bailey and Butler's framework, academic language is characterized as "language that stands in contrast to the everyday informal speech that students use outside the classroom environment" (p. 7). More specifically, it can be characterized at the lexical, syntactic, and discourse levels, and also includes language functions used in the classroom. Stevens, Butler, and Castellon-Wellington (2000) identify three categories of words: 1) high frequency general words used regularly in everyday contexts, 2) nonspecialized academic words that are used across content areas (while not specific to any one content area, they constitute a special register of academic language use as illustrated in the contrast between "show" and "indicate" provided by the respondent in the Solomon and Rhodes survey), and 3) specialized content-area words that are unique to specific disciplines. At the syntactic level, academic language includes complex grammatical structures such as embedded clauses and preference for nominalization. At the discourse level, academic language has been described as "intertextual" (Gibbons, 1998)—that is, students must integrate oral and written discourse in classroom activities. The challenge of negotiating oral and print domains lies in their varying linguistic features. Textbook language, for example, has greater lexical density and syntactic complexity than oral classroom discourse (Schleppegrell, 2001).

The term "language function" takes on an expanded scope in these attempts to define academic language proficiency. Perhaps we can now best characterize functions such as "inviting" or "complementing" as social language functions, while those functions used in classrooms by students to learn and demonstrate mastery of academic content as academic language functions. Several investigations have begun to enhance our understanding of academic language functions in K-12 classrooms. Short (1994), for instance, in analyzing middle school social studies classes, found that teachers and students used the following language functions: *comparison, definition, description, evaluation, exemplification, explanation, justification,* and *sequencing.* In addition, teachers *asked recall questions, gave directions, encouraged, clarified/restated, rephrased, extended, previewed,* and *reviewed.* More recently, Bailey et al., (2001) observed fourth and fifth grade science classrooms to analyze the academic language functions used by both teachers and students. Teachers primarily used four language functions: *assessment, comparison, description,* and *explanation.* Student talk consisted of five academic language functions: *commenting, comparison, description, explanation,* and *questioning.*

In a 2-year ethnographic study, Duff (2001) investigated the discourse contexts for mainstreamed ESL students in two 10th grade social studies classes in Canada. Results of the study revealed that, for the ESL students to succeed in class, they needed to participate in a variety of reading and writing activities that required them to express a range of critical perspectives on social issues and to enter into "quick-paced" classroom discussions and interactions. In order to interact effectively in this discourse context, students needed not only knowledge of current local and world current events, but also of the popular culture of mainstream Canadian high school students to understand references to television programs, teen magazines (and celebrities), and sports teams. Based on her results, Duff suggested three broad areas for intervention with mainstreamed ESL students such as those who participated in the study. The first two underscore the need for teachers to teach academic literacy skills. Duff recommends greater emphasis on listening and speaking skills. The ESL students in her study had difficulty with the oral "texts" of the classroom. Both the ESL students and the mainstream students reported having problems understanding one another. Second, Duff found that there was very little explicit attention to text structures and vocabulary that students read, heard, or were asked to produce. Acknowledging that her final suggestion deviates from "... the usual prescriptions and practices" (p. 120) for integrated language and content instruction, Duff notes that the ESL students in her study not only needed in-depth knowledge of textbook content, but also "a repertoire" of newsworthy current events and knowledge of North American popular culture and the confidence and "... accompanying sense of entitlement or license to speak about their concerns, backgrounds, issues, and views" (p. 120).

Cummins (2000b) adds the dimension of intercultural identity to considerations of academic language proficiency, a concern underscored by Duff's findings in which the ESL students in her study found themselves marginalized, often mocked and laughed at for their mispronunciations or incorrect uses of grammar. Cummins maintains that our aim must be more than "... a technical issue of how to implement appropriate forms of literacy and content instruction when students have weaker language skills. It is equally or more a question of how to create within the classroom and school an interpersonal space that affirms students' developing sense of self" (p. 163). Walqui (2000) keys in as well on the social and cultural contexts of schooling, arguing that structural obstacles, particularly at the secondary level, such as fragmented school days and age-grade inflexibility, inhibit students' academic success. These sociocultural dimensions may somewhat parallel work in critical literacy, in particular Benesch's (2001) work in critical EAP in postsecondary contexts.

Mohan's knowledge framework (Mohan, 1986; Mohan, Leung, & Davison, 2001) offers another lens through which to define academic language proficiency. The framework works within the general perspective of systemic functional linguistics; it provides a perspective on language as a medium of learning that, according to Mohan, differs from but is complementary to genre approaches. It views language as discourse in the context of social practice, a characterization also made by Johns (1997b). In Mohan's view, social practice is a combination of knowledge (theory) and action (practice). The theory aspect of activity includes knowledge structures like classification, principles, and evaluation; the practice aspects of activity include knowledge structures such as description, sequence, and choice. Mohan believes that teachers and students can use knowledge structures as "... hinges between content issues and language issues" (Mohan, Leung, & Davison, 2001, p. 114). Furthermore, he notes, knowledge structures might provide the means for a common agenda for language teachers and content specialists.

Tang (1997) reported on the application of some components of the knowledge framework in a seventh grade social studies class in which the teacher organized the content of the textbook according to knowledge structures and then prepared graphic organizers for students that summarized the contents of the chapters and helped students to see the connections across topics. In various activities to practice the language and the content, the teacher explicitly taught the linguistic and cohesion devices of text/knowledge structure. Students completed tasks in which they constructed graphics from expository prose and wrote expository prose from graphics. Similarly, Early (2001) reported on a Vancouver, British Columbia school district's approach to achieving schoolwide emphasis on integrated language and content instruction using Mohan's knowledge framework in combination with principles of social constructivist learning. The case study revealed that the approach was successful in drawing teachers' awareness to the role of language as a medium of learning.

Strategy instruction is another avenue for making the complex, abstract cognitive structures of academic content more transparent. Influenced by CALLA, Chamot and O'Malley's (1987) well-known approach, teachers in integrated language and content settings have come to recognize the value of systematic strategy instruction. Kinsella (1997) observed that teachers have become too concerned with access to content and have failed to teach students strategies to demystify academic learning. She recommends strategies for autonomous learning like techniques for active learning, systematic vocabulary acquisition, and study reading. In the same vein, Walqui (2000) places the explicit teaching of academic strategies, sociocultural expectations, and academic norms as one of her ten priorities for designing effective instruction for second language students.

Standards and Accountability

Another vantage point for exploring the notion of academic language is through the standards that have been developed for both the content areas and ESL (Bailey & Butler, 2002). In the United States, standards for the content areas have been developed by professional associations such as the National Council of Teachers of Mathematics, the first to release content standards in 1989. In the language arena, ESL standards for school-age learners have been developed in Australia, Canada, England, and the United States in recent years (McKay, 2000). Content-area and ESL standards reflect what students should know and be able to do within the various subjects, and, therefore, make assumptions about uses of academic language.

Bailey and Butler (2002) examined the implicit and explicit statements of requisite language in the content standards of four U.S. states with large ESL populations (California, Florida, New York, and Texas). Their analysis of the science standards, for example, revealed common language functions and descriptors among the four states. Academic language functions that appeared in all four sets of science standards at the elementary level were: *analyze, compare, describe, observe,* and *record*. The New York science standards at sixth grade, for instance, state that students should be able to *explain* seasonal changes on Earth. They must be able to create an Earth model and *describe* the arrangement, interaction, and movement of the Earth, moon, and sun (Bailey & Butler, 2002). At the middle school level, four academic language functions were found in common across the science standards: *compare, explain, identify,* and *recognize*. At the high school, three functions were shared across the four sets: *describe, explain,* and *recognize*.

ESL standards make assumptions about requisite language skills that second language learners must attain. TESOL's *ESL Standards for Pre-K-12 Students* specify the language competencies needed by English language learners in elementary and secondary schools: "... to become fully proficient in English, to have unrestricted access to grade-appropriate instruction in challenging academic subjects, and ultimately to lead rich and productive lives" (TESOL, 1997, pp. 1–2). The *ESL Standards* consist of three goals: 1) to use English to communicate in social settings; 2) to use English to achieve academically in all content areas; and 3) to use English in socially and culturally appropriate ways. Bailey and Butler (2002) also analyzed the nine standards contained within the *ESL Standards*. Across the three grade level clusters, students are expected to know and be able to use a wide array of language functions. Academic language functions that could be found across all three goals and all three grade level clusters are: *express, imitate, listen, negotiate, participate, request,* and *respond*. Within the standards that focus on academic language, functions in common across the grade level clusters include: *analyze, contrast, define, elaborate, hypothesize, justify, paraphrase,* and *summarize*. Functions that are unique to the social language standards are: *clarify, communicate, describe, elicit, engage, restate, recite,* and *talk*.

Findings from these analyses of selected content-area and ESL standards illuminate the explicit and implicit assumptions of academic language use expected of school-age learners and, therefore, deepen our understanding of the complexities of language as a medium of learning. They also raise issues for further examination. For example, Bailey and Butler (2002) point out that the verbs *describe* and *clarify*, categorized under social uses of language (not academic) in the *ESL Standards*, were language functions used for academic purposes in their observations of science classrooms (Bailey et al., 2001). Similarly, as noted, the function *describe* was prominently featured in the example from the New York state science standards. Thus, while standards may provide useful resources for identifying the features that underlie academic language proficiency, Bailey and Butler (2002) caution that standards must be validated against actual classroom uses of academic language and, hence, echo McKay's (2000) call for a sound theoretical base for the construction of standards for ESL. Furthermore, Butler and Bailey's results remind us not to characterize language proficiency as a dichotomy between social and academic language, but rather to view it as a developmental continuum for school-age English language learners.

The forces that brought about the trend toward standards-based instruction also emphasize accountability and high stakes testing. Gottlieb (2000) noted that, in the United States, "The success of the standards-based reform movement depends on the accurate and equitable measurement of students' achievement, which must be tied to challenging academic content" (p. 167). The issue is a complicated one for English language learners, particularly as noted, because current assessment measures generally do not tap academic language. Stevens, Butler, and Castellon-Wellington (2000) found that while the language proficiency and content tests used in their study overlapped in terms of high-frequency general vocabulary and grammatical structures, the vocabulary and sentence structures that appeared on the content test were more complex. They contained nonspecialized academic words, specialized content words, more embeddings, and test language. This point is underscored by a finding from the van Eerde et al. (2001) study in Holland, where classroom observation captured one of the second language learners, Hennia, actively participating in whole group interaction in the math class and orally demonstrating understanding of a key concept of graphing, but failing to demonstrate mastery later on when tested on the same concept on a paper and pencil math test.

Butler and Stevens (2001) stress that academic language emerges as a critical factor in assessing content knowledge because it is the vehicle for acquiring the knowledge being assessed. Academic language proficiency measures are necessary, they maintain, to: 1) make decisions about a second language student's readiness for taking standardized content tests; 2) to apply in research on test accommodations in order to determine the appropriacy of specific accommodations for students at different levels of language proficiency; and 3) to measure student growth in academic language.

Implementation of the standards also provides a vehicle through which to view classroom application of academic language. Bunch et al. (2001) reported on a university-school collaboration in which middle school English language learners were placed in mainstream social studies classes specifically designed to meet the needs of underprepared students of linguistically and culturally diverse backgrounds. In the project, teachers and students use a chart based on the *ESL Standards* (TESOL, 1997) and the national foreign language standards to plan instruction that capitalized on opportunities for identifying, modeling, and guiding practice of academic language skills. For example, in the unit "How Do Historians Know about the Crusades?" one group of students made an oral presentation in which they explained how the Crusaders defended against attack; they also wrote expository essays in which they used the discourse of social studies to describe, explain, justify, and persuade. All the activities were designed as progress indicators for ESL Goal 2: "Students will use English to obtain, process, construct, and provide subject matter information in spoken and written form" (TESOL, 1997).

A MODEL OF ACADEMIC LITERACY FOR INTEGRATED LANGUAGE AND CONTENT INSTRUCTION

This chapter has considered two main areas of research and activity in integrated language and content teaching by 1) examining some of the necessary conditions for CBI

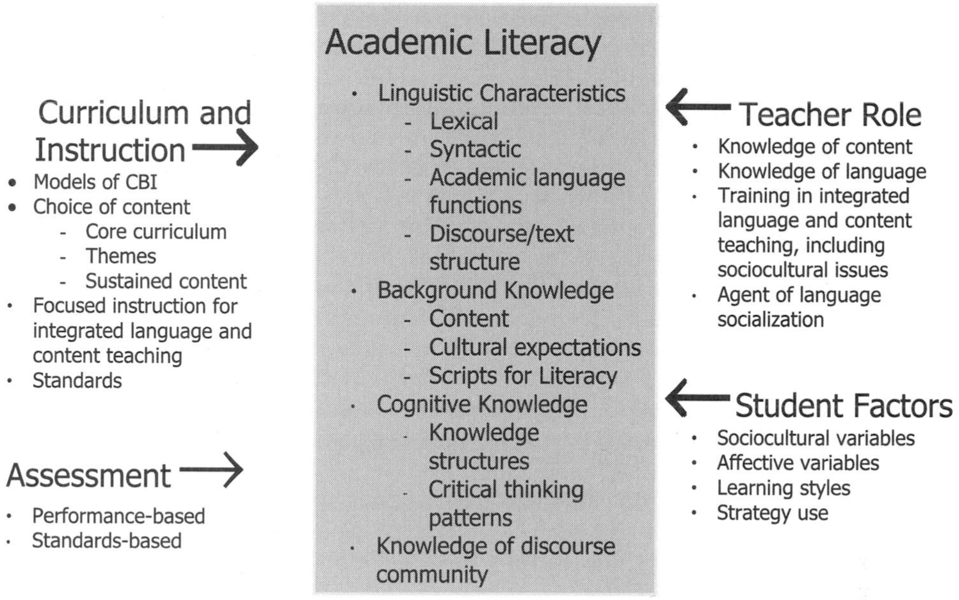

Academic Literacy

- Linguistic Characteristics
  - Lexical
  - Syntactic
  - Academic language functions
  - Discourse/text structure
- Background Knowledge
  - Content
  - Cultural expectations
  - Scripts for Literacy
- Cognitive Knowledge
  - Knowledge structures
  - Critical thinking patterns
- Knowledge of discourse community

Curriculum and Instruction →

- Models of CBI
- Choice of content
  - Core curriculum
  - Themes
  - Sustained content
- Focused instruction for integrated language and content teaching
- Standards

Assessment →

- Performance-based
- Standards-based

← Teacher Role

- Knowledge of content
- Knowledge of language
- Training in integrated language and content teaching, including sociocultural issues
- Agent of language socialization

← Student Factors

- Sociocultural variables
- Affective variables
- Learning styles
- Strategy use

FIG. 38.1. A Model of Academic Literacy for Integrated Language and Content Instruction.

such as models, curricular implementation, instructional interventions, and teacher preparation, and 2) reviewing descriptions of academic literacy from the extant adult EAP literature and exploring the developing work in academic language proficiency for school-age learners. Informed by this work, Figure 38.1 presents a model of academic literacy for integrated language and content instruction that takes into account the CBI and EAP traditions in order to produce a more powerful understanding of integrated approaches. The model incorporates the work of the many researchers and practitioners reviewed in this chapter who have contributed key pieces to our understanding of characteristics of academic literacy.

The centerpiece of the model, academic literacy, is comprised of (at least) four components. The first component is linguistic characteristics that include understandings of the lexicon (i.e., general vocabulary, nonspecialized academic vocabulary, and content-specific or technical terminology), syntactic structures, academic language functions, and discourse/text structures. The second component consists of the background knowledge that learners bring to bear on learning, including the learners' degree of familiarity with the content under study, cultural expectations, and scripts for literacy based on prior or current academic exposure to educational settings. The third component includes the cognitive knowledge inherent in the learning process; this entails the knowledge structures that reveal the systematic relationship between the content and the form and patterns in which it is presented (e.g., hierarchical structures, temporal relationships among events), and patterns of critical thinking that experts (teachers) model and apprentices (students) practice. In the fourth component, knowledge of the discourse community, learners develop their understanding of the specific content area (e.g., biology, mathematics) or what Short (2002) referred to as the "habits of the mind" of biologists, mathematicians, or any practitioners within a particular discourse community.

Contributing to the development of academic literacy for integrated language and content instruction are the cornerstones of curriculum and instruction, assessment, and, of course, the teacher and the student. Curriculum and instruction must necessarily include the models selected for content-based instruction, choice (and rationale) for the content, instructional practices that should reflect language, content, and study skill objectives, and (depending on the setting) standards appropriate for the subject area and level of the students to guide instruction. Assessment, a key cornerstone of the model, is in place to collect essential information about student performance through the use of multiple measures—both informal and formal—to determine student achievement and/or whether learners meet standards (where relevant).

The teacher, depending on the model selected, is a language teacher, a content teacher, language and content teachers working collaboratively, or, in the case of elementary school, a teacher handling both roles. In integrated language and content instruction, teachers, to borrow Hawkins' (2001) notion of "layering" of teacher knowledge, must necessarily have both content and language knowledge and the requisite training that allows them to plan and deliver instruction that will enhance academic literacy. In this role, they also assume the role of agent of language (and academic) socialization practices that will increase their second language students' opportunities for academic success. To this mix, student factors such as sociocultural (e.g., family background, Ll literacy practices, etc.) and affective variables (i.e., attitudes and motivation) are added. And, while all integrated instruction should incorporate strategy training, the students' learning styles and strategy use repertoires become factors as the learners mediate the complex learning process that is entailed in the development of academic literacy.

The model of academic literacy for integrated language and content instruction presented in this chapter attempts to be expansive enough to cover both second and foreign language teaching contexts across educational levels, with components of the model applying differentially to different educational settings and student populations. The common ground for the blending of CBI and EAP traditions is content—challenging subject matter, in whatever form, core curricula, themes, or sustained content. Crandall's (1994) statement is pertinent: "...students cannot develop academic knowledge and skills without access to the language in which that knowledge is embedded, discussed, constructed, or evaluated. Nor can they acquire academic skills in a context devoid of content" (p. 256). The increased spotlight on K-12 ESL populations may have accelerated accountability, but enhanced understanding of the necessary conditions for developing academic literacy has the possibility to strengthen all types of integrated language and content instruction for learners at all levels.

NOTES

1. Stoller and Grabe's framework is described in detail in the next section of this chapter.
2. Increasingly, materials specially designed for preparing teachers for integrated language and content instruction are becoming available. See *Making Content Comprehensible for English Language Learners: The SIOP Model* (Echevarria, Vogt, & Short, 2000); *Handbook of Undergraduate Second Language Education* (Rosenthal, 2000); *Dual Language Instruction: A Handbook for Enriched Education* (Cloud, Genesee, & Hamayan, 2000); *Language Minority Students in the Mainstream Classroom* (Carrasquillo & Rodriguez, 2002); and the Hawkins (2001) and Snow (2001) chapters in *Teaching English as a Second or Foreign Language* (Celce-Murcia (Ed.), 2001) .

REFERENCES

Adamson, H. D. (1993). *Academic competence: Theory and classroom practice: Preparing ESL students for content courses*. New York: Longman.

Bailey, A. L., & Butler, F. A. (2002). *An evidentiary framework for operationalizing academic language for broad application to K-12 education: A design document*. (Final deliverable to OERI, Contract No. R305B960002-02). University of California, Los Angeles: National Center for Research on Evaluation, Standards, and Student Testing (CRESST).

Bailey, A. L., Butler, F. A., LaFramenta, C., & Ong, C. (2001). *Towards the characterization of academic language* (Final deliverable to OERI/OBEMLA, Contract No. R305b60002). University of California, Los Angeles: National Center for Research on Evaluation, Standards, and Student Testing (CRESST).

Belcher, D., & Braine, G. (Eds.). (1995). *Academic writing in a second language: Essays on research and pedagogy.* Norwood, NJ: Ablex.

Benesch, S. (2001). *Critical English for academic purposes: Theory, politics, and practice.* Mahwah, NJ: Lawrence Erlbaum Associates.

Benesch, S. (Ed.). (1988). *Ending remediation: Linking ESL and content in higher education.* Washington, DC: TESOL.

Bigelow, M., & Ranney, S. (2001, May). *Learning how to keep the language focus in content-based instruction.* Paper presented at the Second International Conference on Teacher Education, University of Minnesota, Minneapolis, MN.

Blakely, R. (1997). The English language fellows program: Using peer tutors to integrate language and content. In M. A. Snow & D. M. Brinton (Eds.), *The content-based classroom: Perspectives on integrating language and content* (pp. 274–289). New York: Longman.

Brinton, D. M., & Holten, C. A. (2001). Does the emperor have no clothes? A re-examination of grammar in content-based instruction. In J. Flowerdew & M. Peacock (Eds.), *Research perspectives on English for academic purposes* (pp. 239–251). Cambridge, UK: Cambridge University Press.

Brinton, D. M., Snow, M. A., & Wesche, M. B. (2003). *Content-based second language instruction—Michigan Classics Edition.* Ann Arbor, MI: University of Michigan Press.

Brinton, D. M., Snow, M. A., & Wesche, M. B. (1989). *Content-based second language instruction.* New York: Newbury House.

Bunch, G. C., Abram, P. L., Lotan, R. A., & Valdes, G. (2001). Beyond sheltered instruction: Rethinking conditions for academic language development. *TESOL Journal, 10*(2/3), 28–33.

Butler, F. A., & Stevens, R. (2001). Standardized assessment of the content knowledge of English language learners K-12: Current trends and old dilemmas. *Language Testing, 18*(4) 409–427.

Bycina, D. (1986). Teaching language through content: English for science and technology at USC. *CATESOL News, 18*(3), 13.

Carrasquillo, A. L., & Rodriguez, V. (2002). *Language minority students in the mainstream classroom* (2nd ed.). Clevedon, UK: Multilingual Matters.

Celce-Murcia, M. (Ed.). (2001). *Teaching English as a second or foreign language* (3rd ed.). Boston: Heinle & Heinle.

Chamot, A. U., & O'Malley, J. M. (1987). The cognitive academic language learning approach: A bridge to the mainstream. *TESOL Quarterly, 21*(2), 227–249.

Cloud, N., Genesee, F., & Hamayan, E. (2000). *Dual language instruction: A handbook for enriched education.* Boston: Heinle & Heinle.

Crandall, J. (Ed.). (1987). *ESL through content-area instruction.* Englewood Cliffs, NJ: Prentice-Hall.

Crandall, J. (1994). Strategic integration: Preparing language and content teachers for linguistically and culturally diverse classrooms. *In strategic integration and language acquisition: Theory, practice, and research* (pp. 255–274). Washington, DC: Georgetown University Press.

Crandall, J. (1998). Collaborate and cooperate: Teacher education for integrating language and content instruction. *FORUM, 36*(1), 2–9.

Crandall, J., & Kaufman, D. (Eds.). (2002). *Content-based instruction in higher education settings.* Alexandria, VA: TESOL.

Cummins, J. (1981). The role of primary language development in promoting educational success for language minority students. In *Schooling and language minority students: A theoretical framework* (pp. 3–49). Sacramento, CA: Office of Bilingual Bicultural Education, California State Department of Education.

Cummins, J. (1984). *Bilingualism and special education: Issues in assessment and pedagogy.* Clevedon, UK: Multilingual Matters.

Cummins, J. (2000a). Academic language learning, transformative pedagogy, and information technology: Towards a critical balance. *TESOL Quarterly, 34,* 537–548.

Cummins, J. (2000b). Negotiating intercultural identities in the multilingual classroom. *The CATESOL Journal, 12*(1), 163–178.

Davison, C., & Williams, A. (2001). Integrating language and content: Unresolved issues. In B. Mohan, C. Leung, & C. Davison (Eds.), *English as a second language in the mainstream: Teaching, learning, and identity* (pp. 51–70). Harlow, Essex, UK: Longman.

Donley, K. M., & Reppen, R. (2001). Using corpus tools to highlight academic vocabulary in SCLT. *TESOL Journal, 10*(2/3), 7–12.

Duff, P. A. (2001). Language, literacy, content, and (pop) culture: Challenges for ESL students in mainstream classes. *Canadian Modern Language Review, 58*(1), 103–132.

Early, M. (2001). Language and content in social practice: A case study. *Canadian Modern Language Review, 58*(1), 156–179.

Echevarria, J., Vogt, M., & Short, D. J. (2000). *Making content comprehensible for English language learners: The SIOP model.* Needham Heights, MA: Allyn & Bacon.

Flowerdew, J., & Peacock, M. (Eds.). (2001). *Research perspectives on English for academic purposes.* Cambridge, UK: Cambridge University Press.

Gianelli, M. C. (1997). Thematic units: Creating an environment for learning. In M. A. Snow & D. M. Brinton (Eds.), *The content-based classroom: Perspectives on integrating language and content* (pp. 142–148). New York: Longman.

Gibbons, P. (1998). Classroom talk and learning of new registers in a second language. *Language and Education, 12*(2), 99–118.

Goldstein, L., Campbell, C., & Cummings, M. C. (1997). Smiling through the turbulence: The flight attendant syndrome and other issues of writing instructor status in the adjunct model. In M. A. Snow & D. M. Brinton (Eds.), *The content-based classroom: Perspectives on integrating language and content* (pp. 331–339). New York: Longman.

Gottlieb, M. (2000). Standards-based, large-scale assessment of ESOL students. In M. A. Snow (Ed.), *Implementing the ESL standards for pre-K-12 students through teacher education* (pp. 167–186). Alexandria, VA: TESOL.

Grabe, W., & F. Stoller. (1997). Content-based instruction: Research foundations. In M. A. Snow & D. M. Brinton (Eds.), *The content-based classroom: Perspectives on integrating language and content* (pp. 158–174). New York: Longman.

Hajer, M., & Koole, T. (2001). Introduction to the project. *Interaction in the multilingual classroom: Processes of inclusion and exclusion.* Working papers from the Dutch organization for scientific research (NWO) project. Utrecht, The Netherlands: Utrecht University, Department of Linguistics.

Hawkins, B. (2001). Supporting second language children's content learning and language development in K-5. In M. Celce-Murcia (Ed.), *Teaching English as a second or foreign language* (3rd ed.), (pp. 367–383). Boston: Heinle & Heinle.

Heyden, T. (2001). Using sustained content-based learning to promote advanced ESL writing. *TESOL Journal, 10*(4), 16–20.

Iancu, M. (1997). Adapting the adjunct model: A case study. In M. A. Snow & D. M. Brinton (Eds.), *The content-based classroom: Perspectives on integrating language and content* (pp. 149–157). New York: Longman.

Jacobs, H. H. (1990). The growing need for interdisciplinary curriculum content. In H. H. Jacobs (Ed.), *Interdisciplinary curriculum: Design and implementation* (pp. 1–11). Alexandria, VA: Association for Supervision and Curriculum Development.

Johns, A. M. (1997a). English for specific purposes and content-based instruction: What is the relationship? In M. A. Snow & D. M. Brinton (Eds.), *The content-based classroom: Perspectives on integrating language and content* (pp. 363–366). New York: Longman.

Johns, A. M. (1997b). *Text, role, and context: Developing academic literacies.* Cambridge, UK: Cambridge University Press.

Jordan, R. R. (1997). *English for academic purposes: A guide and resource book for teachers.* Cambridge, UK: Cambridge University Press.

Kasper, L. F. (Ed.). (2000). *Content-based college ESL instruction.* Mahwah, NJ: Lawrence Erlbaum Associates.

Kaufman, D. (1997). Collaborative approaches in preparing teacher for content-based and language-enhanced settings. In M. A. Snow & D. M. Brinton (Eds.), *The content-based classroom: Perspectives on integrating language and content* (pp. 175–186). New York: Longman.

Kerans, M. E. (2001). Simulating the give-and-take of academic lectures. *TESOL Journal, 10*(2/3), 13–17.

Kinsella, K. (1997). Moving from comprehensible input to "learning to learn" in content-based instruction. In M. A. Snow & D. M. Brinton (Eds.), *The content-based classroom: Perspectives on integrating language and content* (pp. 46–68). New York: Longman.

Krueger, M., & Ryan, F. (1993). *Language and content: Discipline- and content-based approaches to language study.* Lexington, MA: Heath.

Lapkin, S. (2002). Reformulation, collaborative dialogue and L2 learning: A Canadian example. *Applied Linguistics Forum, 22*(2), 1–9.

Larsen-Freeman, D. (2000). *Techniques and principles in language teaching* (2nd ed.). Oxford, UK: Oxford University Press.

Lorenz, E. B., & Met, M. (1988). *What it means to be an immersion teacher.* Rockville, MD: Office of Instruction and Program Development, Montgomery County Public Schools.

Lyster, R., & Ranta, L. (1997). Corrective feedback and learner uptake: Negotiation of form in communicative classrooms. *Studies in Second Language Acquisition, 19,* 37–66.

McKay, P. (2000). On ESL standards for school-age learners. *Language Testing, 17*(2), 185–214.

Met, M. (1998). Curriculum decision-making in content-based second language teaching. In J. Cenoz & F. Genesee (Eds.), *Beyond bilingualism: Multilingualism and multilingual education* (pp. 35–63). Clevedon, UK: Multilingual Matters.

Mohan, B. A. (1986). *Language and content.* Reading, MA: Addison-Wesley.

Mohan, B., Leung, C., & Davison, C. (2001). *English as a second language in the mainstream: Teaching, learning, and identity.* Harlow, UK: Longman.

Murphey, T. (1997). Content-based instruction in an EFL setting: Issues and strategies. In M. A. Snow & D. M. Brinton (Eds.), *The content-based classroom: Perspectives on integrating language and content* (pp. 117–131). New York: Longman.

Murphy, J. M., & Stoller, F. L. (2001). Sustained-content language teaching: An emerging definition. *TESOL Journal, 10*(2/3), 3–5.

No child left behind. (2001). Title III: Language instruction for limited English proficient and immigrant students. 107th Congress, 1st Session, December 13, 2001. (Printed version prepared by the National Clearinghouse for Bilingual Education.) Washington, DC: The George Washington University, National Clearinghouse for Bilingual Education.

Pally, M. (2000). *Sustained content teaching in academic ESL/EFL.* Boston: Houghton Mifflin.

Peterson, P. W. (1997). Knowledge, skills, and attitudes in preparing teachers for content-based and language-enhanced settings. In M. A. Snow & D. M. Brinton (Eds.), *The content-based classroom: Perspectives on integrating language and content* (pp. 158–174). New York: Longman.

Richard-Amato, P. A. (2003). *Making it happen: From interactive to participatory language teaching: Theory and practice* (3rd ed.). New York: Longman.

Richards, J. C., & Rodgers, T. S. (2001). *Approaches and methods in language teaching* (2nd ed.). Cambridge, UK: Cambridge University Press.

Rosenthal, J. W. (2000). *Handbook of undergraduate second language education.* Mahwah, NJ: Lawrence Erlbaum Associates.

Rosser, C. (1995). Anne Frank: A content-based research class. *TESOL Journal, 4*(4), 4–6.

Schleppegrell, M. (2001). Linguistic features of the language of schooling. *Linguistics and Education, 12*(4), 431–459.

Short, D. J. (2002). Language learning in sheltered social studies classes. *TESOL Journal, 11*(1), 18–24.

Short, D. J. (1998, March). *Teacher discourse in social studies.* Paper presented at the annual meeting of the American Association for Applied Linguistics, Seattle, WA.

Short, D. J. (1994). Expanding middle school horizons: Integrating language, culture, and social studies. *TESOL Quarterly, 28*(3), 581–608.

Skutnabb-Kangas, T., & Toukomaa, P. (1976). *Teaching migrant children's mother tongue and learning the language of the host country in the context of the sociocultural situation of the migrant family.* Helsinki: The Finnish National Commission for UNESCO.

Snow, M. A. (2001). Content-based and immersion models for second and foreign language teaching. In M. Celce-Murcia (Ed.), *Teaching English as a second or foreign language* (3rd ed.) (pp. 303–318). Boston: Heinle & Heinle.

Snow, M. A., & Brinton, D. (1988). The adjunct model of language instruction: An ideal EAP framework. In S. Benesch (Ed), *Ending Remediation: Linking ESL and content in higher education* (pp. 33–52). Washington, DC: TESOL.

Snow, M. A. (1998). Trends and issues in content-based instruction. *Annual Review of Applied Linguistics, 18,* 243–267.

Snow, M. A., & Brinton, D. M. (Eds.). (1997). *The content-based classroom: Perspectives on integrating language and content.* New York: Longman.

Snow, M. A., & Kamhi-Stein, L. D. (2002). Teaching and learning academic literacy through Project LEAP. In J. Crandall & D. Kaufman (Eds.), *Content-based instruction in higher education settings* (pp. 169–181). Alexandria, VA: TESOL.

Snow, M. A., & Kamhi-Stein, L. D. (1997). Teaching academic literacy skills: A new twist on the adjunct model. *Journal of Intensive English Studies, 11,* 93–108.

Snow, M. A., Met, M., & Genesee, F. (1989). A conceptual framework for the integration of language and content in second/foreign language instruction. *TESOL Quarterly, 23,* 201–217.

Solomon, J., & Rhodes, N. (1996). Assessing academic language: Results of a survey. *TESOL Journal, 5,* 5–8.

Stevens, R. A., Butler, F. A., & Castellon-Wellington, M. (2000). *Academic language and content assessment: Measuring the progress of ELLs.* University of California, Los Angeles: National Center for Research on Evaluation, Standards, and Student Testing (CRESST).

Stoller, F. L. (2002, April). *Content-based instruction: A shell for language teaching or a framework for strategic language and content learning?* Paper presented at the annual meeting of Teachers of English to Speakers of Other Languages (TESOL), Salt Lake City, UT.

Stoller, F. L., & Grabe, W. (1997). A Six T's approach to content-based instruction. In M. A. Snow & D. M. Brinton (Eds.), *The content-based classroom: Perspectives on integrating language and content* (pp. 78–94). New York: Longman.

Stryker, S. B., & Leaver, B. L. (Eds.). (1997). *Content-based instruction in foreign language education: Models and methods.* Washington, DC: Georgetown University Press.

Swain, M. (2001). Integrating language and content teaching through collaborative tasks. *Canadian Modern Language Review, 58*(1), 44–63.

Swain, M. (1988). Manipulating and complementing content teaching to maximize second language learning. *TESL Canada Journal, 6*(1), 68–83.

Swain, M., & Lapkin, S. (1998). Interaction and second language learning: Two adolescent French immersion students working together. *Modern Language Journal, 83,* 320–337.

Swales, J. M. (1990). *Genre analysis: English for academic and research settings.* Cambridge, UK: Cambridge University Press.

Swales, J. M., & Lindemann, S. (2002). Teaching the literature review to international graduate students. In A. M. Johns (Ed.), *Genre in the classroom: Multiple perspectives*. Mahwah, NJ: Lawrence Erlbaum Associates.

Tang, G. (1997). Teaching content knowledge and ESL in multicultural classrooms. In M. A. Snow & D. M. Brinton (Eds.), *The content-based classroom: Perspectives on integrating language and content* (pp. 69–77). New York: Longman.

Tedick, D. J., Jorgengen, K., & Geffert, T. (2001). Content-based language instruction: The foundation of language immersion education. *The ACIE Newsletter, 4*, 1–8. University of Minnesota: Center for Advanced Research on Language Acquisition.

TESOL. (1997). *ESL standards for pre-K-12 students*. Alexandria, VA: Author.

van Eerde, D., Hajer, M., Koole, T., & Prenger, J. (2001). Promoting math and language learning in interaction. *Interaction in the multilingual classroom: Processes of inclusion and exclusion*. Working papers from the Dutch organization for scientific research (NWO) project. Utrecht, The Netherlands: Utrecht University, Department of Linguistics.

Walqui, A. (2000). *Access and engagement: Program design and instructional approaches for immigrant students in secondary school*. McHenry, IL and Washington, DC: Delta Systems and The Center for Applied Linguistics.

Wesche, M. B. (Ed.). (2001). French immersion and content-based language teaching in Canada [Special issue]. *Canadian Modern Language Review, 58*(1).

Wesche, M. B. (1993). Discipline-based approaches to language study: Research issues and outcomes. In M. Krueger & F. Ryan (Eds.), *Language and content: Discipline- and content-based approaches to language study* (pp. 57–82). Lexington, MA: Heath.

Wesche, M. B., & Skehan, P. (2002). Communicative, task-based, and content-based language instruction. In R. B. Kaplan (Ed.), *The Oxford handbook of applied linguistics* (pp. 207–228). Oxford, UK: Oxford University Press.

Wong Fillmore, L., & Snow, C. E. (2002). What teachers need to know about language. In C. T. Adger, C. E. Snow, & D. Christian (Eds.), *What teachers need to know about language* (pp. 7–53). McHenry, IL and Washington, DC: Delta Systems Co. and The Center for Applied Linguistics.

Zamel, V., & Spack, R. (1998). Negotiating academic literacies: Teaching and learning across languages and cultures. Mahwah, NJ: Lawrence Erlbaum Associates.

39

Instructed Language Learning and Task-Based Teaching

Rod Ellis
University of Auckland

INTRODUCTION

A distinction is often drawn between 'instructed' and 'naturalistic' second language (L2) learning (see, for example, Pica, 1983). However, defining these two types of learning is problematic. In terms of *setting*, the distinction is relatively straightforward; instructed learning occurs in a classroom or, perhaps, in a self-access center, whereas naturalistic learning occurs in everyday contexts of language use where the L2 is the medium of communication. In terms of *motive*, however, the distinction is less straightforward, for in both instructional and naturalistic settings learners can choose to function as learners or users and treat the target language as an object or a tool. In terms of the *processes* involved in L2 learning, the distinction is even more problematic, as the same processes are likely to arise in both settings to a greater or lesser extent. In this chapter, instructed language learning will be taken to refer to the L2 learning that takes place in a classroom setting.

Instruction constitutes an attempt to intervene in the process of language learning. This intervention can be of two broad types. In *direct intervention*, the instruction specifies what it is that learners will learn and when they will learn it. This takes place via what White (1988) has called a Type A Curriculum, characterized by a structural syllabus consisting of a graded list of items to be learned and an accuracy-oriented methodology. In *indirect intervention*, the purpose of instruction is to create conditions where learners can learn experientially through learning how to communicate in the L2. This takes place via a Type B Curriculum consisting of a series of "tasks" that motivate communication among the classroom participants. Direct intervention is aimed at "skill-getting," an investment for future use, as Widdowson (1998) puts it. Indirect intervention seeks to integrate 'skill getting' into 'skill using,' the two occurring simultaneously. This chapter will examine research that has addressed the acquisitional outcomes of these two types of instruction.

DIRECT INTERVENTION IN L2 LEARNING

The key questions here are; (1) Do learners learn the specific L2 features/skills they receive instruction in? and (2) Are some forms of direct intervention more effective than others? These questions can be addressed by examining any level of language (pronunciation, vocabulary, grammar, discourse structure, and functions) in any of the four language skills (listening, speaking, reading, and writing). For reasons of space, this chapter will limit consideration to grammar (a traditional focus for direct interventional programs) and will consider, in particular, whether teaching grammar enables L2 learners to use the targeted features in their communicative speech.

The Effectiveness of Grammar Instruction

The first question—whether learners learn the grammatical features they are taught—is of considerable practical and theoretical importance. From a practical point of view, teachers (and policy makers) need to know whether trying to teach specific grammatical forms is worth the effort. Its theoretical significance lies in claims advanced by Krashen (1981) and Schwartz (1993) that grammar can only be acquired unconsciously through natural exposure, a view that is antithetical to a direct approach to instructional intervention. These claims were motivated originally by research that demonstrated that learners acquire grammatical features in a more or less fixed 'natural' order and also that they invariably pass through a series of transitional stages in acquiring each feature (see R. Ellis 1994, chap. 3). They are reinforced by current connectionist accounts of L2 learning (e.g., N. Ellis, 1996, 2002), according to which L2 knowledge is not represented implicitly in the form of rules but as an elaborate network of connections that is built up through massive exposure to sequences of language in context. What both the 'natural route' and the 'connectionist' view of L2 learning have in common is that acquisition is viewed as a very gradual process, involving constant restructuring of the interlanguage grammar. Such a view does not appear to be consonant with attempts to intervene directly in interlanguage development. If it takes time (often months) for a learner to fully internalize a grammatical form, what chance is there of instruction of limited duration (usually no more than a series of lessons) having any effect?

In fact, determining whether grammar instruction is effective has proven a difficult question to answer. One reason for this is that it is not clear what 'effective' means. One possible meaning is 'ability to use' but this raises the further problem of whether this refers to performance in experimentally elicited use of the target feature (e.g., a discrete-point test) or in communication (either written or oral). Another possible meaning of 'effective' is 'advancing learners along the natural route of L2 acquisition.' A third possible definition of 'effective' is 'to show awareness of the correct form.' To demonstrate that instruction is effective in this sense it is necessary to show that learners understand a grammatical form, even if they cannot use it correctly. We will explore whether instruction is 'effective' in each of these different senses.

There is now ample evidence to show that grammar instruction can help learners to perform grammatical features more accurately in experimentally elicited performance. Long (1983) reviewed a number of early studies and concluded that learners who received form-focused instruction outperformed those who did not. Norris and Ortega (2001) carried out a meta-analysis of some 51 studies that utilized either 'selected response' or 'constrained constructed response' as the measure of learning. They report an effect size of 1.46 and 1.20 respectively for these two types of measure, indicating that, overall, form-focused instruction is effective when the learning outcomes are measured in these ways. Furthermore, the beneficial effects of instruction are also durable, as evident in delayed posttests. One conclusion to be drawn from the research, then, is that learners can benefit from instruction in specific grammatical features if their goal is to perform well on discrete-point tests like the TOEFL.

The evidence relating to the effects of grammar instruction on learners' ability to use the targeted features in communicative language use (especially unplanned oral language use) is somewhat meager. This reflects the difficulty researchers have in designing instruments to elicit spontaneous use of specific L2 features (see Loscky & Bley-Vroman, 1993, for a discussion of this issue). Norris and Ortega could only locate eight studies that included a measure of 'free constructed response.' Instruction appears to have a much reduced effect when the learning outcome is measured in this way, the effect size being less than half of that for 'selected response' and 'constrained constructed response.' They note that "particular outcome measure types may result in very different observations about the effectiveness of a treatment" (p. 199). In R. Ellis (2002), I examined 11 studies that included a measure of free oral production. Instruction was found to have a significant effect in only six of these. However, this effect was also evident in delayed posttests and, in fact, in two of the studies, was stronger in these. Two conclusions are in order. First, grammar instruction does not always result in more accurate use of the targeted features in free oral production. Clearly, more research is needed to discover when instruction 'works' for communicative language use and when it does not. Second, when an effect is found it is durable.

Grammar instruction does not enable learners to 'beat' the natural route of acquisition. Studies comparing instructed and naturalistic learners (e.g., Pica, 1983; Pavesi, 1986; R. Ellis, 1989) report the same order of acquisition for grammatical morphemes and the same sequence of acquisition for syntactic structures such as English relative clauses and German word order rules. These findings led Pienemann (1985) to advance the 'teachability hypothesis', which states that for instruction to be effective it needs to target features that lie within the developmental stage next to that which the learner has already reached. Pienemann's own research (e.g., Pienemann, 1989) lent support to this hypothesis. However, a more recent study (Spada & Lightbown, 1999) challenges it. Using Pienemann's account of five developmental stages for English questions forms, they exposed learners to an input flood of question forms at Stages 4 and 5, predicting that learners at Stage 3 would be better placed to benefit from this than learners at Stage 2. However, it was the latter who benefited most from the instruction, although only by advancing to Stage 3. This study, then, indicates that instruction does not alter the natural route of acquisition but that it may not be necessary to ensure that it is fine-tuned to the proximate developmental stage of individual learners. This is encouraging to teachers as it suggests that they may not need to engage in the laborious task of identifying learners' precise developmental stages as a basis for instruction. A general conclusion of these studies is that instruction enables learners to progress more rapidly along the natural route.

Finally, the effectiveness of instruction can be gauged by its success in helping learners to understand grammatical features—that is, the extent to which they develop an explicit understanding of rules. This is usually determined either by means of a grammaticality judgment test or by asking learners to verbalize a rule. Research by Fotos (1993, 1994) indicates that both direct and indirect consciousness-raising aimed at developing explicit knowledge are effective in promoting awareness of grammatical features, both in terms of learners' ability to judge the grammaticality of sentences and also their ability to subsequently notice the features in input. Norris and Ortega (2001), however, found that the magnitude of the effect of instruction when assessed through 'metalinguistic judgment' was much less than that for 'selected response' or 'constrained constructed response' although notably higher than that for 'free constructed response.' Also, the validity and reliability of grammaticality judgment tests has been called into question (see R. Ellis, 1991a). Few studies have investigated the effects of instruction on learners' ability to verbalize grammatical rules so no conclusions can be drawn. However, there would appear to be only a weak relationship between this ability and learners' general language proficiency (Alderson, Clapham, & Steel 1997). In conclusion, the extent to which instruction can help learners to an explicit understanding of grammatical structures remains uncertain as indeed does the value of instruction directed at this type of L2 knowledge.

To summarize, the research to date indicates:

1. Grammar instruction results in greater accuracy in testlike performance.
2. However, it is much less likely to lead to improved accuracy in spontaneous oral language use.
3. Grammar instruction does not enable learners to beat the natural route but it is effective in helping them to progress more rapidly along it.
4. It may not be necessary to fine-tune grammar instruction to the learner's developmental stage.
5. Grammar instruction can contribute to learners' metalingual understanding of L2 grammar rules but doubts exist as to the utility of this kind of knowledge.
6. When grammar instruction does have an effect, this effect is durable.

The Relative Effectiveness of Different Types of Instruction

Given that direct instructional intervention has been shown to be effective, at least in the case of grammar, the next obvious question is whether some kinds of direct intervention work better than others. To answer this question it is necessary to identify a set of instructional options. Long (1991) distinguishes two broad approaches to form-focused instruction (FFI), which he refers to as 'focus-on-forms' and 'focus-on-form.' The former requires a planned approach to FFI (i.e., the prior selection of a specific form for treatment). Learners are required to treat forms as discrete entities that can be accumulated systematically one at a time. Such an approach, Long claims, is incompatible with what is known about the nature of L2 acquisition. In contrast, the latter involves attention to form in 'tasks' (i.e., activities that are primarily meaning-centered), as, for example, when a communication problem arises and attempts are made to negotiate meaning in order to resolve it. As defined by Long, then, 'focus-on-form' is a characteristic of indirect rather than direct instructional intervention. Here, therefore, we will consider only options relating to 'focus-on-forms,' reserving discussion of 'focus-on-form' to later when indirect instruction is considered. Table 39.1 describes the main focus-on-forms options.

Instruction typically involves combinations of options. For example, a fairly typical grammar lesson might begin by asking learners to read a dialogue in which examples of the form have been italicized (Implicit Instruction/Enhanced Input). This might by followed with a formal presentation of the form to be taught (i.e., Explicit Instruction/Didactic). The students could be asked to complete a number of exercises of the fill-in-the-blank kind (Production Practice/Controlled) before finally attempting a role-play to provide an opportunity to use the form they have been practicing in free production (Production Practice/Functional). In the production stages of the lesson the teacher might point out and correct any errors the students make (Negative Feedback/Explicit). However, in researching the effects of FFI, it is desirable to try to isolate the different options in order to evaluate their contribution to learning. Unfortunately, as Norris and Ortega (2001) point out, this has not always been the way that researchers have proceeded, making it difficult to draw firm conclusions about the effectiveness of specific instructional options.

A number of studies have sought to compare the relative effectiveness of explicit and implicit instruction. These were examined in Norris and Ortega's meta-analysis, with instructional treatments being coded as 'explicit' if 'rule explanation comprised

TABLE 39.1

The Main Options in Focus-on-Forms Instruction

Option	Description
1. Explicit instruction	Instruction that requires students to pay deliberate attention to the targeted form with a view to understanding it.
a. Didactic	Students are provided with an explanation of the form.
b. Discovery	Students are provided with L2 data that illustrate the form and are asked to work out how the form works for themselves.
2. Implicit instruction	Instruction that requires learners to infer how a form works without awareness.
a. Non-enhanced input	Students are asked to memorize L2 data that illustrate the form.
b. Enhanced input	The L2 data is presented to the students without any special attempt to draw their attention to the targeted form.
	The targeted form is highlighted in some way (e.g., using italics) to induce noticing.
3. Structured input	Instruction requires learners to process L2 data that has been specially designed to induce 'noticing' of the targeted form and that can only be comprehended if the targeted form has been processed.
4. Production practice	Instruction requires learners to produce sentences containing the targeted form.
a. Controlled	Students are given guidance in producing sentences containing the targeted form (e.g., by filling in blanks in sentences or transforming sentences).
b. Functional	Students are required to produce their own sentences containing the targeted form in some kind of situational context.
5. Negative feedback	Instruction consists of feedback responding to students' efforts to produce the targeted structure.
a. Implicit	The feedback models the correct form without explicitly indicating that the student has made an error.
b. Explicit	The feedback makes it clear to the student that an error has been made.

any part of the instruction' and as 'implicit' when 'neither rule presentation nor directions to attend to particular forms were part of the treatment' (p. 167). Explicit instruction proved to be significantly more effective than implicit instruction. However, they note that the measurement of learning outcomes in many of the studies favored explicit learning (i.e., in 90% of the studies they examined, learners' knowledge of the targeted structures was measured through experimentally elicited responses rather than in communicative use). They also note that the implicit treatments were typically operationalized in very restrictive ways (e.g., through instructions to learners to memorize a set of sentences) whereas the explicit treatment often involved other instructional options. For these reasons caution needs to be exercised in concluding that explicit instruction is more effective than implicit.

There is also the important question of how best to provide explicit instruction. Table 39.1 suggests a distinction between 'didactic' and 'discovery' based approaches. The former involves the direct explanation of grammar points. The latter involves the use of various types of consciousness-raising tasks (see Rutherford, 1987; R. Ellis, 1997a) that guide learners into discovering a grammatical rule by providing them with L2 data to analyze and instructions about how to set about this. A number of studies have compared these two approaches. Fotos and Ellis (1991) found that while both were effective in promoting understanding of a grammatical rule, as measured by a grammaticality judgment test, the didactic option worked best. However, they speculated that this might be because the students in this study were unfamiliar with working in groups, as was required by the discovery option. Fotos (1993) conducted a more extensive study with learners who were well rehearsed in group work. She found that both approaches worked equally well. She argues that the discovery option is to be considered preferable because it also affords opportunities for students to communicate in the target language when they do the tasks in groups. Another reason for preferring discovery tasks is that learners find them more intrinsically motivating (Mohamed, 2001). However, as I have pointed out elsewhere (R. Ellis, 1991b), consciousness-raising tasks have their limitations. Because they are directed at 'understanding' grammar, not using it, their utility rests on claims that explicit knowledge of the L2 facilitates the acquisition of implicit knowledge, which, while theoretically defensible, has not been empirically demonstrated. Also, talking about grammar may not appeal to all learners (e.g., young children).

The relative effectiveness of structured input and production practice has also attracted the attention of researchers. VanPatten (1996) argues that interlanguage development occurs as a response to learners processing input not from their efforts at production, although the latter may help them to automatize forms they have already internalized. He proposes that attempts to intervene directly in interlanguage development be accomplished through "input processing instruction." This consists of (1) explicit instruction directed at helping learners overcome 'default' processing strategies (e.g., treating the first noun in a sentence like 'The dog was bitten by Mary' as the agent of the verb) and (2) structured input as described in Table 39.1. VanPatten and his co-researchers carried out a number of studies designed to compare the effects of input processing instruction and 'traditional instruction' involving production practice. Learners receiving input-processing instruction outperformed those receiving traditional instruction on comprehension posttests and did as well on production posttests. Furthermore, the effectiveness of input processing instruction owed more to the structured input component than to the explicit instruction (VanPatten & Oikennon, 1996). Subsequent studies (e.g., Allen, 2000) have failed to show a clear advantage for structured input over production practice, whereas others (e.g., Erlam, 2001) have found that production practice that forces attention to form-meaning mappings can be more effective. VanPatten (2002), however, argues that studies that have failed to demonstrate an advantage for input-processing instruction did so either because they failed to address structures subject to default processing strategies or were methodologically flawed. Irrespective of whether input-processing instruction is superior, the research does show that the structured input option is effective in promoting learning, whether this is measured in terms of comprehension or production. This finding suggests the need to revise current approaches to grammar teaching to make fuller use of this option. In particular, structured input would seem to be an appropriate option for computer-delivered instructional materials.

Of all the options described in Table 39.1, functional grammar teaching receives the strongest empirical support. Studies by Harley (1989), Day and Shapson (1991), Lyster (1994), and Murunoi (2001) all testify to the effectiveness of this option. Furthermore, the effectiveness is evident in measures of learning derived from both testlike and more communicative performance. Also, the success of the instruction does not appear to be dependent on the choice of target form. Hawkins and Towell (1996) argue that form-focused instruction is likely to be more effective if the targeted feature is "simple and easily-explained" (p. 208) but, in fact, in some of the studies cited earlier, the target structure was highly complex. For example, Day and Shapson investigated French hypothetical conditionals and Murunoi targeted English articles, both of which are notoriously complex and difficult to learn, even as explicit L2 knowledge. Some caveats are in order, however. In many of the studies, functional production practice was combined with explicit explanation. In the case of Murunoi, functional instruction with and without explicit explanation was compared, with the former proving the more effective. Also, a feature of most of these studies is that the instruction provided was very extensive in nature. In Harley's study, for example, the instruction lasted 8 weeks and in Day and Shapson it lasted 5–7 weeks. In most teaching contexts it is difficult to imagine that teachers will have so much time to devote to a single grammatical feature.

The role of negative evidence in L2 acquisition is controversial. From one theoretical perspective it is seen as contributing significantly because learners lack the acquisitional mechanisms to learn purely from positive evidence (Bley-Vroman, 1989). Truscott (1999), however, has argued that correcting learners' errors has no effect on learners' acquisition of new L2 forms. Negative feedback has been examined in both descriptive and experimental studies. Seedhouse (2001) offers a comprehensive account of the various strategies teachers employ to repair learners' linguistic errors. He reports that teachers show a strong dispreference for direct and overt negative feedback and instead opt for various forms of indirect, mitigated feedback. In other words, teachers prefer 'implicit' to 'explicit' feedback (see Table 39.1). This raises the important question as to the relative effectiveness of these two options. Seedhouse argues that teachers would do better to choose the explicit option. He comments:

> Teachers are avoiding direct and overt negative evaluation of learners' linguistic errors with the best intentions in the world, namely to avoid embarrassing and demotivating them. However, in doing so, they are interactionally marking linguistic errors as embarrassing and problematic. (pp. 368–369)

This may offer an explanation for why negative feedback fails to effect changes in learners' interlanguages, as claimed by Truscott. However, experimental studies (e.g., Carroll & Swain, 1993) suggest that negative feedback, especially of the explicit kind, does contribute to learning. While quite a lot is known about how teachers provide negative feedback, few conclusions are currently possible about whether it works or about what kind works best.

It should be clear from this account of the research that has investigated the relative effectiveness of different options for focus-on-forms instruction that any conclusions must be tentative. The research indicates the following:

1. Explicit instruction may be more effective than implicit instruction when learning is measured in testlike performance.
2. Consciousness-raising tasks catering for discovery-based explicit instruction are as effective as didactic explicit instruction at developing explicit L2 knowledge and also afford opportunities for meaning-centered communication.
3. Irrespective of whether input-processing instruction is more effective than production-based instruction, structured input clearly contributes to L2 learning and may prove a useful option for the development of self-instructional materials.
4. Functional grammar teaching results in learning whether this is measured in testlike or more communicative performance.
5. Negative feedback may contribute to learning especially if it is pitched at a level appropriate to the learner's developmental stage.

Research on Direct Interventions and Language Pedagogy

Much of the research previously discussed was carried out to test the claims of different theories of L2 acquisition and only secondarily to address practical issues to do with teaching. As Mitchell (2000) points out, this is problematic in the current educational climate, where outcome-driven educational models predominate and policy makers want to be told what 'works.' In such a context, research that provides evidence that can be used as a basis for making instructional decisions is required. In this respect, Mitchell concludes that research that has investigated direct intervention through focus-on-forms does not measure up very well:

> ...applied linguists are not at present in a position to make firm research-based prescriptions about the detail of 'what works' in FL grammar pedagogy. There has been considerable research activity.... However, the research has been diverse in its theoretical foundations and procedures, patchy in scope, and has led to some mixed patterns of findings. (p. 296)

Borg (1998) reaches a similar conclusion but argues that the problem lies with the reliance on experimental research. He proposes that research efforts be redirected at teachers' craft beliefs about grammar teaching and their actual teaching practices. While such an approach may provide valuable insights into what constitutes 'good practice' (as teachers understand this) it will not tell us what works. For that, as Mitchell emphasizes, we need carefully designed process-product studies.

Mitchell and Borg are perhaps overly harsh on the experimental research to date. As the above review suggests, it does afford some conclusions, albeit often tentative ones. There is clear evidence that focus-on-forms is effective and there are clues as to what types work best (see the earlier summaries).

INDIRECT INTERVENTION IN L2 LEARNING

A good example of indirect intervention in L2 learning is content-based language instruction. In immersion programs (see Johnson & Swain, 1997, for reports on a sample of such programs) the L2 is used as the medium of instruction for a range of subjects in the school curriculum and so is learned as part and parcel of mastering academic content. The results of evaluations of these programs are encouraging. As Genesee (1987) documents, immersion learners achieve high levels of general language proficiency and are able to interact confidently in the L2. They also develop excellent L2 reading skills. However, their production often continues to be marked by grammatical inaccuracies and they do not acquire much in the way of sociolinguistic competence. The explanation commonly offered for this is that the classroom context does not afford sufficient opportunities for "pushed output" (Swain, 1985). For example, student output has been shown to consist of single words or short phrases with little opportunity for extended discourse. Another reason is that the students' are so focused on message content that they do not attend to form and consequently fail to acquire grammatical features that lack saliency (e.g., verb tense endings). To remedy this problem, content-based instruction was modified to include direct intervention by means of supplementary focus-on-forms instruction involving functional grammar teaching, as in Harley (1989) and Day and Shapson (1991) (see previous section). Such instruction, however, is time consuming and incompatible with the noninterventional principles of content-based instruction. For this reason, an alternative solution involving focus-on-form (i.e., attention to form in the context of meaning-centered instruction) has been proposed. Researchers have consequently turned their attention to examining what opportunities for focusing on form arise in immersion classrooms (see, e.g., Lyster & Ranta, 1997) and also the kinds of instructional activities and methodological procedures that can promote a focus-on-form (e.g., Swain, 1988).

Indirect intervention is also evident in proposals for task-based instruction. Tasks are defined as activities where (1) meaning is primary, (2) there is some communication problem to solve, (3) there is some relationship to real-world activities, (4) task completion has some priority, and (5) the assessment of the task is in terms of outcome (Skehan 1998, p. 95). However, although tasks are intended to induce a primary focus on meaning, the importance of a focus-on-form has also been emphasized. The following sections outline the rationale for task-based teaching and offer a brief review of current research.

The Rationale for Task-based Instruction

Proposals for task-based instruction arose out of the conviction that it was not possible to specify what a learner would learn in linguistic terms. Thus, as Prabhu (1987) argued, it was necessary to abandon the preselection of linguistic items in any form and instead specify the content of teaching in terms of holistic units of communication, that is, tasks. In this way, he claimed, it would be possible to teach "through communication" rather than "for communication." Prabhu's procedural syllabus was a first attempt to develop a syllabus on such grounds. The syllabus consisted of a set of tasks, sequenced according to difficulty. Interestingly, it was developed for use in secondary schools in southern India, a challenging context for what was an innovatory approach to language teaching.

A somewhat different approach to task-based teaching has been advanced by Long (see Long, 1985; Long & Crookes, 1992). Like Prabhu, Long explicitly grounds his proposal on a theory of L2 acquisition but the theory differs in one key respect. Whereas Prabhu views language acquisition as an implicit process that takes place when learners are grappling with the effort to communicate, Long emphasizes the need for learners to attend to form consciously while they are communicating—what he calls 'focus on form.' Tasks then have to be designed in ways that will ensure a primary focus on meaning but also allow for incidental attention to form. Long also advances proposals for using tasks in courses for specific purposes. He distinguishes between what he calls target tasks and pedagogic tasks and argues that to ensure the relevancy of a task-based syllabus, the starting point is a needs analysis to establish the target tasks that a specific group of learners need to be able to perform. For Long, 'task' is the ideal unit for specifying the content of specific purpose courses because it most closely reflects what learners need to do with the language.

It can be seen, then, that the rationale for task-based syllabuses draws on a variety of arguments. First and foremost it is premised on the theoretical view that the instruction needs to be compatible with the processes involved in L2 acquisition. Second, as in the case of Prabhu, the importance of learner 'engagement' is emphasized; tasks, as long as they provide a 'reasonable challenge', will be cognitively involving and motivating. Third, as in the case of Long, tasks serve as a suitable unit for specifying learners' needs and thus for designing specific purpose courses.

However, there have also been objections leveled at task-based courses. First, the central claim that learners do not learn the specific grammatical structures that they are taught through direct intervention is incorrect. In the previous section, we saw that there is clear evidence to show that instruction consisting of a focus-on-forms does result in learning, especially when this is measured in testlike performance but, also, importantly, in spontaneous oral production. The noted failure of traditional syllabuses may have had more to do with how the syllabuses were implemented (i.e., with their methodology) than with their design. It should be noted, however, that the dismissal of this claim does not necessarily invalidate task-based instruction, as this may still prove a more efficient way of promoting L2 acquisition than traditional approaches. Second, the finding that immersion program fail to achieve high levels of grammatical and sociolinguistic competence also cast doubt on the overall effectiveness of a meaning-centered approach. Sheen (1994) observes that, if immersion programs have failed in these respects despite the thousands of hours of instruction they afford, one can only be skeptical of what might be achieved by the far fewer hours available in a second or foreign language course based on tasks. Again, though, this does not invalidate task-based instruction but merely points to a limitation, which may be remediable by introducing a 'focus-on-form.' However, Sheen is right to point to lack of clear empirical support for either the effectiveness of task-based instruction or its relative superiority.

To sum up, task-based syllabuses have been promoted by SLA researchers and educationalists as an alternative to linguistic syllabuses on the grounds that (1) linguistic syllabuses are not effective in promoting acquisition and (2) task-based syllabuses conform to what is known about acquisitional processes. However, (1) has been challenged and in part at least would seem to be wrong while (2) remains a theoretical claim as yet without strong empirical support. This is not to say, however, that task-based syllabuses have no role to play in language teaching. Indeed, there are strong theoretical grounds for them (see Skehan, 1998).

Task-Based Research

The goal of task-based research is to identify "psycholinguistically motivated task characteristics" that "can be shown to affect the nature of language produced in performing a task in ways which are relevant to SL processing and SL learning" (Crookes, 1986). Research based on the Interaction Hypothesis (Long, 1996) aims to find out which types of tasks are most likely to lead to the kind of meaning negotiation hypothesized to promote language acquisition. Researchers have investigated a variety of task variables and have been able to show that tasks that are two-way as opposed to one-way (Pica & Doughty, 1985), that have split rather than shared input (Newton, 1991), and where the outcome of a task is closed rather than open (Crookes & Rulon, 1985) and divergent rather than convergent (Duff, 1986) result in higher levels of meaning negotiation. Other research has focused on the nature of the learner's participation in a task, examining whether tasks performed in small groups or in lockstep with a teacher led to greater meaning negotiation (Pica & Doughty, 1985). More recently, researchers have turned their attention to tasks that require learners to produce output. Drawing on Swain's (1985) Output Hypothesis, Izumi (2002), for example, conducted a study that found that learners engaged in a reconstruction task requiring them to produce English relative clause constructions were more likely to notice these constructions and learn them than learners who completed a comprehension task where the same constructions were graphically enhanced.

An alternative approach to investigating tasks has drawn on theories of language competence and of speech production. Skehan (1998) has suggested that language competence is comprised of lexis, including formulaic expressions such as 'I don't know,' and grammatical rules. Native speakers make use of these two different types of knowledge by means of a dual processing system, drawing on both lexicalized and grammatical processing but varying in which type they rely on in a given activity according to the communicative pressure they experience and their need to be precise. Skehan argues that when required to perform spontaneously, L2 learners are likely to depend on lexicalized processing but when required to formulate messages more precisely they will utilize their rule-based knowledge. He suggests that it may be possible to identify the design features that lead learners to place a differential emphasis on fluency (i.e., performance free of undue pauses and false starts), complexity (i.e., the use of a wide range of grammatical structures), and accuracy (i.e., the correct use of grammatical structures). Variables so far investigated include the familiarity of the information to be communicated, whether the task is dialogic or monologic, the degree of structure of the information, the complexity of the outcome and the extent to which information has to be transformed from one form to another (Skehan, 2001).

Dialogic tasks produce greater accuracy than monologic tasks. Tasks with a complex outcome promote greater complexity. Tasks where the information to be conveyed is clearly structured promote fluency.

Some researchers have based their research on Levelt's model of speech production (Levelt, 1989). This identifies three stages in speech production: (1) conceptualization, when the purpose and semantic content of a message is determined, (2) formulation, when the speaker maps grammatical and phonological features onto the preverbal message, and (3) articulation, when the phonetic plan produced by (2) is converted into actual speech. Wendel (1997) has used this model to distinguish two types of planning—strategic or offline planning (i.e., the planning that takes place when learners are given time to plan a task prior to performing it) and online planning (i.e., the planning that occurs while learners are actually performing the task). Thus, strategic planning, according to Wendel, involves conceptualization; online planning, in contrast, is directed at formulation and articulation and manifests itself through monitoring. Bygate (1996) also utilizes Levelt's model to account for what effect asking learners to repeat a task has on task performance.

The contribution that strategic, pretask planning makes to task-based performance has been examined in a number of studies. In an early study, R. Ellis (1987) found that this kind of planning resulted in increased accuracy in the use of English regular (but not irregular) past tense forms. Other studies (e.g., Crookes, 1989), however, suggest that the effects of strategic planning are more evident in enhancing fluency and complexity than accuracy. Ortega (1999) reviews a number of planning studies, concluding that the evidence that planning contributes to greater accuracy is mixed. Her own study of learners of L2 Spanish found a positive effect for noun-modifiers but not for articles. One explanation for these mixed findings is that strategic planning only leads to greater accuracy if learners have time to monitor their actual performance of the task, as suggested by Wendel (1997). Yuan and Ellis (2003) investigated this hypothesis in a study that compared the effects of strategic and online planning. They found that strategic planning resulted in greater fluency and complexity while online planning led to increased accuracy and complexity. It would seem, then, that there is a trade-off between fluency and accuracy, with learners prioritizing one or the other, depending on the kind of planning they engage in.

Not all task-based research has been motivated by theories based on a computational model of L2 learning (i.e., a model that views learning in terms of the mental processing of input and output). A number of recent studies have drawn on Vygotskian accounts of language learning. These view learning as socially constructed. When L2 learners have the opportunity to interact with other users of the language (e.g., a teacher, a native speaker, or another learner) they are able to perform functions in the language that they cannot perform by themselves. With time and practice they internalize these functions, learning to perform them independently. In this way, learning involves a progression from the inter- to the intramental as learners shift from object and other regulation to self-regulation. Vygotskian theory also emphasizes how learners shape the goals of any activity to suit their own purposes. Recently, this theoretical perspective has led to task-based studies that investigate 'scaffolding' and 'collaborative dialogue', the supportive interactions that arise when learners communicate with others (e.g., Swain, 2000) and also to studies that demonstrate how the task-as-workplan is interpreted and reshaped by learners in actual performance (Coughlan & Duff, 1994). There have also been attempts to show how learners and native speaker interlocutors vary in the way they perform a single task depending on the learners' developmental stage (Aljaafreh & Lantolf, 1994; Nassaji & Swain, 2000). Platt and Brooks (2002) discuss the notion of "task engagement" within a sociocultural theoretical framework, arguing that this enhances learners' motivation to accomplish a task and results in 'transformation' when they switch from relatively undirected to more focused activity and, thereby create a context in which learning can take place.

This review of task-based research addressed unfocused tasks (i.e., tasks designed to elicit general communicative use of the L2). However, there have also been a number of studies that have investigated focused tasks (i.e., tasks designed to elicit communicative use of specific L2 features). Newton and Kennedy (1996), for example, provide evidence to suggest that it is possible to predict the linguistic forms that will be used when particular tasks are performed. They found that the discourse genre (i.e., description versus persuasion) elicited by tasks influenced the linguistic forms used. Bygate (1999) has also demonstrated that the processing involved in performing a narrative and an argumentation task led to learners making different linguistic choices. Also, varying a task condition (i.e., shared versus split information) can influence learners' choice of linguistic forms.

By switching attention to form during the performance of a task, teachers can incorporate form-focused instruction into meaning-centered activities methodologically, rather than through task design as in the ways previously described. This branch of task-based research has been motivated by developments in SLA theory that stress the importance for acquisition of the conscious 'noticing' of forms in the input for (Schmidt, 2001). Nobuyoshi and Ellis (1993) and Ellis and Takashima (1999) demonstrated that it is possible to push learners into using a particular grammatical form (past tense) if they receive requests to clarify utterances containing an error in this structure. Other studies have examined the effects of negative feedback in the form of 'recasts' (i.e., reformulations of learners' deviant utterances or parts of them) on L2 acquisition. Doughty and Varela (1998), for example, report a study that examined the effect of recasting utterances whenever learners made an error in the use of English past tense forms in the context of reporting science experiments. They found that this treatment resulted in both improved accuracy in the use of the past tense and in movement along the sequence of acquisition for this structure. However, as Nicholas, Lightbown, and Spada (2001) conclude, the effectiveness of recasts in promoting acquisition may depend on whether it is clear to the learners that the recast is a reaction to the accuracy of the form, not the content, of their utterances. Current research is directed at discovering how recasts aid acquisition. Leeman (2003), for example, conducted a study that suggested that it is the enhanced salience of specific forms that recasts afford rather than the negative evidence following errors that is important for learning. Overall, research has shown that task procedures can be manipulated to induce the use of specific features and also that focused feedback, such as recasts, can bring about changes in learners' interlanguage grammars.

In the case of the studies referred to earlier the focus-on-form was proactive (i.e., it was predetermined to allow the researcher to investigate a specific type of intervention). However, even when no such intervention has been planned, the participants in a task may temporarily suspend attention to meaning in order to focus on form. In this case the focus-on-form is entirely incidental. It can be achieved in a number of ways: when teachers respond to learner errors (Lyster & Ranta, 1997), when they draw learners' attention to the usefulness of specific forms in the task they are performing (Samuda, 2001), or when learners themselves ask questions about form as when they collaboratively try to solve some linguistic problem in order to complete a task (Swain & Lapkin, 1998). It can arise both in the negotiation of meaning, triggered by a communication problem, or in the negotiation of form, when participants take time out from communicating to treat language as an object and function as teachers or learners rather than language users. A feature of this incidental focus-on-form is that it is extensive rather than intensive in nature. That is, within the context of a single communicative task, a number of different linguistic forms (phonological, lexical, grammatical, or discoursal) are likely to be attended to but each focus-on-form episode is only very brief. In this respect, incidental focus-on-form differs from focus-on-forms instruction, where relatively few linguistic features are treated but intensively. A key question is whether focus-on-form detracts from the overall communicativeness of a task but studies to date (e.g., Ellis, Basturkmen, & Loewen, 2001) suggest that this does not happen.

In summary, task-based research affords information about how the design of tasks and their implementation can affect learner performance and L2 acquisition:

1. The negotiation of meaning is enhanced if the information provided by the task is split and the outcome required is closed or convergent.
2. Task design can influence whether learners rely primarily on their lexicalized or rule-based knowledge of the L2 with the result that either fluency or complexity is prioritized.
3. Task design can also influence the specific linguistic forms that learners employ when they perform a task.
4. Providing opportunities for strategic planning of a task performance promotes fluency and complexity of language use. In contrast, providing time for online planning (monitoring) leads to greater accuracy.
5. A focus-on-form, directed at specific linguistic features and induced proactively into a task performance by means of the negotiation of meaning (e.g., requests for clarification and recasts), promotes L2 acquisition.
6. Incidental focus-on-form also arises naturally in task-based interactions without necessarily disturbing the communicative flow and addresses a broad range of linguistic features.

This information can assist in the development of a task-based approach to language teaching.

Research on Indirect Interventions and Language Pedagogy

There is substantial evidence from evaluations of immersion programs to suggest that indirect interventions are effective in developing L2 proficiency. As yet, there is less evidence to support task-based instruction, although there are strong theoretical grounds for its advocacy. In particular, indirect intervention, with its emphasis on learning through communication, is likely to result in linguistic knowledge that is deployable (i.e., that learners can actually access when asked to engage in real-life communication). However, there are caveats that give cause for hesitancy in recommending this instructional approach. First, it may not result in high levels of linguistic and sociolinguistic competence, as noted earlier, although this may be remediable by means of proactive and incidental focus-on-form. Second, because of its relative newness, there is no received set of principles on which to base the design of a course for indirect intervention. Third, such an approach may be too radical for some teaching contexts, especially if the teachers and students view classroom learning as necessarily analytical. Fourth, it is not clear how an indirect interventional approach can cater for self-directed language learning, as it depends very largely on social interaction. In the case of task-based research, there is a clear need for shift from laboratorylike studies to the careful evaluation of both its implementation and the learning outcomes in real classrooms.

CONCLUSION

Instruction plays a major role in both foreign and second language learning. While it may not be necessary to achieve competence in the L2 it undoubtedly helps. Nor should instructed learning be seen as a poor alternative to naturalistic learning for there is plenty of evidence to show that it is as, if not more, effective. The crucial question is, therefore, not whether instruction works but rather what kind of instruction works best. This chapter has been an exploration of this question. The research to date does not provide definite answers. It is not possible to declare that direct intervention is superior to indirect intervention or vice versa. Nor is it possible to declare that one type of focus-on-forms instruction results in better learning than another. Nor is it possible to specify how best to design a task-based course or how to implement it in ways that will maximize learning. Despite these uncertainties, the research is not without value. While it may not justify 'prescriptions' (and thus may disappoint policy makers) it does offer a number of "provisional specifications" (Stenhouse, 1975) and, as I have argued elsewhere (R. Ellis, 1997b) this is all we should expect of research. Its true value lies, perhaps, in helping teachers to understand that "second language classrooms should be characterized by a variety of activities, with an emphasis on those which engage students in meaningful interaction, but with an awareness on the part of the teacher that some attention to language form is also necessary" (Lightbown, 2000, p. 433). This may sound self-evident to many teachers but, as Lightbown points out, if this so, it is partly because research on instructed language learning has helped to make it so.

REFERENCES

Alderson, J., Clapham, C., & Steel, D. (1997). Metalinguistic knowledge, language aptitude, and language proficiency. *Language Teaching Research, 1*, 93–121.

Aljaafreh, A., & Lantolf, J. P. (1994). Negative feedback as regulation and second language learning in the Zone of Proximal Development. *The Modern Language Journal, 78*, 465–483.

Allen, L. (2000). Form-meaning connections and the French causative: An experiment in processing instruction. *Studies in Second Language Acquisition, 22*, 69–84.

Bley-Vroman, R. (1989). The logical problem of second language learning. In S. Gass & J. Schachter (Eds.), *Linguistic Perspectives on Second Language Acquisition.* Cambridge, UK: Cambridge University Press.

Borg, S. (1998). Teachers' pedagogical systems and grammar teaching: A qualitative study. *TESOL Quarterly, 32*, 9–38.

Bygate, M. (1996). Effects of task repetition: Appraising the development of second language learners. In J. Willis & D. Willis (Eds.), *Challenge and change in language teaching.* Oxford: Heinemann.

Bygate, M. (1999). Task as the context for the framing, re-framing, and unframing of language. *System, 27*, 33–48.

Carroll, S., & Swain, M. (1993). Explicit and implicit negative feedback: An empirical study of the learning of linguistic generalizations. *Studies in Second Language Acquisition, 15*, 357–366.

Coughlan, P., & Duff, P. A. (1994). Same task, different activities: Analysis of a SLA task from an activity theory perspective. In J. Lantolf & G. Appel, (Eds.), *Vygotskyan approaches to second language research* (pp. 173–194). Norwood, NJ: Ablex.

Crookes, G. (1986). Task classification: A cross-disciplinary review. Technical report No. 4. Honolulu: Center for Second Language Classroom Research, Social Science Research Institute, University of Hawaii.

Crookes, G. (1989). Planning and interlanguage variability. *Studies in Second Language Acquisition, 11*, 367–383.

Crookes, G., & Rulon, K. (1985). Incorporation of corrective feedback in native speaker/non-native speaker conversation. Technical Report No. 3. Honolulu: Center for Second Language Classroom Research, Social Science Research Institute, University of Hawaii.

Day, E., & Shapson, S. (1991). Integrating formal and functional approaches to language teaching in French immersion: An experimental study. *Language Learning, 41*, 25–58.

Doughty, C., & Varela, E. (1998). Communicative focus on form. In C. Doughty & J. Williams (Eds.), *Focus on form in classroom second language acquisition* (pp. 114–138). Cambridge, UK: Cambridge University Press.

Duff, P. (1986). Another look at interlanguage talk: Taking task to task. In R. Day (Ed.), *Talking to learn: Conversation in second language acquisition* (pp. 147–181). Rowley, MA: Newbury House.

Ellis, N. (1996). Sequencing in SLA: Phonological memory, chunking, and points of order. *Studies in Second Language Acquisition, 18*, 91–126.

Ellis, N. (2002). Frequency effects in language processing: A review with implications for theories of implicit and explicit language acquisition. *Studies in Second Language Acquisition, 24*, 143–188.

Ellis, R. (1987). Interlanguage variability in narrative discourse: Style shifting in the use of the past tense. *Studies in Second Language Acquisition, 9*, 1–20.

Ellis, R. (1989). Are classroom and naturalistic acquisition the same? A study of the classroom acquisition of German word order rules. *Studies in Second Language Acquisition, 11*, 305–328.

Ellis, R. (1991a). Grammaticality judgments and second language acquisition. *Studies in Second Language Acquisition, 13,* 161–186.

Ellis, R. (1991b). Second language acquisition and language pedagogy. Clevedon, UK: Multilingual Matters.

Ellis, R. (1994). The study of second language acquisition. Oxford, UK: Oxford University Press.

Ellis, R. (1997a). SLA research and language teaching. Oxford, UK: Oxford University Press.

Ellis, R. (1997b). Explicit knowledge and second language pedagogy. In L. Van Lier & D. Corson (Eds.), *Encyclopedia of language and education, Vol. 6: Knowledge about language.* Dordrecht, The Netherlands: Kluwer Academic.

Ellis, R. (2002). Does form-focused instruction affect the acquisition of implicit knowledge? A review of the research. *Studies in Second Language Acquisition, 24,* 223–236.

Ellis, R., & Takashima, H. (1999). Output enhancement and the acquisition of the past tense. In R. Ellis (Ed.), *Learning a second language through interaction* (pp. 173–188). Amsterdam: Benjamins.

Ellis, R., Basturkmen, H., & Loewen, S. (2001). Learner uptake in communicative ESL lessons. *Language Learning, 51,* 281–318.

Erlam. R. (2001). *A comparative study of the effectiveness of processing instruction and output-based instruction on the acquisition of direct object pronouns in L2 French.* Unpublished paper, University of Auckland, New Zealand.

Fotos, S. (1993). Consciousness-raising and noticing through focus on form: Grammar task performance versus formal instruction. *Applied Linguistics, 14,* 385–407.

Fotos, S. (1994). Integrating grammar instruction and communicative language use through grammar consciousness-raising tasks. *TESOL Quarterly, 28,* 323–351.

Fotos, S., & Ellis, R. (1991). Communicating about grammar: A task-based approach. *TESOL Quarterly, 25,* 605–628.

Genesee, F. (1987). *Learning two languages.* Rowley, MA: Newbury House.

Harley, B. (1989). Functional grammar in French immersion: A classroom experiment. *Applied Linguistics, 10,* 331–359.

Hawkins, R., & Towell, R. (1996). Why teach grammar? In D. Engel & F. Myles (Eds.), *Teaching grammar: Perspectives in higher education.* London: AFLS/CILT.

Izumi, S. (2002). Output, input enhancement, and the noticing hypothesis. *Studies in Second Language Acquisition, 24,* 541–577.

Johnson, K., & Swain, M. (Eds.), (1997). *Immersion education: International perspectives.* Cambridge, UK: Cambridge University Press.

Krashen, S. (1981). *Second language acquisition and second language learning.* Oxford, UK: Pergamon.

Leeman, J. (2003). Recasts and second language development. *Studies in Second Language Acquisition, 25,* 37–63.

Levelt, W. (1989). *Speaking: From intention to articulation.* Cambridge, UK: Cambridge University Press.

Lightbown, P. (2000). Classroom SLA research and second language teaching. *Applied Linguistics, 21,* 431–462.

Long, M. (1985). A role for instruction in second language acquisition: Task-based language teaching. In K. Hyltenstam & M. Pienemann (Eds.), *Modelling and assessing second language acquisition* (pp. 377–393). Clevedon, UK: Multilingual Matters.

Long, M. (1991). Focus on form: A design feature in language teaching methodology. In K. de Bot, R. Ginsberg, & C. Kramsch (Eds.), *Foreign language research in cross-cultural perspective* (pp. 39–52). Amsterdam: Benjamins.

Long, M. (1996). The role of the linguistic environment in second language acquisition. In W. Ritchie & T. Bhatia (Eds.), *Handbook of second language acquisition* (pp. 413–468). San Diego: Academic Press.

Long, M., & Crookes, G. (1992). Three approaches to task-based syllabus design. *TESOL Quarterly, 26,* 27–56.

Long, M. (1983). Does second language instruction make a difference? A review of the research. *TESOL Quarterly, 17,* 359–382.

Loscky, L., & Bley-Vroman, R. (1993). Grammar and task-based methodology. In Crookes, G., & Gass, S. (Eds.), *Tasks and language learning: Integrating theory and practice* (pp. 123–167). Clevedon, UK: Multilingual Matters.

Lyster, R. (1994). The role of functional-analytic language teaching on aspects of French immersion students' sociolinguistic competence. *Applied Linguistics, 15,* 263–287.

Lyster, R., & Ranta, L. (1997). Corrective feedback and learner uptake: Negotiation of form in communicative classrooms. *Studies in Second Language Acquisition, 19,* 37–66.

Mitchell, R. (2000). Applied linguistics and evidenced-based classroom practice: The case of foreign language grammar pedagogy. *Applied Linguistics, 21,* 281–303.

Mohamed, N. (2001). Teaching grammar through consciousness-raising tasks: Learning outcomes, learner preferences, and task performance. Master's thesis, Department of Applied Language Studies and Linguistics, University of Auckland.

Murunoi, H. (2001). Focus on form through interaction enhancement. *Language Learning, 50,* 617–673.

Nassaji, H., & Swain, M. (2000). A Vygotskian perspective on corrective feedback in L2: The effect of random versus negotiated help on the learning of English articles. *Language Awareness, 9,* 34–51.

Newton, J. (July, 1991). Negotiation: Negotiating what? Paper given at SEAMEO Conference on Language Acquisition and the Second/Foreign Language Classroom, RELC, Singapore.

Newton, J., & Kennedy, G. (1996). Effects of communication tasks on the grammatical relations marked by second language learners. *System, 24*, 309–322.

Nicholas, H., Lightbown, P., & Spada, N. (2001). Recasts as feedback to language learners. *Language Learning, 51*, 719–758.

Nobuyoshi, J., & Ellis, R. (1993). Focused communication tasks. *English Language Teaching Journal, 47*(2), 203–210.

Norris, J., & Ortega, L. (2001). Effectiveness of L2 instruction: A research synthesis and quantitative meta-analysis. *Language Learning, 50*, 417–528.

Ortega, L. (1999). Planning and focus on form in L2 oral performance. *Studies in Second Language Acquisition, 21*, 108–148.

Pavesi, M. (1986). Markedness, discoursal modes, and relative clause formation in a formal and informal context. *Studies in Second Language Acquisition, 8*, 38–55.

Pica, T. (1983). Adult acquisition of English as a second language under different conditions of exposure. *Language Learning, 33*, 465–497.

Pica, T., & Doughty, C. (1985). The role of group work in classroom second language acquisition. *Studies in Second language Acquisition, 7*, 233–248.

Pienemann, M. (1985). Learnability and syllabus construction. In K. Hyltenstam & M. Pienemann (Eds.), *Modelling and assessing second language Acquisition*. Clevedon, UK: Multilingual Matters.

Pienemann, M. (1989). Is language teachable? Psycholinguistic experiments and hypotheses. *Applied Linguistics, 10*, 52–79.

Platt, E., & Brooks, F. (2002). Task engagement: A turning point in foreign language development. *Language Learning, 52*, 365–400.

Prabhu, N. S. (1987). *Second language pedagogy*. Oxford, UK: Oxford University Press.

Rutherford, W. (1987). *Second language grammar: Learning and teaching*. London: Longman.

Samuda, V. (2001). Guiding relationships between form and meaning during task performance: The role of the teacher. In M. Bygate, P. Skehan, & M. Swain (Eds.), *Researching pedagogic tasks: Second language learning teaching, and testing* (pp. 119–114). Harlow, UK: Longman.

Schmidt, R. (2001). Attention. In P. Robinson (Ed), *Cognition and second language instruction*. Cambridge, UK: Cambridge University Press.

Schwartz, B. (1993). On explicit and negative data effecting and affecting competence and linguistic behavior. *Studies in Second Language Acquisition, 15*, 147–163.

Seedhouse, P. (2001). The case of the missing "no"; The relationship between pedagogy and interaction. *Language Learning, 51*, Supplement 1, 347–385.

Sheen, R. (1994). A critical analysis of the advocacy of the task-based syllabus. *TESOL Quarterly, 28*, 127–157.

Skehan, P. (1998). *A cognitive approach to language learning*. Oxford, UK: Oxford University Press.

Skehan, P. (2001). Tasks and language performance assessment. In M. Bygate, P. Skehan, & M. Swain (Eds.), *Researching pedagogic tasks: Second language learning, teaching, and testing* (pp. 167–185). Harlow, UK: Longman.

Spada, N., & Lightbown, P. (1999). Instruction, first language influence, and developmental readiness in second language acquisition. *The Modern Language Journal, 83*, 1–22.

Stenhouse, L. A. (1975). *An introduction to curriculum research and development*. London: Heinemann.

Swain, M. (1985). Communicative competence: Some roles of comprehensible input and comprehensible output in its development. In S. Gass & C. Madden (Eds.), *Input in second language acquisition* (pp. 235–252). Rowley, MA: Newbury House.

Swain, M. (1988). Manipulating and complementing content teaching to maximize second language learning. *TESL Canada Journal, 6*, 68–83.

Swain, M. (2000). The output hypothesis and beyond: Mediating acquisition through collaborative dialogue. In J. Lantolf (Ed), *Sociocultural theory and second language learning* (pp. 97–114). Oxford, UK: Oxford University Press.

Swain, M, & Lapkin, S. (1998). Interaction and second language learning: Two adolescent French immersion students working together. *Modern Language Journal, 82*, 320–337.

Truscott, J. (1999). What's wrong with oral grammar correction? *Canadian Modern Language Review, 55*, 437–456.

VanPatten, B. (1996). *Input processing and grammar instruction in second language acquisition*. Norwood, NJ: Ablex.

VanPatten, B. (2002). Processing instruction: An update. *Language Learning, 52*, 755–803.

Vanpatten, B., & Oikennon, S. (1996). Explanation versus structured input in processing instruction. *Studies in second language acquisition, 18*, 495–510.

Wendel. J. (1997). *Planning and second language production*. Unpublished doctoral dissertation, Temple University, Japan.

White, R. (1988). *The ELT curriculum*. Oxford, UK: Blackwell.

Widdowson, H. (1998). Skills, abilities, and contexts of reality. *Annual Review of Applied Linguistics, 18*, 323–333.

Yuan, F., & Ellis, R. (2003). The effects of pretask planning and online planning on fluency, complexity, and accuracy in L2 monologic oral production. *Applied Linguistics, 24*, 1–27.

40

Discourse-Based Approaches: A New Framework for Second Language Teaching and Learning

Marianne Celce-Murcia
University of California, Los Angeles
Elite Olshtain
Tel Aviv University

PURPOSE/FOCUS

The main objective of this chapter is to propose that discourse-based approaches to second language teaching and learning should be central to the process of enabling learners to become competent and efficient users of a new language. While learning another language, students need to develop discourse skills in that language; to function in new contexts and in new interpersonal relations; and to attend to linguistic, cultural, and social factors that may be completely unfamiliar. Modern language pedagogy is constantly searching for new ways to facilitate this developmental process; this chapter discusses a framework designed to serve this aim.

The chapter focuses primarily on the responsibilities that teachers, practitioners, and curriculum developers need to take in order to work within a discourse framework. Our position is based on the necessity for such a framework if the field is going to fully integrate the recent trend toward returning to a 'focus on form' within communicative language teaching. This trend began with Long's work (1983, 1991), was further expanded in Doughty and Williams (1998), and continues to spur new research in the field (Ellis, 2000; Ellis, Basturkmen, & Loewen, 2001). This chapter shows that focus on form, which is primarily meaning focused, can best be achieved within a discourse framework that is pragmatically driven.

Before we can discuss discourse-based approaches to language teaching, we need to agree on a definition of discourse. What is discourse? It is difficult to define discourse concisely. We propose the following working definition. Discourse is:

> ...an instance of spoken or written language that has describable internal relationships of form and meaning that relate coherently to an external communicative function or

729

purpose and a given audience/interlocutor. Furthermore, the external function or purpose can only be determined if one takes into account the context and participants (i.e., all the relevant situational, social, and cultural factors) in which the piece of discourse occurs. (Celce-Murcia & Olshtain, 2000, p. 4)

It is our position that discourse and context are critical notions for all aspects of language pedagogy and all areas of research and development having to do with language teaching and learning. We reflect this philosophy in our discussions of discourse-based approaches to language pedagogy here and elsewhere (Celce-Murcia & Olshtain, 2000; Olshtain & Celce-Murcia, 2001).

In this chapter we propose to do the following:

1. Show how discourse-based approaches have developed from two earlier strands of research; namely, work in discourse analysis and in communicative approaches to language teaching and learning.
2. Show how a number of so-called controversies can be usefully re-envisioned and resolved with reference to discourse-based approaches.
3. Argue that discourse-based approaches impact all aspects of language instruction (teaching materials, course design and content, teaching procedures, assessment of learner achievement, etc.).

HOW DISCOURSE-BASED APPROACHES FIT WITHIN CURRENT METHODOLOGY

Discourse-based approaches have developed from two prior strands of research: (1) work in discourse analysis, and (2) work in communicative approaches to language teaching and language learning. Over the past 30 years, discourse analysis has developed in part as a reaction to the sentence-level paradigm, long dominant in the influential school of theoretical linguistics developed by Chomsky (1957, 1965, 1972). Both anthropological linguists such as Hymes (1967, 1972), who invented the term "communicative competence," and socially oriented linguists like Halliday (1994)—often in collaboration with Hasan (e.g., Halliday & Hasan, 1976, 1989)–have challenged the narrowness of Chomsky's model of language and the innate mechanisms that he posits for language acquisition. Instead, they have argued that language has social and cultural origins that help us understand its form, function, and acquisition.

Some discourse analysts have dealt exclusively with oral data (e.g., Schegloff, Ochs, & Thompson, 1996) whereas others have dealt primarily with written texts (e.g., Swales, 1990; Hoey, 1991). In principle, discourse analysis can deal with all modes of human communication (including spoken, written, gestural, and nonverbal); individual researchers have had specific analytic preferences, giving rise to a number of approaches to discourse analysis such as genre analysis (e.g., Swales, 1990; Hyland, 2002), conversation analysis (e.g., Sacks, Schegloff, & Jefferson, 1974; Atkinson & Heritage, 1984), rhetorical structure theory (e.g., Mann & Thompson, 1988), cohesion analysis (e.g., Halliday & Hasan, 1976), and critical discourse analysis (Fairclough, 1995; Pennycook, 1995; Luke, 2002). What all of these approaches have in common is that they analyze entire coherent segments of language, not simply sentences taken out of context and viewed in isolation (as is the case in Chomskyan linguistics). This means that the focus of concern in discourse analysis has been features of language that one examines over stretches of discourse, such as how topic continuity is maintained, how reference to entities and to temporal frames is maintained, how ellipsis is to be accounted for, how textual connections (grammatical and lexical, explicit and implicit) should be described, how stance and identity are constructed through discourse, and so on. Grammar (i.e., sentence structure and morphology) is relevant to the extent that it contributes to the understanding and description of such concerns (Celce-Murcia, 1991, 2002).

Proponents of communicative language teaching developed their proposals to teach language as communication and for communication (e.g., Brumfit & Johnson, 1979; Widdowson, 1978) in reaction to the failure of "building block" methods of language teaching such as grammar-translation and audiolingualism. Building block methods hold that if you teach sounds and letters—that form words and morphological inflections, which in turn form sentences—learners can then use these bits and pieces of language to communicate. The past (and current!) failures of such approaches, along with some of the early work in discourse analysis, initially led some language teaching methodologists (e.g., Krashen, 1981) to argue that it would be best to drop all explicit teaching of language structures (building blocks) in favor of focusing on communication. Materials were then produced that were organized around notions such as time, space, number, and so forth, and social functions such as requests, apologies, complaints, and the like. (van Ek, 1976; Wilkins, 1976) rather than grammatical structure. A geat deal of attention was given to developing communicative activities and tasks, exposing learners to authentic materials, teaching performance-enhancing strategies to learners, and focusing instruction on the use of the target language to communicate messages or to learn content of some sort in the belief that the structures of the target language would be acquired as a by-product of such instruction.

The results of early communicative methodology and classical immersion education, both of which focused on content rather than form, demonstrated that such approaches produce learners who have good receptive skills but whose production is fluent yet inaccurate (Harley, 1989; Larsen-Freeman & Long, 1991). In other words, language learners participating in such programs do NOT acquire the structures of the target language to the same extent that children do when learning their first language and the resulting structural by-product that they do acquire is often highly imperfect—especially at the morphological level (Lightbown & Spada, 1999).

Such failures indicate that language teachers need to understand the complex and integrated nature of communicative competence, which consists minimally—Hymes' model is much more complex—of linguistic competence, sociocultural competence, discourse competence, and strategic competence (Canale, 1983). When viewed as an integrated whole, these competencies are not independent and unordered. Rather the core competence is discourse competence, with sociocultural competence (knowledge of social factors, cultural norms, and other pragmatic information that influences choice and sequence of language forms) providing the requisite top-down background knowledge and with linguistic competence (the building blocks) providing the bottom-up resources. Strategic competence (Canale & Swain, 1980; Celce-Murcia, Dörnyei, & Thurrell, 1995) refers to how well language users can deploy the knowledge and resources at their disposal—along with communication strategies—in order to communicate their intended meanings or interpret their interlocutor's messages. Discourse competence—the core competence—is an integrated ability that one needs in order to make use of one's sociocultural and linguistic competence to select or interpret words, phrases, and sentence structures that produce coherent and cohesive segments of language that appropriately communicate an intended meaning to a specific audience.

Given that discourse is the central competency if one's pedagogical objective is communicative competence, pedagogical discourse analysis must become central in all subdisciplines contributing to language pedagogy (i.e., methodology, language teacher training, materials development, syllabus design, second language acquisition research, classroom research, and language assessment).

IMPORTANT DEVELOPMENTS IN LANGUAGE PEDAGOGY: CURRENT CONTROVERSIES

In this section we discuss a number of so-called pedagogical controversies. However, we do not juxtapose the positions that others have taken in the past in order to argue for one option over the other; instead, in each case, we view the two options as endpoints on continua in the discourse framework—both endpoints contributing to a new integrated approach to language teaching, grounded in discourse.

Fluency and Accuracy

In the preceding section we pointed out that the students enrolled in classical immersion education programs, which teach content (but not form) in the second language, become fluent but inaccurate users of their target language over time. The opposite result is also possible: Many learners in building-block approaches can perform fairly well on standardized tests like the TOEFL (Test of English as a Foreign Language, developed and administered by the Educational Testing Service, Princeton, New Jersey) yet are unable to engage in a simple conversation in the target language with anything approaching normal fluency (i.e., interacting according to target language conventions and speaking comprehensibly at an average rate without long pauses or undue hesitation). Of course, there are also many language learners who are neither accurate nor fluent when using their second language—even after many years of instruction. To achieve the goal of training more second language learners who are both fluent and reasonably accurate, it is imperative that professionals adopt an approach in which they work at the discourse level but can, as needed, deal explicitly with any area that is causing problems (pronunciation, vocabulary, grammar, culture, rhetoric, etc.). After the teacher deals with the problem(s) that impede clear communication, the students can then return to the production and/or reception of the discourse that the activity or task requires. (It may, of course, be useful for the teacher to prepare the students linguistically and/or culturally prior to a challenging task and/or to deal with selected problems at different stages while the students are doing the task.)

Comprehensible Input and Comprehensible Output

Krashen (1981) is a language teaching methodologist in the communicative pedagogy camp who has argued that the only requirement for language acquisition is the learner's exposure to (and intake of) a great deal of comprehensible input in the target language. In other words, the more one listens to or reads materials in the target language that one can understand, the more one acquires of the target language. However, Swain (1985) and Swain and Lapkin (1998), among others, have shown that the truest indicator of language acquisition is the ability of the learner to produce comprehensible output, that is, to speak and write messages in the target language that are comprehensible to a specified recipient while the learner is engaging in a communicative activity. This means that learners must be given many opportunities to interact in their second language and to practice their productive as well as their receptive language skills in meaningful contexts at the level of discourse. The discourse level is where language comprehension, production, and acquisition take place (they do not take place at the level of the sound, word, or sentence taken in isolation). In reality, both comprehension (i.e., interpretation of speaker/writer message and intent) and production (i.e., constructing spoken or written messages that convey one's intended communication) are important facets of language teaching in discourse-based approaches (Celce-Murcia, 1995a, 1995b).

Implicit and Explicit Learning/Teaching

Another controversy in language pedagogy has been the debate over whether the language building blocks (and, by extension, also cultural information, learning strategies, and patterns of sequential organization in discourse) should be taught implicitly or explicitly. Implicit pedagogy exposes learners to discourse that is naturally (or artificially) rich in the forms or features that the teacher wants the learner to acquire. Explicit pedagogy makes the learners aware of the target forms or features via explanation, rules, or special highlighting that the teacher provides in the context of appropriate discourse. Research and practice suggest that, in general, younger learners and low proficiency learners may benefit more from implicit instruction (Celce-Murcia, 1985) whereas older and more advanced learners can benefit more from explicit instruction (Lightbown & Spada, 1999; Larsen-Freeman & Long, 1991). However, learners at any age or level are different with respect to these pedagogical practices, which suggests that by focusing on discourse the teacher can satisfy those learners preferring implicit strategies, but also, by zooming in to deal with details within the context of the discourse being interpreted or produced, the teacher will satisfy those learners in need of more explicit instruction.

Top-down and Bottom-up Processing

Discourse processing models that use the notions of top-down and bottom-up processing have been used widely in describing the reading process (e.g., Rumelhart, 1977; Stanovich, 1980). However, we see these notions as being applicable to each language skill if the skills are taught from a discourse perspective. Thus top-down processing involves contextual factors such as sociocultural knowledge and task assessment for producing or interpreting discourse, whereas bottom-up processing are the productive or interpretative choices one makes regarding the words, phrases, and sentence structures comprising the discourse of the task. At the discourse level, effective performance of each language skill demands that the user monitor both top-down and bottom-up knowledge: Is my message coherent and understandable to the listener(s)/potential reader(s)?—top down. Is my pronunciation understandable and not a source of confusion to the listener(s)?—bottom up. Can I understand the gist of what this writer has written?—top down. Can I understand the words that my teacher has underlined in the passage I am reading?—top down and bottom up!

The preceding example is instructive because it shows us that much of the time discourse processing is simultaneously top-down and bottom-up (Grabe, 1991). The student who asks such a question can best resolve it by using bottom-up strategies such as word recognition, part of speech recognition, word decomposition for meaning, and so on. He or she should also use top-down strategies such as contextual cues, considering the general subject matter of the passage, and the like. A strategic integration of top-down and bottom-up processing will improve any skill; thus it is ironic that reading skill instruction has often been dominated by methods that are either exclusively bottom-up (i.e., phonics) or exclusively top-down (i.e., whole language). Discourse-based approaches allow teachers to help learners process language using both top-down and bottom-up methods judiciously.

Cognitive and Sociocultural Approaches to Language Pedagogy

Perhaps the teaching of the writing skill is where one can observe most clearly the differences between a cognitive and a sociocultural approach to language pedagogy. Researchers who favor a cognitive approach (Flower, 1972; Olson, 1977; Ong, 1982) espouse techniques such as doing background reading, outlining, and careful rhetorical organization prior to drafting a piece of writing. Researchers who favor a sociocultural approach (Myers, 1987; Nystrand, 1982) espouse techniques such as oral brainstorming, group discussions, negotiation of audience, and so on prior to drafting a piece of writing, and they also encourage peer feedback and revision in response to such input.

By gearing writing pedagogy to the discourse level, both of these perspectives can be accommodated (Johns, 1997). It is very useful to read relevant materials on a topic before one engages in writing on that topic. It is also useful to discuss one's ideas and to hear the ideas of others prior to writing. Writing that is done by a lone individual tends to involve a great deal of cognition and reflection. Writing that is done as a collaborative task by two or more writers involves more interaction and social activity. Both types of writing benefit from acknowledging that producing an effective piece of writing is a process that should involve preparation, multiple drafts, input from peers and/or teachers, and so on. Ideally, the input that learners receive on a piece of writing is both top-down (e.g., your title doesn't make sense) and bottom-up (e.g., the verb tense is wrong here) so that they can improve their written discourse at all levels before the writing task is considered complete.

Authentic and Adapted Materials

The communicative approach to language teaching has long maintained that learning materials should be authentic and natural; such materials have not been generated for purposes of language teaching but for other communicative purposes. Authentic materials can come from many different sources such as newspapers, magazines, books, stories, maps, charts, graphs, plane/train/bus schedules, comic strips/books, cartoons, ads, menus, recipes, radio/TV broadcasts, movies, and so on. Although there are copyright issues involved in using some types of authentic materials, teachers—if they fully acknowledge the source—can generally use such materials in their own classroom for a specific purpose (i.e., not for profit or publication unless explicit written permission is given). However, such adaptation takes time and thus teachers pressed for time often resort to using textbooks that contain artificial language constructed by the author(s) for specific pedagogical purposes. Dialogues and stories, two widely used discourse-level materials, can be either authentic or artificial.

We recommend that all language learning materials be as authentic as possible. However, some authentic materials are simply too complex for lower proficiency learners. In such cases, we appeal to Ur's (1984) notion of "imitation authentic" materials. This means that the teacher should start with some authentic discourse (a recorded dialogue or a recorded or written story) and then make adaptations that will not change the overall meaning or organization of the message conveyed but that will make the material more accessible to the students who will be using it to learn and practice their second language. When learners are advanced, it is neither necessary nor desirable for teachers to make any such changes. Advanced learners can and should use unsimplified authentic materials as the basis for interpreting and producing discourse in the target language.

IMPLEMENTATION OF DISCOURSE-BASED APPROACHES AND SUPPORT FOR THE AUTHORS' POSITION

Discourse-based approaches to language teaching allow for target language engagement that focuses on meaning and real communication. Such real communication can, of course, be carried out in speech or in writing with a variety of communicative goals. Learners of different age groups and different levels of language proficiency should have, according to such an approach, many opportunities for natural exposure to the target language during the course of study, as well as many opportunities to use the language for meaningful purposes.

Our approach is based on a core language curriculum that takes into consideration the linguistic, sociocultural, and pragmatic functions of language. As such, it is compatible with two currently important influences in current language pedagogy: focus on form (Doughty & Williams, 1998) and pragmatics (Kasper & Blum-Kulka, 1993). Thus, while placing adequate emphasis on language form and its relation to communicative purposes, our approach also enhances pragmatic understanding of the relevant social and cultural contexts within which communication takes place.

Language learning can occur in instructed or natural settings. Our approach is most relevant to instructed settings where there is a planned curriculum (or where a curriculum develops within a given instructional program) and where practitioners take responsibility for the teaching process and the teaching environment. Furthermore, students in such settings are expected to develop awareness of the role they need to undertake if the process is to be successful. The instructional setting can be within a school, at the workplace, or in a course offered in the afternoon or evening for people who enroll based on their personal interests.

We will first seek support for our position in the focus-on-form literature. According to Long (1991), engagement in meaning has to precede understanding of linguistic form; it is only after meaning is understood that the function of any linguistic form can be grasped. Since our approach is discourse-based and focused on given pieces of discourse within relevant contexts, meaning precedes form by definition. Whether we are dealing with a written text for a specific purpose or whether we are enacting a role-play activity that prepares learners for a given type of natural interaction in the real world, meanings are always discussed and focused on before the forms are explained and/or practiced. A discourse-based approach leads to grammatical knowledge that is well embedded in pragmatics and context.

In trying to understand how pragmatic features relate to grammatical knowledge, we note that many scholars have viewed pragmatics as an autonomous area. In our approach, however, there is a close link between pragmatics and grammar since the focus is on discourse and communication. Following Bardovi-Harlig (1999), we examine the relation between pragmatics and grammar carefully and encourage teachers and learners to become aware of this relation.

Thus, for example, an encounter with progressive and perfect aspect used within a narrative told in the past tense can be facilitated using an authentic piece of discourse such as the following:

"The Case of Koko"

1. In the 1980s researchers at Stanford University were trying
2. to teach American Sign Language to Koko, a female gorilla.
3. Koko was well cared for and was surrounded by interesting objects.
4. Her caretakers continually exposed her to signs
5. for the foods and toys in her environment...
6. One day she was hungry but couldn't find any bananas.
7. She went to the researcher and made a good approximation
8. of the sign for 'banana.'
9. Koko was rewarded with a banana and the research team knew
10. that she had made the connection
11. between a sign and the object it represented.

(Celce-Murcia & Larsen-Freeman, 1999, p. 173)

Here the main story line is presented in the simple past tense while background information is signaled by use of the progressive aspect (lines 1 and 2); the climax or moral of the story is signaled by use of the perfect aspect (lines 10 and 11). Simply reading and understanding the story allows learners to identify the main plot, the background information, and the climax as important features of the narrative. Subsequently, the learners can be led to realize that the tense-aspect forms used in the story are related to these three narrative functions. Such teaching/learning, which is embedded in discourse and context, is likely to help learners eventually become both fluent and accurate users of the target language.

This example illustrates that our position combines exposure to authentic language with focus on form and that it requires explicit learning and explicit pedagogy (see also Celce-Murcia & Hilles, 1988; Hinkel & Fotos, 2002). Instruction provides shortcuts to understanding and internalizing new knowledge that eventually leads to more effective production. This is particularly true for older and more advanced learners, as was mentioned earlier. However, if incorporated into a discourse-based approach, instruction evolves naturally from the negotiation of meaning in discourse and can easily be adjusted to the age of the learner and his or her level of knowledge. DeKeyser (1995) found that explicit teaching of grammar rules was most effective when students induced their own rules based on discourse and contextual information. We suggest, therefore, that language instructors focus on form in contextualized discourse followed by explicit instruction that encourages learners to discover the rules. It is our belief, for example, that even in classically problematic cases such as that of speakers of Japanese trying to understand and acquire the English article system (Butler, 2002), consistent focus on discourse and context can facilitate the acquisition of such elusive forms.

Age and level of knowledge may also be relevant to preferences related to emphasis on pragmatics and grammar. As Kasper and Rose (2002, p. 190) point out, "... while the acquisitional direction from pragmatics to grammar characterizes the early (especially untutored) stages of pragmatic development, the reverse appears to be the case with more advanced learners who 'have grammar.'" Discourse-based approaches allow the teacher to shift from pragmatics to grammar as learners advance in their acquisition of the language.

Discourse-based approaches favor the continuing integration of top-down and bottom-up processing. This can best be illustrated in lessons that teach students to read for information. As Johns (1994) claims, when reading for information in a second language, students need to access the information and thus tend to concentrate on the message rather than the code. Yet, according to our position, when the message is not clear to readers or when they need to confirm comprehension as they move along through the text, bottom-up strategies are very important in activating learners' knowledge of the code to resolve such difficulties.

The following is an example of a short passage taken from a reader for advanced ESL learners (Olshtain, Feuerstein, & Schcolnik, 1988: 21):

On Origin and Species
Robert W. Langacker (1974)

1 It has sometimes been maintained that primitive peoples speak primitive languages.
2 In fact, however, there is no correlation between the degree of cultural advancement
3 and complexity of linguistic structure. The language of primitive people can be every
4 bit as complex and rich in expressive power as any European language. Anything that
5 can be said in one language can be said in any other, though perhaps more clumsily.
6 Claims that 'primitive' languages have very small vocabularies, that they have no grammar,
7 that most of their words are onomatopoetic, that they cannot express abstract ideas,
8 and so on are just plain false. The Eskimos have words for specific varieties of snow
9 but no generic, more abstract term (like our 'snow') that embraces all

10 varieties of it. This does not mean that they are incapable of abstract thought
11 or that their language is impoverished; it simply means that snow is more
12 important to them than to us, or that their linguistic categorization in this area
13 of experience is more detailed than ours.

For this particular passage, the focus on the title that readers are typically told to activate may not be very helpful for top-down processing. Instead, the teacher should guide the students to read the first sentence (i.e., the topic sentence) in order to find out that the passage is really about so-called primitive languages. Since the major aim when reading such an expository text is to gain new information—in this case "What do we know about so-called primitive languages?"—the students will read the text and try to get the facts. Yet, sooner or later, they will need to relate the meaning of bottom-up, language-specific features to the stance of the author, for example, the use of the present perfect passive verb form and the meaning of the verb maintain (a position or claim) along with the use of the adverb sometimes. It is the selection of these linguistics features by the writer that alerts the reader to the fact that the writer does not agree with the claim encoded in the 'that' clause in the opening statement. Similarly, the use of the two conjunctive adverbs "In fact, however, ..." to start the second sentence signals an opposing position that the writer is about to present, which refutes the position stated in the first sentence. The discussion of the manner in which these linguistic features serve to open the passage and signal information flow will help readers to develop metacognitive strategies using both top-down and bottom-up processing and to become more effective readers.

For discourse-based approaches to reading, both text-pragmatics (Coulthard, 1994, p. 104) and text-semantics are important at every level. Text-pragmatics describe the interactional relationship between the writer and the reader within discourse, while text-semantics focus on information structure within the text. Grammatical features of reference and logical sequence are key elements in signaling text structure and need to be acquired as parts of any discourse unit.

McCarthy and Carter (1994) suggest that the use of text-frames for teaching English as a second or foreign language is compatible with a discourse-based approach since text-frames are a tool not only for elucidating the macrostructure of a text but also for teaching a variety of internal features of the text. In the previous reading passage, the text could be presented in terms of text-frames indicating: (a) some claims/statements are made by people (sentence 1); (b) there is evidence that refutes these claims (sentence 2); (c) the facts are (lines 3–5); and therefore the claims (lines 6–8) are false; (d) Eskimos present a good example (lines 8–10) of the facts presented in (c), and (e) there is a good explanation (lines 10–13) that shows why (a) is not acceptable. At each such frame in the information structure, the grammatical features should be related to the writer's position. Such an approach can further enhance the development of efficient reading skills.

In this section of the chapter we have tried to show how discourse-based approaches have bearing on the different areas of language learning/teaching and how they are compatible with a focus-on-form position combined with a focus-on-pragmatics stance. What needs to be added is that discourse-based approaches also underlie a view of language curriculum design that places the social context of learning and language use at the center: "A discourse-oriented curriculum (Celce-Murcia & Olshtain, 2000, p. 185) places special emphasis on three areas: context, text types, and communicative competence."

The following presents a model developed with reference to the three main areas mentioned: context, text types, and communicative goals. The model is appropriate for multilingual societies or communities (examples are discussed in detail in Olshtain & Nissim-Amitai, in press). In a multilingual context, curriculum considerations need to respect heritage and ethnic languages on the one hand, while ensuring proficiency and high-level literacy in mainstream languages on the other. These considerations are needed to ensure the learners' social mobility via the mainstream language and to enhance group and individual identity via maintenance of the home language. The discourse-based approach is particularly relevant to such contexts.

There is no doubt that one's language plays a central role in one's identity and feelings of belonging; the language also represents a culture and a host of discourse worlds that are compatible with that culture. When a school aims to develop and implement a multicultural curriculum, it is important to plan a system for the sharing of discourse worlds among the various language groups. Such sharing can ensure respect and appreciation for the different cultures in the community and promote positive views regarding otherness.

Let us assume that we are talking about a small ethnic group in a larger community, who speak language X at home and within the family context but use language Y, the mainstream language, for school activities and all other communicative purposes with the community at large. They also use language Z (English or another language of wider communication) for more international communication. A discourse-based curriculum for this population would be sensitive to the communicative needs the students have in each of the three languages. It would draw content from discourse worlds typical to the three languages and would incorporate this content using text types and learning contexts that reflect real situations outside the classroom. A discourse-based investigation of the social, cultural, and linguistic functions of different text types in the three languages would be the basis for curriculum planning.

With respect to narratives, for instance, it would be important to establish those features typical of how stories are told, what type of interpretations are expected of the reader, what expectations the writer or speaker may have with regard to the impact of the story, what background knowledge is assumed, and what is left for the reader or listener to supply from his or her own experience. It is exposure to such textual and pragmatic features that can truly enrich the world of discourse for all learners in a multicultural/multilingual setting.

Since it is obvious that from a practical point of view one cannot aim at equal language proficiency in all the languages used in the multilingual context, it is very important to define a threshold level that the curriculum will aim at for each language that is compatible with the communicative needs of the learners. How such a threshold level is defined for each language will depend mainly on the patterns of language use in society. Here it is obvious that a discourse-based approach to curriculum design is vital to the decision-making process. The most important goal of a multiculutral/multilingual curriculum is to allow the graduates of the program the degree of social mobility and language choice that suits their personal aspirations.

In sum, context, text types, and communicative goals are the cornerstones not only of curriculum development but of a discourse-based approach to language pedagogy. Teachers, textbook writers, language testers, and other related practitioners need to draw on discourse analysis and attend to these cornerstones when planning and implementing language programs.

CONCLUSIONS/FUTURE DIRECTIONS

In view of the preceding discussion, we feel that there should be some new emphases in language teaching and research:

New teaching priorities should include:

1. Adapting the curriculum (materials, content, procedures, assessment) to the communicative needs of the learners, which involves making discourse analysis an integral part of needs assessment.

2. Designing programs and using discourse-based materials that emphasize the skills and the language that the learners truly need in the target language.
3. Defining realistic and explicit expectations regarding the levels of ability and fluency learners should achieve (as opposed to some abstract level of language proficiency, e.g., a specific score on the TOEFL); this involves making discourse analysis an integral part of language testing.

Some current approaches to language teaching/learning definitely qualify as discourse-based approaches, if properly implemented, such as English for specific purposes (e.g., Johns & Price-Machado, 2001), literature-based approaches (e.g., McKay, 2001), content-based and immersion instruction (e.g., Snow, 2001), and experiential and negotiated language learning (e.g., Eyring, 2001). Note that in this chapter we have consistently referred to discourse-based approaches in the plural since many different types of language courses are compatible with our discourse-based framework: There is no one single discourse-based approach.

There have been a number of books arguing for the importance of discourse in language teacher education (Hatch, 1992; McCarthy, 1991; McCarthy & Carter, 1994; Nunan, 1993; Celce-Murcia & Olshtain, 2000). There have also been recent major efforts to make discourse analysis an integral part of language assessment (see McNamara, Hill, & May, 2002, and Young, 2002, for developments in applying discourse analysis to oral assessment and Connor & Mbaye, 2002, for a discourse-based perspective on writing assessment).

Research questions for which we need better answers include:

1. How best can teachers be trained (or retrained) to implement a discourse-based approach? How much discourse analysis do they need? What kind? What happens to them in the process of change?
2. How can careful analysis of classroom language or pair/groupwork in progress enhance our understanding of the teaching/learning process?
3. Are learners better able to transfer what they learn in the classroom to the real world using discourse-based approaches? Do they take better responsibility for their own learning?
4. Do discourse-based approaches lead to better language ability and/or increased motivation to use the language?

We have begun to address some of these issues and to answer some of these questions in this chapter. Likewise, many researchers have begun to make inroads in some of these research areas (see McGroarty, 2002). However, a great deal of work still needs to be done, and we encourage colleagues who are convinced of the value of discourse-based approaches to second language teaching to contribute to the ever-growing collection of teaching suggestions and research findings in this area.

REFERENCES

Atkinson, J. M., & Heritage, J. (Eds.) (1984). *Structures of social action: Studies in conversation analysis.* Cambridge, UK: Cambridge University Press.

Bardovi-Harlig, K. (1999). Exploring the interlanguage of interlanguage pragmatics: A research agenda for acquisitional pragmatics. *Language Learning, 49,* 677–713.

Brumfit, C., & Johnson, K. (1979). *The communicative approach to language teaching.* Oxford, UK: Oxford University Press.

Butler, Y. G. (2002). Metalinguistic knowledge and English article use. *Studies in Second Language Acquisition, 24*(3), 451–480.

Canale, M. (1983). From communicative competence to communicative language pedagogy. In J. Richards & R. Schmidt (Eds.), *Language and communication* (pp. 2–27). London: Longman.

Canale, M., & Swain, M. (1980). Theoretical bases of communicative approaches to second language testing and teaching. *Applied Linguistics, 1*(1): 1–47.

Celce-Murcia, M. (1985). Making informed decisions about the role of grammar in language teaching. *TESOL Newsletter, 29*(1): 9–12.

Celce-Murcia, M. (1991). Discourse analysis and grammar instruction. *Annual Review of Applied Linguistics, 11*, 135–151.

Celce-Murcia, M. (1995a). Discourse analysis and the teaching of listening. In G. Cook & B. Seidlhofer (Eds.), *Principle and practice in applied linguistics: Studies in honor of H. G. Widdowson* (pp. 363–377). Oxford, UK: Oxford University Press.

Celce-Murcia, M. (1995b). On the need for discourse analysis in curriculum development. In P. Hashemipour, R. Maldonado, & M. van Naerssen (Eds.), *Studies in language learning and Spanish linguistics: Festschrift in honor of Tracy D. Terrell* (pp. 200–213). New York: McGraw-Hill.

Celce-Murcia, M. (2002). Why it makes sense to teach grammar in context and through discourse. In E. Hinkel & S. Fotos (Eds.), *New perspectives on grammar teaching in second language classrooms* (pp. 119–134). Mahwah, NJ: Lawrence Erlbaum Associates.

Celce-Murcia, M., Dörnyei, Z., & Thurrell, S. (1995). Communicative competence: A pedagogically motivated model with content specifications. *Issues in Applied Linguistics, 6*, 5–35.

Celce-Murcia, M., & Hilles, S. (1988). *Techniques and resources in teaching grammar.* Oxford, UK: Oxford University Press.

Celce-Murcia, M., & Larsen-Freeman, D. (1999). *The grammar book: An ESL/EFL teacher's course,* (2nd ed.) Boston: Heinle & Heinle.

Celce-Murcia, M., & Olshtain, E. (2000). *Discourse and context in language teaching: A guide for language teachers.* New York: Cambridge University Press.

Chomsky, N. (1957). *Syntactic structures.* The Hague, Netherlands: Mouton.

Chomsky, N. (1965). *Aspects of the theory of syntax.* Cambridge, MA: MIT Press.

Chomsky, N. (1972). *Language and mind,* (2nd ed.) San Diego: Harcourt Brace.

Connor, U., & Mbaye, A. (2002). Discourse approaches to writing assessment. *Annual Review of Applied Linguistics, 22*, 263–278. New York: Cambridge University Press.

Coulthard, M. (Ed.). (1994). *Advances in written text analysis.* London: Routledge & Kegan Paul.

DeKeyser, R. M. (1995). Learning second language grammar rules: An experiment with a miniature linguistic system. *Studies in Second Language Acquisition, 17*(3), 379–403.

Doughty, C., & Williams, J. (Eds.). (1998). *Focus on form in classroom second language acquisition.* Cambridge, UK: Cambridge University Press.

Ellis, R. (2000). Making the classroom acquisition rich. In R. Ellis (Ed.), *Learning a second language through interaction,* (pp. 211–230). Amsterdam: Benjamins.

Ellis, R., Basturkmen, H., & Loewen, S. (2001). Preemptive focus on form in the ESL classroom. *TESOL Quarterly, 35*(3), 407–432.

Eyring, J. (2001). Experiential and negotiated language learning. In M. Celce-Murcia (Ed.), *Teaching English as a second or foreign language,* (3rd ed). (pp. 333–344). Boston: Heinle & Heinle.

Fairclough, N. (1995). *Critical discourse analysis: The critical study of language.* London: Longman.

Flower, L. S. (1972). Reader-based prose: A cognitive basis for problems in writing. *College English, 41*(1), 19–37.

Grabe, W. (1991). Current developments in second language reading research. *TESOL Quarterly, 25*(3), 375–406.

Halliday, M. A. K. (1994). *An introduction to functional grammar,* (2nd ed.). London: Edward Arnold.

Halliday, M. A. K., & Hasan, R. (1976). *Cohesion in English.* London: Longman.

Halliday, M. A. K., & Hasan, R. (1989). *Language, context, and text: Aspects of language in a sociosemiotic perspective.* Oxford, UK: Oxford University Press.

Harley, B. (1989). Functional grammar in French immersion: A classroom experiment. *Applied Linguistics, 10*(3), 331–359.

Hatch, E. (1992). *Discourse and language education.* New York: Cambridge University Press.

Hinkel, E., & Fotos, S. (Eds.). (2002). *New perspectives on grammar teaching in second language classrooms.* Mahwah, NJ: Lawrence Erlbaum Associates.

Hoey, M. (1991). *Patterns of lexis in text.* Oxford, UK: Oxford University Press.

Hyland, K. (2002). Genre: Language, context, and literacy. *Annual Review of Applied Linguistics, 22*, 113–135. New York: Cambridge University Press.

Hymes, D. (1967). Models of the interaction of language and social setting. *Journal of Social Issues, 23*(2), 8–38.

Hymes, D. (1972). On communicative competence. In J. B. Pride & J. Holmes (Eds.), *Sociolinguistics: Selected readings* (pp. 269–293). Harmondsworth, UK: Penguin.

Johns, A. M. (1997). *Text, role, and context: Developing academic literacies.* Cambridge, UK: Cambridge University Press.

Johns, A. M. & Price-Machado, D. (2001). English for specific purposes: Tailoring course to student needs—and to the outside world. In M. Celce-Murcia (Ed.), *Teaching English as a second or foreign language,* (3rd ed.) (pp. 43–54). Boston: Heinle & Heinle.

Johns, T. (1994). The text and its message. In M. Coulthard (Ed.), *Advances in written text analysis* (pp. 102–116). London: Routledge & Kegan Paul.

Kasper, G., & Blum-Kulka, S. (1993). *Interlanguage pragmatics.* New York: Oxford University Press.

Kasper, G., & Rose, R. (2002). *Pragmatic development in a second language.* Language Learning monograph series. Oxford, UK: Blackwell.

Krashen, S. D. (1981). *Second language acquisition and second language learning.* Oxford, UK: Pergamon.

Langacker, R. (1974). *Language and its structure.* New York: Harcourt Brace.

Larsen-Freeman, D., & Long, M. (1991). *An introduction to second language acquisition research.* London: Longman.

Lightbown, P., & Spada, N. (1999). *How languages are learned* (2nd ed.). Oxford, UK: Oxford University Press.

Long, M. H. (1983). Does second language instruction make a difference? A review of research. *TESOL Quarterly, 17*(3), 359–382.

Long, M. H. (1991). Focus on form: A design feature in language teaching methodology. In K. de Bot, R. Ginsberg, & C. Kramsch (Eds.), *Foreign language research in cross-cultural perspective* (pp. 39–52). Amsterdam: Benjamins.

Luke, A. (2002). Beyond science and ideology critique: Developments in critical discourse analysis. *Annual Review of Applied Linguistics, 22,* 96–110. New York: Cambridge University Press.

Mann, W., & Thompson, S. A. (1988). Rhetorical structure theory: A framework for the analysis of texts. *Text, 8*(3), 243–281.

McCarthy, M. (1991). *Discourse analysis for language teachers.* Cambridge, UK: Cambridge University Press.

McCarthy, M., & Carter, R. (1994). *Language as discourse: Perspectives for language teaching.* New York: Longman.

McGroarty, M. (Ed.). (2002). *Annual review of applied linguistics,* Volume 22. New York: Cambridge University Press.

McKay, S. (2001). Literature as content for ESL/EFL. In M. Celce-Murcia (Ed.), *Teaching English as a second or foreign language,* (3rd ed). (pp. 319–332). Boston: Heinle & Heinle.

McNamara, T., Hill, K., & May, L. (2002). Discourse and assessment. *Annual review of applied linguistics, 22,* 221–242. New York: Cambridge University Press.

Myers, M. (1987). *The shared structure of oral and written language and the implications for teaching reading, writing, and literature.* In J. R. Squire (Ed.), *The dynamics of language learning* (pp. 121–146). Urbana, IL: ERIC.

Nunan, D. (1993). *An introduction to discourse analysis.* Harmondsworth, UK: Penguin.

Nystrand, M. (1982). Rhetoric's "audience" and linguistics' "speech community": Implications for understanding writing, reading, and text. In M. Nystrand (Ed.), *What writers know* (pp. 1–28). New York: Academic Press.

Olshtain, E., & Celce-Murcia, M. (2001). Discourse analysis and language teaching. In D. Schiffrin, D. Tannen, & H. E. Hamilton (Eds.), *The handbook of discourse analysis* (pp. 707–724). Oxford, UK: Blackwell.

Olshtain, E., Feuerstein, T., & Schcolnik, M. (1988). *Cloze for reading comprehension.* Tel Aviv: Am Oved.

Olshtain, E., & Nissim-Amitai, F. (in press). Curriculum decision making in a multilingual context. *International Journal of Multilingualism, 1*(1), Clevedon, UK: Multilingual Matters.

Olson, D. R. (1977). From utterance to text. *Harvard Educational Review, 47,* 257–281.

Ong, W. (1982). *Orality and literacy.* London: Methuen.

Pennycook, A. (1995). *Cultural politics of English as an international language.* London: Longman.

Rumelhart, D. E. (1977). Toward an interactive model of reading. In S. Dornic (Ed.), *Attention and performance.* (Vol. 6, pp. 573–603). New York: Academic Press.

Sacks, H., Schegloff, E. A., & Jefferson, G. (1974). A simplest systematics for the organization of turn-taking in conversation. *Language, 50*(4), 696–753.

Schegloff, E. A., Ochs, E., & Thompson, S. A. (Eds.). (1996). *Interaction and grammar.* Cambridge, UK: Cambridge University Press.

Snow, M. A. (2001). Content-based and immersion models for second and foreign language teaching. In M. Celce-Murcia (Ed.), *Teaching English as a second or foreign language,* (3rd ed). (pp. 303–318). Boston: Heinle & Heinle.

Stanovich, K. E. (1980). Toward an interactive-compensatory model of individual differences in the development of reading fluency. *Reading Research Quarterly, 16*(1), 32–71.

Swain, M. (1985). Communicative competence: Some roles of comprehensible input and comprehensible output in its development. In S. M. Gass & C. G. Madden (Eds.), *Input in second language acquisition* (pp. 235–254). Rowley, MA: Newbury House.

Swain, M., & Lapkin, S. (1998). Interaction and second language learning: Two adolescent French immersion students working together. *The Modern Langue Journal, 82,* 320–337.

Swales, J. (1990). *Genre analysis: English in academic and research settings.* Cambridge, UK: Cambridge University Press.

Ur, P. (1984). *Listening and language learning.* Cambridge, UK: Cambridge University Press.

van Ek, J. A.(1976). *The threshold level for modern language learning in schools.* London: Longman.

Widdowson, H. G. (1978). *Teaching language as communication.* Oxford, UK: Oxford University Press.

Wilkins, D. (1976). *Notional syllabuses.* Oxford, UK: Oxford University Press.

Young, R. (2002). Discourse approaches to oral language assessment. *Annual Review of Applied Linguistics, 22,* 243–262. New York: Cambridge University Press.

41

Computer-Assisted Language Learning

Carol A. Chapelle
Iowa State University

In 1983 at the TESOL Convention in Toronto, Canada, a relatively small group of technology enthusiasts met to discuss professional issues concerning the use of technology for language teaching and learning. Out of that meeting came a decision to refer to this area as "computer-assisted language learning," or CALL. In 1983 the issue of technology in L2 teaching was marginal at best to the profession of L2 teaching as a whole. In the years since the 1983 meeting, technology issues in L2 teaching have spread from the margins, and in the minds of some, are central to current theory and practice in L2 teaching. Even those who do not see technology as a central concern would probably agree that applied linguists need to recognize the ways in which technology affects their work.

As CALL has moved from the margins into the mainstream, the acronym that was agreed on by a small number of people in 1983 has been modified, contested, and discarded by some in what Rose calls "an ongoing power struggle among various factions to privilege their meanings and interpretations above those of others" (Rose, 2000, p. 8). Whatever the political and intellectual shortcomings of the acronym in the ever-changing world of information and communication technologies, this acronym is used in institutions within the profession such as journals and professional organizations to denote the broad range of activities associated with technology and language learning. More important than the specific acronym used to denote this activity is the need to conceptualize and investigate technology-based pedagogy in a way that can inform practice. In this chapter, I will outline the reasons that some applied linguists argue that technology is central to the concerns of the discipline today and I will discuss issues of CALL pedagogy and evaluation.

THE ROLE OF TECHNOLOGY

Applied linguists working in language teaching and research routinely draw on computer technology for a variety of purposes to the point that technology becomes integral to applied linguists' concerns such as communication and language learning. In a paper that problematizes the seeping of technology into the mainstream language-related activity, Bruce and Hogan (1998) portray a world in which the technology is an invisible but integral aspect of language use, and therefore where knowledge of technology is assumed of anyone who wishes to participate. Their point is that language professionals need to recognize how technology is deployed strategically by the competent language user if they are to teach the language learner about and through technology. As Cummins (2000) put it, "we should acknowledge the fundamental changes that IT is bringing to our societies and seek ways to use its power for transformative purposes" (Cummins, 2000, p. 539).

What are the fundamental changes that technology has brought and will bring to society? There is no shortage of speculation on this question. See, for example, Warschauer (2000) for speculation related to English language teaching. However, those who attempt to conceptualize the world of technology take different perspectives. The technologist sees rapid advances in technological developments that transform all aspects of life, especially communication and education. In the future vision of technologist Kurzweil (1999), more communication will take place between humans and computers than will take place between humans, in part due to advances in technologies for language recognition. A social pragmatist moderates this perspective with anecdotes about how technology really works—or fails to work—in the real world, and with analysis of how human communication is accomplished within organizations (Brown & Duguid, 2000). The critical analyst takes still another perspective, viewing technology as a force that is neither neutral nor inevitable, and therefore requires careful analysis and deliberate action. The plea of the critical analyst is for educators to move beyond a shallow, technically oriented discussion of technology in education and society to analysis of the values inherent in the use of technology for communication and education (Bowers, 2000).

Implications for applied linguists can be found somewhere within the mix of these diverse perspectives. The technologist argues persuasively that teachers and researchers should be educated about technological possibilities that could improve or change their work, and that the changes are sweeping and rapid. At the same time, the social pragmatist perspective reminds us not to be so focused on the future that we fail to see today's reality: Real options for technology in a particular setting need to be conceptualized in view of the experience of others and in view of teachers' context and experience. The critical perspective adds that teachers and researchers should be critically aware of the connection between technology and culturally bound ideologies. What the three diverse perspectives share is a conviction that technology is a force to be dealt with, particularly by people concerned with communication, business, education, and cultural implications of seemingly neutral practices. The impact of technology in applied linguistics can be seen concretely through examination of some of the differences that it makes for language learners and language teachers.

Language Learners

Recent publications in applied linguistics (e.g., Rassool, 1999; Crystal, 2001) have pointed out that the English language that learners use on the Internet is different in some important ways from what they needed to be able to use in the past. Crystal analyzed the registers that he calls "Netspeak," concluding that "[t]he electronic medium ... presents us with a channel which facilitates and constrains our ability to communicate in ways that are fundamentally different from those found in other semiotic situations" (Crystal, 2001, p. 5). The language that is required in the technology-shaped registers of English use suggests that the English that learners need is different from what it was before these new semiotic situations were created through the introduction of e-mail, discussion lists, chats, and the like.

Different registers for language use directly implies that the communicative language ability for the 21st century is systematically changing. As Rassool concludes from her analysis of the language in the world of technology, "[u]ltimately, communicative competence refers to the interactive process in which meanings are produced dynamically between information technology and the world in which we live..." (Rassool, 1999, p. 238). Accordingly, Warschauer suggests that rather than skill in reading and writing, language learners need to acquire competence in "reading/research" and writing/authorship" (Warschauer, 2000, p. 521): "We cannot simply choose our tools (i.e., to write longhand, use a typewriter, a word processor, or e-mail) in order to be literate participants. Instead, the technology chooses us; it marks us as full, marginal, or nonparticipating..." (Bruce & Hogan, 1998, p. 271).

For many learners, the opportunities opened through communication on the Internet have sparked new motivation for using the target language with peers, who are readily accessible (Lam, 2000). As a consequence, these new registers created through technology and the communicative language ability required for engaging in them successfully are anything but obscure and remote to the lives of language learners. Instead they are the vehicle through which learners can express themselves and receive genuine responses to their contributions.

Language Teachers

Language teachers need to concern themselves with the language needs of their learners, and in some cases, even to introduce learners to the range of potential activities for language practice. At the same time, technology is changing the jobs of language teachers through the changes it prompts in the language itself, the opportunities for studying language, and the options available for teaching language.

The language. Technology is only one impetus for the enormous and rapid changes in the English language that are occurring today. In a forward-looking set of readings called *Analyzing English in a Global Context* (Burns & Coffin, 2001), the authors explore the phenomenon of language change. The technology that greases the wheels of globalization is noted by at least one author in that volume, who notes "... with increasing use of electronic communication much of the social and cultural effect of the stability of print has already been lost, along with central "gatekeeping" agents such as editors and publishers who maintain consistent, standardized forms of language" (Graddol, 2001, p. 27). The case is more dramatically expressed and more thoroughly studied for English than it is for other languages, but the point for all language teachers is that the new forms of electronic communication are creating the need for new forms at all linguistic levels, and therefore conventions are being quickly adopted, making the subject we teach more of a moving target than it ever has been.

The study of language. The study of language resulting in authoritative grammars was for many years accomplished through a combination of observation and reflective analysis, relying on native speakers' judgments. In English, Longman's authoritative descriptive grammar of English (Quirk et al., 1972) was based on such a methodology. The recent Longman grammar (Biber, et al., 1999) is based on empirical analysis of electronic corpora. Replacing intuition-based approaches with data-based approaches puts the native and non-native speaker of English on more even ground when it comes to researching English grammar. Moreover, the view of grammar that the corpus linguist gets, Conrad (2000) predicts, will have other important implications for language teaching.

Tasks for learners. Three important changes in language teaching are evident from the introduction of technology. First, the range of tasks that teachers can develop for their learners has expanded dramatically from the in-class and homework tasks that comprise most language teaching syllabi to a range of tasks for learning through computer-mediated communication (such as e-mail or chats) and those entailing interaction between the learner and the computer (such as listening with hypermedia support or concordancing). The new technology-based tasks stretch the former boundaries of registers in which written and spoken language typically occur, and expand the potential participants in any task (Salaberry, 2000; Murray, 2000). Second, technology-based language testing is changing the character of language tests in ways that are important for the classroom (Roever, 2001). Whereas in the past some learners might question the value of some CALL activities, many such activities are now seen as helpful in preparing for high-stakes tests that are delivered online (Taylor et al., 1999). This is only one of the many implications of computer-assisted testing for language teaching. Third, a look at any of the journals on technology and language teaching will demonstrate that language teachers use the technology not only for teaching but also for investigating their learners' use of the software (e.g., Allum, 2002).

The Profession

The changes in language use and language teaching have implications for how and what future teachers are taught in programs for teacher education. Critics of the ways in which technology is introduced in teacher education point out the need to go beyond mechanical aspects of how to make Web pages, for example, to help students develop a deep understanding of the many roles and meanings of technology in education (e.g., Bowers, 2000). In language education the lessons would include at least critical analysis of the characteristics of electronic communication and cultural implications of computing. Reflecting on an investigation of computer-mediated communication in an MA TESOL class, Kamhi-Stein notes the importance of the concrete experience future teachers have while they are students:

> [I]f ESL teachers are to use technology effectively for teaching in the future, they must use it for learning while they are students. Limiting technology experiences to one course or to one area of teacher preparation is insufficient for developing teachers who can use technology creatively and flexibly. (Kamhi-Stein, 2000, p. 424)

Kamhi-Stein's approach is clearly an important component in an overall education that needs to provide students with opportunities to gain knowledge about how to develop Web pages, to critically reflect on and analyze technology in the classroom and in society particularly as it affects language learners, and to learn the lessons of the profession about the development, use, and evaluation of technology for language learning.

CALL PEDAGOGY

The expanding presence of technology in L2 use, L2 teaching, and L2 teacher education has continually provided impetus for developing pedagogy that takes advantage of technology. One logical place to begin would be to look toward the research on L2 classroom teaching and instructed SLA to seek principles that might apply to CALL. However, doing so reveals significant gaps in what a CALL pedagogy would need relative to the insights offered by classroom SLA research. The design and use of CALL can be more like classroom materials than like classroom teaching, but the pedagogy associated with teaching materials is somewhat less sophisticated than one would like as a basis for CALL. Moreover, CALL activities can and probably should be different from books and other traditional materials, and therefore pedagogy should be conceived differently too. A third area that might be considered in formulating CALL pedagogy is the research and practice that comes from past experience in CALL that has attempted to identify evidence for potentially beneficial features of instruction.

A promising approach for seeking some middle ground comes from researchers who develop principles for L2 teaching based on principles of L2 acquisition. Pica describes the basis for such a middle ground between materials developers and SLA researchers as based on their interests in the cognitive and social processes of L2 learning:

> From the cognitive perspective, among the most prominent [interests] are L2 comprehension, planning, and production; motivation; and attention to, and awareness of, L2 meaning and form. Social processes include various forms of communication and interaction, ranging from collaborative dialogue to instructional intervention, with mediation through negotiation of meaning. (Pica, 1997, p. 56)

CALL pedagogy has been articulated on the basis of these social and cognitive concerns about L2 learning (Chapelle, 1998; Doughty & Long, 2002). For example, within Doughty and Long's approach, one methodological principle specifies that learners should be provided with rich input (rather than impoverished input that might result from simplified texts). This principle might be put into practice in a variety of ways, but in CALL the suggestion is that the use of corpora and concordancing could be used to provide such input. Other principles provide guidance about how the teacher would have the learner work with the corpora in task-based learning.

Aspects of CALL pedagogy are in the process of being developed through this type of work, and through research attempting to identify the most effective ways of operationalizing the many possibilities for input and interaction that CALL offers. The basic assumption in CALL pedagogy is that the learners should be working with texts and on tasks that require them to attend to the meaning of the language. Some components of pedagogy that have been explored beyond the "meaning first" principle deal with how learners can be prompted to attend to particular aspects in the linguistic input, and how interactions can help learning.

Getting Learners to Notice

One hypothesis that has come from theory and research is that as learners work on meaning-focused tasks, they need to notice the language to have any hope of learning it (Long, 1996; Gass, 1997; Skehan, 1998). The strongest form of this hypothesis suggests "... that subliminal language learning is impossible, and that [what might be learned] is what learners consciously notice" (Schmidt, 1990, p. 149). This noticing hypothesis has been investigated with mixed results in classroom instruction and in paper-based learning materials (Doughty & Williams, 1998). In CALL, however, the opportunities for prompting noticing are different. For example, in one CALL study a linguistic form (the relative clause) was highlighted to help learners notice this form in a text that learners were reading for meaning (Doughty, 1991). In addition, the program provided interaction help with the relative clauses. Another found vocabulary gains for second language learners when they had access to hyperlinked annotations, which provided the opportunity not only to notice the vocabulary that they had trouble with, but also to get help (Chun & Plass, 1996). In these studies, the learners were not only directed to notice the form, but they were also given the opportunity to receive clarification or explanation of the form, consistently and on demand.

Another CALL study compared the opportunity for noticing alone with the opportunity for noticing with help. DeRidder (2002) investigated the conditions under which learners acquired vocabulary from four versions of a reading, each of which varied the ways in which the learners were prompted to notice the vocabulary. One text contained glossed words that were also highlighted on the screen. In a second text, the words were glossed words but there was no highlighting. A third text contained highlighted words without glosses, and the fourth contained no highlighting or glosses. One would assume that the learners would notice the words that were highlighted, but results indicated that highlighting alone was not related to acquisition of vocabulary (DeRidder, 2002); in order to make a difference the highlighted words also needed to be glossed.

Another way of prompting noticing and perhaps learning of vocabulary is through repetition of a grammatical form or lexical phrase. Studies of CALL have suggested that vocabulary repeated in the input is more likely to be acquired by the learner (e.g., Kon, 2002; Desmarais, Duquette, Renié, & Laurier, 1998), but these results were found in post hoc analysis, and ideally future research could design materials specifically intended to offer more evidence in addition to guidance concerning the number of repetitions and would be ideal.

What Kind of Input Modification?

A second hypothesis that comes from research on classroom materials and classroom-based tasks is that modification of the linguistic input will enhance comprehension and therefore has the potential of affecting acquisition. In research based on paper materials, modification has meant changing the original text either through simplification, elaboration, or marginal glosses. The research has indicated a clear advantage for elaborations (i.e., adding to the text) over simplification for higher level comprehension, that is, inference rather than comprehension of facts from the text (Yano, Long, & Ross, 1993). This finding is useful as a starting point for CALL, but the issue is different because a choice does not need to be made between the original text and another version.

> In a hypermedia environment, the learner can have access to the authentic text in addition to whatever form of help is needed to clarify the meaning. Since the help is provided dynamically in *addition to the text rather than instead of it*, it would seem appropriate for CALL pedagogy to reinterpret results from classroom research to investigate principles of input enhancement for CALL. (Chapelle, 2003. p. 52)

In CALL, therefore, the problem is not to decide whether to simplify or elaborate the input, but rather to explore any means available to help the learner to comprehend the input. In CALL, this means that a wide array of options exist including images, L1 translation, L2 dictionary definitions, and simplification. Findings across a number of studies indicate that this type of modification of linguistic input in CALL helps learners to acquire the target vocabulary and grammatical forms (e.g., Hegelheimer, 1998). However, the ways in which hypertext is used to modify the input is an issue that requires more careful investigation. A paper-based study comparing methods of annotation provided some useful findings in this regard. Watanabe (1997) compared vocabulary annotation techniques by asking learners to give L1 definitions of words that they were supposed to have learned while reading. He concluded that "[e]ven if explanations are inserted for unfamiliar words [i.e., through elaborative annotations], and the explanations are comprehensible, unless the students notice the connections between the two, effective learning cannot be expected" (p. 303). This conclusion, which is consistent with other studies of modification (e.g., Chaudron, 1983), may indicate the need for local word and phrase-level annotations in many cases, and exploration of ways of representing complex syntactic information in a way that is clarifying to learners.

Investigating the Effects of Modified Input

The fascinating array of options offered by hypermedia input modifications needs to be investigated in research that identifies ideal pedagogical strategies, but to do so, research methods are needed to document and analyze the choices that learners make. The protypical research design is quasi-experimental, comparing the achievement of learners who have been given materials with one type of modified input to that of learners who have been given materials with another type of modification or no modification. The problem with such research for hypermedia is that learners do not necessarily take advantage of the hypermedia options made available to them. Placing learners in a condition in which hypermedia is available for them to use to obtain modified input does not mean that they will choose to do so. In CALL research, therefore, some researchers attempt to document the learners' interaction with the materials. For example, in a study by Plass, Chun, Mayer, and Leutner (1998), each time learners selected one of the hypermedia annotations available to them while they were reading, the computer recorded the selection. The researchers were then able to correlate annotation selection with performance on individual words for which selections had been made. The results indicated that the more types of annotations (i.e., both visual and verbal) learners looked up, the better they tended to do on the words on the posttest.

Conceptualizing Interaction in CALL

Many of the findings in SLA and classroom research center around the idea that interaction is valuable for language development. However, this work has focused primarily on interaction among learners, teachers, and proficiency language users. Suggestions to adapt insights from this research to learner-computer interaction (e.g., Chapelle, 1997) meet with concern by those who consider the latter to be so different from the former to draw any links (Salaberry, 1999; Harrington & Levy, 2001). Ellis' (1999) discussion of interaction and the theorized reasons for its value is useful in sorting out the underlying explanations from the form of observable interactions. Ellis (1999) distinguishes the interaction that is "used to refer to the interpersonal activity that arises during face-to-face communication" (p. 3) with that which "can also refer to the intrapersonal activity involved in mental processing" (p. 3). Both types of interaction can take place in CALL tasks as the computer is used for a medium of communication or as a means of providing meaningful linguistic input. However, the computer can also act as the partner with which the learner interacts. Table 41.1 summarizes the types of interaction and the three perspectives outlined by Ellis.

With the potential interactions and their benefits laid out, it becomes possible to draw on the construct(s) of interaction to theorize and investigate the value of various types of CALL activities. Indeed, a number of studies have applied the insights from the interaction hypothesis, sociocultural theory, and depth of processing theory to the study of various CALL tasks. Based on theory about the value of modified input, Hsu (1994) investigated the extent to which requests for input modification in a listening task were related to improvement in learners' listening comprehension of specific phrases in the input. She found moderate correlations between requests and improvement as measured on a dictation test. Belz (2001) drew on sociocultural theory to investigate learners' participation in language classes linked between the United States and Germany. Guided by the practices of sociocultural researchers, Belz examined transcripts of the learners' interactions, projects, interviews, and observations to identify factors in the sociocultural setting that affected the important aspects of the practice that the learners were expected to engage in. These examples of research

TABLE 41.1

Benefits of Three Types of Interaction from Three Perspectives Based on Ellis, 1999 (from Chapelle, 2003)

		Perspectives on the Value of Interaction		
Basic types of interactions		Interaction hypothesis	Sociocultural theory	Depth of processing theory
Inter-	between people	Negotiation of meaning	Co-constructing meaning	Prompting attention to language
	between person and computer*	*Obtaining modified input*	*Obtaining help for using language*	Prompting attention to language
Intra-	within the person's mind	Attending to linguistic form	Stimulating internal mental voice	Cognitive processing of input

*Ellis (1999) did not discuss interaction between person and computer.

drawing on theoretical perspectives on the value of interaction suggest alternative ways of tackling evaluation of CALL.

EVALUATION OF CALL

Most CALL developers and users 20 years ago thought of evaluation of CALL in terms of checklists used to check off particular ideal characteristics of a CALL activity (Susser, 2001). Such checklists were typically focused on an interactive computer program and some speculation about how it might be used with a particular class. Whatever the merits of the checklist, today evaluation is seen from more diverse perspectives. In an attempt to characterize a sample of research papers published in journals on CALL and in edited books, Levy (2000) categorized the papers as representing the following topics: computer-mediated communication (CMC), artifact, hybrid, environment/comparative evaluation, teacher education, hypertext/reading, and other (p. 177). He found that only about one third (28%) of the "new research" had to do with measuring learning gains. Despite the variety of areas taken up in the CALL journals and books, most applied linguists would probably agree that among the critical areas of study for CALL should be empirical evaluation of the extent to which students learn language from working on CALL. As CALL evaluators conceive of their work as more complex than checking off categories, a number of issues arise, several of which are outlined next.

Evaluation for Whom?

Whereas some might look to checklists as a means of evaluating CALL, others claim to be interested in studies comparing CALL with "traditional" classroom learning. The problems inherent in attempting to compare CALL to classroom learning have been discussed extensively in the professional literature, and yet the idea of CALL-class comparisons dies hard, perhaps because of the large number of constituents potentially interested in the issue (see Chapelle, 2001, for discussion). Some have argued that administrators, publishers, and the public need to have such proof that technology-mediated learning is indeed time well spent for language learners. The fact that the march toward technology-filled classrooms does not wait for such research results may suggest that this argument is overstated. However, even some language

TABLE 41.2

Three Approaches to Developing Useful Research Questions About CALL
(Based on Chapelle, 2003)

Audience	Focus on...	Results
Software developers and lab coordinators	the software	Indicate the most successful software design strategies.
Teachers and students	the learner	Indicate successful strategies for using software.
Teachers	the task	Indicate the best ways to structure learning tasks.

teachers have suggested that such comparisons are useful in their lesson planning and decision making.

The variety of opinions expressed on the issue of CALL evaluation points strongly toward the need to consider the audience for evaluation. As summarized in Table 41.2, software developers, lab directors, teachers, and students have some genuine use for evaluation that focuses on the software, the learner, and the pedagogical tasks, respectively. The purported need for comparisons of computer-assisted versus classroom instruction by administrators is less defensible in view of the way in which decisions about funding for computer labs are made—on the basis of space, funding, and local politics rather than on research. Research intended to offer insights for those who work closely with CALL has to be conducted using appropriate methods for discovering relevant facts about CALL and its use. Rejecting the CALL versus classroom paradigm requires theory, such as the theories concerning interaction outlined previously, that can suggest approaches for examining relevant aspects of CALL use. The most interesting but challenging aspect of evaluating CALL on the basis of such theories is that it requires analysis of data revealing the process of CALL use.

Interaction Theory and Learning Processes

The theoretical perspectives on the three types of interactions offer some guidance for studying learning processes in CALL. The observable records of learners' work on CALL tasks are called "working style data—consistent, observable behavior displayed by students as they worked on [computer-based] L2 tasks" (Jamieson & Chapelle, 1987, p. 529) or "CALL texts" (Chapelle, 1994). These terms, in addition to "tracking data," "computer logs," and "process data," all refer to the data that are documented in order to study learners' work on CALL. Such data might include sequences of interaction such as the learner's incorrect response to a question, feedback indicating the response was wrong, and a second response (e.g., Chanier et al., 1992). It might consist of a linguistic production to a peer in a chat room, a sign of laughter (e.g., "hee-hee"), and a second attempt at the production (Negretti, 1999; Pellettieri, 2000). These sequences can consist of language alone or, more commonly, through a combination of language and other forms such as mouse clicks. Research has drawn on interactionist theory to investigate whether the three hypothesized benefits were evident.

Negotiation of meaning. Based on interactionist theory suggesting the value of negotiation of meaning in task-oriented L2 conversation (Pica, 1994; Long & Robinson, 1998), researchers have investigated the quality of communication tasks by seeking evidence for learners' negotiation of meaning. Research on face-to-face classroom tasks provides guidance for developing communication tasks such as the one Blake (2000) investigated using 50 intermediate learners of Spanish. Data indicating negotiation included sequences such as the following:

A:	Cuales son en común? [What are in common?]	(Trigger)
B:	Como se dice comun en ingles? no comprehende [How do you say "common" in English? no understand]	(Indicator)
A:	Común es cuando algo y una otra algo son el mismo; entiendes mi explicacion? ["Common" is when something and another thing are the same; do you understand my explanation?]	(Response)
B:	Si, gracias . . . [Yes, thank you . . .]	(Reaction)

This analysis draws on the methods used for identifying sequences of negotiation of meaning. The first turn shown acts as the trigger that initiates the sequence by introducing a word that the second participant does not know. The second move is an indicator that draws attention to the problem, lack of knowledge of "común." The response explains the meaning, and the reaction acknowledges the explanation. Using these methods developed by those studying the L2 conversation from the perspective of the interactionist hypothesis, researchers have found that under some conditions the CMC tasks can prompt the type of negotiation of meaning that is believed to be valuable.

Obtaining modified input. A number of studies have looked at the effects of offering learners modified input, and can therefore be interpreted in view of the interactionist hypothesis. For example, Borrás and Lafayette (1994) investigated the optional L1 (English) subtitles as a means of modifying the input. One group of French learners used computer-assisted video materials with access to subtitles and a second group used the same materials without subtitle options. The subtitle condition allowed students the option of choosing to see English subtitles for the aurally presented French as they requested. A speaking task following the video required learners to address questions about the content of the video. The fact that the learners who had participated in the subtitle condition outperformed those who had not had access to subtitles suggested that the subtitles had indeed acted as one would expect modified input to do. Other studies have found similarly positive results when learners are able to obtain modified input to help them provide access to meanings of the vocabulary through hypermedia.

Attending to linguistic form. The *use* of hypermedia annotations might also be interpreted from the perspective of "intraperson" interaction, that is, within the learner's mind. The control-treatment research design that places learners in a modified input condition or a plain text condition assumes that those who are given the provision for modification will benefit from it. However, the hypothesis developed from the perspective of intraperson interaction requires evidence that the learner has attended to the linguistic form (Schmidt, 1990, 1992). Hegelheimer and Chapelle (2000) suggest that such evidence comes from sequences such as the following:

The computer displays:	BRUSSELS, Belgium—They had to struggle a bit to open some **recalcitrant** bottles of champagne, but finance	
The student acts:	<clicks on "recalcitrant">	(possibly indicating noticing)
The computer displays:	recalcitrant—Definition: formal adjective; refusing to obey or be controlled, even after being punished: recalcitrant behavior	

Like any measure, the mouse clicks on vocabulary are not "proof" of noticing but rather an indicator that might reasonably be inferred to indicated noticing under some conditions. As mentioned earlier, studies investigating interaction are probably most defensible as studies of intrapersonal interaction. Plass, Chun, Mayer, and Leutner (1998) put the issues as follows: "Because the student's look-up behavior may change from word to word, the only way to test the hypothesis is to use vocabulary items, not students, as the units of observation" (Plass et al., 1998, p. 30).

These three examples of the study of interaction from an interactionist perspective, of course, are not the only type relevant to CALL researchers. In view of the range of issues of interest to software developers, learners, and teachers, a variety of methods is needed. Learners might benefit from knowing more about learner strategies, the study of which typically draws on introspective methods that ask learners to report their thoughts and motivations as they work on CALL or afterwards. Teachers may be interested in assessing quality of writing (rather than negotiation of meaning) in CMC tasks as Swaffar (1998) did through examination of four rhetorical types:"1) descriptive sentences, 2) sentences that express opinions, 3) sentences that have logical features to substantiate opinion, and 4) sentences that establish a logical argument for a point of view" (p. 155). These were used to assess what she called "strategic discourse management," which is intended to provide evidence for "level of thinking" (p. 155). Other attempts to examine the language of CMC in terms of quality need to be explored, perhaps through the methods developed for the study of task-based learning through assessment of fluency, accuracy, and complexity (Skehan, 1998). In examining online conversation, Lamy and Goodfellow (1999) look for evidence of "reflective conversation" in which learners explicitly refer to the language and their learning, in contrast to "social conversation" in which no evidence of attention to language and learning appears. This and other approaches (e.g., Renié & Chanier, 1995) might be considered to be consistent with the perspectives on interaction summarized in Table 41.1, but work remains to better understand the basis of the many research practices in CALL.

CALL IN APPLIED LINGUISTICS

Some collections in applied linguistics do not contain a chapter on technology. If one is included, it is typically placed at the end of the collection—at the margins. If the vision of the technology enthusiasts is accurate, future collections in applied linguistics will not need a separate chapter on technology because technology will be implicated in all the work across chapters, that is, it will be invisible. Before this happens, if indeed it does, it seems that it would be to the benefit of all to have a period in which technology remains the focus of explicit investigation in applied linguistics. Levy's (2000) analysis of the issues investigated in the study of CALL pointed out the "distinct thread" in the very diverse types on inquiries reported: "[f]or the CALL researcher, technology always makes the difference; the technology is never transparent or inconsequential" (Levy, 2000, p. 190). I have suggested in this chapter that this visibility of the technology is critical at this point in time for three reasons. Technology plays a significant role in virtually all matters of concern to applied linguists. CALL pedagogy needs to be developed as distinct from but related to pedagogy for classroom teaching and learning through other materials. Evaluation of CALL needs to be developed in view of its purpose and audience, drawing on and expanding existing theory and research on learning.

REFERENCES

Allum, P. (2002). CALL in the classroom: The case for comparative research. *ReCALL Journal, 14*(1), 146–166.

Belz, J. A. (2001). Institutional and individual dimensions of transatlantic group work in network-based language teaching. *ReCALL, 13*(2), 213–231.

Biber, D., Johansson, S., Leech, G., Conrad S., & E. Finegan (1999). *The longman grammar of spoken and written English*. London: Longman.

Blake, R. (2000). Computer-mediated communication: A window on L2 Spanish interlanguage. *Language Learning and Technology, 4*(1), 120–136.

Borrás, I., & Lafayette, R. C. (1994). Effects of multimedia courseware subtitling on the speaking performance of college students of French. *The Modern Language Journal, 78*, 61–75.

Bowers, C. A. (2000). *Let them eat data: How computers affect education, cultural diversity, and prospects of ecological sustainability*. Athens, GA: The University of Georgia Press.

Brown, J. S., & Duguid, P. (2000). *The social life of information*. Boston: Harvard Business School Press.

Bruce, B. C. & Hogan, M. P. (1998). The disappearance of technology: Toward an ecological model of literacy. In D. Reinking, M. C. McKenna, L. D. Labbo, & R. D. Kieffer (Eds.), *Handbook of literacy and technology: Transformations in a post-typographic world* (pp. 269–281). Hillsdale, NJ: Erlbaum.

Burns, A., & Coffin, C. (Eds.), (2001). *Analyzing English in a global context*. London: Routledge & Kegan Paul.

Chanier, T., Pengelly, M., Twidale, M., & Self, J. (1992). Conceptual modelling in error analysis in computer-assisted language learning systems. In M. L. Swartz & M. Yazdani (Eds.), *Intelligent tutoring systems for foreign language learning*, (pp. 125–150). Berlin: Springer-Verlag.

Chapelle, C. A. (2003). *English language learning and technology: Lectures on teaching and research in the age of information and communication technology*. Amsterdam: Benjamins.

Chapelle, C. A. (2001). *Computer applications in second language acquisition: Foundations for teaching, testing, and research*. Cambridge, UK: Cambridge University Press.

Chapelle, C. (1998). Multimedia CALL: Lessons to be learned from research on instructed SLA. *Language Learning and Technology, 2*(1), 22–34.

Chapelle, C. A. (1997). CALL in the year 2000: Still in search of research agendas? *Language Learning and Technology, 1*(1), 19–43.

Chapelle, C. (1994). CALL activities: Are they all the same? *System, 22*(1), 33–45.

Chaudron, C. (1983). Research on metalinguistic judgments: A review of theory, methods, and results. *Language Learning, 33*, 343–377.

Chun, D. M., & Plass, J. L. (1996). Effects of multimedia annotations on vocabulary acquisition. *The Modern Language Journal, 80*, 183–198.

Conrad, S. (2000). Will corpus linguistics revolutionize grammar teaching in the 21st century? *TESOL Quarterly, 34*(3), 548–560.

Crystal, D. (2001). *Language and the internet*. Cambridge, UK: Cambridge University Press.

Cummins, J. (2000). Academic language learning, transformative pedagogy and information technology: Towards a critical balance. *TESOL Quarterly, 34*(3), 537–548.

DeRidder, I. (2002). Electronic glosses revisited. In J. Colpaert, W. Decoo, M. Simons, & S. Van Bueren (Eds.), *Proceedings of the tenth international CALL conference: CALL Conference 2002—CALL professionals and the future of CALL research*, (pp. 65–76). Antwerp: University of Antwerp.

Desmarais, L., Duquette, L., Renié, D., & Laurier, M. (1998). Evaluating learning interactions in a multimedia environment. *Computers and the Humanities, 22*, 1–23.

Doughty, C., (1991). Second language instruction does make a difference: Evidence from an empirical study of SL relativization. *Studies in Second Language Acquisition, 13*, 431–469.

Doughty, C., & Long, M. (2002). Optimal psycholinguistic environments for distance foreign language learning. Paper presented at the Distance Learning of the Less Commonly Taught Languages Conference, Arlington, Virginia, February 1–3.

Doughty, C., & Williams, J. (1998). Pedagogical choices in focus on form. C. Doughty & J. Williams (Eds.), *Focus on form in classroom second language acquisition*, (pp. 197–261). Cambridge, UK: Cambridge University Press.

Ellis, R. (1999). *Learning a second language through interaction*. Amsterdam: Benjamins.

Gass, S. (1997). *Input, interaction, and the second language learner*. Mahwah, NJ: Lawrence Erlbaum Associates.

Graddol, D. (2001). English in the future. In A. Burns & C. Coffin, (Eds.), *Analyzing English in a global context*, (pp. 260–37). London: Routledge & Kegan Paul.

Harrington, M., & Levy, M. (2001). CALL begins with a "C": Interaction in computer-mediated language learning. *System, 29*(1), 15–26.

Hegelheimer, V. (1998). *Effects of textual glosses and sentence-level audio glosses on reading comprehension and vocabulary recall*. Unpublished doctoral dissertation. Department of Educational Psychology, College of Education, University of Illinois.

Hegelheimer, V., & Chapelle, C. A. (2000). Methodological issues in research on learner-computer interactions in CALL. *Language Learning and Technology, 4*(1), 41–59.

Hsu, J. (1994). *Computer-assisted language learning (CALL): The effect of ESL students' use of interactional modifications on listening comprehension.* Unpublished doctoral dissertation, Department of Curriculum and Instruction, College of Education, Iowa State University.

Jamieson, J., & Chapelle, C. (1987). Working styles on computers as evidence of second language learning strategies. *Language Learning, 37,* 523–544.

Kamhi-Stein, L. D. (2000). Looking to the future of TESOL teacher education: Web-based bulletin board discussions in a methods course. *TESOL Quarterly, 34*(3), 423–455.

Kon, C. K. (2002). The influence on outcomes of ESL students' performance strategies on a CALL listening comprehension activity. Unpublished master's thesis, Department of English, Iowa State University.

Kurzweil, R. (1999). *The age of spiritual machines: When computers exceed human intelligence.* New York: Viking.

Lam, W. S. E. (2000). L2 literacy and the design of the self: A case study of a teenager writing on the Internet. *TESOL Quarterly, 34*(3), 457–482.

Lamy, M-N., & Goodfellow, R. (1999). Reflective conversation in the virtual language classroom. *Language Learning and Technology, 2*(2), 43–61

Levy, M. (2000). Scope, goals, and methods in CALL research: Questions of coherence and autonomy. *ReCALL, 12*(2), 170–195.

Long, M. H. (1996). The role of linguistic environment in second language acquisition. W. C. Ritchie & T. K. Bhatia (Eds.), *Handbook of second language acquisition,* (pp. 413–468). San Diego: Academic Press.

Long, M. H., & Robinson, P. (1998). Focus on form: Theory, research, and practice. C. Doughty & J. Williams (Eds.), *Focus on form in classroom second language acquisition,* (pp. 15–41). Cambridge, UK: Cambridge University Press.

Murray, D. (2000). Protean communication: The language of computer-mediated communication. *TESOL Quarterly, 34*(3), 457–482.

Negretti, R. (1999). Web-based activities and SLA: A conversation analysis research approach. *Language Learning and Technology, 3*(1), 75–87.

Pellettieri, J. (2000). Negotiation in cyberspace: The role of *chatting* in the development of grammatical competence in the virtual foreign language classroom. In M. Warschauer & R. Kern, (Eds.), *Network-based language teaching: Concepts and practice,* (pp. 59–86). Cambridge, UK: Cambridge University Press.

Pica, T. (1997). Second language teaching and research relationships: A North American view. *Language Teaching Research, 1*(1), pp. 48–72.

Pica, T. (1994). Research on negotiation: What does it reveal about second language learning conditions, processes, and outcomes? *Language Learning, 44*(3), 493–527.

Plass, J. L., Chun, D. M., Mayer, R. E., & Leutner, D. (1998). Supporting visual and verbal learning preferences in a second language multimedia learning environment. *Journal of Educational Psychology, 90*(1), 25–36.

Quirk, R., Greenbaum, S., Leech, G., & Svartvik, J. (1972). *A grammar of contemporary English.* London: Longman.

Rassool, N. (1999). *Literacy for sustainable development in the age of information.* Clevedon, UK: Multilingual Matters.

Renié, D. & Chanier, T. (1995). Collaboration and computer-assisted acquisition of a second language. *Computer-Assisted Language Learning, 8*(1), 3–29.

Roever, C. (2001). Web-based language testing. *Language Learning and Technology, 5*(2), 84–94.

Rose, E. (2000). *Hyper texts: The language and culture of educational computing.* Toronto: The Althouse Press.

Salaberry, R. (2000). Pedagogical design of computer-mediated communication tasks: Learning objectives and technological capabilities. *Modern Language Journal, 84*(1), 28–37.

Salaberry, R. (1999). CALL in the year 2000: Still developing the research agenda. A commentary on Carol Chapelle's ACALL in the Year 2000: Still in search of research paradigms. *Language Learning and Technology, 3*(1), 104–107.

Schmidt, R. (1992). Awareness and second language acquisition. *Annual Review of Applied Linguistics, 13,* 206–226.

Schmidt, R. W. (1990). The role of consciousness in second language learning. *Applied Linguistics, 11*(2), 129–158.

Skehan, P. (1998). *A cognitive approach to language learning.* Oxford, UK: Oxford University Press.

Susser, B. (2001). A defense of checklists for courseware evaluation. *ReCALL Journal, 13*(2), 261–276.

Swaffar, J. (1998). Assessing development in writing: A proposal for strategy coding. In J. Swaffar, S. Romano, P. Markley, & K. Arens, (Eds.), *Language learning online: Theory and practice in the ESL and the L2 computer classroom,* (pp. 155–176). Austin: Labyrinth Publications.

Taylor, C., Kirsch, I., Eignor, D., & Jamieson, J. (1999). Examining the relationship between computer familiarity and performance on computer-based language tasks. *Language Learning, 49*(2), 219–274.

Warschauer, M. (2000). The changing global economy and the future of English teaching. *TESOL Quarterly, 34*(3), 511–535.

Watanabe, Y. (1997), Input, intake and retention: effects of increased processing on incidental learning of foreign vocabulary, *Studies in Second Language Acquisition, 19,* 287–307.

Yano, Y., Long, M. H., & Ross, S. (1993). The effects of simplified and elaborated texts on foreign language reading comprehension. *Language Learning, 25,* 297–308.

42

L2 Learning Strategies

Neil J. Anderson
Brigham Young University

STATEMENT OF FOCUS

Perceptive second/foreign language (L2) learners are those who are aware of and use appropriate strategies for learning and communicating in a second language. The purpose of strategy use is to improve performance in the learning and use of ones' second language. Strategies are the *conscious* actions that learners take to improve their language learning. Strategies may be observable, such as observing someone take notes during an academic lecture to recall information better, or they may be mental, such as thinking about what one already knows on a topic before reading a passage in a textbook. Because strategies are conscious, there is active involvement of the L2 learner in their selection and use. Strategies are not isolated actions, but rather a process of orchestrating more than one action to accomplish an L2 task. It may be helpful to view strategy use as an orchestra. Rarely does an instrument sound good alone. However, when combined with other instruments, beautiful music results. Although we can identify individual strategies, rarely will one strategy be used in isolation. Strategies are related to each other and must be viewed as a process and not as a single action.

Einstein offers a very interesting definition of insanity: doing the same thing over and over again and expecting different results. Research consistently shows that less successful language learners often use the same strategies over and over again and do not make significant progress in their task. They do not recognize that the strategies they are using are not helping them to accomplish their goal. These less successful learners seem to be unaware of the strategies available to them to successfully accomplish a language task. Successful L2 learners have a wider repertoire of strategies and draw on a variety of them to accomplish their task of learning a language.

The purpose of this chapter is to examine the research on L2 learning strategies within the context of current language teaching methodologies, to consider important developments in L2 strategy research, to identify current directions, and to anticipate the future of L2 strategy research. A single chapter of this nature cannot possibly go into the depth that a researcher or teacher needs on the role of language learning strategies. Researchers and teachers are encouraged to do additional reading on their own by consulting the references cited in this chapter. Perhaps the most extensive bibliography on language learning strategies can be found electronically at http://linguistics. byu.edu/faculty/andersonn/learningstrategies/LearningStrategies.html. Consulting works on this list may better prepare researchers and teachers as we all work together to better understand the role of strategies in L2 learning.

L2 LEARNING STRATEGIES WITHIN THE CONTEXT OF METHODOLOGIES

Since the mid-1970s, close attention has been given to the role of strategies in L2 learning (Anderson, 1991; Cohen, 1990, 1998; Hosenfeld, 1979; Naiman, Fröhlich, & Todesco, 1975; O'Malley & Chamot, 1990; Oxford, 1990, 1993, 2002; Rubin, 1975; Stern, 1975; Wenden, 1991, 2002; Wong-Fillmore, 1979). The early research identified the primary strategies that good learners use while engaged in language learning tasks. Five primary strategies were consistently addressed in these early studies: (1) memorization strategies, (2) clarification strategies, (3) communication strategies, (4) monitoring strategies, and (5) prior knowledge strategies. All this pointed to a new generalization that could be made about L2 learning, when learners actively use strategies to accomplish their language learning goals.

A language teaching methodology typically assumes that if the language teacher follows the steps outlined, the effort will result in effective learning by students in the class. Methodologies often assume that everyone learns the same way. Oxford (1993) and Nunan (1991) each point out that no single method can meet the needs of all learners. The fact that individual learners use a variety of strategies and approach learning a language differently is not taken into careful consideration within the context of most of the methods for language teaching.

Within the context of methodologies, strategies play a central role in two approaches: Styles and Strategies-Based Instruction (SSBI) and the Cognitive Academic Language Learning Approach (CALLA). SSBI is an approach to language teaching that places learning style and language learning strategy instruction as a central goal in this learner-centered approach. Learning styles are the general approach one takes to learning; the ways that we prefer to organize and retain information. Teaching learners to be aware of their learning style is known as Style-Based Instruction. For example, you may learn best by listening (auditory), looking at printed material (visual), or by moving around (kinesthetic). Strategies are the specific things that one does to learn. Strategies are typically linked to a learning style. For example, an auditory learner may apply a strategy of reading aloud to hear a text. A visual learner may draw a graphic organizer to help visualize the organization of a reading passage. A kinesthetic learner may walk around while studying new vocabulary written on flash cards. Research data suggest that there is a link between the language learning strategies and learning styles (Rossi-Le, 1995).

An SSBI approach to language teaching has two primary goals: styles and strategy instruction, and style and strategy integration. Style and Strategy instruction involves the explicit instruction of learning styles and strategies so that learners know about their preferred style of learning and how, when, and why to use the strategy. Style and strategy integration involves embedding learning style and strategies into all classroom activities so that learners have contextualized practice. The practice provides reinforcement of the concepts learned during explicit instruction.

Cohen, Weaver, and Li (1997) report on one key research project. The specific focus of their research was to examine the impact of Strategies-Based Instruction (SBI) on speaking for university-level, foreign-language learners. Fifty-five intermediate level learners of French and Norwegian participated in the study. Thirty-two students received explicit SBI while the remaining 23 served as a control group receiving no explicit strategy instruction. A pretest/posttest design was used to determine whether SBI influenced gains in students' oral proficiency over a 10-week term. One unique feature of this research is that the subjects were asked to report their strategy use on three specific speaking tasks. These tasks included: (1) self-description, (2) story retelling, and (3) city description. After completing all three speaking tasks, the subjects responded to a strategies checklist prepared for each task. The checklist was designed to capture subjects' strategy usage during three stages: (1) preparation for accomplishing the task, (2) self-monitoring during execution of the task, and (3) self-reflection following the task. In addition, subjects completed the *Strategy Inventory for Language Learning*. A subsample of 21 subjects provided retrospective think-aloud protocols to justify their frequency of strategies reports. ANCOVA results showed that both groups made gains in their oral language proficiency. This should not be surprising since we would hope that regular language instruction results in proficiency gains. The ANCOVA results indicate that the experimental group outperformed the control group on the third task, city description. Cohen, Weaver, and Li report that SBI "seems to have contributed to the students' ability" (p. 14) to produce the necessary language to perform the tasks. Overall this research suggests that SBI can have an impact on language learners in the classroom.

Additional understandings of SSBI are needed to more fully comprehend the impact of styles- and strategies-based instruction. Very little research has been conducted to examine the full extent to which learners acquire strategies within a SBI approach. Also, researchers must ask whether engaging learners in an SBI approach results in higher levels of language proficiency among the learners? Can we explicitly teach learners to draw on their learning style strengths and then apply the appropriate strategies for accomplishing language learning tasks? Can we teach learners to move beyond their learning style preferences so that they can then apply strategies for learning that are not linked to their preferred learning style?

O'Malley and Chamot (1990) proposed the Cognitive Academic Language Learning Approach (CALLA). As this approach has evolved since its inception, it has combined four primary elements for successful language teaching: (1) academic content for language learning, (2) learning strategies, (3) standards-based education, and (4) portfolio assessment. One assumption of this approach is that L2 acquisition is accelerated by an explicit focus on strategies.

Chamot and O'Malley (1994) emphasize that the CALLA framework integrates research from several previous studies and puts it into practice. Their extensive research has resulted in the metacognitive model of strategic learning and the framework for learning strategies instruction.

In spite of the three and one-half decades of research, recent research by Dörnyei and Skehan (2003) points out that "learner differences, such as aptitude, style, and strategies, as a sub-area of second language acquisition, and applied linguistics more generally, have not been integrated into other areas of investigation, and have not excited much theoretical or practical interest in recent years" (p. 589). Clearly, more research is needed on the influence of individual differences and language learning.

IMPORTANT DEVELOPMENTS IN L2 STRATEGY RESEARCH

Five important developments have contributed to the success of L2 learning strategy research: (1) the identification, classification, and measurement of language learning strategies, (2) the distinction between language use and language learning strategies, (3) the relationship between strategies and L2 proficiency, (4) the transferability of strategies from first language (L1) tasks to L2 tasks, and (5) the explicit instruction of language learning strategies.

The Identification, Classification, and Measurement
of Language Learning Strategies

Research by Hsiao and Oxford (2002) clearly supports the notion that L2 strategies can be classified in a "systematic manner" (p. 377). Language learning strategies have been classified into seven major categories: cognitive strategies (e.g., identifying, retention, and storage of learning material as well as retrieval, rehearsal, and comprehension), metacognitive strategies (e.g., preparing and planning, identifying, monitoring, orchestrating, and evaluating strategy use), mnemonic or memory-related strategies (e.g., memorization strategies), compensatory strategies (e.g., circumlocution strategies such as using a word you do know to describe the meaning of a word or phrase you do not know), affective strategies (e.g., strategies for reducing anxiety), social strategies (e.g., strategies for interacting with others), and self-motivating strategies (e.g., self-encouragement, relaxation, and meditation, eliminating negative influences, creating positive influences). There is some overlap between affective strategies and self-motivating strategies. Oxford (1990, 2001) refers to the first six of these categories, while other researchers (Chamot & O'Malley, 1994; Chamot et al., 1999; Cohen, 1996a; Weaver & Cohen, 1997) use a fewer number. Work by Dörnyei (2001) focuses on self-motivating strategies.

A recent research article provides empirical data into how best to classify language learning strategies. Hsiao and Oxford (2002) compared classification theories of language learning strategies. Their research involved 517 college English as a Foreign Language (EFL) learners from Taiwan. Participants took the *Strategy Inventory for Language Learning* (SILL) that had been translated into Chinese. Fifteen strategy classifications were developed and tested based on classification systems proposed by Oxford (1990), Rubin (1981), and O'Malley & Chamot (1990). The research findings support the classification of L2 learning strategies into six distinct categories: cognitive strategies, metacognitive strategies, memory strategies, compensatory strategies, affective strategies, and social strategies. These six categories correspond to Oxford's six dimensions of strategy classification.

Among the tools available for identifying, classifying, and measuring L2 strategies, the most frequently cited and used include standardized inventories, think-aloud protocols, and reflective journals. Researchers are urged to triangulate the research design so that more than one of these tools is used.

Standardized inventories. The most widely used inventory for L2 strategy research is Oxford's (1990) *Strategy Inventory for Language Learning* (SILL). Oxford and Burry-Stock (1995) report on the successful use of this inventory in gathering data on language learning strategies. One great advantage of the SILL is that reliability and validity data are available. Oxford (1996) reports on the psychometric qualities of the SILL. Reported reliabilities for the ESL/EFL SILL range from .86 to .91 when learners respond to the questionnaire in their second language (English). Translated versions of the SILL have been used in many research projects. Reliability coefficients increase when learners respond in their L1 to .91 to .94. Whether administered in the subjects' L1 or L2, the SILL has high reliability.

Validity for the SILL is likewise high. When strategy use is compared with language performance, evidence strongly favors the SILL. Oxford reports a variety of studies that link strategy use and performance in general language proficiency, oral language proficiency, grades in language courses, proficiency self-ratings, and professional language career status.

Oxford is currently developing a task-based version of the SILL that would be administered in conjunction with specific L2 tasks. This could be a very important contribution to the L2 strategy research.

One additional inventory that shows great promise is a more recent instrument developed by Mokhtari and reported in Mokhtari and Sheorey (2002) and Sheorey and Mokhtari (2001). The *Survey of Reading Strategies* (SORS) focuses on metacognitive strategy use within the context of reading. The SORS was based on a separate metacognitive reading strategy survey developed for native speakers on English, the Metacognitive-Awareness of Reading Strategies Inventory (MARSI). The SORS measures three categories of reading strategies: global reading strategies (e.g., having a purpose for reading, using context to guess unfamiliar vocabulary, confirming or rejecting your predictions), problem-solving strategies (e.g., adjusting reading rate, focusing when concentration is lost), and support strategies (e.g., taking notes while reading, highlighting important ideas in the text). Mokhtari and Sheorey report reliability for the MARSI but not for the SORS. Because it has just recently been completed, more studies need to be conducted using this instrument to determine whether the SORS is as stable of an instrument as the MARSI from which it was based.

Additional inventories for identifying L2 learner strategies can be found on the Internet. *Language Strategy Use Survey*, by Andrew D. Cohen and Julie C. Chi: <http://carla.acad.umn.edu/profiles/CohenPapers/Lg_Strat_Srvy.html> and the Young Learners' Language Strategy Use Survey by A. D. Cohen and R. L. Oxford at <http://carla.acad.umn.edu/profiles/CohenPapers/Young_Lg_Strat_Srvy.html>.

Think-aloud protocols. Think-aloud protocols or verbal report data have been used in many L2 strategy research projects to identify strategies used by language learners (Anderson, 1991; Anderson & Vandergrift, 1996; Cohen, 1996b; Cohen & Olshtain, 1993; Gass & Mackey, 2000). Protocols allow the researcher insights into the language learning process that would not be available without their use. One of the greatest strengths of think-aloud protocols is that researchers are able to gather data on the process of strategy use. We can capture the sequence of strategies that language users implement to complete language tasks.

Cohen and Scott (1996) suggest three categories of verbal reports: self-report, self-observation, and self-revelation. Self-report is a statement of typical behavior. Responses to questionnaires are a form of self-report. Self-observation is used simultaneously to completing a language task or within a very short time after completing the task. Self-revelation data refer to unanalyzed thoughts. Think-aloud protocols typically fall into this category. One key to the successful use of think-aloud protocols is to gather the data as close to the event as possible. Thus, the strategies identified will be those actually used.

Reflective journals. For several years, the use of journals (or diaries) has been advocated as a tool for student reflection (Oxford et al., 1996). Riley and Harsch (1999) outline a research project to compare Japanese learners of English strategy use in ESL and EFL environments. One of the primary tools they used to gather data was a strategy journal. The journal served as a tool to explore learner awareness, development, and use of language learning strategies as well as what effect guided reflection has on the development of language learning strategies.

One common feature of the work of those involved in learner reflective journals is the encouragement for teachers to give learners prompts to select from in making their entry. If you are specifically focusing on language learning strategies you want the learners to make journal entries that focus on their strategy use and not other aspects of the language learning process.

The Distinction Between Language *Use* and Language *Learning* Strategies

Cohen (1996a) makes the distinction between language use and language learning strategies. This distinction can be useful for L2 researchers and teachers. Cohen indicates "*language use* strategies focus primarily on employing the language that learners have in their current interlanguage" (p. 2). Under this umbrella term, the following strategies apply: retrieval strategies (e.g., strategies used to recall learned material;

similar to Oxford's memory strategies), rehearsal strategies (e.g., strategies used to practice vocabulary or grammar structures), cover strategies (also known as compensation strategies, e.g., strategies used to get around missing knowledge), and communication strategies (e.g., strategies used to express a message). Cohen continues by indicating "*language learning* strategies have an explicit goal of assisting learners in improving their knowledge in a target language" (pp. 1–2). Language learning strategies include strategies in four common categories: cognitive, metacognitive, social, and affective as illustrated earlier.

Although I have listed this as an important development in L2 strategy research, essentially no research has been conducted with L2 learners to determine if this categorization of strategies is valid. Hsiao and Oxford (2002) point out that "in daily reality the strategies for L2 learning and L2 use overlap considerably" (pp. 378–379). The way that Cohen (1996a) classifies strategies within these two categories (language use strategies: retrieval strategies, rehearsal strategies, cover strategies, and communication strategies; language learning strategies: cognitive, metacognitive, social, and affective) suggests that employing cognitive and metacognitive strategies only occurs during the learning phase and not the use phase of language. This seems to be shortsighted. As learners move from learning to use they free up cognitive capacity from thinking about the language to knowing how to use it. They are now in a position to implement more cognitive and metacognitive strategies.

The Relationship Between Strategies and L2 Proficiency

The research conducted to date has been consistent in linking levels of L2 proficiency to strategy use. Proficient L2 learners have been found to have a wider repertoire of strategies and draw on them to accomplish L2 tasks. At the same time, research supports the concept that less proficient L2 learners draw on a smaller number of strategies and do so in a less effective manner (Anderson, 1991; Dreyer & Oxford, 1996; Ehrman & Oxford, 1990, 1995; Green & Oxford, 1995). Proficiency can explain from .30 to .78 of the variance in strategy use. There is a strong relationship between strategy use and L2 proficiency.

One thing that researchers and teachers must keep in mind is that there are no good or bad strategies; there is good or bad application of strategies. Anderson's research (1991) shows that effective and less effective learners reported using the same kinds of strategies. The difference is in how the strategies are executed and orchestrated. Therefore, we cannot suggest that successful L2 learners use good strategies and less effective learners use poor or bad strategies. With a value judgment placed on strategies it would appear that all teachers have to do is teach poor learners the "good strategies" that successful learners use. Unfortunately, it is not that simple. The ways that effective learners use strategies and combine them makes the distinction between them and less effective learners. Cohen (1998) supports this concept. He states, "with some exceptions, strategies themselves are not inherently good or bad, but have the potential to be used effectively" (p. 8).

Transferability of Strategies from L1 Tasks to L2 Tasks

Wolfersberger (2001) conducted exploratory research to examine the transfer of composing processes and to determine whether L2 proficiency had any effect on the transfer of the L1 composing processes to L2 composing. Three high intermediate- and three high beginning-level Japanese learners of ESL participated in the research. All were considered experienced writers in Japanese based on responses to a writing survey prepared by Wolfersberger. The data collection involved three stages: (1) a background questionnaire, (2) two think-aloud composing sessions, and (3) post-composing session interviews. The results show that the three high beginning-level writers used different writing strategies when composing in their L1 and L2. All three subjects reported thinking in Japanese while writing their essays in English. Five primary differences appeared during their writing tasks: (1) general translation for words and ideas into English, (2) back-translating their English text in order to help interpret its meaning, (3) finding the vocabulary to express the ideas produced in the L1, (4) dealing with challenges in lack of English grammatical knowledge, and (5) correcting spelling errors in English. These five are primarily language concerns that did not appear while the subjects were writing in Japanese. The three high intermediate writers used similar strategies while composing in both English and Japanese. They reported being at ease in both languages while engaging in the writing tasks. There was transfer of strategies while engaged in writing in both languages. Wolfersberger reports that these results support a threshold hypothesis for L2 writing as has been reported for L2 reading (Clarke, 1980).

Wolfersberger's research helps inform L2 researchers and teachers about the role of transfer of strategies from L1 to L2 learning tasks. We can move forward by carefully considering how L2 acquisition can be accelerated through helping learners draw more on their L1 skills.

Explicit Instruction of Language Learning Strategies

Nunan (1996, 1997) provides a good rationale for integrating explicit instruction of language learning strategies into the classroom curriculum: "[L]anguage classrooms should have a dual focus, not only teaching language content but also on developing learning processes as well" (1996, p. 41). The primary purpose of instruction is to raise learners' awareness of strategies and then allow each to select appropriate strategies to accomplish their learning goals.

Research consistently shows that the most effective strategy instruction occurs when it is integrated into regular classroom instruction (Cohen, 1998; Oxford & Leaver, 1996). Some language programs prepare special strategy lessons that are presented.

Brown (2002) provides a very practical guide, firmly based on the L2 strategy research, on how to approach the teaching of language learning strategies in the classroom. Teachers and learners are guided through the language learning strategy process in an effective and organized fashion. One benefit to the research would be for teachers to apply the concepts outlined in the book and measure the effect of the instruction on language learning.

Rees-Miller (1993, 1994) calls into question the concept of strategy instruction. She suggests that because of the mixed results that have been obtained from various research studies that teachers should be more cautious in accepting the concept of learner-strategy training. Factors that she suggests that teachers must take into account include learners' cultural backgrounds, age, educational background, life experience, affective factors, and the learners' and teachers' beliefs about language learning. Certainly all of these factors are important for teachers to consider. As Chamot and Rubin (1994) point out in response to Rees-Miller's article, all of these variables influence individual strategy use. They remind us, as pointed out in the definition of strategies earlier in this chapter, that a strategy is not used in isolation, but rather in an orchestrated manner with other strategies as part of a process. This should not suggest that strategy instruction is not effective, but rather give teachers increased insight into the various factors they should take into consideration when strategy instruction is undertaken.

Also, Eslinger's research (2000) suggests that there may be a natural tendency to grow in strategy use without explicit instruction. She suggests that implicit strategy learning should be given closer attention.

CURRENT DIRECTIONS IN L2 STRATEGY RESEARCH

Strategy Research Within the Language Skills

Researchers and teachers have traditionally approached the language skills through listening, speaking, reading, and writing. Larsen-Freeman (2001) suggests that "grammaring" is a fifth skill area that deserves our attention. Significant research has been conducted on the use of specific strategies in each of these language skill areas.

Listening Strategies. Vandergrift is perhaps the researcher most actively engaged in strategy research within the context of L2 listening (Vandergrift 1997, 1999, 2002). In his 2002 published research, he reports on a metacognitive strategy awareness project undertaken with 420 children in 17 different Grade 4-6 classes in Canada. The L2 learners are learning French. What makes this study noteworthy is that it is the first study published that focuses on listening strategy use of children. All classes responded to at least one of three tasks and a guided reflection activity. Data were collected from classes rather than from individuals because of the age of the participants. Teachers recorded all student responses. The three tasks engaged the learners in (1) listening for what to feed animals, (2) listening to descriptions of five families and matching the descriptions with pictures, and (3) listening to answering machine messages and matching activities on the checklist with the name of the person who suggested it. After each of these tasks, teachers engaged the class in reflective exercises to determine how the listeners approached the tasks and what they learned in French. Results indicate that students have a high level of awareness of their strategies for listening to materials in French. They were able to successfully identify the strategies that they had used while engaged in the listening tasks. In particular, learners' use of metacognitive strategies of planning, monitoring, and evaluation during the listening was clear. Vandergrift emphasizes the importance of teaching language content as well as learning processes. This was one of the additional benefits of the research with these young learners.

In addition to this key research study, additional research on the role of strategies and listening has been conducted. The research of O'Malley and Chamot (1990), Goh (1997), Cheng (2002), and Chien and Kao (2002) all add to our understanding of the important role that strategies play during the language task of listening.

Speaking Strategies. Cohen and Olshtain (1993) have applied retrospective think-aloud protocols to get L2 learners to report the ways in which they "assess, plan, and execute" their spoken utterances. The researchers videotaped 15 L2 learners participating in role-play situations with a native speaker of English. Six speech act situations were provided for each learner (two apologies, two complaints, and two requests). After each set of two speech acts, the video was repeated for the learners, who then responded in their L1 to a set of questions about what they were thinking during the role-plays. One of the strengths of this research is the use of the retrospective protocols. The videotape provided the source of the recall stimulus. The learners were not asked to remember great amounts of material before providing the protocol. The tasks were structured so that after each speech act pair the strategies for the two speech acts could be reported. Cohen and Olshtain generalize from the data to classify learners from this study into one of three types of learners: metacognizers, avoiders, and pragmatists. The results indicate that in using strategies to perform speech acts, the subjects utilized four primary strategies: (1) planning to use specific vocabulary and grammatical structures, (2) thinking in two languages, (3) using a variety of different strategies in searching for language forms, and (4) not paying much attention to grammar or to pronunciation. This research supports the claims that learners can be aware of their strategies and report them to researchers and teachers. This awareness facilitates language learning. Additional research related to learner's strategies during speaking tasks can be found in the research of Dörnyei (1995).

Reading Strategies.   Sheorey and Mokhtari (2001) and Mokhtari and Sheorey (2002) are conducting significant research on the metacognitive reading strategies of L2 learners. They have developed a new instrument named the *Survey of Reading Strategies* (SORS) designed to measure the metacognitive reading strategies of L2 readers engaged in reading academic materials. One of the first studies published that used the SORS reports on the strategies of 152 native English-speaking students and 152 ESL students. The focus of the study was to examine the differences in reading strategy usage between native speakers and non-native speakers of English. They asked three primary research questions: (1) Are there any differences between ESL and U.S. students in their perceived strategy use while reading academic materials? (2) Are there any differences between male and female ESL and U.S. students, respectively, in their perceived strategy use while reading academic materials? (3) Is there a relationship between reported strategy use and self-rated reading ability?

Results show that the ESL students reported a higher use of strategies than the U.S. students. The ESL students reported using a greater number of support reading strategies, which should not be surprising. We would expect learners of English to need more support strategies. When the data were examined overall no significant differences were reported between the male and female readers in this study. However, there was one significant difference in the use of the strategy of underlining information in the text for ESL learners. The female ESL students reported using the strategy more frequently than the male ESL students. Finally, students who had a higher self-reported reading rating reported using a higher frequency of reading strategies than those readers who gave themselves a lower rating. Sheorey and Mokhtari (2001) report that "skilled readers ... are more able to reflect on and monitor their cognitive processes while reading. They are aware not only of which strategies to use, but they also tend to be better at regulating the use of such strategies while reading" (p. 445). This research contributes a great deal to our understanding of the reading strategies of L2 readers.

Anderson (1991) highlights that "strategic reading is not only a matter of knowing what strategy to use, but also the reader must know how to use a strategy successfully and orchestrate its use with other strategies. It is not sufficient to know about strategies; a reader must also be able to apply them strategically" (pp. 468–469). Additional research on reading strategies can be found in the works of Block (1986, 1992), Carrell, Pharis, and Liberto (1989), Janzen (1996), Knight, Padron, and Waxman (1985), and Song (1998).

Writing Strategies.   Two recent research projects in Taiwan highlight the continued interest in learning about strategies used by L2 writers (He, 2002; You & Joe, 2002). He's research involved 38 Taiwanese college-level writers. These writers were divided into two groups: mastery-orientation (intrinsic motivation to improve writing) or performance-orientation (extrinsic motivation to be better than other writers) classes. The purpose of the division was to determine if the learner's goal orientations would influence the learner's strategy use. Results indicated that the writers in both groups reported using strategies classified into five categories: planning, monitoring/evaluation, revising, retrieving, and compensating strategies. Writers in the mastery-orientation group had a higher frequency of reported strategies in the monitoring/evaluation, revising, and compensating categories. The mastery group also produced better essays than the performance-orientation group. Finally, revising strategies and mastery orientation served as two significant predictors of successful writing. What makes this study of interest is that there is an integration of strategy use with writers' goal orientations.

You and Joe (2002) designed a research study to examine incoherence in EFL learners' writing. They examined the strategies that writers used in solving problems of incoherence in their work. Nine college-level writers were engaged in this research project. After writing a composition, the writers were each interviewed and asked to describe their writing strategies in sections of the essay that were incoherent. Three reasons were identified for the incoherence in these writers' essays. First, the subjects failed to apply the writing strategies that they were aware of for handling difficulties in writing. Second, the writers had a limited number of strategies that they implemented during their writing. Finally, given the limited amount of time for the writing task, writers did not feel they had sufficient time to monitor their strategies and produce the required composition. These nine writers lacked metacognitive strategies, in particular the strategies of planning (e.g., preparing for a writing task), monitoring (e.g., being aware of strategy use during writing), and evaluating (determining if the strategies being used are helping to accomplish the writing goal), in order to improve their performance.

We continue to learn about L2 strategies, particularly when the research is focused on a specific language skill. These two studies represent the growing research in writing. Other articles on L2 strategy use and writing include Anderson (2003), Bosher (1998), Leki (1995), and Paulus (1999).

"Grammaring" Strategies.   Consistent with what we have discussed related to L2 learning strategies, the role of strategies in the teaching of L2 grammar has focused more on the teacher's pedagogical strategies than on learner's strategies for learning the grammar of a language. Larsen-Freeman (2001, 2003) emphasizes that we go beyond teaching "grammar" to teaching learners the skill of "grammaring": "Grammar teaching is not so much knowledge transmission as it is skill development. In fact, it is better to think of teaching 'grammaring,' rather than 'grammar'" (p. 255). Sharwood Smith (1993) suggests that "enhanced input" allows learners to focus on elements of grammatical structures that are targeted by the teacher. Krashen (1985) and Ellis (1994) have advocated making input comprehensible for learners. Ellis (2002) suggests that input to become intake "noticing" is the necessary condition. Focusing learner's attention on specific aspects of grammar is the pedagogical strategy to get learners to learn grammar.

What is greatly lacking in the research are studies that specifically target the identification of the learning strategies that L2 learners use to learn grammar and to understand the elements of grammar. Clearly more research is needed on "grammaring" strategies of L2 learners.

The Role of Metacognition and L2 Strategy Research

McDonough (1999) asks a provocative question of whether there is a hierarchy of strategies for language learning. His review of a part of the literature suggests that this is an area of possible future research that should be considered. Of the various categories of strategies identified through strategy research, does any one category play a more significant role than the others? I hypothesize that the metacognitive strategies play a more significant role because once a learner understands how to regulate his or her own learning through the use of strategies, language acquisition should proceed at a faster rate.

Vandergrift (2002) emphasizes the essential role of metacognitive strategies: "Metacognitive strategies are crucial because they oversee, regulate, or direct the language learning task, and involve thinking about the learning process" (p. 559). O'Malley and Chamot (1990) strengthen the importance of the role of metacognitive strategies when they state that "students without metacognitive approaches are essentially learners without direction or opportunity to plan their learning, monitor their progress, or review their accomplishments and future learning directions" (p. 8).

Metacognition can be defined simply as thinking about thinking (Anderson, 2002). It is the ability to make your thinking visible. It is the ability to reflect on what you know and do and what you do not know and do not do. Metacognition results in critical but healthy reflection and evaluation of your thinking that may result in making specific changes in how you learn. Metacognition is not simply thinking back on an event, describing what happened, and how you felt about it.

Understanding and controlling cognitive processes may be one of the most essential skills that classroom teachers can develop in themselves and the students with whom they work. Rather than focusing students' attention only on issues related to learning content, effective teachers can structure a learning atmosphere where thinking about what happens in the learning process will lead to stronger learning skills. Developing metacognitive awareness may also lead to the development of stronger cognitive skills as well.

Work by Skehan (1989), Vann and Abraham (1990), and Wenden (1998) points out that explicit teaching of language learning strategies does not ensure a successful learning experience. Learners need to be metacognitively aware of what they are doing. Learners need to connect their strategies for learning with their purpose for learning.

FUTURE DIRECTIONS IN L2 STRATEGY RESEARCH

I believe that three areas deserve increased attention in L2 strategy research in the coming years: (1) the relationship between language learning strategies and learning styles, (2) strategy use in second language learning contexts versus foreign language learning contexts, and (3) the role of computers in L2 strategy research.

The Relationship Between Language Learning Strategies and Learning Styles

We cannot look at language learning strategies in isolation. Strategies are linked to the individual learner's learning style.

Cohen (2000) suggests that in an ideal world teachers would be aware of learners' styles and the wide variety of strategies that are used for these styles. Teachers would accommodate learners to help them progress as quickly as possible in their task of learning the language. This ideal world is not likely to exist any time in the near future. Teachers must therefore teach learners how to self-assess their learning styles and strategy usage and to then help them monitor these issues themselves. Researchers can play a significant role in exploring the explicit links between learners' use of strategies and their preferred learning styles.

Strategy Use in Second Language Learning Contexts Versus Foreign Language Learning Contexts

Riley and Harsch (1999) explored the use of language learning strategies through strategy journals. One major finding from their research was that learners in second language settings as compared to those in foreign language settings report using different strategies. Riley and Harsch report that the second language learners in their study reported using more metacognitive strategies than the foreign language learners. The foreign language learners reported using more cognitive strategies than the second language learners. Riley and Harsch conclude that the environment influences the learners' need to use certain kinds of strategies.

Research can play a significant role in exploring the use of L2 strategies in different learning environments. In addition to research on the similarities and differences between strategy use in ESL and EFL environments, researchers can consider what role the use of strategies play in academic versus social language use contexts. To better understand strategy use, we must explore how strategy use changes when conditions for language use change.

The Role of Computers in L2 Strategy Research

Computer-assisted strategy assessment is a rich source of potential data still not actively utilized by L2 researchers and teachers. Hyte (2002) and Kohler (2002) have conducted very interesting research projects examining the use of the computer in metacognitive strategy training. Hyte studied the influence of metacognitive strategy training for language learning within the context of computer-assisted language learning (CALL). Two hundred thirty-nine second language learners of Spanish participated in her study. An experimental group (n = 120) received metacognitive training integrated within their CALL training. The control group (n = 119) did not receive the metacognitive strategy training. Hyte found that there was a significant difference between the two groups in terms of their listening strategies. Learners in the experimental group scored higher than those in the control group. One interesting finding was that learners in the control group reported a higher use of metacognitive strategies than learners in the experimental group. Hyte concludes that the metacognitive training increased the awareness of the learners in the experimental group such that they more accurately reported their strategy use.

Kohler's research (2002) was designed to investigate the effects of metacognitive strategy training on lower-achieving second language learners. Seventy learners of Spanish as a foreign language represented the lower-achieving 30% of a randomly selected larger group. The 70 subjects were divided into two groups. One group received metacognitive strategy training in class on through 20 CALL lessons. The second group served as a control group receiving no strategy training.

Results indicate that the subjects who received the metacognitive language learning strategy training significantly increased their listening comprehension, vocabulary, and phrases mastered. No significant differences were found in grammar usage and performance in specific language tasks between the two groups. Subjects who received the strategy training indicated higher perceived value of the training and use of metacognitive language learning strategies than those subjects from the control group.

One area of research that deserves additional focus is how learners use strategies while engaged in CALL tasks. For example, we need to investigate the strategies that learners use while reading online as opposed to the traditional hard copy reading strategies. Are there any differences in the use of language learning strategies when learners approach language learning through CALL environments versus traditional classroom settings? These are issues that need directed attention by researchers in the near future.

CONCLUSION

Will Rogers is credited with the saying that common sense ain't necessarily common practice. Perhaps what I have addressed in this chapter appears to be common sense to some readers. I believe that in many respects it is, but the reality is that what is common sense related to L2 learning strategies research is not common practice among researchers and language teachers.

There is still much research that needs to be completed for us to better understand the role of strategies and language learning. I hope that we can see a renewed research focus on the use of strategies in these areas.

REFERENCES

Anderson, N. J. (1991). Individual differences in strategy use in second language reading and testing. *Modern Language Journal, 75*, 460–472.

Anderson, N. J. (2002). *The role of metacognition in second/foreign language teaching and learning*. ERIC Digest. Washington, DC: ERIC Clearinghouse on Languages and Linguistics. Retrieved August 8, 2002, from www.cal.org/ericcll/digest/0110anderson.html

Anderson, N. J. (2003). Metacognition in writing: Facilitating writer awareness. In A. Stubbs & J. Chapman (Eds.), *Rhetoric, uncertainty, and the university as text: How students construct the academic experience* (pp. 10–30). Canadian Plains Research Center, University of Regina: Regina, Canada.

Anderson, N. J., & Vandergrift, L. (1996). Increasing metacognitive awareness in the L2 classroom by using think-aloud protocols and other verbal report formats. In R. L. Oxford (Ed.), *Language learning strategies around the world: Crosscultural perspectives* (pp. 3–18). National Foreign Language Resource Center. Manoa: University of Hawaii Press.

Block, E. (1986). The comprehension strategies of second language readers. *TESOL Quarterly, 20*, 163–194.

Block, E. (1992). See how they read: Comprehension monitoring of L1 and L2 readers. *TESOL Quarterly, 26*, 319–342.

Bosher, S. (1998). The composing processes of three Southeast Asian writers at the post-secondary level: An exploratory study. *Journal of Second Language Writing, 7*, 205–241.

Brown, H. D. (2002). *Strategies for success: A practical guide to learning English*. White Plains, NY: Pearson Education.

Carrell, P. L., Pharis, B. G., & Liberto, J. C. (1989). Metacognitive strategy training for ESL reading. *TESOL Quarterly, 23*, 646–678.

Chamot, A. U., Barnhardt, S., El-Dinary, P. B., & Robbins, J. (1999). *The learning strategies handbook*. New York: Longman.

Chamot, A. U., & O'Malley, M. (1994). *The CALLA handbook: Implementing the cognitive academic language learning approach*. White Plains, NY: Addison Wesley Longman.

Chamot, A. U., & Rubin, J. (1994). Comments on Janie Rees-Miller's "A critical appraisal of learner training: Theoretical bases and teaching implications." *TESOL Quarterly, 28*, 771–776.

Cheng, C. H. (2002). Effects of listening strategy instruction on junior high school students. In J. E. Katchen (Ed.), *Selected papers from the Eleventh International Symposium on English Teaching/Fourth Pan Asian Conference*. Taipei, Taiwan, November 8–10, 2002, pp. 289–297.

Chien, C. N., & Kao, L. H. (2002). Effects of metacognitive strategy on listening comprehension with EFL learners. In J. E. Katchen (Ed.), *Selected papers from the Eleventh International Symposium on English Teaching/Fourth Pan Asian Conference*. Taipei, Taiwan, November 8–10, 2002, pp. 298–307.

Clarke, M. A. (1980). The short circuit hypothesis of ESL reading: Or when language competence interferes with reading performance. *The Modern Language Journal, 64*, 203–209.

Cohen, A. D. (1990). *Language learning: Insights for learners, teachers, and researchers*. New York: Newbury House.

Cohen, A. D. (1996a). *Second language learning and use strategies: Clarifying the issues*. CARLA Working Paper Series #3. Minneapolis, MN: The University of Minnesota.

Cohen, A. D. (1996b). Verbal reports as a source of insights into second language learner strategies. *Applied Language Learning, 7*, 5–24.

Cohen, A. D. (1998). *Strategies in learning and using a second language*. New York: Longman.

Cohen, A. D. (2000, October). *The learner's side of ESL: Where do styles, strategies, and tasks meet?* Paper presented at the Southeast TESOL Meeting, Miami, Florida.

Cohen, A. D., & Olshtain, E. (1993). The production of speech acts by EFL learners. *TESOL Quarterly, 27*, 33–56.

Cohen, A. D., & Scott, K. (1996). A synthesis of approaches to assessing language learning strategies. In R. L. Oxford (Ed.), *Language learning strategies around the world: Crosscultural perspectives* (pp. 89–106). Honolulu: University of Hawaii, Second Language Teaching and Curriculum Center.

Cohen, A. D., Weaver, S. J., & Li, T. Y. (1997). *The impact of strategies-based instruction on speaking a foreign language*. Minneapolis, MN: Center for Advanced Research on Language Acquisition (CARLA), University of Minnesota.

Dörnyei, Z. (1995). On the teachability of communication strategies. *TESOL Quarterly, 29*, 55–85.

Dörnyei, Z. (2001). *Motivational strategies in the language classroom*. Cambridge, UK: Cambridge University Press.

Dörnyei, Z., & Skehan, P. (2003). Individual differences in second language learning. In C. J. Doughty & M. H. Long (Eds.), *Handbook of second language acquisition*. Oxford, UK: Blackwell.

Dreyer, C., & Oxford, R. L. (1996). Learning strategies and other predictors of ESL proficiency among Afrikaans speakers in South Africa. In R. L. Oxford (Ed.), *Language learning strategies around the world: Crosscultural perspectives* (pp. 61–74). Honolulu, HI: University of Hawaii Press.

Ehrman, M., & Oxford, R. L. (1990). Adult language learning styles and strategies in an intensive training setting. *Modern Language Journal, 74*, 311–327.

Ehrman, M., & Oxford, R. L. (1995). Cognition plus: Correlates of adult language proficiency. *Modern Language Journal, 79*, 67–89.

Ellis, R. (1994). An instructed theory of second language acquisition. In N. Ellis (Ed.), *Implicit and explicit learning of languages* (pp. 79–114). London: Academic Press.

Ellis, R. (2002). Methodological options in grammar teaching materials. In E. Hinkel & S. Fotos (Eds.), *New perspectives on grammar teaching in second language classrooms* (pp. 155–179). Mahwah, NJ: Lawrence Erlbaum Associates.

Eslinger, C. E. (2000). *A more responsive mind: A study of learning strategy adaptation among culturally diverse ESL students*. Unpublished master's thesis, Brigham Young University, Provo, Utah.

Gass, S., & Mackey, A. (2000). *Stimulated recall methodology in second language research*. Mahwah, NJ: Lawrence Erlbaum Associates.

Goh, C. (1997). Metacognitive awareness and second language listeners. *ELT Journal, 51*, 361–369.

Green, J., & Oxford, R. L. (1995). A closer look at learning strategies, L2 proficiency, and gender. *TESOL Quarterly, 29*, 261–297.

He, T. H. (2002). Goal orientations, writing strategies, and written outcomes: An experimental study. In J. E. Katchen (Ed.), *Selected papers from the 11th International Symposium on English Teaching/Fourth Pan Asian Conference*. Taipei, Taiwan, November 8–10, 2002, pp. 198–207.

Hosenfeld, C. (1979). A learning-teaching view of second language instruction. *Foreign Language Annals, 12*, 51–57.

Hsiao, T. Y., & Oxford, R. L. (2002). Comparing theories of language learning strategies: A confirmatory factory analysis. *Modern Language Journal, 86*, 368–383.

Hyte, H. D. (2002). *The effects of computer-based metacognitive strategy training for adult second language learners*. Unpublished master's thesis, Brigham Young University, Provo, Utah.

Janzen, J. (1996). Teaching strategic reading. *TESOL Journal, 6*(1), 6–9.

Knight, S. L., Padron, Y. N., & Waxman, H. G. (1985). The cognitive reading strategies of ESL students. *TESOL Quarterly, 19*, 789–792.

Kohler, D. B. (2002). The effects of metacognitive language learning strategy training on lower-achieving second language learners. Unpublished doctoral dissertation, Brigham Young University, Provo, Utah.

Krashen, S. (1985). *The input hypothesis*. London: Longman.

Larsen-Freeman, D. (2001). Teaching grammar. In M. Celce-Murcia (Ed.), *Teaching English as a second or foreign language* (pp. 251–266). Boston: Heinle & Heinle.

Larsen-Freeman, D. (2003). *Teaching language: From grammar to grammaring*. Boston: Heinle & Heinle.

Leki, I. (1995). Coping strategies of ESL students in writing tasks across the curriculum. *TESOL Quarterly, 29*, 235–260.

McDonough, S. (1999). A hierarchy of strategies? In S. Cotterall & D. Crabbe (Eds.), *Learner autonomy in language learning: Defining the field and effecting change* (pp. 51–60). Frankfurt, Germany: Peter Lang.

Mokhtari, K., & Sheorey, R. (2002). Measuring ESL students' awareness of reading strategies. *Journal of Developmental Education, 25*(3), 2–10.

Naiman, N., Fröhlich, M., & Todesco, A. (1975). The good second language learner. *TESL Talk, 6*, 68–75.

Nunan, D. (1991). *Language teaching methodology: A textbook for teachers*. New York: Prentice-Hall.

Nunan, D. (1996). Learner strategy training in the classroom: An action research study. *TESOL Journal, 6*(1), 35–41.

Nunan, D. (1997). Does learner strategy training make a difference? *Lenguas Modernas, 24*, 123–142.

O'Malley, J. M., & Chamot, A. U. (1990). *Learning strategies in second language acquisition*. New York: Cambridge University Press.

Oxford, R. L. (1990). *Language learning strategies: What every teacher should know*. New York: Newbury House Publishers.

Oxford, R. L. (1993). Individual differences among your ESL students: Why a single method can't work. *Journal of Intensive English Studies, 7*, 27–42.

Oxford. R. L. (1996). Employing a questionnaire to assess the use of language learning strategies. *Applied Language Learning, 7*, 25–46.

Oxford, R. L. (2001). Language learning styles and strategies. In M. Celce-Murcia (Ed.), *Teaching English as a second or foreign language* (3rd ed.), (pp. 359–366). Boston: Heinle & Heinle.

Oxford, R. L. (2002). Sources of variation in language learning. In R. B. Kaplan (Ed.), *The Oxford handbook of applied linguistics* (pp. 245–252). New York: Oxford University Press.

Oxford, R. L., & Burry-Stock, J. A. (1995). Assessing the use of language learning strategies worldwide with the ESL/EFL version of the *Strategy Inventory for Language Learning. System, 23*, 153–175.

Oxford, R. L., & Leaver, B. L. (1996). A synthesis of strategy instruction for language learners. In R. L. Oxford (Ed.), *Language learning strategies around the world: Crosscultural perspectives* (pp. 227–246). National Foreign Language Resource Center. Manoa: University of Hawaii Press.

Oxford, R. L., Lavine, R. L., Felkins, G., Hollaway, M. E., & Saleh, S. (1996). Telling their stories: Language students use diaries and recollection. In R. L. Oxford (Ed.), *Language learning strategies around the world: Crosscultural perspectives* (pp. 19–34). National Foreign Language Resource Center. Manoa: University of Hawaii Press.

Paulus, T. (1999). The effect of peer and teacher feedback on student writing. *Journal of Second Language Writing, 8,* 265–289.

Rees-Miller, J. (1993). A critical appraisal of learner training: Theoretical bases and teaching implications. *TESOL Quarterly, 27,* 679–689.

Rees-Miller, J. (1994). The author responds. *TESOL Quarterly, 28,* 776–781.

Riley, L. D., & Harsch, K. (1999). Enhancing the learning experience with strategy journals: Supporting the diverse learning styles of ESL/EFL students. Proceedings of the HERDSA Annual International Conference, Melbourne, Australia. http://herdsa.org.au/vic/cornerstones/pdf/Rikley.PDF

Rossi-Le, L. (1995). Learning styles and strategies in adult immigrant ESL students. In J. Reid (Ed.), *Learning styles in the ESL/EFL classroom* (pp. 118–125). Boston: Heinle & Heinle.

Rubin, J. (1975). What the "good language learner" can teach us? *TESOL Quarterly, 9,* 41–51.

Rubin, J. (1981). Study of cognitive processes in second language learning. *Applied Linguistics, 11,* 118–131.

Sharwood Smith, M. (1993). Input enhancement in instructed SLA. *Studies in Second Language Acquisition, 15,* 165–179.

Sheorey, R., & Mokhtari, K. (2001). Differences in the metacognitive awareness of reading strategies among native and non-native readers. *System, 29,* 431–449.

Skehan, P. (1989). *Individual differences in second language learning.* London: Arnold.

Song, M. (1998). Teaching reading strategies in an ongoing EFL university reading classroom. *Asian Journal of English Teaching, 8,* 41–54.

Stern, H. H. (1975). What can we learn from the good language learner? *Canadian Modern Language Review, 31,* 304–318.

Vandergrift, L. (1997). The strategies of second language (French) listeners: A descriptive study. *Foreign Language Annals, 30,* 387–409.

Vandergrift, L. (1999). Facilitating second language listening comprehension: Acquiring successful strategies. *ELT Journal, 53,* 168–176.

Vandergrift, L. (2002). It was nice to see that our predictions were right: Developing metacognition in L2 listening comprehension. *The Canadian Modern Language Review, 58,* 555–575.

Vann, R. J., & Abraham, R. G. (1990). Strategies of unsuccessful language learners. *TESOL Quarterly, 24,* 177–198.

Weaver, S., & Cohen, A. D. (1997). *Strategies-based instruction: A teacher-training manual.* CARLA Working Paper Series #7. Minneapolis, MN: University of Minnesota, The Center for Advanced Research on Language Acquisition.

Wenden, A. L. (1991). *Learner strategies for learner autonomy.* New York, NY: Prentice-Hall.

Wenden, A. L. (1998). Metacognitive knowledge and language learning. *Applied Linguistics, 19,* 515–537.

Wenden, A. L. (2002). Learner development in language learning. *Applied Linguistics, 23,* 32–55.

Wolfersberger, M. (2001). *The effects of second language proficiency on the transfer of first language composing processes to second language writing.* Unpublished master's thesis, Brigham Young University, Provo, Utah.

Wong-Fillmore, L. (1979). Individual differences in second language acquisition. In C. J. Fillmore, W-S. Y. Wang, & D. Kempler (Eds.), *Individual differences in language ability and language behavior* (pp. 203–228). New York: Academic Press.

You, Y. L., & Joe, S. G. (2002). A metacognitive approach to the problem of incoherence in EFL learners' writing. In J. E. Katchen (Ed.), *Selected Papers from the 11th International Symposium on English Teaching/Fourth Pan Asian Conference.* Taipei, Taiwan, November 8–10, 2002, pp. 599–610.

VI

Second Language Testing and Assessment

Guest Editors:

Tim McNamara
Annie Brown
Lis Grove
Kathryn Hill
Noriko Iwashita
University of Melbourne

Introduction

Tim McNamara
University of Melbourne

The Social Turn in Language Assessment

Language assessment is an institutional practice, whether it takes the form of large-scale proficiency tests or curriculum-related assessment. Until recently most published research in language testing has focused on proficiency tests, particularly two international tests of English for Academic Purposes (EAP), used to facilitate the admissions processes of universities in English-speaking countries: the American Test of English as a Foreign Language (TOEFL) and the British/Australian International English Language Testing System (IELTS). The emphasis in this research is on guaranteeing the quality of the inferences about test-takers implied in test scores: This process is known as test score validation, and it draws on concepts and techniques from psychometric theory, whose terminology and procedures (particularly in the area of statistical analysis of test data) can appear formidably complex for the nonspecialist. Although the language proficiency tested in such tests is the target of second language learning programs, proficiency assessment (albeit in minor key) has not always been well integrated into the language learning process, as teachers have found its terminology and its requirements, developed in other institutional contexts and to serve other institutional needs, both technical and onerous. Even where (as is increasingly the case) curriculum reform involves attention to assessment, and has led to the development of assessment methods more sympathetic to the needs of teachers and learners, language assessment is still carried out to serve primarily institutional purposes, and the role of the teacher is to gather data for administrative purposes of accountability or the fulfillment of policy. It can thus still be seen by language teachers as the practice of others. The institutional character of language testing has been disguised from researchers in language testing by the discourse of the principal contributing disciplines to language testing, linguistics, psychology, and measurement, with their overtly asocial character. Tests have focused on the measurement of individual knowledge and individual skill, and theories of proficiency have been social in a very limited sense, even when they address issues of communicative competence.

In the last decade and more, however, a growing critical focus on the character of applied linguistics as a whole has found its echo in language testing, which has experienced what we might call a "social turn." This turn is associated with both theoretical and policy-related developments. In terms of theory, these include a new concern for values and social consequences in validity theory; epistemological debates about the socially situated nature of knowledge; and a specific questioning of the individualistic focus in current conceptualizations of language proficiency. In terms of policy, they include a renewed role for assessment in managerialist educational and training systems; and the advent of what is known as critical language testing.

First, theories of validity in educational assessment have increasingly stressed the social context and meaning of assessments, and have required that interpretations of the ability of students be seen in the context of the social values implied in such assessments, and in the light of the social practices engendered by them. These issues have been most comprehensively addressed in the work of Messick (1989), and their influence on the field, originally somewhat muted in the influential original presentation of Messick's ideas in the work of Bachman (1990), have begun to be felt strongly. Second, the ferment about the epistemology of research in the social sciences (cf. Lynch, 1996) (also reflected in Messick's discussion of validity), has led to changes in the methodology of validation research so that it is no longer based solely on the traditional procedures of psychometrics but now includes various forms of discourse analysis and other qualitative research methods, particularly introspection. Third, work in discourse analysis on the co-construction of performance, particularly in spoken language, has challenged the individualistic focus of received conceptualizations of language proficiency, which saw language performance as a projection of individual competence, rather than seeing it as distributed and collaborative. Fourth, the managerialist emphasis on accountability in curriculum reform has led to the creation of powerful overarching scales and frameworks for guiding the language assessment practices of teachers, and these have led to an increasing focus on the differences between teacher assessments and formal tests developed within the psychometric tradition. Finally, the critical perspective on applied linguistics associated most clearly with the work of Pennycook (2001) has found its response in the development by Shohamy of the field of critical language testing (Shohamy, 2001), which attempts to bring to the fore the political and social agendas involved in language assessment practice.

- The social context of language assessment is addressed in detail in chapter 43, "Social and Political Context of Language Assessment by **Antony Kunnan**." Kunnan specifies four dimensions of the context in which language testing takes place: "the political and economic, the educational, social and cultural, the technological and infrastructure, and the legal and ethical," and relates these to Messick's widened conceptualization of validity. Kunnan presents detailed examples of issues confronting language testing related to each of these dimensions: for example, the (sometimes covert) role of tests in the service of dubious social policies; issues of fairness and test bias in standardized tests containing a language-based testing component; the differential impact on test-takers of new technologies used for the delivery of tests; the legal rights of test-takers, including those with disabilities; and the response of the language testing profession to a new sense of their social and professional responsibilities in the form of the development of a code of ethics.

- In chapter 44, "Validity and Validation in Language Testing," the discussion by **Alan Davies** and **Cathie Elder** is by turns speculative and empirical (cf. Davies, 1992). Davies, long one of the most independent and iconoclastic thinkers in Applied Linguistics, discusses the nature and requirements of test validity, and sets Messick's thinking on validity within his own critically evaluative framework. Davies' work on validity in language testing long predates the influence of Messick in the field, and the paper thus presents an encounter between an older and a more currently influential tradition. He argues that the process of validation of test scores is a potentially endless search for the Holy Grail of validity; Elder demonstrates in detail what this involves in her account of the validation of a test of English for Academic Purposes, setting out the scope, results, and limits of a complex program of validation research.

• A somewhat different focus on the 'social' is present in chapter 45, "A Look Back at and Forward to What Language Testers Measure by **Micheline Chalhoub-Deville** and **Craig Deville**, who discuss in detail the third of the earlier points, the co-constructed character of performance in language tests, and the intellectual and practical challenges this poses for current theories of proficiency. Their discussion of the construct of language proficiency is located in the context of a survey of how currently available textbooks on language testing treat issues in measurement. They argue that the most distinctive feature of language testing, when compared with other areas of educational measurement, with which it shares much, is the conceptualization of its measurement target, language proficiency.

• In chapter 46, "Research Methods in Language Testing," **Tom Lumley** and **Annie Brown** also address measurement issues within the context of current theories of validity in their discussion of research methods in language testing. Messick's validation framework includes the need for empirical investigation to support claims about the interpretability of test scores. They draw attention to the widening range of research methods used in carrying out such investigations. They begin with a survey of quantitative methods including traditional psychometric methods such as correlation and analysis of variance, moving on to deal with techniques of increasing statistical sophistication derived from theories including Item Response Modelling, Rasch measurement, Structural Equation Modelling and Generalizability Theory. They then discuss a range of qualitative approaches. These include loosely ethnographic methods including interviews and observation; discourse-based methods, particularly the use of Conversational Analysis, for examining the interaction in various types of oral assessments; and introspection, the analysis of concurrent or stimulated recall protocols in order to examine rater cognition and test-taker strategies. Discourse analysis emerges as an important lever for change in language testing research, this time in the area of research methodology, complementing its role as a trigger point for the epistemological issues and questions of construct raised in the previous chapter.

• The contribution of discourse studies to language assessment is also prominent in chapter 47, "Testing Languages for Specific Purposes," by **Dan Douglas**. He defines a number of persistent issues in research on specific purpose tests. Two of them tie in closely to issues raised in the previous papers. The first is the nature of specific purpose language proficiency, and the tendency of the structuralist heritage in applied linguistics to isolate 'language' from 'context,' in this case the context of real-world specialist knowledge that forms one dimension of specific purpose language. Although it is at some level possible to conceptualize language knowledge and subject-matter knowledge as separable, it is not clear that this is either coherent theoretically or practically relevant in many of the specific purpose contexts Douglas discusses. Certainly, current theories of discourse would make such a separation problematic. Second, Douglas appeals to work in discourse analysis, particularly the work of Sally Jacoby (Jacoby, 1998), to justify his call for reference to "indigenous" criteria in the reporting of achievement on specific purpose tests. In her dissertation work, Jacoby studied a team of experienced and novice physicists rehearsing conference papers prior to presentation, and analyzed the naturally occurring or "indigenous" criteria being appealed to implicitly or explicitly in feedback to team members about the strengths and weaknesses of their individual presentations. These criteria made no special place for language, even though several graduate student members of the team were non-native speakers with, in many cases, rather limited proficiency in English. The feedback did not differentiate between native and non-native speakers, except in marginal ways. This surprising fact, that the criteria actually being oriented to in performance did not single out aspects of language proficiency, has obviously important implications for the earlier issue of the conceptualization of specific language proficiency, as well as suggesting that research on such naturally occurring "assessment" activities in the target setting may be relevant to establishing valid criteria for language assessments.

• The need for a shift of research attention to the underrepresented area of classroom assessment is the principal argument in chapter 48, "Classroom Teacher Assessment of Second Language Development: Construct as Practice by **Constant Leung**. Leung contrasts teacher assessment with standardized testing. Following Lynch (2001), he defines teacher assessment as "the noticing and gathering of information about student language use in ordinary (noncontrived) classroom activities, and the use of that information to make decisions about language teaching without necessarily quantifying it or using it for reporting purposes." This locally focused definition of assessment represents a radical challenge to the tradition of institutional language testing: it is not about measurement; it does not serve administrative functions; it does not adhere to psychometric canons. Its aim is to improve pedagogy. Leung attempts to define its status and nature, and to articulate a research and development agenda. He locates the primary focus for this in the development in teachers of "professional knowledge, responsive pedagogy, and reflexive practice." The question remains as to how to get the necessary institutional muscle behind such a development, given that institutional goals are not normally formulated in such terms, certainly not in traditional theorizing of assessment, even in the most progressive theories of validity. There is a possibly unbridgeable gap here, which underlines one dimension of the many difficulties involved in implementing more socially aware language assessment.

REFERENCES

Bachman, L. (1990). *Fundamental considerations in language testing*. Oxford, UK: Oxford University Press.

Davies, A. (1992). Speculation and empiricism in applied linguistics. *Melbourne Papers in Language Testing* 1(2): 1–18.

Jacoby, S. W. (1998). Science as performance: Socializing scientific discourse through conference talk rehearsals. Unpublished doctoral dissertation, University of California, Los Angeles.

Lynch, B. K. (1996). *Language program evaluation*. Cambridge, UK: Cambridge University Press.

Lynch, B. K. (2001). Rethinking assessment from a critical perspective. *Language Testing, 18*(4): 333–349.

Messick, S. A. (1989). Validity. In Linn, R. L. (Ed.), *Educational measurement* (3rd ed.). (pp. 13–103). New York: Macmillan.

Pennycook, A. (2001). *Critical applied linguistics: A critical introduction*. Mahwah, NJ: Lawrence Erlbaum Associates.

Shohamy, E. (2001). *The power of tests: A critical perspective on the uses of language tests*. Harlow, Essex: Longman.

43

Language Assessment From a Wider Context

Antony John Kunnan
California State University, Los Angeles

INTRODUCTION

Most individuals who have been required to take language tests know that tests are part of the sociopolitical setup of a community. Yet, language assessment is characterized as a field that is primarily concerned with the psychometric qualities of tests and one in which test developers/researchers ignore the socioeconomic-political issues that are critically part of tests and testing practice[1]. It is not that these perspectives have not been known earlier. In fact, about two decades ago, Cronbach (1984) pointed out that "testing abilities has always been intended as an impartial way to perform a political function—that of determining who gets what" (p. 5). Bachman (1990) also succinctly stated that "tests are not developed and used in a value-free psychometric test tube; they are virtually always intended to serve the needs of an educational system or of society at large" (p. 279). In addition, Hanson (1993) characterized the intentions and social benefits of testing:

> Most tests are intended to contribute to social ends that are generally reckoned as beneficial, such as equal opportunity, honesty, law-abiding behavior, acquisition of knowledge and skills, identification and development of individual interests and talents, knowledge, and skills for the mutual benefit of the individual and society. (p. 6)

Examining the intentions and social benefits of language testing in the 20th century, Spolsky's (1995) pioneering and eye-opening treatise entitled *Measured Words* was critical of the whole enterprise:

> Since the days of World War I, psychometric principles and practices have come to dominate the testing of foreign language proficiency, and a movement that initially blossomed in the United States has spread throughout the world. As long as testing was confined to helping students learn or to determining the qualifications of individuals seeking employment, there was a strong ethical case to be made for it, as the end justifies the means. But, from its beginnings, testing has been exploited also as a method of control and power—as a way to select, to motivate, to punish. The so-called objective test, by

virtue of its claim of scientific backing for its impartiality, and especially when it operates under the aegis and with the efficiency of big business, is even more brutally effective in exercising this authority. (p. 1)

He also called for a different approach to understanding the motivations and impact of tests.

It is only by taking full account of the institutional or political context that one can appreciate how the psychometric controversies have distracted attention from more serious social (or antisocial) motivations and impact. (p. 1)

Having set up the framework, Spolsky (1995) convincingly showed the influence of personal, institutional, political, and economic policies on the development of language testing in the United States (particularly in the development of the Test of English as a Foreign Language at Educational Testing Service, Princeton) and in the United Kingdom (at the University of Cambridge Local Examinations Syndicate), often overriding appropriate educational and ethical practice.

Using a similar framework, Shohamy (2001) found compelling evidence in three case studies (a reading test, an Arabic test, and an English test) that the "power of tests and their detrimental forces" can alter the intentions of those who introduce tests. McNamara (1998) also noted that tests are used as a disciplinary tool by political institutions for example, as an arm of policy reform and control in fields as broad as education, vocational training, immigration, and citizenship[2].

This chapter follows these researchers in spirit. I examine tests and testing practice from a wide context in order to more fully determine whether and how these tests are beneficial or detrimental to society. The wide "context", constructed from reflection and research in the last two decades, includes the political and economic, the educational, social and cultural, the technological and infrastructure, and the legal and ethical.

TEST VALIDITY AND TEST FAIRNESS: OPENING UP THE "CONTEXT"

In the late 1980s, Messick (1989) revolutionized test validity discussions by arguing for a unified view of validity. Specifically, he asserted that validity should be considered as a unified concept (in contrast to the three traditional validity types: content validity, predictive and concurrent criterion-related validity, and construct validity developed and applied in earlier decades) with a superordinate role for construct validity. He postulated that test validity refers to the "appropriateness, meaningfulness, and usefulness of the specific inferences made from test scores" (p.8) and that the unified validity framework could be constructed "by distinguishing two interconnected facets of the unified validity concept. One facet is the source of justification of the testing, being based on appraisal of either evidence or consequence. The other facet is the function or the outcome of the testing, being either interpretation or use" (Messick, 1989, p. 20)

In this view of validity, Messick also explicitly advanced a critical role for value implications and social consequences, particularly evaluation of intended and unintended social consequences of test interpretation and use, as part of test validity. This was the first time that values implications and social consequences were brought from the back room (where test developers had conveniently ignored them) and included as part of test validity. This view has now been instantiated in the *1999 Standards* (AERA, APA, NCME, 1999). The examination of the social value of tests as well as their unanticipated consequences or side effects, especially if such effects were traceable to sources of invalidity of test score interpretation, received support from this view. Many researchers welcomed this significant development as a possible sign of a new beginning in a hitherto psychometrically driven field and such discussions are widespread today (see paper in Cumming & Berwick, 1996; Kunnan, 1998; and Chapelle, 1999). Messick's view of test validity also triggered the reworking of the role of test reliability and has led many researchers to argue that test reliability evidence should be used as evidence that contributes to test validity (Chapelle, 1999; Kunnan, 2000).

Similarly, after Messick's view was widely circulated, the importance of fairness has also been understood better. The 1999 *Standards* acknowledged the critical importance of fairness as a goal in testing by devoting a whole chapter to fairness for the first time. Its vision is as follows:

> A full consideration of fairness would explore the many functions of testing in relation to its many goals, including the broad goal of achieving *equality of opportunity* in our society. It would consider the technical properties of tests, the ways test results are reported, and the factors that are validly or erroneously thought to account for patterns of test performance for groups and individuals. A comprehensive analysis would also examine the regulations, statutes, and case law that govern test use and the remedies for harmful practices. (p. 73; emphasis added)

Further more, the *Standards* specifically defined three categories of fairness: fairness as lack of bias, fairness as equitable treatment in the testing process, and fairness as equality in outcomes of testing.

Willingham and Cole (1997) offered another perspective, but their focus was noticeably different: Their focus was on comparable validity, the validity of score interpretations for all individuals and groups. Their three criteria for fair tests were comparable opportunity for test-takers to demonstrate relevant proficiency, comparable testing tasks and scores, and comparable treatment of test-takers in test interpretations and use. Incorporating these two definitions and Messick's interest in values and social consequences through his unified validity framework, Kunnan (2004) proposed a fairness framework that positions fairness as the ultimate goal in testing[3]. The main qualities of the framework are construct validity, absence of bias, access, administration, and social consequences. These concepts inform the "Wider Context" concept.

THE WIDER CONTEXT

The wider context of tests and testing practice refers mainly to the collection of traditions, histories, customs, professional practices, and academic, social, and political institutions of a community. This collection can then be identified loosely as the political and economic, the educational, social and cultural, the technological and infrastructure, and the legal and ethical contexts of a community in which a test operates (Figure 43.1). Other contexts that may also play a role in a community but which are not explicitly shown in Fig. 43.1 include race and ethnicity, gender, class, caste, religion, sexual orientation, entertainment, and so on. As shown in the figure, the main contexts surround, overlap, and enmesh each other and it is into this milieu that a test is thrust when it is commissioned. It is then developed, administered, scored, reported, and researched and decisions are made based on test scores for this community[4]. This conceptualization also implies that we need to use this wider context in debating and evaluating tests and testing practice but does not exclude any of the technical aspects of language testing practice, such as validity, reliability, standard-setting, and the like from being used in such evaluations[5].

The Political and Economic Context

The political and economic context of language assessment has not been—until very recently—overtly acknowledged, and relative silence on this front has contributed

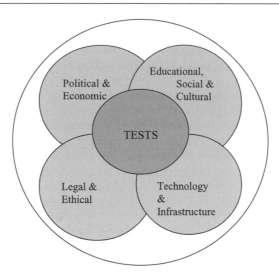

FIG. 43.1. The wider context of tests and testing practice.

to the notion that language testing is an apolitical discipline (see Spolsky, 1995; McNamara, 1998; Shohamy, 2001, for notable exceptions). An examination of school-level testing and testing for immigration and citizenship will be discussed along these lines.

The Politicization of School-Level Testing

In the United States, there has recently been a huge growth in publications and public discussions on school-level standardized testing, so much so that electoral campaigns and platforms have become a key stage for such debates[6]. Elected officials (such as the president, state governors, mayors, and school superintendents) often take the first opportunity to underscore their desire to impose standardized testing on schools in their jurisdiction in the guise of public accountability.

Large-scale standardized testing is now the main component that drives the concept of public school accountability. This is largely because until recently most school did not require tests for grade-level promotion or high school graduation. Instead, schools depended on teacher grades for courses and students were promoted to the next grade automatically. College-bound students took additional courses and standardized tests such as the SAT for admission to colleges and universities. The official accountability argument goes as follows: If parents knew how well their children were doing, then educators, policymakers, and the public would know how well their schools were doing. Financial incentives would then be offered to schools that have met or exceeded their goals or punitive action would be taken against schools that do poorly.

President Bush's education agenda added negatively to this state of affairs when he signed the *No Child Left Behind (NCLB) Act of 2001*, which requires all states to introduce testing in science, mathematics, and (English language) reading for Grades 3 through 8. It is based on four basic principles: stronger accountability for results, increased flexibility and local control, expanded options for parents, and an emphasis on teaching methods that have been proven to work. In terms of increased accountability, the Act requires states to implement statewide accountability systems covering all public schools and students on state standards in reading and mathematics, annual testing for all students in Grades 3–8, and annual statewide progress objectives ensuring that all groups of students reach proficiency within 12 years. Results of such tests are required to be broken out by poverty, race, ethnicity, disability, and limited English proficiency to ensure that no group is left behind. School districts and schools that fail to make adequate yearly progress (AYP) toward statewide proficiency goals will, over time, be subject to improvement, corrective action, and restructuring measures. Schools that meet or exceed AYP objectives or close achievement gaps will be eligible for State Academic Achievement Awards. This overtly stated goal masks the Bush administration's related concept of awarding parents tuition fees (known as the School Voucher Program) if they choose to remove their children from failing public schools and place them in private schools[7].

Whereas there is general support for the accountability argument from educators and parent groups, (which is driven by dissatisfaction with instructional and grading practices and social promotion through grade levels), the mechanism of using standardized testing to achieve this end has been challenged by education groups, including civil rights organizations, as well as individuals. For example, according to Heubert and Hauser (1999), "for more than 20 years the National Association for the Advancement of Colored People has called the use of testing as a sole criterion for the nonpromotion of students and the use of competency testing for high school graduation 'another way of blaming the student victim'" (p. 45). The Mexican American Legal Defense and Educational Fund has filed a lawsuit in Texas against the use of the Texas Testing of Academic Skills, which claims that, in the words of Heubert and Hauser (1999), "the test denies diplomas to students without sufficient proof that the test does not correspond to what is actually taught in schools in many minority communities" (p. 46). Similarly, the National Association of Bilingual Education argues, according to Heubert and Hauser (1999) "students should be assessed with appropriate, performance-based tests, and English language learners should not be assessed with tests that are inappropriate at their level of language competency" (p. 46). At the individual level, Linn, Baker, and Betebenner (2002) present arguments that the states' content standards, the rigor of their tests, and the stringency of their performance standards vary greatly, thus posing substantial challenges to schools, school districts, and states.

Overall, there is a disjuncture between elected officials and opinion polls, on the one hand, and major educational groups and academic researchers regarding school-level testing on the other hand. However, school-level tests continue to be used as policy instruments by elected officials[7]. Whatever direction this policy takes in the near future, test use will continue to be a highly politicized issue, as ultimately whether and how tests are used is largely decided by elected officials in school boards, governments, and legislatures, and finally in courts; in most cases without much regard to opinions from educators and academic researchers. As Cronbach (1980) put it, "the public intends to judge specific test uses for itself, directly or through courts and legislatures" (p. 100).

Testing for Immigration and Citizenship: Political and Economic Gatekeeping

Political and economic interests have been at the center of gatekeeping in the high-stakes arena of immigration and citizenship. In most countries, language abilities (in the official language of the country) have been required of potential immigrants. Often, the overt goal of assessing language proficiency and the associated intention of providing free language instruction is not the real reason for the testing policy. The real objective may be "racial exclusion," as in the case of the dictation test in Australia and in the case of intelligence tests in the United States in the early 20th century.

In the case of Australia, language tests were used as part of the immigration requirement as early as 1901 as part of the "White Australia" policy. The first test was a dictation test in a European language (or any "prescribed language") to a potential immigrant in such a way that the immigrant (if not from the British Isles) could be excluded. As a result of rigorous application of this policy from 1902 to 1946, only 125,000 members of "the alien races" (Asians and "colored") were admitted to the country. In 1956, the dictation test given in any European language was changed to an English dictation test. In the 1990s, first the ACCESS and then the STEP tests were introduced to assess English language proficiency of professionals prior to registration or immigration of those seeking permanent residence. However, standard setting was influenced by immigration policy that was intended to be benign but sometimes indefensible in practice. According to Hawthorne (1997), the standard set on the ACCESS test restricted immigration in terms of English language ability but the standard on the STEP test was set in such a way as to enable Chinese students already in Australia (after the events of Tiananmen Square) to continue their stay: "The case of the STEP test offers a dramatic illustration of the increasing use of language testing by Australian authorities to achieve political purposes . . . The federal government was able to impose control over a politically volatile situation; the Australian legal system was cleared of an unmanageably large backlog of refugee applications; and young PRC, Pakistani, Sri Lankan, and other asylum seekers were transformed into a relatively educated and acculturated skilled migrant intake—commencing their legal permanent residence in Australia supported by a functional basis of English" (pp. 257–258).

Rather similarly, the use of intelligence tests for immigration in the 1920s had a "racial exclusion" objective in The United States. The earliest language testing was the English Competence examination prepared by the College Entrance Examination Board in 1930. According to Spolsky (1995), this test was intended to deal with a loophole in the Immigration Act of 1924: "Carl Brigham gave evidence in Congress on the deleterious effects of permitting non-Nordic immigrants to 'contaminate the American gene pool'" (p. 55). Spolsky (1995) cites Brigham's racist intentions: "We must frankly admit the undesirable results which would ensue from a cross between the Nordic in this country with the Alpine Slav, with the degenerated hybrid Mediterranean, or with the Negro, or from the promiscuous intermingling of all four types . . . Immigration should not only be restrictive but highly selective" (p. 37). In addition, according to Spolsky (1995), the nexus between the government and testing agencies was clear: "It is important to note that the purpose of this test . . . was in fact political and restrictive, namely to enforce an immigration act intended to close the gates to 'undesirables.' A well-established testing agency wrote it at government request" (p. 59).

More recently, the political and economic interests of New Zealand government were evident in the way it introduced the IELTS in 1995. As Read (2001) notes, "the test which would determine whether applicants in the target categories had a minimum level of English proficiency, defined as Level 5 in the General module. Principal applicants were required to pass the test in all four skills before arriving in New Zealand. Other members of the family (or 'nonprincipal applicants') aged 16 and over were also expected to achieve the same level. However, they could be admitted to the country without doing so, upon payment of a fee of NZ$20,000 each. The fee was refundable as follows: a full refund would be given if IELTS Level 5 was achieved within three months of arrival; the sum of NZ$14,000 would be refunded if the required level was reached from three to twelve months after arrival. After that, the full NZ$20,000 was to be retained by the government" (p. 192). Read (2001) goes on to state that the government realized that this high fee was having a negative effect on potential business investor applicants, [and] as an intermediate measure the level of attainment for refund was lowered to Level 4. Later in 1998, the NZ$20,000 fee was abolished and was replaced with a fee ranging from NZ$1,700 to NZ$6,650, which was to entitle the applicants to ESL tuition for a 3-year period.

Many countries also have language tests for citizenship. In the United States, in order to become a citizen, one of the requirements is that the applicant "must understand English and be able to read, write, and speak ordinary English unless the applicant is 50 years or older and have lived in the country for 20 years" (Immigration and Naturalization Service [INS])[9]. Although this requirement is stated clearly, what is unclear is how it is operationalized, as there does not seem to be a standard testing protocol or procedure. The INS examiners who conduct the final interview also conduct the civics test and the English test, along with other duties such as examining documents. Unlike the civics part, which is made up of a body of knowledge that is described in the citizenship study materials, the English test is not described in terms of a proficiency level or can-do statements and is therefore left to the interpretation of the examiner, allowing obvious variations in the test. Anecdotal information collected from citizenship applicants indicates the test may consist of any of the following: The applicant may be asked to write a sentence in English (such as "Today is a beautiful day"), read the civics questions aloud and answer the questions in English ("Who was the first president of the United States?"), or answer questions on everyday matters in English ("Where do you live?")[10]. Such variation in any test would be cause for concern; in this high-stakes test, it is a vexing problem that needs immediate attention.

In the 1990s, new language tests have become part of the requirements for application for citizenship in many countries such as Estonia, Germany, Latvia, and Lithuania. According to Shohamy (2001), the test of Latvian required of all residents including Russians, many of whom have lived their entire lives in Russian-speaking communities in Latvia, is an example of a test used to discriminate against minority ethnic groups: " . . . in 1996, a report showed a drastic decline in the number of Russians residing in Latvia . . . While the language test may not be the only reason for the decline, it clearly contributed significantly to ethnic cleansing" (p. 89).

From these examples, it is imperative for language testers to examine the social consequences of such policies, particularly in terms of what would happen to the applicants who do not pass the test and therefore cannot become citizens. Would they have to continue to live in such countries as second-class citizens because of their inability to achieve an acceptable level of language ability or return to their "homelands"? More fundamental questions could be asked of immigration tests: What is the purpose of such a test? Is the purpose to encourage applicants to learn the local language or identify their deficiencies so that they can take the language classes they need? Or, is the purpose to expressly deny rights and powers to residents who have not mastered the local language to an acceptable level and by extension have not assimilated to the local community and country? Similar questions have been raised in the context of testing immigrants in Canada (Cumming, 1997).

The Educational, Social, and Cultural Context

Standardized language tests are common in the educational, social, and cultural contexts. They are used for a variety of educational and career-related purposes that include competency, admission, and employment. Key concerns that have been raised about these tests are primarily regarding their educational and social consequence: test bias and washback.

Standardized Tests and Washback

Standardized tests have become most popular in U.S. education in. Scores on the SAT that assesses verbal and quantitative ability and/or SAT-II (subject areas) or the ACT are required for admission to U.S. colleges[11]. Similarly, students who are nonnative speakers of English and who wish to apply for admission to U.S. and Canadian colleges and universities are required to demonstrate their English language ability by taking and providing scores on the Test of English as a Foreign Language (TOEFL) or the International English Language Testing System (IELTS). At the graduate level, applicants are generally required to demonstrate their preparedness for study by providing scores on graduate-level aptitude tests (that assess English language reading and writing ability in addition to quantitative skills) such as the Graduate Record Examination or on professional tests such as the Graduate Management Test.

In keeping with the accountability concept, the state of California introduced the California High School Exit Examination (CAHSEE) in English from 2003–2004. According to the State Education Code, the purpose of the CAHSEE is to ensure that students who graduate from high school can demonstrate grade-level competency in the state content standards for reading, writing, and mathematics. The exam has two parts, English-language arts and mathematics, and students of the class of 2006 must pass both portions of the test to receive their high school diploma. Although the independent evaluation of the test reports that the test development, administration, scoring, and reporting is flawless, the report documents through one table that teachers spent 45 hours on test preparation and in one short paragraph that a small DIF study was conducted for Hispanic test-takers.[12]

In 1998, anticipating the national accountability concept, California introduced standardized tests that assesses students from Grades 2 to 11 in a variety of subjects including English reading and writing, mathematics, and science. The impact of this test has generally been negative particularly in terms of washback: Teacher anecdotes have indicated that they have to "teach to the test" for about two months prior to the test and that the curriculum has in general become "test-driven" with less time devoted to activities that are not part of the test. Furthermore, there have been complaints that the test is not aligned to the stated curriculum, a clear problem of content representativeness/coverage. This is a result of many factors, including the situation that different school districts have slightly different curricula and different school districts have slightly different timelines for completion of topics, units, and concepts. It is clear, therefore, that more systematic washback studies need to be conducted although the limitations and dangerous consequences of such standardized tests have been regularly raised[13]. The value of these high-stakes educational tests to California society depends on construct validity, and the absence of bias and positive washback of the tests on instruction.

Achieving Fairness Through Test Bias Studies

Fair access to education and employment has required test bias investigations on standardized tests. Although such investigations are not always mandatory, they are advisable in multicultural, multilingual test-taking populations where a test may be considered biased when it produces systematic differential performance among test-takers from *the same ability group* but from different subgroups of interest (such as age, academic major, gender, race and ethnicity, nationality, native language, religion, and test-takers with disability). Such systematic differential performance may be due to the presence of construct-irrelevant test characteristics in a test (or in test items) or relevant secondary item characteristics. Irrelevant item characteristics may be found in different components of a test: language variety, directions, content, response process, administration, and scoring, reporting, interpretation toward a particular subgroup. Thus, differences in test performance for a designated subgroup of interest (DSI) might result in differences in meaning of test scores such that the validity of the test scores would be seriously in doubt. In summary, test bias could occur when two groups of test-takers with equal ability show a differential probability of a correct response. Furthermore, as test bias investigations are based on comparable test-takers matched with respect to the primary construct the test is measuring, a large difference in performance may mean the test is measuring additional constructs differently across the groups. The additional construct(s) could be either intended secondary constructs or nuisance constructs that have crept into the test.

According to the 1999 *Standards*, there are two sources of bias: content-related and response-related. Content-related bias is related to the following aspects of testing:

1. *Content representativeness:* In an achievement test, it is possible there may be less than desirable alignment between the curriculum and the test items leading to content underrepresentativeness or construct irrelevance. A slightly different type of content bias may also be identified in cases where the topic or subject matter or events, places, and situations that are construct-irrelevant are different or unfamiliar to a DSI (such as test-takers from different academic major, gender or cultural or educational background subgroups).

2. *Language variety:* The language of the test can be a source of bias, particularly if a DSI uses a language variety different from the language variety of a test (such as a DSI uses British or Australian English instead of American English that is used in the test to measure English language ability).

3. *Offensive content and language:* This type of bias refers to content or language used in a test that is controversial or inflammatory to a DSI, demeaning or offensive to members of a DSI, depicting members of a DSI as having stereotypical occupations (i.e., Chinese launderer, White professionals, Black porters, Hispanic laborers, female secretaries or nurses) or in stereotypical situations (i.e., boys as successful in math, girls needing help with math) or material that does not provide adequate representation of all DSI. This type of bias also includes terms and expressions that are offensive or inappropriate, such as "he" to include male as well as female members, "man" as in policeman instead of police officer, "fireman" instead of firefighters, and "disabled workers" instead of workers with disability.

Response-related source of bias is related to the following aspects of testing:

1. *Response-format:* This type of bias refers to the format used in a test such as the item format as well as the response format (essay writing, short-answer, multiple-choice, true-false, etc.). It also includes test directions, scoring rubrics, or test-taking procedure that may be ambiguous or confusing to a particular DSI.

2. *Differential performance:* This type of bias refers to differences in performance on a test between two subgroups (for example, age, gender, race/ethnicity, geographic, or other DSI)[13].

3. *Standard setting:* When a test is used for standard setting (that is, selection and prediction), evidence is gathered to check whether the relationship between the test score and the criterion score (used for standard setting) is biased for a DSI.

Many standardized language tests have been the subject of test bias studies. Most of the attention has been on the following areas: language variety, language content, response format, differential performance, and standard setting (see Kunnan, 2000, for a list of studies). Such investigations have helped test developers and researchers understand the role of social and cultural factors in the performance of different test-taker groups although the limited role of such studies in terms of fairness has also been pointed out (Camilli & Shepard, 1997; Kunnan, 2000).

The Technology and Infrastructure Context

The importance of this context has become clearer in the last decade than ever before due to the rapid use of high technology in testing such as computers and the Internet.

A key concern with the use of technology often articulated is whether test-takers have access to and knowledge of the technology necessary for success on a test.

Technology and Access

In low-technology-use areas, where machine scoring has replaced human scoring, it is likely that this is coupled with the promotion of multiple-choice test items and the use of machine-scorable cards that enable machine scoring (such as most U.S. based tests). While recording responses to test items on a machine-scorable card might be easy for test-takers who are used to this format, test-takers who are not used to it might find it rather confusing and unnecessarily tricky from two points of view: the use of multiple choices for each test item and the recording of responses. Thus, it is critical that test developers are aware of how familiar test-taking groups (in their targeted population) are with multiple-choice test items and whether they are able to record their responses.

Similarly, in the case of tape-mediated tests (such as the Test of Spoken English or the Simulated Oral Proficiency Tests), talking into an audio tape recorder in response to an unseen voice that asks for responses is another problematic test format. Test-takers who are unfamiliar with this format will have difficulty dealing with it (especially starting and completing responses within the time allocated for each response). Furthermore, from a social and cultural point of view, it may seem inappropriate to particular test-taking groups to talk into a tape recorder, especially in tests that claim to assess communicative language ability.

In high-technology-use areas, computers may be used in all aspects of test development, administration, scoring, and reporting. In test administrations using computers (such as the computer-based TOEFL), a test-taker would receive test items on the computer screen that have been either based on item difficulty and person ability estimates (if the test section is a computer-adaptive test) or based on a set order of items (as in a computer-based test or a paper-and-pencil test). Either way, the test-taker would need to have the requisite computer keyboarding and mouse movement skills (clicking, scrolling, highlighting, etc.) in order to read the test items and to record the answers. This calls into question the issue of test access if the test is required of test-takers in places where such computer skills and computer-based tests are relatively new or nonexistent.

For example, the administrators of the computer-based TOEFL (which replaced the paper-and-pencil TOEFL) had to deal with this issue as the test is offered worldwide, including places in which high-technology use is new or nonexistent. As the test administrators were aware of the test access issue, a computer-familiarity study of potential TOEFL test-takers was conducted prior to launching the test (Taylor et al., 1998). This study enabled the test administrators to be confident that most test-takers who might take the computer-based TOEFL have sufficient familiarity with keyboarding and mouse skills and that those who do not could benefit from a free tutorial that test-takers could take prior to taking the test. This solution is acceptable for test-takers who come forward to take the tutorial and the test, but it would not be sufficient if the very thought of having to take a computer-familiarity tutorial and computer-based test inhibited a sizable number of test-takers in a particular area from taking the test. This example shows how the use of high technology has to be understood and managed in areas where such technology may not be commonplace among test-takers.

Other related issues also need to be considered. Cost is a concern when paper-and-pencil versions of tests are replaced with computer-based tests; geographical access is another, as a computer-based test may only be available in test centers located in cities[15]. Furthermore, comparability of test versions (computer-based and paper-and-pencil) is also a matter of concern. Thus, if these are major concerns, then technology with computer-based testing may raise more questions than answers.

The Legal and Ethical Context

Test-takers and test score users need a remedial procedure whenever a test is shown to be in violation of established practice or a regulation. For example, if there are problems with any aspect of a test (indefensible construct validity, absence of bias, lack of access, administration, scoring, score-reporting, etc.) or if any existing regulations have been violated that has a direct impact on test-takers, remedial measures should be available to test-takers or any affected persons or agencies. Furthermore, if decisions made on test scores that are in doubt can be reversed as in nonhigh stakes tests, then any of the following remedial measures might satisfy affected test-takers: re-scoring, re-totaling, or re-taking of the test for free or a small fee. In cases when decisions are not easily reversible or test-takers are affected adversely, legal action may be the only recourse.

Legal Framework in the U.S.

In the United States, legal frameworks based on the Constitution, federal civil rights statutes, and judicial decisions apply to standardized tests (including language tests) in educational, licensure, employment, and professional arenas. Test score interpretations and decisions based on scores can be challenged on three grounds by test-takers or interested parties. They are the discrimination challenge based on the basis of test-takers' race, color, national origin, or gender; the due process challenge based on inadequate notice of test requirements or a challenge of the test's curricular validity; and the disability challenge based on legislation passed to protect Americans with disabilities.

The discrimination challenge: In terms of the discrimination challenge, three types of claims can be made to a court: (1) A test is intentionally discriminating against test-takers (who are a particular class of people) on the basis of race, color, national origin, or gender. This challenge is based on the equal protection clause in the 14th Amendment of the U.S. Constitution that forbids public employers from engaging in acts of discrimination. (2) A test preserves the effects of prior discrimination. (3) A disparate impact claim. This claim can be made when different test-taker groups receive different scores (such as female and male or from different race/ethnic groups). State and public school agencies that receive federal funding are prohibited from discriminating against students based on federal statutes[16].

The due process challenge: High-stakes tests that are not found to be discriminating against protected classes may still be illegal under the due process provision of the 5th and 14th Amendments of the U.S. Constitution. The claims under this provision may be either that the test-takers did not receive sufficient advance notice or adequate notice of the test or that the test-takers did not receive instruction on the test knowledge and skills (also known as curricular validity). In terms of the adequate notice provision, test score users or similar agencies are expected to provide adequate notice. This has been interpreted by courts to mean anywhere between 1 to 4 years of advance notice before a test becomes effective, so that the test-takers have adequate opportunity to learn the relevant knowledge or skills. In terms of curricular validity, there have been disagreements as to how educational agencies can demonstrate what students have been taught. Some argue that the formal written school or district curriculum can be used to match the knowledge and skills measured in the test. Others argue that it is not the formal written curriculum that should be used to check curricular validity but the instructional curriculum of the classroom. Test researchers have also made the same argument: They prefer to examine whether test-takers have had the "opportunity to learn" the knowledge and skills in the classroom rather then merely matching test knowledge and skills with a formal written curriculum.

Accommodations for test-takers with disabilities: Test accommodations for test-takers with disabilities were given a major push in the form of three pieces of legislation as part of a political and social agenda: Section 504 of the Rehabilitation Act of 1973, the Americans with Disability Act (ADA) of 1990, and the Individuals with Disabilities Educational Act (IDEA) of 1991 and 1997. Of these, the ADA of 1990 prohibits not only discrimination against individuals with disabilities but also relates to the opportunities for individuals to obtain employment and education[17].

Following these legislative actions, the 1999 *Standards* and the *Code of Fair Testing Practices in Education* (Joint Committee on Testing Practices, 1988) recommend that test accommodations should be made available for test-takers with disabilities. In the 1999 *Standards*, the chapter titled "Testing Individuals with Disabilities" identifies individuals with disabilities "as persons possessing a physical, mental, or developmental impairment that substantially limits one or more of their life functions" (p. 101). And, it urges "test developers and users to become familiar with (U.S.) federal, state, and local laws, and court and administrative rulings that regulate the testing and assessment of individuals with disabilities" (p.101). U.S. federal regulations and testing guidelines, therefore, mandate that tests should not discriminate against test-takers with disabilities but must be valid measures, measuring the ability to be tested and not the disability. While this mandate for testing and test accommodations is evident, IDEA regulations and Section 504 contain an important proviso: "...except where those skills are the factors that the test purports to measure" (Burns, 1998, p. 9). This is important because in some cases the disability itself might be the focus of the test. However, neither the regulations nor the testing guidelines provide or suggest the exact test accommodations to be offered to test-takers with specific disabilities. This leaves many critical issues to be sorted out by test developers, administrators, and users, and finally, by courts.

In the past, test-takers with disabilities were identified only as persons with visual, hearing, or physical impairments. Test-takers with visual impairments were provided a Braille version of a test, test-takers with hearing impairments received a written version of test directions, and test-takers with physical impairments were offered the services of a scribe. In recent years, however, learning disabilities have gained more attention, and appropriate test accommodations (such as extended time and format change) have been designed for this group of test-takers. In fact, in 1994–1995, out of about 5 million test-takers with disabilities, a little more than 50% are learning disabled. What is critical to recognize is that as people with disabilities are heterogeneous, test accommodations need to fit the needs of the individuals if the test accommodation has to be valid as well as meaningful. The most popular type of accommodation is time accommodation: test scheduling, time management, extended time, and reduced time. A chief concern of this test accommodation is whether the validity of the test-score interpretations is altered when the extended time given is varied for test-takers with and without disabilities.

ADA-related challenges: Prior to the passage of the ADA of 1990 and the IDEA of 1991 and 1997, legal cases filed by test-takers with disabilities or disability rights groups were based on the two challenges discussed earlier. Post-ADA legal cases have generally been related to learning disabilities (rather than physical disabilities) and this is probably due to the fact that the majority of test-takers with disabilities are now from this group. But in the various rulings, courts have not provided clear directions on many critical matters like test accommodations (such as extended time). Pitoniak and Royer (2001) state, "The results of these cases do not present a consistent picture, owing to courts' struggling with both how to determine whether a learning disability exists and what that disability means in terms of the affected individual's rights" (p. 63). In summary, as legal challenges in testing are relatively new, court opinions do not offer clear directions as to how to proceed with many matters, including how to avoid discriminatory testing practice, how to identify individuals with disabilities, or what test accommodations are appropriate for different physical and learning disabilities[18].

Ethics and Professional Standards: The Way Forward

With legal standards and regulations constantly under attack and reinterpretation by courts, it is obvious that legal recourse for unsound professional practice may not always help and is often too late from the test-takers' point of view. Thus, sound professional practice needs to be promoted and one way of doing this would be to focus on ethical practice for testing professionals. However, according to Spolsky (1995), from the 1910s to the 1960s, social, economic, political, and personal concerns among key language-testing professionals in the United States and the United Kingdom dominated boardroom meetings and decisions. But in the last two decades, ethical concerns have emerged in the research literature. Spolsky (1981) argued that tests should be labeled like drugs, "Use with care." Stevenson (1981) urged language testers to adhere to test development standards that are internationally accepted for all educational and psychological measures. Canale (1988) suggested a naturalistic-ethical approach to language testing, emphasizing that language testers should be responsible for ethical use of the information they collect. Stansfield (1993) argued that professional standards and a code of practice are ways to bring about ethical behavior among testers. Alderson et al. (1995) reviewed principles and standards but concluded "language testing still lacks any agreed standards by which language tests can be evaluated, compared, or selected" (p. 259). Corson (1997), broadly addressing applied linguists, made a case for the development of a framework of ethical principles by considering three principles: the principal of equal treatment, the principle of respect for persons, and the principle of benefit maximization.

In the last few years, momentum has gathered through publications such as the special issue of *Language Testing* guest-edited by Alan Davies (1997) and conferences such as the Language Assessment Ethics Conference (see Kunnan, 2002). Narrowing the discussion to applied ethics, Hamp-Lyons' (1997) asked what the principle was against which the ethicality of a test was to be judged. To offer guidance in this matter, the International Language Testing Association (ILTA) recently published a report of the Task Force on Testing Standards (1995) and the ILTA's Code of Ethics (2000) that lays out broad guidelines of how professionals should conduct themselves.

As a way of forward, then, the key question for assessment ethics should be: How should ethical test development and test use be promoted? The answer is that there are indirect and perhaps difficult ways. One way is to develop appropriate group ethics through the development of professional standards (for researchers, practitioners, and students) as recently provided by ILTA's Code of Ethics. This Code could be used in developing, researching, maintaining, and evaluating tests as well as in training graduate students although it may not be universally applicable and adjustments may need to be in certain communities.[19]

CONCLUSION

This chapter discusses language tests and testing practices by situating them within four main wider contexts. The four contexts discussed here do not preclude the relevance of other contexts that may be useful in other discussions. This chapter also explicitly puts forward the notion that tests are best understood when a wider interdisciplinary perspective is used in debating and evaluating tests and testing practice. As Spolsky (1995) asserts, "In the study of fields like language testing and teaching, scholars need to be ready to draw not just on the obvious theoretical disciplines that underpin applied linguistics, such as the various language sciences and education, but also on fields like economics, political science, and sociology that furnish methods of investigating the context in which language and education exist" (p. 3).

I would like to conclude with McNamara's (2000) beautiful theater analogy that perfectly captures my own interest in the wider context and the spirit of this chapter: At a moment of dramatic intensity in the theater, the glare of a single spotlight can isolate an individual actor from his or her surroundings. The spotlight focuses the spectators' attention on the psychological state of the character being portrayed. Temporarily at least, the surroundings, including other actors present, are rendered invisible for the audience. Until fairly recently, thinking about language assessment was like this. It focused exclusively on the skills and abilities of the individual being assessed . . . But what does this spotlight of this individualizing perspective exclude? What lies behind, around? Imagine the spotlight going off to be replaced by normal stage lighting: The other actors on the stage are revealed. Now imagine the performance continuing, but the house lights coming up, so that the audience is revealed. Imagine finally the side curtains behind pulled back and the stage removed to expose all the personnel working behind the scenes. The individual performer is now exposed as forming part of a larger collective activity . . . (p. 67).

NOTES

1. As I am making no distinction in this chapter between tests and assessments, I am using tests interchangeably with assessments and testing interchangeably with assessment.
2. General critiques of U.S. educational testing include Gould's *The Mismeasure of Man*, (1981) Crouse and Trusheim's *The Case against the SAT* (1988), and more recently Lemann's *The Big Test* (1999).
3. In this view, 'a fair test' is not necessarily one in which a test-taker is awarded a better score.
4. In Fig. 43.1, the four main contexts are presented in neatly overlapping circles. In reality, it is likely that one or two contexts may overlap fully or only be tangentially involved. Much depends on the how and why a test is commissioned, developed, administered, scored, reported, researched, and used by the community in which the test operates. Moreover, the main contexts need not always be configured in the manner shown. In particular communities, depending on the local situation, the main contexts of interests could be social and political or economic and technological, or legal and political, etc.
5. Davidson and Lynch, (2002) in their book *Testcraft* use the concept of mandate, which they define as a constellation of forces that shape the design of a test: theory, curriculum, politics, money, answerability (to higher powers), etc.
6. Most of the examples in this chapter are from the United States this is where the author works but this does not mean that the "Wider Context" perspective promoted in the chapter is restricted to the United States. This framework could be used for evaluation of tests and testing practices of any community.
7. Most commentators read private schools to mean faith-based (meaning, religious and Christian) schools which is very much in line with the Republican President Bush's agenda.
8. It must be noted that California teachers are not directly involved in any of the standardized tests used in the state. The CAHSEE, the CELDT, or the California Achievement Test 6 are all produced by testing companies thus increasing the divide between teaching and testing and teachers and tests.
9. The INS has been reorganized and renamed the Bureau of Citizenship and Immigration Services (BCIS). See the website for details: http://www.immigration.gov/graphics/index.htm retrieved on 5/27/2003.
10. This website provides a list of about 200 unconnected English sentences for the written English test, much like a set of sentences in an old-fashioned dictation test; test-takers are cautioned that other sentences may be on the test: http://www.ins.usdoj.gov/graphics/services/natz/natzsamp.htm retrieved on 1/23/2003.
11. At the time of writing, the College Board, which owns the SAT, is planning to revise the test. The new test will have Critical Reading (an increase in the reading part and the elimination of the word analogies section), an Essay Writing section (a new addition), and the Mathematics section.
12. See website for HUMRRO's (2002) independent evaluation of the CAHSEE: http://www.cde.ca.gov/statetests/cahsee/eval/2002/2002humrro.html retrieved on 1/25/2003.
13. The FairTest: The National Center for Fair and Open Testing at the following website has many arguments on these lines: www.fairtest.org.
14. A caveat regarding this type of bias is that outcome differences do not automatically mean that the test is biased but the burden is on the test developer to demonstrate that biased test items are not causing the differential performance.
15. It was reported in U.S. press that the Computer-based TOEFL, which had been launched in sub-Saharan Africa in 2000, soon had to be replaced with the paper-and-pencil version due to problems of geographical access after many university and college professors in departments of African studies in the United States (known as Africanists) complained to ETS about this.

16. This is a uniquely American legal provision due to legal (for example, slavery) and illegal discrimination of several groups of people (Native Americans, African Americans, Hispanic Americans, and Asian Americans) practiced for centuries in the country.
17. Similar laws are on the books in the United Kingdom the European an Union, and India.
18. See Bersoff (1981) and Fulcher & Bamford (1988) for legal challenges that are possible in the United States and United Kingdom. Also, see Kunnan (2000) for a list of court cases related to testing in the United States and Lippi-Green (1997) for court cases related to employment-related language use and discrimination in the United States.
19. See Singer (1991) for discussion on universal prescriptivism and relativism.

REFERENCES

Alderson, J. C., Clapham, C., & Wall, D. (1995). *Language test construction and evaluation*. Cambridge, UK: Cambridge University Press.
American Educational Research Association, American Psychological Association, National Council for Measurement in Education (1999). *Standards for educational and psychological testing*. Washington, DC: Author.
Bachman, L. F. (1990). *Fundamental considerations in language testing*. Oxford, UK: Oxford University Press.
Bersoff , D. (1981). Testing and the law. *American Psychologist, 36,* 1,047–1,056.
Burns, E. (1998). *Test accommodations for students with disabilities*. Springfield, IL: Thomas.
Camilli, G., & Shepard, L. (1994). *Methods for identifying biased test items*. Thousand Oaks, CA: Sage.
Canale, M. (1988). The measurement of communicative competence. *Annual Review of Applied Linguistics, 8,* 67–84.
Chapelle, C. (1999). Validity in language assessment. *Annual Review of Applied Linguistics, 19,* 254–272.
Corson, D. (1997). Critical realism: An emancipatory philosophy for applied linguistics? *Applied Linguistics, 18,* 166–188.
Cronbach, L. (1980). Validity on parole: How can we go straight? New directions for testing and measurement: Measuring achievement over a decade. Proceedings of the 1979 ETS Invitational Conference (pp. 99–108). San Francisco: Jossey-Bass.
Cronbach, L. (1984). Essentials of psychological testing [fourth Edition]. New York: Harper & Row.
Crouse, J., & Trusheim, D. (1988). *The case against the SAT*. University of Chicago Press.
Cumming, A. (1997). Does language assessment facilitate recent immigrants' participation in Canadian society? *TESL Canada 11,* 117–133.
Cumming, A., & Berwick, R. (1996). Validation in language testing. Clevedon, UK: Multilingual Matters.
Davidson, F., & Lynch, B. (2002). *Testcraft*. New Haven, CT: Yale University Press.
Davies, A. (1997). (Guest Ed.) Ethics in language testing. *Language Testing, 14,* 3.
Fulcher, G., & Bamford, R. (1996). I didn't get the grade I need: Where's my solicitor? *System, 24,* 437–448.
Gould, G. (1981). The mismeasure of man. New York: Norton.
Hamp-Lyons, L. (1997). Ethics in language testing. In C. Clapham & D. Corson (Eds.), Language testing and assessment. *Encyclopedia of language and education, Vol. 7,* Dordrecht, The Netherlands: Kluwer.
Hanson, F. A. (1993). *Testing testing: Social consequences of the examined life*. Berkeley, CA: University of California Press.
Hawthorne, L. (1997). The political dimension of English language testing in Australia. *Language Testing, 14,* 248–260.
Heubert, J., & Hauser, R. (Eds.) (1999*). High stakes: Testing for tracking, promotion, and graduation*. Washington, DC: National Academy Press.
International Language Testing Association. (1995). Task Force on Testing Standards. Author.
International Language Testing Association. (2000). Code of Ethics. Author.
Joint Committee on Testing Practices. (1988). *Code of Fair Testing Practices in Education*. Author.
Kunnan, A. J. (1998). Approaches to validation. In A. J. Kunnan (Ed.), *Validation in language assessment* (pp. 1–14). Mahwah, NJ: Lawrence Erlbaum Associates.
Kunnan, A. J. (2000). *Fairness and justice for all*. In A. J. Kunnan (Ed.), *Fairness and validation in language assessment* (pp. 1–13). Cambridge, UK: Cambridge University Press.
Kunnan, A. J. (2002). (Ed.) *Proceedings of the Language Assessment Ethics Conference*, Pasadena, CA.
Kunnan, A. J. (2004). Test fairness. In M. Milanovic, C. Weir, & S. Bolton (Eds.), *European Year of Language Conference Papers, Barcelona* (pp. 27–48). Cambridge, UK: CUP.
Lemann, N. (1999). *The big test*. New York: Farrar, Straus & Giroux.
Linn, R., Baker, E. & Betebenner, D. (2002). Accountability systems: Implications of requirements of the *No Child Left Behind Act of 2001*. *Educational Researcher 31,* 3–16.
Lippi-Green, R. (1997). *English with an accent*. London: Routledge.
Messick, S. (1989). Validity. In R. Linn (Ed.), *Educational measurement*. 3rd edition. (pp. 13–103). New York: Macmillan.
McNamara, T. (1998). Policy and social considerations in language testing. *Annual Review of Applied Linguistics, 18,* pp. 304–319.

McNamara, T. (2000). *Language testing*. Oxford, UK: Oxford University Press.

Pitoniak, M., & Royer, J. (2001). Testing accommodations for examinees with disabilities: A review of psychometric, legal, and social policy issues. *Review of Educational Research, 71*, 53–104.

Read, J. (2001). The policy context for English testing for immigrants. In C. Elder et al., (Eds.), *Experimenting with uncertainty: Essays in honor of Alan Davies* (pp. 191–199). Cambridge, UK: Cambridge University Press.

Shohamy, E. (2001). *The power of tests*. London, UK: Longman.

Singer, P. (1991). (Ed.), *A companion to ethics*. Oxford, UK: Blackwell.

Spolsky, B. (1981). Some ethical questions about language testing. In C. Klein-Braley & D. Stevenson (Eds.), *Practice and problems in language testing* (pp. 5–21). Frankfurt: Verlag Peter Lang.

Spolsky, B. (1995). *Measured words*. Oxford, UK: Oxford University Press.

Stansfield, C. (1993). Ethics, standards, and professionalism in language testing. *Issues in Applied Linguistics, 4, 2*, 189–206.

Stevenson, D. K. (1981). Language testing and academic accountability: On redefining the role of language testing in language teaching. *International Review of Applied Linguistics, 19*, 15–30.

Taylor, C., Jamieson, J., Eignor, D., & Kirsch, I. (1998). *The relationship between computer familiarity and performance on computer-based TOEFL test tasks*. TOEFL Research Report 61. Princeton, NJ: ETS.

Willingham, W., & Cole, N. (1997). *Gender and fair assessment*. Mahwah, NJ: Lawrence Erlbaum Associates.

44

Validity and Validation in Language Testing

Alan Davies
University of Edinburgh
Catherine Elder
Monash University, Australia

INTRODUCTION

The concept of validity, which concerns the truth-value of a test and its scores, is both powerful and precarious: powerful because it dominates all aspects of language testing; and precarious because it responds uneasily to four challenges. These are first, the challenge of the appeal to logic and to syllogistic reasoning; second, the challenge of the claims of reliability; third, the challenge of the local and the universal; and fourth, the challenge of the unitary and the divisible. In this chapter we will first discuss the concept of validity, making use of these three causes of concern; we will then take up the issue of validation and examine with exemplification how far different approaches to validation meet the requirements of validity. It is through validation that validity is established, which means that validity is only as good as its validation procedures.

VALIDITY

The Appeal to Logic

Our concern in this chapter is with validity and validation in language testing. However, it may help clarify the argument if we begin with a note on how the term is used in philosophical logic. Validity is an old song for philosophers. They define validity in the following ways:

> A deductive argument is valid whenever its conclusion necessarily follows from the premises; if the premises of the argument are true, then its conclusion cannot be false; the conclusion too must be true. (Angeles, 1981, p. 310)

Traditional logic studies the validity of syllogistic arguments while modern logic identifies as valid those arguments which accord with truth-preserving roles. Any argument is valid if and only if the set consisting of its premises and the negation of its conclusion is inconsistent. (Marcus, 1995, p. 894)

In other words, an argument is valid if its premises and its conclusion are consistent with one another; or to put it negatively, an argument is valid if its premises and the negation of its conclusion are inconsistent with one another.

When choosing a language test for a particular setting (such as medicine), this mode of argument can be exemplified thus:

- This is a test of medical Languages for Specific Purposes (LSP).
- We are in an appropriate medical setting in which to use the test.
- Therefore the test is likely to be valid in this setting.

The negation of its conclusion would be that this test is not valid for its purpose, which would be inconsistent with the previous premises.

For us, what matters in these definitions of validity via logic is the nature of validity construed as an argument. Validity is self-contained: Its definition is reflexive ("validity is validity") just like those other great abstractions: beauty, truth, justice. No doubt that is why when Keats attempted to explain beauty, the best he could achieve was:

"Beauty is truth, truth beauty"—that is all
Ye know on earth, and all ye need to know.

The analogy to justice is particularly instructive since justice (like validity) is unattainable directly and must be reached for via law: It is as though lawyers recognize that while they aim at justice, they have to be content to achieve a remedy that is available in law. There is indeed a view that states that true justice is simply unattainable because there are too many factors that would need to be taken into consideration. And so, just as justice has to be approached via the law, so in the same way, validity can only be accessed via validation.

The Claim of Reliability

If the truth-value of a test is said to be its validity, the reliability of a test indicates its consistency. The relationship of reliability and validity is not unlike that between Form and Meaning in language studies. Meaning, we say, is what matters and yet, without Form, Meaning disappears. In the same way, Validity is what gives a test its life, its uniqueness as a measure, but to do that, to exist as an entity, it needs reliability. It is for this reason that Lado wrote, "Reliability . . . is general rather than specific. If the scores on a test are steady, that is, reliable, they are reliable regardless of what we test" (Lado, 1961, p. 31). Reliability, we say, is necessary but not sufficient: sufficiency depends on validity. Looked at this way, reliability appears as a separate, parallel (if junior) quality of a test, supporting validity but somehow independent of it. Hence Lado's comment about the generality of reliability: It provides the framework, the structure on which validity depends and builds.

Another currently fashionable way of explaining the relationship is to see reliability as part of validity. Being reliable (or consistent) may not be exciting, but in a test, as in life, it can offer a modicum of security, and therefore of meaning—even when its validity status is unclear. But a modicum only, for although it offers generality, that generality is repetitive and recursive, whereas validity offers newness and change. Reliability is said to represent agreement between similar measures of the same test such that, for whatever reason, scores derived from different test sessions or different ratings will be similar, whereas validity resides in agreement between different measures of the same trait (and, to be convincing, in lack of agreement with measures of another trait).

It makes sense to recognize this similarity dimension of reliability as contributing to the overall validity portfolio, which is how validity is now typically viewed (Bachman, 1990; Chapelle, 1999; Winter, 2000). Being similar is a start, as it were, it shows that replication is possible: but it tells us little about the construct that the test models. For that we must look at difference, at the new, at the explorations validity allows us to make. For statisticians, there is a fixed relationship between reliability and validity such that the maximum validity of a test is actually the square root of its reliability (Bellack & Hersen, 1984, p. 48). Thus, the higher a test's reliability, the greater the possibility for validity. This relationship is not, however, reciprocal: If one could "demonstrate that a measure has good validity, its reliability can be assumed and becomes a secondary issue" (Bellack & Hersen, p. 48). Indeed, current discussions of interpretivist approaches to test validity (Lynch, 2003) claim precisely this, that reliability is not as necessary as has been traditionally assumed.

The Local and the Universal

Much of the argument in language testing over the last period mirrors the argument in the wider social science and humanities area, that between the enlightenment (or universal) view that humanity (and experience) can be understood in similar ways and the relativist (or local) view that contexts are not just apparently but fundamentally different. This is the argument from postmodernism, which has insisted over the last 40 years or so that it is unacceptable to assume that one size fits all. With regard to test validity, these approaches manifest themselves as the positivist and the interpretivist, as Lynch (2003) explains. Lynch maintains, "Different research paradigms such as positivism and interpretivism require different validity frameworks" (Lynch, 2003, p. 153). Positivist validity typically uses correlational information between the test and an agreed criterion. The question asked within this paradigm is "Are we measuring the relevant trait or construct?" (Lynch, 2003, p. 151). Interpretivist validity, on the other hand, asks the opposite question: What is it that we are testing? Unlike positivist validity frameworks, interpretivist frameworks do not insist on reliability: "Ultimately, establishing validity from an interpretivist perspective involves achieving consensus across multiple audiences and sources of evidence" (Lynch, 2003, p. 154).

How far tests are appropriate only in a specific (or local) context and how far they can be used more widely (or universally) continues to be debated. Brown and Goodman (2001) point up the issue: "Validity claims always occur in and are tied to specific contexts. Nevertheless, Habermas thinks that they transcend the contingencies of their local genesis to make universal claims. To make a claim to validity is, for Habermas, always to presuppose universality, that is to suppose that any rational person would be motivated to agree" (p. 206).

Transcending their specific contexts must mean that in some sense validity does reside in the test instruments. After all, on what principled grounds does one choose this test (Test A) rather than that test (Test B) to develop and employ? How do we know which one is more likely to provide the kinds of information we seek regarding score inferences? It must surely be the case that Test A and Test B are distinguishable on some principled basis before one or the other is put into use for decision making, learning, or whatever purpose the test claims to serve. And that principled basis must have something to do with validity. In other words, over time, tests in use (such as TOEFL or IELTS) accrue information about the scores that candidates have achieved on them and the inferences that have been drawn. This information allows us to say that one test has provided more helpful inferences than the other and it is not just a trick of semantics, therefore, to say that one test is more valid than the other for a particular purpose.

If of course we are constructing a new test then we have no such information to go on and must rely on the inferences gained from the first test scores to make a judgment about the test. And, indeed, it is now commonly accepted that validity is everywhere a property of the conclusions, interpretations, or inferences that we draw from tests and not a property of the tests themselves, that is, no test is *tout court* "valid." Such a view is not just current orthodoxy. Lado opined that "validity is not general but specific" (1961, p. 31). And in the same vein, and in the same decade as Lado (1961), Tyler (1963) argued for local validity: "A good rule when using tests to select people is: get information about their specific validity, what they accomplish in a particular situation" (p. 93).

This is a view echoed by Anastasi (1988): "The validity of a test cannot be reported in general terms. No test can be said to have 'high' or 'low' validity in the abstract. Its validity must be established with reference to the particular use for which the test is being considered" (p. 139).

The Unitary and the Divisible

Validity, then, concerns the extent to which a test provides us with true information about persons, always with regard to the situation of its use. It is now regarded as a unitary concept. In order to allow the test constructor to make a statement about the test's validity, some accessible methodology of investigation is necessary. Otherwise, validity remains a matter of belief, a kind of magic. And so, in spite of the unitary view now taken of validity, it has to be operationalized through the usual suspects of content and construct validity, concurrent and predictive validity, although, as we have seen, the current fashion is to talk not about plural validities but about multiple sources of evidence for validity. As Messick points out, "excessive reliance on only one kind of validity evidence (as, in the past, on only one kind of so-called validity) is unlikely to be seriously endorsed for long" (1988, p. 35). To the usual suspects we need to add reliability; some will want to include face validity. However, the joker is the validity added by Messick (1989) as a result of the wider cultural climate of social and ethical turns. He wrote of the role of test consequence: for some this has come to be called consequential validity. Here, for the first time judgment is made not just by design and intention and existing networks, but by future possibilities and unexpected consequences (collected, of course, post hoc). There are serious objections to this. It is analogous to saying here is an alarm clock; it keeps very good time; however, because it could be used to trigger a bomb (an unexpected consequence) it behooves us to monitor those who purchase the alarm clock and the uses they make of it. Surely a distinction needs to be drawn between, for example, weapons such as bombs, which are designed with the sole purpose of inflicting harm and, say, motor cars, which in some circumstances may be used by suicide bombers to carry out terrorist attacks. To what extent are the manufacturers of the motor cars responsible for what, after all, are unintended consequences of the machines they have produced?

Test specificity, the accumulation of evidence, these, we have seen, are not new demands. What Messick adds, and it is an important addition, is to make the link between testing arguments and the wider social and ethical turns. McNamara (2000) considers this development as representing "a renewed theory of test validation." This takes account of the impact of the test itself and the changes produced by its implementation.

Two main changes have taken place with regard to how validity can be operationalized. The first is that the scope of evidence gathered and taken into account has widened. The second is that there is a broad antipositivist groundswell of scepticism about the meaning and value of traditional correlational evidence (e.g., O'Loughlin, 2001). As we will see, such evidence is still collected and taken seriously—but it is now only part of the validity story, and for exactly the same reason that reliability, which relies entirely on correlational evidence, is now itself put into question (Swain, 1990; Moss, 1994; Gipps, 1994) or at least downplayed in classroom contexts, where the focus is on enhancing learning, rather than on buttressing high stakes decisions.

Classical validity studies looked in different and unrelated directions. Content validity was the appeal to specialist knowledge of the field under test ('English grammar,' 'Japanese for tour-guides,' 'French for chefs'). Both predictive validity and concurrent validity used correlations to examine how close the test was to existing (and acceptable) criteria, predictive to a variable to be accessed in the future, concurrent to a variable already available. And construct validity, that "most central type of validity" (Lynch, 2003, p. 151), concerns, as Bachman explains, "the extent to which performance on tests is consistent with prediction that we make on the basis of a theory of abilities or constructs" (Bachman, 1990, p. 255). There is also that nonprofessional validity, face validity, the appeal to the layperson who is not equipped to examine the test (and the inferences of its scores) in terms of its professional content and meaning. Face validity is routinely dismissed as unimportant but lay views do matter, even though they will differ, because the lay are just as much stakeholders as are the professionals. Indeed, in some instances, a test's limited appeal may result in reduced engagement with the test-taking event on the part of test-takers, thereby limiting the accuracy of test scores as measures of ability (Elder & Lynch, 1998). And there is the further point: As some of the stakeholders (for example, government departments) commission tests to implement policies they have adopted, if the test does not 'speak' to them in a language they understand, it will not go ahead.

Each approach in the classical tradition had failings, especially on its own. Predictive and concurrent validity were bedeviled by the lack of certainty as to whether the external criterion was itself a valid one and how to interpret significant but low correlations. Content validity was not dependent on statistics and it did give everyone the comfortable feeling that they were on home ground, but not for long. Since content validity operated at the level of surface similarities between field and test, it was difficult to demonstrate a convincing correspondence between test tasks and real-world tasks (Davies, 1984) and to encompass sufficient detail in a test to be able to claim representativeness (Alderson, 1988). An alternative approach to content validity was to theorize it. Messick points out that "except for simple domains...the notion of a domain or behavioural class is a construct" (1988, p. 39) and Fulcher argues that using content validity as a major criterion in test design and evaluation has been mistaken (1999, p. 221).

Messick's particular achievement has been to characterize validity as a simple and coherent question: "This question has various aspects related to evidence about, rationales for, interpretations of, and uses of a particular test in a specific social context" (Cumming, 1996, p. 4). However, Messick insists on a unified approach to validity in which "appropriateness, meaningfulness, and usefulness of score-based inferences are inseparable and . . . the unifying force is empirically grounded construct interpretation" (1988, p. 35). To that extent Messick was primarily concerned with validity as a theoretical concept rather than with validation in its practical operation.

Messick's conceptual clarity can be analyzed less charitably. Since validity can only be achieved through validation, using logic, judgment, and empirical evidence, it may be suggested that what Messick does is to offload all the problems of validity onto validation, leaving validity as an abstract and essentially empty concept. Indeed, he adds to the problems of validity by extending its scope into the social and the ethical. Kunnan (2000) goes further in proposing that validity should be regarded as only one component of ethicality, along with access and justice. Indeed, Bachman reminds us that "historically, the notion of construct validity grew out of efforts in the early 1950s by the American Psychological Association to prepare a code of professional ethics, part of which would address the adequacy of psychological tests" (Bachman, 1990, p. 255).

However, professional test constructors must always steer a middle course between the potential hypocrisy of claiming to be ethical and the acceptance of responsibility for the impossible demands of unexpected consequences (Davies, 1997). What professions exist to do is to combine field expertise with a proper moral and social concern to act responsibly in normal settings. As it happens, we do not think Messick was so reckless as to open the floodgates of consequential validity in this way, concerned, as he was, to "improve validity by test design" (Messick, 1996, p. 247) but it does appear possible that his theorizing has been extended and misapplied by the proponents of critical language testing (Shohamy, 2001; Pennycook, 2001).

To an extent, what Messick has done is to issue a warning, a kind of government health warning for test consumers. Like land mines, he is saying, tests have continuing lives. Take care! Be on your guard! (Lynch, 2003, p. 164; and see Spolsky, 1995). This is how Cumming explains Messick's message in Table 44.1, making use of Messick's own "Progressive Matrix of construct validation (1989)."

He writes "Ultimately, Messick proposes that the social consequences of test use must be appraised, combining the considerations raised in all three previous cells of his matrix, to assess the long-term effects that actually occur from implementation of a test, for example, the washback of tests on educational practices or more broadly the realizations of specific values related to the construct of interest on whole societal systems" (Cumming, 1996, p. 7).

Making construct validity the validity of choice may create problems. Just as construct validity was an attempt to imbue correlational and content validity with wider responsibilities, so in more recent times, classical construct validity has itself been found inadequate because, however perfect or 'beautiful' the construct may be in itself, its effects may be unacceptable. (A good example from a different field would be the system or construct of prison reform proposed by the Utilitarian philosopher Jeremy Bentham. He invented the Panopticon, a Model or Silent Prison, designed in such a way that prisoners were forbidden to speak and isolated from one another but under constant observation by the warders. As a means of detaining prisoners at minimum cost, the design was admirable; it was also inhuman. (It is said of the Model or Silent Prison at Port Arthur in Tasmania that the idea was that the prisoners would be given plenty of opportunity to consider their deeds and their fate. Many went mad from the enforced silence and solitude).

Hence the push to consider effects, to widen the pool of evidence, hence the consequential basis of validity what has come to be called "consequential validity." What

TABLE 44.1

Cumming's Interpretation of Messick's Progressive Matrix of Construct Validation

	Test Interpretation	*Test Use*
Evidential Basis	1. Construct validity	2. Construct validity + Relevance/utility
Consequential Basis	3. Construct validity + Value implications	4. Construct validity + Relevance/utility + Value implications + Social consequences

this does that is different is to round up all available sources of evidence under the auspices of construct validity, adding the relevance/utility, value implications, and social consequences to the established content, concurrent, predictive, and construct approaches. To that extent consequential validity is inductive, opening itself up to tests as social facts and as institutionalized interventions. Lynch asks the hard question:

> How far does the responsibility for the consequences of tests extend? If negative conse-
> quences are the result of otherwise valid test measurement (construct relevant test-score
> variance), is the test still valid? Is this the test developer's responsibility? Questions like
> these make the relationship between validity and ethics (as well as the social and political
> nature of both) all the more apparent. And the fact that Messick's framework raises these
> questions demonstrates its usefulness as a bridge between positivist validity typologies
> and interpretivist approaches to assessment validity.... (Lynch, 2003, p. 153)

The Old and the New

As we have seen, what we have called the precariousness of the validity concept is evidence of its abstract nature. That being so, validity can be defined, established, and measured only operationally. That is why discussion of validity quickly turns into a consideration of validation. And so, contrary to the competing voices claiming different approaches to and definitions of validity, what the dispute is really about is validation. In other words, there is general agreement about validity: What is in dispute is how to establish it, how to do validation. This explains why, very early in her account of validity, Chapelle (1999) can slide between validity and validation, blurring the distinction: "The definition of validity affects all language test users because accepted practices of test validation are critical to decisions about what constitutes a good language test for a particular situation" (p. 254).

Even the celebrated distinction between the 'old' and the 'new' validity questions (Tyler, 1963) does not represent a real difference of view of the meaning of validity since what is (again) in contention is how to establish validity, in other words, how to do validation.

The 'old' validity question was: To what extent does this test measure what it purports to measure? whereas the 'new' validity question asked: Just what is it that this test does measure? The 'old' approach is at bottom a deductive approach: There is an agreed criterion and what the test at issue aims to do is to represent or simulate that criterion. Interestingly, for such a direct test–criterion relationship the concept of validity is multi(factorial) in the sense that there are different (and unrelated) avenues to its establishment, thus content, concurrent, predictive, construct. All avenues provide evidence, evidence that does not necessarily cohere as one judgment. Like the 'old' question the 'new' validity question is interested in what the test stands for, what it means, what inferences may be drawn from the scores derived from it. The 'old' version thinks it knows; the 'new' does not. For this reason the 'new' offers an inductive approach. As we have seen, it looks for a range of types of information, all of which are criterial since there may be different criteria, on the one hand seeking predictive information and on the other, providing feedback on learners' behavior. Furthermore, the approach, paradoxically, is unitary, in the sense that all sources of evidence (including reliability) belong together, contributing to the overall evaluation of the test's validity. What this suggests is that although validity is a unitary concept, what happens in validation is the search for a range of information contributing to the validity judgment of the test. Since that may lead to contradictory evidence, decision makers have a choice, either to redesign or revise the test so as to remove the contradictions or to accept them and make explicit just how the test relates to each of the chosen criteria. For example, contradiction is likely between impact on the educational system and selection efficiency for promotion to higher levels of education or to coveted appointments.

VALIDATION

The Scope of Validation

We now turn to the process of test validation, and to the question of whether validation efforts, on which the burden of proof for validity rests, can ever be deemed sufficient. One thing that is certain is that the permissible evidence and the forms it comes in are growing. A survey of validation studies in language testing (Hamp-Lyons & Lynch, 1998) documents a paradigm shift away from more positivistic forms of inquiry involving statistical analysis of test scores toward more naturalistic approaches focusing on the nature of the test encounter and the qualities of the performance elicited from it. Kunnan's (1998) collection of papers presented at one of the many Language Testing Research Colloquia on the theme of validity also bears witness to this broadening scope of validity inquiry and includes several papers on such issues as test-taker feedback and test-taking processes, which were not previously seen as central. Among the newer and increasingly popular methodologies used for test validation is introspection, which is the subject of an entire volume by Green (1998) and is used to reveal what informs test-taker choices and rater decisions. Discourse analysis has also found favor as a means of illuminating the quality of speech elicited in oral proficiency interviews (see McNamara, Hill, & May, 2002, for an overview). *Studies in Language Testing* monographs in language testing put out by UCLES Cambridge (Milanovic, 1995) offer some rich accounts of the newer approaches to validation, some of which combine both quantitative and qualitative techniques. Notable among these is that of O'Loughlin (2001), which brings together evidence from different research traditions to explore the equivalence of live- and tape-based forms of *access:*, a vocational test of English used as a means of stemming the flow of skilled immigrants to Australia during a period of economic recession in the early 1990s. The approaches taken include a more traditional quantitative analysis of score patterns to determine whether scores derived from a live- and taped-based test can be mapped on a common scale, along with quantitative and qualitative analyses of test discourse and a narrative account of test-taking processes from multiple stakeholder perspectives. The conclusion is that the two testing modalities are measuring different constructs and cannot be used interchangeably. However, even such a thorough analysis is insufficient according to Shohamy (2001) who, drawing support from Messick's concern with the values underlying test constructs and Bourdieu's notion of symbolic power, argues that validation efforts should go even further to deconstruct the broader meaning of tests as institutional practice. Hawthorne (1997) is similarly dissatisfied with test internal investigations asserting that in high-stakes tests such as the one investigated by O'Loughlin: "Where the measurement of language proficiency is clearly a pretext for achieving some broad political procedures, construct validation processes which are concerned with what the test purports to measure may be an insufficient means of ensuring the test's ethicality" (p. 58).

This raises the important question of how much evidence is enough to claim that a test is valid for its purpose, or indeed whether language testers can ever rest easy on this score. Although Messick's framework is often invoked, most published articles single out a particular aspect of a test's validity, leaving open the question of whether validity limitations in one area might be compensated for by strong evidence for validity with respect to another aspect of the test's meaning or use. A notable exception is Fulcher's (1997) study of an English language placement test, which documents a number of different approaches to examining the reliability and validity of an English as a Second Language (ESL) placement test and concludes that the instrument fulfills its purpose "as well as can be expected within the context" (p. 137). Fulcher's study brings home strongly the point that validity is a local and relative affair. Another attempt at a multifaceted approach is that offered by Guerrero (2000), who organizes his critical review of the Four Skills Exam (FSE) used in New Mexico to measure the Spanish language proficiency of bilingual educators around the various cells in Messick's framework. He finds the test wanting in almost every area and reports that the test has since been replaced by another one, following "overdue legislative action" (p. 418). It would be helpful to know whether all of the FSE's shortcomings were taken into account in this legal decision, or, whether, say, the lack of evidence for the test's reliability was seen as primary. One also wonders about the validity of the new and improved test, La Prueba, given Guerrero's suggestion that, ultimately, the validity of teacher certification tests requires evidence that the teachers who pass them are providing "meaningful instruction to the growing number of English language learners in our schools" (p. 419). Such evidence may be elusive and in any case must be gathered AFTER a test has become operational, which means that validity must be taken on trust at the outset of any new testing initiative.

In an attempt to impose some order on what might seem an unwieldy and eclectic enterprise, Read and Chapelle (2001) propose a framework that links validity and validation to three aspects of a test's purpose, namely the intended score inferences (Messick's construct validity and value implications), score uses (Messick's relevance and utility), and their intended impacts (Messick's social consequences). They work through the various dimensions of this framework with reference to eight different vocabulary measures, proposing that validation studies are needed to support construct definitions (with different kinds of evidence required according to whether these definitions are 'trait', 'behaviorist' or 'interactionist' in their orientation), the methods of reporting scores (either multiple or global) and the audience for test presentation (whether students, administrators, the general public, or the scholarly community). The framework does not however accord priority to any aspect of validity. Moreover, consequential validity, as they describe it, remains both daunting and inchoate, requiring investigation of what each of the specified audiences makes of the information it receives and whether these interpretations result in better diagnosis, better decision making, or sounder theorizing.

The Validation Argument

Although it seems that the sources, kinds, and amounts of validation evidence necessarily vary according to test purpose and context and to the view of language that underpins the test design, there is general agreement that validation is a kind of argument comparable to a legal defense. According to McNamara (2000) there are two stages involved, each requiring consideration of evidence. First, there is the test score, which is code for a claim about the candidate's ability based on inference (comparable in his formulation with the charge laid against the suspect on the basis of available clues). Then comes the subsequent investigation of the reasonableness of this claim (comparable to the legal trial, where the evidence for the charge is subjected to scrutiny). The importance of the second stage hinges on the consequences of the first stage, which may sometimes be dire (resulting in possible failure or exclusion in the case of tests, and a fine, imprisonment, or worse in the case of the police charge). The higher the stakes, the greater the need for a formal defense. The legal defense takes the form of a reasoned argument supported by a trail of evidence and so too does the test validation process. The argument and evidence chain is built around a series of hypotheses concerning a) what the test tasks or items are measuring and how appropriate they are for this purpose, b) the inferences drawn from test scores, c) the uses to which these scores will be put, and d) the consequences that are expected to ensue from the test's implementation.

A Validation Case Study

To illustrate the nature of the validation process and the reasoning that underpins it we now offer a brief work-in-progress account of validation activities surrounding a particular assessment procedure. This case study serves to illustrate the complexities of the process, but also the ambiguity of outcomes that, it is argued, makes Messick's notion of validity as a *unitary* construct somewhat difficult to operationalize.

The test we have chosen is a Diagnostic English Language Needs Assessment (DELNA) used in the University of Auckland, New Zealand, for the purpose of a) identifying first-year undergraduates in an English medium university who may be at risk in their academic study owing to limited English, b) determining the areas in which such students are likely to experience problems, and then c) guiding them toward appropriate means of language support in order to enhance their chances of success (Elder & Von Randow, 2002). The test is administered to students, whether native or non-native speakers of English, who cannot show formal evidence of English language proficiency in the form of either a specified score on the IELTS test (or recognized equivalent) or a designated level of performance in English or some other writing-intensive subject offered as part of the end-of-school certificate used as a basis for admitting students to the university. DELNA is a two-tiered procedure: The first tier, made up of an academic vocabulary and text-editing component, which takes less than 20 minutes to complete, is designed as a filter for the purpose of exempting more literate students from further diagnosis. High scoring students are simply informed that their performance is satisfactory and that language skills are unlikely to hamper their academic progress. The second tier is for those who perform below a specified threshold on Tier One. This second tier includes a listening, reading, and writing component drawn from an English as an Additional Language (EAP) test developed for an ESL population at the University of Melbourne[1] and takes just under 3 hours to complete. Its purpose is to assess students' academic reading, listening, and writing skills in greater depth, so that their strengths and weaknesses can be highlighted. Performance is reported on a 6-point scale, with a descriptive profile generated for each skill area and a recommendation for the student about possible avenues for English support where these are deemed necessary.

Although the second tier diagnostic component has already been validated for use with international students at another institution, the conditions surrounding the introduction and implementation of the entire DELNA battery raise some important local validity issues, which are currently being explored. In keeping with current conceptualizations of validity as a process of logical argumentation, each foray into validity is formulated as a hypothesis.

Case Study Hypotheses

In what follows, we examine our case study in terms of a series of questions (linked to one or more cells in Messick's matrix) accompanied by one or more hypotheses, each contributing to our validation argument. The questions and accompanying hypotheses are set out below:

How effective is Tier One as a screening device? (Relevance/utility)

H.1 Students performing above a specified threshold will perform satisfactorily on all of the second tier diagnostic components.

How suitable is the existing diagnostic test for the broader population to which it is now being administered? (Construct validity)

H.2 All test components will function uniformly for the different populations of test-takers.

Is the new writing task eliciting relevant academic literacy skills? (Construct validity/relevance/utility)

H.3 Essays rated high will contain a higher incidence of linguistic and discoursal features, which have been found to be characteristic of academic prose in various disciplinary areas.

Are score interpretations and cutoffs on the writing task consonant with academic values? (Value implications, Relevance/utility)

H.4 Academics from different disciplines will accept the writing tasks as representative of the language demands placed on students in their discipline.

H.5 The standards they use to judge the adequacy of samples of academic writing will conform with those applied by the language experts who have been trained to rate the scripts.

Are the existing test-reporting mechanisms meaningful to users? (Relevance Utility)

H.6 Students, language instructors, and faculty administrators will be able to interpret and make use of the test results for relevant test purposes.

How well do the various test components predict subsequent academic performance? (Relevance/utility, Construct validity)

H.7 Academic language proficiency (as measured by DELNA) will be significantly related to performance in the academic domain (as measured by GPA)

Are the outcomes of the DELNA initiative consonant with its intended purposes? (Social consequences)

H.8 The student population will benefit from the information that the test provides.

Testing the Hypotheses

The first hypothesis pertains to the accuracy of the cutoffs on the first tier used to exempt the more able students from the subsequent diagnostic component. The hypothesis to be tested here is as follows:

H.1 Students performing above the specified threshold will perform satisfactorily on all of the second tier diagnostic components.

This process involves getting students to take all DELNA components and using logistic regression techniques to determine an optimum threshold on Tier One above which there is the minimum number of false positives (i.e., students who perform well on Tier One but unsatisfactorily on Tier Two) and false negatives (students who perform poorly on Tier One and well on Tier Two). The false positives are more of a concern than the false negatives since the latter are identified as false in the second round of testing. This is an ongoing process with the threshold adjusted as additional data come to hand. Given that the correlations between Tier One and Tier Two components are less than perfect (ranging from 0.78 to 0.81 on successive administrations) there is inevitably some error associated with these predictions and there is a trade-off between raising the bar to a point where false positives are eliminated altogether and the cost savings that come from lowering the threshold and thereby exempting larger numbers of students from the more resource-intensive diagnostic assessment, which includes a double-marked writing component.

Validation efforts have also been directed to exploring the suitability of DELNA for the very diverse population of candidates, which includes recent immigrants from a range of different countries, indigenous students who may or may not be native speakers of English, and the majority European population, most of whom were born and educated in New Zealand. (Recall that the diagnostic components of the procedure were developed for an ESL population at another institution.) The purpose of the investigation was to detect sources of possible bias or unfairness in the test relating to factors independent of the construct. Such issues are now regarded as integral to test fairness (e.g., AERA, APA, NCME, 1999). The hypothesis underlying this investigation is as follows:

H.2 All test components will function uniformly for the different populations of test-takers.

Note that uniform functioning has nothing to do with differences in mean ability scores for the different groups, but rather with systematic differences that emerge *after* any inter-group differences in ability have been taken into account. A technical bias analysis of group-by-item interactions yielded evidence of differential item functioning on all test components except vocabulary, but how these apparent biases should be dealt with is unclear, because some of the biased items (e.g., grammatical accuracy) were reckoned to be indicative of real differences in ability between the groups rather than of construct-irrelevant variance (Elder, McNamara, & Congdon, 2003). A technical bias analysis (as noted by Elder, 1997; Kunnan, 1997; Gipps, 1994, among others) is an insufficient basis for drawing conclusions about test validity and fairness. While some changes to the test have been made as a result of this bias analysis, it is also clear that any potential unfairnesses linked to assessing this diverse population of test-takers on a common measure need to be weighed against the cost and administrative problems of introducing separate measures for native and non-native students. These different groups of test-takers can only be identified via self-report against an arbitrary criterion and students may in any case resist being assigned to one or other category.

Further validation studies are being undertaken with respect to a new writing task, which it is hoped can replace the one developed for University of Melbourne students. The new task is more efficient, taking only 30 minutes rather than almost an hour to complete and might be seen as more validly representing the target domain of academic writing in that the response is closely linked to a specified quasiacademic input rather than involving open-ended argument based on personal opinion (Moore & Morton, 1999). There was also less evidence of bias on this task when scored holistically than on the longer analytically scored writing component. (Of course, as noted by Hamp-Lyons, 1991, holistic scoring is less useful for diagnostic purposes, so again there is a trade-off between validity and absence of bias and the relevance and utility of the task for its intended purpose.)

An additional validation study that is currently being undertaken involves a close analysis of test-taker scripts generated from this task and explores the following hypothesis:

H.3 Essays rated high will contain a higher incidence of linguistic and discoursal features that have been found to be characteristic of academic prose in various disciplinary areas.

The analysis (Thomborson, 2003) focuses particularly on nominalization and involves both quantitative and qualitative comparisons. It confirms that 'good' (i.e., high scoring) writers are more likely to use these nominalizations and use them to better effect than the poor writers. However, this kind of linguistic analysis is unlikely to convince the nonlinguistic members of the academy who may have different views about what academic writing entails. Further hypotheses are being investigated in order to explore the validity of the test as a predictor of the ability to handle the language demands of academia.

H.4 Academics from different disciplines will accept the writing tasks as representative of the language demands placed on students in their discipline.

H.5 The standards they use to judge the adequacy of samples of academic writing will correspond to those applied by the language experts who have been trained to rate the scripts.

These hypotheses are being investigated in a study involving academics from three broad disciplinary areas who are invited both to rate a set of scripts spanning a range of proficiency levels and to introspect about the criteria they have applied and to offer their views as to the adequacy of the writing task for its intended purpose. This approach (see also Cushing Weigle, Boldt, & Valsecchi, 2003) is somewhat different from the standard-setting procedures normally undertaken that involve pooling of judgments with the aim of forcing consensus on the issue of cut-offs. The differences of opinion that have emerged when lecturers from different disciplines are left to their own devices (Smith, 2003) raise serious questions as to whether a single writing task can capture the highly variable language demands of academia and, indeed, whether there is such a thing as a uniform standard of satisfactory language performance that can be separated from other content-based requirements and the multitude of individual interpretations as to what a satisfactory academic essay entails.

Nevertheless, although the perspective of the subject-specialists provides a useful reality check, giving too much credence to academics from nonlanguage disciplines may be unfair and unhelpful in that their training arguably equips them better to assess mastery of content than to make judgments about language as a vehicle for demonstrating this mastery. As for the single writing task, given that there are limitations on available resources, one would need to embark on a further validation study to weigh up the reliability and washback effects of using a single task assessed by two raters against the use of two different academic writing tasks assessed by a single rater, which is all that current resources will allow.

The more traditional forms of evidence based on the tests' predictive power are alluring in that they offer a seemingly more manageable means of evaluating a test's utility for its intended purpose. The hypothesis underlying predictive validation studies is as follows:

H.6 Language proficiency will be significantly related to performance in the academic domain.

This hypothesis was sustained in this particular context of use. For those assessed in 2002, the correlation between the combined Listening, Reading, and Writing score and end-of-semester grades was around 0.32, indicating that language proficiency accounted for just under 10% of the variance in academic performance. There was some variation in the strength of these correlations according to skill, with reading more strongly related to GPA than listening and writing. There was also, as one might predict, considerable variation in the strength of the English/GPA relationship according to faculty, with language proficiency appearing to play a more important role in, for example, Arts, with a correlation of around 0.4, than in Science where it fell to just under 0.2. Interestingly, the shorter writing task, in spite of the problems revealed by the research mentioned earlier, proved to be a better predictor of GPA across all faculties than the longer argument essay. These correlations, while moderate at best, were in all cases statistically significant. They attest to the utility of DELNA as a predictor of subsequent performance although there are obviously (and rightly so!) many factors other than language that come into play. There also appears to be a threshold of proficiency at or below that students are highly likely to fail in one or other of their first-year subjects. While this needs to be confirmed by tracking students in successive years of the program, it offers a useful basis for determining which students might perhaps be required rather than simply advised to undertake further English language instruction.

Another aspect of test use that is worthy of investigation pertains to the meaningfulness of score reporting mechanisms for the various participants in the DELNA initiative. There has been considerable work undertaken to refine the rating scales for use by assessors, but the meaningfulness of the profiles for test-takers and other end users has yet to be established. The assumption underlying the current reporting mechanisms is that

H.7 Students, language instructors, and faculty administrators will be able to interpret and use test results in appropriate ways.

A survey of users indicated that some were less interested in a profile than in a score or a grade accompanied by a brief recommendation regarding the kind of intervention required. Thus it has been decided to use different reporting mechanisms for different users, with students and ESL teachers receiving a descriptive report on the strengths and weaknesses and faculty coordinators receiving an overall bandscore and recommendations for action that will assist them in planning and resource provision for their students. Of course, the decision as to how to combine the various test components in arriving at an overall score rests on a value judgment that must itself be validated. There is also a danger that such a score could be used as a basis for barring students from taking certain subjects (turning what is meant to be a diagnostic tool into a de facto selection device). This is an unintended consequence that would constitute a threat to the test's validity.

A further important dimension of validity needs to be considered given that the ultimate purpose of DELNA is to enhance the quality of the educational experience and, ultimately, improve academic outcomes. The hypothesis to be investigated in this regard relates to the impact of the testing program on the stakeholders, including the students who take the test. It can be formulated thus:

H.8 Students will benefit from the information the test provides.

Just what kind of evidence needs to be gathered in support of such a hypothesis will depend on how one defines the notion of benefit. Uptake of language support options by students diagnosed to be at risk? More sophisticated, transferable, English skills for at-risk students taking advantage of available support? Or higher marks and/or lower failure rates in particular academic subjects? Uptake of support may depend on a range of factors, such as motivation, or the amount of time that students have at their disposal to spend on extra English, which have little to do with the information that the test provides. Investigating language gains achieved by low-scoring DELNA students after an intensive period of language support is a complex undertaking, and it is difficult to know how long one should wait before deciding whether or not a particular support option is having the desired effect. A recent evaluation study (Lynberg, 2003) has focused on the effectiveness of a language support course that is integrally linked to subject-specific demands in a business course. Data gathered after only one semester of study revealed a noticeable improvement in the quality of written work among the DELNA students who attended the relevant tutorials. The content-based instruction was also perceived by participants as extremely valuable in helping them interpret and respond to the demands of the particular subject area. Whether these language proficiency improvements have resulted in greater engage-ment with study or better academic performance than would otherwise have been achieved however remains open to question. A series of case studies documenting the experience of first-year immigrant students undertaken by Bright (2003) has shown that such students adopt highly variable strategies in pursuing their academic goals, and that language proficiency, although perceived by the students to be important, may be less influential than attitudinal and sociocultural factors, which are far more difficult to pinpoint.

Validating DELNA in terms of its effectiveness in identifying students' needs and its impact on study strategies and study outcomes is a daunting undertaking because of the difficulty of disentangling test impact from the many other institutional and social influences that are played out in students' lives and that influence their choices and actions in complex ways (Wall, 2000). In any case, if we return to the legal analogy, it could be argued that to include the consequences of a given procedure within the scope of a validation exercise is to confuse the verdict with the sentence. The sentence, and also the extent of rehabilitation or recidivism, may vary in response to factors that are not directly related to the charge, such as the person's prior history of criminal activity, but the verdict of guilty or not guilty (or, in our case, literate or otherwise) and the burden of proof for that verdict remains the same.

The Limits of Validation

The earlier account of validation efforts in relation to a particular language test raises a number of issues regarding the validation process. First, it is clear that validation entails more than a set of technical procedures undertaken while developing a test. (In fact, we have given scant attention to these procedures in our account because we are focusing on using a previously validated test in a new environment.) Whereas the traditional attention to internal consistency and criterion-linked correlational analyses remain fundamental, they may be insufficient grounds for defending inferences drawn from test scores because they do not deal sufficiently with the test's use in a particular context for particular populations and specific purposes, with the values of the various stakeholders (including test-takers and end users) and with the relationship between the test's intended purpose and its ultimate impact or consequences. A range of other sources of evidence are therefore sought and the earlier example has provided some indication of the kind of studies that might be conducted in the interests of gathering such evidence for a particular context of use. The fact that such studies are ongoing supports the notion that validity is not tucked up in the test itself but rather resides in the meanings that are ascribed to the test scores. These meanings are dynamic rather than static, changing along with shifting attitudes and practices in the relevant context of test use. Since none of the studies described is sufficient in its own right, it makes sense to gather all the aspects of validity under a single unified validity umbrella as Messick has done. However, while Messick's conceptualization of validity has arguably provided a stronger theoretical base for validity inquiry, we still lack a means of combining the various elements of Messick's framework in a principled and meaningful way, as Chapelle (1999) and Kunnan (chap. 43, this volume) also point out.

Furthermore, discussions as to what validity is or what it needs to encompass leave unanswered the question of what constitutes *adequate* evidence of validity in situations where there are limited time and resources available. Is a test invalidated by a weak link in the chain of evidence as Haertel (1999) among others, has suggested? Or are some sources of evidence to be considered primary? Do actions or interpretations based on misunderstandings of a test's purpose invalidate other outcomes that fit with the test's purpose? The processes described earlier certainly tell us more about the test and the inferences that can or cannot be drawn from test scores, but the decision as to whether the test is good enough, or what kind of improvements are necessary or desirable or indeed whether we need the test at all, remain open to debate. The broadened scope of validity inquiry comes at a price. It offers richer and more multifaceted accounts of test properties and score meanings but at the same time transforms validity into a kaleidoscope of images that configure differently for each viewer. Gone is the perhaps fictional certainty that the validity coefficient once offered, leaving us with no truth other than that which is constructed in the minds of test stakeholders including those charged with validating the test.

One test consequence that is seldom explored in discussions of test validation is the self-serving role of a language test, such as the one described previously, in furnishing research and publication opportunities for applied linguistic scholars. Although research conferences and publications have an important peer review function and may serve to enhance the quality and rigor of the validation process, one could also argue that the current tendency to complexify the task of validation has served the research community well, while in some sense ignoring the very real need of test administrators to justify the decisions they need to make about selection, certification, and/or resource allocation.

The Way Forward

Returning to the legal analogy we conclude by reflecting on the fact, also noted by McNamara (2000), that whereas the arbiters in a legal trial are the jurors and ultimately the judge who considers the legitimacy of charges laid by other parties, the instigator of test validation is more often than not the test developer. The test developer may well have a vested interest in the outcome and his or her reluctance to seek evidence against intended test interpretations means that validation studies often have a confirmatory bias (Cronbach, 1988). If the notion of test validity and the processes of test validation discussed in this chapter are to be regarded as credible, rather than dismissed as the arcane practices of a self-serving élite, they need to be simplified or at least rendered more transparent to test users. In addition, more attention needs to be paid in test validation efforts to documenting the test design, delivery, and reporting decisions that have arisen from validation studies, so that the utility of this process is more obvious to the outsider. For example, was the decision to do away with the subject-specific modules of the IELTS test a result of the findings of research (e.g., by Clapham, 1996) or was it a decision based largely on cost considerations? And what is the relationship between ETS-sponsored research on TOEFL-related issues and the design of the Next Generation TOEFL? How will the findings of current research on the impact of both the IELTS and the TOEFL program be acted on? Will it result in changes to test design or simply in caveats that delimit the responsibilities of testing agencies in relation to test-related teaching practices and score-related decisions made by institutions? Do expanded notions of test validity mean that responsibilities for test validation are also more widely distributed as Chalhoub-Deville and Turner (2000) suggest? How can stakeholders be alerted to these responsibilities and what sanctions can or should be applied to those who fail to discharge them? If discussions about new dimensions of validity and new ways of validation are to do more than warm the air, the language testing community needs to come clean about not just the processes involved in the business of test validation but also to build up what Hamp-Lyons (2000) refers to as "case law," documenting the conclusions they come to about how much validation is enough in different testing situations and how different sources of evidence are weighed in overall judgments about the adequacy of assessment tools, the appropriacy of their uses, and the legitimacy and fairness of their impacts.

VALIDITY AND VALIDATION

In this chapter we have considered the relationship between the concept of validity and the practice of validation. We have highlighted the contribution of Samuel Messick to our understanding, both in his presentation of validity as a unitary concept and in the blueprint he presents for the pursuit of validation from multiple perspectives. Validity is the abstract test construct; validation, through the assembling of multiple sources of information including empirical evidence, judgments, and logical appreciation, operationalizes validity. So much is straightforward: validation operationalizes validity. However, this does not resolve the dilemma at the heart of validity; how to combine into a coherent whole the different insights offered by validation: in other words how to give the multiple sources of information that validation provides, the unity that validity needs.

NOTES

1. The test is known as Diagnostic English Language Assessment (Language Testing Centre, 1991).

REFERENCES

Alderson, J. C. (1988). New procedures of validating proficiency tests of ESP? Theory and practice. *Language Testing, 5*(2), 220–232.

Anastasi, A. (1988). *Psychological testing* (6th ed.). New York: Macmillan.

Angeles, P. A. (1981). *Dictionary of philosophy*. New York: Barnes & Noble.

American Educational Research Association, American Psychological Association, National Council for Measurement in Education (1999). *Standards for educational and psychological testing*. Washington DC: Author.

Bachman, L. (1990). *Fundamental considerations in language testing*. Oxford, UK: Oxford University Press.

Bellack, A. S., & Hersen, M. (1984). *Research methods in clinical psychology*. New York: Pergamon.

Bright, C. (2003). The language experiences of NESB students in their first year of a tertiary business or social sciences course. Unpublished master's thesis. Department of Applied Language Studies and Linguistics, University of Auckland.

Brown, R. H., & Goodman, D. (2001). 'Jurgen Habermas' theory of communicative action: An incomplete project. In G. Ritzer & B. Smart (Eds.), *Handbook of social theory* (pp. 201–216). London: Sage.

Chalhoub-Deville, M., & Turner, C. (2000). What to look for in ESL admission tests: Cambridge certificate exams, IELTS, and TOEFL. *System, 28*, 523–539.

Chapelle, C. (1999). Validity in language assessment. *Annual Review of Applied Linguistics, 19*, 254–272.

Clapham, C. (1996). *The development of IELTS: A study of the effect of background knowledge on reading comprehension*. Cambridge, UK: Cambridge University Press.

Cronbach, L. J. (1988). Five perspectives on validity argument. In H. Wainer & H. I. Braun (Eds.), *Test validity* (pp. 3–17). Hillsdale, NJ: Lawrence Erlbaum Associates.

Cumming, A. (1996). Introduction: The concept of validation in language testing. In A. Cumming & R. Berwick (Eds.), *Validation in language testing* (pp. 1–14). Clevedon, UK: Multilingual Matters.

Cushing Weigle, S., Boldt, H., & Valsecchi, M. I. (2003). Effects of task and rater background on the evaluation of ESL student writing: A pilot study. *TESOL Quarterly, 37*(2), 345–355.

Davies, A. (1984). Simple, simplified, and simplification: What is authentic? In J. C. Alderson & A. H. Urquhart (Eds.), *Reading in a foreign language* (pp. 181–198). London: Longman.

Davies, A. (1997). Demands of being professional in language testing. *Language Testing, 14*(3), 328–339.

Elder, C. (1997). What does test bias have to do with fairness? *Language Testing, 14*(3), 261–277.

Elder C., & Lynch, B. (March, 1998). Public perceptions of basic skills tests and their ethical implications. Paper presented at the 20th Language Testing Research Colloquium, Monterey, CA.

Elder, C., McNamara, T., & Congdon, P. (2003). Rasch techniques for detecting bias in performance assessments: An example comparing the performance of native and non-native speakers on a test of academic English. *Journal of Applied Measurement, 14*(1), 181–197.

Elder, C., & Von Randow, J. (November, 2002). Report on the 2002 Pilot of DELNA at the University of Auckland. Auckland, New Zealand: Department of Applied Language Studies and Linguistics, University of Auckland.

Fulcher, G. (1997). An English language placement test: Issues in reliability and validity. *Language Testing, 14*(2), 113–138.

Fulcher, G. (1999). Assessment in English for academic purposes: Putting content validity in its place. *Applied Linguistics, 20*(2), 221–226.

Gipps, C. (1994). *Beyond testing.* London: The Falmer Press.

Green, A. (1998). *Verbal protocol analysis in language testing research.* Cambridge, UK: Cambridge University Press.

Guerrero, M. (2000). The unified validity of the fours skills exam. *Language Testing, 17*(4), 397–421.

Haertel, E. H. (1999). Validity argument for high stakes testing. *Journal of Educational Measurement: Issues and Practice, 18*(4), 5–9.

Hamp-Lyons, L. (1991). Basic concepts. In L. Hamp-Lyons (Ed.) *Assessing second language writing in academic contexts* (pp. 5–15). Norwood, NJ: Ablex.

Hamp-Lyons, L., & Lynch, B. K. (1998). Perspectives on validity: A historical analysis of language testing conference abstracts. In A. J. Kunnan (Ed.), *Issues in language testing research: Conventional validity and beyond* (pp. 253–277). Mahwah, NJ: Lawrence Erlbaum Associates.

Hamp-Lyons, L. (2000). Social professional and individual responsibility in language testing. *System, 28,* 579–591.

Hawthorne, L. (1997). The political dimension of English testing in Australia. *Language Testing, 14*(3), 248–260.

Kunnan, A. (1997). Connecting fairness and validation. In A. Huhta, V. Kohonen, L. Kurki-Suomo, & S. Luoma (Eds.), *Current developments and alternatives in language assessment* (pp. 85–105). Jyväskylä, Finland: University of Jyväskylä.

Kunnan, A. (1998). *Validation in language assessment. Selected papers from the 17th Language Testing Research Colloquium, Long Beach, CA.* Mahwah, NJ: Lawrence Erlbaum Associates.

Kunnan, A. J. (2000). Fairness and justice for all. In A. J. Kunnan (Ed.), *Fairness and validation in language assessment. Selected papers of the 19th Language Testing Research Colloquium, Orlando, Florida* (pp. 1–10). Cambridge, UK: Cambridge University Press.

Lado, R. (1961). *Language testing.* London: Longman.

Language Testing Centre. (1991). The University of Melbourne ESL test. Final Report. Melbourne: University of Melbourne.

Lynberg, L. (2003). A brief overview: Bachelor of business an international management support program. Unpublished report (11 pp.). University of Auckland, New Zealand.

Lynch, B. K. (2003). *Language assessment and program evaluation.* Edinburgh, Scotland: Edinburgh University Press.

Marcus, R. B. (1995). Validity. In T. Honderich (Ed.), *The Oxford companion to philosophy* (p. 894). Oxford, UK: Oxford University Press.

McNamara, T. F. (2000). *Language testing.* Oxford, UK: Oxford University Press.

McNamara, T. F., Hill, K., & May, L. (2002). Discourse and assessment. *Annual Review of Applied Linguistics, 22,* 221–242.

Messick, S. (1988). The once and future uses of validity: Assessing the meaning and consequences of measurement. In H. Wainer & H. I. Braun (Eds.), *Test validity* (pp. 33–45). Hillsdale, NJ: Lawrence Erlbaum Associates.

Messick, S. (1989). Validity. In R. L. Linn (Ed.), *Educational measurement* (pp. 13–103). (3rd Ed.). New York: Macmillan.

Messick, S. (1996). Validity and washback in language testing. *Language Testing, 13*(2), 241–256.

Milanovic, M. (Ed.). (1995). *Studies in language testing,* Vols 1–15. Cambridge, UK: Cambridge University Press.

Moore, H., & Morton, J. (1999). Authenticity in the IELTS academic module writing test: A comparative study of task 2 items and university assignments. In R. Tulloh (Ed.), *International English language testing system.* Research Report 2. Canberra, Australia: IELTS.

Moss, P. A. (1996). Enlarging the dialogue in educational measurement: Voices from interpretive research traditions. *Educational Researcher, 25*(1), 20–28.

O'Loughlin, K. (2001). *The equivalence of direct and semidirect speaking tests.* Cambridge, UK: Cambridge University Press.

Pennycook, A. (2001). *Critical applied linguistics: A critical introduction.* Mahwah, NJ: Lawrence Erlbaum Associates.

Read, J., & Chapelle, C. (2001). A framework for second language vocabulary assessment. *Language Testing, 18*(1), 1–32.

Shohamy, E. (2001). *The power of tests: A critical perspective on the uses and consequences of language tests.* London: Longman.

Smith, S. (2003). Standards for academic writing: Are they common across disciplines? Unpublished master's thesis. University of Auckland, New Zealand.

Smith, S. (in press). Standards for academic writing: Are they common across disciplines? Unpublished master's thesis, Department of Applied Language Studies and Linguistics, University of Auckland, New Zealand.

Spolsky, B. (1995). *Measured words.* Oxford, UK: Oxford University Press.

Swain, M. (1990). Second language testing and second language acquisition: Is there a conflict with traditional psychometrics? In J. Alatis (Ed.), *Linguistics, language teaching, and language acquisition* (pp. 401–412). Georgetown University Round Table. Washington, DC: Georgetown University Press.

Thomborson, B. (2003). The use of nominalization as an aspect of EAP in a test of writing. Unpublished doctoral dissertation, University of Auckland, New Zealand.

Tyler, L. (1963). *Tests and measurements.* Englewood Cliffs, NJ: Prentice-Hall.

Wall, D. (2000). The impact of high stakes testing on teaching and learning: Can this be predicted or controlled? *System, 28,* 499–509.

Winter, G. (2000). A comparative discussion of the notion of "validity" in qualitative and quantitative research. *The Qualitative Report, 4*(3,4), 1–13, http://www.nova.edu/ssss/QR/QR4-3/winter.html

45

A Look Back at and Forward to What Language Testers Measure

Micheline Chalhoub-Deville
Craig Deville
The University of Iowa

INTRODUCTION

Our charge for this chapter is to write about measurement issues in second language (L2) testing. To do this we begin by presenting a definition of measurement that guides much of our thinking and discussion. We apply the definition to an examination of topics found in language testing textbooks published since 1961. We focus primarily on how language testers have depicted the construct of second language ability and performance over the years, and we trace the past development and point to a plausible future of the field's view of what we measure and how. Finally, we conclude by advocating increased attention to validity arguments that focus on how test scores are actually used.

A major part of the chapter focuses on how the L2 construct definition has evolved over time. The review starts with Lado's (1961) L2 representation and moves through the various models to the present day and includes emerging calls for considering interactional competence in language testing. In discussing interactional competence, we seek primarily to problematize the issues raised by this model. Given the survey character of the chapter, it is not feasible to deliberate in detail on these issues, but interested readers can consult Chalhoub-Deville (2003). Finally, it is important to mention that in the present review we do not seek to promote any one model, but to explicate the orientation and the contribution of each model to the measurement of language testing.

DEFINITION OF MEASUREMENT

Measurement, assessment, evaluation, and testing are terms that are sometimes used interchangeably in everyday language, and at other times are utilized by authors to denote distinct ideas, intents, and practices (e.g., compare Bachman, 1990, and Lynch,

2001). We adopt a definition of measurement in the present chapter that situates it as part of testing, which in turn can serve broader assessment and/or evaluation purposes. In addition, our definition reflects a more conventional perspective and not alternative paradigms as described by Lynch (2001), McNamara (2001), and Shohamy (2001).

A critical first step then is to clarify what we mean by measurement. Thorndike and Hagen (1977) state that:

> Measurement in any field always involves three common steps: (1) identifying and defining the quality or attribute that is to be measured, (2) determining a set of operations by which the attribute may be made manifest and perceivable, and (3) establishing a set of procedures or definitions for translating observations into quantitative statements of degree or amount. (p. 9)

This definition will serve as an organizer for much of the chapter, in which we review how language testers have dealt with measurement topics in published textbooks over the years. This definition is also mirrored in Bachman's (1990) discussion of measurement. Bachman defines measurement as "the process of quantifying the characteristics of persons according to explicit procedures and rules" (p. 18). The two definitions overlap considerably. They both state that the process of measurement involves a description of the construct attributes or characteristics to be measured, and it entails the delineation of the operations or procedures to be followed to elicit the requisite test-taker behavior indicative of the construct. Furthermore, both definitions of measurement include the application of methods for quantifying the attribute exhibited by test-takers, that is, methods for obtaining meaningful test scores. As mentioned, our focus in this chapter will be on the first two aspects of the measurement process. This focus reflects what we observed in the language testing textbooks that we examined. Additionally, the topic of quantification methods is addressed in Chapter 46 of this volume.

Understanding and working through this three-step process is incumbent on any language test developer or analyst. As in any field, experts can and do disagree with respect to both the practice and theory involved in each step. For example, some might initiate the development of a new test by clearly defining and specifying what is to be measured and for what purpose, and then, deciding which items, tasks, and concomitant scoring procedures best reflect the construct definition and specification. Others might begin with a global model of language proficiency that, in essence, combines construct, task, and scoring definition in one package (see the following discussion of hierarchical scales). There are no hard and fast rules for these steps, but testers must explicitly or implicitly go through this process whenever they construct assessments and interpret scores from them.

LANGUAGE TESTING TEXTBOOKS REVIEWED

In an attempt to understand how language testers have covered the three aspects of measurement, we reviewed language testing textbooks that have been published since Lado's 1961 seminal volume, which was a time when the field of language testing was first emerging (Carroll, 1986). Our intent in this chapter is not to provide an exhaustive listing of the language testing textbooks or to indicate the extent certain texts are used in graduate courses (e.g., Bailey & Brown, 1996), but instead to identify a representative sample of books and use them to explicate how the field has viewed measurement issues over the years.

The review focuses on language testing textbooks because such volumes are intended to address basic considerations involved in measurement. Edited volumes (e.g., Kunnan, 1998; Hurley & Tinajero, 2001) are not included as they typically comprise articles/chapters that concern themselves more with elaborating a certain aspect of measurement and do not necessarily afford a representative treatment of measurement issues. In addition, textbooks with a more specialized focus (e.g., Underhill, 1987; Read, 2000; Buck, 2001; Davidson & Lynch, 2002) are not considered. While such textbooks might address the measurement aspects described earlier, including them would have rendered the review task unwieldy.

Language testing textbooks were reviewed and a determination was made as to whether the textbooks addressed specific measurement content or issues (see Table 45.1). The content/issue categories used in the review emerged from the definition of measurement, as described earlier, and after a careful study of the table of contents in numerous language testing and several general measurement textbooks (e.g., Nitko, 2001). Although one can argue that categorizing these textbooks according to their own table of contents is circular, one must keep in mind that the categories are dynamic in the sense that they are derived from textbooks published over a 40-year span. As such, the categories are not confined to a particular era. The review of the volumes was performed independently by the two authors and where differences surfaced, decisions were made after discussion.

Specifically, the *Definition of the Construct or Attributes* entails the following categories:

- *History*—An account of trends, movements, periods in the field (e.g., Madsen, 1983).
- *Purpose/Type*—The variety of situations, contexts, decisions, and uses of test scores, for example, diagnostic, achievement, proficiency, placement, screening, norm- and criterion-referenced, direct- and indirect testing (e.g., Hughes, 1989).
- *Skills, Components, and Models*—A description of language models, classroom syllabi, skills/modalities, components (e.g., vocabulary, grammar, pronunciation) that denote attributes to be measured (e.g., Lado, 1961).

As for *Operations to Elicit Behavior*, these include:

- *Development/Administration*—Considerations for effective test preparation and administration (e.g., Valette, 1967).
- *Methods/Forms*—Characteristics and impact of various testing methods such as cloze, multiple-choice, interviews, and so on, employed to elicit examinee behavior (e.g., Heaton, 1975).
- *Resources*—Taking into account available resources when developing, administering, scoring, and interpreting language tests; practicality concerns (e.g., Harris, 1969).
- *Projects*—Documentation of research and development work on a given language testing project that serves to explicate specific issues (e.g., Davies, 1990).

Finally, *Rules/Procedures for Quantification* comprise:

- *Validity*—Explication of validation procedures (e.g., Bachman, 1990).
- *Reliability*—Approaches to document the consistency and dependability of the test scores and/or ratings obtained (e.g., McNamara, 1996).
- *Fairness/Advocacy*—Practices that support using assessment to better serve instructional and learning needs (e.g., Fradd & McGee, 1994).
- *Scores*—How scores are aggregated and reported using procedures such as z-scores, t-scores, percentiles, cutoff points, descriptive profiles (e.g., Brown, 1996).

TABLE 45.1
Textbooks Reviewed and Their Categorizations

	Identify/Define Construct			Operations to Elicit Behavior				Rules and/or Procedures for Quantification					
	History	Purpose	Model	Project	Development	Methods	Resources	Validity	Reliability	Fairness	Scores	Rating	Analysis
Lado (1961)		X	X	X		X	X	X	X		X	X	X
Valette (1967)		X			X	X		X	X		X	X	X
Harris (1969)		X	X			X	X	X	X		X	X	X
Clark (1972)		X	X			X		X	X			X	
Heaton (1975)		X	X		X	X		X	X	X	X	X	X
Valette (1977)		X			X	X		X	X		X	X	X
Carroll, B. J. (1980)		X	X		X	X	X	X	X		X	X	X
Finocchiaro & Sako (1983)	X	X	X		X	X	X	X	X		X	X	X
Omaggio (1983)		X	X	X		X		X	X		X	X	
Madsen (1983)	X	X	X		X	X		X	X		X	X	X
Carroll, B. J., & Hall (1985)		X	X		X	X	X	X	X		X	X	X
Shohamy (1985)	X	X	X	X	X	X		X	X	X	X	X	X
Brindley (1986)	X	X	X		X			X	X	X	X	X	X
Henning (1987)		X	X		X	X		X	X	X	X	X	
Brindley (1989)		X	X	X	X			X	X	X	X	X	
Hughes (1989)		X	X		X	X		X	X	X	X	X	X
Bachman (1990)		X	X		X	X	X	X	X	X	X	X	X
Davies (1990)	X	X	X	X	X			X	X	X			
Weir (1990)	X	X	X	X	X	X	X	X	X	X	X	X	
Weir (1993)		X	X		X	X	X	X	X	X	X	X	
Cohen (1994)		X	X		X	X		X	X	X	X	X	X
Fradd & McGee (1994)	X	X	X		X	X	X	X	X	X	X	X	
Alderson, Clapham, & Wall (1995)		X	X	X	X	X	X	X	X	X	X	X	X
Bachman & Palmer (1996)	X	X	X	X	X	X	X	X	X	X	X	X	X
Brown (1996)	X	X	X	X	X	X	X	X	X		X	X	X
Genesee & Upshur (1996)		X	X	X	X	X	X	X	X	X	X	X	X
McNamara (1996)	X	X	X	X	X	X	X	X	X	X	X	X	X
McNamara (2000)	X	X	X	X	X	X	X	X	X	X	X	X	X
Brown & Hudson (2002)	X	X		X	X	X	X	X	X	X	X	X	X
Hughes (2003)	X	X	X	X	X	X	X	X	X	X	X	X	X

818

- *Rater/Ratings*—A discussion of rater training and/or development and administration of rating scales (e.g., Alderson, Clapham, and Wall, 1995).
- *Analysis*— Test and item analysis; classical test and/or item response theory (e.g., Henning, 1987).

These categories overlap and distinctions among them, as mentioned earlier, can be tenuous. For example, some might argue that the test purpose, the definition of the skills or model, and the test method overlap—a diagnostic speaking test for beginning learners that emphasizes pronunciation of specific phonemes might constrain the choice of test method. Furthermore, some may question the appropriateness of assigning particular features, for example, Validity, to Rules and Procedures for Quantification instead of to Definition of the Construct. We readily acknowledge the slipperiness of the categorizations but maintain their usefulness as a heuristic for examining measurement issues in the L2 testing textbooks.

As to be expected, textbooks varied in the amount of space allocated to measurement topics covered. For example, while in some volumes (e.g., Bachman, 1990), the topic of validity accounts for 50 pages; in other books, such as Madsen (1983), that topic is covered in a few paragraphs. Some topics, such as fairness/advocacy, have gained attention only more recently. In addition, it is understandable that earlier textbooks did not review historical developments or present illustrative projects in language testing as the field was in its infancy then. Except for the topics/categories just mentioned, virtually all of the textbooks covered the other categories to varying degrees of comprehensiveness.

Obviously it is not possible to talk about all the textbooks listed in Table 45.1 (several are discussed in some detail below with respect to how they define L2 ability and performance), but we do wish to single out several because of the uniqueness of the information they present. Alderson, Clapham, and Wall (1995), in their book *Language Test Construction and Evaluation*, end each chapter with illustrative information as to how the principles of test development they present are actually practiced by various examination boards in the United Kingdom. Although readers might think that such examples do not apply in local contexts of more modest resources, they will find the information to be extremely useful (and sometimes surprising!). Much of what larger testing organizations do can indeed be undertaken on a smaller scale in local contexts.

In addition, the authors include three chapters that deserve special mention. The first is on the training of examiners and administrators. Whereas many of the textbook authors listed in Table 45.1 discuss rater reliability, the Alderson, Clapham, and Wall volume provides a much more comprehensive discussion of the issues surrounding the training of the various participants responsible for evaluating test-takers. They also include specific tips to raters when assessing different skills. A chapter covering posttest score reports—and one from Brown and Hudson (2002)—represent, as far as we know, the only discussions of this topic in our field. The authors point out that validating test score interpretations also means assisting multiple audiences and/or constituents to understand those scores by providing them with meaningful, appropriately tailored reports. Finally, the Alderson, Clapham, and Wall chapter on standards in language testing is also unique to the textbooks reviewed, presenting a valuable review of various codes of practice of which test developers should be aware.

Brown's *Testing in Language Programs* (1996) offers an excellent introduction to basic quantitative measurement and statistical concepts and procedures, and would be a good first book for students pursuing this area of study. He presents much of the material in the context of language testing and programs, thus contextualizing the concepts and making them more accessible. In addition, each chapter contains useful review questions and application exercises with answers in an appendix.

Generally, Brown's discussion of these sometimes complex issues is straightforward and on target. We especially liked his review of standard setting, an important topic that is often neglected in texts. Some chapter material is somewhat dated (e.g., the discussion of validity) and would need to be supplemented with additional readings.

The Genesee and Upshur (1996) text, *Classroom-based Evaluation in Second Language Education*, distinguished itself because of its intended audience. The text is written with an eye directed toward classroom language teachers' needs regarding assessment. The authors discuss testing in the larger framework of instructional evaluation. In addition, the book stands out because of its coverage of nontraditional forms of assessment such as portfolios and conferencing, and how these fit into an evaluation scheme.

A COMPARISON WITH GENERAL MEASUREMENT TEXTBOOKS

A survey of several widely used general measurement textbooks (e.g., Thorndike, 1997; Linn and Gronlund, 2000; Nitko, 2001) reveals an overlap—but considerable difference in emphasis—of the topics addressed in these texts and their counterparts in the field of language testing. A notable difference between these two groups of textbooks is the focus on the construct. Understandably, virtually all the language testing textbooks devote considerable space to discussing, defining, and operationalizing the language construct. The general measurement books, on the other hand, tend to focus more on issues of scoring and quantifying. The discrepancy in focus is to be expected as the audience of the general measurement textbooks is relatively heterogeneous with regard to their fields of study. Consequently, the intent of the authors of these textbooks is to provide readers with a set of "generic" skills and tools that can be employed in developing and analyzing tests across content domains. In language testing textbooks, however, it is essentially a mandate to explicate the nature of the L2 construct and the corresponding operationalization, whereas the coverage of tools used to quantify and analyze test scores receives less attention.

In the remainder of this chapter we focus our discussion on the various L2 models that have been prominent in the language testing textbooks and literature over the years and briefly touch on the issues of operationalization and quantification approaches as they pertain to the models. We acknowledge that our use here of the term 'model' to refer to the various approaches to defining and evaluating the language construct—language skills, ability, proficiency, performance, and so forth—is somewhat indiscriminate. We deliberately did this to avoid the impression of a pecking order of theory, comprehensiveness, or popularity.

LANGUAGE CONSTRUCT AND OPERATIONALIZATION

Ability-Based Construct Definition

Researchers have defined L2 ability in different ways at different times. During the so-called precommunicative era (McNamara, 1996), Lado (1961) represents the ability or knowledge that underlies test-takers' performance within a structuralist approach. Language knowledge is essentially examined in terms of skills (reading, writing, listening, and speaking, with an emphasis on the receptive skills) and elements (e.g., grammatical structure, lexicon, pronunciation, cultural meaning). Lado's perspective of what should be measured focuses on competence (Chomsky, 1965), and not on performance or ability to use the language (Hymes, 1972).

Carroll (1961) differentiates between what he calls discrete-point and integrative testing, emphasizing the importance of the latter. In his reflections on language testing in the 1960s, Carroll (1986) advocates that "language tests should measure those aspects of language performance that call upon skills in putting together utterances or written statements in more or less real-life situations, or in understanding or reading connected speech or text" (pp. 123–124). His call for performance-based testing underscores two features or attributes: (1) a more integrative method of measurement, and (2) the real-life or authentic aspect of testing.

Oller (1979), among others, takes up the baton and extends the idea of integrative testing—not by contrasting it to discrete-point testing, as Carroll did—but by specifically tying the integrative notion (and methods) to a theory of psychological language processing and use. He refers to this idea as pragmatic expectancy grammar. According to Oller, pragmatic expectancy grammar "causes the learner to process sequences of elements in a language that conform to the normal contextual constraints of that language" (p. 38). This theory of language processing led Oller to advocate such integrated testing methods as dictation and cloze. And although such integrative testing methods can be problematic to score (see Deville & Chalhoub-Deville, 1993), they do represent an important effort to link construct theory with test method.

One can characterize Oller's view of language processing and use as integrative but essentially cognitive in nature. His language theory and testing methodology largely ignore the social and interpersonal aspects of language use in real-life, interactive contexts. This point is elaborated by Cummins (1983). Nonetheless, Oller's work distinguishes itself in that it represents an early attempt in language testing to richly and systematically explicate the psychological and linguistic processes that underlie language use by linking construct theory and test operationalization, albeit in a somewhat restricted context.

Canale and Swain (1980) emphasize not only linguistic but also pragmatic knowledge as critical components of the L2 construct. The authors introduce sociolinguistic competence as a prominent feature in their model of communicative competence in language teaching and testing, along with grammatical and strategic competence. Later, Canale (1983) adds discourse competence to the model. In their distinction between competence and performance, Canale and Swain choose to emphasize issues pertaining to the knowledge of language in terms of components and do not deliberate on how these components come together to result in performance.

Although Canale and Swain present a more comprehensive view of language ability, they, like Lado (1961), essentially follow Chomsky's (1965) representation of abstract knowledge, and not Hymes' (1972) broader view, that is, ability to use that knowledge in specific contexts. As Ellis, (1994) points out, however, "although Canale and Swain prefer to exclude 'ability to use' from their definition of 'competence,' they argue in favor of including sociolinguistic, discourse, and strategic knowledge within its compass" (p. 158). In other words, while it may be possible to view grammatical competence simply in terms of knowledge (see Rea-Dickins, 1991, for a contrary viewpoint), it is more difficult to conceptualize the other competences, especially sociolinguistic and discourse competence, as divorced from a particular performance context. Nevertheless, the Canale and Swain model essentially features cognitive, psycholinguistic elements.

Bachman (1990) and Bachman and Palmer (1996) take into account earlier work in communicative language ability and use, particularly that by Canale and Swain, in formulating their communicative language ability (CLA) model. The CLA model meets Carroll's (1986) call for both integrative and real-life measurement by attempting to model not only language knowledge but language use as well. The model posits an interaction among language knowledge, topical knowledge, affective schemata, and individual characteristics together with the test task. According to the model, this interaction is mediated through strategic competence. Bachman and Palmer (1996) indicate that strategic competence represents "higher order executive processes that provide a cognitive management function in language use, as well as in other activities" (p. 70).

Bachman (1990) and Bachman and Palmer's (1996) inclusion of strategic competence represents the field's best attempt to forge a relationship between language knowledge and language use. (For an excellent discussion of strategic competence, see Douglas, 2000). As Alderson (2000) points out, however, "[t]his aspect of language ability is arguably the least developed in their [Bachman and Palmer's] framework" (p. 166). For example, Bachman (1990) states that his representation of strategic competence is cognitive in nature and is based on Faerch and Kasper's (1983) model of communicative strategies. Yet Bachman and Palmer (1996) present strategic competence as metacognitive strategies "derived largely from Sternberg's description of the metacomponents in his model of intelligence" (p. 82). Although the representation of strategic competence in terms of goal setting, planning, and assessment strategies is essentially the same in both books, the lack of clarity in the theoretical underpinnings of this construct and its questionable usefulness in terms of both test development and the measurement of language ability are troublesome.

What is important to our discussion is the consistent view that this element of the CLA model is cognitive—rather than interactional—in its orientation. Moreover, the representation of affect in CLA, which is a significant addition to Bachman and Palmer's (1996) model, is essentially cognitive in nature. According to Bachman and Palmer, affect schema is viewed not as integral to interactional communication but as background knowledge/experience that can be a double-edged sword, capable of hindering or helping a learner's performance.

In conclusion, Bachman and Palmer's treatment of strategic competence and affect is in terms of cognitive demands on the individual. Whereas they do address the social nature of language in their discussion of task demands, much of their model deals with the stored knowledge within an individual test-taker. Bachman and Palmer would, therefore, agree with Sharwood Smith (1994) that "[performance] has, of course, sociolinguistic relevance, but social factors are not the immediate concerns..." (p. 111). The CLA model is essentially a psycholinguistic representation of performance.

While a psycholinguistic/cognitive approach to modeling, evaluating, and understanding performance is clearly legitimate, another that emphasizes interactional and sociolinguistic elements is also worthy of consideration. We discuss such an approach later, but first we turn our attention to hierarchical definitions of language proficiency.

Hierarchical Construct Definition

The Foreign Service Institute (FSI) scale, American Council on the Teaching of Foreign Languages (ACTFL) Guidelines, International Second Language Proficiency Ratings (ISLPR), and Common European Framework all illustrate a hierarchical approach to representing the L2 construct (see North, 2000, for an extensive discussion of these and other scales). By delineating functions, contexts, and degrees of accuracy across different ability levels, these frameworks are most ambitious in their attempts to define the language construct. These hierarchical models share many features (e.g., their behavior/task orientation) but also differ in important ways (e.g., intended users, research base). The present discussion will focus on one of the models, the ACTFL Guidelines.

The widespread impact of the Guidelines on instructional material and oral proficiency testing is commonly acknowledged (Omaggio, 1983, 1986). Also well documented are the criticisms of these Guidelines (Chalhoub-Deville, 1997). A prevalent criticism is the lack of theoretical base and empirical evidence to support the hierarchical representation of the construct. Additionally, the Guidelines have been depicted as a hodgepodge of task descriptions and levels of performances and abilities that attempt to offer information to multiple audiences—teachers, students, test developers, interviewers, and score users—but which leave many wanting additional information and guidance. A criticism relevant to the present discussion is the lack of modeling that links test-takers' performances to either abilities or a real-life language use paradigm.

On the surface the ACTFL Guidelines seem to emphasize authenticity and real-life performance tasks expected to be encountered by learners in the target language culture. However, the tasks and situations included in the Guidelines are generic and were selected by a committee without any systematic investigation into actual student needs and eventual use. Such a needs analysis would be problematical indeed since students vary considerably in their needs and goals of language use. Yet, until such studies are undertaken, scores based on ACTFL-like tasks remain hard to interpret and generalize.

Language use on these tasks is not the sole focus of proficiency proponents. Given that the primary users of the proficiency Guidelines are schools and universities, where discrete abilities lend themselves more readily to instruction and assessment, such ability components achieve virtually the same importance as language use (see Omaggio, 1983, 1986). ACTFL tasks are viewed as tapping and/or eliciting specific ability and skill components that vary across different proficiency levels (Higgs & Clifford, 1982). Language components such as vocabulary, grammar, pronunciation, fluency, and sociolinguistic knowledge play an important role in the Guidelines' descriptions of what learners at different levels can do.

One would expect that this emphasis on performance and implicitly on the abilities underlying performance calls for systematically modeling these abilities (e.g., Chalhoub-Deville, 1995a, 1995b). Such is not the case, however. The proficiency movement's contribution via the ACTFL Guidelines is its promotion of an integrated and contextualized approach to language teaching, learning, and assessment—not a model of the language construct. Also, inattention to explicating capacity for language use linking ability and performance is not, however, a problem specific to the ACTFL Guidelines, but, as indicated earlier, is endemic to most representations of the communicative language construct. Finally, much like the other models discussed thus far, the Guidelines advocate a cognitive representation of the test-taker's proficiency. For example, while speaking performances evaluated using the ACTFL Guidelines are typically obtained via a trained interviewer, collaborative interaction is not modeled in the Guidelines. Performance is attributed solely to the test-taker. This position has been questioned by several researchers (e.g., Brown, 1998, 2003) and is vigorously opposed by proponents of an interactionalist model (see Johnson, 2001, discussed next).

Performance-Based Construct Definition

As we have seen, many language testers, as a reaction to the structuralist approach to language ability, differentiated between discrete-point and integrative tests (or indirect versus direct; or testing language usage versus use; etc.). Although this distinction was meaningful and helpful at the time, researchers more recently have begun to examine different approaches to measurement within the framework of performance-based assessment. McNamara (1996) provides the most extensive discussion of issues related specifically to language performance assessment. In his book, he distinguishes between two types of performance assessment practice:

1. an application of the techniques of performance assessment developed in non language contexts, which we will call the *work sample* approach; and
2. a tradition that sees performance in a second language as a complex *cognitive* achievement, involving integration of a number of psycholinguistic processes. (p. 6, italics in original)

Along these lines, McNamara also points out the difference in a weak versus a strong approach to the assignment and evaluation of scores derived from language performance assessments. The weak approach is commonly associated with the cognitive type of performance assessment and focuses on inferences about the test-taker's language abilities. This approach is employed with virtually all of the models of language ability discussed thus far. Conversely, the strong approach is associated with the work sample type of assessment and takes its cue from personnel psychology. This approach finds some application in the areas of language for specific and/or academic purposes. The strong approach's primary criterion for the evaluation of the test-taker is how well he or she has accomplished a given task. Consideration of the test-taker's language ability is relevant only inasmuch as it contributes to overall performance on the task.

Scores from the cognitive or psycholinguistic practice of performance assessment are linked—to varying degrees—to an explicit or implicit theory of language ability, and the test developer's, evaluator's, and researcher's efforts are guided accordingly by this theory. With respect to performance on work sample types of tasks, interest in scores as indicators of just language abilities is mitigated. Modeling performance within the strong approach requires a more comprehensive representation of ability, one that includes linguistic as well as nonlinguistic factors. In addition, these factors interact in complex ways with attributes of the context to affect performance. Within the strong approach, the degree of successful task fulfillment might be determined in part by language ability, and in part by other cognitive, affective, as well as social factors. Nevertheless, both the weak and strong approaches make inferences about the internal—primarily cognitive—constructs an individual brings to the task.

As rich as the strong perspective of language ability and performance is, understanding and modeling the many factors remains elusive. Attempts to do so, such as Munby's (1978) framework—with its extensive lists of skills, subskills, and enabling skills—have been criticized (e.g., Skehan, 1984). The next model we discuss, although also based on language performance, emphatically and purposefully stresses the social nature of language, and provides the field with a very different perspective of the L2 construct.

Interaction- and Discourse-Based Construct Definition

Interaction- and discourse-based competence is a relatively recent approach to defining language knowledge and performance. Kramsch (1986, 1998), whose work has been influential in this area, introduces the term 'interactional competence' to denote the social nature of language interaction and the notion of communication as the co-construction of participants:

> Whether it is face-to-face interaction between two or several speakers or the interaction between the reader and the written text, successful interaction presupposes not only a shared knowledge of the world, the reference to a common external context of communication, but also the construction of a shared internal context or "sphere of inter-subjectivity" that is built through the collaborative effort of the interactional partners. (1986, p. 367)

Although this definition describes interaction as part of oral and written communication, in reality this approach relies almost solely on analyses of speech data often collected in natural settings. As such, the interaction- and discourse-based approach to competence is concerned primarily with speech communication. On a positive note, this focus offers us a somewhat tapered view of language, allowing us to concentrate our attention on one modality, analyze how speech is realized in natural settings, and use this information to bolster our understanding and assessment of interaction. On the other hand, this same tapered view limits our capability to some degree to look at language across the four skills. To be sure, however, because the interaction- and discourse-based view of language demands that we examine the many vagaries of the social context and consider how communication is co-constructed among participants, it is just as complex and challenging—and promising—as any other model.

Young (2000) builds on Kramsch's work stating that interactional competence deals with recurring, that is stable episodes of interaction in context among participants. He refers to these episodes as discursive practices. Young identifies six interactional resources that participants make use of in a given context to co-construct their communication. These resources include (1) sequences of speech acts or rhetorical scripts; (2) register (in terms of lexical and syntactic structures as well as the semantic relations typical in a given practice); (3) turn taking patterns; (4) topic management (e.g., topic nomination and topic shift); (5) participation configuration; and, (6) designation of boundaries among and transition across discursive practices. In discussing these resources, Young emphasizes that the way the resources are utilized is not set in advance but is dependent on the particulars of the dynamic social context.

Recently, Young (2000), Swain (2001), and Johnson (2001) have urged language testers to incorporate this interactional perspective into the measurement process. Johnson's book offers the most comprehensive discussion of a discourse analytic approach to understanding and evaluating language performance. Her research refutes claims that the interview technique, specifically the Oral Proficiency Interview (OPI), elicits conversational features (e.g., topic management, turn-taking, question type, etc.) that correspond to those occurring in nontesting conversations. In essence, Johnson sees OPI-like discourse in the same vein as Kramsch (1986) sees classroom discourse. Both types of discourse tend to be asymmetric, negotiation-reduced, teacher- or tester-controlled. Moreover, the OPI's discourse can be likened to what Kramsch (1998) calls "topic-centered" communication, which is characteristic of essay writing where the main focus is on the transmission of a message. This "topic-centered" exchange in the OPI is to be contrasted with "people-centered" communication, in which discourse is constructed not only to transmit information, but also to mutually engage the participants and to negotiate meaning. In conclusion, these authors point out that the OPI and other conventional tests, "which have to break down language into functions, structures, and accuracy levels, have their purpose, but they do not show learners how to achieve the synthesis necessary to adapt to new conversational partners, new cultural contexts, new situations" (Kramsch, 1986, p. 370).

Proficiency, communicative competence, communicative language ability, and interactional competence models may, at first glance, seem to represent nuanced differences of the same construct. These models tend to focus on abilities the learner brings to the testing situation and consider contextual factors as well. Such surface similarities, however, mask fundamental differences in how language use is conceptualized. Because interactional competence researchers view language, social contexts, and the co-construction of meaning as inextricable, they maintain that interactional competence is an alternative model to the previously discussed language ability models. Young (2000), for example, addresses the issue of how communicative competence differs from interactional competence. He writes that whereas "communicative competence has been interpreted in much of the testing literature as a trait or bundle of traits that can be assessed in an individual, interactional competence is co-constructed by all participants in a discursive practice and is specific to that practice" (p. 9). The idea that performance can be attributed to an individual test-taker's array of internal, cognitive competences or abilities is rejected in favor of a model that views the interaction between the dynamic language exchange of participants and external social context as the primary determinant of performance. Interested readers are encouraged to consult Johnson's (2001) model, which she refers to as Practical Oral Language Ability, for a discussion of how such a model can find application with language testers.

Whereas language testing models discussed in the previous sections might be characterized as reflecting theories of cognitive language abilities, and are intended to be comprehensive and general, the interactional competence approach is primarily a social model of performance or practice, which is local and context dependent. According to the latter model, there are no static abilities inherent in and applied by all learners that conveniently sit still while we measure them. Instead, following Vygotsky (see McNamara, 1997, or Swain, 2001, for a brief introduction to Vygotsky's ideas, or Johnson, 2001, for a more comprehensive discussion of Vygotsky and others), knowledge and learning are engendered by the social transactions in which we engage and are therefore "*local*: They apply to a given discursive practice and either do not apply or apply in a different configuration to different practices" (Young, 2000, p. 10, italics in original).

With respect to the three aspects of measurement defined earlier, the interactional competence model can have implications for our depiction of the construct (as already discussed), the operationalization of that construct, that is, test development, and the scoring and interpretation of test performances. In terms of test development, if we are to take seriously the claim made by interactionalists or co-constructionists that language performance is local and that we cannot assume constructs of individual competence, then we need an accurate picture of how language is generated between or among participants in the setting of interest. Such a picture would facilitate the development of simulated tasks and evaluation of performance. As McNamara (1997) writes, in essence what we need is a "close analysis of naturally occurring discourse and social interaction [to] reveal the standards that apply in reality in particular settings" (p. 457). This calls for conducting language ethnomethodological studies and/or extensive needs analyses in order to describe and establish those standards (e.g., Douglas & Myers, 2000). Analysts would have to study many plausible interactions from the target language use context, a task requiring special skills that many language testers possess only to a limited degree. Collaborative efforts with researchers in other areas of applied linguistics and with content experts (e.g., Jacoby & McNamara, 1999) would be needed.

Evaluating test-takers' performances according to this model offers a conundrum. Generally speaking, we administer tests to, assign scores to, and make decisions about individuals for purposes such as selection, placement, assignment of grades/marks, and the like. If we view language as co-constructed, how can we disentangle an individual's contribution to a communicative exchange in order to provide a score or assess a candidate's merit for a potential position? Some have suggested that all participants in the interaction be scored, but it is unclear how doing this will help us arrive at a 'better' score for the participants. If we wish to pursue this approach in language testing, we will need to reconcile the demand for individual scores and group performances. Perhaps we will need to rethink how we assign—and ultimately interpret—test scores. Furthermore, with respect to scoring, proponents of the interactional competence model would reject the use of hierarchical or fixed/generic proficiency scales across contexts. The proponents maintain that such scales presuppose an ordering of abilities and/or skill thought to be internal to test-takers and to be responsible for the generation of language. The interactional competence supporters would prefer scales that take into account the dynamics of the interaction process. Again, this model would oblige us to rethink how we characterize, construct, use, and interpret language rating scales.

Because the interactional competence model is relatively new and has yet to be applied or investigated widely, the jury remains out with regard to the usefulness and appropriateness of this approach for language testers. Both Young (2000) and

Johnson (2001) see interactional competence as a model of language practice, not of language abilities. In addition, Vygotsky's ideas are primarily meant to explain and model learning, so although such a model may seem sensible when investigating L2 learning and acquisition, it may prove intractable for the purpose of assessment. Despite these potential limitations, we resolutely maintain that this approach deserves further consideration and application.

Summary of L2 Construct Representation

This section summarizes the evolving representation of the L2 construct. Our review documents that the majority of the L2 models have adopted a cognitive orientation to representing the construct. Also to be noted is the ever-expanding representation of the construct as newer models incorporate the knowledge and thinking garnered from past researchers and scholars. The review concludes by focusing on interactional competence. A question raised by this last representation of the L2 construct is whether ideas advanced by interactional competence proponents can be reconciled with and incorporated into established L2 models. Interactional competence researchers advocate a reconceptualization of existing theories of language ability and performance because cognitive and interactional models represent fundamentally different orientations to defining and investigating the construct. This issue, as well as others raised earlier, present the field with a challenging alternative to how we think about the L2 construct—one that shouldn't be dismissed without earnest reflection and discourse.

ABILITY TO USE TEST SCORES

The focus in the present chapter has been on representations of the L2 construct that have gained recognition in the language testing field. As pointed out, the manner in which testers define the L2 construct often leads to the way they operationalize that construct. We have chosen in this chapter to concentrate on how language testers conceptualize their constructs as that is what sets them apart from other measurement experts. In this final section we turn our attention to issues concerning the use and interpretation of L2 test scores.

The long history of interest in performance-based assessment has amplified L2 researchers' attention to not only linguistic, but also to nonlinguistic cognitive, affective, and social factors that have an effect on test scores. Consequently, modeling of language use has become increasingly complex. Although such modeling is critical for meaningful interpretation and appropriate generalization of scores, until we achieve greater understanding of such variables as metacognition, affect, and co-construction, their place in the *measurement* of performance remains tenuous. Our position is not to discount the need for the inclusion of such factors in a comprehensive model of ability and performance, but to question the soundness of incorporating them into test specifications when their measurement is so elusive. We have already pointed out the dilemmas associated with the co-construction approach. In terms of the other factors, numerous researchers have already pointed out how difficult the research and assessment of metacognition (e.g., Ellis, 1994; Anderson & Krathwohl, 2001) and affect (Carroll, 1991; Porter, 1991) can be. We therefore argue that it is reasonable to take a somewhat conservative, but responsible, position. As Alderson and North (1991) note:

> This [conservatism] implies not only that language testing researchers and test developers need humility, and an understanding that resistance to change is not necessarily obstructionism, but also that we need in language testing perhaps to explore more carefully the nature of innovation, in order to better understand how to optimize our instruments and procedures and their impact on their environment. (p. ix)

A conservative position, however, should not be employed as a smokescreen for not engaging in systematic investigations that help improve our understanding of the role these slippery factors play in L2 ability and performance. This understanding can then direct how we might incorporate such factors into language tests in order to better understand what our test scores mean.

The meaningfulness and appropriateness of test scores are, of course, issues of validity (Messick, 1989). With respect to validation, we must begin by asking ourselves what we wish test scores to tell us about test-takers. Are we, for example, primarily interested in what test scores tell us about performance relative to our construct definition, or more so in a candidate's merit for a job or position? This dichotomy is illustrated in the infamous reproach McNamara received from a medical educator while conducting research that led to the development of the Occupational English Test: "Oh, so you're only interested in language, not communication" (McNamara, 1997, p. 452). As stated earlier, this tension in evaluating language performance led McNamara to distinguish between a weak approach to validation, whereby the focus is simply on a candidate's language ability, and a strong approach, whereby a more comprehensive model of task fulfillment is investigated. One might argue, however, that the goal of both approaches is to formulate (or confirm/falsify) an abilities-based theory or model of language ability and performance—the difference being essentially the degree of comprehensiveness.

Another way of conceiving validation would be to prioritize what we wish to say about test-takers (Shepard, 1993). Validation efforts will likely result in confusing and contradictory information unless we prioritize the uses and interpretations of our test scores. How we intend to use test scores should guide us in how we interpret them. Is our first concern to examine decisions we make and actions we take with respect to examinees? Or is our primary concern the relation of test scores to a theory of language or to a set of similar tasks? We argue that it is the use of test scores that should take precedence in validity arguments. As Kane (2001, p. 334) states: "The distinction here is not among different kinds of validity or even different types of validity evidence, but among different types of interpretations." Anytime test scores are used to make important decisions about examinees, the catchall bin of construct validity should prioritize evidence concerned with the particular use of/decision from test scores.

We believe there is an imbalance in validity arguments that favors test score interpretation and inference—with respect to content/tasks and/or global, theoretical models of ability—instead of test use, that is, examining local, practical decisions made and actions taken based on scores. For example, Douglas (2000, pp. 257–258) presents a very apt and appropriate metaphor for construct validation, referring to the process as creating a "validity mosaic." He lists ten avenues for investigation of the construct, nine of which are essentially theory-driven and one that is related to the specific use of the test scores. (In fairness to Douglas, he cautions his readers that no such list is exhaustive, and that any validity mosaic is malleable.) No question, it is easier and safer to construct validity arguments about a theory than about decisions and actions.

Attention is warranted as well to practice-driven validation with an emphasis on supporting our uses/decisions and their consequences. We are by no means suggesting that language testing become atheoretical or that test development be task-driven (e.g., see Chalhoub-Deville, 2001). Structured, discerning investigations into the relationship of test-taker performance to a model of ability and/or to a domain of tasks is desirable, but not at the expense of an uncompromising examination of our decisions about test-takers. We language testers, our constituents, and even our theories/models may all be better served if we devote increased attention to the more pragmatic—and sometimes more mundane—consideration of better understanding our assessment tools, our use of test scores, and the consequences.

Finally, we would like to draw attention to score reporting. A critical—but often neglected—aspect of measurement, test score interpretation, and especially test use, is how we document score information and relay this to intended users. Brown and Hudson (2002) realize the importance of reporting, saying:

> One of the most important lessons we have learned . . . is that feedback is crucial; this involves more than just feedback to the students, but also to teachers, administrators, parents, etc. In addition, we have to come to realize that feedback should not just be top-down, but a two-way communication. (pp. 278–279)

Multiple audiences, who have varying needs and perspectives and who interpret and use test score information with their particular needs in mind, give rise to the necessity of communicating test score information in inventive but appropriate ways.

The value and usefulness of our scores are directly related to how we disseminate test score information to users (see Wainer, Hambleton, & Meara, 1999). When we fail to communicate test results effectively, we diminish the validity of our test scores. It is crucial to understand how test users negotiate meaning from scores reported by test developers/institutions. Systematic investigations into how scores are reported and used can be utilized to enhance practice- and purpose-oriented validity evidence.

REFERENCES

Alderson, J. C. (2000). *Assessing reading*. Cambridge, UK: Cambridge University Press.

Alderson, J. C., Clapham, C., & Wall, D. (1995). *Language test construction and evaluation*. Cambridge, UK: Cambridge University Press.

Alderson, J. C., & North, B. (1991). Introduction. In J. C. Alderson & B. North (Eds.), *Language testing in the 1990s: The communicative legacy* (pp. vii–xvii). London: Macmillan/Modern English Publications.

Anderson, L. W., & Krathwohl, D. (Eds.). (2001). *A taxonomy of learning, teaching, and assessing*. New York: Longman.

Bachman, L. F. (1990). *Fundamental considerations in language testing*. Oxford, UK: Oxford University Press.

Bachman, L. F., & Palmer, A. S. (1996). *Language testing in practice*. Oxford, UK: Oxford University Press.

Bailey, K. M., & Brown, J. D. (1996). Language testing courses: What are they? In A. Cumming & R. Berwick (Eds.), *Validation in language testing* (pp. 236–256). Clevedon, UK: Multilingual Matters.

Brindley, G. (1986). *The assessment of second language proficiency: Issues and approaches*. Adelaide: National Curriculum Resource Centre.

Brindley, G. (1989). *Assessing achievement in the learner-centred curriculum*. Sydney: National Centre for English Language Teaching and Research.

Brown, A. (1998). Interview style and candidate performance in the IELTS oral interview. Paper presented at the 20th Language Testing Research Colloquium, Monterey, CA.

Brown, A. (2003). Interviewer variation and the co-construction of speaking proficiency. *Language Testing, 20*, 1–25.

Brown, J. D. (1996). *Testing in language programs*. Upper Saddle River, NJ: Prentice-Hall.

Brown, J. D., & Hudson, T. (2002). *Criterion-referenced language testing*. Cambridge, UK: Cambridge University Press.

Buck, G. (2001). *Assessing listening*. Cambridge, UK: Cambridge University Press.

Canale, M., & Swain, M. (1980). Theoretical bases of communicative approaches to second language teaching and testing. *Applied Linguistics, 1*(1), 1–47.

Canale, M. (1983). On some dimensions of language proficiency. In J. W. Oller, Jr. (Ed.), *Issues in language testing research* (pp. 333–342). Rowley, MA: Newbury House.

Carroll, B. J. (1980). *Testing communicative performance: An interim study*. Oxford, UK: Pergamon.

Carroll, B. J. (1991). Response to Don Porter's paper: 'Affective factors in language testing.' In J. C. Alderson & B. North (Eds.), *Language testing in the 1990s: The communicative legacy* (pp. 41–45). London: Macmillan.

Carroll, B. J., & Hall, P. J. (1985). *Make your own language tests: A practical guide to writing language performance tests*. Oxford, UK: Pergamon.

Carroll, J. B. (1961). Fundamental considerations in testing for English proficiency of foreign students. In *Testing the English proficiency of foreign students* (pp. 31–40). Washington, DC: Center for Applied Linguistics.

Carroll, J. B. (1986). LT + 25, and beyond? Comments. *Language Testing, 3*, 123–129.

Chalhoub-Deville, M. (1995a). Deriving oral assessment scales across different tests and rater groups. *Language Testing, 12*, 16–33.

Chalhoub-Deville, M. (1995b). A contextualized approach to describing oral language proficiency. *Language Learning, 45*, 251–281.

Chalhoub-Deville, M. (1997). Theoretical models, assessment frameworks, and test construction. *Language Testing, 14*, 3–22.

Chalhoub-Deville, M. (2001). Task-based assessments: Characteristics and validity evidence. In M. Bygate, P. Skehan, & M. Swain (Eds.), *Researching pedagogic tasks: Second language learning, teaching, and testing* (pp. 210–228). Harlow, UK: Pearson Education Limited.

Chalhoub-Deville, M. (2003). Second language interaction: Current perspectives and future trends. *Language Testing, 20*, 369–383.

Chomsky, N. (1965). *Aspects of the theory of syntax*. Cambridge, MA: MIT Press.

Clark, J. L. D. (1972). *Foreign-language testing: Theory and practice*. Philadelphia: The Center for Curriculum Development, Inc.

Cohen, A. (1994). *Assessing language ability in the classroom* (2nd ed.). Boston: Heinle & Heinle.

Cummins, J. P. (1983). Language proficiency and academic achievement. In J. W. Oller, Jr. (Ed.), *Issues in language testing research* (pp. 108–126). Rowley, MA: Newbury House.

Davies, A. (1990). *Principles of language testing*. Oxford, UK: Basil Blackwell.

Davidson, F., & Lynch, B. K. (2002). *Testcraft: A teacher's guide to writing and using language test specifications*. New Haven, CT: Yale University Press.

Deville, C., & Chalhoub-Deville, M. (1993). Modified scoring, traditional item analysis, and Sato's caution index used to investigate the reading recall protocol. *Language Testing, 10*, 117–132.

Douglas, D. (2000). *Assessing languages for specific purposes*. Cambridge, UK: Cambridge University Press.

Douglas, D., & Myers, R. (2000). Assessing the communication skills of veterinary students: Whose criteria? In A. Kunnan (Ed.), *Fairness in language testing: Selected papers from the 1997 Language Testing Research Colloquium* (pp. 60–81). Cambridge, UK: Cambridge University Press.

Ellis, R. (1994). *The study of second language acquisition*. Oxford, UK: Oxford University Press.

Faerch, C., & Kasper, G. (1983). Plans and strategies in foreign language communications. In C. Faerch & G. Kasper (Eds.), *Strategies in interlanguage communication* (pp. 20–60). London: Longman.

Finocchiaro, M., & Sako, S. (1983). *Foreign language testing: A practical approach*. New York: Regents.

Fradd, S. M., & McGee, P. L., with Wilen, D. K. (1994). *Instructional assessment: An integrative approach to evaluating student performance*. Reading, MA: Addison-Wesley.

Genesee, F., & Upshur, J. A. (1996). *Classroom-based evaluation in second language evaluation*. Cambridge, UK: Cambridge University Press.

Harris, D. P. (1969). *Testing English as a second language*. New York: McGraw-Hill.

Heaton, J. B. (1975). *Writing English language tests: A practical guide for teachers of English as a second or foreign language*. London: Longman.

Henning, G. (1987). *A guide to language testing: Development, evaluation, research*. Rowley, MA: Newbury House.

Higgs, T., & Clifford, R. (1982). The push toward communication. In T. V. Higgs (Ed.), *Curriculum, competence, and the foreign language teacher* (pp. 57–79). The ACTFL Foreign Language Education Series, vol. 13. Lincolnwood, IL: National Textbook Company.

Hughes, A. (1989). *Testing for language teachers*. Cambridge, UK: Cambridge University Press.

Hughes, A. (2003). *Testing for language teachers* (2nd ed.). Cambridge, UK: Cambridge University Press.

Hurley, S. R., & Tinajero, J. V. (Eds.). (2001). *Literacy assessment of second language learners*. Boston: Allyn & Bacon.

Hymes, D. H. (1972). On communicative competence. In J. B. Pride & J. Holmes (Eds.), *Sociolinguistics: Selected readings* (pp. 269–293). Harmondsworth: Penguin.

Jacoby, S., & McNamara, T. (1999). Locating competence. *English for Specific Purposes, 18*, 213–241.

Johnson, M. (2001). *The art of nonconversation: A re-examination of the validity of the oral proficiency interview*. New Haven, CT: Yale University Press.

Kane, M. (2001). Current concerns in validity theory. *Journal of Educational Measurement, 38*, 319–342.

Kramsch, C. (1986). From language proficiency to interactional competence. *The Modern Language Journal, 70*, 366–372.

Kramsch, C. (1998). *Language and culture*. Oxford, UK: Oxford University Press.

Kunnan, A. J. (Ed.). (1998). *Validation in language assessment*. Mahwah, NJ: Lawrence Erlbaum Associates.

Lado, R. L. (1961). *Language testing: The construction and use of foreign language tests: A teacher's book*. New York: McGraw-Hill.

Linn, R. L., & Gronlund, N. E. (2000). *Measurement and assessment in teaching* (8th ed.). Upper Saddle River, NJ: Prentice-Hall.

Lynch, B. K. (2001). Rethinking assessment from a critical perspective. *Language Testing, 18*, 351–372.

Madsen, H. S. (1983). *Techniques in testing*. Oxford, UK: Oxford University Press.

McNamara, T. (1996). *Measuring second language performance*. London: Longman.

McNamara, T. (1997). 'Interaction' in second language performance assessment: Whose performance? *Applied Linguistics, 18*, 446–466.

McNamara, T. (2000). *Language testing*. Oxford, UK: Oxford University Press.

McNamara, T. (2001). Language assessment as social practice: Challenges for research. *Language Testing, 18*, 333–349.

Messick, S. (1989). Validity. In R. L. Linn (Ed.), *Educational measurement* (3nd ed.) (pp. 13–103). New York: American Council on Education and Macmillan.

Munby, J. (1978). *Communicative syllabus design*. Cambridge, UK: Cambridge University Press.

Nitko, A. J. (2001). *Educational assessment of students* (3rd ed.). Upper Saddle River, NJ: Prentice-Hall.

North, B. (2000). *The development of a common framework scale of language proficiency*. New York: Peter Lang.

Oller, J. W., Jr. (1979). *Language tests at school: A pragmatic approach*. London: Longman.

Omaggio, A. C. (1983). *Proficiency-oriented classroom testing*. Washington, DC: Center for Applied Linguistics.

Omaggio, A. C. (1986). *Teaching language in context: Proficiency-oriented instruction*. Boston: Heinle & Heinle.

Porter, D. (1991). Affective factors in language testing. In J. C. Alderson & B. North (Eds.), *Language testing in the 1990s: The communicative legacy* (pp. 32–40). London: Macmillan.

Rea-Dickins, P. (1991). What makes a grammar test communicative? In J. C. Alderson & B. North (Eds.), *Language testing in the 1990s: The communicative legacy* (pp. 112–131). London: Macmillan.

Read, J. (2000). *Assessing vocabulary*. Cambridge, UK: Cambridge University Press.

Sharwood Smith, M. (1994). *Second language learning: Theoretical foundations*. London: Longman.

Shepard, L. A. (1993). Evaluating test validity. In L. Darling-Hammond (Ed.), *Review of Research in Education, 19* (pp. 405–450). Washington, DC: American Educational Research Association.

Shohamy, E. (1985). *A practical handbook in language testing for the second language teacher*. Tel-Aviv: Tel-Aviv University.

Shohamy, E. (2001). Democratic assessment as an alternative. *Language Testing, 18*, 373–291.

Skehan, P. (1984). Issues in the testing of English for specific purposes. *Language Testing, 1*, 202–220.

Swain, M. (2001). Examining dialogue: Another approach to content specification and to validating inferences drawn from test scores. *Language Testing, 18*, 275–302.

Thorndike, R. L., & Hagen, E. P. (1977). *Measurement and evaluation in psychology and education* (4th ed.). New York: Wiley.

Thorndike, R. M. (1997). *Measurement and evaluation in psychology and education* (6th ed.). New York: Macmillan.

Underhill, N. (1987). *Testing spoken language: A handbook of oral testing techniques*. Cambridge, UK: Cambridge University Press.

Valette, R. M. (1967). *Modern language testing: A handbook*. New York: Harcourt Brace.

Valette, R. M. (1977). *Modern language testing* (2nd ed.). New York: Harcourt Brace.

Wainer, H., Hambleton, R. K., & Meara, K. (1999). Alternative displays for communicating NAEP results: A redesign and validity study. *Journal of Educational Measurement, 36*, 301–335.

Weir, C. W. (1990). *Communicative language testing*. New York: Prentice-Hall.

Weir, C. W. (1993). *Understanding and developing language tests*. New York: Prentice-Hall.

Young, R. F. (March, 2000). Interactional competence: Challenges for validity. Paper presented at the Annual Meeting of the Language Testing Research Colloquium, Vancouver, Canada.

46

Research Methods in Language Testing

Tom Lumley
Annie Brown
University of Melbourne

INTRODUCTION

A common stereotype of the language testing researcher is that he or she is essentially a statistician who employs a daunting array of procedures, often obscure to outsiders, to attack or defend the quality of language tests, with scant regard for more humanistic issues or a full range of validity concerns. Certainly a great amount of language testing research is quantitatively based, employing an increasingly sophisticated range of statistical procedures, as perusal of the journal *Language Testing*, for example, easily confirms. Spolsky (1995) and Lemann (1999) discuss the triumph of reliability in all areas of educational measurement including language testing in the United States, over much of the last century, while McNamara (2001, p. 334) has recently claimed that "language testing is arguably the most positivist in orientation of all areas of applied linguistics." Assessment involves measurement, which requires the use of numerical data (in the form of scores or ratings), and language testing research is concerned centrally with the defensibility of these numbers, which implies a positivistic paradigm.

Nevertheless, in the last decade or so there has been a broadening of scope in the kind of issues investigated in language assessment research, with a concomitant expansion in the research methods used to investigate them. There has been a move from positivistic research focusing on properties of tests and scores toward a broader and more critical examination of a wide range of validity issues embracing construct definition as well as language testing practice and policy. This has required the use of an increasing variety of (broadly) qualitative approaches to problems that arise in language assessment contexts, involving, for example, more consultation with stakeholders and more sophisticated approaches to analyzing both the product and the process of language testing. Such developments have to a considerable extent resulted from expanded models of validity (e.g., Linn, Baker, & Dunbar, 1991; Messick, 1989, 1994, 1996; Moss, 1994) in educational assessment more generally, which have brought with them greater attention to the consequences of language assessment. There has been increasing questioning and problematization of notions and consequences of language testing and assessment (see, for example, Hill & Parry, 1994; Lynch, 2001; McNamara, 2001; Shohamy, 2001a, 2001b). Instrumental in relating Messick's conceptualization of validity to language testing has been Bachman's work (Bachman, 1990; Bachman & Palmer, 1996). The broadening of concerns in language testing research is exemplified by the inclusion in the recent *Encyclopedia of Language and Education* of a chapter on qualitative approaches to test validation (Banerjee & Luoma, 1997), by Shohamy's (2001a) critical perspective on language testing, and by Kunnan's chapter (chap. 46, this volume) "Language Assessment from a Wider Context." Conceptual issues in language assessment, including those relating to development of frameworks or theories, test design, discussion of policy, and understanding of processes, necessarily rely on argument and the complexity of multiple points of view, and raise problems that challenge a positivistic paradigm and which no degree of quantitative sophistication can resolve.

The essential point here is that language testing and assessment research now necessarily relies on a variety of research methods, quantitative and qualitative, that increasingly complement each other. It is impossible to ignore the role of quantitative data and appropriately sophisticated statistics in test validation; however, aspects of validity including the process, impact, and consequences of assessment deserve equal attention and require investigation using appropriately different and varied research methods.

Statement of Purpose

In this chapter we aim to introduce the reader to some of the most commonly used methodological approaches to research in language testing in recent years, including methods long established as well as new approaches and current directions. Although we recognize that any classification of methodologies into types is simplistic at best, we distinguish here research concerned primarily with scores (labeled here, for the sake of convenience, "quantitative methods") from research that we consider to be concerned mainly with issues other than scores ("qualitative methods")[1]. The remainder of this chapter will therefore be organized under these two headings.

QUANTITATIVE METHODS

Language testing implies measurement, which is necessarily quantitative. Much research in language testing examines test scores and ratings to investigate the internal qualities of tests (addressing issues of both reliability and validity) and the validity of the inferences made using those scores.

Language testing practice long relied on classical test theory, borrowed from the field of psychological testing (Anastasi, 1976; Bachman, 1990) to investigate the qualities of tests, with reliability a principal concern. One issue was the internal consistency of tests: the extent to which the test items correlate with each other and hence collectively define a single measurable trait or dimension. A narrow interest in the reliability of tests is rarely the major focus of research studies these days, although it is still necessary to estimate the reliability of test scores or ratings in order to support other claims, whether these claims relate to the quality of a new test or item type, or to tests used for research in areas of applied linguistics other than language testing itself. The reliability of the scoring procedures, for example, was an issue in Alderson, Percsich, and Szabo's (2000) study of a proposed test item type in which test-takers are required to reorganize a sequence of sentences or paragraphs so as to construct a coherent text. Reliability also remains an issue in research studies dealing with more established tests, as in J. D. Brown's (1999) study of sources of error in the Test of English as a

Foreign Language (TOEFL), which focused specifically on the reliability of the whole TOEFL test and that of its subtests.

Until recently, the predominant view of validity was of separable kinds, including content, construct, and criterion-related validity (Anastasi, 1976; Bachman, 1990). Whereas content validity was (and is) seen as a matter of judgment and argument, score data formed the basis for investigations of the nature of the construct and of criterion-related validity. Broadly speaking, the statistical approaches used in these studies involve measures of correlation, or convergence of data, on the one hand, and of difference, or divergence, on the other.

In recent decades, the range of statistical procedures available for the examination of the internal measurement properties of tests, contributing to better understanding of both reliability and validity, has expanded beyond classical procedures to include item-response theory (Baker, 1997; Henning, 1984, 1987), the related Rasch measurement (Bond & Fox, 2001; McNamara, 1996; Wright & Masters, 1982; Wright & Stone, 1979), Generalizability Theory (G-Theory) (Brennan, 1983; Shavelson & Webb, 1991) and structural equation modeling (SEM) (Bae & Bachman, 1998; Kunnan, 1998). The chapter will look first at classical statistics before discussing other procedures.

Correlation

Correlations between different measures have always been a major point of concern in quantitatively based language testing research. The number of studies in which correlational analyses (such as Pearson product-moment, Spearman rank correlations and regression analyses, all part of classical test theory[2]) are used is enormous. Correlations, which examine similarity among measures, can provide information about practical issues such as the equivalence of different tests or test forms, the ability of a test to predict performance on another measure, or the behavior of raters, as well as more theoretical issues such as the dimensionality of a test's construct.

At a simple level, scores by test-takers on different forms of a single test (intratest correlation) may be compared, in order to determine whether each form provides similar information about the test-taker. This can help to establish whether all test-takers face equivalent challenges in test difficulty, regardless of which test form they have taken, and hence the extent to which results from different test forms are directly comparable. A typical use of correlation occurs in Beglar and Hunt (1999): High correlation coefficients were used to support the authors' claim that two new versions of parts of the Vocabulary Levels Test (Nation, 1983, 1990) could be considered as parallel, or equivalent.

Intertest comparisons involve studies of concurrent or predictive validity (both forms of criterion-related validity). Correlations are used to compare scores on a test under investigation with some other criterion, such as a score on a different test (concurrent validity), or perceptions of success on a later course of study or in employment (predictive validity). Such studies offer the simplest indication of how closely performance on one (often new) measure compares to a different, criterion measure, often an existing instrument already accepted as a measure for a similar purpose. This issue is relevant when theoretical advances lead to the development of new kinds of language tests. For example, Henning, Schedl, and Suomi (1995) compared scores from the old version of the Test of Spoken English (TSE) with scores on a new prototype. Their finding of a fairly high correlation between scores on the two versions suggested that both versions assess a similar construct, although without addressing the question of what the construct is.

Scores on two subtests may also be compared, in order to determine whether, say, an objectively scored or short test (probably cheaper and easier to administer, with potentially higher reliability) is a good predictor of scores on a subjectively scored test (probably more expensive and less reliable). During the development stages of an EAP test, correlation statistics were also used (Clapham & Alderson, 1996) to show that the proposed grammar component of the test overlapped considerably with the reading component, and yielded little if any additional information. In this case, the desire to avoid unfavorable washback led to a decision not to include the grammar component in the new test; in another situation, where the stakes are lower, efficiency (i.e., cost considerations) would dictate removal of the reading test. Correlational studies have also been used to defend the use of a simulated (tape-mediated) test of oral proficiency (SOPI), by showing a high correlation between scores on the SOPI and those on a face-to-face oral proficiency interview (OPI) (e.g., Stansfield & Kenyon, 1992). A potential problem in studies based solely on correlations, as various writers (e.g., Bachman, 1990) have pointed out, is that simple correlations between scores on two different instruments are not sufficient evidence that either is a valid measure of the construct or ability the test aims to assess, nor do they allow statements to be made about which is more valid.

Where a test aims to predict future performance, as in a selection test for university entrance, as part of the validation process, test results may be correlated with subsequent university grades. Clapham (1996) reported correlations between students' scores on the Academic Reading module of an entrance test and ratings by university tutors of students' general English ability at the end of their first year at university, as evidence of the predictive validity of the reading test score. In another kind of predictive study, Powers, Schedl, and Wilson (1999) used different types of regression analyses (also based on correlation) to examine the relationship between test-takers' scores on the revised Test of Spoken English (TSE) and ratings indicating listeners' ability to understand what the test-takers were trying to communicate.

A different branch of investigation, also based on correlations, and arising from the increasing use of subjective assessment in language testing, compares the ratings provided by different types of raters. Correlational studies allow the investigation of how background factors may affect the level of agreement (and hence the potential impact on test-takers) among raters of different kinds. These factors include (in academic contexts) raters' language teaching experience, such as ESL versus English as L1 (e.g., J. D. Brown, 1991; O'Loughlin, 1992), and (in occupation-specific language tests) their professional background, such as tour guides versus language teachers (A. Brown, 1995) or health professionals versus ESL specialists (Lumley, 1998). The results of these studies can offer an indication of how closely scores from one group of raters substitute for scores from raters of a different background, giving information relevant to the validity as well as the reliability of the assessment results.

In addition to practical issues such as those discussed earlier (dealing with choice of test or test form and choice of rater), correlations also offer information on the more theoretical issue of test dimensionality, an important aspect of construct validation. If a language test claims to assess something described as "second language proficiency," this assumes that we can conceive of "second language proficiency" in broad terms as a single (or holistic) dimension, along which all learners can be placed. Such an assumption is necessary if measurement is to take place, although it is clear that "because of the nature of human learning, all educational tests are likely, to some degree, to be multidimensional" (Blais & Laurier, 1995, p. 74), involving different components (or dimensions) of knowledge and ability (e.g., grammatical knowledge, pronunciation, range of technical vocabulary, clarity of writing) that may develop at different rates in individuals. Correlational studies, more complex than those referred to earlier, can give information on the degree of unidimensionality or multidimensionality observed in the tests under investigation. Such studies assist researchers to make and evaluate claims about the measurement properties of the tests and the ways in which test results are to be interpreted.

Established statistical procedures used in construct validation research include multitrait multimethod analysis (Bachman, 1990; Buck, 1990; Campbell & Fiske, 1959) and factor analysis (Bachman et al., 1994). Both confirmatory and exploratory factor analysis have been used in language testing research in attempts to define factors that account for consistency and variation in language test scores. High correlations among scores (convergence) suggest a single (or overall) dimension of measurement, whereas variation (or divergence) among scores on different subtests (or assessment criteria) supports claims that different components of language ability (such as grammar, vocabulary, organization) can be separately assessed. For example, Boldt and Oltman (1993) examined the statistical relationship among Test of Spoken English (TSE) scores with the measurement constructs (pronunciation, grammar, fluency, and overall comprehensibility) that the scores aimed to reflect. In a study designed to evaluate the usefulness of reporting separate scores for different aspects of test performance, Fulcher (1997) used factor analysis to examine the degree of convergence and divergence among scores given for different test components (writing, structure, and reading) in an English language placement test.

Correlation is also the basis for a recently developed, rather complex set of statistical procedures, Structural Equation Modeling (SEM), described by Kunnan (1998, p. 298) as "a coming together of several models: multiple regression, path analysis and factor analysis." SEM is particularly useful in trying to explain factors that influence test results, including those considered both relevant and irrelevant to the constructs that tests aim to assess, with the general goal of improving our understanding of what it is that language tests actually measure. Recent studies employing SEM have investigated the relationship between test-takers' use of strategies and second language test performance (Purpura, 1997, 1998, 1999) and the relationship between test-taker background and test performance (Kunnan, 1995).

Difference

In contrast to correlation, which is primarily concerned with similarity among measures, the other general group of approaches to analyzing test data involves investigating difference. A wide variety of statistical approaches investigating difference in test data are used to address issues relating to construct validity. One area of interest concerns differences in performance by different groups of test-takers, or differences in performance by the same group on different tests or test forms. Many are based on analysis of the magnitude and significance of variance observed in scores from two or more groups (analysis of variance (ANOVA), and related statistics). Such studies raise questions of whether, or to what degree, these differences are relevant to the construct the test aims to assess, whether modifications to test design are likely to lead to improved (i.e., more valid) language tests, or whether a particular test is relevant or fair for specified groups of test-takers. They therefore have importance in consideration of issues such as the ethics and consequences of test use.

One branch of study focuses on trying to explain differences in scores observed for different test tasks. Thus, Sasaki (2000) examined the influence of schemata activated by culturally familiar words on students' cloze test-taking processes. She identified two groups of test-takers with no difference in age, length of instruction in English or English reading ability, and then used t-tests to compare performance by the two groups when each was administered a different version of a cloze test. She found that inclusion in the test of words more likely to trigger familiar schemata led to improved test performance. In the context of speaking assessment, Iwashita, McNamara, and Elder (2001) used MANOVA and ANOVA to examine whether variation in test performance (as measured by ratings) could be related to differences in task characteristics. For example, they considered the effect on measures of accuracy and fluency when test-takers were confronted with tasks predicted to be more or less demanding. This work is interesting for the range of researcher expectations that were not fulfilled, its general lack of support for previous research findings aiming to identify components of task difficulty, and its confirmation of the hugely problematic nature of attempts to reliably predict influences on task difficulty (cf. also Hamp-Lyons & Mathias, 1994).

A second focus is on differences in observed performance by test-takers of different kinds. For example, Clapham (1996) used ANOVA to investigate whether subject-specific reading passages offered equal advantage to test-takers of different subject backgrounds. She identified little advantage in the inclusion of subject-specific reading modules, and the test was revised accordingly. ANOVA was also used by Hamilton et al. (1993) to examine differences in performance levels of different groups of native and non-native speakers of English on an EAP reading and writing test used by universities as a selection test for non-native speakers. They found that native speakers of different backgrounds performed neither homogeneously, nor especially highly, on the test, and concluded that there was inherent bias in the system toward native speakers, who were not required to take the test.

Examination of differences in group performance can also shed light on bias in tests. Item bias, or Differential Item Functioning (DIF), can be said to exist when the test scores of one group of test-takers is higher than those of another group, for reasons unrelated to the construct being assessed (Elder, 1998; Holland & Wainer, 1993), thus threatening the validity of claims made on the basis of test performance. DIF analysis is employed to investigate bias in test items against particular groups of test-takers, such as those from different language or educational backgrounds. For example, Ryan and Bachman (1992) used the Mantel-Haenszel procedure (derived from a simple test of difference, the chi-square test) to compare responses by test-takers of Indo-European and non-Indo-European language background on two tests, finding that many of the items showed DIF in favor of one group of test-takers or the other, raising questions about the construct measured by each test. Further insights into the complexity of bias were provided by Elder (1996), who used the Mann Whitney procedure and the Mantel-Haenszel procedure to investigate performance by school-age students of Italian, Greek, and Chinese to establish whether students with a home background in one of these languages outperformed those with no such background. Her finding that the tests varied in the extent to which they advantaged one group or the other raised questions about what the test construct should be in such tests and also highlighted the difficulty of providing fair assessments for students of different backgrounds.

Item Response Theory and Rasch Measurement

Over the past two decades the range of statistical procedures used in language assessment validation research has expanded dramatically. Arguably the most important development has been the increasingly widespread acceptance of item response theory (IRT) (Hambleton, Swaminathan, & Rogers, 1991; Henning, 1984, 1987; Henning, Hudson, & Turner, 1985; Woods & Baker, 1985) and the related Rasch measurement in place of, or in addition to, classical theory, not only for test analysis but also for research expanding our understanding of how tests function. Baker's (1987) doctoral dissertation was the first application of IRT to language test data, and the forerunner of many more studies using IRT to examine aspects of test functioning. IRT models are especially useful for equating the difficulty of different test forms, in item banking (Pollitt, 1984) and in the construction of computer-adaptive tests (CAT) (e.g., Brown & Iwashita, 1996; Chalhoub-Deville, 1999), where large numbers of test items are required, each of whose measurement properties (such as difficulty) should be known in detail, in order to construct efficient and reliable tests of required difficulty levels.

Rasch measurement (Bond & Fox, 2001; Linacre, 1989; Wright & Masters, 1982; Wright & Stone, 1979), also referred to as a one-parameter item response model, although deriving from different mathematical principles, is named after the Danish mathematician Georg Rasch, and has assumed enormous importance in educational assessment, including, more recently, language assessment (McNamara, 1996). Most simply, IRT and Rasch analysis uses data from candidate responses to test items to posit a single dimension of measurement, typically language ability (or a component, such as vocabulary knowledge). The analysis then provides a variety of measures (expressed in probabilistic terms) that indicate how well the data fit this single dimension. These forms of analysis can identify items that elicit test-taker responses that are unexpected, divergent or "misfitting," on the basis of 'fit' statistics providing information analogous to (classical) point-biserial statistics (Henning, 1987; Henning, Hudson, & Turner, 1985). On a theoretical level, these 'fit' statistics can provide evidence for the unidimensionality of a test (as in studies of specific-purpose listening tests by de Jong and Glas (1987) and McNamara (1991). More practically, results of such studies can be used to identify unsuitable test items.

Multi-faceted Rasch measurement (Linacre, 1989), a refinement of Rasch analysis, examines the relationship among relevant elements (or facets) of a language test. Multi-faceted Rasch measurement is of increasing value in studying performance-based assessment, which involves, in addition to the candidate and the test items, features of the performance, the rating scale, and the rater (McNamara, 1996, p. 9). Typical facets that may be examined include item (or task) difficulty, candidate background, and rater harshness as well as candidate ability. Studies employing Rasch analysis (e.g., McNamara, 1996; McNamara & Adams, 1994; McNamara & Lumley, 1997; Pollitt & Hutchinson, 1987; Weigle, 1998) have drawn attention to the importance of understanding the role raters play in language assessment. Studies have focused not only on reliability of raters, but have provided ways of examining levels of consistency and harshness of individual raters on different occasions and over varying periods of time (Congdon & McQueen, 2000; Lumley, 2000; Lumley & McNamara, 1995) as well as differences between groups of raters from different backgrounds (A. Brown, 1995; Hill, 1997; Zhang, 1998). Perhaps the most significant achievement of Rasch analysis has been conclusive documentation of the many ways in which rater behavior can vary, as well as to identify some of the kinds of measures (such as training and multiple rating) that can be taken to assist in managing this variation. For example, A. Brown (1995) used Rasch measurement to show how raters with teaching and tour guiding backgrounds applied different components of rating scales in a test of spoken Japanese for tour guides. She found that raters from different backgrounds used the individual scales differently, although there was no effect on overall scores. Such findings can assist in the selection of raters. In another context, Weigle (1994) used Rasch measurement to investigate the effectiveness of training for raters of ESL writing in a university context by comparing ratings made by a group of raters before and after training, providing convincing evidence for the need for rater training, while also showing that there are limits to its effectiveness.

In addition to examining rater and item behavior, Rasch measurement allows bias analyses to be carried out, investigating other aspects of the testing situation. For example, McNamara and Lumley (1997) used the bias statistics produced by the computer program FACETS (Linacre & Wright, 1992–1996) to investigate the impact on ratings given on a speaking test when raters perceived audiotaped recordings of speaking test interactions to be less than perfectly audible, or when interlocutors appeared to be less than fully competent, highlighting the role of rating conditions in test validity. In a study focusing on how items should be combined to create a fair test, Takala and Kaftandjieva (2000) used a Rasch model to analyze DIF for males and females in an L2 vocabulary test. They looked not only at the test as a whole, but at individual items and clusters of items, suggesting the need for item banks to incorporate this information, and to use it to improve the way items are selected for individual test-takers.

Generalizability Theory

One final statistical methodology to be mentioned in this section that has gained particular prominence in recent years is Generalizability Theory (G-Theory) (Shavelson & Webb, 1991), which is based on analysis of variance. As its name suggests, it provides information about how reliably we can generalize information obtained from a single testing event. G-Theory allows the estimation of the sources of variance in test scores, and hence a way of ascertaining whether, for example, test-taker ability or variability in rater standards is more important in accounting for differences in test scores. J. D. Brown and colleagues have conducted numerous studies employing G-Theory over many years: J. D. Brown (1984) investigated the effect of variations in the numbers of items and passages on the dependability (analogous to reliability) of a reading test for engineers, giving information on the optimal number required for reliable assessment; Brown and Bailey (1984) examined the effect of different numbers of raters and of scoring categories on the dependability of writing scores, again providing information that can assist in developing efficient and reliable measurement; Brown and Ross (1996) used a series of G-studies in their investigation of the reliability of subtests of the TOEFL and their contribution to the dependability of scores on the overall TOEFL battery; and J. D. Brown (1999) examined the relative effects of items, subtests, and language backgrounds on the level of error in the TOEFL. Bachman, Lynch, and Mason (1995) have also investigated the utility of G-Theory in investigating variability in tasks and rater judgments, making the important suggestion that greater dependability is achieved by increasing the number of tasks taken by test-takers than the number of raters.

It will be clear from this survey, necessarily far from exhaustive, that the uses of quantitative analyses vary considerably, ranging from issues such as informing choices between test methods to pointing out serious potential inequities in test use. Both the focus of investigation and the ways in which findings are used depends necessarily on the interests of the researchers. A broader focus and a more complex picture will emerge in the second section of the chapter.

QUALITATIVE APPROACHES

Introduction

Although language testing research typically involves the analysis of score data, recent years have seen an increase in the use of qualitative research methodologies to examine issues of interest in test validation and language testing research in general. McNamara, Hill, and May (2002) attribute this increase in the range of research methods to a cross-fertilization of research in language testing and other areas of applied linguistics, and to the challenge to the positivist epistemology of applied linguistics generally. Others (e.g., Banerjee & Luoma, 1997; Bachman, 2000) attribute it to the widening conceptualization of validity in the assessment literature in general, and language testing in particular. As in other areas of educational measurement, validity is no longer viewed as a set of measurable phenomena (based in the traditional categories of construct, content, predictive and concurrent validities) but as an integrated and holistic judgment that is based on the collection of evidence from a number of different areas (Messick, 1988, 1989). In this revised conceptualization, the main concern is the validity of the inferences made about test-takers on the basis of their scores, that is, the meaning of scores. The enterprise is made more complex through the increased recognition of a need to employ alternative methods of assessment, including portfolios (Hamp-Lyons & Condon, 2000), teacher-designed tasks, observation, and self-assessment (Brown & Hudson, 1998). What validity investigations require, as Banerjee and Luoma (1997) point out, is a thorough understanding of tests, both product and process. It is in this area where qualitative approaches are of particular value.

One type of research methodology that has become increasingly prevalent in language testing research in recent years is discourse analysis. In their state-of-the-art article on "discourse and assessment," McNamara, Hill, and May (2002) attribute this trend to the central role afforded assessments of oral proficiency within the current communicative approach to language teaching and testing. Although early research focused almost exclusively on the American OPI, discourse analytic research is now undertaken in relation to a wide range of oral test formats. It has been used to address such questions as how proficiency can be characterized and to what extent test performance is an adequate reflection of authentic, nontest performance. The role of discourse analysis in language testing research will be discussed in more detail in the next section.

Another qualitative research methodology that has seen a recent growth in use in language testing research is introspection in the form of verbal report analysis (also called protocol analysis). Verbal report analysis, drawn from the field of cognitive psychology, responds to a concern with understanding the strategies involved in test-taking and rating and represents a move away from earlier approaches to the examination of test constructs that relied primarily on expert judgment. Prior to its use in language testing research, verbal report analysis had appeared in the SLA literature in relation to cognitive strategies in second language learning (Faerch & Kasper, 1987). It had also been used to examine rating behavior in the context of L1 essay writing (Huot, 1988, 1993). In the context of language testing, verbal report studies of test-taker cognition have examined the ways in which test-takers process language input (for example, when reading texts in a foreign language or when listening to spoken language in a listening test) and how they respond to test items. More recently, following on from studies of first language composition marking, research has focused on how raters react to texts, both spoken and written, produced under test conditions. The use of verbal report methodology will be discussed in more detail later.

A third and rapidly expanding area of research in language testing can also be attributed to more recent conceptualizations of validity that expand the notion to include an analysis of the context in which tests are used and the role they play in society (Shohamy, 1997, 2001a). In this view, also championed by Messick, tests are not isolated events that have no impact outside the test room but are social and political tools whose impact must be evaluated as part of the validation of the test. This increasing concern with the impact or social consequences of test use— consequential and systemic validity—is attested by recent volumes of the journal *Language Testing*, one devoted to the topic of ethics in language testing (1997, Vol. 14, 3), and the other to washback, the impact of tests on instruction (1996, Vol. 13, 3). Research concerned with the consequences of test use tends to draw heavily on ethnographic research methods such as observation, interviews, and questionnaires, with stakeholders in the test under examination as the main source of data. Impact studies, as they are termed, are typically case studies of single-test implementations.

In the remainder of this section, because of their current popularity as research methods, we will examine in more detail these three types of methodology described earlier: discourse analysis, introspection, and ethnographic methods. In the discussion of each, we will focus on the questions that they have addressed, and the methodologies used. Readers are referred to the studies described and to other sources for more detailed discussions of the methodologies, including questions of methodological validity.

Discourse Analysis

Over the last two decades the analysis of test discourse has become an increasingly important research methodology, particularly in relation to tests of second language speaking proficiency. As McNamara, Hill, and May (2002) comment in their overview of "discourse and assessment," "If structural linguistics was the source of the views on language of the formative period of postwar language testing, best represented in the work of Lado (1961), then discourse analysis has taken its place for the assessment of oral language."

Discourse analysis was first used in language testing research to critique the archetypal oral test, the ACTFL OPI (Clark & Gifford, 1988). In a now classic paper, van Lier (1989) criticized the OPI for its lack of authenticity as a 'conversational' event, commenting in particular on the lack of empirical analyses of test discourse. In the decade following the publication of van Lier's article, discourse analyses of oral interview data began to appear with increasing frequency, culminating most recently with a collection of articles (Young & He, 1998) involving a range of oral interview tests in a range of languages and addressing the question of validity from a number of perspectives. A general consensus has emerged from these and other analyses that, although oral interview interaction shares some features with nontest conversation, it is essentially a distinct and institutional form of interaction, and that because of its nonsymmetrical nature, it is limited in the extent to which it can provide an indication of nontest conversational performance (Johnson, 2001; Johnson & Tyler, 1998; Lazaraton, 1991, 1992; Perrett, 1990; Ross & Berwick, 1992; Young & Milanovic, 1992).

Although this is perhaps not an unexpected finding, it is nevertheless important as it raises the question of what can and what should be assessed in a performance assessment of oral proficiency. In particular, the question arises of the extent to which it is either appropriate or possible to assess interactional skills such as conversational management and turn-taking skills in assessments of second language proficiency.

Discourse analysis is, of course, not a single method reflecting a single approach to the data. The question of how to analyze and characterize the discourse is dependent on the research question itself, and will be informed by relevant theories. Perrett's (1990) examination of oral interview discourse, for example, analyzed oral interviews using a Systemic Functional Linguistics framework to show how social constraints imposed there (defined in terms of the systemic functional categories of field, tenor, and mode) resulted in a lack of authenticity. Young and Milanovic (1992) addressed the same question from the perspective of Dominance Theory. Their analysis revealed that, in comparison with noninterview conversation, oral interview discourse was highly asymmetrical with respect to dominance, contingency, and goal orientation. Interviews were found to be characterized by greater reactiveness on the part of the candidates and greater goal orientation on the part of the interviewers. Ross (1992) used Speech Accommodation Theory (see Giles, Coupland, & Coupland, 1991), a social psychological approach to language, to examine the ways in which interviewers accommodated their speech to their interlocutor (i.e., the candidate), and Lazaraton (1991, 1992, 1997) showed the usefulness of Conversation Analysis in comparing the structure of oral interviews with that of conversation. More recent studies, such as those by Johnson and Tyler (1998) and Johnson (2001) have been informed and guided by sociocultural theory.

Although the characteristics of oral interview discourse vis-à-vis nontest interaction remain a major focus of concern, discourse analysis has also been used to address a range of other questions, such as the way in which interviewer or candidate variables affect performance, or variation in performance due to the manipulation of aspects of the test such as the task type, the conditions under which the performance is elicited, or the mode of testing.

Turning first to the candidate, one question of obvious interest is how different levels of performance (i.e., proficiency) can be characterized. In his analysis of OPI performance, Young (1995) compared the discourse produced by candidates at intermediate and advanced levels in terms of features such as changing topic, talking at length, reactiveness, and gaining the floor (performance features that he considers to be relevant to measures of communicative proficiency). The only difference that emerged between the levels was that intermediate learners tended to answer questions briefly, taking them at face value, whereas advanced students were more likely to take the floor and elaborate. Young concludes, on the basis of this finding, that the interview format masks the display of relevant skills. Perhaps more important for the validity of the inferences that are drawn about candidate's ability to perform in nontest situations, he also points out that such differences may be due not to proficiency per se but to cultural understandings of appropriate interview behavior, a finding that has been echoed in other studies such as A. Brown (2003) and He (1998). A study by Yoshida-Morise (1998) revealed that interviewees at different levels of proficiency used different types of communication strategies. While Young's and Yoshida-Morise's analyses focused on interactional aspects of interview test performance, a recent study (Brown et al., 2003) involved detailed linguistic analysis of the monologic performance of candidates on a range of computer-administered speaking tasks proposed for new TOEFL in order to compare the quality of candidate output in independent and integrated speaking tasks and across different levels of proficiency.

Although the studies described above are concerned with characterizing different levels of proficiency, others have been concerned with the effect on candidate performance of background variables such as gender (O'Loughlin, 2002; Young & Milanovic, 1992), native language (Ross, 1998; Young & Halleck, 1998), personality (Berry, 1997) or familiarity with the interlocutor (Katona, 1998; O'Sullivan, 2002). Such studies are concerned with possible test bias. Ross (1998), for example, found that students from a Japanese background were more likely to produce simple, "factual" responses, which was likely to result in them being identified as having lower proficiency and being awarded lower ratings.

The greater understanding of the co-constructed nature of oral interview discourse and the increasing importance of interactional aspects of performance in assessments of oral proficiency, have stimulated a research interest in the impact of interviewer behavior on test-taker performance, and the implications that arise for test fairness. Lazaraton (1996a, 1996b) and Brown and Lumley (1997), for example, identified a number of accommodative behaviors in the speech of examiners and speculated on the effect they might have on the candidate's subsequent behavior. A. Brown (2003, 2004) showed how the same candidate is perceived as stronger or weaker in interviews with two different interviewers as a result of the interviewers' different interactional styles. Ross (1996) related differences in interviewer style to their ethnicity and language background, although O'Loughlin (2002) did not find the differences in style (in terms of indicators of support and rapport) that he predicted between male and female interviewers.

Discourse analysis is particularly useful in examining the functioning of innovative test methods. It has been used in examinations of performance on paired orals (O'Sullivan, 2002; Swain, 2001) or group orals (Berry, 1995; Fulcher, 1996), which incidentally saw an increase in popularity in part because of the findings that interview discourse is asymmetrical and inhibitive of candidate initiative-taking. Other research into task effects that involves discourse analysis includes O'Loughlin's (1995) detailed comparison of two alternative test modes, face-to-face and taped-based. In his analysis he focused on the lexical density of the texts produced in the two formats. Although steps were put in place to ensure comparability across the two formats and the two tests were operationally treated as equivalent, a thorough analysis of the test discourse revealed that they were qualitatively very different. Wigglesworth (1997) examined the effect that different amounts of planning time had on test performance. Iwashita, McNamara, and Elder (2001) used Skehan's task characteristic framework to examine the quality of test performances according to the cognitive complexity of the tasks (see Skehan, 1998).

One of the drawbacks to discourse analysis as an approach to test validation is the complexity of the transcription procedure and analysis: Discourse analysis can be extremely time-consuming. O'Sullivan, Weir, and Saville (2002) propose an alternative approach to the content validation of oral interviews using checklists that, they claim, can answer "the basic question" concerning validity (i.e., whether the expected/intended functions are actually present) but also task-type functioning, performance across levels, comparison of paired/examiner formats, and differences among interviewers. However, as they point out, a "degree of training and practice" is necessary to ensure a reliable and consistent outcome (O'Sullivan, Weir, & Saville, 2002, p. 46).

Introspection

Although introspective techniques for data collection were scorned during the many years when behaviorist theories dominated research in the social sciences, since the early 1980s they have gradually come back into favor (Ericsson & Simon, 1980, 1993; Faerch & Kasper, 1987). Within the field of applied linguistics, they were used initially to examine language learning and language use strategies (see Oxford, 1990, for example). This led to their use of language testing research to examine the strategies employed by participants in language tests, by test-takers and raters. Recent books such as Green (1998) attest to the usefulness of verbal report studies in language testing research.

Introspection has been used to examine the strategies employed by test-takers to derive answers to test items. Cohen (1998) provides a useful overview of research into test-taking strategies. Early studies were concerned with particular types of item, such as cloze (Cohen, 1984; Homburg & Spaan, 1981). More recently, they have focused on skills testing; for example, studies by Buck (1990, 1991) and Gruba (1999) examined listening and viewing (video-mediated listening), and Cohen (1994) performance on integrated reading-writing tasks involving summarizing. Dollerup, Glahn, and Hansen (1994) used introspection to examine the strategies employed by test-takers in an EAP context when completing multiple-choice reading questions, whereas Wu (1998) focused on multiple-choice listening comprehension questions. Dollerup, Glahn, and Hansen argue that the data provided in the verbal reports not only allowed them to identify the types of strategy used by test-takers when responding to the test questions (an important aspect of item quality), but also gave insights into the ways in which students' foreign language reading proficiency could be improved. Anderson et al. (1991) combined think-aloud data with test item analysis and statistical item data, arguing that such triangulation gives insights not only into test-taking strategies but also their relationships with item characteristics and performance.

Over the last decade, following on from studies of first language composition rating, there has been a growing interest in examining the cognitive process employed by raters of second language production. Whereas most studies to date have been concerned with the assessment of writing (e.g., Cumming 1990; Cumming, Kantor, & Powers, 2001; Lumley, 2000, 2002; Vaughan, 1991; Weigle, 1994; Zhang, 1998), there has more recently been an interest in using the methodology to examine assessments of speaking (e.g., Meiron, 1998; A. Brown, 2000; Brown et al., 2003). These studies have investigated such questions as how raters go about assigning a holistic rating to a performance, what aspects of the performance they privilege, whether experienced or novice raters rate differently, the status of self-generated criteria, and how raters deal with problematic performances. In general, they have revealed that raters are influenced not only by the quality of the performance in relation to the features described in the scales, but also by what they themselves bring to the rating process through their background and training. They have shown that while training does have some effect in constraining raters' reactions to test performances, it cannot iron out all differences.

Whereas most verbal report studies have involved operational tests, and as such examined the use of test-specific rating criteria, Brown et al. (2003) argue that asking expert informants (i.e., experienced teachers) to assess performances without reference to specific criteria has the potential to inform the empirical development of rating scales, thus ensuring that the content of the scales is really relevant to task performance and experts' judgments of proficiency.

Just as discourse analysis involves a variety of approaches and methods, so protocol analysis also involves a range of different elicitation techniques. Data may be elicited in real time during the activity under consideration (such as rating), or retrospectively, such as immediately after a test task. Because of the online nature of speaking assessment, a retrospective verbal report methodology has been found to be more useful than a concurrent one.

For their use in language testing research, verbal report studies initially relied almost exclusively (as well as sometimes uncritically) for credibility on the work of Ericsson and Simon (1980, 1987, 1993). More recent studies have taken a more critical view of what can be learned from consulting participants about aspects of the language assessment process (Cumming 1990; Cumming, Kantor, & Powers, 2001; Lumley, 2000, 2002). An extensive discussion of the limitations and advantages of using think-aloud data elicited during the process of rating a set of writing scripts is given in Lumley (2000). It is clear that introspection can provide only a very partial picture of any cognitive processes, that major parts of such processes may simply be inaccessible to description, and that the act of providing introspective data may disturb or alter the cognitive process under consideration. Nevertheless, employed with proper care, this methodology offers the potential for insights into processes employed by raters and test-takers that would not be available by any other means.

Ethnographic Methods

Ethnographic methods, which essentially involve a description of events within particular contexts, and are generally described as including observations, interviews, and questionnaires, are by no means a recent introduction to language testing research. The growth in popularity of tests of languages for specific purposes in the 1980s and 1990s led to a need for information about target language use that was used to inform task design and content. The process of collecting this information is termed a *needs analysis*. Weir (1983, 1988), McNamara (1990, 1996), and Douglas (2000) provide comprehensive overviews of the role of the needs analysis in specific-purpose test design where, in order to match the test design to the purpose for which the test is intended, methods such as direct observation of people in the target context, as well as questionnaires and interviews may be used. Ethnographic methods such as these are also employed in language program evaluations (Lynch, 1996; Weir & Roberts, 1994), in addition to tests, particularly in formative evaluations where the aim is to gather information that will lead to improvements in the program rather than simply measuring effectiveness in terms of test scores.

Where ethnographic methods do reflect a new and important strand in language testing research, as mentioned earlier, is in the examination of the social consequences, or impact, of test use. Shohamy (2001a, 2001b) lists as some of the questions that should be (and are increasingly being) asked in such studies:

- How are tests used by decision makers?
- How are scores being interpreted?
- Are language tests used according to their intended purposes?
- What are the consequences of tests?
- Are tests used fairly?
- What is the impact of tests on learning and teaching?

In tests designed to assess achievement in relation to a specific curriculum, changes in the assessment procedures can have a profound impact on the teaching of that subject. Studies that have examined the impact of newly introduced achievement assessments include one by Shohamy (1993) that made use of a range of ethnographic methods (observation of classrooms before and after the test's introduction, interviews with teachers, and a series of student questionnaires, as well as review of teaching materials) to examine the ways in which the introduction of a new test of Arabic affected the practices of teachers and students. A study by Wall and Alderson (1993) was concerned with the impact of a new O-Level examination in Sri Lanka. Cheng (1997) documented the changes that occurred in both teaching practice and in materials following the announcement of revisions to the Hong Kong Certificate of Education Examination, and in China, Li (1990) examined the impact on school teaching of the introduction of a new English test used to select students for university entrance and taken by approximately 3 million candidates every year.

The studies described above were concerned with the impact of tests used to assess achievement against a specified curriculum. Test impact is also a concern in relation to proficiency tests, particularly as they may narrow the teaching of language in preparatory courses to (in the extreme version) a focus on strategies for answering questions. In a study of the impact of TOEFL on the teaching of English, Alderson and Hamp-Lyons (1996) found that this concern was justified in some cases (where teachers taught very narrowly to the test) but not in others. As a consequence, they argue that washback of any particular type is not a consequence of the test per se but of the individuals (both teachers and learners) who are required to engage with it. Research undertaken in relation to the International English Language Testing System (IELTS) test as part of the IELTS validation program (see for example, Tulloh, 1999, 2003; Woods, 1998) is an example of how a series of single-institution studies can together contribute to a 'big' picture of the social consequences of tests used on a worldwide basis.

We turn next to a discussion of some of the most commonly used ethnographic methodologies in language testing research, namely self-report data such as questionnaires, surveys and interviews, and observation.

Questionnaires and Surveys

Questionnaires and surveys have long played a role in language testing research as a means of gathering (typically quantitative) background information on test candidates (or raters) in order to examine the relationship of particular variables to test outcomes. Even though they are commonly analyzed quantitatively, they tend be viewed as one type of ethnographic data. A large-scale study of school language learning (Brown, Hill, & Iwashita, 2000) gathered data on the amount and quality of home exposure and amounts, periods of instruction and type of instruction in order to compare school foreign language learning outcomes in four languages. Elder (1996) also gathered information on the amount and quality of home exposure among "background" speakers of the language being taught in order to examine the role of this prior exposure on test performance. Berry (1997) drew on survey data in order to classify learners as extroverted and introverted in order to examine the influence of personality on oral test performance. Numerous other studies combine the use of questionnaire data with test score analysis in order to examine the impact of specific variables on performance on the test.

Depending on the degree of freedom permitted for responses, questionnaires may also contribute qualitative data. As noted earlier, questionnaires play a major role in the gathering of data when undertaking a needs analysis to support the development of tests for specific purposes. There are a number of reports of the use of expert informants in the development of tests for professional and academic purposes (e.g., A. Brown, 1994; Elder, 1993; Lumley & Brown, 1996, 1998; McNamara, 1990).

Questionnaires and surveys have also been used to evaluate tests once they have been introduced. Studies by Wall, Clapham, and Alderson (1994) and Bradshaw (1990) both used questionnaires to evaluate newly introduced placement tests. A. Brown (1993) showed how test-takers themselves can provide useful feedback in posttest questionnaires, providing a different perspective from that of teachers. As one aspect of the validation of a new Japanese proficiency test, trial subjects were asked to respond to a series of questions about the test. Brown illustrates how this information was integrated with information on item functioning and incorporated into the test revision process. Lewkowicz (2000) asked university students about their perceptions of the authenticity in and the relative usefulness of two tests, the TOEFL and a locally developed EAP test. The study raised questions about the assumed importance of authenticity to test-takers. Lumley and Stoneman (2000) used questionnaires to examine students' attitudes not toward a test but toward test preparation materials. Interestingly, students' views on the usefulness of the materials were markedly different from those of the teachers.

Finally, questionnaire data has also been used to examine questions such as what examination boards do and how they see themselves and their tests (Alderson, Clapham, & Wall, 1995). Questionnaires were used to elicit information about exam syllabuses, exam construction, procedures for validation, administration, marking procedures, results, and examination revision and quality control. Although the data were largely quantifiable and analyzed accordingly, open-ended questions allowed respondents to give a clear picture of the exam boards' practices.

Interviews

Interviews have much in common with open-ended questionnaires, and are commonly used where qualitative descriptions of learning and assessment contexts are required. They can take many forms and, depending on the aims of the research, may be more or less structured, allowing more or less freedom to follow up individual responses or topics. Lynch (1996) in his book on language program evaluation provides a useful introduction to different types of interview.

Interviews are frequently used in classroom contexts, for example, as one component of ethnographic surveys of teacher assessment practices, which remain undertheorized (Teasdale & Leung, 2000) despite the many purposes they serve (Brindley, 1998). Chronicles of their use, mainly descriptive, have become more common with the increasing attention paid to the variety of modes of language assessment in the classroom (especially the primary school classroom) in recent years, as a recent volume of *Language Testing* (2000, Vol. 17,2) devoted to "Assessing young language learners" attests. The study by Rea-Dickins and Gardner (2000) in that volume used a "structured [interview] protocol ... to probe in depth the key issues of English language assessment at Key Stage One of the National Curriculum" (p. 219). Interviews also formed a prime source of data, along with classroom observation, in a large-scale study of the classroom assessment procedures used by early primary school teachers of ESL learners across Australia (Breen et al., 1997). The study, conducted over a number of months, was concerned with the relationship between everyday teaching, the various assessment methods and practices employed by teachers, and the array of scales available to report on both first and second language development. In another study aiming to elaborate the constructs used by teachers in their assessments of primary school children's language development, Leung and Teasdale (1997) used semistructured interviews to relate teachers' reactions to video footage of primary school students' performances with the reporting scales of the British National Curriculum.

Interviews are also commonly used to elicit views of raters and candidates about both test-taking and rating, as an alternative or supplement to verbal reports. For example, in his investigation of the process of assessing second language writing, Lumley (2000, 2002) supplemented verbal protocol data provided by raters with interviews in which they were asked to identify possible difficulties in uses of the rating scales or difficulties they had encountered in rating and to comment on the use of think-aloud protocols. These interviews were able to provide additional insights into the rating process, but also into the status of the think-aloud data forming the main component of the study. Other researchers including Weigle (1994) and Zhang (1998) have also used interviews with raters to supplement investigations using essentially cognitive methodologies such as verbal reports.

Observation

Observation may be an end in itself or may be used in conjunction with (to provide a context for) follow-up interviews, as in the studies described above. Observation has been used to examine how teachers carry out classroom assessment (Breen et al., 1997; Leung & Teasdale, 1997; Rea-Dickins, 2001; Rea-Dickins & Gardner, 2000), as well as to describe the processes or observable behaviors involved in test-taking or assessing. Classroom observations can take many forms; Lynch (1996) provides a useful description. Whereas there are several published frameworks such as the Communicative Orientation of Language Teaching, or COLT (Spada & Fröhlich, 1995), these have typically been developed for use for particular purposes. Generally, a framework will either need to be adapted from an existing framework or developed specifically for each research study in order to capture most effectively appropriate observations. Gattullo (2000), for example, in a study of formative assessment in primary school ELT classrooms in Italy, adapted a framework of assessment events and processes developed by Torrance and Pryor (1998) for analysis of the data. The washback study carried out by Wall and Alderson (1993) was one of the first test validation studies to employ classroom observation, while TOEFL test preparation course classrooms formed the focus of observations in Alderson and Hamp-Lyons' (1996) washback study. Observation is commonly also used in the design stages of specific purpose assessments; it formed one of the first stages in a project to develop a language and teaching skill self-assessment instrument for teachers of English in Korean primary schools (Jin, McNamara, & Brown, 2002), where existing frameworks were adapted to capture Korean and English language use by both teachers and students.

CONCLUSION

This chapter shows that research in language testing, although still essentially quantitative in many respects, involving as it often does the analysis of test scores, increasingly involves qualitative methodologies that it draws from a range of related disciplines. These include, in addition to educational measurement, cognitive and social psychology, education, and social sciences in general. Research is increasingly looking outside the test itself to its impact (consequences, including washback) in the context where it is used.

The survey presented here provides a representative view of commonly used approaches to research in language testing and questions that they are employed to address. It is by no means exhaustive, however, and readers are referred to journals devoted to language testing research, such as *Assessing Writing, Language Assessment Quarterly* (from 2004), *Language Testing, Language Testing Update,* and *Melbourne Papers in Language Testing,* the bibliography of the International Language Testing Association (ILTA) (Banerjee et al., 1999), to research reports and other publications produced by testing agencies, and to proceedings of conferences, especially the annual Language Testing Research Colloquium. They are also directed more broadly to research and publications in Applied Linguistics in general.

NOTES

1. The reader is referred to Davies et al. (1999) for brief definitions of a broad range of terms used in language testing.
2. See Hatch and Lazaraton (1991) for explanations of these and other classical statistics.

REFERENCES

Alderson, J. C., & Hamp-Lyons, L. (1996). TOEFL preparation courses: A study of washback. *Language Testing, 13*(3), 280–297.

Alderson, J. C., Clapham, C., & Wall, D. (1995). *Language test construction and evaluation.* Cambridge, UK: Cambridge University Press.

Alderson, J. C., Percsich, R., & Szabo, G. (2000). Sequencing as an item type. *Language Testing, 17*(4), 422–447.

Anastasi, A. (1976). *Psychological testing.* New York: Macmillan.

Anderson, N. J., Bachman, L. F., Perkins, K., & Cohen, A. (1991). An exploratory study into the construct validity of a reading comprehension test: Triangulation of data sources. *Language Testing, 8*(1), 41–66.

Bachman, L. F. (2000). Language testing at the turn of the century: Assuring that what we count counts. *Language Testing, 17*(1), 1–42.

Bachman, L. F., & Palmer, A. S. (1996). *Language testing in practice.* Oxford, UK: Oxford University Press.

Bachman, L. F. (1990). *Fundamental considerations in language testing.* Oxford, UK: Oxford University Press.

Bachman, L. F., Davidson, F., Ryan, K., & Choi, I. C. (1994). *An investigation into the comparability of two tests of english as a foreign language: The Cambridge-TOEFL comparability study.* Cambridge, UK: Cambridge University Press.

Bachman, L. F., Lynch, B., & Mason, M. (1995). Investigating variability in tasks and rater judgments in a performance Test of Foreign Language Speaking. *Language Testing, 12*(2), 238–257.

Bae, J., & Bachman, L. F. (1998). A latent variable approach to listening and reading: Testing factorial invariance across two groups of children in the Korean/English two-way immersion program. *Language Testing, 15*(3), 380–414.

Baker, R. (1987). An Investigation of the Rasch Model in its Application to Foreign Language Proficiency Testing. Unpublished doctoral dissertation, University of Edinburgh.

Baker, R. (1997). *Classical test theory and item response theory in test analysis,* Language Testing Update, Special Report 2. Lancaster, UK: Lancaster University.

Banerjee, J., Clapham, C., Clapham, P., & Wall, D. (Eds.) (1999). *The ILTA language testing bibliography 1991–1999.* Available at http://www.surrey.ac.uk/ELI/ilta/ilta.html

Banerjee, J., & Luoma, S. (1997). Qualitative approaches to test validation. In C. Clapham, & D. Corson, (Eds.), *Encyclopaedia of language and education. vol 7: Language testing and assessment* (pp. 275–287). Dortrecht, The Netherlands: Kluwer.

Beglar, D., & Hunt, A. (1999). Revising and validating the 2000 Word Level and University Word Level Vocabulary Tests. *Language Testing, 16*(2), 131–162.

Berry, V. (1997). Personality characteristics as a potential source of language test bias. In A. Huhta, K. Sajavaara, & S. Takala (Eds.), *Language testing: New openings* (pp. 115–122). Jyväskylä, Finland: University of Jyväskylä.

Berry, V. (1995). *A qualitative analysis of factors affecting learner performances in group oral tests.* Paper presented at the 17th Language Testing Research Colloquium, Long Beach, CA.

Blais, J. G., & Laurier, M. D. (1995). The dimensionality of a placement test from several analytical perspectives. *Language Testing, 12*(1), 72–98.

Boldt, R. F., & Oltman, P. K. (1993). *Multimethod construct validation of the Test of Spoken English.* TOEFL Research Report RR-46. Princeton, NJ: Educational Testing Service.

Bond, T. G., & Fox, C. M. (2001). *Applying the Rasch model: Fundamental measurement in the human sciences.* Mahwah, NJ: Lawrence Erlbaum Associates.

Bradshaw, J. (1990). Test-takers' reactions to a placement test. *Language Testing, 7*(1), 13–30.

Breen, M. P., Barratt-Pugh, C., B., Derewianka, H., House, C., Hudson, T., Lumley, & M. Rohl (1997). *Profiling ESL children: How teachers interpret and use national and state assessment frameworks.* Vols 1–3. Canberra: Department of Employment, Education, Training & Youth Affairs.

Brennan, R. L. (1983). *Elements of generalizability theory.* Iowa City, IA: The American College Testing Program.

Brindley, G. (1998). Outcomes-based assessment and reporting in language learning programmes: A review of the issues. *Language Testing, 15*(1), 45–85.

Brown, A. (1994). LSP testing: The role of linguistic and real-world criteria. In R. Khoo (Ed.), *LSP: Problems and prospects* (pp. 202–215). Singapore: SEAMEO-Regional Language Centre.

Brown, A. (1993). The role of test-taker feedback in the development of an occupational language proficiency test. *Language Testing, 10*(3), 277–303.

Brown, A. (1995). The effect of rater variables in the development of an occupation-specific language performance test. *Language Testing, 12*(1), 1–15.

Brown, A. (2000). An investigation of the rating process in the IELTS speaking module. In R. Tulloh (Ed.), *Research Reports 1999, Vol. 3* (pp. 49–85). Sydney: ELICOS.

Brown, A. (2003). Interviewer variation and the co-construction of speaking proficiency. *Language Testing, 20*(1), 1–25.

Brown, A. (2004). Discourse analysis in language testing. In D. Boxer & A. Cohen, (Eds.), *Studying speaking to inform second language learning,* (pp. 253–282). Clevedon, UK: Multilingual Matters.

Brown, A., Hill, K., & Iwashita, N. (2000). Is learner progress in LOTE learning comparable across languages? In C. Elder (Ed.), Defining standards and monitoring progress in learning languages other than English. *Australian Review of Applied Linguistics, 23*(2), 35–60.

Brown, A., & Iwashita, N. (1996). Language background and item difficulty: The development of a computer-adaptive test of Japanese. *System, 24*(2), 199–206.

Brown, A., Iwashita, N., McNamara, T., & O'Hagan, S. (2003). An examination of rater orientations and test-taker performance on English for academic purposes speaking tasks. Unpublished project report. Princeton, NJ.: Educational Testing Service.

Brown, A., & Lumley, T. (1997). Interviewer variability in specific-purpose language performance tests. In A. Huhta, V. Kohonen, L. Kurki-Suonio, & S. Luoma (Eds.), *Current developments and alternatives in language assessment: Proceedings of LTRC 96.* (pp. 137–150). Jyväskylä: University of Jyväskylä.

Brown, J. D. (1984). A norm-referenced engineering reading test. In A. K. Pugh & J. M. Ulijn (Eds.), *Reading for professional purposes: Studies and practices in native and foreign languages* (pp. 213–222). London: Heinemann.

Brown, J. D. (1991). Do English and ESL faculties rate writing samples differently? *TESOL Quarterly, 25*(4), 587–603.

Brown, J. D. (1999). The relative importance of persons, items, subtests, and languages to TOEFL test variance. *Language Testing, 16*(2), 217–238.

Brown, J. D., & Bailey, K. M. (1984). A categorical instrument for scoring second language writing skills. *Language Learning, 34*(2), 21–42.

Brown, J. D., & Hudson, T. (1998). Alternatives in language assessment. *TESOL Quarterly, 32*(4), 653–675.

Brown, J. D., & Ross. J. (1996). Decision dependability of subtests, tests, and the overall TOEFL. In M. Milanovic & N. Saville (Eds.), *Performance testing, cognition and assessment: Selected papers from the 15th Language Testing Research Colloquium, Cambridge and Arnhem* (pp. 231–265). Cambridge, UK: Cambridge University Press and University of Cambridge Local Examinations Syndicate.

Buck, G. (1990). *The testing of second language listening comprehension.* Unpublished doctoral dissertation, University of Lancaster.

Buck, G. (1991). The testing of listening comprehension: An introspective study. *Language Testing, 8*(1), 67–91.

Campbell, D. T., & Fiske, D.W. (1959). Convergent and discriminant validation by the multitrait-multimethod matrix. *Psychological Bulletin, 56*, 81–105.

Chalhoub-Deville, M. (1999). *Issues in computer-adaptive testing of reading proficiency.* Cambridge, UK: Cambridge University Press and University of Cambridge Local Examinations Syndicate.

Cheng, L. (1997). How does washback influence teaching? Implications for Hong Kong. *Language and Education 235, 11*(1), 38–54.

Clapham, C., & Alderson, J. C. (Eds.) (1996). *Constructing and trialing the IELTS test.* IELTS Research Report 3. Cambridge, UK: The British Council, The University of Cambridge Local Examinations Syndicate, and the International Development Program of Australian Universities and Colleges.

Clapham, C. (1996). *The development of IELTS: A study of the effect of background knowledge on reading comprehension.* Cambridge, UK: University of Cambridge Local Examinations Syndicate and Cambridge University Press.

Clark, J. L. D., & Gifford, R. T. (1988). The FSI/ILR/ACTFL proficiency scales and testing techniques: Development, current status, and needed research. *Studies in Second Language Acquisition, 10,* 129–147.

Cohen, A. D. (1984). On taking language tests: What the students report. *Language Testing, 1*(1), 70–81.

Cohen, A. D. (1994). English for academic pruposes in Brazil: The issue of summary tasks. In C. Hill & K. Parry (Eds.), *From testing to assessment: English as an international language* (pp. 174–204). London: Longman.

Cohen, A. D. (1998). Strategies and processes in test-taking and SLA. In L. Bachman & A. Cohen (Eds.), *Interfaces between second language acquisition and language testing research* (pp 90–111). Cambridge, UK: Cambridge University Press.

Congdon, P. J., & McQueen, J. (2000). The stability of rater severity in large-scale assessment programs. *Journal of Educational Measurement, 37*(2), 163–178.

Cumming, A. (1990). Expertise in evaluating second language compositions. *Language Testing, 7*(1), 31–51.

Cumming, A., Kantor, R., & Powers, D. E. (2001). *Scoring TOEFL essays and TOEFL 2000 prototype writing tasks: An investigation into raters' decision making and development of a preliminary analytic framework.* TOEFL Monograph Series, MS-22. Princeton, NJ: Educational Testing Service.

Davies, A., Brown, A., Elder, E., Hill, K., Lumley, T., & McNamara, T. F. (1999). *Dictionary of language testing: Studies in language testing, 7.* Cambridge, UK: Cambridge University Press/University of Cambridge Local Examinations Syndicate.

de Jong, J. H. A. L., & Glas, C. A. W. (1987). Validation of listening comprehension tests using item response theory. *Language Testing, 4*(2), 170–194.

Dollerup, C., Glahn, E., & Hansen, C. R. (1994). 'Sprogtest': A smart test (or how to develop a reliable and anonymous EFL reading test). *Language Testing, 11*(1), 65–82.

Douglas, D. (2000). *Assessing languages for specific purposes.* (Cambridge Language Assessment Series.) Cambridge, UK: Cambridge University Press.

Elder, C. (1993). How do subject specialists construe classroom language proficiency? *Language Testing, 10*(3), 235–254.

Elder, C. (1996). The effect of language background on "foreign" language performance: The case of Chinese, Modern Greek, and Italian. *Language Learning, 46*(2), 233–282.

Elder, C. (1998). What counts as bias in language testing? *Melbourne papers in Language Testing, 7*(1), 1–42.

Ericsson, K. A., & Simon, H. A. (1980). Verbal reports as data. *Psychological Review, 87,* 215–251.

Ericsson, K. A., & Simon, H. A. (1987). Verbal reports on thinking. In C. Faerch & G. Kasper, (Eds.), *Introspection in second language research* (pp. 24–53). Clevedon, UK: Multilingual Matters.

Ericsson, K. A., & Simon, H. A. (1993). *Protocol analysis: Verbal reports as data* (2nd ed.). Cambridge, MA: MIT Press.

Faerch, C., & Kasper, G. (Eds.). (1987). *Introspection in second language research.* Clevedon, UK: Multilingual Matters.

Fulcher, G. (1996). Testing tasks: Issues in task design and the group oral. *Language Testing, 13*(1), 23–52.

Fulcher, G. (1997). An English language placement test: Issues in reliability and validity. *Language Testing, 14*(2), 113–39.

Gattullo, F. (2000). Formative assessment in ELT primary (elementary) classrooms: An Italian case study. *Language Testing, 17*(2), 278–288.

Giles, H., Coupland, N., & Coupland, J. (Eds.). (1991). *Contexts of accommodation: Developments in applied sociolinguistics.* Cambridge, UK: Cambridge University Press.

Green, A. (1998). *Verbal protocol analysis in language testing research: A handbook, Studies in Language Testing, 5.* Cambridge, UK: Cambridge University Press and University of Cambridge Local Examinations Syndicate.

Gruba, P. (1999). The role of digital video media in second language listening comprehension. Unpublished doctoral dissertation, The University of Melbourne.

Hambleton, R. K., Swaminathan, H., & Rogers, H. J. (1991). *Fundamentals of item response theory.* Newbury Park, CA: Sage.

Hamilton, J., Lopes, M., McNamara, T., & Sheridan, E. (1993). Rating scales and native speaker performance on a communicatively oriented EAP test. *Language Testing, 10*(3), 337–354.

Hamp-Lyons, L., & Condon, W. (2000). *Assessing the portfolio: Principles for practice, theory, and research.* Cresskill, NJ: Hampton Press.

Hamp-Lyons, L., & Mathias, S. P. (1994). Examining expert judgments of task difficulty on essay tests. *Journal of Second Language Writing, 3*(1), 49–68.

Hatch, E., & Lazaraton, A. (1991). *The research manual: Design and statistics for applied linguistics.* New York: Newbury House.

He, A. W. (1998). Answering questions in LPIs: A case study. In R. Young & A. W. He (Eds.), *Talking and testing: Discourse approaches to language proficiency interviews* (pp. 101–116). Amsterdam: Benjamins.

Henning, G. (1984). Advantages of latent trait measurement in language testing. *Language Testing 1*(2), 123–133.

Henning, G. (1987). *A guide to language testing: Development, evaluation, research.* Cambridge, MA: Newbury House.

Henning, G., Schedl, M., & Suomi, B. K. (1995). *Analysis of proposed revisions of the test of spoken English.* TOEFL Research Report No. 48, ETS RR 95-1. Princeton, NJ: Education Testing Service.

Henning, G., Hudson, T., & Turner, J. (1985). Item response theory and the assumption of unidimensionality for language tests. *Language Testing, 2,* 141–154.

Hill, C., & Parry, K. (Eds.). (1994). *From testing to assessment.* London: Longman.

Hill, K. (1997). Who should be the judge? The use of non-native speakers as raters on a test of English as an international language. In A. Huhta, V. Kohonen, L. Kurki-Suonio, & S. Luoma (Eds.), *Current developments and alternatives in language assessment* (pp. 275–290). Jyväskyla: University of Jyväskyla.

Holland, P. W., & Wainer, H. I. (1993). *Differential item functioning.* Hillsdale, NJ: Lawrence Erlbaum Associates.

Homburg, T. J., & Spaan, M. C. (1981). ESL reading proficiency assessment: Testing strategies. In M. Hines & W. Rutherford (Eds.), *On TESOL '81* (pp. 25–33). Washington, DC: TESOL.

Huot, B. A. (1988). *The validity of holistic scoring: A comparison of the talk-aloud protocols of expert and novice holistic raters.* Unpublished doctoral dissertation, Indiana University of Pennsylvania.

Huot, B. A. (1993). The influence of holistic scoring procedures on reading and rating student essays. In M. M. Williamson & B. A. Huot (Eds.), *Validating holistic scoring for writing assessment: Theoretical and empirical foundations* (pp. 206–236). Cresskill, NJ: Hampton Press.

Iwashita, N., McNamara, T., & Elder, C. (2001). Can we predict task difficulty in an oral proficiency test? Exploring the potential of an information-processing approach to task design. *Language Learning 21,* 401–436.

Jin, K-A., McNamara, T., & Brown, A. (2002). *Developing an assessment tool and training program for Korean middle school English teachers: Classroom communicative competence project.* Seoul: Korea Institute of Curriculum and Evaluation.

Johnson, M. (2001). *The art of nonconversation: A re-examination of the validity of the oral proficiency interview.* New Haven CT: Yale University Press.

Johnson, M., & Tyler, A. (1998). Re-analyzing the OPI: How much does it look like natural conversation? In R. Young & A. W. He (Eds.), *Talking and testing: Discourse approaches to language proficiency interviews* (pp. 27–51). Amsterdam: Benjamins.

Katona, L. (1998). Meaning negotiation in the Hungarian oral proficiency examination of English. In R. Young & A. W. He (Eds.), *Talking and testing: Discourse approaches to the assessment of oral proficiency* (pp. 239–267). Amsterdam: Benjamins.

Kunnan, A. J. (1998). An introduction to structural equation modeling for language assessment research. *Language Testing, 15*(3), 295–352.

Kunnan, A. J. (1995). *Test-taker characteristics and test performance: A structural modeling approach.* Cambridge, UK: University of Cambridge Local Examinations Syndicate and Cambridge University Press.

Lado, R. (1961). *Language testing.* London: Longman.

Lazaraton, A. (1991). *A conversation analysis of the structure and interaction in the language interview.* Unpublished doctoral dissertation, University of California, Los Angeles.

Lazaraton, A. (1992). The structural organisation of a language interview: A conversation analytic perspective. *System, 20,* 373–386.

Lazaraton, A. (1996a). Interlocutor support in oral proficiency interviews: The case of CASE. *Language Testing, 13,* 151–172.

Lazaraton, A. (1996b). A qualitative approach to monitoring examiner conduct in the Cambridge Assessment of Spoken English (CASE). In M. Milanovic & N. Saville (Eds.), *Performance testing, cognition, and assessment: Selected papers from the 15th Language Testing Research Colloquium* (pp. 18–33). Cambridge, UK: Cambridge University Press.

Lazaraton, A. (1997). Preference organization in oral proficiency interviews: The case of language ability assessments. *Research on Language and Social Interaction, 30*(1), 53–72.

Lemann, N. (1999). *The big test: The secret history of the American meritocracy.* New York: Farrar, Strauss & Giroux.

Leung, C., & Teasdale, A. (1997). What do teachers mean by speaking and listening? A contextualised study. In A. Huhta, V. Kohonen, L. Kurki-Suonio, & S. Luoma (Eds.), *Current developments and alternatives in language assessment: Proceedings of LTRC 96* (pp. 291–326). Jyväskyla: University of Jyväskyla.

Lewkowicz, J. (2000). Authenticity in language testing: Some outstanding questions. *Language Testing 17*(1), 43–64.

Li, X. (1990). How powerful can a language test be? The MET in China. *Journal of Multilingual and Multicultural Development, 11*(5), 393–404.

Linacre, J. M., & Wright, B. (1992–1996). *FACETS.* Chicago, IL: MESA Press.

Linacre, J. M. (1989). *Many-faceted Rasch measurement*. Chicago, IL: MESA Press.

Linn, R. L., Baker, E. L., & Dunbar, S. B. (1991). Complex, performance-based assessment: Expectations and validation criteria. *Educational Researcher, 20*(8), 15–21.

Lumley, T. (1998). Perceptions of language-trained raters and occupational experts in a test of occupational English language proficiency. *English for Specific Purposes, 17*(4), 347–367.

Lumley, T. (2000). *The process of the assessment of writing performance: The rater's perspective.* Unpublished doctoral dissertation, The University of Melbourne.

Lumley, T. (2002). "Assessment criteria in a large-scale writing test: What do they really mean to the raters?" *Language Testing, 19*(3), 246–276.

Lumley, T., & Brown, A. (1996). Specific-purpose language performance tests: Task and interaction. In G. Wigglesworth & C. Elder (Eds.), *The testing cycle: New perspectives. Australian Review of Applied Linguistics Series S.* No. 13. (pp. 105–136). Canberra: ANU Printing Services.

Lumley, T., & Brown, A. (1998). An investigation of the authenticity of discourse in a specific-purpose language performance test and its relevance to test validity. In E. S. L. Li & G. James (Eds.), *Testing and evaluation in second language education* (pp. 22–33). Hong Kong: Language Centre, Hong Kong University of Science and Technology.

Lumley, T., & McNamara, T. F. (1995). Rater characteristics and rater bias: Implications for training. *Language Testing, 12*(1), 54–71.

Lumley, T., & Stoneman, B. (2000). Conflicting perspectives on the role of test preparation in relation to learning. *Hong Kong Journal of Applied Linguistics, 5*(1), 50–80.

Lynch, B. K. (1996). *Language program evaluation: Theory and practice.* Cambridge Applied Linguistics Series. Cambridge, UK: Cambridge University Press.

Lynch, B. K. (2001). Rethinking assessment from a critical perspective. *Language Testing, 18*(4), 351–372.

McNamara, T. F. (1990). *Assessing the second language proficiency of health professionals.* Unpublished doctoral dissertation, University of Melbourne.

McNamara, T. F. (1991). Test dimensionality: IRT analysis of an ESP listening test. *Language Testing, 8*(2), 45–65.

McNamara, T. F. (1996). *Measuring second language performance.* London: Longman.

McNamara, T. F. (2001). Language assessment as social practice: Challenges for research. *Language Testing, 18*(4), 333–350.

McNamara, T. F., & Adams, R. J. (1994). Exploring rater characteristics with Rasch techniques. In *Selected papers of the 13th Language Testing Research Colloquium (LTRC).* Princeton, NJ: Educational Testing Service.

McNamara, T. F., & Lumley, T. (1997). The effect of interlocutor and assessment mode variables in offshore assessments of speaking skills in occupational settings. *Language Testing, 14*(2), 140–156.

McNamara, T., Hill, K., & May, L. (2002). Discourse and assessment. *Annual Review of Applied Linguistics, 22*, 221–242.

Meiron, B. E. (1998). *Rating oral proficiency tests: A triangulated study of rater thought processes.* Unpublished master's thesis, University of California at Los Angeles.

Messick, S. (1988). The once and future issues of validity: Assessing the meaning and consequences of measurement. In H. Wainer & H. I. Braun (Eds.), *Test validity.* Hillsdale, NJ: Lawrence Erlbaum Associates.

Messick, S. A. (1989). Validity. In R. L. Linn (Ed.), *Educational measurement* (3rd ed.). (pp. 13–103). New York: Macmillan.

Messick, S. A. (1994). The interplay of evidence and consequences in the validation of performance assessment. *Educational Researcher, 23*(2), 13–23.

Messick, S. A. (1996). Validity and washback in language testing. *Language Testing, 13*(3), 241–256.

Moss, P. A. (1994). Can there be validity without reliability? *Educational Researcher, 23*(2), 5–12.

Nation, P. (1983). Testing and teaching vocabulary. *Guidelines, 5*, 12–25.

Nation, P. (1990). *Teaching and learning vocabulary.* Boston: Heinle & Heinle.

O'Loughlin, K. (1992). Do English and ESL teachers rate essays differently? *Melbourne Papers in Language Testing, 1*(2), 19–44.

O'Loughlin, K. (1995). Lexical density in candidate output on direct and semidirect versions of an oral proficiency test. *Language Testing, 12*(2), 217–237.

O'Loughlin, K. (2002). The impact of gender in oral proficiency testing. *Language Testing, 19*(2), 169–192.

O'Sullivan, B. (2002). Learner acquaintanceship and oral proficiency test pair-task performance. *Language Testing, 19*(3), 277–295.

O'Sullivan, B., Weir, C. J., & Saville, N. (2002). Using observation checklists to validate speaking-test tasks. *Language Testing, 19*(1), 33–56.

Oxford, R. (1990). *Language learning strategies: What every teacher should know.* New York: Newbury House.

Perrett, G. (1990). The language testing interview: A reappraisal. In J. H. A. L. de Jong & D. K. Stevenson (Eds.), *Individualizing the assessment of language abilities* (pp. 225–238). Clevedon, UK: Multilingual Matters.

Pollitt, A., & Hutchinson, C. (1987). Calibrating graded assessments: Rasch partial credit analysis of performance in writing. *Language Testing, 4*(1), 72–92.

Pollitt, A. (1984). *Item banking. Issues in Educational Assessment Occasional Papers.* Edinburgh, UK: Her Majesty's Stationery Office.

Powers, D. E., Schedl, M. A., & Wilson, S. (1999). Validating the revised test of spoken English against a criterion of communicative success. *Language Testing, 16*(4), 399–425.

Purpura, J. E. (1997). An analysis of the relationships between test-takers' cognitive and metacognitive strategy use and second language test performance. *Language Learning, 42*(2), 289–325.

Purpura, J. E. (1998). Investigating the effects of strategy use and second language test performance with high- and low-ability test-takers: A structural equation modeling approach. *Language Testing, 15*(3), 333–379.

Purpura, J. E. (1999). *Learner strategy use and performance on language tests: A structural equation modeling approach.* Studies in Language Testing Series, Vol. 8. Cambridge, UK: University of Cambridge Local Examinations Syndicate and Cambridge University Press.

Rea-Dickins, P., & Gardner, S. (2000). Snares or silver bullets: Disentangling the construct of formative assessment. *Language Testing, 17*(2), 215–243.

Rea-Dickins, P. (2001). Mirror, mirror on the wall: Identifying proceses of classroom assessment. *Language Testing, 18*(4), 429–462.

Ross, S. (1996). Formulae and inter-interviewer variation in oral proficiency interview discourse. *Prospect, 11*(3), 3–16.

Ross, S. (1992). Accommodative questions in oral proficiency interviews. *Language Testing, 9,* 173–186.

Ross, S. (1998). Divergent frame interpretations in oral proficiency interview interaction. In R. Young & A. W. He (Eds.), *Talking and testing: Discourse approaches to the assessment of oral proficiency* (pp. 333–353). Amsterdam: Benjamins.

Ross, S., & Berwick, R. (1992). The discourse of accommodation in oral proficiency interviews. *Studies in Second Language Acquisition, 14,* 159–176.

Ryan, K. E., & Bachman, L. F. (1992). Differential item functioning on two tests of EFL proficiency. *Language Testing, 9*(1), 12–29.

Sasaki, M. (2000). Effects of cultural schemata on students' test-taking processes for cloze tests: A multiple data approach. *Language Testing, 17*(1), 85–114.

Shavelson, R. J., & Webb, N. M. (1991). *Generalizability theory: A primer.* Newbury Park, CA: Sage.

Shohamy, E. (1993). *The power of tests: The impact of language tests on teaching and learning.* Washington, DC: The National Foreign Language Center at Johns Hopkins University.

Shohamy, E. (1997). Testing methods, testing consequences: Are they ethical? Are they fair? *Language Testing, 14*(3), 340–349.

Shohamy, E. (2001a). *The power of tests: A critical perspective on the uses of language tests.* New York: Pearson Education Ltd.

Shohamy, E. (2001b). Democratic assessment as an alternative. *Language Testing, 18*(4), 373–391.

Skehan, P. (1998). *A cognitive approach to language learning.* Oxford UK: Oxford University Press.

Spada, N., & Fröhlich, M. (1995). *COLT: Communicative Orientation of Language Teaching observation scheme: Coding conventions and applications.* Sydney, Australia: National Centre for English Language Teaching and Research.

Spolsky, B. (1995). *Measured words.* Oxford UK: Oxford University Press.

Stansfield, C. W., & Kenyon, D. M. (1992). Research on the comparability of the oral proficiency interview and the simulated oral proficiency interview. *System, 20*(3), 347–364.

Swain, M. (2001). Examining dialogue: Another approach to content specification and to validating inferences drawn from test scores. *Language Testing, 18*(3), 275–302.

Takala, S., & Kaftandjieva, F. (2000). Test fairness: A DIF analysis of an L2 vocabulary test. *Language Testing, 17*(3), 323–340.

Teasdale, A., & Leung, C. (2000). Teacher assessment and psychometric theory: A case of paradigm crossing? *Language Testing, 17*(2), 163–184.

Torrance, H., & Pryor, J. (1998). *Investigating formative assessment: Teaching, learning, and assessment in the classroom.* Buckingham, UK: Open University Press.

Tulloh, R. (Ed.). (2003). *International English Language Testing System Research Reports 2003, Vol 4.* Canberra: IELTS Australia.

Tulloh, R. (1999). *International English Language Testing System Research Reports 1999, Vol. 3.* Sydney: ELICOS.

van Lier, L. (1989). Reeling, writhing, drawling, stretching, and fainting in coils: Oral proficiency interviews as conversations. *TESOL Quarterly, 23,* 480–508.

Vaughan, C. (1991). Holistic assessment: What goes on in the rater's mind? In L. Hamp-Lyons (Ed.). *Assessing second language writing in academic contexts* (pp. 111–125). Norwood, NJ: Ablex.

Wall, D., & Alderson, J. C. (1993). Examining washback: The Sri Lankan impact study. *Language Testing, 10*(1), 41–69.

Wall, D., Clapham, C., & Alderson, J. C. (1994). Evaluating a placement test. *Language Testing, 11*(3), 321–244.

Weigle, S. C. (1994). Effects of training on raters of ESL compositions. *Language Testing, 11*(2), 197–223.

Weigle, S. C. (1998). Using FACETS to model rater training effects. *Language Testing, 15*(2), 263–287.

Weir, C. J. (1983). *Identifying the language needs of overseas students in tertiary education in the United Kingdom.* Unpublished doctoral dissertation, University of London Institute of Education.

Weir, C. J. (1988). The specification, realisation, and validation of an English language proficiency test. In A. Hughes (Ed.), *Testing English for university study.* ELT Document 127 (pp. 45–110). Oxford, UK: Modern English Press.

Weir, C., & Roberts, J. (1994). *Evaluation in ELT*. Oxford, UK: Blackwell.

Wigglesworth, G. (1997). An investigation of planning time and proficiency level on oral test discourse. *Language Testing, 14*(1), 85–106.

Woods, S. (Ed.) (1998). *International English Language Testing System Research Reports 1997, Vol. 1*. Sydney: ELICOS.

Woods, A., & Baker, R. (1985). Item response theory. *Language Testing, 2*(2), 117–140.

Wright, B. D., & Masters, G. N. (1982). *Rating scale analysis*. Chicago, IL: MESA Press.

Wright, B. D., & Stone, M. H. (1979). *Best test design*. Chicago, IL: MESA Press.

Wu, Y. (1998). What do tests of listening comprehension test? A retrospection study of EFL test-takers performing a multiple-choice task. *Language Testing 15*(1), 21–44.

Young, R., & He, A. W. (1998). *Talking and testing: Discourse approaches to the assessment of oral proficiency*. Amsterdam: Benjamins.

Yoshida-Morise, Y. (1998). The use of communication strategies in language proficiency interviews. In R. Young & A. W. He (Eds.), *Talking and testing: Discourse approaches to the assessment of oral proficiency* (pp. 205–238). Amsterdam: Benjamins.

Young, R. (1995). Conversational styles in language proficiency interviews. *Language Learning, 45*, 3–42.

Young, R., & Halleck, G. B. (1998). "Let them eat cake!" or how to avoid losing your head in cross-cultural conversations. In R. Young, & A. W. He (Eds.), *Talking and testing: Discourse approaches to the assessment of oral proficiency* (pp. 355–382). Amsterdam: Benjamins.

Young, R., & Milanovic, M. (1992). Discourse variation in oral proficiency interviews. *Studies in Second Language Acquisition, 14*(4), 403–424.

Zhang, W. (1998). *The rhetorical patterns found in Chinese EFL student writers' examination essays in English and the influence of these patterns on rater response*. Unpublished doctoral dissertation, Hong Kong Polytechnic University.

47

Testing Languages for Specific Purposes

Dan Douglas
Iowa State University

INTRODUCTION

After a review of the "state of the art" in specific purpose language testing in my book on assessing languages for specific purposes (Douglas, 2000), I concluded with a discussion of four "interesting but troublesome" issues that arose from the review: the nature of the input in specific purpose tests, engaging communicative language ability and specific purpose language ability, devising assessment criteria relevant to target language use situations, and the use of general versus specific purpose language tests. In discussing the first issue, I argued for the use of extended input from genuine sources and the use of trained interlocutors in role-plays, and expressed a concern about the ultimate lack of pragmatic reality in simulations (what might be called the "there is no airplane" syndrome, referring to a well-known test for air traffic controllers). Under the heading of engagement, I suggested that even in tasks rich in target language use (TLU) situational features, it was possible that very little negotiation of meaning or creation of discourse was required by the test-taker, thus limiting the degree to which interactional authenticity was engaged. Thirdly, I argued for the inclusion of TLU-relevant assessment criteria in at least the interpretation of test performance if not in the actual rating of performances themselves, and for the inclusion of specific purpose background knowledge in the construct of specific purpose language ability. And finally, I reviewed what I perceived as a tendency in the field to move toward the more general end of the specificity continuum and emphasized the reasons for specific purpose testing: That language performances vary with context and specific purpose language is precise. I concluded the book with a view of a rich future for specific purpose language testing as we grapple with our attempts to understand and measure "the complex abilities language users require to function in specific purpose contexts where precision, clarity, range, and flexibility of language use are increasingly called for as requirements for participation in academic, vocational, and professional life" (p. 282).

In this chapter, I want to move beyond where I left off in 2000 and consider where we are now in specific purpose language assessment, touching on these same issues, though perhaps not always directly. I will refer frequently to three publications important to specific purpose testing: a special issue of *System* (28(3), 2000) on language testing, a special issue of *Language Testing* (18(2), 2001) based on papers from a conference on Language for Special Purpose (LSP) testing held at Hong Kong Polytechnic University early in 2000, and a *festschrift* honoring Alan Davies on his retirement (Elder et al., 2001). These three collections raise a number of current issues in LSP testing as well as describing recent work in research and development. I will begin with a brief discussion of the very notion of specific purpose language testing, arguing that it is getting harder and harder to distinguish specific purpose tests from more general language tests, particularly since the publication of Bachman and Palmer (1996) and Douglas (2000)—specific purpose language testing is seen as a special case of communicative testing. This leads to a problem of "blurred boundaries" (Elder, 2001, p. 149): between specific purpose and general tests, between domains of language use, and between components of language ability. Beginning the chapter proper, I will first review a crucial theoretical discussion that has been going on for some time regarding the nature of specific purpose language and the need, desirability, and indeed, the possibility of specific purpose tests. Next, I will review current research initiatives including needs analysis and TLU analysis, various effects of input on test performance, and raters and rating criteria. I will then review current test revision and development efforts that illustrate both the vitality and the variety of specific purpose assessment. I will conclude with a personal view of the issues that we must deal with in moving the field of specific purpose testing forward.

Specific Purpose Tests Defined

Is there such a thing as specific purpose language testing? I have argued (Douglas, 2000) that specific purpose language testing is a special case of communicative language testing in that they share a number of critical features, including the notions of language performance, specific contexts of use, and communicative capacity (Weir, 1990). In fact, it would be difficult to find a language proficiency test anywhere in the world today whose developers do not claim that it represents to some degree or other aspects of performance and context of use, and measures capacity for communicative language use. Indeed, we might ask ourselves whether the traditional distinction between "general purpose" and "specific purpose" tests is still valid, and if so, what a general purpose test is. In a subsequent publication, I have also argued (Douglas, 2001) that very often general purpose test content and methods are derived from theories of language acquisition and use or from theoretical understandings of measurement, whereas specific purpose tests are more often than not based on an analysis of the TLU situation and employ both content and methods derived from the analysis. However, it is not clear that these analyses are truly exclusive to specific purpose testing any more. Since Bachman and Palmer (1996) presented a model for test development that requires attention to, among other things, validity, authenticity, and interactiveness, as well as a thorough analysis of the target language use situation, the distinction between specific purpose tests and more general purpose language tests is blurred even further: even by the time *Assessing Languages for Specific Purposes* was published, it was becoming hard to find any sort of test that was not based on an analysis of a TLU situation. I proposed a continuum of specificity with quite general purpose tests, such as Test of English as a Foreign Language (TOEFL), at one end and quite narrowly defined tests, such as the test of Proficiency in English for Air Traffic Control, at the other, but practitioners will be hard pressed to actually agree on where on such a continuum any given test might be placed. Finally, I argued that true specific purpose tests must share a focus on an interaction between language knowledge and specific purpose background knowledge and that background knowledge, far from being a factor leading to "construct irrelevant variance" (Messick, 1989, p. 35), or error, may be an essential aspect of the construct of specific purpose language ability. This, I think, remains an essential defining characteristic of specific purpose tests—the specificity of our tests lies in the nature of the construct that we wish to make inferences about on observing test-takers' performances on the test tasks—it is how we define the construct specific purpose language ability that defines specific purpose language testing. As Fulcher (2000) puts it, "Some aspects of context may need to be defined as construct rather than error if they are found to be part of the meaning of test scores" (p. 491). This is the essence of specific purpose language testing—a willingness, indeed necessity, to include nonlinguistic elements in defining the construct to be measured. This includes an area of great potential interest in specific purpose testing: the use of assessment criteria derived at least in part from an analysis of the target language use situation. I have proposed (Douglas, 2000, 2001) that we should base not only test content and format on an analysis of the target situation, but also the criteria by which we judge specific purpose test performances, employing the notion of indigenous assessment criteria put forward by Jacoby and McNamara (1999).

There are two related issues here: whether or not we include specific purpose background knowledge in the construct of language ability, and whether we are measuring language use in specific contexts or success in achieving specific communicative purposes. With regard to the first issue, Davies (2001) states categorically that "LSP testing cannot be about testing for subject specific knowledge. It must be about testing the ability to manipulate language functions appropriately in a wide variety of ways" (p. 143). He is surely correct in that we Applied Linguists are not in the business of assessing, for example, how much of engineering or language teaching methodology people know. Nevertheless, in measuring language knowledge in professional, vocational, or academic contexts, we may indeed decide to include specific purpose background knowledge in the construct to be measured on the grounds that it is very difficult to separate language knowledge from the content that it conveys. As Bachman and Palmer (1996) have argued, when we are testing experienced engineers or teachers, we may assume background knowledge as a given, but when we are testing novices, a possible lack of background knowledge can be a source of error in our measurement of language for specific purposes. In such a case we may need a test of background knowledge to sort out the two traits.

The second issue, whether we are assessing test-takers' ability to use language in specific contexts or whether we are assessing ability to perform specific tasks in target language use situations, is described by McNamara (1996) as "weak" and "strong" performance hypotheses and continues to give us headaches today. In 1996, McNamara recommended the weak performance hypothesis on the grounds that what we language testers are best at is making inferences about language ability. However, subsequent research (e.g., Lumley, 1998; Jacoby & McNamara, 1999) has cast doubt on our ability to separate language ability from performance. McNamara himself has acknowledged this in an e-mail exchange:

> I'm not sure we should be restricting ourselves to the 'weak' end of the continuum I proposed, but it also means that the criteria for assessment become critically important . . . We should be using our best understanding of the nature of face-to-face communication as the basis for deciding on these criteria. In this we should be looking to colleagues outside our own field to help us understand—and what they tell us, for example about the shared burden of communicative success, is problematic for procedures designed to report on 'individual language ability.' I'm not sure where we go, but I do know we have a problem.
>
> LTEST-L, April 10, 2001

In a related discussion (Douglas, 2000), I proposed that until we understand better the relationship between language knowledge and background knowledge, we are better off in specific purpose testing not to try to separate the two but to interpret test performance in terms of a composite construct of specific purpose language ability that includes both specific purpose language knowledge and field specific content knowledge. Thus, an important research challenge of the coming decades is to try to understand better the relationship between these two aspects of specific purpose language ability. Clapham (1996) has shown us the difficulties we face in this enterprise: It is very difficult even to define what makes a text field specific, and in addition, texts appear to vary in their degree of specificity within themselves, with some sections being more specific than others. This is a present and future challenge for researchers in specific purpose language testing.

In this section, I have discussed a number of issues that center around the definition of a specific purpose test. As Elder (2001) has pointed out, the uncertainty about the boundaries between target language domains, between test and nontest situations, and between components of language ability intended to be measured, all stem from a systemic uncertainty about the nature of specific purpose language itself, and consequently about the nature of specific purpose language testing. Indeed, this indeterminacy is reflected in the similarly blurred boundaries between specific purpose and general purpose teaching practices that were "unexpectedly uniform from context to context" (Cumming, 2001, p. 223) among teachers Cumming interviewed with respect to the assessment of writing in academic programs. All this leads me to wonder whether we are not asking the wrong questions when we consider the distinction between specific purpose and general purpose tests, or whether "English for academic purposes" is part of ESP or not, for example. In Douglas (2000), I proposed a continuum of specificity based on "the amount of background knowledge required for carrying out test tasks, and the narrowness of interpretations which may be made on the basis of test performance" (p. 14), and Cumming (2001) also discusses the specific/general purpose distinction in terms of a continuum (p. 213). This indeed blurs boundaries between and within specific and general purpose tests. But such, perhaps, is the nature of the language testing enterprise and indeed of language itself. I will argue next that a case can be made for defining a construct of specific purpose language, but, although I do not propose to argue it here, I do wonder whether any case can be made for the existence of general purpose language.

Specific Purpose Language?

For years in specific purpose language testing, we have referred, somewhat unthinkingly perhaps, to testing "English for air traffic control," "scientific German," or "technical Japanese," as if these were definable dialects. Davies (2001) reminds us that there is an important distinction between a dialect and a register: Dialects are acquired as native languages whereas registers may be acquired for specific purposes at any time in life and, when the purpose is no longer of relevance to us, the register can be dropped. After reviewing Clapham's and others' research on the effect of background knowledge, Fulcher (1999) concludes that we cannot justify testing "academic English" but only that we are testing "English in an academic context" (p. 234). Davies (2001) echoes this sentiment, arguing that we cannot make a theoretical case for the existence of language for specific purposes, that there are practical problems with implementing such tests, and that in any case specific purpose language tests seem not to predict future performance much better than more general tests. He maintains that there are sound pragmatic reasons for employing tests that appear to the test-takers and score users to reflect the communicative tasks they are interested in performing in English, and that as such, specific purpose language tests have a "beneficial effect on learners and teachers" (p. 144). This view brings us logically, it seems to me, to a "face validity view" of specific purpose language testing in which general English is dressed in a specific purpose context. This, I think, would be wrong, not because the notion of face validity is inherently wrong but because it rests on an argument that there is no theoretical basis for specific purpose language.

For the most part, those who argue that there is not such a thing as specific purpose language base their arguments on empirical studies suggesting that specific purpose knowledge plays a very small role in the measurement of language ability in specific purpose language tests (cf. Alderson & Urquhart, 1985; Hale, 1988; McNamara, 1990; Jensen & Hansen, 1995; Papajohn, 1999). The difficulty with these studies is not that they were poorly carried out but that the contextual and linguistic characteristics investigated in each vary so much as to make a generalization about the effect of specific purpose language difficult to maintain. Davies (2001) nevertheless argues that the existence of language for specific purposes has never been demonstrated and that therefore specific purpose language testing is atheoretical. His distinction between dialect and register I am not so sure about. I see language acquisition as a special case of a general capacity for language use and both dialects and registers acquired and discarded as part of social behavior—this is related to the discourse domains hypothesis that Selinker and Douglas have been attempting to make a case for some years now (Selinker & Douglas, 1985; Douglas & Selinker, 1985). Our argument is that languages are learned in contexts, and as Chapelle (1998) has argued, the interaction between trait and context changes the nature of both. If we agree with this notion, then it seems to me that logically there must be such a thing as specific purpose language and I wonder whether the distinction between dialect and register, as it relates to specific purpose language, is really important. Tarone (2001) argues that what matters is variation with respect to context, which she calls "variable capacity" (Tarone, 1998) rather than "competence." This sounds very much like what Widdowson has called "capacity," and Halliday (1994) calls "meaning potential," as I discuss later. Tarone notes that both native and non-native speakers of languages have to acquire new registers as they participate in new discourse communities, and this is in line with my own view of language acquisition as a special case of general language use. If we cannot define specific purpose language as a measurable property, as Fulcher (1999) calls us to do, there will continue to be a problem with specific purpose language testing.

I find it somewhat paradoxical that Davies (2001) argues that specific purpose language testing, indeed specific purpose language itself, is an atheoretical concept but that it can be justified on pragmatic grounds—what Fulcher (1999) has called the "face validity argument" (p. 234)—for I would argue the reverse: that specific purpose language testing is justified on theoretical grounds, taking an interactionalist view of construct definition, but that it is often not actually carried out for pragmatic reasons—it is too expensive or impractical to produce the variety of field specific tests that theory would justify. As Fulcher (2000) suggests, an important task for specific purpose language researchers in coming decades will be to "identify the level of generalizability that is permitted in making inferences from scores across variable features of tasks" (p. 491). Fulcher goes on to ask how far down the variationist road language testing will go in the future, allowing that "in practice it is likely that the position adopted on the cline [of specificity] of any specific test will be related to test purpose and the needs of score users" (p. 491). Hamp-Lyons and Lumley (2001) agree with this view: "Tests have multiple audiences, but the one that is most likely to drive design decisions is the score user" (p. 130). This would appear to be another defining feature of specific purpose language tests—the degree to which test results can be interpreted with respect to the specific needs of groups of score users.

LINGUISTIC COMPETENCE AND SPECIFIC PURPOSE LANGUAGE

In addition to the current arguments about the nature, indeed existence of specific purpose language, a number of researchers in specific purpose language testing have recently proposed the centrality of linguistic competence (Clapham, 2000a, 2000b; Davies, 2001; Fulcher, 1999; Widdowson, 2001) and have recommended that somehow tests of linguistic knowledge be included in the assessment of specific purpose communicative ability. In particular, Widdowson argues strongly that we should not even try to measure communicative language ability since, on the one hand, it is a dynamic, complex process that appears incapable of being pinned down long enough to be measured, and on the other our means of measurement, which depend on static, apparently unrelated components, are in principle incapable of measuring communication. He suggests that we instead attempt to test only the most salient features of communication on which the others depend or are derived from. Thus, he proposes that linguistic knowledge be restored to a central place in the inventory of components to test, not as in, for example, the Chomskian paradigm, where linguistic competence is seen as a somewhat self-contained formal property of sentences in isolation, but as an integral part of a more general ability to communicate, integrating the other components in relation to a context of use. Widdowson incorporates Halliday's (1994) notion of *meaning potential*, contextually realized meanings that are inherent in the lexicogrammatical code that we call linguistic knowledge, and argues that only when we assess "the extent to which learners have internalized the communicative potential in language" (p. 19) will we be on the right track. This notion of meaning potential is related, it seems to me, to that of "capacity" that Weir proposed earlier as a defining feature of communicative language testing, and which Widdowson himself argued for before that. Widdowson discusses communicative potential in a way relevant to specific purpose language testing by rejecting the Hymes-Canale/Swain-Bachman/Palmer frameworks as going both too far and not far enough. Too far in the sense that in the thirty years since Hymes first proposed a componential view of language knowledge, the frameworks for describing communicative language ability have become more and more complex, adding more and more components; not far enough in that they have never specified the dynamic relationships among the components as they are used in communication. It seems to me that the challenge to specific purpose language researchers in the coming decades will be to explore the consequences of the proposal of the centrality of linguistic competence for the construct of specific purpose language ability and the impact it may have for specific purpose test development. It has been suggested, for example, that the Rule Space Model offers a means for analyzing test content and linking it to performance data (Buck & Tatsuoka, 1998) that might usefully be further explored in this regard.

Research

I'd like to turn now to a brief review of current research in testing language for specific purposes. The projects I refer to are only representative of a great deal of work being done around the world and not a definitive catalog, but the review is intended to give an idea of the nature of research being conducted. I should point out, too, that although some of the projects described here are not based on highly specific purpose tests, the investigations themselves do bear on issues of interest to specific purpose language testers. There are four categories of research that I will review here, some of which have been discussed earlier: the nature of the test input, analysis of the target language use situation, the nature of the assessment criteria, and backwash (also known as washback or impact).

The Nature of the Input

A listening comprehension test developed as part of the Hong Kong English Language Benchmark Test is the vehicle for a study of differences between audio and video input (Coniam, 2000). The stimulus consists of authentic discussion on educational themes such as a panel discussion or professional seminar in a range of contexts, including task content that reflects the culture of the target audience and differences between spoken and written discourse. Coniam concluded that audio input was preferred: whereas test-takers perceived no advantages for either format and performed similarly on both, a majority preferred audio to video—some found the visuals distracting. In another test development effort, video has been the chosen medium for input: Feak and Salehzadeh (2001) are developing a listening test for international teaching assistants. After reviewing the research literature, which was inconclusive regarding advantages of using video over audio input, Feak and Salehzadeh turned the question "Why use video?" around to "Why continue to use audio?" They are attempting to employ video carefully to complement the auditory signal rather than distracting from it. The issues raised with regard to visual and audio input have implications for our views of the authenticity provided by video, and there has been considerable research recently on the advantages and disadvantages of video input in specific purpose language tests, with inconclusive results overall. No doubt the preference for video or audio input depends, as do most aspects of language testing, on the purpose and uses of the tests as well as the construct being measured.

Pino-Silva, of the Language Department, Universidad Simón Bolívar in Venezuela, is working on a series of small-scale studies dealing with computerized reading comprehension tests. He is looking particularly at the perception of ESP students of the advantages of computerized reading comprehension tests, including the relationship between reading online and test performance, as well as test/retest performance on computer versus paper-and-pencil tests. The differences between reading online and from printed texts is especially important as more and more specific purpose language tests are being put on computers and the Web, and more research is certainly needed to help us interpret test performance in light of the nature of the input medium.

The Analysis of the Target Language Use Situation

Purpura is conducting research that will have relevance to testing with regard to the specific language needs of students doing their master's in the School of International Policy and Administration (SIPA) at Columbia University, where there is a foreign language requirement related to the region they expect to work in. The intent of Purpura and his colleagues is to examine to what degree this requirement is appropriate, given the students' perceived needs and wants. They are also examining to what degree the foreign language programs at Columbia are providing foreign language instruction appropriate to the future career goals of SIPA students. The project is in the qualitative data-gathering stage: Staff have interviewed current students, alumni, administrators, language teachers, and SIPA teachers and will be interviewing end users (employers). Based on the interviews, they are devising structured questionnaires for their survey.

O'Sullivan, at the University of Reading has been conducting research studies related to the Test of English for Educational Purposes (TEEP). In 1999, a project funded by the University of Reading, and implemented by Weir and O'Sullivan, replicated the original needs analysis conducted by Weir (1983), and found that the original results were still relevant. This is not really surprising as the context of language use has changed little in the intervening years, although the growing use of computer-mediated communication technology must surely have an effect on academic language use. Another aspect of this effort was research that focused on task-related factors such as the question of the effect on written performance of the provision, or lack of provision of scaffolding (O'Sullivan, Slaght, & Pallant, 2001). This research is associated with revisions to TEEP described next.

Analysis of Assessment Criteria

Elder, at the University of Auckland, is working on the development of a post-admission diagnostic test of EAP for NS and NNS undergraduates. Research related to this project focuses on two issues: a) the difficulty of setting benchmarks given differences between the views of faculty members from different disciplines and ESL experts regarding what constitutes adequate performance, and b) whether the same set of assessment criteria can provide valid information about NS and NNS test-takers on post-admission diagnostic EAP bias and threshold setting. Once again, this is related to the issue of assessment criteria in specific purpose language testing.

Eggly, Musial, and Smulowitz (1999) studied the relationship between medical residents' performance on two tests, both at the less-specific end of the specificity continuum—the Test of English for International Communication (TOEIC) and the Speaking Proficiency in English Assessment Kit (SPEAK)—and patient satisfaction, faculty and colleague evaluations, and in-training exam scores. They found significant relationships between the tests and the performance measures, such that faculty, colleagues, and patients perceived their language skills to be deficient, although the residents had very high proficiency scores as a group (the TOEIC mean was 904 out of 990 whereas the SPEAK mean was 272 out of 300). This finding is similar to that of McNamara (1996) with regard to the more highly specific Occupational English Test (OET)—whatever the test was measuring, it wasn't what the score users were interested in—and highlights the need for incorporating information about assessment criteria in the target situation in our test specifications.

Backwash

Green is conducting backwash research into the role of the IELTS Writing test in EAP provision at the University of Surrey-Roehampton, comparing courses directed at IELTS preparation with "pre-sessional" preparation courses provided by universities that draw more directly on academic writing needs analyses and so may have a 'broader' scope. He is investigating differences between course types and relating these to outcomes, including test score gains and perceptions of learning. Does teaching-to-the-test lead to greater or faster score gains? And at what cost to EAP training?

Test Revision Projects

Three test revision projects reflect current trends in specific purpose language testing—the tendency noted by Douglas (2000) toward less specificity may be stabilizing. A European consortium of business management schools, Community of European Management Schools (CMS), offers a pan-European master's degree in economics and business administration in which students must demonstrate proficiency in two European languages. Quite some time ago, the consortium developed a set of specific purpose tests to assess candidates' proficiency in their chosen languages. Currently, the main European language test forms are developed annually, whereas the lesser taught languages are developed on an as-needed basis (two versions) and re-used for several testing sessions, and recently, the team charged with assessment has been working to link the tests to the Council of Europe Framework for Teaching and Testing.

The TEEP revision project referred to in the earlier section on research has led to a completely new tape-mediated test of speaking, currently undergoing a final trial, and which was due to be added to the existing battery in autumn of 2001 (O'Sullivan, 2001). The main TEEP paper, which consisted of reading, listening, and writing tasks, has also been the subject of a major revision. O'Sullivan and Slaght (2001) have reviewed and updated the specifications of the test and have recently introduced the first of a series of updated versions. This revision has seen the introduction of more contemporary topics, while a rigorous trialing process has greatly enhanced the test's reliability. In addition to reviewing the procedures for writing and evaluating TEEP items, the Revision Project also integrated the results of a series of specifically designed research studies that focused on task-related factors such as the question of the effect on written performance of the provision, or lack of provision of scaffolding (O'Sullivan, Slaght, & Pallant, 2001). The major addition to the TEEP is the inclusion of a grammar paper. This paper has been the subject of a joint project between TERU and the Centre for Research in Testing, Evaluation and Curriculum in ELT (CRTEC), the University of Surrey-Roehampton (Weir et al., 2001).

In a project that has been ongoing since 1997 (Jamieson et al., 1997), Educational Testing Service is undertaking a major revision of the TOEFL. The main motivations for the revision project include developments in the field of language testing away from discrete-point, multiple-choice tasks, toward more integrative, communicative tasks, and concerns among test users that students were being admitted to university programs with high scores on the current TOEFL who had insufficient written and spoken communication skills. The project was based on an extensive research and design phase, during which TOEFL staff and outside consultants from the fields of applied linguistics, language assessment, and higher education, considered trends in international student admissions and intensive English program enrollments, examined developments in technologies for test delivery, scoring, and reporting, reviewed the literature on communicative competence and communicative language testing, and commissioned papers elaborating communicative constructs in academic reading, writing, listening, and speaking. Prototype tests have been developed and plans are for the New TOEFL to be introduced initially in a low-stakes version to be marketed to English language programs. A particular feature of the new test is a focus on extended production tasks, integrated with reading and listening input. For example, test-takers will read an excerpt from an academic text and then write an essay based on one or more of the points in the text, or listen to a lecture on an academic topic and provide a spoken summary.

Recent/Current Test Development Projects

For me, perhaps the most exciting part of preparing this paper has been learning about the vibrant activity in specific purpose language test development—there is a lot going on all over the world. I sent out a message on the TESP-L, EST-L, and LTEST-L online discussion lists, asking for information about ongoing test revision and development projects. I received more than 30 replies and have categorized the information under the broad headings of tests for academic and vocational purposes. The list of tests below is thus not exhaustive or even randomly representative of all the activity going on in specific purpose language testing, but it is nevertheless a fascinating glimpse of some exciting developments in our field. [Note: Unless otherwise noted, all references are personal e-mail communications.]

Academic Tests

There are a number of tests of academic English for science and technology: English for chemical engineering at Abu Dhabi Men's College; reading, vocabulary, and technical report writing in EST at Kwangju Institute of Science and Technology in Korea; writing, listening, and editing assessment in biochemistry at Yonsei University, also in Korea; article reading tests in biology and chemistry at the University of Guam; and alternative assessments for students in dentistry and various other sciences at the University of Hong Kong. A number of tests of academic business English are being developed at Kyiv University; a large-scale project in France will introduce a national foreign language exam for students of all subjects (other than literature and language) in French universities, under the auspices of the Centre Régional Interuniversitaire de Formation En Langues (CRIFEL); a test of English for policy studies is under development at Kwansei Gakuin in Japan; and a computer-based test of oral proficiency for international teaching assistants (ITAs) is under development at Purdue University in the United States. In another large-scale project, English placement tests have been developed in the fields of agriculture, forestry, applied chemistry and microbiology, marketing, chemistry, mathematics, biology, drama, medicine, pharmacy, and veterinary medicine at the University of Helsinki.

Vocational Tests

Two commercial ventures include entry and exit achievement tests to accompany online business English courses published by Pearson Education and an online business language test, the Business Language Testing Service (BULATS), offered in a number of European languages, and developed by the University of Cambridge Local Examination Syndicate (UCLES) and the Association of Language Testers in Europe (ALTE). A research and development team at Hong Kong Polytechnic University, in association with the Hong Kong Society of Accountants, is working on an online test of English for professional accountants, currently known as the Context-led English Language Assessment System (CLELAS). Vocational language testing in the medical professions includes the Communication Skills assessment that is part of the Clinical Skills Assessment of foreign-trained physicians by the Educational Council for Foreign Medical Graduates (ECFMG), and an Australian test of English communication skills for overseas-trained nurses who wish to practice in Australia, sponsored by the Queensland Nursing Council and developed and administered by staff at the Centre for Applied Linguistics and Languages at Griffith University. Other vocational language tests include an online English test for trainee aircraft maintenance workers in Saudi Arabia; an online English test for engineers in Japan, under the auspices of the Institute for Professional English Communication; a European initiative under a NATO Standard Agreement to test the military English ability of officers and civilian personnel for service at NATO Headquarters in Brussels or participation in peace-keeping operations with military personnel from other countries; and a Taiwanese version of the Listening Summary Translation Examination (LSTE) for law enforcement personnel (Wu & Stansfield, 2001). Stansfield and colleagues are also developing a court interpreters written examination to screen candidates for the more expensive oral examination.

CONCLUSION

So, what is the state of the art of languages for specific purposes testing? Like other areas of Applied Linguistics (Larsen-Freeman, 2000), specific purpose language testing is still an emerging discipline whose practitioners are grappling with definitions, boundaries, and methods. I have argued that specific purpose language testing is defined by the nature of the construct to be measured, which includes both specific purpose language and background knowledge. While, as Davies (2001) points out, we are not in the business of measuring specific purpose content knowledge, it is also true that we know very little about the interrelationship between language knowledge and the content it is used to convey. Thus, it will be necessary to take background knowledge into account in the interpretation of specific purpose language test performance even if it is not explicitly measured by our tests. It may also be, as Fulcher (2000) has suggested, that other aspects of the context, such as purpose, tone, or genre, for example, may need to be included in the construct definition to the extent that they are seen to be part of the meaning of scores on specific purpose language tests. In this regard, we need, as McNamara (2001) reminds us, to pay more attention to the criteria we employ to judge performances on specific purpose language tests, listening to practitioners in the professional and academic fields within which we are producing tests for what they have to tell us about the criteria they use in judging performances in their fields. Some of these may be directly useful in constructing rating scales, whereas others may be of more use in the interpretation of test performances. Finally, we need to come to grips with our understanding of specific purpose language itself, particularly in light of the challenge put forward by Davies (2001), Fulcher (1999), and Clapham (2000a), among others, that specific purpose testing is linguistically atheoretical but that it is justified on pragmatic, face validity grounds. I have argued that we need to find a way to describe specific purpose language in a way that allows for its measurement in our tests, perhaps in a paradigm similar to what Tarone (1998) has called *variable capacity* or what Widdowson (2001), invoking Halliday (1994), refers to as *meaning potential*—"the extent to which learners have internalized the communicative potential in language" (p. 94)—and which he suggests is best measured as contextualized linguistic competence. This issue will continue to be a point of investigation for language for specific purposes practitioners for some time to come.

In addition to these fundamental, definitional issues, specific purpose language testing continues to require empirical studies of what makes spoken and written texts field specific (cf. Clapham, 1996), of the degree of generalizability of test performance (Fulcher, 1999), of the effect of test delivery technologies on test performance, and of the impact of specific purpose language testing on specific purpose language teaching and materials.

Finally, given the rich and vibrant test revision and development work going on all around the world, the hopeful vision at the end of Douglas (2000) of a rich future for specific purpose language testing would appear to be justified.

ACKNOWLEDGMENTS

I thank the numerous colleagues who sent me information about ongoing research and development projects in specific purpose language testing.

REFERENCES

Alderson, J. C., & Urquhart, A. (1985). The effect of students' academic discipline on their performance on ESP reading tests. *Language Testing, 2*, 192–204.
Bachman, L., & Palmer, A. (1996). *Language testing in practice.* Oxford, UK: Oxford University Press.
Buck, G., & Tatsuoka, L. (1998). Application of the rule-space procedure to language testing: Examining attributes of a free response listening test. *Language Testing, 15*(2), 119–157.
Chapelle, C. (1998). Construct definition and validity inquiry in SLA research. In L. Bachman & A. Cohen, (Eds.), *Interfaces between second language acquisition and language testing research,* (pp. 32–70). Cambridge, UK: Cambridge University Press.
Clapham, C. (2000a). Assessment for academic purposes: Where next? *System, 28,* 511–521.
Clapham, C. (2000b). Assessment and testing. *Annual Review of Applied Linguistics, 20,* 147–161.
Clapham, C. (1996). *The development of IELTS: A study of the effect of background knowledge on reading comprehension.* Cambridge, UK: Cambridge University Press.
Coniam, D. (2000). The use of audio or video comprehension as an assessment instrument in the certification of English language teachers: A case study. *System, 29*(1), 1–14.
Cumming, A. (2001). ESL/EFL instructors' practices for writing assessment: Specific purposes of general purposes? *Language Testing, 18*(2), 207–224.

Davies, A. (2001). The logic of testing languages for specific purposes. *Language Testing, 18*(2), 133–148.

Douglas, D. (2000). *Assessing languages for specific purposes*. Cambridge, UK: Cambridge University Press.

Douglas, D. (2001). Language for specific purposes assessment criteria: Where do they come from? *Language Testing, 18*(2), 171–186.

Douglas, D., & Selinker, L. (1985). Principles for language tests within the "discourse domains" theory of interlanguage: Research, test construction, and interpretation. *Language Testing, 2,* 205–226.

Eggly, S., Musial, J., & Smulowitz, J. (1999). The relationship between English language proficiency and success as a medical resident. *English for Specific Purposes, 18*(2), 201–208.

Elder, C. (2001). Assessing the language proficiency of teachers: Are there any border controls? *Language Testing, 18*(2), 149–170.

Elder, C., Brown, A., Grove, E., Hill, K., Iwashita, N., Lumley, T., McNamara, T., & O'Loughlin, K. (Eds.), (2001). *Experimenting with uncertainty—Essays in Honour of Alan Davies.* Cambridge, UK: Cambridge University Press.

Feak, C., & Salehzadeh, J. (2001). Challenges and issues in developing an EAP video listening placement assessment: A view from one program. *English for Specific Purposes, 20,* Supplement 1, 477–493.

Fulcher, G. (1999). Assessment in English for academic purposes: Putting content validity in its place. *Applied Linguistics, 20*(2), 221–236.

Fulcher, G. (2000). The 'communicative' legacy in language testing. *System, 28,* 483–497.

Hale, G. (1988). *The interaction of student major-filed group and text content in TOEFL reading comprehension.* TOEFL Research Report 25. Princeton, NJ: Educational Testing Service.

Halliday, M. (1994). *An introduction to functional grammar.* London: Edward Arnold.

Hamp-Lyons, L., & Lumley, T. (2001). Assessing language for specific purposes. *Language Testing, 18*(2), 127–132.

Jacoby, S., & McNamara, T. (1999). Locating competence. *English for Specific Purposes, 18*(3), 213–241.

Jamieson, J., Jones, S., Kirsch, I., Mosenthal, P., & Taylor, C. (1997). *TOEFL 2000 framework: A working paper.* Princeton, NJ: Educational Testing Service.

Jensen, C., & Hansen, C. (1995). The effect of prior knowledge on listening-test performance. *Language Testing, 12,* 99–119.

Larsen-Freeman, D. (2000). Second language acquisition and applied linguistics. In W. Grabe (Ed.), *Annual review of applied linguistics 20* (pp. 165–181). Cambridge, UK: Cambridge University Press.

Lumley, T. (1998). Perceptions of language-trained raters and occupational experts in a test of occupational English language proficiency. *English for Specific Purposes, 17, 347–367.*

McNamara, T. (1990). Item response theory and the validation of an ESP test for health professionals. *Language Testing, 7,* 52–76.

McNamara, T. (1996). *Measuring second language performance.* London: Longman.

McNamara, T. (2001). Language assessment as social practice: Challenges for research. *Language Testing, 18,* 333–349.

Messick, S. (1989). Validity. In R. L. Linn (Ed.), *Educational measurement* (pp. 13–23). New York: Macmillan.

O'Sullivan, B. (2001). TEEP speaking component. Testing and Evaluation Research Unit, University of Reading.

O'Sullivan, B., & Slaght, J. (2001). TEEP revision project. Testing and Evaluation Research Unit, University of Reading.

O'Sullivan, B., Slaght, J., & Pallant, A. (2001). (manuscript). *Exploring the effect of scaffolding on written performance.* Testing and Evaluation Research Unit, University of Reading.

Papajohn, D. (1999). The effect of topic variation in performance testing: The case of the chemistry TEACH test for international teaching assistants. *Language Testing, 16*(1), 52–81.

Selinker, L., & Douglas, D. (1985). Wrestling with 'context' in interlanguage studies. *Applied Linguistics, 6*(2), 190–204.

Tarone, E. (1998). Research on interlanguage variation: Implications for language testing. In L. Bachman & A. Cohen (Eds.), *Interfaces between second language acquisition and language testing research* (pp. 71–89). Cambridge, UK: Cambridge University Press.

Tarone, E. (2001). Assessing language skills for specific purposes: Describing and analysing the 'behaviour domain.' In C. Elder, A. Brown, E. Grove, K. Hill, N. Iwashita, T. Lumley, T. McNamara, & K. O'Loughlin (Eds.), *Experimenting with uncertainty: Essays in honour of Alan Davies* (pp. 53–60). Cambridge, UK: Cambridge University Press.

Widdowson, H. (2001). Communicative language testing: The art of the possible. In C. Elder, A. Brown, E. Grove, K. Hill, N. Iwashita, T. Lumley, T. McNamara, & K. O'Loughlin (Eds.), *Experimenting with uncertainty: Essays in honour of Alan Davies* (pp. 12–21). Cambridge, UK: Cambridge University Press.

Weir, C. J., O'Sullivan, B., Green, A., & Slaght, J. (2001). TEEP grammar component. Joint project, the Testing and Evaluation Research Unit, the University of Reading and Centre for Research in Testing, Evaluation and Curriculum in ELT, the University of Surrey-Roehampton.

Weir, C. (1990). *Communicative language testing.* New York: Prentice-Hall.

Weir, C. (1983). *Identifying the language needs of overseas students in tertiary education in the United Kingdom.* Unpublished doctoral dissertation, University of London.

Wu, W.-P., & Stansfield, C. (2001). Towards authenticity of task in test development. *Language Testing, 18*(2), 187–206.

48

Classroom Teacher Assessment of Second Language Development: Construct as Practice

Constant Leung
King's College, University of London

INTRODUCTION

Classroom-based teacher assessment of second language development has been the subject of a great deal of interesting and at times polemical discussion in recent years. One area of interest is concerned with the claims of distinctive usefulness and pedagogic value made by proponents of classroom-based teacher assessment as an alternative approach to the more conventional forms of standardized language testing. There has also been a lot of interest in the quality and soundness of classroom-based teacher assessment in terms of validity and reliability and other issues traditionally associated with standardized testing. In addition, the arguments for critical language assessment has added a number of new issues such as ethical values, political responsibility, and democratic principles to the discussion. The main purpose of this chapter is to present an overview of some of the constitutive issues concerning pedagogically oriented classroom-based teacher assessment, and some suggestions for further articulation and formulation of the research and development agenda.

The discussion will argue for a view of teacher assessment that is intrinsically tied to a built-in requirement for expanding professional knowledge, responsive pedagogy, and reflexive practice. It will be proposed that teacher practice should be seen as a key site for research and development. The privileging of teacher practice represents an epistemological turn as well as a starting point for reflexive examination. This chapter will draw on works from the fields of second language testing/assessment and educational assessment more generally. Researchers and writers have used the terms 'assessment,' 'evaluation,' and 'testing' in a number of different and/or overlapping senses; every effort will be made to minimize terminological ambiguity.

FINDING A WAY THROUGH CONCEPTUAL DIFFERENCES AND COMMON CONCERNS

The term classroom-based teacher assessment, from now on teacher assessment, has been associated with a range of different but often overlapping conceptualizations and practices in different contexts. The following are some examples:

• Alternative assessment—Huerta-Macías, for instance, argues that "[a]lternative assessment ... provides alternatives to traditional testing" and these alternatives include "checklists of student behaviors ... journals, reading logs ... work samples and teacher observations and anecdotal records" (1995, p. 9); the centrality of teacher action and teacher involvement in alternative assessment can be clearly seen when she states that alternative assessment procedures are "non-intrusive to the classroom because they do not require a separate block of time to implement ... " and " ... the ... day-to-day activities that a student is engaged in (e.g., writing, role play, group discussion) are the basis for alternative assessment" (1995, p. 9).

• Authentic assessment—García and Pearson (1994, pp. 357–358) state that the goal of authentic assessment is "to gather evidence about how students are approaching, processing, and completing "real-life" tasks in a particular domain. Authentic classroom assessment can include ... anecdotal records ... teacher-student conferencing ... and portfolios of student work...." They add that " ... authentic classroom assessment requires teachers to observe the participants (students), respond to their performance, and plan instruction accordingly" (1994, p. 359).

• Classroom assessment—TESOL (1998, p. 3) states that "classroom assessment are those that are interwoven into instruction, often created and delivered by ESL/bilingual teachers"; it also suggests elsewhere in the same title that "classroom assessments mirror the language(s) and content of instructional practices" and "classroom assessments enable students to demonstrate their learning in multiple ways from multiple perspectives, thus serving as learning experiences themselves" (1998, p. 7).

• Educational assessment—Gipps (1994, p. 123) states that "teacher assessment is essentially an informal activity: the teacher may pose questions, observe activities, evaluate pupils' work in a planned and systematic or ad hoc way...."

• Formative assessment—Black and Wiliam (1998b, p. 2) suggest that assessment includes "all those activities undertaken by the teachers, *and by their students in assessing themselves,* which provide information to be used as feedback to modify the teaching and learning activities in which they are engaged. *Such assessment becomes "formative assessment" when evidence is actually used to adapt the teaching work to meet the needs'* of students" (original italics).

• Informal assessment—Rea-Dickins (2001, p. 434) suggests that "much routine classroom teaching activity allows teachers to make decisions about their learners—e.g., how much a learner knows, and how much progress a learner is making—and may be influential in determining what is taught next and how that material is taught, thereby constituting an important core in classroom assessment practice."

• Statutory assessment—In England, teacher assessment is "an essential part of the national curriculum assessment and reporting arrangement" at the end of elementary school and teachers are advised that "tests provide a standard "snapshot" of attainment ... while teacher assessment, carried out as part of teaching and learning in the classroom, covers the full range and scope of the programs of study, and takes account of evidence of achievement in a range of contexts, including that gained through discussion and observation" (Qualifications and Curriculum Authority [QCA], 2001).

The terminological and discoursal differences can be seen to represent different theoretical and practical orientations. For instance, the seemingly formative-cum-summative, instrumental, and record-keeping conceptualization presented by official curriculum and assessment authorities such as QCA (2001) is clearly quite different from the strongly pedagogic orientation suggested by Rea-Dickens, and Black and Wiliam. However, there appears to a common core meaning underlying the terminological differences—that is, nonstandardized local assessment carried out by teachers in the classroom.

Additionally there seems to be a shared understanding that teachers need classroom-based information about individual students, even where formal test scores are available. Genesee and Upshur (1996, p. 5) illustrate the argument in this way:

> Imagine that Pedro scored 19 on a class test. By itself, Pedro's score is meaningless. We cannot tell from this score alone whether Pedro has done well. Moreover, if he has done poorly, we cannot discern the reason from his score alone. Therefore, we cannot decide whether to proceed with our teaching as planned or to take another course of action more appropriate for Pedro.

Furthermore, arguments for teacher assessment recognize that standardized testing does not necessarily provide valid information accurately and reliably about students' ability or performance in a specific domain, particularly at the level of the individual. Gipps (1994, p. 6) raises the issue of the limiting effect of the tendency to conceptualize construct (in the psychometric tradition) as comprising one single underlying attribute or skill when many, if not most, language abilities or skills are multidimensional. For instance, if a standardized reading test operationalizes reading as "comprehension of simple sentences," then the other aspects of a student's ability to read in context in a wider sense are left out. Pedagogically the possible consequence of curriculum narrowing of limited construct dimensionality, through washback, is not difficult to see. In education systems with ethnic and linguistic diversity, García and Pearson (1994) point out that in test construction the norming process tends to (a) underrepresent linguistic minority groups and (b) eliminate test items that have low correlation with the total test score, thus getting rid of those items on which minority students may perform well (cf. Bachman, 2000). Wiliam (2001b, p. 18) shows the potential unreliability of standardized test scores at the individual level: for a test with scaled scores with 100 as the average score and a standard deviation of scores of 15, "with a reliability of 0.75 . . . someone who scores 115 . . . might really have a true score of just 100 . . . or as high as 130 . . . we must be aware that the results of even the best test can be wildly inaccurate for individual students. . . . "

So educationally and pedagogically there is a good case for teacher assessment to play at least a complementary role, to borrow a phrase from Linn, Baker, and Dunbar (1991, p. 16), to standardized testing. The important task now is to consider what constitutes epistemologically appropriate questions for teacher assessment. For the purpose of this discussion teacher assessment is understood as, building on Lynch (2001, p. 358), the noticing and gathering of information about student language use in ordinary (noncontrived) classroom activities, and the use of that information to make decisions about language teaching without necessarily quantifying it or using it for reporting purposes. It is hoped that this deliberately low-key perspective on teacher assessment will help focus attention on the core issues centered around the relationship between assessment and pedagogy.

ASSUMPTIONS, CLAIMS, AND CRITICAL RESPONSES

The usefulness of teacher assessment is generally accepted but there are questions as to the status and the nature of the information it produces. The strong claims of validity and reliability advanced by proponents of teacher assessment such as Gipps and Huerta-Macías are contested. Huerta-Macías (1995, p. 9), for instance, argues that these concerns, traditionally associated with psychometric approaches, should be recast as aspects of trustworthiness: "An instrument is deemed to be *trustworthy* if it has *credibility* (i.e., truth value) and *auditability* (i.e., consistency)." On this account credibility appears to be associated with real-life classroom tasks and activities such as "writing, self-editing, reading, participation in collaborative work...' (Huerta-Macías, 1995, p. 9); the syllogism is as follows: Real-life tasks are credible, credibility is validity, therefore real-life tasks are valid. Consistency or reliability is regarded as a consequence of being valid:

> ...if a procedure is valid, then it is reliable in that it will consistently produce the same results if audited or replicated. The probability is very high, for example, that a student's written retelling of a story will share the same or at least highly similar characteristics in his writing from one week to the next. Two instructors or even the same instructor who is trained in the use of a holistic evaluation scale will more than likely find two pieces, written one week apart by a student, will exhibit like characteristics. (Huerta-Macías, 1995, p. 9)

Gipps (1994, pp. 123–124) presents her views on validity and reliability as follows:

> The information which the teacher thus obtains may be partial or fragmentary...But repeated assessment of this sort, over a period of time, and in a range of contexts *will* allow the teacher to build up a solid and broadly based understanding of the pupil's attainment. Because of these characteristics teacher assessment may be seen as having a high validity in relation to content and construct...If the assessment has sampled broadly across the domain and in depth within it then the assessment is likely to be generalizable (within that domain)....

> Where traditional reliability measures are not appropriate we need to drop reliability and...use...*comparability*, which is based on consistency. The level of comparability demanded for any assessment will be related to its use: for example, if performance assessment is used for accountability purposes then great care will need to be taken to ensure comparability; for teacher assessment for formative purposes comparability is of lesser concern. Consistency leading to comparability is achieved by assessment tasks being presented in the same way...assessment criteria being interpreted in the same way...(Gipps, 1994, p. 171).

Brown and Hudson (1998, p. 655), in a discussion on the usefulness of different kinds of second language tests and teacher assessment, agree that attributes such as *credibility* and *auditability* contribute to the notion of *trustworthiness* in teacher assessment; but they insist that *trustworthiness* so defined is not enough. In their view teachers conducting classroom assessment "must make every effort to structure the ways they design, pilot, analyze, and revise the procedures so the reliability and validity of the procedures can be studied, demonstrated and improved" (Brown & Hudson, 1998, p. 656).

In a similar vein, Cohen (1994) suggests that when teachers evaluate their own assessment instruments they should look at different aspects of their reliability and validity. For instance, with reference to reliability, Cohen (1994, p. 36) suggests that "the reliability of a test concerns its precision as a measuring instrument" and that "three different types of factors contribute to the reliability of language assessment instruments: test factors, situation factors, and individual factors." Attention is drawn to formal means of investigating test factors such as the internal consistency of test items. It seems quite clear that this view of validity and reliability locates teacher assessment within the broader concept of performance testing. (For a discussion on validation criteria of performance assessment see Linn, Baker, & Dunbar, 1991.) However, given that teacher assessment is regarded in this discussion as complementary to and not an extension of standardized testing, it would seem more pertinent to ask on what basis can teacher assessment claim validity and reliability and whether this question is indeed germane.

One way of making sense of this kind of questioning is to understand a particular difference in the epistemological concerns of psychometric measurement and teacher assessment—psychometrics treats the attribute to be sampled as a property of the individual, which is quantifiable at any one time, whereas teacher assessment has to take account of the interactive nature of student performance in the classroom, which is dynamic and co-produced with the teacher and others. (The issues raised by A. Brown (1995) and McNamara (1997) on the interactive nature of performance tests are relevant here.)

The views expressed by Rea-Dickens, Black, and Wiliam[1] and others[2] cited earlier would suggest that what they have in mind is a form of teacher assessment that is integrated into the ordinary teaching and learning activities. Gipps (1994, p. 13) suggests that teacher assessment (in her terms, "trickle up testing"):

> ... is essentially nonstandardized and involves a wide range of activity but its purpose is to gather information for use in decision making in the classroom ... and the teacher is assessor, user, and interpreter of results, i.e., s/he has an interactive role. The results are used by teachers to identify students' needs ... [and] by students for feedback on their learning ...

More observationally, Rea-Dickins (2001, p. 437) suggests that teacher assessment may be "plotted at different points along a more 'formal' to 'informal' continuum." The more formal assessments would include preplanned stand-alone assessment activities carried out for reporting or summative purposes, but the teacher would nevertheless provide scaffolding for the students during the assessment activities. The informal assessments would take place as part of teaching and learning with "strategic teacher intervention—by questioning, seeking clarification ... pushing some learners' forward in their understanding and language learning" (Rea-Dickins, 2001, pp. 437–438).

The alternative conceptualization of validity and reliability suggested by Huerta-Macías and others has in fact been recognized within the psychometric perspective. For instance, Haertel (1992, p. 986), in a discussion on what he calls "instructional uses of student performance measurement," suggests that, teacher assessment tasks "may be highly motivating for students and may be more closely tied to curriculum and instruction than are typical objective tests" and, given the focus on teaching and learning at the local classroom level, "reliability and efficiency in scoring are relatively unimportant. . . . " From a psychometric point of view it is not difficult to follow Haertel's line of reasoning. There are at least three reasons. First, each teacher assessment task is unique because it is virtually impossible to reproduce any particular assessment task in the same way or under the same conditions since the task and the conditions are not controlled in the first place. Second, teacher assessment tasks are rarely used without variation (see previous point) beyond a particular class or group of students (therefore "objective" comparability of scores or outcomes is not an issue). Third, "important decisions are unlikely to hinge on the precise ranking of the [students]" (Haertel, 1992) because the focus is on teaching and learning. Furthermore, it is recognized that in day-to-day classroom work teachers generally have multiple sources of information about their students, and misinterpretation of teacher assessment outcome can be easily corrected.

This relaxation of reliability for "instructional uses of student performance measurement" may be seen as concessions offered on account of the low-stakes and "home-made" nature of teacher assessment from a psychometric perspective of high-stakes testing. In a sense, this is a form of tacit acknowledgment that teacher assessment is not the same thing as psychometric testing, therefore there is no point in insisting on applying the same basis of validation. Lynch (2001, p. 361), in a discussion on a critical perspective on language assessment, suggests that "the use of qualitative methods would not be simply a methodological choice, but an epistemological and ontological one, entailing a view of language as something that is created and exists in the act of our using, inquiring, and interpreting, not as an independent, objective entity waiting to be discovered and measured." Along similar lines, Wiliam (2001a, p. 172) argues that "... much of the investigation that has been done into authentic assessment of performance has been based on a 'deficit' model, by establishing how far, say, the assessment of portfolios of students' work, falls short of the standards of reliability of standardized multiple-choice tests. An alternative approach is, instead of building theoretical models and then trying to apply them to assessment practices, we try to theorize what is actually being done."

TEACHER ASSESSMENT: TEACHER MEDIATION

If teacher assessment is part of the teaching and learning process, then it follows that its quality and value crucially depend on what (kinds of) pedagogically oriented information is being sought and what basis of judgment is being invoked by the teacher in that process. These questions are related to the idea of construct. Bachman and Palmer (1996, p. 89) suggest that in test development it is important to define the test construct because the activity of defining it "makes explicit the precise nature of the ability we want to measure, by defining it abstractly." For example, reading can be defined as the ability to read with comprehension unconnected sentences or to read and understand sentence and whole text level meaning. In teacher assessment the issue of construct is considerably more complicated. The teacher, qua assessor, acts as a mediated representation of construct when working with and interpreting their own assessment criteria or published assessment scale descriptors. In most, if not all, institutional settings teachers exercise considerable amount of asymmetric power over students in regulative and pedagogic decision making in terms of both day-to-day classroom construction of the curriculum and longer term trajectories of student progress. This power inequality makes it all the more important to explore teachers' mediation of construct and assessment criteria both theoretically and empirically.

In one sense the notion of mediation is concerned with the basis of teacher judgment. A conventional way of looking at this is to ask whether teachers operate according to clearly defined criteria of what students know or can do, that is, criterion-referenced assessment. The key argument for criterion-referenced assessment is that there should be clarity about the relationship between what is being assessed and what the assessment means. At first glance it may seem that teacher assessment should be criterion-referenced because this may help clarify what the teacher should attend to. However, it is generally the case that the criteria in a criterion-referenced assessment scheme are set out in advance of the assessment activities. The teacher's job, qua assessor, is to look for the requisite evidence. It can be argued that the kind of teacher assessment being discussed here may not fit easily into this conceptual framework. If teacher assessment is part of the ordinary teaching-learning process, the teacher has to respond to all kinds of contingent student responses. For instance, in a story-writing task, based on previous acting out and role play, some students show signs that they are finding it difficult to use reported speech and this may lead to an impromptu teaching session on grammar. In this situation, any teacher intention to assess aspects of story writing would be displaced. It is not clear how possible it is for the teacher, any teacher, to operate the full range of prespecified criteria that would cover all possible aspects of student learning, modes of participation, and learning strategies, to name but a few possible issues that can emerge in the teaching and learning process that might impact on teacher assessment; the fluid, socially dynamic, and sometimes unpredictable nature of classroom activities would preclude this possibility. A teacher cannot in good faith impose an assessment agenda on classroom events when teaching and learning are the declared purpose. In any case, when they are not acting as official invigilators or examiners, teachers often intervene in assessment activities to assist learning. This is not to say that teachers should not work with clearly defined criteria. The point is that one cannot assume that noncontrived classroom events would always provide the necessary opportunities to sample the language use (or any other kind of "evidence") required for the intended criterion-referenced assessment.

Wiliam (2001a, pp. 172–173) suggests that an alternative to criterion-referenced assessment, is construct-referenced assessment, which is glossed as follows:

> The innovative feature of such assessment is that no attempt is made to prescribe learning outcomes. In that it is defined at all, it is defined simply as the consensus of the teachers making assessments. The assessment is not objective, in the sense that there are no objective criteria for a student to satisfy . . . the assessment system relies on the existence of a construct (of what it means to be competent in a particular domain) being shared by a community of practitioners. . . .

The high-stakes Ph.D. examination, according to Wiliam, is an example of this kind of assessment. The University of London regulations, for instance, stipulate that to pass the examination a Ph.D. thesis must make a contribution to original knowledge by discovering new facts or by the use of critical power. This would appear to be a criterion at first sight. However, in fact not all new facts are rated equally at Ph.D. level. In a thesis concerned with the nature of teacher-student interaction, counting up the total number of words uttered by all participants in a particular lesson may show a new fact, but by itself it is unlikely to count for much. Indeed notions such as 'original' and 'critical,' even 'contribution,' are subject to interpretation. When two examiners agree to pass a thesis they do so "not because they derive similar meanings from the regulation, but because they already have in their minds a notion of the required standard" (Wiliam, 2001a).

This concept of construct-referencing is useful because it provides an epistemologically helpful basis for further critical exploration of the complexities in pedagogically oriented teacher assessment. The most important issue raised by this concept is what constitutes professional or communal consensus alluded to by Wiliam. Teachers' professional knowledge and the way they use this knowledge in assessment practices are now being brought into focus. Seen in this light, there are at least two aspects of teacher assessment that require further exploration: institutional or community practice and individual teacher qua assessor practice. These are actually overlapping phenomena in real life. At this stage, however, it would seem helpful to look at them separately to show how they may impact on teacher assessment.

We will look at institutional or community practice first. The notions of institution and community are understood loosely here; an institution is a school or a department within a school and a community is a group of teachers who share some common understanding and approaches to assessment within a school, a subject area, or even a particular phase of education.[3]

INSTITUTIONAL AND COMMUNITY PRACTICE

Clarke and Gipps (2000, p. 38) observe that a number of public educational systems, such as Australia and England, have introduced national curriculum frameworks and assessment schemes that require teachers to both teach and assess according to published content and benchmarks, and yet "little is known about the actual processes of assessment." One of the focuses of attention of their work was on how elementary and secondary teachers in England carried out their ongoing teacher assessment, which enabled them to make an overall judgment on the level of attainment at the end of a school year or at the end of a Key Stage.[4] They report that "mathematics and science departments in secondary schools adopt rather formal approaches to ongoing assessment (e.g., end of module tests, regular classroom tests), whereas English departments and [elementary] teachers tend to use more informal, formative methods (e.g., pupil self-assessment, regular notetaking, use of pupil portfolios)" (Clarke & Gipps, p. 44). This kind of findings points to the fact that teachers in specific disciplines or subject departments and different phases of schooling may adopt different practices and use different kinds of information and procedures.

Brindley (1998, 2001) investigates a number of issues concerning the assessment of the Certificates in Spoken and Written English, a nationally accredited competency-based curriculum and assessment framework designed for adult migrants in Australia. This framework provides teachers with four levels of "'can-do' statements of the outcomes of learning ... in oral interaction, reading and writing (e.g., *can participate in a casual conversation ...*)" (Brindley, 1998, p. 60). The assessment tasks are produced and administered by teachers. As part of his study Brindley looked at six particular writing tasks intended to assess two particular competencies at Certificate III level and found "major differences in rater severity ... a person's chances of being awarded [either one of the competencies] would be reduced by approximately 45 percent if his or her script were judged by the most severe rater instead of the most lenient" (Brindley, 1998, p. 63). This kind of findings suggests that even with a group of teachers who are working within the same curriculum and assessment framework there can be greater differences in terms of their judgments, possibly reflecting a range of different interpretations of criteria.

The National Curriculum in England operates a set of common scales for (the subject) English for all students, irrespective of their language background except for the first (lowest) level.[5] Indeed, until the recent introduction of the additional modified Level 1 to accommodate second language beginners (Qualifications and Curriculum Authority [QCA], 2000), all students were meant to be assessed according to the common national scales. The curriculum framework and the assessment arrangement generally did not (and still does not to a large extent, see Endnote 3) encourage teachers to draw a clear distinction between English as a mother tongue and English as an Additional/Second Language (EAL/ESL). In an exploratory study of teacher models of speaking and listening Leung and Teasdale (1997b) reported that when a group of EAL teaching staff, all serving in the same local education authority but assigned to different schools, were asked to comment and to judge some noncontrived classroom performances of students from diverse language backgrounds from another school area on video, they appeared to operate constructs such as "native-speaker like," "accent," and "task focus," which were not in the official level descriptions (see Appendix 1 for Levels 1–4 descriptions). This kind of finding points to the possibility of teacher-invoking constructs other than those set out in the published assessment scales.

It would seem that there is a great deal to be learned about teacher assessment practices within even the relatively well-established curriculum and assessment schemes. The publication and standardization of curriculum and assessment statements does not by itself lead to shared practice or perception. There appears to be variability in both procedures and criteria of assessment. This draws attention to the need for further development in both institutional assessment organization and procedure, and collective teacher qua assessor practice. At this point we will turn to some of the even less visible issues of teacher knowledge, beliefs, and values at the level of individual teacher qua assessor practice.

INDIVIDUAL PRACTICE

The practice of teacher assessment becomes even more complex if we try to understand what happens when teachers assess, without conscious planning, as part of ordinary classroom interaction with students, that is, when they consider themselves to be teaching. Breen (1997, p. 96) refers to this kind of assessment graphically as "assessment on the run." The online and fleeting nature of this kind of formative assessment makes it very difficult to know what construct, in other words, what question(s) or what abilities, are being foregrounded and how they are interpreted. For instance, an assessment descriptor such as "pupils talk about matters of immediate interest" (Department for Education and Employment [DfEE] and Qualifications and Curriculum Authority [QCA], 1999) is very broad and teachers need to interpret its meaning in terms of classroom spoken language. For some time now it has been generally recognized that students bring to curriculum and assessment tasks their understanding and interpretation of what is to be done (often with others) in specific contexts; therefore assessment has to take account of this agentive aspect of student performance (Murphy, 1996). If it is also accepted that, in view of the contingent, dynamic, and yet intensely active (and interactive) nature of classroom activities, teachers are not passive instruments of curriculum and assessment schemes, then it follows that there is a very good reason to ask questions about how teachers construe their assessment activities and student performance. This difficulty is, of course, a problem for the researcher, not for the teacher as assessor. After all, the teacher is already happily, so to speak, operating in the classroom and has a good sense of what is happening. However, if teacher assessment is to be understood better, it would be useful to explore the aspects of curriculum content and theories of knowledge and learning (folk or formal) being foregrounded in these moments of assessment by teachers. A number of relevant theoretical and empirical studies will be looked at in the next section.

In a case study of assessment of speaking and listening in English within the National Curriculum in England, Leung and Teasdale (1997a) and Leung (1999) carried out semistructured interviews with teachers in two elementary schools to explore their representations of spoken English. The interviews were carried out in three phases. The first phase was focused on the teachers' interpretations of the first four levels on the official National Curriculum scale (Department for Education [DfE], 1995), without reference to the students in their own linguistically diverse classes. The second phase interviews elicited views and evaluative comments from the teachers, from memory, on some of their students' spoken English performance. In the final interviews the teachers were invited to watch video clips of ordinary noncontrived activities of the students in their classes and at the end of each clip the teachers were asked to comment on what they saw in relation to the use of spoken English. Of particular interest to this discussion are the comments on the specific students made by the teachers after each video segment in the final phase interviews. The following five teacher comments are highly suggestive of a set of complex, experience-informed, and episodic narrativelike reasoning:

a) Interview context: Having watched a short video clip of a particular child in classroom situations, the teacher informant was asked to elaborate on the child's reluctance to listen and respond, a feature noticed and mentioned by the teacher informant in the first place.

Very much personalities, very much tied to her personality sometimes children you can see that they are not understanding because they don't respond when you say something . . . with Nosheen it's not that she can't understand it's just she won't give herself time to really reflect on what she's been asked to do and I think that's the personality thing. (Leung, 1999, p. 233)

b) Interview context: Having watched a short video clip of a particular child working with other children, the teacher informant was asked to comment.

Sushma's understanding is not bad. Her mother doesn't speak much English, but her father is excellent. He is a leader in the community and his understanding and standard is very good. (Leung, 1999, p. 234)

c) Interview context: Having watched a short video clip of a particular child talking to another child, the teacher informant was asked to comment.

Interesting that she, em, said to Sadhna at one point 'Sadhna,' and she said this perfect sentence, which obviously she has heard lots, 'Sadhna, can I have . . .' something to do with buttercups. And the next sentence the words 'what him had.' So it's interesting again, the variations of awareness of a sentence which has been dependent on, which she has learned and internalized and she's become quite dependent on say, whereas she is wanting to speak more spontaneously and she's getting mixed up, but it is still excellent the fact that she has got that far. (Leung, 1999)

d) Interview context: On seeing a video clip showing a child trying hard to explain something to her friend, the teacher informant commented.

. . . to me a lot of that just proves the point that a lot of children get to Level 2, it's a very wide range of skills that they've got to acquire and it's before they get to Level 3, which is difficult, and this is a problem we get with most of the Asian children. So they stay at 2 for quite a long time, so we get a big range in that level. (Leung, 1999)

e) Interview: On seeing a video clip, the teacher interviewee commented that a particular pupil was able to understand very little until recently. She was invited to elaborate on that point.

Yeah, well she didn't know what was going on, whereas now looking at that tape I could see that she was trying to really interact with the other children. She was trying to join in. She most probably just didn't know what copying meant, when Saeeda said 'don't copy mine' or something and she said like 'yes' or whatever it was. But she most probably doesn't know what copying meant, but she was doing the right things. She knew it was a question and she obviously just wanted to interact.' (Leung, 1999, p. 235)

These comments suggest that the teacher informants were working with categories such as personality, family, sentence-level grammar from a (possibly untheorized) second language acquisition perspective, and different expectations of language development and sequence of development for second language students. These categories cannot be traced back to the level descriptions in the published National Curriculum English scales (see Appendix 1). The narrativized nature of some of the comments suggests that the teacher informants did not see the use or the learning of spoken language as just a school- or classroom-engendered activity; there is a strong sense that the total life experience of the student, as perceived by the teachers, was being brought into the picture. Breen (1997, p. 98) reports a broadly similar finding in a study of ESL assessment by elementary teachers working in Australia and cites this teacher statement as representative of the 25 teachers in the study: "What I observe and how they talk to me. A lot of it is observation and how they're relating to one another, how they're playing in the shops and how they're mixing."

The point about teachers attending to the 'whole child' has also been raised by Torrance and Pryor (1998). In their study of teacher assessment in elementary schools in England, they note that teachers tended to sit or stand with a particular group in class (whereas the rest got on with their work) and

> while the purpose ... was ostensibly to observe and question, often the opportunity arose to intervene and extend or "scaffold" the group's learning ... the teacher often appeared to be using a Vygotskian guided discovery approach to learning ... observing and questioning the group as they worked, but also intervening to support learning when appropriate ... (Torrance & Pryor, 1998, p. 29)

This Vygotskian approach, however, seemed to be more practice-based than a theoretically articulated position because the teachers concerned also spoke about learning in Piagetian terms of good management of learning tasks. Torrance and Pryor also observe that teacher assessment was seen by many of their teachers as a means of obtaining information about a child's knowledge and progress to plan forward and

> ... concern for the "whole-child" was noted with respect to making ipsative judgments about progress in the classroom—what had done before, whether what they were doing now represented real progress—irrespective of whether or not it met a criterion for a particular level of achievement ... (Torrance & Pryor, 1998, pp. 36–37).

In recent years elementary teachers in England have been encouraged to familiarize themselves with formal aspects of the English language and to teach explicitly the structural elements of English, including sentence-level grammar. Terms such as 'phonemes,' 'nouns,' and 'structure' have entered into the public curriculum discourse in highly visible forms through the official teaching programs (see, for example, Department for Education and Employment [DfEE], 1999). In an exploration of teachers' language knowledge, Gardner and Rea-Dickins (2001, p. 169), as part of their work on assessment of English language learners in mainstream classes, report that, among other things, in their data "only a limited set of such terms are available for confident use to some teachers." An example of this observation can be seen in the following teacher utterance when the teacher concerned was commenting on what she was trying to assess in a classroom question-and-answer exchange with a student about a visit to another school:

> ... understanding different **question forms**. The "what" particularly the "how" they found very difficult. And there's lots of ... there's *tell me about* ... that's not so much a question, *did you enjoy?*, *would you like to*. .... (Gardner & Rea-Dickins, 2001)

The teacher's attention was focused on the students' knowledge and understanding of different ways of asking questions. Gardner and Rea-Dickins point out that the teacher concerned appeared to be aware of the difference between form and function but the lack of an explicit language model and the associated metalanguage made it difficult for her to express her points directly. It seems quite clear that the teacher knew that 'tell me about ... ' was not in an interrogative form but was performing a question function. The issue here is not about that particular teacher's knowledge, but this observation points to the fact that teachers' own professional knowledge about the content of official curriculum and assessment schemes may not be taken for granted. Indeed, these studies raise a question about the role of professional development for teachers, particularly where several assessment schemes or frameworks, statutory and/or optional, are in place. In a study of the influence of teachers' working contexts on their use of ESL assessment frameworks in Australia, Rohl (1997, p. 88) reports that "where teachers had a choice of frameworks, they used those for which they had received professional development."

MOVING BEYOND PARADIGM-BOUND
CLAIMS AND STRICTURES

Whereas there is a great deal of potential pedagogic merit in teacher assessment, its formative (or perhaps more aptly, informative) value cannot be assumed just because of its apparent 'naturalness,' 'real-lifeness,' and 'directness' in the order of things in the classroom. The appeal to these qualities, as Huerta-Macías' and Gipps' arguments appear to have suggested, is in a sense a defensive strategy against criticisms stemming from a psychometric perspective on conventional notions of validity and reliability. Brown and Hudson's (1998, p. 656) injunction that "designers and users of alternative assessments must make every effort to structure the ways they design, pilot, analyze, and revise the procedures so the reliability and validity of the procedures can be studied, demonstrated, and improved" is understandable if the concern is with using teacher-made assessment for public accountability and student comparison purposes. In pedagogically integrated teacher assessment of individual students, the concerns for psychometric properties are not a priority. Indeed Lynch's (2001) discussion would suggest that different sets of epistemological and ontological questions should be asked for this kind of teacher assessment. The concept of construct-referenced assessment (Wiliam, 2001a) is useful in that it opens the way to an examination of the kind of information teachers seek and the basis of their decision making. In other words, it is precisely the 'naturalness' and 'real-lifeness' of teacher reasoning and teacher action that need examination.

The earlier discussion would suggest that in terms of institutional or community and individual practices there are at least three kinds of questions that require some immediate attention:

- What do teachers do when they carry out teacher assessment?
- What do teachers look for when they are assessing?
- What theory or "standards" do teachers use when they make judgments and decisions?

These questions should be posed with reference to real practitioner communities. If teacher assessment is to be understood as construct-referenced assessment situated in specific social and educational environments, then it would not be meaningful to attempt to address these questions as context-free phenomena at this stage of development. For instance, assessment descriptors such as "pupils show understanding of the ways in which meaning and information are conveyed in a range of texts" (Department for Education and Employment [DfEE], 1999, p. 57) necessarily take on a local interpretation. The available research evidence seems to indicate that there is a great deal of variability within individual education systems and among teachers within a locality. A well-recognized measure to reduce variability is to introduce or to increase the role of group moderation—teachers discussing samples of student work and attempting to achieve some degree of consensus, particularly in contexts where teachers are meant to use published criteria (and where the outcome of teacher assessment is also used for official or quasi-official recording and reporting purposes). Clarke and Gipps (2000, p. 40) argue that if we are "... 'to warrant assessment-based conclusions" without resorting to highly standardized procedures ... then we must ensure that teachers have common understandings of the criterion performance ... this can be developed through group moderation."

Group moderation can clearly play an important part in promoting some degree of consistency in the outcomes of teacher assessment. In general group moderation tends to be a part of the formal apparatus or infrastructure of official assessment systems. Everyday, ad hoc, nonreported teacher assessment that is key to effective teaching and learning is rarely, if ever, assisted by the facility of group moderation. However, the central idea behind group moderation, that is, teachers discussing their points of view and professional decisions about students' work, is potentially very useful in building up a shared understanding and practice within a community of teachers. The opportunities afforded by preservice teacher education and particularly in-service staff development programs can be used for this purpose. However, if teacher assessment is going to make a genuine contribution to the quality of teaching and learning, then it is necessary to move beyond achieving some sort of professional consensus among peers (which may be based on irrelevant or, worse, ill-informed opinions). McNamara (2001, pp. 344–345) argues that

> The role of the language testing researcher in aiding this process can include:
>
> - working to develop the articulation of constructs in assessment frameworks in such a way that they are potentially of maximum benefit to teachers in this process of reflection and evaluation of the detail of individual performance;
> - researching effective procedures for promoting critical reflection on learner performance by teachers, for example, by developing techniques and opportunities for reflection that can be carried out in 'real time' during classroom activity, and comparing them with "slowed down" procedures that require the recording of performance and subsequent analysis and evaluation for diagnostic purposes.

There is a strong intimation of a researcher-teacher collaborative approach to research that creates processes in which teachers are providers of data and active agents in professional development. In other words, teacher assessment development programs should be, among other things, concerned with expanding and/or helping to harness teachers' professional knowledge and know-how in relevant fields.

Three examples of the type of teacher assessment research and development work that may begin to address the issues raised by McNamara will be discussed here. All three are attempts to engage with some specific aspects of teacher assessment practice in the National Curriculum in England by making use of actual classroom data or professional knowledge and experience in professional development activities with trainee or practicing teachers. The first example is concerned with the assessment of spoken English. The second relates to assessment of written English and the third to teachers' understanding of the authority of the use of assessment scales for different purposes.

Example 1

The assessment of listening and speaking in English in elementary school is meant to be carried out by the teacher in ordinary classroom activities. Evidence reported earlier would suggest that teachers draw on criteria outside the current assessment scheme (Leung, 1999; Leung & Teasdale, 1997a, 1997b; Teasdale & Leung, 2000). Furthermore, the narrativized observational accounts offered by teachers are highly indicative of a view of students' use of English as straightforward evidence of what the students know, that is, the competence residing inside the individual. In other words, the interactive nature of classroom language and the part played by the teachers in shaping the interactions, and therefore the students' language use, appear to be hidden from view. One way of foregrounding the socially constructed and socially constrained nature of classroom language use is to look at some classroom interaction data and to draw attention to the teacher's part in shaping the students' use. The following is an example of the type of data that can be used[6]:

(Context of the activity: the teacher is trying to encourage the students to recall what happened in the previous numeracy session.)

T:	Oh dear dear dear dear dear! Do you remember we had some little pots like this on the table and how many coins did I tell you to choose to start with?
Ps:	Two!
T:	Two, so you chose two coins
Pupil 26:	We were
T:	No no da da dat And then what did you have to do?
Ps:	Draw them!
T:	You drew round them and then what did you do?
Pupil 27:	Had to count them.
T:	We had to
Ps:	Count them
T:	To see how, did you say how many? How
Ps:	Much
T:	Much! To see how much we've got. Let's do this one, look I've chosen a
Ps:	Five
T:	Five pence. How do I know it's a five pence?
Ps:	'Cos it's got five on it!
T:	'Cos it's got a five on it. And then what is this one?
Ps:	A two!
T:	And how do I know it's a two then?
Ps:	'Cos it's got a two on it!
T:	Right now, how many do we have to count on this time?
Ps:	Five!
Ps:	(echo) Five!
T:	Five. How many counts? How many counts on this one?
Ps:	Two!
Ps:	(echo) Two!
T:	Right let's do it all together, are you ready?

By describing and analyzing this short extract of the teacher–pupil interactions, it is possible to draw attention to, among other things, the teacher-directed nature of the interaction, the particular kind of framing of pupil responses, and the restricted nature of the students' language use. This kind of analysis could lead to wider discussions on the prevalence of the I(nitiation)-R(esponse)-F(eedback) pattern of classroom communication and alternatives that may engender richer language use (e.g., van Lier, 1996, 2000).

Example 2

This example is concerned with the assessment of written English. It has been widely accepted by elementary teachers working in multiethnic and multilingual schools that English language learners tend to be assessed at Level 2 English for a long time before they move up (see the relevant teacher remarks cited earlier in Leung, 1999). The following two written texts were produced by elementary students; Text 1 was written by an English language learner:

Text 1:
Once upon a time I was sleping in my bed room. Then suddely I feel over and I feelt a crown on my hede. And I was in Buckingham palace. Hooray hooray I

am a Qween. Bring me my food. yummy yummy dinner. Then she put her dres on. Then she went for a woock. And then she cam back home.

Text 2:
Once in the night I had a dream that I was Queen for the day. early next morning I woke up and I was still half a sleep and I banged in to the skirting board. I saw a crown fall in to the skirting board. I saw a crown fall of my head I said, 'wow, I'm Queen,' I yelled. I went to play with my xylophone it had all different kinds of jewel on it and diamonds on it. I went to London and then suddenly Buckingham Palace guards came and put swords up to my neck and said, 'who are you' and I said tiny voice I'm Queen Christina and get those filthy swords of of me 'certainly your highness. and they all kissed my hand and as soon as I got in I washed my hands with soap to get the grubi kissis of my hands. Then I opened up buckingham Palace and I had thousands of Jewels and that was the end of my day of being Queen.

Both texts were rated by the teacher (of the two students) as Level 2 written English (see Appendix 2 for level descriptions). By comparing and contrasting the language features and content of these two pieces of writing, it is possible to draw attention to, among other things, the interpretation of level description meaning; the differences between the two pieces in terms of grammatical accuracy, social and cultural knowledge, and knowledge of genre; the use of a mother tongue-normed assessment scale for students from diverse linguistic backgrounds, and the meanings of the assessment levels.

Example 3

The third example is concerned with teachers' understanding of the authority and the use of assessment scales for different purposes. A teacher recorded this in her audio-journal after an introductory session on the Australian-based ESL Scales (Curriculum Corporation, 1994), which was/is not widely used in England:
(The teacher started the diary by explaining that the students, aged 8 or 9, were regarded as at National Curriculum English Level 1; the normal expectation is for 7-year-olds to be at Level 2. She also explained that she was working with the students to develop their literacy in English and she had not been involved in the assessment of these children using the National Curriculum scales.)

Well I began reading the levels we were given [by the staff development tutor], and [the level descriptions] put me off really to start with because Level B1 it said beginning writing, I couldn't reconcile beginning writing with the fact that these children are 8 or 9 years old and all have been writing at least a year . . . and that definitely influenced the way I looked at that, uhm I quickly flipped through it, I could see that they were beyond that. I had a little look at Level B2, again a little bit longer, the suggestions of evidence, again I could see pretty quickly they've got beyond that as well. I suspected this to be the case, after all they were a good Level 1 under the English scheme. Looking at Level B3 I took a little longer over this because it says things like communication, write simply about topics of personal significance, write simply, write sentences that made a coherent statement, I began to think that perhaps I was getting close to my children. (Tape pause.)

I still couldn't get it out of my head that this Level B3 couldn't be relevant to my children because they weren't beginners in the time sense of the word. They've all got B3.5 and B3.6 but B3.7 they had some of these, they could do some of these but not all, and there seemed to be quite a difference in the level of expertise needed between some of these, for instance, the one which was based on write sentences, based on repetitive sentences, modelled patterns, they could all do that and certainly Kamal, he'd done an awful lot of that in his last year with me. And yet at the end they were to use basic punctuation to separate out ideas, capitals to start a sentence, full-stop to end, and Hilda definitely wasn't doing that. She's only got one full-stop in the middle of the page and one at the end of the page. She's got sentences in the middle which have no full-stop. So I did find that, I felt that the difference between the levels I'd expect to see those things in young children was quite different from what I'd expect to see them in an older child. (See Appendix 3 for relevant ESL Scales descriptors.)

This teacher's account can be used to trigger discussion on the differences between what McKay (2001) refers to as long-term and short-term assessment. In short-term assessment it is likely that the teacher would wish to pay close attention to the discrete items or performance indicators within a level description, for example, "recognize and respond to common signs, brand names, and advertisements and logos" (Curriculum Corporation, 1994, p. 64). One of the purposes for short-term assessment would be to look at students' achievement "in the task, the unit of work, or on the course of work" (McKay, 2001, p. 18). Pedagogically long-term assessment is concerned with students' progress over time to identify overall areas of strength and weakness, to plan for "teaching and learning to aim for end-of-school-study success" (McKay, 2001, p. 19). For long-term assessment, an assessment scale is more like a model of development. The levels within a scale represent a sort of route map that sets out the overall picture of progress. In this sense the individual components within a level matter less than the overall 'levelness.' Another possible topic of discussion would be the authority and the soundness of assessment scales. Some teachers may find the sequence of progression and/or the component parts of a particular level or stage ill-fitting in terms of their perceptions of students' performance. Any observed discrepancy can be used to open up explicit discussions on whether teachers' own professional experience and practically gained knowledge should have any role to play in interpreting and analyzing assessment scales and, in a more critical guise, whether published assessment schemes should be assessed and evaluated by teachers.

These are examples of some of the possibilities that have emerged in a specific educational context. Different or changing circumstances will produce different types of issues and possibilities. The important point here is that locally identified issues are worked on with reference to theory and principles drawn from the wider networks of research and scholarship. The researcher is positioned as an interested outsider whose claim to empirical knowledge crucially depends on access to actual and teachers' perceptions of classroom practice. This kind of researcher–teacher collaboration clearly has a professional development dimension with teachers' views and practices serving as starting points of discussion, not as "problems" to be fixed through in-service development activities. One of the roles of the researcher, qua professional development facilitator, in this context is to provide opportunities of critical engagement with information and theories emanating from relevant fields of research and education. And, equally important for this discussion, it requires the researcher to pay attention to teachers' ways of seeing and doing things as a primary research datum, not as points of information to be assimilated as data or rejected as irrelevant noise with reference to a pre-adopted theoretical model.

All this represents an epistemological departure from the practice of framing research within established paradigms and theoretical models in the psychometric tradition. Attending to teachers' professional knowledge and practice in this way systematically would contribute toward understanding the "construct" in construct-referenced assessment, a phenomenon that is far from clearly understood. This kind of understanding is vital for the development of a grounded, dynamic, and contextually sensitive research agenda. What is being suggested here is not some sort of value-free exercise whereby anything goes in the name of empiricism! This call for working with local teachers' assessment practice and perceptions as points of departure, providing teachers with access to wider theories and research literature, offering opportunities for critical discussion and reflection, and observing and charting these phenomena as part of research, is intended to contribute to the quality of teaching and learning.

CONCLUDING REMARKS

The strength and the value of pedagogically oriented classroom teacher assessment lie in its integration with the normal processes of teaching and learning. It can provide useful close-up information on student learning in context. The information generated can also be used indirectly to inform development or change in pedagogy and curriculum, and to provide feedback to students. In this sense, it plays an important and indispensable educational role that is quite different from standardized testing. On this view, it can be argued that teacher assessment is *sui generis* and therefore the evaluation criteria traditionally associated with psychometric testing such as reliability and validity are not necessarily and automatically relevant, especially when the outcomes of teacher assessment are not used for public comparison and reporting purposes.

The notion of construct-referenced assessment provides an interesting epistemological turn that can lead to a re-framing of questions to be asked. Instead of asking "How valid and reliable is teacher assessment?" as a form of testing, the questions are now "What do teachers look for in their classroom assessment?" and "How useful is the information produced by this kind of assessment for thinking about learning and teaching?". A related shift in orientation is the need to attend to the local as much as the universal or the general. All teaching and learning takes place in highly specific contexts—different participants, age groups, time periods, educational and social environments, and so on—and teacher assessment takes place within a unique mix of individuals and circumstances in each instance. This acknowledgment of the local argues for the building up of a close-up knowledge of a representative range of teacher practices before attempting generalizations, or to return to the point made by Wiliam (2001a, p. 172) cited earlier: "We try to theorize what is actually being done." Therefore at this stage of development it is important to ask the questions of teacher assessment raised here in relation to groups or communities of teachers working in broadly identifiable domains such as disciplines/subject areas or phases of education.

Linn, Baker, and Dunbar (1991, p. 17) argue that, with reference to what they refer to as complex, performance-based assessment, "High priority needs to be given to the collection of evidence about the intended and unintended effects of assessments on ways teachers and students spend their time and think about the goals of education. It cannot just be assumed that a more "authentic" assessment will result in classroom activities that are more conducive to learning." Recontextualizing this statement to the present discussion, it may well be said that one should not assume that just because teacher assessment takes place in natural and real classroom contexts, it will automatically yield pedagogically useful information or lead to higher quality learning or teaching. Much depends on teacher knowledge and action, both at the level of an individual practitioner and as a member of a community of practice. The research agenda for teacher assessment, seen in this light, should investigate what teachers look for and do when they carry out classroom assessment, how they use the information yielded for teaching purposes, and how this kind of research knowledge can be used in professional development.

APPENDIX 1

National Curriculum Subject English (DFE, 1995, p. 26)

Speaking and Listening Levels 1–3

Level 1

Pupils talk about matters of immediate interest. They listen to others and usually respond appropriately. They convey simple meanings to a range of listeners, speaking audibly, and begin to extend their ideas or accounts by giving some detail.

Level 2

Pupils begin to show confidence in talking and listening, particularly where the topics interest them. On occasions, they show awareness of the needs of the listener by including relevant detail. In developing and explaining their ideas they speak clearly and use a growing vocabulary. They usually listen carefully and respond with increasing appropriateness to what others say. They are beginning to be aware that in some situations a more formal vocabulary and tone of voice are used.

Level 3

Pupils talk and listen confidently in different contexts, exploring and communicating ideas. In discussion, they show understanding of the main points. Through relevant comments and questions, they show they have listened carefully. They begin to adapt what they say to the needs of the listener, varying the use of vocabulary and the level of detail. They are beginning to be aware of standard English and when it is used.

APPENDIX 2

National Curriculum (subject) English (DfEE & QCA, 1999, p. 59)

Writing Levels 1–2

Level 1

Pupils' writing communicates meaning through simple words and phrases. In their reading or their writing, pupils begin to show awareness of how full stops are used. Letters are usually clearly shaped and correctly orientated.

Level 2

Pupils' writing communicates meaning in both narrative and non-narrative forms, using appropriate and interesting vocabulary, and showing some awareness of the reader. Ideas are developed in a sequence of sentences, sometimes demarcated by capital letters and full stops. Simple, monosyllabic words are usually spelt correctly, and where there are inaccuracies the alternative is phonetically plausible. In handwriting, letters are accurately formed and consistent in size.

APPENDIX 3

ESL Scale Level B3 Beginning Writing (Curriculum Corporation, 1994, p. 47)

B3.7

Writes several coherently linked sentences using basic structures and well-known vocabulary.

Evident when students, for example:

- Write sentences based on simple repetitive, modeled patterns ('I play ...,' 'I go to lunch ...,' 'I go to home').

- Write sentences reflecting spoken English in vocabulary and structure (Yesterday I ... ,' then I ... ').
- Write 'run-on sentences' ('At school we work and at school we play and at school we read and at school ... ').
- Link sentences using common conjunctions (and, then, but).
- Write sentences using basic subject-verb-object patterns ('I study maths').
- Use common language patterns learned in class ('I can ,' 'he is ... ').
- Use the language of instruction for writing simple procedures (simple imperatives: draw, cut, stop, run).
- Write sentences using past tense verbs and adverbial phrases of time ('In holidays I went ... ').
- Use words commonly related to a topic (holiday, stay home, play).
- Use some standard English letter patterns when writing new words (scool for school, wite for white, sow for saw).
- Use basic punctuation to separate ideas (capitals to start a sentence, full stop to end a sentence).

NOTES

1. For further discussion on assessment and learning, see Black and Wiliam (1998a) and Black (2001).
2. Indeed, even the statement on teacher assessment by the QCA, an official curriculum and assessment authority in England, can be seen in this light.
3. The background reference is the work of Lave and Wenger (1991).
4. In England compulsory schooling is divided into four Key Stages—KS1covers ages 5–7, KS2 8–11, KS3 12–14, and KS4 15–16.
5. A set of modified Level 1 descriptors, together with two pre-Level 1 levels, were introduced recently to accommodate early stage English as an additional/second language students (QCA, 2000). These EAL-modified levels appear to have been written with very young children in mind. The assumption appears to be that once the students have passed the very early stages of learning English, they can be assessed according to the mother tongue-normed scales (DfEE & QCA, 1999). However, English language learners enter the school system at all ages.
6. This data is drawn from the Leverhulme Numeracy Program, a 5-year research program (1997–2002) that focuses on student attainment in numeracy and is based at King's College in London. The researchers are Alison Tomlin and Brian Street (King's College, London) and Dave Baker (Brighton University).

REFERENCES

Bachman, L. F. (2000). Modern language testing at the turn of the century: Assuring that what we count counts. *Language Testing, 17*(1), 1–42.

Bachman, L. F., & Palmer, A. S. (1996). *Language testing in practice.* Oxford, UK: Oxford University Press.

Black, P. (2001). Formative assessment and curriculum consequences. In D. Scott (Ed.), *Curriculum and assessment* (pp. 7–23). Westport, CT: Ablex.

Black, P., & Wiliam, D. (1998a). Assessment and classroom learning. *Assessment in Education, 5*(1), 7–73.

Black, P., & Wiliam, D. (1998b). *Inside the black box.* London: King's College London.

Breen, M. P. (1997). The relationship between assessment frameworks and classroom pedagogy. In M. Breen, C. Barratt-Pugh, B. Derewianka, H. House, C. Hudson, T. Lumley, & M. Rohl (Eds.), *Profiling ESL children: How teachers interpet and use National and State assessment frameworks* (Vol. 1, pp. 91–128). Canberra: DEETYA.

Brindley, G. (1998). Assessing in the AMEP: Current trends and future directions. *Prospect, 13*(3), 59–73.

Brindley, G. (2001). Outcomes-based assessment in practice: Some examples and emerging insights. *Language Testing, 18*(4), 393–407.

Brown, A. (1995). The effect of rater variables in the development of an occupation-specific language performance test. *Language Testing, 12*(1), 1–15.

Brown, J. D., & Hudson, T. (1998). The alternatives in language assessment. *TESOL Quarterly, 32*(4), 653–765.

Clarke, S., & Gipps, C. (2000). The role of teachers in teacher assessment in England 1996–1998. *Evaluation and Research in Education, 4*(1), 38–52.

Cohen, A. (1994). *Assessing language ability in the classroom.* (2nd ed.). Boston: Heinle & Heinle.

Curriculum Corporation. (1994). *ESL scales.* Melbourne: Curriculum Corporation.

Department for Education. (1995). *English in the national curriculum.* London: DfE.

Department of Employment and Education, & Qualifications and Curriculum Authority. (1999). *English: The national curriculum for England*. London: DfEE and QCA.

García, G. E., & Pearson, P. D. (1994). Assessment and diversity. In L. Darling-Hammond (Ed.), *Review of Research in Education, 20* (pp. 337–391). Washington, DC: American Educational Research Association.

Gardner, S., & Rea-Dickins, P. (2001). Conglomeration or chameleon? Teachers' representations of language in the assessment of learners with English as an additional language. *Language Awareness, 10*(2&3), 161–177.

Genesee, F., & Upshur, J. A. (1996). *Classroom-based evaluation in second language education*. Cambridge, UK: Cambridge University Press.

Gipps, C. (1994). *Beyond testing: Towards a theory of educational measurement*. London: Falmer Press.

Haertel, E. (1992). Performance measurement. In M. C. Alkins (Ed.), *Encyclopedia of Educational Research* (6th ed., Vol. 13, pp. 984–989). New York: Macmillan.

Huerta-Macías, A. (1995). Alternative assessment: Responses to commonly asked questions. *TESOL Journal, 5*, 8–11.

Lave, J., & Wenger, E. (1991). *Situated learning, legitimate peripheral participation*. Cambridge, UK: Cambridge University Press.

Leung, C. (1999). Teachers' response to linguistic diversity. In A. Tosi & C. Leung (Eds.), *Rethinking language education: From a monolingual to a multilingual perspective* (pp. 225–240). London: Centre for Information on Language Teaching and Research.

Leung, C., & Teasdale, A. (1997a). Raters' understanding of rating scales as abstracted concept and as instruments for decision making. *Melbourne Papers in Language Testing, 6*, 45–70.

Leung, C., & Teasdale, T. (1997b). What do teachers mean by speaking and listening: A contextualised study of assessment in the English National Curriculum. In A. Huhta, V. Kohonen, L. Kurki-Suonio, & S. Louma (Eds.), *New contexts, goals, and alternatives in language assessment* (pp. 291–324). Jyväskylä: University of Jyväskylä.

Linn, R. L., Baker, E. L., & Dunbar, S. B. (1991). Complex, performance-based assessment: Expectations and validation criteria. *Educational Researcher, 20*(8), 15–21.

Lynch, B. (2001). Rethinking assessment from a critical perspective. *Language Testing, 18*(4), 333–349.

McKay, P. (2001). *Innovation in English language assessment: Looking towards long-term learning*. Paper presented at the Innovation and Language Education—Selected Refereed Papers from the International Language in Education Conference, 2000, Hong Kong.

McNamara, T. (1997). 'Interaction' in second language performance assessment: Whose performance? *Applied Linguistics, 18*(4), 446–466.

McNamara, T. (2001). Language assessment as social practice: Challenges for research. *Language Testing, 18*(4), 333–349.

Murphy, P. (1996). Integrating learning and assessment—The role of learning theories? In P. Woods (Ed.), *Contemporary issues in teaching and learning* (pp. 173–193). London: Routledge & Kegan Paul.

Qualifications and Curriculum Authority. (2001). *Teacher assessment*. London: QCA. Available at http://www.qca.org.uk/ca/tests/ara/ks2_assessment.asp.

Qualifications and Curriculum Authority. (2000). *A language in common: Assessing English as an additional language*. London: QCA.

Rea-Dickins, P. (2001). Mirror, mirror on the wall: Identifying processes of classroom assessment. *Language Testing, 18*(4), 429–462.

Rohl, M. (1997). The influence of teachers' working contexts on their use of assessment frameworks. In M. Breen, C. Barratt-Pugh, B. Derewianka, H. House, C. Hudson, T. Lumley, & M. Rohl (Eds.), *Profiling ESL children: How teachers interpet and use National and State assessment frameworks* (Vol. 1, pp. 67–90). Canberra: DEETYA.

Teasdale, A., & Leung, C. (2000). Teacher assessment and psychometric theory: A case of paradigm crossing? *Language Testing, 17*(2), 163–184.

TESOL. (1998). *Managing the assessment process: A framework of measuring student attainment of the ESL standards*. Alexandria, VA: Teachers of English to Speakers of Other Languages.

Torrance, H., & Pryor, J. (1998). *Investigating formative assessment; Teaching, learning, and assessment in the classroom*. Maidenhead, UK: Open University Press.

van Lier, L. (1996). *Interaction in the language curriculum: Awareness, autonomy, and authenticity*. London: Longman.

van Lier, L. (2000). From input to affordance: Social-interactive learning from an ecological perspective. In J. P. Lantolf (Ed.), *Sociocultural theory and second language learning.* (pp. 245–259). Oxford, UK: Oxford University Press.

Wiliam, D. (2001a). An overview of the relationship between assessment and the curriculum. In D. Scott (Ed.), *Curriculum and assessment* (pp. 165–181). Westport, CT: Ablex.

Wiliam, D. (2001b). Reliability, validity, and all that jazz. *Education, 3*(13), 17–21.

VII

Identity, Culture, and Critical Pedagogy in Second Language Teaching and Learning

Introduction

In the 1950s, 1960s, and 1970s, second language (L2) teaching and learning were largely seen as having to do with the formal properties of language, such as grammar, lexicon, and pronunciation. In the 1980s, however, researchers and practitioners began to recognize that learning a second language involves a great deal more than attaining L2 linguistic proficiency. In her study of culture and the individual, Rosaldo (1984) points out that the constructs of personhood, identity, culture, and language are intertwined in the social milieu where people live and the reality that they construct. According to Rosaldo, culture shapes and binds an individual's or a group's social and cognitive concepts.

The study of identity and culture, and critical perspectives on L2 pedagogy are relatively late arrivals on the scene of language teaching and learning. In general, research into these abstract facets of second language are concerned with construction of identity in various social and linguistic contexts, culture as the way of life of a people, the social frameworks that evolve within a group or a larger society (Hinkel, 1999). On the other hand, researchers believe that language use may have little to do with the true causes of human behavior and often serves to mask them.

By the 1980s and 1990s, research on L2 teaching and learning also added a focus on the social contexts in which second languages are taught and learned. In recent years, multidisciplinary studies on culture have been carried out in various domains of applied linguistics, sociolinguistics, and language policy. The environments in which languages are learned and taught often serve as research grounds where the impact on L2 learning of learners' identities, culture, and predominant approaches to language teaching can be examined. The new venues of investigation began to address the many complex issues of social identity, culture, and power that are inextricably intertwined.

A large number of publications emerged to describe and analyze the profound impact of sojourn and immigration and the vital need for L2 learning on individuals' views of themselves and their environments. For example, Peirce (1995) explains that social identity can be understood in terms of how people see themselves and their social roles in relation to others, as well as the ways in which they understand their past, present, and future.

In research on social contexts of language teaching and learning, the concepts of identity and culture are not static, but complex, perpetually evolving, and sensitive to such diverse social constructs as social status, education, language contact, current and shifting ideologies, and historical and political legacies. A different perspective on how one's identity can be bound up with language lies in the combined macro- and microanalytic approach. The sociocultural view of research presents a broad picture of how language contributes to the formation of identity and culture within the social contexts and the politics of power and how cultural identity is continually threatened by economic, political, and power-balance insecurities.

The three chapters in Part VII emphasize that language or a language variety is fundamentally tied to the construction of identity of individuals, as members of social groups. For example, such languages as English, which has become a lingua franca, have been themselves altered and "nativized" in various parts of the world. As an outcome, the nativization of language gives rise to new varieties, new discourses, and linguistic identities that emerge at the conflation of a language's past and present.

- In Chapter 49, "Considerations of Identity in L2 Learning," **Thomas Ricento** considers sociocultural aspects and processes of identity construction and change. In recent years, many innovative studies in Applied Linguistics have focused on the sociocultural rather than psychological dimensions of identity, and Ricento's perspective primarily encompasses the research on the complex connections among language, identity, and social discourses bound up with relations of power. Thus, identity is proposed to be a contingent process that pivots on the dialectic relations between learners and the various worlds and experiences. Since an individual identity is not fixed but is transformed by experience, the transnational character of various immigrant communities can have many implications for language pedagogy and learning. Ricento emphasizes that common and often popular assumptions that immigrants who arrive in the United States have the goal of assimilating and losing their native language and culture do not apply. In L2 teaching, the identities of L2 learners are deeply connected to their membership in distinct, but frequently interrelated, communities.
- In Chapter 50, "Teaching and Researching Intercultural Competence," **Michael Byram** and **Anwei Feng** present a sociolinguistic and ethnosemantics point of view to promote culture teaching and learning in education. They emphasize that in education and learning of culture, the issues of values and ideology play a prominent role, and thus, language teaching susceptible to political and social influences necessarily entails political education and the many considerations of "neohumanist" practices, and cultural relativity. Both teachers and learners need to see as critical the findings of attitudes and motivation research, as well as the complex relationships between teaching styles, materials, methods, and learners' ability to adopt new perspectives. In all, Byram and Feng point out that the cultural dimension and intercultural competence in language teaching has grown to become a new emphasis in language teaching and learning. On the other hand, whereas attaining intercultural competence may be seen as positive, it also necessitates the development of critical awareness and the pursuit of democratic processes and values.

The issue of power and its maintenance and distribution in language teaching and learning, and in the wider society represents a key consideration in critical pedagogy. This domain of critical analysis focuses on how and in whose interests knowledge is promulgated and teaching is carried out. Ideally, critical pedagogy envisions the goals of learning and education as directed toward the emancipation of the learner. One of the main tenets of critical pedagogy is that the very enterprise of teaching in general, and language teaching in particular, constitute a part of the system of beliefs and values that have the combined effect of maintaining an unequal distribution of power in the society.

- In Chapter 51, "Critical Pedagogy in L2 Learning and Teaching," **Suresh Canagarajah** states clearly that teaching language to students from many minority groups is a political activity that for far too long L2 teachers and researchers have had an "idyllic" view of their work. Canagarajah argues that, when L2 teaching is seen as a means for providing students linguistic and communicative skills, they simply overlook the fact that this activity is motivated by geopolitical realities. Thus, according to Canagarajah, the dominant principles in language teaching have long served to hide the controversial means toward ideological ends within the social power structure. Critical pedagogy is not merely a set of ideas or theories, but a way of carrying out language teaching and learning motivated by a clear-cut attitude toward classrooms as a part of a wider society. Canagarajah asserts that students and teachers alike must be prepared to understand how teaching and learning are part and parcel of the social contexts of power and identify the ways to unmask the implications of power in teaching. The purpose of critical pedagogy is to transform the means and ends of learning and to construct more egalitarian, equitable, and ethical educational and social environments untainted by power and domination. Canagarajah defines the term "critical" as intended to contrast with such terms as "detached, objective, dispassionate, instrumental, practical, and descriptive" that have been used to describe "noncritical" traditions of the L2 enterprise.

REFERENCES

Hinkel, E. (Ed.). (1999). *Culture in second language teaching and learning.* Cambridge, UK: Cambridge University Press.

Peirce, B. N. (1995). Social identity, investment, and language learning. *TESOL Quarterly, 29*(1), 9–31.

Rosaldo, M. (1984). Toward an anthropology of self and feeling. In R. Shweder & R. LeVine (Eds.), *Culture theory* (pp. 137–157). Cambridge, UK: Cambridge University Press.

49

Considerations of Identity in L2 Learning

Thomas Ricento
University of Texas, San Antonio

INTRODUCTION

My focus in this chapter will be on the sociocultural dimensions and processes of identity formation and transformation as they relate to the varied contexts of second language learning. A great deal of attention has been paid to this topic in recent years in the literatures of second language learning and applied linguistics. In this chapter, I will highlight important theoretical and methodological approaches that have helped to expand and enrich our understanding of commonly used terms in second language acquisition (SLA) theory such as motivation, native speaker, and second language proficiency. My focus will be on the sociocultural rather than psychological dimensions of identity, as this is the area in which the greatest innovation has taken place in applied linguistics research.

Much of the research I will describe concerns the ways in which identity is constituted through and by language, and how these processes occur within broader social discourses with their inscribed power relations. Applied linguists and second language acquisition (SLA) researchers have developed frameworks for exploring how a learner's identity influences, and is influenced by, the various settings in which learning takes place. Within sociocultural approaches (e.g., Bakhtin, 1986; Bourdieu, 1991; Lantolf, 2000; Le Page & Tabouret-Keller, 1985; Ochs, 1988; Schecter & Bayley, 1997; Vygotsky, 1978), identity is not viewed as a fixed, invariant attribute in the "mind" of the individual learner. Rather, identity is theorized as a contingent process involving dialectic relations between learners and the various worlds and experiences they inhabit and which act on them. Since individual identity is not a fixed attribute, it is inaccurate to ascribe totalizing group-based identities and behaviors based on language, ethnicity, religion, or national origin. It is neither descriptively accurate nor pedagogically useful to classify, for example, Japanese students as diffident, introverted, and nonlinear thinkers, as has often been the case in previous positivistic research (see Kubota, 1999, for discussion on this point). Although a particular cultural group may share common beliefs and practices, the representation of these beliefs and practices as ethnic *traits* perpetuates stereotypical thinking about the 'other' that is often based on cultural constructions imposed by 'outsiders' through various contact processes: conquest, intermarriage, absorption (see, for example, Said, 1993, and Willinsky, 1998, on the legacies of imperialism). These sociocultural constructions of the 'other' may eventually come to be seen as self-evident not only by the 'outside' group but to varying degrees and in various guises by the culture thus described as well. Furthermore, attempts to legitimize the 'other' usually results in the reaffirmation of normative categories in which the 'normal' (for example, heterosexuality or Western ways of thinking) is counterpoised to the 'other' (for example, homosexuality or Oriental ways of thinking).

Glynn Williams (1999) argues that in American sociology, ethnicity became a dichotomized construct of the normative/standard group—a unitary citizenry speaking a common language (us)—and non-normative/nonstandard groups—including those speaking other languages—(them). This naturalizing of a sociological construct (ethnicity) informs the widely held popular view promoted by Western scholarship that 'reasonable' (modern) people should naturally become part of the culture of the state (or the transnational world) and speak 'its' language, whereas 'irrational' (traditional) people will tend to cling to their 'ethnic language and culture.' Yet, the prevalence of cultural hybridity and multilingualism throughout the non-Western (and, increasingly, Western) world suggests that received views are no longer descriptively adequate. In SLA and Applied Linguistics research, attribution of group-based, ethnic characteristics has tended to perpetuate difference in negative terms vis-à-vis Western, and especially Anglo-American, norms and expectations (see Pennycook, 1998, for an extended discussion on this point; and Dwight Atkinson, 1999, for analysis and discussion of the role of culture in second language acquisition research and pedagogy). Therefore, characterizations of, for example Japanese, let alone 'Asian' students, are likely to be more harmful than helpful to language educators. Nor can one's social or cultural identities or affiliations be predicted by the language(s) that person speaks.

IDENTITY AND SLA RESEARCH

Approaches to identity in (SLA) research have changed considerably over the past decades, reflecting shifts in thinking about how and why second and foreign language learning takes place, and especially the nature and effects of interactions between the learner and contexts of learning. It is useful to understand why these changes in approach occurred in order to contextualize current thinking about identity and language learning.

Early work in SLA was influenced by the theories of social identity developed by Tajfel (1981). Tajfel understood social identity as being derived from an individual's membership in a social group (or groups). If an individual's emotional needs were not met by their identification with a particular group, that person could change their group affiliation(s), although that might not always be possible. Drawing on this work, Giles and Johnson (1981, 1987) developed their ethnolinguistic identity theory in which language was posited as a prominent marker of group membership and social identity. If a change in group membership involved linguistic adaptation, one result could be subtractive bilingualism or even language erosion and loss over time. The connections between language and identity have been explored as well by interactional sociolinguists, such as Gumperz (1982) and Heller (1982, 1987, 1995). In this research, both the choice of language (code) and the use of the code in particular ways signal "social relationships based on shared or unshared group memberships" (Heller, 1982, p. 5). Gumperz (1982, p. 66) used the terms "we code" to characterize the minority, in-group language, and "they code" to characterize the majority, out-group language. Gumperz notes that code switching is used to signal various group memberships and identities. In SLA research, identity was conceptualized as a group attribute. A key concept in several theories is that of *social distance*, a concept that was operationalized in John Schumann's Acculturation Model (1976, 1978). Distance here was used in an abstract (even metaphorical) sense to indicate the degree of similarity between two cultures. Schumann hypothesized that the greater the social distance between two cultures, the more difficulty the learner would have in acquiring the target language, whereas the smaller the social distance, the more likely the learner would be successful in acquiring the target language. Schumann assumed that less social distance entailed greater social solidarity between two cultures. In other words, the degree to which the learner *identifies* with another culture, the more motivated he or she will be to acquire that culture's language.

Although Schumann's model provided language educators with useful metaphors to guide their practice and seemed to comport with many of their intuitions about the whys and wherefores of successful SLA, it has not stood up to empirical scrutiny, in part because it attempts to control for dynamic, interactive processes that are not easily isolated or measured. In fact, even on its own terms, Schumann's hypothesis is not upheld. Analysis of Schumann's original data shows that his primary informant, "Alberto," *was* progressing toward more frequent use of targetlike forms despite his relative isolation and distance from native speakers of English in the United States (Berdan, 1996).

Another model from SLA research of relevance to any discussion of identity was proposed by Gardner and Lambert (1972). These researchers studied foreign language learners in Canada, the United States, and the Philippines to determine the role played by attitude and motivation in language learning. Based on their research, they divided clusters of attitudes into two basic types of motivation: instrumental and integrative. Instrumental motivation reflects targeted, pragmatic purposes for learning a language, such as for career advancement, to study in another country, to pass an important exam, and so on. Integrative motivation comes about when a learner has a desire to integrate themselves within the second language cultural group, to become a part of that society. Lambert found that integrative motivation was associated with high scores on proficiency tests in a foreign language. The conclusion was that a high degree of integrative motivation tended to correlate better with successful L2 acquisition than did instrumental motivation, although there could be exceptions. Other scholars soon reported contrary findings. Lukmani (1972) investigated the English acquisition of Marathi-speaking Indian students and found those with higher instrumental motivation scored high in tests of English proficiency. Au (1988) reviewed 27 studies that employed the integrative-instrumental construct and found that the measurement of motivation and the theory behind these measurements were questionable. Modifications to the theory were proposed, including one by Graham (1984) who argued that integrative assimilation could be broken down into integrative and assimilative motivation. Integrative motivation concerns a language learner's desire to learn the target language to be able to communicate with, or find out about, members of the target language culture, and does not imply direct contact with the target language group. In contrast, assimilative motivation is the desire to become an indistinguishable member of the target speech community, and usually requires prolonged contact with that community (in Brown, 1994, p. 155). The important point to note here is the presupposition that a learner should be comfortable with and positively disposed toward a target culture group in order to successfully acquire the language, and if the learner *identifies* with that culture, he or she will more likely be motivated to acquire the target language. One problem with these approaches is that they presuppose (often unwittingly) an exclusively *assimilationist* model in which the price of acceptance into a host culture is the loss of one's identity, or at the least the adoption of dual identities. Another possibility, to be discussed in the next section, is that identities in multilingual contexts are transformed, complex, dynamic, and variable.

The bias in much of the SLA research from the 1960s through the 1980s presupposed the conflictual aspects of language contact. Borrowing from the cultural anthropological literature (e.g., Foster, 1962, Hall, 1959), applied linguists tended to characterize L2 learning as a "clash of consciousness" Mark Clarke (1976, p. 380) likened second language learning to schizophrenia in which "social encounters become inherently threatening, and defense mechanisms are employed to reduce the trauma." Acculturation was described by Brown (1994, p. 171, relying on the research of Larson & Smalley, 1972) as proceeding through four stages: euphoria, culture shock, culture stress, assimilation or adaptation to the new culture and acceptance of the "new" person that has developed. Recent qualitative research, including first-person accounts in the form of personal narratives (to be discussed later), provides a far more complex picture of what can happen in second language contact situations.

To summarize earlier work in SLA research, there was little emphasis on the interaction of an individual's multiple memberships based on gender, class, race, linguistic repertoire, or on how these memberships were understood and played out in different learning contexts (although see McNamara, 1997, for a discussion of the continuing relevance of Tajfel's theories in SLA research). Furthermore, the motivation of L2 learners was often measured in relation to optimal models of positive identification leading to assimilation of some type, or to less than optimal models leading to varying degrees of failure to assimilate and, as a result, failure to acquire nativelike fluency in the target language. It is no accident that the use of dichotomous and scalar *etic* variables from psychology and sociology coincided with the positivistic, structural paradigms that guided (and continue to guide) SLA research (see Pennycook, 1989, and Lantolf, 1996, for a discussion of positivism in Applied Linguistics research). As new theories from poststructuralist and critical paradigms became influential in Applied Linguistics research, the characterizations of learners and the contexts in which learning occurs changed dramatically.

RECENT APPROACHES TO IDENTITY IN SLA RESEARCH

Language, Identity, and Investment

In a series of articles (1995, 1997), a special-topic issue of *TESOL Quarterly* (31(3), 1997), and a monograph (2000), Bonny Norton has developed a number of ideas with important consequences for second language acquisition theory. In a richly contextualized qualitative study involving five female immigrant language learners in Canada, Norton (2000, p. 5) shows how learner identity influences motivation and, ultimately, acquisition of a second language. Norton uses the term identity "to reference how a person understands his or her relationship to the world, how that relationship is constructed across time and space, and how the person understands possibilities for the future." At least two aspects of SLA theory are called into question by Norton. First, she claims that SLA theorists "have not developed a comprehensive theory of identity that integrates the language learner and the language learning context . . . furthermore, they have not questioned how relations of power in the social world impact on social interaction between second language learners and target language speakers" (p. 4). She cites the work of Monica Heller (1987) who demonstrates the central role of language in the negotiation of a person's sense of self at different points in time and in different contexts, and in allowing a person access (or lack thereof) to powerful social networks that give learners the opportunity to speak. Following Foucault (1980), Norton takes the position that "power does not operate only at the macro level of powerful institutions such as the legal system, the education system and the social welfare system, but also at the micro level of everyday social encounters between people with differential access to symbolic and material resources—encounters that are inevitably produced within language" (Norton, 2000, p. 7).

Another important influence on Norton's work comes from French sociologist Pierre Bourdieu, whose work on the relation between identity and symbolic power is invoked to help explain how hierarchies based on social status influence the "right to speech," which Norton translates from the French to mean the "right to speak," as well as the "power to impose reception" (Bourdieu, 1977, p. 75). Bourdieu's notion of cultural capital is particularly relevant for research in language and identity. According to Bourdieu and Passeron (1977), cultural capital refers to the "knowledge and modes of thought that characterize different classes and groups in relation to specific sets of social forms" (cited in Norton, 2000, p. 10). Norton uses the term *investment* to characterize the complex motives and desires that language learners may have vis-à-vis a target language. According to Norton, "if learners invest in a second language, they do so with the understanding that they will acquire a wider range of symbolic and material resources, which will in turn increase the value of their cultural capital" (p. 10). Furthermore, because learners have complex social histories and multiple desires, "they are constantly organizing and reorganizing a sense of who they are and how they relate to the social world. Thus an investment in the target language is also an investment in a learner's own identity, an identity which is constantly changing across time and space" (p. 11).

The implications of this approach for SLA research can be summarized. First, the assumption that SLA researchers and educators should operate with is that "speech, speakers, and social relationships are inseparable" (Norton, 1997, p. 410). Therefore, theories and research in SLA that do not take into full account the social aspect of language learning and use cannot be taken seriously. Second, an individual's identity in L2 contexts is mediated by the reactions of others to that individual's social and cultural position, which, in turn, can influence that individual's motivation to learn in ways that are not predictable using standard psychological or sociological categories and variables mentioned earlier in this chapter. Norton's (2000) study of immigrant female language learners in Canada demonstrates the different effects of diverse and complex social interactions on the learners' acquisition and use of English.

Norton's idea of *investment* has been used by other researchers in diverse settings. McKay and Wong (1996) found that the needs and desires of language learners determined their investment in learning the target language. Angelil-Carter (1997) found it useful to break down the concept of investment into specific domains of learning, such as literacies, or other discourses "that are dislodged and reconstructed over time and space" (p. 268). Along these lines, Starfield (2002) shows how in postapartheid South Africa differential ability to use linguistic features of authority within the essay-text genre results in one (White) student's ability to construct a powerful, authoritative textual and discoursal identity for himself, whereas another (Black) student, who relies on the words of recognized authorities in the discipline, is labeled a plagiarizer. The successful student relies on his highly developed 'textual' capital; the unsuccessful student fails to negotiate an authoritative "self as author" (p. 121).

Language, Identity, and Gender

The study of language and gender in linguistics coincided with the growth of the feminist movement in the 1970s. Early work by Lakoff (1975) and Thorne and Henley (1975) stimulated several decades of research on the relations among sex, power, and language. This research has been subsumed under the headings *deficit*, *dominance*, and *difference*. Within the deficit framework, women were characterized as deficient in their use of language compared to men (e.g., Lakoff, 1975). Thus, Lakoff argued, women used more tag questions (e.g., *You're coming to dinner tomorrow, aren't you*?), hedges, certain 'feminine' adjectives and expressions, and so on compared to men. Lakoff argued that these linguistic structures reflected females' relative insecurity and inferior social position in relation to males. In the dominance model (e.g., Fishman, 1983; West & Zimmerman, 1983; Zimmerman & West, 1975), patterns of male-female interactions in conversation were analyzed. By measuring the amount of talk, nature and frequency of interruptions, number of questions asked, number of turns taken, and ability to introduce and maintain conversational topics, these researchers provided quantitative evidence to support the claim that male-female conversational patterns mirrored broader social power imbalances. Specifically, they found that in mixed gender conversations, men talked and interrupted more than women, occupied more of the conversational 'floor,' and were more successful in controlling the topic of conversation. The third paradigm, the gender differences model, argued that men and women were socialized in different cultures (male and female) in which they learned different rules for appropriate verbal interaction (e.g., Maltz & Borker, 1982; Tannen, 1990). According to Tannen, women are socialized to be concerned about maintaining social relations and solidarity in their conversations, whereas men are socialized to be more focused on the informational aspects of conversation, concerned more about their status than on the feelings of their interlocutors.

Applied linguists interpreted findings in the difference approach as supporting their claims that female learners have superior learning strategies compared to men (e.g., Oxford, 1993). SLA researchers influenced by the two cultures approach found, for example, that men interact to produce more output (Gass & Varonis, 1986) and that female NSs were likely to ask more helpful questions and to negotiate meaning in a more consistent way than male NSs (Pica et al., 1991).

Critical work in the 1990s (e.g., Cameron, 1992; Eckert & McConnell-Ginet, 1999; Gal, 1991; Trömel-Plötz, 1991) showed the ways in which earlier research tended to essentialize 'women' and 'men' and failed to consider the effects of different interactional contexts in diverse cultural settings. The shortcomings of the deficit, dominance, and difference paradigms in language and gender research stem, in large part, from the conceptualization of gender as a series of personal traits or attributes rather than as a socially constructed set of relations and practices (Pavlenko & Piller, 2001, p. 22). Within critical, and especially postmodern, theory gender is not viewed as a static (or stable) attribute, but rather as "a system of social relations and discursive practices" (p. 23). Therefore, gender itself as a social variable is mediated by other social variables, such as race, social class, educational background and experience, cultural norms, and so on. Understood in this way, gender itself is neither exclusively (or always) enabling or disabling in terms of language acquisition, learning, or use.

Pavlenko and Piller (2001, p. 17) cite several researchers (e.g., Ehrlich, 1997; Woolard, 1997) who have pointed out the growing gap between the study of SLA and bilingualism and the study of language and gender. To remedy this situation, they propose to bring together the disparate literatures of second language acquisition and bilingualism, and the study of language and gender into a new framework they label multilingualism, second language learning, and gender. In doing this, Pavlenko and Piller describe four areas of research that could comprise such a field of inquiry and report important findings within each area. Three of these four areas are of particular importance to L2 educators and will be described here.

The first area is 'Gendered access to linguistic resources in multilingual contexts.' The research Pavlenko and Piller present is concerned with the ways in which gender privileges access to second language skills in different societies. For example, they cite research by Goldstein, (1995), Harvey (1994), Hill (1987), Holmes (1993), Lofton (1996), Losey (1995), Spedding (1994), Stevens (1986), and Swigart (1992) that shows the ways in which men have access to the symbolic capital of a second language, whereas women are restricted by various gatekeeping practices from gaining access to majority language education and the workplace (p. 24). Pavlenko and Piller also cite research that shows how men are disadvantaged by ideologies of language and gender from achieving success in L2 learning (e.g., Günthner, 1992; Moon, 2000).

The second area of research findings in this proposed new paradigm concerns 'Gendered agency in second language learning and use.' The research grouped under this heading explores the intrinsic relationship between gender and agency in the process of L2 learning and use. According to Pavlenko and Piller (2001, p. 29):

> This view implies that in some cases L2 users may decide to learn the second, or any additional, language only to a certain extent, which allows them to be proficient, but without the consequences of losing the old and adopting the new ways of being in the world. In other contexts, their L2 learning may be accompanied by a full transition to the new linguistic community and L1 loss. And yet in others they may resist the language that positions them unfavorably.

Examples of these three possible outcomes are provided. Of particular interest to ESL/EFL educators are studies that show that women around the world are learning English as a means of liberating themselves from the confines of patriarchy (Kobayashi, 2000; Matsui, 1995; Solé, 1978). Other research shows how women are motivated to learn a second language in order to improve their social and economic status (e.g., Gal, 1978; McDonald, 1994).

The third area described by Pavlenko and Piller is 'Critical and feminist pedagogy.' Of particular interest in this area is gender representation in teaching materials. Borrowing from linguistic research on the various ways in which the English language represents gendered social relations and hierarchies (e.g., Graddol & Swann, 1989), applied linguists and TESL/TEFL specialists have analyzed how these representations are reproduced in ESL textbooks. For example, content analyses of ESL textbooks published in the 1970s and 1980s revealed stereotyped male and female roles and promoted the use of masculine generics such as 'he,' 'man,' or 'mankind' (Hartman & Judd, 1978; Porreca, 1984; Sunderland, 1992). Other more recent studies have found stereotypical portrayals of gender roles in EFL textbooks published in Japan (McGregor, 1998) and Russian textbooks published in the United States (Shardakova & Pavlenko, 2004). Cynthia Nelson (1999) argues that queer theory, as opposed to the straight/gay binary, offers the possibility of problematizing the very notion of sexual identities in ESL/EFL classrooms. Nelson comments that "a queer approach recognizes that sexual identities are not universal but are done in different ways in different cultural contexts, and it calls for a close look at how identities are produced through day-to-day interactions" (pp. 377–378).

Language, Identity, Race, and Ethnicity

Ethnicity, like race, is a sociological construct that both reflects and serves various sociopolitical interests. One's ethnicity may be ascribed, chosen, contested, and/or contingent. As Heller (1987) points out, ethnicity is a product of opposition because persons growing up in a homogeneous society would not define themselves nor be defined as ethnic. Within postmodern scholarship, ethnicity is understood as being produced in specific circumstances of social, economic, and historical relations of power that are reinforced and reproduced in everyday social encounters (Norton, 2000, p. 13). In concurrence with Rockhill (1987), Norton (2000, p. 13) takes the position that "ethnicity, gender, and class are not experienced as a series of discrete background variables, but are all, in complex and interconnected ways, implicated in the construction of identity and the possibilities of speech."

Recently, this position has been explored in a variety of L2 contexts. A number of studies and special-topic issues of journals (e.g., *Linguistics and Education, 8*(1,2), 1996; *Journal of Sociolinguistics, 3*(4), 1999; *The International Journal of Bilingualism, 5*(2), 2001) have examined the complex relations between choice of code and learner identity in defined contexts. An important finding has been that the language(s) (and language varieties) one speaks are not necessarily markers of a particular ethnic identity. Depending on where, when, and how a second or third language is acquired, a speaker's identification with that language (and the culture with which it is identified) will vary in often unpredictable ways. This is demonstrated in the research of Rampton (1995, 1999a, 1999b); Leung, Harris, and Rampton (1997); Blackledge and Pavlenko (2001); Pavlenko (1998), among others. To capture the complexity of learner identity in ESL contexts, Leung, Harris, and Rampton (1997, p. 418) suggest that the terms 'native speaker' and 'mother tongue' be changed to 'language expertise,' 'language inheritance,' and 'language affiliation.' Instead of asking "Is the learner a native speaker of Punjabi?", the teacher should ask "What is the learner's linguistic repertoire? Is the learner's relationship to these languages based on expertise, inheritance, affiliation, or a combination?" (p. 418). In an ethnographic study of a Sikh community in England, Hall (2002) explores the contrast between Punjabi as a reified political symbol and the ways in which Sikh teenagers actually use Punjabi in different contexts and for different purposes. Hall (2002, p. 114) notes that as these teenagers move through the social worlds that constitute their everyday lives "[they] actively construct linguistic practices that make use of a mixture of linguistic forms and styles in relation to influences, expectations, and interests that are situational and shifting. Sikh teens assess and reassess the value of Punjabi as they participate in different types of social interaction, media consumption, and cultural events." In a critical ethnographic study of Francophone African youths studying ESL in an urban Canadian setting, Ibrahim (1999, p. 349) argues that these youths enter "a *social imaginary*—a discursive space in which they are already imagined, constructed, and thus treated as Blacks by hegemonic discourses and groups... This imaginery... influences what and how these students linguistically and culturally learn... [i.e.,] Black stylized English, which they access in hip-hop culture and rap lyrical and linguistic styles."

Two special issues of *Linguistics and Education* titled "Education in Multilingual Settings: Discourse, Identities, and Power" (Martin-Jones & Heller, 1996) explore "the role of education in the production and reproduction of cultural identity and social inequality in multilingual communities" (p. 4). A common framework to the research presented, borrowed from Bourdieu (1977, 1982), is *legitimate language*. The editors have chosen multilingual settings as particularly revealing sites to explore the role played by schools in the production and reproduction of social identities and unequal relations of power, since the "language practices of educational institutions are bound up in the legitimization of relations of power among ethnolinguistic groups" (p. 128). The editors also correctly point out that these processes must be contextualized within broader historical processes of colonialism, postcolonialism, globalization, and nationalist and minority rights movements (e.g., Grillo, 1989; May, 2001; Phillipson, 1992; Tollefson, 1991). The articles in Volume I focus on the ways in which participants in different educational activities contribute (often unwittingly) to the (re)production of hegemonic relations through their bilingual or monolingual discursive practices in the postcolonial nations of Botswana, Burundi, Hong Kong, and Malta, along with England. The research in Volume II focuses on the ways in which participants in educational settings contest the legitimacy of discursive practices and the prevailing symbolic order in Canada, England, Brazil, and Australia.

The findings of this research suggest that the roles played by dominant groups in multilingual educational settings have direct and indirect consequences on language acquisition processes. For example, if greater value is attached to language x than language y, this will be conveyed through classroom interactions (how do participants express their attitudes and beliefs about a language, and its speakers, through their discourses), curricular choices (which language is used for instruction, which language has value for particular educational paths), linguistic behavior (which variety of a language is valued or devalued, and how are these perceived evaluations reflected in learners' linguistic repertoires), learners' identities (how do learners see themselves positioned in relation to other languages and cultures), and motivations (is the learner positively or negatively motivated to learn the language, generally, and for what purposes). The research presented in Martin-Jones and Heller (1996) offers an important theoretical and methodological framework for investigating relations between power, identity, and second language learning.

Native Speaker, Non-native Speaker, and Identity

A great deal of SLA and foreign language (FL) research has focused on mismatches between the learner's culture and target language culture to account for the learner's inability to achieve "nativelike" proficiency in a second or foreign language. The use of the term "nativelike" by researchers and practitioners reveals a widely (often implicitly) held view that the native speaker is the norm toward which language learners should strive to emulate. Robert Phillipson (2000, p. 98) notes the terms native/non-native themselves are "offensive and hierarchical in that they take the native as the norm, and define the Other negatively in relation to this norm." Ironically, as Widdowson (1994) points out, although persons socialized in their L1 as native speakers will possess an insider's knowledge of many facets of that language, the reality is that the vast majority of English Language Learners (ELLs) in the world today are instructed by non-native speakers (NNSs). Furthermore, English is now more commonly spoken as a second, rather than first, language by bilinguals and is used more frequently for intercultural communication between non-native speakers than between native speakers (see Crystal, 1997). This trend will accelerate for the foreseeable future (see David Graddol's "The decline of the native speaker," 1999). The implications of these facts for approaches to understanding the goals and processes of language learning in second and foreign language contexts are profound. Not only are traditional criteria for language competence and proficiency rapidly becoming outdated as "global" languages such as English occupy specialized niches and have achieved the status of indigenized varieties in many countries such as India, Singapore, and Nigeria (see Kachru, 1982, 1986), but identification with a "home" culture has decreasing relevance for the vast majority of ESL/EFL speakers.

The legacies of colonialism (see Canagarajah, 1999; Pennycook, 1998; Phillipson, 1992; Ridge, 2000) that too often inform Applied Linguistics research and English Language Teaching (ELT) have begun to be systematically uncovered and critiqued in recent years. One aspect of this legacy has been the problematizing of the subordinate positioning of ELL vis-à-vis NS in many contexts worldwide, a process characterized as 'Othering' by Kubota (2001). Responses (negative and positive) to 'Othering' and to the experiences, in general, of NNS in various settings have been explored in collections (e.g., Braine, 1999; Norton, 1997), in many articles and chapters (e.g., Brutt-Griffler & Samimy, 1999; Canagarajah, 2000; Flowerdew, 2000; Kubota, 1999, 2001; Leung, Harris, & Rampton, 1997; Lin, Wang, Akamatsu, & Riazi, 2002; Liu, 1999; Morgan, 2002; Pavlenko, 1998, 2001; Piller, 2002; Rampton, 1990; Spack, 1997), and monographs (e.g., Canagarajah, 1999; Davies, 1991; Medgyes, 1994; Norton, 2000; Pennycook, 1998; Rampton, 1995).

A methodology that is particularly suited to exploring the topic of identity for L2 users is the personal narrative or life history. A number of important studies have used this technique to explore L2 users' introspective accounts of their experiences "crossing" into other cultures and languages. In their exploration of first-person narratives of late/adult bilingual writers, Pavlenko and Lantolf (2000, p. 157) claim that "first-person accounts in the form of personal narratives provide a much richer source of data than do third-person distal observations." Whereas the tradition of hermeneutic research in SLA has focused mainly on the 'here-and-now' or 'in process' descriptions of the second language learning process by learners and researchers, Pavlenko and Lantolf's goal is "to establish 'retroactive' first-person narratives as a legitimate source of data on the learning process by teasing out in a theoretically informed way insights provided by the life stories of people who have struggled through cultural border crossings" (p. 158). Based on their analysis of the autobiographical work of several American and French authors of Eastern European origin, all of whom learned their second language (in which they work) as adults, Pavlenko and Lantolf identify particular sites of reconstruction of identity. Following Pavlenko (1998), they use self-translation as a unifying metaphor that entails a phase of continuous loss followed later by an overlapping second phase of gain and reconstruction. The initial phase of loss is segmented into five stages (pp. 162–163):

1. loss of one's linguistic identity ("careless baptism," according to Hoffman, 1989).
2. loss of all subjectivities.
3. loss of the frame of reference and the link between the signifier and the signified.
4. loss of the inner voice.
5. first language attrition.

The phase of recovery and (re)construction encompasses four critical stages:

1. appropriation of others' voices.
2. emergence of one's own new voice, often in writing first.
3. translation therapy: reconstruction of one's past.
4. continuous growth "into" new positions and subjectivities.

Pavlenko and Lantolf conclude that "it is ultimately through their own intentions and agency that people decide to undergo or not undergo the frequently agonizing process of linguistic, cultural, and personal transformation documented in the preceding narratives" (p. 171). They point out, however, that such a decision may be influenced by many factors, including the person's positioning in the native discourse and the power relations between the discourses involved. This research is relevant to SLA theory in that it suggests that "'failure' to attain 'ultimately' in a second language is an issue that arises from the imposition of the third-person objectivist perspective informed by a particular linguistic ideology based on the NS/NNS dichotomy" (p. 170). One's linguistic competence in a new culture reflects a process of transformation rather than one of replacement, in which the ultimate outcome represents an identity that is not exclusively anchored in one culture/language or another. As Pavlenko and Lantolf put it, "crossing a border is about 'renarratizing' a life" (p. 174).

While Pavlenko and Lantolf explore the autobiographies of late/adult bilingual writers, Lin, Wang, Akamatsu, and Riazi (2002) in a special topic issue of the *Journal of Language, Identity, and Education* ("Celebrating local knowledge on language and education," Canagarajah (Ed.), 2002) explore the life histories of applied linguists whose experiences as English language learners began much earlier. These language educators use the technique of the collective story (see Richardson, 1985) where the personal/biographical and the sociological/political intersect. Their purpose is to explore and analyze "our encounters and experiences with English in our own life trajectories just as we are constructing them and performing through them new voices, expanded identities, and alternative subject positions" (p. 296). The authors, who studied English from childhood in different parts of Asia—mainland China, colonial Hong Kong, Japan, and Iran—completed their doctoral studies in English language education in Canada in the early 1990s. Having presented their biographies to a mainstream audience at the 2001 TESOL convention, the authors decided to further explore their writings by "reflexively analyzing them, linking them to current discourses of language learning and identity, and local production of disciplinary knowledge in applied linguistics" (p. 300). Although each author's trajectory was unique, they collectively identify a similar storyline that they divide into four stages: English from initially being a more or less irrelevant or external language for instrumental purposes (getting good grades, entering into a good school, getting a good job, climbing the socioeconomic ladder) to becoming an intimate language for self-expansion and enrichment, for exploration of new horizons and new knowledge and understanding of different peoples and the world. In order to destabilize the pervasive hierarchy of racial, cultural, and linguistic relations, the authors argue it is necessary to deconstruct the dichotomized and essentialized categories of Self and Other rooted in colonialist discourse and manifested in classifications such as native, native-like, and non-native English speakers. In a move toward re-imagining and altering these discourses, the authors propose a paradigm shift from doing TESOL (Teaching English to Speakers of Other Languages) to doing TEGCOM (Teaching English for Globalized Communication). Rather than assume (as the name and discourses of TESOL do) that it is the "Other-language" speaker who needs "pedagogical treatment," the authors suggest that we should imagine a TEGCOM class in which all learners are monolingual "native English speakers" who need to be instructed in the ways of using English for cross-cultural communication (e.g., cross-cultural pragmatic skills and awareness) in specific contexts (e.g., for conducting business in Japan, China, or Iran).

CONCLUSIONS AND FUTURE DIRECTIONS

As should be evident at this point, the essentializing of L2 learners as members of a national culture or language group has been widely (and rightly) criticized by critical and postmodern scholars in recent years. As Rosaldo (1993, p. 217) has noted, cultural identities are "always in motion, not frozen for inspection." Yet, as Hansen and Liu (1997, p. 572) point out, despite the fact that many researchers have acknowledged the dynamic nature of social identity, they still use methods—questionnaires, observations, interviews, and so forth—that "do not allow for dynamism, as they are typically one-time occurrences." Although these methods should not be abandoned, additional methods discussed in this chapter (e.g., first-person narratives, collective stories, longitudinal studies, in-depth interviews, and ethnographic research), should be employed in the study of identity in L2 and FL settings. These methods have generated a rich source of data and have deepened and widened our understanding of the complexity of identity, showing the limitations of dichotic oppositional categories such as native/non-native, proficient/limited proficiency, assimilated/alienated, Western/Oriental in the interpretation of human motivations and desires. Spack (1997, p. 773) points out that "when teachers and researchers exercise the power to identify, we actually may be imposing an ethnocentric ideology and inadvertently supporting the essentializing discourse that represents cultural groups as stable or homogeneous entities." She suggests that rather than asking "What should we name students?", we should ask "Should we name students?" She suggests that we follow the lead of critical cultural anthropologists who argue that those who have been the objects of analysis can now "speak for themselves, represent their own lives" (Friedman, 1994, p. 71).

Issues of naming and labeling apply equally in the case of seemingly neutral terms, such as 'Mother Tongue.' The articles in Ricento and Wiley (2002) show the ways in which this term has been appropriated, rejected, or reappropriated for different ideological and political purposes. However, by analyzing the texts and discourses of different subjectivities, there is the possibility to identify "third places" (Kramsch, 1993) in which new/re-articulations of our identities through linguistic and cultural contact experiences can be explored. An excellent example of such a move is found in the work of the South African scholar Sinfree Makoni. Makoni (cited in Pennycook, 2002, pp. 25–26) argues that "unless African languages are disinvented, some ways of conceptualization of the social world consistent with European missionary imperialism will be sustained into the next century...disinvention argues that African languages in their current ways of conceptualization are European scripts." Pennycook suggests that disinvention, rather than reification, of languages "might lead us to address questions of language in education rather differently, not focusing so much on reified notions of dominant languages and mother tongues as on trying to understand the complex and hybrid mixtures of semiotic tools that are actually used" (p. 26).

There are many exciting possibilities in the study of identity and L2 learning. One area that is receiving attention recently is the transnational character of many immigrant communities and the implications for language pedagogy and learning. Pita and Utakis (2002) examine the economic, political, social, cultural, and linguistic dimensions of the Dominican community in New York City. They argue that in order to function effectively in their lives, members of this community require enriched bilingual bicultural programs, as opposed to just ESL, to promote parallel development so that students can succeed in either country. With reference to the Dominican community in New York, old assumptions that immigrants come to the United States to assimilate and lose their ancestral language and culture do not apply. Educators who deal with this and similar populations need to understand that the identities of their L2 learners are deeply connected to their status as members of distinct, but interrelated, communities, in which bilingualism (as opposed to monolingualism) is the norm.

Finally, ESL and EFL teachers have a responsibility to consider how their pedagogical practices enable or challenge prevailing social hierarchies. McMahill (2001) describes how she was able to stimulate class discussions on women's issues in Japan using the topic of mother/daughter relationships. McMahill describes how these EFL learners can appropriate English as a weapon for self-empowerment for women in Japan and for women of color in the world. Another example of the possibilities of a critical pedagogy is found in Canagarajah (1999). The author provides insights into the ways that teachers and students in a postcolonial setting (Sri Lanka) can negotiate the challenges posed to their identity, community membership, and values, by the vernacular and English. The research approaches and findings presented in this chapter suggest starting points for critical, self-reflexive inquiry about how our practices as teachers might better serve the complex interests, desires, and identities of our second and foreign language students around the world.

REFERENCES

Angelil-Carter, S. (1997). Second language acquisition of spoken and written English: Acquiring the skeptron. *TESOL Quarterly, 31*, 263–287.
Atkinson, D. (1999). TESOL and culture. *TESOL Quarterly, 33*, 625–654.
Au, S. Y. (1988). A critical appraisal of Gardner's social-psychological theory of second language learning. *Language Learning, 38*, 75–100.

Bakhtin, M. (1986). *Speech genres and other late essays*. Austin, TX: University of Texas Press.

Berdan, R. (1996). Disentangling language acquisition from language variation. In R. Bayley & D. R. Preston (Eds.), *Second language acquisition and linguistic variation* (pp. 203–244). Amsterdam: Benjamins.

Blackledge, A., & Pavlenko, A. (2001). Negotiation of identities in multilingual contexts. *The International Journal of Bilingualism, 5*, 243–257.

Bourdieu, P. (1977). The economics of linguistic exchanges. *Social Science Information, 16*, 645–668.

Bourdieu, P. (1982). *Ce que parler veut dire* [What spending means]. Paris: Fayard.

Bourdieu, P. (1991). *Language and symbolic power*. London: Polity Press.

Bourdieu, P., & Passeron, J. (1977). *Reproduction in education, society, and culture*. London/Beverly Hills, CA: Sage.

Braine, G. (Ed.) (1999). *Non-native educators in English language teaching*. Mahwah, NJ: Lawrence Erlbaum Associates.

Brown, H. D. (1994). *Principles of language learning and teaching*. Englewood Cliffs, NJ: Prentice-Hall.

Brutt-Griffler, J., & Samimy, K. (1999). Revisiting the colonial in the postcolonial: Critical praxis for non-native-English-speaking teachers in a TESOL program. *TESOL Quarterly 33*, 413–431.

Cameron, D. (1992). *Feminism and linguistic theory* (2nd ed.). London: Macmillan.

Canagarajah, A. S. (1999). *Resisting linguistic imperialism in English teaching*. Oxford, UK: Oxford University Press.

Canagarajah, A. S. (2000). Negotiating ideologies through English: Strategies from the periphery. In T. Ricento (Ed.), *Ideology, politics, and language policies: Focus on English* (pp. 121–132). Amsterdam: Benjamins.

Canagarajah, A. S. (Ed.) (2002). Celebrating local knowledge on language and education. Special Issue, *Journal of Language, Identity, and Education, 1*(4).

Clarke, M. A. (1976). Second language acquisition as a clash of consciousness. *Language Learning, 26*, 377–390.

Crystal, D. (1997). *English as a global language*. Cambridge, UK: Cambridge University Press.

Davies, A. (1991). *The native speaker in applied linguistics*. Edinburgh: Edinburgh University Press.

Eckert, P., & McConnell-Ginet, S. (1999). New generalizations and explanations in language and gender research. *Language in Society, 28*, 185–201.

Ehrlich, S. (1997). Gender as social practice: Implications for second language acquisition. *Studies in Second Language Acquisition, 19*, 421–446.

Fishman, P. (1983). Interaction: The work women do. In B. Thorne, C. Kramarae, & N. Henley (Eds.), *Language, gender, and society* (pp. 89–102). Rowley, MA: Newbury House.

Flowerdew, J. (2000). Discourse community, legitimate peripheral participation, and the non-native-English-speaking scholar. *TESOL Quarterly, 34*, 127–150.

Foster, G. M. (1962). *Traditional cultures*. New York: Harper & Row.

Foucault, M. (1980). *Power/knowledge: Selected interviews and other writings 1972–1977* (C. Gordon, trans.). New York: Pantheon.

Friedman, J. (1994). *Cultural identity and global process*. London: Sage.

Gal, S. (1978). Peasant men can't get wives: Language and sex roles in a bilingual community. *Language in Society, 7*, 1–17.

Gal, S. (1991). Between speech and silence: The problematics of research on language and gender. In M. Di Leonardo (Ed.), *Gender at the crossroads of knowledge* (pp. 175–203). Berkeley: University of California Press.

Gardner, R. C., & Lambert, W. E. (1972). *Attitudes and motivation in second language learning*. Rowley, MA: Newbury House.

Gass, S., & Varonis, E. (1986). Sex differences in NS/NNS interactions. In R. Day (Ed.), *Talking to learn: Conversation in second language acquisition* (pp. 327–351). Rowley, MA: Newbury House.

Giles, H., & Johnson, P. (1981). The role of language in ethnic group formation. In J. C. Turner & H. Giles (Eds.), *Intergroup behavior* (pp. 199–243). Oxford, UK: Basil Blackwell.

Giles, H., & Johnson, P. (1987). Ethnolinguistic identity theory: A social psychological approach to language maintenance. *International Journal of the Sociology of Language, 68*, 69–99.

Goldstein, T. (1995). "Nobody is talking bad": Creating community and claiming power on the production lines. In K. Hall & M. Bucholtz (Eds.), *Gender articulated: Language and the socially constructed self* (pp. 375–400). London: Routledge & Kegan Paul.

Graddol, D. (1999). The decline of the native speaker. In D. Graddol, & U. H. Meinhof (Eds.), *English in a changing world. The AILA Review, 13*, 57–68.

Graddol, D., & Swann, J. (1989). *Gender voices*. Oxford, UK: Blackwell.

Graham, C. R. (March, 1984). Beyond integrative motivation: The development and influence of assimilative motivation. Paper presented at the TESOL Convention, Houston, Texas.

Grillo, R. (1989). *Dominant languages: Language and hierarchy in Britain and France*. Cambridge, UK: Cambridge University Press.

Gumperz, J. J. (1982). *Discourse strategies*. Cambridge, UK: Cambridge University Press.

Günthner, S. (1992). The construction of gendered discourse in Chinese-German interactions. *Discourse & Society, 3*, 167–191.

Hall, E. (1959). *The silent language*. Garden City, NY: Doubleday.

Hall, K. (2002). Asserting "needs" and claiming "rights": The cultural politics of community language education in England. *Journal of Language, Identity, and Education, 1,* 97–119.

Hansen, J. G., & Liu, J. (1997). Social identity and language: Theoretical and methodological issues. *TESOL Quarterly, 31,* 567–576.

Hartman, P., & Judd, E. (1978). Sexism and TESOL materials. *TESOL Quarterly, 12,* 383–393.

Harvey, P. (1994). The presence and absence of speech in the communication of gender. In P. Burton, D. Kushari, & S. Ardener (Eds.), *Bilingual women: Anthropological approaches to second language use* (pp. 44–64). Oxford: Berg.

Heller, M. (1982). *Language, ethnicity, and politics in Quebec.* Unpublished doctoral dissertation, University of California, Berkeley.

Heller, M. (1987). The role of language in the formation of ethnic identity. In J. Phinney & M. Rotheram (Eds.), *Children's ethnic socialization* (pp. 180–200). Newbury Park, CA: Sage.

Heller, M. (1995). Language choice, social institutions, and symbolic domination. *Language in Society, 24,* 373–405.

Hill, J. (1987). Women's speech in modern Mexicano. In S. Philips, S. Steele, & C. Tanz (Eds.), *Language, gender, and sex in comparative perspective* (pp. 121–160). Cambridge, UK: Cambridge University Press.

Hoffman, E. (1989). *Lost in translation: A life in a new language.* New York: Dutton.

Holmes, J. (1993). Immigrant women and language maintenance in Australia and New Zealand. *International Journal of Applied Linguistics, 3,* 159–179.

Ibrahim, A. (1999). Becoming black: Rap and hip-hop, race, gender, identity, and the politics of ESL learning. *TESOL Quarterly, 33,* 349–369.

Kachru, B. B. (1982). *The other tongue: English across cultures* (2nd ed.). Chicago: University of Illinois Press.

Kachru, B. B. (1986). *The alchemy of English: The spread, functions, and models of non-native Englishes.* Oxford: Pergamon Press.

Kobayashi, Y. (March, 2000). Young Japanese women's perceptions about English study. Paper presented at the TESOL Conference, Vancouver, Canada.

Kramsch, C. (1993). *Context and culture in language teaching.* Oxford, UK: Oxford University Press.

Kubota, R. (1999). Japanese culture constructed by discourses: Implications for applied linguistics research and ELT. *TESOL Quarterly, 33,* 9–35.

Kubota, R. (2001). Discursive construction of the images of U.S. classrooms. *TESOL Quarterly, 35,* 9–38.

Lakoff, R. (1975). *Language and woman's place.* New York: Harper & Row.

Lantolf, J. P. (1996). SLA theory building: "Letting all the flowers bloom!" *Language Learning, 46,* 713–749.

Lantolf, J. P. (2000). *Sociocultural theory and second language learning.* Oxford, UK: Oxford University Press.

Larson, D. N., & Smalley, W. A. (1972). *Becoming bilingual: A guide to language learning.* New Canaan, CN: Practical Anthropology.

Le Page, R. B., & Tabouret-Keller, A. (1985). *Acts of identity: Creole-based approaches to ethnicity and language.* Cambridge, UK: Cambridge University Press.

Leung, C., Harris, R., & Rampton, B. (1997). The idealised native speaker, reified ethnicities, and classroom realities. *TESOL Quarterly, 31,* 543–560.

Lin, A., Wang, W., Akamatsu, N., & Riazi, A. M. (2002). Appropriating English, expanding identities, and re-visioning the field: From TESOL to teaching English for Glocalized communication (TEGCOM). *Journal of Language, Identity, and Education, 1,* 295–316.

Liu, J. (1999). Non-native-English-speaking professionals in TESOL. *TESOL Quarterly, 33,* 85–102.

Lofton, J. (April, 1996). "Women's knowledge" and language choice at the Fourth Cultural Congress in Otavalo, Ecuador. In N. Warner, J. Ahlers, L. Bilmes, M. Oliver, S. Wertheim, & M. Chen (Eds.), *Gender and belief systems. Proceedings of the Fourth Berkeley Women and Language Conference, April 19–21* (pp. 447–454). Berkeley, CA: University of California.

Losey, K. (1995). Gender and ethnicity as factors in the development of verbal skills in bilingual Mexican American women. *TESOL Quarterly, 4,* 635–661.

Lukmani, Y. (1972). Motivation to learn and language proficiency. *Language Learning, 22,* 261–274.

Maltz, D., & Borker, R. (1982). A cultural approach to male-female miscommunication. In J. Gumperz (Ed.), *Language and social identity* (pp. 196–206). Cambridge, UK: Cambridge University Press.

Martin-Jones, M., & Heller, M. (Eds.) (1996). Education in multilingual settings: Discourse, identities, and power [Two-part special issue]. *Linguistics and Education, 8.*

Matsui, M. (1995). Gender role perceptions of Japanese and Chinese female students in American universities. *Comparative Education Review, 39,* 356–378.

May, S. (2001). *Language and minority rights: Ethnicity, nationalism, and the politics of language.* Edinburgh Gate: Pearson Education.

McDonald, M. (1994). Women and linguistic innovation in Brittany. In P. Burton, K. Dyson, & S. Ardener (Eds.), *Bilingual women: Anthropological approaches to second language use* (pp. 85–110). Oxford, UK: Berg.

McGregor, L. (Ed.) (1998). Gender issues in language teaching [Special Issue]. *The Language Teacher, 22.*

McKay, S. L., & Wong, S. C. (1996). Multiple discourses, multiple identities: Investment and agency in second language learning among Chinese adolescent immigrant students. *Harvard Educational Review, 3,* 577–608.

McMahill, C. (2001). Self-expression, gender, and community: A Japanese feminist English class. In A. Pavlenko, A. Blackledge, I. Piller, & M. Teutsch-Dwyer (Eds.), *Multilingualism, second language learning, and gender* (pp. 307–344). Berlin: Mouton de Gruyter.

McNamara, T. (1997). What do we mean by social identity? Competing frameworks, competing discourses. *TESOL Quarterly, 31*, 561–567.

Medgyes, P. (1994). *Non-natives in ELT*. London: Macmillan.

Moon, S. (2000). Ideologies of language and gender among Korean ESL students and South American ESL students: Shaping language learning processes. *Gender Issues in Language Education: Temple University Japan Working Papers in Applied Linguistics, 17*, 148–163.

Morgan, B. (2002). Critical practice in community-based ESL programs: A Canadian perspective. *Journal of Language, Identity, and Education, 1*, 141–162.

Nelson, C. (1999). Sexual identities in ESL: Queer theory and classroom inquiry. *TESOL Quarterly 33*, 371–391.

Norton Pierce, B. (1995). Social identity, investment, and language learning. *TESOL Quarterly, 29*, 9–31.

Norton, B. (1997). Language, identity, and the ownership of English. *TESOL Quarterly, 31*(3), 409–430.

Norton, B. (2000). *Identity and language learning: Gender, ethnicity, and educational change*. Edinburgh Gate: Pearson Education.

Norton, B. (Ed.) (1997). Language and identity [Special issue]. *TESOL Quarterly, 31*(3).

Ochs, E. (1988). *Cultural and language development: Language acquisition and language socialization in a Samoan village*. New York: Academic Press.

Oxford, R. (1993). Gender differences in styles and strategies for language learning: What do they mean? Should we pay attention? In J. Alatis (Ed.), *Strategic interaction and language acquisition: Theory, practice, and research* (pp. 541–557). Washington, DC: Georgetown University Press.

Pavlenko, A. (1998). Second language learning by adults: Testimonies of bilingual writers. *Issues in Applied Linguistics, 9*, 3–19.

Pavlenko, A., & Piller, I. (2001). New directions in the study of multilingualism, second language learning, and gender. In A. Pavlenko, A. Blackledge, I. Piller, & M. Teutsch-Dwyer (Eds.), *Multilingualism, second language learning, and gender* (pp. 17–52). Berlin: Mouton de Gruyter.

Pavlenko, A. (2001). "In the world of the tradition, I was unimagined": Negotiation of identities in cross-cultural autobiographies. *The International Journal of Bilingualism, 5*, 317–344.

Pavlenko, A., & Lantolf, J. P. (2000). Second language learning as participation and the (re)construction of selves. In J. P. Lantolf (Ed.), *Sociocultural theory and second language learning* (pp. 155–177). Oxford, UK: Oxford University Press.

Pennycook, A. (1989). The concept of method, interested knowledge, and the politics of language teaching. *TESOL Quarterly, 23*, 589–618.

Pennycook, A. (1998). *English and the discourses of imperialism*. London: Routledge & Kegan Paul.

Pennycook, A. (2002). Mother tongues, governmentality, and protectionism. *International Journal of the Sociology of Language, 154*, 11–28.

Phillipson, R. (1992). *Linguistic imperialism*. Oxford, UK: Oxford University Press.

Phillipson, R. (2000). English in the new world order. In T. Ricento (Ed.), *Ideology, politics, and language policies: Focus on English* (pp. 87–106). Amsterdam: Benjamins.

Pica, T., Holliday, L., Lewis, N., Berducci, D., & Newman, J. (1991). Language learning through interaction: What role does gender play? *Studies in Second Language Acquisition, 13*, 343–376.

Piller, I. (2002). Passing for a native speaker: Identity and success in second language learning. *Journal of Sociolinguistics, 6*, 179–206.

Pita, M. D., & Utakis, S. (2002). Educational policy for the transnational Dominican community. *Journal of Language, Identity, and Education, 1*, 317–328.

Porreca, K. (1984). Sexism in current ESL textbooks. *TESOL Quarterly, 18*, 705–724.

Rampton, B. (1990). Displacing the 'native speaker': Expertise, affiliation, and inheritance. *ELT Journal, 44*, 97–101.

Rampton, B. (1995). *Crossing: Language and ethnicity among adolescents*. London: Longman.

Rampton, B. (1999a). Deutsch in inner London and the animation of an instructed foreign language. *Journal of Sociolinguistics, 3*, 480–504.

Rampton, B. (1999b). Styling the other: Introduction. *Journal of Sociolinguistics, 3*, 421–427.

Ricento, T., & Wiley, T. G. (Eds.) (2002). Revisiting the mother-tongue question in language policy, planning, and politics. *International Journal of the Sociology of Language, 154*.

Richardson, L. (1985). *The new other woman*. New York: The Free Press.

Ridge, S. G. (2000). Mixed motives: Ideological elements in the support for English in South Africa. In T. Ricento (Ed.), *Ideology, politics, and language policies: Focus on English* (pp. 151–172). Amsterdam: Benjamins.

Rockhill, K. (1987). Gender, language, and the politics of literacy. *British Journal of Sociology of Education, 18*, 153–167.

Rosaldo, R. (1993). *Culture and truth: The remaking of social analysis* (2nd ed.). Boston: Beacon Press.

Said, E. (1993). *Culture and imperialism*. New York: Knopf.

Schecter, S. R., & Bayley, R. (1997). Language socialization practices and cultural identity: Case studies of Mexican-descent families in California and Texas. *TESOL Quarterly, 31*, 513–541.

Schumann, J. H. (1976). Social distance as a factor in second language acquisition. *Language Learning, 26*, 135–143.

Schumann, J. H. (1978). *The pidginization process: A model for second language acquisition.* Rowley, MA: Newbury House.

Shardakova, M., & Pavlenko, A. (2004). Identity options in Russian textbooks. *Journal of Language, Identity, and Education, 3*(1), 25–46.

Solé, Y. (1978). Sociocultural and sociopsychological factors in differential language retentiveness by sex. *International Journal of the Sociology of Language, 17*, 29–44.

Spack, R. (1997). The rhetorical construction of multilingual students. *TESOL Quarterly, 31*, 765–774.

Spedding, A. (1994). Open Castilian, closed Aymara? Biilngual women in the Yungas of La Paz (Bolivia). In P. Burton, K. Dyson, & S. Ardener (Eds.), *Bilingual women: Anthropological approaches to second language use* (pp. 30–43). Oxford, UK: Berg.

Starfield, S. (2002). "I'm a second language English learner": Negotiating writer identity and authority in sociology one. *Journal of Language, Identity, and Education, 1*, 121–140.

Stevens, G. (1986). Sex differences in language shift in the United States. *Sociology and Social Research, 71*, 31–34.

Sunderland, J. (1992). Teaching materials and teaching/learning processes: Gender in the classroom. *Working Papers on Gender, Language, and Sexism, 2*, 15–26.

Swigart, L. (1992). Women and language choice in Dakar: A case of unconscious innovation. *Women and Language, 15*, 11–20.

Tajfel, H. (1981). *Human groups and social categories.* Cambridge, UK: Cambridge University Press.

Tannen, D. (1990). *You just don't understand: Women and men in conversation.* New York: Morrow.

Thorne, B., & Henley, N. (1975). *Language and sex: Difference and domination.* Rowley, MA: Newbury House.

Tollefson, J. (1991). *Planning language, planning inequality.* London: Longman.

Trömel-Plötz, S. (1991). Review essay: Selling the apolitical. *Discourse and Society, 2*, 489–502.

Vygotsky, L. S. (1978). *Mind in society.* Cambridge, MA: Harvard University Press.

West, C., & Zimmerman, D. (1983). Small insults: A study of interruptions in cross-sex conversations between unacquainted persons. In B. Thorne, C. Kramarae, & N. Henley (Eds.), *Language, gender, and society* (pp. 102–117). Rowley, MA: Newbury House.

Widdowson, H. G. (1994). The ownership of English. *TESOL Quarterly, 28*, 377–389.

Williams, G. (1999). Sociology. In J. A. Fishman (Ed.), *Handbook of language and ethnic identity* (pp. 164–180). Oxford, UK: Oxford University Press.

Willinsky, J. (1998). *Learning to divide the world: Education at empire's end.* Minneapolis: University of Minnesota Press.

Woolard, K. (1997). Between friends: Gender, peer group structure, and bilingualism in urban Catalonia. *Language in Society, 26*, 533–560.

Zimmerman, D., & West, C. (1975). Sex roles, interruptions, and silences in conversations. In B. Thorne & N. Henley (Eds.), *Language and sex: Difference and dominance* (pp. 105–129). Rowley, MA: Newbury House.

50

Teaching and Researching Intercultural Competence

Michael Byram
Anwei Feng
University of Durham

INTRODUCTION

Three main perspectives are identifiable in teaching for intercultural competence and communication, even though there is inevitable overlap among them:

1. Culture teaching is moving toward an ethnographic perspective.
2. Culture teaching is moving toward a critical perspective.
3. Culture teaching focuses on preparation for residence in another country, often without attention to language learning.

The first two perspectives are found in the work that arises from general education, in schooling or higher education. The third is associated more with the world of work, business, and commerce.

Increased interest in teaching has also led to more research. The relationship between the two is complex and sometimes uneasy. We shall see in the discussion of approaches to teaching that the pursuit of intercultural competence brings language teachers, who might have seen their purpose as developing skills (the four linguistic skills and culture as the "fifth dimension" Damen, 1987), into close contact with moral and political education as they deal with values and education for democracy. Teaching culture can quickly become a matter of conviction and ideology with hopes and intentions that may or may not be underpinned by research. This is not to say, however, that research is value-free, and in the second part of this chapter we shall present a distinction between research and scholarship that helps to demonstrate that research also needs to be evaluated not only in terms of validity and reliability but with an awareness of the values that it inevitably embodies.

CONTEXT AND LANGUAGE AND CULTURE TEACHING

Most of the recent literature on teaching culture has apparently arisen from the increasing importance attached to context in theoretical discussions in sociolinguistics, cultural studies teaching, and intercultural communication. Gudykunst and Kim (1992) argue that in intercultural interactions two types of context come into play: external context and internal context. The former refers to the settings or locations where the interaction takes place and the meanings the society attaches to them. Whereas the latter, internal context, is the culture the interactants bring to the encounters. In intercultural communication, misunderstanding is much more likely to occur because the internal contexts, that is, the ways interactants use to perceive the situations and each other and the meanings they associate with the settings can differ greatly from one culture to another. Thus, it is essential for language learners to be effective in culture learning.

Such views are shared by Kramsch (1993) who summarizes the discussions of the notion of context along five lines: linguistic, situational, interactional, cultural, and intertextual. She argues that teachers need to help learners of foreign languages discover potential meanings through explorations of the context of the discourse under study. The more contextual clues learners can identify, the more likely their learning becomes meaningful. The fruits of this view can now be seen in contemporary collections of articles and monographs describing classroom methods that focus on the interplay between language and culture (e.g., Fantini, 1997; Lo Bianco, Liddicoat, & Crozet, 1999; Byram & Grundy, 2002; Moran, 2001; Morgan & Cain, 2000).

ETHNOGRAPHIC APPROACHES

The extensive discussions on context have resulted, first of all, in the systematic adoption of an ethnographic approach to culture learning and teaching. In the past few decades, the ethnographic approach has gained currency in the literature of sociolinguistics. Particularly since Hymes (1974) proposed an ethnographic framework that takes into account various factors involved in speaking, the ethnographic approach has been adopted repeatedly by sociolinguistic researchers to conduct empirical studies into the interrelationships between language and society (e.g., Hill & Hill, 1986; Milroy, 1987; Lindenfeld, 1990). Sociolinguists usually define ethnography as a disciplined way to observe, ask, record, reflect, compare, analyze, and report. Hymes (1981) further notes that:

> Of all forms of scientific knowledge, ethnography is the most open, the most compatible with a democratic way of life, the least likely to produce a world in which experts control knowledge at the expense of those who are studied. The skills of ethnography are enhancements of skills all normal persons employ in everyday life.... It (ethnography) mediates between what members of a given community know and do, and accumulates comparative understanding of what members of communities generally have known and done. (p. 57)

Ethnography has attracted language educators partly because access to countries where a target language is spoken has become increasingly easier for language learners and partly because language educators and scholars have ever more realized that language teaching can benefit from application of other disciplines rather than drawing solely on theoretical linguistics. The value of ethnography is particularly noticeable as the literature on culture learning and cultural studies teaching has grown in recent years. Discussions about the close relationship between language and sociocultural patterns in the literature of cultural studies, anthropology, and sociolinguistics have prompted language education scholars such as Paulston (1974), McLeod (1976), Damen (1987), and Byram (1989a) to examine the relevance of anthropological, sociolinguistic, and cultural studies methodology for language and culture teaching. Coupled with social changes of the late 20th century that are encapsulated in the words *globalization* and *internationalization*, an increasing number of educational institutions particularly in the industrialized countries have developed programs for students to study abroad. Most of these programs are claimed to be part of the agendas to internationalize educational systems (Murphy-Lejeune, 2002; Kauffmann et al., 1992) and many have the dual purposes of improving proficiency in the target language and developing their intercultural competence and ethnographic skills (Byram, 1989b; Coleman, 1995; Roberts et al., 2001).

Ethnographic Study in Naturalistic Settings

An ethnographic perspective in language education, first of all, takes naturalistic settings, that is, real-world situations, as most effective and central to culture learning. This view is most illustrated in the literature on study abroad. According to Murphy-Lejeune (2002), in 1996, UNESCO estimated that the number of internationally mobile students reached 1,400,000 worldwide and projected an increase of 50,000 students each year in the years to come. Among these students a large number study abroad for educational purposes whereas many are obliged to study abroad for economic and political reasons. The ethnographic experience of these internationally mobile students attracts the attention of researchers of various disciplines including those in language and culture learning and acquisition. Research findings, particularly those obtained from in-depth interviews, often show a close relationship between students' ethnographic experience and their intellectual development (including development of learners' linguistic competence) (Dyson, 1988; DeKeyser, 1991), international perspectives and positive attitudes toward otherness (Carlson et al., 1990; Kauffmann et al., 1992; Murphy-Lejeune, 2002). In her article on interviews of 50 students who spent a year in a European country other than in their own, Murphy-Lejeune (2003, p. 113) states that the experience is generally positively felt by many interviewees as an adaptation process. This process does not always bring about a drastic change in personality but it evidently leads to a "personal expansion, an opening of one's potential universe."

Many language educators see these study-abroad programs as opportunities not only to develop learners' linguistic competence but their cultural awareness and intercultural competence. Armstrong (1984) researched more than a hundred high school students who participated in a 7-week language study program in Mexico and found that the stay positively influenced the students' attitude toward the host culture and the target language and led to a higher level of cultural awareness. In the European context, the proximity of countries with different languages and the advantages of living in a multilingual continent, have led to major increases in the number of young learners experiencing other cultures that can be exploited with an ethnographic approach (Byram & Snow, 1997).

Having studied the effects of studying abroad on university-level students, Jurasek (1996) concludes that in learning another language it is important for a learner to engage in the ethnographic process of observing, participating, describing, analyzing, and interpreting. This engagement is much more significant than the product of the study itself. He further suggests that as a consequence of such an approach learners will gain increased awareness with regard to perception and perspective and improve their ability to a lesser or greater extent of recognizing what things might look like from the perspective of members of another culture. Perhaps, the most comprehensive ethnographic program for language students is the one that was designed and carried out by researchers at a British university (see Roberts et al., 2001; Barro et al., 1998). The program was conducted over a period of 3 years in three distinct phases: the presojourn acquisition of ethnographic methods and concepts, the during-sojourn ethnographic fieldwork, and the postsojourn write-up of a monograph.

Most ethnographic projects such as this and study-abroad programs described earlier have reportedly produced positive impact on learners in terms of intercultural awareness, interest in otherness, intellectual and personal development. Nevertheless, some research findings indicate that negative experience in foreign countries can reinforce stereotypes (Coleman, 1997, 1998) and some students even feel that the year abroad is a "lost year" as they lose contact with their home school and their fellow students (Lewis & Stickler, 2000). In response to these, education scholars and institutions have used or experimented with various measures to help achieve the specified aims. These include formal training of students before residence abroad, as in Roberts et al. (2001), regular visits by home institutions, and regular report or diary writing by students (Lewis & Stickler, 2000). Most of the measures are reported to be effective in bringing about positive outcomes.

Ethnographic Study in Structured Settings

Recent literature on ethnography has also expanded to professional development and culture teaching in a structured language classroom. Language education researchers have explored a range of ways in which teachers as well as learners can be encouraged to "live an ethnographic life," depending on the context of learning and resources available. Both research findings and theoretical discussions demonstrate a strong interest in the ethnographic perspective for culture learning and teaching, whether it takes place in the country where the target language is spoken or in a structured language classroom.

In discussing ethnography for culture teaching and learning in language education, many scholars maintain that teachers first of all need to be ethnographers themselves capable of dealing with cultural issues with understanding and sensitivity. It is mistaken to assume that teachers can competently provide explanations of complex issues to their students by simply drawing on text information and personal experience. Damen (1987) is one of the keen promoters of ethnography for professional development of language teachers and for culture teaching in language classrooms. She suggests seven steps for teachers, preservice or in-service, to plan an individual ethnographic project. She names the procedure "pragmatic ethnography" because she states that the procedure is to "serve personal and practical purposes and not to provide scientific data and theory" (p. 63). Although this model does not explicitly suggest that the teacher ask the students to use the same approach to culture learning, there is potential for doing so and the teacher is encouraged to link their ethnographic learning experience with teaching practice.

Literature documenting language teachers' attempts to study their students' perceptions of language learning, attitudes, and classroom behavior using an ethnographic approach is increasing (Canagarajah, 1993; Atkinson & Ramanathan, 1995; Barkhuizen, 1998). The findings of most of these studies shed new light on materials selection, lesson planning, and classroom teaching as Damen expects. That is the very reason why Holliday (1994) argues that each time a language teacher meets a new group of students or a curriculum planner enters a new institution they should apply ethnographic skills to discovering the "hidden agendas" and life objectives of their students. It is the hidden objectives of their students that determine whether they accept or reject the curricular innovations and the teaching and learning methodology used by the teacher. In a later article, Holliday (1996) further states that in ethnographic studies into teaching English as an international language a teacher should not restrict research to empirical research on verbal data but develop a "sociological imagination," the ability to locate themselves and their actions (as a teacher cum researcher) critically within a wider community or world scenario.

In recent years, even more significant is the fact that many attempts have been made to equip students with ethnographic techniques to conduct language-and-culture projects themselves in their own classrooms and neighboring communities. Robinson-Stuart and Nocon (1996) report an experimental study they carried out in an American university. In this study, the students studying Spanish as a foreign language were trained to employ ethnographic interview skills to study the local Spanish speakers. Both quantitative and qualitative results reveal that most language students benefited cognitively, affectively, and intellectually as they demonstrated a more positive attitude toward the cultural perspectives of local target language speakers, showed more interest in learning the target language, and practiced the life skill of active listening. Byram and Cain (1998) describe an experiment carried out in two schools in France and England using an ethnographic approach, and argue for greater efforts in exploring other disciplines such as anthropology, sociology, and ethnography in language teaching practice. Carel (2001) reports a project that made use of information technology to develop in students cultural sensitivity and intercultural competence in the classroom. For this, she designed and implemented an interactive computer courseware package that enabled students to use ethnographic skills to observe and analyze cultural phenomena, do virtual fieldwork, and reflect on their own culture and their previous views of the target culture. Similarly, a project in Bulgaria has explored the ways in which the skills of the ethnographer in collecting and analyzing data and studying their meanings comparatively with data from one's own culture, can be brought into the classroom (e.g., Topuzova, 2001). In his monograph, Corbett (2003) also argues for ethnography as one of the most important features of the intercultural approach. As ethnographic skills such as observing, interviewing, analyzing, and reporting are all vital skills for students when they encounter otherness firsthand, they need to be trained and incorporated into language curricula. He offers practical suggestions and methods to conduct interviews, to make use of resources and to explore cultures in general using an ethnographic approach. Finally, Fleming (1998, 2003) shows how drama teaching, as a unique form of classroom teaching, can be linked with ethnographic methodology to enable learners to see others' behavior and their own through the eyes of "made strangers," a process of active participant observation and reflection.

The potential of the Internet for virtual ethnography seems obvious but has not yet been fully explored. One particularly interesting project combines the use of the immediacy of the Internet and a constructivist pedagogy whereby one student group is linked to another and both compare and contrast their responses to culture-specific phenomena, relate these to sociological data, and begin to discover patterns of beliefs, values, and behaviors in the other's society and culture (Furstenberg et al., 2001).

CRITICAL APPROACHES

Culture Teaching and Political Education

It is widely acknowledged by educationists and language researchers that education is never neutral and foreign language education has a political role to play in any education system of the world. Many language scholars and educators therefore argue that foreign language teachers should take social and political responsibilities in the education of the young in the contemporary world. Byram (1997), for example, places political education firmly at the center of his model for intercultural communicative.

He suggests that insights from citizenship education, education for democracy, human rights and peace education, and cultural studies can be drawn to establish criteria of evaluation and mediation between cultures. Byram and Risager (1999) further elaborate this stance with data from their empirical studies in two European countries. They show how geopolitical changes affect language educators' perceptions of language teaching and analyze and recommend ways to respond to these changes in language education.

In her monograph on critical citizenship, Guilherme (2002) puts even greater and more explicit emphasis on the political dimension for foreign language and culture education. The critical model she proposes integrates three components that are all politically based. First, she argues for human rights education and education for democratic citizenship through opposing philosophies to promote critical cultural awareness in teaching a foreign language and culture. The second component is an interdisciplinary one that consists of cultural studies, intercultural communication, and critical pedagogy. The third comprises a series of "operations." pedagogical strategies that function at various levels in terms of local, national, and global geopolitics and in relation to "existential" references, namely attitudes, values, and beliefs. She suggests, however, that integration, particularly critical pedagogy, in foreign language/culture education, although important and attempted in some studies, requires further research.

As an initial step toward a critical perspective in language and culture teaching, quite a few monographs have been written recently to provide theoretical underpinnings and practical ideas for foreign language teacher training. A common feature of these writings is their attempts to deal explicitly and critically with the social, political, and ideological aspects in language and language learning and teaching. Nieto (1999, 2002) addresses issues of cultural diversity and identity in relation to language education in American classrooms and suggests community and classroom activities in settings ranging from multicultural classrooms to district or national levels. In carrying out these activities, in-service and preservice language educators are encouraged to reflect on their practice and perceptions of language teaching and learning, conduct ethnographic field work, and experience the critical perspective through activities such as curriculum design. Reagan and Osborn (2002) link foreign language education with critical pedagogy and propose what they call the "metalinguistic content" for foreign language education, moving beyond pragmatic pedagogical concerns to the social and political domains relevant to language teaching.

The purpose for some of these writers is not only to make learners take new perspectives and reflect on their own, but to focus on some principled and universal "meanings," in order to avoid the relativism of postmodernism. Corbett sees this as "neohumanist," placing respect for individuals at the heart of the enterprise:

> The intercultural learner moves amongst cultures, in a process of continual negotiation, learning to cope with the inevitable changes, in a manner that is ultimately empowering and enriching. The home culture is never denied nor demeaned, yet the intercultural learner will find his or her attitudes and beliefs challenged by contact with others, and the process of interaction will lead to the kind of personal growth characterised by 'progressive' curricula. (2003)

Culture Taught as a Dialogic Process

An important feature of a critical perspective in language education is the dialogic approach that emphasizes a teacher-student relationship of mutual respect, freedom of expression, and dialogic sharing. A dialogic approach to language and culture teaching moves away from the traditional concept of teaching knowledge as an "I/It" phenomenon (I teach it, you learn it) to a teaching method that problematizes the very concepts under study (Tomic, 2000). These include the concepts of "culture" itself, "cultural identity," "carriers of culture," and "nonverbal communication" (Hoffman, 1999; Woodward, 1997; Scollon & Scollon, 1995). Tomic argues that in culture teaching and learning it is the individual's voice that has more resonance than the "culture." Language learners undergo the empowering process as they realize that each person's voice counts.

Based on the view that language and culture learning is a dialogic process of inter-action with others, Morgan and Cain (2000) conducted a project that aimed to enable secondary students in two schools of two countries (England and France) to learn about each other's culture and their own and learn how to decenter and take the other's perspective. The articles in Fenner (2001) also represent a dialogic perspective in dealing with culture in a classroom context. Based on theories exploring the inter-relationship between text and reader and reading and writing processes as dynamic dialogues, the authors examine the interactions between the learners themselves, the cultures involved, learners and teachers, and texts and readers. Common to all the articles is the fact that the practices they present are based on classroom activities using authentic texts ranging from literary texts and drama to Internet materials.

The authenticity of texts for intercultural teaching is important. It is true that many of the texts or discourses traditionally defined as authentic texts are produced by native speakers for the consumption of other native speakers of that language. It is thus not difficult to find in the literature that some argue against using authentic texts in a language classroom on the ground that it is almost impossible for the classroom to provide the contextual conditions for the authentic language data to be authenticated by learners. However, intercultural authenticity (Feng & Byram, 2002) regards the issue of inauthentic context not as an obstacle but as an opportunity to explore the language and culture, including the context, from all angles through dialogues. First, it can encourage students' voices, not silence them, by asking what their initial response to and interpretation of the discourse is. Second, it can lead to discussions of the context, the possible intended audience, and the intended meaning. And third, it may enable both the students and the teacher to gain a multifaceted perspective through negotiations and mediation.

Culture Taught as Knowledge Subject to Scrutiny

The most conventional and also the most criticized perspective of culture teaching is what critics call the facts-oriented approach in which culture is basically viewed as civilization, the "big C" culture, as well as everyday lives, the "small c" culture (Oswalt, 1970; Brooks, 1975; Chastain, 1976). In this facts-oriented approach, culture is normally dissected into small segments that are listed as topics for teaching. Many critics take this approach as inappropriate or even damaging, arguing that it ignores the fact that the major component of what we call the culture "is a social construct, a product of self and other perceptions" (Kramsch, 1993, p. 205). It may well lead to the teaching of stereotypes.

Nonetheless, the facts-oriented perspective in teaching culture is not entirely aban-doned, particularly in language teaching situations where learners have limited op-portunities to expose to otherness and relatively fewer resources to explore the target culture. In effect, many language scholars in these contexts have been making constant efforts to address the theoretical concerns of this approach and to develop it into a "critical model." Hu and Gao (1997), for example, argue that the majority of millions of foreign language learners in China are too ignorant of the basic formulaic facts of the culture they are studying. The knowledge of the facts is undoubtedly necessary as a starting point for culture learning. They warn of the risks and negative implications in teaching stereotypical knowledge as they point out that facts only will inevitably lead to superficial learning and may enhance stereotypes and ethnocentrism. To deal with this paradox, they propose an approach where first learners are taught stereotypical knowledge (to build an open "bridge" in their figurative terms). Immediately, this knowledge is put under scrutiny, by providing learners with a variety of representations of the cultural product or concept under discussion. This is to make learners aware that there are hidden "barriers" along the seemingly straight, easy-to-cross "bridge." The repetition of the process will effectively make learners culturally sophisticated and eventually obtain the "key" to becoming intercultural speakers.

In a similar line of thought, Doyé (1999) puts forward a "strategy for cultural studies" for foreign language classrooms that starts with stereotypical information. The 12-step procedure, in summary, engages learners in exploring preknowledge, creating cognitive dissonance, replacing stereotypical images, exploiting related sources of information and nonverbal communication, comparing others with own, and moving beyond the culture of the target language. This process not only enriches learners' knowledge by studying the culture from different angles, but also improves their skills in comparing and discovering by exploring related sources, and enables them to become open-minded and critical, by reflecting on their 'natural' way of looking at others and perhaps their own.

CULTURE TEACHING AND CULTURE TRAINING

The work reviewed so far has general educational purposes as well as the intention to develop learners' practical competences. We have seen that Hymes stressed the democratic character of ethnography, and we have seen the increase in the relationship of culture teaching to critical pedagogy with its democratic principles and focus on critical analysis. The location for this work is above all the foreign or second language classroom in schools or universities, and this has two important implications.

The first of these is that language and culture are seen as inseparable in the learning process; students learn a language and its cultural implications, even where they are learning it as a lingua franca. They learn to communicate in a new language and this in itself is part of the experience of decentering, which gives them a fresh perspective, a critical perspective, on the taken-for-granted world that surrounds them. Their competence is both intercultural and communicative (Byram, 1997). The second implication is that teachers of languages who might have previously seen themselves as developing in their learners' skills and knowledge, perhaps with a hope that this would lead to attitude change, now find themselves engaged with values.

In practice, the significance of this democratic, educational dimension can be watered down, as teachers prepare their learners for examinations that do not, and perhaps should not, attempt to assess the effect of values and moral education on learners. One of the effects of contemporary emphasis on "quality and standards" in most education systems is to reinforce "teaching to the test." Language teachers who are culturally minded would understandably adopt an ad hoc approach to teaching culture as it appears during their focus on linguistic matters; this is the worst-case scenario. When contextual factors are favorable, they would, at their best, design a syllabus to teach culture systematically through the use of cultural awareness activities and discussion of critical incidents. In these situations, the practical activities for language classrooms designed in Damen (1987), Tomalin and Stempleski (1993), and Fantini (1997) are typically used.

It is also important to bear in mind this difference between principle and practice as we turn to the third general perspective in our review: work that trains people for sojourns in other countries. Here, in principle, the emphasis is on skills and knowledge for practical purposes, but the educational effects in practice can also include the decentering and challenge that leads to reassessment of the taken-for-granted world. On the other hand, the distinction between training for intercultural competence without a focus on language learning, and the combination of language and culture learning in general education is usually clear. Culture teaching in this perspective focuses exclusively on the specific information of the country where the sojourner is going for a short or long stay and offers specific communication patterns, the do's and don'ts, for living and working in that context. The approach does not usually take the language level of the sojourner into account and is used particularly for short training programs for personnel going abroad for business and studying purposes. Numerous texts with titles such as *Living in Japan*, *Communicating with Arabs*, *Studying and Living in the USA* and so on are written as resource books for culture specific study.

The theoretical basis for this work is largely psychological. Bennett's model for the development of intercultural sensitivity (1993) is often cited, and Ward, Bochner, and Furnham (2001) is a recent review and analysis of psychological theory in this field. An alternative approach is to focus on the linguistic foundation for intercultural relationships. Trainers in this approach try to ensure that, irrespective of whose language is being used, learners become aware of the significance of speech acts, turn taking, register directness/indirectness, and so on. Often the assumption is that learners will not have time to acquire a new language, will use a lingua franca, usually English, and therefore need to understand these other features to become sensitive to the nature of the communication. Here the underlying theoretical basis is a comparative linguistic analysis of discourse, most significantly represented in the work of Scollon and Scollon (1995), and presented in its practical implications in Pan, Scollon, and Scollon (2002).

The analysis of work on cross-cultural training would need a chapter in itself, and insofar as this work does not focus on language teaching and learning, would be beyond our scope. There are many handbooks and manuals (e.g., Fowler & Mumfort, 1995, 1999; Cushner & Brislin, 1997; Kohls & Knight, 1994). Many of these have been produced in the United States where the notion of cross-cultural training has been strong, but in the last decade there has been an increasing interest in Europe too. The work of Hofstede (1991) and Trompenaar (1993) is widely cited, and there are practical handbooks and guides increasingly available (e.g., Gibson, 2000; Hofstede, Pederson, & Hofstede, 2002). There are also many materials that remain copyrighted and not widely available for commercial reasons. The main thrust of all this work has been to prepare people to go to other countries, but it also has relevance in giving those who are immigrant to a country an introduction and a program of transition.

What is evident and carefully documented in Dahlen's (1997) critique of the way these interculturalists "package" knowledge of culture, is that there is a close relationship with the business world and with the marketplace. Dahlen argues that this leads to an approach to culture that is a commodification of a dated concept of culture, concluding with some irony:

> More generally, there is a need for conversations between interculturalists and academics for mutual benefit.

Perhaps one bridge is offered by recent work that explores the implications for language learning of a sociocultural theory of mind (Lantolf, 2000a). Here the perspective taken is that learning is mediated by interaction with other people in a given sociocultural context, and that we can better understand the learning of other languages by analyzing how that interaction takes place. The significance for culture teaching and training is yet to be determined, but it suggests that research is needed to analyze the ways in which people learn other cultures and learn about other cultures in interaction with people who embody them. It is to the research agenda in general, that we turn next.

APPROACHES TO RESEARCH

Researching Foreign Language Teaching and Learning

The research questions that can be asked about culture learning in a foreign language learning context depend partly on whether the researcher is seeking explanation or understanding (von Wright, 1971). From an explanation perspective, hypotheses about the relationships among culture learning and other aspects of learning and teaching can be quickly established, for example:

- The relationship between 'the' foreign culture, or perceptions of it, and the motivation for learning.
- The relationship between language learning and attitudes to and/or perceptions of other cultures and peoples.
- The relationship between teaching techniques and/or methodologies and knowledge about other cultures.
- The relationship between learning (about) another culture and learners' perceptions of and/or attitudes toward their own culture.
- The relationship between culture teaching (or absence thereof) and vocabulary learning.
- The relationship between culture learning and the development of specific social identities, particularly national identity.

The best researched account of culture learning is undoubtedly the search for explanation of relationships between learners' understanding of other cultures and their motivation and achievement in language learning. In early research by Gardner and Lambert (1972), the notion of "integrative" motivation—the desire to learn a language to be in some sense closer to speakers of the language—was considered the best basis for success. Later research (Dörnyei, 1998) has shown that "instrumental" motivation can be more important than "integrative," depending on the social context in which languages are learnt. Later research has also shown that many other factors need to be taken into consideration, not least the impact of classroom conditions (Dörnyei, 2001). Where a language is dissociated in learners' perceptions from all links with native speakers—as may be the case with English as an International Language—then "instrumental" or "pragmatic" motivation will be the better concept for explaining achievement.

On the other hand, integrative motivation expressed as a positive interest in peoples and cultures associated with a language is still a significant area of research. This aspect of motivation—it is only one aspect of a very complex issue—is also related to research on attitudes. In both cases, assumptions that there are linear and unidirectional causal relationships between attitudes or motivation on the one hand and achievement in language learning on the other are misplaced. It is for this reason that researchers have constructed complex models that attempt to show the inter-relationships among attitudes, motivations, self-concepts, environmental factors, and instructional factors. The complexity of such models may appear, to applied linguists and teachers, to limit severely their usefulness for teaching, and when Dörnyei and Csizer (1998) offer "ten commandments for motivating language learners" based on research, these might appear intuitively self-evident. However, the significance of culture learning is reinforced by their inclusion of "familiarize learners with the target language culture."

Whatever the precise formulation of the hypothesis, the causal relationship between language learning and teaching and culture learning in the form of insights and attitudes is one that has been researched, albeit sparingly. Byram, Esarte-Sarries, and Taylor (1991) investigated the effects of different styles of language and culture teaching on learners' perceptions and understanding of a national culture. Their conclusions were disappointing in the sense that they could find no discernible effect of teaching, but a strong presence of other factors from outside the classroom and the school. More recently, Australian researchers have investigated the relationship of teaching to attitude formation, which again is disappointing in that there seems to be no causal relationship between teaching and positive attitudes (Ingram & O'Neill, 2002).

There is therefore a major area in the relationships between teaching and understanding of and attitudes toward self and other, own and foreign cultures that needs much more research. Such research could be informed and enriched by other work on culture learning. Much of this is comparative in methodology, comparing, for example, culture-specific views and reactions to communicative language teaching (in China and 'the West,' Rao, 2002), in Colombia and the United States (Schulz, 2001). There is a particularly well-mined seam of research on vocabulary differences between, for example, English and Chinese (Cortazzi & Shen, 2001) or English and German (Olk, 2002) or French and English (Boers & Demecheleer, 2001). In most cases, research that thus analyzes speakers' understanding of apparently similar vocabulary draws out implications for teaching and learning.

There are also analyses of differences in other aspects of communication: different cultural values and communication styles (FitzGerald, 2003), or different discourse strategies (Orsoni, 2001).

Research that is focused on understanding rather than explanation may not always appear to have immediate relevance to Applied Linguists and language teachers, particularly when it deals with phenomena outside the classroom. This is nonetheless an important area because it situates language and culture learning in social contexts. Lantolf (1999, 2000a, 2000b) has argued for a theoretical position that recognizes the value of understanding processes of culture learning from the perspective of learners in informal learning contexts. Pavlenko and Lantolf (2000) have used personal stories as a basis for analyzing "second language learning as participation and the (re)construction of selves." There are recent studies which analyze problems of "identity loss" as children learn languages (Downes, 2001; Jo, 2001) or "identity maintenance" for children of minority groups learning their heritage language (Mills, 2001). The particular role of the textbook in supporting learners' identity has also been analyzed (Arbex, 2001).

The learners in some of these studies are from minority groups or find themselves in an identity-threatening situation. There is also a growing research interest in the impact of language and culture learning on the cultural identities of learners in majority groups, especially when they spend time in another country to improve their learning (Crawshaw, Callen, & Tusting, 2001; Jordan, 2001). Related research investigates the interplay among social context, perceptions of self, and language learning (Miller, 2003).

Scholarship and Foreign Language Teaching

Work that we classify as scholarship, is that which is concerned with intervention in the status quo of foreign language learning in order to develop it in a certain direction, and is far more frequent than research. Whereas the quality of research will be judged by criteria of clarity of conceptual analysis, validity and reliability of data, rigor in interpreting and drawing conclusions from data, scholarly work is often judged by the power of the argument and the rhetoric that sustains it, by the relevance of the argument to a given time and place, and by the support cited from research. Argument about "what ought to be" may depend more or less closely on research and the analysis of "what is." Proposals for future directions may be judged, irrespective of research, as realistic or unrealistic/ideal. Scholarship reflects, more than research, the relationship of language learning and teaching to the social conditions in which it is located. As the contemporary world changes to a state of globalization, for example, arguments about culture learning have changed too.

Contemporary scholarship is therefore concerned with and a reflection of social and political contents, and the responses of theorists and social commentators. In Germany, for example, Kramer has argued for attention to a "cultural studies" dimension to the teaching of English that has its roots in the critical social analysis of Raymond Williams and Stuart Hall in England (Kramer, 1997). Kramer argues that the study of English (*Anglistik*) needs to respond to the new ways in which people live their lives, engage in their culture, in a time of rapid change. The study of language and culture should address questions of "how we live" and also "how we ought to live," thus introducing an explicitly ethical dimension to teaching and learning. Starkey, too, introduces a strong ethical dimension by arguing that language and culture teaching should take note of and introduce human rights education into its aims and purposes (Starkey, 2002).

Changing social conditions are reflected in the work of Kramsch and Zarate. The former argues, like Kramer, for new purposes and re-definitions of language study to respond to "epistemological shifts occurring in academia" (Kramsch, 1995, p. xiv) and her argument that language study creates "a third place," a privileged and questioning location, where learners gain special insights into their own and others cultures, has become widely accepted. Zarate (2003), too, redefines the nature and purposes of language and culture learning, stressing the significance of in-between or border locations and the need for language teaching to respond to the particular challenges of European integration, as nation–states and national identities fuse and change.

Such authors present new perspectives and purposes. By doing so they open up new questions for research and scholarship. For example, researchers might explore the self-understanding of learners and teachers living in these newly defined conditions. Scholars who are interested in intervention and development work can find guidance in their planning from these new purposes, and new teaching objectives that follow from them.

There are some signs of this in intervention and development work already, although the relationship of classroom practice to pedagogical aims and ethical questions is not frequent enough. We reviewed recent publications abstracted in *Language Teaching* and concluded that intervention and development work is currently often focused on the problems of difference and distance, and how to overcome them. Culture learning is perceived as even less feasible if confined to the classroom than language learning. Culture learning needs to be experiential and experience of difference has to be at the center of learners' and teachers' attention.

Unsurprisingly, new communication technologies are promoted as a means of overcoming distance and giving learners experience of interacting with native speakers. E-mail contacts (Liaw & Johnson, 2001; Belz, 2001; Jogan, Heredia, & Aguilera, 2001), electronic conferencing (Truscott & Morley, 2001) and the Internet as a source of information (Herron et al., 2002; Gruber-Miller & Benton, 2001) are representative of this trend.

Tandem learning, originally developed as a means of enhancing linguistic competence, is a means of creating opportunities for culture learning (Rohrbach & Winiger, 2001; Kötter, 2001). Where possible visits and exchanges are offered to language learners for the same purposes, there are similar attempts to create culture learning (Gohard-Radenkovic, 2001; Harbon, 2002; Breugnot, 2001).

Implicit in these approaches is the assumption that interaction with people who embody a culture, who are native speakers of a language, is crucial. This then leads to debate and argument for (and against) the use of native speakers as teachers (Hinkel, 2001; Jiang, 2001). The debate about the advantages of non-native and native speakers with respect to teaching language (Medgyes, 1994) is thus beginning to be extended to teaching culture, and the related question of the relationship between teachers' experience of other cultures and their introduction of a cultural dimension into their teaching is being investigated (Aleksandrowicz-Pedich & Lazar, 2002).

Analysis of the cultural content of textbooks is a well-established area and insofar as it has begun to develop theoretically well-founded criteria, might be better classified as research into the effects of teaching on learners' perceptions (Sercu, 2000). Reports on the difficulties of using textbooks written in one country when teaching in another (Yakhontova, 2001) are, however, like reports of difficulties of using Western communication technology in non-Western countries (Smith, 2001; Takagaki, 2001). Feng and Byram (2002) adopt a more intercultural perspective in content analysis, and argue for intercultural representation in selecting textbook materials and analysis of intention and interpretation in handling authentic texts in the classroom.

Research and Scholarship in Second Language Teaching and Learning

The distinction between foreign and second language learning is often considered by those concerned with Second Language Acquisition research as unimportant. Research on bilingual education where students learn through the medium of another language than their first or dominant language would not make a distinction between learners who are immigrants to another country and learning through the official language of that country, and learners who simply go to a school where it has been decided to teach them through the medium of another language. However, it is important when thinking about the cultural issues involved because of the inevitability of some kind of culture learning when learners live in another culture, which they do not have if they are exposed to language learning only in the classroom. The learning of English is a special case in many countries because of the dominance of English-language media, and the inevitable exposure to manifestations of U.S. American culture.

Where some Second Language Acquisition research does make a distinction is between tutored and untutored learning, the latter often being the experience of adult immigrants whereas child immigrants are provided with formal, tutored language learning opportunities (Perdue, 2000). Nonetheless, this research seeks to answer questions about the acquisition of language as a system, what paths are taken by learners, what relationships there are among attitudes and motivation factors, why they stop learning so that their language fossilizes. Further questions that need to be asked concern how people, children and adults, acquire the concepts of their new cultural environment, the "keywords" that distinguish one language from another (Wierzbicka, 1997) the "rich points" of a culture (Agar, 1991). As Lantolf puts it:

> Although it may be possible for people to develop an intellectual understanding and tolerance of other cultures, a more interesting question, perhaps, is if, and to what extent, it is possible for people to become cognitively like members of other cultures; that is, can adults learn to construct and see the world through culturally different eyes. (1999, p. 29)

Lantolf then provides a useful survey of research that has examined the acquisition of lexis and metaphors, but points out that this is still at an early stage.

Another recent development is beginning to extend the range of interest of Second Language Acquisition in the way we have suggested is necessary. Norton (2000) argues that language acquisition is influenced by social relationships, by the social identities that immigrants are allowed to develop by the society in which they live. By careful case studies, she shows that the questions concerning the rate of acquisition, motivation, fossilization, precisely those questions that focus on language as a system, can be better explained by attention to the social conditions and the social identities present in the experience. Miller (2003) has carried out similar work with children, studying the cases of ten immigrant children in Australia in-depth to analyze the ways in which their self-representations impact on their language acquisition.

A further recent development approaches these questions through an attempt to understand the experience, particularly of adult language learners. Pavlenko (1998) has analyzed autobiographical accounts of language learning, notably in what she describes as "acclaimed literary masterpieces" whose authors have demonstrated a particular sensitivity and ability to recall and reflect on their learning experience. What is particularly interesting is that, although she starts with a focus on Second Language Acquisition and a search for further insight into the acquisition of language as system, she ends with questions about identity, about the possible incompatibilities of living in two languages.

In second language learning, then, there are more questions than answers, and research is only just beginning, but the distinction between "pure" research and "committed" scholarship, is just as valid, and in the next section we turn to the question of taking a position and the consequences that follow.

Taking a Position and Identifying Research Needs

One of the purposes of a review article or chapter is to evaluate, and not only present, research and scholarship. Where there is no disagreement about the purposes of research, then the task is to clarify criteria for good theories and make judgments about which research best meets those criteria. This seems to be the case in research on Second Language Acquisition (Long, 2000), which takes its lead from some forms of research in the natural sciences. The question is to decide which theories provide the best understanding of how second languages are acquired.

Evaluation of intervention and development work is less simple because there often remain implicit purposes, because the accounts of what is done are not sufficiently detailed, and because experimental conditions are not rigorous. Here, then, teachers read teachers' accounts and rely on their professional intuition and judgment. This is not without value since internalized professional criteria are not arbitrary; they reflect current theories as transmitted in teacher education. At the same time, of course, they remain often unarticulated and therefore not open to review and revision.

Evaluation of scholarship that is focused on "what ought to be" and argues for a particular position—such as those mentioned earlier associated with Kramsch, Kramer, and Zarate—is a more complex issue. There are no simple criteria beyond those of logical, clear and well-supported argument. Behind these, there is often a philosophical position, an ideology of axioms concerning the bases of human interaction, beliefs about the nature of human beings, and the societies they form. Discussion of aims and purposes of culture and language teaching and learning at this level is quickly seen to be related to judgments of values and desirable education.

In her discussion of the ways in which language teaching should change in universities in the United States, as a consequence of "major upheavals that are shaking at the foundation of the old idea of the university," Kramsch argues that "relevance" is a crucial issue, that there is:

> Renewed pressure on universities to serve national political and economic interests of the time by justifying their choice of the knowledge they produce and transmit, and by demonstrating its relevance to the current needs of society. Foreign languages are particularly vulnerable to this pressure. (1995, p. xvi)

She argues that language should be taught as social practice and that we should teach "meanings that are relevant both to the native speakers and to our students." If these are representative views then language and culture study is, first, a means to other ends and, second, an acquisition of knowledge of relevant meanings. Kramsch goes on, however, to say that learners can be made to reflect on their own social upbringing and cultural values as a consequence of study. The overlap between scholarship and teaching thus becomes evident and takes us back to our earlier discussion of critical approaches to teaching.

We have thus seen that where culture teaching-and-learning takes place in an educational context, questions of values and ideology are inevitable. Once this is accepted, there are implications for the evaluation of research and scholarship that go beyond technical discussions of best theories. This means that, if the position outlined earlier—let us call it language and political education—is accepted, then research and scholarship on culture teaching and learning can be judged not only in terms of its rigor and clarity, but also in terms of the contribution it makes to understanding current practice and developing new, "neohumanist" practices, while bearing in mind the issues of cultural relativity. Thus to take the example of motivation research, as well as investigating the impact of integrative motivation, there should be research that investigates the relationship between teaching styles, materials, methods, and the ability to take new perspectives, to be critical, to understand, and act according to the principles of democratic citizenship.

An alternative to this ideology-driven approach to evaluation is to identify gaps in the research. The most obvious, when research on culture learning is compared with that on language learning, is the lack of work on acquisition. Sercu (2004, p. 84) points out that empirical research on the acquisition of intercultural competence "is still very limited, and at any rate far more limited than that of studies investigating second language acquisition," and in fact she is obliged to analyze work that focuses mainly on language acquisition in her survey. She nonetheless presents a discussion of the variables that would have to be taken into consideration in acquisition studies: teacher variables, learner variables, teaching materials, and assessment processes. This approach assumes however that culture acquisition can be treated in the same way as language acquisition. It may not be quite so simple, not least because of the difficulty of delineating the "object" to be acquired, which is much easier with language.

An alternative perspective for language learning that might be extended to culture learning is suggested by the distinction made by Sfard (1998) between the acquisition metaphor and the participation metaphor. Pavlenko and Lantolf (2000) apply this to language learning. The acquisition metaphor presents learning as the ability to internalize knowledge as an object, as a commodity. Thus, language learning is conceptualized as the internalization of rules and specific linguistic entities. The participation metaphor makes us think of learning as "a process of becoming a member of a certain community" (Sfard, 1998, p. 6).

The use of this metaphor of participation (combined with acquisition as Sfard says) is particularly apposite for culture teaching provided that the critical dimension of teaching is not forgotten. Culture learning can thus be conceptualized as socialization, by the teacher as mediator, into another culture. The teacher acts as mediator between learners and those who are already members of the language-and-culture group of which they seek understanding. At the same time, if it is axiomatic for the teacher that learners should reflect critically and analytically on their own culture, the participation and socialization process is not focused exclusively on other cultures. For it is not the purpose of teaching, we would contend, to change learners into members of another culture, but to make them part of the group who see themselves as mediators, able to compare, juxtapose, and analyze.

CONCLUSION

Our review has shown that activity in teaching and researching the cultural dimension and intercultural competence in language teaching has developed rapidly in the last decades. We have also argued that this work cannot avoid engagement with and challenges to values and ideas, and that this is, if not a new direction for language teachers and researchers, at least a new emphasis. It reminds us that language teaching has always been susceptible to political and social influences, whether it was the use of English teaching in Germany in the 1920s to boost the self-esteem of German pupils (Neuner, 1988, p. 36), or the use of English teaching in former colonial countries to re-assert Western hegemony (Phillipson, 1992; Pennycook, 1994, 1998). It suggests however that the contribution might also be positive—the development of critical awareness, the pursuit of democratic processes and values—while reminding us that even these need to be challenged.

The increase in the volume of work does not inevitably mean an improvement in quality, and there is a need to develop more systematically a program of research rather than ad hoc efforts that may not have a lasting effect. This is the task for the research and teaching community.

REFERENCES

Agar, M. (1991). The biculture in bilingual. *Language in Society, 20*, 167–181.

Aleksandrowicz-Pedich, L., & Lazar, I. (2002). Cross-cultural communicative competence in teaching English as a foreign language: Research project in four European countries (Estonia, Hungary, Iceland, and Poland). In T. Siek-Piskozub (Ed.), *European Year of Languages 2001*. Proceedings of the Third CER-FIPLV Conference, 26–28 September 2001, Poznan, Poland. Poznan: Adam Mickiewicz University.

Arbex, M. (2001). La diversité culturelle dans les méthodes de FLE uilisées au Brésil. *Dialogues et Cultures, 44*, 92–98.

Armstrong, G. K. (1984). Life after study abroad: A survey of undergraduate academic and career choices. *The Modern Language Journal, 68*, 1–6.

Atkinson, D., & Ramanathan, V. (1995). Cultures of writing: An ethnographic comparison of L1 and L2 university writing/language programs. *TESOL Quarterly, 29(3)*, 539–568.

Barkhuizen, G. P. (1998). Discovering learners' perceptions of ESL classroom teaching/learning activities in a South African context. *TESOL Quarterly, 32(1)*, 85–108.

Barro, A., Jordan, S., & Roberts, C. (1998). Cultural practice in everyday life: The language learner as ethnographer. In M. Byram & M. Fleming (Eds.) *Language learning in intercultural perspective: Approaches through drama and ethnography* (pp. 76–97). Cambridge: Cambridge University Press.

Belz, J. A. (2001). Institutional and individual dimensions of transatlantic group work in network-based language teaching. *ReCALL, 13(2)*, 213–231.

Bennett, M. J. (1993). Towards ethnorelativism: A developmental model of intercultural sensitivity. In R. M. Paige (Ed.), *Education for the intercultural experience* (pp. 21–71). Yarmouth, ME: Intercultural Press.

Boers, F., & Demecheleer, M. (2001). Measuring the impact of cross-cultural differences on learners' comprehension of imageable idioms. *ELT Journal, 55(3)*, 255–262.

Breugnot, J. (2001). L'institution scolaire en France et en Allemagne: différences et proximités. *Les Langues Modernes, 3*, 13–20.

Brooks, N. (1975). The analysis of language and familiar cultures. In R. Lafayette (Ed.), *The cultural revolution in foreign language teaching: Reports of the Northeast Conference on the Teaching of Foreign Languages* (pp. 19–31). Lincolnwood, IL: National Textbook.

Byram, M. (1989a). *Cultural studies in foreign language education*. Clevedon, UK: Multilingual Matters.

Byram, M. (1989b). A school visit to France: Ethnographic explorations. *British Journal of Language Teaching, 27(2)*, 99–103.

Byram, M. (1997). *Teaching and assessing intercultural communicative competence*. Clevedon, UK: Multilingual Matters.

Byram, M., & Cain, A. (1998). Civilisation/cultural studies: An experiment in French and English schools. In M. Byram & M. Fleming (Eds.), *Language learning in intercultural perspectives* (pp. 32–44). Cambridge, UK: Cambridge University Press.

Byram, M., Esarte-Sarries, V., & Taylor, S. (1991). *Cultural studies and language learning: A research report*, Clevedon, UK: Multilingual Matters.

Byram, M., & Fleming, M. (Eds.) (1998). *Language learning in intercultural perspectives*. Cambridge, UK: Cambridge University Press.

Byram, M., & Grundy, P. (2002). *Context and culture in language teaching and learning*. Clevedon, UK: Multilingual Matters.

Byram, M., & Risager, K. (1999). *Language teachers, politics, and cultures*. Clevedon, UK: Multilingual Matters.

Byram, M., & Snow, D. (1997). *Crossing frontiers: The school study visit abroad*. London: Centre for Information on Language Teaching.

Canagarajah, A. S. (1993). Critical ethnography of a Sri Lankan classroom: Ambiguities in student opposition to reproduction through ESOL. *TESOL Quarterly, 28*(4), 601–626.

Carel, S. (2001). Students as virtual ethnographers: Exploring the language culture connections. In M. Byram, A. Nichols, & D. Stevens (Eds.), *Developing intercultural competence in practice* (pp. 146–161). Clevedon, UK: Multilingual Matters.

Carlson, J., Burn, B., Useem, J., & Yachmowicz, D. (1990). *Study abroad: The experience of undergraduates*. Westport, CT: Greenwood.

Chastain, K. (1976). *Developing second language skills: Theory to practice*. (2nd Ed.). Chicago: Rand McNally.

Coleman, J. A. (1995). The current state of knowledge concerning students residence abroad. In G. Parker & A. Rouxeville (Eds.), *The year abroad: Preparation, monitoring, evaluation* (pp. 17–42), London: CILT.

Coleman, J. A. (1997). Residence abroad within language study. *Language Teaching, 30*(1), 1–20.

Coleman, J. A. (1998). Evolving intercultural perceptions among university language learners in Europe. In M. Byram & M. Fleming (Eds.), *Language learning in intercultural perspectives* (pp. 45–75). Cambridge, UK: Cambridge University Press.

Corbett, J. (2003). *An intercultural approach to english language teaching*. Clevedon, UK: Multilingual Matters.

Cortazzi, M., & Shen, W. W. (2001). Cross-linguistic awareness of cultural keywords: A study of Chinese and English speakers. *Language Awareness, 10*(2/3), 125–142.

Crawshaw, R., Callen, B., & Tusting, K. (2001). Attesting the self: Narration and identity change during periods of residence abroad. *Language and Intercultural Communication, 1*(2), 101–119.

Cushner, K., & Brislin, R. W. (Eds.) (1997). *Improving intercultural interactions: Modules for cross-cultural training programs. Vol. 2*. Thousand Oaks, CA: Sage.

Dahlen, T. (1997). *Among the interculturalists*. Stockholm: Stockholm Studies in Social Anthropology.

Damen, L. (1987). *Culture learning: The fifth dimension in the language classroom*. Reading, MA: Addison-Wesley.

DeKeyser, R. M. (1991). Foreign language development during a semester abroad. In B. F. Freed (Ed.), *Foreign language acquisition research and the classroom* (pp. 104–119). Lexington, MA: Health.

Dörnyei, Z. (1998). Motivation in second and foreign language learning. *Language Teaching, 31*(3), 117–135.

Dörnyei, Z. (2001). *Motivational strategies in the language classroom*. Cambridge, UK: Cambridge University Press.

Dörnyei, Z., & Csizér, K. (1998). Ten commandments for motivating language learners: Results of an empirical study, *Language Teaching Research, 2*(3), 203–229.

Downes, S. (2001). Sense of Japanese cultural identity within an English partial immersion programme: Should parents worry? *International Journal of Bilingual Education and Bilingualism, 4*(3), 165–180.

Doyé, P. (1999). *The intercultural dimension: Foreign language education in the primary school*. Berlin: Cornelsen.

Dyson, P. (1988). *The year abroad*. Report from the Central Bureau for Educational Visits and Exchanges. Oxford University Language Teaching Centre.

Fantini, A. E. (1997). *New ways in teaching culture*. Alexandria, VA: TESOL.

Feng, A. W., & Byram, M. (2002). Authenticity in college English textbooks: An intercultural perspective. *RELC Journal, 33*(2), 58–84.

Fenner, A. (2001). *Cultural awareness and language awareness based on dialogic interaction with texts in foreign language learning*. Strasbourg Cedex, France: Council of Europe Publishing.

FitzGerald, H. (2003). *How different are we?* Clevedon, UK: Multilingual Matters.

Fleming, M. (1998). Cultural awareness and dramatic forms. In M. Byram & M. Fleming (Eds.), *Language learning in intercultural perspectives* (pp. 147–157). Cambridge, UK: Cambridge University Press.

Fleming, M. (2003). Intercultural experience and drama. In G. Alred, M. Byram, & M. Fleming (Eds.). *Intercultural experience and education*. Clevedon, UK: Multilingual Matters.

Fowler, S. M., & Mumfort, M. G. (Eds.) (1995). *Intercultural sourcebook: Cross-cultural training methods. Vol. 1*. Yarmouth, ME: Intercultural Press.

Fowler, S. M., & Mumfort, M. G. (Eds.) (1999). *Intercultural sourcebook: Cross-cultural training methods. Vol. 2*. Yarmouth, ME: Intercultural Press.

Furstenberg, G., Levet, S., English, K., & Maillet, K. (2001). Giving a virtual voice to the silent language of culture: The Cultura project. *Language Learning and Technology, 5*(1), 55–102. Available at http://llt.msu.edu

Gardner, R. C., & Lambert, W. E. (1972). *Attitudes and motivation in second-language learning*. Rowley, MA: Newbury House.

Gibson, R. (2000). *Intercultural business communication*. Berlin: Cornelsen and Oxford.

Gohard-Radenkovic, A. (2001). Comment évaluer les compétences socioculturelles de l'étudiant en situation de mobilité? *Dialogues et cultures, 44*, 52–61.

Gruber-Miller, J., & Benton, C. (2001). How do you say MOO in Latin? Assessing student learning and motivation in beginning Latin. *CALICO Journal, 18*(2), 305–338.

Gudykunst, W. B., & Kim, Y. Y. (Eds.). (1992). *Readings on communicating with strangers: An approach to intercultural communication*. New York: McGraw-Hill.

Guilherme, M. (2002). *Critical citizens for an intercultural world.* Clevedon, UK: Multilingual Matters.

Harbon, L. A. (2002). Stories of raw green chillies and unlocked cupboards. *Babel (AFMLTA), 36*(3), 23–38.

Herron, C., Corrie, C., Dubreuil, S., & Cole, S. (2002). A classroom investigation: Can video improve intermediate-level French language students' ability to learn about a foreign culture? *The Modern Language Journal, 86*(1), 36–53.

Hill, J. C., & Hill, K. C. (1986). *Speaking Mexicano.* Tucson: University of Arizona Press.

Hinkel, R. (2001). Sind 'native-speakers' wirklich die besseren Fremdsprachenlehrer? *Info-DAF, 28*(6), 585–599.

Hoffman, D. M. (1999). Culture and comparative education: Towards decentring and recentring the discourse. *Comparative Education Review, 43*(4), 464–488.

Hofstede, G. (1991). *Cultures and organizations.* London: McGraw-Hill.

Hofstede, G. J., Pedersen, P. B., & Hofstede, G. (2002). *Exploring culture: Exercises, stories, and synthetic cultures.* Yarmouth, ME: Intercultural Press.

Holliday, A. (1994). *Appropriate methodology and social context.* Cambridge, UK: Cambridge University Press.

Holliday, A. (1996). Developing a sociological imagination: Expanding ethnography in international English language education. *Applied Linguistics, 17*(2), 234–255.

Hu, W. Z., & Gao, Y. H. (1997). *Waiyu Jiaoxue yu Wenhua* (Foreign Language Teaching and Culture). Changsha: Hunan Education Press.

Hymes, D. H. (1974). *Foundations in sociolinguistics: An ethnographic approach.* Philadelphia: University of Pennsylvania Press.

Hymes, D. H. (1981). Ethnographic monitoring. In H. Trueba, G. Guthrie, & K. Au (Eds.), *Culture and the bilingual classroom: Studies in classroom ethnography* (pp. 56–68). Rowley, MA: Newbury House.

Ingram, D., & O'Neill, S. (2002). The enigma of cross-cultural attitudes in language teaching: Part 2. *Babel (AFMLTA) 36*(3), 17–22, 37–38.

Jiang, W. (2001). Handling 'culture-bumps.' *ELT Journal, 55*(4), 382–390.

Jo, H-Y. (2001). 'Heritage' language learning and ethnic identity: Korean Americans' struggle with language authorities. *Language, Culture, and Curriculum, 14*(1), 26–41.

Jogan, M. K., Heredia, A. H., & Aguilera, G. M. (2001). Cross-cultural e-mail: Providing cultural input for the advanced foreign language student. *Foreign Language Annals, 34*(4), 341–346.

Jordan, S. A. (2001). Writing the other: Transforming consciousness through ethnographic writing. *Language and Intercultural Communication, 1*(1), 40–56.

Jurasek, R. (1996). Using ethnography to bridge the gap between study abroad and the on-campus language and culture curriculum. In C. Kramsch (Ed.), *Redefining the boundaries of language study* (pp. 221–251). Boston: Heinle & Heinle.

Kauffmann, N., Martin, J., & Weaver, H. with J. Weaver (1992). *Students abroad: Strangers at home.* Yarmouth, ME: Intercultural Press.

Kohls, L. R., & Knight, J. M. (1994). *Developing intercultural awareness: A cross-cultural training handbook* (2nd Ed.). Yarmouth, ME: Intercultural Press.

Kötter, M. (2001). MOOrituri te salutant? Language learning through MOO-based synchronous exchanges between learner tandems. *Computer Assisted Language, Learning, 14*(3-4), 289–304.

Kramer, J. (1997). *British cultural studies.* München: Wilhelm Fink.

Kramsch, C. (1993). *Context and culture in language teaching.* Oxford, UK: Oxford University Press.

Kramsch, C. (1995). *Redefining the boundaries of language study.* Boston: Heinle & Heinle.

Lantolf, J. P. (1999). Second culture acquisition: Cognitive considerations. In E. Hinkel (Ed.), *Culture in second language teaching,* Cambridge, UK: Cambridge University Press.

Lantolf, J. P. (2000a). Second language learning as a mediated process. *Language Teaching, 33,* 79–96.

Lantolf, J. P. (2000b). Introducing sociocultural theory. In J. P. Lantolf, (Ed.), *Sociocultural theory and second language learning.* Oxford, UK: Oxford University Press.

Lewis, T., & Stickler, U. (2000). 'While they are out there . . .' Using diaries to structure independent learning during a period of residence abroad. In N. McBride & K. Seago (Eds.), *Target culture—target language?* (pp. 206–232). London: Centre for Information on Language Teaching and Research.

Liaw, M-L., & Johnson, R. J. (2001). E-mail writing as a cross-cultural learning experience. *System, 29*(2), 235–251.

Lindenfeld, J. (1990). *Speech and sociability at French urban marketplaces.* Amsterdam: Benjamins.

Lo Bianco, J., Liddicoat, A. J., & Crozet, C. (Eds.) (1999). *Striving for the third place.* Melbourne: Language Australia.

Long, M. (2000). Second language acquisition theories. In M. Byram (Ed.), *Routledge encyclopedia of language teaching and learning.* London: Routledge & Kegan Paul.

McLeod, B. (1976). The relevance of anthropology to language teaching. *TESOL Quarterly, 10*(2), 211–220.

Medgyes, P. (1994). *The non-native teacher,* London: Macmillan.

Miller, J. (2003). *Audible difference.* Clevedon, UK: Multilingual Matters.

Milroy, L. (1987). *Observing and analysing natural language.* Oxford, UK: Basil Blackwell.

Mills, J. (2001). Being bilingual: perspectives of third generation Asian children on language, culture and indentiy. *International Journal of Bilingual Education and Bilingualism, 4/6,* 383–402.

Moran, P. (2001). *Teaching culture: Perspectives in practice.* Boston: Heinle & Heinle.

Morgan, C., & Cain, A. (2000). *Foreign language and culture learning from a dialogic perspective*. Clevedon, UK: Multilingual Matters.

Murphy-Lejeune, E. (2002). *Student mobility and narrative in Europe: The new strangers*. London: Routledge & Kegan Paul.

Murphy-Lejeune, E. (2003). An experience of interculturality: Student travellers abroad. In G. Alred, M. Byram, & M. Fleming (Eds.), *Intercultural experience and education* (pp . 101–113). Clevedon, UK: Multicultural Matters.

Neuner, G. (1988). Towards universals of content in the foreign language curriculum: A cognitive-anthropological approach. *Language, Culture, and Curriculum, 1*(1), 33–52.

Nieto, S. (1999). *The light in their eyes: Creating multicultural learning communities*. New York: Teachers College Press.

Nieto, S. (2002). *Language, culture, and teaching: Critical perspectives for a new century*. Mahwah, NJ: Lawrence Erlbaum Associates.

Norton, B. (2000). *Identity and language learning: Gender, ethnicity, and educational change*. Harlow: Longman.

Olk, H. M. (2002). Translating culture: A think-aloud protocol study. *Language Teaching Research, 6*(2), 121–144.

Orsoni, J-L. (2001). Pistes de travail pour un comparaison des discours en portugais du Brésil et en français. *Etudes de Linguistique Appliquée, 121* 101–110.

Oswalt, W. H. (1970). *Understanding our culture: An anthropological view*. New York: Holt, Rinehart & Winston.

Pan, Y., Scollon, R., & Scollon, S. (2002). *Professional communication in international settings*. Malden, MA: Blackwell.

Paulston, C. (1974). Linguistic and communicative competence. *TESOL Quarterly, 8*(4), 347–362.

Pavlenko, A. (1998). Second language learning by adults: Testimonies of bilingual writers. *Issues in Applied Linguistics, 9*(1), 3–19.

Pavlenko, A., & Lantolf, J. P. (2000). Second language learning as participation and the (re)construction of selves. In J. P. Lantolf (Ed.), *Sociocultural theory and second language learning*. Oxford, UK: Oxford University Press.

Pennycook, A. (1994). *The Cultural politics of english as an international language*. London: Longman.

Pennycook, A. (1998). *English and the discourses of colonialism*. London: Routledge & Kegan Paul.

Perdue, C. (2000). Untutored language acquisition. In M. Byram (Ed.), *Routledge encyclopedia of language teaching and learning*. London: Routledge & Kegan Paul.

Phillipson, R. (1992). *Linguistic imperialism*. Oxford, UK: Oxford University Press.

Rao, Z. (2002). Chinese students' perceptions of communicative and non-communicative activities in the EFL classroom. *System, 30*(1), 85–105.

Reagan, T. G., & Osborn, T. A. (2002). *The foreign language educator in society: Towards a critical pedagogy*. Mahwah, NJ: Lawrence Erlbaum Associates.

Roberts, C., Byram, M., Barro, A., Jordan, S., & Street, B. (2001). *Language learners as ethnographers*. Clevedon, UK: Multilingual Matters.

Robinson-Stuart, G., & Nocon, H. (1996). Second culture acquisition: Ethnography in the foreign language classroom. *The Modern Language Journal, 80*(4), 431–449.

Rohrbach, R., & Winiger, E. (2001). Tandem statt Unterricht. *Babylonia, 3*, 64–68.

Schulz, R. (2001). Cultural differences in student and teacher perceptions concerning the role of grammar instruction and corrective feedback: USA-Colombia. *The Modern Language Journal, 85*(2), 244–258.

Scollon, R., & Scollon, S. W. (1995). *Intercultural communication*. Oxford, UK: Blackwell.

Sercu, L. (2004). Researching the acquisition of intercultural communicative competence in a foreign language: Setting the agenda for a research area. In O. St. John, K. van Esch, & E. Shalkwijk (Eds.), *New insights in foreign language learning and teaching*. Frankfurt: Peter Lang.

Sercu, L. (2000). *Acquiring intercultural communicative competence from textbooks*. Leuven: Leuven University Press.

Sfard, A. (1998). On two metaphors for learning and the danger of choosing just one. *Educational Researcher, 27*(2), 4–13.

Smith, R. (2001). Group work for autonomy in Asia: Insights from teacher research. *AILA Review, 15*, 70–81.

Starkey, H. (2002). *Democratic citizenship, languages, diversity, and human rights*. Strasbourg: Council of Europe.

Takagaki, Y. (2001). Des phrases mais pas de communication. Problème d'organisation textuelle chez les non-Occidentaux: le cas des japonais. *Dialogues et Cultures, 44*, 84–91.

Tomalin, B., & Stempleski, S. (1993). *Cultural awareness*. Oxford, UK: Oxford University Press.

Tomic, A. (2000). A critical pedagogy for teaching intercultural communication to language learners. In N. McBride & K. Seago (Eds.), *Target culture—target language?* London: CILT.

Topuzova, K. (2001). British and Bulgarian Christmas cards: A research project for students. In M., Byram, A., Nichols, & D., Stevens, (Eds.), *Developing intercultural competence in practice*. Clevedon, UK: Multilingual Matters.

Trompenaar, S. F. (1993). *Riding the waves of culture*. London: Nicholas Brealey Publishing.

Truscott, S., & Morley, J. (2001). Cross-cultural learning through computer-mediated communication. *Language Learning, 24*(1), 17–23.

von Wright, G. H. (1971). *Explanation and understanding*. London: Routledge & Kegan Paul.

Ward, C., Bochner, S., & Furnham, A. (2001). *The psychology of culture shock* (2nd ed.). London: Routledge & Kegan Paul.

Wierzbicka, A. (1997b). *Understanding cultures through key words. English, Russian, Polish, German, and Japanese* Oxford, UK: Oxford University Press.

Woodward, K. (1997). *Identity and difference.* London: Sage.

Yakhontova, T. (2001). Textbooks, contexts, and learners. *English for Specific Purposes, 20*(5), 397–415.

Zarate, G. (1991). The observation diary: An ethnographic approach to teacher education. In D. Buttjes & M. Byram (Eds.), *Mediating languages and cultures: Towards an intercultural theory of foreign language education* (pp. 248–260), Clevedon, UK: Multilingual Matters.

Zarate, G. (2003). Identities and plurilingualism: Preconditions for recognition of intercultural competences. In M. Byram (Ed.), *Intercultural competence.* Strasbourg: Council of Europe.

Critical Pedagogy in L2 Learning and Teaching

Suresh Canagarajah
Baruch College, City University of New York

Critical pedagogy entered the second language (L2) scene quite belatedly, at least in comparison to its sister disciplines literature, composition, and education. Marxist orientations to the material and ideological implications of learning were already being discussed around the 1970s by Williams (1977) in literature, Ohmann (1976) in composition, and Giroux (1979) in education. Although teaching a colonial language to students from many minority language groups is a controversial activity fraught with political significance, L2 professionals largely adopted an idyllic innocence toward their work. This attitude was shaped by the structuralist perspective on language (which orientated to proficiency as the rule-governed deployment of abstract value-free grammar), behaviorist orientation to learning (which assumed that the calculated exposure to linguistic stimuli would facilitate competence among docile students), and the positivistic tradition to language acquisition research (which stipulated that a controlled observation of learning in clinically circumscribed settings would reveal the processes of acquisition that help construct the methods and materials for successful learning). L2 teaching was motivated by the pragmatic attitude of equipping students with the linguistic and communicative skills that would make them socially functional. With hindsight, critical practitioners would now argue that these apolitical disciplinary principles were indeed motivated by geopolitical realities. English Language Teaching, or ELT, (as sponsored by cultural agencies like the United States Information Agency and the British Council) became an important activity after decolonization and around the Cold War when English language was perceived as a more effective medium of hegemony (see Phillipson, 1992). The dominant principles in the discipline, therefore, served to mask the controversial material and ideological ends of ELT pedagogy (Pennycook, 1989, 1994a).

It is around the late 1980s and early 1990s that we begin to see the stirrings of a critical orientation to L2 learning in the mainline journals in the field (see Pennycook, 1989; Peirce, 1989; Auerbach, 1993; Benesch, 1993; Canagarajah, 1993a, 1993b). To list such developments as decolonization, the Cold War, and ethnic revivalism as the social conditions that determine the emergence of this pedagogical orientation is to adopt an unnecessarily reductive approach. Suffice it to say that this was a hectic time of intellectual questioning and discursive reconstruction in the academy. With the modernist values of the Enlightenment tradition being challenged, there was a range of critical theories coming into prominence from diverse socially marginalized groups. Although the period prided itself as being "post" everything (as displayed in the choice of labels for its popular discourses—poststructuralism, postmodernism, post-Marxism, postcolonialism), other affected groups were right to question the smug multicultural ethos emerging in the West (see Bahri, 1997; Prendergast, 1998). Feminism, critical race theory, subaltern studies, and queer theory inspired a more radical critique of the models of diversity in fashion.[1] As for L2 pedagogy, all this represented a healthy climate of research and application. The school didn't have the dogmatic character that marked the critical orientations in its sister disciplines. It also moved away from the deterministic brands of thinking that Marxism imposed on previous models of education. Thus critical pedagogy in L2 has always been sympathetic to the agency of subjects; the shaping influence of culture, discourse, and consciousness (and not just of economic and material conditions) on learning activity; the relative autonomy of specific social domains to critically negotiate the machinations of economic and political structures; and the power of local settings like the classroom to develop cultures of resistance to larger political forces. All of these positions may be rejected by certain versions of Marxism (see Canagarajah, 1999a, pp. 27–35). For this reason, it was worth the wait. The field began to ask critical questions of L2 learning from multiple, flexible, and broad angles or orientation, unlike the disciplines that practiced critical pedagogies before the 1970s.

Given this history, it is difficult to define critical pedagogy in our field according to a static body of ideas or a limited set of philosophical axioms. In fact, it is dangerous to define it so. Theories can narrow down the perspectives from which the learning activity should be interpreted. While theories are enabling (in opening our eyes to the issues that matter in a specific activity), they can also be limiting. This is not to deny the well-known axiom that there is nothing as practical as a theory—that is, any activity or practice is informed by a body of assumptions, and demands certain explanatory frameworks to make sense of it. Personally, I prefer to adopt a tool box approach to theory. We must feel free to pick and choose among the available critical theories as relevant for the diverse students, classrooms, and communities we are working with. To define critical pedagogy, then, we should turn to the other end of the theory/praxis dichotomy and orientate to it as a form of practice. Critical pedagogy is not a set of ideas, but a way of "doing" learning and teaching. It is a practice motivated by a distinct attitude toward classrooms and society. Critical students and teachers are prepared to situate learning in the relevant social contexts, unravel the implications of power in pedagogical activity, and commit themselves to transforming the means and ends of learning, in order to construct more egalitarian, equitable, and ethical educational and social environments. In this sense, the term *critical* contrasts with terms like detached, objective, dispassionate, instrumental, practical, and descriptive, which have informed "noncritical" traditions of L2 practice from the modernist philosophical perspective.[2]

If we define critical pedagogy (CP) in such a practice-oriented manner, we may infer that it is not just another method or school for teaching L2. The temptation for many instructors is to treat CP as one more method among the many we have, ranging from grammar-translation to learner strategy training. Others treat CP as a special school, such as the cognitive process, contrastive rhetoric, or English for Academic Purposes (EAP) approaches in the teaching of writing. However, CP is a fundamentally different way of doing L2 learning and teaching. Everything in pedagogical activity gets transformed in the process. To practice CP, we must situate all the activities, skills, proficiencies, and standards in the social context and interrogate them in relation to power. To use a cliched term, CP affords a new "paradigm" for teaching L2. Given these assumptions, it is possible to apply the adjective "critical" to any domain of pedagogy with predictable results. Although we already have a string of labels with the adjective attached to it—such as critical contrastive rhetoric (Kubota, 1999), critical classroom discourse analysis (Kumaravadivelu, 1999), critical writing (Canagarajah, 1993a), critical applied linguistics (Pennycook, 2001), and critical EAP (Benesch, 2001)—we don't have to stop there.

Although critical practitioners may apply this orientation to everything in L2 learning activity, it is possible to review here only the prominent traditions of research practice that have been reported in the professional literature. I must confess, however, that many of the assumptions and orientations of CP have seeped into the profession in a pervasive manner (as it certainly should) that it is becoming difficult to identify CP as a distinct persuasion anymore. Many teachers/researchers have begun to situate their practice in configurations of power without labeling their work as CP. It is possible, then, that some of the scholars I review here may feel more at home in other chapters of the handbook, on identity, culture, or language acquisition. However, since their research/teaching practice is sensitive to power, they still help develop a CP orientation to L2.

I begin by exemplifying critical research in certain well-known areas of L2 pedagogy.[3] I have to leave out areas like language socialization, classroom discourse, attitudes and motivation, identity, teacher education, and language policy planning for other chapters that focus exclusively on them. In the second section, I move on to identify the central issues that scholars wrestle with in critical research and interpretation. New researchers have to mind these ongoing debates as they undertake their own studies. In the final section, I review the methods that critical researchers adopt to study issues of power in language learning. As I will explain, research on CP is itself motivated by critical assumptions, constituting a unique approach of "critical research." I conclude with a consideration of the unique rhetorical challenges that concern critical researchers as they attempt to represent their findings in scholarly publications, inspiring them to discover genres that are consistent with their philosophical assumptions.

AREAS OF RESEARCH INTEREST

Critical Academic Literacy

More research reports in CP relate to practices of reading and writing than to other areas like speaking and listening. Perhaps there is the unstated assumption that the more spontaneous acts of speaking and listening don't conveniently provide the space for critical reflection in order to question and alter manifestations of power in interpersonal interactions. Reading and writing, being slightly detached activities, have provided more possibilities for intervention. Even in the latter, there are more reports relating to macro-textual domains than those on the use of grammar or vocabulary. Though we have a well-established critical tradition on orientating to sentence-level rules from the time of critical linguistics (see Fowler & Kress, 1979) and stretching up to more recent forms of critical discourse analysis (see Fairclough, 2000; Gee, 2000), there are very few research projects using this approach in classroom learning. Although exemplary articles on how critical linguistics can help classroom language learning are available (see Fairclough, 2000), they haven't inspired active research.

The few case studies that focus on grammar-level issues in literacy (perhaps indirectly influenced by the critical linguistics school) provide some useful leads that can be pursued by other critical practitioners. Using news reports during the Gulf War, Brian Morgan (1998) enables immigrant students to interpret the way lexical items, the grammatical status of words, and syntactical choices construct meanings that favor the North American position in this conflict. The collocation of words used to describe both parties in this conflict are shown to lack neutrality. This sensitivity enables students to read critically and unravel the ideological interests that motivate language in these news reports.

In an example of how we can move from critique to transformation, Min-zhan Lu (1994) shows how a peculiar grammatical modal used by a Chinese-Malaysian student indicates a move toward creative language use. The student uses the construction "can able to" consistently—in a rule-governed way. The structure seems to connote for her "ability from the perspective of the external circumstances" (Lu, 1994, p. 452). Although she is aware of the modal "can," she finds that this is loaded with a volitionist connotation that is more typical of the western sense of agency. She wants to express the need to achieve independence despite community constraints (as informed by her personal experience of coming to study in the United States, despite the family's view that the place of a woman is inside the home). Lu doesn't immediately accept this "nonstandard" usage. She makes this an opportunity to discuss with students the ways in which English grammar assumes ideological positions that may not be suitable for the interests of other speakers. She then encourages her students to explore what other creative alternatives they may have for negotiating an expression of their unique meanings through English language. Surprisingly, some students opt to use the "nonstandard" usage within quotation marks, or with a footnote mentioning the need for this unusual modal, to show their critical and creative language usage. There is more scope for studies on how students can be made sensitive to ideological values in texts and encouraged to make grammatical choices critically.

More studies have been conducted on the extra-sentential aspects of text construction than on sentence-level grammar. This power-sensitive textual critique was built on the excellent descriptive work of the schools of English for Academic Purposes, Genre Analysis, and English for Specific Purposes. Through a careful observation of communication in academic settings and analyses of texts produced in scholarly communities, these schools have unraveled the hidden conventions that characterize the genre of academic literacy. However, their work is motivated by the pragmatic attitude that, while these conventions may be value-ridden and favor the ideologies of the dominant English speech communities, these are the conventions that students of all languages have to know in order to succeed in the academic setting. Benesch (1993) has taken this pragmatism to task. She has shown that leaving the underlying values and interests of this genre unquestioned is itself an ideological position and is by no means neutral. Critical practitioners have argued for the need to teach students the ways in which these conventions serve to limit membership in the academic community (Canagarajah, 1993a). They have shown the ways in which the typical academic posture of detachment and objectivity excludes other ways of knowing that are more empathic and personal, including writings that are more involved and narrative, as in the case of women and other minority communities (see Belcher, 1997; Benesch, 1993; Canagarajah, 2002b). They have argued for the need to negotiate competing writing traditions for more independent expression, rather than mimicking academic conventions. Insights have been borrowed from critical compositionists in the L1 circles (i.e., Bizzell, 1992) to develop such a pedagogy. Benesch (1999, 2001) reports on attempts to motivate L2 students to read and write critically in academic settings, questioning their own assumptions and those of the experts in different fields.

Moving beyond grammar and text to more rhetorically based issues, the ways in which students can adopt transformative practices to construct variant discourses has been explored only recently with the theorization of "voice" in feminist circles. It is more mature/professional multilingual writers (such as ESL teachers and academic scholars) who have provided examples of how they have struggled with the multiple discourses from their backgrounds to create a space for alternative styles in the academic text or to appropriate the established conventions for their more radical purposes. This new line of research constitutes largely narrative, personal, and reflective case studies (see Belcher & Connor, 2001; Casanave & Vandrick, 2003). Xiao Ming Li (1999) reflects on the conflicts she faced between her formal Chinese ethos and the highly individuated American academic writing. Her attempts to adopt American or Chinese conventions in their own terms led to academic marginalization. It was when she developed the confidence to draw from the strengths of both traditions and adopt a "third" discourse that her voice was taken seriously by the academic audience. Her theorization is similar to the report of Kramsch and Lam (1999) who study several multilingual writers to show how the "third spaces" they construct in their textual world serve to creatively complicate accepted conventions and empower these writers for critical expression.

We must note that studies on reading/writing are now not limited to the text, but adopt a more holistic approach in situating textual reception and production in social processes. Using the term *literacy practice* studies, scholars in this tradition address issues of power and difference with great complexity. Whereas well-known studies in this tradition focus on literacy in the L1 context, the field is expanding to include multilingual students. A recent collection of ethnographic studies by Street (2001) brings out some familiar themes in this tradition: how the literacy encouraged in the classroom doesn't always meet the real-world needs of students; how the dominant methods of teaching literacy don't relate well to the local traditions of literacy acquisition; and how the learners appropriate what is taught by teachers and other sponsors of literacy for divergent local uses and purposes. On the whole, these studies serve to remind educators that rather than imposing their own vision of what kinds of literacy are needed for learners and how they should be taught to them (albeit for the enlightened purpose of empowering them), it is more important to listen to local communities (especially in periphery contexts) to understand their motivations. In a similar vein, Pennycook (1996) situates the writing of Chinese students in social context to show how the perception of plagiarism in their writing can be explained from their socialization into modes of thinking and communicating that value the place of authoritative texts in their society. In a case study that will remain a model for holistic inquiry into literacy acquisition, Paul Prior (1998) compares the initiation of two ESL graduate students into disciplinary writing. Critical to the success of both students is the way they manage to negotiate the influences from the multiple channels of communication from family, work, and society into accomplishing their purposes in their academic writing. The more successful student is not only more receptive to these influences, but also displays the confidence to negotiate her personal interests with those of the authoritative discourses in the discipline. The less successful student forms a dependent relationship with her faculty advisor.

A research approach that expands the analysis of L2 texts to cultural context and remains indigenous to ESOL is contrastive rhetoric (see Kaplan, 1966; Connor, 1996). However, critical practitioners have had to broaden this approach to address issues of power. The limitation of contrastive rhetoric (at least in some of the traditional versions) is that although cultural difference is respected, it is not situated in power. Contrastive rhetoricians seem to be saying: "With the knowledge that all discourses/cultures are equal, we can move on to adopt the established conventions for a specific context." However, discourses are not equal. In specific social contexts, certain discourses are privileged. Continuing to use them uncritically only serves to uphold their power. The established discourses colonize other communities, providing inferior status to their forms of writing and shaping their thinking (see Canagarajah, 1996). Additionally, contrastive rhetoricians define the cultural differences of other communities in stereotypical and homogeneous terms (thus "essentializing" them).

They also define cultures in biased terms, using the dominant culture is the norm in their description. Other cultures serve as foils for the dominant culture (i.e., they are "othered"), with the implication that they are of secondary status (see Kubota, 1999). Such rhetorical descriptions suppress the complexity, historical dynamism, and even internal conflicts within these cultures. In fact, with English enjoying hegemonic status globally, it is naïve to treat students from other cultures as employing an uncontaminated "native" discourse. In the light of such orientations to culture in writing, critical practitioners have researched the following:

- Situate the "culture" displayed in L2 writing in contexts of history and power to show that the hybridity in these texts reflects a complex process of resistance and appropriation of local and globally powerful cultures (Kubota, 1999).
- Explore the process by which students shuttle between local and "target language" communities in their writings in L1 and L2, critically negotiating cultures in the process (Canagarajah, 2000);
- Analyze the products of such negotiation and shuttling to show how texts may adopt a critical orientation on both discourses, with varying levels of rhetorical and ideological effectiveness (see Canagarajah, 2002a, pp. 118–121).

Encouraged by such research, critical practitioners now argue for the need to make L2 writers critique their own discourses as well as that of English in order to practice a critical writing that negotiates cultures. Trying to represent their "native" culture in L2 texts or conforming to Anglophone culture one-sidedly don't reflect a critical positioning of the writer in the text.

Learning Processes, Strategies, and Styles

Critical research has also challenged the stereotypes about the preferred learning styles of ESOL students. We have heard it said that students from traditional communities (in Asia, Africa, and Latin America) prefer memorization, rote learning, and product-oriented pedagogies. The favored approaches in the field are of course process-oriented. Holliday defines the ideal conditions for language learning endorsed by the ELT research tradition as follows: "This learning group ideal sets the conditions for a process-oriented, task-based, inductive, collaborative, communicative English language teaching methodology" (1994, p. 54). The ELT research and professional circles treat this as "the optimum interactional parameters within which classroom language learning can take place" (Holliday, 1994, p. 54). Myron Tuman (1988) describes how the change toward process-oriented approaches of writing in the American academy is unconditionally treated as a more progressive pedagogical development. It is not surprising then that some ESL teachers display a missionary zeal in enforcing such learning strategies in their classrooms. They sincerely think that they are empowering foreign students and developing a more democratic learning environment. Western experts conducting teacher development in traditional Asian learning environments have attempted to impose process-oriented pedagogies in the place of the prevailing product-oriented ones (see Pennington, 1995).

Critical practitioners have questioned this learning group ideal of ELT. They have opened up several useful lines of thinking on the process/product debate in L2 learning. Product-oriented approaches cannot be dismissed as dysfunctional in all contexts. Several scholars have pointed out that there is a real need for ESL students in some learning situations to desire a knowledge of the rules and conventions of English (see Leki, 1991). As Lisa Delpit (1995) has pointed out in the case of African American students, for those who don't know the established codes, insisting on a more indirect acquisition of grammar through creative activities may prove confusing and irrelevant. Whereas process strategies work well for mainstream students who already have some knowledge of the socially valued codes, it may result in letting minority students sink or swim on their own. Furthermore, older students who come to western institutions for college or graduate-level education may favor a form-oriented learning, unlike younger learners who can benefit more from an inductive or immersion approach (Leki, 1995). Some recent ethnographies from communities with limited material/educational resources (thus, featuring large classrooms and few textbooks for students) show that a product-oriented pedagogy is quite effective in developing literacy in English (see Muchiri et al., 1995; Wright, 2001). Teachers make the best of a pedagogical situation when they are the sole educational resource.

Several other scholars have given more social and psychological complexity to the learning styles of ESL students by situating product-oriented learning in context. Pennycook (1996) points out that the memorization techniques of the Chinese students he worked with were motivated by a respect for others who have previously put those ideas in more effective ways. It is not taking other people's words, but how they are used that is important. The fresh contexts in which Chinese students use these words show their creativity. After all, in the postmodern context of intertextuality, we recognize that all of us borrow words from elsewhere for our purposes and, at any rate, the words we use already come with the meanings given by history and society.

Furthermore, product-oriented learning may have oppositional significance (Canagarajah, 1993b; Resnick, 1993; Muchiri et al., 1995). Resnick (1993), for example, argues that in the context where Puerto Rican ESL students are caught between cultural/ideological identification with Spanish nationalism and the economic reality of North American market benefits, they make a compromise by adopting a product-oriented learning. Through this approach they are making the statement that they don't envision using English for everyday communicative purposes. They need English (or more specifically, the certification of proficiency in English) to vie for jobs and other utilitarian purposes.

Those who treat a product-oriented learning as encouraging a passive and conforming attitude are going too far in stereotyping ESL students. First, everyone has the agency to adopt diverse forms of thinking; no one is culturally determined to be only quiescent. Critical practitioners show that critical thinking can be expressed in many different forms. Sometimes, silence or taciturnity can be motivated by oppositional attitudes (Schenke, 1991). Students refrain from participating in communicative activities in the classroom as they see no relevance to their everyday life. This is an active form of refusal, and not conformity. Of course, sometimes they unquestioningly conform to teachers' expectations (although they sense a threat to their cultural and ideological integrity) because they recognize that they are compelled to earn credit in ESL in order to attain their other objectives in life (Chick, 1986). The best defense for them is a mechanical reproduction of notes and rules in examinations without an internalization of the values or communicative facility in the language. Other forms of indirect opposition may involve parody, satire, and humor (see Canagarajah, 1990, 1993c). Anthropologists point to subtle behavior traits through which people from disempowered communities express their protest as they don't want to provoke the dominant groups by overt opposition (see Scott, 1990). Foot dragging, cheating, name calling, mimicking, and stealing are forms in which they express opposition behind the backs of those in authority. Therefore, in our research, we must become more sensitive to subtler ways in which the critical thinking of our students may manifest itself. Not always do minority students have the luxury of openly expressing idiosyncratic views in the name of individualism—as privileged students are disposed to do.

To understand the subtle learning strategies students adopt in order to negotiate unfavorable pedagogies, we have to analyze the classroom more deeply, taking into consideration the many sites and relationships that elude the public spaces and authority figures (i.e., teachers, researchers, administrators) in typical classroom research. In classroom ethnographies in a variety of pedagogical contexts, I have come to identify spaces/interactions that students define as separate for themselves. I call these spaces *classroom underlife* (Canagarajah, 1997). Other researchers in L2 contexts have identified a similar site, though they don't use the same label or framework of analysis (see Chick, 1986; Rampton, 1995; Martin-Jones & Heller, 1996). They may constitute micro-level interactions like gossip, passing of notes, and unauthorized conversations and topics behind the back of the teacher. Or they could be practiced in larger level interactions in small group discussions, e-mail or chat rooms in the computer-mediated classes, and graffiti in textbooks and notebooks passed around among the students. In most cases, these sites are constructed in locations that are treated as outside the surveillance of authority figures.

The rationale for activities in classroom underlife can be explained in many ways. Mary Louise Pratt (1991) explains this site as motivated by a need for solidarity, relief, and protection for students from the ideological assaults and reproductive threats of the school. Robert Brooke (1987) borrows Goffmanesque social psychology to explain this as a needed site for students to construct alternate identities that differ from those shaped by the school. Although these orientations look at classroom underlife as largely passive, defensive, or individualistic, my research shows that there is also a subversive, collective, and resistant function as students construct values, identities, and relationships that encourage a transformative orientation toward learning and society (see Canagarajah, 1995, 1997). For me, these spaces are largely oppositional to the ideologies and interests of authority figures in the educational domain. Whereas the public sites of the classroom enforce a narrower range of legitimized discourses, and pressure students to adopt uniform identities, safe houses provide them a space for the display of more complex discourses and mixed identities. Rather than being deviant and distractional, these sites are profoundly educational as students reframe and reinterpret authorized curricula, textbooks, and discourses to favor their own contexts and interests.

Given such complexity in learning processes, there is a significant line of research inquiry into the effects of ESL textbooks published in Anglo-American communities (informed by their preferred learning group ideal). Deborah Cameron (2002) and David Block (2002) argue that there is a current tendency for publishers to adopt uniform learning styles and discourses in ELT textbooks in the name of globalization and its presumed homogeneity in the required languages and discourses. Block sarcastically charges them for promoting "McCommunication." Such textbooks are understandably not informed by the communicative needs and cultural practices of local student groups. The consequences of using such materials have been well articulated by critical researchers. There is a reproductive effect (as the values and codes are spread locally) in classes where students and teachers are less critical in their learning (Raj, 1982). In some others, there is a clash of discordant discourses as the expectations of the publishers and host community don't match, affecting the motivation and interest of the students (Canagarajah, 1993b; Gray, 2002). In still others, there is resistance and appropriation as ideologically better informed teachers and students reinterpret or localize the discourses of the textbook for their own purposes (see Canagarajah, 1993c; Martin, in press).

In the area of methods, too, the profession has validated approaches that suit the preferred learning styles of western communities. Although new methods are periodically publicized with great fanfare, bolstered by claims of effectiveness and pedagogical success, they are largely versions of the same process paradigm. In more recent times, such approaches as task-based teaching, learner-strategy training, student-centered pedagogies, and learner-autonomy practices seem to take us further along the process-oriented paradigm. Fortunately, we are in a position to recognize now that "there is no best method" (Prabhu, 1990). Kumaravadivelu (1994) rightly argues that we should abandon the notion that there are preconstructed methods that can be implemented wholesale in the classroom and can assure pedagogical success. We have to now think of responding more directly to the needs and learning styles of our students, sensitive to the cultures and social conditions relevant to the classroom context, as we adopt pedagogical practices that are suitable. It is possible that we may eclectically draw from previously defined methods. However, this is better than coming to the classroom with a predisposition toward a specific method because it has been touted as universally relevant and successful. Kumaravadivelu (1994) calls these new pedagogical realizations as constituting the *postmethod condition*.

The postmethod realization is important for several reasons. Critical practitioners have pointed out that methods are ideological—contrary to the myth that methods are value-free instruments for pragmatic purposes. As Pennycook (1989) has pointed out, methods are loaded with a range of "interests." Apart from the economic interests of textbook publishers and the ideological interests of the communities exporting these methods elsewhere, there are the interests of researchers who are separated from classrooms and practitioners. Pennycook has pointed out the interesting demography in our field that, while practitioners are largely females, scholars/researchers are largely male. In the context of periphery communities, the export of these authoritative methods (backed by the credentials of the elite institutions and scholars in the West) has led to stifling the professionalism of local practitioners. The postmethod condition would empower periphery practitioners to develop teaching approaches that are more relevant to their pedagogical contexts, rather than depending on the center for methods that are considered authoritative.

Target Language?

As they become sensitive to the diverse discourses represented in the classroom and attempt to accommodate them in the learning process, critical researchers are concerned about the target language proficiency teachers should strive for among ESL students. It used to be commonly accepted that the dominant dialects spoken by the "native speakers" was the target (i.e., Standard American English, or the dominant dialects of South East England). The local varieties spoken in postcolonial communities were considered transitional interlanguages and pidgins or corrupt forms of creoles and "broken English."

Such traditional assumptions have been effectively challenged since Kachru (1986) displayed the system and logic of nativized Englishes. Since then, non-native teachers have called on ELT professional circles to live up to the values of descriptive linguistics, which teaches us that there are no linguistic bases for considering one dialect as superior to the other, that local dialects reflect the sociocultural contexts of their development, and that they are functional for the communities that use them (representing their identity, solidarity, and worldview). We are now in the process of redefining dichotomies such as native speaker/non-native speaker and standard dialect/nonstandard dialect. A problem with these notions is that they assume that the native speaker and his or her language as the norm (Singh, 1998). As such, they display a comparative fallacy (see Cook, 1999). We are moving toward the egalitarian position that English is a plural language with a system that accommodates different norms and grammars in different regions; that we are all native speakers of this pluralized global English; and that we should develop alternate terminology for native/non-native speaker that avoids notions of birth or blood relationships with a language (perhaps terms that focus purely on proficiency, such as expert and novice speakers of various dialects?).

These developments would be of purely theoretical interest, if not for several social changes that validate them. With postmodern forms of hybrid communication, inspired by processes of globalization, transnational communities, and web-based interactions, we are more sensitive to the fluidity in languages, discourses, and registers. We recognize the need for proficiency in multiliteracies to be competent in postmodern reading/writing practices (Cope & Kalantzis, 2000). Skills in negotiating diverse dialects of English become important in the global village. More important, we recognize that "non-native speakers" are fast outpacing in number the native speakers of the inner circle (Graddol, 1999). These realizations generate new imperatives regarding the place of diverse dialects in the language classroom (Holliday, in press).

Critical practitioners have unraveled the economic and ideological motivations behind the valorization of standard English and the authority of the native speakers in language pedagogy. What has come to be called the *native speaker fallacy* (see Phillipson, 1992) justifies the preferred position of native speaker teachers in the employment market. The authority of native varieties permit textbook publishers to produce uniform materials for classrooms all over the world. These assumptions make it difficult to accommodate postcolonial Englishes and cultures in the language classroom, bolstering the function of standard English as a tool for ideological domination. Other scholars have gone into the pedagogical implications of imposing standards of "native speaker" communities in classrooms elsewhere. In the context of South African classrooms, Peirce (1989) argues that standard English provides unequal subject positions to speakers of the local dialect "People's English." An instructional system based on alien norms disempowers students, filling them with feelings of inferiority. She goes on to narrate how local teachers have begun to use texts written in local dialects to increase the relevance of the language and to explore issues and interests that concern the local community. I have reported elsewhere how students from marginalized/rural backgrounds in Sri Lanka see little relevance for standard American English as they have no prospects for going abroad to use this dialect (Canagarajah, 1993b). They also sense that such language and discourse pose conflicts for their cultural integrity as they are confronted with values that are alien. Although this develops a perfunctory, product-oriented attitude to English language learning, the students also go on to use local dialects in surreptitious ways in underlife discourse to practice a dialect that is more meaningful for them.

Researchers have pointed out how some of the local variants demonstrate students' attempts to appropriate English. It might be said that any language has to be taken over by the speaker, adapted to local conditions, filled with local values, and used with independence and confidence in order for one to develop a voice in it. What appears as ungrammatical or nonidiomatic usage may in fact be creative adaptations of the language for one's own purposes. Note in Lu's (1994) example pointed out earlier, how the Chinese-Malaysian student is developing a grammatical structure that is ideologically better suited to serve her interests. In a telling observation, Lu points out that the rest of the class later used the modal half-jokingly. As they used it more often, the modal took on a life of its own. Such are the ways new dialects are born.

Another study, by Eva Lam (2000), shows how the use of local variants doesn't hinder proficiency in socially and professionally valued dialects. In an ethnography of a Chinese American student, Almon, she shows how a student who is tongue-tied in the ESL class (because of its insistence on standard English), is very expressive in the Internet. He writes e-mail to fans of Japanese pop music, develops a web page in English to talk about his interests, and visits chat rooms to interact with other second language speakers. His confident and creative use of diverse dialects of English develops the motivation to strengthen his acquisition of the preferred dialect in the classroom. The relevance of the language in extra-classroom contexts of interaction inspires him to master standard English in the classroom. As Lam's study shows, a repertoire of variant dialects is important for many today to be functional in the post-modern world. Rather than developing a mastery of a specific code, students need the interactional skills to negotiate dialect differences with their interlocutors. For this purpose, an awareness of diverse dialects is a resource that should be educationally validated. Rather than teaching standard dialects one-sidedly, it might be more important to develop a repertoire of dialects—with an awareness of their values, structure, and their contextual appropriateness in different situations.

Discussions of target language should go further to include the place of the first languages ESL students speak. Gone are the days when we treated the L1 as needing to be suppressed if one is to become a proficient speaker of an L2. The dominant assumption was that L1 interfered with and hindered L2 acquisition. We know from recent research that skills and language awareness developed in L1 can transfer positively to L2 (Cummins, 1991), that a validation of the student's L1 can reduce the inhibitions against English and develop positive affect to enhance acquisition (Auerbach, 1993), and that a multilingual self can be formed of diverse languages without dysfunctional consequences for the students (Kramsch, 2000). Skuttnab-Kangas (1992) considers it a violation of linguistic human rights to teach English in isolation from the first languages of the students. She argues that an ELT pedagogy based on English-only in the classroom can lead to the gradual devaluation of L1 and decline in proficiency. It can convey to students the inequality of languages, with a low estimation of their L1. This unequal relationship of languages in the ESL classroom can get reproduced outside. This can lead to the vernaculars declining in currency and status, with English continuing its hegemony worldwide.

Researchers on language acquisition outside the class have pointed out that, in natural contexts, English is acquired together with L1 in many multilingual and post-colonial communities (Sridhar, 1994). In fact, *codeswitching* is an important medium of communication in such communities. It might be said that codeswitching has more communicative functionality than unmixed English in these contexts. However, typically, codeswitching is not tolerated in ESL classes. The dominant notions of linguistic purity still prevent practitioners from permitting language mixing in the classroom. Codeswitching, however, may appear as another form of appropriating English for local purposes according to local values. As we saw in the previous section, students' spontaneous acts of codeswitching in classrooms may show a natural desire to develop communicative competence in a discourse that is more relevant and meaningful for them. Many scholars are now moving to the position that codeswitching may constitute a valid medium of communication in its own right and that we should give this some attention in our pedagogy (see Canagarajah, 1995; Heller & Martin-Jones, 2001).

The reality of hybrid languages reminds teachers that multilingual students shuttle between communities in their everyday life. (We now recognize that under the influence of globalization and the Internet, even dominant speakers of English in the "native communities" have to move fluidly between communicative contexts that demand a competence in different codes.) In this context, it is important to consider how ESL pedagogy can teach skills of linguistic negotiation that enables students to move across languages and communities. Teaching English without reference to the first language of the students may disempower them in the multilingual life in the postmodern world. It may also be treated as a vain attempt to reduce the hybridity of personal and social life with an imposition of English Only. Multilingual speakers may use their proficiency in languages for critical expression in the communities they shuttle between. I have reported elsewhere how some Sri Lankan faculty members shuttle between the vernacular and mainstream academic communities in their research writing (see Canagarajah, 2002b). In writing in Tamil to the local scholars, they adopt a largely narrative and personalized discourse with their claims developed indirectly; however, compared to other typical articles in Tamil, they adopt a relatively more objective and argumentative approach in order to challenge local scholars from what they perceive as unclear formulations of the thesis or ad hominem arguments. When they write in English, we can see a shift to a more explicit and detached development in deference to the conventions in mainstream research articles. However, they display more involvement and develop a "nativized" voice in this discourse to challenge what they see as the mechanical, value-free, and noncommittal discourse of scientific positivism. In this way, they draw from their multilingual competence the resources to challenge both the native and the mainstream communities. Such communicative activities prove the hidden power in multilingual speakers to use the resources from competing languages to develop a critical point of view. As postcolonial scholars like Bhabha (1994) have theorized, the "in-betweenness" of multilingual/multicultural subjects develops in them a peculiar "double vision" to adopt multiple viewpoints on the languages they use.

ISSUES OF CONTESTATION

As space prevents me from providing an exhaustive review of the evolving literature on critical research in diverse fields of L2 learning, it is prudent to identify the central issues that concern this line of inquiry. Although many scholars don't make these concerns clear or adopt an explicit position on them, inevitably they have to navigate these issues as they practice critical teaching and research. Internal debates continue among critical practitioners, and new researchers entering this field have to consider how they would position themselves in relation to these issues. We can formulate these central concerns as follows:

Structure and Agency. Critical practitioners rightly take into consideration abstract arrangements of social organization, political establishment, economic infrastructure, and ideological complexes for the ways they condition students to think and behave in conformity to the status quo (see Phillipson, 1992). However, this emphasis shouldn't be allowed to eclipse the power of individuals to see through the designs of the powerful, critique the status quo, and work toward structural change. The danger is that sometimes human agency is romanticized to such an extent that the subtle and persistent workings of social structure are simplified (see Zamel, 1997). We have to be open to the possibility that structure and agency will interact with each other dialectically in an ongoing and relentless fashion, without foreclosing the possibility for human agents to resist social institutions.

Reproduction and Transformation. Our position on the previous debate may influence how we view possibilities for transforming or reproducing discourses and structures. Reproductionist studies show the power of economic and ideological forces to shape the thinking of individuals or workings of institutions in an all-encompassing fashion (Bourdieu & Passeron, 1977). They alert us to the pervasive and subtle way in which power controls all domains of life, but this may lead to a deterministic view of society and individuals. Others have felt the need, therefore, to emphasize that people and institutions enjoy a relative autonomy from larger structures to find spaces for diverse degrees of opposition and change (Giroux, 1983).

History and Desire. It is possible to consider the workings of power as an external manifestation through history and society. From this perspective, we would critique power objectively (Rajagopalan, 1999). However, it is important to see that our own consciousness, subjectivity, and desire are shaped by diverse histories of domination. There is a need, therefore, to be reflexive in analyzing how the marks of domination and struggle are manifested in our thinking and behavior (Schenke, 1991). We have to unravel the workings of power not only externally in history, but also in subjectivity.

Opposition and Resistance. Since the dynamic between history and desire, or reproduction and transformation, is so complex, student response to domination can differ widely. Whereas some may accommodate to values and structures that are unfavorable to them, others will react against them, but this reaction can also be divergent. Many researchers find it important to distinguish *resistance*, which displays ideological clarity and commitment to collective action for social transformation, from mere *opposition*, which is unclear, ambivalent, and largely passive (see Canagarajah, 1993b; Giroux, 1983). The latter is largely a vague, instinctive behavior that fails to sustain consciousness raising or mobilize groups for concerted social action.

Macro- and Micro-levels of Intervention. What is the effective level of pedagogical intervention that would lead to lasting changes? Some scholars focus on changing educational policies by lobbying established structures such as boards, organizations, and administrators. Among them are those who would hold the state and other political authorities responsible for initiating pedagogical change (Skuttnab-Kangas, 2002). Although this line of work shouldn't be ignored, we mustn't underestimate the power of local level changes that happen in classrooms everyday (Canagarajah, 1999b). If we accept the relative autonomy of institutions, we shouldn't be surprised that teachers and students enjoy spaces for significant critical thinking and action even in a context marked by unfair conditions. The local changes can in fact transcend their immediate context to unsettle larger institutional structures.

Student Autonomy and Teacher Control. Some critical practitioners consider teachers as the enlightened intellects who should lead their students toward critical thinking and practice by exerting their authority. Students do have to be challenged sometimes to open their eyes to issues of inequality and exploitation (see hooks, 1989). Others have pointed out that students (especially those from marginalized backgrounds) come with personal experience and direct insights from their life that should shape a critical practice relevant to them. Furthermore, teachers should be humble enough to learn liberatory values and thinking from their students (see Canagarajah, 1997). In fact, teachers who come from a privileged background and identify with educational authorities may discover their own ideological limitations and complicity with power. However, as in the other constructs, we should learn to balance both orientations in our pedagogy. Teachers and students may collaborate constructively for change (Canagarajah, 1999a, pp. 193–197).

Voice and Access. Should critical practitioners provide marginalized students access to the dominant codes or, rather, empower their own vernaculars for educational and professional purposes? Some would consider teaching dominant codes (such as "standard English" or mainstream literacy conventions) as reifying their hegemony (Skuttnab-Kangas, 1992). Therefore, they would favor encouraging the use of marginalized codes in mainstream contexts. Others would argue that without a mastery of the dominant codes minority students cannot survive in the educational and professional world (see Street, 2001, for studies that explore different sides of this debate). Although we should acknowledge the claims of both positions, we needn't reduce linguistic proficiency to univocal codes and discourses (i.e., a case of either vernacular or dominant codes). It is good for students to be multilingual. Learning dominant codes with a critical attitude can go hand in hand with negotiating spaces for the vernacular discourses in the mainstream.

Inclusion and Interrogation. How should we set about changing curricula and textbooks? Should we fight for more inclusive representation, with marginalized cultures and communities given equal importance as dominant cultures (see Gray, 2002; Peirce, 1989)? Or should we say that it is idealistic to expect such a level of diversity, and simply encourage students to critique biased/limited representations in the existing curricula? The latter approach sounds more pragmatic in a context where economic and market interests shape curricular decisions. However, there are creative ways in which students' cultures can be incorporated into the learning agenda. Students can themselves bring texts from their families and neighborhoods for discussion in the class. Vernacular resources can also be developed in the classroom from students' own talk and writing (see Auerbach et al., 1996).

CRITICAL RESEARCH METHODS AND REPORTING

Critical research differs from descriptive approaches (as in descriptive linguistics or descriptive ethnography), which adopt a detached, objective, value-free orientation to knowledge. Critical approaches align themselves with the post-Enlightenment philosophical tradition in situating research in the social context to consider how knowledge is shaped by the values of human agents and communities, implicated in power differences, and favorable for democratizing relationships and institutions (see Pennycook, 1994b). Therefore, a critical approach questions the separation of constructs such as the following (where the second term in each pair is treated as constituting the valid approach in traditional research):

• *Theory and method:* In descriptive approaches, research methods are considered atheoretical. They are treated as practical instruments or value-free procedures to attain objective knowledge. They are considered neutral and transparent, suitable for gaining an undistorted view of reality, but CP treats methods as ideological (see Pennycook, 1989). Methods come with their own orientations to reality, informed by values that offer certain selective perspectives. As such, methods are partial (in both senses of the term: incomplete and biased) as I will exemplify through the sociolinguistic interview method discussed next. From this perspective, each method comes with its own implicit theories of knowledge and social relations (Peirce, 1995b).

• *Interpretation and data:* In descriptive research, data is considered hard and raw—that is, factual, pure of bias, and devoid of values. After the data is collected with the use of objective instruments and procedures, the more subjective interpretive procedure is supposed to follow, but CP assumes that the data presupposes an interpretation. It is already collected by human agents with certain presuppositions about their research objectives from specific contexts of experience. CP would advise that we reflexively analyze the data to make explicit the interpretation presupposed by it in order to develop generalizations that are of greater validity, rather than imposing selective interpretations in the guise of scientific neutrality.

• *Subjective and objective:* Descriptive research considers it possible to detach ourselves from the matter studied to develop an objective approach to inquiry. CP would consider all research as colored by the intentions, experiences, values, and predispositions of researchers. Even those conducted by impersonal instruments (i.e., data generated and analyzed by a computer software) show the marks of human agency as the software is written and the data fed by human beings. CP would encourage researchers to engage more frankly with the research process in order to bring out both the strengths and limits of one's own involvement in the study (see Harding, 1991).

• *Contextual and universal:* Although all research is situated in a specific context, the objective of descriptive research is to filter out the particularities of the process in order to generate facts and constructs of universal validity. However, CP would acknowledge that all research is situated and that it is important to appreciate the particularity of each study in order to realistically assess the relativity of one's findings and generalize more cautiously (see hooks, 1989; Prior, 1998). Of course, there are unique insights generated by the specificity of a research context that contributes to the richness of each research experience. The haste to universalize the study/findings may suppress local insights of more far reaching value.

• *Applied and disinterested:* Traditional research has taken pride in conducting research for purely descriptive purposes. Concerns about how to apply this knowledge are supposed to pollute the objectivity and purity of research. However, for CP, research is conducted for the difference it will make for social betterment and human development. There are strong ethical values that motivate research. Rather than corrupting the research experience, such practical concerns give a deeper commitment and ethical framework that would enhance the meaning of one's research. In fact, there have always been ulterior motivations (not made explicit) in the so-called pure sciences (Nandy, 1990). Knowledge has always been implicated in social and political processes. If we don't engage in its uses, knowledge would be appropriated for unethical purposes by default.

There is a small range of emerging research approaches that accommodate a critical orientation to inquiry. *Critical ethnography* treats the classroom/school as a cultural site and inquires into the ways in which culture may serve as a dominating or empowering force in pedagogy (see Canagarajah, 1993b). *Action research* enables teachers to critically reflect on their classroom experience, as they manage their teaching and research to complement each other (Nunan, 1990). A variant of this is *Participant Action Research*, which encourages the teacher to collaborate with students, giving them a greater role in designing the pedagogy and research, in order to produce knowledge relevant to their interests (Auerbach, 1994). *Self-reflexive studies* encourage the subject to become a researcher of his or her own learning/teaching experience, as one's own struggles and responsive strategies are a rich source of knowledge if they can be elicited and interpreted in a disciplined way[4] (Belcher & Connor, 2001). *Critical Language Socialization* situates processes of second language acquisition (SLA) in sociopolitical context (see Peirce, 1995a; Kramsch & Lam, 1999). It is not impossible to tailor other established research approaches, such as discourse analysis, language planning/policy studies, or literacy studies to take on the critical assumptions outlined here.

Whereas critical practitioners in ESL have begun to design research projects that accommodate these orientations, not many of them are alert to the fact that research reporting can itself impose values uncongenial to critical research. It is possible that the established genres of the research article may not always be suitable for reporting studies that adopt critical approaches. The dominant IMRD (Introduction/Method/Results/Discussion) structure is more amenable for reporting descriptive studies informed by Enlightenment values, enabling a detached, inductive, controlled, and authorially imposed version of the findings (see Canagarajah, 1996). Other emergent genres of research reporting adopt:

• *Reflexivity,* in representing the personal shaping of the findings, in light of the changing biases, subject positions, and involvement of the researcher (see Wright, 2001).
• *Narrativity,* for a more indirect, context-bound, and personal form of theorization (see Canagarajah, 2001b; Belcher, 1997).
• *Multivocality,* for textualizing the plural perspectives and voices of different informants, researchers, participants on the same pedagogical feature (see Chopra, 2001).
• *Authorial collaboration,* in involving the participants/informants in the representation of the findings (see Auerbach et al., 1996; Lin et al., 2002).

- *Open-endedness*, in dramatizing the tensions in interpretation and data from the field, and encouraging the readers to form alternate paradigms of interpretation (see Robinson-Pant, 2001).

It is important for the researcher to develop a mode of textual representation that is sensitive to issues of power and difference. Compared to fields like ethnography or even L1 composition studies, where there is a heightened sense of textual creativity, ESL research reports appear to be more regulated—possibly because the main research journals in the field are still influenced by modernist values.

CONCLUSION

Defining critical pedagogy or research in terms of a static set of rules or axioms, especially by scholarship removed from local practices, would lead to ossified paradigms that constitute a "p.c." (politically correct) approach. Perhaps the best way to define critical pedagogy is as a heuristic, made up of the conceptual tensions described in the second section above.[5] The questions posed by these conflicting issues should be answered in relation to the conditions characterizing specific pedagogical contexts as we develop an appropriate teaching and research practice ground up. However, this open-endedness shouldn't be romanticized. It is possible that some of the other features in my characterization of theory and practice in L2 critical research—especially, the rejection of the noncommittal pragmatism in teaching and a positivistic detachment in research—may sound too insistent and uncompromising for some. Such a discriminating characterization is important to safeguard against the increasingly cliched use of "empowerment" and "critical" in the professional discourse. As critical pedagogy loses its marginal (even "pariah") status in the field, we have to be alert against the reverse trend of transforming it into a cheap fad—or into another income-generating pedagogical industry.

NOTES

1. For an introduction to these schools of thinking, see Harding, 1991; Prendergast, 1998; Bhabha, 1994; Nelson, 1999, respectively.
2. For a detailed and accessible introduction to critical pedagogy, see Canagarajah, 2002a, pp. 1–8.
3. I am assuming in this discussion that learners of English as a second or foreign language experience unequal power status. If we accept that English is a globally powerful language (enjoying more status and resources than any other language in the world today) then those who come from other language groups to learn this as a second language are in an unequal relationship to it linguistically. Though their minority status may vary from a purely economic, academic, or professional point of view, it is possible to assert that learners of English as a second language experience unequal power relationships from a linguistic standpoint.
4. For exemplary studies see, Casanave & Vandrick, in press; Lin et al., 2002; Kramsch & Lam, 1999.
5. We should also keep in mind the other important dialectic introduced in the beginning of the article, i.e., theory and practice. I also explored the differing levels of effectiveness of process and product in different pedagogical contexts.

REFERENCES

Auerbach, E., with Barahona, B., Midy, J., Vaquerano, F., Zambrano, A., & Arnaud, J. (1996). *Adult ESL literacy from the community to the community: A guidebook for participatory literacy training.* Mahwah, NJ: Lawrence Erlbaum Associates.

Auerbach, E. R. (1994). Participatory action research. *TESOL Quarterly, 28*, 693–697.

Auerbach, E. R. (1993). Reexamining English only in the ESL classroom. *TESOL Quarterly, 27*(1), 9–32.

Bahri, D. (1997). Marginally off-center: Postcolonialism in the teaching machine. *Colllege English, 59*(3), 277–298.

Belcher, D. (1997). An argument for nonadversarial argumentation: On the relevance of the feminist critique of academic discourse to L2 writing pedagogy. *Journal of Second Language Writing, 6*(1), 1–21.

Belcher, D., & Connor, U. (Eds.) (2001). *Reflections on multiliterate lives.* Clevedon, UK: Multilingual Matters.

Benesch, S. (1993). ESL, ideology, and politics of pragmatism. *TESOL Quarterly, 27*(2), 705–717.

Benesch, S. (1999). Thinking critically, thinking dialogically. *TESOL Quarterly, 33*(3), 573–580.

Benesch, S. (2001). *Critical English for academic purposes.* Mahwah, NJ: Lawrence Erlbaum Associates.

Bhabha, H. (1994). *The location of culture.* New York: Routledge & Kegan Paul.

Bizzell, P. (1992). *Academic discourse and critical consciousness.* Pittsburgh: University of Pittsburgh Press.

Block, D. (2002). "McCommunication:" A problem in the frame for SLA. In D. Cameron & D. Block, (Eds.), *Globalization and language teaching* (pp. 117–133). London: Routledge & Kegan Paul.

Bourdieu, P., & Passeron, J. P. (1977). *Reproduction in education, society, and culture.* London: Sage.

Brooke, R. (1987). Underlife and writing instruction. *College Composition and Communication, 38,* 141–153.

Cameron, D. (2002). Globalization and the teaching of "communication skills." In D. Cameron & D. Block, (Eds.), *Globalization and language teaching* (pp. 67–82). London: Routledge & Kegan Paul.

Canagarajah, A. S. (1990). Negotiating competing discourses and identities: A sociolinguistic analysis of challenges in academic writing for minority students. (Doctoral dissertation, University of Texas at Austin, 1990). *Dissertation Abstracts International, 51,* 3398.

Canagarajah, A. S. (1993a). Up the garden path: Second language writing approaches, local knowledge, and pluralism. *TESOL Quarterly, 27*(2), 301–306.

Canagarajah, A. S. (1993b). Critical ethnography of a Sri Lankan classroom: Ambiguities in opposition to reproduction through ESOL. *TESOL Quarterly, 27*(4), 601–626.

Canagarajah, A. S. (1993c). American textbooks and Tamil students: A clash of discourses in the ESL classroom. *Language, Culture, and Curriculum, 6*(2), 143–156.

Canagarajah, A. S. (1995). Functions of code switching in the ESL classroom: Socialising bilingualism in Jaffna. *Journal of Multilingual and Multicultural Development, 16*(3), 173–196.

Canagarajah, A. S. (1996). Nondiscursive requirements in academic publishing, material resources of periphery scholars, and the politics of knowledge production. *Written Communication, 13*(4), 435–472.

Canagarajah, A. S. (1997). Safe houses in the Contact Zone: Coping strategies of African American students in the academy. *College Composition and Communication, 48*(2), 173–196.

Canagarajah, A. S. (1999a). *Resisting linguistic imperialism in English teaching.* Oxford, UK: Oxford University Press.

Canagarajah, A. S. (1999b.) On EFL teachers, awareness, and agency. *ELT Journal, 53*(3), 207–214.

Canagarajah, A. S. (March, 2000). Understanding L2 academic writing as codeswitching. Paper presented in the 34th Annual Convention of TESOL, March 14–18, Vancouver.

Canagarajah, A. S. (2001b). The fortunate traveler: Shuttling between communities and literacies by economy class. In D. Belcher & U. Connor (Eds.), *Reflections on multiliterate lives* (pp. 23–37). Clevedon, UK: Multilingual Matters.

Canagarajah, A. S. (2002a). *Critical academic writing and multilingual students.* Ann Arbor, MI: University of Michigan Press.

Canagarajah, A. S. (2002b). *A geopolitics of academic writing.* Pittsburgh: University of Pittsburgh Press.

Canagarajah, A. S. (2003). A somewhat legitimate, and very peripheral participation. In C. P. Casanave & S. Vandrick (Eds.), *Writing for scholarly publication: Behind the scenes in language education* (pp. 197–210). Mahwah, NJ: Lawrence Erlbaum Associates.

Casanave, C. P., & Vandrick, S. (Eds.) (2003). *Writing for scholarly publication: Behind the scenes in language education.* Mahwah, NJ: Lawrence Erlbaum Associates.

Chick, K. (1986). Safe-talk: Collusion in apartheid education. In H. Coleman (Ed.), *Society and the language classroom* (pp. 21–39). Cambridge: Cambridge University Press.

Chopra, Priti. (2001). Betrayal and solidarity in ethnography on literacy: Revisiting research homework in a north Indian village. In B. V. Street (Ed.), *Literacy and development: Ethnographic perspectives* (pp. 78–92). London: Routledge & Kegan Paul.

Connor, U. (1996). *Contrastive rhetoric: Cross-cultural aspects of second language writing.* Cambridge: Cambridge University Press.

Cook, V. (1999). Going beyond the native speaker in language teaching. *TESOL Quarterly, 33*(2), 185–210.

Cope, B., & Kalantzis, M. (Eds.). (2000). *Multiliteracies: Literacy learning and the design of social futures.* London: Routledge & Kegan Paul.

Cummins, J. (1991). Interdependence of first- and second-language proficiency in bilingual children. In E. Bialystok (Ed.), *Language processing in bilingual children* (pp. 70–89). Cambridge: Cambridge University Press.

Delpit, L. (1995). *Other people's children: Cultural conflict in the classroom.* New York: New Press.

Fairclough, N. (2000). Multiliteracies and language: Orders of discourse and intertextuality. In B. Cope & M. Kalantzis (Eds.), *Multiliteracies: Literacy learning and the design of social futures* (pp. 162–181). London: Routledge & Kegan Paul.

Fowler, R., & Kress, G. (1979). Critical linguistics. In R. Fowler, B. Hodge, G. Kress, & A. Trew (Eds.), *Language and control* (pp. 185–213). London: Routledge & Kegan Paul.

Gee, J. P. (2000). New people in new worlds: Networks, the new capitalism, and schools. In B. Cope & M. Kalantzis (Eds.), *Multiliteracies: Literacy learning and the design of social futures* (pp. 43–68). London: Routledge & Kegan Paul.

Giroux, H. A. (1983). *Theory and resistance in education: A pedagogy for the opposition.* South Hadley: Bergin.

Giroux, H. A. (1979). Writing and critical thinking in the social studies. *Curriculum Inquiry,* 291–310.

Graddol, D. (1999). The decline of the native speaker. *AILA Review, 13,* 57–68.

Gray, J. (2002). The global coursebook in English language teaching. In D. Cameron & D. Block, *Globalization and language teaching* (pp. 151–167). London: Routledge & Kegan Paul.

Harding, S. (1991). *Whose science? Whose knowledge? Thinking from women's lives.* Ithaca, NY: Cornell University Press.

Heller, M. and Martin-Jones, M. (Eds.). (2001). *Voices of authority: Education and linguistic difference.* Westport, CT: Ablex.

Holliday, A. (1994). *Appropriate methodology and social context.* Cambridge, UK: Cambridge University Press.

Holliday, A. (in press). *The struggle to teach English as an international language.* Oxford, UK: Oxford University Press.

hooks, bell. (1989). *Talking back: Thinking feminist, thinking black.* Boston: South End Press.

Kachru, B. B. (1986). *The alchemy of English: The spread, functions, and models of non-native Englishes.* Oxford, UK: Pergamon.

Kaplan, R. B. (1966). Cultural thought patterns in intercultural education. *Language Learning, 16,* 1–20.

Kramsch, C., & Lam, W. S. E. (1999). Textual identities: The importance of being non-native. In G. Braine (Ed.), *Non-native educators in English language teaching* (pp. 57–72). Mahwah, NJ: Lawrence Erlbaum Associates.

Kramsch, C. (2000). Social discursive constructions of self in L2 learning. In J. Lantolf (Ed.), *Sociocultural theory and second language learning* (pp. 133–153). New York: Oxford University Press.

Kubota, R. (1999). An investigation of L1-L2 transfer in writing among Japanese university students: Implications for contrastive rhetoric. *Journal of Second Language Writing, 7*(1), 69–100.

Kumaravadivelu, B. (1994). The postmethod condition: (E)merging strategies for second/foreign language teaching. *TESOL Quarterly, 28*(1), 27–48.

Kumaravadivelu, B. (1999). Critical classroom discourse analysis. *TESOL Quarterly, 33*(3), 453–484.

Lam, E. W. S. (2000). L2 literacy and the design of the self: A case study of a teenager writing on the Internet. *TESOL Quarterly, 34*(3), 457–482.

Leki, I. (1991). The preferences of ESL students for error correction in college-level writing classes. *Foreign Language Annals, 24,* 203–218.

Leki, I. (1995). Coping strategies of ESL students in writing tasks across the curriculum. *TESOL Quarterly, 29*(2), 235–260.

Li, X-M. (1999). Writing from the vantage point of an outsider/insider. In G. Braine (Ed.), *Non-native educators in English language teaching* (pp. 43–56). Mahwah, NJ: Lawrence Erlbaum Associates.

Lin, A., Wang, W., Akamatsu, N., & Riazi, M. (2002). Appropriating English, expanding identities, and re-visioning the field: From TESOL to teaching English for glocalized communication (TEGCOM). *Journal of Language, Identity, and Education, 1*(4), 295–316.

Lu, M-Z. (1994). Professing multiculturalism: The politics of style in the contact zone. *College Composition and Communication, 45*(4), 442–458.

Martin, P. (in press) Talking knowledge into being in an upriver primary school in Brunei. In A. S. Canagarajah (Ed.), *Negotiating the global and local in language policies and practices.* Mahwah, NJ: Lawrence Erlbaum Associates.

Martin-Jones, M., & Heller, M. (1996). Language and social reproduction in multilingual settings. *Linguistics and Education, 8*(1&2), 127–137.

Morgan, B. (1998). *The ESL classroom.* Toronto: University of Toronto Press.

Muchiri, M. N., Mulamba, N. G., Myers, G. & Ndoloi, D. B. (1995). Importing composition: Teaching and researching academic writing beyond North America. *College Composition and Communication, 46*(2), 175–198.

Nandy, A. (Ed.). (1990). *Science, hegemony, and violence.* Oxford, UK: Oxford University Press.

Nelson, C. (1999). Sexual identities in ESL: Queer theory and classroom inquiry. *TESOL Quarterly, 33*(3), 371–392.

Nunan, D. (1990). Action research in the language classroom. In J. C. Richards & D. Nunan, (Eds.), *Second language teacher education.* Cambridge, UK: Cambridge University Press.

Ohmann, R. (1976). *English in America: A radical view of the profession.* Oxford, UK: Oxford University Press.

Peirce, B. N. (1995a). Social identity, investment, and language learning. *TESOL Quarterly, 29*(1), 9–32.

Peirce, B. N. (1995b). The theory of methodology in qualitative research. *TESOL Quarterly, 29*(3), 569–576.

Peirce, B. N. (1989). Towards a pedagogy of possibility in teaching of English internationally. *TESOL Quarterly, 23*(3), 401–420.

Pennington, M. (1995). The teacher change cycle. *TESOL Quarterly, 29,* 705–732.

Pennycook, A. (1989). The concept of "method", interested knowledge, and the politics of language teaching. *TESOL Quarterly, 23*(4), 589–618.

Pennycook, A. (1994a). *The cultural politics of English as an international language.* London: Longman.

Pennycook, A. (1994b). Critical pedagogical approaches to research. *TESOL Quarterly, 28*(4), 690–693.

Pennycook, A. (1996). Borrowing others' words: Text, ownership, memory, and plagiarism. *TESOL Quarterly, 30,* 201–230.

Pennycook, A. (2001). *Critical applied linguistics.* Mahwah, NJ: Lawrence Erlbaum Associates.

Phillipson, R. (1992). *Linguistic imperialism.* Oxford, UK: Oxford University Press.

Prabhu, N. S. (1990). There is no best method–Why? *TESOL Quarterly, 24*(2), 161–176.

Pratt, M. L. (1991). Arts of the contact zone. *Profession 91* (33–40). New York: MLA.

Prendergast, C. (1998). Race: The absent presence in composition studies. *College Composition and Communication, 50,* 36–53.

Prior, P. (1998). *Writing/disciplinarity: A sociohistoric account of literate activity in the academy.* Mahwah, NJ: Lawrence Erlbaum Associates.

Raj, J. (1982). WASP ideology: The kernel of the American Kernel Lessons. *Lanka Guardian, 5*(11), 15–18.

Rajagopalan, K. (1999). Of EFL teachers, conscience, and cowardice. *ELT Journal, 53*(3), 200–206.

Rampton, B. (1995). *Crossing: Language and ethnicity among adolescents.* London: Longman.

Resnik, M. C. (1993). ESL and language planning in Puerto Rico. *TESOL Quarterly, 27*(2), 259–273.

Robinson-Pant, A. (2001). Women's literacy and health: Can an ethnographic researcher find the links? In B. V. Street (Ed.), *Literacy and development: Ethnographic perspectives* (pp. 152–170). London: Routledge & Kegan Paul.

Scott, J. C. (1990). *Domination and the arts of resistance.* New Haven CT: Yale University Press.

Schenke, A. (1991). The "will to reciprocity" and the work of memory: Fictioning speaking out of silence in ESL and feminist pedagogy. *Resources for Feminist Research, 20,* 47–55.

Singh, R. (Ed.) (1998). *The native speaker: Multilingual perspectives.* New Delhi: Sage.

Skutnabb-Kangas, T. (1992). Linguistic human rights and minority education. *TESOL Quarterly, 28*(4), 625–628.

Skutnabb-Kangas, T. (2002). Marvelous human rights rhetoric and grim realities: Language rights in education. *Journal of Language, Identity, and Education, 1*(3), 179–206.

Sridhar, S. N. (1994). A reality check for SLA theories. *TESOL Quarterly, 28*(4), 800–805.

Street, B. V. (Ed.), (2001). *Literacy and development: Ethnographic perspectives.* London: Routledge & Kegan Paul.

Tuman, M. C. (1988). Class, codes, and composition: Basil Bernstein and the critique of pedagogy. *College Composition and Communication, 39*(1), 42–51.

Williams, R. (1977). *Marxism and literature.* Oxford, UK: Oxford University Press.

Wright, M. W. (2001). More than just chanting: Multilingual literacies, ideology, and teaching methodologies in rural Eritrea. In B. V. Street (Ed.), *Literacy and development: Ethnographic perspectives* (pp. 61–77). London: Routledge & Kegan Paul.

Zamel, V. (1997). Toward a model of transculturation. *TESOL Quarterly, 31*(2), 341–351.

VIII

Language Planning and Policy and Language Rights

Guest Editor:

Richard B. Baldauf, Jr.
University of Queensland

Introduction

Richard B. Baldauf, Jr.
University of Queensland

In this section of the *Handbook*, a framework for and overview of the important research issues for language policy and planning are presented. Following an introductory chapter that examines some general key issues and provides a possible framework for the types of activities that define the field, five chapters cover each of the archetypal activity types: status planning, corpus planning, language-in-education planning, prestige planning, and critical approaches to language planning, with particular emphasis on minority language rights. Within each of these areas, important recent research directions for language teaching and learning are discussed. The recent publication of two new journals in the field, *Current Issues in Language Planning* and *Language Policy*, the founding of a number of discipline-related journals, and the publication of books that take a critical perspective on language planning is indicative of the field's new-found sense of vitality.

Initially, **Richard Baldauf** (chap. 52) confronts the relevance of a section on language policy and planning (LPP) for a handbook devoted to research on language learning and teaching. Although large scale, usually national, planning—often undertaken by governments and meant to influence, if not change, ways of speaking or literacy practices within a society—may seem remote and only marginally relevant to the other issues being discussed in this *Handbook*, Baldauf argues that relevance to research on language teaching and learning exists on at least two counts:

- First, broadly speaking, language policies and the subsequent implementation planning that occur at least partially provide the structure or policy context for language learning and teaching and contribute to defining what counts as research.
- Second, at a more micro level, decisions that administrators and/or teachers make about who teaches what language, in what manner, for what purpose, and to whom, have small-scale policy consequences as these decisions either reinforce policy or begin to undermine it, thereby contributing to the development of new policy.

The chapter goes on to provide a brief historical context for the more theoretical perspective that is outlined as a possible framework for understanding the discipline. A brief overview of the goals that make up four of the activity types typically used to define the discipline (i.e., status planning, corpus planning, language-in-education planning, and prestige planning) then follows.

It is noted that other ways of defining the discipline are possible (e.g., language management) and that although the four sets of activity types and their goals make sense for descriptive pedagogical purposes, this makes them, of necessity, overly simplistic. In practice, language policy and planning goals normally are multiple and more complex, often cutting across activity types and sometimes coming into conflict with one another.

In the second part of the chapter, Baldauf explores three key general issues that need to be considered when thinking about the various activity types related to language policy and planning, those being:

- *Levels of language planning.* Much of the research cited in the chapters in this section has as its focus polity or macro level language policy and planning. Although such research has an important impact on second language learning and teaching by setting agendas and through the allocation of resources, language policy and planning can also occur at other levels—meso and micro—although these two remain underrepresented in the literature. Some micro examples are discussed.
- *Over and covert language planning.* Language policy and planning can either be overt (explicit, planned) or covert (implicit, unplanned)—or may not be done at all. Although the notion of "unplanned" planning, or the failure to address language issues, may seem in the context of language planning to be an oxymoron, such (in)decisions have a major impact on how languages are learned and taught, and some of these issues are explored in this section.
- *Critiques of language planning.* As a classic case of applied linguistics, it is possible to critique language policy and planning from either an applied or a theoretical perspective. It is argued that neither practitioners (who should be informed by principals and by research, but who may be caught up in the necessities of political expediency) nor those more inclined to theoretical analysis (who should be taking some account of what is possible, but who may instead be interested in creating solutions for virtual problems) may be satisfied by some disciplinary approaches. Contextualization and a focus on the micro are two directions that planners are moving in to strengthen the field.

In the second chapter in this section, **Theo van Els** (chap. 53) examines what is known about status planning, where the concern is with the status of languages as second languages, that is, with such high-level planning questions as "Which second languages should be known, learned, and taught?", "What aspects of the language(s) chosen should be known, learned, and taught, that is, which variety and to what level?", "Who should learn them and to whom should they be taught?", and "When should learning begin and under what circumstances?", and the particular needs for second languages that lie beneath such choices. These issues are illustrated in particular by examples from the Netherlands and Europe more generally.

The chapter argues that there are four aspects related to the status of second languages.

1. Their status for their own communicative purposes.
2. Their role as second languages—as a lingua franca or as a language of instruction.
3. Their role as immigrant or ethnic minority languages.
4. The degree to which promotion of a second language impacts on linguistic or language rights.

These aspects all need to be taken into account when making status planning decisions. Van Els argues, however, that whatever the status purposes, status planning decisions should be based on community needs. The chapter focuses on the nature of needs and how these needs can be identified and therefore planned for through status planning. Van Els argues that there is an adequate knowledge base and theoretical framework to tackle all status problems in the field of second language learning and teaching, but that there still seems to be a preference for uninformed laymen (politicians) developing policies without any recourse to empirical findings or advice.

In the third chapter in this section, **Anthony Liddicoat** (chap. 54) examines what is known about corpus planning and its relation to language teaching and research. Corpus planning—with its focus on the nature of the language to be taught and learned—is the activity area most dependent on linguistic input for its methodology, but it is shaped by status planning decisions; its output contributes in a major way to language-in-education planning; and it may contribute to, or benefit from, the prestige that a language has in the community. Liddicoat initially describes in some detail the research foundations for the corpus planning process (i.e., condification— graphization, grammatication and lexication, and elaboration—lexical development, stylistic development, renovation), providing examples related both to polities and languages. Having an understanding of this process provides a basis for the production of corpus planning products, more specifically syllabus development and materials development. It is at this point that the language teaching and learning implications of corpus planning become most evident, particularly as teachers are often involved in syllabus and materials development and modification for use in classrooms.

In the fourth chapter in this section, **Richard Baldauf** and **Robert B. Kaplan** (chap. 55) examine language-in-education policy and planning, sometimes known as acquisition policy. It is noted that language-in-education policy and planning often constitutes the sole language planning activity in many polities, but that such activities are limited in their impact by slow rates of dissemination, a limited audience, and often a lack of resources. Although language-in-education planning occurs most often in schools, it also implicates less systematic teaching situations in the community or the workplace.

The chapter goes on to examine seven key language-in-education policy goals (i.e., access policy, personnel policy, curriculum policy, methodology and materials policy, resourcing policy, community policy, evaluation policy) and four key language-in-education planning goals (i.e., language maintenance, language reacquisition, foreign/second language learning, language shift) by looking at examples of the implementation of these goals in three polities: Japan, Sweden, and North Korea. A number of general implications for language-in-education are then drawn from these descriptions and those from other similar polity studies available in the published literature.

In the fifth chapter in this section, **Dennis Ager** (chap. 56) discusses prestige or image planning. Noting that as this is not a well developed area within LPP, Ager suggests that it may initially be helpful for readers to look at three examples: Wales, Malaysia, and Quebec. The examination of LPP in these polities suggests that there may be three separate activities that underlie prestige planning. First, image (prestige) seems to be related to ethnic or civic identity (real or imagined) and the promotion of a language, as in the case of Quebec. Second, image seems to be used to describe a method of implementing and manipulating language policy as in Wales. Finaly, image has something to do with motive and the activities of language planners themselves and the communities they plan for, as in Malaysia and increasingly Quebec. Each of these three notions of image is explored in detail, bringing in further examples to illustrate these categorizations. In the final section, Ager illustrates how various aspects of motivation related to powerful states and powerless communities contribute to language policy development. Issues of prestige or image have implications for research into the teaching and learning of languages and for the implementation of minority language rights.

In the final chapter in this section, **Stephen May** (chap. 57) explores the interconnections between LPP and minority language rights (MLR), sometimes referred to as linguistic human rights. The chapter discusses the often complex and contested nature of the interaction between LPP and MLR, highlighting the wider sociohistorical, sociocultural and sociopolitical analysis of LPP, particularly as it relates to the question of the status, use, and power of minority languages in the modern world. This approach contrasts with the apolitical, ahistorical, and technicist paradigm that has characterized LPP, particularly in its early development. Although this modernist, constructivist approach to developing national languages was seen as a strength in developing national languages, it has lead to the pejorative positioning of minority languages and their speakers and to the consequent development of research on MLR. The chapter outlines the concerns of MLR advocates in the context of language ecology and linguistic human rights paradigms.

The particular research issues that May addresses in the chapter include: language shift and loss; language ecology; nationalism, minoritization, and historical constructionism; language replacement and social mobility; linguistic human rights; tolerance- and promotion-oriented language rights; and developments in international and national law. May argues that as a result of these research influences, language planners and policymakers are now addressing more overtly the political and ideological aspects of LPP as well as their consequences for minority languages. In the micro planning sense, these issues are also finding their way more explicit into the language teaching and learning literature.

This section provides a comprehensive overview of language planning as a field and the critiques that have been made of it in the context of research in second language teaching and learning.

52

Language Planning and Policy Research: An Overview

Richard B. Baldauf, Jr.
University of Queensland

INTRODUCTION

The relevance of a section on language policy and planning for a handbook devoted to research on language learning and teaching could well be questioned. This is especially the case as many applied linguists define language planning in terms of large-scale, usually national, planning, often undertaken by governments and meant to influence, if not change, ways of speaking or literacy practices within a society (Kaplan & Baldauf, 1997, p. 3). Although such issues may seem remote and only marginally relevant to the other issues being discussed in this *Handbook*, it can be argued that language planning and policy is relevant to research on language teaching and learning on at least two counts. First, broadly speaking, the language policies and the subsequent implementation planning that occur, at least partially provide the structure or policy context for language learning and teaching and contribute to defining what counts as research. Second, at a more micro level, decisions that administrators and/or teachers make about who teaches what language, in what manner, for what purpose, to whom have small-scale policy consequences as these decisions either reinforce policy or begin to undermine it, thereby contributing to the development of new policy. Therefore, it behooves us to examine the research about language policy and planning processes to develop an understanding of how such practices impact language learning and teaching.

This section of the *Handbook* on language planning is set out as follows. This chapter examines some of the more general theoretical issues that contribute to providing a framing context for language policy and planning. It is followed by chapters that examine four aspects that are generally considered to comprise the field: status planning (about society), corpus planning (about language), language-in-education (or acquisition) planning (about learning) and (most recently) prestige planning (about image). Finally, planning of any sort is about the distribution of resources and power, and the final chapter in this section examines the important social contextual aspects of language planning, especially the impact that such policy and planning has on minority language rights. Initially, however, it is useful to start with some definitions and a conceptual overview.

LANGUAGE PLANNING MODELS

Some Definitions

Although it can be demonstrated that a number of the concepts related to language policy and planning began to develop in the work of the Prague School out of the need for Czech language standardization and development that arose as part of the emergence of the new Czechoslovakian Republic after the World War I (see, e.g., Neustupný & Nekvapil, 2003), language management, as it came to be called, did not initially develop wider currency. Instead, the discipline of language planning—called language engineering by some early practitioners—developed anew in the 1950s out of the similar, but more widespread, needs for large-scale government language planning in the new, decolonizing independent states, particularly those in East Africa—Ethiopia, Kenya, Tanzania, Uganda, and Zambia—(Fox, 1975) and in South and Southeast Asia—the Indian subcontinent, Indonesia, Malaysia, and the Philippines (see e.g., Fishman, 1974). In one of the earliest volumes specifically devoted to the new discipline (Rubin & Jernudd, 1971, p. xvi), language planning was defined as the deliberate, future-oriented systematic-change of language code, use and/or speaking, undertaken by some organization mandated for such purposes—most visibly by governments (see e.g., Baldauf & Kaplan, 2003)—in some social situation, that is, in a community of speakers. Language planning often is directed by, or leads to, the promulgation of language policy(s).

The discipline of language planning differentiates between language policy (the plan) and language planning (plan implementation) although the two terms are frequently used interchangeably in the literature. The former, language policies, are bodies of ideas, laws, regulations, rules, and practices intended to achieve some planned language change. Such policy may be realized in very formal or overt ways, through language planning documents and pronouncements (e.g., constitutions, legislation, policy statements), which may have either symbolic or substantive intent. Alternately, policy may be inferred from more informal statements of intent (i.e., in the discourse of language, politics, and society), or policy may be left unstated or covert. Language planning, in the subcategory sense, focuses on the implementation of these plans (Kaplan & Baldauf, 2003).

Although language planning in the 1950s and 1960s was an out growth of the positivistic economic, linguistic, and social science paradigms that dominated the three post-World War II decades, by the 1970s, it was apparent that language problems were not unique to developing nations but were much more widely applicable to *macro* (i.e., state-level) language problems and situations. Since the 1990s, critical approaches to the discipline and the broader context of the discipline have become more important (see Ricento, 2000a, and Tollefson, 2002, for somewhat different historical perspectives), as those involved with the discipline have taken on issues such as language ecology (e.g., Kaplan & Baldauf, 1997; Mühlhäusler, 2000), language rights (e.g., May, 2001), and the place of languages other than English (e.g., Maurais & Morris, 2003; Pennycook, 1998; Ricento, 2000b).[1]

AN EVOLVING LANGUAGE PLANNING FRAMEWORK

As one might expect, over the last 35 years a number of those involved in language planning have put forward their ideas about what might constitute a model for language policy and planning (e.g., Ferguson, 1968; Fishman, 1974; Haarmann, 1990; Haugen, 1983; Neustupný, 1974), whereas others (e.g., Annamalai & Rubin, 1980; Bentahila & Davies, 1993; Nahir, 1984) have contributed to understanding the discipline by concentrating on language planning goals. Kaplan and Baldauf (1997) have argued that these ideas need to be framed within an ecological context, whereas Hornberger (1994) was the first to explicitly bring the model and goals strands together in a single framework. Kaplan and Baldauf (2003) have developed a revised and expanded version of the framework and have provided a number of illustrative examples from the Pacific basin for each of the goals. However, despite all of this theory-oriented activity, most language planning and policy practitioners probably would agree that insufficient research has been done to allow a complete and accurate model of the discipline to be constructed.

Still, it is useful to reflect on what is known. When thinking about the things that contribute to a model, both policy (i.e., form) and planning (i.e., function) components need to be considered as well as whether such policy and planning is or will be overt (explicit) or covert (implicit) in terms of the way it is decided and put into action. It is also useful to understand that language policy and planning occurs at different levels—the macro, the meso, and the micro—and that these may have differential effects on research on language learning and teaching. In addition, when language policy and planning is undertaken, there is a significant underlying historical and social component that helps to frame ongoing work. (See the polity studies in Kaplan and Baldauf, 2003, or individual polity studies in *Current Issues in Language Planning* for examples.)

A framework reflecting these issues, which is elaborated in greater detail in the sections that follow, is set out in Table 52.1. More specifically, the framework suggests that the practice of language policy and planning may be one of four types: status planning (about society), corpus planning (about language), language-in-education (acquisition) planning (about learning), or prestige planning (about image). Each of these four types of language planning can be realized from two approaches: a policy approach—with an emphasis on form: basic language and policy decisions and their implementation; or a cultivation approach—with an emphasis on the functional extension of language development and use. These eight language planning perspectives are best understood through the goals planners set out to achieve. However, it is important to understand that most of the goals in this framework are not independent of one other, that is, policy-planning goals normally lead to goals related to cultivation-planning support. A particular language planning matter may also have embedded in it several different goals, which may even be contradictory, for example, the widespread introduction of a strong foreign language (like English) may potentially conflict in the school curriculum with goals related to the importance of local and regional language maintenance. Nor are goals normally implemented in isolation, but as part of a broader (even if covert or unstated) set of objectives.

Finally, although a framework such as this is useful as a pedagogical device for explaining the scope of and some possible sequences for language planning, it should not be taken literally as a map of either how to do language planning or what happens in real language planning situations. In addition, as the subsequent chapters in this section show, there still is not complete agreement within the field on the terminology that is to be used or how various concepts are to be defined and applied (also see, Kaplan & Baldauf, 1997, p. 14). Rather, this chapter should serve as a starting point for understanding the discipline and the issues that confront policymakers and planners involved in research on second language learning and teaching.

Having set out a possible framework for the discipline, let us now briefly examine each of the four types of policy and planning goals and then the issue of the social context in which such goals exist. The brief descriptions provided in this chapter

TABLE 52.1

An Evolving Framework for Language Planning Goals by Levels and Awareness

Approaches to Goals	Policy Planning (on form)	Cultivation Planning (on function)	Levels Planning Processes and Goals					
			Macro		Meso		Micro	
			Awareness of Goals					
			Overt	Covert	Overt	Covert	Overt	Covert
Productive Goals Status Planning (about society)	Goals *Status Standardization* • Officialization • Nationalization • Proscription	Goals *Status Planning* Revival • Restoration • Revitalization • Reversal Maintenance Interlingual communication • International • Intranational Spread						
Corpus Planning (about language)	*Standardization* • Graphization • Grammatication • Lexication Auxiliary Code • Graphization • Grammatication • Lexication	*Corpus Elaboration* Lexical modernization Stylistic modernization Renovation • Purification • Reform • Stylistic simplification • Terminological unification Internationalization						
Language-in-Education Planning (about learning)	*Policy Development* Access policy Personnel policy Curriculum policy Methods & materials policy Resourcing policy Community policy Evaluation policy	*Acquisition Planning* Reacquisition Maintenance Foreign/second language Shift						
Receptive Goal Prestige Planning (about image)	*Language Promotion* • Official/Government • Institutional • Pressure group • Individual	*Intellectualization* • Language of science • Language of professions • Language of high culture						

Note. Adapted from R. B. Kaplan & R. B. Baldauf, Jr. (2003). *Language and Language-in-Education Planning* (p. 202), Dordrecht, The Netherlands: Kluwer.

outline the broad nature of language policy and planning. These five topics then are developed in the subsequent chapters with a more specific focus on research in learning and teaching.

Status Planning Goals

Status planning consists of those social goals that are external to the language and that a society must make about the environment or language ecology in which a language(s) is used. As van Els (chap. 53, this volume) points out, detailed status planning, especially as it relates to language learning and teaching, is a process that is well understood, but is a relatively neglected activity in practice. The goals of status planning relate either to the policy planning—about the form of language(s), that is, status standardization (officialization, nationalization and proscription) or to cultivation planning about functions, that is, the revival (restoration, revitalization, reversal), maintenance, interlingual communication (international, intranational) and spread of languages (see e.g., Haugen, 1983).

Corpus Planning Goals

Corpus planning is directed at those linguistic goals related to language itself that need to be made to codify, standardize, or modify and elaborate a language(s). These goals relate either to policy planning about the linguistic form of the language(s), that is, corpus standardization and auxiliary code standardization (graphization including orthographic reform, grammatication, lexication), or to cultivation planning about enhancing linguistic functions, that is, lexical modernization, stylistic modernization, renovation (purification, reform, stylistic simplification, terminological unification), and internationalization. Language renovation may involve language purification, that is, the removal of foreign (lexical) influences or the adherence to the classical forms and lexicon of a language. Written forms of a language, by definition, are more standardized and purified than the corresponding oral forms. Although the application of technical linguistic skills is central to meeting corpus planning goals, corpus planning also involves making choices or selecting alternatives that have a social aspect and that must be resolved for such planning to be successful. (See, e.g., Baldauf, 1990; Clyne, 1997; Haugen, 1983). Liddicoat (chap. 54, this volume) examines how corpus planning relates to language learning and teaching.

Language-In-Education (Acquisition) Planning Goals

Language-in-education planning is the area most explicitly related to language learning and teaching. It focuses on those user-related learning decisions that need to be made to develop language education programs and teach a language(s) for various purposes. These goals relate to policy planning about the form of a language learning program(s), that is, access policy, personnel policy, curriculum policy, methods and materials policy, resourcing policy, community policy; evaluation policy; or to cultivation planning for enhancing language teaching functions, that is, reacquisition, maintenance, foreign language/second language, and shift. Although language-in-education planning should co-occur with the other planning types, this frequently does not happen, and language-in-education planning, through schooling, can become the sole language change agent. (See e.g., Baldauf & Ingram, 2003; Cooper, 1989; Ingram, 1990; Kaplan & Baldauf, chap. 55, this volume; Paulston & McLaughlin, 1994; Spolsky, 1978).

Prestige Planning Goals

Prestige planning is directed at those goals related to the image a language needs to develop to promote and intellectualize that language(s). These goals relate either to policy planning by those individuals or groups that have or take the responsibility to create the image of the language(s), that is, language promotion (via official/government, institutional, pressure group, individual), or to cultivation planning by enhancing the functional image and status of the language in key language domains, that is, intellectualization (language of science, language of professions, language of high culture). Prestige planning represents a separate receptive or value function range of activities to status, corpus, and language-in-education planning, which are productive activities that influences how the three former planning activities are acted on and received. Prestige or efficiency of organizational impact levels influences the success of a language plan and the uses to which languages are put (see, Ager, 2001; chap. 56, this volume; Haarmann, 1990).

Language Planning and Language Rights

As the definition previously provided by Rubin and Jernudd (1971) has indicated, language planning is not just a technical exercise involving status, corpus, language-in-education, and prestige planning but occurs in a social context. Kaplan and Baldauf (1997) have referred to this context as a language ecology noting that when one changes one language in an ecology, the other languages in that ecology are also affected and usually changed in some manner. As with other ecologies, power relationships exist and groups using one language may dominate or exclude or may tolerate or promote other languages. This occurs not only at the macro policy level, but also in institutions, including schools and classrooms. It is, therefore, an issue that is important for language policymakers and planners interested in language learning and teaching to consider.

Initial language policy and planning projects, with their positivistic beliefs and focus on problem solutions, did not provide much critique of, nor explicit focus on, the broader context. In part this was because it was assumed that broadly based planning teams would bring expertise that would take contextual matters like language rights into account as part of the development of the best possible policy and planning implementation for a given situation (see e.g., Jernudd & Baldauf, 1987). However, in recent years the resultant problem of the "insiders' paradox" has become more apparent, that is, the difficulties that planners have in dealing with the real political and linguistic issues of the day while being able to take an unbiased view of their own planning (Baldauf & Kaplan, 2004). Critical studies of the context and the impact of policy and planning have grown and attracted a lot of scholarly attention, well beyond the formal domains of language planning and policy. Professional bodies like TESOL have set up subsections—Sociopolitical Concerns—to develop this area as it relates to their profession (e.g., Hall & Eggington, 2000). May (chap. 57, this volume) provides an overview of these issues as they apply to the language policy and planning context.

LANGUAGE MANAGEMENT FRAMEWORK

As indicated in the introductory section, this view of a language planning framework is not the only way of conceptualizing the discipline. Another compatible perspective to the description of how languages are planned and managed is the language management approach. Although the most recent discussions of this approach relate to Quebec (e.g., Cormier & Guilloton, 2001; Jernudd & Neustupný, 1987; also see Neustupný, 1983, 1985), the material presented here is briefly summarized from an introduction to the classical case of Czechoslovakia, now the Czech Republic (see, Neustupný & Nekvapil, 2003).

In the context of language management, *management* refers to a wide range of acts of attention to "language problems." Initially these problems were conceptualized as occurring in the narrow linguistic sense, but according to current practice areas such as discourse, politeness, intercultural communication, proofreading, speech therapy, or literary criticism are implicated. The basic features of language management may be summarized as follows:

- Management may be *simple*—dealing with specific, often individual problems—or *organized*—involving multiple participants in the discussion (potential ideological) of the management process.
- Management is a process in which *deviation* from some particular norm (or expectation) is *noted* and *evaluated*, an *adjustment plan* selected, and then *implemented*.
- Linguistic management is nested within communicative management, which is nested within socioeconomic management, that is, one cannot change language forms (e.g., gender-loaded words) unless communicative and socioeconomic management also occurs.
- Language management recognizes that decisions and plans are based on interests and power relations within the community (Jernudd, 1996; Neustupný, 1996).

Neustupný and Nekvapil (2003) state that language management can occur at a number of different levels (from micro to macro) and that this approach is compatible with other evolving language planning frameworks, but argue that it is more comprehensive, that is, it is more explicit about what needs to be done in order to arrest language and communication problems. More specifically, once deviation from some particular norm is noted and evaluated, there are a number of strategies, based on a "Hymesian model" (Neustupný, 1987, 1997) that exist and are subject to language management (the eight being: participant, variety, situational set, function, setting, content, frame, and channel). These provide processes to understand and/or bring about language change.

LEVELS OF LANGUAGE PLANNING

Work published on language policy and planning, including much of the research cited in the accompanying chapters, has focused on polity or macro-level language policy and planning. Although such research has an important impact on second language learning and teaching by setting agendas and through the allocation of resources, language policy and planning can also occur at a number of different levels—macro, meso, and micro—although the latter two remain underrepresented in the literature. However, because actual planning at the macro level is very much a political process (Baldauf & Kaplan, 2003)—at least in the first instance—for many researchers and practitioners, it is planning at the meso[2] and particularly the micro level where they could be most involved.

There are those, of course, who would argue that almost by definition language policy and planning is a classic case of macro-sociolinguistics or macro-applied linguistics. From this perspective, it is difficult enough to provide a coherent framework for language planning at the polity or macro level without trying to extend the model to smaller scale studies (Davies, 1999). This view is reflected in much of the published literature that relates to a description or evaluation of some aspect of polity-level policy or planning (Baldauf, 2002). Furthermore, it can be argued that "the impact that language planning and policy has depends heavily on meso and micro level involvement and support" (Kaplan & Baldauf, 2003, pp. 201–202; also see Kaplan & Baldauf,

1997). That is, that there is a need for language policy and planning, if it is to be successful, to extend down through the system—for example, the creation of macro policy (e.g., the development of the Australian Language and Literacy Policy) has an impact on classrooms and on teachers (Breen, 2002), and is an extension of research at the macro level.

Therefore, small-scale language policy and planning problems discussed in the literature typically refer to an analysis of macro issues arising from the language problems to be found in nation states. Normally there is little or no suggestion that independent micro-level policy should be developed or that planning should extend beyond what is required to implement macro policy. Rather, it is the impact of macro polity policy or its refinement (or the lack thereof) on micro situations that is being examined (Baldauf, 2004). In contrast to this, micro language policy should originate at the micro and not the macro level. Micro planning refers to cases where businesses, institutions, groups, or individuals create what might be recognized as a language policy and plan to utilize and develop their language resources. Such a policy is not directly the result of some larger macro policy, but is a response to the needs of individuals or groups, their own "language problems," their own need for language management. It is difficult to identify studies of micro language policy and planning in the literature. Perhaps this is because such work currently is not valued because it doesn't belong to an "authentic" research genre, or perhaps because business and other micro sites are less open to public scrutiny (and therefore academic analysis) than governmental entities, or perhaps because publication occurs in "business-related" journals under different headings (Baldauf, 2004).

Some examples of studies (or proposals for studies) at the micro level include the suggestion that Irish language learning and teaching in Northern Ireland needs to be fostered independently at the local level (Mac Giolla Chriost, 2002), that a focus on sojourner status by parents and children was an effective contextual language planning strategy for maintaining Japanese for bilingual children whose parents were of Japanese background (Yoshimitsu, 2000), or that problems with the bilingual materials produced by the banking sector in Los Angeles indicated there was a substantial failure on the part of banks to serve their non-English speaking clientele (Kaplan, Touchstone, & Hagstrom, 1995; Touchstone, Kaplan, & Hagstrom, 1996). Corson's (1999) analysis of school contexts provides an excellent starting point for anyone concerned with developing school-based (micro) language planning and policy. It provides a detailed discussion and a set of questions for micro language planners interested in developing school-based policy in first language (L1), second language (L2), literacy, oracy, bilingual or multilingual education programs. For those taking a language management approach, the macro–micro divide is less problematic for while language management may be *organized*, it may be, and in fact often must be, *simple* as well.

Thus, although language planning is frequently viewed as a macro activity, it is normally extended to micro situations for implementation, but it also can be applied as an independent process in a variety of language learning and teaching situations. Research on such micro aspects is generally lacking, but would contribute to a better understanding of both policy implementation and the solution of micro policy problems.

OVERT AND COVERT LANGUAGE PLANNING

Another important characteristic of language planning is that policy and planning can be either be overt (explicit, planned) or covert (implicit, unplanned) or may not be done at all. While the notion of "unplanned" planning or the failure to address language issues, may seem in the context of language planning, to be an oxymoron, it is not, because such (in)decisions have a major impact on how languages are learned and taught. Much of what passes for planning occurs informally, off the record, and sometimes without much explicit thought by those involved. Baldauf (1994) has called this "unplanned language planning" because language policy decisions are being taken without thinking explicitly about them or their consequences. Baldauf (1994) and Kaplan and Baldauf (1997, pp. 298–299) suggest there are four reasons why considerations of formal planning need to consider the informal or unplanned. These can briefly summarized as:

• Planned and unplanned features often coexist is the same context and the unplanned can alter or pervert the planning process. In Papua New Guinea (Swan & Lewis, 1990), Côte d'Ivoire (Djité, 2000), Tunisia (Daoud, 2001), and South Africa (Heugh, 2003) some aspects of language (and languages) are planned, whereas others are not, and the failure to address the latter distorts the policy and planning processes and outcomes.

• The absence of some activity (i.e., language planning) often provides information about the activity. In relation to diglossic language use in social and political situations, examples one might look at include: in Papua New Guinea where English is the official language, Tok Pisin is ignored in policy terms (Swan & Lewis, 1990), or Côte d'Ivoire (Djité, 2000) where the promotion and valorization of autochthonous languages and Popular French are ignored in policy terms in relation to Standard French. In Malaysia, Ozóg (1993) asserts that the focus on Bahasa Melayu in the National Language Policy and the inability to talk about English for reasons of national harmony have limited Malays' access to the language at a time when the language is important for economic and scientific advancement. (In 2003, English was reintroduced to teach some content areas in all schools in Malaysia.)

• Language policy and planning activities are power related and may be invoked to ensure social control rather than to implement desirable language change. For example, Sommer (1991) examines the power exercised by bureaucracies in shaping language plans to suit political needs, whereas Souaiaia (1990) and Daoud (2001) discuss how the political interests of the elites has effected the progress of Arabicization in the Maghreb.

• Much micro language planning is unplanned because most people or groups feel quite competent—often based on their native-speaker competence—to become involved in such language activities. The two articles by Kaplan, Touchstone, and Hagstrom (1995) and Touchstone, Kaplan, and Hagstrom (1996) concerning bilingual banking brochures in Los Angeles are illustrative of this point.

However, Eggington (2002, p. 405) argues that discussion at this level tends to "cast rather benign attributes on this phenomenon" and that it is also important to look at the underlying motivations and ideologies that are being revealed when "unplanning" occurs. He suggests that there are two somewhat overlapping categories of unplanning in language policy and planning that need to be examined, those being:

• Unplanned language planning as social engineering planning that is often used as a nonconsultative, ideologically driven, top-down process that provides simplistic solutions to virtual problems. Eggington (2002, pp. 408–412) illustrates the nature of such problems using the specific examples from the right and the left of the sociopolitical spectrum—the *Official English* movement in the United States, and the *language rights movement* found in many international contexts. He argues that the assumptions that underlie these "problems" are questionable—that is, English is not threatened in the United States, nor will the opportunities for children to learn their parents' idiom in schools save those languages from extinction. He concludes that such ideologically driven "fixes" to perceived language problems, may in some cases exacerbate the problems and lead to a host of unintended consequences.

- Unplanned language planning conducted by nonspecialists examines decisions about what language to use in a particular situation, for example, in a multinational project or to address the minority language needs of children in schools. Although it can be argued that from a power ideologies perspective that the selection of English in such situations would be motivated by hegemonic considerations, Eggington (2002, p. 415) suggests that an equally valid hypothesis would be that language is selected to meet communicative needs.

Thus, rather than being an oxymoron, these arguments suggest that unplanned language planning is an important phenomenon to consider, because it provides one of the reasons why there has been a growing critical focus on language policy and planning activity, including issues of language rights (see May, chap. 57, this volume).

CRITIQUES OF LANGUAGE PLANNING

As this chapter demonstrates, language planning and policy is perhaps the classic case of applied linguistics. But, the balance between the applied and the theoretical that this implies does not sit easily with neither practitioners, who should be informed by principals and by research, but who may be caught up in the necessities of political expediency, nor those more inclined to theoretical analysis, who should be taking some account of what is possible, but who may instead be interested in creating solutions for what Eggington (2002) calls virtual problems. However, this underlying tension means that beyond issues related to the "insiders paradox" mentioned previously, and issues related to context and language rights (see May, chap. 57, this volume), there have been some general critiques of language planning as a discipline, particularly from a postmodern perspective (e.g., Luke, McHoul, & Mey, 1990; Tollefson, 1991) and more recently in terms of ecolinguistics (Kibbee, 2003). Some of the postmodern critiques of practice-based language planners and language planning can be said to be based around the following issues (Fishman, 1994, p. 91):

- Language planning is conducted by elites that are governed by their own self-interest—for example, in Côte d'Ivoire (Djité, 2000) or the Maghreb (Souaiaia, 1990).
- Language planning reproduces rather than overcomes sociocultural and econo-technical inequalities—the classic case being South Africa (Heugh, 2003; Kamwangamalu, 2001).
- Language planning inhibits or counteracts multiculturalism—for example, in the European Union (Phillipson & Skutnabb-Kangas, 1999; cf. van Els, 2001).
- Language planning espouses worldwide Westernization and modernization leading to new sociocultural, econotechnical and conceptual colonialism—for example, in Hong Kong (Pennycook, 1998).
- Ethnographic research is the most appropriate methodology for avoiding the traps posed by the previously mentioned shortcomings.

Fishman (1994, p. 97) has argued that these five critiques focused mainly on theoretical issues related to an analysis of language planning theory rather than on an analysis of practice and that "very little language planning practice has actually been informed by language planning theory." He also points out that although issues of language rights of minorities are important, the solutions suggested or implied by these critiques should not replace one kind of exploitation of minorities with another nor replace one existing minority with a new minority created by the process intended to redress current injustice. Language planners need to contribute to the empowerment of the disadvantaged and the education of the advantaged. But, languages will be planned, and:

> language planning will be utilised by both those who favor and those who oppose whatever the socio-political climate may be. This is a truth that neo-Marxist and post-structuralist critics of language planning never seem to grasp and, therefore, they never seem to go beyond their critique as decisively or as productively as they state their critique. (Fishman, 1994, p. 98)

In addition, Tollefson (2002, pp. 419–420) suggests that there are two further criticisms of language policy and planning that relate to local impact. These can be said to have had a more substantial impact on the field, as they relate more directly to practice. These are:

- The failure to realize the complexity of problems, to adequately analyze the impact of local context on policies and plans, and, therefore, the failure of policies to achieve their lofty goals.
- Lack of attention paid to language practices and attitudes of communities affected by macro language policies and planning.

Those interested in language planning have moved to accommodate these issues, and more recent studies of language planning have had more limited aims and have begun to focus on micro problems where context can be more easily incorporated.

SUMMARY AND CONCLUSIONS

This chapter has provided a brief overview of the discipline of language policy and planning and an indication of some of its intersections with the research on learning and teaching. It has been argued that language policy and planning is a dynamic field for application and study. As a discipline, it has moved from being a methodology for solving language problems in developing nations to a way of examining language problems in general. It has moved from a focus on societal and linguistic concerns to add the dimensions of language-in-education (acquisition) planning and prestige planning to its scope of activities. It has moved from taking context as an internal variable to be manipulated only as part of the planning process to increasingly making it an external one for that is the basis for critique. It has begun to move from an exclusive focus on large-scale language problems to look at language problems in smaller, more everyday contexts, including businesses and schools. It has recognized that it is not only overt policy and planning, but covert or "unplanned" policy, or even the failure to take any policy decisions at all, that affects the nature of language, including the teaching and learning context. Furthermore, there is a recognition of the central role that politics plays in language policy and planning decisions. In addition, Tollefson (2002) suggests that in the future, language planners need to take more notice of the role that legal frameworks play in determining what kinds of policies and practices are possible in particular polities. He also argues that language planners need to establish closer links with sociology and with the discourses of ideology and identity. It is also likely that the issue of language rights will be a central question for language planners to consider.

In the chapters that follow, the four types of language policy and planning outlined in the framework are discussed in detail. The final chapter in the section examines the context of language policy and planning with a particular focus on language rights.

NOTES

1. As Baldauf (2002) indicates, the published literature related to language policy and planning is quite numerous but is spread across a broad range of publications with only a few key journals or book series focusing specifically on the discipline. For example, the *Linguistics and Language Behavior Abstracts* database for 1973–1998 contains about 6,000 references to language policy and/or language planning, whereas I have developed a database containing between two and three times that many articles. The articles cited in this chapter are therefore only indicative of the literature. To avoid duplication, many specific references to issues and areas introduced in this chapter, but developed in the other five chapters in this section, can be found in those chapters. Some key journals for the discipline include: the *International Journal of the Sociology of Language* (1974–), the *(New) Language Planning Newsletter* (1975–), *Terminogramme/Revue d'Aménagement Linguistique* (c. 1975–), *Language Problems & Language Planning* (1977–), the *Journal of Multilingual and Multicultural Development* (1980–), *Current Issues in Language Planning* (2000–), *Language Policy* (2002–). Journals like the *TESOL Quarterly* have had special issues related to aspects of language planning.
2. See Williams (1994) for a macro/meso/micro example relating to the anglicization of Wales.

REFERENCES

Ager, D. (2001). *Motivation in language planning and language policy.* Clevedon, UK: Multilingual Matters.

Annamalai, E., & Rubin, J. (1980). Planning for language code and language use: Some considerations in policy formation and implementation. *Language Planning Newsletter 6*(3), 1–4.

Baldauf, R. B., Jr. (1990). Language planning: Corpus planning. In R. B. Kaplan (Ed.), *Annual review of applied linguistics, 10* (pp. 3–12). New York: Cambridge University Press.

Baldauf, R. B., Jr. (1994). "Unplanned" language policy and planning. In W. Grabe (Eds.), *Annual review of applied linguistics, 14* (pp. 82–89). New York: Cambridge University Press.

Baldauf, R. B., Jr. (2002). Methodologies for policy and planning. In R. B. Kaplan (Ed.), *Oxford handbook of applied linguistics* (pp. 391–403). Oxford, UK: Oxford University Press.

Baldauf, R. B., Jr., & Ingram, D. (2003). Language-in-education planning. In *International encyclopedia of linguistics, Vol. 2* (2nd ed., pp. 412–416). Oxford, UK: Oxford University Press.

Baldauf, R. B., Jr., & Kaplan, R. B. (2003). Who are the actors? The role of (applied) linguists in language policy. In P. Ryan & R. Terborg (Eds.), *Language: Issues of inequality* (pp. 19–40). Mexico City: CELE/ Autonomous National University of Mexico.

Baldauf, R. B., Jr., & Kaplan, R. B. (2004). Language policy and planning in Botswana, Malawi, Mozambique and South Africa: Some common issues. In R. B. Baldauf & R. B. Kaplan (Eds.), *Language planning and policy in Africa, Vol 1: Botswana, Malawi, Mozambique and South Africa,* (pp. 1–17). Clevedon, UK: Multilingual Matters.

Baldauf, R. B., Jr. (in press). Micro language planning. In D. Atkinson, P. Bruthiaux, W. Grabe, & V. Ramanathan (Eds.), *Studies in applied linguistics: English for academic purposes, discourse analysis, and language policy and planning (Essays in honour of Robert B. Kaplan on the Occasion of his 75th Birthday).* Clevedon, UK: Multilingual Matters.

Bentahila, A., & Davies, E. E. (1993). Language revival: Restoration or transformation. *Journal of Multilingual and Multicultural Development, 14,* 355–374.

Breen, M. (2002). From a language policy to classroom practice: The intervention of identity and relationships. *Language and Education, 16,* 260–283.

Clyne, M. (1997). *Undoing and redoing corpus planning.* Berlin/New York: Mouton de Gruyter.

Cooper, R. L. (1989). *Language planning and social change.* Cambridge, UK: Cambridge University Press.

Cormier, M. C., & Guilloton, N. (2001). Interventions sociolinguistique et practiques langagières: L'Office de la langue française de 1961 à 2001 [English translation]. *Terminogramme, 101–102.*

Corson, D. (1999). *Language planning in schools.* Mahwah, NJ: Lawrence Erlbaum Associates.

Daoud, M. (2001). The language planning situation in Tunisia. *Current Issues in Language Planning, 2,* 1–52.

Davies, A. (1999). Review of Kaplan, R. B. & Baldauf, R. B., Jr. (1997). *Language planning from practice to theory. Australian Review of Applied Linguistics, 22*(1), 121–124.

Djité. P. G. (2000). Language planning in Côte d'Ivoire. *Current Issues in Language Planning, 1,* 11–46.

Eggington, W. (2002). Unplanned language planning. In R. B. Kaplan (Ed.), *Oxford handbook of applied linguistics* (pp. 404–415). Oxford, UK: Oxford University Press.

Ferguson, C. A. (1968). Language development. In J. A. Fishman, C. A. Ferguson, & J. Das Gupta (Eds.), *Problems of developing nations* (pp. 27–36). New York: Wiley.

Fishman, J. A. (1974). Language planning and language planning research: The state of the art. In J. A. Fishman (Ed.), *Advances in language planning*. The Hague, The Netherlands: Mouton.

Fishman, J. A. (1994). Critiques of language planning: A minority languages perspective. *Journal of Multilingual and Multicultural Development, 15*, 91–99.

Fox, M. J. (1975). *Language and development: A retrospective survey of Ford Foundation language projects, 1952–1974* (2 vols.). New York: Ford Foundation.

Haarmann, H. (1990). Language planning in the light of a general theory of language: A methodological framework. *International Journal of the Sociology of Language 95*, 109–129.

Hall, J. K., & Eggington, W. G. (2000). *The sociopolitics of English language teaching.* Clevedon, UK: Multilingual Matters.

Haugen, E. (1983). The implementation of corpus planning: Theory and practice. In J. Cobarrubias & J. A. Fishman (Eds.), *Progress in language planning: International perspectives* (pp. 269–289). Berlin: Mouton de Gruyter.

Heugh, K. (2003). *Language policy and democracy in South Africa: The Prospects of equity within rights-based policy and planning.* Stockholm, Sweden: Centre for Research on Bilingualism, Stockholm University.

Hornberger, N. (1994). Literacy and language planning. *Language and Education, 8*, 75–86.

Ingram, D. E. (1990). Language-in-education planning. In R. B. Kaplan (Eds.), *Annual review of applied linguistics, 10* (pp. 53–78). New York: Cambridge University Press.

Jernudd, B. H. (1996). Language planning. In H. Goebl, P. H. Nelde, Z. Starý, & W. Wölck (Eds.), *Kontaktlinguistik* (pp. 833–842). Berlin: de Gruyter.

Jernudd, B. H., & Baldauf, R. B., Jr. (1987). Language education in human resource development. In B. K. Das (Ed.), *Human resource development* (pp. 144–189). Singapore: RELC.

Jernudd, B. H., & Neustupný, J. V. (1987). Language planning: For whom? In L. Laforge (Ed.), *Proceedings of the International Colloquium on Language Planning* (pp. 69–84). Quebec, Canada: Les Presses de l'Université Laval.

Kamwangamalu, N. M. (2001). The language planning situation in South Africa. *Current Issues in Language Planning, 2*, 361–445.

Kaplan, R. B., & Baldauf, R. B., Jr. (1997). *Language planning from practice to theory.* Clevedon, UK: Multilingual Matters.

Kaplan, R. B., & Baldauf, R. B., Jr. (2003). *Language and language-in-education planning in the Pacific Basin.* Dordrecht, The Netherlands: Kluwer.

Kaplan, R. B., Touchstone, E. E., & Hagstrom, C. L. (1995). Image and reality: Banking in Los Angeles. *Text, 15*, 427–456.

Kibbee, D. A. (2003). Language policy and linguistic theory. In J. Maurais & M. A. Morris (Eds.), *Languages in a globalising World* (pp. 47–57). Cambridge, UK: Cambridge University Press.

Luke, A., McHoul, A., & Mey, J. L. (1990). On the limits of language planning: Class, state and power. In R. B. Baldauf, Jr. & A. Luke (Eds.), *Language planning and education in Australasia and the South Pacific* (pp. 25–44). Clevedon, UK: Multilingual Matters.

Mac Giolla Chriost, D. (2002). Language planning in Northern Ireland. *Current Issues in Language Planning, 3*(4), 425–476.

Maurais, J., & Morris, M. A. (Eds.). (2003). *Languages in a globalising world.* Cambridge, UK: Cambridge University Press.

May, S. (2001). *Language and minority rights: Ethnicity, nationalism and the politics of language.* New York: Longman.

Mühlhäusler, P. (2000). Language planning and language ecology. *Current Issues in Language Planning 1*, 306–367.

Nahir, M. (1984). Language planning goals: A classification. *Language Problems & Language Planning, 8*, 294–327.

Neustupný, J. V. (1974). Basic types of treatment of language problems. In J. A. Fishman (Ed.), *Advances in language planning* (pp. 37–48). The Hague, The Netherlands: Mouton.

Neustupný, J. V. (1983). Towards a paradigm for language planning. *Language Planning Newsletter, 9*(4), 1–4.

Neustupný, J. V. (1985). Problems in Australian–Japanese contact situations. J. B. Pride (Ed.), *Cross-cultural encounters: Communication and mis-communication* (pp. 44–84). Melbourne, Australia: River-Seine Publications.

Neustupný, J. V. (1987). *Communicating with the Japanese.* Tokyo: The Japan Times.

Neustupný, J. V. (1996). Current issues in Japanese-foreign contact situations. *Kyoto Conference on Japanese Studies 1994* (Vol. II; pp. 208–216). Kyoto: International Research Center for Japanese Studies.

Neustupný, J. V. (1997). Teaching communication or teaching interaction. *Intercultural Communication Studies* (Kanda University of International Studies) *10*, 1–13.

Neustupný, J. V., & Nekvapil, J. (2003). Language management in the Czech Republic. *Current Issues in Language Planning, 4*(2), 95–278.

Ozóg, C. K. (1993). Bilingualism and national development in Malaysia. *Journal of Multilingual and Multicultural Development, 14*, 59–72.

Paulston, C. B., & McLaughlin, S. (1994). Language-in-education policy and planning. In W. Grabe (Eds.), *Annual review of applied linguistics, 14* (pp. 53–81). New York: Cambridge University Press.

Pennycook, A. (1998). *English and the discourses of colonialism*. London and New York: Routledge.

Phillipson, R., & Skutnabb-Kangas, T. (1999). Englishisation: One dimension of globalisation. *AILA Review, 13*, 19–36.

Ricento, T. (2000a). Historical and theoretical perspectives in language policy and planning. In T. Ricento (Ed.), *Ideology, politics and language policies: Focus on English* (pp. 9–24). Amsterdam: Benjamins.

Ricento, T. (2000b). (Ed.). *Ideology, politics and language policies: Focus on English*. Amsterdam: Benjamins.

Rubin, J., & Jernudd, B. H. (1971). Introduction: Language planning as an element in modernization. In *Can language be planned? Sociolinguistic theory and practice for developing nations* (pp. xiii–xxiv). Honolulu: East West Center/University of Hawaii Press.

Sommer, B. (1991). Yesterday's experts: The bureaucratic impact on language planning for aboriginal bilingual education. In A. Liddicoat (Ed.), *Language planning in Australia* (pp. 109–134). Canberra: Applied Linguistics Association of Australia.

Souaiaia, J. (1990). Language, education and politics in the Maghreb. *Language, Culture and Curriculum, 3*, 109–123.

Spolsky, B. (1978). *Educational linguistics: An introduction*. Rowley, MA: Newbury House.

Swan, J., & Lewis, D. L. (1990). Tok Pisin at university: An educational and language planning dilemma in Papua New Guinea. In R. B. Baldauf, Jr. & A. Luke (Eds.), *Language planning and education in Australasia and the South Pacific* (pp. 210–233). Clevedon, UK: Multilingual Matters.

Touchstone, E. E., Kaplan, R. B., & Hagstrom, C. L. (1996). "Home, sweet casa"—Access to home loans in Los Angeles: A critique of English and Spanish home loan brochures. *Multilingua, 15*, 329–349.

Tollefson, J. W. (1991). *Plannning language, planning inequality*. London: Longman.

Tollefson, J. W. (2002). Limitations of language policy and planning. In R. B. Kaplan (Ed.), *Oxford handbook of applied linguistics* (p. 416–425). Oxford, UK: Oxford University Press.

van Els, T. J. M. (2001). The European Union, its institutions and its languages: Some language political observations. *Current Issues in Language Planning, 2*, 311–360.

Williams, C. H. (1994). Development, dependency and the democratic deficit. *Journal of Multilingual and Multicultural Development, 15*, 101–127.

Yoshimitsu, K. (2000). Japanese school children in Melbourne and their language maintenance efforts. *Journal of Asian Pacific Communication, 10*, 255–278.

53

Status Planning for Learning and Teaching

Theo van Els
Radboud University Nijmegen

INTRODUCTION

Although a distinction is often made between *second* and *foreign* language learning and teaching, based on different didactic procedures, as the example of The Netherlands illustrates, there are only few societies in which the distinction actually applies. Dutch learned by Turkish immigrants is a clear instance of second language learning, but the learning of Turkish by autochthonous Dutch speakers may be either foreign or second language learning, depending on what relationships the learner in question has with the Turkish minority. On the other hand, the learning of English by speakers of Dutch is normally considered foreign language learning—English having no official second language status in the country—but this language is so predominant in day-to-day life that the learner receives a great deal of extracurricular support beyond that gained through classroom teaching.

In the present chapter this distinction is not made, rather the whole field is referred to as second language learning and teaching, although for reasons of space the focus is on planning for languages that are basically external to the society in question. However, roughly speaking, what is said about planning for foreign languages, mutatis mutandis, also applies more generally.

This chapter with its focus on status planning only examines part of second language learning and teaching planning. Corpus planning issues such as syllabus and materials development, language-in-education planning or didactic issues concerning the learning and teaching of second languages, and prestige planning are dealt with in chapters 54 by Liddicoat, 55 by Kaplan and Baldauf, and 56 by Ager, respectively. Here the concern is with the status of languages as second languages, that is, with such high-level planning questions as "Which second languages should be known, learned, and taught?", "What aspects of the language(s) chosen should be known, learned, and taught, that is, which variety and to what level?", "Who should learn them and to whom should they be taught?", and "When should learning begin and under what circumstances?" and the particular needs for second languages that lie beneath such choices.

Status planning for second language learning and teaching—the focus of this chapter is not the same as, nor does it require, a national languages policy or a national *second* language(s) policy. The former, for example, regulates the position, the use, or the preservation of a nation's language(s). What, for instance, are the rights of the speakers of the language(s) not designated as *national* language(s)? The latter kind of policy specifies regulations or measures regarding the position of and use of second languages in the country; thus, it may regulate the use of second languages in courtrooms, by foreigners (van Els, 1994, p. 36).

Although the chief point of departure is traditional national level second language status planning, some attention is also given to the macro-level of supra-national or interstate planning. Whenever the argument is supported with examples, the chapter shows a bias toward the European scene, in particular the European Union on the one hand and The Netherlands on the other.

STATUS PLANNING: GENERAL ASPECTS

Before examining second language status planning, some terminological clarification is required. It has become customary to distinguish among *status planning, corpus planning*, and *acquisition planning*, referred to by some as *language-in-education planning* or *educational planning* (see e.g., Ager, 2001, p. 5; Spolsky & Shohamy, 2000; Kaplan & Baldauf, chap. 55, this volume). This distinction is not always consistently made, in particular one finds that *language-in-education planning* overlaps with the other two categories. For example, the *Dutch National Action Program for Foreign Languages* is called an example of acquisition planning by Spolsky and Shohamy (1997, p. 101), whereas by implication Lambert (2000, p. 172) classifies it as an example of status planning. Or, Spolsky and Shohamy (2000, pp. 13–14), explicitly subsume under acquisition policy the specification of "which segment of the population (such as all or part of the school population or of a specific occupational group) should spend a defined amount of time acquiring defined levels of competence in specific languages;" whereas, except for the definition of the specific "amount of time to be spent;" these activities could be classified as belonging to *status planning for learning and teaching*. In this chapter only choices of which language to teach form part of and are treated as the main issue in *status planning for learning and teaching*, which also includes the subsequent choices regarding, for example, to what level and by whom the language(s) selected should be learned. However, terminological correctness is not pursued at any cost, and the chapter may transgress into *language-in-education planning* at times as a consequence.

Status of Second Languages

The status of second languages can be said to have four aspects to it. First, there is the status that languages have, so to speak, for "themselves," both in internal and external communication. Languages compete with each other, that is, some languages are preferred over others for communication purposes between speakers of different languages. Internally, in multilingual communities, a language may be assigned the status of (one of) the national language(s) and externally a language may be selected to serve as *the* means of international communication. Status planning for languages of that kind is not a topic that is central to our discussion. However, the *prestige* or *weight* that a language carries in comparison to other languages is certainly a factor to be taken into account in status planning for learning and teaching.

Second, there is the status that languages may be assigned in their role as *second* languages, from the perspective of their *use* in countries outside the *home* country. There are two particular functions (i.e., those of lingua franca and language of instruction) that need to be discussed to define what relevance this kind of status may have for the learning and teaching of the languages in question.

A lingua franca, strictly speaking, is "a medium of communication between people or groups of people each speaking a different native language" (Gnutzmann, 2000, p. 357). Two types may be distinguished: a *pidginlike* type, which commonly has a mix of elements from different languages, very often based on one of the former colonial languages (i.e., English, French, or Spanish) and one or more indigenous languages, and second, a particular language type. English is a case in point when it is used for international communication as often there are no native speakers taking part in the communication. In such situations, non-native users tend to take over the "ownership" of the language and to adapt it according to their own needs and linguistic capacities (e.g., simplifying vocabulary and syntax) thereby becoming "minority shareholders in the global resource" that international English has become (Graddol, 1997, p. 23). English as it is used between non-native and native speakers of the language is definitely not the lingua franca variant.

The wide distribution of English as a lingua franca is important in planning considerations because the ownership situation—nobody's exclusive 'possession'—makes it a very suitable candidate for acceptance as second-language-for-all. However, it would be a mistake to think that it could fulfil the diverse range of second-language needs on its own.

The second function that English has in many countries where the language is not indigenous, is that of *language of instruction* in the educational system. Many youngsters receive all their instruction in (an)other language(s) than the one they were born into. This is even more the case when those born into local and regional dialects deviating considerably from the standard language are included. However, there is only one particular case that will be examined—choosing a non-native language of instruction that serves other than general educational purposes.

This occurs when instruction in most or all of the nonlanguage school subjects is given in one of the second languages of the prevailing curriculum, because one expects that in that way a higher command of the respective second language may be achieved—either more quickly or efficiently—than in regular second language classes. This approach, referred to as Content-based Instruction (CBI) or Content and Language Integrated Learning (CLIL) by some or classified as bilingual education by others (as it has much in common from a didactic point of view), has recently attracted a lot of attention in some Western European countries. The choice of the particular second language for CBI forms part of the field of status planning for learning and teaching, but the reasons why CBI is selected to speed up the learning and teaching of the second language in question, or the didactic ways in which CBI lessons are conducted are not.

The third aspect relates to *immigrant* or *ethnic minority languages*. There are two perspectives from which these languages may be of interest in status planning for second language learning and teaching. One is that of the languages themselves, the other is that of their speakers. From the former perspective, immigrant languages are in competition with all the other "foreign" second languages when planning decisions are to be taken. Such languages, no doubt, may represent a greater (communication) need for the planning country in question, because relations with their home countries gain in importance, simply by the presence of considerable numbers of immigrant speakers of these languages. The latter perspective, that is, of the immigrant language speakers, concerns them as *consumers* or *customers* of second language learning and teaching provisions, because their position differs from that of their autochthonous compatriots. Immigrant children sustain an extra language learning load because of their ethnic language background. On the positive side, it may be very helpful for the planning country to avail itself of the special language competence that immigrants bring with them to fulfill the country's second language needs, but this raises the question of why set up teaching programs in such languages for autochthonous citizens, if the relevant linguistic competence is already available in the community (Lambert, 1994, p. 50). On the other hand, immigrants should not be treated as different from their co-citizens if they are to achieve equal opportunities. They have a right to attain the same levels of education as other citizens, but if their second—that is, in the strict sense of *foreign*—language qualifications are less than those of their compatriots, it may be a serious setback to their socioeconomic possibilities.

This leads us to the fourth, and final, aspect, linguistic or language rights (see May, chap. 57, this volume) and the related topic of *linguistic imperialism* that sometimes is bracketed with it. Both topics have only restricted relevance in the status planning for second language learning and teaching context.

It is quite understandable that nation-states should try to achieve as prominent a position as possible for their language in interstate communication. Language promotion may range from such *mild* forms as offering help in curriculum and materials development to the more imperialistic extremes—where others are forced to learn and use the language while having their first language(s) suppressed—which were not unusual during the colonial and postcolonial period (see e.g., Phillipson, 1992). The view, however, that the present-day prominent international position of English is mainly to be attributed to devious imperialistic behavior on the part of the British and the Americans has been challenged (see e.g., Fishman, Conrad, & Rubal-Lopez, 1996; Spolsky & Shohamy, 1999). The main argument for adopting languages as second languages in (post) colonial situations starts from a consideration of the needs of the people from abroad, the non-natives, both as individuals and as a group. In this context, linguistic rights as they are defined in such documents as the draft "Universal Declaration of Linguistic Rights" and in the "European Charter for Regional and Minority Languages" (see e.g., Ager, 2001, pp. 34, 93; Phillipson & Skutnab-Kangas, 1999) are not really applicable to *second* language learning and teaching because linguistic rights are concerned with the use, maintenance, development, and learning of *native*—usually minority—languages and related cultures by those born into these languages and cultures. It is also a fallacy to think that in order to maintain European plurilinguality, people should be made to learn the minor languages, even if they have no personal need for them (see, van Els, 2002, p. 347).

Factors Relevant to the Status Planning Process

The prime preoccupation in status planning for second language learning and teaching is the choice of the second languages that need to be learned and taught. The second languages that are provided for in the educational system should be selected in such a way that the country's current and future needs for second languages are satisfied in an optimal way. Needs, therefore, are an important factor to consider in the status planning process; moreover, it is of the utmost importance to be very specific about *what* these needs are and *to what extent* they are felt in the country. Such questions as "How great is the demand for each individual second language?" or "Does every citizen have a need for the same linguistic skills, or the same level of command of those skills?" or "Is there a stable needs pattern?" must be answered before solutions can be proposed in national policy to questions like "Is it necessary for all citizens or just for specific professional groups to receive instruction in a particular second language?" or "How many languages, and which languages, are required?" To arrive at satisfactory answers to such questions, needs research is vital.

However, even if needs analysis research findings are to be the most significant source for a national policy, due consideration must be taken of things like the language policies advocated by neighboring countries, the level of difficulty of individual second languages, or the availability in the educational system of suitable teaching materials and adequately trained teachers. National policy decisions based only on needs data, however carefully gathered and analyzed, may well fail to meet the desired objectives.

Levels and Types of Status Planning Decisions

Second language status policies may differ in a great many respects. In the process leading up to a final policy statement, a variety of types of decisions have to be taken, based on individual and group expertise.

First, the possible *decision-making "agents"* in the process have to consider the various aspects on which decisions are based, even when using a restricted definition of second language status planning focusing on what to learn and teach. This question includes issues like: Whether or not to learn and/or teach (a) second language(s) at all, which language(s) to what level(s) by/to whom, and which varieties or aspects of the language(s) to select. The most obvious decision-making agents for formulating a national second language learning and teaching policy include: the pupils, their parents or caretakers, the teachers, the school authorities, the local and/or regional authorities, the school inspectors, and the national government. Roughly speaking, there are three levels: the *school*, the *region*, and the *nation*, each with their sub-levels (see e.g., van Els, 1993, p. 9, 1994, p. 36); others identify the major agents as individuals, communities, and states (Ager, 2001, p. 6). The authority that the decisions made at these levels have, clearly differs—decisions of individual teachers have an impact only within their classrooms, whereas regional decisions hold for all schools within a region and national decisions for all schools in the country.

In planning for second language learning and teaching on a national scale the first issue to settle is where or with whom or at which level the authority lies with respect to the various decisions that have to be made. A national policy holds a clear pronouncement on the distribution of planning authority, both with respect to *who* carries authority for what and *what kind* or type of authority that is. But, a policy truly *national* in the above sense is not to be seen as synonymous with a fully *centralized* policy. Centralization refers to the degree to which policy decisions are made at the national level and that varies by country depending on history, traditions, and geographic and demographic make-up of the country—for example, the number of inhabitants and the ethnic stratification of the population. However, subject-related arguments for government interference also exist. Because of their present international surroundings, European countries all have a national ruling that one or more second languages should be offered in all secondary schools. Some countries have a national specification as to the minimum number of second languages that pupils should actually learn; others even have a ruling as to which specific second language(s) everybody should be taught. The degree of specification is largely determined by the quality of the insight policymakers have into the various policy-relevant factors. (See later sections on "Second Language Needs" and "Other Factors.")

The introduction of the notion of *degrees of specification* leads to a discussion of the second issue in this section, that is, *types* of planning statements. For example, in the following list of statements, there is an increasing degree of specification:

- That there should be second language learning and teaching in schools.
- That schools should offer a particular number of second languages for the pupils to take.
- That pupils should learn a particular number of languages.
- That specific languages should be offered.
- That pupils should learn particular languages.

Specificity is one feature that may lead to distinctions between types of decisions; another such feature is the degree of obligation or compulsion that decisions imply for the learners. Big differences exist among countries regarding the degree to which second language learning is an obligatory subject for pupils, ranging from the freedom to choose not to learn any second languages to the obligation to go through centrally defined curricula with centrally run final examinations in a specified number of second languages (e.g., Lambert, 1997, p. 82).

SECOND LANGUAGE NEEDS

There has been little principled discussion in the second language learning and teaching planning literature of the needs issue (van Els, 1994, p. 37). The fairly recent *Encyclopedia of Language and Education*, which has a separate volume on "Language Policy and Political Issues in Education" (Wodak & Corson, 1997), doesn't have a separate chapter on the subject of needs, treating it only in passing (see Christ, 1997a). The more recent *Encyclopedia of Bilingualism and Bilingual Education* (Baker & Prys Jones, 1998) mentions it very briefly. In the latter case, as in many others, the subject of needs is only brought up in connection with the work of the Modern Languages Programme of the Council of Europe, which employs a very limited interpretation of that notion.

The notion of needs draws on typical arguments summarized by van Els, Bongaerts, Extra, Van Os, and Janssen-van Dieten (1984) in favor of the learning of second languages first collected by Rivers (1968, pp. 8–9); the advantages of second language learning usually cited represent a curious collection:

- It aids intellectual development.
- It aids cultural development by bringing pupils into contact with the literature written in other languages.
- It enriches pupils' personalities by bringing them into contact with other customs, norms, and ways of thinking.
- It deepens the understanding of the way in which language, also the native language, works.
- It enables pupils to communicate with speakers of a different language.
- It contributes to better international relations.

They are all—it should be stressed—valid arguments in favor of learning second languages. A closer look at them, however, shows immediately that the list, restricted as it is, contains arguments falling into a number of different categories, which can be hard to balance against one another when difficult choices have to be made. For example, when one has to make a case for the introduction of second language teaching into a school system at the expense of another subject for which some of the same arguments are equally valid, or especially when a choice between languages has to be made. Only in cases when in general terms an argument has to be made for second language learning as such—as in the United States or Great Britain, whose national language has such a wide distribution that there does not seem to be any desperate need of acquiring competence in any other language—is a random accumulation of arguments such as these helpful.

In the next section we first discuss the various types of needs that we think should—and may fruitfully—be distinguished. From Rivers' (1968) list it is clear that there are other factors other than needs that may be brought up as arguments for second language learning. These are dealt with in the subsequent section "Other Factors." In a separate subsection, the question of how needs can be empirically investigated is examined.

Types of Needs

So far we have assumed that needs have to do with the underlying—whether explicitly recognized or latently felt—wants, drives, deficits, or other motivating factors that make an individual require a command of a particular second language and, thus, serve as urgent motives to learn the language. However, it is more complex than that. In recent reviews of the concept, it has been shown that the term is open to several interpretations. For example, Clark (1999, p. 539) points out that the term has also been used for learner characteristics (e.g., age, motivation, preferred learning style) that may affect the learning process, whereas others also understand it to mean "what learners will need to do in the learning situation in order to learn" (Brindley, 2000, p. 438; see also Clark, 1999). It is highly preferable, however, to restrict the use of the term to the drives and wants that require an individual to learn a second language. Other interpretations that may represent aspects and factors in the learning process, in as far as they are relevant to status planning, will be accommodated in our model under the category of "Other Factors Besides Needs." Other aspects and factors, such as learning styles and motivation, clearly should find a place in language-in-education planning or in prestige planning.

Returning to the subject of needs in the restricted sense of the term, arguments for second language learning, such as the ones given previously, are all in one way or another statements of needs, however distantly. It is not uncommon, when attempts at defining or categorizing needs are undertaken, to divide needs into pairs of polar opposites, like *individual* versus *societal* or *national*. From a planning point of view, such divisions are not very useful, as societal needs cannot be separated from individual needs—societal needs are always transformable into, that is, have been derived from, the individual needs of (a number of) members of that society. In essence, all educational needs are individual. On the other hand, not all individual needs are also societal; they only take on a societal dimension when society declares needs of (groups of) individuals important enough to take them into account when formulating a national educational policy. In the same way, other common polar opposite pairs (e.g., *nonutilitarian*, *cultural*, or *formative* versus *utilitarian*, *directly useful*, or *capitalizable*) do not provide any clear-cut distinctions. Furthermore, talking about the issues in these terms may lead people to carelessly equating *utilitarian* with *political* and *practical* (Phillips, 1989, p. xiv).

In sum, from the distinctions proposed, inadequate as they are, it becomes clear that needs, when taken in their restricted sense, may be very different in character. However, these distinctions do not supply a categorization that could form a proper basis for status planning discussions. A more helpful criterion for distinguishing between needs than the ones used so far, lies in the degree of communicative competence required to fulfill a need (see van Els et al., 1984, p. 162; van Els, 1994, pp. 37–38). On the basis of that criterion, three broad categories of needs may be distinguished:

1. *Communicative needs*: one may want to be competent in a particular second language in order to be able to communicate effectively with speakers of that language.

2. *Language competence-related needs*: one may want to become familiar, for example, with the way of life, culture, and, more specifically, the literature of another people with a differing language; competence in the second language in which that culture is embedded and in which the literary texts are written, is not, strictly speaking, a prerequisite to fulfill this need.

3. *Needs distantly, or not at all, related to language competence*: one wants to acquire particular social and/or intellectual skills of a general nature, such as empathy and rational thinking; such general educational objectives may be pursued equally well, or possibly better, through the learning and teaching of a variety of other school subjects than second languages.

The three categories of needs—which together can easily accommodate all the needs underlying Rivers' (1968) arguments—show different degrees of relationship with actual second language competence with the relationship becoming more indirect and more diffuse as one proceeds down the list. With needs of the third category, the relationship is very tenuous—there are many other ways to satisfy the needs than by being made to learn a second language. With those of the first category, there is no way around acquiring some degree of actual competence in the second language(s), although this may not apply to the needs of the second category. Literary texts can best be read in the original language, which presupposes a high command of the second language making it very common for people to read them in translation. A better understanding of speakers of other languages in general and their cultures may be brought about by providing for the learning and teaching of just one second language, no matter which one, even when it is taught through mother-tongue instruction.

The great advantage of applying the criterion of actual second language competence is that it clarifies the issue considerably when choices between second languages have to be made or when the cause of second language teaching as such in the school curriculum has to be defended against other subjects. Only if needs of the first category can be demonstrated, can a clear case be made for second language teaching as such. That is why it is so hard in a country like the United States to secure a place for second language teaching in the secondary school curricula. Although as a package Rivers' (1968) arguments may be valid or convincing, they fail to clinch the argument for second languages in schools for Americans who are in a position to use their native tongue in large parts of the world. When abroad, they (are given the impression that they) can cope without any competence in any second language (see e.g., Lambert, 1994, p. 55). In most countries of the world, on the other hand, the question is not so much "Should we learn a second language?" but rather "Which language(s), how many of them, and which skills should be learned to what levels of competence?" In such cases, first category needs are more important than those in the other two categories.

However, the conclusion just drawn should not be misunderstood. It should not lead people to think that category two and three needs can be treated as *quantité négligeable*. They may be very valuable objectives to realize in second language teaching, and in status planning they should be accounted for, even if needs of the first category have led to a choice of one particular second language. Therefore, needs research cannot and should not be restricted to investigating only category one needs, but should be set up in such a way that the need for actual second language competence is determined as unequivocally as possible.

Needs Research

What the needs just discussed all have in common is that they reside in and originate from the individual as (prospective) second language user. From that point of view the needs factor differs fundamentally from all the Other Factors discussed in the next section. The other factors are all either external to the individual person or, in as far as they are internal, they relate to the individual as a learning person, not as a user of (second) languages. In developing a status plan for second language learning and teaching, data related to all factors must be collected empirically and taken into consideration. However, this chapter is restricted to research into needs as they have been previously defined.[1]

Because research into needs would seem to be a necessary complement to status planning for second language learning and teaching, it is surprising that such research is a relatively late development and, moreover, has been a rare phenomenon even in recent times. Early summaries were presented by Bausch, Bliesener, Christ, Schröder,

& Weisbrod (1978, pp. 375–405) and Christ (1980, pp. 87–102) and the state of the art until about 1980—regarding a number of European countries, the United States, and Australia—was discussed at an international gathering of experts in 1982 (see van Els & Oud-de Glas, 1983). Christ's (1991, pp. 48–53) brief summary or more recent review articles by Clark (1999) and Brindley (2000) provide few recent references.

What research there is has been mostly conducted in the context of second language teaching for business and commerce, that is, in connection with special purpose programs. It is striking how few countries seem to have had recourse to empirical investigations of the nation's second language needs; notable exceptions being The Netherlands in the late 1970s (van Els et al., 1984, p. 166), the Belgian replication of the Dutch investigations in the early 1980s (Verdoodt & Sente, 1983) and, to some extent, Finland in the second half of the decade (Takala, 1993). In Australia, where the development of an all-encompassing national languages policy has been given much attention, empirical assessment of the second language needs was not the basis of the status planning proposals in that field (see e.g., Clyne, 1991).

It also seems significant to note how seldom these investigations are included in research reviews (e.g., Arrouays, 1990; Brindley, 1989, 2000; Clark, 1999; Phillips, 1989). Exceptions are to be found in publications stemming from or inspired by the National Foreign Language Center in Washington, DC (see e.g., Lambert, 1997; Spolsky & Shohamy, 1997, 2000). Needs analysis and research are still associated almost exclusively by many with the work performed in connection with the Modern Languages Programme of the Council of Europe. This very influential program and its philosophy are presented following a discussion of some general aspects relating to needs research design. A lengthier introduction into needs research design is to be found in van Els & Oud-de Glas (1983, pp. 3–12) and in Van Hest & Oud-de Glas (1991, pp. 7–21).

When examining the need for communicative competence, it is necessary to have further defined:

- What we understand by *communicative competence*.
- Who is in need of *communicative competence*.
- What exactly *to be in need of* means.

Communicative competence is generally understood in its wider and "richer" meaning first developed in some detail in the context of the Council of Europe program (see e.g., Trim, 1994; Van Ek, 2000; Van Ek & Alexander, 1975). There is not only linguistic competence involved (i.e., the ability to use the rules of the language adequately), but also an additional set of five competences, namely:

- *Sociolinguistic*: an awareness of the ways in which such conditions as setting and relationships between communication partners determine the choice of language forms.
- *Discourse*: the ability to construct and interpret written and oral texts.
- *Strategic*: the ability to cope with gaps in the language user's command of the language.
- *Sociocultural*: an awareness of the ways in which the context of language use affects the choice of language forms.
- *Social*: the ability to use general social strategies.

Without debating the merits of distinguishing this particular set of (sub)components, the point being made is that when assessing the need for communicative competence, a richer concept than just *linguistic* is being examined. Moreover, if it is done properly, there is no necessity to separately assess other aspects, such as *sociocultural* or *strategic* competence. Such an approach means that in needs research one cannot restrict oneself to investigating only the linguistic content (i.e., phonological, grammatical, or lexical content), nor to describing communicative competence in terms of the four macro-skills (i.e., speaking, writing, listening, and reading). Rather, one relies on a *situational* and *functional* description of language, such as the one that formed the model of specification for the behavioral second language teaching objectives developed in the context of the Council of Europe program. In the model, the following components are specified (see Van Ek & Alexander, 1975, p. 5; Van Ek, 2000):

- The *situations* in which the second language user will find himself, including the *topics* occurring in them and the relevant *settings*, and *social* and *psychological roles*.
- The *language activities* or the *skills* the user will engage in.
- The *language functions* to be fulfilled, such as giving information or turning down an offer.
- The *notions* that the user will have to handle.
- The *language forms*, such as lexical or syntactic elements.
- An indication of the *degree of skill* needed.

In a research model that relies mainly on a situational and functional description, situations are indicated in which the second language may be used and also the functions that the user must be able to perform. This leads to questionnaire items like writing a short businesslike letter (in relation to e.g., holidays or a hobby) or giving or receiving oral instructions or advice specifically related to one's work. This type of questions is very helpful from two different perspectives: the nonspecialist can actually understand them, but the answers offer material for detailed linguistic analysis.

Who it is whose needs should be investigated depends on the aim and scope of the research project. One may be interested in finding out about the needs of particular sectors of society, of particular individuals or groups of individuals, but one may also be interested in establishing a nationwide picture. The thing to keep in mind is that the subject of the needs investigated does not necessarily coincide with the person(s) questioned.

What constitutes the *object* of needs research is not as straightforward as it may seem, even if there is agreement that the analysis should result in a description of what aspects of communicative competence are sought, to what level, under what circumstances, and when. Different needs research projects and related discussions tend to approach the problem from a number of different perspectives. A common practice is not to describe the need per se, but to follow a narrower definition of the term, namely, need as *lack* of competence, that is, to focus on "the gap between the foreign language competence required and the amount of foreign language competence available on the part of the language user" (Van Hest & Oud-de Glas, 1991, p. 10). In addition, German scholars often make a distinction between *Bedarf* and *Bedürfnisse* (see Christ, 1991, p. 50), which Clark (1987, p. 106) defines as "socially agreed objective needs" and "individually determined subjective needs" respectively. The difference, however, between the two is not so much a difference in kind—which terms such as objective and subjective suggest—as in status. Other perspectives that people have taken vary most notably along the following two axes:

- A *time axis*, that is, actually experienced needs (present) versus expected needs (future).
- An *awareness axis*, that is, actually felt needs (explicit) versus hidden, not-felt needs (latent).

As for the time axis, if one is planning for the future, it is insufficient to rely on a simple description of present experience. As for the awareness axis, an assessment by (groups of) individuals of their own present and future felt needs may not lay bare language needs that may well be essential to them personally—or to the organization or nation to which they belong—but of which they are not aware. It is a well-known fact that people tend to avoid, either consciously or unconsciously, getting into communication situations for which they fear they lack the appropriate language skills. Finally, the language competence required as a consequence of strategic decisions regarding opening up new commercial markets for a firm or new political alliances for a country is not likely to be something that individuals are aware of personally. In this context, Van Hest & Oud-de Glas (1991) speak of (the need for) language competence as a *key asset*.

As for *needs research methods*, there are, basically, three possible routes to take in order sto arrive at an assessment of the need for language competence:

- Collecting *factual data* on the language(s) in question, as, for example, its international status and the number of its speakers.
- Collecting *people's opinions* on present or future second language performance.
- Recording of *actual second language performance* in relevant language use situations.

The first route, that is, the gathering of indicators indicative of communicative needs, is a very indirect way to gain an insight into actual language competence needs and, therefore, usually involves a great deal of interpreting of the findings. A recent example based on such factual data is *The Nuffield Languages Inquiry* in Great Britain (Nuffield Foundation, 2000), a large-scale investigation undertaken at the request of the government into both the country's second languages needs and its present language capability. Besides an intensive program of interviews aimed at gaining information on people's experiences with and the advice of experts on second language use, major surveys were conducted of data indicative of second language use in the public and the private sectors. Merkx (2000) provides another example where estimates and findings concerning government and business manpower needs for personnel trained in second languages and area studies play a prominent role.

The third route, that is, the recording of actual second language use, is the least commonly followed. Recording of sufficient and sufficiently relevant samples of actual second language use is usually very difficult to achieve and is, moreover, very costly. Most projects, therefore, heavily rely on methodology of the second route, that is gathering information on present and/or future second language use from people who have direct experience with the second language domains. The people with that kind of experience may be divided into two groups. One may interrogate the individuals who are in need of second language competence, that is, the so-called *users*, but one may also interrogate persons who are in direct contact with the users, for example, employers or personnel managers, that is, the so-called *requirers*.

Other Factors

Besides the obviously important needs factor, other numerous and diverse factors have to be taken into account in status planning, either because they have an intrinsic value of their own or because they present an obstacle to achieving a particular learning objective. They may be usefully grouped into four categories, although it is necessary to point out that there is no strict separation between the factors and that sometimes there is overlap with the needs category. These factors are briefly summarized in the following sections.

Language Policy Factors

There are internal and external language policy factors to be considered. The *internal* languages situation of a country, where a number of languages—whether indigenous or nonindigenous—are spoken, requires primary attention. Learning another language of the country is often given priority over learning a second language from abroad. Moreover, the choice of a second language(s) may be made dependent on what languages the country has internally. The position of French, for example, as a second language is likely to be different in The Netherlands than in Belgium, where the language also has the status of national language, and, therefore, serves another national purpose as well. It has also been argued that learning the languages of ethnic minorities as second languages by members of the majority may further the cause of the minority groups of the country and promote national cohesion. This, some would say, could be a strong argument for breaking up the traditional second languages curriculum, for example, in a country like The Netherlands where Frisian might be given greater prominence. (Van der Avoird, Broeder, & Extra, 2001, p. 232.)

However, primacy may be given to the *external* languages situation, which may have a number of language-related aspects that impact on national status planning for second language learning and teaching. The focus is not so much the pressure that foreign countries put on other nations to pay proper attention to the learning of their languages, but the need for intercultural communication. The needs as of the receiving nation should be the decisive factor, not the interest that the native speakers of a particular language have in promoting their language for international communication (see e.g., Ammon, 2000).

Another factor may be the desire to make special provision for learning the languages spoken in neighboring countries, irrespective of the status of those countries or of their languages in the rest of the world. Moreover, a country also has to take into account the language situation of the international alliances and organizations it belongs to, in particular the (second) languages policies pursued by such organizations. Cases in point are provided by the situation in the European Union (EU) where the learning of EU languages, in particular those of the neighboring countries, is strongly advocated and, to some extent, also supported to promote mobility and cohesion. Such a policy is the natural corollary of the decision that the monolingual option is not an acceptable basis for greater European integration (see Ager, 2001, p. 72).

As to the extent to which the *institutional* language policy of international organizations should be taken into account in *national* planning for second language learning and teaching it should have an impact on national second language planning only in as far as it engenders an actual second language competence need for the country. From this perspective it is hardly relevant whether a choice is made for a monolingual or a plurilingual international institutional model. The only decisive fact is the amount of second language competence the country's representatives require to be able to function adequately in the institutions in question. On the whole, the number of people actually representing a country forms only a small proportion of its population and their competence needs, while high, are, therefore, comparatively negligible.

Linguistic Factors

Languages are related to each other to different degrees—members of families of languages may be very closely related. The greater the distance between individual languages, the fewer features of vocabulary and syntax they share and, in general, the heavier the learning load for those who have to acquire a competence in the respective second language. *Language distance* is a factor, therefore, that may have to be taken into account in status planning because of its learnability and cross-linguistic transfer impact (see e.g., Odlin, 1989). Given space in the curriculum, choices between languages that otherwise show a comparable needs pattern may be made based on the time needed to obtain the required competence level or the degree to which the learning of the language in question may facilitate the subsequent acquisition of skills in other related languages. For similar reasons, in cases where there is very little need for specific second language teaching, the introduction of a planned language, like Esperanto, or a lingua franca has been advocated (see e.g., Christ, 1997a, p. 130).

Psychological Factors

A number of aspects of bilingualism and second language learning are relevant when policy choices have to be made regarding, for example, which second language to teach first, whether more languages can be learned simultaneously (and, if so, how many), and at what age to start second language teaching. Besides the competence needs factor, the optimal age for learning second languages is an important factor to be taken into consideration.

Other such psychological considerations, related to language distance, are the perceived ease or difficulty of learning particular languages and subskills. As for the former, the learning of Japanese, or for that matter French, offers more obstacles to native speakers of Dutch than the learning of English or German. However, that degree of difficulty does not correlate directly with degree of structural (dis)similarity between the languages because people's *perceptions of learning difficulty* can be important. For example, although German may be considered to be linguistically more closely related to Dutch than English, Dutch secondary school pupils generally hold German to be the more problematic language (Oud-de Glas 1997, p. 44). However, this perception is not shared by older generations, who believe that German is the easier language to learn. When it comes to the relative difficulty of learning the subskills, there is a generally held assumption that acquiring the productive skills of speaking and writing is more difficult than acquiring listening and reading. However, the policymaking relevance of this may be counterbalanced by another psychological factor, namely, that learners, also the less gifted, tend to be more motivated to learn the productive skills, in particular, speaking.

Educational Factors

Aspects of the educational context may have an overriding influence on the process of status planning. Perhaps the most important of such factors is that the time available for second language teaching is nearly always limited, especially in secondary education systems, where a great many other subject areas claim a place in the curriculum. The time constraint is particularly pressing in countries where the demand for second languages is great. Under those circumstances there is usually much less room for adopting a noncommittal attitude toward questions regarding which languages to offer, whether to make learning them obligatory, and at what age to make pupils start learning second languages (See "Specific Aspects of Actual Status Planning Decisions" for more on obligation and articulation).

Other important and very obvious educational factors lie in the availability of suitable teaching materials and adequately trained teachers. Lacking these, introducing a second language in the school curriculum makes no sense. The well-documented, very disappointing results of the British experiment with French in primary schools have in part been attributed to the lack of suitable teaching materials and to the methodology adopted (Buckby, 1976, p. 345).

A NATIONAL SECOND LANGUAGE LEARNING
AND TEACHING POLICY

The ultimate aim of status planning for second language learning is the formulation of a second language learning and teaching policy with a national scope. Specifically with a view to exploring the development of a national policy, the next two sections return to the roles that both needs and other factors have to play, before several features of a truly national policy are discussed.

A National Needs Picture

When devising a national policy, information on the needs of the country should be drawn from as great a variety of sectors, sources, and respondents in a society as possible. Empirically based needs research, if properly conducted, yields a picture of the needs of both individual persons and specific groups of individuals, for example, the vocational needs of employees of particular industries or the personal needs of the general public. If, on the basis of such findings, a second language teaching in general education policy has to be formulated for the country as a whole, a separate effort has to be made to infer the national needs pattern required for that purpose. The different needs data, possibly representing diverging needs patterns, have to be integrated into an overall, national needs picture. Simply combining the data from various, often dissimilar, sources concerning various, often conflicting, fields of activity and interest is unlikely to produce a usable result. For example, the vocational needs for second languages, collected from extensive interview sessions, may have to be weighed against leisure time needs, based on statistical data from the tourist industry. The decisions as to how much weight to allot in a national needs pattern to the needs of such interest groups as business and commerce, culture and arts, and general interest are political decisions. A national needs pattern never transpires automatically from research findings.

Weighing Up All Policy Factors

When in second language learning and teaching planning a proper assessment of the national needs pattern has been arrived at, the moment has come to consider the contribution that other factors make to the planning process. Such factors can impact the planning outcome, interacting in all sorts of ways depending on the specific circumstances under which a national policy has been devised. Two examples from The Netherlands demonstrate this point.

First, with regard to the teaching of English, there is no doubt whatsoever that all Dutch nationals need to acquire a usually fairly high command of the language. Taken by itself the needs side suggests that all Dutch citizens should learn English and, what is more, should learn it as early as possible. Such considerations have also been the basis for the decision to select English for the more or less exclusive position of the first language to be taught to all primary school pupils in the country. However, the self-evident preferred position of English in the Dutch educational system has been queried (De Bot, 2000). The omnipresence of English in Dutch society is, in itself, very supportive of the acquisition of English, both from the point of view of actual competence acquisition and, also, from the point of view of motivation. On the one hand, in a sense there is no escaping picking up the language; on the other hand, the need for it is so evident to everyone that the Dutch require few external motivational incentives to learn it. Therefore, De Bot proposes that (part of) the time now devoted to primary school English would be better spent on either German or French. In the light of the massive national need for languages, the room in schools for second language teaching is comparatively limited and what room there is should, therefore, be allocated with care.

The other example concerns the introduction several years ago of the so-called *partial qualifications* for French and German in upper secondary education. In a nationwide investigation of the second language needs of the country—conducted in the late 1970s and revisited in the late 1980s—convincing evidence was found for not only an overwhelming need for English but also a considerable need for French and German, especially among sectors of society catered to by upper secondary education (see Oud-de Glas, 1983; van Els & Van Hest, 1992). In an attempt to reconcile the generally agreed desirability to make all three languages obligatory subjects for everyone in upper secondary education—on the one hand, a return to the situation that had once been the practice and on the other hand the scarcity of curricular time—only *partial qualifications* were made obligatory for French, and German, that is, only reading comprehension, the skill for which the universities had expressed a preference, was included in the set of final examination requirements for the languages in question. However, what seemed to be a perfect compromise has not been the success that educational planners had expected. Opposition to the partial qualification solution has grown in the few years since it was introduced to such a degree that abolition of the concept is on the present political agenda. It is unnecessary in this discussion to expand on the reasons for its rejection by teachers. In developing a seemingly obvious and rationalistic compromise, the planners had overlooked the views and feelings that the professionals in the field, a major factor in the educational context, had on what constitutes language competence and on how second languages must be taught.

A National Policy

In previous sections, "Types of Needs" and "Needs Research," a number of things were mentioned that concern national planning for second language learning and teaching, that is, the national plan should state which decision-making agents have which specific planning responsibilities for what planning issues and to what degree of specificity. Some of the aspects of this are discussed in more explicit terms in the following section, but there is one feature of a truly national policy that still needs to be discussed.

In general, planning statements tend to be limited in scope. Many, actually, focus exclusively on (general) secondary education. There may also be specific attention for the less commonly taught languages (LCTs). A truly national policy, however, sets out to be all-encompassing, both with regard to the demand for second languages—it should not only deal with the academic need for languages—and with the supply of second languages and second language teaching. Thus, not only the facilities provided in secondary education should be considered, but the whole gamut of all educational sectors, including nongovernment-funded private language instruction (see e.g., Christ, 1991, p. 66). This is not to say that drawing up proposals for secondary education only is illegitimate in itself, but in doing so one should be aware of how this sector relates to all other sectors in which second language teaching is provided. In many countries the demand for second language competence is so great that catering for it only in secondary education is out of the question. A case in point, again, is The Netherlands (see van Els & Van Hest, 1992, p. 33; for another quite different example in Tunisia see Daoud, 2001).

Statistics on second language provision in the school systems, that is, primary and lower and upper general secondary education, for a great many European countries, can be found in a recent publication of the European Union (see Eurydice, 2001). Because private initiatives outside the school system, such as language courses offered by enterprises or local authorities, are not covered, a full insight into the second language learning and teaching policy of the countries involved cannot be gained from the publication. Bergentoft (1994) presents a comparative survey of second language teaching in a number of European countries, including Russia and Japan, but it is equally focused on the government-sponsored sectors of mainly secondary education and, thus, doesn't give a full picture either.

National second language teaching policies, that is, policies with a wider coverage than just the primary, secondary, and higher sectors of the regular school system, are very rare. For example, in Finland, where second language teaching policy has been an issue of great importance since the early 1960s, the policy proposals have only dealt with the regular school system, in particular primary and secondary education. An interesting feature of the Finnish effort has been that, on the basis of needs analyses, educational measures have been proposed aimed at achieving explicitly stated national quantitative and qualitative targets (Latomaa & Nuolijärvi, 2002; Sajavaara, 1997; Takala, 1993, p. 59). Therefore, there are only a few instances that may be called national in the sense that they are also oriented toward out-of-school, mainly adult, learning of languages (see e.g., Lambert, 1997, p. 80). The most recent instance is the Nuffield Languages Inquiry with recommendations for second language learning and teaching in England and Wales, which, for example, explicitly calls on the government to take strategic responsibility for lifelong language learning (Nuffield Foundation, 2000).

The Australian national languages policy that was developed in the late 1980s, primarily to support the language-in-education policies developed by the States (Ager, 2001, p. 95; Clyne, 1991; Lo Bianco, 1987). It had a wider coverage than second language learning and teaching, taking as its central focus the internal languages situation of the country, in particular the place and function of the languages other than English (LOTE). The central principle of the national policy was that Australia is a multilingual society that has renounced the pursuit of the ideal of the one-language-only nation, but revisions to this policy since 1991 have put a greater emphasis on English (Kaplan & Baldauf, 2003, p. 143). The major policy instrument is the stimulation of as many language learning opportunities as possible, both within and outside of the regular school system.

The final instance that deserves mention is the *National Action Programme on Foreign Languages* of The Netherlands drawn up around 1990 (van Els & Van Hest, 1992; see also, e.g., Lambert, 1994, 1997; van Els, 1993, 1994). Although the *National Action Programme* is a set of second language policy recommendations, that cover both school system and out-of-school educational provision and that were developed in relation one with the other, they were not formulated as a fully integrated document standing in its own right. Nevertheless, the full set of recommendations became official government policy in 1992 with the establishment of a Task Force commissioned to implement the recommendations (see Tuin & Westhoff, 1997). The distinguishing features of the Dutch enterprise are not only its scope, but also its being based to a large extent on the outcomes of empirical needs research. The Dutch undertaking, which has attracted quite a bit of international attention (see e.g., Christ, 1997b; Spolsky & Shohamy, 1997), arose from a conference held at the instigation of national organizations in business and commerce and organized by the Dutch government. Almost simultaneously, that is, in the late 1980s, a similar conference took place in France (see Arrouays, 1990), which was not government convened and which did not lead to a similar national action plan.

SPECIFIC ASPECTS OF ACTUAL STATUS PLANNING DECISIONS

There are number of specific aspects of the actual planning process that deserve further treatment in the status planning context, but only two, namely, the obligatory/

nonobligatory question and the need for articulation across levels for (a) particular language(s) are discussed. Other aspects deserving attention include:

- International perspectives on second language planning, in particular the need that growing international mobility has created for making second language competence comparable and, therefore, measurable across national educational systems and across languages, for example, the *Common European Framework* (see Trim, 2000) and *European Language Portfolio* (see Dobson, 2000).
- The role that so-called language-enablers might play in national second language planning, for example, the use of the internet or several kinds of translation services (see Lambert, 2000, p. 181).

Obligatory or Nonobligatory Second Language Learning

As previously indicated, great differences exist between countries in the degree to which second language learning is made obligatory for the learners in the school system depending on the national policy decision as to which decision-making agent the authority is assigned to regarding *how many* and *which language(s)* to learn. The wide array of different national arrangements that result all can be justified and none is preferable, as long as the assignment of decision-making authority is based on a proper weighing up of all the policy factors. However, the issue of diversification requires some further discussion.

Diversification is sometimes a hotly debated issue in discussions about how many and which languages ought to be offered to, and/or should be chosen by, pupils or, for that matter, schools, in primary and especially secondary education (see e.g., Christ, 1991; Phillips, 1989; van Els, 1988, p. 59, 1994, p. 40). *Diversification* refers to expanding the number of languages offered and implies extending the freedom of choice for the learners. Various forms of diversification may be distinguished. For instance, it may apply both to the obligatory and to the nonobligatory segment of the second language curriculum. As is the case in many countries, there may be an obligation for all pupils in secondary education to learn at least one second language, while at the same time the choice of that language is left to the learners. Furthermore, when there is an increase in the demand in a country for second languages, that may be translated into an expansion of the number of languages offered to pupils and/or programs in schools to choose from. Such a policy is often advocated and justified mainly on the argument that the learners themselves know best where their interests lie and that over time their specific individual choices taken together will yield the outcome that is optimally suited to the country's needs pattern. But, when all the evidence points to an overall need for learning one particular language—English being a case in point in many countries—what purpose is served by leaving it to individual learners to choose another second language that is against their own interest?

There are other questions that could be raised in connection with what seems to be a good idea in principle. Even in the circumstance where the need for second language learning remains unspecified or that the need is rather diffuse with respect to which specific language(s) would serve the country's purposes best, offering a seemingly unlimited number of languages may not be the best answer. For one thing, when there is so much choice, clear ideas about aims and levels to be achieved in any of these languages may be lacking and may not seem to be an urgent matter. Moreover, offering many optional languages may lead to a fragmentation of the attention that each of these languages receives, in particular in such matters as the development of teaching materials, the training of qualified teachers and the required research effort. The notion of diversification, although very attractive at first sight, may produce actual outcomes that belie the high hopes that usually accompanied its introduction (see, e.g., Phillips, 1989, p. xi). Instead of offering as many optional languages as possible for schools and/or pupils to choose from, as an easy way out, (at one time the national curriculum of England and Wales offered a choice of 19 languages—see e.g., Clark, 1989, p. 119), it normally would be better to articulate more precisely what the country's second language needs are. Comparing the highly decentralized American approach with the highly centralized Dutch approach to second language learning and teaching planning, in particular for secondary education, Lambert (1997) suggests that the Americans "would be well advised to examine the Dutch example closely to determine afresh whether the pattern of total disaggregation of planning and decision-making so prevalent in America is fully effective" (p. 28).

Planning Second Languages Articulation

Planning for what the Americans call *articulation* and the British call *progression* is critically important. In the analyses of the Nuffield Languages Inquiry it is concluded that there is a lack of coherence in the governmental approach to the field of second language teaching in the educational system. What is needed is a rational path of learning from primary school to university and beyond (Nuffield Foundation, 2000). As Lambert (2000) notes, an effective second language learning and teaching plan "should include all levels and forms of instruction and use" (p. 184). We have already stressed that a truly national policy deserving of that name should cover all sectors in which language education is provided, that is, it should be all-encompassing. In the planning process, the focus should be on the architecture of the system, that is, on "what the building blocks are and how they can be assembled." Lambert (1994) blames the disappointing results of American second language teaching on the ineffectual structure of the system, not on "how we teach" (p. 49). Elsewhere he speaks of "the essentially laissez-faire system in the United States" (Lambert, 1997, p. 85). Disregarding or ignoring the existence of the potential contributions each sector makes to second languages may lead to losses of several types. In many countries there is a strong tendency to more or less exclusively look to either secondary or higher education to satisfy whatever second language needs have been revealed (see e.g., van Els, 1994, p. 40; Lambert, 1994, p. 49). This often leads to overtaxing the possibilities of the educational sector in question, both quantitatively and qualitatively. That is to say, on the one hand, one expects to be able to accommodate additional languages where the available space has already been taken up by other languages; this, not uncommonly, leads to the decision to widen the number of optional languages. On the other hand, the longitudinal aspect of planning is often overlooked, that is, the achievements as well as potential of both preceding and following sectors are fully neglected (see, also, De Bot & van Els, 2000). The devastating effects of this phenomenon in a number of the second language teaching projects in primary education are well documented. A case in point is how the absence of proper longitudinal planning between primary and secondary school curricula has greatly thwarted the development of the teaching of English in primary schools, as, for example, in The Netherlands.

Finally, too often the sector in question is required to deliver language competencies that it is not qualified to offer. Thus, general secondary education also may be expected to cater to needs that are specifically vocational in kind, or for higher levels of competence that would be better taught in higher education. A lot could be gained in educational systems across the world, if proper consideration was given in second language planning to such structural aspects.

CONCLUSIONS AND FUTURE DEVELOPMENTS

The focus of this chapter has been on the major high-level questions of status planning for second language learning and teaching and the ways that answers should be sought to those questions. A select number of such questions from the research literature have been examined suggesting that a complete enough picture can be presented of the essential issues in status planning for second language learning and teaching, of their comparative importance, and of their relationships to each other when actual planning decisions have to be made. A sufficient knowledge base and an adequate theoretical framework exist to tackle all status planning problems in the field of second language learning and teaching.

All education is basically aimed at satisfying learning needs of individuals and groups of individuals. What constitutes needs for second languages and how such needs are to be defined has been elucidated in a number of research projects. We now know how to investigate such needs and how to achieve an empirical basis for a needs-oriented second language learning and teaching plan. The road from needs data to such plans, however, is not a direct one. The chapter also highlights the important contribution that other factors (i.e., linguistic, psychological, or educational) besides needs make. Enough is known about their role in second language learning and teaching to weigh—at least in principle—their impact on actual second language teaching programs and, thus, to be able to decide how far conclusions based on an analysis of the needs picture should be adjusted.

The chapter highlights two additional findings. First, there is very little empirical research into needs or into the nature, scope, and interaction of the other factors. Second, the theoretical framework outlined in the chapter has hardly ever been used to plan second language activities anywhere in the world. A poignant example of this is the fact that again and again when a particular sector of a national educational system plans a new second language teaching curriculum, the planners do this with complete disregard to the relevant curricula of other sectors.

Thus, although the theoretical framework is available and we have the means and the instruments to assemble all the materials needed for well-founded policy statements for second language learning and teaching, very little along those lines has been attempted in the past and the prospects for the future are hardly encouraging. Of course, some progress has been made in the past few decades; there are signs of a growing awareness of the need for a rational approach to curricular changes. But the normal practice in second language learning and teaching planning—as in all educational planning, for all we know—still is for uninformed laymen to develop policies without any recourse to empirical findings or expert advice. Even in The Netherlands, one of the pioneers in the field when it developed its *National Action Programme* for second language teaching, the latest adaptations in the national curricula for primary and secondary education have been introduced in the old, well-established, amateurish way that many thought had been left behind for good. How long will it take before people in responsible status planning positions realize that having had personal experience with education does not as such qualify one to make properly founded policy decisions?

NOTES

1. Research activity covers a wider range of topics than those that are discussed in this chapter, and these have also been used as the basis for status planning purposes. Recent examples include the *Nuffield Languages Inquiry* (Nuffield Foundation, 2000) conducted in the United Kingdom and a number of studies in the United States reported on by Merkx (2000).

REFERENCES

Ager, D. (2001). *Motivation in language planning and language policy.* Clevedon, UK: Multilingual Matters.
Ammon, U. (2000). Die Rolle des Deutschen in Europa [The role of German in Europe]. In A. Gardt (Ed.), *Nation und Sprache. Die Diskussion ihres Verhältnisses in Geschichte und Gegenwart [Nation and language. A discussion of their relation in past and present]* (pp. 471–494). Berlin: de Gruyter.

Arrouays, M. (1990). Les finalités de l'enseignement des langues dans l'enseignement secondaire [The objects of the teaching of languages in secondary education]. *Les Langues Modernes, 84,* 7–29.

Baker, C., & Prys Jones, S. (1998). *Encyclopedia of bilingualism and bilingual education.* Clevedon, UK: Multilingual Matters.

Bausch, K.-R., Bliesener, U., Christ, H., Schröder, K., & Weisbrod, U. (Eds.). (1978). *Beiträge zum Verhältnis von Fachsprache und Gemeinsprache im Fremdsprachenunterricht der Sekundarstufe II. [Contributions on the relation between technical language and general language in upper secondary education].* Bochum, Germany: Ruhr Universität.

Bergentoft, R. (1994). Foreign language instruction: A comparative perspective. In R. Lambert (Ed.), *Language planning around the world: Contexts and systemic change* (pp. 17–46). Washington, DC: National Foreign Language Center.

Brindley, G. (1989). The role of needs analysis in adult ESL programme design. In R. Johnson (Ed.), *The second language curriculum* (pp. 63–78). Cambridge, UK: Cambridge University Press.

Brindley, G. (2000). Needs analysis. In M. Byram (Ed.), *Routledge encyclopedia of language teaching and learning* (pp. 438–441). London: Routledge.

Buckby, M. (1976). Is primary French really in the balance? *The Modern Language Journal, 60,* 340–346.

Christ, H. (1980). *Fremdsprachenunterricht und Sprachenpolitik [Foreign-language teaching and language policy].* Stuttgart, Germany: Klepp.

Christ, H. (1991). *Fremdsprachenunterricht fuer das Jahr 2000. Sprachenpolitische Betrachtungen zum Lehren und Lernen fremder Sprachen [Foreign-language teaching for the year 2000. Language political considerations on the teaching and learning of foreign languages].* Tübingen, Germany: Verlag.

Christ, H. (1997a). Language policy in teacher education. In R. Wodak & D. Corson (Eds.), *Encyclopedia of language and education: Language policy and political issues in education* (Vol. 1; pp. 219–227). Dordrecht, The Netherlands: Kluwer.

Christ, H. (1997b). Foreign-language policy from the grass roots. In T. Bongaerts & K. de Bot (Eds.), *Perspectives on foreign-language policy. Studies in honour of Theo van Els* (pp. 129–141). Amsterdam: Benjamins.

Clark, J. (1987). *Curriculum renewal in school foreign language learning.* Oxford, UK: Oxford University Press.

Clark, G. (1989). Diversification and the national curriculum: Policy and provision. In D. Phillips (Ed.), *Which language? Diversification and the national curriculum* (pp. 119–132). London: Hodder & Stoughton.

Clark, J. (1999). Needs analysis. In B. Spolsky (Ed.), *Concise encyclopedia of educational linguistics* (pp. 539–540). Amsterdam: Elsevier.

Clyne, M. (1991). *Community languages. The Australian experience.* Cambridge, UK: Cambridge University Press.

Daoud, M. (2001). The language situation in Tunisia. *Current Issues in Language Planning, 2,* 1–52.

De Bot, K. (2000). An early start for foreign languages (but not English) in the Netherlands. In R. Lambert & E. Shohamy (Eds.), *Language policy and pedagogy. Essays in honor of A. Ronald Walton* (pp. 129–138). Philadelphia: Benjamins.

De Bot, K., & van Els, T. (2000). Linking levels in foreign language teaching through a common frame of reference. In R. Cooper, E. Shohamy, & J. Walters (Eds.), *New perspectives and issues in educational language policy. In honour of Bernard Dov Spolsky* (pp. 197–208). Amsterdam: Benjamins.

Dobson, A. (2000). European language portfolio. In M. Byram (Ed.), *Routledge encyclopedia of language teaching and learning* (pp. 204–206). London: Routledge.

EURYDICE, (2001). *Foreign language teaching in schools in Europe.* Brussels, Belgium: European Commission.

Fishman, J., Conrad, A., & Rubal-Lopez, A. (Eds.). (1996). *Post-imperial English. Status change in former British and American colonies, 1940–1990.* Berlin: Mouton de Gruyter.

Gnutzmann, C. (2000). Lingua franca. In M. Byram (Ed.), *Routledge encyclopedia of language teaching and learning* (pp. 356–359). London: Routledge.

Graddol, D. (1997). *The future of English? A guide to forecasting the popularity of the English language in the 21st century.* London: British Council.

Kaplan, R. B., & Baldauf, R. B., Jr. (2003). The language planning situation in Australia. In R. B. Kaplan & R. B. Baldauf, Jr. (Eds.), *Language and language-in-education planning in the Pacific basin.* Dordrecht, The Netherlands: Kluwer Academic.

Lambert, R. (1994). Problems and processes in U.S. foreign language planning. *The Annals of The American Academy of Political and Social Science, 532,* 47–58.

Lambert, R. (1997). *Horizon Taal* and language planning in the United States. In T. Bongaerts & K. de Bot (Eds.), *Perspectives on foreign-language policy. Studies in honour of Theo van Els* (pp. 79–87). Amsterdam: Benjamins.

Lambert, R. (2000). Adult use and language choice in foreign language policy. In R. Cooper, E. Shohamy, & J. Walters (Eds.), *New perspectives and issues in educational language policy. In honour of Bernard Dov Spolsky* (pp. 171–196). Amsterdam: Benjamins.

Latomaa, S., & Nuolijärvi, P. (2002). The language situation in Finland. *Current Issues in Language Planning, 3,* 95–202.

Lo Bianco, J. (1987). *National policy on languages.* Canberra: Australian Government Publishing Service.

Merkx, G. (2000). Foreign language and area studies through Title VI. Assessing supply and demand. In R. Lambert & E. Shohamy (Eds.), *Language policy and pedagogy. Essays in honor of A. Ronald Walton* (pp. 93–110). Philadelphia: Benjamins.

Nuffield Foundation (2000). *Where are we going with languages?* London: Author.

Odlin, T. (1989). *Language transfer. Cross-linguistic influence in second language acquisition.* Cambridge, UK: Cambridge University Press.

Oud-de Glas, M. (1983). Foreign language needs in the Netherlands. In T. van Els & M. Oud-de Glas (Eds.). *Research into foreign language needs* (pp. 151–170). Augsburg, Germany: Augsburg Universität.

Oud-de Glas, M. (1997). The difficulty of Spanish for Dutch learners. In T. Bongaerts & K. de Bot (Eds.), *Perspectives on foreign-language policy. Studies in honour of Theo van Els* (pp. 41–54). Amsterdam: Benjamins.

Phillips, D. (Ed.). (1989). *Which language? Diversification and the national curriculum.* London: Hodder & Stoughton.

Phillipson, R. (1992). *Linguistic imperialism.* Oxford, UK: Oxford University Press.

Phillipson, R., & Skutnab-Kangas, T. (1999). Minority language rights. In B. Spolsky (Ed.), *Concise encyclopedia of educational linguistics* (pp. 51–54). Amsterdam: Elsevier.

Rivers, W. (1968). *Teaching foreign language skills.* Chicago: University of Chicago Press.

Sajavaara, K. (1997). Implementation of foreign-language policy in Finland. In T. Bongaerts & K. de Bot (Eds.), *Perspectives on foreign-language policy. Studies in honour of Theo van Els* (pp. 113–128). Amsterdam: Benjamins.

Spolsky, B., & Shohamy, E. (1997). Planning foreign-language education: An Israeli perspective. In T. Bongaerts & K. de Bot (Eds.), *Perspectives on foreign-language policy. Studies in honour of Theo van Els* (pp. 99–111). Amsterdam: Benjamins.

Spolsky, B., & Shohamy E. (1999). *The languages of Israel. Policy, ideology and practice.* Clevedon, UK: Multilingual Matters.

Spolsky, B., & Shohamy, E. (2000). Language practice, language ideology, and language policy. In R. Lambert & E. Shohamy (Eds.), *Language policy and pedagogy. Essays in honor of A. Ronald Walton* (pp. 1–41). Philadelphia: Benjamins.

Takala, S. (1993). Language policy and language teaching policy in Finland. In K. Sajavaara, S. Takala, R. Lambert, & C. Morfit (Eds.), *National foreign language planning: Practices and prospects* (pp. 54–71). Jyväskylä, Finland: Jyväskylä University, Institute for Educational Research.

Trim, J. (1994). Some factors influencing national foreign language policymaking in Europe. In R. Lambert (Ed.), *Language planning around the world: Contexts and systematic change* (pp. 1–15). Washington, DC: National Foreign Language Center.

Trim, J. (2000). Common European framework. In M. Byram (Ed.), *Routledge encyclopedia of language teaching and learning* (pp. 122–124). London: Routledge.

Tuin, D., & Westhoff, G. (1997). The task force of the Dutch National Action Programme as an instrument for developing and implementing foreign-language policy. In T. Bongaerts & K. de Bot (Eds.), *Perspectives on foreign-language policy. Studies in honour of Theo van Els* (pp. 21–34). Amsterdam: Benjamins.

Van der Avoird, T., Broeder, P., & Extra, G. (2001). Immigrant minority languages in the Netherlands. In G. Extra & D. Gorter (Eds.), *The other languages of Europe* (pp. 215–242). Clevedon, UK: Multilingual Matters.

Van Ek, J. (2000). Threshold level. In M. Byram (Ed.), *Routledge encyclopedia of language teaching and learning* (pp. 628–631). London: Routledge.

Van Ek, J., & Alexander, L. (1975). *The threshold level in a European unit/credit system for modern foreign language learning by adults.* Strasbourg, France: Council for Cultural Co-operation.

van Els, T. (1988). Towards a foreign language teaching policy for the European Community: A Dutch perspective. *Language, Culture and Curriculum, 1,* 53–65.

van Els, T. (1993). Foreign language teaching policy: Some planning issues. In K. Sajavaara, S. Takala, R. Lambert, & C. Morfit (Eds.). *National foreign language planning: Practices and prospects* (pp. 3–14). Jyväskylä, Finland: Jyväskylä University, Institute of Educational Research.

van Els, T. (1994). Planning foreign language teaching in a small country. *The Annals of the American Academy of Political and Social Science, 532,* 35–46.

van Els, T. (2002). The European Union, its institutions and its languages: Some language political observations. *Current Issues in Language Planning, 2,* 311–360

van Els, T., Bongaerts, T., Extra, G., Van Os, C., & Janssen-van Dieten, A.-M. (1984). *Applied linguistics and the learning and teaching of foreign languages.* London: Edward Arnold.

van Els, T., & Oud-de Glas, M. (Eds.). (1983). *Research into foreign language needs.* Augsburg, Germany: Ausburg Universität.

van Els, T., & Van Hest, E. (1992). *The Dutch National Action Programme on Foreign Languages: Recommendations and policy reactions.* The Hague, The Netherlands: Ministry of Education.

Van Hest, E., & Oud-de Glas, M. (1991). *A survey of the techniques used in the diagnosis and analysis of foreign language needs in trade and industry.* Brussels, Belgium: Commission of the European Communities.

Verdoodt, A., & Sente, A. (1983). Interest shown by secondary school pupils in modern languages and adult language needs in Belgium. In T. van Els & Oud-de Glas M. (Eds.), *Research into foreign language needs* (pp. 263–283). Augsburg, Germany: Ausburg Universität.

Wodak, R., & Corson, D. (Eds.). (1997). *Encyclopedia of language and education.* Dordrecht, The Netherlands: Kluwer Academic.

54

Corpus Planning: Syllabus and Materials Development

Anthony J. Liddicoat
Griffith University

INTRODUCTION

Corpus planning focuses on those elements of language planning that are linguistic and internal to language (Baldauf, 1990; Bamgbose, 1989). Corpus planning, together with status planning and language-in-education (or acquisition) planning and more recently prestige planning, is one of the core areas of language planning (Cooper, 1989; Kaplan & Baldauf, 1997, 2003; Baldauf, chap. 52, this volume). Although this division is both conventional and also hermeneutically useful for dealing with different underlying goals, processes, and concepts, these components articulate with and are influenced by each other. Status planning makes demands of the linguistic code being planned: As new sets of functions are allocated to languages, this has an impact on the code itself, which has to be able to be used in new domains and to communicate about new topics (Cooper, 1989). Therefore, changes at the societal level, have consequences at the linguistic level, and status planning drives corpus planning (see e.g., North Korea in Kaplan & Baldauf, 2003). In addition, corpus planning is implemented largely through education, and corpus planning decisions affect the form of the language that is used and valued within an educational system. Matters of language prestige may also have an impact on the extent to which some aspects of corpus planning are accepted in a speech community.

This chapter will examine corpus planning from a general perspective, but with a specific emphasis on how corpus planning articulates with language-in-education planning on the assumption that "education is an important variable in most language planning situations" (Baldauf, 1990, p. 22). In corpus planning, education becomes a significant variable in its implementation when the language being planned is disseminated through schooling (Haugen, 1983). In order for this to happen, the language needs to be included in syllabi and materials in which the results of corpus planning are given a pedagogical form. The discussion here will begin by considering the processes involved in corpus planning and then consider the products that emerge from these processes and the issues relevant for their use in educational settings.

CORPUS PLANNING PROCESSES

The process of corpus planning is conventionally divided into processes of codification and processes of elaboration (or cultivation) (Eastman, 1983; Haugen, 1983; Kaplan & Baldauf, 1997). Codification refers to the selection and standardization of a linguistic norm. Elaboration involves developing the linguistic resources of the language for dealing with new domains of language use and for thematizing new realities. Although the application of technical linguistic skills is central to corpus planning, corpus planning involves more than simple linguistically based decision making. Most important, successful corpus planning must take into consideration the political and social consequences of linguistic decision making (Cooper, 1989; Hagège, 1983).

Codification

Codification involves formalizing a set of linguistic and usually literate norms (Haas, 1982; Haugen, 1983; Woods, 1985). This involves determining which dialect/variety of the language will serve as the basis for the standard language and reducing the amount of variation in the language to create a more regular and uniform linguistic structure. The selection of the norm on which a standard language is to be developed has political consequences, which may involve empowering or consolidating the power of some groups (that is, native speakers of the chosen norm) and disempowering or marginalizing others who do not speak the language (Luke, McHoul & Mey, 1990).

The selection of a norm may come about where no overt language planning has occurred, as in the case of selecting southeastern English, Paris French, Amsterdam Dutch, or Tokyo Japanese as the basis of national standard. In these cases, the political, economic, or social power exerted by these centers has driven the standardization process. However, in many cases the selection of the norm is the result of direct, overt language planning. In both cases, the selection of the norm is the result of decisions that are not purely linguistic, but that are influenced by economic, social, and political factors (Hagège, 1983). Serbo-Croatian (the official language of the former Yugoslavia) had two standard variants, known as Ekavian and Ijekavian distinguished in the pronunciation (and writing) of the vowel in small number of words as either *e* or *(i)je*: for example, *bel* vs *bijel* (*бел* vs *бийел*) meaning "white." The former variant is native to the area around Belgrade, the latter elsewhere in Serbia and in other areas, notably Bosnia and Croatia. In June 1996, the Republika Srpska declared the nonindigenous Ekavian spellings to be the only official form (Dragosavljević, 2003). The choice of an Ekavian norm was motivated by a linguistically based cleavage: Ekavian was seen as Serbian, Ijekavian as Croatian/Muslim, even though the Ekavian–Ijekavian dichotomy had never been ethnically based (Dragosavljevic, 2000, 2003). The decision to select only the Ekavian norm was motivated by a nationalist desire to symbolize a Serbian identity and to distinguish Bosnian Serbs linguistically from other Bosnians. The decree was eventually overturned (in September 1998) in favor of official status for both variants and both scripts again for nationalistic reasons: Too strong an association between Ekavian and Serbian identity undermined Serbian identities of Ijekavian speakers and fears that prestigious literary works written by Serbs in Ijekavian would be identified with Croatian (Dragosavljevic, 2003).

The central focus of codification is the written language, although features of spoken language are sometimes deliberately planned. However, even where there is no overt language planning aimed at establishing spoken norms, these tend to develop from the basis of the written standard (Hagège, 1983). The development of a standard language where no such language has existed before alters the language ecology found within a society (Mühlhäusler, 1996). In particular, standardized written languages develop an authority that is not usually enjoyed by nonstandardized and unwritten forms of language and become prescriptions for "good" language use (McGroarty, 1996). In fact, standardization and the spread of a single authoritative variety through education leads to the development of a prestige written language that is acquired primarily through education (Milroy & Milroy, 1985; McGroarty, 1996).

The work of codification is usually divided into three separate activities, which have been termed by Haugen (1983):

- *Graphization*: the development of a writing and orthographic system.
- *Grammatication*: the development of a standard grammar.
- *Lexication*: the development of a standard lexicon and terminology.

Graphization

Graphization involves the development, selection, and modification of scripts and of the orthographic conventions of the language. In the world's languages, three basic types of writing systems are usually identified: alphabet systems where each symbol represents a sound, syllabaries where each symbol represents a syllable, and logographic scripts in which each symbol represents a unit of meaning (e.g., Eastman, 1983). The reality is, however, that scripts cannot be categorised strictly into one of these categories (Unger, 1996). Moreover, some languages have mixed scripts, such as Japanese, which combines two syllabaries (*hiragana* and *katakana*) with a set of logographic symbols (*kanji*).

Graphization involves a decision about whether to adapt an existing script for the language to be written or whether to develop a new script for that particular language (Annamalai & Dahal, 1986). The advantage of using an existing script is that the script that already exists is supported by existing infrastructure and technology and has the potential for transferability in the learning of other languages. However, the development of a new script can be an important cultural artifact for a language group and can function as a marker of linguistic identity for users of the script. These motivations can be seen in the graphization movements of West Africa in the 19th century that sought to establish unique writing systems based primarily on indigenous graphic forms (Dalby, 1968).

A large number of existing scripts are alphabetic, including both established scripts extended to new languages and newly developed scripts (e.g., Bassa and Bambara alphabets in West Africa). Alphabetic scripts are particularly useful for languages that have a large number of possible syllables as they minimize the number of syllables needed to represent the language. Nonetheless, a number of languages have created syllabaries (e.g., Kpelle, Loma and Vai syllabaries in West Africa, *Far Soomaali* syllabary in Somalia) and a few have adapted existing syllabaries to their language (e.g., Ainu in Japan). The case of Ainu is interesting because the *katakana* syllabary that has been adopted is designed for a language with a basic CV syllabic pattern with very few codas. Ainu, however, permits a wide range of CVC syllables that cannot easily be represented by *katakana*. In order to represent syllable final consonants, Ainu makes use of a subscript version of a katakana symbol beginning with the appropriate consonant. This is also the case for CV combinations not available in the *katakana* syllabary that are written with a *katakana* symbol representing the consonant and a subscript vowel symbol. It is therefore possible that an Ainu word with a CVC structure will be written with three *katakana* symbols each of which actually represents only a single phoneme in a quasi-alphabetic subsystem, for example, チェㇷ゚ *chep* "fish" = chi+e+pu.

The question of the best writing system to use for a particular language is not uncontroversial. Cooper (1989) has identified two sets of criteria that may be used to evaluate the effectiveness of a script: psycholinguistic criteria and sociolinguistic criteria. Psycholinguistic criteria include how easy the script is to learn, how easy it is to use in reading and writing, how easily it can be used to transfer skills to another language, and how easy it is to reproduce with current technology. These criteria may be in conflict with one another and the interpretation of the criteria themselves is very much determined by the underlying theoretical construction of the nature of literacy (Berry, 1977; Cooper, 1989). Sociolinguistic criteria include the relationship between the script and aspects of a group's religious, political, ethnic, or nationalist aspirations, the functionality of the script within the linguistic ecology, the prestige of the script within the society, and the symbolic associations people make with the script (cf. also Annamalai & Dahal, 1986; Eastman, 1983; Mühlhäusler, 1996). Cooper (1989) argues that sociolinguistic criteria are in fact much more important than psycholinguistic criteria in determining the level of acceptance of a script.

Script selection can be a marker of political, social, or national identity (Hagège, 1983) and various orthographic changes have as their motivation an issue of political or social identity. The replacement of Arabic script by Latin script in Turkish, for example, was motivated in part by the inadequacies of the existing orthography. However, the decision to replace rather than reform the existing orthography was motivated by a desire to affirm the westernization and secularization of the country as important national goals and to distance modern Turkey from its Islamic Ottoman past (Bazin, 1983). Similarly, in North Korea, the replacement of a mixed writing system involving phonologically based indigenous *hangul* characters and ideographic Chinese characters with a pure *hangul* system was argued by North Korean language planners as a necessary step in facilitating the acquisition of literacy. However, at the same time, the removal of Chinese characters also had a nationalist function in emphasizing Korean cultural identity and freedom from external cultural influence, while at the same time, developing distinctiveness between North Korean written in "culturally pure" *hangul* and South Korean, which retained the use of Chinese characters (Kumatani, 1990). In the former USSR, the replacement of Latin and Arabic scripts by Cyrillic during the Stalinist era served to reinforce a sense of unified national identity and to weaken the cultural distinctiveness of minority groups in the context of a movement toward Russification of the Soviet Union (Imart, 1983–1984).

It may be the case that the selection of a standard orthography for a language may involve selection from among a number of existing nonofficial scripts. This was the case, for example, for the adoption of an official script for Somali in 1973. At the time of choosing an official script, Somali had been written in a number of different ways by different groups within the country (Andrzewski, 1983). The most widely used script appears to have been *Far Soomaali* an indigenous syllabary developed in the 1920s, which had been diffused through adult literacy campaigns. A Latin-based orthography had also been developed by Somali linguists and, although not as widely diffused as *Far Soomaali*, it was supported by a culturally important elite. In addition, Arabic was used by some (Islamic) writers of Somali, although a standardized Arabic orthography had not emerged and there was a great deal of variation in the use of Arabic script. This meant that, at the time of independence, the issue of choosing a script was highly politicized, with different groups promoting different scripts for nationalist, modernizing, or religious reasons. The selection of the Latin-based script as the standard orthography for Somali was, in the end, the result of the political influence of a modernizing, secularist, anti-traditionalist group in the government of the time (Andrzewski, 1983).

Changes of script, especially dramatic ones, do not come without a cost in terms of creating a cultural rupture. Where one script is replaced by another and only the new script is taught in basic education, access to material produced before the script reform is restricted unless a substantial program of transliteration of older publications is undertaken (Bazin, 1983). Such programs of extensive transliteration are rare and the end result is that older writings in the language become restricted to specialists who have been educated in both the old script and the new (Annamalai & Dahal, 1986).

In a similar vein, the adoption of the Cyrillic script as the official script of the Bosnian Serb Republika Srpska in 1996 and the abolition of Latin script resulted from a desire to maximize linguistic links with Serbia proper and to establish linguistic distinctiveness between Bosnian Serbs and Bosnian Croats and Muslims, who used Latin script (Dragosavljevic, 2003).

In cases where a script has been in use, it may be felt by the society that some modification of the script is desirable. Such modifications are usually the result of a perception that the current script system is too difficult to acquire or that the current script does not adequately represent the language. An important example of script reform in order to make a writing system easier to acquire can be seen in the various movements in Japanese and Chinese to simplify writing systems based on Chinese characters. In the case of Japan, the emphasis on script reform has been to reduce the number of Chinese characters (*kanji*) in everyday use (Unger, 1996). In Japan, this has been accomplished by publishing lists of approved *kanji*, beginning in 1934 with the *Hyojun Kanji Jihyo* (Standard *Kanji* List) of 2,528 characters and being further reduced in the 1946 *Toyo* (current use) *kanji* list of 1,850 characters. The *Toyo* list was further supplemented in 1949 by a list of permissible readings simplifying the complexities involved in the pronunciations of the characters and recommendations about approved character shapes in printing, harmonizing printed and written forms of some characters (Seeley, 1991; Unger, 1996). These reforms have undergone gradual relaxation since the end of the 1950s and the approved *kanji* list, which has undergone some expansion, is seen as recommending a minimum number of *kanji* for educated use, rather than a maximum limit (Unger, 1996). In the Peoples Republic of China, the emphasis in script reform has been on the simplification of the forms of the characters themselves, particularly on the reduction of the numbers of strokes required for writing characters. As Coulmas (1983) notes, however, the simplification of Chinese characters has been of more benefit to writers than to readers and although characters have become easier to write, the simplification has also meant a loss of distinctiveness for readers.

Once a script has been chosen, corpus planners are also faced with issues of how to represent the sounds of the language using that script: that is, what spelling conventions will be adopted. Such decisions are not simply motivated by the best fit between the sounds of the language and symbols of the script. Where a subordinated language and a dominant language share the same script, the decision has to be made as to whether the sound–symbol correspondences for the two languages should be the same. For example, in developing a writing system for an indigenous language of Spanish-speaking South America, the syllables /ka/, /ku/ and /ki/ may be written as *ka, ku, ki* as in Awa Pit (Ecuador, Colombia) or alternatively the Spanish-influenced spellings *ca, cu, qui* as in Quechua. The former system has the advantage of a consistency of sound–symbol correspondence for the velar /k/, whereas the latter corresponds with the standard conventions of the dominant language, even though those conventions stem from historical developments in Spanish that are not relevant to Quechua. Kephardt (1992) distinguishes between a *minimizing* approach to orthography, which seeks to reduce the sound–symbol differences between languages (i.e., *ca, cu, que*), and a *maximizing* approach, which develops a distinctive set of sound–symbol correspondences for the language for which a new system is being developed (i.e., *ka, ku, ke*).

However, the choice of sound–symbol conventions, like the choice of script, is complex and many nonlinguistic factors can be important. For example, a *minimizing* approach to orthography may be seen as conveying the prestige or social value of the dominant variety to the newly developed system, as facilitating acquisition of the dominant system, or as avoiding possible stigmatization if the language is perceived to be unusual or unlike other languages. In Samoa in the 1960s, the removal of the symbols ' and ?, which represented a glottal stop and a long vowel respectively, was based in part on a desire to make the language appear more "normal" as such symbols were not found in other languages, especially English (So'o, 1997). At the same time a minimizing approach may lead to literacy difficulties if the underlying phonologies for the systems involved are too widely different. For example, Dunn (2000) reports that the use of Russian combinatory rules in the Cyrillic orthography used for Chukchi is an important contributor to low literacy levels in that language as the complexity of the system makes literacy in Russian and a knowledge of Russian orthographic rules a prerequisite for literacy in Chukchi.

Spelling systems may also be revised, usually because the spelling conventions that exist in the language are felt to be too complex or too anomalous, or because they no longer accurately reflect current pronunciations. Webster's attempts at reforming American English spelling in the wake of independence are in part an attempt to simplify and regularize the conventions of English spelling. Many of Webster's proposals represented quite radical departures from the previous conventions: for example, *proov* for *prove*, *hiz* for *his*, *det* for *debt*, *hed* for *head*. In the end, however, very few of the proposed changes proved acceptable to American speakers of English and the resulting reform introduced only minor differences between U.S. and U.K. usage (Ayto, 1983). In some cases of proposed spelling reform, the existence of complexities and anomalies have actually been advanced as arguments against reform. This was the case with the attempt to reform French spelling in the 1990s, where the reforms were attacked because the regularization of the language was seen as undermining the language itself (Baddeley, 1993). It was argued by some critics that the difficulties of language are the sign of its strength and quality, and mastering the difficulties demonstrates intelligence or social worth. The attempt at spelling reform has so far failed completely (Ager, 1996; Schiffman, 1996).

Grammatication

When a language develops new functions and in particular when a language comes to be used for writing, education, and supraregional communication, there is a need to formulate a standard variety of the language (Ferguson, 1988). Essentially the development of a standard grammar involves the reduction of the social and/or regional variation found in the existing spoken language ecology and formulating a set of grammatical rules that will function as the agreed version of the language to be used in literate contexts. The first stage in codifying a language is to select the variety or varieties on which the standard language will be based. The variety selected is usually a variety that has prestige either because it has important symbolic associations or because it is the language of an elite group with the social, economic, or political power to establish their variety as the standard. Commonly, the standard language is developed around the educated language use of the capital city.

The development of the standardized grammar for a language with no traditional standard begins as a descriptive enterprise: Linguists record the grammatical structure found in the designated dialect. The codification of a set of grammatical structures and their publication as an official grammar of the language, imbues the codified structures with authority and establishes a norm against which other usage is measured. The codified grammar, therefore, can become the arbiter of usage, not a reflection of it. At the same time, the establishment of a standard variety implies the establishment of nonstandard varieties: varieties that existed prior to standardization, but that differ from the prescribed standard (Milroy & Milroy, 1985). Such varieties may become stigmatized as "incorrect" versions of the standard language rather than as autonomous patterns of usage. The resulting grammar, however, is usually treated as a prescriptive grammar, not a descriptive one. The process of codification, therefore, takes instances of language used in a particular variety as the basis for the codification of a grammar (Byron, 1976; Rubin & Jernudd, 1971), prestandard language usage becomes the basis for the standard language.

In the process of codification, it may be possible for new rules to enter into the language. In English, the development of the standard written form of the grammar was characterized by a movement to make the grammar of English better conform to the grammar of Latin. Rules were introduced proscribing previous patterns of language use on the justification that such rules did not exist in Latin: for example, split infinitives, sentence final prepositions, and object pronouns as copula complements. The aim in this case was aesthetic: the grammar of Latin was deemed to be elegant and the changes in English were to increase its elegance (Wardhaugh, 1999).

Lexication

The codification of the lexicon develops in much the same way as grammatication. The main task here is to establish the core lexicon of the language, the agreed meanings of individual words and their stylistic and thematic conventions of usage (Haugen, 1983). The work of lexication is the publication of the codified forms and meanings in a dictionary (Kaplan & Baldauf, 1997). As with the development of a grammar, the development of a dictionary typically begins as a descriptive enterprise based on actual patterns of usage, but results in the establishment of authoritative prescriptions that can then affect usage (Liddicoat, 2000). The lexicon of a language that has recently been assigned a new function through status planning, may be well endowed with the lexical resources needed to discuss indigenous technologies, concepts, and behaviors; however, it may not be equally well equipped lexically to function in new domains and functions. As such, the process of creating a dictionary for such a language often includes not only the codification of the lexicon, but also its elaboration.

Elaboration

Status planning decisions often mean that a language comes to be used for functions and in domains that had not previously been the case for this language. Where this happens, the language does not typically have the linguistic resources, in terms of vocabulary and text types, to communicate effectively in these new areas. This does not mean that the language is unable to communicate new topics and ideas, but rather it lacks a specialized register with terms and ways of using language specifically developed for the new area of use (Gonzales, 2002). When the development of new linguistic resources becomes an object of language planning, this is known as elaboration. Elaboration work concerns the development of new lexical items and the development of new registers and text types (stylistic development), however, most attention in language planning is given to the development of new lexical items (Kaplan & Baldauf, 1997). Elaboration can also be used to cover some corpus planning activities that are not associated with functional change, but with a change in the sociolinguistic context in which the language is used. Such corpus planning work, which includes elements such as linguistic purism, nondiscriminatory language, and stylistic simplification, can be considered to be types of language renovation.

Lexical Development

Lexical development, sometimes called lexical modernization, involves creating new terminologies to enable users of a language to use the language in a wider range of contexts than had previously been the case. A chief concern in lexical development is to ensure intertranslatability between standard languages, and especially between English, as a key world language of science and technology, and other languages. Although such intertranslatability may seem desirable for many reasons, the process of developing a modernized lexicon privileges particular (European) systems of knowledge over others. Mühlhäusler (2000) has argued that this may be accelerating the loss of non-European systems of knowledge, and classificatory and epistemological systems through a process of homogenizing terminological systems and valuing certain types of knowledge as *modern* and *technological* while devaluing others as *traditional* or *folk*.

The development of new terminology involves decisions about how the new terminology is to be created, and there are two basic ways in which this can be done: (1) an existing term can be adopted, or (2) a new term can be created. At the time an official term is needed, it may be the case that people have been talking and writing about the relevant concept or the artifact before a term has received official approval. Where such pattern of use occurs and where there is a consensus about the terminology among users, it is usually much easier to adopt the current usage rather than to introduce a new term and persuade people to abandon the existing term. This option, however, is not always used by language planners because the existing term may not conform with other language policy objectives, for example, linguistic purism, and a replacement term may be developed. Where there is no clear consensus in the current usage, language planners are faced with the choice of either identifying one existing term to adopt as the official term or developing a new term. In other language planning contexts, it may be the case that there is no usage of a particular term because the term has not previously been needed. In this case, adopting an existing term is not an option and a new term will need to be developed. In some language planning cases, it may be that terms are not developed unless there is a perceived need for the term for communicating in a particular domain. In other cases, however, factors other than communicative need are important. The development of a full range of technical terms may actually be seen as a matter of prestige for the language, as Fellman and Fishman (1977) report has been the case for Hebrew lexical development.

Where the decision is made to create a new term, there is then a decision to be made about how the new term will be created and again there are options: (a) borrow a term from another language, or (b) develop a term using the existing linguistic stock of the language.

If a term is borrowed, language planners need to decide on the source language. In some cases, borrowings are taken from the internationalized lexicon of a particular subject area: usually the terms with currency in English. This often has the advantage that specialists working in many disciplines may be familiar with the internationalized lexicon of their field and, therefore, already know and use these terms and adopting the borrowing may be no more than confirming current usage (Jernudd, 1977). Such decisions may also be felt to be appropriate where people routinely need to work in both the local language and a world language in their discipline and a technical vocabulary that is in harmony with the internationalized vocabulary may be felt to be efficient both for those working in the area and students who are being inducted into it. Terms may be borrowed in the form in which they are found in the donor language with minimal adaptation to the phonology and orthography of the donor language, as in the case of *le sandwich* or *le parking* in French, or may be nativized to the host language as in the case of *sanduche* sandwich or *cuásar* quasar in Spanish. In cases where the phonology of the donor and host languages are quite different, nativization may lead to major restructuring of the borrowed word *teeberu* (table), *ranchi* (lunch), or *oosutoraria* (Australia) in Japanese.

In other cases, political factors may be influential in the choice of the source language. For example, in the Soviet Union, Russian provided most of the technical vocabulary for minority languages and Russian technical vocabularies were imposed by centralized language planning on minority languages (Lewis, 1972). The imposition of Russian meant that the technical vocabularies of the minority languages was uniform and this uniformity has to some degree facilitated preparation of education materials (Cooper, 1989). At the same time, the Russianization of the vocabulary strengthened the position of Russian and was in harmony with Stalin's policy of Russification of the Soviet Union (Lewis, 1972).

In Bahasa, Indonesia, language planners have taken borrowings from multiple sources. In this case, language planners tend to use European languages, especially English as a source for lexical items in the sciences and technology, but use Sanskrit, a language from which Indonesian has historically borrowed words, for the more culturally salient areas of literature, arts, and scholarship (Lowenberg, 1983). In choosing borrowings from these sources, language planners capitalize on the symbolic associations these languages have: Sanskrit's traditional authority and associations with the Indonesian golden age of the 7th to 14th centuries, Arabic's associations with Islam, and English's associations with modernity and internationalism. In this distribution of the sources of borrowings, Indonesian language planners are reflecting a need for a balance in the process of elaboration between the traditional and the modern (Fishman, 1983).

Borrowing a term from another language is not, however, always desirable or appropriate. In particular borrowed terms may not be well integrated into the lexicon as they may not have associations with other lexical items in the same semantic field or they may not have meanings that are readily apparent. Given these problems, many language planners opt to create new terms from existing elements of the language by expanding the range of meanings of an existing lexical item, by creating a new term using the derivational morphology of the language, or by translating the loan into the language morpheme by morpheme (calquing). Such new words have the advantage of being authentic and recognizable as words of the language into which they are being introduced.

Once lexical forms have been developed, they need to be disseminated for the corpus planning work to be effective. It is usual in most societies for lists of terminologies to be published, but publication per se does not ensure that the terminologies will be used and additional dissemination efforts, such as use in education and the media or incentives to use the terminologies, are needed.

Stylistic Development

The development of conventions for using a language for new functions and in new domains is not simply a matter of lexical and grammatical codification and elaboration. Lexicon and grammar are deployed to create texts. When texts are regularly produced in a particular culture, regular and identifiable patterns of text structure emerge and become normative for the production of such texts. Languages develop discourses and text types appropriate to the domains in which they are used, and as new domains are added to the communicative repertoire of the language, new discourses and new text types become relevant. Stylistic development aimed at introducing new discourses and new text types is therefore an important element of language planning (Kaplan & Baldauf, 1997).

Stylistic development can be considered in terms of the development of both a set of linguistic resources and conventions for expressing particular subject matters (registers) and the development of sets of textual conventions for organizing and presenting information (genres). Register, in part, depends on grammatication and terminological elaboration as a register requires the relevant lexical and grammatical resources for expressing content (Kaplan & Baldauf, 1997). However, register also depends on the emergence of particular conditions of use for lexis and grammar.

Stylistic development, although linguistically important, has not typically been given a high profile in language planning research (Kaplan & Baldauf, 1997). In part this seems to result from the difficulty inherent in such planning, particularly as a top-down process. Stylistic development appears to be a more organic process in which conventions of register and genre emerge from practice rather than being developed before practices can be instituted. The features of specific-purpose genres, both in terms of register and rhetorical structure, are not so much precodified but rather they emerge within specific discourse communities as these communities communicate about their subject matters (Swales, 1992). Individuals can also play a very important role in the emergence of style. For example, Anwar (1980) has suggested that in Indonesia, Sukarno's personal style and usage helped to set the norms for the emerging national language, whereas Gonzalez (2002) traces the origins of a Philipino academic style and register for psychology to the influence of Virgilio Enriquez at the University of the Philippines. Genres, therefore, grow out of networks of communicative practice in which texts are developed to meet contextualized, subject-specific communicative purposes, and generic features of texts evolve over time as the communicative needs of the discourse community evolve. It is for this reason that the pre-establishment of stylistic features is problematic: such action, by establishing conventions outside an actual communicative context, represent language planning at a remove from and potentially unrelated to language use in that they furnish prescriptions for texts for which a social use has not yet been established, and for which clear communicative purposes have not emerged. Although it is possible that emerging genres will draw on textual features of the same genre used by the same discipline in another language (especially English), the emerging genres may also be influenced by the cultural conventions of the language within which they are written. The interrelationship between discipline-specific textual features and established culturally based communicative practices is complex and affects all the structural levels of texts (Liddicoat, 1997). As such, preplanning of genres will find it difficult to predict which discipline factors and which cultural factors will become important in the emerging genres, although prestige planning can have an impact on this process (see Ager, chap. 56, this volume).

It has been argued that the appropriate way to plan for stylistic development is to encourage the use of the language for various new subject matters to provide a context in which genres and registers can emerge organically. Gonzalez (1990) argues that the process of stylistic development should begin at tertiary level, with a creative minority of scholars who would pioneer communicative practice that would then be diffused into the lower levels of schooling. Alternatively it has been argued that stylistic development should be a bottom-up process beginning in primary school with simpler genres and simpler language and diffusing upward through the education system, gaining in complexity as it goes (Nik Safiah, 1987).

A related strategy has been to provide incentives for the use of the language in prestigious domains in order to develop the genres and registers of the domains and to provide models for subsequent language use: for example, Chidambaram (1986) reports the use of cash prises for civil servants for high quality use of Tamil in official correspondence.

Renovation

Language renovation is a form of corpus planning that is undertaken when no functional change has occurred in the language. In the case of renovation, the language is modified in order to achieve a broader social or political goal by exploiting the symbolic potential of language.

Purism.   One common form of renovation is found in linguistic purism (or purification) that seeks to remove words of foreign origin from the language and replace them, where necessary, with words developed from the native linguistic stock (Thomas, 1991). The terminology *purism* and *purification* indicates a perception in such language planning that languages can be "pure" in some sense.

The usual rationales for purism include notions of better communication, improved aesthetic qualities, or arguments based on social needs: a pure language is better for communication because loans from other language create problems for intelligibility; a pure language has values of wholeness, homogeneity, and correctness; or it may be felt that foreign elements weaken or divide the community and promote disunity (Jernudd, 1989; Thomas, 1991). Language purity is not, however, an objective linguistic phenomenon and is primarily ideologically driven. Purism movements tend to grow out of periods of rapid social change including nationalistic movements: Language becomes a symbol of nationalist aspirations—for example, purism in German (Kirkness, 1975), there is a perception of loss of national status—for example, purism in French (Schiffman, 1996), or when there is a desire to mark a separated identity—for example, purism in Croatian (Mikula, 2003).

There are a number of strategies that governments and other organizations can take in introducing a policy of purification, either individually or in combination (Jernudd, 1989):

- Censorship: monitoring public language and controlling use of proscribed elements. It has no direct effect on the inventory of the language. Censorship works to discourage particular uses, however, prohibitions on using a word in publicly sanctioned contexts does not meant that the word will no longer be used in private contexts.
- Eradication: removing proscribed elements from dictionaries and other publications. The removal of words from dictionaries and other publications, however, does not have a direct impact on use.
- Prevention: stemming the tide of incoming words. This requires an official institution to produce new words for new concepts or products as they enter the culture, before a name arises spontaneously.
- Replacement: providing acceptable alternatives to proscribed words by reviving of archaic words, adopting of dialectal forms, creating new words from native elements, or developing calques.

Nondiscriminatory Language.   Another influential form of renovation has been the movement to develop nondiscriminatory language, most notably the development and dissemination of gender-neutral language forms. Feminist politics has developed a view of language that emphasizes the role of language in creating and perpetuating gender stereotypes and views language as a means of oppression. The language planning response to this has been to propose changes to the form of the language that reflects or encodes gender equality (Pauwels, 1998). The movement began as a grassroots movement, with feminist writers and groups proposing new forms and usages. However, the general proposal for a *gender inclusive language* has now been accepted by many governments, who are now introducing top-down language planning. The program for developing gender neutral language has been a corpus planning exercise that has involved replacing words and structures that are perceived as gendered with alternative (often new) lexical items using the following strategies:

- Gender neutralizing: removal of overt indications of gender, for example replacing *chairman* with *chair* or *chairperson*.
- Gender-splitting: marking gender overtly to signal the participation of both genders in the various professions, for example, Spanish *medico/medica* (doctor), *profesor/profesora* (teacher), *abogado/abogada* (lawyer).
- Gender reduction: removing overt gender markings for one gender as in the case of using masculine terms for all genders in French *le capitaine* (captain), *l'avocat* (lawyer).
- Gender reversal: replacing a masculine form with a feminine form as in the use of generic *she* in place of, or together with, generic *he*.

Different strategies are chosen by different communities as a solution to the perceived problem of gendered language and the solution adopted is influenced by the cultural and linguistic context in which such planning is undertaken.

Stylistic Simplification.   In many communities there has been a realization that the language used in some domains is very complex and may exceed the literacy levels of many of the people who need to have access to this language. This has emerged as a particular problem in areas where an understanding of rights and responsibilities is important, as in contracts, taxation, law, etc. In recognition of this problem, some societies have undertaken renovation work in the form of stylistic simplification in order to reconstitute overly complex language in a more readable and comprehensible form. Stylistic simplification has been a particular focus in English-speaking societies where it is often known as plain English. Plain English emphasizes stylistic features such as shorter sentences, less complex vocabulary and syntax, more iconic organization, and decreased redundancy (Eagleson, 1991). Although much work has gone into the development of plain English documents, the results of this work have so far not made significant gains in improving text comprehension. In fact, there are arguments that stylistic simplification is in itself not adequate for meeting the goals such language planning sets. Sless (1995), for example, argues that formal stylistic rules are not the answer to communication problems; but, rather, there is a need to consider more widely what good communication means. In particular, Sless argues that formal simplicity may not affect a reader's ability to use the information in the text, because the difficulty is often conceptual as well as linguistic and that stylistic simplicity may make reader's problems in understanding a conceptually complex but linguistically simple document appear more related to defects of the reader than to problems of communicating complex content.

CORPUS PLANNING PRODUCTS

The products of corpus planning can be considered to be the various artifacts (documents, texts, etc.) produced by language planners for the codification and/or elaboration of the language and for the implementation of corpus planning in the society. Although these documents and texts are not limited to educational contexts, the following discussion will focus on those products of the corpus planning process used for education: specifically, syllabi and materials. These corpus planning products reflect a link between corpus planning and language-in-education planning (See Kaplan, & Baldauf, chap. 55, this volume), as syllabi and materials do not simply develop the linguistic code, but develop the linguistic code to meet educational objectives. As such, the products of corpus planning for schools must go beyond issues of codification and description and present the language in pedagogically useful and appropriate ways.

Syllabus Development

The relationship between syllabus development and corpus planning is complex in that the implementation of corpus planning requires a syllabus to be developed for use of the planned language in schools, whereas at the same time, the development of syllabi may require further corpus planning to meet the needs of the course content being developed. In the context of the implementation of corpus planning, syllabus development provides a context for language use through selecting and grading content for the teaching that will occur in the language (Nunan, 1988). It is in the context of the syllabus that materials are developed and new corpus planning needs are identified. The nature of materials development and further corpus planning derives from the nature and extent of the syllabi to be developed. A syllabus may be developed purely for second language teaching or it may be developed for the teaching of some or all curriculum areas at some or all levels of education. These syllabi need to be stated in a form that can be disseminated among teachers and education systems, and as such the syllabus documents themselves can be considered a product of the corpus planning process. Whatever the syllabus or range of syllabi chosen, the effective implementation of the syllabus depends on the nature and supply of teaching materials. Those teaching materials most directly related to corpus planning work will be considered in the remainder of this chapter.

Materials Development

The development of educational materials is central to corpus development in vernacular languages programs throughout the world and in the implementation status planning decisions that have brought languages new functions and domains of use. Some of this development is found in activities more traditionally included in corpus planning, such as producing grammars and dictionaries; however, most activity is normally devoted to the production of more specifically school-based materials such as readers, textbooks, and other classroom materials. The development of classroom materials is particularly a matter of urgency where a previously unwritten language is being introduced into the school curriculum and is being used for initial literacy development. The need is clear. A literacy program cannot function without texts, so a first step in developing any literacy program must be to ensure that there are texts to be read.

The materials required for the implementation of language planning are quite extensive and include language-focused materials such as dictionaries, grammars, spelling books, etc.; literacy-development materials such as readers; and content-based materials such as textbooks for the range of subjects taught in the language.

Materials development as corpus planning should ideally be seen as a late stage of language planning, which is undertaken in conjunction with language planning and after certain language-in-education decisions have been made. In particular, educational goals and objectives need to be determined and a syllabus needs to be designed in order to provide a context in which materials development can be undertaken. The development of appropriate materials needs to be located within a pedagogical framework rather than relying on a process of creating *ad hoc* materials and then trying to slot them into syllabi and pedagogical objectives. This idea, however, leads to a practical problem: There is a tension between the need to plan and the need to implement and sometimes the timetables for the two processes are in conflict as the result of a need to get programs into place quickly.

It is possible to identify three basic approaches to materials design:

• Experts as producers: experienced educators and/or linguists are commissioned to produce materials by a government or commercial materials developer. This is the usual model for materials development in many parts of the world, especially for larger, well-established languages that provide adequate markets for commercial materials. In some contexts, government agencies take a central role in the development of materials for smaller languages that have a place in the national education system.

• Users as producers: teachers themselves develop materials for newly implemented language programs. One common strategy for developing vernacular language materials is to organize workshops in which teachers produce literacy materials by writing stories in the language. This process has been described for Pacific languages such as Tuvaluan, Kiribati, Tongan, etc. (Liddicoat, 1990) and for the indigenous languages of Namibia (Tomlinson, 1995).

• Speakers as producers: speakers of the language develop material, usually in collaboration with linguists or teachers, who may or may not know the language. This is sometimes an initiative of government or it may be a grass-roots initiative from within the community: for example, for materials development in Otomí/Ñahñú in Mexico (Lastra, 2001) and for KadazanDusun language of Sabah (Lasimbang & Kinajil, 2000). Any materials development program may be based either on one such approach or on a combination of approaches.

In many discussions of corpus planning, the establishment of a grammar and dictionary are seen as key outcomes of the corpus planning process (Eastman, 1983; Garvin, 1993; Haugen, 1983). For the purposes of language codification, the production of a single grammar and a single dictionary encapsulating the norms of the newly codified language is indeed important, as the aim is the establishment of a single authoritative norm for the language. However, when the results of corpus planning come to be implemented, it is more appropriate to consider the production of several grammars and dictionaries rather than one all-purpose work. This is because the role and scope of dictionaries and grammars as tools of codification is quite different from those required for teaching and learning.

One basic distinction that can be made in the case of grammars is between descriptive grammars that seek to present and account for the existing structural features of a language and pedagogical grammars that have an educational focus (Liddicoat & Curnow, 2004; Odlin, 1994). However, even within the framework of a pedagogical grammar, it is important to consider finer distinctions between academic grammars designed for linguistics and for tertiary-level study, grammars for teachers of the language and grammars for learners of the language at various age levels (Dirven, 1990; Westney, 1994) and grammars for first language teaching and for second/foreign language teaching in all of these contexts. In each type of grammar, different content, explanations, organizational principles, and theoretical perspectives may be required to fit the grammar for different purposes and different audiences.

Within an educational context, however, not all possible types of grammars will be necessary and decisions about the development of various types of grammars should reflect the syllabus and curriculum in which the grammar will be used. As such, a learner grammar would not be a high priority in a communicative language program in which the emphasis is on providing comprehensible input rather than on grammatical instruction, although a teacher grammar may be an important resource even in this context.

Similar considerations exist in the case of dictionaries with again a range of different types of dictionaries being possible (Landau, 1989). Important considerations in corpus planning concern the extent of the coverage of the dictionary, the age of users, and the number of languages involved. These factors are connected with the domains of use for the dictionary.

The extent of the language covered by a dictionary is important. A dictionary can aim to cover as much of the lexicon of the language as possible, and in the establishment of a codified lexicon for a language this is important. However, a complete dictionary of the language is not useful or practical in all contexts. This is, of course, recognized by established dictionary makers, who produce full, shorter, and pocket versions of dictionaries for different markets. Large-coverage dictionaries, such as the *Oxford English Dictionary*, are useful as reference materials but are of limited practicality for classroom use, where a smaller dictionary with a more restricted coverage is more useful. A large-coverage dictionary of any language encapsulates the magnavocabulary of that language, a vocabulary that exceeds the actual vocabulary of any individual speaker (Ong, 1982) and although the magnavocabulary is of use in some contexts, the scope of such dictionaries can be counterproductive in others, including the classroom. A further type of limited coverage dictionary is the subject-specific dictionary, such as dictionaries of legal, medical, and scientific terminology. Subject-specific dictionaries are targeted at specialist and neophyte groups of users and seek to establish norms of use with that field and are sometimes characterized by longer definitions and more encyclopedic content (Haiman, 1980; Landau, 1989; Wierzbicka, 1995).

The extent of coverage of a dictionary interacts with the age of users. Younger learners do not require high coverage dictionaries but, rather, more limited dictionaries of high frequency words. The problem with developing such dictionaries in the early stages of corpus planning lies in the problems of establishing frequency counts in languages that do not have an established literate tradition and so such dictionaries necessarily begin on an ad hoc basis. In the initial stages of school literacy development, a dictionary as such is of limited use and texts with a more limited range and targeted scope, such as spelling books, are needed. A spelling book can be distinguished from a dictionary in that it presents only orthographic forms without definitions, thereby implying that the entries have known, or at least easily knowable, meanings. Such books function as models for the orthographic system of language and do not have the checking function that is associated with dictionaries.

The languages in which a dictionary is written is a particularly important issue for language education. A monolingual dictionary implies a group of users who are high-proficiency speakers of the language, who require a dictionary for reference in order to access an expanded version of the vocabulary of the language. If the only dictionary available for pedagogical use is a monolingual dictionary, such a dictionary is of very limited use in contexts where the students are not first language speakers of the language. A bilingual dictionary, in contrast, implies a context of second/foreign language acquisition and a group of users who are not highly proficient in one of the language used and who need to check translation equivalents between languages. Bilingual dictionaries may be unidirectional—implying knowledge of the language of the headword is at a lower level than the knowledge of the language of the explanation, or bidirectional—implying no direction of transfer of information or primacy of one language. The choice of languages in a bilingual dictionary is important where this dictionary is the sole dictionary of the language. If the dictionary is written in a language with high prestige but low levels of use within the culture in which it is being used, the dictionary is of limited practical use, although it may have a high symbolic status and be associated with greater levels of prestige for the language (Liddicoat, 2000). Landau (1989) makes the point that bidirectional dictionaries are not usually designed for a single audience, but rather each language section is usually designed for native speakers of the language of the head words.

Where stylistic development is a target for corpus planning, one possible means for doing this is through the productions of manuals of rhetoric or style (Gonzalez, 2002). Such manuals of rhetoric or style exist for many languages; however, they are problematic. Prescriptive style manuals may not reflect the actual conventions of writing within a given language and culture, but rather reflect an idealized or intuited state of writing practice that deviates from the actual writing conventions practiced. Research-based accounts of genre and rhetoric such as those proposed by Swales (1992) and Trimble (1985) may, however, be useful where a corpus of relevant texts exists and for the teaching of established patterns of academic or professional literacy.

In the process of language intellectualization (Gonzalez, 2002), the need for class-room materials extends beyond the basic artifacts of the linguistic corpus (that is, dictionaries and grammars). Although these obviously do have a place in language education, there are many other types of materials that are needed in order to provide the resources necessary for language education. Languages that are in the process of being introduced into the education system also need to be supported by textbooks, literacy materials, and increasingly by information and communication technology resources. These materials are in a sense secondary to the core work of corpus planning as they presuppose the establishment of orthographic, grammatical, and textual norms as their starting point. As such, basic corpus planning provides the input for the development of other materials; the language developed through corpus planning then must be shaped by the pedagogical theories, cultural practices, and other variables of the local educational system.

In some language planning contexts, materials development may take the form of creating, for example, a whole textbook in the language; however, such large-scale developments are not always feasible, especially in the short term. One common procedure for developing materials in languages that as yet have not been used in education is the development of single-type activities, such as language exercises, or collections of spoken, written, or visual texts that are presented without an specification of how they are to be used. Such materials can be produced centrally and disseminated by teachers, or they may be produced by individual teachers or groups of teachers. The advantage of single-type materials lies in the time and economic advantages of producing small-scope materials, although in a context of a general paucity of materials the ad hoc nature of such materials may lead to difficulties in implementing a coherent and complete program.

In some cases, the development of school materials in vernacular languages focuses on the development of initial literacy materials, without similar levels of development for more advanced students. As such, there is a risk that the same materials may be re-used at a range of levels and, as such, may prevent older children from expanding their literacy levels (e.g., the case of Jaru in Australia, cited by Lo Bianco & Rhydwen, 2001) The development of vernacular literacy materials for school use can have an impact on the ecology of the language for which such materials are developed. In some communities, the only literacy materials available are schoolbooks; and, as such, literacy in a vernacular might be solely a school-based activity, with no niche for vernacular literacy elsewhere in the society. The lack of a viable context for using literacy in the vernacular outside school may, in fact, undermine the value of the vernacular that such programs were often designed to reinforce.

CONCLUSION

Although corpus planning is concerned with those elements of language that are internal to language itself, and the methods of corpus planning draw centrally on the technical methods of linguistics, any understanding of corpus planning must go beyond considerations of the technical and examine the context in which corpus planning occurs. For corpus planning, two broad contexts need to be considered: the sociopolitical context in which planning is done and the educational context through which corpus planning is implemented. Changes to language form are drawn from and affect the sociopolitical context, and the symbolic value attached to language(s) in a society is an important factor in developing appropriate and acceptable forms with that society. Similarly, corpus planning has implications for the development of education in the language planned, and the educational requirements for implementing corpus planning may themselves require additional corpus planning work and/or the modification of corpus planning products to meet educational objectives. Corpus planning for national development and corpus planning for education appear to represent two different levels of corpus planning work with different needs and goals and equal consideration needs to be given to both levels of work for the corpus plan to be effective.

REFERENCES

Ager, D. (1996). *Language policy in Britain and France: The processes of policy*. London & New York: Cassel.

Andrzewski, B. W. (1983). Language reform in Somalia and the modernisation of the Somali vocabulary. In I. Fodor & C. Hagège (Eds.), *Language reform: History and future* (pp. 69–84). Hamburg, Germany: Buske.

Annamalai, E., & Dahal, B. M. (1986). Creating and changing a writing system: Social, economic, pedagogical and linguistic criteria for choice. In E. Annamalai, B. H. Jernudd, & J. Rubin (Eds.). *Language planning: Proceedings of an institute* (pp. 390–404). Mysore, India: Central Institute of Indian Languages.

Anwar, K. (1980). *Indonesian: The development and use of a national language*. Yogyakarta, Indonesia: Gadjah Mada University Press.

Ayto, J. (1983). English: Failures of language reforms. In I. Fodor & C. Hagège (Eds.), *Language reform: History and future* (pp. 85–100). Hamburg, Germany: Buske.

Baddeley, S. (1993). The 1990 French spelling reforms: An example to be followed? *Journal of the Simplified Spelling Society, 2*, 3–5.

Baldauf, R. B., Jr. (1990). Language planning and education. In R. B. Baldauf, Jr. & A. Luke (Eds.), *Language planning and education in Australasia and the South Pacific* (pp. 319–334). Clevedon, UK: Multilingual Matters.

Bamgbose, A. (1989). Issues for a model of language planning. *Language Planning & Language Problems, 13*, 24–34.

Bazin, L. (1983). La réforme linguistique en turquie. In I. Fodor & C. Hagège (Eds.), *Language reform: History and future* (pp. 155–177). Hamburg, Germany: Buske.

Berry, J. (1977). "The making of alphabets" revisited. In J. A. Fishman (Ed.), *Advances in the creation and revision of writing systems* (pp. 3–16). The Hague, The Netherlands: Mouton.

Byron, J. (1976). *Selection among alternates in language standardisation*. The Hague, The Netherlands: Mouton.

Chidambaram, M. (1986). The politics of language planning in Tamil Nadu. In E. Annamalai, B. H. Jernudd, & J. Rubin (Eds.), *Language planning: Proceedings of an institute* (pp. 338–359). Mysore, India: Central Institute of Indian Languages.

Cooper, R. L. (1989). *Language planning and social change*. Cambridge, UK: Cambridge University Press.

Coulmas, F. (1983). Writing and literacy in China. In F. Coulmas & K. Ehlich (Eds.), *Writing in focus* (pp. 239–254). Berlin: Mouton.

Dalby, D. (1968). The indigenous scripts of West Africa and Surinam: Their inspiration and design. *African Language Studies, 9*, 156–197.

Dirven, R. (1990). Pedagogical grammars. *Language Teaching, 23*, 1–18.

Dragosavljevic, A. (2000). Language policies and academic responses: The Ekavian debate in Republika Srpska. *Australian Slavonic and East European Studies, 14* (1–2), 1–27.

Dragosavljevic, A. (2003). Language planning in Republika Srpska. In A. J. Liddicoat & K. Muller (Eds.), *Perspectives on Europe: Language issues and language planning in Europe* (pp. 141–152). Melbourne: Language Australia.

Dunn, M. (2000). Planning for failure: The niche of standard Chukchi. *Current Issues in Language Planning, 1*, 389–399.

Eagleson, R. D. (1991). Plain English: Some sociolinguistic revelations. In S. Romaine (Ed.), *Language in Australia* (pp. 362–372). Cambridge, UK: Cambridge University Press.

Eastman, C. M. (1983). *Language planning: An introduction*. San Francisco: Chandler & Sharp.

Fellman, J., & Fishman, J. A. (1977). The Hebrew academy: Solving terminological problems. In J. Rubin, B. H. Jernudd, J. Das Gupta, J. A. Fishman & C. A. Ferguson (Eds.), *Language planning processes* (pp. 79–95). The Hague, The Netherlands: Mouton.

Ferguson, C. A. (1988). Standardisation as a form of language spread. In P. Lowenberg (Ed.), *Language spread and language policy: Issues, implications, and case studies* (pp. 119–132). Washington, DC: Georgetown University Press.

Fishman, J. A. (1983). Modelling rationales in corpus planning: Modernity and tradition in images of the good corpus. In J. Cobarrubias & J. Fishman (Eds.), *Progress in language planning: International perspectives* (pp. 107–118). Berlin: Mouton.

Garvin, P. L. (1993). A conceptual framework for the study of language standardisation. *International Journal of The Sociology of Language, 100/101*, 37–54.

Gonzalez, A. (1990). Evaluating bilingual education in the Philippines: Towards a multidimensional model of evaluation in language planning. In R. B. Baldauf, Jr. & A. Luke (Eds.), *Language planning and education in Australasia and the South Pacific* (pp. 319–334). Clevedon, UK: Multilingual Matters.

Gonzalez, A. (2002). Language planning and intellectualisation. *Current Issues in Language Planning, 3*, 5–27.

Haas, W. (1982). *Standard languages: Spoken and written.* Manchester, UK: Manchester University Press.

Hagège, C. (1983). Voies et destins de l'action humaine sur la langue. In I. Fodor & C. Hagège (Eds.), *Language reform: History and future* (pp. 1–68). Hamburg, Germany: Buske.

Haiman, J. (1980). Dictionaries and encyclopedias. *Lingua, 50*, 329–357.

Haugen, E. (1983). The implementation of corpus planning: Theory and practice. In J. Cobarrubias & J. A. Fishman (Eds.), *Progress in language planning: International perspectives* (pp. 269–289). Berlin: Mouton.

Imart, G. (1983–1984). Développement et planification des vernaculaires: L'expérience soviétique et le tiers monde. In I. Fodor & C. Hagège (Eds.), *Language reform: History and future* (pp. 1–68). Hamburg, Germany: Buske.

Jernudd, B. H. (1977). Linguistic sources for terminological innovation. In J. Rubin, B. H. Jernudd, J. Das Gupta, J. A. Fishman, & C. A. Ferguson (Eds.), *Language planning processes* (pp. 215–236). The Hague, The Netherlands: Mouton.

Jernudd, B. H. (1989). The texture of language purism. In B. H. Jernudd & M. J. Shapiro (Eds.), *The politics of language purism* (pp. 1–19). Berlin: Mouton de Gruyter.

Kaplan, R. B., & Baldauf, R. B., Jr. (1997). *Language planning: From practice to theory.* Clevedon, UK: Multilingual Matters.

Kaplan, R. B., & Baldauf, R. B., Jr. (2003). *Language and language-in-education planning in the Pacific basin.* Dordrecht, The Netherlands: Kluwer.

Kephardt, R. (1992). Reading Creole English does not destroy your brain cells. In J. Siegal (Ed.), *Pidgins, Creoles and nonstandard dialects in education* (pp. 67–86). Clayton, Australia: Applied Linguistics Association of Australia. [Occasional Paper #12]

Kirkness, A. (1975). *Zur Spracheinigung im Deutschen: Eine historische Dokumentation 1789–1871.* Tübingen, Germany: Naar.

Kumatani, A. (1990). Language policies in North Korea. *International Journal of the Sociology of Language, 82*, 87–108.

Landau, S. I. (1989). *Dictionaries: The art and craft of lexicology.* Cambridge, UK: Cambridge University Press.

Lasimbang, R., & Kinajil, T. (2000). Changing the language ecology of KadazanDusun: The role of the KadazanDusun language foundation. *Current Issues in Language Planning, 1*, 415–424.

Lastra, Y. (2001). Otomí language shift and some recent efforts to reverse it. In J. A. Fishman (Ed.), *Can threatened languages be saved?* (pp. 142–165). Clevedon, UK: Multilingual Matters.

Lewis, E. G. (1972). *Multilingualism in the Soviet Union: Aspects of language policy and its implementation.* The Hague, The Netherlands: Mouton.

Liddicoat, A. J. (Ed.). (1990). *Vernacular languages in South Pacific education.* Melbourne, Australia: National Languages Institute of Australia.

Liddicoat, A. J. (1997). Texts of the culture and texts of the discourse community. In Z. Golebiowski & H. Borland (Eds.), *Academic literacy across disciplines and cultures* (pp. 38–41). Melbourne, Australia: Victoria University of Technology.

Liddicoat, A. J. (2000). The ecological impact of a dictionary. *Current Issues in Language Planning, 1*, 424–430.

Liddicoat, A. J., & Curnow, T. J. (2004). Language descriptions. In A. Davies & C. Elder (Eds.), *Handbook of applied linguistics* (pp. 25–53). Oxford, UK: Blackwell.

Lo Bianco, J., & Rhydwen, M. (2001). Is the extinction of Australia's indigenous languages inevitable? In J. A. Fishman (Ed.), *Can threatened languages be saved?* (pp. 391–422). Clevedon, UK: Multilingual Matters.

Lowenberg, P. H. (1983). Lexical modernisation in Bahasa Indonesia: Functional allocation and variation in borrowing. *Studies in the Linguistic Sciences, 13*(2), 73–86.

Luke, A., McHoul, A. W., & Mey, J. (1990). On the limits of language planning: Class, state and power. In R. B. Baldauf, Jr. & A. Luke (Eds.), *Language planning and education in Australasia and the South Pacific* (pp. 25–44). Clevedon, UK: Multilingual Matters.

McGroarty, M. (1996). Language attitudes, motivation and standards. In S. L. McKay & N. H. Hornberger (Eds.), *Sociolinguistics and language teaching* (pp. 3–46). Cambridge, UK: Cambridge University Press.

Mikula, M. (2003). Croatia's independence and the language politics of the 1990s. In A. J. Liddicoat & K. Muller (Eds.), *Perspectives on Europe: Language issues and language planning in Europe* (pp. 109–123). Melbourne, Australia: Language Australia.

Milroy, J., & Milroy, L. (1985). *Authority in language: Investigating language prescription and standardisation.* London: Routledge & Kegan Paul.

Mühlhäusler, P. (1996). *Language ecology: Linguistic imperialism and language change in the Pacific region*. London: Routledge.

Mühlhäusler, P. (2000). Language planning and language ecology. *Current Issues in Language Planning, 1*, 306–367.

Nik Safiah, K. (1987). Language cultivation, the school system and national development: The case of Bahasa Malaysia. In B. K. Das (Ed.), *Language education in human resource development* (pp. 58–69). Singapore: RELC.

Nunan, D. (1988). *Syllabus design*. Oxford, UK: Oxford University Press.

Odlin, T. (1994). Introduction. In T. Odlin (Ed.), *Perspectives of pedagogical grammar* (pp. 1–22). Cambridge, UK: Cambridge University Press.

Ong, W. J. (1982). *Orality and literacy: Technologizing of the word*. London: Methuen.

Pauwels, A. (1998). *Women changing language*. London, Longman.

Rubin, J., & Jernudd, B. H. (1971). Introduction: Language planning as an element of modernization. In J. Rubin & B. H. Jernudd (Eds.), *Can language be planned? Sociolinguistic theory and practice for developing nations* (pp. xiii–xxiv). Honolulu: University of Hawaii Press.

Schiffman, H. F. (1996). *Linguistic culture and language policy*. London: Routledge.

Seeley, C. (1991). *A history of writing in Japan*. Leiden, The Netherlands: E. J. Brill.

Sless, D. (1995). The plain English problem. *Australian Language Matters, 3*(4), 3, 4–5.

So'o, A. M. (1997). Developing vernacular literacy in Western Samoa: Reading problems and their planning implications. Unpublished master's thesis: Australian National University, Canberra, Australia.

Swales, J. (1992). *Genre analysis: English in academic and research settings*. Cambridge, UK: Cambridge University Press.

Thomas, G. (1991). *Linguistic purism*. London: Longman.

Tomlinson, B. (1995). Work in progress: Textbook projects. *FOLIO 2*(2), 14–17.

Trimble, L. (1985). *English for science and technology*. Cambridge, UK: Cambridge University Press.

Unger, J. M. (1996). *Literacy and script reform in occupation Japan*. New York: Oxford University Press.

Wardhaugh, R. (1999). *Proper English: Myths and misunderstandings about language*. Oxford, UK: Basil Blackwell.

Westney, P. (1994). Rules and pedagogical grammar. In T. Odlin (Ed.), *Perspectives on pedagogical grammar* (pp. 72–96). Cambridge, UK: Cambridge University Press.

Wierzbicka, A. (1995). Dictionaries vs encyclopaedias: How to draw the line. In P. W. Davis (Ed.), *Alternative linguistics: Descriptive and theoretical modes* (pp. 289–315). Amsterdam: Benjamins.

Woods, J. D. (1985). *Language standards and their codification: Processes and application*. Exeter, UK: University of Exeter Press.

55

Language-in-Education Policy and Planning

Robert B. Kaplan
University of Southern California (Emeritus)
Richard B. Baldauf, Jr.
University of Queensland

INTRODUCTION

Language-in-education planning, sometimes referred to as *acquisition planning* (Cooper, 1989), is one of four types of language policy and planning, the others being status planning, corpus planning, and prestige planning. Kaplan and Baldauf (1997) have suggested that language-in-education planning should be an outcome of national language planning (i.e., status planning and corpus planning) with prestige planning contributing as a motivational factor. However, in the real world, language-in-education planning often constitutes the sole language planning activity in many polities, a situation far more common than the one in which it is a neat outgrowth of national language planning. Some authors like Corson (1999) have focused on this tendency, demonstrating how schools can provide a platform from which all language-in-education activities could proceed.

However, beyond the obvious systematic discontinuities that result from stand-alone language-in-education planning, other problems that flow from the inherent nature of such planning include:

- *Slow dissemination*: language dissemination through the education system is a long-term affair, requiring several generations to reach a significant segment of the population.
- *Limited audience*: activity of national educational authorities is restricted to that agency and its dependent schools, teachers, and functions, and has little or no effect on language planning activities occurring simultaneously in other agencies, either governmental or private.
- *Lack of resources*: the education sector is often under-resourced for the tasks it fulfills.

When language-in-education planning becomes the focal activity, it is sometimes charged with education-oriented status (van Els, chap. 53, this volume) and corpus planning—beyond the normal syllabus and education-oriented materials and text-book creation activities that may accompany such planning (see, Liddicoat, chap. 54, this volume). Faced with this set of constraints (including commonly the absence of status and corpus planning specialists), activities such as the preservation and/or resurrection of moribund language(s) (see e.g., Liddicoat & Bryant, 2001), or intel-lectualization (modernization) of indigenous language(s) (Gonzalez, 2002) for use as languages of education (e.g., in Indonesia, Malaysia, the Philippines, or South Africa) can implicate a heavy investment of time and resources. Although such activities may, given sufficient time, contribute to renewed language vitality, they often implicate a top-down process where language change emanates from tertiary education or from education more generally and is diffused to society as a whole.

Although language-in-education planning is most visible and most closely associ-ated with goals for language and literacy learning in formal educational settings (i.e., schools; see Ingram, 1989; Paulston & McLaughlin, 1994, for earlier reviews), it also im-plicates the less systematic teaching of heritage/community languages (Hornberger, 2004) and activities related to literature and cultural learning, religion, communicative media, and work-related goals.

For language-in-education policy planning, the policymakers' problem is to define and facilitate choices that are relevant to individuals' interests and needs—to encour-age active participation (see Prestige and Image Planning, chap. 56, this volume)—while at the same time ensuring that the general education benefits and societal needs are being met in the defining political climate. However, the success of meeting these goals depends largely on policy decisions related to the teachers, the courses of study, and the materials and resources to be made available. As suggested by Baldauf (Chap. 52, this volume), there are seven interrelated policy goals that can be said to influence the success of language-in-education driven policy development:

- Access policy (Who learns what when?).
- Personnel policy (Where do teachers come from and how are they trained?).
- Curriculum policy (What is the objective in language teaching/learning?).
- Methodology and materials policy (What methodology and what materials are employed over what duration?).
- Resourcing policy (How is everything paid for?).
- Community policy (Who is consulted/involved?).
- Evaluation policy (What's the connection between assessment on the one hand and methods and materials that define the educational objectives on the other?).

Unfortunately, these goals are not always systematically addressed, thereby greatly complicating cultivation planning (i.e., program implementation). This is made fur-ther problematic by the heterogeneity found in most polity populations, making it imperative that successful language cultivation embraces several of these goals simul-taneously. The four language-in-education cultivation planning goals, which relate to the policy or form-related planning goals, are:

- Language maintenance (For whom—majority or minority language/bilingual education?).
- Language reacquisition (What languages are slated for revival; why?).
- Foreign/second language learning (What foreign languages (FLs) are taught; why?).
- Language shift (How are language populations induced/forced to change?).

Given the political nature of much language-in-education planning (Baldauf & Kaplan, 2003) and its contextual embeddedness in the language ecology of particular situations, this chapter is organized around an examination of the situations in three polities—Japan, Sweden, and North Korea—where these language-in-education planning goals have been a predominant factor in language policy development and in the changing or maintaining (i.e., the cultivation) of the language.

LANGUAGE-IN-EDUCATION PLANNING IN JAPAN

The Japanese language has no legal status in Japan. The current national constitution makes no mention of language matters. Indeed, there has been only limited governmental language planning to speak of in all of Japan's previous history except for the pre-World War II imperial period. It has simply been taken for granted that all Japanese speak Japanese, and that there is no language problem in need of attention (Kaplan & Baldauf, 2003, chap. 2). It is important to understand, as Neustupný, and Tanaka (2003, p. 17) write, "Japanese society still maintains a very strong Modern (i.e., not Postmodern) component, with attendant isolation from the rest of the world."

However, that is not to say that there has been absolutely no language planning. On the contrary, at the beginning of the Meiji Restoration there was a great deal of concern on two counts: (a) in the written language, there was considerable style diversity, with the more academic registers employing great numbers of Chinese characters, thus making written language inaccessible to the majority of the population (see Kaplan & Baldauf, 2003, chap. 3 for similar concerns in North Korea); (b) in the spoken language, there was considerable dialect variation and there was a significant gap between spoken and written language. Through the final decades of the 19th century and the first decades of the 20th century, several alternatives were widely debated—reducing the number of Chinese characters, eliminating Chinese characters entirely, or adopting a Roman alphabet (Coulmas, 2002). This debate, however, took place largely among intellectuals, and it was only in 1903 that the Ministry of Education endorsed the first *Modern Standard Japanese* textbooks, thereby lending some weight to the development of a standard variety.

Japanese military success in the 1894–1895 Sino-Japanese war and the 1904–1905 Russo-Japanese war significantly increased militarism and nationalist feeling, and in emulation of the situation in the West, a popular desire and strong movement for the development of a *national language* [*kokugo*] arose (Twine, 1991; Yamada, 1992). In 1923, as part of the standardization process required for the development of such a national language, the Interim Committee on the National Language (*Rinji Kokugo Chosakai*) published a list of 1,963 Chinese characters for general use. It also was decided that the oral standard would be the speech of educated Tokyo residents. Rural dialects were perceived as delaying the learning of the standard, but also as relics of the old order—they had to be eliminated. This standardizing activity was conducted largely through the educational system. Thus, from about 1910 to about 1945, the Japanese government became heavily involved in language-in-education policy, because education provided the means to inculcate several generations of students into what Japan perceived as its manifest destiny in Asia. The languages of the impoverished and outnumbered Ainu, as well as of the Okinawans, were banned as part of turning these people into conforming Imperial subjects.

As Japan conquered and occupied areas of the Asian-Pacific region during this period, the evolving language policy did not stop with the Japanese Islands, but was extended to Taiwan (Formosa 1895), Korea (1905), the South Sea Islands (1914), Manchuria (1932) and it subsequently became a feature of the Greater East Asia Co-Prosperity Sphere (Coulmas, 2002). Education needed to be provided in these conquered territories, and the government became centrally concerned with promulgating Japanese language, Japanese values, and "Japaneseness" throughout those polities—that is, stressing moral education and the importance of Japanese national language (*kokugo*—not *nihongo*) using an assimilationist policy (Kaplan & Baldauf, 2003: Rhee, 1992). The idea developed that Japanese should be the common language of East Asia and indeed should be recognized as a leading world language. However, since the end of World War II, Japanese language spread policy (Hirakata, 1992) has had to rely on persuasion rather than force.

After World War II, language policy became a matter of political contention in the years of the U.S. occupation (Unger, 1996). Language planning was perceived as an exclusively governmental prerogative, and the absolute control of primary and secondary education and substantial control of tertiary education, rested entirely with *Monbusho*—the Ministry of Education (Shimaoka, 1999). A simplified writing system became the objective, although still inhibited by debates between traditionalists and liberal proponents of simplification. But, for the new post-war democratic ideal to take root, a transparent writing system accessible to all was essential as a precondition for total literacy, broad political participation, and democratic citizenship.

As a result, reducing the number of Chinese characters became an imperative of social change. In 1948, the vestigial Council on the National Language produced, for general use, a list of 1,850 Chinese characters (the Toyo list). With the end of the occupation and the election of the Liberal Democratic Party, the simplification debate continued, and between 1966 and 1981 the Toyo list was often amended, resulting in a new list in 1981 that added some 95 characters to the 1948 list. By the 1990s, economic factors had become more important; although it was generally conceded that the state had control over written language, and character lists drawn up by the Japan Industrial Standards Organization and the International Standards Organization include more characters than the government's official list. Indeed, software developers also seemed to pay little attention to the concerns of the government.

Although an organization known as the Japanese National Language Research Institute (*Kokuritu Kokugo Kenkyuzyo*) was established under the jurisdiction of the Ministry of Education in 1948 "to conduct scientific surveys on the Japanese language and the linguistic life of the Japanese people in order to create reliable bases for rationalization of the Japanese Language" (National Language Research Institute, 1998, p. 1), the Institute was not a language planning body. It was a research body, licensed only to make recommendations to the Ministry of Education and has contributed little to language-in-education planning.

More recent language-in-education debates have centered on the role of English in Japan. For example, Japan's then (March 30, 1999) Prime Minister Keizo Obuchi, appointed a commission charged with defining Japan's goals in the 21st century. Note that it was the Prime Minister, a political figure, who appointed the Commission, and note that the charge of the Commission, though couched in altruistic terms, was essentially political in the sense that the Prime Minister was seeking to build a political agenda. The final report of the commission entitled, *The Frontier Within: Individual Empowerment and Better Governance in the New Millennium*, was delivered to Prime Minister Obuchi on January 18, 2000. The discussion of English, and of foreign language teaching more broadly, constitutes a minor theme in the report—less than 2% of the total report. The report boldly recommends making English the second official language of Japan, but the question of how all this activity would be financed is not addressed. This recommendation created a tempest of discussion in the Japanese press—indeed, in the world press—but with the untimely death of Prime Minister Keizo Obuchi (in May 2000), the report essentially disappeared from view in favor of the much larger issues surrounding Japan's current economic situation. The furor of public debate has died down. The teaching of English (and to a lesser extent of other foreign languages) remains as it was, vested in the Ministry of Education and implemented through the schools.

LANGUAGE-IN-EDUCATION POLICY

Access Policy

In Japan, since the end of World War II, all children have been required to study English. Initially, English was introduced in middle school, but it has gradually expanded in both directions; introduction in elementary school is currently (post-2002) being implemented, and students normally continue English studies into tertiary education. The national college entrance examination, taken by virtually all high school graduates, contains an English segment, and national university law requires eight credits in one foreign language, usually English. Many major corporations operate their own English schools. In addition, there are thousands of private English language schools (*Juku*) that make English education an important preoccupation of Japanese students beyond their formal schooling. Thus, access to English is both required and sustained for most students. Despite universal access, it is generally acknowledged that outcomes are relatively negligible. Most students can accomplish whatever they need to in Japanese; English is simply a boring academic subject.

Personnel Policy

English (or any other language) teachers are drawn from a wide variety of tertiary institutions, which are under the control of the Ministry of Education, making teacher training fairly standardized across the country. Entry to the profession is via a multiple-choice examination administered by the board of education in each locality. However, there seems to be little uniform control of language proficiency among teachers. Many teachers have relatively limited control of the language they are expected to teach, leading to fairly conservative teaching; that is, teachers teach what they can—decontextualized grammar and vocabulary, the latter intended to inculcate as many words as possible (minimum 1,000 words by the end of junior high school), but without any sense of their connotative meanings or of their frequency and distribution.

The Japan Exchange and Teaching (JET) Program, launched in 1987, aims to improve foreign language teaching of English in Japan while also promoting international exchange and "internationalization" of Japan's regions. Inviting young university graduates to Japan originally to teach English, for a maximum of up to 3 years, or to be attached to a local government office, this program has grown enormously in numbers and countries concerned, with a total of some 5,800 JET participants from 37 countries in Japan during 1999–2000; the bulk still comes from the English-speaking world. The wider educational enterprise in Japan is enormous with a steeply pyramidal structure that has 42,484 schools (from elementary to University), 20,710,746 students (out of a population of about 126,550,000) and 1,017,541 teachers (see, Kaplan, 2000).

Curriculum Policy

The system is very top-down, and the community has little input into policy. The Ministry of Education dictates curriculum policy that is disseminated in periodic directives known as *Courses of Study*. The most recent directives, promulgated in 1993 for junior high schools and in 1994 for senior high schools, emphasize communicative abilities and international understanding. They are intended to:

- Give more importance to listening and speaking without neglecting reading and writing.
- Focus teaching more clearly in specific items so that it may be more effective.
- Foster a positive attitude toward mastery of a foreign language among learners, help them become good speakers of a foreign language, and enhance their understanding of foreign countries by developing their interest in language and culture both at home and abroad (Shimaoka, 1999, p. 90).

However, given that lower secondary school provides 3 hours per week of instruction in each of 3 years and upper secondary school also provides 3 hours of instruction per week in each of 3 years with 1 additional hour in the first or last year (625 hours of instruction over 6 years), it is unreasonable to assume that learners will emerge from the system as good speakers of a foreign language.

Methodology and Materials Policy

The Ministry of Education spells out the English teaching curriculum in great detail with respect to grammar and vocabulary selection, and authorizes textbooks, meeting certain criteria, which foreign language learners are required to use. Although teachers are free to adjust these textbooks to the level and needs of their students, authorized textbooks must:

- Include the four skills—listening, speaking, reading, and writing—as separate activities.
- Adopt a flexible arrangement of grammatical items to be taught.
- Include the 507 vocabulary items suggested by the Ministry within a total of approximately 1,000 items.

Early foreign language methodology, going back to the early Meiji era, was based on the grammar-translation approach, because communication with native speakers was not an issue. In 1923, Harold Palmer created the Institute for Research in Language Teaching (IRLT) to promote the "oral approach." However, English was disparaged during the years between 1939 and 1945, and English-language teaching virtually disappeared from the Japanese educational system. After World War II, when English was reinstated in the educational system, teachers were encouraged to pay more attention to the oral aspects of language teaching. In 1952, with a gift from the Ford Foundation, the English Language Educational Council (ELEC) was created. Several U.S. linguists played key parts in the development of ELEC; namely, Charles C. Fries and Freeman Twaddell, among others. They were responsible for the wide introduction of the "oral approach" into Japanese education. Because this activity coincided with the development and availability of inexpensive tape recorders, so that recorded native-speaker models became readily available, the oral approach became entrenched. Both IRLT and ELEC provided regular conferences and workshops to train teachers and to enhance in-service education. More recently, such organizations as JACET (Japanese Association of College English Teachers) and JALT (Japanese Association of Language Teachers, an affiliate of international TESOL) have taken over much of the activity of conducting conferences to introduce new developments in the field and of providing workshops for training teachers.

Evaluation Policy

The Ministry of Education has long sponsored an English proficiency test (*Eiken*) designed to provide information internally within the educational system and externally to the business world by identifying individuals deemed to be proficient in English, but technically, this test is seriously flawed. Furthermore, it is actually independent of the methodologies and materials used in English language teaching.

In more recent years, both the educational and the business sectors have begun to use the U.S.-based Test of English as a Foreign Language (TOEFL), and the Test of English for International Communication (TOEIC), as well as the U.K.-based International English Language Testing Service (IELTS) battery. Although more valid and prestigious, these international tests have no connection with the methods and materials used in EFL teaching in Japan.

The test required of aspiring teachers, because it is prepared and administered in different localities, is neither valid nor reliable in a technical sense. Hence, there is no reliable evaluation of foreign language outcomes.

Resourcing Policy

Japan's gross domestic product (GDP) (as of 1998) was $2,903 trillion (U.S. dollars) with a per capita figure of $23,100 (U.S. dollars). Education is largely subsidized by the government, although private schools at all levels (including *juku*) that charge tuition have been developing. It is unclear what proportion of the education budget is spent directly on language education, on the training of language teachers, and on language assessment. Japanese education is a very large enterprise, completely funded and controlled by the Ministry of Education. Thus, the percentage of GDP allocated to various aspects of education, including language education, must be substantial.

LANGUAGE-IN-EDUCATION CULTIVATION PLANNING

Language Maintenance

In Japan, there is no recognition of the need for any language except Japanese. It is, absolutely, the majority language. Officially, there are no minority languages. There are substantial populations of speakers of Korean and Chinese, as well as a small population of Ainu; in recent years substantial numbers of migrant workers have arrived in Japan from Bangladesh, Brazil, the Middle East, Nepal, Pakistan, and the Philippines, not to mention Australia, the United Kingdom, and the United States. There is, however, no state support for the teaching of minority languages, and there is little probability that such programs for the children of foreign workers will be established in the near future.

At the same time, it must be recognized that Japan is a polydialectal society (Kaplan & Baldauf, 2003; Yamada, 1992).[1] From the Meiji period until the mid-1970s, there was a perceived need to establish both a national means of communication accessible to all and a unified sense of national identity. The state language policy promoted the national language (*kokugo*)[2] and the eradication of local dialects (*hogen*). A reversal of policy occurred in the mid-1970s, and the new policy has continued through the 1980s and 1990s. Recent Ministry prescriptions for the teaching of *kokugo* at primary and secondary level explicitly state that children should learn to understand the differences between their local dialects and *kokugo* and should learn to use each appropriately in speech, according to setting and circumstances; the common language is always to be used for written work. There is no groundswell to preserve local dialects; on the contrary, dialect revival remains largely at the level of "hometown song festivals and novelty key-rings" (Tokugawa Munemasa, cited in Carroll, 2001, p. 203). Bidialectal teaching is not endorsed; indeed, the school emphasis lies largely in tolerance of local dialects. The assumption is that students will learn local dialects at home; however, the nearly century-long dialect eradication effort has succeeded, and parents brought up in that environment do not have the local dialects nor do children learn the dialects at home or in the community (Carroll, 2001). (A notable exception is Okinawan, which has persisted and which is passed on intergenerationally.) Thus, instead of replacing dialects with the standard common language, code-switching has become the ideal (Shibatani, 1990, p. 187).

Language Reacquisition

In Japan there is currently some interest in revivifying Ainu. The impoverished and outnumbered Ainu were turned into Japanese Imperial subjects in the period of militarization; the nation needed their services in the army during World War II, and to serve in the military it was essential that they spoke Japanese. The Ainu language has only recently been recognized as an area worthy of study (see e.g., DeChicchis, 1995; Maher, 1997). Ainu is essentially a dead language, although there is a community of some 15,000 Ainu people living largely in Hokaido as well as some 1,500 in southern Sakhalin Island (Russia). There are virtually no native speakers left, and the few remaining are very elderly. The best that can be hoped for in this context is an historical preservation, or possibly a small population of second-language speakers of Ainu in a context in which the language has an extremely limited number of registers. Only in very recent years has there been action to recognize the Ainu people; Ainu culture can now be taught, but only to Ainu people. The Ainu language is not included in the school curriculum.

Foreign/Second Language Learning

In Japan, since the U.S. occupation (1945–1952), the foreign language most widely taught has been English. More than 95% of all age groups in junior and senior high school study English, although foreign language study is not required. The study of Chinese, French, German, and other foreign languages is conducted primarily at the tertiary level, although the study of Classical Chinese is available as an elective in senior high school, but is considered part of Japanese language education. The objective of foreign language education is stated in the directives of the Ministry of Education:

> To foster a positive attitude towards mastery of a foreign language among learners, help them become good speakers of a foreign language, and enhance their understanding of foreign countries by developing their interest in language and culture both at home and abroad (Shimaoka, 1999, p. 90; see discussion under curriculum policy).

Language Shift

In a country like Japan, in which complete control of the educational system is vested in the Ministry of Education, and in which the objectives of government are based on a perceived need to establish both a national means of communication accessible to all and a unified sense of national identity, the state language policy necessarily promoted the national language (*kokugo*). Given the persistence of these practices for more than a century (1868–1978), and the addition after 1926 of the powerful support of *Nippon Hôsô Kyôkai*—Japan Broadcasting Corporation (NHK; Carroll, 1995), the outcome was predictable; that is, a population highly literate in the national language to the exclusion of local dialects and foreign languages. As Twine (1991) has noted:

> Leaders gradually came to recognize that what was needed in the wake of the tremendous social upheavals following the Meiji Restoration was the fashioning and refining of that

language into an instrument which would serve the nation both as a means of achieving its various planned reforms and as a focus of national pride. (p. 9)

The Ministry of Education is also vested in the notion that the teaching of Japanese reading and writing should precede the study of foreign languages. The idea of Japan as a homogeneous society is a popular one, particularly in the discourse of those considered *nihonjinran* (a group dedicated to the preservation and purity of the Japanese language). Part of this widespread notion is the idea that becoming fluent in any other language makes one "less Japanese"; an idea implicating subtractive bilingualism (Kaplan, 2000).

LANGUAGE-IN-EDUCATION PLANNING IN SWEDEN

Language-in-education planning in Sweden has a long history that Winsa (2000, p. 108) argues has been underpinned by sociopolitical and ideological motives, rather than by pedagogical objectives. As a society that has viewed itself as lying on the periphery of the Continent—the real Europe that provides the source of high culture—Swedish language policy has been "based on access to international communication, control of communities speaking languages/vernaculars other than Swedish, the influence of theology and religious ideologies, the development of the society and the institutionalisation of education and knowledge." Thus, despite the fact that Sweden has no monolingual constitutional requirement, Swedish is the only de facto national language (except more recently for Sami in the Sami Parliament) and the official spoken standard is that of the well-educated living in the capital region.

For centuries, language planning has been the basis for gaining political control of various language groups in Sweden. During the 17th century when the Swedish empire was at its greatest extent, the Swedish kings controlled Finland, the Baltic States, the coastal parts of western Russia, the northern part of Germany and some former Danish provinces in the south, and Danish-Norwegian provinces in the west. These areas included 14 spoken languages plus a greater number of varieties and at least 7 sanctioned written languages. This diversity probably encouraged a strong interest in standardization of high Swedish and lead to the use of a sociopolitical diglossia, which excluded the use of local vernaculars from official domains and public institutions, as a means of subjugating the various language communities (Winsa, 2000). However, by 1809 all these outlying areas had been lost, and the territorial basis for modern Sweden was formed.

With the coming of the Protestant Reformation, the vernacular Bible and the Swedish language was used to spread the faith, and this use across various communities contributed to the gradual standardization of high Swedish. By the end of the 17th century, the Lutheran Church had launched a literacy campaign, supported by a Church Law in 1686 that mandated that no illiterate was allowed to take Holy Communion and no unconfirmed person was allowed to marry, a policy leading to high levels of community literacy (in Swedish). The establishment of formal schools—grammar schools in 1571 and cathedral (secondary schools) from 1611 (although mainly for the upper classes)—also shifted language use toward the high variety at the expense of Danish and Swedish dialect varieties in the south and minority languages like Sami or Finnish in the north. Although Swedification began much later in the northern part of the country, the exclusion of Sami and Finish from education and the public sector meant that an outsider "would hardly notice that the area is trilingual" (Winsa, 2000, p. 153).

In the 1950s, Sweden experienced the beginnings of a large influx of immigrants and by the 1990s there were a million resident immigrants (over 12% of the country's population). Since 1965, the teaching of Swedish as a Second language (Sw2) has been provided as a right for all immigrants. In 1975, the constitution was changed to include a paragraph that stated that the cultures of linguistic, religious, and ethnic minorities should be promoted, and, thus, bilingualism was officially supported. Since 1977, programs of Mother Tongue Instruction (MTI) (later called home language instruction) have been available, but these are voluntary and currently in decline. Since the 1990s, these programs have been shifted from the central government to the municipalities, who have been able to define their own policies and amount of funding for MTI. Despite this apparent support for multilingualism and these liberal pronouncements and programs that speak of "integration," Winsa (2000, p. 194) characterizes Swedish language policy as assimilationist. Many Swedes still have a monolingual cultural identity—as distinguished from their acceptance of the need for a multilingual foreign language capacity—and this puts continuing pressure to assimilate on both traditional minority and immigrant language users. This recent activity has been influenced by Sweden's desire to be included in the European Union and by the political requirements of such membership.

LANGUAGE-IN-EDUCATION POLICY

Access Policy

Sweden provides free and open access to its educational system, and 9 years of attendance (until age 16) is required. A 3-year program of senior secondary school is optional, but it is estimated that about 98% of students voluntarily continue their studies. Although funding for places in higher education has some limits, about 30% of students attend a Swedish college or university within 5 years of high school graduation (Nuwer, 2002). In terms of languages, Swedish or Sw2 are required of students throughout their schooling, whereas English can begin as early as preschool, but is required from mid-elementary school. A modern language may also start in preschool, but is required in junior secondary school. An additional modern language may also be added in junior secondary school. MTI is available throughout the school years, depending on the options available or selected. Those options, simplified from Lainio (2000) for this discussion, allow students, especially those taking Finnish, to engage with the language in a number of different ways (i.e., as MTI, as a language choice, as a secondary school language option). As Fig. 55.1 indicates, languages are an important part of the curriculum, and eligibility and requirements at the school level depend on such things as funding, teacher availability, or number of students available (e.g., five for most MTI groups) to make a class group.

At the tertiary level, the language of instruction is usually Swedish, but much of the literature for courses is in English. However, in the sciences, in prestige areas, for research degrees, and particularly at the post-graduate level, English is becoming more widespread, leading to a concern that a Swedish (L)–English (H) diglossia may be developing (Berg, Hult, & King, 2001).

Personnel Policy

Entrance to teaching is well regulated and teachers must study for a 3.5-Year (for lower grades) or 4.5-year (for higher grades) diploma that specifies the specialization and status of the qualification. However, in the fields of minority and immigrant languages "teacher training courses have not met the demands for teachers in the field, so many teachers providing the [MTI] programs are inadequately trained. [MTI] . . . problems are exacerbated by the large number of minority languages in any one school, and in many cases, by the small number of pupils with the same [first language] L1 in a particular area" (Boyd, 1999, p. 74).

```
Age      1   2   3   4   5   6   7   8   9  10  11  12  13  14  15  16  17  18  19
Grade                        Pre  1   2   3   4   5   6   7   8   9   I      II  III
Language

Swedish          ------------------------------------------------------------------?
Swedish L2            (------------)-------------------------------------------------?
English               (------------)(---------------)---------------------------------?
Modern Lang 1              (----------------------------)-----------------------------?
Modern Lang 2*                                          (-----)(----------------------? )
MTI³        ((---------------------)(-----------)(-------------------)(---------------)(---------- ? ))
```

-----?   Compulsory, or must legally be offered when chosen.
(-------) Optional, during one or more years, need not be offered.
(----?) Optional, till year X.
((-----)) Optional through the whole school program.
* May involve additional study of English or Sw2.

FIG. 55.1. Language options and eligibility for minority and majority language instruction in Swedish public schools. Adapted from Lainio (2000). "The Protection and Rejection of Minority Language in the Swedish School System," *Current Issues in Language and Society*, 7, 32–50.

Curriculum Policy

The teaching of languages has quite clear objectives. First, all students are meant to become fluent in Swedish so they can fully participate in Swedish society. Second, the curriculum also seeks to develop a sound technical knowledge of English as a spoken and written lingua franca for international communication. Students must also develop either mother tongue language skills (where appropriate) or study one or two additional foreign languages as part of their compulsory schooling.

Methodology and Materials Policy

Sweden has chosen to adopt a formal standardized curriculum from preschool through compulsory school up to Grade 9, with national syllabi and formalized educational objectives. The municipalities have some freedom to decide how the objectives are implemented, and no particular teaching method is required (Nuwer, 2002). Lainio (2000) indicates that second language teaching methodology (unspecified) has become a common approach to teaching Swedish in many municipalities because many classes contain speakers of very mixed background. He adds, however, that such second language (L2) teaching is "low prestige among politicians and parents, and to some extent, teachers of other subjects, who are unaware of the importance of L2 instruction" (p. 45). Parents have yet to be convinced of the benefits of bilingual education. The introduction of English for all, with it greater emphasis on communication, has also had an impact on the teaching of foreign languages, moving them away from the grammar-translation notions that previously underpinned foreign language study.

Evaluation Policy

Although municipalities are fully responsible and accountable for educational decisions, the National Agency for Education (NAE) is responsible for school accreditation and standards from preschool through high school. To ensure quality outcomes, pupils are evaluated on the required curriculum (including languages) in their 5th and 9th years of compulsory schooling and the NAE tracks educational development in districts, provides consultancy help, disseminates results, supports research, etc. (Nuwer, 2002).

Resourcing Policy

In line with the importance given to education, education in state schools is free at every level from preschool to university, subject to some restrictions related to age (beyond 45 at university) and length of time for Sw2 instructional programs and for university degrees. For compulsory schooling (Grades 1 to 9), school-related expenses are also paid. Although the state schools are of very high quality, since the law was changed in 1992 about 3% of pupils have chosen to attend private schools in Sweden (some of which are language-and/or ethnic-based schools, including a number of Finnish bilingual schools), mainly in urban areas. A voucher system requires municipalities to pay 75% of the average per pupil cost to these schools, as long as the schools meet state-mandated NAE requirements (Cabau-Lampa, 1999; Nuwer, 2002).

Educational support for immigrants is based on the premise that they should have the same access to educational entitlements as the native-born population, with some additional resources being provided to support linguistic and cultural choice. In theory, immigrants can maintain their language (through MTI) and culture or adopt Swedish norms. Free adult classes in Swedish are also provided. These support policies apply quite widely to anyone born abroad or who has a parent born abroad (Boyd, 1999).

Community Policy

Historically, education, whether by the state or the church, has been very centralized and not consultative. Although the current syllabus and programs are very top-down in some respects in their implementation, the NAE encourages the input of parents, and surveys of stakeholders (parents, teachers/administrators, students) are taken to ascertain changes in attitudes and satisfaction/dissatisfaction with the Swedish school system (Nuwer, 2002). MTI programs and the more recent ability to open private schools has also provided minority and immigrant language speakers with choices related to language and cultural studies.

LANGUAGE-IN-EDUCATION CULTIVATION PLANNING

Language Maintenance

Standard Swedish is the predominant language of the country and is in some respects gaining in its dominance, although some believe the continued growth of English poses a long-term threat. The general trend in the minority communities in Sweden is a rapid decline in the number of bilingual speakers (there are few if any non-Swedish monolingual speakers) with second-or third-generation Swedish-Finns, the largest minority community, being Swedish-dominant or Swedish-only users. Although there are MTI programs available to support minority language maintenance, participation rates in them are in general declining. The European Union is also having an increasing impact on language maintenance. Although there is an increased requirement to support minority and immigrant languages and the availability of EU funding for projects, the European structures also create a new layer of supra-national languages that are important to learn—hence, the relatively recent requirement for all students to learn a foreign language other than English. Although that foreign language may be a minority or immigrant language, in general this development has disadvantaged the maintenance of smaller and minority languages.

Language Reacquisition

Language reacquisition is not a priority in Sweden. Winsa (2000) reports that most non-mutually intelligible varieties of Swedish are now extinct and only a small number of people speak the remaining varieties. There was a small revival effort in the 1960s, but it did not gain wide acceptance, perhaps because there were no media models or obvious situations for using such language varieties. Some local school plans stress local varieties, but the aim seems to be to strengthen local identity rather than to reintroduce the varieties.

MTI programs are meant to support maintenance, rather than reacquisition, of languages like Sami or Meänkieli/Finnish. Although bilingual schooling, cross-border contacts, and better status for these languages in northern Sweden provides some hope of their maintenance and/or reacquisition, many of the five Sami languages, in particular, are endangered and are becoming relics of identity. The Sami Parliament has not given language issues a high priority. In these circumstances, only North Sami, the predominant variety in Norway, seems likely to survive. Meänkieli/Finnish is also in decline, both in domains of use and in numbers of speakers.

Boyd (1999) points out that one of the major problems with MTI—whether in Sw2, minority, or immigrant languages—is that "much of the instruction in the compulsory school [Grades 1–9] . . . has been organized along the lines of remedial education, requiring pupils to leave their regular classes for one or more lessons a week. L1 instruction has taken place primarily after school hours, when children are tired and have other activities that compete with it (p. 74)." Both pedagogically and attitudinally, such provision undermines MTI.

Foreign/Second Language Learning

English is the dominant foreign language taught in Sweden, taking over from German that dominated until the end of World War II (German remains the next largest foreign language studied). Since 1962, English has been a compulsory subject for all pupils in schools, thus democratizing languages, moving them away from being a grammar and translation-based subject for the elite. In 1994, students were required to study an additional language (i.e., French, German, or Spanish) except for foreign born or minority students who were able to elect to study their first language. In their final year of compulsory schooling and in upper secondary school, pupils may elect to learn a third foreign language or take additional studies in one of the languages they are already studying (Cabau-Lampa, 1999).

Language Shift

As the brief overview of Swedish history indicates, the religious bureaucracy and government policy has, over a long period of time, encouraged the use of standard high Swedish by making it the only language of religion, government, and government institutions. Although the formal coercion to shift to Swedish has disappeared (and has been replaced by formal support for minority languages), underlying community attitudes do not seem to have changed, nor are there opportunities to use these languages or varieties. There is, therefore, a continuing shift to Swedish as the dominant language and a shift to use English more widely for a variety of purposes.

LANGUAGE-IN-EDUCATION PLANNING IN NORTH KOREA

Ideally, as noted in the introduction, language-in-education policy ought to be a product of national language policy. In the real world, this relationship rarely occurs, and language-in-education policy often constitutes a stand-alone, singular effort to plan language. In North Korea, this "ideal" situation exists, and events in North Korea demonstrate the potential dangers that such an all-encompassing approach can have.

North Korea as an independent political entity came into existence on August 15, 1948, after the defeat of the Japanese who had occupied Korea until 1945 and the failure of the subsequent reunification talks between the USSR, the United States, the United Kingdom, and the two Koreas. From that time to the present, the government of North Korea has undertaken official, sustained, conscious efforts to shape the Korean language to the political needs of a socialist state. The government has accepted the sociopolitical value of a national language as the major means for implementing socialist policy and for directing the thinking and behavior of the populace. Obviously, the language served as well to represent the will of the Party to the citizenry. Language planning at the highest levels of government was directed by the objectives of socialist state-building. National language policy gave rise to language-in-education policy.

It has been argued that language policy development in postwar North Korea may be roughly divided into three periods: The Preparation Period (1945–1953), The Transition Period (1954–1963), and The *Munhwae* (Cultured Language) Period (1964 to the present)—these titles obviously assigned after the fact. The Preparation Period was most clearly characterized by a massive national literacy campaign. In 1945, some 30% of the population was believed to be illiterate in any language. In order to solve the perceived problem—that is, the elimination of illiteracy—in November 1947 the Peoples' Committee (later the North Korean Peoples' Committee) adopted the Winter Illiteracy Eradication Movement in Rural Areas, a 4-month long program running from December 1947 to March 1948. The government decreed that all persons between 12 and 50 years of age would participate. A second campaign followed immediately on the heels of the first. The entire population was involved either as teachers or as learners. Special night classes were mounted in every workplace and village. The Youth Organization, the Women's League, and the Peasant's League were mobilized. Although primary emphasis was placed on literacy, the program also offered an ideal opportunity for ideological education as well. Simultaneously, the government mounted the Movement for Total Ideological Mobilization for Founding the Nation. The government claimed that it had achieved total literacy within 4 years (i.e., by 1949).

In order to achieve total literacy, the language needed to be simplified, because the learning of the Hangul alphabet was one thing, but the learning of thousands of Chinese characters was quite another. Thus, the government initiated a program to eliminate Chinese characters from the language. This activity turned out to be more complex than literacy education and ideological training, and the campaign spilled over into the second period. (As previously discussed, a similar undertaking occurred in Japan from the time of the Meiji restoration.)

Following the Korean War cease fire in July 1953, language planning (intended "to mobilize everything for economic reconstruction of the socialist fatherland") became an essential part of the comprehensive national rehabilitation programs under the Three-Year Economic Rehabilitation and Development Plan (1954–1956). The objective of this activity was to standardize the language, an activity that was seen to require the promulgation of a grammar and a dictionary and the promulgation of standard rules for the *Romanization of Korean and the Koreanization of Foreign Words.* This period saw the production of:

- *Korean Orthography (Cosene chelcapep)*, disseminated in 1954.
- *Writing Loan Words (Oylaye phyokipep)* in 1956/1958.
- *Korean Language Grammar 1 (Cosene munpep 1)* in 1960.
- *Korean Dictionary (Cosenmal sacen)* in 1960/1962.

The transition that is recognized in the name of the period was a transition from *old* Korean (i.e., the Korean of the colonial period [i.e., the Japanese occupation] and of the variety used in the South) to the *new* Korean (i.e., a variety permitting the language to function as a socialist cultural weapon).

In 1963, the term meaning *cultured nature and attitude* (*munhwaseng*) was introduced as the most important element for the Korean language standard; this term quickly became simply *cultured language* (*munhwae*)—the name given to standard Korean by Kim Il Sung in 1966. This third period was significantly concerned with intellectualization (modernization) of the language—that is, with prestige planning. It is interesting to note the gradual migration of interpretation from "the modern speech of the middle class in Seoul," to "modern speech most commonly spoken by Koreans" to "the language of workers and revolutionaries in Pyongyang." This meaning migration defines the enormous language planning work conducted in the North in the 2 decades between 1945 and 1965. That work involved both corpus planning and status planning. All of this preliminary activity came to fruition in the third period—one that exploited intellectualization and modernization.

Kim Il Sung's leader's words (*kyosi*—literally, "enlightened teaching") from his speeches in the mid-1960s and thereafter became the ultimate rationale for all subsequent language planning activity in North Korea. (See, especially, Kim, 1977.)

- Kim believed people of the same racial makeup, the same culture, living in the same territory, could not be considered a nation if they spoke different languages—thus, the need for a *nationalistic*, *pure* standard.
- He further held that people speaking the same language but living under different political systems can be seen as belonging to the same nation—thus, leaving open an opportunity for reunification of the two Koreas.
- He reversed the earlier total proscription of Chinese characters on the grounds that they continued to be used in the South, and, thus, that banning them would remove one of the common bonds between the two Koreas—again leaving open an opportunity for reunification of the two Koreas.[3]
- He defined the teaching of Chinese characters as part of foreign language education and banned their use in national language classes and in school textbooks—a case of having your cake and eating it, too.
- He severely criticised South Korean language practices on the grounds that influences from Chinese, Japanese, and English were allow to coexist with Korean, thereby threatening the eventual extinction of Korean.
- He further criticised South Korean for the undemocratic gap between spoken and written language resulting from a skewed distribution of power.
- He also criticised South Korean as sexist because it retained features that marked women as subordinate to men.

On the bases of these views, Kim steered Korean language planning, insisting that the first principle of developing *Munhwae* was that the language must be nationalistic (including words deriving from dialects of Korean, which were seen as a rich source of *pure* lexicon).

LANGUAGE-IN-EDUCATION POLICY

Access Policy

In North Korea, national language planning activity has dominated the language-in-education planning process. The objective was to produce socialist equality within the population and to eliminate the intellectual class. It was, therefore, essential to involve the entire population. That objective was introduced in the early literacy campaigns, in which all persons between 12 and 50 years of age were simply required to participate. The entire population was involved either as teachers or as learners—that is, college students and teachers became literacy teachers and special schooling for adults was provided at every level of the societal structure. At present, all children are required to attend 11 years of basic education. Advanced educational opportunities are determined by the needs of the state. But the language policy did not extend only to Hangul; in December 1946, the Preliminary Peoples' Committee also mandated Russian language schools in major cities, and by 1948 the study of Russian was made compulsory at middle school level. All upper level officials of the Party were required to be fluent in Russian. English, of course, was banned at the time of the Korean War. Kim later changed his mind as he came to see that the time for one worldwide socialist state had not yet come. He was disillusioned by the Sino-Soviet disputes based on national interest rather than socialist principle. In 1964, the North Korean Workers' Party issued an edict promoting foreign language education, and English was introduced into the secondary school curriculum on a 50/50 basis with Russian, students having no say in the choice. By 1980, English had become the undisputed foreign language with 80% of students studying it. In 1992, following the collapse of the USSR, Russian was completely eliminated from the curriculum, and English became the only mandated foreign language taught.

Personnel Policy

In North Korea, as previously noted, teachers for the masses were drawn initially from the ranks of college students and teachers. Over time, teacher education became more institutionalized; at present, teachers are trained at the Institute of Higher Education and Kim Hyong Juk Advanced Teacher-training College.[4] However, the first criterion for every teacher was party loyalty. To a large extent, the system operated on the assumption that education is a political activity and any (educated) native speaker is a competent teacher. Teaching Hangul required acceptance of the linguistic criteria laid down in the dictionaries, grammars, and orthographies produced essentially between 1950 and 1980. In the earlier period, when Russian was a compulsory foreign language, Russian teachers were imported from the Soviet Union. Some foreign languages are currently taught, but they are taught by Korean citizens rather than by imported native speakers. Chinese characters are taught in foreign language courses by Korean citizens; because Chinese characters were initially purged from North Korean Hangul and subsequently reinstated at the specified number of 3,000, widespread teaching of Chinese characters has not been necessary.[5] Ironically, although English has become the most popular foreign language, it too is taught by North Korean teachers.

Curriculum Policy

The early need for rapid transition to full literacy was coupled with patriotic (nationalistic) and socialist dogma. The use of Hangul-only as the language of government, education, and cultural activities was made mandatory. One of the purposes of extensive lexical activity was to standardize and codify words that had been introduced during a decade of socialist state development (e.g., 'workers' party,' 'people's army,' 'people's front,' 'people's economy,' 'people's liberation war,' and 'soviet') and to alter the meanings of other words (e.g., 'capitalist,' which took on all of the negative semantic connotations common in socialist literature), all based on Marxist/Leninist principles (Kim, 1977). Kim Il Sung insisted that future dictionaries must be based on the principle of self-reliance; thus, in so far as possible, rejecting foreign words and replacing them with "native" words. The idea of basic lexicon on the principle of the speech of the people (*inminseng*) was accepted in order to achieve the unification of speech and writing and to promulgate easily understood and quickly accepted words in place of difficult foreign items. The first principle of developing *Munhwae* was that it must be nationalistic (including words deriving from dialects of Korean, which were seen as a rich source of 'pure' lexicon). That first principle necessitated purification—the removal of 'foreign' influences. Language curriculum (without reference to the language being taught) served to inculcate communist ideology.[6] In practice, the State Education Commission draws up both long- and short-term plans for the promulgation of educational policy and for the development of teaching materials. The State Academy for Research in Education develops educational programs and teaching materials that are subsequently published by the State's educational publishing houses, subject to final approval by the State Education Commission. Changes in textbooks are developed by the National Commission for the Revision of Textbooks, again subject to approval by the Commission (Chang, 1994).

Methodology and Materials Policy

North Korea is so tightly closed a society that published materials take a long time to reach the outside world, if they ever do. North Korea is an "impenetrable society with a totally controlled press [and substantial] restrictions on travel in and out of the country" (Cumings, 1990, p. 53). It should come as no great surprise that little has been published on the North Korean educational system, let alone on language teaching. (There is a 1990 study of education in North Korea (Huh, 1990, cited in Jae, 2002), but it is in Hangul and neither available to nor readable by the authors of this chapter.) Although materials are not accessible, it is possible to speculate that English (or any other foreign language for that matter) is not taught to achieve communicative competence. As Jae (2002) points out, "[l]essons on grammatical rules, pronunciation, and the like—never mind pragmatics of sociolinguistic conventions—take a back seat to lessons on ideology. Moreover, North Korea's English textbooks give priority to the *Juche*[7] ideology over such topics as the English-speaking peoples and their culture (p. 50)." As Baik and Shim (1995) suggest, North Korean secondary English textbooks are written in order to embellish the reality in North Korea and to totally distort reality outside North Korea to legitimize and maintain the present regime. Thus, although it is impossible to discuss method or materials in any detail, it is possible to speculate about the intent and more immediate objectives of language instruction. The methodology is probably a mixture of grammar-translation and an early version of audiolingualism. The intent is political indoctrination in the socialist ideology of the state.

Evaluation Policy

Given that little is known about assessment policy in North Korea, and given that education in foreign languages appears to be independent of communicative competence, it seems possible to speculate that assessment policy as such is perhaps rather slight and probably highly conventional. It is also possible to speculate that the material tested covers state policy rather than language structure. With respect to the teaching of Korean, it is again possible to speculate that assessment is perhaps notional. There is no indication that writing as a distinct skill is taught. Pronunciation, grammar, and reading are perhaps taught and assessed conventionally. Thus, if there is a connection between methods and materials on the one hand and assessment on the other, that connection is not transparent. In practice, evaluation consists of "discovering whether the pupil's education by the teacher . . . is properly conducted" (Chang, 1994, p. 3159). There is a final secondary examination, constructed by municipal and district education committees.

Resourcing Policy

Little is known about the details of the development of the North Korean national budget. GDP, as of the most recent available figures (1998), is $21.8 billion (U.S. dollars) GDP per capita is $1,000 (U.S. dollars) and the rate of growth is 5%—as compared with South Korea, GDP $584.7 billion (U.S. dollars; 12 times as great), GDP per capita $12,600 (U.S. dollars; 12 times as great), rate of growth 6.8%—placing North Korea among the world's poorest nations. But North Korea has the largest standing military in the world, and it has reportedly suffered greatly from shortages of food resulting from drought and other natural causes. Given this situation, and given the understanding that language education is an important part of government policy, it is possible to assume that language education is relatively high on the list of governmental priorities, but that resources available are significantly constrained. Chang (1994, p. 3158) reports that the North Korean government has funded education over a 11-year period as suggested in the following:

Government expenditure on education in 1,000s of won [estimated average rate of exchange over the period 1.00 (U.S. dollar)] = 2.1 won

1. 20,333,000	Educational grants in the amount of $7,524 (U.S. dollars) on
2. 22,203,600	average cover the cost of education from K to
3. 24,018,600	university; in 1991 an average grant for a primary
4. 26,158,000	school student was $163 (U.S. dollars) for a high school
5. 27,328,830	student $199 (U.S. dollars) and for a university student
6. 28,396,000	$476 (U.S. dollars) per year. If average income may be
7. 30,085,100	estimated at $1,000 (U.S. dollars) per year, the grants are
8. 31,660,900	substantial. However, compared to educational
9. 33,382,940	expenditures in other countries, the investment
10. 35,513,480	in education by the North Korean government
11. 36,909,240	is not impressive.

The percentage expended on foreign language education, or for that matter on the teaching of the national language, is unknown.

LANGUAGE-IN-EDUCATION CULTIVATION PLANNING

Language Maintenance

In North Korea, only one language really counts: The North Korean version of Korean, as written in revised Hangul. From the 1950s, the government has promoted the exclusive use of Hangul in all sectors of the society. It has purged Chinese characters (but not completely), it has revised the syntax of the language, the orthography of the language, and the lexicon. In the lexicon it has purged all vestiges of the Japanese occupation, it has purged all vestiges of the benighted capitalist perceptions, and it has created new lexicon along socialist lines as well as supportive of the cult of adulation of Kim Il Sung. The "sanitized" version has been consistently perceived as a powerful tool for the achievement of the socialist policies of the government. There are no minority languages, so it hasn't been necessary to deal with problems arising from competing languages. Regional varieties of Korean (North Korean dialects) have been, on the one hand, seen as sources of authentic Korean lexicon, whereas, on the other hand, they have been seen as requiring standardization and assimilation into the "national" variety. Foreign languages, discussed in the following, have played only a relatively minor role in language planning.

Language Reacquisition

As noted previously, North Korea is monolingual. No other languages hold any status; indeed, there aren't any competing languages. It is important to note that, contrary to trends elsewhere (e.g., the European Union), the government has diligently striven to create a monumentally monolingual society with a single objective. Because language is perceived as a tool of socialist state building, other languages are of no consequence except as they contribute to the basic principle. Although foreign languages are taught, they are taught for political purposes—as exemplified in the bit of text cited in endnote 7 "we learn English [or any other language] for our revolution." Thus, the competing demands faced by language planning bodies in other polities are irrelevant in North Korea.

Foreign/Second Language Learning

In the early stages of the development of North Korea, Russian was the only foreign language available and learning it was mandatory. Russian language schools were established in major cities, and by 1948, the study of Russian was made compulsory at middle school level. All upper level officials of the Party were required to be fluent in Russian. But, as Kim Il Sung became disillusioned with the Soviet Union, especially after the death of Stalin in 1953, Russian lost its place and was gradually replaced by English. In 1964, the North Korean Workers' Party issued an edict promoting foreign language education, and English was introduced into the secondary school curriculum on a 50/50 basis with Russian. By 1980, English had become the undisputed first foreign language with 80% of students studying it. In 1992, following the collapse of the USSR, Russian was completely removed from the curriculum, and English became the only mandated foreign language taught. English was introduced on the rationale that it was necessary for access to science and technology but, in actual fact, it has not served that end to any significant extent. As Baik (cited in Jae, 2002) has pointed out, "it is extremely doubtful—North Korea being arguably the most tightly controlled country in the world—that foreign materials in English, scientific or otherwise, are freely imported into the country and then made readily available to the general public (p. 49)." English—indeed, all foreign languages—are taught by North Korean teachers. Knowledge of 3,000 Chinese characters is required of all students through foreign language courses taught by North Korean teachers. In addition, Chinese as a foreign language is gaining in popularity. Aside from English and Chinese, it is possible to study French, German, or Japanese.

Language Shift

In North Korea, there has been a shift to literacy and to increasing monolingualism. First literacy and subsequently the "revised" *Munhwae* (Cultured Language)—a product of Kim Il Sung's thought—were imposed on the North Korean people through the total mobilization of the social structure including the Youth Organization, the Women's League, and the Peasant's League. As a consequence, the entire population of North Korea has been shaped into a monumentally monolingual society with a single objective. All other dialects of Korean spoken in North Korea have been extinguished. Foreign language learning is rigorously controlled by the state. Because of the restructuring of Hangul in the North, some Korean linguists are concerned that the variety employed in the South and that employed in the North are gradually becoming mutual incomprehensible.

CONCLUSIONS

The three illustrative case studies included in this chapter provide concrete instances of how the policy and planning aspects of language-in-education policy and planning goals are implemented in these polities. Had space permitted, it would have been possible to examine the powerful impact that language-in-education planning has had in other parts of the world; for example, in Côte d'Ivoire (Djité, 2000) where the requirement to use French in schools has limited the development of Popular French and autochthonous languages; in Finland (Latomaa & Nuolijärvi, 2002) where language-in-education programs support Finnish–Swedish bilingualism and access to a wide range of foreign languages; in Israel (Spolsky & Shohomy, 1999) where Hebrew has been revived to create a national language, but where Arabic is taught in schools and the demand for English is increasing; in Paraguay (Gynan, 2001) where Spanish and Guarani bilingualism and education have been the battle ground between the political left and right; in South Africa (Kamwangamalu, 2001) where teaching African languages in schools, that served apartheid by denying access to Afrikaans and English, is now struggling to be revalorized to support equity and identity; or in Tunisia (Daoud, 2001) where Arabicization in schools has to contend with the problem of multiple standards of the language as well as the strong colonial language French and an increasingly attractive English.

From these and other instances of language-in-education policy, a number of more general issues are implicated for language-in-education goals, including:

- Political nature of goal selection process (also see, Baldauf & Kaplan, 2003).
- Lack of professional language and literacy input to policy or planning goals (also see, van Els, chap. 53, this volume).
- Lack of community consultation or input in most language-in-education decisions.
- Focus of attention on national languages and their development.
- Standardization effects of teaching (national) languages through schools.
- General lack of support for language maintenance for minority languages or dialects.
- Active suppression of some languages or varieties and/or the failure to support the continued use or acquisition of others (also see May, chap. 57, this volume).
- Impact of institutional use (e.g., established churches, religious use) on language choice.
- Continued prominence of former colonial languages.
- Increasing impact of English on educational systems.
- Inadequacy of training for many teachers (both in terms of language and methods).
- Problem of adequately funding language programs to meet individual and societal needs.

These points demonstrate that although language-in-education planning is only one component of language planning, it often plays a central role in language directions and development in polities around the world.

NOTES

1. The main local dialects are Tohoku (Northern Japan), Kanto (Tokyo area), Kan-sai (Kyoto/Osaka area), Shimane/Tottori (Shikoku, Hiroshima, and San-in), Kyushu (Northern Kyushu), Kagoshima (Southern Kyushu), and Okinawan.

2. Dialect differences were mitigated by the use of a generalized variety of Tokyo dialect—spoken *kyootuu-go*, and written *hyoozyuun-go*.
3. As early as 1959, however, students in Grades 8 through 10 learned Chinese characters and Sinitic terms. By 1968, 1,500 characters were required in upper-level middle schools, and an additional 500 characters were required in high-level technical schools. In 1971, a textbook on Chinese writing appeared using 3,323 characters. In 1972, *Kuk-Hanmun Tokbon* (A Mixed-Script Reader) appeared for college students, including 2,000 characters taught in middle and high school and an additional 1,000 characters, the intent being to permit the expression of high-level concepts in modern Korean (Hannas, 1995, p. 255).
4. The Korean educational system consists basically of a 2-year kindergarten (starting at age 4), a 4-year primary school and a 6-year secondary school. (Counting only the second year of kindergarten, the system provides a total 11 years of education.) This system is mandatory and free. Beyond basic education, there is a 4 to 6 year-university system in parallel with a 4-year Institute of Higher Education, and a series of 3-year specialized institutions (i.e., industry, agriculture, fisheries) as well as a 6-year medical school (Chang, 1994).
5. Jae (2002) reports that Chinese seems to be gaining in popularity as a foreign language, but no information appears to be available on the extent of Chinese language education.
6. Jae (2002, p. 50) cited the following example from a secondary English textbook:

> Teacher: Now close your books everybody. Han Il Nam, how do you spell the word *revolution*?
> Student: r-e-v-o-l-u-t-i-o-n.
> Teacher: Very good, thank you. Sit down. Ri Choi Su, what is the Korean [word] for *revolution*?
> Student: *Hyekmyeng*.
> Teacher: Fine, Thank you. Have you any questions? [No questions arise.]
> Teacher: Well, Kim In Su, what do you learn English for?
> Student: For our revolution.
> Teacher: That's right. It's true that we learn English for our revolution.

7. *Juche* may be defined roughly as "self-reliance" as interpreted by Kim Il Sung and proclaimed as party policy in 1955, following Joseph Stalin's death in 1953, as North Korea began to limit its relationship with the USSR and as Kim Il Sung asserted his power and independence. *Juche* forms the guiding ideology of the country—everyone has control over his or her own destiny; accordingly the people are responsible for, and are the prime movers of, the social and economic program of the state. Kim attempted to propagate *Juche* through the Non-Aligned Nations movement in the hope that he would be recognized as a world leader, a genius, a hero, and a statesman.

REFERENCES

Baldauf, R. B., Jr., & Kaplan, R. B. (2003). Language policy decisions and power: Who are the actors? In P. M. Ryan & R. Terborg (Eds.), *Language: Issues of inequality* (pp. 19–37). Mexico City: Universidad Nacional Autónama de México.

Baik, J. M., & Shim, R. J. (1995). Language, culture and ideology in the English textbooks of two Koreas. In M. L. Tickoo (Ed.). *Language, and culture in multilingual societies: Viewpoints and visions* (pp. 43–59). Singapore: SEAMEO Regional Language Center.

Berg, E. C., Hult, F. M., & King, K. A. (2001). Shaping the climate for language shift? English in Sweden's elite domains. *World Englishes, 20*, 305–319.

Boyd, S. (1999). Sweden: Immigrant languages. In B. Spolsky (Ed.), *Concise encyclopedia of educational linguistics* (pp. 73–74). Amsterdam: Elsevier.

Cabau-Lampa, B. (1999). Decisive factors for language teaching in Sweden. *Educational Studies, 25*, 175–186.

Carroll, T. (1995). NHK and Japanese language policy. *Language Problems & Language Planning 19*, 293–271.

Carroll, T. (2001). *Language planning and language change in Japan.* Richmond, Surrey, UK: Curzon.

Chang, G-C. (1994). Korea, Democratic People's Republic of: System of education. In T. Husén & T. N. Postlethwaite (Eds.), *International encyclopedia of education* (2nd Ed., pp. 3155–3158). Exeter, UK: Pergamon.

Cooper, R. L. (1989). Acquisition planning. In *Language planning and social change* (pp. 157–163). Cambridge, UK: Cambridge University Press.

Corson, D. (1999). *Language policy in schools.* Mahwah, NJ: Lawrence Erlbaum Associates.

Coulmas, F. (2002). Language policy in modern Japanese education. In J. W. Tollefson (Ed.), *Language policies in education: Critical issues* (pp. 203–223). Mahwah, NJ: Lawrence Erlbaum Associates.

Cumings, B. (1990). *The two Koreas: On the road to reunification?* New York: Foreign Policy Association.

Daoud, M. (2001). The language situation in Tunisia. *Current Issues in Language Planning, 2*, 1–52.

DeChicchis, J. (1995). The current state of the Ainu language. In J. C. Maher & K. Yashiro (Eds.), *Multilingual Japan: Journal of Multilingual and Multicultural Development, 16*, 103–124.

Djité, P. G. (2000). Language planning in Côte d'Ivoire. *Current Issues in Language Planning, 1,* 11–46.

Gonzalez, A. (2002). Language planning and intellectualization. *Current Issues in Language Planning, 3,* 5–27.

Gynan, S. N. (2001). Language planning and policy in Paraguay. *Current Issues in Language Planning, 2,* 53–118.

Hannas, W. C. (1995). Korea's attempts to eliminate Chinese characters and the implications for Romanizing Chinese. *Language Problems & Language Planning, 19,* 250–270.

Hirakata, F. (1992). Language-spread policy of Japan. *International Journal of the Sociology of Language, 95,* 93–108.

Hornberger, N. H. (Ed.). (2004). Heritage/community language education: U.S. and Australian perspectives. *International Journal of Bilingualism and Bilingual Education.* [Special Issue]

Huh, D-C. (1990). *Kyoyuk kwacheng* [School Curriculum]. In H.-C. Kim (Ed.), *Pwukhanul kyoyuk [Education in North Korea].* Seoul: South Korea Ulyumwunhwasa.

Ingram, D. E. (1989). Language-in-education planning. In R. B. Kaplan (Ed.), *Annual Review of Applied Linguistics, 10: A broad survey of the entire field of applied linguistics* (pp. 53–78). New York: Cambridge University Press.

Jae, J.-S. (2002). The *Juche* ideology: English in North Korea. *English Today, 69,* 47–52.

Kamwangamalu, N. M. (2001). The language planning situation in South Africa. *Current Issues in Language Planning, 2,* 361–445.

Kaplan, R. B. (2000). Language planning in Japan. In L. S. Bautista, T. A. Llamzon, & B. Sibayan (Eds.), *Parangalcang Brother Andrew: Festschrift for Andrew Gonzales on his sixtieth birthday* (pp. 277–287). Manila, The Philippines: Linguistic Society of the Philippines.

Kaplan, R. B., & Baldauf, R. B., Jr. (1997). *Language planning from practice to theory.* Clevedon, UK: Multilingual Matters.

Kaplan, R. B., & Baldauf, R. B., Jr. (2003). *Language and language-in-education planning in the Pacific Basin.* Dordrecht, The Netherlands: Kluwer.

Kim, S. I. (1977). *The thesis on socialist education.* Pyongyang, North Korea.

Lainio, J. (2000). The protection and rejection of minority and majority languages in the Swedish school system. *Current Issues in Language and Society, 7,* 32-50.

Latomaa, S., & Nuolijärvi, P. (2002). The language situation in Finland. *Current Issues in Language Planning, 3,* 95–202.

Liddicoat, A. J., & Bryant, P. (Eds.). (2001). Language planning and language revitalization. *Current Issues in Language Planning, 2*(2&3).

Maher, J. (1997). Linguistic minorities and education in Japan. *Educational Review, 49,* 115–127.

National Language Research Institute. (1998). *An introduction to the National Language Research Institute.* Tokyo: Author.

Neustupný, J. V., & Tanaka, S. (2003). English in Japan: An overview. In V. Makarova (Ed.), *ELT: The case of Japan.* (pp. 3–34) Muenchen, Germany: Lincom Europa.

Nuwer, H. (2002). Sweden. In R. Marlow-Ferguson (Ed.), *World education encyclopedia,* (Vol. 3; pp. 1318–1332). Farmington Hills, MI: Dale Group.

Paulston, C. B., & McLaughlin, S. (1994). Language-in-education policy and planning. In W. Grabe (Ed.), *Annual Review of Applied Linguistics, 14: Language policy and planning* (pp. 53–81). Cambridge, UK: Cambridge University Press.

The Prime Minister's Commission on Japan's Goals in the 21st Century. (2000). *The frontier within: Individual empowerment and better governance in the new millennium.* Retrieved November 18, 2000, at http://www.kantei.go.jp/jp/21century/report/pdfs [In English].

Rhee, M.-J. (1992). Language planning in Korea under Japanese colonial administration. *Language, Culture and Curriculum, 5,* 87–97.

Shibatani, M. (1990). *The languages of Japan.* Cambridge, UK: Cambridge University Press.

Shimaoka, T. (1999). Japanese language education policy. In B. Spolsky (Ed.), *Concise encyclopedia of educational linguistics* (pp. 86–91). Amsterdam: Elsevier.

Spolsky, B., & Shohamy, E. (1999). *The languages of Israel: Policy, ideology and practice.* Clevedon, UK: Multilingual Matters.

Twine, N. (1991). *Language and the modern state: The reform of written Japanese.* London: Routledge.

Unger, J. M. (1996). *Literacy and script reform in occupation Japan: Reading between the lines.* New York: Oxford University Press.

Winsa, B. (2000). Language planning in Sweden. In R. B. Baldauf, Jr. & R. B. Kaplan (Eds.), *Language planning in Nepal, Taiwan and Sweden* (pp. 107–203). Clevedon, UK: Multilingual Matters.

Yamada, Y. (1992). The national language development of Japan. In A. Q. Perez & A. Santiago (Eds.), *Language policy and language development of Asian countries* (pp. 56–72). Manila, The Philippines: Pambansang so Lingguistikang Pilipino.

56

Prestige and Image Planning

Dennis E. Ager
Aston University

INTRODUCTION

Although there has been some discussion of prestige and image planning in the literature during the last 15 years (e.g., Ager, 1999, 2001; Haarmann, 1990; Omar, 1998), it is an area that is not as well developed, described, and understood as the traditional areas of status and corpus planning, or the more recent language-in-education (acquisition) planning. It may, therefore, be useful to begin by examining three examples of what most people accept as image planning. These examples then lead us to think image planning might be, in fact, three separate activities: promoting a language, manipulating image as a method of implementing language policy, and something deeper to do with the motives of language planners themselves. From an examination of each of these activities, we could, hopefully, try to set out the relationship between society, language, and what planners do.

WALES

In the United Kingdom, the 1993 Welsh Language Act, updating the 1967 Act of the same name, set up a Welsh Language Board (WLB) whose main duty would be to plan for the Welsh language in Wales. In 1996, the Board published a strategy document outlining how it intended to promote the language. The document had four sections:

1. Increasing numbers of Welsh speakers.
2. Providing opportunities to use the language.
3. Changing the habits of language use.
4. Strengthening Welsh as a community language.

The first section is clearly about helping the education system to teach Welsh as a second or foreign language; the second about the status of the language; and the fourth has been implemented, among other ways, by setting up *mentrau iaith*, or small groups of amateurs to encourage a whole variety of very local initiatives. The third section is intriguing: It is of a different order. The WLB's overall aim in this section was

1035

to nurture confidence among Welsh speakers, by improving its image, and by seeking to change the linguistic habits of those who use it (Welsh Language Board, 1996).

Knowing that 17.5% of the Welsh population had defined themselves as Welsh speakers in the 1991 Census, and following the traditional marketing sequence, the Board first commissioned a survey to identify attitudes toward Welsh language planning (WLB, 1996). It found that 71% supported using the Welsh language; 88% believed that the language is something to be proud of; there was a widespread consensus (75%) that Welsh and English should have equal status in Wales; 82% believed that bilingual road signs were a good idea; 83% agreed that every public body should be able to deal with people in both Welsh and English alike; and 45% thought that the private sector did not use enough of the Welsh language. Against these signs of goodwill, only 51% believed that Welsh had a future in their own area; 3%, who had been fluent Welsh speakers while at school, had lost the use of the language since that time; confidence in using the language was highest in intimate and domestic circumstances and minimal when contacting bodies such as local councils or the (privatized) utilities. Half the fluent Welsh speakers would fill in the vehicle registration form in English because they thought the English version was clearer. Such attitudes indicate very clearly a lack of confidence in the language and an expectation that its main focus of use would be more and more in the home rather than the public sphere. Yet there was a fund of goodwill that provided a basis for work on influencing feelings and attitudes about Welsh in such a way that hope could be given to its speakers for a broader than domestic future.

The strategy the WLB adopted was to promote the use of the language by young people; to ensure that services could be provided that would use the language; and to influence the media. These considerations led to Objectives 13 to 17 of the Board's strategy, of which Objectives 13 and 14(a) seem to be specifically about image planning, as is the second half of Objective 17:

13. to increase the number of young people who use Welsh naturally as a medium of communication
14. (a) to nurture confidence among Welsh speakers to increase their use of the language
    (b) to ensure that Welsh speakers use the services provided for them
15. to ensure that services provided in Welsh are easily available for the public to use
16. to promote the use of Welsh by ensuring the appropriate provision of Welsh language programmes
17. to promote the use of Welsh by ensuring the appropriate provision of published books, magazines and papers, and by seeking to ensure these are widely read.

Language planning in Wales, as it has been conducted through the WLB, is a matter of persuasion and influence, rather than control. There are teeth, and there are indeed provisions for control: The Board can insist on bodies and organizations making Welsh Language Schemes, and has done so for a large number of public and private organizations. It has preferred to act, as far as possible, in a consensual and cooperative way. But the practical results the Board is looking for are intended to happen as a result of image manipulation: If the image is changed, then Welsh will come to be used more widely, and Wales can get closer to the ideal of a bilingual society. In 2000, a second WLB report on the state of the language found that there remained problems: despite oversampling Welsh speakers in the survey (43% could speak the language, although the cells were reduced to the correct proportion of 17.5% speakers in the final results), 28% of the population were still either indifferent to the language or opposed to its use. One half the nonspeakers were not interested in learning Welsh; only one

TABLE 56.1

Percentages of Individuals From England, Scotland, and Wales Identifying With Geopolitical Entities

Which two or three of these, if any, would you say you most identify with?

	Great Britain	England	Scotland	Wales
This local community	41	42	39	32
This region	50	49	62	50
England/Scotland/Wales	45	41	72	81
Britain	40	43	18	27
Europe	16	17	11	16
The Commonwealth	9	10	5	3
The global community	8	9	5	2
None of these	*	*	0	0
Don't know	2	2	1	0

Note. Multiple answers were allowed.

From www.mori.com

* = small sample sizes.

fourth would make the effort to attend a class. There remains a somewhat tenuous link between feelings of nationalism and both actual language use and the desire to use the language, because more than 75% of the sample considered themselves to be Welsh. Indeed, Welsh nationalism is strong: 81% of a representative sample in a different survey identified with Wales, as against only 62% with Scotland and 41% with England in these countries (see Table 56.1). Despite the well-known centrality of language in the Welsh nationalism that has kept alive the idea of an autonomous Wales for centuries, the language is still not regarded as essential to Welshness. Image planning for language through the WLB seems to be intended as a method of bringing about that Welshness.

MALAYSIA

In the case of "new" nations, the issue for language planning is often one of ensuring image building for the indigenous language. The identity of the new nation may be in doubt; it has been colonized, oppressed, or its differences from the major nation of which it formed a part hidden. Malay in Malaysia is a case in point (Omar, 1998). Omar looks particularly at the problems facing the creation of an image repertoire for Malay as opposed to English in domains such as science, the professions, high culture and refined social interaction, international diplomacy, and high literature. Since independence in 1957 when strong language-in-education planning was implemented, Malay has been increasingly used until now undergraduate courses are taught in the language and some 30% of doctoral theses at the University of Malaya were written in the language between 1989 and 1995. Scientists in Malaysia still face the challenge that all other languages do, including major European ones: despite growing use of Malay, to achieve international recognition and career advancement it is necessary to publish in English. In the professions, there is a similar tension. There are already home-grown lawyers, accountants, doctors, dentists—these groups are comfortable using Malay, but need English to interact with colleagues in other parts of the world (Omar, 1998, p. 57). Malay, although used as a lingua franca of the region, is not identified with modern high culture. According to Omar, there may indeed be linguistic reasons why the language is little used in this area: Malay is much more marked than English in terms of sociolinguistic levels. Nonetheless, in high prestige domains such as diplomacy, at the international level, Malay is used when Malaysia, Indonesia, and Brunei meet with one another to discuss affairs that pertain to them only. Otherwise, English is used. In the media, it is a real challenge for Malay creative writers to rise much above what they have achieved so far. The situation facing Malay is that English has a very high image. Omar's overall view is that despite the growth in the use of Malay, Malay enjoys lower prestige and is generally not chosen because it does not provide similar economic value as English. Omar seems to consider, therefore, that image building, although a necessary component of language policy and planning and certainly a main feature of official attitudes, is unlikely to be successful while society does not find adequate economic value in the high-status domains necessary to achieve a positive image for the language. Image planning, here, is a matter of motive. Language planners, and the Malay speakers as a community, need to find the inspiration and the urge to convince themselves that Malay is a satisfactory alternative to English in the high-status domains. To change the image of the language and to conduct image planning successfully, planners need to find an appropriate motivating ideology, which has not been done yet.

QUEBEC

The language situation in Canada, and particularly in Quebec, is probably the most studied of any in the world. Image planning has long been a main concern of the planners in Quebec. They seem to see Quebec less as a province within a federation and more as an independent nation-state. The view seems to be that image manipulation will reflect this ideal, and that the task is to encourage the population to assume an ideal, rather than an actual, identity. To an extent, this is language planning by an elite for (its own view of) society. Not that planners would have seen things in this elitist way: the motivating ideology has been that French and French-speakers were the oppressed minority and needed to create a new identity in order to reject the political reality of domination by Anglophones. Indeed, the general view among most commentators is that the language management approach used in Quebec has as its basis a bottom-up approach to solving language problems (see e.g., Jernudd & Neustupny, 1987).

The Quebec language planners urge the French-speaking Quebeckers to value their own language, as a symbol of their own identity. What their own language might be caused the first problem for the idea of image planning: Is it the French of Paris or the French of Montreal that should be encouraged? Parisian French has high status; French speakers in France (50% of all speakers of French in the world) value it highly; elite speakers in Quebec tamely follow this, as do elite speakers of the language everywhere. But Quebec French is not Parisian French, and encouraging the mass of Quebec speakers to value a foreign variety of their own language could only mean denigrating their own—replacing oppression by English speakers by oppression from Paris. This aspect of the image problem has still not been altogether resolved for Quebec, even though robustly rejected at the political and economic levels.

A second image problem arose as pressure mounted for political independence from the Canadian federation. If French was to be recognized and valued as the language of ethnic French Quebeckers, where did that leave the other inhabitants of Quebec? How could a sense of national pride and a desire to encourage civic nationalism be encouraged among non-French speakers, including the first peoples, allophones, non-French-speaking immigrants, civic minorities? Could French be the common language for all, imitating the role of English in the United States where it is the cement that binds rather than the flag of separation? Again, this is an unsolved problem as planners in Quebec desperately try to shift the focus from ethnicity to citizenship. Thus, in Quebec, image planning has not yet proved an absolute success, even though here, image planning is a matter of planning for identity.

THREE WAYS OF LOOKING AT IMAGE

These examples indicate that, when we come to look at the way image planning has been used by language planners, we are in fact dealing with at least three different meanings of the term. First, image has to do with reflecting *identity* (real or imagined), as in Quebec, whether the term is interpreted as ethnic identity or as civic identity. Second, image seems to be used to describe a *method of implementing* language policy, as in Wales. Third, image has something to do with the *motives* of planners, and of the communities they plan for, for doing language planning in the first place, as in Malaysia, and as Quebec is gradually realizing. Let us deal with these three uses of image in order.

IMAGE AND IDENTITY

As an area of study, language planning and policy (henceforth LPP) requires under- standing of and sympathy with a number of disciplines. Some of these are clearly social, involving such issues as types of social community or category and the na- ture of the sociopolitical, economic, and cultural environment within which planning takes place, not to mention, in some well-known instances such as Northern Ireland or Brittany, simple matters of geography and the physical environment. Other rele- vant disciplines are part of political science: political behavior; planning processes; the distinctions between mundane and necessary instrumental and managerial ac- tivities like developing graphization or deciding terminology and more elevated, or more ideological, attempts to restore or reinvigorate a language that has dropped out of use. Economics is also important. The cultural practices of the group are sig- nificant: religion, its high and popular culture, its ideals, its myths, and its history. A sociolinguistic assessment of the interplay of languages, language varieties, and communities in the relevant society is crucial. These disciplines—the sociological, the political, the economic, the cultural, the sociolinguistic—enable us to understand the areas to which LPP is then applied: the status of a language, its corpus, its acqui- sition. But it is the social psychology of the relevant community of users, involving issues of behavior and attitudes, the way individuals respond to complex stimuli and, particularly, the nature of group and intergroup relations, that sheds light on the fun- damentals: why some LPP proposals have been made, why some are unthinkable, why some are effective and others fall by the wayside. Planning that falls by the way- side, that is rejected by the target group, is pointless, no matter how well-researched or technically brilliant. Success in language planning is about succeeding in influ- encing language behavior, whether this is behavior in using language, identified in the phrase language-as-instrument, or behavior toward language, often described as language-as-object. It is this that moves us beyond Cooper's (1989) definition of an accounting scheme for LPP. Cooper asked the question: What actors attempt to influ- ence what behaviors of which people for what ends under what conditions by what means through what decision-making processes with what effect? We should add the question: Why?

The importance of influencing behavior is not always clear, although even the oldest practical language planners like the French Academy know that practical mea- sures may well be useless unless hearts and minds are convinced. "Every planning effort . . . has to rely on a kind of psychological background which favours an effective implementation of planning goals and which, ultimately, is the most crucial variable for a long-term success of planning" (Haarmann, 1990, p. 104; see also Kaplan & Baldauf, 1997, pp. 50–51). Haarmann, concerned with language planning as a process, a continuous activity of controlling language variation under changing social conditions, developed the idea to a three-part classification of three separate functional ranges of planning: status, corpus, and prestige. Status and corpus planning were productive, whereas prestige planning was "receptive, required for both status and corpus planning, and required by both the actors and the targets of planning" (p. 105). For him, "any kind of planning has to attract positive values, that is, planning activities must have such prestige as to guarantee a favorable engagement on the part of the planners, and, moreover, on the part of those who are supposed to use the planned language" (p. 104). In effect, Haarmann saw language planning as a serious attempt to achieve success in influencing behavior, considered that what mattered was the (social) psychology that drove both planners and the targets of planning, and was convinced that the prestige attributed to the (linguistic) object of planning, both by planners and by the recipients of the planning, was fundamental to this success: *elementary*, in his terminology. Haarmann put language promotion, progressively more efficient as it was carried out by individuals, pressure groups, institutions, and by governments, on the same level as activities in corpus and status planning.

Although drawing out and providing a role for prestige planning, this tripartite distinction is still not altogether satisfactory. Perhaps we need to explore further the idea of prestige and what it might imply. In the literature and in common parlance, four terms are involved: status, prestige, identity, and image.

The *status* of a language in a particular society is its position or standing relative to other languages. To an extent, this is matter of observable fact, well analyzed and illustrated in the original concept of diglossia (Ferguson, 1959). Status can be measured by assessing the number and nature of the domains in which the target language is used. High-status domains—the elite, Parliament, the judiciary, education, the forces of law and order—use the high-status language (H) that is essentially the public language of the state. Low-status languages (L) are used in domestic situations, for private purposes, and among groups that wish to distinguish themselves from those holding power, or that are marked as powerless when they are unable to deploy linguistic skills in the high-status language.

Prestige describes the attitude of members of that society toward this language relationship, and usually implies an attitudinal scale with one language (or language variety) having higher prestige than another. Attitude is not necessarily so clearly a matter of fact as is status and is more difficult to measure even through such techniques as sociopsychological surveys. Attitude involves three elements:

1. An awareness of the factual situation (e.g., the contrast between H and L).
2. An emotional stance toward it (e.g., a feeling that H is desirable).
3. The desire to take some action in relation to the situation (e.g., learn to use H).

Citizens of a particular state are fully aware that one language (or language variety) has higher status than another, but may not necessarily accord it higher prestige. In most cases they will, of course: A high-status language used in the public domain has high prestige, and in Britain and France standard languages like English and French will be prestigious as well as enjoying high status. But Welsh has long had high prestige in (some parts of) Wales, even though generally it was not used in the higher status domains until devolution in 1998. Conversely, even after it has been used in the Welsh Assembly, its prestige rating is still not high in all parts of Wales.

The second pair of terms can be similarly contrasted. The *identity*, of the speakers of a language, is how they see themselves, the social personality they allocate to their own group. Like status, this is, to an extent, a matter of measurable sociohistorical fact. Their own view of their own history, the accepted myths of the relevant society or community, its social structure, its religion, its media, and its social leaders combine to mean that it is not necessary to explain every reference to members; that Americans can expect to find very similar reactions to September 11th everywhere in the United States; that Scotsmen will feel pride when they see bagpipes or eat haggis. The relative status of the language(s) through which this fellow-feeling is realized in a community, its language ecology, is part of that community's identity, and both status and identity can be measured or at least described factually.

The term *image* reflects this identity, in the same way that prestige reflects status. The image of a language or of the speakers of a language is how that identity is perceived, whether by its own speakers or by others. An attitude, like prestige, *image* represents something less tangible, less easily measurable, which may have behavioral consequences. This attitude may be internal, that adopted by members of the society using the language or set of languages, or it may be external, an attitude adopted by people outside that society toward that society and its language. There is a neat parallelism inherent in these terms: status is to prestige what identity is to image.

Given that diverse terminology is a problem for LPP and its contributing disciplines in general, it is perhaps not surprising that each of these four terms suffers from considerable confusion, among experts, by different disciplines as well as among nonexperts. The distinctions are rarely clear: status and prestige are often used to mean the same thing. Identity and image are often confused. For us, though, the status of a language is part of a community's identity, part of its social structure; the prestige that a community allocates to a language is part of the image of itself that community has; it is part of its attitudinal structure. Similarly, the identity of a community is a fact, but it is the image of that identity that can be positive or negative, and can be quite different for members of the community than for those outside.

What can language planners interested in prestige planning do? There is a difference between planning for the real or concrete aspects of language use (status and identity) and planning for the unreal or social-psychological aspects (image and prestige). Language planners and particularly policymakers in government or other credible authority, accustomed to social or economic policy issues, often concentrate their efforts on confirming or changing what they regard as real issues: the status of a language, its corpus, or, most frequently, its acquisition. A language may, thus, be accepted into the public domain by legislative fiat, as happened with Scottish Gaelic in 1998; its spelling may be required to follow certain rules by governmental or nongovernmental authorities like publishers or copy editors, as happened (unsuccessfully) with French in 1990; the teaching of a language may be subject to official direction, both as to what may be taught and how the job can be done (as when the United Kingdom National Curriculum specifies both the spelling and the teaching of English). Thus, using traditional LPP techniques, language *status* can be changed, fairly easily. Direct attempts to change prestige are fairly rare, with the Welsh Language Board's "nurturing confidence" significant among them; but they are conceivable. Doing prestige planning without doing status planning is even rarer.

Can planners change the image of a group's identity? The contrast between feelings of nationalism in France and those in the United Kingdom makes the difficulties clear. France did not achieve its present territory until 1860, but from 1789 on, there is little doubt that nation, state, language, and the name France/French have been synonymous for all but a very small minority of the French: The image of the nation was fixed by the Revolution, even though subsequent changes in the underlying reality of identity have been quite large. The United Kingdom is made up of four nations: England, Wales, Scotland, and Northern Ireland. It took from 1301, when English kings took over Wales, to 1536 before the administration was united, to 1830 before the judicial systems were combined. Although royal power combined the two countries with Scotland in 1603 under the name Great Britain, it took until 1707 before the parliaments united. The Scottish educational and the judicial systems still remain different from those of England and Wales. It took from 1801, when Ireland was added under the name the United Kingdom, to 1922 for the realization to dawn that the two nations were culturally separate. As a result, British people living in the United Kingdom are still often at a loss to decide whether they feel more British than English/Welsh/Scottish/Irish or vice versa. In 1999, on the Moreno nationalism scale, in England 17% felt English, not British and 15% more English than British; 14% British, not English and 11% more British than English; 37% equally British and English (*The Guardian*, Nov. 28, 2000). The language is English, not British. British social planners have struggled and are struggling to define identity, and an attempt in 2000 to alter the self-perception, the image people recognize, by incorporating changes brought about by immigration to Britain failed miserably. Yet no one denies that the British are as patriotic as anyone else—only 7% felt no national sense of belonging. The reality of *identity* has changed, but changing the *image* (self-perception) of that identity has been and is very difficult. It can change, although it has taken 3 centuries for the Stuarts' attempts to make people feel more British than English or Scottish to make some headway.

Both image and prestige are psychological attitudes. Attitudes can be affected by propaganda, by deliberate planning, even though the process might be long and difficult. Let us assume that Quebec wishes to change the identity of its territory, from being an ethnically determined province to an independent state welcoming other ethnicities. To change the image of the territory for its inhabitants from being a home for native French speakers only to one welcoming non-French-speaking migrants requires a lot more than simply changing the rules, as the examples of Britain and France both show. It is not sufficient simply to create an independent Ireland by separation from the United Kingdom: it needs further work to establish a positive self-image for the new country, as continuing emigration seemed to show, even up to the 1980s. Both image and prestige change need a basis of factual change in identity and status, but changes in status and identity do not necessarily bring about changes in image or prestige. If you make Gaelic in Ireland a standard language in education, its prestige does not immediately rise. Expecting a different Quebec identity to arise without changing the image of French as the language (only) of the ethnic French, and expecting the prestige of French to rise without changing its status; or planning a rise in prestige for Gaelic without making it useable in education first, are nonstarters.

So according to our definitions, the status of a language and the identity of its speakers are features of the linguistic and social systems of a society—both can be changed by planned actions and sometimes by unplanned ones. (Relative) prestige and (relative) image are attitudes adopted by people—planning is conceivable for both, can affect both, but is again much harder for image than for prestige. There is perhaps a warning here: For planning to be successful, both prestige and image may need to be changed. Both are (usually) closely connected: language is a core value for most societies. Changing the prestige of French in Quebec is excellent, but by itself that will not change the nature of Quebec society. French has to be used and valued by non-native-French speakers for a change in image to occur. Making Welsh useable in the public domain and raising its prestige is only half the battle. To make the Welsh feel Welsh, image has to change, even if the identity does not. Not for nothing do some language planners concede that planning language is planning society.

Similarly, corpus planning and acquisition planning are supposedly basically factual matters, real features of the political system or the educational structures of the society, involving decisions that planners can make. But changes in spelling, in the identity of the language, are now almost impossible to effect in the established languages: the prestige of the language is fixed, but so is its image as a core element of the relevant identity. Changes in acquisition planning, in the status of the language (putting Gaelic in the curriculum of Ireland), are easy to effect. But changes in the prestige of the languages do not necessarily follow.

IMAGE AND METHOD

Promoting a Language to Bolster the Self-image (Identity) of Speakers

Reversing Language Shift.   A first, and perhaps the main, group of cases where image manipulation is used as a method of planning, rather than as a psychological equivalent to identity or as a motive, is reversing language shift (RLS; Fishman, 1991, 2001). Catalan in Spain, French in Quebec, Irish in Ireland, and Hebrew both before the creation of the state of Israel and afterward may stand as examples of the methods employed. In both of the first two cases the language had low prestige, seemed to be in decline, and the self-image of its speakers was a mixture of pride in their identity and of a sort of despair that the future held little hope for that identity. In both cases planners had a mixture of aims, not by any means limited to language planning. In Catalonia the planning conducted by Jordi Pujol and his Convergence and Unity Party (CiU) was mainly oriented toward establishing the political distinctiveness of the territory after the end of the Franco regime. The methods were mainly political and concentrated on the creation of the national myth, associating Catalan with the history of Catalonia and Catalan cultural uniqueness. LPP was oriented toward ensuring the use of Catalan in the high-status public domains (normalization) as well as in education. In Quebec, too, the purpose of the Parti Québécois was primarily political although this time the methods were more social and economic, concentrating on the creation of a factual and particularly an economic independence both from Canada and, almost as important, from the power of the United States. In both cases, social planning saw the relative status of the language as a fundamental, and education in the language as a prime method of ensuring the success of the planning of society that was envisaged. Both sets of planners were supposedly fully aware of the importance of image, and both sets included a range of methods aimed at developing positive images to underline and reinforce the practical measures.

Irish and Hebrew are rather different cases, where the language acted as a symbol of newly acquired nationhood and was intended to underline the identity of that nation. In the case of Irish, the self-image of the target population had suffered because of the presence of an overwhelmingly powerful neighbor that had conquered them, whose language had been used in the high-status roles for centuries. The task for the Gaelic League in 1880 was to ensure that the image of Irish was raised sufficiently to ensure it could move into these roles and be accepted there. Hebrew is a fundamentally different case. Here it was not a matter of reaction against one dominant language or powerful neighbor, but of creating a national myth from the religious unity that already existed and from a number of associated social and economic myths associated with the ideas of Zionism. In the process, the languages that were rejected were not only those of powerful neighbors or supporters, like German, but also languages like Judeo-Spanish or Yiddish, which had symbolized Jewishness for certain groups and that could well have been adopted in this role for the nascent nation and state, but which lost out for different reasons. Eventually, this would result in the development of the political nation, with the eventual result that the Hebrew language has now become the language of the State of Israel. The method was political and amounted to ensuring that Hebrew was viewed positively, while the others were not.

Fishman (2001), revisiting his earlier studies on reversing language shift, invited a range of scholars to describe the current situation of individual languages and to comment on theories and approaches. The Fishman approach relies on fostering an ethnolinguistic community (X-ians) using their language (X-ish) within an environment of Y-ians and their language (Y-ish). Full success can only come when there exists a community of X-ians, transmitting X-ish to their offspring: RLS cannot be based on acts of charity by outsiders (Fishman quotes the case of New Zealanders learning Maori through sympathy with the Maori plight). His recipe for action is, in our terms, internal image planning: "to stress the role of X-ish in family, intimacy, and ethnocultural authenticity in local identity. Rendering kith and kin into important allies (even on a cross-border basis) is more important initially (and for a long time thereafter) than conquering outer space" (Fishman, 2001, p. 475).

Bourhis (2001), in his chapter on Quebec, explores the concept of ethnolinguistic vitality developed in the years leading to the adoption of the Charter of the French Language in 1977. His view is that processes such as language shift cannot really be studied in a sociostructural vacuum, and that an assessment of the relative vitality of ethnolinguistic groups is an essential preliminary to any language planning. Ethnolinguistic vitality, that which makes a group likely to behave as a distinctive and collective entity within the intergroup setting (p. 102), derives from demographic factors such as the absolute numbers of people in the group, their birthrate and immigration/emigration situation, together with their distribution; from institutional support and control factors such as whether the language is used in education and government services; and from status factors originating in the group's history, its economic and social status and that of its language. Planning tried to support French on all these fronts: in terms of numbers, by attracting immigrants toward French and ensuring that education in French was protected; in terms of institutional control, by ensuring that Francophones obtained control, and that French was used in, not merely education, government services, and politics, but particularly the world of work and the economic world. In image planning, the stress was placed on making people aware of the negatives: the low status of French in demography (declining fertility and the Anglicization of new immigrants) and in institutional control, particularly in the world of work. "It is the Xmen analysis of the weak position of French (in these areas) which provided the ideological mobilising tool (threat to French survival) that convinced the Francophone majority that RLS was vital for the survival of their language" (p. 111).

Riagain's (2001) analysis of Ireland is concerned to show that language developments and language policy are related to, if not simply a part of, economic and social planning and variables.

> The social uses of language owe their specifically social value to the fact that they are organised in systems of social interaction which reproduce the system of social differences. The state plays a very dominant role in shaping the socioeconomic development and thus it is necessary to examine policies which relate to economic, and social (particularly education) issues, and whose intent was not at all language oriented, but which greatly affect the operation of language policy. (p. 212)

The unique shape and character of Irish language policy since 1922 relies on the fact that it was the Irish state that dealt with the minority language problem by trying to reestablish Irish as the national language. On the face of it, the policy has been successful: whereas in 1851 the percentage of persons claiming to speak Irish in census returns was 29.1%; in 1996 it was 41.1%. The national increase is primarily caused by improvement since the 1920s in the proportion of young adults speaking Irish: for those ages 20 to 24, from 15.8% in 1926 to 51.7% in 1996. These figures mask the fact that language surveys "suggest that only about 5% of the national population use Irish as their first or main language. A further 10% use Irish regularly but less intensively in conversation or reading.... these levels would appear to have remained stable over recent decades" (Riagáin, 2001, p. 201). Government policy since 1922 has been to make Irish compulsory in the schools, so that the average child studies the language for 13 years. There are about 100 Irish-language immersion schools, and in English-language mainstream schools, Irish is studied as a subject. In terms of social classes, however, the group that includes the elite now makes educational decisions that involve the adoption of a strategy that increasingly does not include higher-level Irish or any Irish at all. In Riagáin's view, it is the changes in Irish society, particularly since 1960, which have brought this about. The new economic policy elaborated over the 1970s and 1980s "placed emphasis on export markets and foreign industrial investment" (p. 207), changing from the predominantly agricultural small businesses where the requirement of a knowledge of Irish for government employment and for entry to the professions affected few people. As a consequence of the growth of tertiary education this socioeconomic change required, in 1973 "Irish ceased to be a compulsory subject for examinations or a requirement for entry to the public service" (p. 207). Even in the Gaeltacht where first-language Irish speakers predominate, employment in agriculture dropped from nearly three fourths of males in 1961 to less than one half in 1981 with the consequence being that the Irish-speaking networks diminished in number and intensity. As a consequence of these societal changes, current government policy looks more toward institutional parallelism, the provision of certain basic state services in and through Irish, than toward fully functional bilingualism—a move toward language maintenance and away from language revival. It may well be that the original ideological impulse for image planning, the need to establish the independence of Ireland as a state and to counter the dominance of English, has been modified in a number of ways. Ireland now no longer has need of its own language to assert its own identity and to give itself a satisfactory self-image.

Catalan in Catalonia has generally been regarded as a success story in terms of language maintenance and revival, with Catalan at Stage 1 of Fishman's Graded Intergeneration Disruption Scale (GIDS). Against this background, Strubell (2001) notes that census data for 1996 shows that comprehension of Catalan is approaching 100%, with rises of 11.3 percentage points from 1986 in speaking, 11.9 points in reading, and 14.4 points in writing. By age-group, in 1996, 90.4% of those aged 15 to 29 could speak the language, whereas the percentage dropped to 61.9% for those over 64. For those of school age, the rise was from 77.9% in 1986 to 83.6% in 1996. New arrivals, too, are learning Catalan. The revival of Catalan has been a consistent policy of the Generalitat, responsible for a series of Linguistic Acts culminating in 1998 with "a message of the political will ... to continue impelling the process of recovery and presence of Catalan in all fields and all segments of social life and a commitment on the part of the Catalan institutions to the language of the country" (p. 272). The legislation contains quotas and sanctions.

Nonetheless, Strubell notes a need to relegitimize the policy, so it is legitimate to ask whether the planning has really been a success. Opposition to it dates back to 1981 and was particularly virulent between 1993 and 1997. Replies by intellectuals had little effect on public opinion and the organization committed to promoting the language had been dissolved. Until recent times, the main motivating factor has been past oppression (from the Franco regime), but this now has less and less explanatory appeal. Social pressure for the integration of newcomers (more than 90% of whom are Spanish-speaking) has been replaced by institutional pressure, and Strubel notes passivity and lack of interest that both political leaders and the Catalan community display toward the future of the language and change in linguistic habits. Such a significant change is the language attitudes of the young, where there seems to be a perception that Catalan is fostered by those in power, favoring a minority simply because Catalan is its family language. Catalan is not the clearest sign of identity among young people who fully identify themselves as Catalans. Another, even more significant, change is the increasing bilingualization of the population, where most Catalans nowadays speak Spanish with little or no accent, thus even leading to conversations between Catalan-speaking strangers often taking place in Spanish (Strubel, 2001, p. 266). Perhaps too much stress has been laid on changing identity through legislation, and not enough on the required image change!

Spolsky and Shohamy (2001) analyzed the position of Hebrew. They wondered whether the unique case of the language is really one of RLS, given the 1,000-year history of language maintenance through religious education and retained, active, literacy. Revival as a spoken language was closely tied to secularized and secularizing Zionism, which concentrated on a Hebrew nation, for Hebrews, and rejected at once the ways of the goyim (gentiles) and their languages and of the Jews (yidn) and their language, Yiddish. The ideological principle was to use Hebrew in public and to ensure intergenerational transmission in the kibbutzim. The consequence has been success for Hebrew, but at the cost of replacing the Arabic introduced into the region 1,000 years earlier, which itself had displaced Aramaic, which had replaced Hebrew and the 40 or more languages brought in by Jewish immigrants. Spolsky and Shohamy see the revitalization of Hebrew as a matter probably best explained as occurring in three areas of language practice (of speaking and teaching Hebrew among secular Jews in particular around 1890 to 1913); of language ideology (of the Zionist movement), and of language policy (of the British Mandate government of the interwar years, which accepted Hebrew as the educational language for that community and its schools). Planning has covered all four of our areas: identity, image, language status, and language prestige. The result has been a confirmation of a new identity and a new status for the language, a case of success for Hebrew through the practical elimination of contenders.

Certainly in relation to these four examples, and possibly more widely in RLS, there seems to be a contrast between those who see LPP as a matter of adding functionality, particularly in the public language and in education, and those who aim at total social change through planning a new image for a language. Image as a method is different for each group. In the first case (Quebec French), the main method is revolution, or as near to it as planners can get. These planners are only interested in language if it acts as a symbol and a point around which the troops can rally, and only care for corpus change if it strengthens the political case. The language is a battle flag. Image planning in Quebec, rooted in economic and social planning and aiming, not at a new sociocultural environment, but at an improved position for French speakers within the existing one, has been successful for the language, while the aims for autonomy and independence have been very nearly achieved. In the second case (Irish), methods involve increased visibility for the language, making sure it is hauled out of the museum and placed on the street. Corpus change is fundamental. Catalan has had considerable success as far as the original image manipulation plans of the activists are concerned, even if the eventual result may now present different problems arising from this very success. It, too, aimed at total change in the sociocultural environment. Finally, Hebrew is a complete success story of language image planning, resulting in the creation of a new nation. Although Ireland, too, has had a successful experience of image planning in the political sphere, and the national political entity has achieved both internal and external recognition and acceptance, and society has thus changed completely, language planning as a method has been much less successful.

One must nonetheless conclude that Fishman's hope for peaceful coexistence and an acceptance of pluralism on the part of language activists may be difficult to achieve, given the conflictual nature of all four of these situations. The image planning that has worked has done so when territorial, political, and economic independence were also involved, in Ireland and Israel. In the same two countries there has been a strong association between ethnicity and language, too. In the case of Quebec, although the ethnic French Québeckers may be convinced, other parts of the population are less so (aboriginals, immigrants) and Quebec has not yet cut itself off from its Federation. In Catalonia, peaceful coexistence with Castilian speakers is not a complete reality, despite Pujol's definition of a Catalan as someone who lives in Catalonia. In all these situations, image manipulation as a method of ensuring change has worked among the ethnic group. The problems lie in extending this image manipulation outside the ethnic group. However, as the next section indicates, LPP for internal image change is by no means restricted to minority groups or to the powerless within society: far from it.

Major Standard Languages. The continuing effort put into ensuring a positive image for major standard languages provides another set of examples. In such cases, the language is promoted in order to maintain, confirm, or defend the identity as seen by the planners. France is well known as a country where significant internal language planning of the defensive type has been in operation for centuries (Ager, 1999). Much of this planning was implemented in a fairly brutal way, through oppression, condemnation, or punishment. Policy and planning at the time of the Revolution concentrated on banning the regional languages, not for reasons of image, but as a political need to destroy regional power and the power of those forces such as the Church, which supported regionalism. Most of the image construction since that time, whether internal or external, has rested on the idea of the superiority of French as the language of the center. But associated with this idea is the ideology of superiority under attack: The language of culture, in which Paris, alone in the world, represents the idea of high culture; the language of democracy, which alone can represent true political ideals; and the language of universality, which alone can fight for human rights for all mankind. Language ideology has used the analogy of a military campaign waged against the barbarians at the gates. It is for this reason that education has been the principal arena in which image manipulation was conducted, although from time to time, there have been changes in deciding who exactly the enemy was. At the time of the French Revolution, the enemy was the regional languages, kept out of the school grounds. During the 19th century, it was low-prestige social varieties, kept out by the use of the written language and a very closely circumscribed definition of culture. In more recent times, the enemy has been American English, associated with free trade and globalization when these are done by other than French companies, whether private or owned by the state. José Bové's symbolic (and practical) attacks on McDonalds restaurants strike a sympathetic chord among the French at all levels of society, although one rather doubts whether similar attacks on croissanteries in the Far East would be quite so well received. Certainly attacks on France's and Europe's farm policy by the African farmers who are ruined by it are rarely mentioned by Bové. The Toubon Law of 1994 strengthened the idea of education as the bastion and of the French Academy as the guardian of the French language. And because of the insecurity associated with the need to protect this impossible ideal of perfection, French government after French government has poured money into protecting the image of the French language.

Britain, too, has in recent years shifted from implicit language policy where the issue was simply not raised because it was so self-evident that the language of Shakespeare was infinitely superior to all others, to a point where explicit defense of standard English seemed necessary. As the language of an island and then of an empire, English had no need of protection—effortless superiority was and remained the ideology. Regional languages were curios, of interest to specialists, but it was clearly to the benefit of the inhabitants of those outlandish regions that for their own good they should acquire and use English as quickly as possible (Grillo, 1989). The same approach was good for Africans, who clearly needed civilization, in English, which would enable them to improve their own lot. By contrast to the French, the ideologizing motive was not one of opposition to the languages of regions, of social classes, or of conquered nations—indeed, considerable effort and money was expended in preserving, recording, and protecting these. But the thought never entered anyone's head that the higher public domains could use anything other than English, that education could use any language other than English, or that training in English as the language of the elite (Public School English) should not receive the highest prestige. The self-image was one of effortless superiority, and the image held by others, too, confirmed and still confirms this attitude toward the international language of diplomacy and commerce. Explicit British language policy has only arrived in the late 20th century as attacks on this self-image have come from two directions. The great standard English debate of the late 1980s pointed to the enemy within, made up of politically motivated teachers, regionalists, and migrants whose collective opposition to good English in the schools would apparently destroy the language and the country with it (Honey, 1997; Marenbon, 1987). The other source of attacks on English and its image come from Phillipson in *Linguistic Imperialism* (1992), Pennycook in *The Cultural Politics of English as an International Language* (1994) and others who attack the neocolonialism of English language teaching or the global triumphalism of Crystal in *English as a Global Language* (1997). Crystal, of course, hotly rejects this accusation and deplores it as ideologically fueled.

Fossilization.   There is another group of examples in which the self-image of a community is of importance and where the issue of domains of use becomes even more salient. Some languages and language varieties have become so associated with particular domains, of cultural importance to the relevant community, that change is unthinkable. Any modernization of the language or script involved in the Classical Arabic used for holy writings in Islam has become impossible. Not merely is the Koran the word of God, but so is the language in which it is written. Indeed the methods of learning are also, for some, sacrosanct. There have been, and still are, difficulties associated with the use of recent translations of the Bible in various Christian groups, too. Even in Britain many Anglicans appear to believe that the King James Prayer Book of 1622 is the only acceptable form in which prayers may be offered, whereas priests who reject hymns like *Jerusalem* because of the nationalism of the words—quite inappropriate in today's world—are regarded as mavericks by some but hotly defended by others. Linguistic differences, and differences of script, underline or reflect differences of religion. In Northern Ireland, Catholic politicians from Sinn Fein use a different dialect and pronunciation (of English) from Protestant politicians (McCafferty, 2001). Indeed, Schiffman (1996, pp. 64–67) lists 13 examples of areas of the world where religious differences are mirrored by language and language policy differences, from Belgium to India, from Korea to Sri Lanka. The same approach to language planning is noticeable among the cultural nationalists of Wales. Here, the language is an untouchable museum piece. Any attempt to modernize, to encourage slang, to tolerate borrowings, or to represent changing social realities is rejected out of hand. Folklore reigns supreme. In such cases, the self-image of the community is fixed in the use of the particular language variety, but the importance and centrality of religion and other key, core values of the relevant community are such that there is no question of any change to identity. Image is a method for ensuring the confirmation of that identity, and preserving it unchanged.

Promoting a Language to Influence Its Image and That of Its Speakers

Diplomacy Through Language. Two obvious examples of diplomacy through language are the languages of nations defeated in World War II: German and Japanese (Ager, 2001, pp. 57–66). In both cases the nations concerned saw a need to modify the attitudes toward themselves that other societies held, and saw that one way in which a more positive view might be achieved would be to encourage an understanding of both the artistic and cultural achievements of their own societies and of their languages, seen as cultural systems and mechanisms enabling access to the societies. The approach, fired by the wish to ensure a positive approach for the country, was to encourage the teaching and learning of German or Japanese outside Germany and Japan. To do this, resource policy was extensively called on. The Goethe Institut and the Japan Foundation are both well-endowed organizations, using governmental money and plans to provide language teaching directly or to foster it, together with cultural appreciation, in many parts of the world. The former has 135 branches in 76 countries; the latter concentrates on activities like international exchanges and the fostering of academic studies of Japan in schools and universities abroad.

Encouraging Language Spread. Promotion of language is by no means restricted to these two examples: indeed, most countries try hard to manipulate the image others have of them through their language policy for the external world. The United Kingdom's British Council recently commissioned a report on the likely future for English and for its own activities in language teaching (Graddol, 1997). Graddol's report was not well received by opponents like Phillipson or Pennycook, and accusations of triumphalism concentrated on the conclusions where Graddol pointed to the effect of small forces, strategically placed . . . careful strategic planning, far-sighted management, thoughtful preparation, and focused action now could indeed help secure a position for British English language services in the 21st century (p. 62). This was seized on as proof positive of the deviousness, manipulation, and craftiness of the British Council, and its intention to keep the superior position of English. Not that the British Council, and its parent organization, the British Government, were the only language with such policies. For Kibbee (2001, p. 71), writing in a special issue of *Terminogramme* on Geostrategies for Languages, you can see a similar concern among French planners trying to maintain the domination of French in the national education systems of (France's) former colonies, particularly in sub-saharan Africa, and its even more threatened situation in international agencies and organizations (UNO, European Union, Olympic Games, and so forth). Kibbee accuses both the British and the French of racing for market share above all, with both of them fostering languages and policies that can only lead to the destruction of smaller and less powerful languages. Kibbee states, however, that both are deliberately placing themselves among the oppressed and marginalized on the grounds that they are defending linguistic diversity or might themselves be crushed by changing military or economic forces. Kibbee's comment was that such fears were hardly credible. He had equally harsh words for the ecolinguists whose only concern with disappearing languages was that this reduction in linguistic diversity and the concomitant disappearance of peoples would lead to the disappearance of their own research grants, not to mention that defending minority languages in certain situations in the Third World was the equivalent of asking people to risk the economic future of their children.

IMAGE AS MOTIVE

What drives planners to plan, and why is it that the people whose behavior is supposed to be changed should be willing to submit themselves to such manipulation?

The question—Why?—is slightly more complicated than Cooper's—for what ends? If we simply consider the ends of planning, then we could stop at the point of noting that planners intend to use language in Parliament or to teach it in Grade 4. But why these particular decisions at this particular point in time? With what purpose are these ends chosen? Ager (2001) has considered this issue in some detail and found that motivation for the planning of language behavior is, in fact, best analyzed as a three-part psychological and social phenomenon, involving not merely ends, purposes, or goals, but also people's attitudes toward them and a more general category of psychological impulses associated with identity. A particular planning or policy decision does not depend solely on the aims and goals planners set themselves, nor solely on their attitudinal structure, necessarily reflecting that of the sociopolitical environment within which they work. In addition to these, it also depends on the self-image planners have of themselves on the identity they think relevant for themselves, and for the group whose behavior they intend to influence. A particular planning decision can often be traced back to a particular point in the process of identity creation and defense. This third element has long been hinted at and even openly examined: it has to do with the nature of the self and particularly on how this self is created and defended.

Most work on motives for planning mentions a number of general psychological motives such as identity or insecurity. Thus, for example, Tšrnquist-Plewa (in Barbour & Carmichael, 2000) states, "The democratic developments initiated in Poland, Hungary, the Czech Republic, and Slovakia after 1989 gave them a chance of building national identities where the state and institutions play an important integrating part...language and ethnic origin are today crucial for national identification" (p. 218). Thus, too, Greece and Turkey demonstrate how language and national identity are becoming ever more closely related in much of Europe (Trudgill in Barbour & Carmichael, 2000, p. 263). Many of these motives, particularly those labeled identity, have a somewhat dubious history in political movements like Fascism and its more modern development toward extreme nationalism: In the Balkans as elsewhere in Europe, it is possible to see the profoundly anti-democratic consequences of the politics of narrow constructions of identity, which privilege the single common denominator of statist ethnicity over region, religion, human rights, shared histories, and even shared languages (Carmichael in Barbour & Carmichael, 2000, p. 239). But again, to declare that such a process of identity construction or defense is itself the motive is insufficient without the two other, more precise, elements of goals and attitudes.

Motivation, for us, is first, a process of dynamic identity construction within which image development can be a phase. We propose successive phases of construction as (the discovery of) identity, (the use of political) ideology (as a component part), (the manipulation of) image, insecurity, the defense or maintenance of identity, the maintenance or correction of social inequality, integration (with a contiguous language), instrumentalism and, in the worst cases, possible despair (at the lack of a future for that particular identity and language). What is more, this list of basic motives seems applicable to all three levels of actor involved in the planning process: the individual, powerless communities, and states, even though it has normally been applied to groups and has given rise to social identity theory. To this extent, we make no distinction between individuals and groups, regarding all such organisms as sharing the process of identity construction and defense as outlined. This development of social identity theory, outlined in Ager (2001), takes into account these major axioms:

1. That identity develops through stages of social categorization, identity creation, social comparison, and psychological distinctiveness.
2. That it is created by awareness of membership of an ingroup and non-membership of an outgroup; the concomitant distinctiveness of such groups.

3. That social comparison is a prime factor in attitudes toward others.
4. That those creating their social identity move toward the positive and high status rather than toward the negative, low status groups.

It also responds to the main criticism of social identity theory, that it is static, by stressing the dynamic and constantly developing process of creating and recreating group identity (Chambers, 1995, pp. 250–253).

The picture then needs to be further clarified by also considering this issue of the ends of language planning. These seem to vary greatly in their precision: in addition to the great and grandiose (make Wales bilingual, eliminate Americanisms from French), there are the concrete (teach Corsican, incorporate Breton-language schools into the state system) and the downright detailed (include the spelling of which in the National Curriculum in England at age 5). At the very least, these ends of language planning can be categorized into three types in a taxonomy, similar to the vision, mission, and targets of quality planning: the general ideal, the concrete objective, and the precise target. It is possible to distinguish between the type of ideal that seemed particularly important to individuals from those that seemed so for powerless communities and again for powerful, or autonomous, states. For individuals, the frequency with which there occurred superordinate ideals of coherence of identity, or of cooperation, sometimes leading to compromise were identified. For powerless communities, the importance of ideals of conflict, but also of cooperation and compromise were noted. For states, ideals of social cohesion, elitism or social mosaicity, on the internal level, are matched by competition or even conflict on the external level. Such superordinate ideals have often been labeled social mobility, affiliation, or assimilation when weak or soft group boundaries are involved, or, at the other extreme, social competition, vitality, rejection, or autonomy when rigid or hard group boundaries are noted.

Ager (2001) looked at how to assess how strong the three aspects of motivation were. Neither for motives nor for goals was it possible to discover precise measures of strength that could be used to compare one with another: rather, the measurement process was limited to one of categorization. It is perfectly possible to measure the strength of policies or planning decisions themselves by assuming that declared and overt policies are stronger than undeclared and covert ones. Declared and overt policies are visible because they are enshrined in legal texts, formal decisions, or court judgments; covert ones are represented simply by what people do or the attitudes they adopt. It is on this basis that British government sources can claim that Britain has no language policy. But a policy of rejection or discrimination is nonetheless real although not openly stated, and language shift or the adoption of a new communicative mechanism is likewise a fact.

This analysis of motivation is still not enough. It might account for some types of real planning for status: the acceptance of a language in a high-prestige domain. It does not account for image planning: for encouraging non-French speakers in Quebec or non-Welsh speakers in Wales to learn the language. In order to understand motivation fully, the picture needs to be developed further by looking at people's attitudes and their attitudinal structure. The attitudinal structure of the actors with reference to both their first language (L1) and any relevant second language (L2) or other language needs exploration, so the total language ecology of the relevant society is a factor. Ager (2001) was particularly interested to measure language attitudes in such a way that they could be summarized meaningfully. This was done by establishing four measurement scales of excellence, vitality, attractiveness, and readiness for action, and allocating markers of strength (1 to 3) to each according to the findings of opinion polls or interviews, sometimes assessing attitudes from what society's leaders have said or what representative figures have put forward.

TABLE 56.2

Language Policies Pursued by Powerless Communities and Powerful Autonomous States

Identity sequence	Motivation of Powerless Communities (1) and Powerful States (2)								
	Attitudinal Structure								Goals:
	Excel		Vitality		Attract		Action		*Ideal, objective, target*
	L1	L2	L1	L2	L1	L2	L1	L2	
Identity (personal)									
Identity (social) Algeria Spoken Classical Arabic (2)	1	3	1	1	1	3	1	3	Cohesion/accept L1 spoken, promote L2 Classical
Ideology UK (2)	3	1	3	1	3	1	3	1	Elitism/ignore diversity
France (2)	3	1	3	1	3	1	3	3	Cohesion/repress diversity
Image Germany (2)	3	1	3	1	3	1	3	1	Competition/foster German
Japan (2)	3	1	3	1	3	1	3	1	Competition/seek favorable image
Insecurity Neologism in French (2)	1	3	1	3	2	1	3	3	Conflict/xenophobia
Maintain identity Welsh (1)	3	3	1	3	3	2	2	1	Conflict/seek equal rights with English; archaic purism
Defend identity Catalan (1)	3	1	3	2	3	1	3	1	Conflict/defend L1 by attacking L
Maintain inequality anti-Roma (2)	3	1	3	1	3	1	3	1	Conflict/repress Roma
Correct inequality Australia (2)	3	3	3	1	3	3	3	3	Moasic/multilingualism
Integrate Koreans in Japan (1)	1	3	1	3	1	3	1	3	Compromise/shift from L1 to L2
Improve instrumentality Québec (2)	1	3	1	3	3	3	3	3	Conflict/reformist purism
Despair Ainu (1)	1	3	1	3	1	3	1	3	Compromise/shift from L1 to L2

Note. ∗ = Motives and attitudinal structures

3 = Strong positive attitude; value language highly; prepared to act

1 = Indifferent attitude toward language and its eventual disappearance

Adapted from table in Ager, D. (2001). *Motivation in Language Planning and Language Policy* (p. 135), Clevedon, UK: Multilingual Matters.

This provided three elements of motivation: the psychological, the attitudinal, and the practical, and each of these three "elements" of motivation has distinct and in some cases measurable stages, levels, or scales of strength. By examining the variations of these, it is possible to identify different types of motivation and pinpoint how the manipulation of image fits into an overall scheme.

This discussion led to a representation and comparison of motives graphically in presentations like that of Table 56.2, where the examples relate to language policies pursued by powerless communities and powerful, autonomous states.

Language planners, whether individuals, communities and groups, or politically autonomous governments, have a variety of motives and rarely make these fully explicit. Aims are rarely unique; most language planning activities and policies have mixed aims. Nor are language planning aims divorced from general aims for society. All language planning and policy is an attempt to influence social behavior in realms other than language alone.

But, as Haarmann (1990) points out, language planners do not plan for failure. They hope for success in influencing individuals and societies. To be successful means following the identity sequence, exploring the point at which the idea of the prestige of a communication system will be most effective, and planning to capture that point. Promoting a language or language variety, trying to confirm or improve its status in society and, hence, the prestige in which it is held, means regarding it as in some way superior to other languages and language varieties. This may be done either so that the identity or self-image of those who speak the language is enhanced and some advantage may thus accrue to them; or so that the image others have of the language and its users is positively influenced, again for the benefit of those who use the language.

REFERENCES

Ager, D. E. (1999). *Identity, insecurity and image. France and language.* Clevedon, UK: Multilingual Matters.

Ager, D. E. (2001). *Motivation in language planning and language policy.* Clevedon, UK: Multilingual Matters.

Barbour, S., & Carmichael, C. (Eds.). (2000). *Language and nationalism in Europe.* Oxford, UK: Oxford University Press

Bourhis, R. (2001). Reversing language shift in Québec. In J. A. Fishman (Ed.), *Can threatened languages be saved?* (pp. 101–141). Clevedon, UK: Multilingual Matters.

Chambers, J. K., (1995). *Sociolinguistic theory.* Oxford, UK: Blackwell.

Cooper, R. (1989). *Language planning and social change.* Cambridge, UK: Cambridge University Press.

Crystal, D. (1997). *English as a global language.* Cambridge, UK: Cambridge University Press.

Ferguson, C. A. (1959). Diglossia. *Word, 15,* 325–340

Fishman, J. A. (1991). *Reversing language shift: The theoretical and empirical foundations of assistance to threatened languages.* Clevedon, UK: Multilingual Matters.

Fishman, J. A. (2001). *Can threatened languages be saved?* Clevedon, UK: Multilingual Matters.

Graddol, D. (1997). *The future of English?* London: The English Company.

Grillo, R. D. (1989). *Dominant languages. Language and hierarchy in Britain and France.* Cambridge, UK: Cambridge University Press.

Haarmann, H. (1990). Language planning in the light of a general theory of language: A methodological framework. *International Journal of the Sociology of Language, 86,* 103–126.

Honey, J. (1997). *Language is power. The story of standard English and its enemies.* London: Faber & Faber.

Jernudd, B. H., & Neustupny, J. V. (1987). Language planning for whom? In L. Laforge (Ed.), *Proceedings of the international colloquium on language planning* (pp. 71–84). Québec: Les Presses de L'Université Laval.

Kaplan, R. B., & Baldauf, R. B., Jr. (1997). *Language planning from practice to theory.* Clevedon, UK: Multilingual Matters.

Kibbee, D. A. (2001). Les géostratégies des langues et la théorie linguistique. In J. Maurais & M. A. Morris (Eds), Géostratégies des Langues [Geostrategies for Languages]. Special issue of *Terminogramme, 99–100,* 69–80.

Marenbon, J. (1987). *English, our English: The new orthodoxy examined.* London: Centre for Policy Studies.

McCafferty, K. (2001). *Ethnicity and language change. English in (London) Derry, Northern Ireland.* Amsterdam: Benjamins.

Omar, A. H. (1998). Language planning and image building: The case of Malay in Malaysia. *International Journal of the Sociology of Language, 130,* 49–65.

Pennycook, A. (1994). *The cultural politics of English as an international language.* London: Longman.

Phillipson, R. (1992). *Linguistic imperialism.* Cambridge, UK: Cambridge University Press.

Riagáin, P. O. (2001). Irish language production and reproduction 1981–1996. In J. A. Fishman (Ed.), *Can threatened languages be saved?* (pp. 195–214). Clevedon, UK: Multilingual Matters.

Schiffmann, H. F. (1996). *Linguistic culture and language policy.* London: Routledge.

Spolsky, B., & Shohamy, E. (2001). Hebrew after a century of RLS efforts. In J. A. Fishman (Ed.), *Can threatened languages be saved?* (pp. 350–363). Clevedon, UK: Multilingual Matters.

Strubell, M. (2001). Catalan a decade later. In J. A. Fishman (Ed.), *Can threatened languages be saved?* (pp. 260–283). Clevedon, UK: Multilingual Matters.

Welsh Language Board. (1996). *Promoting and facilitating the use of Welsh. A strategy for the Welsh language.* Cardiff, Wales: Author. Available from www.bwrdd-yr-iaith.org.uk

Welsh Language Board. (2000). *State of Welsh language research report. March/April 2000.* Cardiff, Wales Author.

57

Language Policy and Minority Language Rights

Stephen May
University of Waikato, Hamilton, New Zealand

INTRODUCTION

This chapter explores the interconnections between language policy and planning (LPP)[1] and minority language rights (MLR), also referred to in the literature as linguistic human rights (LHR). MLR, which for the purposes of this chapter also include LHR, may be described as the linguistic and wider social and political rights attributable to speakers of minority languages, usually, but not exclusively, within the context of nation-states. This definition is, in turn, based on the usual distinction between so-called minority and majority languages employed in the language rights literature; a distinction that is based not on numerical size, but on clearly observable differences among language varieties in relation to power, status, and entitlement.[2]

The particular focus of the chapter is on the often complex and contested history surrounding the individual trajectories of LPP and MLR and how these trajectories have intersected over time, beginning with the development of LPP as an identifiable field of research and policy in the early 1960s. This focus will also highlight the importance of adopting a wider sociohistorical, sociocultural, and sociopolitical analysis of LPP, particularly in relation to ongoing questions surrounding the status, use, and power of minority languages in the modern world, along with the material implications of these questions for those who continue to speak such languages.

A key reason why such a broader sociohistorical, sociopolitical research approach is necessary is because for much of its history, linguistics as an academic discipline has been preoccupied with idealist, abstracted approaches to the study of language—with the synchronic at the expense of the diachronic, with *langue* at the expense of *parole*. In short, language has too often been examined in isolation from the social and political conditions in which it is used. As Pierre Bourdieu (1991), the French sociologist and social anthropologist, comments ironically of this process: "bracketing out the social... allows language or any other symbolic object to be treated like an end in itself, [this] contributed considerably to the success of structural linguistics, for it endowed the 'pure' exercises that characterise a purely internal and formal analysis with the charm of a game devoid of consequences" (p. 34). Or as Jacob Mey (1985) observes, "linguistic models, no matter how innocent and theoretical they may seem to be, not only have distinct economical, social and political presuppositions, but also consequences.... Linguistic (and other) inequalities don't cease to exist simply because their ... causes are swept under the linguistic rug" (p. 26).

This ahistorical, apolitical approach to language has also been a feature of sociolinguistics, albeit to a lesser extent, and, surprisingly perhaps, of many discussions of LPP as well. The last is particularly surprising exactly because one might have reasonably expected any analysis of language policies and practices to engage critically with the wider social and political conditions—and, crucially, their historical antecedents—that have shaped them.

EARLY LANGUAGE POLICY AND PLANNING

The tendency toward this *presentist* approach (May, 2002) to language policy was most evident in the early phase of LPP (1960s–1970s). During this period, LPP was seen by its proponents as a nonpolitical, nonideological, pragmatic, even technicist, paradigm (for a useful overview, see Ricento, 2000). Its apparently simple and straightforward aim was to solve the immediate language problems of newly emergent postcolonial states in Africa, Asia, and the Middle East. Status language concerns at this time, thus, focused in particular on establishing stable diglossic language contexts in which majority languages (usually, ex-colonial languages, and most often English and French) were promoted as public languages of wider communication. If promoted at all, local languages—minority languages, in effect—were seen as being limited to private, familial language domains.[3] Although concern was often expressed for the ongoing maintenance of minority languages, the principal emphasis of LPP at this time was on the establishment and promotion of "unifying" national languages in postcolonial contexts, along the lines of those in Western, developed contexts (see, for example, Fishman, 1968a, 1968b, 1968c; Fox, 1975; Rubin & Jernudd, 1971).

What was not addressed by these early efforts at LPP were the wider historical, social, and political issues attendant on these processes, and the particular ideologies underpinning them. As Luke, McHoul, and Mey (1990) observe, while maintaining a "veneer of scientific objectivity" (something of great concern to early language planners), LPP "tended to avoid directly addressing social and political matters within which language change, use and development, and indeed language planning itself, are embedded" (pp. 26–27).

This omission was problematic for a number of reasons. First, it did not question or critique the very specific historical processes that had led to the hierarchizing of majority and minority languages in the first place. These processes are deeply imbricated with the politics of modern nationalism and its emphasis on the establishment of national languages and public linguistic homogeneity as central, even essential, tenets of both modernization and Westernization (see section on Nationalism, minoritization, and historical construction(ism)). Consequently, the normative ascendancy of national languages was simply assumed, even championed, by early advocates of LPP, and all other languages were compared in relation to them. This is highlighted by the various language typologies developed at the time, such as Kloss (1968), which attempted to rank languages in relation to their relative "suitability" for national development. Bourdieu (1991) observes of this tendency within linguistics more broadly:

> To speak of *the* language, without further specification, as linguists do, is tacitly to accept the *official* definition of the *official* language of a political unit. This language is the one which, within the territorial limits of that unit, imposes itself on the whole population as the only legitimate language ... The official language is bound up with the state, both in its genesis and its social uses ... this state language becomes the theoretical norm against which all linguistic practices are objectively measured. (p. 45; emphases in original)

Second, the notion of linguistic complementarity, so central to early language planning attempts at establishing "stable diglossia," was itself highly problematic. Linguistic complementarity, as understood by early language planners, implied at least some degree of mutuality and reciprocity, along with a certain demarcation and boundedness between the majority and minority languages involved. Situations of so-called stable diglossia, however, are precisely *not* complementary in these respects. Rather, the normative ascendancy of national languages—and by extension, international languages such as English—specifically *militates* against the ongoing use, and even existence, of minority languages. As Dua (1994) observes of the influence of English in India, for example, "the complementary of English with indigenous languages tends to go up in favour of English partly because it is dynamic and cumulative in nature and scope, partly because it is sustained by socio-economic and market forces and partly because the educational system reproduces and legitimizes the relations of power and knowledge implicated with English" (p. 132).

In other words, if majority languages are consistently constructed as languages of "wider communication"; whereas minority languages are viewed as (merely) carriers of "tradition" or "historical identity," it is not hard to see what might become of the latter. Minority languages will inevitably come to be viewed as delimited, perhaps even actively unhelpful languages—not only by others, but also often by the speakers of minority languages themselves. This helps to explain why speakers of minority languages have increasingly dispensed with their first language(s) in favor of speaking a majority language—a process of language shift or replacement that is a prominent concern of current sociolinguistic analysis (see following section, Language shift and loss).

It is these wider concerns with the pejorative "positioning" of minority languages, and their speakers, that have led to the subsequent development of minority language rights. Advocacy of minority language rights has been principally expressed to date via two broad, although closely interrelated research paradigms: language ecology and linguistic human rights. In what follows, I will outline the key concerns of minority language rights' advocates and discuss these concerns in relation to the language ecology and linguistic human rights paradigms.

LANGUAGE SHIFT AND LOSS

Advocacy of minority language rights arises out of three principal concerns. The first has to do with the consequent exponential decline and loss of many of the world's languages. Indeed, of the estimated 6,800 languages spoken in the world today (Grimes, 2000), it is predicted on present trends that between 20% and 50% will "die" by the end of the 21st century (Krauss, 1992, 1995).[4] As has already been suggested, language decline and loss occur most often in bilingual or multilingual contexts in which a majority language—that is, a language with greater political power, privilege, and social prestige—comes to replace the range and functions of a minority language. The inevitable result is that speakers of the minority language "shift" over time to speaking the majority language.

The process of language shift described here usually involves three broad stages. The first stage sees increasing pressure on minority language speakers to speak the majority language, particularly in formal language domains, as seen most commonly in the "diglossic" language contexts discussed earlier. This stage is often precipitated and facilitated by the introduction of education in the majority language, itself often a central feature of the language-in-education planning dimension of LPP (see Baldauf & Kaplan, chap. 55, this volume). It leads to the eventual decrease in the functions of the minority language, with the public or official functions of that language being the first to be replaced by the majority language. The second stage sees a period of bilingualism, in which both languages continue to be spoken concurrently. However, this stage is usually characterized by a decreasing number of minority language speakers, especially among the younger generation, along with a decrease in the fluency of speakers, as the minority language is spoken less and employed in fewer and fewer language domains. The third and final stage—which may occur over the course of two or three generations, and sometimes less—sees the replacement of the minority language with the majority language. The minority language may be remembered by a residual group of language speakers, but it is no longer spoken as a wider language of communication (Baker & Prys Jones, 1998).

A well-known alternative formulation of this process, which also usefully charts a minority language's private and public functions in relation to the nation-state (see section on Nationalism, minoritization, and historical construction(ism)), is found in Joshua Fishman's "Graded Intergenerational Disruption Scale" (see 1991, pp. 81–121). In this 8-point scale, Stage 1 is seen as the most secure position for a minority language (with the proviso that intergenerational family transmission continues to occur), whereas Stage 8 is seen as the least secure. The various stages may be paraphrased as:

- Stage 1: Some use of the minority language (ML) in higher level educational, occupational, governmental, and media realms.
- Stage 2: ML used in lower governmental and media spheres.
- Stage 3: Use of the ML in the work sphere, involving (informal) interaction between ML and other language speakers.
- Stage 4: ML use as medium of instruction in education.
- Stage 5: Informal maintenance of literacy in the home, school, and community.
- Stage 6: Intergenerational family transmission of the ML.
- Stage 7: Although the ML continues to be spoken, most speakers of the ML are beyond childbearing age.
- Stage 8: Remaining speakers of a ML are old and usually vestigial users.

Of course, such language loss and language shift have always occurred—languages have risen and fallen, become obsolete, died, or adapted to changing circumstances in order to survive—throughout the course of human history. But never to this extent, and never before at such an exponential rate. Some sociolinguistic commentators have even described it as a form of *linguistic genocide* (Day, 1985; Skutnabb-Kangas, 2000). Such claims may seem overwrought and/or alarmist, but they are supported by hard data. For example, a survey by the U.S. based Summer Institute of Linguistics, published in 1999, found that there were 51 languages with only one speaker left, 500 languages with fewer than 100 speakers, 1,500 languages with fewer than a 1,000 speakers, and more than 3,000 languages with fewer than 10,000 speakers. The survey went on to reveal that as many as 5,000 of the world's 6,000 languages were spoken by fewer than 100,000 speakers each. It concluded, even more starkly, that 96% of the world's languages were spoken by only 4% of its people (Crystal, 1999a, 1999b).

These figures graphically reinforce an earlier suggestion made by Michael Krauss (1992, 1995) that, in addition to the 50% of languages that may die within the next century, a further 40% of languages are threatened or endangered. Given the processes of language shift and decline just outlined, and the current parlous state of many minority languages, it is not hard to see why. Even some majority languages are no longer immune to such processes, not least because of the rise of English as a global language (Crystal, 1997a, 1997b). Thus, if Krauss is to be believed, as few as 600 languages (10%) will survive in the longer term—perhaps, he suggests, even as few as 300.

LANGUAGE ECOLOGY

In response, proponents of MLR often adopt a *language ecology* perspective. Language ecologists (see, for example, Harmon, 1995; Maffi, 2000, 2001; Mühlhäusler, 1990, 1996, 2000; Nettle & Romaine, 2000) argue that the current parlous state of many of the world's languages is analogous to processes of biological/ecological endangerment and extinction; indeed, is far greater than the threat of extinction facing animal and plant species. Unless this process of language loss is seriously and urgently addressed, they argue, the world's linguistic "gene pool," along with the cultural knowledge associated with these languages, will be irremediably diminished. The parallels that are drawn by language ecologists between linguistic diversity and biodiversity have their merits, particularly in the clear resonances between the two processes. Thus, Steven Pinker (1995) observes that "the wide-scale extinction of languages [currently underway] is reminiscent of the current (though less severe) wide-scale extinction of plant or animal species" (p. 259). Likewise, James Crawford (1994) argues that each "fall[s] victim to predators, changing environments, or more successful competitors," each is encroached on by "modern cultures abetted by new technologies," and each is threatened by "destruction of lands and livelihoods; the spread of consumerism and other Western values . . ." (p. 5). Conversely, some commentators have observed that when biodiversity is high, so too are cultural and linguistic diversity (see Harmon, 1995; Maffi, 2000, 2001).

But despite the usefulness of these parallels, there are significant limitations to language ecology arguments as well. One is an obvious tendency to present a *preservationist* and *romanticist* account of minority languages and their loss—amounting, in effect, to an overly Utopian view of language and language change (for recent critiques along these lines, see Blommaert, 2001; Brutt-Griffler, 2002; May, 2004). The usual response to this perceived Utopianism is what might best be described as *resigned language realism*—that as much as we might not like the process of language shift and loss, there is little, if anything we can do about it. Edwards (1984, 1985, 1994, 2001) perhaps best exemplifies this latter position within current sociolinguistic commentary (see also Bentahila & Davies, 1993; Coulmas, 1992; Eastman, 1984).

Another limitation is that the language ecology paradigm actually reinforces, albeit unwittingly, the inevitability of the evolutionary change that it is protesting about. This is because although biological/ecological metaphors are useful in highlighting the scale and seriousness of the potential loss of languages to the world, they also contribute, ironically, to the equanimity with which potential language loss on such a scale is usually greeted. In effect, such metaphors reinforce, by implication, a widely held view that language loss is an inevitable part of the cycle of social and linguistic *evolution*. Thus, one could view the loss or death of a language as simply a failure on its part, or its speakers, to compete adequately in the modern world where, of course, only the fittest languages can (and should) survive (see, for example, Ladefoged, 1992).

As a result, what tends to be lost from sight are the wider political power relations that underlie language loss—or linguistic genocide, as Skutnabb-Kangas (2000) would have it[5]—and the wider processes of social, cultural, and political displacement of which it inevitably forms a part. Language loss is not only, perhaps not even primarily, a linguistic issue—it has much more to do with power, prejudice, (unequal) competition, and, in many cases, overt discrimination and subordination. As Noam Chomsky (1979) asserts, "Questions of language are basically questions of power" (p. 191). Thus, it should come as no surprise that the vast majority of today's threatened languages are spoken by socially and politically marginalized and/or subordinated groups. These groups have been variously estimated at between 5,000 and 8,000 (Stavenhagen, 1992) and include within them the 250 to 300 million members of the world's indigenous peoples (Davis, 1999; Tully, 1995), perhaps the most marginalized of all people groups. As Crawford (1994) notes, language death seldom occurs in communities of wealth and privilege, but rather to the dispossessed and disempowered. Moreover, linguistic dislocation for a particular community of speakers seldom, if ever, occurs in isolation from sociocultural and socioeconomic dislocation as well (Fishman, 1995). The loss of a minority language almost always forms part of a wider process of social, cultural, and political displacement.

NATIONALISM, MINORITIZATION, AND HISTORICAL CONSTRUCTION(ISM)

This brings us to the second principal concern that underlies the advocacy of MLR—why certain languages, and their speakers, have come to be *minoritized* in the first place. Advocates of MLR argue that the establishment of majority/minority language hierarchies is neither a natural process nor primarily even a linguistic one. Rather, it is a historically, socially, and politically *constructed* process (Hamel, 1997a, 1997b; May, 2000a, 2001, 2002, 2003), and one that is deeply imbued in wider (unequal) power relations. Following from this, if languages, and the status attached to them, are the product of wider historical, social, and political forces, we can discount the process of *natural selection* that a biological account would seem to imply. There is, thus, nothing "natural" about the status and prestige attributed to particular majority languages and, conversely, the stigma that is often attached to minority languages, or to dialects.

There are two specific points at issue here. The first concerns what actually distinguishes a majority language from a minority language or a dialect. This distinction is not as straightforward as many assume. For example, the same language may be regarded as both a majority *and* a minority language, depending on the context. Thus, Spanish is a majority language in Spain and many Latin American states, but a minority language in the United States. Even the term *language* itself indicates this process of construction, because what actually constitutes a language, as opposed to a dialect for example, remains controversial (see Mühlhäusler, 1996; Romaine, 2000). Certainly, we cannot always distinguish easily between a language and a dialect on *linguistic* grounds, because some languages are mutually intelligible, while some dialects of the same language are not. The example often employed here is that of Norwegian, because it was regarded as a dialect of Danish until the end of Danish rule in 1814. However, it was only with the advent of Norwegian independence from Sweden in 1905 that Norwegian actually acquired the status of a separate language, albeit one that has since remained mutually intelligible with both Danish and Swedish. Contemporary examples can be seen in the former Czechoslovakia, with the (re)emergence in the early 1990s of distinct Czech and Slovak varieties in place of a previously common state language. While in the former Yugoslavia, we are currently seeing the (re)development of separate Serbian, Croatian, and Bosnian language varieties in place of Serbo-Croat, itself the artificial language product of the post-Second World War Yugoslav Communist Federation under Tito.

What these latter examples clearly demonstrate is that languages are "created" out of the politics of state-making, not—as we often assume—the other way around (Billig, 1995). Independence for Norway and the breakup of the former Czechoslovakia and Yugoslavia have precipitated linguistic change, creating separate languages where previously none existed. The pivotal role of political context, particularly as it is outworked at the level of the nation-state, might also help to explain the scale of the projected language loss discussed earlier. One only has to look at the number of nation-states in the world today, at approximately 200, and the perhaps 300 or so languages that are projected to survive long term, to make the connection. That many of these languages are already recognized as either national or regional languages, or are currently spoken by groups who wish them to become so, serves only to strengthen this connection further (see Gellner, 1983, pp. 43–50). Such is the narrow concentration of "officially recognized" languages that around 120 nation-states have actually adopted either English, French, Spanish, or Arabic as their official language, while another 50 have a local language as the language of the state (Williams, 1996). In addition, Mackey (1991) notes that there are 45 languages that are accorded regional status. In short, currently less than 1.5% of the world's languages are recognized officially by nation-states.

And this brings us to the second key point at issue here: the central and ongoing influence of nation-state organization, and the politics of nationalism, to processes of national (and international) language formation and validation, along with the linguistic hierarchies attendant on them. In this respect, the model of the linguistically homogeneous nation-state—the "ideal" linguistic model adopted in early LPP efforts—is actually only a relatively recent historical phenomenon, arising from the French Revolution of 1789 and the subsequent development of European nationalism.[6] Previous forms of political organization had not required this degree of linguistic uniformity. For example, empires were quite happy for the most part to leave unmolested the plethora of cultures and languages subsumed within them—as long as taxes were paid, all was well. The Greek and Roman Empires are obvious examples here, while New World examples include the Aztec and Inca Empires of Central and South America respectively. More recent historical examples include the Austro-Hungarian Empire's overtly multilingual policy. But perhaps the clearest example is that of the Ottoman Empire, which actually established a formal system of *millets* (nations) in order to accommodate the cultural and linguistic diversity of peoples within its borders (see Dorian, 1998). Nonetheless, in the subsequent politics of European nationalism (which, of course, was also to spread throughout the world), the idea of a single, common, *national* language (sometimes, albeit rarely, a number of national languages) quickly became the leitmotif of modern social and political organization.

How was this accomplished? Principally via the political machinery of these newly emergent European states, with mass education playing a central role (Anderson, 1991; Gellner, 1983). The process of selecting and establishing a common national language usually involved two key aspects: *legitimation* and *institutionalization* (May, 2001; Nelde, Strubell & Williams, 1996). Legitimation is understood to mean here the formal recognition accorded to the language by the nation-state—usually by the constitutional and/or legislative benediction of official status. Institutionalization, perhaps the more important dimension, refers to the process by which the language comes to be accepted, or taken for granted in a wide range of social, cultural, and linguistic domains or contexts, both formal and informal. Both elements, in combination, achieved not only the central requirement of nation-states—cultural and linguistic homogeneity—but also the allied and, seemingly necessary, banishment of "minority" languages and dialects to the private domain.

If the establishment, often retrospectively, of chosen "national" languages was, therefore, a deliberate and deliberative political act, it follows that so, too, was the process by which other language varieties were subsequently "minoritized" or "dialectalized" by and within these same nation-states. These latter language varieties were, in effect, *positioned* by these newly formed states as languages of lesser political worth and value. Consequently, national languages came to be associated with modernity and progress, while their less fortunate counterparts were associated (conveniently) with tradition and obsolescence. More often than not, the latter were also specifically constructed as *obstacles* to the political project of nation-building—as threats to the unity of the state—thus, providing the raison d'être for the consistent derogation, diminution, and proscription of minority languages that have characterized the last 3 centuries of nationalism (see May, 2001, for a full overview; see also Wright, 2000). As

Nancy Dorian (1998) summarizes it: "it is the concept of the nation-state coupled with its official standard language . . . that has in modern times posed the keenest threat to both the identities and the languages of small [minority] communities" (p. 18). Florian Coulmas (1998) observes, even more succinctly, that "the nation-state as it has evolved since the French Revolution is the natural enemy of minorities" (p. 67).

Proponents of MLR argue that the emphasis on cultural and linguistic homogeneity within nation-states, and the attendant hierarchizing of languages, are thus neither inevitable nor inviolate—particularly in light of the historical recency of nation-states, and the related, often arbitrary and contrived, processes by which particular languages have been accorded "national" or "minority" status respectively. These arguments about the historical and geopolitical situatedness of national languages also apply at the supranational level. In particular, a number of prominent sociolinguistic commentators have argued that the burgeoning reach and influence of English as the current world language, or *lingua mundi*, is the result of an equally constructed historical process. First, there was the initial preeminence of Britain and the British Empire in establishing English as a key language of trade across the globe. Second, there has been the subsequent sociopolitical and socioeconomic dominance of the United States, along with its current preeminent position in the areas of science, technology, media, and academia (see Ammon, 1998, 2000). And third, there have been recent geopolitical events such as the collapse of the former Soviet Union, and much of communist Central and Eastern Europe along with it, which have further bolstered the reach and influence of English (see Holborow, 1999; Maurais & Morris, 2003; Pennycook, 1994, 1998a, 1998b, 2000; Phillipson, 1992, 1998, 2003).

As with the construction of national languages, the current ascendancy of English is also invariably linked with modernity and modernization, and the associated benefits that accrue to those who speak it. The result, MLR proponents argue, is to position other languages as having less "value" and "use" and by extension, and more problematically, to delimit and delegitimize the social, cultural, and linguistic capital ascribed to "non-English speakers"—the phrase itself reflecting the normative ascendancy of English. The usual corollary to this position is that the social mobility of the minority language speakers will be further enhanced if they *dispense* with any other (minority) languages.

LANGUAGE REPLACEMENT AND SOCIAL MOBILITY

Research in support of MLR highlights that the promotion of national languages and/or English is, because of the social and political processes just outlined, almost always couched in terms of *language replacement*—that one should/must learn these languages *at the expense of* one's first language. Consequently, the promotion of cultural and linguistic homogeneity at the collective/public level has come to be associated with, and expressed by, individual monolingualism. This amounts to a form of linguistic social Darwinism and also helps to explain why language shift/loss/decline has become so prominent.

Central to these language replacement arguments is the idea that the individual social mobility of minority language speakers will be enhanced as a result. Relatedly, minority language advocates are consistently criticized for consigning, or ghettoizing minority language communities within the confines of a language that does not have a wider use, thus, actively constraining their social mobility (see, for example, Barry, 2000; Edwards, 1994; Schlesinger, 1992). Little wonder, such critics observe, that many within the linguistic minority itself choose to ignore the pleas of minority language activists and instead "exit" the linguistic group by learning another (invariably, more dominant) language. It is one thing, after all, to proclaim the merits of retaining a particular language for identity purposes, quite another to have to live a life delimited by it—foreclosing the opportunity for mobility in the process. We can broadly summarize the logic of this argument as follows:

- Majority languages are lauded for their *instrumental* value, whereas minority languages are accorded *sentimental* value, but are broadly constructed as obstacles to social mobility and progress.
- Learning a majority language will, thus, provide individuals with greater economic and social mobility.
- Learning a minority language, although (possibly) important for reasons of cultural continuity, delimits an individual's mobility; in its strongest terms, this might amount to actual ghettoization.
- If minority language speakers are sensible they will opt for mobility and modernity via the majority language.
- Whatever decision is made, the choice between opting for a majority or minority language is constructed as oppositional, even mutually exclusive.

These arguments appear to be highly persuasive. In response, however, MLR proponents argue that the presumptions and assumptions that equate linguistic mobility *solely* with majority languages are themselves extremely problematic. For a start, this position separates the instrumental and identity aspects of language. Under this view, minority languages may be important for identity but have no instrumental value, whereas majority languages are construed as primarily instrumental with little or no identity value. We see this in the allied notions, evident in early LPP attempts, of majority languages as *vehicles* of modernity, and minority languages as (merely) *carriers* of identity. However, it is clear that *all* language(s) embody and accomplish both identity and instrumental functions for those who speak them. Where particular languages—especially majority/minority languages—differ is in the *degree* to which they can accomplish each of these functions, and this, in turn, is dependent on the social and political (not linguistic) constraints in which they operate (Carens, 2000; May, 2003, 2004). Thus, in the case of minority languages, their instrumental value is often constrained by wider social and political processes that have resulted in the privileging of other language varieties in the public realm. Meanwhile, for majority languages, the identity characteristics of the language *are* clearly important for their speakers, but often become subsumed within and normalized by the instrumental functions that these languages fulfill. This is particularly apparent with respect to monolingual speakers of English, given the position of English as the current world language.

On this basis, MLR advocates argue that the limited instrumentality of particular minority languages at any given time need not always remain so. Indeed, if the minority position of a language is the specific product of wider historical and contemporary social and political relationships, changing these wider relationships positively with respect to a minority language should bring about both enhanced instrumentality for the language in question and increased mobility for its speakers. We can see this occurring currently, for example, in Wales and Catalonia, with the emergence of these formerly subjugated languages into the public domain—particularly via, but by no means limited to, education (May, 2000b, 2002).

Likewise, when majority language speakers are made to realize that their own languages fulfill important identity functions for them, both as individuals and as a group, they may be slightly more reluctant to require minority language speakers to dispense with theirs. Or to put it another way, if majority languages do provide their speakers with particular and often significant individual and collective forms of linguistic identity, as they clearly do, it seems unjust to deny these same benefits, out of court, to minority language speakers.

And this brings us to the final principal concern of MLR—the legal protections that can potentially be developed in order to enhance the mobility of minority language speakers while at the same time protecting their right to continue to speak a minority language, *if they so choose*. It is here that the influence of the linguistic human rights (LHR) paradigm is most prominent.

LINGUISTIC HUMAN RIGHTS

The linguistic human rights research paradigm argues that minority languages, and their speakers, should be accorded at least some of the protections and institutional support that majority languages already enjoy (see, for example, Kontra, Skutnabb-Kangas, Phillipson, & Várady 1999; Skutnabb-Kangas & Phillipson, 1995; Skutnabb-Kangas, 1998, 2000, 2002). These arguments are also echoed in much of the academic legal discourse that has developed in recent years with respect to minority group rights more broadly, (see Capotorti, 1979; de Varennes, 1996a, 1996b; Thornberry, 1991a, 1991b, 2002). A central distinction in both discourses is one made between national minority groups and indigenous peoples on the one hand, and ethnic minority groups on the other. The former may be regarded as groups that are historically associated with a particular territory (i.e., they have not migrated to the territory from elsewhere) but because of conquest, confederation, or colonization are now regarded as minorities within that territory. The latter may be regarded as voluntary migrants and (involuntary) refugees living in a new national context (see Kymlicka, 1995; May, 2001 for further discussion).

Three key tenets of international law can be applied to the further development of linguistic human rights in relation to these two broad minority groupings. The first principle, which is widely accepted, is that it is not unreasonable to expect from national members some knowledge of the common public language(s) of the state. This is, of course, the central tenet underpinning the current public linguistic homogeneity of modern nation-states. However, LHR advocates assert that it is also possible to argue, on this basis, for the legitimation and institutionalization of the languages of national minorities within nation-states, according to them at least some of the benefits that national languages currently enjoy. LHR proponents qualify this by making it clear that the advocacy of such minority language rights is *not* the language replacement ideology in reverse—of replacing a majority language with a minority one. Rather, it is about questioning and contesting why the promotion of a majority (national) language should necessarily be *at the expense* of all others. By this, they argue, the linguistic exclusivity attendant on the nationalist principle of cultural and linguistic homogeneity can be effectively challenged and contested.

A second principle is that in order to avoid language discrimination, it is important that where there is a sufficient number of other language speakers, these speakers should be allowed to use that language as part of the exercise of their individual rights as citizens. That is, they should have the *opportunity* to use their first language if they so choose. As Fernand de Varennes (1996a) argues, "the respect of the language principles of individuals, *where appropriate and reasonable* [italics added], flows from a fundamental right and is not some special concession or privileged treatment. Simply put, it is the right to be treated equally without discrimination, to which everyone is entitled" (p. 117). Again, this principle can clearly be applied to minority language speakers within particular nation-states. Ostensibly, this can also be applied to majority language speakers on the same grounds. However, a crucial caveat needs to be added here. The formal promotion of a minority language does not preclude the ongoing use of the majority language, given that it is most often dominant anyway in all key language domains. Thus, what is being promoted is, again, not a new monolingualism in the minority language—indeed, this is usually neither politically nor practically sustainable—but the possibility of bilingualism or multilingualism. In other words, the majority language is not generally being precluded from the public realm here, nor proscribed at the individual level, nor are majority language speakers actually penalized for speaking their language.[7] Rather, monolingual majority language speakers are being asked to *accommodate* to the ongoing presence of a minority language and to recognize its status as an additional language of the state—a process that has elsewhere been described as *mutual accommodation* (May, 2001).

The third principle arises directly from the previous one—how to determine exactly what is "appropriate and reasonable" with regard to individual language preferences. Following the prominent political theorist, Will Kymlicka (1995), May (2001) has argued, for example, that only national minorities can demand *as of right* formal inclusion of their languages and cultures in the civic realm. However, this need not and should not preclude other ethnic minorities from being allowed *at the very least* to cultivate and pursue unhindered their own historic cultural and linguistic practices in the private domain (for a dissenting view see Skutnabb-Kangas, 2000).[8]

TOLERANCE- AND PROMOTION-ORIENTED LANGUAGE RIGHTS

In relation to language, this last principle has been articulated by Kloss (1977) as the distinction between *tolerance-oriented* and *promotion-oriented* rights. Tolerance-oriented language rights ensure the right to preserve one's language in the private, nongovernmental sphere of national life. These rights may be narrowly or broadly defined. They include the right of individuals to use their first language at home and in public, freedom of assembly and organization, the right to establish private cultural, economic, and social institutions wherein the first language may be used, and the right to foster one's first language in private schools. The key principle of such rights is that the state does "not interfere with efforts on the parts of the minority to make use of [their language] in the private domain" (Kloss, 1977, p. 2).

Promotion-oriented rights regulate the extent to which minority language rights are recognized within the *public* domain, or civic realm of the nation-state. As such, they involve "public authorities [in] trying to promote a minority [language] by having it used in public institutions—legislative, administrative and educational, including the public schools" (Kloss, 1977, p. 2). Again, such rights may be narrowly or widely applied. At their narrowest, promotion-oriented rights might simply involve the publishing of public documents in minority languages. At their broadest, promotion-oriented rights could involve recognition of a minority language in all formal domains within the nation-state, thus allowing the minority language group "to care for its internal affairs through its own public organs, which amounts to the [state] allowing self government for the minority group" (1977, p. 24).[9]

What tolerance- and promotion-oriented rights usefully highlight is that one can still distinguish effectively between the linguistic entitlements of different minority groups, while maintaining a broad commitment to the extension of linguistic human rights to all minority language groups. In other words, distinguishing between the rights of national and ethnic minorities still affords the latter far greater linguistic protection than many such groups currently enjoy—that is, *active* linguistic protection by the state for the *unhindered* maintenance of their first languages. This protection is applicable at the very least in the private domain and, "where numbers warrant," a principle again drawn from international law, potentially in the public domain as well.

Extending greater ethnolinguistic *democracy* to minority language groups, via LHR, does not thus amount to an argument for ethnolinguistic *equality* for all such groups. Similarly, a call for greater ethnolinguistic democracy clearly does not amount to asserting linguistic equivalence, in all domains, with dominant, majority languages. Majority languages will continue to dominate in most, if not all, language domains, because, as should be clear by now, that is the nature of their privileged sociohistorical, sociopolitical position(ing). Conversely, arguing that only national minorities can claim minority language rights, as of right, is *not* an argument for simply ignoring the claims of other ethnic groups (see May, 2001, 2003 for an extended discussion).

Developments in International and National Law

As a result of LHR arguments, and the wider debates about minority rights of which they form a part, a more accommodative approach to the language rights of minorities has begun to emerge in both international and national law, particularly since the end of the Cold War. At the supranational level, a number of key examples of recent legislation demonstrate this. One is the Draft Universal Declaration of Linguistic Rights (1996) accepted in Barcelona in June 1996 (after many years of preparation and numerous previous drafts) and since handed over to UNESCO for further deliberation. In the draft Declaration it is argued that *explicit* legal guarantees be provided for the linguistic rights of individuals, language communities (in effect, national minorities and indigenous peoples), and language groups (other minority ethnic groups). This includes the right of the individual "to the use of one's language both in private and in public" (Article 3.1). It also includes the right of linguistic communities to have the necessary resources at their disposal "to ensure that their language is present to the extent they desire at all levels of education within their territory: properly trained teachers, appropriate teaching methods, text books, finance, building and equipment, traditional and innovative technology" (Article 25). What is not clear, or at least not yet, is the extent to which nation-states will be *obliged* to act on these statements of general intent once the Declaration is finally adopted and ratified. Given the pattern of qualified "discretion" for nation-states, evident in most other international legislation, the answer must be that the Draft is likely to be revised along these more ambiguous lines before being finally accepted (see also Skutnabb-Kangas, 2000, pp. 543–549).

Another example where exactly the same question applies can be found in the (1993) United Nations Draft Declaration on the Rights of Indigenous Peoples. The Draft Declaration was formulated during a 10-year period by the Working Group on Indigenous Populations (WGIP), in turn a part of the United Nation's Sub-Commission on the Prevention of Discrimination and Protection of Minorities. It amounts to a strong assertion of indigenous rights, including promotion-oriented language rights. Article 15 states, for example, that "all indigenous peoples have ... the right to establish and control their educational systems and institutions providing education in their own languages, in a manner appropriate to their cultural methods of teaching and learning." However, the Draft has since been subject to a formal review by the U.N. Commission on Human Rights Working Group (CHR), prior to its adoption and ratification—a process that began in November 1995 and is still ongoing at the time of writing. Given the many substantive objections raised by states in the process of this review (see Barsh, 1996; Feldman, 2001; Thornberry, 2002), the Draft Declaration is also likely to be considerably amended by the time it reaches its final form, almost certainly toward the dilution of its tenets rather than their enforcement.

Recent pan-European law also reflects these competing tensions between, on the one hand, a greater accommodation of promotion-oriented minority language rights, and on the other, the ongoing reticence of nation-states to accept such a view. The (1992) European Charter for Regional or Minority Languages is one such example. It provides a sliding scale of educational provision for national and regional minority languages that ranges from a minimal entitlement for smaller groups—preschool provision only, for example—through to more generous rights for larger minority groups such as primary and secondary language education. Again, however, nation-states have discretion in what they provide, on the basis of both local considerations and the size of the group concerned. These European nation-states also retain considerable scope and flexibility over which articles of the Charter they actually choose to accept in the first place. In this respect, they are only required to accede to 35 out of 68 articles, although 3 of the 35 articles must refer to education. A similar pattern can be detected in the (1994) Framework Convention for the Protection of National Minorities, which was adopted by the Council of Europe in November 1994 and finally came into force in February 1998. The Framework Convention allows for a wide range of tolerance-based rights toward national minorities, including language rights. It also asserts at a more general level that contributing states should "promote the conditions necessary for persons belonging to national minorities to maintain and develop their culture, and to preserve the essential elements of their identity, namely their religion, language, traditions and cultural heritage" (Article 2.1). That said, the specific provisions for language and education remain sufficiently qualified for most states to avoid them if they so choose (Thornberry, 1997, Troebst, 1998).

These generally positive developments have also been paralleled, at least to some extent, within the laws of (some) nation-states. Let us take just two examples here, both related to indigenous peoples. In Brazil the adoption in 1988 of a new constitution recognized for the first time the indigenous Indians' social organization, customs, languages, beliefs, and traditions, along with the right of native title to their lands (*Constituição* Chapter VIII, Art. 231; Brasil, 1996; see also Hornberger, 1997). Norway also moved in 1988 to revise its constitution in order to grant greater autonomy for the indigenous Sámi, after a century of enforcing a stringent 'Norwegianization' (read assimilationist) policy toward them. As the amendment to the Norwegian Constitution stated: "It is incumbent on the governmental authorities to take the necessary steps to enable the Sámi population to safeguard and develop their language, their culture and their social life" (cited in Magga, 1996, p. 76). The effects of this new amendment are most apparent in the regional area of Finnmark, in the northernmost part of Norway, where the largest percentage of the Sámi live. The formal recognition accorded to the Sámi has led to the subsequent establishment of a Sámi Parliament in Finnmark (in 1989), while the Sámi Language Act, passed in 1992, recognized Northern Sámi as its official regional language (see Corson, 1995; Huss, 1999; Magga, 1995, 1996; Magga & Skutnabb-Kangas, 2001; Todal, 1999).

These national developments in legislating for LHR are clearly significant although, as with parallel developments in international law, they are still largely dependent on the largesse of the individual nation-states involved. Although there may be no watertight legal guarantees here, there *is* nonetheless an increasing recognition within international and national law that significant minorities within the nation-state have a *reasonable* expectation to some form of state support along these lines (de Varennes, 1996a). In other words, whereas it would be unreasonable for nation-states to be required to fund language and education services, for example, for all minorities, it is increasingly accepted that where a language is spoken by a significant number within the nation-state, it would also be unreasonable not to provide some level of state services and activity in that language. Certainly, the long-held practice of states making no accommodations to minority language demands is not so readily defensible in today's social and political climate. Ignoring such demands is also unlikely to quell or abate the question of minority language rights, as it might once have done. Indeed, it is much more likely to escalate them. Under these circumstances, "any policy favouring a single language to the exclusion of all others can be extremely risky ... because it is then a factor promoting division rather than unification. Instead of integration, an ill-advised and inappropriate state language policy may have the opposite effect and cause a *levée de bouclier* [general outcry]" (de Varennes, 1996a, p. 91).

CONCLUSIONS AND CAVEATS

These theoretical, policy, and legislative developments with respect to minority language rights have brought us a considerable way from early debates surrounding the formulation and implementation of LPP. The subsequent development of the language ecology and linguistic human rights paradigms has redirected attention to the underlying, often highly discriminatory, processes that stigmatize and undermine minority languages and their speakers—not only linguistically, but also culturally, socially, economically, and politically. Accordingly, even when language rights are not the principal focus of attention, more recent research and policy in LPP is increasingly having to address these concerns (see, for example, Kaplan & Baldauf, 1999). Certainly, as Ricento (2000) observes, much of the cutting edge research in LPP now deals directly with its limitations (May, 2001; Schiffman, 1996), as well as its potential for promoting social change (Freeman, 1998; Hornberger, 1998; May, 2001, 2003).

In both instances, the nationalist principle of cultural and linguistic homogeneity, and the language replacement ideology invariably attendant on it, have been brought increasingly into question. The principal challenge that emerges from this critique is the need to rethink nation-states in more linguistically plural and inclusive ways. As we have seen, advocates of minority language rights argue that a key means by which this can be achieved is via the extension of tolerance-oriented language rights and, where appropriate, promotion-oriented language rights for minority language groups. Such a process allows for the prospect of more representational multinational and multilingual states by directly contesting the historical inequalities that have seen minority languages, and their speakers, relegated to the social and political margins. As James Tollefson (1991) has observed of these developments:

> the struggle to adopt minority languages within dominant institutions such as education, the law, and government, as well as the struggle over language rights, constitute efforts to legitimise the minority group itself and to alter its relationship to the state. Thus while language planning reflects relationships of power, it can also be used to transform them. (p. 202)

For Tollefson and other advocates of MLR, changing the language preferences of the state and civil society, or at least broadening them, would better reflect the cultural and linguistic demographics of most of today's multinational and multilingual states. Not only this, it could significantly improve the life chances of those minority language individuals and groups who are presently disadvantaged in their access to, and participation in public services, employment, and education, because linguistic consequences cannot be separated from socioeconomic and sociopolitical consequences, and vice versa. Likewise, changing "the rules of the game" that automatically presume an exclusive relationship among dominant languages, modernity, and mobility should make the process of maintaining minority languages a little easier.

Even so, it should also be clear that achieving a greater recognition and acceptance of minority languages, and their speakers, remains a formidable task, not least because of the extent of minority language shift and loss already in train. The challenge for LPP, and its academic analysis, is accordingly to dispense with the largely ahistorical, apolitical, and synchronic or presentist approach that so dominated its origins in order to engage directly and critically with the wider social and political conditions—and, crucially, their historical antecedents—that have invariably framed and shaped such policies. As Jan Blommaert (1999) argues, a synchronic analysis to LPP takes no account of human agency, political intervention, power, and authority in the formation of particular (national) language ideologies. Nor, by definition, is it able to identify the establishment and maintenance of majority languages as a specific "form of practice, historically contingent and socially embedded" (p. 7). And yet, as advocates of minority language rights quite clearly highlight, it is exactly these contingent, socially embedded, and often highly unequal practices, that have so disadvantaged minority languages, and their speakers, in the first place.

These MLR arguments resonate closely with important related research on the ideological influences of language policy (Blommaert, 1999; May, 2001; Ricento, 2000; Schiffman, 1996; Schmid, 2001; Woolard, 1998). As a result of this combination of research influences, more recent LPP scholarship (see, for example, Baldauf & Kaplan, 2003) is increasingly addressing the overtly political and ideological aspects of language policy and planning, along with its often deleterious consequences for minority language speakers. Whether this new academic direction for LPP is sustained and, more important perhaps, whether the long-standing pejorative position (and positioning) of minority language speakers will improve, remains to be seen.

NOTES

1. Language policy usually refers to the development of policy; language planning refers to its implementation. However, the two are often used interchangeably in the literature (see Baldauf, chap. 52, this volume), and I will follow this latter convention in this chapter.
2. That said, such a distinction needs to be treated with some caution because the dichotomy inevitably understates the complex *situatedness* of particular language varieties with respect to power relations (see Coulmas, 1998; Pennycook, 1998a, 2000).
3. Even when certain local languages, such as Malay or Indonesian, were selected as national languages, this simply created an additional diglossic layer. In effect, these newly promoted minority languages quickly coming to dominate remaining local languages in much the same way as majority, colonial languages (see Kaplan & Baldauf, 1997; Baldauf & Kaplan, 2003).
4. Obviously, language death, or the extinction of a language, occurs when the last speaker of that language dies. But, in effect, once a language ceases to be spoken by a *community* of speakers, it has effectively already perished (see Baker & Prys Jones, 1998, p. 150).
5. The term *linguistic genocide* is often viewed as highly problematic by skeptics of minority language rights—as too emotive and conspiratorial. Skutnabb-Kangas argues, in response, that terms such as *language death* and *language loss*, which many of these skeptics prefer, have significant problems of their own—not least the notable absence of agency or responsibility. Language "loss" or "death" does not just happen, nor is it natural and/or inevitable. Rather, it is *always* socially, culturally, and politically situated within a wider nexus of (often highly unequal) power relations between, and within, language groups (see also Section on Nationalism, minoritization, and historical construction(ism)).
6. A precursor to the rise of European nationalism in this respect can also be found in the colonialism of the 16th and 17th centuries, particularly in the privileging of, for example, English, Portuguese, and Spanish in the Americas by their respective colonial powers (see Blaut, 1993; Mignolo, 1995).
7. The examples where this has occurred as the result of a minority language policy remain extremely rare. The post-Soviet language policies of Latvia and Estonia, however, may be said to fall into this category. This is because the significant majority Russian-speaking population in these areas have been denied citizenship rights since independence unless they can demonstrate a conversational ability in Latvian or Estonian (see de Varennes, 1996a).
8. Skutnabb-Kangas is generally more skeptical of the national/ethnic minority distinction, particularly given its potential to delimit the language entitlements of the latter.
9. Kloss's distinction between tolerance- and promotion-oriented language rights is also broadly comparable to one drawn by Churchill (1986), in his typology of minority language policy approaches within the Organization of Economic Cooperation and Development, between the maintenance of languages for private use versus the widespread institutional recognition of languages (for an extended discussion, see May, 2001, chap. 5). Another comparable distinction is that made by Coulombe (1993) between laissez-faire and sustaining language policies.

REFERENCES

Ammon, U. (1998). *Ist Deutsch noch internationale Wissenschaftssprache? Englisch auch für die Lehre an den deutschsprachigen Hochschulen.* Berlin: Mouton de Gruyter.
Ammon, U. (Ed.). (2000). *The Dominance of English as the language of science: Effects on other languages and language communities.* Berlin: Mouton de Gruyter.

Anderson, B. (1991). *Imagined communities: Reflections on the origin and spread of nationalism* (Rev. ed.). London: Verso.

Baker, C., & Prys Jones, S. (Eds.) (1998). *Encyclopedia of bilingualism and bilingual education*. Clevedon, UK: Multilingual Matters.

Baldauf, R. B., Jr., & Kaplan, R. B. (2003). Who are the actors? The role of (applied) linguists in language policy. In P. Ryan & R. Terborg (Eds.), *Language: Issues of inequality* (pp. 20–41). Mexico City: CELE/Autonomous National University of Mexico.

Barry, B. (2000). *Culture and equality: An egalitarian critique of multiculturalism*. Cambridge, MA.: Harvard University Press.

Barsh, R. (1996). Indigenous peoples and the U.N. Commission on Human Rights: A case of the immovable object and the irresistible force. *Human Rights Quarterly, 18*, 782–813.

Bentahila, A., & Davies, E. (1993). Language revival: Restoration or transformation? *Journal of Multilingual and Multicultural Development, 14*, 355–374.

Billig, M. (1995). *Banal nationalism*. London: Sage.

Blaut, J. M. (1993). *The colonizer's model of the world: Geographical diffusionism and Eurocentric history*. New York: Guilford.

Blommaert, J. (Ed.). (1999). *Language ideological debates*. Berlin: Mouton de Gruyter.

Blommaert, J. (2001). The Asmara Declaration as a sociolinguistic problem: Notes in scholarship and linguistic rights. *Journal of Sociolinguistics, 5*(1), 131–142.

Bourdieu, P. (1991). *Language and symbolic power*. Cambridge, UK: Polity Press.

Brutt-Griffler, J. (2002). Class, ethnicity and language rights: An analysis of British colonial policy in Lesotho and Sri Lanka and some implications for language policy. *Journal of Language, Identity and Education, 1*(3), 207–234.

Capotorti, F. (1979). *Study on the rights of persons belonging to ethnic, religious and linguistic minorities*. New York: United Nations.

Carens, J. (2000). *Culture, citizenship and community: A contextual exploration of justice as evenhandedness*. Oxford, UK: Oxford University Press.

Chomsky, N. (1979). *Language and responsibility*. London: Harvester.

Churchill, S. (1986). *The education of linguistic and cultural minorities in the OECD countries*. Clevedon, UK: Multilingual Matters.

Constituição da República Federativa do Brasil (CF/88) (1996). São Paulo, Brazil: Editora Revista dos Tribunais.

Corson, D. (1995). Norway's "Sámi Language Act": Emancipatory implications for the world's indigenous peoples. *Language in Society, 24*, 493–514.

Coulmas, F. (1992). *Language and economy*. Oxford, UK: Blackwell.

Coulmas, F. (1998). Language rights: Interests of states, language groups and the individual. *Language Sciences, 20*, 63–72.

Coulombe, P. (1993). Language rights, individual and communal. *Language Problems and Language Planning, 17*, 140–152.

Crawford, J. (1994). Endangered native American languages: What is to be done and why? *Journal of Navajo Education, 11*(3), 3–11.

Crystal, D. (1997a). *English as a global language*. Cambridge, UK Cambridge University Press.

Crystal, D. (1997b). *The Cambridge encyclopedia of language* (2nd ed.). Cambridge, UK: Cambridge University Press.

Crystal, D. (1999a, November). The death of language. *Prospect*, pp. 56–59.

Crystal, D. (1999b, October 25). Death sentence. *The Guardian*, pp. 62–3.

Davis, W. (1999, August). Vanishing cultures. *National Geographic*, pp. 62–89.

Day, R. (1985). The ultimate inequality: Linguistic genocide. In N. Wolfson & J. Manes (Eds.), *Language of inequality* (pp. 163–181). Berlin: Mouton de Gruyter.

de Varennes, F. (1996a). *Language, minorities and human rights*. The Hague, The Netherlands. Kluwer Law International.

de Varennes, F. (1996b). Minority aspirations and the revival of indigenous peoples. *International Review of Education, 42*, 309–325.

Dorian, N. (1998). Western language ideologies and small-language prospects. In L. Grenoble & L. Whaley (Eds.), *Endangered languages: Language loss and community response* (pp. 3–21). Cambridge, UK: Cambridge University Press.

Dua, H. (1994). *Hegemony of English*. Mysore, India: Yashoda Publications.

Eastman, C. (1984). Language, ethnic identity and change. In J. Edwards (Ed.), *Linguistic minorities, policies and pluralism* (pp. 259–276). London: Academic Press.

Edwards, J. (1984). Language, diversity and identity. In J. Edwards (Ed.), *Linguistic minorities, policies and pluralism* (pp. 277–310). London: Academic Press.

Edwards, J. (1985). *Language, society and identity*. Oxford, UK: Basil Blackwell.

Edwards, J. (1994). *Multilingualism*. London: Routledge.

Edwards, J. (2001). The ecology of language revival. *Current Issues in Language Planning, 2*, 231–241.

Feldman, A. (2001). Transforming peoples and subverting states: Developing a pedagogical approach to the study of indigenous peoples and ethnocultural movements. *Ethnicities, 1*(2), 147–178.

Fishman, J. (1968a). Sociolinguistics and the language problems of the developing countries. In J. Fishman, C. Ferguson, & J. Das Gupta (Eds.), *Language problems of developing nations* (pp. 3–16). New York: Wiley.

Fishman, J. (1968b). Some contrasts between linguistically homogeneous and linguistic heterogeneous polities. In J. Fishman, C. Ferguson, & J. Das Gupta (Eds.), *Language problems of developing nations* (pp. 53–68). New York: Wiley.

Fishman, J. (1968c). Language problems and types of political and sociocultural integration: A conceptual postscript. In J. Fishman, C. Ferguson, & J. Das Gupta (Eds.), *Language problems of developing nations* (pp. 491–498). New York: Wiley.

Fishman, J. (1991). *Reversing language shift: Theoretical and empirical foundations of assistance to threatened languages.* Clevedon, UK: Multilingual Matters.

Fishman, J. (1995). Good conferences in a wicked world: On some worrisome problems in the study of language maintenance and language shift. In W. Fase, K. Jaspaert, & S. Kroon (Eds.), *The state of minority languages: International perspectives on survival and decline.* Lisse, The Netherlands: Swets & Zeitlinger.

Fox, M. J. (1975). *Language and development: A retrospective survey of Ford Foundation language projects 1952–1974.* New York: Ford Foundation.

Freeman, R. (1998). *Bilingual education and social change.* Clevedon, UK: Multilingual Matters.

Gellner, E. (1983). *Nations and nationalism: New perspectives on the past.* Oxford, UK: Basil Blackwell.

Grimes, B. (Ed.). (2000). *Ethnologue: Languages of the world* (14th ed.). Dallas, TX: SIL.

Hamel, R. (1997a). Introduction: Linguistic human rights in a sociolinguistic perspective. *International Journal of the Sociology of Language, 127,* 1–24.

Hamel, R. (1997b). Language conflict and language shift: A sociolinguistic framework for linguistic human rights. *International Journal of the Sociology of Language, 127,* 105–134.

Harmon, D. (1995). The status of the world's languages as reported in the *Ethnologue. Southwest Journal of Linguistics, 14,* 1–28.

Holborow, M. (1999). *The politics of English: A Marxist view of language.* London: Sage.

Hornberger, N. (1997). Literacy, language maintenance, and linguistic human rights: Three telling cases. *International Journal of the Sociology of Language, 127,* 87–103.

Hornberger, N. (1998). Language policy, language education, language rights: Indigenous, immigrant, and international perspectives. *Language in Society, 27,* 439–458.

Huss, L. (1999). *Reversing language shift in the far north: Linguistic revitalization in Northern Scandinavia and Finland.* Uppsala, Sweden: Acta Universitatis Upsaliensis.

Kaplan R. B., & Baldauf, R. B., Jr. (1997). *Language planning: From practice to theory.* Clevedon, UK: Multilingual Matters.

Kaplan, R. B., & Baldauf, R. B., Jr. (1999) *Language planning in Malawi, Mozambique and the Philippines.* Clevedon, UK: Multilingual Matters.

Kloss, H. (1968). Notes concerning a language-nation typology. In J. Fishman, C. Ferguson, & J. Das Gupta (Eds.), *Language problems of developing nations* (pp. 69–85). New York: Wiley.

Kloss, H. (1977). *The American bilingual tradition.* Rowley, MA: Newbury House.

Kontra, M., Skutnabb-Kangas, T., Phillipson, R., & Várady, T. (Eds.). (1999). *Language: A right and a resource. Approaches to linguistic human rights.* Budapest, Hungary: Central European University Press.

Krauss, M. (1992). The world's languages in crisis. *Language, 68,* 4–10.

Krauss, M. (1995). Language loss in Alaska, the United States and the world. Frame of reference. *Alaska Humanities Forum, 6*(1), 2–5.

Kymlicka, W. (1995). *Multicultural citizenship: A liberal theory of minority rights.* Oxford, UK: Clarendon Press.

Ladefoged, P. (1992). Another view of endangered languages. *Language, 68,* 809–811.

Luke, A., McHoul, A., & Mey, J. (1990). On the limits of language planning: Class, state and power. In R. B. Baldauf, Jr. & A. Luke (Eds.), *Language planning and education in Australia and the South Pacific* (pp. 25–44). Clevedon, UK: Multilingual Matters.

Mackey, W. (1991). Language diversity, language policy and the sovereign state. *History of European Ideas, 13,* 51–61.

Maffi, L. (Ed.). (2000). *Language, knowledge and the environment: The interdependence of biological and cultural diversity.* Washington, DC: Smithsonian Institution Press.

Maffi, L. (2001). *On biocultural diversity: Linking language, knowledge, and the environment.* Washington, DC: Smithsonian Institution Press.

Magga, O. (1995). The Sámi Language Act. In T. Skutnabb-Kangas & R. Phillipson (Eds.), *Linguistic human rights: Overcoming linguistic discrimination* (pp. 219–233). Berlin: Mouton de Gruyter.

Magga, O. (1996). Sámi past and present and the Sámi picture of the world. In E. Helander (Ed.), *Awakened voice: The return of Sámi knowledge* (pp. 74–80). Kautokeino, Norway: Nordic Sámi Institute.

Magga, O., & Skutnabb-Kangas, T. (2001). The Saami languages. *Cultural Survival Quarterly, 25*(2), 26–31.

Maurais, J., & Morris, M. (2003). *Languages in a globalising world.* Cambridge, UK: Cambridge University Press.

May, S. (2000a). Uncommon languages: The challenges and possibilities of minority language rights. *Journal of Multilingual and Multicultural Development, 21*(5), 366–385.

May, S. (2000b). Accommodating and resisting minority language policy: The case of Wales. *International Journal of Bilingual Education and Bilingualism, 3*(2), 101–128.

May, S. (2001). *Language and minority rights: Ethnicity, nationalism and the politics of language*. London: Longman.

May, S. (2002). Developing greater ethnolinguistic democracy in Europe: Minority language policies, nation-states, and the question of tolerability. *Sociolinguistica, 16*, 1–13.

May, S. (2003). Misconceiving minority language rights: Implications for liberal political theory. In W. Kymlicka & A. Patten (Eds.), *Language rights and political theory* (pp. 123–152). Oxford, UK: Oxford University Press.

May, S. (2004). Rethinking linguistic human rights: Answering questions of identity, essentialism and mobility. In D. Patrick & J. Freeland (Eds.), *Language rights and language "survival": A sociolinguistic exploration*, (pp. 35–53.) Manchester, UK: St Jerome Publishing.

Mey, J. (1985). *Whose language? A study in linguistic pragmatics*. Amsterdam: Benjamins.

Mignolo, W. D. (1995). *The darker side of the Renaissance: Literacy, territoriality, and colonization*. Ann Arbor: University of Michgan Press.

Mühlhäusler, P. (1990). "Reducing" Pacific languages to writings. In J. Joseph & T. Taylor (Eds.), *Ideologies of language* (pp. 189–205). London: Routledge.

Mühlhäusler, P. (1996). *Linguistic ecology: Language change and linguistic imperialism in the Pacific region*. London: Routledge.

Mühlhäusler, P. (2000). Language planning and language ecology. *Current Issues in Language Planning, 1*, 306–367.

Nelde, P., Strubell, M., & Williams, G. (1996). *Euromosaic: The production and reproduction of the minority language groups in the European Union*. Luxembourg: Office for Official Publications of the European Communities.

Nettle, D., & Romaine, S. (2000). *Vanishing voices: The extinction of the world's languages*. Oxford, UK: Oxford University Press.

Pennycook, A. (1994). *The cultural politics of English as an international language*. London: Longman.

Pennycook, A. (1998a). The right to language: Towards a situated ethics of language possibilities. *Language Sciences, 20*, 73–87.

Pennycook, A. (1998b). *English and the discourses of colonialism*. London: Routledge.

Pennycook, A. (2000). English, politics, ideology: From colonial celebration to postcolonial performativity. In T. Ricento (Ed.), *Ideology, politics and language policies: Focus on English* (pp. 107–120). Amsterdam: Benjamins.

Phillipson, R. (1992). *Linguistic imperialism*. Oxford, UK: Oxford University Press.

Phillipson, R. (1998). Globalizing English: Are linguistic human rights an alternative to linguistic imperialism? *Language Sciences, 20*, 101–112.

Phillipson, R. (2003). *English-only Europe/Challenging language policy*. London: Routledge.

Pinker, S. (1995). *The language instinct*. London: Penguin.

Ricento, T. (2000). Historical and theoretical perspectives in language policy and planning. In T. Ricento (Ed.), *Ideology, politics and language policies: Focus on English* (pp. 9–24). Amsterdam: Benjamins.

Romaine, S. (2000). *Language in society: An introduction to sociolinguistics* (2nd ed.). Oxford, UK: Oxford University Press.

Rubin, J., & Jernudd, B. (Eds.). (1971). *Can language be planned? Sociolinguistic theory and practice for developing nations*. Honolulu, HI: University of Hawaii Press.

Schiffman, H. (1996). *Linguistic culture and language policy*. London: Routledge.

Schlesinger, A. (1992). *The disuniting of America: Reflections on a multicultural society*. New York: Norton.

Schmid, C. (2001). *The politics of language: Conflict, identity, and cultural pluralism in comparative perspective*. Oxford, UK: Oxford University Press.

Skutnabb-Kangas, T. (1998). Human rights and language wrongs—a future for diversity? *Language Sciences, 20*, 5–27.

Skutnabb-Kangas, T. (2000). *Linguistic genocide in education—or worldwide diversity and human rights?* Mahwah, NJ: Lawrence Erlbaum Associates.

Skutnabb-Kangas, T. (2002). Marvellous human rights rhetoric and grim realities: Language rights in education. *Journal of Language, Identity and Education, 1*(3), 179–206.

Skutnabb-Kangas, T., & Phillipson, R. (1995). Linguistic human rights, past and present. In T. Skutnabb-Kangas & R. Phillipson (Eds.), *Linguistic human rights: Overcoming linguistic discrimination* (pp. 71–110). Berlin: Mouton de Gruyter.

Stavenhagen, R. (1992). Universal human rights and the cultures of indigenous peoples and other ethnic groups: The critical frontier of the 1990s. In A. Eide & B. Hagtvet (Eds.), *Human rights in perspective* (pp. 135–151). Oxford, UK: Blackwell.

Thornberry, P. (1991a). *International law and the rights of minorities*. Oxford, UK: Clarendon Press.

Thornberry, P. (1991b). *Minorities and human rights law*. London: Minority Rights Group.

Thornberry, P. (1997). Minority rights. In Academy of European Law (Ed.), *Collected courses of the Academy of European Law* (Vol. VI, Book 2, pp. 307–390). The Hague, The Netherlands: Kluwer Law International.

Thornberry, P. (2002). Minority and indigenous rights at "the end of history." *Ethnicities, 2*(4), 515–537.

Todal, J. (1999). Minorities within a minority: Language and the school in the Sámi areas of Norway. In S. May (Ed.), *Indigenous community-based education* (pp. 124–136). Clevedon, UK: Multilingual Matters.

Tollefson, J. (1991). *Planning language, planning inequality: Language policy in the community*. London: Longman.

Troebst, S. (1998). *The Council of Europe's Framework Convention for the protection of national minorities revisited*. Flensburg, Germany: European Centre for Minority Issues.

Tully, J. (1995). *Strange multiplicity: Constitutionalism in an age of diversity*. Cambridge, UK: Cambridge University Press.

Williams, C. (1996). Ethnic identity and language issues in development. In D. Dwyer & D. Drakakis-Smith (Eds.), *Ethnicity and development: Geographical perspectives* (pp. 45–85). London: Wiley.

Woolard, K. (1998). Introduction: Language ideology as a field of inquiry. In B. Schieffelin, K. Woolard, & P. Kroskrity (Eds.), *Language ideologies: Practice and theory* (pp. 3–47). New York: Oxford University Press.

Wright, S. (2000). *Community and communication: The role of language in nation state building and European integration*. Clevedon, UK: Multilingual Matters.

Author Index

Numbers in *italics* indicate pages with complete bibliographic information.

A

Aarts, J., 399, *405*
Abbate, J., 16, *24*
Abelar, Y., 519, *523*
Abraham, R. G., 767, *771*
Abrahamsson, N., 420, *434*, 447, *451*
Abram, P. L., 706, *709*
Abu-Akhel, A., 513, *523*
Achiba, M., 325, *330*
Ackerman, P. L., 446, *448*
Adams, H., 245, *254*
Adams, R. J., 839, *853*
Adamson, H. D., 695, 702, *708*
Adelstein, A., 420, *433*
Adelsward, V., 131, *131*
Adger, C. T., 58, *60*
Aebersold, J., 576, *577*
Afflerbach, P., 566, *579*
Agar, M., 118, 123, *131*, 923, *926*
Ager, D., 962, *968*, 972, 974, 975, 982, 986, *989*, 998, *1009*, 1035, 1047, 1049, 1050, 1051, 1052, *1053*
Agnello, F., 460, *467*
Agnihotri, R. K. J., 74, 77, *83*
Aguilera, G. M., 922, *928*
Ainscough, V., 147, 148, *151*
Akahane-Yamada, R., 505, *525*

Akamatsu, N., 903, 904, *908*, 945, 946, *948*
Alanen, R., 442, *448*, 677, 678, 679, *687*
Alderson, J., 109, *112*, 567, 572, *577*, 608, *610*, 716, *726*, 791, *793*, 799, *811*, 818, 819, 822, 827, *829*, 834, 836, 846, 847, 848, *849, 851*, *854*, 861, *867*
Aleksandrowicz-Pedich, L., 923, *926*
Alexander, L., 979, 980, *991*
Alexander-Kasparik, R., 19, *23*
Aljaafreh, A., 338, 339, 345, *350, 351*, 723, *726*
Al-Khatib, M., 616, 621, *625*
Allen, B. M., 10, *21*
Allen, J. P. B., 245, *252*
Allen, L., 185, *189*, 358, *371*, 718, *726*,
Allington, R., 574, *577*
Allison, D., 90, *98*, 108, *112*
Allison, R., 164, *167*
Allum, P., 746, *754*
Allwood, J., 513, 519, *523*
Allwright, D., 225, *238*, 245, 246, 250, *252*
Alsagoff, L., 287, *298*
Altarriba, J., 514, *523*
Altenberg, B., 397, *405*
Alvarez, H., 35, *41*
Alvarez-Torres, M. J., 676, 681, 686, *688*
Amanti, C., 37, 38, *41, 42*
Ammon, U., 982, *989*, 1062, *1069*
Anastasi, A., 798, *811*, 834, 835, *849*

Q

Qiang, W., 248, *255*
Qualifications and Curriculum Authority, 870, 871, 876, 887, *888*
Queen, R., 19, *23*
Quesada-Inces, R., 647, *650*
Quezada, M. S., 536, *543*
Quintanilha, T., 588, *595*
Quirk, R., 159, *172*, 289, *298*, 397, *408*, 546, *561*, 745, *755*
Quiroz, B., 20, *24*

R

Rabinowitz, J., 429, *435*
Radencich, M. C., 19, *23*
Radnofsky, M. L., 185, 186, 188, *193*
Rafiqzad, K., 158, *172*
Rahman, T., 164, *172*
Raimes, A., 598, 599, 605, 609, 610, *613*
Raj, J., 938, *949*
Rajagopalan, K., 942, *949*
Ramanathan, V., 185, 186, 188, *189, 193*, 381, *391*, 602, 610, *613*, 914, *926*
Ramirez, D., 536, *543*
Rampton, B., 185, 186, *193*, 209, *220*, 490, 496, *502*, 902, 903, *908, 909*, 938, *949*
Ranard, D. A., 541, *543*
Randazza, L. A., 491, *500*
Ranney, S., 700, *709*
Ranta, L., 274, *280*, 370, *372*, 445, 446, *452, 453*, 476, *482, 522, 525*, 558, *561*, 674, 675, 684, 685, *689*, 698, *710*, 720, 724, *727*
Rao, G. S., 164, *172*
Rao, Z., 645, *650*, 667, *670*, 921, *929*
Rapoport, R. N., 241, *255*
Rassool, N., 744, 745, *755*
Ravem, R., 267, *280*
Raymond, P. M., 577, *579*
Rayson, P., 548, *561*, 622, 623, *626, 627*
Read, J., 508, *526*, 594, *595*, 784, *794*, 803, *813*, 817, *831*
Read, V., 118, *133*
Rea-Dickins, P., 821, *831*, 848, *854*, 870, 873, 879, *888*
Reagan, T. G., 916, *929*
Reason, P., 242, *255*
Reber, A., 441, *452*
Red, D. L., 385, *391*
Reder, L. M., 203, *206*, 441, *450*
Reder, S., 404, *408*
Redington, M., 442, *452*
Reed, J. M., 442, *452*
Rees-Miller, J., 763, *771*

Reichelt, M., 602, *613*
Reichle, E. D., 447, *449*
Reid, J., 89, *98*, 147, *152*, 600, 607, *610, 613*, 618, 619, 620, 622, 625, *628*, 660, 666, *670*
Reid, W. A., 243, *255*
Reinhart, S. M., 105, *112*
Relkin, N. R., 447, *451*
Rendon, P., 38, *41*
Renie, D., 748, 753, *754, 755*
Renou, J. M., 444, *453*
Renouf, A., 396, 402, *408*, 622, *628*
Reppen, R., 87, 92, 94, *96*, 394, 395, 396, 399, 401, 402, 403, *406, 408*, 548, *560*, 698, *709*
Resnick, D. P., 531, 532, *543*
Resnick, L. B., 531, 532, *543*
Resnik, M. C., 937, *949*
Reynolds, S., 654, 655, 656, 657, 658, 668, *670*
Rhee, M.-J., 1016, *1034*
Rhodes, D., 538, 539, *542*
Rhodes, N., 702, *711*
Rhydwen, M., 1008, *1010*
Riagain, P. O., 1044, 1045, *1054*
Riazi, A. M., 903, 904, *908*, 945, 946, *948*
Ricento, T., 906, *909*, 958, *970*, 1056, 1068, 1069, *1072*
Richard-Amato, P. A., 694, *711*
Richards, J., 87, 90, *96*, 139, *152*, 245, 246, 249, *254, 255*, 265, *280*, 551, *561*, 645, *650*, 653, 654, 657, 661, 663, 664, 665, *670*, 694, *711*
Richards, K., 187, *190*, 246, *253*
Richardson, L., 904, *909*
Rickard, T. C., 441, *453*
Rickford, J., 291, 295, 296, *298*
Ridge, S. G., 903, *909*
Riggenbach, H., 210, 211, 214, *220*
Riley, G., 568, *579*
Riley, L. D., 761, 767, *771*
Riney, T., 427, 428, 431, *435*
Ringbom, H., 403, *408*, 622, 623, 625, *628*
Rintell, E., 317, 326, *331, 333*
Riordan, L., 234, 235, *239*
Risager, K., 916, *927*
Rist, R., 187, *193*
Ritchie, W. C., 158, 161, *168, 172*, 226, *239*
Ritter, F. E., 441, *450*
Rivera, A., 38, *41*
Rivera, C., 19, *24*
Rivera, K., 75, *84*
Rivers, W., 976, 978, *991*
Rivers, W. P., 187, *193*
Robb, T. N., 572, *579*
Robbins, J., 760, *769*
Robbins, M., 440, *454*

Subject Index

5R